The Oxford Handbook of
The Indian Economy in the 21st Century

The Oxford India Handbooks are an important initiative in academic publishing. Each volume offers a comprehensive survey of research in a critical subject area and provides facts, figures, and analyses for a well-grounded perspective. The series provides scholars, students, and policy planners with a balanced understanding of a wide range of issues in the social sciences.

Other Titles in the Series

HANDBOOK OF POLITICS IN INDIAN STATES
Regions, Parties, and Economic Reforms
Sudha Pai (Editor)

HANDBOOK OF POPULATION AND DEVELOPMENT IN INDIA (OIP)
A.K. Shiva Kumar, Pradeep Panda, and Rajani R. Ved (Editors)

HANDBOOK OF URBAN INEQUALITIES
Darshini Mahadevia and Sandip Sarkar

HANDBOOK OF GENDER
Raka Ray (Editor)

HANDBOOK OF CLIMATE CHANGE AND INDIA
Development, Politics, and Governance
Navroz K. Dubash (Editor)

HANDBOOK OF MODERNITY IN SOUTH ASIA
Modern Makeovers
Saurabh Dube (Editor)

HANDBOOK OF PSYCHOLOGY IN INDIA
Girishwar Misra (Editor)

THE RIGHT TO INFORMATION ACT 2005
A Handbook
Sudhir Naib

GLOBALIZATION AND DEVELOPMENT
A Handbook of New Perspectives (OIP)
Ashwini Deshpande (Editor)

HANDBOOK OF MUSLIMS IN INDIA
Empirical and Policy Perspectives
Rakesh Basant and Abusaleh Shariff (Editors)

HANDBOOK OF ENVIRONMENTAL ECONOMICS IN INDIA
Kanchan Chopra and Vikram Dayal (Editors)

HANDBOOK OF AGRICULTURE IN INDIA (OIP)
Shovan Ray (Editor)

HANDBOOK OF ENVIRONMENTAL LAW
P.B. Sahasranaman

HANDBOOK OF LAW, WOMEN, AND EMPLOYMENT
Policies, Issues, Legislation, and Case Law
Surinder Mediratta

HANDBOOK OF HUMAN DEVELOPMENT
Concepts, Measures, and Policies
Sakiko Fukuda-Parr and A.K. Shiva Kumar (Editors)

HANDBOOK OF ENVIRONMENTAL DECISION MAKING IN INDIA
An EIA Model
O.V. Nandimath

HANDBOOK OF URBANIZATION IN INDIA (SECOND EDITION) (OIP)
K.C. Shivaramakrishnan, Amitabh Kundu, and B.N. Singh

MAKING NEWS
Handbook of the Media in Contemporary India (OIP)
Uday Sahay (Editor)

HANDBOOK OF INDIAN SOCIOLOGY (OIP)
Veena Das (Editor)

MANAGING BUSINESS IN THE 21ST CENTURY
A Handbook (OIP)
Anindya Sen and P.K. Sett (Editors)

The Oxford Handbook of The Indian Economy in the 21st Century

Understanding the Inherent Dynamism

Edited by
ASHIMA GOYAL

OXFORD
UNIVERSITY PRESS

OXFORD
UNIVERSITY PRESS

Oxford University Press is a department of the University of Oxford. It furthers the University's objective of excellence in research, scholarship, and education by publishing worldwide. Oxford is a registered trademark of Oxford University Press in the UK and in certain other countries

Published in India by
Oxford University Press
22 Workspace, 2nd Floor, 1/22 Asaf Ali Road, New Delhi 110002, India

First Edition published in 2014
Digitally Printed in 2023

ISBN-13: 978-0-19-809753-2
ISBN-10: 0-19-809753-0

Typeset in 10.5/13.2 Minion Pro
by Excellent Laser Typesetters, Pitampura, Delhi 110 034
Printed at Manipal Technologies Limited, Manipal

For Kinara, and other children of India,
who will inherit the 21st Century

Contents

III. THE OPEN ECONOMY

IV. INCLUSION: EQUALITY AND OPPORTUNITY

V. GOVERNANCE

VIII. FACTORS: TECHNOLOGY, LABOUR, FINANCE

Tables and Figures

Tables

Figures

Foreword

This collection represents a substantial contribution to the scholarship on the Indian economy. It is unique in several respects. I have not seen any other book on the Indian economy in recent years which deals with such a wide variety of issues which have an impact on India's future in the 21st century, including governance, corruption, politics in a federal setting, social issues such as caste and gender, as well as urban informal and unorganized sectors in rural India. The focus on dynamism and the constraints that arise in the process of change also gives this book a fresh perspective.

I would recommend this book as an essential reading for all those, in India and abroad, who are interested in India's economic prospects. The volume is very educative and should also be a good resource for those working on, studying and designing policies in India. It is written in a largely non-technical and therefore accessible style. Being non-ideological and fact-based makes it extremely well rooted in context and better abled to assess several unique and puzzling features of India's reform path.

Several important issues covered in the Handbook, such as new technologies, innovation, and detailed analysis of governance and institutions are also not available in any of the current collections on the Indian economy. Deeper analysis of India's political and economic institutions in these and other areas is necessary to understand the failures of governance. As the introduction argues, since India started with universal franchise, Indian political institutions were highly inclusive. But caste and communal divides, and discretionary doles to public at state expense, could be used to create vote banks. Together with large ministerial powers to allocate public resources without adequate accountability, and an inherited top-down bureaucratic structure, the so-called 'inclusion' of the poor in development plans did not lead to delivery of uniform level of high quality public services through the country.

Persistent poverty encouraged political fragmentation and a subsidy culture to maintain vote banks. But post-reform higher growth, judicial and NGO activism, are making the failures of governance clear. Pressures are building for institutional change to address these bottlenecks. The analysis of the failure of governance in several critical areas, of vital importance to the people, contained in this Handbook, with essays from highly distinguished academics and public intellectuals will definitely contribute to these pressures. Let us hope that a maturing democracy like ours will, over time, deliver the inclusive economic institutions required to support catch-up growth.

New Delhi
4 July 2013

BIMAL JALAN

PREFACE

The concept of this book took shape in late 2011. Even as we set about studying the roots of India's dynamism, the economy itself gasped, heaved, bounced, and floundered. Given the long years of disappointing performance, many sceptics saw this as a return to reality.

But moderation in growth made an analysis of the foundations of dynamism all the more relevant. Careful research-based inputs from the many contributors paint a picture of transformative changes too substantial to be reversed, and a process set in motion that has its own logic. States now compete, offering different development models. But research also brought out Indian exceptionalism, and how easier external reforms had been an excuse to neglect essential domestic reform. This manifested in fresh problems such as sticky inflation and governance failures, calling for deeper new analysis in moving on, as the book does, from underdevelopment and reforms to dynamic change and constraints that emerge in the process.

Since it was envisaged as a handbook, it had to have comprehensive, in-depth, and forward-looking analysis of essential aspects to give it lasting value. Conceptual clarity had to go together with knowledge of contextual detail. This meant orchestrating a large number of authors, all established experts in their fields, who were also independent and non-ideological. It was a wonderful experience to discover the depth and breadth of commitment to such fact-based research in India, both inside and outside the country, and the willingness to cooperate in producing a pure public good. Or perhaps it was just the challenge of Indian complexity that triggered such impressive participation.

Reading a more diverse set of papers was a great learning experience for me, as I am sure it will be for the reader. The broader coverage helped to extract the deeper institutional features driving change. The theme of political inclusion that was yet to lead fully to economic inclusion and empowerment, set in the introduction, was found to play out in many different areas of the economy. Indian democracy was messy, but it was deepening steadily, and developing the necessary institutions. It was like finding a thread that unraveled much of the complexity.

The authors, with very few exceptions, graciously accepted strict deadlines, comments and revisions, despite their packed schedules. The author-set was large enough to draw interesting generalizations. Faculty in management institutions tended to believe what they taught, and planned their time and commitments well. But those they taught, and who were now in industry, were often too busy to follow precepts they had learnt. (Some) pure academics tended to be superbly creative with promises also. Last-minute dropouts did create gaps. Unforeseen delays occurred but were an opportunity to find substitutes with a greater interest in the project, and that ended up strengthening the handbook.

A researcher has perforce to spend much time working alone. A major discovery from a project like this is finding the strong community to which one belongs, and which co-creates in so many ways. It is like Midnight's Children finding a medium through which they can converse.

The community created was not merely the authors, but so many who contributed in diverse ways. I am grateful to Jugnu Ansari, Ravi Anshuma, Sanchit Arora, Leslie Armijo, P.G. Babu, Mousumi Das, Errol D'souza, Sandhya Garg, Saurabh Ghosh, Rekha Jain, Raghbendra Jha, Nirupam Mehrotra, Arup Mitra, Jiban Mukhopadhyay, Puran Mongia, Sripad Motiram, Rahul Mukherji, Sudipto Mundle, Sudha Narayanan, Rama Pal, Ramkishen Rajan, K.V. Ramaswamy, Sudhakar Reddy, Y.V. Reddy, Chandrashekhar S., Jayati Sarkar, Kunal Sen, S.P. Sharma, Sanjay Singh, Nisha Taneja, Pushpa Trivedi, and C. Veeramani who read and commented on parts of the manuscript. Reshma Aguiar and Vaishnavi provided excellent support in the correspondence and organization of material.

There is a rich debate in India on the process it is going through, to which academic and industry associations, think tanks, the press and other media contribute. Occasional participation in this was a good source of insights for me, as was participation in government and other committees. IGIDR itself provides the facilities, time, space and independence that make this kind of work possible. All those associated with setting IGIDR up and keeping it going deserve warm thanks.

I also wish to thank the team at OUP for sparking my interest in the project, their commitment to the project and the time and energy required to bring the project to fruition.

And last but not the least I thank my family for giving me the emotional anchor, the unstinting support, and the necessary distraction. Just in this period, an amazing expansion to the family added two generations, giving much joy but forcing me to work efficiently, and try to make every moment count.

INTRODUCTION AND OVERVIEW

ASHIMA GOYAL

The Book's Approach

The background for the book is India's ongoing liberalizing reforms. What worked and why, and the likely future path, are the vital issues that it addresses. Sustained high growth has delivered an almost 2 trillion dollar economy and transformed the lives of a billion people. Even so, analysis is often backward looking and has yet to fully make the transition from the economics of under development to that of an emerging market (EM).[1] High growth and poverty are mentioned together in a country viewed as mired in many problems and with malfunctioning institutions so that only external factors can make a difference. But then both the dynamism and the difficulties that the economy is facing remain a mystery. For example, trend growth rates were higher but their volatility created a new puzzle. This collection gives the idea of change and dynamism at the centre stage. Then the chances of being trapped in dated habits of thought are reduced, although the bottlenecks that emerge as change occurs can also be analysed.

There is also analysis at the other extreme, which treats the economy as fully developed so that it just has to copy advanced economy practices. But

[1] As the economy left behind the Hindu rate of growth, interest and research on it multiplied. Some recent collections of independent scholarly work on India are Basu (2011), Basu and Maertens (2010), Ghate (2012), Goyal (2012a), Jha (2011) and successive *India Development Reports* from Indira Gandhi Institute of Development Research (IGIDR). Balakrishnan (2011) highlights interventions that worked. Panagariya's (2008) book on India also analyses post-reforms dynamism in India.

care is warranted since the context is important. India was always open to international ideas, although it was a closed economy for a long time. It may have been acceptance of inappropriate ideas that doomed it to years of stagnation. The import-substituting big-push model of development adopted at the time of Independence was the frontier knowledge of the time. The Bombay School of Economics, which supported market-led growth much before markets became fashionable, was neglected. As a strong domestic lobby supporting a closed economy and government-led growth formed, the democratic consensus required for change was slow to develop. But the change in global ideas and obvious domestic stagnation eventually led to liberalizing reforms. Since over reaction could occur, the global financial crisis (GFC) was a timely reminder of the flaws of unregulated markets.

Ideological positions tend to resist learning—so assessment of current and future liberalizing reforms often continues to be dogmatic. But countries that had the fastest sustained rate of growth followed a pragmatic reform path suited to context rather than a pure-market or government-led approach.[2] Pragmatic reforms require a deep knowledge of the economy and careful fact-based research. Rather than a standard reform path, knowledge of specific issues is required. This is what the book draws on and puts together. The large body of Indian scholars and experts contributing to the book has balanced views, a deep understanding of India, and appropriate frameworks of analysis, subjected to rigorous testing.

Textbooks study equilibria but dynamics are rarely equilibrium phenomena. A rapidly transforming economy offers an opportunity to study out of equilibrium behaviour but to make full use of it, sometimes even to arrive at the correct questions, perspectives of policymakers and market participants are helpful. The book also draws on these. Inclusion and respect for diversity is as important in studying an economy as it is for the economy itself. Research and facts are very important for policy, but the questions asked must be relevant and diverse approaches should be used. Academic silos and analytical uniformity were partly responsible for a failure to understand the risks that led to the GFC.[3]

[2] Srinivasan (2011) presents arguments that favour the first and Bhaduri (2010) argues the case for the second. Even so, theirs are sophisticated and nuanced analyses. The policy dialogue tends to take more simplified and extreme positions.

[3] For example, as formal models and doctorates in economics came to dominate the Bank of England, details of the financial market's functioning came to be regarded as unfashionable, so relevant knowledge was lost (Tett 2012).

While the book reports on a large body of relevant research, brings readers to research frontiers and tells them what more to read, the focus on dynamism means that it often leaves readers with new questions requiring further research. So a researcher is both informed and equipped for future work. An economy as complex as India has to be approached from different angles. Hence, the book offers a wide range of relevant topics, including those on the political economy and social structure. Often there are multiple approaches to a topic. Even so, the book differs from a standard collection of essays in being more comprehensive and in a deeper, research-based analysis of issues. This makes it a good source to understand the interplay between dynamism and constraints in the specific Indian situation.

Some of the interesting paradoxes that the book explores include labour laws and infrastructure, which were said to restrain manufacturing and exports, but both the latter did well in some respects, although services dominated in a non-standard growth pattern. Interest groups were said to be forcing a low-level trap, based on handouts, but a state like Bihar broke out in one of the fastest rates of growth. Inflation was said to be a sign of overheating, requiring a reduction in demand, but as demand cuts reduced growth and inflation remained sticky, the role of structural features and the importance of the agricultural supply response became clear. High government debt and deficits are said to raise risks but high potential revenue growth gives India an advantage compared to many post-GFC developed countries. The financial sector was said to be backward but proved more stable than many advanced international centres. The country was said to be inured to corruption but then the remarkable countrywide protests against it are puzzling, and show real change is possible.

Examining these and other issues contributes to a finer understanding of the interaction between domestic strengths, external opportunities, and government interventions, helping in identifying feasible interventions that work. A common insight from a number of chapters is that while obvious controls may have gone, empowerment through genuine decentralization is still a work-in-progress. Inclusive ground-level institutions are the key to future progress. There are some good initiatives, but much remains to be done.

Dynamism in India

After stagnating for much of the post-Independence period, India has shown considerable dynamism in processes and outcomes since the mid-1980s.[4] As the inefficiencies and stasis of the control regime became obvious, the requisite critical mass of domestic opinion began to support change.[5] Some reforms were implemented in the 1970s and the 1980s. But the crisis of 1991, when the nation had to borrow from the International Monetary Fund (IMF), allowed substantial reduction of external controls. Indian reforms were in the direction of the standard Washington consensus of 'stabilize, privatize and liberalize', but differed in degree. The reforms' major successes were sectors with some opening-out and competition. Liberated private energies had incentives to act upon and standards to reach. Absolute poverty fell but inadequate inclusion meant that the benefits did not spread widely, and inequality increased.

The IMF was repaid early (1994) and the country was free to design its own path. This turned out to be an advantage. A series of emerging market crises in the 1990s led to a rethink on the consensus itself. It became clear that financial liberalization should be cautious and follow crisis proofing; better regulation should maintain yet restrain competition; and institutions should support productive inclusion in second-generation reforms. Extreme versions of the view that liberalizing reforms alone drove Indian growth, regard domestic institutions as so dysfunctional that only external forces can make a difference. But over dependence on external drivers also creates risk, and a large country like India cannot be driven only by external factors.

Moreover, research shows that successful developers did not necessarily implement any variant of the consensus. The Spence Commission (2008) examined 13 economies, which, in the period after 1950, grew at above 7 per cent for more than 25 years. Of these, 9 were from Asia. Their common characteristics included openness, macroeconomic stability, high saving and investment rates, and market allocation of resources. Governments were capable—pragmatic and flexible—rather than ideological. While willing to intervene in markets to promote exports through industrial policies and to manage exchange rates (with the use of selected capital controls and reserve accumulation), they were flexible enough not to get locked into distorting policies, to anticipate and change policies as required for growth. Resource mobility and urbanization were supported.

[4] This section draws on Goyal (2013). Some of these ideas were presented at a CDS-NMML conference in New Delhi in 2012. I thank my discussant E. Shridharan and other participants for very useful discussions.

[5] At a 2011 Skoch function, to felicitate his contributions to reforms, Montek Singh Ahluwalia named his many superiors in government who supported reforms and said that without them, he would not have dared to act.

Public investment in infrastructure accounted for 5 to 7 per cent of the gross domestic product (GDP) or more. Specific contextual interventions and the microeconomic incentives created were important. External drivers alone did not create growth. And openness did not imply blind application of market-friendly reforms.

After crossing a minimum threshold, normally low-income countries grow rapidly, provided they have the flexibilities mentioned earlier. China had its fastest rate of growth after its GDP per capita in purchasing power parity (PPP) terms crossed US$ 1,747 in 1992. Japan's and the US's experience were similar. India crossed US$ 1,800 in 1999. Both India and China have 1 billion plus population, both had similar low per capita incomes when they followed a strategy of closed government-led import substitution, yet India's opening-out came about 10 years after China. So China's experience offers useful pointers for India's future path.

Although India persisted on an increasingly inappropriate path for a long time, certain strengths were built up. For example, its skilled English-educated labour allowed it to catch the outsourcing wave. The planning process did create a diverse economy—a major current strength that the reforms enhanced. They added export demand to strong domestic demand as some manufacturing became globally competitive. The changes added up to a critical mass. Networks of markets and associations became dense, reducing transaction costs, as learning occurred and quality improved. It was no longer only the government undertaking initiatives for society. Non-governmental organizations (NGOs) and corporates became active as well.[6] Other positive factors include the demographic profile and investment in infrastructure that reached 7 per cent of GDP with plans to take it up to 9 per cent. So India should have many years of robust catch-up growth left. But compared to China's performance, India's catch-up growth has been volatile. Why?

Both countries followed pragmatic policies far from standard reform prescriptions. Their gradual growth-oriented approaches gave the flexibility to respond to outcomes—like the conscious Chinese strategy of 'crossing the river while feeling the stones'. For example, the public sector could shrink as the private grew, thus avoiding the wrenching social tensions of the sudden Russian privatization. Both countries continued with capital account controls, but since China had little domestic industry

[6] See Bhattacharya (2012) for private initiatives based on dynamic social responsibility and business model that are improving the delivery of essential services such as water and health, which the government has failed to provide.

or trade unions, foreign direct investment (FDI) could drive its opening and allow it to focus on manufacturing exports. Since India had more private local industry, and rigid labour laws, some restrictions remained on FDI. The largest flows it attracted were foreign portfolio inflows (FPIs) that contributed to the development and reform of capital markets and financial services, in which it had a comparative advantage. Liberalization favoured equity over debt flows—FPIs may be volatile but they are at least risk-sharing, so that outflows during adverse shocks are reduced.

Macroeconomic Policy

Openness, despite its contribution to diversification and catch-up, was also a source of shocks—the reform years saw major oil and food price shocks, the East Asian crisis, and the GFC. Risk-on, risk-off portfolio flows, with volatility due to external factors, made financing the current account deficit difficult. Catch-up growth is normally faster than industrial country growth but it only defines a potential or trend growth rate. Savings generally rise with growth as firms get cash rich and tax revenues boom. China's savings rate reached the 50s. India's savings rate reached the 30s, and, together with an incremental capital–output ratio of 4, and a sustainable balance of payments current account deficit (CAD) of 3 per cent, peak savings defined a potential growth rate of 9 to 10 per cent.[7] Annual entrants to the labour force and the transition to higher productivity jobs provided required labour inputs. But counter-cyclical macroeconomic policy had to maintain the actual rate of growth in the face of shocks, even while reforms continued to sustain the potential rate. Policy failures on the supply side and in smoothing shocks explain why growth fell below potential, and inflation rose, even after the threshold per capita level was crossed (Goyal and Arora 2012).

Critical bottlenecks emerged because the policy did not address structural features, such as improving agricultural productivity and marketing, and facilitating the removal of infrastructural constraints. As a consequence, given the high share of food consumption, food inflation raised wages and general inflation. The dominant share of employment continued to be in low-productivity rural and informal sectors where wages are sensitive to food inflation. Wages, salaries, and subsidies dominated government spending. This also fell more on non-traded goods and sustained

[7] With a CAD of 3 per cent, US$ 250 billion could come from foreign savings.

the demand for food. But in this sector, structural rigidities prevented an expansion of supply, while monetary tightening reduced demand and raised costs for the industry. Poor governance also raised these costs. High inflation without financial inflation hedges increased the demand for gold imports and widened CAD to unsustainable levels as savings in financial assets fell.

Chinese domestic savings were high and the government could leverage these for large infrastructure spending from the 1990s. This constituted a large fiscal stimulus that maintained Chinese growth during and after the GFC. A country of 1 billion plus, undergoing rapid catch-up growth, requires infrastructure. India, which is 10 years behind China, was expected to go into a similar infrastructure cycle in the 2000s.

But low returns on past government investments and many continuing populist schemes left the government with positive deficits and a debt–GDP ratio which was not low. The fiscal consolidation necessary to reassure mobile capital in a more open economy was achieved through a reduction in public investment all through the first decade of reforms, especially since the reduction of import tariffs reduced the tax–GDP ratio. The government borrowed even for consumption—there was a revenue as well as a fiscal deficit. The neglect of investment in infrastructure further raised costs and created bottlenecks for private endeavours.

When the private sector did not adequately fill the gap and infrastructure constraints became pressing, the government did pursue public–private partnerships more actively in infrastructure. Some tax reforms raised revenue but innovative forms of private participation and financing were still required to get around the finance constraint. Poor financial intermediation of savings, despite two decades of reforms, prevented high domestic savings from funding infrastructure.

Although there are ambitious plans to raise spending on infrastructure to 1 trillion dollars over the Twelfth Plan (2012–17), more than half of this will have to come from the private sector. The private sector did participate and targets were exceeded through the boom years, but investment collapsed below target in 2009–10, helping precipitate an overall slowdown. The cause was policy inconsistency and a failure of the government apparatus to gear up for providing the clearances required. The new scale of investment exceeded government capacity. Private participation was difficult without a drastic improvement in procedures, since delays impact private balance sheets.

Political constraints may explain the Indian government's neglect of investment and governance while relying on foreign inflows to continue subsidies in the post-reforms period. Inadequate policies are followed because of political considerations, not out of ignorance. Poor governance and failures in the education system and in healthcare delivery may be symptoms of deeper issues that must first be resolved.

Institutions

Studies of the industrial revolution have shown the importance of institutions for transformations into modern economies (Ashton 1948; North 1982; North and Weingast 1989). Acemoglu and Robinson (2012) (henceforth AR) argue that since inclusive institutions generate creative destruction and innovation that sustain wealth, such institutions create the best conditions for the success of a nation. The British, however, left India with institutions whose aim was extraction, not public service. But in their geography-based argument, extractive institutions were built when colonial powers did not want to settle in a country because of poor climate. But the British did stay in India for hundreds of years and built courts, railways, and universities.

It was probably the desire for strong central control of heterogeneous provinces, in a large country, that led them to establish a centralized Indian civil service which later became the Indian Administrative Services. No other country has such a service. It retains the superiority and distance of the ruling elites. Together with multiple levels of government and agencies, it lowers accountability to the local populace.

In addition, the prevailing philosophy of economic controls allowed the government to use and further increase the extractive powers of the institutions they inherited. As AR point out, newcomers to power face few constraints in maintaining extractive institutions for gain. In India, top-down planning aided such a process even though political institutions adopted at Independence were highly inclusive.

Britain itself had a very slow and careful extension of suffrage but India started with universal suffrage. In a poor populous democracy, inclusion and removing poverty were always political slogans. But other features, such as a large share of illiterate voters, and voting based on caste, religion, and region, prevented real inclusion. The possibility of creating political vote blocks in a heterogeneous electorate, without thick democracy to eliminate corrupt practices, led to vote buying and populist policies targeting specific groups. Such state-led redistribution schemes also created opportunities for personal enrichment of lower-level politicians and bureaucrats, and this soon became the main motive, with funding the political parties as the minor aim.

Since the origin and rationale of the caste system was economic, it was widely expected to die out with modern economic development (see Gupta 2000 and Béteille 2008). The caste system had changed through the ages in response to economic pressures. But in post-Independence stagnation, caste-based policies for creating vote banks sustained the caste system. Extractive institutions that lowered growth also strengthened castes.[8] Thus, caste allowed politicians to get away with stagnation, and stagnation further strengthened caste, but it was now a political identity and not the historical system of economic organization.[9]

Dominant development ideas aggravated the effect of the heterogeneous electorate. Rath (2012) argues that due to the focus on planning, the government even persuaded a constitutional body, charged with making grants-in-aid to bring states to a uniform level of public services, to cede grant-making powers to the Planning Commission. But the Planning Commission made transfers according to plans to build industry, thus taking attention away from general public services for the average citizen, on which the first Finance Commission had focused. Once established, the planning structure persisted and continued to dominate even in a market-led economy. The disempowerment of the average citizen is a generic pattern discovered in many different areas throughout the book.

A state must be strong to be effective, but for it to create wealth for society as a whole, inclusive institutions must temper its power. Although strong political centralization allowed the Chinese state to coordinate resources for growth, AR expect that the blocks, which a dominant state puts on innovation, for fear of loss of power, will eventually limit such growth.

Even if catch-up is successful, there is the problem of sustaining growth after that. World Bank studies, based on the PPP method, characterize low income countries as those with a per capita Gross National Income

[8] There are signs that a higher post-reforms growth is reducing caste distinctions. Kapur et al. (2010) found that lower castes were now eating ritual upper caste foods in festivals in the villages that they studied. Prasad and Kamble (2012) report on research that finds dalits succeed most in new and caste-neutral occupations—reform opportunities suit dalit entrepreneurs. For example, they found that Delhi's Azadpur fruit and vegetable mandi did not have a single dalit *adhatiya* or middleman, since traditional castes dominate these occupations.

[9] Dipankar Gupta made the latter point. I thank him and Satish Deshpande for a useful discussion on this topic.

(GNI) of less than US$ 975 in PPP terms. In the lower-middle-income group GNI lies between US$ 976 and 3,855; in the upper-middle-income group it is between US$ 3,856 and US$ 11,905. Above that are the high-income groups. Once a country crosses into the upper-middle-income group, a number of studies show that growth rates tend to decline by about 2 percentage points. This threshold varies between US$ 7,000 and 17,000. There is a 50 per cent chance that a middle-income country will stay in that group, caught in the 'middle income trap'. By 2015, China is expected to cross the US$ 17,000 mark.[10] Most analysts expect a slowdown in its rate of growth. A slowdown comes from a fall in productivity growth and is less in more open economies with higher consumption shares.

Democratic pressures may restrain the growth rate sometimes, but if they strengthen institutions and competition, they will help it eventually escape the middle-income trap. But inclusive economic institutions must raise the productivity of the average Indian citizen even as they release creativity and innovation. Interests were not the primary cause of Indian stagnation.[11] The ideas of government control and structural aspects, such as castes, strengthened extractive institutions. Only as internal political and external pressures gradually change laws and make economic institutions more oriented towards the productivity of the many, can substantial change occur. The real dynamism that the Indian economy is showing is the beginning of this process.

Inclusive Economic Institutions

It is useful to examine the historical process of building inclusive economic institutions in the UK in order to benchmark changes in Indian institutions. UK succeeded in economic inclusion because diverse political groupings had emerged, such as upwardly mobile commercial farmers, a variety of manufacturers, and Atlantic traders. There was a history of parliaments, rule of law, and power sharing that had already weakened absolute power. By the standards of the time, the Parliament empowered a broad and strong coalition against Stuart absolutism. The rule of law removes the special privileges that elites routinely enjoy, prevents illegal activities by the government, and safeguards rights that apply equally to all. In this it differs from much of history.

[10] This literature is surveyed in Cai (2012). For a discussion of the minimum threshold, see Goyal (2004, 2001).

[11] Bardhan (1984) first made the argument that the multiple interests that the government had to placate kept Indian growth low.

More inclusive political institutions made economic institutions more inclusive and eventually led to the industrial revolution. The Parliament could be petitioned and was likely to implement petitions that collected many signatures. Domestic monopolies were abolished in 1640. After 1688, the Parliament strengthened property rights eroded under the Stuarts. Obscure property rights were simplified and made secure, encouraging private participation in infrastructure building.[12] The Parliament prevented arbitrary taking away of rights. It began to promote manufacturing, rather than taxing and restricting it. The hated 'hearth tax' (AR: 194), which fell largely on industry, was abolished in 1689. New parliamentarians from Manchester and Birmingham wanted cheap food and low wages. So the Corn Laws, which banned grain import, kept prices high, and benefited large landowners, were repealed in 1846.

The education system was made more accessible to the masses. The Education Act of 1870 made the government responsible for the systematic provision of universal education, made free of charge in 1891. The school-leaving age was raised and special provisions were made for children from poor families. The Liberal Party, in the early years of the twentieth century, began providing public services, such as health and unemployment insurance, government-financed pensions, and minimum wages. As a result, taxes rose many times and fell more on the wealthy.

The consequences of inclusive economic institutions are competitive entry, low broad-based taxes, absence of arbitrariness in policy, and public services that enhance human capital equitably. Can latecomers accomplish all this faster? Leaders can choose to implement some of these policy sets early. For example, many Asian countries focused on primary education even at low per capita income levels. This is partly responsible for high Chinese growth.

Institutions can change at a critical juncture that disrupts the existing economic or political balance. The change can be in the direction of more extraction or more inclusion. Although historical accidents shape institutional trajectories, the emergence and empowerment of broad and diverse interests including merchants and businessmen who can benefit from creative destruction, also influences the direction taken. Inclusive ground conditions raise the probability that the path taken will be in the right direction. Diverse interests prevent any one group from usurping power. Even in the absence of leaders, broad supportive interests can deliver

[12] Property rights are multidimensional. Unclear definitions that limit certain kinds of commercial activities are illustrated by problems in conversion of agricultural land to industrial purposes in India.

the required change (AR). Institutions are also social norms or expected patterns of behaviour, which are subject to, especially rapid change.

Economic Inclusion in India

This process of inclusive political institutions leading to inclusive economic institutions, which allows productivity to rise, remains inadequate in India. Inclusion was always a slogan and strategies for inclusion were consciously adopted even as reforms were implemented. Narasimha Rao made this clear in a speech in 1992, pointing out that India would follow a middle path between free markets and state interventions—markets would be freed but anti-poverty alleviation and welfare measures would be intensified. However, leakage-prone transfers that enriched support groups and were a source of political funding continued to dominate. Poor governance enervated delivery of the public services necessary to empower the masses, while the organization of administration, which reported to the Centre, vitiated accountability. Populist fixing of user charges in an era of cost shocks contributed to deterioration in the quality of public services, while forced private provision of these services made the economy high cost (Goyal 1999).

But the country has for long had the rule of law and private property even though implementation and systems remain inadequate. As the executive failed to deliver good governance, there was increasing court activism. For example, the orders of the Supreme Court (SC) sought to improve air quality in New Delhi and to investigate corruption in the allocation of natural resources. Legal changes also furthered more inclusion. NGOs and the middle class acquired clout through the mechanism of public interest litigations (PILs) and the Right to Information (RTI)[13] Act. The Right to Education Act was part of more rights-based activism. Fiscal Responsibility and Budget Management (FRBM) legislation restrained the government's ability to spend.

Popular protest against corruption sought to reduce the government's discretion over resources—a major source of kickbacks. Independent constitutional bodies, such as the Election Commission, the Finance Commission, and the Controller and Auditor General (CAG), became more active in preventing misuse of political power. This deepening of horizontal democracy, beyond just elections, is pushing for better governance.

[13] Organizations, such as Association for Democratic Reform and Praja, are getting politicians to disclose their assets and police records. They make report cards on elected representatives' performance.

The coalition that gained from government-led redistribution dominated for a long time because of heterogeneity and poverty. But course corrections did occur in critical junctures, such as the crises in 1991. Opening out perhaps occurred as the forces that gained from growth strengthened, and reforms strengthened them further.

So, India, in 2013, met many of the ground conditions identified for institutional change, including pluralism of interests, a vibrant business class, and gradualism of reforms. The reforms made the government more business-friendly although the balance between extraction of revenue and encouraging business growth is yet to be found. Markets that induce a virtuous cycle of more efficient allocation of resources, acquisition of education and skills, and technological innovations, are all there. As a result, economic institutions are also slowly becoming more inclusive.

New opportunities created by growth are available to more people. So demands for better public services in health, education, and infrastructure rise since these facilitate use of the opportunities. These pressures make 'active inclusion', defined as inclusion which creates conditions for many to contribute to and participate in growth (Goyal 2012b), more acceptable politically. Government intervention remains essential, since there are externalities that limit private investment. But the intervention should improve public services, thus increasing rewards to work. This is uniquely suited to the Indian catch-up growth and increasingly youthful demographic profile, while pure transfers may be necessary for the shrinking group of persistent poor.

Since public investment is now too low to be further cut, the way towards fiscal consolidation is organizational efficiency and better targeting and composition of subsidies. Technology-enabled direct distribution to the poor has the potential to reduce leakages, and free resources for more public goods. An expanding cake can accommodate more claims, but without the correct interventions, inequality can rise with growth. China reached Latin American levels of inequality starting from a system without divergence in private wealth. Democratic pressures for inclusive growth may help India avoid such an outcome if that inclusion becomes effective.

Governance and Public Service Delivery

Restructuring of the government administration is long overdue and is essential for better public services. Poor quality of basic public goods, such as air and water quality are responsible for poor health and nutrition outcomes. These, together with poor infrastructure and harassment in permissions, licences, and certifications, hinder private activity.

Successive expenditure reform commissions have made useful suggestions for reorganizing and reducing overlaps, conflicts, and delays associated with multiple agencies and establishing clear accountability. These have been accepted by the Cabinet but not implemented. As the chapters in the section on governance bring out, some of the multiplicity came from superimposing a centralized planning structure on a constitutional structure. There was a tendency to start new programmes and create new bodies without a clean exit from old ones.

Problems with infrastructure clearances since 2009 highlight the bottlenecks that multiple agencies create. Discretion in natural resource allocation and acquisition led to allegations of corruption and a backlash from civil society, while lack of consistency and clarity in policy discouraged investment. Many laws, unchanged since colonial times, give too much power to the administration. Since no one can follow unreasonable laws, everyone can be found guilty, giving a tool to the corrupt or unreasonable official to extort. But ill-defined laws victimize administrators themselves. For example, a clause in the Prevention of Corruption Act (1988) defines criminal misconduct by a public servant to include obtaining a pecuniary advantage from anyone where no public interest is involved. Ensuring this is difficult in a market economy. All these laws need to be re-drafted. Clearer responsibilities will enhance outcomes and reputations of public servants.

Jalan (2013) points out, that ministries ballooned in the era of coalition governments in order to give coalition partners a share in the spoils of government. He suggests a simple systemic reform that will reduce the power of small parties to demand a ransom—extend the anti-defection bill from individuals to parties. So if a party leaves a government in midstream, its seats will be up for re-election.

The most critical Indian policy initiatives require the centre and the states to coordinate well together. Agriculture, health, education, policing, and making India one market are all on the concurrent list of the Constitution. Excessive centralization under the British[14] was initially strengthened due to concerns about national integration. The Constitution mandated an inter-state Council but a strong central government in

[14] The centralized federalism of the British 1935 Government of India Act was largely adopted in the Indian Constitution (Granville 2002).

the early years and the emphasis on planning denied it any weight. As the political system fragmented and regional parties came up, the states obtained more political freedom, but coordination between the centre and the states became very poor. Tax reforms, such as the Goods and Services Tax (GST) conducive to an integrated market, are held up for lack of support by some big consumer states who fear they will lose revenue.

Decentralization needed to be strengthened in the Constitution, and this was attempted with the seventy-third and seventy-fourth amendments on direct local-level democracy in the 1990s, but implementation remains uneven with some states able to use clauses to resist effective devolution of funds, functions, and functionaries to local bodies. Central schemes that created parallel bodies also reduced funds available for such devolution. Local capacity-building, standardized systems, awareness, and monitoring are also required for responsiveness to local needs while avoiding capture by local elites.

Policymakers at the centre focused more on opening up, because this was something they could do without persuading the states to come along. Even so, it was required because India was too closed an economy. But, after 2011, foreign inflows (FIs) slowed down because of domestic policy bottlenecks as well as external risks. FIs will not keep coming in unless domestic supply bottlenecks are removed. So the difficult task of working with the states to improve the supply side has to receive priority. These are examples of the emerging bottlenecks that nations that were able to sustain growth successfully addressed. FIs can be a risky short-term palliative for required domestic reforms. The report of the financial sector legislative reform commission, which seeks to give more power to politicians to liberalize FIs, could have this effect. Politicians have a short-term horizon.

There are some good recent initiatives, however. Recent Finance Commissions' incentives have improved state finances and could be extended to other Planning Commission and central transfers. International experience shows that discipline plus transfers work in a federal structure to improve public services while preventing budgetary indiscipline. The 2012 restructuring of large and recurring state electricity distribution companies' (discoms') debt has this combination and may therefore improve their functioning. Another strategy that has worked is through enabling policies at the centre that encourage yardstick competition in the states. As some states allow FDI in retail, labour laws may be changed and power distribution may be reformed to do better, inspiring others to follow. This happened with the adoption of value added tax (VAT). As states that implemented it gained revenue, others followed. No one wants to be left behind. But dialogue must also complement incentives, for example, to get agreement on GST. Regular meetings should evolve new policy initiatives, not just communicate a policy decision.

Better governance is helping state governments get re-elected. An increasingly aware electorate will reward the centre for incentivizing better public services. Civil society has to push awareness on these issues, not lobby for special schemes. Politicians tend to act only when their own interests are involved. With this essential realignment of interests, more competition, better institutions, and incentive structures can act together resulting in effective 'active' inclusion.

Preventing Extortion and Creating Inclusion: Telecom

As growth increases their value, discretion in the allocation of natural resources becomes a major source of corruption and extortion. The cellular mobile story illustrates the problems and how institutions evolved, with some setbacks, to address the issues. Inclusive economic institutions limit extortion through either public taxation or private corruption.

Mobile telephony became a major success story after 2000, when license fee was lowered. In 1992, private operators were allowed and licenses were granted over 1994–5. Foreign partners brought in the latest technology. The government made sure that there was competition by allotting licenses to more than one provider in a circle. But it was after the Telecom Regulatory Authority of India (TRAI), set up in 1997 and reconstituted in 2000, and a move from a fixed fee to a revenue-sharing model, that the sector really took off. This meant all the risk was not borne by firms, and the government's share depended on the profits made.

India moved from just 5 million telephone subscribers in 1991 to 37 million in 2001 and more than 900 million subscribers in 2012. Competition gave India one of the world's lowest tariffs, and millions of poor people benefited from inclusive innovations that mobiles made possible. Despite a decline in protection and competitive entry, many new businesses did very well.[15]

In 2008, minister A. Raja, a DMK coalition partner in the UPA government, who was given the remunerative telecom ministry, allocated more 2G (voice) mobile licenses at a low price on a first-come, first-served basis. When, in 2010, 3G (data and internet services) auctions raised

[15] Outcomes like these go against Kohli's (2012) argument that reforms were pro-business rather than pro-market. It is true, however, that poor business services handicap small businesses since they are more dependent on public goods.

large amounts, the government's auditor (CAG) alleged a huge loss to the exchequer from the 2G allocation. In 2012 the SC cancelled the old allocation and ordered new 2G auctions. But there was very little competitive bidding in the later auction rounds, which were held with a high reserve price, and the realization was much below expectations. This cast doubt on the CAG figure that had triggered a series of corruption allegations. The rollout of 3G services was also slow, as indebted companies pulled back.

The SC clarified, in response to a Presidential query, that resource allocation was a policy decision and therefore a prerogative of the executive. While auction was not essential, the allocation should be in the 'common good'. The SC could intervene if an allocation did not satisfy the criteria of 'fairness and non-arbitrariness',[16] as in the case of Raja's arbitrary allocations.

Industry will always lobby to minimize what it pays the government. But high upfront costs are passed on to consumers. Slow rollout reduces future revenue to the government, and affects the welfare of subscribers. Major gains from natural resources should go to the people in the shape of low prices for the products that they consume, not to companies or to the government.

The National Telecom Policy, 2012[17] recognized the potential of mobiles as 'an instrument of empowerment', facilitating a number of inclusive innovations. It laid down principles based on this to guide decisions for balancing the interests of consumers, service providers, and government revenue. A simpler and better-enabling policy regime can ride on technological developments in convergence to enable flexible private participation for the missing last mile connectivity and the development of a supporting ecosystem. Good broadband infrastructure and implementation is the key. Then cloud computing and cheap smartphones can multiply internet use in India, creating many externalities.

Auctions have the desirable property of removing the government's discretion in allotting natural resource. But they must not be designed to be revenue maximizing. A single-step auction-based allocation, with a low reserve price, and part of the payment to come from future royalties, could avoid both discretion in allocation and large upfront costs that reduce subsequent development. Adequate competition can ensure that the prices

[16] See news reports on the SC judgement, for example, *Times of India*, 28 September 2012.

[17] Uploaded on the Department of Telecommunications website, http://www.dot.gov.in/, in June 2012.

remain low and service quality improves, while a wary civil society and judiciary make corruption difficult.

As growth raised the value of natural resources and potential extortion the checks and balances of Indian democracy and a more-empowered public, exposed the corruption, held up the allocations, and lowered the growth rate. Institutions are responding in ways that are making extortion more difficult. Corrupt ministers have had to resign and face court cases. The price is worth paying as part of the process of building more robust, corruption-proof institutions and procedures, which may not happen in countries where power is absolute—the Bo Xilai case may have revealed only the tip of widespread corruption in China. But judicial activism can easily result in judicial over-reach, especially since the judiciary has no executive powers and little economic expertise, so the SC qualification was a useful validation of the constitutional separation of powers.

Reducing Monopoly: Agricultural Marketing

The telecom story illustrates governance issues as well as the importance of competition. Reducing monopoly is also a precondition for inclusive economic institutions. Monopoly in agricultural marketing has weakened agricultural supply response. The structure of government interventions in agriculture, established around the time of the major droughts in the mid-1960s, has continued, largely unchanged, since then. They were based on input subsidies, higher output prices supported by government procurement prices, and a monopoly to state marketing boards, to develop markets and to support procurement that fed a subsidized public distribution system (PDS). Together with the new green revolution technology, these initiatives led to a large rise in production, making the nation self-sufficient in food grain production.

Although the idea was to help farmers by developing markets that did not yet exist, production stagnated over time as monopolies developed and markets were segmented. The agricultural produce marketing committee (APMC) Acts do not allow transactions outside the market yard of regulated markets. Since market committees that lose from competition, issue licenses for trade, the conflict of interest prevents expansion of marketing options. Average mandated fees are around 10 per cent, although there is a range. Commission agents are said to be a source of political funding. Fees meant for developing infrastructure have been diverted—most markets do not have cold storage and grading facilities. Governance is poor, professionalism is lacking, and regular elections are not held for the APMCs—all this must change. Estimated value addition and commercial processing are both low.

Trade in food products suffers from other distortions. The Essential Commodities Act, enacted in 1955 in response to World War II scarcities, imposes limits on stocking food grains. State-level differential tax regimes, policies, and laws also artificially segment markets. Private traders require permits to transport food grains out of a state, or even a district. The National Permit System does not apply to trucks. Multiple clearances add to problems—environment laws and agricultural input interventions also sanction physical checks on trucks. The average time required to cross an inter-state border is two hours. Such checks are especially costly for perishable products. Adopting Goods and Services Tax (GST) will remove many of these irritants. Even without that, the Constitution allows market facilitating agreements between two or more states under Article 252.

Estimates from the government's own committees, of gains from harmonization and unification of these markets are large.[18] About 30–40 per cent of fruits and vegetables are said to be wasted. If this waste can be curtailed and transportation costs reduced, farmers will get higher prices even while consumers pay less. Incentives for production will improve. That food inflation accompanies higher recent agricultural growth rates suggests that the government's agricultural interventions need a rethink. With the rise in per capita incomes and more effective minimum wages, there is a diversification of the food basket. More demand for fruits and vegetables is making the PDS less relevant since it cannot cover all these. It was part of an intervention strategy, based on food grains, which, even in 2010, accounted for only 24 per cent of the food basket. It is general agricultural marketing that has to improve now. Rising productivity and employment in production of items, such as fruit, vegetables, and protein items, for which demand rises with incomes, is the way to achieve

[18] A large number of government committees and reports have addressed the issue. These include the report of a 2010 Commission on Centre–State Relations, a Draft National Competition Policy, Working Group of the Twelfth Five-year Plan on Agriculture Marketing Infrastructure (http://planningcommission.nic.in/aboutus/committee/wrkgrp12/agri/weg_rep_market.pdf; accessed in January 2013), an Inter-ministerial Group on Inflation (http://finmin.nic.in/workingpaper/IMG%20on%20Inflation.pdf; accessed in January 2013), a National Academy of Agricultural Sciences (NAAS) 2011–12 report on agriculture (http://www.indiawaterportal.org/sites/indiawaterportal.org/files/state-of-indian-agriculture-report-naas-2011-2012.pdf; accessed in January 2013).

sustainable growth. Precision farming, that scientifically measures inputs, has been able to save precious water and other inputs and yield large productivity gains in some areas (Bhattacharya 2012).

Better supply chains will enable more substitution of the costly and ineffective PDS with cash transfers or food coupons, thus ensuring targeting with lower leakages and corruption, and encouraging more private initiatives in a virtuous loop. With less procurement required, the government's need to force a monopolistic marketing structure to help its procurement will reduce. Although the Food Security Bill, passed by the Cabinet in 2013 but yet to become an Act, extends food subsidy to almost 70 per cent of the population—all those who do not pay income tax—it does give more freedom to states on the mode of delivery, allowing cash transfers.

The large difference between Indian consumer and wholesale price indices is partly due to inefficiencies in retail, which provides employment and therefore is a source of political patronage.[19] Fear of creative destruction that could upset existing power bases has prevented change, but it is beginning and gathering force. Unproductive rent-seeking elements can be absorbed in more productive activities relatively quickly. A large number of agents involved in corrupt activities soon found more constructive activities in Bihar with a regime change (Witsoe 2012).Weakening APMC will also facilitate other innovations, such as negotiable warehouse receipts, bank credit against such receipts, and support for construction of warehouses and storage facilities.

Sustained high food inflation, since 2007, and its spillover into general inflation forced some action to improve productivity and marketing in agriculture. By 2013 about 17 states permitted direct marketing and took marketing of perishables out of APMC. Contract farming was permitted but, as yet, covered only 1 per cent of the cultivated area. Private wholesale markets have not come up. Since a market creates externality, the state does have a role in developing these. One solution may be to allow easier private entry in *mandis*—permission should not depend on existing members.

As the number of those who stand to gain from more rises, change in restricting laws will take place, setting in motion a virtuous cycle. FDI in retail may contribute to these forces and in improving back-end

[19] Ashok Gulati mentioned his estimate of commission agents in Delhi's Azadpur Mandi to be 45,000 (personal communication).

operations but itself requires better markets for, and easier movement of, produce.[20]

The Lessons

Although external liberalization was gradual, it was easier than many essential internal changes since more domestic interest groups were involved in the latter. Internal changes also took place in the financial sector in the 1990s. Large sets of domestic participants lost their livelihoods as new structures were established and the controller of capital issues was abolished. So such change is not only feasible—it is also critical. Opening out alone is myopic since foreign capital will eventually flow out if domestic bottlenecks are not addressed.

Post-Independence, dominant development ideas interacted with the inherited structure and institutions to create stagnancy. Institutions weakened by ideas and structure could be hijacked by interests, but interests were not the primary cause of stagnation. They took advantage of poor systems. Although the structure and ideas became engraved in institutions that affected outcomes,[21] a change in ideas, and a rise in the proportion who benefit from growth, have strengthened institutions. Interests that benefit from inclusive economic institutions are becoming dominant.

These constitute India's inherent dynamism.

More external participants contribute to broadening the set of groups benefiting from growth. These push for institutions that enable productivity, not just redistribution or extortion. The process is messy and prolonged, but systems and incentives are improving. As wider social awareness and support makes activists turn from their traditional anti-industry and redistribution-based platforms to reforms that create inclusive economic institutions, it can help right choices to be made at critical junctures leading to more productive employment and equality.

It is possible to vet each reform proposal on the criterion of active inclusion. For example, consider the argument that reservations have not created equity so they are required in all types and hierarchies of activities. Reservations were originally introduced for 10 years. They have lasted for 60 years but have still not delivered. Their effective implementation is difficult since such groups account for more than half the population.

[20] Nayar (2011) argues that the forces of globalization are pushing India towards forming one market.

[21] Goyal (2011) calls this the structure, ideas, institutions, and outcomes (SIIO) paradigm.

An important lesson from vote banks and economic stagnation of the past, is that caste-based policies must give way to better general public services in a new India. The solution of equipping disadvantaged groups with relevant skills becomes feasible as many intermediate occupations appear in a higher growth economy. Schools, roads, and hospitals may be more effective than reservations. Equality of opportunity and skill-based access to jobs may deliver social justice with progress, even as direct benefit transfers or negative income taxes protect a well-identified narrow set of persistent poor as price and allocation distorting subsidies are reduced. Better air and water quality may improve nutritional outcomes more than elaborate, expensive, and distorted government interventions in food procurement and distribution.

Coming back to our China comparison, wages seem to be rising earlier in India than they did in China. If this is accompanied by productivity-enhancing inclusion, and, together with openness, will encourages innovation, India's growth path may differ from China's in a better balance between domestic demand and exports. India's growth has been more volatile, but may be more sustainable over a longer horizon.

Structure of the Book

The book is divided into eight sections of three to five chapters each. As in the introductory analysis of factors important for dynamism, the sections start with aspects of structure and reforms, changes in macroeconomic policies that followed reforms, inclusion, governance, and outcomes in different areas and sectors. The issue of better governance and empowerment of the citizen is a recurrent theme through the book. Factors contributing to this are the real sources of Indian dynamism.

Each chapter gives a reader-friendly, up-to-date overview of the research and thinking in the area, while bringing out changes, recent challenges, and the potential future path. Section I assesses factors behind the acceleration in India's growth at the sector and states levels; and a comparative contribution of domestic and external factors in reforms. Section II brings out change and continuity in the country's macroeconomic frameworks and policies, while section III analyses new issues with respect to capital flows, trade structure, and regional agreements that become important in a more open economy.

Section IV on 'Inclusion: Equality and Opportunity', examines the evolution of thinking on inclusion, the failures and successes in reducing poverty and inequality, improving education, health, and food security, and the potential for better design of interventions. Section V takes up the major challenges in governance. Although much remains to be done in relation to the government itself, there are signs of a steady strengthening of institutions with progress in regulation, in court activism, and in corporate governance. Section VI turns to infrastructure—another major bottleneck for India—notes problems, such as multiplicity of agencies but also steady progress in the design of contracts, private participation, collective action, and in industrial policy initiatives that try to compensate for other constraints. Section VII offers an in-depth analysis of sectors: agriculture, industry, and services including the informal sector, the constraints, and the sources of dynamism, including innovation, in each. Section VIII turns to factors of production: bringing out the contribution of labour, finance, and technology. New internet and communication technologies have a significant role in India's growth story.

Structure and Reforms

Each chapter in this section analyses different aspects of reforms. The first takes up the unusual sectoral structure of India's growth and diversity in states' performance; the second attributes reform successes to the consensus in favour of openness, and failures to blocks that restrict further opening out; but the third emphasizes the relative importance of domestic reforms and macroeconomic policy in relation to further external liberalization.

Laveesh Bhandari and Sumita Kale study the underlying factors behind the acceleration in India's economic growth. The 'dipstick' reforms of the 1980s paved the way for more substantive policy changes in the 1990s and beyond. Their success emboldened reformers to carry out a deeper set of changes when the opportunity arose, and revealed to the political class the large benefits from a more open and productive economy. Studies reviewed establish the link between growth, productivity, and reforms. The services sector has been the engine of growth for the economy, with different sub-sectors taking the lead in different time periods as each responds to a policy change, for example, bank nationalization in the 1970s and the construction boom in the 2000s. However, industrial reforms have not resulted in sustained high growth due to constraints in land, labour, and infrastructure. States have followed diverse trajectories, initial conditions in each leading to differential responses to central reforms. Growth and governance are now crucial to electoral outcomes, so political economy makes such reforms a focal point for the path ahead. The chapter points out inconsistencies in standard views on Indian growth and suggests that sectors, states, the unusual structure of India's growth, and changing leads and lags are useful issues for further research.

Rahul Mukerji characterizes India's growth path as a tipping-point transformation that depended on substantial changes in policy ideas within the government and the technocracy—the East Asian authoritarian path was not feasible. A tipping point connotes a model of gradual change resembling an earthquake where endogenous changes over a long period can create large-scale transformation for predominantly endogenous reasons. The evolution of economic ideas from state-driven import substitution towards globalization and deregulation from the mid-1970s enabled the executive to initiate far-reaching changes in economic policies during and beyond the balance of payments crisis in 1991. India had responded very differently to a similar shock in 1966 when the dominant policy ideas favoured autarky and government control. Even though ideational changes enabled substantial policy changes beyond 1991, powerful vested interests still block further reforms. The chapter details both the change and the obstacles that stand in its way and points to further research on how ideas become critical—can a policy elite drive ideational change, or do those ideas have to be more widely accepted in a democracy?

Pulapre Balakrishnan suggests that rethinking is required on suiting reforms to context, with more importance given to domestic reforms. The euphoria over the 1991 economic reforms appeared justified as there was very high growth for 5 years, starting from 2003. However, in a drastic change the promise of double-digit growth has been replaced, since 2008, with the prospect of persistent inflation and lower growth. This chapter identifies the proximate causes of this turn, arguing that domestic factors rather than the state of the global economy will determine whether India will regain the growth trajectory from which it has slipped, since liberalizing reforms per se have a limited reach, whatever be their relevance in specific spheres. The discussion on reforms tends to be delinked from its macroeconomic context—the latter is regarded as only of short-run relevance. The chapter suggests that the macroeconomic policy has impacted growth and an increased study of the interaction between the two will yield dividends.

The Macroeconomy

The reforms saw the macroeconomic framework change from one that was relevant to a closed, financially repressed economy to an open economy with greater freedom for markets. Fiscal dominance also reduced. But transitions were gradual and sequenced, giving time for developing supporting institutions and for the market deepening. Fluctuations in inflation and in capital inflows created major policy challenges. Both labour and the finance to support it were available in an economy in transition, facilitating growth, but supply shocks and poor governance raised costs of production that could not be easily contained. The chapters in this section address these issues.

Deepak Mohanty assesses the relative contribution of demand and supply shocks to Indian inflation. India is a moderate inflation country, with the 60-year long-term average inflation rate being 6.7 per cent, notwithstanding occasional spikes. Inflation performance improved significantly in the 2000s, with the average dropping to 5 per cent. However, inflationary pressures have resurfaced since 2009–10, following the GFC. From the supply side, high global crude oil prices, coupled with exchange rate depreciation and changes in dietary preferences towards protein items in the face of low supply elasticity, accentuated inflationary pressures. From the demand side, high fiscal deficit, imbalance in aggregate demand towards consumption, a significant increase in real wages in the informal sector, and rise in medium-term inflation expectations added to inflation persistence. Associated uncertainties make managing inflation in an economy recovering from a downturn more complex. Nonetheless, consequent to monetary policy action, inflation moderated during 2012–13, though it remained above the Reserve Bank of India's (RBI's) comfort level of around 5 per cent. But both growth and potential growth fell strongly and output remained below potential for an extended period. While monetary policy addresses inflation expectations, attending to the structural supply constraints is also essential. The formation of inflation expectations in India is a major black box requiring more research.

The fiscal and monetary authorities of a country are joined by balance sheet identities. Romar Correa uses these to analyse different types of fiscal and monetary policy coordination. The national income accounting framework used is mostly theory-free except explicitly for the Fisher relation linking interest rates to expected inflation and implicitly the idea that agents in an economy are price setters. The assets and liabilities of households, firms, and banks, along with identities, comprise an economic system. In input–output relations between components of net worth, items like budget deficit, which is one side of the balance sheet of one arm of the government, is not necessarily important. The framework makes it possible to distinguish between two institutional configurations. In the first, both the Government of India and the RBI are codependent and intimately linked with the private sector of the economy. In the second, the RBI is independent and the economy is liberalized with no more than prudential norms like Basel-type stipulations in place. Financial intermediation is important here. Demands of a low interest rate regime are more stringent in the former than in the latter. The cash reserve ratio and a bank liquidity ratio figure as stabilizing devices. In a dynamic economy, the future unfolds in surprising ways. It follows the fiscal authorities and RBI needs to be open to fresh data and recalculate solutions accordingly. The chapter brings out the relatively neglected balance sheet links between fiscal and monetary authorities. Since assets and liabilities must add up across sectors, one sector must be willing to hold another sectors' liabilities. What makes it willing is analysed. More than the deficit itself, markets seem to worry about financing large public sector borrowings. This is an interesting research issue.

Kanagasabapathy K., Rekha A. Bhangaonkar, and Shruti Pandey explore the many changes in Indian money markets and monetary policy transmission. RBI's monetary policy framework is characterized by multiple objectives, a multiple indicator approach, and use of multiple instruments, combining adjustments in the policy rate with a complex use of liquidity management operations. In this milieu, the impact of monetary policy can be viewed from the rate channel and a quantum channel and an interplay of both. An issue addressed by this chapter is whether the two channels were complementary to each other after 2001, when the new system of liquidity management reached maturity. An analysis of policy easing and tightening phases through the period shows that a policy-easing phase results in higher output growth and lower inflation in the subsequent tightening phase and vice versa. Consumer price inflation is however found to be sticky in the last two phases analysed.

An empirical analysis confirmed the linkage between repo- and market-related short- and long-term rates. The repo rate had a more pronounced influence on one-year government securities and on lending rates. On the quantum side, a bi-causal relationship is observed between repo and liquidity. An insignificant positive relationship was observed between the repo rate and non-food credit. Work on and linkages between short-term interest rates are both relatively advanced. This chapter pushes our understanding of transmission to longer term credit markets where more work is required.

The Open Economy

Is India's engagement with, and benefits from the global economy going to be substantially different from those of China? Should it try to follow China's path or forge a new path? The China story is well understood—a Lewisian absorption of surplus labour in labour-intensive manufacturing exports helped by an under-valued exchange rate, good infrastructure, basic education, poor labour rights, and low wages. We have surplus labour but none of the other conditions. We have opened out to portfolio capital flows and developed capital markets before China did, and, in the current global environment, maintaining an exchange rate peg is difficult. But regional integration and strategic industrial policy may offer India new options. The chapters in this section shed light on these and other open economy issues.

Soumyen Sikdar attempts to understand that to what extent external liberalization, of both current and capital accounts, has contributed to the dramatic improvement in India's growth performance over the past quarter century. The effectiveness of four major channels through which greater global integration is supposed to boost economic performance are examined in the light of empirical work done in this area.

Current account openness has contributed by significantly reducing the cost of importing intermediate inputs and technical knowledge. The services sector, helped by the telecom revolution, has efficiently exploited burgeoning global demand for business process services and has become the chief driver of growth. The demand-pull effect has been much weaker for manufacturing. Chinese competition is responsible no doubt, but persistent domestic inefficiency and serious infrastructural deficiencies are equally important. Agriculture also continues to be hamstrung by supply side constraints in which decline in public investment has played a crucial role.

In exports, a movement up the value ladder is noticeable and import composition too has changed for the better, though much scope for improvement remains. There is evidence of Total Factor Productivity (TFP) growth, particularly in services. FDI has failed to effect any major supply side change and Foreign Portfolio Investment (FPI) has failed to bring down the cost of capital significantly or to stimulate stock market development in general. Domestic investment continues to be predominantly financed by domestic resources. The need to counter exchange rate volatility caused by volatile FPIs has forced RBI to take measures that have impacted growth adversely. External liberalization may have added to regional disparities. The chapter has interesting insights on changes in the composition of Indian trade. The key research issue remains why it has not become part of the global supply chain as in the case of China and East Asia.

Renu Kohli writes that it is difficult for emerging economies to balance benefits and risks of financial integration. India's experience with financial globalization illustrates the challenges even on a cautious, gradualist, and step-by-step path. The chapter attempts a broad-brush look at the opportunities that financial globalization brought via growth, macroeconomic discipline, and financial development, before analysing accompanying volatility and other risks. It considers how challenges from surges in foreign capital flows have been dealt with through an array of macroeconomic and other tools, linking these to broader issues of the effectiveness of macroprudential measures and capital controls. The appraisal ends with a look at future policy directions. A question for further research is the cost of reserves. In China, they are based on a current account surplus, but in India they amount to an expensive taxpayer subsidy of private borrowing. The country ends up borrowing at a high cost and lending cheaply to the US, instead of investing domestically where there are severe infrastructure shortfalls. Since reserves become an indicator of strength and give comfort to global markets they are seldom used—so global complements that can reduce self-insurance need to be explored.

Nagesh Kumar examines trade and regional economic integration. He argues that the reforms pursued since 1991 have led to a much deeper integration of the Indian economy with the global economy in terms of the rising share of merchandize trade, a transformation of services trade, and emergence of the country as one of the most attractive destinations for FDI as well as an important source of FDI flows among the developing world. However, a quantitative analysis suggests that export growth benefited more from expansion of world trade and enhanced competitiveness—the potential of product diversification and market diversification remain to be exploited. Diversification into technology-intensive higher value adding goods or labour-intensive goods could be helpful for sustaining growth of exports while also creating more industrial jobs, and reducing the merchandize trade deficit. Opportunities for strategic import substitution in products like electronic goods need to be exploited to leverage the large market size that has been developed. A special targeting of multinational companies to establish local manufacture through pioneer industry incentives as employed by East Asian countries like Malaysia may be fruitful. Indian moves towards integration with the East Asian economies through a number of bilateral and regional FTAs and the Regional Comprehensive Economic Partnership of East Asia that seeks to create a broader Asia-Pacific regional trade arrangement covering 16 of the region's largest and fastest growing economies, offer Indian industry preferential access to East Asian markets provided by these agreements. Apart from the 'look East policy' the chapter points out a number of Indian strategic initiatives that contributed to successes in pharmaceutical, information and communications technology (ICT), and auto ancillary industries. Industrial policy that is effective, yet avoids the lock-in and distortions that the earlier import substituting regime created, deserves further study.

Inclusion: Equality and Opportunity

Poor access of an average Indian to essential public services is an important reason why reducing poverty was slow in India, and inequality is rising in post-reforms India. The chapters in this section examine the history of government interventions in the social sector, and new initiatives in education, health, food security, and for minorities and backward castes, that show promise for the future.

Raghabendra Jha and Anurag Sharma point out that despite 20 years of economic reforms, poverty and inequality remain issues of enduring concern. In particular, there is substantial disquiet about persistence of mass poverty and perceived rising inequality, even in the presence of accelerated rates of economic growth. Although, during the post-reforms period, inequality has grown and poverty has fallen, according to the existing yardsticks of assessing these, there are legitimate questions about the accuracy of these yardsticks. There is widespread spatial variation in both inequality and poverty. Adequacy of nutrition—the traditional rationale for the poverty line—has not recorded impressive gains. The most important means of lowering poverty is by creating jobs for poor and unskilled workers in both rural and urban sectors on a mass scale, an area in which the economic reforms programme has not had a good track record. The chapter also advances arguments and suggestions for better targeting of anti-poverty interventions, for improving nutritional outcomes, and for reducing inequality. The key research issues that it highlights are those relating to employment and better targeting as a means of lowering poverty.

Shikha Jha and P.V. Srinivasan take up the latter issue with respect to government interventions to deliver food security. Despite a large food grain procurement apparatus and having one of the largest food subsidy programmes in the world run by the government, food insecurity has been high in India. This chapter reviews the trends in food grain production and consumption, and discusses the issues concerning an effective policy design for food security in India. It argues for a holistic approach to reforms by bringing together the costs and benefits of the entire system, taking into account both supply and demand sides. In particular, the chapter highlights key policy choices that could help farmers deal with output and price uncertainty and ensure that poor consumers have adequate access to food. It suggests some policy alternatives for increasing food consumption by the poor and providing incentives to farmers to produce more without distorting the market for food grains. A rationale often given for government-mandated distribution outlets is that markets are thin. The chapter brings out a possible reverse causality that needs to be researched: how government procurement limits private initiatives.

Rukmini Banerji and Wilima Wadhwa argue that a number of conditions have to be met to reap India's demographic dividend, combining employment opportunities with requisite skills in the workforce. The chapter focuses on primary education, since it provides the basic foundations for human capital accumulation. In the last 50 years, universalizing education has been one of the most important policy goals in developing countries. India has also made great strides. Over 95 per cent of the children are enrolled in schools; close to 90 per cent villages have a primary school within a 1 kilometre radius; and teacher absenteeism has been falling. Although educational inputs seem to be in place, evidence on learning outcomes suggests that children are far behind grade-level competency even in basic reading and numeracy skills. The two major trends that characterize the current Indian education system—a move to private schools and the government's thrust on more inputs, are unlikely to result in a major improvement in learning levels. Without immediate acceleration in basic learning levels and large-scale remedial efforts in primary schools, India's demographic advantage will dribble away. But change is possible and that too in a short period of time. The Punjab government collaborated with a NGO in a state-wide programme to boost basic reading and arithmetic. Grade 5 children in Punjab were at the national level when the programme started but in five years, they were more than 20 percentage points ahead. Developing, refining, and spreading interventions that work are critical issues for further work. For example, activity-based learning is transforming primary education in Tamil Nadu government schools and spreading elsewhere (Bhattacharya 2012).

Gita Sen discusses major challenges and possible solutions for health security for all citizens (and non-citizens) which is a major issue of global debate. In India also, the Planning Commission (2010) appointed a High-level Expert Group to point the way to achieving universal health coverage. Given the complex interplay of demographic, epidemiological, economic, and social factors affecting health status and outcomes, and the weaknesses of the health policy over more than five decades, a large majority of the people in the country suffer from one or more aspects of insecurity related to health. The chapter examines the health system and policy challenges through three central dimensions of health insecurity from the perspective of people: whether healthcare is affordable; whether it can be accessed easily; and whether health problems are even acknowledged as such within families and/or the health system. In doing this, it integrates health and population policies, which are often treated in analytical and policy silos. The chapter marshals evidence, provides some international perspective, and then proceeds to examine how policies need to be directed to address each of the three dimensions of health insecurity. A substantive contribution of the chapter is the linking of failures in health policy to the planned regime. It follows that local empowerment in health issues is the way to better outcomes. The chapter raises research questions on mechanism design to avoid the trap of indifference in government provision and profit-gauging in market delivery. For example, is it possible to improve incentives for low-cost delivery by providing limited reimbursements to health providers rather than following the American system of reimbursing insurance companies?

Ashwini Deshpande explores the persistence of caste and other identities in a modernizing India. Translation and impact of momentous recent changes on inter-group disparities has been uneven. Caste inequality shows very strong inter-state variations and some convergence, but no clear relationship between growth and convergence. In other words, it is not necessarily the case that richer or faster-growing states have seen lower caste disparity (or vice versa). Gender-wage gaps are substantial, and these are greater for the lower part of the wage distribution. A decomposition of these gaps between 'explained' and 'residual' indicates that the discriminatory component is greater among the bottom four wage deciles, indicating the presence of a 'sticky floor', rather than a 'glass ceiling' for women. While poverty incidence has reduced, class inequality has increased sharply. In large parts of the country, increasing inequality has fuelled protracted armed insurgency, which has also brought questions of control over forests and natural resources to the fore. This suggests that as the economy becomes more market oriented, the state has to step in decisively to act on a strategy of redistribution, improve public goods, and make the policy framework as well as governance structures accountable, transparent, and inclusive. Since neither reservations nor growth has created convergence, better design of interventions is the substantive issue that the chapter highlights. Inputs from careful quantitative research are essential for this rethinking.

Governance

Improving the government's functioning is critical for remedying the failures discussed in the earlier section. But governance is broader than just government administration and includes systemic incentives, institutions, and the legal framework. The chapters in this section cover the narrow functions of government; the checks and balances; the effectiveness of the executive, legislature, and judiciary; and changes in legal, regulatory, and corporate governance systems. Although much remains to be done, especially in government proper, the chapters demonstrate some strengthening of institutions. Sometimes one set of institutions have compensated for failures in others. For example, courts have forced executive policy and action on environment issues.

Parthasarathi Shome characterizes India's fiscal performance in recent years as unstable, with periods of fiscal conservatism followed by loosening in both taxation and expenditure. When expanding, the authorities tended to set aside established policy, for example, on fiscal responsibility and budget management. Good policies were, however, undertaken in taxation. Distortionary indirect taxes were scaled back while direct taxes were increased through the expansion of the tax and taxpayer base rather than by merely increasing tax rates. Broad-based consumption orientation to taxation was given in the form of a state-level VAT and a central VAT (CENVAT) and there are ongoing efforts to implement a national GST.

The government had less success on the expenditure side. As a ratio to GDP, non-development expenditures overtook development expenditures.

Revenue expenditures rose while capital expenditures plunged. Public sector investment in agriculture declined and, despite some improvement in recent years, remains well below what it was in the 1980s. Small successes in containing some subsidy components on food and fertilizers have been overwhelmed by petroleum subsidies.

Overwhelming challenges of structural policies remain in the tax administration and in expenditure management. Modernizing tax administration is of essence. The use of monitoring and evaluation techniques on expenditure programmes and projects will be crucial. The chapter makes a useful distinction between policy successes and implementation failures. An important research question is why the failures were more pervasive on the expenditure side. A valid point seldom noticed is that India's adjusted tax–GDP ratio is quite high. The current composition of expenditure makes it very difficult to reduce spending—there is hardly any investment left to be cut, and committed expenditures dominate. It follows that better implementation is the key to raising investment, as well as for improving government deficits.

Abhay Pethe, Vaidehi Tandel, and Sahil Gandhi identify governance as the key for meeting ever-increasing infrastructure needs in the context of an urbanizing India. They analyze the nature of urban governance using tools from New Institutional Economics. Urban governance in India is complex, involving a multitude of actors, such as public organizations and agents, private sector, civil society, and citizens. The public goods and service delivery, contingent on the interactions of these actors, suffers from serious shortcomings, such as inefficiencies, differential access, corruption, and leakages. To understand the dynamics, the chapter examines the role of underlying institutions in driving interactions among actors and the persistence of inefficient outcomes by focusing on the nature of multilevel governance, urban land management, and the supervisory space. It finds that the existing urban governance system is unable to deliver public goods and services efficiently because of deficient political institutions that vest too much power with a few authorities, missing institutions for information-dissemination; lack of accountability, and transparency; elite capture; fragmented civil society and an overburdened judiciary; and high political transaction costs that preclude effective competition, cooperation, and conflict resolution among public organizations. More study is required on the dimensions on which urban governance institutions are too many and the dimensions on which they are too few.

In taking up issues in federalism and decentralization, T.R. Raghunandan suggests a possible solution to the multiplicity identified in the previous chapter. In his view, three preconditions are essential for strong and responsive institutions, which are an essential ingredient of a well-functioning democracy. First, they must have a precise and exclusive role. Second, there must be a way for people to hold them accountable for performing that role. More precisely, there should be penalties for non-performance of responsibilities. Third, there must be a clear network of relationships that mesh different institutions together. These might be relationships of command and subordination or relationships of partnership, collaboration, and complementarity. Another important principle is that constitutional institutions should stand on a higher footing than that of institutions created through statutes. Similarly, statutory institutions should have a stronger basis than those that are created through executive order. Raghunandan argues that the failure to follow this principle has created multiple government structures and vitiated the three preconditions. This chapter pushes for more research on the logic of institution design.

A.V. Raja and Francis Xavier Rathinam explore the interplay of regulation, law, and judicial activism in affecting economic activities in India. Regulation has been transformed from a pervasive state control model to one where only selected segments are regulated. What is the role of the legal system in shaping this transformation? The authors assess whether law, and/or regulation, helps in building a stronger governance structure. The two areas chosen for this inquiry are finance and the environment. The analysis shows how the choice of institutions for the social control of economic activity is determined by a combination of political and incumbent industry interests, shaped by judicial activism. In case of the financial sector, the political equilibrium led to a repressed, though stable, financial sector, which was partially liberalized in the recent period as the dynamics of interest groups changed; on environmental matters, the failure of the regulatory apparatus led to judicial review/intervention. The subsequent media coverage exposed the failure of the executive and forced the state to initiate a process towards better implementation of environmental laws. The chapter opens up a rich vein of research on interactions among changing Indian institutions. There may be weaknesses in each, but one tends to compensate, to some extent, for weaknesses in another. So the whole may be stronger than any one part. Are the set of institutions in India rich enough now to push the economy in the right direction?

Jayati Sarkar and Subrata Sarkar examine this question with respect to the evolution of corporate governance after economic liberalization. They overview the committees and codes that shaped governance standards while comparing those standards with international best practices. A corporate governance report card, in terms of trends in key governance indicators, and an overall index is presented for top 500 listed companies. There is a tightening in the distribution of the index over the years implying a convergence in corporate governance standards. Although there is still divergence between policy and implementation, there is some improvement in corporate governance practices also across companies. Governance reforms are in line with international best practices. But better enforcement will improve outcomes. An interesting issue for research is whether specific reforms need to be designed for Indian conditions, such as the dominance of proprietor directors. Or could deviation in norms from global ones improve outcomes? Does the industry feedback, that committees have utilized, help identify and close the loopholes often used in India.

Infrastructure

The slowdown in public investment and the domination of populist transfers in government expenditure meant that it is essential for the private sector to participate in removing India's pressing infrastructure bottlenecks. But this requires policy clarity and coordination across multiple government departments for requisite clearances, as well as for strengthening auction procedures, contracts, firm balance sheets, and corporate governance. Finance is not a constraint for firms with clear strengths, although developing corporate bond markets will help to circulate the risk to those most equipped to hold it. The chapters in this section trace this institution-building process. The section also explores how industrial policy actions can compensate for existing infrastructural bottlenecks.

Inadequate transport infrastructure has constrained Indian growth and development. Yet, at the same time, existing facilities are not adequately utilized for a variety of reasons, including inappropriate pricing, poor regulation, and inefficient operating practices. The underlying reasons include lack of effective investment and pricing policies, legislative measures and the absence of coordinated efforts. In other words, the transport system in India also suffers from severe governance inadequacies. S. Sriraman seeks to understand the current governance structure and its relevance—giving a new approach to providing transport infrastructure and services—that emphasizes not only on policymaking but also effective implementation. A broad framework of an ideal governance mechanism is outlined, followed by a brief description of the institutional framework for governance as it has evolved. The chapter then goes on to examine specific issues with regard to the two dominant modes of transport in India—railways and road transport—and also briefly reports a case study with regard to governance of urban transport in Mumbai. The point that more investment will not solve problems without better systems is an important one. The case studies identify specific problems yet suggest feasible resolutions.

Ram Singh and Param Jit turn to issues involved in creating an extensive as well as efficient infrastructure network required for sustainable high growth. They analyse problems and challenges, such as funding, project delivery and regulatory hurdles. Therefore, apart from augmenting investment, there is need for inter-modular planning of traffic across sectors and optimum pricing of infrastructure services. The chapter offers suggestions for overhauling project delivery systems, and streamlining the regulatory framework so as to expedite the implementation of projects. The traditional public-funding based approach is compared with private funding through public–private partnerships. Other questions are also addressed, such as: the major differences between public–private partnership contracts and traditionally used contracts; their relative advantages and disadvantages; whether public–private partnerships are a superior means of infrastructure procurement; benefits and risks associated with private funding; and Indian experience with public–private partnerships. The public–private partnerships route can help but will require careful designing, monitoring, and regulation of contracts. Policy suggestions are made. The chapter brings out the inevitability of new modes of organization to deliver India's infrastructure and the need for further research on these. An in-depth analysis of public–private partnerships contracts contributes towards this.

Sidharth Sinha argues that there is broad consensus on the role of privatization, or just private participation, in power sector distribution reforms. This is reflected in the recommendations of numerous committees and working groups. However, even after almost two decades of reforms, the extent of private participation is extremely limited and shrinking in scope—from Odisha to Delhi to Bhiwandi. The main conclusion from the analysis is that private participation is not possible without government support and regulatory certainty, especially during the initial transition period. Private participation must also be accompanied by separating of commercial activities and subsidized social mandates. Although some states have achieved significant improvements through state-owned utilities by providing the necessary support and regulatory certainty, it is an open question whether these successes are sustainable in the long run as state governments and leaderships change. Moreover, achieving a separation between commercial and social activities is likely to be difficult without private participation. The chapter paints a picture of disarray but also brings out the examples of few states (Andhra Pradesh and Gujarat) and mechanisms (for example, bidding structures) that have done well. The constraints to more widespread adoption of best practices serve as interesting research questions.

Aradhna Aggarwal turns to the role of special economic zones (SEZs) as a policy of industrialization. Developing countries, being late entrants to industrialization, face numerous production failures and bottlenecks. So markets by themselves cannot lead to efficient outcomes. A state-led policy designed to address these market failures is critical. One such frequently used policy is the creation of SEZs. While SEZs have been associated with significant industrial transformation in China, Korea, Taiwan, and Malaysia, they have failed miserably in many other countries. The chapter examines the formation and evolution of the SEZ policy and its contribution to the process of Indian industrialization in different phases. In doing so, it draws lessons for a recently launched new variety of national investment and manufacturing zones (NIMZs). It examines important dimensions of the policy surrounding NIMZs and identifies the SEZ practices that linger and need to be addressed with urgency if the new zones are to be successful. Since policy solutions are contextual in nature, an experimental approach is required. But continuity of government support over political cycles is also essential. The secret of a successful zone programme lies in a strategic vision, dynamic learning, and political will to implement.

A major insight from the chapter is how the continuing Indian pro-poverty mindset often leads to a blind anti-industry position, when decisive support of the industry and employment generation is the way to reduce poverty. Moreover, policy consistency is important. Special initiatives need to be made independent of the government, which keeps changing its mind. Commercial sustainability with some legal backing may be the way to go—to the extent that special concessions are given, like some sunset clause, or else use of competition—and appropriate regulation to prevent rent-seeking will be required. Tax concessions could be reduced as other constraints ease. An interesting research question is the extent to which the major fluctuations in India's post-crisis export performance are related to policy flip-flops, on export policy in general and on SEZs in particular.

Sectors

The standard growth pattern involves the shrinking of agriculture and the expansion of industry. India is puzzling in that agriculture has shrunk as a share of output but not as much in the share of employment. Industry has grown but less than expected. Services have been the real star, but ICT-enabled and financial services provide employment only to skilled elites. The informal sector remains a large heterogeneous buffer. Despite our labour endowments we have missed integrating with global vertical fragmented export chains, or removing the disadvantages that our small industry sector faces, perhaps because governance-related obstacles to doing business are yet to be adequately lowered. High food price inflation suggests that the growth and composition of agricultural output has been inadequate and improving this is critical to the Indian growth story, just as creating a more continuous ladder of higher productivity employment is critical for equity. Although improvements are still required, there is considerable dynamism as openness and competition enforce better organization, governance, and quality; free trade agreements bring diversification in exports and raw material sourcing; reforms improve financing and ease of doing business. Chapters on agriculture, industry, ICT, and the informal sector, present in this section, expand on these issues. The chapter on industry also discusses the contribution of improved financial services to industry—these services are taken up again in the next section. Since services are such an important part of the India story, they are analysed elsewhere in the book also—such as in the chapter on growth drivers and the chapters on trade.

S. Mahendra Dev, Srijit Mishra, and Vijay Laxmi Pandey contextualize Indian agriculture by evaluating its performance, the roles, challenges, and opportunities for smallholders. They observe a turnaround in recent years (2004/5–2010/11) compared to the immediate post-reforms period (1993/4–2004/5), which had witnessed stagnation in comparison to the pre-reforms period (1981/2–1993/4). The changes in recent years could be attributed, among others, to certain public policy initiatives on investments, research, extension and credit, and also a slew of good monsoons. A matter of concern is the sustainability of smallholder farmers who have difficulty in livelihood sustainability despite being efficient. But there are opportunities that reduce costs and risks and use low external input sustainable agriculture without compromising on production. Despite substantial aggregate and micro-improvements, just in this period, there were sharp peaks in agricultural prices and the terms of trade shifted to agriculture—so improvements came at a high cost. A research question is: what else needs to be done so that the supply response keeps up with demand growth without excessive inflation?

Bandi Ram Prasad argues that economic reforms have provided Indian industry with numerous opportunities to pursue growth, diversification, and global expansion. India even came to be acknowledged as a leading global player. Policy support, changing dynamics of global manufacturing, reforms, and subsequent developments in the financial sector emerged as new sources of dynamism for the industry. The chapter overviews major aspects of industrial growth, and new avenues of resource mobilization enabled by development of financial systems. The link with finance raises interesting research questions, such as risks for large corporates from foreign currency borrowing, the under-servicing of small industry, and further innovations required for infrastructure financing.

Rohit Prasad explores a puzzle. Both business process outsourcing and telecommunications, based on information technologies (IT), are striking success stories of post-liberalization India. However, ICT's performance as a driver of welfare has not matched its performance as a driver of GDP growth: empowering the rural population using voice and data, and promoting domestic research and development (R&D) and manufacturing form part of the unfinished agenda. This is a result of certain conceptual and systemic policy failings. Three of these are highlighted through an analysis of case studies of rural ICT schemes and the policy for preferential access to domestic IT and telecom products: a technology-led development paradigm that under-emphasizes the necessity of complementary 'soft' inputs; unwarranted faith in the market mechanism for awarding projects and ensuring the percolation of their benefits to the common citizen; and unthinking transference of urban solutions to rural areas. In addition, policy bottlenecks that are presenting challenges for the growth of the ICT sector at a time of inflexion are highlighted. These include the auction design for spectrum allocation, the licensing regime, and tax laws related to startup companies. How ICT can make its full potential contribution to India and to inclusion is the very important question the chapter opens up for further work. Designing an intelligent supporting ecosystem is necessary as is paying more attention to context and industry as well as user needs, while preventing possible rent-seeking.

Arup Mitra considers the size, structure, and functioning of the informal sector, the constraints it faces, linkages between the formal and informal sectors, changes particularly after globalization, the job search procedures followed by workers in the informal sector, and the scope for upward mobility. The chapter is based on both secondary and primary data from a field survey.

The relative size of the informal sector is on the rise, particularly after liberalization. Even within the formal sector, casual and contractual employment has been increasing. Sub-contracting practices are being followed extensively. The piece-rate-based payment system restricts benefits to those located at the lower spectrum. Inter-linkages between the sectors exist but they do not seem to be favourable to the informal sector. There are considerable overlaps between informal employment and poverty. Job search practices followed by informal sector workers are often based on informal networks which involve substantial information asymmetry and thus lead to excess supplies of labour in certain pockets of cities. This tends to restrict upward mobility though social capital is indispensable for an entry to the job market. A detailed analysis of factors making for expansion, and those making for stagnation, suggests that further research on the role of education and skill formation in upward mobility is required. Distinguishing between low and high income components of the services sector and the functioning of networks will be useful—what does it take for a stagnant low-income network to transform—is a critical mass of younger, more educated workers sufficient?

Saibal Kar and Meghna Dutta point out while there is substantial analysis of the Indian unorganized sector, studies have predominantly focused on the urban informal manufacturing sector. Its rural counterpart, which covers about 60 per cent of all such units spread over states and union territories, is relatively neglected. These units are also the ones that suffer most from lack of access to formal credit. Their study offers an in-depth analysis of access to finance by rural unorganized sectors in comparison to the agricultural sector. They also obtain a sector-wise and state-wise distribution of volatility of gross value added and fixed assets for various industries within the realm of the rural unorganized sector. Finally, they discuss the role of micro-credit organizations in linking formal credit agencies to unorganized rural units. The chapter is a rare example of careful work on the rural informal sector. A major insight from the chapter is how local distortions tend to be neglected in the reform process. Questions raised for further research include linkages between rural industries and agriculture. Are these activities correlated or do they help diversify risk?

Factors: Technology, Labour, Finance

Technology and innovation have played a large part in India's growth spurt. New technologies drove both outsourcing and telecom. Indian skilled labour could virtually reach the global marketplace, side-stepping infrastructural constraints. Not enough changed for the better in domestic labour markets, however. Many changes in finance improved accessibility for the wealthy and for large corporates, but better democratic access remained a distant dream. Indian banks reformed yet remained stable, continued as the major source of finance for firms, and remained as the preferred choice for the risk-averse domestic saver. The share of household financial saving going to equity and mutual funds actually fell. And the absence of inflation-indexed savings instruments resulted in excessive real estate investments and gold imports. Since innovation was driven from abroad, it suited those with higher incomes and global exposure rather than meeting domestic needs. However, systems strengthened, and finance was no longer a constraint for firms with strong balance sheets.

K.J. Joseph and Kiran Kumar Kakarlapudi explore broad aspects of encouraging innovation and its contribution to development. India has been one of the pioneering developing countries to recognize science, technology, and innovation as key factors in development. A sharp paradigm change is mapped in this chapter on the basis of two different but inter-related issues. The first relates to the link between innovation, growth, and development and the second on facilitating socioeconomic transformation or catching up. The inquiry into the former is located in different heuristic frameworks, including the classical legacies of Marx and Smith, Schumpeter, Arrow, endogenous growth models, technological capability paradigms, and the National Systems of Innovation approach. Of these, the last two are particularly relevant for innovation in developing countries. Enquiry into the second issue revealed that catch-up is more difficult today than ever before notwithstanding new opportunities. The new paradigm of globally integrated innovation involves harnessing all possible external sources for stimulating domestic capability building. Fostering an internationally competitive economy involves liberalized access to embodied technology (capital goods) and FDI and technology, increased reliance on mergers and acquisitions, increasing participation in global innovation networks through R&D in FDI, greater reliance on outward FDI and a new patent policy compliant with international regimes. But inclusive growth involves the creation of institutional architecture at the national, regional, and sectoral levels that is geared towards creating more 'frugal, distributed, affordable, innovation' that produces more 'frugal cost' products and services that are affordable at low-income levels. But this has not worked in the Indian institutional context, giving rise to multiple exclusions. Hence, the chapter calls for a walking-on-two-legs strategy for addressing these varied exclusions.

The differences brought out in the pre- and post-reforms innovation policies will be productive areas for more research. There are interesting hints of unintended consequences. Nehru's temples of science contributed to post-reforms performance because they equipped people with skills (although only a small elite); the big public-sector-led push on physical investment was less successful. There has been more innovation than expected after the reforms, despite withdrawal by the government, but the most successful has been based on products (ICT, mobiles) that suited local skills or needs. Innovation policies need to be fine-tuned to these lessons.

Bibhas Saha and Rupayan Pal focus on some key aspects of the labour market, such as industrial relations and labour market rigidities of the organized sector. With increased product-market competition and rent dissipation, industrial disputes have fallen; increased opportunities also had some calming effects. But labour market rigidities, which can be attributed to an array of legislative and institutional provisions for the organized sector, are to be taken seriously. Recent researches, which have explicitly allowed for changes in legal provisions among the states, systematically uncover unequal effects of liberalization between the states and between the organized and unorganized sectors. The unorganized sector, by and large, has responded positively to reforms and globalization. But the welfare of workers in the unorganized sector has to be addressed, and they have to be empowered to take advantage of new opportunities in a globalized world. The chapter points to the necessity of closing the gap between the formal and informal labour market, by reducing regulatory rigidities in the first, and by improving standards in the second. Even though the centre may be unable to move forward on legislation on this sensitive issue, experimentation, dynamism, and perhaps eventual convergence is possible in the states.

Rajesh Chakrabarti gives an overview of the financial sector in India. For him a financial system is akin to the circulatory system in the human body, tapping and transporting savings throughout the economy, with markets and banks being the two competing and complementary arteries. The Indian financial system that ranks slightly below the median in the

World Economic Forum's rankings has virtually re-booted since the still-ongoing liberalization that started in 1991. The four pillars of a financial system—laws, technology, creditors' rights, and corporate governance—have all undergone, and are still undergoing, major transformations. Financial access and inclusion remain key challenges despite serious efforts and experimentation. The banking system is stable, public-sector dominated, fragmented, and heavily regulated. Financial markets that have witnessed a sea-change since liberalization, still have limited liquidity. The corporate bond market—a key for much-needed infrastructure financing—remains seriously under-developed. The regulatory system is fragmented, rule-based, and, generally speaking, quite conservative. Globalization of the financial system has been steadily increasing with time and while not the most innovation-friendly in the world, it has succeeded in providing stability and averting crises in an increasingly turbulent global financial environment. The chapter's focus on the institutional and legal base brings out the deep-seated transformational changes taking place. There is space for more work on lacunae, such as poor customer service and the simplicity and suitability of products.

T.T. Ram Mohan argues that India's banking system, nearly two decades after the onset of reforms, presents a striking contrast to other systems that have gone through financial liberalization, in having escaped banking crises. At the same time, efficiency in the system has improved. Banking penetration has increased and, in terms of technology, banking has undergone a sea-change. How and why these remarkable outcomes came about are documented in the chapter. Sound macroeconomic management, tight regulation, and government ownership were contributory factors. Strong economic growth, following liberalization in other areas, boosted banks' income and profits. India's calibrated approach to capital account convertibility kept the banking sector from being exposed to volatile flows of capital. Caution on foreign banks, and entry and prudential norms for private ownership, also contributed to stability in the system. Not least, he argues, diversified ownership, with a dominant public sector, stood the Indian banking system in good stead. The challenges of financing India's infrastructural requirements remain, as also the objective of greater inclusion. While the strengths built over two decades of reforms have left India's banks well placed to address these, other issues also remain for research. What are the efficiency properties of the base rate system and what is its possible evolution? Why have private sector banks been able to pull ahead of others in the very recent period? What will be the impact of the slowdown given government-pushed public sector banks' sectoral exposure?

Sanjay Banerji, Krishna Gangopadhyay, Prashant Gupta, and Sushanta Mallick explore financial intermediation and economic development using district-level evidence from Bihar, one of the poorest but fastest-growing states in India. The chapter analyses the relationship between financial intermediation and economic development. They find that the standard index of depth of financial intermediation measured by credit–deposit (CD) ratio is very low in the state (30 per cent) and has little impact on economic development at the aggregate level. However, an analysis of sectoral CD ratios shows that credit allocation to agriculture influences per capita income across districts but similar allocation to industry has almost no impact. This finding is robust to different model specifications, including other financial indicators. But bank branches tend to be significant in explaining variations in per capita income across districts, as reflected through its indirect effect via higher realized credit relative to the planned credit limit. Directed lending towards priority sectors in the form of kisan credit cards also has a significant impact on economic development. However, with regard to the industrial sector, the aggregate impact of the CD ratio is insignificant and a firm-level analysis for the sector also suggests a limited impact of different sources of financing, although companies are heavily dependent on bank borrowing as opposed to equity financing. The chapter paints a valuable picture of finance in an under-developed state. Further research on the role of technology in more rapidly deepening financial intermediation will be useful.

REFERENCES

Acemoglu, D. and J. Robinson (2012), *Why Nations Fail: The Origins of Power, Prosperity and Poverty*. New York: Crown.

Ashton, T.S. (1948), *The Industrial Revolution (1760–1830)*. London: Oxford University Press.

Bardhan, P. (1984), *The Political Economy of Development in India*. Basil Blackwell: Oxford. Expanded edition, New Delhi: Oxford University Press, 1998.

Bhaduri, A. (2010), *Essays in the Reconstruction of Political Economy*. Delhi: Aakar Books.

Bhattacharya, A. (2012), 'Quiet Revolutions', *Business Today*, 19 August.

Balakrishnan, P. (2011), *Economic Reforms and Growth in India: Essays from Economic and Political Weekly*. Hyderabad: Orient Black Swan.

Basu, K. (2011), *The New Oxford Companion to Economics in India*. New Delhi: Oxford University Press.

Basu, K. and A. Maertens (2010), *The Concise Oxford Companion to Economics in India*. New Delhi: Oxford University Press.

Béteille, A. (2008), 'Constitutional Morality', *Economic and Political Weekly*, 43(40): 35–42.

Cai, F. (2012), 'Is There A "Middle-Income Trap"? Theories, Experiences and Relevance to China', *China and World Economy*, 20(1): 49–61.

Ghate, C. (2012), *The Oxford Handbook of the Indian Economy*. New Delhi: Oxford University Press.

Goyal, A. (1999), 'The Political Economy of the Revenue Deficit', in Kirit S. Parikh (ed.), *India Development Report 1999–2000*, pp. 140–51. New Delhi: IGIDR and Oxford University Press.

——— (2001), 'Reasoned Optimism', *The Economic Times*, 19 June.

——— (2004), 'Puzzles in Indian Performance: Deficits Without Disasters', Chapter 12 in K.S. Parikh and R. Radhakrishna (eds), *India Development Report 2004–5*. New Delhi: IGIDR, and Oxford University Press (2005).

——— (2011), 'History of Monetary Policy in India since Independence', *Report for 2010–11 first Professor P.B. Brahmananda Memorial Research Grant Award, 2011*.

——— (2012a), *Macroeconomics and Markets in India: Good Luck or Good Policy?*, UK: Routledge.

——— (2012b), 'An Appraisal of Five Year Plans and the Future', in *Yojana*, special issue on 'An Approach to 12th Five Year Plan—Issues and Challenges', January.

——— (2013), 'Sustaining growth: Interests versus institutions', IGIDR Working Paper 2013-01.

Goyal, A. and S. Arora (2012), 'Deriving India's Potential Growth from Theory and Structure', IGIDR Working Paper No. WP-2012-018. Available at: http://www.igidr.ac.in/pdf/publication/WP-2012-018.pdf (accessed in January 2013).

Granville, A. (2002), 'The Expected and the Unintended in Working a Democratic Constitution', in Z. Hasan, E. Shridharan, and R. Sudarshan (eds), *India's Living Constitution*, pp. 319–43. New Delhi: Permanent Black.

Gupta, D. (2000), *Interrogating Caste: Understanding Hierarchy and Difference in Indian Society*. New Delhi: Penguin Books.

Jalan, B. (2013), *Emerging India: Economics, Politics and Reforms*. New Delhi: Penguin Books.

Jha, R. (2011), *Routledge Handbook on South Asian Economies*. Oxon and NY: Routledge.

Kapur, D., C.B. Prasad, L. Pritchett, and D.S. Babu (2010), 'Rethinking Inequality: Dalits in Uttar Pradesh in the Market Reform Era', *Economic and Political Weekly*, 45(35): 39–49. Available at: http://casi.ssc.upenn.edu/system/files/Rethinking+Inequality+DK,+CBP,+LP,+DSB_0.pdf (accessed on January 2013).

Kohli, A. (2012), *Poverty amid Plenty in the New India*. New Delhi: Cambridge University Press.

Nayar. B.R. (2011), 'Globalization, the State, and India's Halting March to Common Market: The Political Economy of Tax Reform Under Federalism', *India Review*, 10(3): 201–45.

North, D.C. (1982), *Structure and Change in Economic History*. New York: W.W. Norton and Co.

North, D.C. and B.R. Weingast (1989), 'Constitutions and Commitment: Evolution of Institutions Governing Public Choice in 17th Century England', *Journal of Economic History*, 49: 803–32.

Panagariya, A. (2008), *India: The Emerging Giant*. New York: Oxford University Press.

Prasad, C.B. and M. Kamble (2012), 'To empower dalits do away with India's antiquated retail trading system', *Times of India*, Mumbai edition, 5 December.

Rath, N. (2012), 'Economic Origin of Regional and Caste Parties', *Economic and Political Weekly*, 47(30): 24–8.

Spence Commission on Growth and Development (2008), 'The Growth Report: Strategies for Sustained Growth and Inclusive Development', Chair M. Spence. Available at: http://go.worldbank.org/FC797ZNZP0 (accessed in January 2013).

Srinivasan, T.N. (2011), *Growth, Sustainability and India's Economic Reforms*. India: Oxford University Press.

Tett, G. (2012), 'Beware the Next Financial Blindspot', *Financial Times*, 22 November.

Witsoe, J. (2012), 'Everyday Corruption and the Political Mediation of the Indian State: An Ethnographic Exploration of Brokers in Bihar', *Economic and Political Weekly*, 47(6): 47–54.

PART I

STRUCTURE AND REFORM

CHAPTER 1

DRIVERS OF GROWTH

sources and sectors

LAVEESH BHANDARI AND SUMITA KALE*

Economic growth in India has been accelerating steadily since the 1970s, yet most agree that the reforms in 1991 and after have taken the growth path to another level. India has, since, left the Hindu rate of growth far behind, and with growth spread across all parts of the country, laggard states are well on their way to discard the highly demotivating term of 'BIMARU' (or sickly states in north India). Growth has been sustained, has not been limited to urban India, and some also argue that economic growth in rural India continues to lead economic growth, even though agriculture now accounts for a small share of the economy. Sectorally as well, growth has been quite well spread; take, for instance, agriculture—while overall agricultural growth has been far lower than that in other sectors and centred around 2.8 to 3 per cent in the 1990s and the 2000s, there are states, such as Gujarat and Nagaland, that have shown double-digit growth in agriculture for close to a decade. Further, sectors such as transportation, communication, and logistics were not the only ones that grew in double-digits in the last decade, they were also accompanied by strong and sustained growth in other sectors as well such as construction and finance.

The last two to three decades have seen two significant changes, which are arguably closely connected. The first is what has been generally termed

* The authors are grateful to Swati Gupta and Minakshi Chakraborty for their help and to the editor and reviewer for their comments and direction. All errors are ours.

as economic policy reforms that have led to a significant change in the way the state deals with economic activity. And the second is a significant change in technologies being used both inside and outside the country. High growth has therefore spread far and wide (though by no means smoothly). Where did this high growth come from? Which sectors led the changed trajectory?

The answer is not easy to decipher, as the reforms have themselves been quite staggered and uncoordinated.[1] Implementation of announced policy changes has been delayed many times and sometimes it has been quite ineffective. On top of that the underlying data collection mechanisms have remained poor. The net result is that it is very difficult to adequately decipher how reforms impacted India at a microeconomic level. This is not to say that studies have not been attempted. In other words, while evidence on aggregate economic growth having improved is unambiguous, data to pinpoint the *sources of that growth* and acceleration are not as unambiguous, as is shown in this chapter.

This chapter proceeds as follows. The section 'Economic Growth since Independence' provides a base for later sections by first looking into aggregate growth figures in the post-Independence period with special emphasis on the period since 1991. The section that follows, 'Economic Reforms and Economic Growth', reviews the studies that have attempted to link reforms with growth. The next section, 'Productivity and Growth' delves into issues of productivity growth and total factor productivity growth (TFPG) with the following section, 'Inter-state Differences', looking at inter-state differences and whether states are converging and why. The last section gives a conclusion.

Economic Growth since Independence

The Central Statistical Office (CSO) of the Ministry of Statistics and Programme Implementation has been putting out annual National Accounts Statistics which contain key economic variables such as GDP.

[1] The process of reforms has not been smooth, rather it has been stop and go, thanks to interdepartmental and interministerial differences and differences between the states and the Centre, as well as between successive political denominations that have ruled at the Centre and in the states.

The bulk of the studies on growth use these GDP figures from the CSO. The base year changes every few years, though recent practices have been to change them every five years. In other words, GDP figures are estimated in detail every five years, in line with the large sample quinquennial employment and expenditure survey of the National Sample Survey Organisation (NSSO); and the intervening years involve an updation to GDP that requires lesser data inputs. Every time the base year changes, the CSO publishes a document on the latest methods of estimating and updating GDP.[2] A detailed examination of this document reveals—(a) the government is very well aware of the possible limitations of the underlying data sources and circumvents most pitfalls; and (b) GDP in India is probably underestimated, and this downward error is arising out of the government's inability to capture value added in the informal sector. But since the methods of data collection are standard and consistent over time, the underlying data, though somewhat flawed, are good enough for most studies on growth, especially in the absence of alternatives.

While growth has been increasing, the volatility in annual growth rates has reduced significantly as Figure 1.1 shows. Arguably, this is a result of the diversification in the economic activity caused by the reforms. Figure 1.1 reveals a simple story. Growth has varied tremendously year to year since the 1970s. Depending on how one estimates growth and determines the periods and sub-periods, it is possible to get somewhat different results. And some of the differences in interpretation we find in literature are indeed due to differences in time periods being covered. Figure 1.1 shows that: One, growth has been on an increasing path over the last few decades. Two, the improvements in growth not only precede the 1990s, but also the 1980s, and arguably go back to the latter half of the 1970s. And three, the current slowdown may very well be a temporary component of a long-term political-economic cycle. Each of these elements is taken up in later sections.

The Sectoral Picture: Pre-1991

Following the low growth phase in the 1960s and first half of the 1970s, the high growth phase of the 1980s was not limited to a single sector, but all three—agriculture, industry, and services—achieved a higher growth plane (see Figure 1.2).

[2] The latest methodology for the new series is available in CSO (2010).

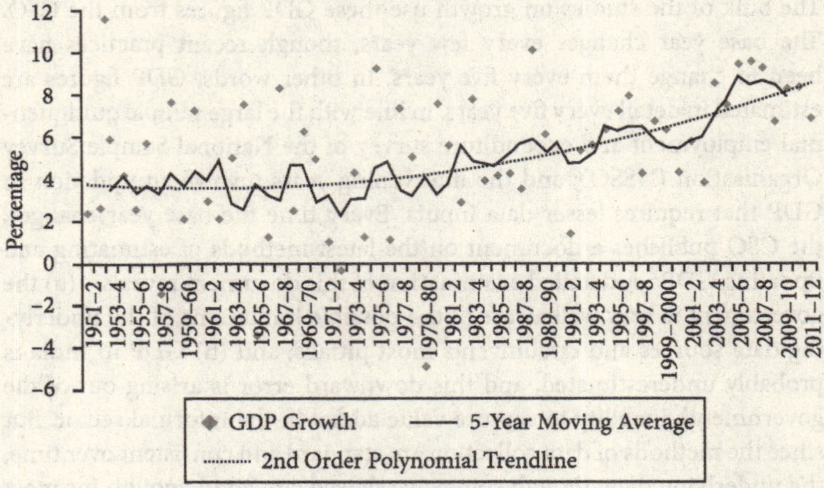

FIGURE 1.1 GDP Growth in India
Source: Authors' estimations from CSO data.

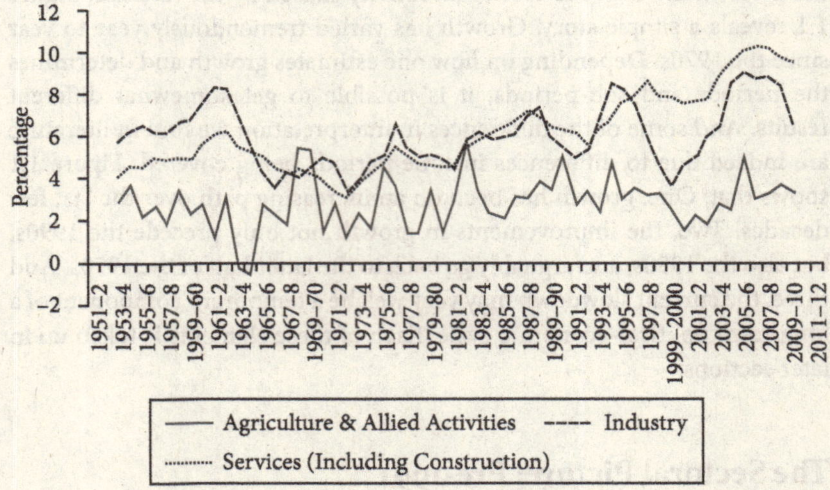

FIGURE 1.2 Sector-wise Growth Rates—5-Year Moving Average
Source: Authors' estimates from CSO data.

Consider agriculture and allied activities first that registered an average growth of 3.1 per cent in the 1980s following the low 1.8 per cent annual average seen in the 1970s. This, it is well known, occurred as the Green

Revolution took hold in Punjab and spread across Haryana and western Uttar Pradesh. Other states also started benefitting from the increased availability of fertilizers and better seeds though maybe not to the same extent as north-western India [see, for instance, Swaminathan (2010)].

Registered manufacturing and electricity were the focus of the early years in planning, but the dividends soon ran out as controls stifled growth. Industry therefore suffered a sharp decline through two decades after seeing high growth in the 1950s. The Janata Party did not do much apart from some support to the small scale sector.[3] Devaluation in the late 1960s was followed by a steady depreciation in the first half of the 1970s (the latter not by design but because the rupee was tied to the depreciating sterling). Though it is not clear whether it was support to small scale industries (SSIs) and other interventions, or reducing the relative value of the rupee, but manufacturing did grow backed by a steady increase in exports [see Mohan (2006) and Panagariya (2008), for instance].

The services sector has for a long time led the Indian economy in terms of size. But it was by no means the growth engine of the Indian economy as it grew roughly at the same rate as manufacturing. The major change occurred in the 1970s with the nationalization of banks. Command and controls contributed to the spread of the banking system and the consequent growth in the financial sector. On the other hand, other sectors such as construction, trade, telecom, business services, and IT did not benefit from any of the technology changes that were occurring in their domains at the time, as the sectors remained protected. The 1980s saw the government recognizing and providing limited support for the first time to the IT and communications sectors. But this delay in the entry of new communication and IT technologies would also have been partly responsible for the delay in the commencement of the high growth phase in the post-reforms period.

Post-1991 Growth

Over the period 1991–2011, the economy grew at an average annual rate of 6.8 per cent. Though significantly higher than the period before, the aggregate figure hides some important aspects (Table 1.1). GDP grew at

[3] It accorded greater protection to small industry by increasing the list of reserved items to 504 in April 1978; it also increased the SSI limit from Rs 10 lakh to Rs 30 lakh capital investment.

a little over 6 per cent in the 1990s but accelerated to slightly over 7 per cent in the first half of the 2000s and then further to a little over 8 per cent in the period after 2006 (it appears to be back to 7 per cent or an even lower figure in the post-2011 phase but we will not get into those issues). The post-reforms churn very quickly corrected itself and the economy appeared to be on a high growth path by the middle of the 1990s; but the acceleration in growth was hit in the second half of the 1990s. There were a number of factors for this—the Asian crisis, post-nuclear test sanctions, stalling of reforms after 1995, and rising fiscal deficits from 1996 were all contributory factors [see Acharya (2002) for a detailed exposition of these factors]. The National Democratic Alliance (NDA) government's years saw an improvement in growth despite some of the worst agricultural years and a tightening of the fisc. The major sectors that were leading India's march towards a high growth economy in the early 2000s were construction, transport, storage, and communication, and financial and business services which also include IT. Each of these was preceded by some important institutional developments. The communications sector gained from the more open policies of the government and the presence of an independent regulator in the form of the Telecom Regulatory Authority of India (TRAI). Together they succeeded in creating an environment

Table 1.1 Sectoral Growth since the 1990s (percentage)

Sectoral CAGR	1991–6	1996–2001	2001–6	2006–11
Agriculture, forestry, and fishing	3.6	2.1	2.3	2.9
Mining and quarrying	4.5	4.5	5.1	4.3
Manufacturing	9.5	4.0	7.5	7.7
Electricity, gas, and water supply	7.8	5.7	6.1	5.5
Construction	3.7	7.7	12.8	7.5
Trade, hotels, and restaurants	9.3	7.1	9.1	7.8
Transport, storage, and communication	7.7	11.5	12.9	13.1
Financing, insurance, real estate, and business services	7.2	8.2	8.4	10.9
Community, social, and personal services	4.7	9.6	5.3	9.6
GDP	6.2	6.0	7.2	8.1

Source: Authors' estimates using data from CSO, Ministry of Statistics and Programme Implementation, GoI.

which enabled free and fair competition, consumer interest was kept foremost, and both entry and exit were allowed while keeping government intervention to a minimum. The construction sector's growth was boosted by housing and highway construction, an outcome of lower interest rates, income tax incentives, more disposable income, and government investment in roads under the Pradhan Mantri Gram Sadak Yojana (PMGSY) and the Golden Quadrilateral programme, among others.

Developments in financial markets in the mid- and later-1990s included the entry and strengthening of two major institutions. First, an independent regulator in the form of the Securities and Exchange Board of India (SEBI) had overcome its teething troubles. Second, perhaps as importantly, new trading technologies introduced by the National Stock Exchange (NSE) created a transparent system of trade; moreover, the spread of electronic communications technologies also had its secondary impact on the financial sector (ATMs and offsite trading terminals being just two examples).

The 1990s finally saw the IT sector come onto its own, both as an exporter[4] and as an employment generator.[5] If there is one institutional element that can be identified as synchronous with the growth in the IT sector, it would be the efforts of NASSCOM. The association is a textbook example of how cooperative lobbying by a highly competitive sector can help in creating and sustaining a far more enabling environment than unilateral action. Some important government decisions pertinent to the IT sector included low tariff on imports of IT hardware, greater depreciation of hardware and software and at the same time ensuring that the industry built for itself a set of quality standards that were in sync with those operating internationally.[6]

A comparison of the overall growth rate and that in manufacturing shows that apart from the first post-1991 period, the manufacturing sector has not been able to significantly pull up aggregate growth in India. This has remained one of the most curious aspects of the reforms and their

[4] Total export revenues earned by this sector grew from Rs 6,723 crore (US$ 1.8 billion) in 1997–8 to Rs 104,500 crore (US$ 23.6 billion) in 2005–6, according to the Eleventh Plan Working Group on Information Technology, Planning Commission.

[5] A number of IT professionals in India increased from barely 50,000 in 1990–1 to about 1.045 million in 2004–5. See Sanjay K. Singh (2006).

[6] For more details refer to Ministry of Information and Technology, available at http://www.mit.gov.in/content/schemes-and-policies-electronic-hardware and http://www.mit.gov.in/content/export-promotion-schemes-dpl-elec (last accessed on 1 August 2013).

impact. The first and the deepest set of reforms—industrial delicensing and relaxation in bottlenecks to international and domestic investment, as well as in international and domestic trade occurred specifically for releasing the manufacturing sector from the stranglehold of government intervention. But the manufacturing sector growth could not take off. Popular discourse has identified labour laws, others mention inspector *raj*[7] and yet others lack of FDI.[8] No doubt each of these institutional constraints have added to costs and therefore constrained manufacturing growth, but at the same time we find that none of these have been able to stifle growth in selected sectors—the automobile manufacturing sector being one example. Over the entire period, the lagging sectors were predictably forestry and logging, agriculture including livestock and mining and quarrying. After the green revolution, the agriculture sector has not received significant investment or policy focus; this shows up in declining agricultural productivity that is taken up later in this chapter.

This section briefly sketched out the shifting trajectory in growth and also alluded to some institutional developments that preceded high growth phases. The next few sections delve into the determinants behind this growth, to understand the impact of reforms, productivity, and political economy on overall growth, and by extension to the sectors that have registered stellar performances. But that is best achieved by first looking into the received wisdom on reforms and how they impacted growth.

Economic Reforms and Economic Growth

Reforms, in short, the changes that work towards amending and improving a system, are an ongoing process in any economy. There are various facets of reforms and this section reviews studies that have attempted to link the *process* of reforms to growth in the Indian economy.

[7] 'World Economic Forum's Global Competitiveness Report 2003-04 ranked India at the fifth place out of 102 countries on the parameter of burden of regulatory inspection. The World Bank's 'Investment Climate Survey' in 2004 estimated that on an average, 11.9 per cent of senior management's time in India was spent in dealing with government agencies. See GoI (2005).

[8] For a review of the FDI policy path in India, the changing definitions, and lack of FDI in the infrastructure sector, see Kulwinder Singh (2006).

When did the growth turnaround begin? We have shown in the previous section that an argument could be made for the latter half of the 1970s. But that is an argument that is rarely made in literature. Deepak Nayyar (2006) makes the point that during the past century, 1951 was the turning point for India's growth performance and since Independence it was 1980 that framed the break point with a growth surge. While the 1980s saw a definite surge in the growth trajectory, studies have not been able to pin the shift down to a particular year.[9] Virmani (2005), for instance, documents the growth phases and contentious debates over the break points in these phases and notes that most studies have pinned the change in growth trajectory to the 1990s, while his earlier papers in 1989 and 1997 showed that growth acceleration predated the New Economic Policy launched in 1991. Further, his analysis for 1950–2002 shows no break point other than 1980–1, showing that the turnaround effectively happened in the 1980s.[10]

What part did reforms play in the higher growth in the 1980s? Even a cursory look at Figure 1.1 shows that it is possible to create many different stories depending upon the periods where growth rates are aggregated.[11] Each of those stories need not be incorrect, but they are rarely indicative of the larger picture. For instance, it would be difficult to disagree with Panagariya (2004) that the high growth in 1988–91 pushed the average growth for the 1980s upwards and the variance of growth in the 1980s was much higher than that in the 1990s. While relaxation of controls was ongoing since the 1970s, the pace of reforms actually picked up in 1985, especially over the period 1985–8. These were important reforms and covered exports, industrial licensing and production (MRTP, cement and aluminium), tax (MODVAT) and management of the real exchange rate.[12] These 'dipstick reforms' of the 1980s were indeed the precursor for the far deeper changes of the 1990s, as they yielded important insights on growth outcomes.

⁹ See Wallack (2003) for the shift in the cut-off year depending on which series of national income was taken.

¹⁰ See also DeLong (2004).

¹¹ A recent paper by Dholakia and Sapre (2011) finds that detecting break dates is sensitive to base year changes, marginal extension of time series, and alteration of the length of the partition. The paper concludes that due to empirical limitations there is no conclusive evidence of break dates and hence cannot help settle the debates over different growth and policy regimes of the Indian economy.

¹² Joshi and Little (1994) note that the exchange rate policy became more active from 1985, 'though the fiction of a fixed basket peg was maintained'.

The consequent impact on trade and manufacturing showed immediately in the second half of the 1980s. Apart from the usual greater business orientation type of arguments, Virmani (2005) points to the importance of credibility. He argues that the credibility of intent of policy change was firm. This was critical in achieving a high rate of growth of private investment. This observation is substantiated through the rise in the annual growth rate of gross fixed capital formation (GFCF) in the 1980s to 6.9 per cent as compared to 4.8 per cent in the previous two decades and higher growth for manufacturing. There is also a view that the key reason behind this increase in growth and reduction in volatility was a shift in the political economy towards a more pro-business policy stance [see, for instance, Rodrik and Subramanian (2004)].

We, however, find it difficult to classify reforms as pro or anti-business. On the one hand, overall economic freedom has increased and entry and exit is easier and independent regulatory entities have been set up and are functioning relatively well. On the other, as many reforms have arguably created greater discretion in the hands of a few, there is some cause to believe that corrupt practices have increased, and there is little evidence of increase in small business activity.

What went wrong in the reforms–growth equation of the 1980s? Despite the growth surge, the very nature of the reforms of the 1980s has in fact been attributed as the determinant of the 1991 crisis faced by the Indian economy. As argued by Joshi and Little (1994), the rise in government expenditures was considerable, with the bulk of this expenditure being on defence, interest payments, and subsidies. Growth in the 1980s was primarily due to unsustainable increases in public expenditures and excessive foreign borrowing that finally ended in the balance of payments crisis of 1991 when the international environment soured. It was because of this that though Bhagwati (1998) accepted the higher rate of growth in the 1980s, he did not consider it a new phase in India's development. Therefore, though the higher rate of growth is accepted by all studies, this was not considered healthy growth, as reforms were lopsided and created more problems than they set out to resolve.

What went right in the reforms–growth equation of the 1980s? Ahluwalia (1994) identifies the changes in the 1980s as 'the result of a process of evolutionary reform'. More importantly, he correctly identifies the changes as 'marginal rather than fundamental'. This was why we term these as 'dipstick reforms' for there was no 'comprehensive shift away from a regime of controls' but they went a long way to make further reforms palatable to a democracy that had grown up with socialism as the dominant paradigm. But there is another argument. Panagariya (2004) argues that it is difficult to perceive any such change in attitude within the government or bureaucrats and quotes some personal instances and communications to underscore the arguments. We believe that this was all a part of the same picture—massive reforms of the 1990s required political support and dipstick reforms were an important element in achieving that political consensus.

What changed in the 1990s in the reforms–growth equation? The key difference from the previous decade was that now the reforms were systemic, coordinated across ministries, and required strong political support. The first and most important set of reforms unarguably occurred in the Ministry of Industry—delicensing and removal of controls on investment being the two most critical changes. Though, as shown earlier, these reforms did not translate into stronger manufacturing growth immediately, they signalled a major change in the policy mindset from the previous decades, as they were accompanied by sustained changes in the Ministry of Commerce with an easing of import barriers and the rupee was also devalued in tandem by the Ministry of Finance.

Whatever the reasoning and analysis, it is indisputable that reforms had set in by the 1990s. The next section explores the mechanism through which the reforms impacted growth—by raising productivity.

Productivity and Growth

Growth in output can stem in a natural way through increase in factor inputs of labour and capital, or through improvements in the efficiency of these inputs; for example, a unit of labour produces more output than before. Reforms would work on growth in output by raising efficiency, by raising the total factor productivity (TFP); Dholakia (2001) shows that the post-1985 growth acceleration is to a very large extent due to improvements in the efficiency of factor use, or TFP: over the period 1960–85, the growth of total factor productivity contributed less than 22 per cent of the overall growth rate, while TFP growth accounted for 48 per cent of overall GDP growth during 1985–2000.

Bosworth et al. (2007) worked on deciphering the link between growth acceleration and TFPG in finer detail. Their analysis was conducted over a four-decade period divided into smaller sub-periods[13]—1960 to 1973, 1973 to 1983, 1983 to 1993, 1993 to 1999, and 1999 to 2004. They find that over 1960–73, nearly all the output growth can be attributed to growth in factor inputs, with nearly two-thirds accounted for by increased employment, and a third by increases in capital per worker. A little over half the small acceleration in growth seen over 1973–83 is attributed to TFPG and the remainder is associated with increased labour inputs or employment. During this period, the determinants of TFPG are the green revolution increasing agricultural TFP and sectoral reallocation of employment towards other sectors. A marginal rise in output growth in 1983–93 over the previous decade's performance can be completely attributed to increased TFP, but this time the gains are concentrated in services and industry (especially manufacturing). Therefore, with growth associated with TFPG, reforms are linked directly to TFPG in this time period.

The period 1993–9 saw annual growth at 7 per cent levels. This was a short period where the impact of reforms of 1991 and thereafter had not fully played out. There was a decline in employment, along with a particularly large jump in labour productivity, mainly in the services sector but which was also evident in other sectors.[14] Finally, the period 1999–2004 saw slower growth in all sectors, with TFP and capital deepening slowing in both services and industry.

Both popular discourse and the authors have identified the slowdown in the early years of the NDA regime due to (a) international conditions, and (b) poor monsoons during the period. Bosworth et al. (2007) further investigate the strong rise in the services sector's TFP and provide another more mundane explanation that output growth in services has been overstated due to an underestimate of services price inflation. However, other studies have delved deeper into the services sector to investigate the high productivity growth, discussed next.

Goldar and Mitra (2008) examined the services sector in depth as their analysis showed that the rise in TPFG at the economy level in the post-1980 period is mainly traceable to the increase that took place in the TFP growth rate in the services sector. Of the 2.4 percentage point increase in growth in the post-1980 period, they attribute about 40 per cent to a faster growth in TFP in services. Going into sub-sectoral performance within

[13] The breakpoints have been chosen in line with data availability from various NSSO survey rounds.

[14] Bosworth et al. (2007) note that this decline in employment is 'puzzling' as they have no explanation for it. It could be stemming from the data limitations in their study.

services, Goldar and Mitra (2008) found that on labour productivity, it was the financial services that saw the highest growth across the years, but when it came to capital productivity, trade, hotels, and restaurants stood out with a very sharp decline in the pre-1980 period being reversed dramatically after 1980. Overall, while TFP rose fastest in financial and business services from the 1970s, the crucial determinants for the post-1980 turnaround were trade, hotels, and restaurants, and public administration and other community services[15] (see Table 1.2). There are severe data caveats and too much should not be read into the rise in productivity of these sectors since the higher TFPG in public administration could stem from the rise in pay scales of public sector employees. Moreover, it is not clear whether the measurement of capital stock and definitions of the sectors have remained consistent over the large time periods being analysed.[16]

Table 1.2 Growth Rates in TFP, Sub-sectors and Services

Sub-sectors of Services	Growth in TFP (% per annum)		
	Pre-1980	Post-1980	1960–1 to 2006–7
Trade, hotels, and restaurants	–3.4	2.9	0.2
Transport, storage, and communication	2.0	3.0	2.2
Financing, insurance, real estate, and business services	2.0	3.9	3.5
Public administration and other community, social, and personal services	1.1	3.5	2.0
Services sector (total)	1.3	3.0	2.1
Memo: Estimates by Bosworth et al. (2007) for aggregate services sector	0.4	2.9	1.7

Source: Goldar and Mitra (2008: 14).

Despite these problems, Goldar and Mitra's results clearly indicate the turning points of financial sector productivity improvements as early to mid-1980s, that of trade and hotels from the mid-1990s, and that of transport, storage, and communications since 2000s (see Figure 1.3).

[15] In public administration, the downsizing of the public sector as well as pay scale hikes for government employees has raised output per worker. This could account for part of the growth in productivity in this sub-sector.

[16] There are severe issues concerning definitions across the years that have caused different researchers to come out with different results.

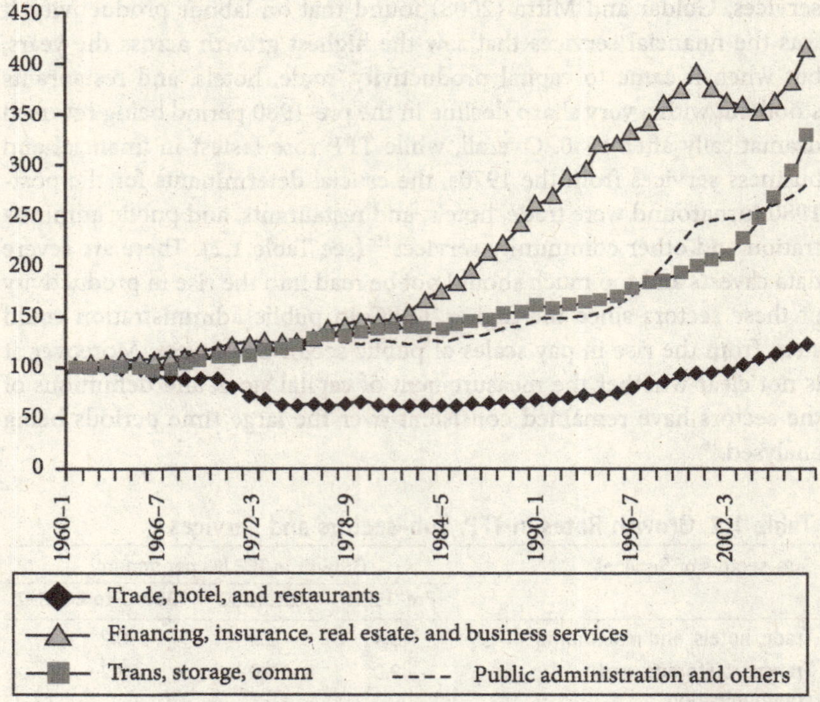

FIGURE 1.3 Total Factor Productivity Index (1960–1 = 100)
Source: Goldar and Mitra (2008: 14).

The lack of event studies, however, prevents us from identifying whether technology infusion in the mid-1980s in the banking sector, or greater international orientation of post-1991 India impacted the trade sector whether infrastructure improvements in the road sector commencing in early 2000s, or for that matter mobile telephony finally spreading in the 2000s can be held responsible for these patterns.

It must be noted that the high growth in productivity in the services sector had a beneficial impact on the other sectors. For instance, industrial productivity growth is related to financial, physical, and social infrastructure (Mitra et al. 2002), and the new skill-intensive activities, particularly in the IT sector that are a part of services, provide significant support to manufacturing productivity growth. Similarly, trade and transport have high linkages supporting both agricultural and manufacturing growth and productivity. In short, high productivity growth in the services sector was also crucial for other sectors.

The impact of reforms in the services sector on manufacturing productivity was analysed by Arnold et al. (2012). They found expectedly that the rise in services sector productivity contributed significantly to manufacturing productivity—but they also found an ordering—banking, telecom, insurance, and transport all led to significant productivity rises in manufacturing firms. Using panel data for 4,000 firms over 1993–2005, they showed that a one standard deviation increase in the aggregate index of services liberalization resulted in a productivity increase of 11.7 per cent for domestic firms and 13.2 per cent for foreign enterprises.

What about productivity in agriculture? Studies show that there has been a moderation in agricultural productivity growth in recent years. Bosworth et al. (2007) find TFPG in agriculture increasing till 1999 but moderating thereafter. The reasons behind the rise were of course the green revolution, improvements in inputs, and labour reallocation away from agriculture, while moderation has been explained by lower returns to government R&D and extension services. On similar lines, Saikia (2009) found that TFPG for agriculture declined in the 1970s, grew in the 1980s, and declined in the 1990s, showing a possible connect with public sector investments.

When it comes to manufacturing, Bosworth et al. (2007) find TFPG for industry slowing and not accelerating in the post-reforms period that they analyse till 2004. However, this has been accepted as a natural phenomenon in economies that are starting from a protected environment; adapting new technology in a liberalized world has a time lag. On the other hand, employment growth has not been commensurate with overall growth, leading to improved labour productivity. However, a note of caution by all researchers investigating industry TFPG is that results are not conclusive: as Kathuria et al. (2010: 1) report, 'Krishna and Mitra (1998), Pattnayak and Thangavelu (2005), Unel (2003) among others find an acceleration in total factor productivity growth (TFPG) in the reform period whereas studies by Trivedi et al. (2000), Srivastava (2000), Balakrishnan et al. (2000) and Das (2004) find a deceleration in TFPG in the 1990s.'

The most recent and comprehensive study on TFPG in manufacturing in India, by Trivedi et al. (2011) systematically lays out all the issues in estimating TFPG in India and one of their results is that for 1980–1 to 2003–4, the contribution of TFPG to output growth for organized manufacturing sector ranged between 13 per cent and 25 per cent depending on which methodology is used. Before analysing the impact of reforms per se on growth, they put forth two issues—it is difficult to isolate the impact of reforms from the other factors which affect TFPG, and there could be time lags only after which the impact of reforms could be felt on TFPG. Despite the caveats they give, their results across various industries and states do indicate increase in TFPG in the post-1990s.

Interestingly, Rodrik and Subramanian (2004) analyse the surge in aggregate factor productivity after 1979, and reject all commonly postulated causes behind this rise in productivity—external and internal liberalization, aggregate demand, public investment, fiscal expansion, and the green revolution. They make the point that the pro-business stance of the government post-1980 led to higher productive utilization of resources. They base their reasoning on a regional analysis to show that states whose governments were allied with the Centre grew faster than the others post-1980, thereby benefitting only those states that already had large formal manufacturing, the focus of the pro-business attitude.

On similar lines, Aghion et al. (2008) argue that there is a differential impact across states when it comes to manufacturing productivity, their main result being that the response to delicensing varies significantly depending on labour market conditions prevailing in different Indian states. The fact that there will be strong state-level factors that are playing a role is quite obvious and needs to be looked at in greater detail; the next section looks into this aspect of regional differences in growth.

Despite all the studies done so far (see Table 1.3 for summary), there is still a lot we do not know. For instance, how has infrastructure impacted growth? While many point to how poor infrastructure is harming growth in India, few studies point to how successes in the sector had a positive impact on growth rates. Since the latter part of the 1990s India has built an impressive network of rural roads, which has constructed a massive telecom network accessed by all including the very poor, and has been able to make almost all children who are at the primary school-going age literate. Few studies are able to tie-in the productivity impact of these social and physical infrastructure developments of the 2000s.

Inter-state Differences

India's 35 states and union territories (UTs) have diverse socioeconomic profiles and despite planning and controls aimed at balanced regional growth, the states were quite far apart even till the 1980s. Did liberalization accentuate these differences or did it provide an environment for

Table 1.3 Key Results on TFPG in India

Author	Time Period	Main Results
Dholakia (2001)	1960–1 to 2000–1	1960–85, TFPG contributed less than 22 per cent of the overall growth rate. 1985–2000 TFPG accounted for 48 per cent of the overall growth.
Bosworth et al. (2007)	1960 till 2004	Effect of TFPG in growth shows post-1983.
Saikia (2009)	1960–2000	TFPG for agriculture declined in the 1970s, grew in the 1980s, and declined in the 1990s, showing a possib e connect with public sector investments.
Goldar and Mitra (2008)	1960–80 and 1980–2004	40 per cent of the 2.4 percentage point increase in growth post-1980 is due to faster services TFPG. Overall, TFP rose the fastest in financial and business services from the 1970s; trade, hotels, and restaurants, and public administration and other community services were crucial for the post-1980 turnaround.
Arnold et al. (2012)	1993–2005	Rising services sector productivity contributed significantly to manufacturing productivity. Banking, telecom, insurance, and transport all led to significant productivity rises in manufacturing firms.
Kathuria et al. (2010)		Review of studies giving conflicting results for manufacturing sector productivity depending on the time period analysed and the methodology used.
Trivedi et al. (2011)	1980–1 to 2003–4	Contribution of TFPG to output growth for the organized manufacturing sector ranges between 13 and 25 per cent depending on which methodology is used.
Rodrik and Subramanian (2004)	1970s to 2000	Surge in aggregate factor productivity after 1979 due to the pro-business stance of the government post-1980, leading to higher productive utilization of resources.
Aghion et al. (2008)	1980–97	Differential impact of delicensing across states on manufacturing productivity, depending on state's prevailing labour markets conditions.

convergence? There is a caveat at the beginning of any regional study in India that an analysis over a long time period, as done for national income, is not possible for all states, especially since data for the newly formed states is not available pre-1993.

Further, studies looking at convergence of states over time have had diverse results depending on factors such as the time period analysed, the number of states in the sample, and benchmarks used for comparison.[17] Focusing purely on the impact of reforms, there are again a number of studies that show that states adopted disparate growth paths post-reforms, for example, Bhattacharya and Sakthivel (2004) found increasing inequality in per capita regional output after 1991, Kar and Sakthivel (2007) used the 'new geography' framework to analyse the impact of reforms on per capita regional output to validate the theory of post-reforms divergence across states. Sachs et al. (2002) worked on the period 1980–98 for 14 states and found that there was overall increasing divergence over the period, with greater divergence during 1992–8. Interestingly, richer states showed convergence over 1992–8, while poorer states in the sample did not. The reason postulated for this divergence by the authors was regional differences in the marginal productivity of investments by sub-sector. This stemmed from the general business environment and also specific geographical factors. Therefore the green revolution benefitted the states of Punjab and Haryana, while services sector reforms benefitted Maharashtra, Tamil Nadu, Karnataka, and Delhi where the initial conditions were favourable for these activities.

Singh et al. (2003) noted that the results on regional inequality were sensitive to the measures of attainment used; hence while analysis using state income showed divergence over the post-reforms period, human development indices did not show the same increase in regional inequality. Liberalization had led to more efficient allocation of private capital, foreign as well as domestic, and while this will lead to a more uneven balance depending on state policies, they found that governments in poorer states such as Madhya Pradesh and Rajasthan had improved, on average, the relative standard of living of their constituents. Their conclusion therefore was that liberalization does not necessarily leave certain states behind.

A more recent study, using club convergence and polarization as the methodology by Kar et al. (2010) shows that there is increasing inequality and polarization into two clubs, that is, over the period analysed

[17] For more details on these studies, see Singh et al. (2003).

1993–2005, some of the middle income states moved up (relatively) and other middle income states fell back creating two separate groups. According to their analysis, the middle income states that fell back are either inland as opposed to coastal states or have political unrest in the form of insurgencies. The reasons given therefore show that reforms have been favourable to those states that have conducive geographies or social structures.

It is difficult to robustly decipher whether states are converging or diverging. Table 1.4 shows state growth divided by the all-India growth rate for each of the sub-periods for the 21 larger states in the country (for actual growth rates, see Appendix A1). A ratio of 1 indicates that the state growth rate was the same as national growth, states with lower growth rates have ratios less than 1 while states whose growth rate exceeded the national growth have ratios greater than 1. The analysis in Table 1.4 shows that there is some correlation with growth from the previous period, but this figure will differ depending on the period considered. At the same time, historically poor states have sometimes grown at a rate that is significantly higher than India, but then fallen back; at the same time there are other states that have fallen for a while, to pick up again. Despite all this, it is evident that states such as Delhi, Maharashtra, Tamil Nadu, Gujarat, and to a lesser extent Karnataka have been performing consistently better than the average since the 1960s. States such as Kerala, Uttarakhand, Chhattisgarh, Tamil Nadu, and to a lesser extent Bihar are among the accelerating states whereas those such as Punjab and Rajasthan appear to be falling behind in terms of growth rates.

A sectoral analysis of state growth reveals an interesting picture in Table 1.5. Taking five-year periods from 1991 to 2010, we find the highest growth sector in these sub-periods changing across time, even as the services sector dominates. In the early 1990s, banking and insurance was the fastest growing sector in eight states, reflecting financial sector reforms that benefitted states like Maharashtra, Karnataka, and West Bengal. In the late 1990s, it was transport, storage, and communication that had the highest growth in nine states, again reflecting telecom reforms benefiting states like Andhra Pradesh and Haryana. The most striking result comes from the early 2000s which reveal the massive thrust on construction through public investments in roads coming through with this sector being the fastest growing one in 15 states. The late 2000s again show diversity as the states moved on different paths. Three sectors—banking and insurance (built upon the boom in household savings), public administration (the pay commissions), and transport, storage, and communication

Table 1.4 Growth of States Relative to India Growth

State	1961–2 to 1970–1	1971–2 to 1980–1	1981–2 to 1990–1	1991–2 to 2000–1	2001–2 to 2010–11
Andhra Pradesh	0.4	1.0	1.1	0.9	1.1
Assam	1.1	0.8	0.5	0.3	0.6
Bihar	0.3	0.9	0.9	0.6	1.1
Chhattisgarh				1.5	2.5
Gujarat	0.9	1.6	0.9	1.1	1.3
Haryana	1.8	1.5	1.0	0.8	1.1
Himachal Pradesh	1.0	0.9	1.0	1.1	0.9
Jammu & Kashmir	1.1	1.3	0.4	0.7	0.7
Jharkhand				1.6	0.7
Karnataka	1.0	1.2	1.0	1.1	1.0
Kerala	1.2	0.5	0.7	0.9	1.0
Madhya Pradesh	0.6	0.5	0.8	0.8	0.9
Maharashtra	0.9	1.6	1.2	1.0	1.3
Odisha		0.8	0.8	0.6	1.1
Punjab	1.6	1.5	1.0	0.7	0.8
Rajasthan	0.8	1.0	1.2	1.0	0.9
Tamil Nadu	0.7	0.8	1.0	1.0	1.2
Uttar Pradesh	0.6	1.0	1.0	0.6	0.8
Uttaranchal				1.7	1.5
West Bengal	0.6	0.9	0.9	1.1	0.8
Delhi	1.5	1.9	1.5	2.4	1.3
India GDP Growth	3.60%	3.50%	5.30%	6.20%	8.10%
Correlation of state growth with previous decade		54.19%	45.80%	68.37%	45.51%

Source: Authors' calculations from CSO data on national accounts.

(predominantly telecom and a greater road network) had the highest growth across six states each, with construction now being the fastest growing sector in just five states.

To conclude, at the state level, manufacturing has been among the leading sectors in very few states, despite the early reforms centring around this sector. Services have led growth in India for a long time and continue

Table 1.5 High Growth Sectors at the State Level

2001–2 to 2005–6 (1999–2000 GSDP series)		2006–7 to 2010–11 (2004–5 GSDP series)	
Highest Growth Sector	No. of States/UTs	Highest Growth Sector	No. of States/UTs
Construction	15	Banking and insurance	6
Transport, storage, and communication	6	Public admin	6
Manufacturing	4	Transport, storage, and communication	6
Mining and quarrying	3	Construction	5
Electricity, gas, and water supply	2	Electricity, gas, and water supply	4
Banking & insurance and insurance query	1	Mining and quarrying	2
Trade, hotels, and restaurants	1	Trade, hotels, and restaurants	2
		Real estate, ownership of dwellings, and business services	1
No. of States/UTs	32	No. of States/UTs	32

Source: Authors' calculations using CSO data on GSDP. See Appendix A1.2 for state-wise details.

to do so even at the state level. Though again which services have been leading differs across states depending on idiosyncratic conditions in the states.

As discussed earlier, researchers have given varied explanations for the disparate growth paths of states. However, whatever the rationale given by various researchers, it is clear that the initial response to liberalization clearly varied across states due to local institutions and economic structures.

There is an additional question that arises of particular importance at a regional level. In a vibrant democracy like India where there are so many political calculations, what do aspirations, growth, and therefore reforms, have to do with being in power? Studies have linked growth performance to voting behaviour and election outcomes. Virmani (2004) argues that the benchmark for growth performance has been rising over the years and voters can discern the gap between what is professed and the actual outcomes on the ground. Gupta and Panagariya's (2011) analysis of the 2009 elections also shows the importance of growth performance for an incumbent party to win. Their results include that personal characteristics of candidates are significant only in states that have shown slow growth and the incumbency factor is much larger in high growth states. In fact, when alternative defining issues are absent, growth is likely to be increasingly central in determining election outcomes. In effect, growth and governance matter much more now than they did before, a point that political parties are beginning to grasp. With a multitude of political parties and split votes, the various forces that pull the state in different directions will dictate the pace of change in the future and therefore the growth trajectory.

***

This chapter aimed at understanding the underlying factors behind the accelerated growth path of the Indian economy. Trends show that the growth surge after the 1990s was deeper and less volatile than in the previous decade, clearly the effect of widespread and more credible reforms. Studies reviewed in this essay show that growth has been the outcome of productivity, which in turn can be linked to the reforms process in certain sub-sectors. However, a finer analysis that links specific events and reforms to such a process has not been initiated so far. In addition, the puzzle in manufacturing growth that has not responded to industrial reforms in a sustained manner also remains to be answered by researchers.

When it comes to reforms and growth, two points are crucial for further analysis from the point of view of India's future growth trajectory. To begin with, though reforms were directed initially at the industry, the sector continues to be plagued by numerous constraints. While on the one hand, the manufacturing sector shows a close relation to the global macro-environment and is deeply affected during slowdowns, researchers have identified many domestic factors that possibly have a hand in restraining higher growth, including infrastructure, especially power shortages, labour laws, inspector raj, and lack of foreign investment interest. Clearly, though India does possess the capability of a vibrant manufacturing sector, this sector has not been able to contribute to its potential towards India's growth. This brings us to the second point: why did the services sector take the lead in India, and can this growth be sustained ahead? While studies have attributed the growth surge in the Indian economy to the rise in the services sector's productivity, this chapter notes that the growth in the services sector in India has been broad-based and not confined to any single sub-sector. Over the last 30 years of high growth in the services sector, different sub-sectors have taken the lead across time. The turning point of financial sector productivity improvements is as early as the mid-1980s, that of trade and hotels from the mid-1990s, and that of transport, storage, and communications since 2000s. *The key tipping point in each case has been some government policy change that facilitated introduction of new technology or investment in the sector.* Services that started at low bases have responded more than proportionately to the liberalized environment and specific policy moves, and the baton has shifted from one sub-sector to another.

This chapter also finds that different states have responded differently to the reforms process, and there are various reasons for this: favourable initial conditions, political alignments with the central government, and electoral outcomes that defined governance. Interestingly, a few studies have also shown that growth and governance are more crucial for electoral outcomes now than ever before. This despite the fact pointed out by many heterodox economists that the emphasis on reforms, growth, and productivity has pushed to the background more important issues of increasing inequality and persistence of poverty.[18]

Yet, there need not be a dichotomy here, as Rakshit (2007) explains. There are two supply side initiatives that will increase efficiency for all sectors, particularly the laggard agriculture and industry sectors, as well as provide employment opportunities for low-skill labour. These are: (a) putting in place an effective credit delivery system, access to finance being a major hurdle for productive investment particularly by small and medium enterprises (in other words, financial inclusion), and (b) massive public investment in irrigation, roads, railways, communication, ports, power, and other infrastructure; this is long overdue. With these two in place, productivity and employment will be boosted across the sectors and economy, making for more sustained equitable growth.

As Kochhar et al. (2006) argue, India has so far followed an idiosyncratic pattern of development, and the past gives little guidance for the future. Yet, it can be said that reforms have so far led to productivity surges and therefore growth across various sectors. What remains is unblocking the infrastructure constraints that are currently holding back the economy, to unleash more broad-based policy changes that will take forward a process that began more than two decades ago.

[18] See Nayyar (2006) and Bhaduri (2007).

Appendix A1.1

Table A1.1 Decadal Growth Rates of NSDP at Constant Prices (percentage)

	1961–2 to 1970–1	1971–2 to 1980–1	1981–2 to 1990–1	1991–2 to 2000–1	2001–2 to 2010–11
Andhra Pradesh	1.6	3.4	5.6	5.6	8.7
Assam	3.8	2.7	2.9	2.0	5.0
Bihar	1.1	3.2	4.7	3.8	9.2
Chhattisgarh				9.3	20.1
Gujarat	3.1	5.6	4.7	6.9	10.2
Haryana	6.3	5.4	5.3	4.7	9.3
Himachal Pradesh	3.5	3.2	5.3	6.9	7.1
Jammu & Kashmir	3.8	4.7	2.1	4.5	5.7
Jharkhand				10.1	5.9
Karnataka	3.6	4.3	5.2	6.8	8.1
Kerala	4.2	1.7	3.6	5.7	8.4
Madhya Pradesh	2.3	1.7	4.4	4.9	7.0
Maharashtra	3.2	5.7	6.4	6.3	10.5
Odisha		2.8	4.3	3.5	9.1
Punjab	5.8	5.4	5.3	4.5	6.6
Rajasthan	2.9	3.5	6.6	6.5	7.3
Tamil Nadu	2.6	2.8	5.3	6.4	9.6
Uttar Pradesh	2.3	3.5	5.1	3.7	6.3
Uttaranchal				10.6	12.2
West Bengal	2.3	3.2	4.8	6.8	6.7
Arunachal Pradesh		7.6	8.2	3.9	8.1
Delhi	5.4	6.5	7.7	14.6	10.6
Goa		6.1	6.8	8.1	8.4
Manipur	7.1	6.1	4.8	4.4	6.2
Meghalaya			5.2	6.4	7.3
Mizoram			10.4	5.0	8.2
Nagaland			7.0	5.6	
Pondicherry		7.1	4.3	13.4	6.9
Sikkim				13.7	9.9
Tripura	2.0	5.3	6.1	7.9	7.9
Andaman & Nicobar			5.2	5.7	10.4
Chandigarh					10.6
India	3.6	3.5	5.3	6.2	8.1

Source: Authors' estimates using CSO data.

Note: Chhattisgarh, Jharkhand, and Uttarakhand's 1990s growth is 1993–4 to 2000–1 since there is no earlier data.

Table A1.2 Highest Growing Sectors at the State Level in the 2000s (percentage)

	2001–2 to 2010–11	2001–2 to 2005–6		2006–7 to 2010–11	
	GSDP Growth Rate	Highest Growing Sector	Growth Rate of Highest Growing Sector	Highest Growing Sector	Growth Rate of Highest Growing Sector
Andhra Pradesh	8.70	Construction	15.8	Banking and insurance	16.6
Assam	5.00	Electricity, gas, and water supply	24.4	Construction	17.4
Bihar	9.20	Construction	25.6	Trade, hotels, and restaurants	22.1
Chhattisgarh	20.10	Manufacturing	15.6	Electricity, gas, and water supply	23.4
Gujarat	10.20	Construction	24.0	Construction	19.9
Haryana	9.30	Transport, storage, and communication	16.1	Trade, hotels, and restaurants	16.3
Himachal Pradesh	7.10	Transport, storage, and communication	17.5	Mining and quarrying	22.7
Jammu & Kashmir	5.70	Transport, storage, and communication	16.3	Mining and quarrying	28.5
Jharkhand	5.90	Manufacturing	21.1	Transport, storage, and communication	15.5
Karnataka	8.10	Mining and quarrying	18.2	Banking and insurance	12.6
Kerala	8.40	Construction	20.8	Transport, storage, and communication	21.2
Madhya Pradesh	7.00	Construction	10.7	Banking and Insurance	18.9
Maharashtra	10.50	Trade, hotels, and restaurants	11.5	Public admin	17.3

(contd.)

Table A1.2 (*contd.*)

	2001–2 to 2010–11	2001–2 to 2005–6		2006–7 to 2010–11	
	GSDP Growth Rate	Highest Growing Sector	Growth Rate of Highest Growing Sector	Highest Growing Sector	Growth Rate of Highest Growing Sector
Odisha	9.10	Manufacturing	20.6	Banking and insurance	17.6
Punjab	6.60	Construction	12.4	Banking and insurance	15.3
Rajasthan	7.30	Construction	16.6	Banking and insurance	14.0
Tamil Nadu	9.60	Construction	14.0	Real estate and business services	16.6
Uttar Pradesh	6.30	Construction	21.2	Public admin	14.9
Uttaranchal	12.20	Mining and quarrying	31.8	Public admin	22.6
West Bengal	6.70	Construction	14.4	Transport, storage, and communication	13.9
Delhi	10.60	Construction	19.3	Electricity, gas, and water supply	24.3
India GDP Growth	8.10	Construction	12.80	Finance, insurance, real estate, and business services	10.90

Source: Authors' estimates using CSO data.

References

Acharya, Shankar (2002), 'India: Crisis, Reforms and Growth in the Nineties', Stanford University Center for Research on Economic Development and Policy Reform Working Paper No. 139.

Aghion, Phillipe, Robin Burgess, Stephen J. Redding, and Fabrizio Zilibotti (2008), 'The Unequal Effects of Liberalization: Evidence from Dismantling the License Raj in India', *American Economic Review* 98(4): 1397–1412.

Ahluwalia, Montek S. (1994), 'India's Economic Reforms', Planning Commission Paper. Available at http://planningcommission.nic.in/aboutus/speech/spemsa/msa012.pdf (last accessed on 2 July 2012).

Arnold, Jens Matthias, Beata Javorcik, Molly Lipscomb, and Aaditya Mattoo (2012), 'Services Reform and Manufacturing Performance Evidence from India', Policy Research Working Paper 5948, The World Bank, January.

Bhaduri, Amit (2007), 'Economic Growth: A Meaningless Obsession?,' India Seminar, January 2007. Available at http://www.india-seminar.com/2007/569/569_amit_bhaduri.htm (last accessed on 28 July 2012).

Bhagwati, Jagdish (1998), 'The Design Of Indian Development', in Isher Judge Ahluwalia and I.M.D. Little (eds), *India's Economic Reforms and Development: Essays for Manmohan Singh*, pp. 23–39. New Delhi: Oxford University Press.

Bhattacharya, B.B. and S. Sakthivel (2004), *Regional Growth and Disparity in India: A Comparison of Pre- and Post-Reform Decades*. Delhi: Institute of Economic Growth.

Bosworth, Barry, Susan M. Collins, and Arvind Virmani (2007), 'Sources Of Growth In The Indian Economy', NBER, Working Paper 12901.

CSO (2010), *New Series of National Accounts Statistics (base year 2004–6)*. New Delhi: Central Statistical Organisation, Ministry of Statistics and Programme Implementation, Government of India, March.

DeLong, J. Bradford (2004), 'India Since Independence: An Analytic Growth Narrative', in Dani Rodrik (ed.), *Modern Economic Growth: Analytical Country Studies*. Available at: http://www.j-bradford-delong.net/ (last accessed on 24 July 2012).

Dholakia, Bakul (2001), 'Sources of India's Accelerated Growth and the Vision of Indian Economy in 2020', *Indian Economic Journal* 49(4, April 2001–June 2002): 27–46.

Dholakia, Ravindra and Ameya Sapre (2011), 'Estimating Structural Breaks Endogenously in India's Post-Independence Growth Path: An Empirical Critique', *Journal of Quantitative Economics* 9(2, July): 73–87.

Goldar, Bishwanath and Arup Mitra (2008), 'Productivity Increase and Changing Sectoral Composition: Contribution to Economic Growth in India', Working Paper Series No. E/291/2008, Institute of Economic Growth, New Delhi.

Government of India (2005), *The Report of the Committee on Streamlining the requirement of Inspection of Industrial Units under Different Acts*. New

Delhi: Ministry of Commerce & Industry, Department of Industrial Policy & Promotion.

——— (2007), *Report of the Working Group on Construction for the 11th Five Year Plan (2007–12)*. New Delhi: Planning Commission.

Gupta, Poonam and Arvind Panagariya (2011), 'India: Election Outcomes and Economic Performance', Paper 7, NCAER Conference on Trade, Poverty, Inequality and Democracy, New Delhi.

Joshi, Vijay and I.M.D. Little (1994), *India: Macroeconomics and Political Economy: 1961–91*. Washington, DC: The World Bank.

Kar, Sabyasachi, Debajit Jha, and Alpana Kateja (2010), 'Club-Convergence and Polarisation of States: A Nonparametric Analysis of Post-Reform India', IEG Working Paper No. 307.

Kar, S. and S. Sakthivel (2007), 'Reforms and Regional Inequality in India', *Economic and Political Weekly*, 42(47): 69–77.

Kathuria, Vinish, Seethamma Natarajan, Rajesh Raj, and Kunal Sen (2010), 'Organized versus Unorganized Manufacturing Performance in India in the Post-Reform Period', MPRA Paper No. 20317.

Kochhar, Kalpana, Utsav Kumar, Raghuram Rajan, Arvind Subramanian, and Ioannis Tokatlidis (2006), 'India's Patterns of Development: What Happened, What Follows', NBER Working Paper No. 12023.

Mitra, Arup, Aristomene Varoudakis, and Marie Ange Veganzones Varoudakis (2002), 'Productivity and Technical Efficiency in Indian States' Manufacturing: The Role of Infrastructure', *Economic Development and Cultural Change* 50(2): 395–426.

Mohan, Rakesh (2006), *Financial Sector Reforms and Monetary Policy: The Indian Experience*. RBI Bulletin, July.

Nayyar, Deepak (2006), 'Indians Unfinished Journey Transforming Growth into Development', *Modern Asian Studies*, 40(3): 797–832.

Panagariya, Arvind (2004), 'India in the 1980s and 1990s: A Triumph of Reforms', IMF Working Papers 04/43, International Monetary Fund.

——— (2008), *India: The Emerging Giant*, USA: Oxford University Press.

Rakshit, Mihir (2007), 'Services-led Growth: The Indian Experience', *Money & Finance*, February: 91–126.

Rodrik, Dani and Arvind Subramanian (2004), 'From "Hindu Growth" to Productivity Surge: The Mystery of the Indian Growth Transition', NBER Working Paper 10376.

Sachs, J.D., N. Bajpai, and A. Ramiah (2002), 'Understanding Regional Economic Growth in India', *Asian Economic Papers*, 1(3): 32–62.

Saikia, Dileep (2009), 'Total Factor Productivity in Indian Agriculture: Some Conceptual and Methodological Issues', MPRA Paper No. 28578.

Singh, Kulwinder (2006), *Foreign Direct Investment in India: A Critical Analysis of FDI from 1991–2005*. New Delhi: Centre for Civil Society.

Singh, Sanjay K. (2006), 'Information Technology in India: Present Status and Future Prospects for Economic Development', *Directions*, May, IIT Kanpur.

Singh, Nirvikar, Laveesh Bhandari, Aoyu Chen, and Aarti Khare (2003), 'Regional Inequality in India: A Fresh Look', *Economic and Political Weekly*, 38(11): 1069–73.

Swaminathan, M.S. (2010), *From Green to Evergreen Revolution: Indian Agriculture: Performance and Challenges*. New Delhi: Academic Foundation.

Trivedi, Pushpa, L. Lakshmanan, Rajeev Jain, and Yogesh K. Gupta (2011), 'Productivity, Efficiency and Competitiveness of The Indian Manufacturing Sector', Development Research Group Studies Series No. 37, Reserve Bank of India.

Virmani, Arvind (2004), 'Economic Growth, Governance and Voting Behaviour: An Application to Indian Elections', Working Paper No. 138, Indian Council for Research on International Economic Relations, Delhi.

———— (2005), 'India's Economic Growth History: Fluctuations, Trends, Break Points and Phases', Occasional Paper, Indian Council for Research on International Economic Relations, New Delhi.

Wallack, Jessica Seddon (2003), 'Structural Breaks in Indian Macroeconomic Data', *Economic and Political Weekly*, XXXVIII(41, 11 October): 4312–15.

CHAPTER 2

POLITICAL ECONOMY OF GROWTH

RAHUL MUKHERJI*

The Indian state has been more penetrated by powerful social actors than many East and South East Asian states.[1] Unlike China, India could neither abolish private enterprise nor could it embrace globalization with the same speed and ferocity. Both, complete state-driven nationalization and state-driven globalization would demand a state which would have much greater command over interest groups such as industrialists, farmers, and trade unions.[2] Policies favouring economic growth and development in India needed to evolve gradually after certain ideas became prominent in policy circles after years of cogitation. This is a model of growth driven by a relationship between the state and society, where the power of the state, even in its commanding moments, was moderated by the power of social actors.

This chapter addresses two questions. First, how did economic policies change to accelerate India's growth trajectory? Economic ideas held by

* This chapter draws from Rahul Mukherji (2009) 'The State, Economic Growth and Development in India', *India Review* 8 (1 January–March): 81–106. The author also thanks a referee for comments. I thank Sumit Ganguly for pointing me towards this project; Ashima Goyal for the invitation, comments, and encouragement; an anonymous reviewer for encouraging feedback; and Ngawang Drakpa for excellent research help. The errors, as usual, rest with the author.

[1] On the Asian developmental states, see Wade (1990), Amsden (1985), Haggard (1990), and Evans (1995).

[2] On the 'dominant coalition' ranged against economic reforms, see Bardhan (1984).

dominant sections of the technocracy and those that captured the imagination of powerful leaders mattered. Over time, these ideas also found support from powerful interest groups. To give one example, even though the birth of import substitution could be understood as an idea that persuaded Jawaharlal Nehru and some other members of the Congress Party who dominated the policy framework after 1955, this idea also appealed to sections of the industrial class over time who favoured industrial controls and protectionism.

Then how did the policy idea of economic self-sufficiency and government control under-girding many of the salient institutions of the Indian economy change, especially after 1991. A tipping point model of ideational change through a brief narration of India's economic history reveals that policy ideas get undermined over a period of time when expectations arising from certain policies are not met. Import substitution industrialization that depended on substituting imports with home production rather than promoting exports neither produced robust industrialization and growth nor did it produce economic self-sufficiency. This sowed the seeds of economic change from around 1975, which accelerated during the 1980s. The Government of India's reports and policy changes suggested that policymakers wanted the government to withdraw from investment decisions and allow entrepreneurs to play a bigger role. At the same time, it became clear to policymakers that globalization or trade needed to be harnessed as a harbinger of growth. While the ideational milieu within the Indian technocracy was far more favourable towards giving private companies and globalization freer play, politics stood in the way.

The balance of payments crisis of 1991 is an important turning point—not because the International Monetary Fund (IMF) came as a meteor from above at a time when India was in dire need for foreign exchange. Such exogenous short-lived meteoric impacts with long-term consequences have often been described as a critical juncture in comparative political economy.[3] An ideational tipping point, on the other hand, is like an earthquake which occurs when endogenous changes gain momentum over a period of time and make an impact only after ideas have reached a certain critical mass or a tipping point. Seismologists cannot exactly predict an earthquake though they can guess when one would be likely within a rough time frame. This is because seismologists can ascertain when tectonic shifts have occurred substantially in a particular direction.

[3] On a critical juncture, see Krasner (1984: 223–45), Pierson (2004: 80), and Gould and Eldridge (1977: 115–51).

This is the time when an earthquake becomes very likely. We find that economic change in India often follows a path similar to the earthquake model rather than the meteor model of change.[4]

An economic earthquake was waiting to occur in 1991 because of rising fiscal deficit, deficit in India's current account, and increased dependence on foreign banks and non-resident Indians for financing the deficit. The government had changed its mind, building on the development experience since the mid-1970s. The exogenous shock in 1991 was not any more severe than the one in 1966. The reason why India returned to economic regulation and autarky in 1966 was that the government was not convinced about the need for reforms at that time. In 1991, on the other hand, the government made a virtue of necessity and steered the economy towards globalization and deregulation taking advantage of dependence on the IMF because the government had a different view about development policies than in 1966. This is because the government's own development experience since the mid-1970s had changed its mind about future economic direction favouring globalization and deregulation.[5] The growth experience of the rest of Asia had played an important part in this story.[6]

Second, this chapter reflects on challenges for India's growth. It points to the fact that the single most important factor that poses a challenge for growth is effective regulation of various sectors of the economy. Many sectors of the Indian economy were largely governed by the state in the past. As the state opened up opportunities to private companies, two kinds of challenges arose. First, in the initial phase, government departments tried hard to throttle private business by tilting the regulatory scales in their favour. We find that private companies were often hurt by the predatory policies of government-owned incumbents. Second, as private companies won regulatory conflicts over time, it was found that some private companies tried to influence regulation to secure a greater share of the market. Even though regulatory evolution produced positive results in areas like telecommunications and the stock market, the challenge is to produce independent and accountable regulators who are fairly detached from the executive and have licensing powers.

India's growth rate began looking more like China's after 2003. It accelerated to over 5 per cent between 1975 and 1990 when India's domestic private sector was given greater room for manoeuvre. This was not a period

[4] On the tipping point, see Pierson (2004: 82–90); Cappoccia and Kelemen (2007: 351); and Mukherji (2013).

[5] On Indian gradualism, see Ahluwalia (2007).

[6] On the two crises, see Mukherji (2013).

when India's engagement with the global economy witnessed a significant rise. The paradigm shift in private sector and trade orientation beyond 1991 has been associated with higher rates of growth, over 6 per cent between 1991 and 2004, and over 8.5 per cent between 2003 and 2007. It is the latter figure that has drew the attention of the world when India became one of the fastest growing economies in the world after China. Even if we take the global financial crisis into account, India has grown at a rate higher than 7 per cent in the new millennium, which is slower only to China and more rapid than economies such as Brazil, Russia, and Singapore. This chapter explores how the surge in growth occurred and what obstacles lay in its path.

The Political Economy of Growth Beyond 1975

India's accelerated economic growth, at a rate higher than 5 per cent in the period from 1975 to 1990, needs to be understood in the context of steady private sector orientation beginning in the mid-1970s, which accelerated in the 1980s. Thoughts about private sector and trade orientation arose in the mid-1970s. In 1975 a special cabinet committee was formed for export promotion (Mukerji 2007; Nayar 2006). A number of influential reports within the Government of India began arguing against the system of physical and financial controls, and the need for export promotion.[7] The Department of Electronics set up within the Prime Minister's Office foresaw the potential for India's exports in software even in the mid-1970s. In the early 1980s, Indira Gandhi was attentive to China's trade-oriented growth and the inability of the Soviet system to meet even its food requirements (Gandhi 1985: 236).

It was politically tougher for Indira Gandhi (1980–4) and her successor and son Rajiv Gandhi (1984–9) to undo the economic legacy built from the 1950s than it was for Deng to undo the legacy of Mao. Private sector-oriented liberalization entailed gradual dismantling of controls over private enterprise. The corporate private sector was highly protectionist. Trade orientation and substantial tariff liberalization could not be

[7] The influential reports included Dagli (1979), Alexander (1978), Hussain (1984), Chakravarty (1985), and Narasimhan (1985).

achieved and India's trade to GDP ratio remained constant between 1980 and 1990 (Kohli 1991: 315–38).

There was substantial opposition to economic deregulation. The Congress Party was largely opposed to private sector orientation. Indian industry had become so accustomed to licensed production within the protected home market that the auto industry even opposed the automatic expansion of its manufacturing capacity when it learned that it was being made to compete with Maruti Suzuki—a joint venture between the Government of India and Suzuki Corporation of Japan (Gokarn and Vaidya 2004: 280–314). The Maruti Suzuki car quickly overtook the sales of India's known brands—Ambassador and Fiat cars, which had not upgraded their technology for decades. Indian industrialists had typically become past masters at 'briefcase politics'—which entailed bribing the government in order to secure production, import, and export licenses. Stanley Kochanek (2007: 417–19) has aptly described how briefcases filled with currency notes were exchanged in return for licenses and other privileges that the government could offer.

Economic deregulation in the 1980s was quite substantial in relation to the legacy of the 1970s, despite the political opposition described earlier. It occurred largely because the government had changed its mind about the role of private companies in India's industrialization. A number of decisions were taken to correct the situation of what was perceived as low levels of industrial productivity. First, some industrial deregulation favouring the Indian private sector was achieved. A few sectors, such as automobile parts and pharmaceuticals, were released from the clutches of industrial licensing—a practice that had come into existence in 1956. These sectors had earlier required government permission before any private sector investment could be made. Second, restrictions for large businesses via the MRTP[8] route were eased. It was now easier to expand capacity or to manufacture a product similar to a licensed product without seeking permission from the government (Kumar and Sen Gupta 2008: 4; Nayar 2006: 1887–8). Third, Rajiv Gandhi was able to move the telecommunications sector in the direction of private sector orientation. He initiated the corporatization of parts of the Department of Telecommunications (DOT) into the government-owned corporate entity—Mahanagar Telephone Nigam Limited (MTNL), despite vehement opposition from

[8] MRTP refers to the Monopolies and Restrictive Trade Policies Act (1969). This act stringently regulated companies that were worth more than Rs 200 million. Rajiv Gandhi raised this limit to Rs 1 billion.

DOT's managers and workers. The government-funded Centre for the Development of Telematics (CDOT) produced technology for telephone switches, which was superior to the one being produced by the public sector company Indian Telephone Industry (ITI). CDOT switches had to contend with opposition from ITI in order to succeed. This technology was licensed to private companies and continues to serve India's rural areas.[9] These efforts produced impressive levels of industrial growth in the mid- to late-1980s that were surpassed only after 2003.

Fourth, Rajiv Gandhi drew the more professional and modern Association of Indian Engineering Industry (AIEI) closer to the government. As a consequence, the erstwhile influential industrialists of the Federation of Indian Chambers of Commerce and Industry (FICCI) who were habituated to obtaining licenses by supplying the ruling party with funds—a practice that was perfected in the 1970s—were relegated to the background. Rajiv Gandhi now consulted AIEI on important matters, provided it with access to government policy, and persuaded a small association to transform itself into an organization that would come to represent larger interests of the Indian industry.[10]

Fifth, the period of domestic deregulation witnessed the emergence of the software sector as an export-oriented sector. This was aided by synergies between the Department of Electronics (DOE) and India's natural comparative advantage, which lay in its cheap English speaking technically competent workforce. The DOE, manned by technocrats with backgrounds similar to the newly qualified middle class entrepreneurs, gradually nudged the government towards providing entrepreneurs with greater choice with respect to imports and obtaining finance for imports essential for exports. It also provided the push to government investment in software technology parks. These parks provided Indian firms with cheap connectivity, office space, and infrastructure, and were a major boost for India's software exports.[11]

Finally, the most important legacy of the Rajiv Gandhi government was background research on economic liberalization that was carried

[9] On the telecom transformation during Rajiv Gandhi's premiership, see Mukherji (2007: 302–4). The Indian Telecom Industries had a tie up with the French company Alcatel at that time.

[10] Sinha (2005: 1–27); Kochanek (2007: 424–27); Pederson (2000: 268–71); and Kantha and Ray (2006: 139–56).

[11] On India's information technology revolution, see Pingle (2000: 127–38); Saxenian (2007: 362–4); and Kapur (2002: 93–102).

out within the Prime Minister's Office, the Ministry of Commerce and Industry, and the Ministry of Finance by skilled technocrats, such as Montek Singh Ahluwalia, Shankar Acharya, Rakesh Mohan, and Vijay Kelkar. This effort was spurred in part by India's own policy failures and in part by the rising growth rates in China and South East Asia. To give one example, Rajiv Gandhi's successor, Prime Minister V.P. Singh, requested his Special Secretary, Montek Singh Ahluwalia, to write a memo on the urgent economic tasks for India if it was to approach South East Asian levels of development. Singh and Ahluwalia had returned from a trip to Malaysia and Prime Minister Singh was stunningly impressed by economic progress made by Malaysia. Ahluwalia's 1990 memo, which was leaked to the press, was the blueprint of reforms that India carried out after 1991 when faced with a severe balance of payments crisis (Shastri 1995: 223–6). This research and changes in the ideational milieu within the government formed the raison d'etre for the half-hearted liberalization of the 1980s. It also prepared India ideationally to deal with the balance of payments crisis of 1991 in a manner that was impossible in 1966 when the ideational environment within government was quite different.[12]

High Growth Trajectory: 1991–Present

It is important to note that trade, investment, and infrastructure reforms of 1991, even though they constituted a break from the past, were largely path dependent. Without the experience of the 1970s and the 1980s, the technocratic conviction required to break the political deadlock in favour of the status quo bias in a moment of financial crisis would not have arisen. India could have acted in 1991 in the same way it did in 1966, which was retreat to reforms in a moment of crisis only to pursue state control and autarky in the long run. The reason why 1991 was different from 1966 was that this time technocratic conviction within the executive branch made a virtue of depending on IMF at the time of the balance of payments crisis and pursued reforms that were tough within the context of India's political

[12] This view is based on discussions with influential technocrats such as Montek Singh Ahluwalia, Shankar Acharya, Rakesh Mohan, and Vijay Kelkar.

economy. This is why it is reasonable to conjecture that India had reached a tipping point in 1991.

Former Finance Minister Manmohan Singh is a distinguished economist whose doctoral dissertation at the University of Oxford was published by Clarendon Press in the early 1960s. At a time when most distinguished development economists were talking about the virtues of import substitution, Singh pointed out through detailed empirical analysis that export promotion was important for India's development.[13] Manmohan Singh had the support of an excellent technocratic team whose research and policy experience during the 1980s generated a sophisticated blueprint for reforms. Singh stated in no uncertain terms in his budget speech in 1991 that the underlying problem was the unsustainability of government spending in the presence of low levels of productivity.[14] Budget deficit contributed to the balance of payments deficit and engendered investor pessimism. Equally significant was the fact that Prime Minister Rao was willing to stick his political neck out in favour of economic reforms. He chose his finance minister and trusted him. He understood that the end of the Cold War required a fundamental restructuring of India's internal and external economic policies.[15]

The policy team took advantage of the crisis to deal with a powerful industrial class largely opposed to significant globalization and deregulation. Indian industry agreed to tariff reductions, devaluation, and easier entry of foreign direct investment (FDI) because the import-substituting industry needed foreign exchange for imports of intermediate goods, and this finance could only be made available by IMF at a time when commercial banks and non-resident Indians had largely withdrawn their money from India. India had merely two weeks of foreign exchange and no alternative sources of funding when it approached IMF in 1991. Indian industry's acquiescence to economic reforms was articulated and promoted effectively by the Confederation of Indian Industry (CII), which was earlier known as AIEI described in the previous section.

Technocrats, who were largely in agreement with IMF on the earlier-mentioned issues, made virtue of necessity and pushed for far-reaching

[13] This view is based on discussions with Jagdish Bhagwati, University Professor, Columbia University. See also, Bhagwati (1998: 23–4, 35–6); Singh (1964); and Sen (1998: 81).

[14] Lok Sabha Debates (24 July 1991: 271–315).

[15] I benefitted from a discussion with former Prime Minister Narasimha Rao in February 2001. See also Bhattacharya (2 July 2011). This view has also been shared by senior technocrats who discussed issues with the author.

reforms in trade, industrial, and foreign investment policies in the first three reform years (1991–3), when India was accepting conditional funds from IMF. Technocrats also begged to differ with IMF. Fiscal deficit was allowed to grow after the first year, as government spending could not be drastically reduced in a poor country. Trade union laws could not be reformed. And market restructuring in areas, such as telecommunications, stock markets, and airlines, were home-grown efforts unaided by World Bank funds.[16] Finance minister Singh declared at the Gabriel Silver lecture at Columbia University in 1995 that India's tryst with globalization was irreversible—no matter which government came to power after the elections of 1996. This prophecy has come true.[17]

What are the drivers of India's growth? Industrial delicensing after 1991 allowed Indian private companies to produce without the need for a license. To give one example, Tata Motors, a company that was not permitted to manufacture cars during the regime of controls, took advantage of delicensing and produced one of India's most popular cars—the Indica. Spurred by their success, Tata Motors purchased global brands such as Rover and Jaguar. And, the company also introduced the world's cheapest car—Nano. Such possibilities could not arise during the regime of controls.

Second, devaluation of the Indian rupee quickly rendered India's software and other exports more competitive. To give just one example, India replaced Japan as Sri Lanka's largest trading partner in 1996 after a period of 60 years. Geography, exchange rates, and improved products made Indian goods such as watches, motor bicycles, cars, and trucks more competitive than their counterparts from Japan. Titan watches replaced their Japanese counterparts and the cheaper Indian Kawasaki Bajaj and Hero Honda bikes replaced the more expensive Kawasaki and Honda bikes from Japan (Kelegama 1999: 95–103; Mukherji 2011: 301–28).

Third, India's increasing competitiveness arose also as a result of competition from foreign markets. Even though India's tariffs are high by the standards of many East and South East Asian countries, the weighted average nominal tariff dropped dramatically from 81.4 per cent in 1991–2 to

[16] These views are based on extensive interviews and a reading of news and transcripts of the executive board meetings of IMF in 1991 and 1992. It should be noted that IMF concentrates more on the fiscal and balance of payments side of the conditional lending whereas the World Bank works with governments on longer term structural adjustment.

[17] On the irreversible nature of reforms, see Nayar (2007: 202–27).

32.9 per cent in 1995–6 and to 18 per cent in 2004–5. India abolished quotas for consumer goods imports in 2001. Tariff liberalization, which was especially successful in the intermediate goods sector, reduced the prices of Indian finished products (Tendulkar and Bhavani 2007: 116–25). Over time, preferential trade agreements with Singapore, Sri Lanka, Thailand, and the Association of South East Asian Nations (ASEAN) also spurred competitiveness (Aggarwal and Mukherji 2008: 235–53).

Fourth, the legacy of the Foreign Exchange Regulation Act, 1974 was overturned after 1991. Non-debt-creating investments of multinational corporations were viewed favourably after 1991. While the quantum of foreign investments increased quite rapidly in relation to the past, such investments were still insignificant when compared with China. A fundamental difference between the Indian and Chinese political economies is that while China could promote foreign investments in the absence of a domestic private sector, in India's case, foreign investments needed to deal with domestic corporations to win regulatory advantages. This was not easy. Of the US$ 48 billion that India received between 1992 and 2002, US$ 24 billion came via the portfolio route and US$ 24 billion via the direct route (Tendulkar and Bhavani 2007: 106–16). This entire amount could have gone to China in a single year. And foreign investments through the portfolio route that arrived in India via stock markets went towards strengthening Indian companies.

A business lobby that supports foreign investment in India is domestic industrialists who need foreign capital and expertise to compete with more cash-rich companies. It was the less well financially endowed companies like Bharti Televentures in India's GSM cellular mobile sector that supported the government over increasing the foreign equity limit from 51 to 74 per cent in 2006 in order to compete with richer companies like Tata and Reliance (Mukherji 2008: 1425–45).

India attracts US$ 30 to US$ 40 billion a year in foreign investment after 2003. This is a substantial advance over the past even though this is less than half the amount that China attracts. The Government of India created the Foreign Investment Promotion Board (FIPB) and has legislated the Foreign Exchange Management Act (FEMA) to streamline investments.[18] A National Investment Board has been established for easing business conditions for investors. In September 2012 the government decided to allow 51 per cent equity in multi-brand retail and 49 per cent in civil

[18] I owe this insight to the yet unpublished doctoral work of my student Sojin Shin.

aviation and it was keen on attracting the same for pension funds, despite substantial political opposition. The government's resolve to attract non-debt creating assets with foreign investment has increased, even though India is substantially more driven by domestic investment than China.

Last but not the least, the entrepreneurial instincts of Indian business, which could take advantage of deregulation, were critical for India's growth. A significant difference between India and China is that while the Chinese economy is still largely driven by government-owned companies, the Indian economy is driven to a much greater extent by its domestic private sector. A quick look at the list of top companies in Indian and Chinese stock markets reveals this pattern quite unambiguously. Indian private sector business houses have offered successful business models that are being discussed in leading business schools of the world.[19]

Sectors, such as software services and business process outsourcing have won India acclaim as the back-office of the world. Americans think of themselves as being 'Bangalored' when their jobs get outsourced to India. India's manufacturing sector has also begun shaping up after 2003. Pharmaceuticals, gems, and jewellery, and automotive parts have emerged as leading sectors. Even though Indian manufacturing lags behind China due to logistical and regulatory bottlenecks, Indian companies are consolidating and multinationalizing their business operations, overcoming domestic bottlenecks, and capturing the international market.

Indian multinationals now have a substantial footprint, which is a far cry from the days when India was scared of neocolonialism exploitation. The Tatas, for example, purchased the Tetley brand for US$ 432 million and became the second largest producer of packaged tea after Unilever's Lipton. Tata consolidated the operations of Tata Steel to be christened as the Best Steel Company in the World accorded by World Steel Dynamics. Thereafter, Tata acquired the Anglo Dutch Corus Steel for US$ 11 billion in 2007, in the fourth largest deal in the history of the industry. The Corus acquisition was preceded by smaller acquisitions in Singapore and Thailand in 2004 and 2005, respectively. There have been substantial foreign acquisitions in sectors, such as automotive parts, IT, consumer goods, and pharmaceuticals since 2004 (Goldstein 2008: 8–12, 18–25).

[19] On the importance of Indian entrepreneurship, see Das (2002) and Kumar (2009). On the India–China comparison on entrepreneurship, see Huang (2010: 233–98). For the relationship between government policy and entrepreneurship in India, see Murthy (2011: 462–72).

INFRASTRUCTURE REFORMS

India reformed its telecommunications sector, airlines, stock markets, and banks. It has so far failed in reforming the power sector and has had middling success in reforming its ports and highways. What is interesting is that with the exception of the power sector all the success stories were home grown and evolved in the context of messy democratic politics. The success stories were driven by the idea of promoting competition for the government-owned incumbents rather than by privatizing them. Oftentimes, these ideas reached a tipping point at the time of a financial crisis and bold changes were introduced thereafter.

India's telecommunications revolution driven by GSM cellular technology is truly spectacular, despite various periodic setbacks. The country added more than 8 million phones every month and its telecommunications services are among the most efficient in the world. It has over 900 million lines with a tele-density of greater than 65 lines per 100 residents. This remarkable success was achieved by promoting competition and by luring private players to compete with government-owned incumbents, rather than by privatizing government assets. India's telecommunications boom, though more widespread in urban areas, has penetrated rural areas as well.

DOT, housed within the Ministry of Communications, was averse to private sector competition. The Prime Minister's Office and the Ministry of Finance gradually persuaded DOT to accept competition from the private sector. Promoting competition, which was aided by the TRAI in 1997 and its further consolidation (2000), was spurred by financial crises. Each time DOT's rent-seeking behaviour brought the private sector to its knees, the Prime Minister's Office moved quickly to upgrade the regulatory framework favouring the private sector (Mukherji 2009: 491–517).

The sector faced a grave crisis when telecommunications minister D. Raja distributed spectrum cheaply in January 2008. The process did not follow due procedure and the minister ignored the advice of the prime minister, the minister of law and the finance minister. A few companies that acquired spectrum cheap resold it for windfall profits. The regulator who did not possess licensing powers could not check the excesses of the telecommunications minister. This process has hurt investor sentiment in recent years. Even though the government erred in issuing licenses, steps were taken to correct the situation. The concerned minister was sent to the high-security Tihar prison in New Delhi and the Supreme Court cancelled all the 122 licenses that had been distributed in a manner that reeked of rent-seeking propensities. The government implemented an auction with a one-time payment of Rs 14,000 crore,[20] which was substantially greater than the Rs 1,658 crore that the operators paid in 2008. Even though there were few takers of spectrum at this price, these moves signalled a political will to reduce rent-seeking and promoting competition.

India's stock markets were reformed via a similar dynamic. The government realized the need for a well-regulated stock market in the aftermath of the balance of payments crisis of 1991. The stock market was viewed as an important institution for directing savings towards industrialization. Moreover, investments were to be driven by the market rather than political or personal preferences. There was an urgent need to curb the opaque and rent-seeking propensities of Indian brokers that demanded computerization and reforms of the payment settlement system. The brokers of the Bombay Stock Exchange (BSE) successfully resisted both till the Ministry of Finance deployed its powers to set up a new National Stock Exchange (NSE). The brokers had underestimated NSE's competitive potential. NSE's success produced reforms in the BSE. But reforms in the settlement system had to wait till the stock market scam of 2001 because these reforms were resisted even by the regulator. The health of Indian companies and its stock markets make India a compelling destination for foreign institutional investors (FIIs) (Echeverri-Gent 2007: 328–58; Goyal 2012b: 63–96).

India's power sector is a dismal reform failure despite the government's best efforts. Farmers considered providing electricity a right in many states and have successfully opposed tariffs. In addition, there is rampant electricity theft in the non-farm sector (Dubash and Rajan 2001: 3367–90; Mukherji 2007: 312–23; Tongia 2007: 109–74). To give one example, fieldwork in Andhra Pradesh in December 2007 revealed that poor and middle-income farmers were in favour of subsidized high-quality electricity rather than the poor-quality free electricity being provided by the Congress government of Dr Rajasekhar Reddy. Free power came at night and distribution companies did not invest adequately in maintenance. Consequently, farmers and animals were being regularly electrocuted at night.

Why did the government make such a political issue out of free electricity? Rich farmers hired labourers at night and could afford the maintenance costs that the state-owned distribution companies did not

[20] 1 crore = 10 million.

provide for farmers who did not pay for electricity. Poor and middle income farmers also opined that the government's claim of having reduced theft could be spurious because agricultural consumption had not been metered. Andhra Pradesh was reputed to have the best governed power sector in India at the time when the interviews were conducted in 2007 (Mukherji 2010: 193–208).

Further, systematic interviews in rural Andhra Pradesh in the summer of 2009 revealed that even poorer farmers were using electric pump sets and benefitting from free electricity. Despite this, there were still a substantial number of farmers (though not a majority) who wished subsidized but better quality electric power. The tragedy was that the politics of populism trumped the politics of development. Progressive tariff could be used to make commercial farmers and industrialists pay for subsidizing poor farmers rather than giving power away for free. But it was politically more expedient to give it away for free to all farmers.

Challenges for Development

India's robust growth needed to involve more people. Its agriculture sector has been in decline since the mid-1990s. Its trade union laws increase the propensity of the Indian industry to remain capital intensive, resulting in unemployment and increased employment in the unorganized sector. Manufacturing industry faces substantial regulatory bottlenecks. Last but not the least, human development in areas such as primary education and health leave a lot to be desired. The result is that even though there has been a decline in the number of people below poverty line, a strategy of more inclusive growth would have achieved poverty alleviation more rapidly.

India is faced with its second agrarian crisis. The first one in the mid-1960s was due largely to the emphasis of the Second and the Third Five-Year plans on heavy capital-intensive industrialization and neglect of public investment in agriculture. India corrected this bias after the late 1960s by giving agriculture its due importance and increasing investment in agricultural technology, inputs, and prices. Middle income and rich peasants in western India produced the green revolution and made the country self-sufficient in food grains (Frankel 2005: 268–92; Varshney 1998).

India's agriculture sector, which feeds more than 60 per cent of the population, grew at a rate of 1.65 per cent between 1996–7 and 2004–5. This is a cause for concern as it may produce a second agrarian crisis. Subsidies, such as free power, price supports, free water, and free fertilizers to rich and middle income families have not been reduced but public investment that uplifts all, has dipped. To give one example, the US$ 15 billion loan waiver for farmers announced in the populist union budget of 2008–9 will not affect a majority of the marginal farmers. Eighty per cent of the marginal farmers did not access formal loans. Drought proofing 60 million hectares of arable land with the same investment would have produced more inclusive results (Chand et al. 2007: 2528–33; Mahajan 2008). Democracies have a propensity to get captured by powerful interest groups, which work to the detriment of larger developmental concerns.

The Industrial Disputes Act 1947 protects less than 10 per cent of India's workforce in a manner that makes it very difficult to retrench unionized workers. Any industrial unit employing more than 100 workers needs to seek the government's permission before firing an employee. Such permission can be difficult to obtain. Unionized workers are largely in the public sector, and private companies try to discourage workers from being unionized. Industry adjusts to regressive labour laws by sub-contracting its commercial operations to smaller units that escape labour laws and by increasing the capital intensity of production. Even though some state governments have been favouring employers in the recent times aided by favourable verdicts by courts, a stable contract between a worker and an employee that protects the worker in return for his labour is yet to evolve. Inclusive growth demands labour-intensive production aided by rational labour laws (RoyChowdhury 2007: 388–411).

India needed to promote a developmental, transparent, and investment-friendly democracy. Industrial regulations in India make it more difficult to make a success of manufacturing investment in India relative to China despite the progress made after 1991. Indian firms can invest in any sector but need state and central government permissions on a variety of issues ranging from land, labour, environment, electricity, water, taxation, and many more. These regulations often become a source of rent-seeking and patronage rather than a speedy and judicious clearance of an investment proposal based on its merits. India is not an easy place to begin business in manufacturing unless one finds a willing state government taking an initiative to make a success of the investment. The process of initiating manufacturing investment needs to be made more transparent and less cumbersome. Second, the Indian industry is negatively served by poor ports and roads and is crippled by power cuts. India's airports have improved in recent years, though.[21]

India's industrialization is beginning to demand more and more land. Industrial land acquisition needed to be based on the consent of the local people. It needed to be preceded by compensation and welfare measures that rendered the acquisition of land for industrial purposes a developmental endeavour. Fertile double-cropped land needed to be largely left alone for cultivation. The current laws give the government substantial powers to acquire land. Forced land acquisition by the government has led to violent unrest in some parts of India.

Land acquisition has been successful in areas where developers have worked with state governments and the local people for gaining consent by attempting to uplift their human conditions. States like Tamil Nadu, Andhra Pradesh, Gujarat, Maharashtra, and Haryana have streamlined these procedures at the sub-national level. Investment-friendly states are able to craft developmental bureaucracies that work more effectively for the local people and investors (Mukherji 2008a). The government is concerned about the issue of acquisition and the Land Acquisition Bill (2011) was passed as an Act in the Lok Sabha on 29 August 2013.

The success of Indian entrepreneurship lay in the fact that it was able to overcome these bottlenecks and grow. The software sector was especially lucky because it needed roads, ports, airports, and power to a much lesser extent than manufacturing. It was aided by India's success in creating efficient telecommunications, stock markets, and financial infrastructure.

* * *

The trajectory of the economic policies favouring India's growth was path dependent. From 1947 to 1975, policy consensus favoured an important role for the state within a relatively closed economy. Private enterprise survived during this period but India's trade declined. Changes in the policy consensus favouring economic deregulation began to appear in the mid-1970s, which prepared the ground for the tectonic policy shifts beyond 1991.

Economic change in India can be likened to an ideational tipping point. India's gradualism can be frustrating but it works through a process by which the government changes its mind building over decades of policy failure and experimentation. Crises often highlight these failures but what

[21] On bottlenecks for business, see Forbes (2002: 129–68). On ports, see Mukherji (2010: 184–93). See also Goyal (11 October 2012a).

looks like discontinuous change has an ideational past which has been building over a long period. The reason why India responded differently to the balance of payments crisis in 1991 than it did to the one in 1966 cannot be understood in terms of external pressure. It needs to be understood in terms of the dominant ideas of the day in 1966 and in 1991. In 1991, India was prepared for globalization and deregulation but in 1966 it was not (Mukherji 2013). Similarly, policy announcements in September 2012 favouring foreign investment reveal that influential sections of the government believe that foreign investment and non-debt creating assets are important resources for India's growth. The government was willing to face substantial political opposition because it felt that this was the right way to go.

Why then has the government failed in so many areas that directly impact India's growth? These are areas where the government is unable to deal with oppositional politics. The concentrated trade union lobby has successfully stalled legislations that would make trade unions more inclusive and more orientated towards productivity. India's industrialization continues to be capital- and knowledge-intensive at a time when over 250 million people survive on less than a dollar a day. If India grows in this way, it will take a longer time to eradicate poverty, illiteracy, and malnutrition. This is a serious challenge and the government is attempting to address it with the National Skills Development Corporation, which is a public–private partnership (PPP) seeking to cash in on India's demographic dividend. The right to education, the right to employment, and the right to information are enforcing the idea of welfare and citizenship (Ganguly and Mukherji 2011: 95–104).

These have to be reinforced with a concerted attack on corruption at all levels. Effective, autonomous, and independent regulators are essential for checking grand corruption. India has a long way to traverse in that direction. The state and civil society have to work in harmony to check corruption and clientelism that reduces the impact of every citizen-friendly government initiative. It is important both for the government to be responsive to a vigilant civil society and for civil society to be responsible for the best interests of good governance.

India's high-growth trajectory, which is essential for development, has become reasonably stable. The debate is not about whether India will grow at 6 per cent or at 4 per cent per annum. The debate is whether India can grow at 8 per cent or 6 per cent even during a global financial crisis. One forgets that less powerful exogenous shocks in the past had driven the country to bankruptcy. This is a substantial achievement. It has been achieved in the context of democratic politics where changes in policy orientation have been slow because it is difficult to produce new winners in the economy by not causing injury to some social groups or classes. Rich farmers, unions, industrialists, and a substantial section of government officials all favoured the status quo that supported a protected economy and the public sector. This coalition is gradually beginning to favour growth and competition as the middle class learns that the competition game is a rewarding one.

The challenge for India's growth and development is to get a larger proportion of the Indian people into its middle class, which is well served by markets and competition. This enterprise demands an active role of the Indian state and will demand support from its society.

Economic change in India was more gradual than in China or in East Asia. Even though India embarked on the process around the same time as China in the late 1970s, the Indian state was relatively weak in its capacity to deal with powerful political constituencies ranged against economic reforms. Over time, however, India's growth resembled China's as it became the second most rapidly growing major economy in the world. That this growth could occur in a cacophonous democracy must surely pose a puzzle for development literature that has celebrated the relationship between an authoritarian state and economic growth. India's growth lags China's but the country has greater capacity to engender growth with consent, even though the path is ridden with many pitfalls.

References

Aggarwal, V. and R. Mukherji (2008), 'India's Shifting Trade Policy: South Asia and Beyond', in V.K. Aggarwal and M.G. Koo (eds), *Asia's New Institutional Architecture*, pp. 215–58. Heidelberg: Springer-Verlag.

Ahluwalia, M.S. (2007), 'Economic Reforms in India since 1991: Has Gradualism Worked?' in Rahul Mukherji (ed.), *India's Economic Transition*, pp. 27–51. New Delhi: Oxford University Press.

Alexander, P.C. (Chair). (1978), *Report of the Committee on Import-Export Policies and Procedures.* New Delhi: Ministry of Commerce.

Amsden, A. (1985), 'The State and Taiwan's Economic Development', in P. Evans, D. Rueschmeyer, and T. Skocpol (eds), *Bringing the State Back In*, pp. 78–106. New York: Cambridge University Press.

Bardhan, Pranab (1984), *The Political Economy of Development in India.* Oxford: Basil Blackwell.

Bhagwati, J. (1998), 'The Design of Indian Development', in I.J. Ahluwalia and I.M.D. Little (eds), *India's Economic Reforms and Development: Essays for Manmohan Singh*, pp. 23–39. New Delhi: Oxford University Press.

Bhattacharya, A.K. (2011), 'The Months the Changes India,' *Business Standard*. New Delhi: 2 July.

Cappoccia, Giovanni and R. Daniel Kelemen (2007), 'The Study of Critical Junctures: Theory, Narrative, and Counterfactuals in Historical Institutionalism', *World Politics*, 59(3): 314–69.

Chakravarty, Sukhamoy (Chair). (1985), *Report of the Committee to Review the Working of the Monetary System*. New Delhi: Reserve Bank of India.

Chand, R., S.S. Raju, and L.M. Pandey (2007), 'Growth Crisis in Indian Agriculture', *Economic and Political Weekly*, 42(26): 2528–33.

Dagli, Vadilal (Chair). (1979), *Report of the Committee on Controls and Subsidies*. New Delhi: Ministry of Finance.

Das, Gurcharan (2002), *India Unbound*. New Delhi: Penguin Books.

Dubash, N. and S.C. Rajan (2001), 'Power Politics', *Economic and Political Weekly*, 36(35): 3367–90.

Echeverri-Gent, J. (2007), 'Politics of Market Micro-Structure', in Rahul Mukherji (ed.), *India's Economic Transition*, pp. 328–58. New Delhi: Oxford University Press.

Evans, Peter (1995), *Embedded Autonomy*. Princeton: Princeton University Press.

Forbes, N. (2002), 'Doing Business in India', in Anne Krueger (ed.), *Economic Policy Reforms and the Indian Economy*, pp. 129–68. New Delhi: Oxford University Press.

Frankel, Francine R. (2005), *India's Political Economy*. New Delhi: Oxford University Press.

Gandhi, Indira (1985), *Selected Speeches and Writings, Volume 4, 1980/81*. New Delhi: Publications Division of the Ministry of Information and Broadcasting.

Ganguly, Sumit and Rahul Mukherji (2011), *India Since 1980*. New York and New Delhi: Cambridge University Press.

Gokarn, S. and R. Vaidya (2004), 'The Automobile Components Industry', in S. Gokarn, A. Sen, and R.R. Vaidya (eds), *The Structure of Indian Industry*, pp. 281–314. New Delhi: Oxford University Press.

Goldstein, A. (2008), 'The Internationalization of Indian Companies', *CASI Working Paper Number* 08–02. Philadelphia: University of Pennsylvania.

Gould, S.J. and N. Eldridge (1977), 'Punctuated Equilibria', *Paleontological Society* 3(2): 115–51.

Goyal, A. (2012a), 'Explaining the Infrastructure Slowdown', *Businessline*. New Delhi: 11 October.

——— (2012b) 'The Future of Financial Liberalization in South Asia', *Asia Pacific Development Journal*, 19(1): 63–96.

Haggard, Stephan (1990), *Pathways from the Periphery*. New York: Cornell University Press.

Huang, Yasheng (2010), *Capitalism with Chinese Characteristics*. New York: Cambridge University Press.

Hussain, Abid (Chair). (1984), *Report of the Committee on Trade Policy*. New Delhi: Ministry of Commerce.

Kantha, Sharmila and Subhajyoti Ray (2006), *Building India with Partnership: The Story of CII 1895–2005*. New Delhi: Penguin Books.

Kapur, D. (2002), 'The Causes and Consequences of India's IT Boom', *India Review* 1(2): 93–102.

Kelegama, S. (1999), 'The Indo-Sri Lanka Trade and Bilateral Free Trade Agreement', *Asia Pacific Development Journal*, 6(2): 87–106.

Kochanek, S. (2007), 'Liberalization and Business Lobbying in India', in Rahul Mukherji (ed.), *India's Economic Transition*, pp. 412–31. New Delhi: Oxford University Press.

Kohli, Atul (1991), *Democracy and Discontent*. New York: Cambridge University Press, pp. 315–38.

Krasner, S.D. (1984), 'Approaches to the State', *Comparative Politics*, 16(2): 223–46.

Kumar, Nirmalya (2009), *India's Global Powerhouses*. Boston: Harvard Business Press.

Kumar, Rajiv and Abhijit Sen Gupta (2008), 'Towards a Competitive Manufacturing Sector', Working Paper Number 203. Indian Council for Research on International Economic Relations, New Delhi.

Lok Sabha Debates (24 July 1991), 10th Series, 1–9. New Delhi: Government of India, pp. 271–315.

Mahajan, V. (2008), 'Farmers Loan Waiver Endangers Financial Inclusion', in *India in Transition*. Philadelphia: Centre for the Advanced Study of India, University of Pennsylvania.

Mukerji, S. (2007), 'State and Industrial Transformation in India', Unpublished MPhil Dissertation. New Delhi: Jawaharlal Nehru University.

Mukherji, R. (2007), 'Managing Competition', in Rahul Mukherji (ed.), *India's Economic Transition*, pp. 300–27. New Delhi: Oxford University Press.

———(2008a), 'Promoting Foreign Investment in India's Telecommunications Sector', *Journal of Development Studies*, 44(10): 1425–45.

——— (2008b), 'Special Economic Zones in India', Institute of South Asian Studies Working Paper 30. Institute of South Asian Studies, Singapore.

———(2009), 'Interests, Wireless Technology and Institutional Change: From Government Monopoly to Regulated Competition in Indian Telecommunications', *Journal of Asian Studies*, 68(2): 491–517.

———(2010), 'Regulation and Infrastructure Development in India', in Vikram Chand (ed.), *Public Service Delivery in India*, pp. 177–225. New Delhi: Oxford University Press.

———(2011), 'Political Economy of the Indo-Sri Lanka Free Trade Agreement', in E. Sridharan (ed.), *International Relations Theory and South Asian Regionalism*, pp. 301–28. New Delhi and New York: Oxford University Press.

Mukherji, R. (2013), 'Ideas, Interests and the Tipping Point: Economic Change in India', *Review of International Political Economy*, 20(2): 363–89.

Narasimhan, M. (Chair). (1985), *Report of the Committee to Examine Principles of a Possible Shift Physical to Financial Controls*. New Delhi: Ministry of Finance.

Narayana Murthy, N.R. (2011), 'India Inc', in Medha M. Kudaisya (ed.), *The Oxford India Anthology of Business History*, pp. 462–72. New Delhi: Oxford University Press.

Nayar, B.R. (2006), 'When Did the Hindu Rate of Growth End?' *Economic and Political Weekly* (13 May): 1885–90.

——— (2007), 'The Limits of Economic Nationalism in India', in Rahul Mukherji (ed.), *India's Economic Transition*, pp. 202–30. New Delhi: Oxford University Press.

Pederson, J.D. (2000), 'Explaining Economic Liberalization in India', *World Development*, 28(2): 265–82.

Pierson, Paul (2004), *Politics in Time*. Princeton: Princeton University Press.

Pingle, Vibha (2000), *Rethinking the Developmental State*. New Delhi: Oxford University Press.

RoyChowdhury, Supriya (2007), 'Public Sector Restructuring and Democracy', in Rahul Mukherji (ed.), *India's Economic Transition*, pp. 388–411. New Delhi: Oxford University Press.

Saxenian, AnnaLee (2007), 'Bangalore: The Silicon Valley of Asia', in Rahul Mukherji (ed.), *India's Economic Transition*, pp. 359–87. New Delhi: Oxford University Press.

Sen, Amartya (1998), 'Theory and Practice of Development', in I.J. Ahluwalia and I.M.D. Little (eds), *India's Economic Reforms and Development: Essays for Manmohan Singh*, pp. 73–84. New Delhi: Oxford University Press.

Shastri, V. (1995), 'The Political Economy of Policy Reform in India', Unpublished PhD Dissertation, pp. 223–26. New York: Cornell University.

Singh, Manmohan (1964), *India's Export Trends and Prospects for Self-sustained Growth*. Oxford: Clarendon Press.

Sinha, A. (2005), 'Understanding the Rise and Transformation of Business Collective Action in India', *Business and Politics*, 7(2): 1–27.

Tendulkar, Suresh D. and T.A. Bhavani (2007), *Understanding Reforms*. New Delhi: Oxford University Press.

Tongia, R. (2007), 'The Political Economy of Indian Power Sector Reforms', in D.G. Victor and T.C. Heller (eds), *The Political Economy of Power Sector Reform*, pp. 109–74. Cambridge: Cambridge University Press.

Varshney, Ashutosh (1998), *Democracy, Development and the Countryside*. New York: Cambridge University Press.

Wade, Robert (1990), *Governing the Market*. Princeton: Princeton University Press.

CHAPTER 3

AFTER LIBERALIZING REFORMS

public policy at a crossroads

PULAPRE BALAKRISHNAN

In the early 1990s, it was suggested that India's economy was at a *crossroads* (see Mookherjee 1992). Implicit in this characterization was the understanding that things could not continue as they had for some decades by then. The immediate provocation for such thinking was the unravelling of the former Soviet Union and, with it, the entire communist archipelago of Eastern Europe. This was to have a major implication for India in terms of economic flows, but at that time this had been recognized most acutely by political scientists. Economists, on the other hand, being susceptible to the allure of theory, saw the end of the Soviet empire as having immediate implications for the economic model that India was to credibly pursue from then on. Economic reforms aimed at liberalizing the policy regime were launched soon after in July 1991. It would, of course, be wrong to suggest that these reforms were freely chosen by the Indian policy establishment. India had been under a quite-severe balance of payments stress for about a year by then. This had led it to approach the International Monetary Fund (IMF); standard prescriptions had followed. From the perspective from which this chapter is written, however, it is immaterial whether the reforms were imposed or freely chosen. The fact is that those responsible for implementing them in India were quite convinced that they were necessary. Now, two decades hence, some of this confidence has evaporated and it is India's policymakers who appear to be at a crossroads.

The state of the economy at present, how we got here, and the direction in which policymakers must now move are the concerns of this chapter.

The Genealogy of Market Reforms in India

Going by policy statements of the Government of India at the time, and the contents of its then Finance Minister Manmohan Singh's much-celebrated budget speech in July 1991, the guiding principle of policy at that juncture was the integration of India's economy with that of the rest of the world. At the same time, the world over, the inevitability of embracing globalization was assumed by reference to the implosion of the former Soviet Union (FSU). The latter event itself was interpreted as evidence of the unsustainability of the autarkic Soviet economic model upon which India had allegedly based her own. Everything, according to those who held this view, pointed to the imperative of granting freer play to market forces. It is important to flag the rather casual reasoning involved in arriving at this conclusion. First, even as the unsustainability of the Soviet economic model was presented as a predictable outcome after the event, FSU's collapse had come entirely unexpectedly to economists.[1] Its roots had perhaps lain more in Gorbachev's policy of *glasnost* or openness, a radical regime shift in the sphere of politics, than in *perestroika* or the restructuring of the economy. This had first cut at the foundations of single-party rule by the communists and the vice-like grip of the bureaucracy and the secret police, spreading to dislodge the more than half a century of ethnic Russian hegemony over the so-called 'union' of nationalities. FSU's unravelling as a political entity had followed, and with it the implosion

[1] Consider the following: 'Every revolution is a surprise. Still, the latest Russian Revolution must be counted among the greatest of surprises. In the years leading up to 1991, virtually no Western expert, scholar, official, or politician foresaw the impending collapse of the Soviet Union, and with it one-party dictatorship, the state-owned economy, and the Kremlin's control over its domestic and Eastern European empires.... Although there were disagreements over the size and depth of the Soviet system's problems, no one thought them to be life-threatening, at least not anytime soon' (Aron 2011). The author goes on to provide economic data ranging from the growth rate to the size of the fiscal deficit to argue that there was nothing inevitable about the collapse of the Soviet Union from an economic point of view.

of the entire Socialist Bloc of Eastern Europe. In hindsight, a potential application of the 'domino theory', albeit in a part of the world far from that for which it had originally been proposed, had remained unimagined for over three decades!

A recognition of politics as the most proximate cause of the collapse of FSU does not for a moment reinstate its economy as having been dynamic, but it does help us see that the forces making for the disintegration of the European socialist world were largely political, and its timing almost entirely determined by them. It is not irrelevant to note that China had, for at least three decades by then, adhered to a highly *dirigiste* model of import-substituting industrialization. And for a decade and a half from 1950, yielded a growth rate not much higher than that of India's (see Balakrishnan 2010: Table 11.2). The argument advanced here that political liberalization may have been the more important factor in the disintegration of FSU is strengthened by reference to the experience of China, where the move to a largely capitalist economic model has been underpinned by a severely repressive political regime, which alone could have contained the political disaffection due to a growing inequality of income and regional imbalance. The second reason why the justification of a regime change based on the Soviet experience would be inappropriate is that in 1991 India was quite far from having been a Soviet-style economy ever. Apart from the total absence of the coercive allocation of labour, perhaps the most significant marker of the erstwhile communist economies, even in 1991, over 80 per cent of GDP in India was generated in a barely regulated private sector, something entirely alien to FSU. Organized manufacturing had been tightly regulated indeed but it had comprised a highly developed private sector and constituted less than a fifth of the economy. By 1991, the Indian corporate sector was also highly organized politically and boasted of a lobby with increasing access to the political class. Where India's economy had a strong resemblance to the Soviet economy, however, was with respect to the foreign-trade regime. Here, import quotas were widespread, and when they were absent, there were tariffs which were among the highest in the world. So it can be said that India, as did FSU, had attempted to industrialize via across-the-board import-substituting industrialization, no matter that some trade liberalization measures had been initiated from the mid-1970s on. However, the broad economic strategy would by itself hardly qualify India as a Soviet clone, for much of East Asia too had pursued what can be termed import-substituting industrialization. But something a little more than mere economic strategy had been in the balance when the policy regime had been chosen by India's political leadership in the 1950s. Foreign capital had not just been discouraged, it had, over time, been more or less expunged from the economy by design. It was this closedness to foreign capital, at times in forms not envisaged in the 1950s, that was to change in 1991. This was the truly radical shift accomplished by the reforms of that year. There is every indication that it was deliberate and intended to be irreversible. In any case, it is a move that has held for close to two decades by now and shows no sign of waning.

Within the overarching objective of integrating India with the rest of the world, specific changes to the policy regime were undertaken. For the sake of convenience, these may be grouped under the rubrics 'internal' and 'external', even as we realize that their elements may overlap and need not always be independent of one another. The principal changes in the former group were the scrapping of investment licensing and amendments made to the Monopolies and Restrictive Trade Practices Act of 1969 originally promulgated to regulate 'large industrial houses'. Among the most visible features of the policyscape for at least a quarter of a century, their disappearance was of considerable symbolic value. As for the changes with respect to India's interface with the rest of the world, three may be noted. First, the tariff rate was reduced across the board, clearly intended to lower the protection enjoyed by the Indian industry. Second, after an early devaluation of the rupee, it was left to float with respect to transactions on the current account. This amounted to allowing a greater role for market forces in determining trade flows. In this context, this could also have been rationalized as necessary when quantitative restrictions on imports were being rescinded. Finally, a simplification of procedures for inward foreign direct and portfolio investments was announced. As a signal of the intention to integrate the country with the global economy, this remained unsurpassed. These changes to the external-policy regime of the economy were unilateral. Other changes were to come into effect in the mid-1990s following India's accession to World Trade Organization (WTO) rules. This was part of a simultaneous move by member countries to a set of rules jointly agreed upon. Prominent elements of this new set were a commitment to phasing-out quotas, legislating a new patent regime granting recognition to product patents, hitherto non-existent in India, and recognizing trade in services. Though these were not ceded unilaterally and came with reciprocal rights—particularly of market access—for India, the move was viewed with deep suspicion by vocal sections of the polity. Arguably, however, the trade and industrial policy reforms of 1991 constituted a greater shock to the economy and were in this sense the more potent of the changes.

The expression 'liberalization, privatization, globalization', or LPG for short, has been used to describe the shift in the policy regime initiated in 1991. But this is misleading and it would be pertinent to demonstrate why.[2] Liberalization, in the form of the trade and industrial policy changes recounted here, was in the forefront of the economic reforms alright, but of privatization there has been very little so far. Evidently the politics of the public sector run far deeper than the superficially differentiated agendas of India's political parties. This we can infer from the fact that alliances of nominally both the right and the left have governed India since but have moved little in the direction of privatization. The approach of India's political class to the public sector appears to be independent of ideology, the reluctance to privatize perhaps reflecting more an unwillingness to let go of a significant lever of power. That privatization had featured so prominently at all in the policy announcements of governments in the early 1990s, only to be dropped as soon as the crisis of 1991 had passed and the economy had stabilized, has encouraged speculation on the role of some external agencies in its inclusion in the agenda for reforms. Finally we come to globalization, the extent of which tends to get exaggerated. User-specificity is a hazard often encountered in the parleying of this term, and not just in India. One might ask if globalization is the adoption of supra-national standards in economic arrangements within a country, or whether it refers to the unrestrained cross-border movement of goods, services, and factors. We can see that either way, far too much by way of globalization is attributed to the reforms of 1991. For a surplus labour economy such as India, true globalization should encompass the possibility of labour emigration. This is restricted by immigration controls in the rest of the world, especially among the labour-scarce economies of Organisation for Economic Co-operation and Development (OECD) which would count as the obvious destination, and not just for Indians, at present. On the other hand, the barriers to adopting certain kinds of global standards are largely internal. Take, for instance, adopting global standards in evaluating the education and health status of the population. For a large country with considerable administrative reach and growing government revenues, which is India, these are not unattainable any longer. However, no move in this direction has been made as part of the reforms of 1991. The reforms themselves were almost entirely in the nature of liberalization

[2] Admittedly, the usage is found more often in the media than among academic economists, but in India by now the media has emerged as an important influence on public opinion.

and had not initially addressed the issues of either human development or social protection.[3] India lags behind much of the world on almost every indicator of human capital and welfare provision. Therefore, while the share of trade in India's GDP has risen, the extent of globalization defined more broadly that has taken place is limited. The one notable move in that direction is that after a gap of four decades or so, India has now once again become exposed to the global flow of financial capital for the first time since 1947.

Another feature of the reforms of 1991 may now be noted. The liberalization that has occurred has taken place mostly in what is constitutionally recognized as the central government's policy space. In the case of foreign trade, central legislation defines policymaking, but this cannot be said of industrial policy. This is so because in India foreign trade is a 'central subject' and trade policy the preserve of the central government. Not so with industrial policy. Here state governments retain substantial powers and a central legislation is not the last word as far as industrial investment is concerned. So while the Industrial Policy Statement of 1991 may have scrapped industrial licensing, fresh proposals for industrial investment continue to be dependent on state governments for other forms of clearances, especially environmental ones. In practice, some states have turned out to be more attentive to such proposals than the others. That this is so is partly revealed by the growing divergence of industrial performance among the states. Yet the scrapping of industrial licensing, once a potential barrier to even a demonstrably profitable capacity expansion, was a significant event, marking the end of an era as far as the policy regime is concerned. Returning to the question of how the reforms of 1991 and after are to be characterized, we might say that we have had 'liberalizing trade and industrial policy reforms'. LPG is not a particularly helpful account of the recent evolution of the economic policy regime in India.

As may be imagined, the politics of regime change is less sure ground for an economist than is its economics. Judging from their writings, however, it does not appear to be a fully mapped territory for political scientists either.[4] The main 'axis of contestation', an expression favoured by one of them (see Sengupta 2008), is whether the economic reforms package of 1991 was only an egregious event in a sequence of market reforms that had

[3] These were to come over a decade after 1991 in the form of the Sarva Shiksha Abhiyan and the National Rural Employment Guarantee Scheme respectively.

[4] See especially Kohli (2006a, 2006b); Pedersen (2000); and Sengupta (2008).

been experimented with earlier by the domestic leadership or whether it was an imposition by global multilateral agencies, notably the IMF. Political scientists may be expected to bring along the element needed for a fuller understanding of regime change, rendering their perspective invaluable. However, even while they may be united by their interests in the origins of reforms, the issue of the factors underlying regime change has not been resolved by them similarly. Among the most recent accounts is that of Sengupta (2008) who rejects the portrayal of reforms 'as the outcome of a linear, cumulative process of "learning"' (Sengupta 2008: 36)[5] among the country's policy elites, preferring instead an account of 1991 as a 'political event'. What is so political about it for her is the defeat of the old paradigm by the Washington Consensus, a manifesto on the ideal economic-policy architecture that was ascendant in the 1990s. In this defeat, a significant role is said to have been played by professional economists of the Indian government who subscribed strongly to the worldview that was emerging as dominant globally. Despite a self-conscious effort to provide a political explanation for the reforms, Sengupta's approach lacks a political economy, being without a sufficient role for domestic political parties, global institutions, and historical events.[6] En route to our providing an account that encompasses these, it is instructive to note the views of two other political scientists.

Pedersen (2000) ascribes an important role in regime change to an emerging economic class whose interests diverged from that of the class that had mostly dominated the private industrial sector in India for almost three decades. Neither mercantilist in outlook nor suspicious in its dealings with the west, this class is said to have had less at stake in the old model and much in the adoption of an open trade and industrial policy regime. This class was constituted by the owners and managers of emerging industrial groups in India. These industries were professionally run, marked by the absence of family influences, and different in their geography in that they were not concentrated in the west and the east.

[5] Though reference is made to the career of the idea in political theory, no evidence is advanced for an argument in the Indian context that provides answers to such a description.

[6] However, her characterisation of the essence of the regime change is worth noting: 'This was far more than a transition from "state" to "market", since much "market reform" had occurred prior to 1991. The most significant aspect of the 1991 reforms is that they signalled a transition to the political ideology of neoliberalism, and to its attendant assumption of a benign (liberal-capitalist) global order' (Sengupta 2008, p. 39). The last observation is particularly apposite.

Southern Indian engineering firms with an interest in the global market were a large constituent. The managers of these industries had links with the global managerial elite and viewed themselves as positioned differently vis-à-vis the west by comparison with the first generation of Indian industrialists after Independence. Pedersen sees this group, which coalesced into the Confederation of Indian Industries (CII), as having been a strong lobby for the kind of reforms which were undertaken in 1991.

Among political analysts, as he describes himself, Kohli's work on the politics of reform is the most grounded, scouring first the policyscape of the 1980s in order to provide a longer view of the regime change of 1991 (see Kohli 2006a, 2006b). While he is astute in recognizing the role of the newly emerged industry associations, Kohli (2006b) is most insightful when he links the change to the collapse of the Soviet Union. The interpretation that regime change in India was inevitable in that the collapse of the Soviet Union meant that free market was the only solution to India's problem we have already discussed. However, Kohli is referring to something more palpable. This is the ending of the strong economic links that the Indian economy had enjoyed with FSU for almost four decades. A pivotal feature of this was rupee trade which had enabled India to buy oil and defence equipment without having to pay foreign exchange, a trade facilitated by the export of tea, textiles, and raw materials. The ending of this possibility, not to mention the drying up of the market constituted by the Eastern European economic block COMECON, had grave implications for the Indian economy. Kohli points to recognition among India's elites that defence equipment would now have to be sourced mainly from the United States. And, more importantly, that a move in that direction would require the opening up of the Indian economy to American capital and goods, a demand the other developing countries of the world had experienced all along. To this important insight we might add the following. With the collapse of FSU, India would have had to export more to an open global market to earn the necessary foreign exchange. And rather, like the historically observed relationship between markets and prosperity, it could not but have been apparent to any unbiased observer at that moment that it would be virtually impossible to be a successful exporter while remaining ensconced behind protective trade barriers. The latter has less to do with any ethical element of reciprocity expected in trade relations, having instead, everything to do with an exporter needing access to globally competitive technology and capital goods which in the first instance can only be imported. Of course, for India in particular there had all along been present an imperative to export to make up the foreign exchange needed to finance its voracious consumption of oil and gold. We may add that adjustment in the form of reducing oil dependence was politically inconceivable, in that the Indian state is far too populist to restrict consumption.

Having surveyed the views of political analysts, we may now sift through them with reference to the history of the Indian economy since 1947. Some form of incipient reforms of the trade and industrial policy regime had begun in the mid-1970s. This continued in dribs and drabs right through till the middle of Rajiv Gandhi's tenure as Prime Minister which lasted till 1989. The intervening two years before 1991 had seen two governments, led by V.P. Singh and Chandrashekar, respectively, which devoted little attention to matters economic as they were more concerned with political survival. However, except for the Rajiv Gandhi era, liberalizing reforms in some areas were mostly accompanied by enhanced restrictions in others, akin to 'two steps forward, one step back'. For instance, Indira Gandhi's mildly liberalizing initiatives in the mid-1970s and the early 1980s were accompanied by a tightening of labour laws, introducing a major barrier to exit in industry. Earlier, the Janata Party led by the politically conservative Morarji Desai, had signalled its intention to liberalize licensing and external commercial policy by appointing the Alexander Committee on Import-Export Policies and Procedures in 1977. However, it granted further concessions to small industry and actively discouraged foreign direct investment (FDI), as may be seen in the highly publicized forced exit of Coca-Cola and IBM. As for the Rajiv Gandhi era, it has been pointed out (see Rodrik and Subramanian 2005) that the effective tariff actually rose during this period, thus neutralizing the removal of import quotas for some products. However, Rajiv Gandhi's role cannot be sufficiently captured by indicators of the restrictiveness of the trade regime. His tenure was on balance a period of reforms. The young prime minister had positioned himself as one who was not afraid of initiating change without rejecting the past in India's economic development. The radical rhetoric talked by Indira Gandhi, and walked by George Fernandes in his brief tenure as the Minister for Industries in the Janata government, was by now a thing of the past. There was a strong sense of using state-of-the-art technology to transform India. Also, without in any way dismantling the public sector, Rajiv Gandhi had provided room for the private. This was most noticeable with respect to information technology and telecommunications. The by now innocuous 'STD booth' was at the moment of its first appearance in the mid-1980s symbolic of some intrepid private entrepreneurs having been allowed to scale the ramparts of a public sector monopoly. Given that after the Nehru era privileging of the public sector had become a marker of left-wing politics, this was a portent. Further, it could not have been missed by the political class that the move had a widely distributed welfare effect that was not without a significant payoff.

The fact of plentiful evidence of a liberalization of the policy regime for over a decade before 1991 is not to deny that the reforms package of 1991 may have been influenced by the IMF. Indeed, the influence is there for all to see. However, it is likely to have been more with macroeconomic reforms. Lowering of tariffs, reducing the budget deficit, and restricting credit and devaluation all bear the hallmark of the Fund's standard stabilization package for a balance-of-payments-constrained economy. That the reduction in the fiscal deficit must clearly have been influenced by the IMF is also suggested by the feature that the sharp cuts initiated in the early years of the 1990s were to be followed by a slipping of targets as soon as the programme with the Fund had been wound up. Public savings promptly turned negligible in the second half of the 1990s (see Balakrishnan 2009). On the other hand, it is unlikely though that the Industrial Policy Statement of 1991 abolishing licensing would have been solely at the behest of the Fund, and, even if it was, the reforms for licensing had been contemplated in Indian government circles for over two decades by then.

In conclusion, it is not particularly difficult to isolate the elements of regime change imposed by external agencies as the price of balance of payments support from those adopted quite willingly by the Indian political leadership, even if it had been hectored by then to do so. The balance of payments crisis had left India with little alternative but to travel, cap in hand, to Washington. This gave the Fund-Bank combine the perfect opportunity to impose its views of an ideal economic architecture on the last major country that had for long resisted its writ. In fact, an opportunity had been missed in 1981 when having been granted the largest ever loan made by the IMF to a member India had refused to take the final tranche of the US$ 5 billion assistance, as the economy had recovered quickly from the impact of the second oil shock. The recovery itself had been made possible by the then Finance Minister Pranab Mukherjee ingeniously tapping non-resident Indians for foreign exchange support. The end of communism in FSU and the wooing of the west by China had left India isolated as a practitioner of extensive restrictions on international trade and capital flows. It should not come as a surprise at all that IMF had weighed-in with its trademark conditionalities, intending that this country's resistance should end forever. However, at least as far an internal liberalization was concerned, this was only the culmination of what had been toyed with hesitantly, for fear of political repercussions, by India's major political parties for some time by then.

The progress of the reforms, both macroeconomic and structural, provides an insight into the role of external agencies relative to that of domestic liberalizing forces. It would be a fair summary to say that next to none of the structural reforms, whether of the 'external' or 'internal' type according to our classification, has been reversed. On the other hand, the principal macroeconomic reforms of permanently reducing the budget deficit, an important element of the IMF package, have more or less been abandoned since the end of the IMF programme in the mid-1990s. The Fiscal Responsibility and Budget Management Act of 2003 has had a shaky start, largely because India's politicians are aware of the restrictions that it places on their established practices, particularly the buying of political allegiance through subsidies while at the same time keeping taxes low. Clearly, budgetary rectitude had been imposed from without in 1991. On the other hand, structural reforms, in evidence at least since the 1980s, were very likely perceived by the political class as potentially contributing to growth, and therefore beneficial to their political future, even if some sectional interests may be hurt in the process. In any case, the role of domestic calculations in at least sustaining structural reforms is evident. However, it is more difficult to place the proposed privatization of public sector enterprises in perspective. The IMF actually refuses to acknowledge the accrual of revenues from privatization as a legitimate form of fiscal correction.

The liberalizing reforms of 1991 stand out in marked contrast to the liberalization episode of 1966 when, faced with a balance of payments crisis, India had first gone to the IMF. Then, a sharp devaluation and some liberalizing reforms were implemented in return for promised balance of payments support. When this did not materialize, Indira Gandhi, smarting under the ignominy of having been outplayed by the international powers that be and goaded by domestic public opinion, had simply reversed the reforms. On the other hand, since 1991 we have thus far had strongly liberalizing governments of all hues at the Centre, each advancing India's continuing integration with the rest of the world. Clearly, something has altered significantly in the sphere of politics and the work of political scientists discussed here helps us understand that change.

From Accelerating Growth to Accelerating Inflation

Strictly speaking, there never was double-digit growth after 1991, only the promise of it.[7] However, the Indian policy establishment was so confident that this would be attained that they behaved as if the economy had actually achieved double-digit growth. This was during the five years starting 2003–4 when the economy averaged around 9 per cent growth per annum. Then it had been assumed that the tipping point had been reached. The confidence was soon to evaporate though. Coinciding with the onset of the global financial crisis, the phase of high growth ended in 2007–8. For three years from 2005–6 the annual growth rate cleared 9 per cent in every year. At that time there was widespread anticipation in policy circles of the economy crossing the double-digit barrier. However, this was not to be. We see from Table 3.1 that 2008–9 saw a slowing of growth to 6.4 per cent. A smart recovery took place over the next two years. However, growth was soon back to 6.9 per cent in 2011–12. The final figures for 2012–13 are yet to come at the time of writing, but provisional estimates place growth at around 5 per cent for the year. It needs to be acknowledged that the average growth rate of over 7 per cent registered since 2008–9 is indeed very high by contemporary global standards. Only, it falls short of the double-digit growth which was being expected by the Indian policy establishment till about three years ago. Be that as it may, the economy has clearly on a lower growth path for about four years by now, and this reversal is of interest by itself.

Recent macroeconomic performance in India is not characterized by slowing growth alone, however. The slowing of growth in India has been accompanied by a rise in the inflation rate. From a situation of generally low inflation during the high growth phase referred to, since 2010 it has come close to reaching 10 per cent per annum. The decline in the rate of growth of output accompanied by a rise in the inflation rate has constituted an unexpected challenge for policymakers. After over a year of aggressive monetary tightening, there was a decline evident in the inflation rate in 2011–12. It may be queried though whether this is permanent, or whether

[7] The average annual growth rate for each decade and for every decade starting the 1950s and for each year during 2000–9 is presented in Balakrishnan (2010: table 4.1).

inflation will revive once growth revives, pointing to the presence of some underlying structural impediment.

The inflationary episode reflected in the data in Table 3.1 provides a clue to understanding the slowing of growth in India after 2008. Before moving on to our explanation, however, it may be noted that the data throw out a challenge to two opposing views of the growth–inflation nexus. First, the combination of slowing growth and rising inflation flies in the face of the idea of a Phillips Curve. If there is a trade-off, we should have witnessed a decline in inflation as growth slowed. Secondly, it is contrary to the diagnosis[8] popular among financial economists that inflation reflects *overheating* of the economy, for we find inflation rising even as growth has slowed substantially. There is, on the other hand, a complete explanation of the observed growth–inflation history that relies on neither account, and I turn to this now.

Table 3.1 Growth, Inflation, and Monetary Policy

	2009–10	2010–11	2011–12
Growth rate	8.4	8.4	6.9
Inflation rate	3.8	9.6	9.1
Food-price inflation	12.6	15.6	8.3
Relative price of food	100	110	108
Interest rate (average repo)	4.8	6	7.9
Credit growth	15.8	21.3	10.2
Industrial growth	5.3	8.2	3.6
Fiscal deficit (percentage of GDP)	6.5	4.8	4.6

Source: 'Economic Survey 2011-12', New Delhi: GoI and 'RBI Bulletin', March 2012.
Notes: 'Relative price of food' is the ratio of the wholesale price index for food articles to the wholesale price index for manufactured goods. The repo rate is the annual average.

There has been a tendency in Indian policy circles to relate the slowing of the economy since 2008 to the global financial crisis. While a priori there is every reason to believe that this is a correct interpretation, we see in Table 3.2 that it is not fully borne out by data. The year-on-year growth in exports is not well correlated with the year-on-year growth of GDP. On

[8] Such a diagnosis of the recent inflation in India made by IMF is contested in Goyal (2013). The author makes her point by referring to the decline in manufacturing growth. However, in Table 3.1 is contained alternative information that makes it difficult to sustain the diagnosis of 'overheating'. The budget deficit of the central government declines quite sharply as inflation accelerates.

the other hand, there is a better fit between growth and the year-on-year growth of agriculture. Secondly, on the whole, export growth is higher since the ending of the high growth phase in 2007–8 while agricultural growth is lower. Exceptional years do exist in the case of both, however. Exports are not the only way in which a global slowing can affect India's economy, though as a source of autonomous demand they are the most immediate. Note from Table 3.2 that the lack of correspondence between exports and growth during this period also carries over to the case of foreign direct investment (FDI) and growth. Note also that by 2011–12 FDI inflows were over a third higher than they were in 2007–8. Altogether then, we find the tendency to rely on global slowing as an explanation for the Indian one, less than convincing. On the other hand, the demand side effect of slowing agricultural growth cannot be ruled out as a factor on the basis of the data.

Table 3.2 Domestic versus Global Factors in the Economic Slowdown

	2007–8	2008–9	2009–10	2010–11	2011–12
Growth of GDP	9.3	6.4	8.4	8.4	6.9
Agricultural growth	5.8	0.1	1.0	7.0	2.5
Export growth	5.9	14.6	-4.8	22.7	14.3
Public investment (percentage of GDP)	8.9	9.4	9.2	8.4	7.9
Inflation	4.7	8.1	3.8	9.6	9.1
FDI inflow (US$ million)	34,835	41,874	37,745	34,847	46,847

Source: Economic Survey, GoI, various issues and RBI Bulletin, May 2012.

What the Inflation Signals

With the virtual disappearance of inflation from Europe and the United States since the 1970s, the dominant view appears to have been established that inflation is related to central bank action. Money growth is not even mentioned, for apparently central bank announcements—or inflation targets specified in its mandate—are sufficient to assume that inflation signals laxity on the part of the central bank. This view has also been encouraged by the feature that most of the central banks in the western hemisphere have been granted both goal and functional autonomy. The facts of the decline of labour militancy and the reduced reliance of the economies of this region on OPEC, both having been historically relevant to inflation there, tend to get ignored. Non-monetarist explanations of inflation no longer find a place in either Anglo-American textbooks or in the international policy discourse heavily guided by the worldview of the global financial sector.[9] The absence of an inflation theory capable of diagnosing the Indian situation has cost its policy establishment dear. Actually, this cost has been self-inflicted for, as already stated, we have a complete understanding of the inflation episode under study. Such an explanation had originated from a study of the experience of the economies of Latin America observed over some decades. The western economist who first recognized a universal potential in this approach, which for convenience we may label structuralist, was Nicholas Kaldor (1971). The starting point of the analysis in this tradition is the disaggregation of the economy into sub-sectors according to the rules of price formation and output determination. Thus, in the short-run—that is the province of macroeconomics anyway—agriculture is characterized by demand-determined prices and supply-determined output while industry is characterized by cost-determined prices and demand-determined output. Two crucial inter-sectoral links are: Agricultural supply is a source of demand for industrial output and agricultural prices are transmitted to industrial prices via wages linked to the cost of living. To complete the macro-model, money is largely credit, and is thus rendered endogenous due to a central bank's targeting of the interest rate to stabilize the financial system. Introducing dynamics within such a system, any continuing excess demand in the market for agricultural goods leads to rising prices that are generalized across the economy via wage bargaining and cost-determined industrial prices. A flexible exchange rate can aggravate an inflationary situation when depreciation feeds inflation via a rising price of imports. As Kaldor had emphasized that the relative price of agriculture plays a role in driving growth and inflation. A rising relative price of agriculture is inflationary as industrial prices are cost-determined. It can at the same time be recessionary, or at least depressive of output, in that it can impose negative income effects on sections of the population that are not entirely compensated for in the rise in agricultural prices. As food is a necessity, with low price elasticity of demand, a rise in its price can crowd-out household expenditure on industrial products. A traded goods sector can ameliorate the effects of a slow growth of agriculture by providing imported food and an external market for industrial products. However, competitiveness, which is necessary to be able to import food in exchange for exports, cannot simply be

[9] See, for instance, Romer (2012).

assumed, or ensured by merely depreciating the exchange rate. Kaldor had proposed just such a model to explain the stagflation that had enveloped the economies of Europe and the United States following the first oil shock of the 1970s (see Kaldor 1976). As we shall soon see, it had considerable traction in the growth–inflation nexus in India over 2010–12.

Table 3.1 presents data on growth, inflation, and relative prices over 2009–12. First, as stated earlier, we can see a pattern of slowing growth and rising inflation. Again, as stated earlier, this is difficult to square with the account of inflation contained in mainstream macroeconomic theory. On the other hand, the structuralist account outlined earlier fares well. Note, first and foremost, that the course of inflation is fully tracked by the change in the price of food. However, this by itself is insufficient to establish that inflation has been driven by price inflation triggered by agricultural supply shortfall. The rise in the price of food might well be part of a general rise in prices, which is the very definition of inflation. It is the movement of the relative price of food that makes plausible, in the context, a structuralist explanation story. The inflation rate may be seen to mirror this movement, even though the strength of the relationship has varied over time. Econometric evidence on the applicability of the structuralist account of inflation to India is available in Balakrishnan (1991) for the period 1950–80 and in Dash (2012) for the period 1970–2010. This evidence, it may be noted, is based on the methodologically stringent non-nested test procedure. In Balakrishnan (1991) evidence is also provided for the negative impact of the relative price of agriculture on industrial production.

The data presented is also sufficient for us to infer the limits of macroeconomic policy in eliminating a food-supply-related inflation. Macroeconomic policy can eliminate inflation driven by the rising price of food only by engineering a recession. When industrial output is demand-determined, restrictive macroeconomic policy can lower industrial growth which in turn lowers the market demand for food, and thus the inflation rate itself. Note, however, that this is an inefficient solution from the point of view of welfare as it is achieved by constricting output and employment growth. Anyhow, the sequence of events is evident from the data in Table 3.1. We find that the Reserve Bank of India has raised the interest (repo) rate steadily over this episode.[10] Industrial output growth

[10] Averaging over the year conceals the fact that the interest rate was raised 13 times during 2010–12.

has been reduced and so has been the inflation rate, though, as already pointed out in a slightly different context, the decline in the latter may be considered less than commensurate.[11] The role of monetary policy in having lowered output growth is indicated by the reduction in credit growth over the period considered. The rise in the interest rate would be expected to do precisely this. Reduced credit growth affects the availability of capital for both production and investment.

While anti-inflationary macroeconomic policy in the form of interest rate hikes may have slowed industrial growth alright, it would be placing far too great a burden of explanation on it to suggest that it also accounts for the slowing of the economy itself. As industrial output accounts for only around a fourth of GDP, a credible explanation must proceed by alluding to a greater economic force. This is to be found in the growth of agriculture and the slowing of public investment, historically two important factors in the growth process in India. It may come as a surprise to many that during the phase of high growth over 2003–8, when it had appeared that the double-digit growth rate barrier was set to be breached, public investment had grown faster than ever since the 1950s (see Balakrishnan 2010: table 3.4). Apart from public investment, agriculture has continued to play an important role in determining the annual changes in the rate of growth of the economy. Consider the following evidence. For the first 17 years since 1991, the direction of change in the annual growth in GDP is correlated more closely with the direction of change in annual agricultural growth than with that of manufacturing and two out of the three categories of services at the two-digit level. Only the growth of 'community and personal services' is more closely linked to the change in the rate of growth of GDP during this period. However, as neither theory nor history suggests a significant role for this category of services when compared to that of agriculture, the correlation observed between growth of the economy and that of 'community and personal services' may be interpreted as being without explanatory potential.

On the other hand, coming back to the episode that we have focused on, we have reason to believe that both slow growth and higher inflation have much to do with the record of agricultural growth. Though agricultural growth was impressive in 2011–12, in all other years it remained

[11] A reason for continuing inflation despite slowing output growth is the low price and income elasticities of the demand for food.

lower than it was in 2007–08, the last year of the high growth phase. In one year it was actually at a standstill. Allowing for lags in the impact of agricultural growth on the rest of the economy its role in influencing the overall growth and inflation trajectory is apparent.

We have already argued that global slowing has little traction as a factor accounting for the slowing of growth in India recently as the economy had made a swift recovery after 2008–9. In particular, exports—the component of GDP most likely to have been affected by the slowing—after a bad showing in 2008–9 when the global financial crisis had peaked, continued to do remarkably well right up to 2011–12. But it is the combination of slowing growth and rising inflation that suggests that the global financial crisis and the consequent slowing of the world economy is not the explanation for these outcomes in India. On balance this can only be explained by reference to domestic developments, and the structuralist approach outlined earlier can be used effectively in such an exercise. Recall that according to it, inflation is caused if agriculture does not grow fast enough in relation to the demand for its output that is generated by growth elsewhere in the economy. Next, if wage incomes are not compensated for inflation, a redistribution takes place and the growth of demand for non-agricultural output is affected adversely. Add to this the possibility that public investment tends to be restrained when inflation rises and growth is doubly affected negatively, this time through a restrictive macroeconomic policy.

In this chapter, I do not explore at length the specific factors underlying food-price inflation in India over the past three years, at least not beyond pointing out that agricultural growth has been indifferent for two consecutive years. However, it needs to be emphasized that the relative price of agriculture may rise, with all its consequences for growth and inflation, even if agriculture were to grow. The question is whether it is growing at the rate required for maintaining price stability. Where the income elasticity of demand for high-value foodstuffs is greater than 1, double-digit growth of GDP will require close to double-digit growth in the output of this segment of agriculture. Such a segment comprises vegetables, fruits, eggs, milk, fish, and meat. While the output of these commodities has very likely grown in recent years, it is unlikely to have matched the growth in the demand for these foods given the rate of non-agricultural growth in 2003–8. Once structural inflation enters the system it is not easily expunged even after growth slows down.

Public Policy at a Crossroads

Though it has been argued here that the global financial crisis has had a very limited role in the slowing of the Indian economy since 2010, the crisis itself is of import for Indian policymakers. Indeed, a fresh approach to public policy is now needed. First, and foremost, there is the implication of the slowing of the world economy for the demand side of growth. The only justification for the almost exclusively supply-side-oriented nature of the economic reforms launched in 1991 could have been that growth was predicated on an assumed expansion of world demand. More heroically it may have been predicated on an assumption of an increasing competitiveness of India's exports which would penetrate world markets. This would then have provided an additional argument for integration with the rest of the world, beyond the anticipated supply side benefits of access to frontier technologies via imports and through FDI. But now when India's export destinations are in the doldrums and the pall does not appear to be lifting, the question of the future source of demand for double-digit growth aspired to needs to be faced. If internal demand is to be granted a more significant role, then attention to agriculture needs to assume a more important place in the policymakers' agenda. It is not that a strategy for agriculture was not ever considered. In fact, the very act of lowering protection to industry via trade liberalization was meant to boost agricultural growth via a terms-of-trade effect.[12] The shift in the terms-of-trade in favour of agriculture did materialize as predicted by theory but faster agricultural growth did not. The reasons why trade liberalization may not be a sufficient strategy for an agricultural revival are elaborated on in Balakrishnan et al. (2008). Here it need only be stated that other measures beyond the opening-up of the economy, central to the reforms launched in 1991, are needed. While public investment is needed, governance in the specific form of ensuring that funds are spent appropriately and that systems actually function is perhaps more important. This is most obvious with respect to irrigation (see Balakrishnan et al. 2008).

However, the structuralist approach outlined earlier alerts us to another aspect when it comes to the role of agriculture. Agriculture itself is becoming a shrinking part of the economy but it crucially impacts the

[12] It was laid out with some clarity by Manmohan Singh in a speech made to fellow economists during his tenure as the Finance Minister. See Singh (1995).

demand for industrial production via the price of food. In the history of the west the declining real price of food has been a major factor in creating a market for industrial consumer goods. The importance of cheap food to sustained growth is demonstrated by the fact that in the three decades since World War II, the real price of food in the United States declined by 75 per cent (see Gopinath and Roe 1997). This was the longest boom enjoyed by western economies in recorded history. Note that by 1945 the United States was the world's richest economy. For India, an economy with a low level of per capita income, the beneficial impact of a sustained decline in the price of food may well be imagined. In this context, it is significant that as may be seen in Table 3.3, this price has actually risen since 1991. Even though the figure for 2010–11 exaggerates the trend somewhat,[13] the movement of food prices in India since 1991 is at variance with that recorded historically in the industrialized economies. It is of relevance to the immediate future of its economy.

Table 3.3 The Real Price of Food since 1991

Year	Price
1991–2	101
1995–6	101
2000–1	110
2005–6	104
2010–11	125

Source: Author's calculation from the price series in RBI: 'Handbook of Statistics on the Indian Economy'.
Note: 'Real price' is the ratio of the wholesale price index for food articles to the wholesale price index for all commodities; index base 1993–94=100.

The demand-generating role of agriculture has not been sufficiently imagined by India's planners, the term being used here in its broadest sense to include also those in charge of policymaking today. As suggested earlier, for agriculture to play this role, it is not only necessary to elicit more food but also to ensure that it comes forth at a lower real price (and ultimately cost). Raising yields become important now. How much trade liberalization can contribute to this can well be imagined. This is even before we have factored-in the consequences of climate change and declining fertility

[13] For annual data on the real price of food since 1993–94, see Balakrishnan (2010, table 4.4).

of land for the global price of food in the future. Finally, the depletion of fossil fuel reserves is leading to the re-allocation of arable land to bio-fuels which reduces the supply of food. The extent to which technology can keep the possibility of rising food prices at bay globally is yet to be known. But one thing is clear. The recent episode of slowing growth and rising inflation that we have experienced in India indicates that policymakers must pause. Public policy can no longer be legitimately confined to expanding the ambit of the private sector. In fact, it is when considering the future of agriculture in India that we are able to see this most clearly. There are a few restrictions, other than periodic export caps, on agricultural activity in the country today. On the other hand, infrastructural bottlenecks abound. Further liberalization is not going to address the issue of cheap food that I have argued is central to faster growth.

I had stated that the global financial crisis had two implications for the future of policy in India. The first, having to do with a greater reliance on internal demand, has been discussed. The second is broader and is set within the realm of ideas. The crisis has, to use the expression coined by managerial economist John Kay, revealed via a means which is the closest we can get to a controlled experiment in economics 'the truth about markets' (Kay 2003). Ever since the work of Arrow and Debreu, we have known that the conditions necessary for a Pareto-efficient competitive equilibrium are seldom, if at all, fulfilled in practice. Revolving around the existence of contingent markets, this critique of the market mechanism may appear remote. However, far from being remote to our day-to-day concerns, we have seen market failure on a gigantic scale at work in the case of the financial crisis of 2007–8. The global financial crisis has had the effect of muting the once vocal demand for financial sector reforms in India. The report of a committee set up by the Planning Commission (2009), arguably by stretching its mandate somewhat, was given a quiet burial after the events of 2008. Capital account convertibility is suddenly no longer seen as absolutely vital. But a fundamental rethinking on public policy is yet to take place. I conclude this chapter by proposing the course that this rethinking ought to take.

First, it is necessary to see the role of trade for what it is. The government alludes (GOI 2012) admiringly to the fact that trade now accounts for over 50 per cent of India's GDP. It is interesting to note that this statement was made at a time when inflation was close to double-digit and manufacturing growth had almost ground to a halt, for reasons that I have provided earlier in this chapter. Two decades after 1991 we are able to see what openness to trade and capital flows can in effect do. The foreign exchange constraint, the bugbear of Indian policymakers in the 1950s, appeared to have been lifted. This is an achievement indeed. But the wage goods constraint, signalled by rising food prices, appears to be still with us after all these years. As we have seen, the real price of food has not budged since the launching of the reforms in1991. And manufacturing, a sector which has been the target of trade liberalization, has not expanded its share of the economy despite the fact that much of the reforms have been addressed at this sector. Clearly something more than just a liberal policy regime is needed to leave India a manufacturing power to reckon with. East Asia's experience suggests that steady expansion of food supply and the expansion of quality education and infrastructure are likely to be important. Note that apart from food the set mostly comprises non-tradeables. The second element in a necessary rethinking of public policy that is needed now is that the government must be disabused of the notion that its economic function has been discharged once it has legislated a fixed ideal of a policy regime, if there is one such ideal across economies and over time. The legitimacy of a government draws from its ability to provide and maintain public goods, by definition beyond the incentival radar of the private sector. The point about public goods is that in the twenty-first century, they extend beyond roads and parks. We now have to deal with 'public bads' in the form of environmental degradation and climate change. Legislating or decreeing policy cannot bring forth necessary public goods. Governance, which is an expression often encountered but seldom defined in the current discourse on the future of India's economy, must be understood as the provision of public goods mainly.

References

Aron, L. (2011), 'Everything You Think You Know About the Collapse of the Soviet Union is Wrong', *Foreign Policy*, July/August. Available at http://www.foreignpolicy.com/articles/2011/06/20/everything_you_think_you_know_about_the_collapse_of_the_soviet_union_is_wrong (last accessed on 24 October 2013).

Balakrishnan, P. (1991), *Pricing and Inflation in India*. New Delhi: Oxford University Press, pp. 31–55.

——— (2009), 'Macroeconomic policy, structural reforms and economic Growth', in *Macroeconomic Management and Government Finances*. New Delhi: Oxford University Press for the Asian Development Bank.

——— (2010), *Economic Growth in India: History and Prospect*. New Delhi: Oxford University Press.

Balakrishnan, P., R. Golait, and P. Kumar (2008), 'Agricultural Growth in India since 1991', DRG Paper No. 27, Mumbai: Reserve Bank of India.

Dash, S. (2012), 'An Empirical Analysis of Inflation in India: 1970–2010', unpublished MPhil dissertation, Thiruvananthapuram: Centre for Development Studies.

Gopinath, M. and T. Roe (1997), 'Sources of Sectoral growth in an Economy Wide Context: The Case of US Agriculture', *Journal of Productivity Analysis* 8: 293–310.

Government of India (GOI) (2012), *Economic Survey* 2011–12. New Delhi: Government of India.

Goyal, A. (2013), 'Propagation Mechanisms in Inflation: Governance as Key', in S. Mahendra Dev (ed.), *India Development Report 2012–13*, pp. 32–46. New Delhi: IGIDR and Oxford University Press.

Kaldor, N. (1971), 'The Role of Industrialisation in Latin American Inflations', Paper originally read at the Latin American Conference held in Gainsville, Florida, February 1971 and reprinted in *Further Essays on Applied Economics*. London: Duckworth.

——— (1976), 'Inflation and Recession in the World Economy', *Economic Journal* 86: 703–14.

Kay, J. (2003), *The Truth About Markets*. London: Penguin Books.

Kohli, A. (2006a), 'The politics of economic growth in India, 1980–2005 Part I: the 1980s', *Economic and Political Weekly*, 41: 1251–259.

——— (2006b), 'The politics of economic growth in India, 1980–2005 Part II: the 1990s and beyond', *Economic and Political Weekly* 41: 1361–70.

Mookherjee, D. (1992), '*Indian Economy at the Crossroads*', *Economic and Political Weekly*, 27: 791–801.

Pedersen, J.D. (2000), 'Explaining economic liberalisation in India: state and society Perspectives', *World Development*, 28: 265–82.

Planning Commission (2009), *Report of the Committee on Financial Sector Reforms*. New Delhi: Planning Commission. Available at http://planningcommission.gov.in/reports/genrep/report_fr.htm (Accessed on 1 June 2012).

Rodrik, D. and A. Subramanian (2005),' From "Hindu Growth" to productivity surge: The mystery of Indian growth transition', *IMF Staff Papers*, 52: 193–228.

Romer, P. (2012), *Modern Macroeconomics*. New York: McGraw-Hill.

Sengupta, M. (2008), 'How the state changed its mind: Power, politics and the origins of India's market reforms', *Economic and Political Weekly*, 43: 35–42.

Singh, M. (1995), 'Inaugural Address, Fifty-Fourth Annual Conference of the Indian Society of Agricultural Economics', Kolhapur, 26 November 1994, reprinted in *Indian Journal of Agricultural Economics*, 50: 1–6.

PART II

THE MACROECONOMY

CHAPTER 4

INFLATION IN INDIA
trends and determinants

DEEPAK MOHANTY*

I have said many, many times that inflation is a sinister beast

—Richard Fisher

India is a moderate-inflation country, though there have been occasional spikes in inflation emanating from the supply and demand sides of the economy. In recent years, after a fairly long period of price stability, inflationary pressures have surfaced since 2009–10 following the global financial crisis. This has naturally prompted monetary policy action from the Reserve Bank of India (RBI). Consequently, while inflation has shown some moderation, growth has also slowed. Falling growth has widened the negative output gap, that is, actual GDP growth is significantly lower than potential growth. However, this is not having the desired moderating impact on inflation, pointing to possible structural factors in the current bout of inflation.

Against this background, I examine the changing nature of the inflation process in India over the years and how monetary policy has been responding to inflation challenges. The chapter is divided into seven sections. The next section presents a literature review on inflation. The section that follows describes the concept and the costs of inflation which is followed by a section that presents the various measures of inflation.

* The views expressed in the chapter are personal. The assistance provided by Praggya Das and Abhiman Das in preparing this chapter is acknowledged.

The next section examines the determinants of inflation. The following section focuses on the recent inflation episode. The last section provides a conclusion with some suggestions on the way forward.

Literature Review

Before I discuss the concept, measures, and determinants of inflation, let me present a brief review of literature, though a substantial part of my own research is covered contextually in the following sections (see Mohanty [2010b, 2010c, 2011a and 2011b]). The relationship between the trends and determinants of inflation in consumer prices vis-à-vis wholesale prices in India has been examined extensively in literature. Their movement has not been uniformly coherent and there are phases when inflation based on the consumer price index (CPI) and the wholesale price index (WPI) has diverged widely (Mohanty 2010a). It is commonly believed that any price shocks in the wholesale market will eventually get transmitted to the retail market with a lag. Also, as consumer prices are a weighted average of domestic and imported goods prices, domestic price inflation as measured by WPI, should cause CPI inflation. However, Goyal and Tripathi (2011) empirically observed that this may not always be the case in India. They argue that at low per capita incomes, average wages respond to food prices, raising costs, and hence domestic prices. Then CPI, for which food is the dominant component, should Granger cause WPI. This reverse causality was established in an estimated new Keynesian Aggregate Supply framework with a wage–price link. The aggregate supply was found to be elastic, but food prices and exchange rate were important determinants for inflation in India.

Empirical findings on the appropriate measure of headline inflation in India, particularly with reference to monetary policy, are not conclusive. Patnaik et al. (2011) examined the suitability of a price index by analysing the price data, NSSO data on expenditure patterns of households, and the composition of different price indices available in India during the last three decades. Among all the available price indices for measuring headline inflation, they however argue in favour of using CPI-IW as against WPI and GDP deflator under present conditions and suggest that the macroeconomic analysis and policy thinking need to move away from a focus on WPI to CPI-IW. Srinivasan (2011) suggested using an aggregated

CPI combining all available CPIs through some statistical adjustments for policy-making, till the new CPI gets stabilized.

This issue is far more complicated while discussing and thinking about the conduct of monetary policy when some central bankers focus on core inflation, that is, a measure of inflation that excludes the rate of increase of prices for certain volatile components in price indexes. The Federal Reserve, for example, pays particular attention to the rate of growth of the core personal consumption expenditure deflator, which excludes food and energy prices (Mishkin 2007). Indeed, available microeconomic evidence on sectoral price rigidity for both the euro area and the US shows that consumer prices tend to be more flexible and volatile precisely in the energy and food sectors (Dhyne et al. 2006; Nakamura and Steinsson 2008), thereby providing empirical support for targeting a measure of core inflation which excludes the latter prices. This leaves the items to be included then as typically services prices or wages (Mankiw and Reis 2007).

Such an exclusion-based method of estimating core inflation has its own limitations. In the Indian context, various core inflation measures and their practical utility is explained in Das et al. (2009). They observed that many estimated core inflation measures in India usually fail to predict future inflation. One of the major criticisms of core inflation measures typically comes from their treatment of food items. In the case of emerging economies where the share of food consumption is high and not all consumers are able to borrow in credit markets to smoothen their consumption, Anand and Prasad (2010) show that an inflation-targeting central bank should target the headline inflation rather than the less volatile core inflation. Recent literature on inflation targeting suggests that targeting headline CPI is welfare-improving relative to core CPI (Catão and Chang 2010).

The inflation dynamics in India in the pre- and post-crisis of 2008 period is marked by some striking features in the temporal behaviour of price levels and their co-movements with the gross domestic product (GDP) and other major macro variables (Rakshit 2011). He observed that most of the usual macro indicators of overall excess demand like GDP growth rates, narrow money, and broad money failed to explain India's inflation process during the Q1:2006–Q2:2010 period. These factors leave unexplained the overwhelming part of the headline as well as the core WPI and CPI inflation; nor are any of the variables found to be statistically significant. This is also true of the output gap, which is considered the most important determinant of inflation in mainstream macroeconomics. Rakshit concludes that since temporal variations in these explanatory variables were fairly large during Q1:2006–Q2:2010, there can be little doubt that the sources of inflation were not macroeconomic in nature. While this result holds for all categories of inflation, other findings highlight the role of sectoral factors in driving them. The multiple sources of India's recent inflation and related policy issues are discussed by, among others, Mishra and Roy (2011) and Basu (2011a, 2011b).

Why Do We Need to Worry About Inflation?

What is inflation? Why do we care so much about inflation? Inflation is a sustained increase in the overall level of prices. Since price stability is a key objective of monetary policy, central banks are obviously concerned with inflation. The question is how do we define price stability? Price stability does not mean zero inflation. It is considered a low and stable order of inflation. Prices of specific goods or services may go up or down relative to the prices of others reflecting changes in productivity or demand and supply conditions. But when the overall price level rises, it has an adverse impact on the real economy. It is a cause of concern for public policy because of the associated costs, especially when a large part of the population has no hedge against inflation. I highlight some of the costs of inflation.

First, high and persistent inflation imposes significant socio-economic costs. Given that the burden of inflation is disproportionately large on the poor, high inflation by itself can lead to distributional inequality. As Keynes said: 'Inflation is the form of taxation which the public find hardest to evade.' Therefore, for a welfare-oriented public policy, low inflation becomes a critical element for ensuring balanced progress. Second, high inflation distorts economic incentives by diverting resources away from productive investments to speculative activities. Third, inflation erodes the purchasing power of money. Fixed-income earners and pensioners see a decline in their disposable income and standard of living. Inflation reduces households' savings as they try to maintain the real value of their consumption. Consequent fall in the overall investment in the economy reduces its potential growth. Fourth, economic agents base their consumption and investment decisions on their current and expected future incomes as well as their expectations on future inflation rates. Persistent high inflation alters inflationary expectations and apprehensions arising from price uncertainty do lead to a cut in spending by individuals and slowdown in investments by corporates which hurts economic growth in the long run.

Fifth, as inflation rises and turns volatile, it raises the inflation risk premia in financial transactions. Hence, nominal interest rates tend to be higher than they would have been under low and stable inflation. Sixth, if domestic inflation remains persistently higher than that of trading partners, it affects external competitiveness through appreciation of the real exchange rate. Finally, as inflation rises beyond a threshold, it has an adverse impact on the overall growth. The Report of the Chakravarty Committee on Monetary Policy (1985), Reserve Bank of India, defined an inflation rate of 4 per cent per annum as tolerable for India. The Reserve Bank's current assessment suggests that the threshold level of inflation for India is in the range of 4–6 per cent (Reserve Bank of India Annual Report 2010–11). If inflation persists beyond this level, it could lower economic growth over the medium term.

It has, therefore, been the objective of the Reserve Bank to contain the perception of inflation in the range of 4–4.5 per cent and to bring it down to 3 per cent over the medium-term, consistent with India's increasing integration with the global economy. For advanced economies, price stability is considered to be at around a 2 per cent per annum inflation rate. For emerging and developing economies, a little higher range of 3–4 per cent is considered tolerable. Hence, the Reserve Bank's medium-term objective is not only consistent with empirical observations but also with global best practices.

MEASUREMENT OF INFLATION

While inflation as a concept is well understood, measuring it poses several challenges in terms of collection of price statistics and compilation of price indices that appropriately reflect the structure of the economy. India has a rich tradition of collecting and disseminating price statistics dating back to 1861 when the Index of Indian Prices was released. Currently, there are seven different primary measures of inflation—the wholesale price index (WPI) and six measures of the consumer price index (CPI). The weighting pattern of various items in these price indices is given in Table 4.1. As is to be expected, given our stage of economic development and per capita income, food has a dominant share in all the price indices. In addition,

GDP deflator and Private Final Consumption Expenditure (PFCE) deflator from the National Accounts Statistics (NAS) provide implicit economywide inflation estimates.

Table 4.1 Weights of Major Groups in Price Indices (percentage)

Major Groups	CPI-R	CPI-U	CPI-C	CPI-IW	CPI-RL	WPI
Food	56.6	35.8	47.6	46.2	66.8	24.3
Pan, tobacco & intoxicants	2.7	1.4	2.1	2.3	3.7	1.8
Fuel & light	10.4	8.4	9.5	6.4	7.9	14.9
Housing	0.0	22.5	9.8	15.3	0.0	
Clothing, bedding & footwear	5.4	3.9	4.7	6.6	9.7	59.0*
Miscellaneous	24.9	28.0	26.3	23.3	11.8	
Excl Food & Energy	33.0	55.8	42.9	47.4	25.3	55.0
General Index (All Groups)	100.0	100.0	100.0	100.0	100.0	100.0

Source: Central Statistics Office (http://mospi.nic.in); Labour Bureau (http://labourbureau.nic.in); Office of Economic Adviser, Ministry of Commerce and Industry (http://www.eaindustry.nic.in).

Note: ** Other items of WPI. Not strictly comparable. It consists of WPI excluding food, fuel, and beverages.*

WPI is a monthly price index released by the Office of Economic Adviser, Ministry of Commerce and Industry (MoCI), Government of India. Item-wise WPI data was released at a weekly frequency earlier. MoCI discontinued the weekly series component wise. It has stopped publishing weekly manufactured products since October 2009 and discontinued the other components from early 2012. The concept of wholesale price had hitherto covered the general idea of capturing all transactions carried out by residents of the country in the domestic market. It is considered as a headline inflation measure because of its national coverage and availability of disaggregated data which facilitate a better analysis of inflation. WPI, however, does not cover prices of services.

Various CPIs, on the other hand, are meant to reflect cost of living conditions for a homogeneous group of consumers based on retail prices. The Labour Bureau, Government of India, releases CPI for industrial workers (IW), CPI for agricultural labourers (AL), and for rural labourers (RL) representing consumer prices for specific segments of the population. In the organized sector, CPI-IW is used as a cost of living index. These indices, however, do not encompass all the segments of the population and as such do not represent a pan-India consumer price behaviour. To overcome this shortcoming, Central Statistics Office (CSO), Ministry of Statistics and Programme Implementation, Government of India introduced, with effect from January 2011, a new CPI series, which has a CPI-rural (CPI-R) series for the entire rural population, a CPI-urban (CPI-U) series for the entire urban population, and a CPI-combined (CPI-C) series representing the entire country. Like WPI, all the consumer price indices are released at a monthly frequency with a time lag of 12 days to one month.

GDP deflator is a comprehensive measure of price index, implicitly derived from national accounts data as a ratio of GDP at current prices to constant prices. While it encompasses the entire spectrum of economic activities including services, it is available on a quarterly basis with a lag of two months since 1996. Moreover, national income aggregates extensively use WPI for deflating nominal price estimates to derive real price estimates.

In India, we still do not have a producer price index (PPI) which measures changes in prices of goods and services received by the producer. For example, an output PPI measures the rate of change in the prices of products (output) sold as they leave the producer while an input PPI measures the rate of change in the prices of inputs of goods and services purchased by a producer. Since the concept of inputs and outputs depends on a particular production process and there are multiple stages of production between primary goods and final goods produced in the country, PPIs are more generally known as stage of processing price indices.

PPI differs from CPI as the prices received by producers differ from the prices paid by consumers on account of various factors, such as excise duty, value-added and sales taxes, distribution costs, and government subsidies. PPI also differs from WPI, which captures the price changes of products in wholesale markets and may include some taxes levied and the distribution costs up to the stage of wholesale transactions.

A representative measure of inflation for the country as a whole and availability of information on inflation at high frequency with a shorter time lag are important for conducting monetary policy. A number of empirical works based on the long-run equilibrium analysis have found that money supply (M_3) and WPI series are co-integrated to a fair extent, thus providing evidence on WPI being more amenable to monetary policy changes. The report of the Working Group on Money Supply (1998) also used WPI as an inflation measure and found that the nominal money demand equation showed long-run price elasticity close to unity.

Even though conventionally WPI inflation has been used as headline inflation, several limitations have emerged in the recent past that complicate a realistic assessment of inflation based essentially on WPI. This underscores the need for a representative measure of inflation for better articulation of the monetary policy with the objective to anchor inflationary expectations. Since an inflation objective has to be pursued by the Reserve Bank, to avoid any conflict of interest, primary statistics on inflation should be generated by another statistical agency. While now we have a comprehensive CPI, for analytical purposes it will be desirable to initiate the process of compiling PPI for India.

Apart from headline inflation, for policy purposes, central banks look at various secondary (derived) measures of inflation to gauge the underlying inflationary pressures. One such indicator of inflationary momentum is annualized month-over-month seasonally adjusted inflation. However, the use of such an indicator for emerging market economies like India has its limitations because it could be quite volatile.

Another way to analyse inflation data is by looking at 'core inflation', which is generally a chosen measure of inflation that excludes more volatile categories like food and energy prices. The main argument here is that the central bank should effectively be responding to movements in the permanent component of the price level rather than temporary deviations. There are many variants of core inflation which try to remove the volatility of price changes by statistical means. These include truncation of commodities based on standard deviation of price changes, trimmed mean, median and other filter based smoothing techniques.

Illustratively, various measures of WPI-based core inflation for 2010–11 and 2011–12 are given in Table 4.2. It can be seen that the core measures show significant month-to-month variations, though the volatility sometimes could be lower compared to the headline measure. Since core inflation is derived from the headline measure, it is not immune to weaknesses in the primary measure of inflation. A prerequisite of a good inflation measure is that it is broader in coverage and the base period is updated frequently reflecting structural changes in the economy.

A standard measure of core inflation, which many central banks report, is headline inflation excluding food and fuel. However, in the Indian context, the derivation of core inflation by exclusion of food and energy from CPI/WPI discards a substantial portion of the commodity basket. So the price movement of the remaining commodities may not be representative of the underlying inflationary trend. Although these prices have substantial effects on the overall index, they are often quickly reversed. But the reversal of volatile prices is sometimes not short-lived. Therefore, determining when to use a core inflation measure versus an overall inflation measure remains a complex issue.

Table 4.2 Various WPI-based Core Inflation Measures*

Month	Headline	Trimmed Mean	Median	Re-weighting	Excluding Fuel & Power	Excluding Food Articles	Excluding Fuel & Power and Food Article
Apr-11	9.7	7.5	5.5	6.1	9.1	9.5	10.0
May-11	9.6	7.9	5.8	6.1	9.1	9.8	10.1
Jun-11	9.5	8.7	6.7	6.6	8.9	9.9	10.1
Jul-11	9.4	8.7	7.5	6.6	8.9	9.6	9.8
Aug-11	9.8	8.7	7.1	6.7	9.2	9.8	10.0
Sep-11	10.0	8.9	8.0	7.0	9.3	10.1	10.4
Oct-11	9.9	8.7	7.5	7.1	9.0	9.8	10.1
Nov-11	9.5	8.5	7.5	7.1	8.4	9.7	10.0
Dec-11	7.7	7.9	7.4	6.6	6.4	9.3	9.7
Jan-12	7.2	7.4	6.3	6.5	5.5	9.0	9.5
Feb-12	7.6	6.8	5.7	6.1	6.2	7.9	8.2
Mar-12	7.7	6.5	5.3	5.8	6.7	7.2	7.3
Apr-12	7.5	6.6	5.9	5.7	6.6	6.8	6.8
May-12	7.5	6.3	5.4	5.6	6.8	6.9	7.0
Jun-12	7.6	6.3	6.3	5.9	6.7	6.9	7.0
Jul-12	7.5	5.9	4.7	5.9	7.4	6.9	6.9
Aug-12	7.6	6.1	5.1	6.0	7.4	7.2	7.0
Sep-12	7.8	6.7	5.9	6.3	7.0	7.8	7.5

(*contd.*)

Table 4.2 (*contd.*)

	Headline	Trimmed Mean	Median	Re-weighting	Excluding Fuel & Power	Excluding Food Articles	Excluding Fuel & Power and Food Article
Financial year: 2011-12							
Range	2.8	2.4	2.7	1.3	3.8	2.9	3.0
Mean	9.0	8.0	6.7	6.5	8.1	9.3	9.6
Std. dev.	1.1	0.8	0.9	0.4	1.4	0.9	0.9
H1: 2012-13							
Range	0.3	0.8	1.6	0.7	0.8	1.0	0.7
Mean	7.6	6.3	5.5	5.9	7.0	7.1	7.0
Std. dev.	0.1	0.3	0.6	0.3	0.3	0.4	0.3

Source: Author's calculations.

Note: **1.5 SD method*: This method excludes all those commodities in which percentage price change is more than mean plus/minus 1.5 standard deviation over mean price change.

Trimmed mean: The trimmed mean procedure estimates price change of all the commodities, arranges them in increasing order, calculates cumulative weight of the series, and cuts the commodities for which cumulative weight is less than 8 per cent or greater than 92 per cent.

Median: This procedure computes price change for all the commodities, arranges them in ascending order, calculates cumulative weight of the new series, and takes the inflation of the first commodity for which cumulative weight is greater than or equal to 50 per cent.

Reweighting: In this method, we compute price change, calculate standard deviation of price change for WPI-All Commodities as well as each commodities over a period of time, calculate historical standard deviation for each commodity as the difference between WPI-All Commodities standard deviation and standard deviation of that commodity. Then, we calculate final weight as the reciprocal of historical standard deviation, multiplied by initial weight.

Determinants of Inflation

The WPI series is available 1952–3 onwards though the base year has undergone revisions from time to time. The monthly year-on-year inflation for the 58 years from 1953–4 to 2011–12 is given in Figure 4.1. A visual impression of Figure 4.1 suggests: First, inflation was quite volatile in the initial three decades of the 1950s, 1960s, and 1970s. But volatility reduced in the subsequent decades even with occasional spikes in inflation. Second, since the high inflationary phase of the mid-1990s, the inflation rate has moderated. It showed remarkable stability coinciding with great moderation globally till early 2008. Third, following the global financial crisis, inflation became volatile again and has remained elevated and sticky since March 2010.

Going by the current experience of elevated inflation of two-and-a-half years, one can trace 10 such episodes in the last 58 years. Out of these 10 episodes, double-digit inflation lasting beyond a year occurred on five occasions. The most prolonged one lasted for 30 months during October 1972 to March 1975. The last such high inflation was in the mid-1990s which lasted 15 months between March 1994 and May 1995. In the most recent bout of inflation, double-digit inflation lasted for five months from March 2010 to July 2010. The Reserve Bank responded to the high inflation phases through available policy instruments.

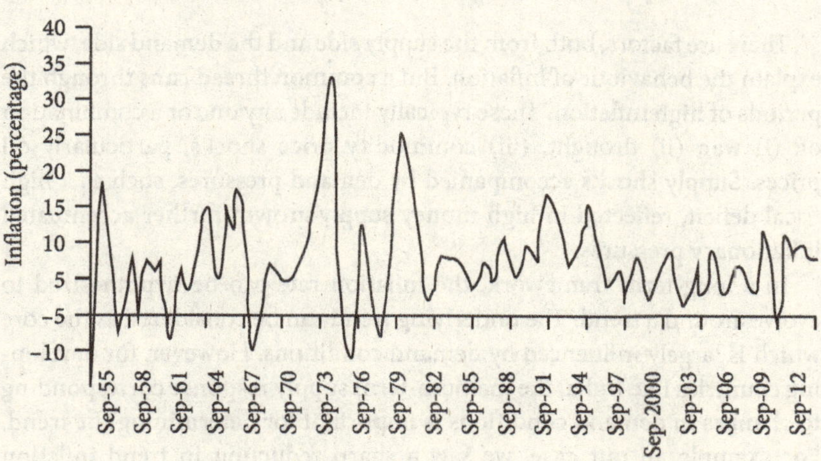

FIGURE 4.1 Long-term WPI-Inflation Movement (year-on-year %)

Source: Office of Economic Adviser, Ministry of Commerce and Industry (http://www.eaindustry.nic.in).

Notwithstanding these episodes of double-digit inflation, it is important to recognize that India has been a moderate inflation country and the average inflation has come down over the last 15 years. For about 60 years during 1953–4 to 2011–12, the monthly annual average inflation was around 6.7 per cent. There was particularly a perceptible drop in the average WPI inflation to 5.6 per cent during 2001–2 to 2010–11 (Table 4.3).

Table 4.3 Decadal Average Inflation

Decades	WPI	CPI-IW	GDP Deflator	PFCE Deflator
1951–2 to 1960–1	2.8	–	1.7	1.6
1961–2 to 1970–1	6.2	–	6.1	6.3
1971–2 to 1980–1	10.3	8.3	9.0	8.4
1981–2 to 1990–1	7.1	9.0	8.6	8.1
1991–2 to 2000–1	7.6	8.7	8.0	8.2
2001–2 to 2010–11	5.6	6.5	5.6	4.9
Apri 2011–March 2013	8.9	8.4	8.0	8.4
		Long-Term Trend		
1951–2 to 2011–12	6.7	8.2*	6.5	6.3

Source: Central Statistics Office (http://mospi.nic.in); Labour Bureau (http://labourbureau.nic.in); Office of Economic Adviser, Ministry of Commerce and Industry (http://www.eaindustry.nic.in).

Note: Inflation based on GDP Deflator and PFCE Deflator are based on the new series (Base 2004–5).

* Estimated over the period from 1971–2 to 2011–12.

There are factors, both from the supply side and the demand side, which explain the behaviour of inflation. But a common thread runs through the periods of high inflation. These typically include any one or a combination of: (i) war, (ii) drought, (iii) commodity price shocks, particularly oil prices. Supply shocks accompanied by demand pressures, such as a high fiscal deficit, reflected in high money supply growth further accentuated inflationary pressures.

In a long-term framework, the inflation rate can be hypothesized to evolve around a trend. The underlying trend can be considered as the core which is largely influenced by demand conditions. However, for developing countries like India, the medium-term supply response corresponding to changes in demand conditions is important for determining the trend. For example, in our case, we saw a sharp reduction in trend inflation during the 2000s on improved supply response following wide-ranging economic reforms and liberalization initiated in the 1990s in the real and financial sectors.

Emphasis on fiscal consolidation, discontinuing the practice of automatic monetization of fiscal deficit, a market determined exchange rate system, and greater reliance on price signals vastly improved the underlying macroeconomic framework. These had a positive impact on our macroeconomic preferences, including a clear drop in the long-term inflation trend and a decline in the volatility of inflation with a step-up in economic growth. Inflationary pressures again resurfaced in 2010–11 with increasing supply constraints, high oil prices, and deterioration in fiscal conditions.

Fluctuations around the trend are determined more by the severity of supply shocks and the nature of policy responses. One of the recurrent supply shocks influencing inflation conditions in India emanates from the agricultural sector due to drought conditions. Food inflation, which has always been a major source of fluctuation in headline inflation, has a significant negative correlation (–)0.5 with two-year average growth in agricultural GDP.

If the supply shock is prolonged and monetary policy remains accommodative for an extended time period, supply-induced inflation tends to get generalized. This is a lesson learnt in macroeconomics following the oil price shock of the early 1970s which triggered worldwide inflation. Hence, policy authorities were wiser in handling subsequent supply shocks by not extending policy accommodation beyond a point. Fiscal deficit was a major factor in determining inflation in the 1980s. With fiscal consolidation after the mid-1990s, monetary growth became more commensurate with the overall economic growth contributing to reduction in inflation (figures 4.2 and 4.3).

A simple but more formal assessment of the determinants of long-term inflation can be considered on the basis of output and money supply. Since agricultural GDP is frequently interrupted by weather conditions, non-agricultural GDP, and money supply can be considered as the more relevant variables in determining the inflation trend. An empirical exercise based on annual data for the 58-year period, 1952–3 to 2010–11, shows that there is a co-integrating long-term equilibrium relationship among inflation, non-agricultural GDP, and money supply.[1]

[1] *In WPI* = 6.15 – 0.75* *(–) 0.5 Non-Agri-GDP* + 0.90* *(–) 0.5* M_3. * Significant at 1%. Corresponding error correction (EC) model including crude oil price and rainfall as exogenous variables is estimated as: *WPI–inflation* = –0.038**EC* + 0.766**growth in money supply* (–1) + 0.063**growth in crude oil price* + 0.139* *deficit in rainfall*. * Significant at 10%.

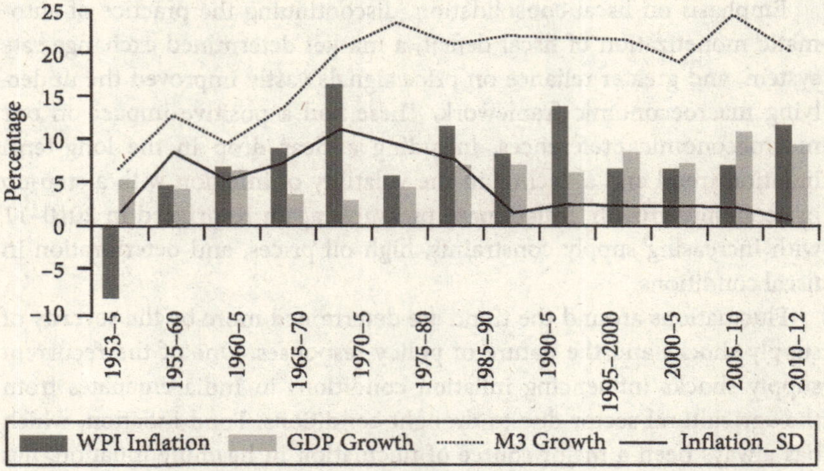

FIGURE 4.2 GDP and M3 Growth, Inflation, and Its Volatility

Source: Reserve Bank if India.

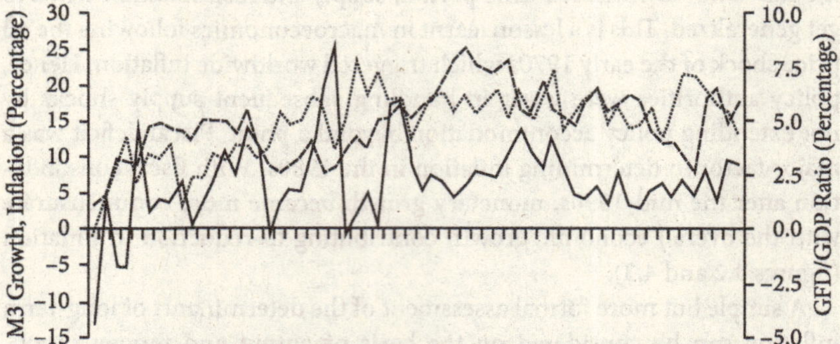

FIGURE 4.3 Fiscal Deficit, Money Growth and Inflation

Source: Central Statistics Office (http://mospi.nic.in); Office of Economic Adviser, Ministry of Commerce and Industry (http://www.eaindustry.nic.in); Reserve Bank of India (http://www.rbi.org.in)

From this exercise, the following inferences can be drawn. First, non-agricultural GDP has a highly significant and negative relationship with inflation, which implies that an increase in non-agricultural GDP representing improved supply conditions will decrease inflation. Second, money supply has a highly significant and positive relationship with inflation. A 1 per cent increase in money supply in the absence of any increase in non-agricultural GDP could lead to a 0.9 per cent increase in inflation. Third, alongside increase in money supply by 1 per cent, if non-agricultural GDP also increases by 1 per cent, it will have a dampening effect on inflation. But still inflation could go up by 0.15 per cent in the long run. Fourth, deviation from the long-run equilibrium is statistically significant and the adjustment towards the long-run equilibrium is faster through changes in non-agricultural GDP.[2] Fifth, there is a two-way causal relationship between money supply and prices.[3]

The Reserve Bank responded to phases of high inflation with policy changes through the available instruments. In the earlier phases, quantity instruments, such as the cash reserve ratio (CRR) were used as a major instrument. In addition, commercial lending rates were raised as those were regulated (Table 4.4 and Figure 4.4).

THE RECENT INFLATION EPISODE

Now I turn to the most recent inflation episode.

After remaining at an average level of around 5 per cent in the 2000s, inflation rose to double-digits in March 2010 and remained elevated and sticky thereafter. It is important to appreciate the background in which the inflation surge occurred. The current phase of high inflation followed the global financial crisis, which affected India's economy, though not with the same intensity as it did the advanced countries. Managing inflation in an economy which is recovering from a downturn is much more complex because of associated uncertainties than managing inflation under normal conditions.

In the initial phase of the crisis, it appeared that emerging market economies (EMEs) were better positioned to weather the storm created by the global financial meltdown on the back of their substantial foreign

[2] The error correction term is negative and the speed of adjustment coefficient for non-agricultural GDP is significant at 1 per cent and that of WPI at 5 per cent with negative signs.

[3] This implies that in the short-run changes in price cause changes in money supply which, in turn, causes changes in prices.

Table 4.4 High Inflation Episodes in India: Causal Factors and Policy Responses

Sr. No.	Period	No. of Months of Double-digit Inflation	Causal Factors	Policy Responses
1.	Apr-56 to Feb-57	11	Drought and decline in agricultural output for two consecutive years Demand pressures, especially investment demand	• Bank rate was raised by 50 basis points (bps) in May 1957
2.	Aug-64 to Feb-65	7	Indo-Pak War Drought	• Bank rate was raised cumulatively by 150 bps by February 1965 • SLR was raised by 5 per cent of NDTL in September 1964
3.	Mar-66 to Nov-67	21	Drought for two successive years Rupee devaluation	• No monetary measures were undertaken
4.	Oct-72 to Mar-75	30	Drought Indo-Pak War First oil price shock Higher global grain and metal prices Large Monetary Expansion even as output decelerated	• Bank rate was increased by 300 bps cumulatively • SLR was raised cumulatively by 4% of NDTL by July 1974. • CRR was raised initially by a cumulative 4 per cent of NDTL by September 1973 (subsequently reduced cumulatively by 2 per cent bps by December 1974) • Net liquidity ratio was increased from 34 to 40 per cent • Minimum lending rates increased successively • Increase in interest rates for food credit, export credit, and selective credit control • Deposit rates increased by 200 bps • Maximum interest rate chargeable increased by 300 bps • Withdrawal of concessionary and automatic refinance facilities
5.	Jun-79 to Aug-81	26	Drought Second oil price shock Global inflation	• Bank rate was raised by 100 bps in July 1981 • CRR was raised cumulatively by 1 per cent of NDTL by August 1981 • Minimum lending rates increased by 300 bps • Interest rates on selective credit control, credit authorization scheme and discounting of bills increased

6.	Nov-90 to Jul-92	21	Drought Increase in the prices of administered items and excise duties Cumulative impact of large fiscal deficit 37 per cent rupee depreciation in 1991–2	• Bank rate was raised cumulatively by 200 bps by October 1991 • Incremental CRR presribed • SLR increased by 0.5 per cent of NDTL • Incremental SLR prescribed • Increase in lending above Rs 2 lakhs by 400 bps and export credit interest rate by 250 bps • Deposits rates above 3 years increased by 200 bps • Revised structure of lending rates prescribed. Restriction on credit to real estate, personal loans including for consumer durables, loans against shares and debentures/bonds • Withdrawal of RBI refinance facilities • Banks to take minimum commitment charges on unutilized limits
7.	Mar-94 to May-95	15	Substantial hike in administered prices Shortfalls in the production of cash crops High fiscal deficit Large monetary expansion	• CRR was raised cumulatively by 1 per cent of NDTL • Deregulation of lending rate for credit over Rs 2 lakh • Maximum term deposit rate increased by 200 bps
8.	Jun-08 to Oct-08	5	High global commodity prices Large credit expansion for 3 years	• Repo rate was raised cumulatively by 125 bps by July 2008 • CRR was raised cumulatively by 0.75 per cent of NDTL by August 2008
9.	Mar-10 to Nov-11	5	Drought Structural demand supply imbalance in protein-based food items Administered price increases Sharp reversal of global commodity prices after fall during global crisis Strong domestic demand	• Forward-looking '*Exit*' since October 2009 • Key policy (repo) rate increased by 375 basis points in 13 times during March 2010–October 2011 • CRR increased by 100 bps • Changes in operating procedures of monetary policy (May 2011)

Source: Authors' calculations.

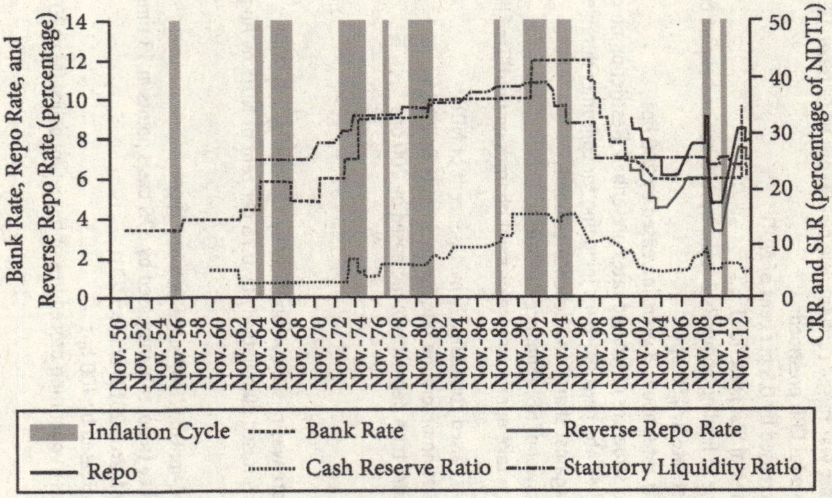

FIGURE 4.4 Inflation Cycle and Policy Instruments

Source: Office of Economic Adviser, Ministry of Commerce and Industry (http://www.eaindustry.nic.in); Reserve Bank of India (http://www.rbi.org.in)

exchange reserve cushion, improved policy frameworks, and a generally robust banking sector and corporate balance sheets. However, any hope about EMEs escaping unscathed could not be sustained after the failure of Lehman Brothers in September 2008 which triggered global deleveraging and heightened risk aversion. Eventually, EMEs were also adversely affected by spillover effects: first through contraction in world trade and then from reversal in capital flows.

India, though initially somewhat insulated from global developments, was eventually impacted significantly by global shocks through all the channels—trade, finance, and expectations. In response, the Reserve Bank swiftly introduced a comprehensive range of measures to limit the impact of the adverse global developments on the domestic financial system and the economy. The Reserve Bank, like most central banks, took a number of conventional and unconventional measures to augment domestic and foreign currency liquidity, and sharply reduced policy rates. In a span of seven months between October 2008 and April 2009, there was unprecedented policy activism. For example: (i) the repo rate was reduced by 425 basis points to 4.75 per cent, (ii) the reverse repo rate was reduced by 275 basis points to 3.25 per cent, (iii) CRR of banks was reduced by a cumulative 400 basis points of their net demand and time liabilities (NDTL) to 5 per cent, and (iv) the total amount of primary liquidity potentially made available to the financial system was over Rs 5.6 trillion or over 10 per cent of GDP. The government also come up with various fiscal stimulus measures.

In October 2009, it was not easy to exit from the excessively accommodative monetary policy stance for two main reasons. First, the year-on-year headline WPI inflation had just barely turned positive and was entirely driven by food inflation. Industrial production had started picking up but exports were still declining. Hence, recovery was not assured. Second, globally, most central banks were in favour of continuing stimulus. On the other hand, domestically, consumer price inflation was high, households' inflation expectations were rising, and surplus liquidity was substantial as reflected in the Reserve Bank's Liquidity Adjustment Facility (LAF) window. These developments had inflationary consequences.

The evolution of the inflation process since the beginning of the exit in October 2009 can be characterized into four different phases: Phase I—October 2009–March 2010; Phase II—April–July 2010; Phase III—August–November 2010; Phase IV—December 2010–November 2011; and Phase V—December 2011–November 2012. As the drivers of inflation changed over the phases, monetary policy's response was calibrated on the basis of changing dynamics of inflation as also the growth–inflation balance and evolving global economic conditions (Table 4.5).

During Phase I (October 2009–March 2010), the year-on-year headline WPI inflation accelerated from under 2 per cent in October 2009 to above 10 per cent by March 2010. A major part of this increase in inflation was attributed to the waning of the base effect. In addition, price pressures largely emanated from food. There was severe deficiency in rainfall during 2009–10, which adversely affected food prices. Moreover, global commodity prices rebounded from the trough reached during the crisis. Fuel prices rose significantly during this period. Manufactured non-food products' inflation also reverted to its medium-term trend.

The Reserve Bank, in its Second Quarter Review of Monetary Policy in October 2009, highlighted the need for exit from crisis-time monetary policy stimulus and withdrew unconventional liquidity support measures and restored the statutory liquidity ratio (SLR) of banks to the pre-crisis level. At the same time, monetary policy had to recognize that economic growth was recovering from the crisis time slowdown and any aggressive monetary tightening at that point would have affected the recovery. Subsequently, in January 2010, CRR was raised by 75 basis points of banks' NDTL, and policy rates were increased for the first time in March 2010 by 25 basis points. The transmission of rate-based monetary policy actions

Table 4.5 Changes in Key Policy Rates

Period	Repo Rate (per cent)		Reverse Repo Rate (per cent)		CRR (per cent of NDTL)		Systemic Liquidity* (₹ Rs illion)
	Magnitude	Frequency	Magnitude	Frequency	Magnitude	Frequency	
October 2009 to March 2010	25	25 bps × 1	25	25 bps × 1	75	50 bps × 1 25 bps × 1	(+)780
April to July 2010	75	25 bps × 3	100	50 bps × 1 25 bps × 2	25	25 bps × 1	(–)10
August to November 2010	50	25 bps × 2	75	50 bps × 1 25 bps × 1	–	–	(–)465
December 2010 to November 2011	225	50 bps × 2 25 bps × 5	225	50 bps × 2 25 bps × 5		–	(–)670
December 2011 to November 2012	(–)50	(–)50 bps × 1	(–)50	(–)50 bps × 1	(–)125 bps	(–)50 bps × 1 (–)25 bps × 3	(–)1045

Source: Reserve Bank of India (http://www.rbi.org.in).

Note: *Systemic liquidity measured by daily average liquidity in LAF; positive indicates surplus (reverse repo) and negative indicates deficit (repo). NDTL: Net Demand and Time Liabilities of Banks.

was weak during the periods of surplus liquidity in the financial system and, therefore, bringing down liquidity levels was a crucial challenge.

Increase in headline inflation during this period, however, caught up with households' inflation expectations. During the initial months of this phase, the major challenge for monetary policy was, on the one hand, to remain supportive of recovery while on the other hand to keep a vigil on the build-up of inflationary pressures which were getting amplified by the deficit in monsoon rainfall. Subsequently, increases in global commodity prices, especially fuel, emerged as a key risk. At the same time, consolidating recovery necessitated a shift in the monetary policy stance from 'managing the crisis' to 'managing the recovery'.

During Phase II (April–July 2010), year-on-year WPI inflation remained stubborn around 10 per cent. It was expected that with a normal monsoon during 2010–11, food inflation would be moderate. But, contrary to expectations, the major driver of inflation in this period was food. In fact, inflation in cereals, pulses, and vegetables was significantly lower in July 2010 as compared with the March 2010 levels indicating that the good monsoon indeed had a moderating impact on these items. However, food inflation did not decline as price pressures were emanating from protein-rich items, such as milk, eggs, meat, and fish, whose output was less responsive to the monsoon. Demand for these items has been growing with increasing per capita incomes and changing dietary patterns. In the absence of an adequate supply response, price pressures were substantial. Another major contributor to an increase in WPI during this period was the increase in administered prices of petroleum products and deregulation of petrol prices in June 2010. The major contribution to inflation thus emanated from food and fuel.

During this period, key policy rates were increased gradually with a narrowing of the LAF interest rate corridor in order to reduce volatility in the overnight interest rate. While the level of inflation had increased, industrial production was showing a declining trend. On the global front, the weak US recovery and concerns over sovereign debt sustainability in the euro area during this period raised fears of a double-dip recession and global commodity prices declined marginally. Moreover, the pressure on inflation during this period emerged largely from food and administered price revisions. Given the limitations of demand management policies to address supply shock induced inflation, monetary policy actions were geared towards normalization of policy rates as well as anchoring inflation expectations. During this period, policy rates were raised thrice and CRR was raised once.

By the end of this period, the liquidity in the system had turned into deficit as was evident from banks borrowing from the Reserve Bank's LAF. Therefore, the effective policy rate showed an additional increase by the width of the LAF interest rate corridor, that is, 100 basis points, as the repo rate became the policy rate. The transition of the liquidity situation from surplus to deficit mode also set the stage for improved monetary transmission.

Phase III (August 2010–November 2010) was marked by the slowing down of price pressures as headline inflation declined to 8.2 per cent by November 2010 from above 10 per cent in the preceding phase. Moderate softening of price pressures during this period also reflected that the monetary policy's calibrated approach was having an impact on demand in a non-disruptive manner. However, inflation expectations remained elevated. Global commodity prices rebound in this period was largely driving industrial raw material prices. But, monetary policy had to be cautious as mixed signs on growth sustainability were becoming evident coupled with a gradual decline in inflation. At the same time, as inflation remained significantly above the comfort level, monetary policy had to act to anchor inflation expectations. Transmission of monetary policy improved significantly during this period as liquidity continued to remain in deficit with a significant increase in banks' borrowing from the repo window. Rates in all the segments of the financial market increased during this period with a more prominent increase in the call money rate.

The moderately declining trend in inflation changed course significantly during Phase IV (December 2010–November 2011): first, on account of a spurt in food inflation as unseasonal rains in some parts of the country caused significant damage to output of vegetables and subsequently on account of stronger than expected pass-through of increase in input costs to output prices. The contribution of non-food manufactured products' inflation to overall increase in WPI rose significantly during this period. Inflation in this group reached a high of 8.5 per cent in March 2011 and remained at or above 7 per cent thereafter indicating generalized price pressures. Consequently, the share of non-food manufactured products inflation rose sharply during this phase.

The drivers of headline inflation changed path after November 2011 in Phase V (December 2011–November 2012). Headline inflation declined significantly from 9.5 per cent in November 2011 to 7.7 per cent in December 2011 and remained sticky at that level thereafter. The decline in inflation was driven by a deceleration in non-food manufactured products' inflation from 8.4 per cent in November 2011 to 4.5 per cent in November

2012. Along with a decline in the inflation of non-food manufactured products, its contribution to price increase during this phase declined and was replaced by increasing price pressures from food (cereal, vegetables, and protein items), primary non-food articles (especially oil seeds), and minerals. During this phase the policy rate was reduced by 50 basis points and CRR was reduced by 175 basis points.

While I have characterized the recent inflation episode into five phases based on the drivers of inflation and the nature of policy response, the fact is that inflation remained persistent above its long-term trend for a period of over two years. In what follows, I attempt a more analytical explanation of inflation persistence.

Monthly WPI inflation data suggest that there was a structural break[4] around the mid-2000s with the inflation rate during the latter half being higher. Average WPI inflation increased from 5.2 per cent in the first half of 2000s to 5.5 per cent in the second half. This was largely contributed by primary food inflation. In fact, the core non-food manufactured products' inflation moderated from 4.2 per cent to 3.9 per cent. What caused the structural break in the mid-2000s? A disaggregated assessment suggests that protein items largely contributed to this change in trend.

Food prices being subject to supply shocks tend to be volatile. For example, the performance of a monsoon has a significant bearing on the trend of domestic food grain prices. Spikes in food prices normally subside as they are transitory. However, an empirical analysis suggests that inflation in protein items has become persistent.[5] This indicates that protein inflation has assumed a structural character and is partly driven by demand factors. Within the protein group, persistence was lower for pulses as well as 'egg, meat and fish', but was markedly higher for milk. Thus, the persistence of protein inflation changed inflation dynamics in the latter half of the 2000s. Increase in demand for protein appears to be an inevitable consequence of rising affluence (Gokarn 2010).[6] This process was further accentuated by a renewed global food price shock during 2010–11. Among processed food items, the persistence of inflation for edible oils was high (Table 4.6 and Figure 4.5).

[4] Estimated by the Bai-Perron test.

[5] Persistence is estimated as the sum of autoregressive coefficients of the inflation series of the relevant items; a coefficient of over 0.5 is considered to be an indication of persistence.

[6] 'The Price of Protein', Inaugural Address at the Special Conference in honour of Dr Kirit Parikh at IGIDR, Mumbai, 26 October 2010.

Table 4.6 Average WPI Inflation (percentage)

Group/ Sub-Group	2001–10	2001–5	2006–10	2010–11	2011–12	H1: 2012–13
WPI	5.4	5.2	5.5	9.6	8.9	7.7
Primary Food Articles (14.3)	5.8	2.4	9.2	15.6	7.3	10.0
Protein (6.4)	6.3	3.5	9.0	19.8	10.3	13.4
Milk (3.2)	6.3	4.5	7.9	20.1	10.3	9.2
Egg, Meat & Fish (2.4)	5.6	2.3	8.8	25.5	12.7	15.7
Industrial Raw Materials (16.2)	7.9	8.4	7.4	17.2	12.3	9.3
Non-Food Manufactured Products (55.0)	4.0	4.2	3.9	6.1	7.3	5.4

Source: Central Statistics Office (http://mospi.nic.in); Office of Economic Adviser, Ministry of Commerce and Industry (http://www.eaindustry.nic.in); Reserve Bank of India (http://www.rbi.org.in)
Note: Figures in bracket indicate weights in WPI.

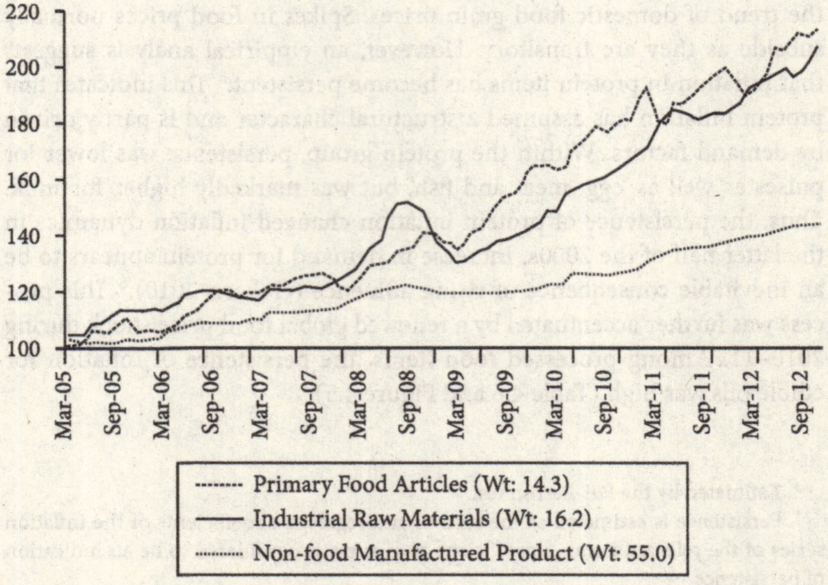

FIGURE 4.5 Price Levels Surge from Early 2009
Source: Ministry of Commerce and Industry (http://www.eaindustry.nic.in).

While the persistence of inflation in protein items has increased, it still has a relatively smaller share in overall WPI inflation. What matters more for the overall inflation trajectory is the non-food manufactured products' inflation which has a higher weight of 55 per cent in WPI. It averaged 4 per cent in the 2000s with a moderation in the second half. Subsequently, there was a sharp increase in 2010–11 and 2011–12. The non-food manufactured products' inflation shows a major structural break towards the middle of 2009–10 around the time global commodity prices rebounded. This has also raised the question: is non-food manufactured products' inflation an imported inflation? Further, analysis suggests that industrial raw material[7] prices also showed a structural break in early 2009 and the average price increase was high and volatile. Moreover, the pass-through from non-food international commodity prices to domestic raw material prices increased particularly in recent years reflecting growing interconnectedness of domestic and global commodity markets. This trend is also corroborated by corporate finance data which show that the share of raw material costs as a percentage of both expenditure and sales has been rising.

Price pressures can emanate from the supply side but it will be difficult to sustain them without rising demand. In this context, important information on recent trends in expenditure patterns and wages is available from the sixty-sixth round of NSSO consumption survey and the Labour Bureau. As per the NSSO survey (sixty-first and sixty-sixth rounds), nominal wage rates of skilled workers in both rural and urban areas increased much faster in the second half of the 2000s than they did in the first half. While real wage rates declined in the first half, they increased significantly in the second half of 2000s. Labour Bureau data suggest sustained increase in rural wages since the later part of 2009–10 (Figure 4.6).

The average annual monthly per capita expenditure both in rural and urban centres increased faster in the second half of 2000s as compared with the first half, both in nominal and real terms. While the share of per capita expenditure in food went down both in rural and urban centres, dietary patterns shifted in favour of protein items whose share went up. Rural consumption is sustained by increase in the wage rates of unskilled rural labourers both in nominal and real terms. In the formal sector, company finance data suggest that the wage bill has risen at a faster rate since the middle of 2009–10.

[7] Includes non-food articles, metallic minerals, other minerals, coal, aviation turbine fuel, high speed diesel oil, naphtha, bitumen, furnace oil, lubricant, electricity for industry, cotton yarn, and paper pulp with a weight of 16.2 in WPI.

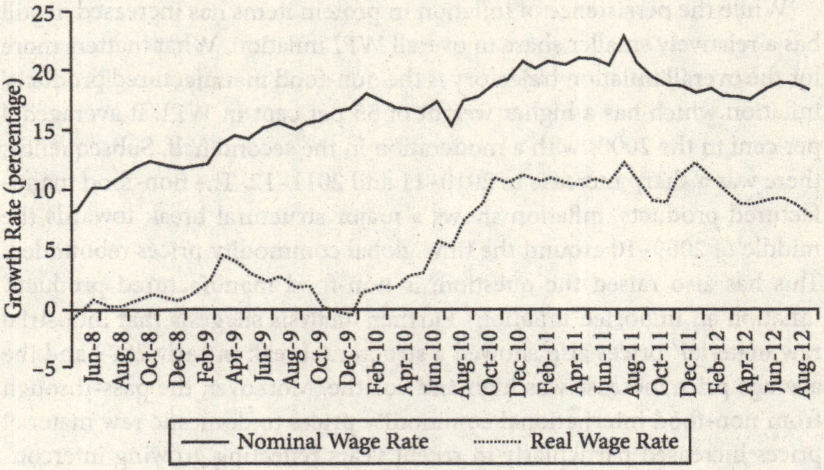

FIGURE 4.6 Average Wage Rate for Rural Labourers (Men)—Annual Growth Rate

Source: Labour Bureau (http://labourbureau.nic.in).

There has also been added stimulus from the crisis-driven fiscal expansion as the fiscal consolidation process was reversed in 2008–9 (Figure 4.7).

In addition, medium- to long-term inflation expectations in the economy have increased. In recent years, the Reserve Bank has been assessing the state of inflation expectations in the Indian economy through several means. It conducts a series of surveys aimed at different economic agents as well as model based inflation forecasts.

Professional forecasters' long-run inflation expectations have been influenced by a trend in actual inflation. In the last quarter of 2007–8, the 5-year (10-year) WPI inflation expectations at 5 per cent (4.5 per cent) was aligned to the Reserve Bank's comfort level. The consumer price (CPI-IW) inflation expectation was slightly higher at 5.5 per cent (5 per cent). With the persistence of near double-digit inflation in 2010 and 2011, medium- and long-term inflation expectations have risen. As per the latest survey conducted in the second quarter of 2012–13, 5-year (10-year) WPI inflation expectations were higher at 6.5 per cent (6 per cent). Similar upward movement in inflation expectations with regard to CPI-IW was also seen. At the same time, the divergence between WPI and CPI-IW has

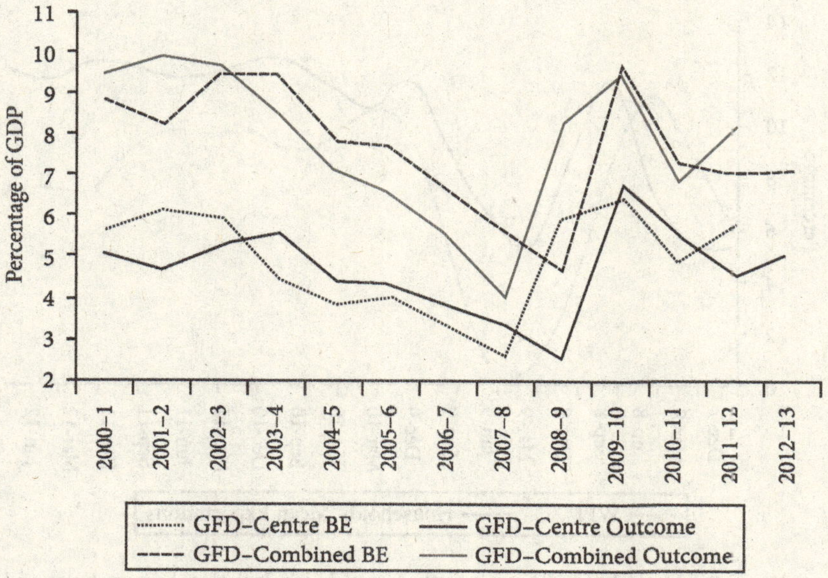

FIGURE 4.7 Rise in Fiscal Deficit Adds to Demand Pressure

also widened underscoring the role of higher food prices in expectations formation (figures 4.8 and 4.9).

***

Let me conclude with some thoughts on improving price statistics and give an analysis on the way forward. In India we have multiple price indices. The divergence between alternative inflation measures complicates the conduct of monetary policy. Accordingly, the Reserve Bank looks at all the measures of inflation, both overall and disaggregated components, in conjunction with other economic and financial indicators, to assess underlying inflationary conditions. In the context of forming monetary policy, it is important to have a robust primary measure of inflation at the national level. In this direction, the compilation of CPI (urban) and CPI (rural) could pave the way for a representative CPI for the country. There is also a need to augment the new WPI series with a service price index to improve its overall coverage. In addition, it will be desirable to initiate steps to develop a producer price index (PPI) for the country. Moreover, the representativeness of the various price indices could be enhanced by frequent updation of the base year so that it reflects structural change in

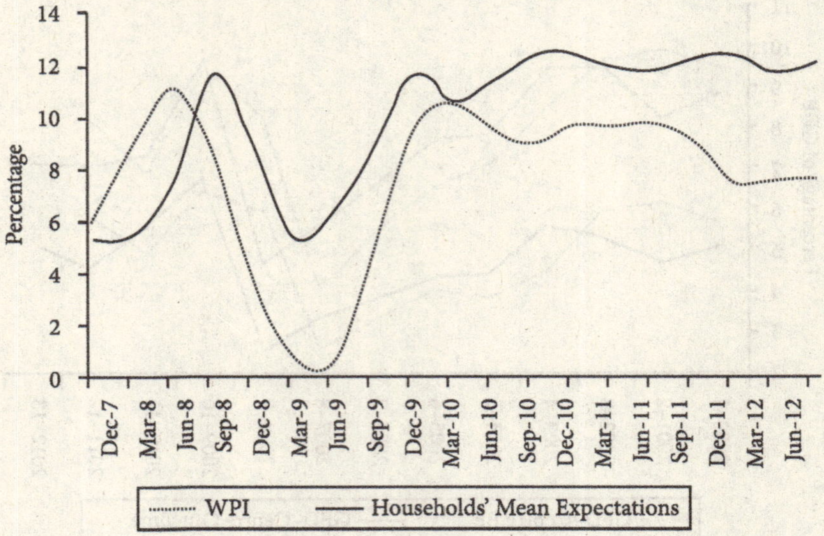

FIGURE 4.8 Households' Three-month Ahead Mean Inflation Expectations and WPI Inflation

Source: Office of Economic Adviser, Ministry of Commerce and Industry (http://www.eaindustry.nic.in); Reserve Bank of India (http://www.rbi.org.in).

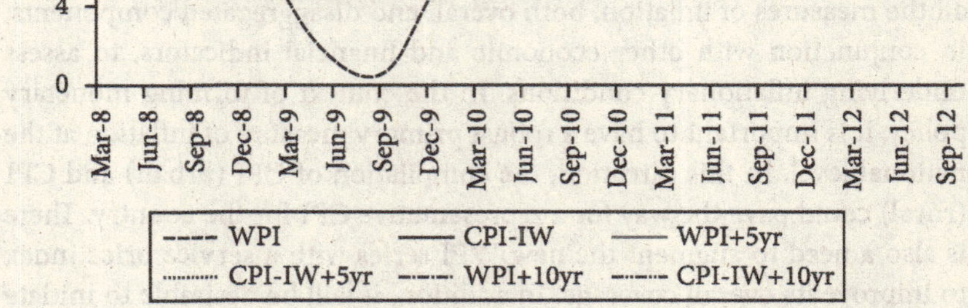

FIGURE 4.9 Professional Forecasters' Long-term Median Inflation Expectations

Source: Labour Bureau (http://labourbureau.nic.in); Office of Economic Adviser, Ministry of Commerce and Industry (http://www.eaindustry.nic.in); Reserve Bank of India (http://www.rbi.org.in).

the economy. As indicated by the former Governor of the Reserve Bank, Dr Subbarao, 'the Reserve Bank has been constantly engaged in the refinements of the various price indices and would continue to provide the necessary support to the government to bring about further improvements in the measurement of inflationary conditions'.[8]

Core inflation is usually estimated by excluding food and energy prices. The rationale for excluding these is that the prices of food and energy tend to fluctuate sharply and such volatility from the supply side, if passed on into the general price index, makes it difficult to interpret the overall trend. Core inflation, being less volatile, is expected to give a better sense of future price trends. In the Indian context, the derivation of core inflation by exclusion of food and energy from CPI or WPI discards a substantial portion of the commodity basket and the price movement of the remaining commodities may not be representative of the underlying inflationary trend. Moreover, if inflation in fuel and food items gets persistent it may not be desirable to exclude them from the core measure. Thus, there is a need for research to identify the appropriate measure of core that can be used for policy calculations to gauge the true underlying price pressure.

There are several factors that influence the inflation trajectory. First is the trend in domestic food prices. Given the current stage of our economic development, the demand for food items, particularly animal proteins, will increase with economic growth and rise in income levels. Second, global commodity prices, particularly oil prices, will have an impact on overall inflation. Third, on the demand side, there is a need to shift aggregate demand away from consumption towards investment to augment the potential output of the economy. Fourth, the level of the fiscal deficit and the quality of government expenditure have significant influence on inflation. Fifth, the stance of monetary policy and its ability to anchor inflationary expectations will matter as to how inflation evolves in the future. Thus, another area of research is identifying the determinants of inflation and how they change over time.

Peoples' belief about future inflation is an important factor in shaping inflation trends. The Reserve Bank's household expectations surveys suggest that such expectations are formed adaptively with learning; but here there is a dominance of food inflation in shaping overall household inflation expectations. Even professional forecasters, who are considered more rational, have moved up their inflation expectations to some

[8] Inaugural address delivered by Dr D. Subbarao, Governor, Reserve Bank of India at the third Annual Statistics Day Conference of the Reserve Bank at Mumbai on 2 July 2009.

extent. This suggests that food inflation is acquiring a structural character feeding into inflation expectations: rather than treating higher food prices as a temporary shock, households are assessing this as a permanent structural factor. This has inflationary implications in terms of a higher wage-price spiral. This has inflationary implications in terms of higher wage-price spiral. If workers' and producers' inflation expectations go up, than the workers' demand for wage increases is more likely to be acceded to by the producer. If such wage increases are in excess of productivity increase, they will be inflationary, making the inflation process persistent and raising the costs of disinflation.

Inflation imposes real costs which are borne disproportionately by different segments of the economy. Poorly anchored inflation expectations make long-term financial planning more complex with potential adverse effects on investment and growth. It is, therefore, important to keep inflation expectations anchored so that consumers do not mark up their long-run inflation expectations by reacting to a short period of higher-than-expected inflation.

Even when supply-side factors dominate inflationary pressures, given the risks of spillovers into a wider inflationary process, there is need for policy response. While monetary policy action address the risk of unhinging inflation expectations, attending to structural supply constraints, particularly in agriculture, ensure that these do not become a binding constraint in the long run making the task of inflation management more difficult.

The medium-term objective of the Reserve Bank is to bring down inflation to 3 per cent consistent with India's broader integration into the global economy. In this direction, monetary policy aims to contain perceptions of inflation in the range of 4–4.5. This objective is consistent with the estimated threshold level of inflation of 4–6 per cent suggesting the absence of a 'new normal' for inflation in India.

References

Anand, R. and E.S. Prasad (2010), 'Optimal Price Indices for Targeting Inflation under Incomplete Markets', NBER Working Paper No 16290, August. Available at: http://www.nber.org/ papers/w16290 (last accessed on 29 October 2013).

Basu, Kaushik (2011a), 'India's Foodgrains Policy: An Economic Theory Perspective', *Economic and Political Weekly*, 46(05): 37–45.

——— (2011b), 'Understanding Inflation and Controlling It', *Economic and Political Weekly*, 46(41): 50–64.

Catão, L. and R. Chang (2010), 'World Food Prices and Monetary Policy', IMF Working Paper WP/10/161. Available at: http://www.imf.org/external/pubs/ft/wp/2010/wp10161.pdf (last accessed on 29 October 2013).

Das, Abhiman, J. John, and S. Singh (2009), 'Measuring Core Inflation in India', *Indian Economic Review*, 44(2): 247–73.

Dhyne, E., L.J. Alvarez, H.L. Bihan, G. Veronese, D. Dias, J. Hoffmann, N. Jonker, P. Lunnemann, F. Rumler, and J. Vilmunen (2006), 'Price Changes in the Euro Area and the United States: Some Facts from Individual Consumer Price Data', *Journal of Economic Perspectives*, 20(2): 171–92.

Gokarn, Subir (2010), 'The Price of Protein', *RBI Bulletin*, November.

Goyal, A. and S. Tripathi (2011), 'New Keynesian Aggregate Supply in the Tropics: Food Prices, Wages and Inflation', *International Journal of Monetary Economics and Finance*, 4(4): 330–54.

Mankiw, N.G. and R. Reis (2007), 'Sticky Information in General Equilibrium', *Journal of the European Economic Association*, 5(2–3): 603–13.

Mishkin, F.S. (2007), 'Headline versus Core Inflation in the Conduct of Monetary Policy', Speech at the Business Cycles, International Transmission and Macroeconomic Policies Conference, HEC Montreal, 20 October. Available at: http://www.federalreserve.gov/newsevents/speech/mishkin20071020a.htm (last accessed on 29 October 2013).

Mishra, Prachi and Devesh Roy (2011), 'Explaining Inflation in India: The Role of Food Prices', mimeo. Washington, DC: IMF and IFFPRI.

Mohanty, Deepak (2010a), 'Measures of Inflation in India: Issues and Perspectives', *RBI Bulletin*, February.

——— (2010b), 'Inflation Dynamics in India: Issues and Concerns', *RBI Bulletin*, April.

———(2010c), 'Perspectives on Inflation in India', *RBI Bulletin*, October.

———(2011a), 'Changing Inflation Dynamics in India', *RBI Bulletin*, September.

——— (2011b), 'Monetary Policy Response to Recent Inflation in India', *RBI Bulletin*, October.

——— (2012), 'The Importance of Inflation Expectations', *RBI Bulletin*, December.

Nakamura, E. and J. Steinssonn (2008), 'Five Facts about Prices: A Re-evaluation of Menu Cost Models', *Quarterly Journal of Economics*, 123(4): 1415–64.

Patnaik, Ila, Ajay Shah, and Giovanni Veronese (2011), 'How Should Inflation be Measured in India?' *Economic and Political Weekly*, 46(16): 55–65.

Rakshit, Mihir (2011), 'Inflation and Relative Prices in India 2006–10: Some Analytical and Policy Issues', *Economic and Political Weekly*, 46(16): 41–54.

Srinivasan, T.N. (2011), 'Recent Bouts of Inflation in India: Policy paralysis?', The Third Shri R.Venkataraman Endowment Lecture, Madras School of Economics, 12 December.

CHAPTER 5

FISCAL AND MONETARY POLICY

outcomes and coordination

ROMAR CORREA*

The Indian economy has always been a conundrum for a macroeconomist. Monetary and fiscal policy typically operate with trade-offs. The most famous is the dictum that you cannot have a high level of activity and low prices at the same time. The corollary is that the consolation for sluggish production of goods and services is a comfortable rate of inflation. It would be simplistic to suggest that the Indian experience completely belies this received wisdom but, in broad historical terms, prior to the epoch of liberalization, there was little doubt that Indian consumers and producers operated well within their possibility frontiers. At the same time, inflation, while never high by international standards, was always a nagging worry. In recent times, after the steady dismantling of controls and invitations to enter and exit sent out, growth rates in some years have been smart. Yet, inflation, while always of concern for an Indian citizen, does not compare unfavourably with the experience of other countries and does not elicit blunderbuss advise from an academic economist (perceptions at the country's central bank [CB] might run in the opposite direction even in the case of a few basis points. At one well-publicized meeting of a technical

* I am grateful to Ashima Goyal for her comments on an earlier draft. The observations of two referees contributed to the final draft. The usual disclaimers apply.

advisory committee to the Reserve Bank of India [RBI], while almost all the members advised a reduction in the cost of borrowing, the governor proceeded to raise the interest rate). RBI's latest annual report shares this befuddlement and is unable to provide an explanation for the stubborn persistence of inflation in the face of a slowdown in growth (RBI 2012).

The single arrow in the quiver of the governor of the modern CB is the short-term interest rate, the bank rate or the federal funds rate. It should be noted, however, that both in practice and precept, RBI has insisted on its freedom to employ multiple instruments to hit its multiple targets. Thus, while the cash reserve ratio (CRR) might exhibit a secular downward trend in keeping with international practice, it is regularly used by RBI in both directions. In general, however, the target is the inflation rate, the assumption being that even if the region around the bull's eye is hit, output will be around its market-clearing level. RBI's procedure consists of an explicit operating target, a policy rate, and a corridor with a 100 basis points spread on either side of the policy rate (RBI 2012). Changes in the call rate that rapidly carry over to lending and borrowing rates must trigger appropriate changes in demand for and supply of funds. Another conflict plays out here. Creditors welcome high interest rates, debtors protest. A low interest rate is conducive to borrowing for the purchase of durables. Yet, an extended period of purchases across the board would lead to a rise in prices. Consequently, central bankers are wary of operating too close to the inflation end of the trade-off. Furthermore, according to RBI, the elasticity of borrowing for investment purposes with respect to the interest rate is small (RBI 2012). In other words, while a low interest rate is sufficient to demand investment goods, it is not necessary. Thus, if pessimism is rife, entrepreneurs will not be forthcoming even if the interest rate was at the floor. The famed zero lower-bound interest rate problem illustrated by Japan in the recent past was an illustration of funds being available for free and no takers.

If the demand (supply of) for funds is interest-inelastic, then 'crowding out', another popular theorem in a macroeconomist's toolkit, does not naturally follow. The notion is that an increase in government expenditure and the concomitant financial support to fund it raises interest rates and dampens private expenditure. If, on the other hand, the private sector is influenced more by a mood of policy paralysis than by the price of credit, then CB and fiscal authorities working in tandem (in this case, a coordinated expansionary policy) can, in fact, lower interest rates. 'Crowding in' is, more often than not, the rule. In that case, the fiscal deficit goes up. Not so, however, if taxes are increased commensurately. In India, the tax-GDP ratio for 2011–12 was low (RBI 2012). Indeed, if taxes go up more than proportionately to expenditure, the balanced budget norm might still be efficacious. In particular, RBI has energetically been trying to impress upon the government the wisdom of cutting back on expenditures that have proved to be a colossal waste. Subsidies are a case in point (Birner et al. 2011). They do not stimulate input use and benefit large farmers. More than 80 per cent of landholdings are small and marginal and their proportion is increasing. Correspondingly, the number of large holdings, that is those over ten hectares, has been declining. While all subsidies can be reduced, those for urea, in particular, can be sharply curtailed. An alternate plan will include the use of nitrogenous fertilizers, targeting small farms when providing subsidies, subsidizing fundamental nutrients, and encouraging technology-based modes of improving crop productivity. Electricity supply for groundwater use can be supported by community-based strategies. The elements will be electricity cooperatives, groundwater management by community groups, and monitoring the quality of electricity by user groups. In Andhra Pradesh, for instance, hard bargaining between labour unions, electricity utilities, and the government facilitated power sector reforms. However, state laws will have to be changed in order to recognize farmers' cooperatives.

We develop our critical appraisal in the rest of the chapter. The next section is a summary of the intellectual background to the subject. What follows is an analytical reconstruction. We return to basic concepts and results that are germane to our discussion. A sub-section gives a modelling language that enables us to distinguish two institutional configurations that might be used to appraise the monetary–fiscal nexus in India. The methodology is distant from the fashionable practice of setting up a set of optimization exercises. Solutions are assumed to be subject to exogenous shocks with known properties. The language is microeconomics. Consequently, some imagination has to be exercised in introducing monetary and financial arrangements into the models. In contrast, with existing balance sheets, our framework is grounded in the empirical reality of actual economies. The modelling strategy *does* allow for decision-making by all classes ex-ante but we proceed with ex post outcomes. From a different end, it might be characterized as hybrid old Keynesian with full dynamics (Lipsey 2012). The components are a CB committed to low inflation and the absence of an expectations-augmented Philips Curve. There is no long-run equilibrium nor a steady-state growth path. The solution of our differential equations does not mean full-employment; so, fiscal policy does not mean crowding out. There is no category of expenditures that are reduced due to an expansionary fiscal policy. The penultimate section is usually the last chapter in a macroeconomics education; the rationale for transparency, truth-telling, and so on, is looked at afresh. The final section concludes.

A Potted Intellectual History

Coordination between the fiscal and monetary authorities (MA) in a country is the opposite of independence of the latter from the former. The different orientations have reflected different moments in the evolution of developed economies. In addition, the doctrine of the CB's independence from fiscal authorities is derived from a particular macroeconomic model. Thus, the output of goods and services is believed to be largely the domain of the private sector, the government stepping in in the case of externalities and public goods. Since markets will deliver efficient relative prices, the monetary authority must track the general price level or, more importantly, its rate of change. The instrument to that end is a short-term policy rate. The expectation of the fiscal authority is budget balance. A less obvious aspect of this package is low-income taxation. Thus, equalizing government expenditure must also be low. Strong reservations about this widespread belief have recently been voiced. From the perspective of the pure theory of taxation, we recall that public economists specify an objective defined in terms of a final distribution of utilities. Thereafter, they work out the system that will induce this distribution, agents responding to the (dis)incentives laid out by the tax system (Fleurbaey 2012). The social welfare function is likely to include an aversion to inequality as an argument as well as a high priority to the worst-off in society. Combined with the Pareto principle, the modern approach combines fairness in models that escape the dilemma of equity versus efficiency. Theories of justice are incorporated which lay emphasis on the distribution of resources rather than well-being. For instance, an approach to equality of resources, egalitarian-equivalence, is recommended on the grounds that, under it, solidarity among members of a society is easier to sustain. Thus, considering all possible preferences in the population, there is no bound to the ratio between the loss of utilities of the better-off to the gain in the utilities of the worse-off in terms of equivalent transfers. Only an absolute priority for the worse-off ensures the desired property.

The so-called new classical framework invoked earlier continues to exert imperialistic sway over the profession. The main reason is the fungibility of the model. It can be, and has been, stretched to absorb whatever aberrations the real world can throw up. However, the underlying presumption is that, absent these frictions, an economy is around a natural level of unemployment. Early attempts to grow out of the model came from countries in Europe before its unification. Faced with prolonged unemployment, and since operating with the short-term interest rate in such a situation is 'akin to pushing on a string', models of monetary and fiscal coordination began to be written. It is worth recalling that the founding fathers of the 'old' classical framework of the Chicago school were more nuanced and pragmatic in their approach to policy. For instance, the defeat of discretion by rules at the hands of Kydland and Prescott was not foretold by their forefathers in Chicago (Moe 2012). Henry Simons' complete model consisted of narrow banks (the theory of which was developed by Milton Friedman) and an active fiscal authority. Under these circumstances, a monetary supply rule will lead to a reduction in the general price level as a result of increased productivity. With Chinese walls in place in the financial system, companies will have recourse to long-term funding and will not face a liquidity crunch in a crisis. An independent CB did not feature in the scheme. The Ministry of Finance will affect the flow of funds in the system by taking decisions with regard to government revenue and expenditure. Fiscal policy will thereby determine monetary policy. In other words, the debt policy of the government will determine the constancy of the price level or money supply. The government will run budget deficits in order to provide sufficient means of payments to keep the price level constant. Conversely, a fixed price level rule will be an explicit guideline for budget balance.

The RBI and the Government of India (GoI), becoming increasingly exposed to global influences, cannot be immune to these intellectual pressures. Thus, inflation targeting, the negative consequences of fiscal deficits, and so on have been given due respect. D. Subbarao seems to believe in the classical dichotomy. Increasing output and employment is the job of the government. His task is to track inflation. In India's case, the special circumstance was the tradition of RBI 'passively' monetizing GoI's fiscal deficit. In the new dispensation it is felt that RBI should be autonomous to pursue, effectively, one goal—inflation—and GoI should go to the market to finance its expenditures. At the same time, we are not aware of RBI operating with even a putative Dynamic Stochastic General Equilibrium (DSGE) model. Rather than a single target, inflation, and a single instrument, the repo rate, the CB of the country insists on a multiple indicators-multiple targets approach. The former implies that the information set of the Indian MA is thick, the latter that the weights on different macroeconomic targets might change from time to time. Indeed, price stability does not command a premium over financial stability at present (Mohanty 2012). Although, along with sovereign debt sustainability, the Subbarao (2012) suggests that the three might be incompatible bedfellows. The common impression is that, prior to the great financial crisis in America and recession in the world, CBs that doggedly followed the inflation rate and fiscal authorities that balanced their budgets like good householders did the trick in delivering low inflation and decent growth to their economies. Then the financial meltdown came. Inflation could not occupy pride of place and MA and fiscal authorities had to come together in dependence of an epoch-marking magnitude. The medium- to long-run expectation is that a slew of controls and regulations and the appointment of watchdogs will reduce the likelihood of financial breakdowns occurring and so macro managers can get back to working with New Classical or New Keynesian models. The response to Hyman Minsky is that the chances of 'it happening again' are slim. *Au contraire*, we propose a framework where the real and the monetary and financial are inextricably linked. For example, government expenditure and taxes that define a deficit follow independent paths in the dynamics of our economy. What matters is the stability of the overall system. Under the rubric of systemic fragility, models inspired by Minsky predate the particularities of this particular crisis. In our view, RBI's generous remit can be extended to systemic stability which includes the overall steady state character of MA and fiscal authorities acting in sync. One of the essential ingredients of the DSGE model is the (expectations-augmented) Phillips Curve. Heterodox economists have been experimenting with Phillips Curves of different shapes. Researchers at RBI, as well, are working with the hypothesis that the relationship between inflation and employment might be non-linear. Specifically, a backward-bending Phillips Curve, proposed by Thomas Palley (2011), is being tested. The top administration at the bank often speaks of a 'threshold level' of the inflation rate. The complete specification is: it can be shown rigorously, using the standard assumptions structure, that up to a point defined as the 'minimum unemployment rate of inflation', the Phillips Curve is a trade-in. Only later, does the familiar picture take shape. MA's duty then is to target the inflation rate that minimizes the rate of unemployment. The foundation of changing Phillips Curves, also laid by Palley, is the price-setting behaviour of firms and workers. It is the relative power of each, jettisoning the assumption of competition, that determines the form of the trade-off.

Getting Back to the Drawing Board

The Law

In the aftermath of the financial crises in the US in 2008, interest in different models was revived. The Federal Reserve did unusual things but all of them were mandated by the American constitution. Accordingly, we return to the RBI Act and examine the Fiscal Responsibility and Budget Management (FRBM) Act which is intended to guide fiscal policy. Like all monetary constitutions, the former does not mention inflation, or indeed the price level; highest in the order of priorities is maintaining the integrity of the payments mechanism. In addition, it is not outside RBI's purview to rediscount paper drawn on and payable in India arising out of the legitimate demands of commerce and trade and agriculture. Indeed, since deposits in banks are falling (some reasons offered for this are reported later), commercial banks might borrow from the CB of the country to finance their positions in assets. The suggestion is to open the discount window beyond its present association with statutory holdings and penal interest rates (Levy Economics Institute of Bard College 2012a). Thereby, all private institutions will be 'in the bank'. The contention is that rate hikes are a blunt instrument to control bank lending. Direct controls like developing collateral standards and issuing cease-and-desist orders are called for. RBI has the power to direct any bank to supply it with credit information about clients notwithstanding extant laws relating to secrecy. It could demand evidence of cash flows that will enable banks to service loans. It is not uncommon for a CB to lend against collateral using a 'haircut' to favour certain classes of assets. In addition, based on information furnished by financial institutions, RBI might provide them direction. The FRBM Act came much later and reflects the fashions of the day. Thus, the first line of the act speaks of inter-generational equity and echoes Ricardian equivalence, a theorem with respectable critics who grow in number and voice. Although not explicit, the work–leisure choice is implicit. High income taxes induce leisure and discourage work. The admonition not to borrow from RBI is immediately tempered with qualifiers. During 2012–13, the government intended to increase the tax-GDP ratio by 0.5 percentage points over the previous year to 10.6 per cent. The measures are a sharp hike of standard excise duty rates from 10 per cent to 12 per cent, widening of the service tax base, and rationalizing customs duty rates. On other hand, the projection for direct tax receipts, corporation tax, and income tax, are 'conservative' (RBI 2012: 59).

Going back to the basics, in the beginning there was government with its two macroeconomic arms, the monetary and fiscal authorities. MA cannot but coordinate with fiscal authorities. So, the RBI Act empowers the central government to supersede RBI's central board.

RBI and GoI: Joined by Balance Sheet Identities

A clarification of the title of the section is called for. In keeping with modern practice, fiscal emissions are subject to the forces of demand and supply. Thus, households and banks will choose to hold government paper depending on risk-return trade-offs. CB is enjoined, as 'banker to the government', to hold the residual paper. Likewise, from the discipline of stock-flow identities, a government deficit might be financed by the issue of government money. No normative statements can be made of an identity. Of concern, though, is the stability of the overall model of which the RBI and GoI stances are a part. A first glimpse of Godley-type modelling is available in an alternative macroeconomics education (Godley and Cripps 1983). Therein, the following identity will be encountered early and some of our equations given later can be appreciated against this yardstick. Final sales, *FE*, equal private sector purchases, *PE*, and government expenditure, *G*. Ignoring the subtleties of inventory adjustments, income, *Y*, equals expenditure, *E*, equals *PE* + *G*. At the same time, national income equals, *YP*, the disposable income of all private institutions plus the net income of the government, *YG*, which are direct and indirect tax revenues minus grants and subsidies and interest outlays on government debt. Putting the two identities together we get $YP - PE = G - YG$. In other words, a private sector surplus equals a government deficit. The FRBM schedule to eliminate all deficits, transforming the revenue deficit to a revenue surplus, must then be reflected upon. The following identities are taken from Godley and Lavoie, 2007.

In the period under consideration, a quarter, a year, time *t*, a firm makes sales to its customers. The value is denoted by *S*. In addition, there are unsold goods, ΔIN, which are purchased with the help of bank loans, *L*. There are no retained earnings. The firm will have incurred a wage bill,

WB, and must pay interest on the outstanding stock of loans, $r_{t-1}.IN_{t-1}$, or $r_{t-1}.L_{t-1}$, where r is the rate of interest on bank loans. The difference between the sources and uses of funds of purchasing firms is entrepreneurial profits, *F*. As noted, we assume that these profits are disbursed to shareholders. Thus:

$$F = S - (WB - \Delta IN + r_{t-1}.IN_{t-1})$$

Macroeconomics can also be done with physical objects. The practice is to think in terms of all firms producing 'widgets', identical physical objects. They are usually depicted in lowercase letters to distinguish them from their nominal counterparts in uppercase letters. Thus, nominal income $Y = p.y$, where p is the price level and y is total production. The unit cost of producing widgets in a period is $UC = WB/y$. The rate of cost inflation, π_c, is the rate of growth in unit costs and if we denote the real rate of interest by i, we have the familiar relationship:

$$(1 + r_{t-1}) = (1 + i_{t-1}).(1 + \pi_{ct-1})$$

Nominal disposable income, *YD*, in the period, consists of, along with the items introduced, the return on deposits held in banks, M_{t-1}, and the return on the holding of government bills, B_{ht-1}. The model distinguishes between the rates of return on these assets. The 'law of one price' does not hold in financial markets but we assume 'no arbitrage' and, therefore, one rate of interest. Nothing but notational clutter is lost. That is to say:

$$YD = F + WB + r_{t-1}.M_{t-1} + r_{t-1}.B_{ht-1}$$

The government collects revenue through a sales tax at the rate $\tau/(1+\tau)$. In equation form, $T = S.\tau/(1+\tau)$. We have a foretaste here of the heralded Goods and Services Tax (GST). In addition, the government also buys a part of the total nominal output, *G*. Fiscal deficit or public sector borrowing requirements, *PSBR*, then turns out to be:

$$PSBR = G - T + r_{t-1}.B_{t-1}$$

As a first glimpse of monetary and fiscal coordination, we assume that both authorities are committed to holding the interest rate constant, buying and selling bills without limit. The change in the supply of bills naturally is:

$$B_t = B_{t-1} + PSBR$$

The supply of bills can be held by households, already incorporated, as well as commercial banks, B_b. CB is the residual purchaser of bills. That is:

$$B_{cb} = B - B_h - B_b$$

Finally, the balance sheet constraint of commercial banks is:

$$B_b = M - L$$

We also define the net bank liquidity ratio as:

$$BLR = B_b/M$$

Putting the equations together we can capture two institutional configurations. The first dynamical system is:

$$\begin{bmatrix} IN_t \\ B_t \end{bmatrix} = \begin{bmatrix} 1-2r_{t-1} & -r_{t-1} \\ 0 & 1+r_{t-1} \end{bmatrix} \begin{bmatrix} IN_{t-1} \\ B_{t-1} \end{bmatrix} + \begin{bmatrix} YD + r_{t-1}.B_{cbt-1} - (1+\tau)/\tau.T \\ G-T \end{bmatrix}$$

Note that both active fiscal intervention as well as RBI support of the bill issue are autonomous drivers of the system. Stability is ensured by the rate of interest being 'small', less than one half. A sufficiently low rate of interest via the Fisher relation spelt out earlier means, given the real rate of interest, a low inflation rate. The result is not inconsistent with the steady state of the Indian economy with low nominal interest rates and a low inflation rate. The contrast with received wisdom is primarily due to the absence of a Phillips Curve trade-off in the model. In addition, the result can emerge from a model in which agents form Keynes-type expectations and MA is perfectly credible (Laidler 2012). In such a framework as long as the real interest rate is determined by the classical explananda of productivity and thrift and markets are assumed to work, a CB can lower the inflation rate by lowering the nominal interest rate. The reason is that the interest rate policy is interpreted as a credible commitment by CB to a time path of inflation. The translation into an equilibrium or an actual inflation rate takes place. A careful reader will observe that the prices here are costs and not the rate of change of the general price level. However, both inflation rates can be incorporated into the model and the result that deflation in at least one price is both necessary and sufficient for stability of the system derived (Correa 2012a). One institutional configuration for achieving this is the narrow banking proposal referred to earlier. A 100 per cent reserve system will be 'failure-proof' as both assets and liabilities of narrow banks will be money or near-money. CB will be able to affect a deflationary policy.

We confirm that we can recover basic stock-flow identities by looking at the stationary solution of the model. Dropping the time subscripts, we get:

$$T - G - r.B_{cb} = -\, rIN + r(M + B_h)$$

We have a variation on the familiar theorem cited, that a government surplus (the left-hand side, see the definition of *PSBR*) must equal a private sector deficit (the right-hand side).

Assume now the apotheosis of financial sector reforms in India with RBI no more 'monetizing the deficit'. Secondly, we highlight liquidity, sometimes the only parameter on the radar of regulatory authorities. With the leader of the club of banks playing a less important role, the balance sheet of a commercial bank turns out to be of central interest. We have:

$$IN_t = (1 - r_{t-1})IN_{t-1} - r_{t-1}(1 - BLR_{t-1})M_{t-1} + YD_t - r_{t-1}.B_{ht-1} - (1 + \tau)/\tau.T$$

The stability requirement of the interest rate is now less stringent. As importantly, the dimension of the system has been reduced. Net bank liquidity requirements could be met by Basel-type requirements rather than the holding of government paper. The household sector holding bills, rather than RBI as a purchaser of last resort, figure in the equation. Pushing harder in the direction of the market regime to which GoI is committed, we might regard deposits in the model as private money. Or, we could introduce the connection between high-powered money supplied to the banks, H_b, and M, the cash reserve ratio, ρ. The stationary solution is:

$$r[IN + (1 - BLR)H_b/\rho] = YD - rB_h - (1 + \tau)/\tau.T$$

Since the equation is a sectoral relationship, the identity between private sector surplus and government deficit does not apply. What we have, instead, is the sum of the surplus of two components of the private sector. On the left-hand side is the net return to the commercial sector and on the right-hand is the surplus of the non-banking private sector. Narasimham's efforts were directed towards maximizing the left-hand side. We might understand now the tension generated by movements in CRR. The Chairman of the State Bank of India, speaking on behalf of all commercial banks, champions the cause of its one-way, downward movement. In that, he has the backing of international experience. Some countries are hitting the zero lower-bound value of rho. RBI, on the other hand, is firm on holding on to this control variable. In the hands of MA, the instrument is, if anything, sticky downward. A resolution might be provided by invoking the Theil-Tinbergen theorem: There must not be more instruments than targets (there cannot be less). If inflation is the target, using both the repo rate as well as CRR seems like overkill. However, as observed earlier, RBI professes to a multitude of targets and will, therefore, want to lay claim to all the instruments it can command. Secondly, a high level of the net bank liquidity ratio goes with a low level of private sector activity (the right-hand side). From a microeconomic perspective the statement seems a truism but the fallacy of division must be guarded against along with the fallacy of composition (Kregel 2012). The question that might be asked is 'Why don't both components of the private sector, banks and firms, imbibe the same spirit of optimism and want to do more business?' To answer the question, recall that diversity of opinion is required for a market and an equilibrium price. A buyer must expect the price to rise, a seller must forecast the opposite. When both hold the same view, the market collapses. RBI must hold the opposite view when all market participants are moving in one direction. The famous illustration by Keynes is relevant. When everybody saves, aggregate income falls. The government must take an opposite position and dissave so that the private sector can save. Thus, it is the case that financial institutions cannot store liquidity and the business sector reduce costs and improve profitability at the same time. At present, the Indian reality is an interesting twist of this result. Despite the 'low' level of the statutory liquidity ratio (SLR), banks have been investing a large part of their deposits in government securities (EPW Research Foundation 2012). It is conjectured that inflation and the consequent demand for hedges like gold and real estate is responsible for the sluggish growth of bank deposits in recent times. In addition, the problem of non-performing assets (NPAs) that will not go away, higher provisioning requirements due to pension liabilities, and Basel III have put pressure on net bank liquidity ratios.

GoI and RBI move between these two systemic orientations. In relatively tranquil times, both will prefer the latter model where, in a sense, private interests are more dominant than the public purpose. We can interpret RBI's emphasis on liquidity, and in the face of the zero-bound interest rate problem, in this light. In less tranquil times, both must be activists and the former description is valid.

Credibility, Reputation, and All That

After years of consensus about the case for transparency, clear announcements of policy, and so on, it is less obvious now that these values are an unmitigated good when it comes to the government. For instance, one line of thinking is to distinguish between the two arms of the state in this regard (Levy Economics Institute of Bard College 2012b). Accordingly, a democratically-elected government cannot/should not formulate its budget in secret. All items in the budget should be open for discussion and subject to transparent audits. On the other hand, a protracted debate on monetary policy by a monetary policy committee is not likely to inspire confidence in financial markets. Behaviouralists will be sympathetic to people not being very predictable (Kareev 2012). The general practice of basing decisions on the most recent outcomes is a reflection of the high payoffs associated with limited data. In particular, in situations that involve interactions with sections of the private sector, not all of whose interests will be congruent with those of the MA, behaving randomly may be to the benefit of all. By international standards, the credibility of the Governor of the RBI must be low because he does not resist the temptation to finance GoI's deficit. Yet, the opposite of the textbook expectation is the case with Dr Subbarao's reputation being among the highest. The reason is that, over the long haul, growth has been moderately high and inflation moderately low. RBI is, consequently, circumspect about communication (Mohanty 2012). A signal, clear to RBI officers, might be ambiguous to members of the private sector. The event of the easing of the cash reserve ratio in March 2012 when inflation was high has been provided as an illustration. One section of the market regarded it as routine, another as a reversal of the weights on the inflation and output objectives in RBI's welfare function.

The set of FRBM rules consist of an annual reduction of the fiscal and revenue deficits culminating in a terminal value in 2008. These are open-loop plans, invariant to unfolding information. However, the convention in India is that, given the demands of credit and employment and activity on the one hand and inflation on the other, both organs of the government are always open to new information. The RBI Governor regularly visits Delhi for meaningful (not cheap) talk with the government. Particularly in an economy churning in different ways, any concerted policy action taken today will set off a chain of responses and events that alter the milieu tomorrow. It is the duty of policymakers to renege on the commitments made in the past! Tying the hands of the CB's Governor in advance in the interest of time consistency might not be a welfare-enhancing procedure. Time-inconsistent discounting means that choice is often intractable (Offer 2012). The unknowability of the future opens up room for genuine discretion. People fall back on established norms that allow them to place a greater weight on social welfare above their immediate interests. Fiat money and taxes are such commitment devices. Fortunately, in recent times authorities in the US and Europe have displayed considerable ingenuity in circumventing constitutionally-ordained constraints in the interest of addressing their respective crises (Wall 2012). The Fed's actions, it is well-known, were quasi-fiscal. The ECB is not permitted to finance governments. However, in what has been called the Sarkozy trade, the French President encouraged commercial banks to borrow from ECB and buy euro area sovereign debt with the proceeds. Closed-loop controls are required. A timetable detracts from the open systems approach to the economy that the RBI and GoI take. Thus, it is sufficient that in each period, a quarter, a year, officials from RBI and GoI sit together and optimize a social welfare function, the outcomes holding till the next meeting. Here again, the case for rules rests on the DSGE model. If, on the other hand, GoI is open to a suite of models, none of which contain a tendency towards market clearing, then both the citizen and the state are best off if policymakers reformulate their decisions period by period (Correa 2011, 2012b). In every fresh round, bygones are regarded as bygones.

* * *

Monetary and fiscal authorities in a nation are joined at the hip. There is no better way of conveying this truth than through national income identities. In the model given here, RBI cannot but accept the residual offerings of the government after private appetites have been slaked. The criterion is systemic stability. Accordingly, the framework is agnostic about fiscal deficits and fiscal balance. In both cases, while there is a consensus that government expenditure must be directed towards green and ecologically-kind investments, less attention is given to progressive taxation. In the model of the text, a sales tax was used but the framework also incorporates income and capital gains taxation. We anticipate a rethink of standard responses to taxes especially when the gap between the rich and the poor within the country and in countries in the world grows to catastrophic levels.

References

Birner, R., S. Gupta, and N. Sharma (2011), 'The Political Economy of Agricultural Policy Reform in India', IFPRI Research Monograph.

Correa, R. (2011), 'On Concurrent Solutions in Differential Games', *Business Systems Review*, 2(1): 17–23.

——— (2012a), 'Cost Inflation and Price Inflation', *South Asian Journal of Macroeconomics and Public Finance*, 1(1): 15–24.

——— (2012b), 'Weak and Strong Time Consistency', *Theoretical Economics Letters*, 2(1): 79–82.

EPW Research Foundation (2012), 'Dilemma of Indian Banking', *Economic and Political Weekly*, 47(1): 119–125.

Fleurbaey, M. (2012), 'Economics is Not What You Think: A Defence of Thee Economic Approach to Taxation', Foundation maison des sciences de l'homme, Paris: Working Paper No. 10.

Godley, W. and F. Cripps (1983), *Macroeconomics*. Oxford: Oxford University Press.

Godley, W. and M. Lavoie (2007), *Monetary Economics*. Basingstoke: Palgrave Macmillan.

Kareev, Y. (2012), 'Advantage of Cognitive Limitations', The Hebrew University of Jerusalem, Discussion Paper #611.

Kregel, J. (2012), 'Diversity and Uniformity in Economic Theory as an Explanation of the Recent Economic Crisis', New York: Levy Institute of Bard College, Working Paper No. 730.

Laidler, D. (2012), 'Two Crises, Two Ideas and One Question', University of Western Ontario RBC Financial Group Economic Policy Research Institute Working Paper No. 2012–14.

Levy Economics Institute of Bard College (2012a). *Beyond the Minsky Moment*. New York: Levy Economics Institute of Bard College.

——— (2012b), *Improving Governance of the Government Safety Net in Financial Crisis*. New York: Levy Economics Institute of Bard College.

Lipsey, R.G. (2012), 'Policy Implications of Alternative Economic Paradigms: Some Surprises from Endogenous Technological Changes', Simon Fraser University Department of Economics Working Paper 12-16.

Moe, T.G. (2012), 'Control of Finance as a Prerequisite for Successful Monetary Policy: A Reinterpretation of Henry Simons's "Rules versus Authorities in Monetary Policy"', New York: Levy Institute of Bard College, Working Paper No. 713.

Mohanty, D. (2012), 'Price Stability and Financial Stability: An Emerging Market Perspective', *Reserve Bank of India Bulletin*, July: 1299–1309.

Offer, A. (2012), 'Self-Interest, Sympathy and the Invisible Hand: From Adam Smith to Market Liberalism', University of Oxford, Discussion Papers in Economic and Social History No. 101.

Palley, T.I. (2011), 'Monetary Policy and Central Banking', Hans Boeckler Foundation, Germany: Macroeconomic Policy Institute Working Paper 8/2011.

Reserve Bank of India (2012), *Annual Report 2011–12*. Mumbai: Reserve Bank of India.

Subbarao, D. (2012), 'Price Stability, Financial Stability, and Sovereign Debt Sustainability: Policy Challenges from the New Trilemma', *Macroeconomics and Finance in Emerging Market Economies*, 5(2): 246–59.

Wall, L.D. (2012), 'Central Banking for Financial Stability: Some Lessons from the Recent Instability in the United States and Euro Area', ADBI Working Paper No. 379, August.

CHAPTER 6

MONETARY POLICY TRANSMISSION IN INDIA

interplay of rate and quantum channels

KANAGASABAPATHY K.,

REKHA A. BHANGAONKAR, AND

SHRUTI J. PANDEY*

A central bank can use quantity or rate as alternative targets/operating instruments and if it chooses one, the other is determined exogenously. Monetary policy in India seems to operate at both ends, liquidity and interest rates, either by intent or by compulsion due to multiple and at times conflicting choices. While the rate channel is somewhat straightforward to understand and study, the quantum channel as it operates get blurred because of multiple objectives of complex liquidity management operations. One of the statements repeatedly finding place in the Reserve Bank

* The authors wish to place on record their sincere thanks to Professor Ashima Goyal and an anonymous referee for insightful suggestions on a earlier draft, Mr Thiagu Ranganathan for his valuable suggestions regarding empirical techniques, Vishakha G. Tilak for valuable assistance in data analysis and graphs, and Rema K. Nair for page formatting.

of India's (RBI) monetary policy statements runs like this: The Reserve Bank will ensure that appropriate liquidity is maintained in the system so that all legitimate requirements of credit are met, particularly for productive purposes, consistent with the objective of price and financial stability. Towards this end, the RBI will continue with its policy of active demand management of liquidity through open market operations (OMO) including the Market Stabilization Scheme (MSS), Liquidity Adjustment Facility (LAF) and Cash Reserve Ratio (CRR), and using all the policy instruments at its disposal flexibly, as and when the situation warrant.[1] Of late this seems to be the case with many central banks in advanced countries too. According to Friedman and Kuttner (2011), central banks no longer set the short-term interest rates that they target for monetary policy purposes in the way described in standard economics textbooks. The explanation for this phenomenon involves several features of how central banks actually implement monetary policy decisions in the current era. Central banks tend to use the policy interest rate and the quantity of reserves not as mutually exclusive operations but use both of them in conjunction with each other and this represents a fundamental departure from decades of thinking about the scope of a central bank's action.

This chapter fundamentally looks at the interplay between the rate and quantum channels of monetary operations since 2001 when the new LAF operating procedure was introduced as the principal liquidity management tool. Literature referred to earlier and RBI's current position is that the policy interest rate should signal the stance of monetary policy, while liquidity may be managed as required using discretionary instruments depending on exogenous movements in overall liquidity conditions. RBI has also recently taken a stand that rate transmission will work better if LAF is operated injecting or absorbing liquidity within a band of plus or minus one percentage point of the liability of the banking system. RBI of late also prefers to keep the system in a deficit mode or liquidity injection mode, as research has shown that rate transmission works better in such a situation. But, the reality is somewhat different. LAF is only one of the liquidity managing instruments. There are other discretionary operations such as OMO, CRR, and foreign exchange operations all affecting bank reserves. In this backdrop, the chapter addresses the broader question that when an easing or tightening stance is taken with regard to policy rate in terms of liquidity management operations, whether the movement in liquidity and its impact works complementary to policy rate changes.

[1] Reserve Bank of India (2007). Third Quarter Monetary Policy Review.

With this objective, we look at the transmission mechanism of rate and quantum channels, the former captured by the influence of policy rate on other market rates and the latter assessed through the impact of a measure of total liquidity representing the combined impact of all discretionary use of investments such as LAF, CRR, OMO, and RBI's foreign exchange operations on interest rates and non-food bank credit. The period covered by the study is April 2001 to May 2012 and the data used are on a monthly basis except for the real gross domestic product (GDP) which is on a quarterly basis.

The chapter is sequenced as follows: following the introduction, the next section briefly narrates the changes in policy framework and operating procedures with reference to rate and quantum channels. The next section makes an effort to divide the reference period into easing and tightening phases of the policy cycle and brings out stylized facts on several relationships highlighting the impact of policy rate changes and liquidity conditions on short-term and medium-term market interest rates and output and prices. The section that follows attempts a review of literature. The next section provides the results and analysis of a Vector Auto Regressive (VAR) model built on Granger Causal relations between a set of variables considered. For this purpose, we first try to establish the linkage and transmission from policy rate to other short- and long-term interest rates. Secondly, we attempt to establish the relationship between policy rate changes and movement in liquidity and their combined impact on the bank lending rate, deposit rate, and non-food credit. The last section provides concluding observations.

Policy Framework and Operating Procedures

In India, RBI has historically maintained the twin objectives of monetary policy as price stability and ensuring adequate flow of credit to the productive sectors of the economy.[2] While these primary objectives continue to govern policy, over the years there has been a transformation in the

[2] Financial stability has been loosely added as an objective of monetary policy in recent years. But this objective is being served more by macro-prudential and regulatory policies of the Reserve Bank of India.

monetary policy framework in India. In that process, the operating instruments and their transmission have become increasingly complex.

Before 1985, the central bank's policy was essentially a credit policy with a plethora of controls on interest rates as also the direction of credit flow to preferred sectors and groups of population. During the mid-1980s to 1997–8 a monetary targeting framework with feedback was followed. However, in the mid-1990s this framework lost its importance because of several other developments along with economic and financial sector reforms. Taking into account the challenges posed by financial liberalization and increasing complexities of monetary management, RBI opted to switch to a multiple indicator approach in 1998–9.[3] This broad-based approach has provided the central bank with enormous flexibility in operating policy instruments.

RBI has also been continuing its efforts to develop the money and government securities markets since the mid-1980s with the introduction of new instruments, such as the commercial paper (CP), certificates of deposit (CD), and later collateralized borrowing and lending obligations (CBLO) which expanded the base of money market. RBI also initiated auction methods for primary issuance of government securities including treasury bills which made the government securities interest rates market related. In parallel, RBI also strengthened institutional infrastructure for trading and settlements which contributed to the growth of the secondary market. All these enabled RBI to use a market-based interest rate and liquidity management with improved transmission of signals.

A snapshot of growth in money and government securities markets during the last about a decade is given in Table 6.1.

In this backdrop, the instruments and related transmission can be viewed in two broad dimensions: first is the interest rate channel and second the quantum channel. While the former is governed by policy rate changes, the latter is captured by liquidity influencing instruments.

Rate Channel

Bank rate is the standard rate at which the central bank is prepared to buy or discount bills of exchange or other commercial eligible paper. In the early stages of liberalization of interest rates in the mid-1990s, RBI

[3] Money supply, M_3, continues to be an informative component, but it is not targeted.

Table 6.1 Growth in Volume of Money/Government Securities Markets

Sr. No.	Nomenclature	Volume in Rs crore		Compound Annual Growth Rate (%)
		2001–2	2011–12	
1.	Call/Notice/Term Money	5,665,108	4,013,031	-3.39
2.	CDs	1,576	419,530	74.79
3.	CPs	7,224	91,190	28.86
4.	CBLO	976,789#	11,155,428	41.61
5.	Market Repo	1,560,510#	3,763,877	13.40
6.	Central Government Securities	1,138,479	3,151,482	10.72
7.	Treasury bills	66,556	334,136	17.51
8.	Total Government Securities (6+7)	1,205,035	3,485,619	11.21

Source: Reserve Bank of India (www. rbi.org.in) & Compiled by Authors.
Note: #: Data pertain to 2004–5.

attempted to activate the bank rate as the benchmark rate along with the introduction of the prime lending rate (PLR). But, with the activation of repo operations, repo rate came to be viewed as a market preferred policy rate. This firmed up further when RBI introduced the full-fledged LAF in June 2000. LAF is characterized by repo and reverse repo operations of the central bank at prescribed rates, which provide a corridor within which the short-term interest rates to operate. However, this procedure had some limitations as there was no single policy rate instrument defined as such, and the operating policy rate alternated between repo and reverse repo rates depending on the prevailing liquidity condition. The absence of a firm corridor led the implicit target rate (call rate) breaching the upper and lower limits under easy liquidity or stress conditions. Taking these shortcomings into consideration, a new operating procedure was put in place in May 2011. Following the recommendations of (Chairman: Deepak Mohanty) a Working Group to Review the Operating Procedure of Monetary Policy, repo rate is recognized as the only policy rate. All other associated rates, such as the reverse repo rate, bank rate/marginal standing facility rate—a kind of Lombard rate—have all been linked to the repo rate at prescribed spreads. In the current context and for the purpose of this chapter, repo rate is used as the policy rate transmitting through other short- and medium-term interest rates.

The Quantum Channel

In the pre-reforms period up to the 1980s, liquidity influencing measures consisted of essentially two instruments—CRR and refinance facilities. When the monetary targeting approach was followed during 1985 to 1997, these two instruments were used to influence primary liquidity, consistent with the targeted money supply. When the framework was changed to multiple indicators, most of the refinance facilities were withdrawn, though some select facilities are still available. Liquidity operations assumed several complexities, though the primary objective of managing liquidity is implicitly to ensure flow of credit to the productive sectors of the economy. Unless liquidity management operations are used in conjunction and in alignment with the policy stance as reflected through rate signals, such liquidity operations may not only counteract the policy's intentions of tightening or easing, but also negate the signalling effect of policy rate changes. For instance, when the policy rate is on a rising path, a cut in CRR can send a wrong signal.

First are LAF operations. Repo is used for injecting liquidity and reverse repo is used for absorption of liquidity. These operations are mostly passive in nature, in the sense that the auctioned amount at the prescribed rates are accepted by RBI.

Second is CRR. In the post-reforms period, the medium-term policy was to gradually reduce CRR to its statutory minimum.[4] But, in response to an unprecedented surge in foreign capital inflows, CRR has been reactivated since December 2006 both as a liquidity management tool and as an instrument for sterilization of the liquidity impact of foreign exchange purchases by RBI. The burden on LAF turned out to be too high and it tended to affect the RBI's balance sheet and profits. Hence, increase in CRR was a less costly option to sterilize capital flows and RBI considered that the cost of sterilization should be shared by the banking system as well.

The third major liquidity management tool is OMO which involves RBI's buying and selling of government securities to regulate liquidity in the system. As RBI is also the debt manager, OMO also facilitates a smooth conduct of the government's borrowing programme particularly since 2006, when RBI was prohibited from participating in primary issuance of government securities.

[4] The statutory minimum was 3 per cent; but an amendment to the RBI Act in 2006 removed this ceiling.

Fourth, in the wake of very large and continuous capital inflows and the need for modulating surplus liquidity conditions of an enduring nature, MSS was introduced in April 2004 to equip RBI with an additional instrument of liquidity management. Under MSS, treasury bills (TBs) and dated securities of the Government of India are issued to the market but these funds were not used for budgetary operations. Money raised under MSS was held in a separate identifiable cash account maintained and operated by the Reserve Bank and the amount held in this account is appropriated only for the purpose of redemption and/or buyback of TBs and/or dated securities issued under MSS. But, in the post-global financial crisis period, MSS securities were desequestrated to accommodate the government's higher borrowing needs. Thus, while MSS was not originally intended as borrowing operations for the government during the crisis, the government exploited the outstanding MSS to expand its budgetary operations through the desequestration process. This to some extent reduced the rollover problem of government debt that would have necessitated fresh borrowings from the market.

Fifth is RBI's foreign exchange market intervention. Though RBI's objective behind such operations is to contain rupee-dollar exchange rate volatility, in effect, it also becomes a part of liquidity management operations, since purchase and sale of foreign exchange have the same influence as OMO in government securities.

Sterilization is a process that attempts to influence the exchange rate without changing the monetary base. It should, however, be noted that the effectiveness of a sterilized intervention is more controversial and ambiguous. By definition, the sterilized intervention has little or no effect on domestic interest rates, since the level of the money supply is left unchanged. However, according to some literature, a sterilized intervention can influence the exchange rate through two channels: the portfolio balance channel and the expectations or signalling channel. Sterilization in India is generally associated with counteracting the liquidity impact at times of buying foreign exchange by the central bank. In late 2011, when RBI was selling foreign exchange to arrest the depreciation of the rupee, it used CRR to neutralize the liquidity impact on the system.

For purposes of analysis in this chapter a measure of 'total liquidity' was compiled by combining the influence of all these instruments during the reference period.

Thus, in multiple objective and multiple instrument frameworks, a single objective may be served by more than one instrument and a single instrument may aim at fulfilling more than one objective as shown in Table 6.2.

Table 6.2 Instruments and their Objectives

No.	Instruments	Intended Objectives	Other Assumed Role in Practice
1.	CRR	To control reserve money and thereby M_3 growth	Cost-free sterilization instrument
2.	LAF-Repo and Reverse Repo	Provide a corridor for short-term money market; in particular call money market	Sterilization instrument at a cost
3.	OMO	To supplement LAF	Debt management objective
4.	MSS	Sterilization	Liquidity management and debt management objective
5.	Forex Market Interventions	Contain volatility of exchange rate	Reserve accumulation and achieve exchange rate objective

Source: Compiled by authors.

In a nutshell, given this analysis of operating framework and instruments, the operations of rate and quantum channels in the Indian context may be viewed as in Figure 6.1.

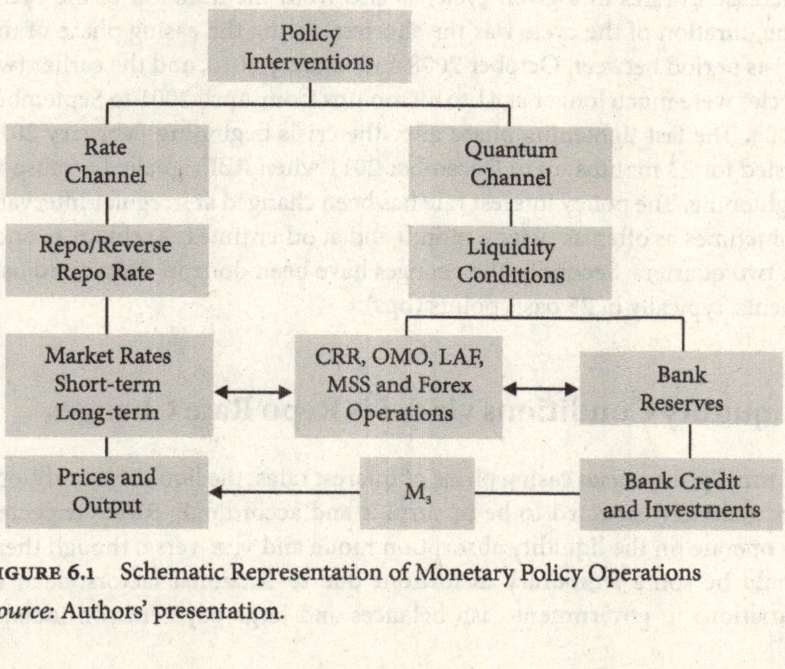

FIGURE 6.1 Schematic Representation of Monetary Policy Operations

Source: Authors' presentation.

Trends during Easing and Tightening Phases: Some Stylized Facts

Interest rate cycles follow changes in the stance of monetary policy and operations from time to time, an easing phase followed by a tightening phase, characterized by falling and rising interest rates respectively. A continuous reduction in the policy rate during a certain period is considered as an easing phase, whereas continued hikes in the policy rate over a period is considered a tightening phase. On this basis, the reference period falls under four phases—two easing and two tightening phases. Phase I runs from April 2001 to August 2004, an easing phase; Phase II from September 2004 to September 2008, a tightening phase; Phase III from October 2008 to January 2010, an easing phase; and Phase IV from February 2010 to December 2011 which is a tightening phase. India is again in an easing phase since about January 2012. During this last phase, RBI used liquidity management tools, such as the CRR more prominently than the policy repo rate.

The intensity of easing or tightening can be gauged by the extent of increase in rates in a given cycle, as also from the duration of the cycle. The duration of the cycle was the shortest during the easing phase of the crisis period between October 2008 and January 2010, and the earlier two cycles were much longer at 41 to 49 months from April 2001 to September 2008. The last tightening phase after the crisis beginning February 2010 lasted for 23 months up to December 2011 when RBI signalled a pause to tightening. The policy interest rate has been changed at irregular intervals, sometimes as often as twice a month and at other times as seldom as once in two quarters. Secondly, the changes have been done in discrete adjustments, typically of 25 basis points (bps).

Liquidity Conditions vis-à-vis Repo Rate Changes

Normally, during an easing phase of interest rates, the liquidity conditions are generally expected to be in surplus and accordingly RBI is expected to operate on the liquidity absorption mode and vice-versa, though there could be some temporary distortions due to frictional factors, such as variations in government cash balances and large payments on income tax due dates. But this was not the case except during the last phase of tightening when RBI was observed to be in liquidity injection mode (Table 6.3 and Figure 6.2).

Table 6.3 Liquidity Operations

Phases	Easing Phase (April 01 to August 04)	Tightening Phase (September 04 to September 08)	Easing Phase (October 08 to January 10)	Tightening Phase (February 10 to December 11)
Time durations (months)	41	49	16	23
Change in CRR	8.00 to 4.50	4.75 to 9.00	6.00 to 5.00	5.75 to 6.00
No. of times change	6	13	3	2
Basis points	-350	425	-100	25
CRR Amount (Net Injection (+)/ absorption (-))	21,650	-274,000	115,621	-148,521
LAF (Net Injection (+)/absorption (-))	-546,520	-529,746	-1,235,742	954,555
OMO (Net Purchase (+)/Net Sales (-))	-121,055	-257,343	171,286	111,350
MSS (Net Injection (+)/absorption (-))	-28,784	-128,001	166,067	7,737
Net RBI Intervention in Forex Market (Rs crore) (Net Purchases (+)/sales (-))	270,623	490,130	-144,034	-57,460
Total Liquidity	-404,085	-698,960	-926,802	867,661

Source: Reserve Bank of India (www. rbi.org.in) & Compiled by Authors.

It should be noted that absorption/injection of liquidity is captured in terms of a measure of total liquidity in this paper as the combined impact on primary liquidity through the discretionary use of instruments of CRR, MSS, LAF, forex operations, and OMO.

It can be observed from Figure 6.2 that irrespective of the tightening or easing phases, overall RBI was in a liquidity absorbing mode till mid-2010 allowing huge surplus liquidity conditions in the system. One main reason for this was the enormous capital inflows followed by RBI's intervention in forex purchases injecting large amounts of liquidity into the system which in turn needed to be absorbed through various means of sterilization.

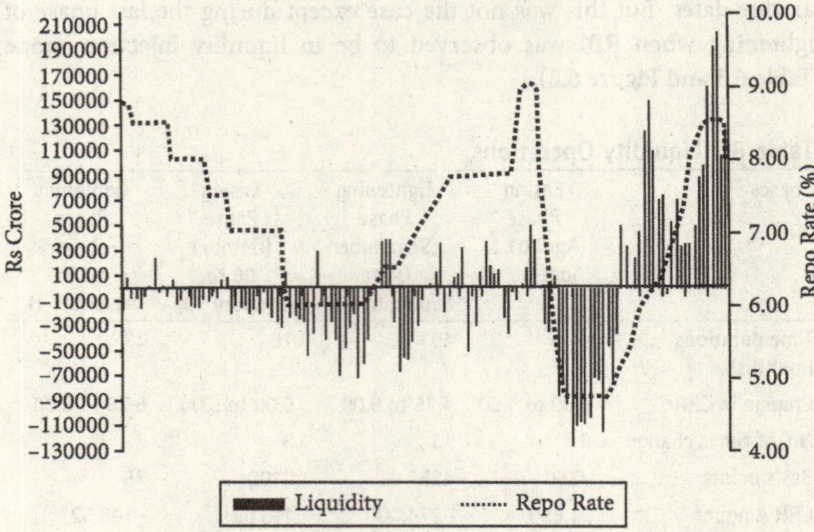

FIGURE 6.2 Movement in Liquidity & Repo Rate

Source: RBI & EPWRF

The total liquidity in the paper is derived as the combined impact on the primary liquidity through the discretionary use of instruments of CRR, MSS, LAF, forex operations and OMO. The RBI attempts to ensure liquidity flows through its discretionary operations in conjunction with autonomous movements in liquidity caused, for instance, due to changing government cash balances and currency in circulation. Through its liquidity management operations, the RBI either offsets or complements the autonomous liquidity flows in order to maintain liquidity at the desired level. The chapter attempts to capture how far such discretionary operations on liquidity were consistent with the easing, tightening of policy rates.

During 2002–3 there was a significant increase in capital inflows in India, and excess capital inflows was managed through day-to-day LAF and OMO, besides other measures, such as building government balances with RBI, particularly through increased issuances of 91-day TBs and limited forex swaps. Given this backdrop, a Working Group on Instruments of Sterilization recommended that the central government issue a special variety of bills/bonds for sterilization purposes (Thorat 2003). In order to operationalize such a new instrument of sterilization and ensure fiscal transparency, a new instrument named the MSS was made functional from April 2004. The introduction of MSS has succeeded broadly in restoring LAF to its intended function of daily liquidity management. RBI used multiple instruments, such as the LAF, OMO, CRR, and securities under MSS to modulate the liquidity in the system. RBI also took recourse to increasing the CRR for banks to withdraw excess liquidity from the system.

The period 2004–5 to 2007–8 continued to witness a huge inflow of foreign capital and RBI had to reckon with its impact on domestic liquidity in several ways. First, the central bank intervened in the foreign exchange market partly to arrest excessive rupee appreciation and partly to build up foreign exchange reserves to more comfortable levels. The foreign exchange reserves increased from US$ 18.5 billion in April 2004 to US$ 314.6 billion in May 2008. RBI also used liquidity management tools, such as CRR and LAF along with the newly introduced MSS to absorb excess liquidity flows into the system through purchase of foreign exchange, termed as sterilization operations. Further, to arrest the inflationary impact, RBI also hiked the policy repo rate. Thus, the repo rate was raised from 6 per cent in April 2004 to 9 per cent in July 2008.

During 2008–9, after the fall of Lehman Brothers, the impact of the global financial turmoil impacted India too, exploding the myth of decoupling of countries like India from global shocks. During the crisis period, RBI had used unconventional instruments to keep the system afloat with abundant liquidity through cuts in CRR, policy interest rates, and through a variety of liberal refinancing instruments.

The system since 2004 therefore was generally experiencing surplus liquidity conditions and hence the interest rates ruled relatively easy throughout till the last quarter of 2010, though market interest rates were responding to policy rate changes. The broad objective of RBI's liquidity management operations was ensuring that liquidity conditions do not hamper the smooth functioning of financial markets and disrupt flows to the real economy (Gokarn 2011). According to Patra and Kapur (2010), during the episodes of excess liquidity (2001 through 2006 and again from 2008:Quarter$_4$ (Q_4) to 2010:Q_2), the reverse repo rate was the effective policy rate. On the other hand, during episodes of monetary tightening/ liquidity shortage (2007:Q_1 to 2008:Q_3 and 2010:Q_3 to 2011:Q_4), the repo rate became the effective policy rate. Thus, the policy rate, during the post-2003 period, switched between repo and reverse repo rates, mostly remained closer to the reverse repo rate due to surplus liquidity conditions.

It can be observed from Figure 6.3 that the overnight call money rate for most of the period till mid-2010 hovered around the reverse repo rate. Ghosh and Bhattacharyya (2009) show the dominance of policy interventions in the overnight money market.

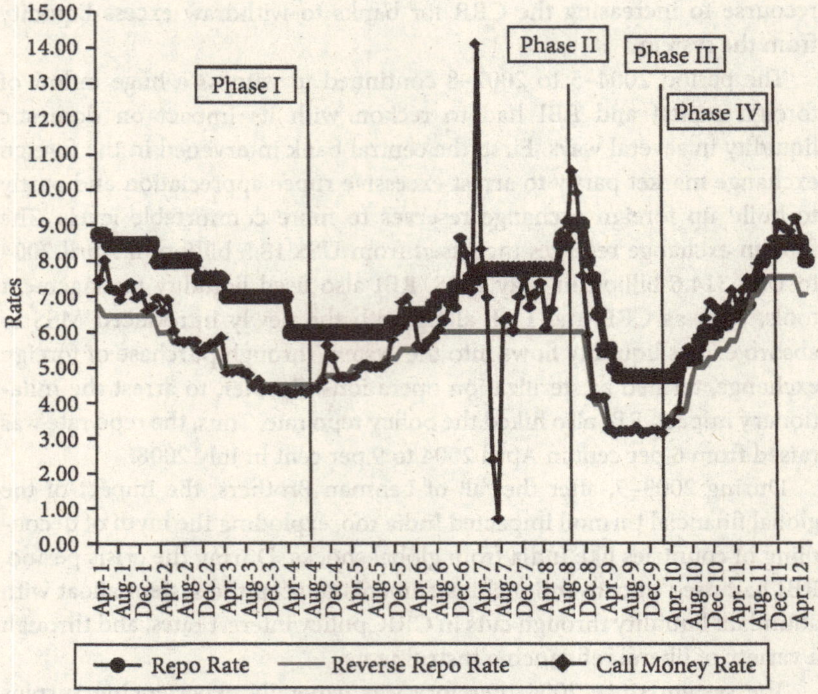

FIGURE 6.3 Repo Rate, Reverse Repo Rate and Call Money Rate
Source: RBI & EPWRF.

Repo Rate and Market Interest Rates

A hike in policy rate was followed by a rise in short-term market rates, such as the call money, 91-day TBs rate, and one year government securities (g-sec) rate and vice versa (Table 6.4). While the one year g-sec rate was more elastic, this impact petered out as the maturity increased, showing that longer term rates are influenced by an additional set of factors like current and future economic activity, output gap, fiscal policy, and the global environment. This was particularly so in the last two phases of the policy cycle. As shown earlier, surplus liquidity conditions that prevailed during most of the reference periods, also contributed to lower long-term interest rates.

Table 6.4 Short-, Medium-, and Long-term Market Rates

	Easing Phase (April 01 to August 04)	bps	Tightening Phase (September 04 to September 08)	bps	Easing Phase (October 08 to January 10)	bps	Tightening Phase (February 10 to December 11)	bps
Repo Rate	8.75 to 6.00	–275	6.00 to 9.00	300	9.00 to 4.75	–425	4.75 to 8.50	375
No. of Times Change	5		9		6		12	
91 T-Bills	7.53 to 4.59	–294	5.00 to 7.60	260	7.03 to 3.78	–325	4.15 to 8.50	435
Call Money Rate	7.53 to 4.36	–317	3.5 to 14.81	1131	17.89 to 2.99	–1490	3.27 to 8.83	556
1 year G-sec	8.94 to 5.26	–368	5.12 to 8.81	369	7.54 to 4.03	–351	4.96 to 8.62	366
10 year G-sec	10.24 to 6.37	–387	6.17 to 8.41	223	7.84 to 7.71	–13	7.77 to 8.50	73
bps (basis points)								

Source: Reserve Bank of India (www. rbi.org.in) & Compiled by Authors.

This could also be attributed to the segmented and still a captive market for government securities from the banking system on account of high statutory liquidity ratio (SLR) and administrative directions applicable to long-term investment institutions, such as insurance companies and provident funds. The ten-year security prices being more sensitive to yield rate changes, markets have a tendency to respond in anticipation to policy rates changes.

Response of Banking Indicators

Commercial banks were observed to have responded to repo rate changes by adjusting both their deposit and lending rates (Figure 6.4).

It appears that while adjusting these rates the banking system tried to keep the spread between deposit and lending rates intact. In fact, the spread seems to have widened in the last phase of the tightening cycle. Commercial banks also tend to adjust their portfolios of assets changing

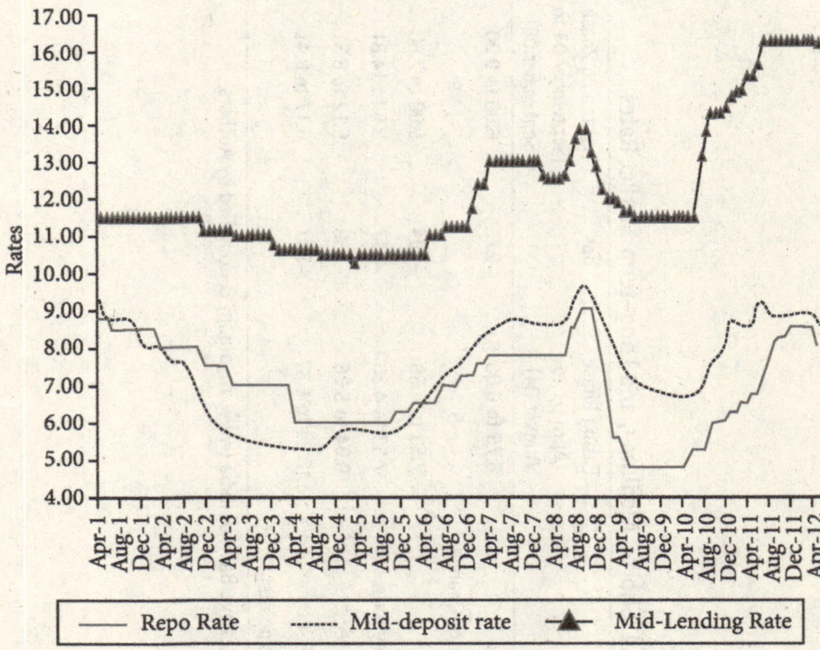

FIGURE 6.4 Trend in Mid-deposit Rates and Mid-lending Rates

Source: RBI.

preferences between credit and investments. Monetary policy affecting banks' willingness to lend is examined either by analysing the banks' portfolio adjustment behaviour or the impact on price and non-price term of lending of banks (Bernanke and Blinder 1992: Romer and Romer 1990).

Banks expanded their credit portfolio by reducing their investments during the second phase of the cycle when the system had huge surplus liquidity. But, this was also the period of fiscal correction. Later to the global financial crisis, banks seem to have reversed this trend and there is a tendency for growth in investment adversely impacting bank credit growth (Figure 6.5). During the recent period, banks seem to have opted for safer avenues of investment resulting in a compositional shift in their asset portfolios. This can be attributed to increasing non-performing loans and the need for banks to build up additional capital in the run up to compliance with stricter Basel III norms. Lower credit growth can also be partly attributed to lower deposit growth in the recent period since April 2011.

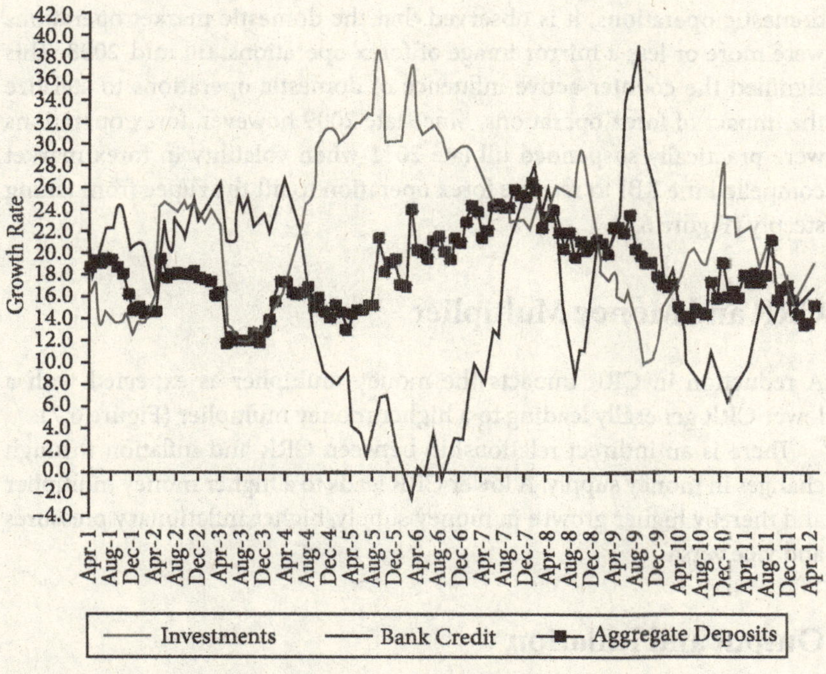

FIGURE 6.5 Trend in Deposits, Credit and Investments
Source: RBI.

Commercial banks' investments consist mostly of statutory liquidity ratio (SLR) investments. However, the banks undertake non-SLR investments which consist of commercial papers, shares and bonds/debentures issued by public sector undertakings, public financial institutions and private corporate sector and other instruments issued by mutual funds. Whereas other instruments issued by mutual funds, public financial institutions, and bond/debentures. These non-SLR investments are mostly credit substitutes and constituted on an average less than 12 per cent of the total assets (as on May 2012). The total banking assets consist of balances with other banks, money at call and short notice, advance to banks, other assets, investments (SLR), bank credit, loans, cash credit and overdrafts, inland bills, and discounted and foreign bills.

Forex Market Operations and other Liquidity Operations

If the liquidity management is split into forex market operations and other domestic operations, it is observed that the domestic market operations were more or less a mirror image of forex operations, till mid-2008. This signified the counter-active influence of domestic operations to sterilize the impact of forex operations. Since late 2009 however, forex operations were practically suspended till late 2011 when volatility in forex market compelled the RBI to resume forex operation to lift the rupee from falling steeply (Figure 6.6).

CRR and Money Multiplier

A reduction in CRR impacts the money multiplier as expected with a lower CRR generally leading to a higher money multiplier (Figure 6.7).

There is an indirect relationship between CRR and inflation through changes in money supply. A lower CRR leads to a higher money multiplier and thereby higher growth in money supply, higher inflationary pressures and vice versa.

Output and Inflation

Apparently, the impact of easing or tightening of policy is with a lag. A policy easing phase results in higher growth and lower inflation in the

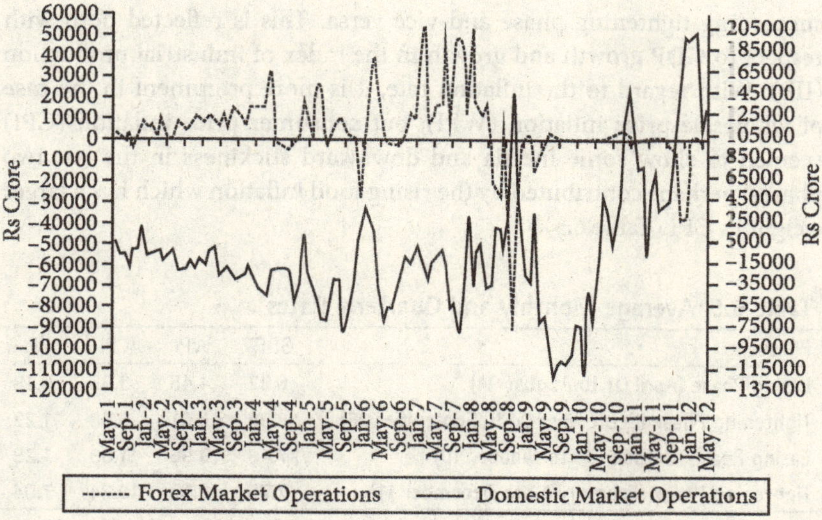

FIGURE 6.6 Forex Market Operations and Other Domestic Operations

Source: RBI & EPWRF

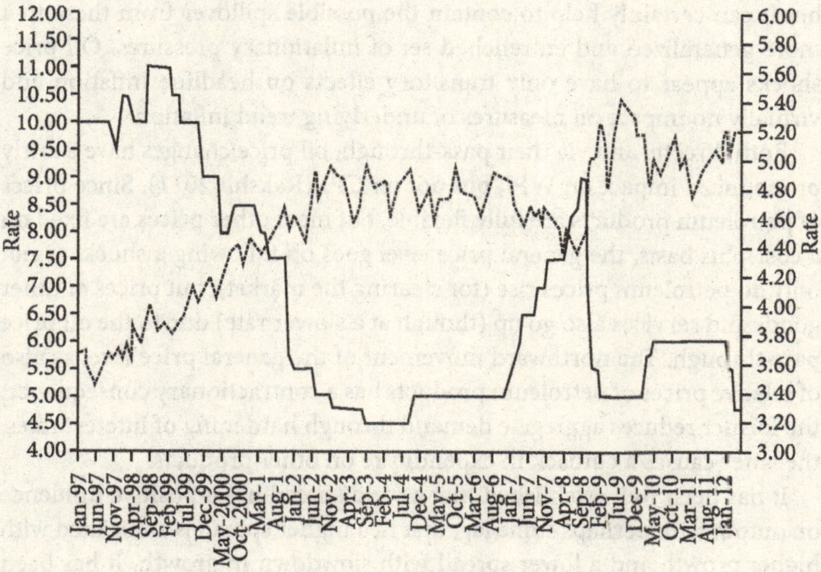

FIGURE 6.7 Movement in CRR and Money Multiplier

Source: RBI.

succeeding tightening phase and vice versa. This is reflected both with respect to GDP growth and growth in the index of industrial production (IIP). With regard to the inflation rate, it is more prominent in the case of wholesale price inflation (WPI); but consumer price inflation (CPI) seemed to show some inertia and downward stickiness in the last two phases, perhaps contributed by the rising food inflation which has a larger weight in CPI (Table 6.5).

Table 6.5 Average Monthly and Quarterly Rates

Phases	GDP*	WPI	CPI	IIP
Easing Phase (April 01 to August 04)	6.32	4.45	3.95	5.48
Tightening Phase (September 04 to September 08)	8.98	6.01	5.88	11.22
Easing Phase (October 08 to January 10)	7.49	3.96	11.05	1.28
Tightening Phase (February 10 to December 11)	7.75	9.57	10.24	7.04

Source: EPW Research Foundation Database (www.epwrfits.in), Compiled by authors.
* Quarterly Average

The tight policy stance may not directly address supply side pressures, but it can certainly help to contain the possible spillover from these to a more generalized and entrenched set of inflationary pressures. Oil price shocks appear to have only transitory effects on headline inflation and virtually no impact on measures of underlying trend inflation.

Both directly and via their pass-through, oil price changes have a fairly pronounced impact on WPI, but not on CPI (Rakshit 2011). Since prices of petroleum products are fully flexible, but most other prices are fixed on a cost-plus basis, the general price level goes up following a shock, as not only do petroleum prices rise (for clearing the market), but prices of other goods and services also go up (though at a slower rate) due to the oil price pass-through. The northward movement of the general price level as also of relative prices of petroleum products has a contractionary consequence: the former reduces aggregate demand through hardening of interest rates, the latter causes a cutback in expenditure on other products.

It has been well established that a yield spread has a positive influence on output with perhaps some lag, that is, a higher spread is associated with higher growth and a lower spread with slowdown in growth. It has been observed that the yield spread of one year and ten year G-sec evidently has an impact on growth in IIP (Figure 6.8). It can be particularly seen that the narrowing of the spread around mid-2008–9 is associated with the slowdown in economic activity following the crisis.

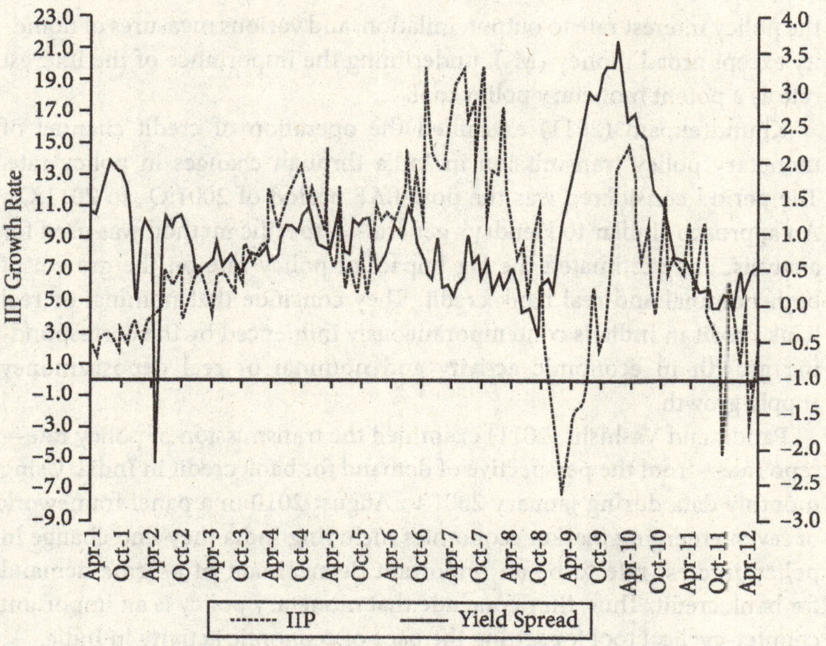

FIGURE 6.8 Movements of IIP Growth and Yield
Source: RBI & EPWRF.

Review of Literature

Literature on monetary transmission in India is apparently at a nascent stage mainly due to the under-developed nature of financial markets and quick structural changes. Also, the policy framework and operating procedures are governed by several competing objectives and purposes. Despite these limitations, attempts have been made earlier to study transmission mechanisms, in particular of rate and credit channels.

Mohanty (2012) used a quarterly structural vector auto-regression (SVAR) model, to find evidence that policy rate increases have a negative effect on output growth with a lag of two quarters and a moderating impact on inflation with a lag of three quarters. The overall impact persists through 8–10 quarters. These results were found to be robust across alternative specifications with different measures of output, inflation, and liquidity. Moreover, significant unidirectional causality was found from the policy interest rate to output, inflation, and various measures of liquidity except broad money (M_3), underlining the importance of the interest rate as a potent monetary policy tool.

Khundrakpam (2011) examined the operation of credit channel of monetary policy transmission in India through changes in policy rate. The period considered was the post-LAF period of 2001:Q_3 to 2011:Q_3. An approach similar to Hendry's general-to-specific method was used for analysis. They estimated the lag impact of policy rate on the growth of both nominal and real bank credit. They conclude that nominal or real bank credit in India is contemporaneously influenced by the corresponding growth in economic activity and nominal or real deposit/money supply growth.

Pandit and Vashisht (2011) examined the transmission of policy rate—repo rate—from the perspective of demand for bank credit in India. Using monthly data during January 2001 to August 2010 in a panel framework of seven emerging market economies including India they find change in policy interest rate to be an important determinant of a firm's demand for bank credit. Thus, they conclude that monetary policy is an important counter-cyclical tool for setting the pace of economic activity in India.

Pandit et al. (2006) using a VAR framework on quarterly panel data of banks for 1997 to 2002 find that the changes in CRR and the bank rate get transmitted to bank lending, with the impact being far more severe on small banks than it is on large banks.

Empirical Analysis through VAR Model

The continuous evolution of the monetary transmission channel necessitates re-recognizing the inter-relation between variables involved in the transmission process. The rate channel in conventional terms operates through a short-term rate influencing the term structure of interest rates, including lending rates, in turn influencing demand for credit and investments and thereby output and prices. The quantum channel can influence interest rates and also the availability of credit and thereby influence output and prices. Though the interest rate channel and quantum channel of monetary transmission are thus defined by past literature, we have made an attempt to emphasize the role of the impact of policy rates on market rates and the transmission to output. Similarly, from the quantum side the impact of total liquidity on non-food bank credit and the relationship between the policy rate and total liquidity are captured though an empirical analysis. Granger Causal relationships among variables were established as a means of deciding the variables involved in the interactive dynamics of monetary transmission. Based on the Granger Causal relation between the variables considered, a Vector Auto Regressive (VAR) model was applied to arrive at the results.

The ability of the VAR framework that treats all variables as simultaneous and endogenous fetches merit in an analysis of monetary transmission (Pandit et al. 2006). Akaike Information Criterion (AIC) was used to ascertain lag length pertaining to the model. In considering lag length as suggested by the Bayesian Information Criterion (BIC), the system suffered from auto correlation in residuals. VAR's stability estimates are checked through the Eigen value stability condition. With a stable VAR, Impulse Response Function (IRF) graphs are plotted and the Cholesky Forecast-Error Variance Decomposition (FEVD) tables arrived at. The variables suffered from unit root and hence were corrected for unit root using the first difference.

The structure of the method adopted and the general form equations are:

$$Y_t = \sum_{i=1}^{n} \alpha_{11} Z_{t-i} + \sum_{j=1}^{n} \alpha_{12} Y_{t-j} + u_{1t} \quad \text{(a)}$$

$$Z_t = \sum_{i=1}^{n} \alpha_{21} Z_{t-i} + \sum_{j=1}^{n} \alpha_{22} Y_{t-j} + u_{2t} \quad \text{(b)}$$

$$Y_t = \beta_{10} + \beta_{11} Z_{t-1} + \beta_{12} Y_{t-1} + \gamma_{12} Z_{t-2} + \varepsilon_{yt} \quad \text{(c)}$$

$$Z_t = \beta_{20} + \beta_{21} Z_{t-1} + \beta_{22} Y_{t-1} + \beta_{23} Y_{t-2} + \varepsilon_{zt} \quad \text{(d)}$$

As the Granger Causal relations involve a bi-directional estimation of the variables,

Y_t = Response variable

Z_t = Policy variable

$\sum_{i=1}^{n} \alpha_{11} Z_{t-i} = n$ is the lag length, and α_{11} is coefficient matrix of lagged observation of Z_t $\sum_{i=1}^{n} \alpha_{12} Y_{t-j} = n$ is the lag length, and α_{12} is coefficient matrix of lagged observation of Y_t β = representing the co-efficient values.

The analysis covers the period from May 2001 to May 2012. The frequency of the data is monthly and the data have been sourced from various RBI sources and as compiled by the EPW Research Foundation.

In Model I, the variables used are repo (*repo rate*), one-year government security rate (*Onegs*), ten-year government security rate (*Tengs*), the mid-bank lending rate (*Lend*), the mid-bank deposit rate (*Deposit*), and the call money rate (*Call*). In building a relationship between short-term and long-term interest rates derived from market and non-market sources, variables were grouped as block 1, *Repo*, *Onegs*, and *Tengs*, block 2, *Repo*, *Lend*, and *Deposit*, and block 3 *Repo* and *Call*. The blocks were independently estimated and the Granger Causal relationship was derived. Further, the blocks were integrated and their Granger Causal relation was re-estimated. Based on the Granger Causal results in the blocks' integrated estimation, VAR equations were re-estimated. As the variables *Lend* and *Deposit* are collinear in nature, they were integrated with other blocks independently (Table A6.1).

Model I: The System of Equations—Rate Channel of Monetary Transmission

$$Onegs_t = f(Onegs_{t-n}, Repo_{t-n}, Call_{t-n}) \quad \text{Eq. 1}$$

$$Tengs_t = f(Tengs_{t-n}, Repo_{t-n}, Deposit_{t-n}) \quad \text{Eq. 2}$$

$$Lend_t = f(Lend_{t-n}, Repo_{t-n}) \quad \text{Eq. 3}$$

$$Deposit_t = f(Deposit_{t-n}, Lend_{t-n}, Repo_{t-n}) \quad \text{Eq. 4}$$

$$Repo_t = f(Repo_{t-n}, Lend_{t-n}) \quad \text{Eq. 5}$$

$$Call_t = f(Call_{t-n}, Repo_{t-n}) \quad \text{Eq. 6}$$

$$LnNonFood_t = f(LnNonFood_{t-n}, Deposit_{t-n}) \quad \text{Eq. 7}$$

Granger Causal Results

Variable 1	*Granger Causes*	*Variable 2*
Repo **	Granger Causes	Onegs
Call **	Granger Causes	Onegs
Repo ***	Granger Causes	Tengs
Deposit **	Granger Causes	Tengs
Repo***	Granger Causes	Lend
Lend **	Granger Causes	Deposit
Repo ***	Granger Causes	Deposit
Lend ***	Granger Causes	Repo
Repo ***	Granger Causes	Call
Deposit **	Granger Causes	LnNonFood

Note: *** Significant at 1% ** Significant at 5% * Significant at 10%.

Impulse Response Function to Change in Repo Rates—
Rate Channel (Model I)

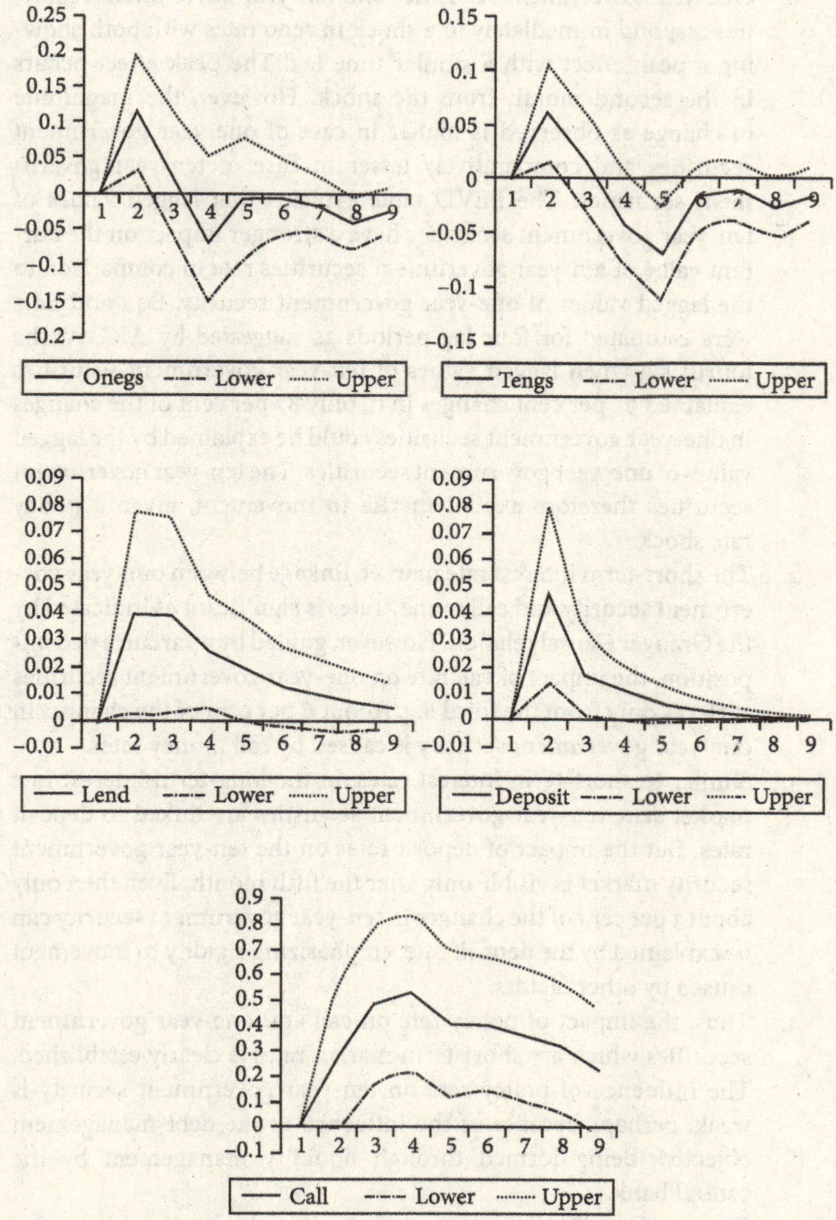

The important observations are:

1. One-year government securities and ten-year government securities respond immediately to a shock in repo rates with both showing a peak effect with a similar time lag. The peak effect occurs in the second month from the shock. However, the magnitude of change as observed is higher in case of one-year government securities and comparatively lesser in case of ten-year government securities. The FEVD table explains that lagged values of ten-year government securities have a stronger impact on the current value of ten-year government securities rate in comparison to the lagged values of one-year government security. Eq.1 and Eq.2 were estimated for four lag periods as suggested by AIC. At the fourth lag when lagged values of ten-year government securities explained 92 per cent changes in it, only 87 per cent of the changes in one-year government securities could be explained by the lagged values of one-year government securities. The ten-year government securities therefore exhibit inertia to movement, given a policy rate shock.
2. The short-term interest rate market, linkage between one-year government security and call money rates is significant as indicated by the Granger Causal relation. However, guided by a variance decomposition, the impact of call rate on one-year government securities surfaces only from the third lag. About 6 per cent of the changes in one-year government security is caused by call money rates.
3. Similar to short-term interest rates, in the long-term interest rate market also, ten-year government securities are linked to deposit rates. But the impact of deposit rates on the ten-year government security market is visible only after the fifth month. Even then only about 3 per cent of the changes in ten-year government security can be explained by the deposit rate, emphasizing rigidity to movement caused by other factors.
4. Thus, the impact of policy rate on call and one-year government securities which are short-term market rates is clearly established. The influence of policy rate on ten-year government security is weak, perhaps because of the influence of the debt management objective being formed through liquidity management by the central bank.
5. Granger Causal relationships suggest that the lending rate influences the deposit rate but reciprocation is not observed. Both the

lending and deposit rates peak at the second lag to a shock in repo rate but both rates behave quite differently. When the lending rate achieves a stable position lasting for about over a month, the deposit rate drops immediately after it reaches the peak effect.

6. Repo rate influences the lending rate only from the third lag explaining 5 per cent of the changes in lending rates. With about 97 per cent changes in lending rates being explained by their own lagged values, lending rates are stubborn to policy rate changes. In the case of deposit rates, at the second lag when the peak effect is observed, 5 and 4 per cent of the changes are attributed to repo rate and deposit rate. In other words, of the peak effect only 91 per cent of the changes in deposit rate are contributed by its lagged values.
7. A widely spread response curve is observed for call money rates with the peak effect observed after the fourth month. At the peak effect, about 86 per cent of the changes in call money are explained by the lagged values of call money and 14 per cent of the changes are explained by repo rate. This indicates that call money and repo rates operate in a close nexus with each other with repo rates influencing call rates in a unidirectional manner as indicated by the Granger Causal relation. This shows that the new operating target of the weighted call money rate which has been recently introduced can be successfully pursued by the central bank.
8. In considering the VAR relationship between non-food credit and deposit rates, the lag length as suggested by AIC was two time periods. The impact of repo rates on non-food credit, however, is steady at 3 per cent through eight lag periods.

In Model II, the variables used are repo (*repo rate*), total liquidity (*TLq*), and the natural log value of non-food credit (*LnNonFood*). The relationships developed between the variables are guided by the Granger Causal relationship (Table A6.2).

Model II: The System of Equations—Quantum Channel of Monetary Transmission

$$Repo_t = f(Repo_{t-n}, Tlq_{t-n}) \qquad \text{Eq. 8}$$

$$TLq_t = f(TLq_{t-n}, Repo_{t-n}, LnNonFood_{t-n}) \qquad \text{Eq. 9}$$

$$LnNonFood_t = f(LnNonFood_{t-n}, Repo_{t-n}, TLq_{t-n}) \qquad \text{Eq. 10}$$

Granger Causal Results

Variable 1	*Granger Causes*	*Variable 2*
*Repo ****	*Granger Causes*	*TLq*
*TLq **	*Granger Causes*	*Repo*
*LnNonFood ***	*Granger Causes*	*TLq*
*TLq **	*Granger Causes*	*LnNonFood*
*Repo ***	*Granger Causes*	*LnNonFood*

Note: *** Significant at 1% ** Significant at 5% * Significant at 10%.

Impulse Response Function of Repo Rate—Quantum Channel (Model II)

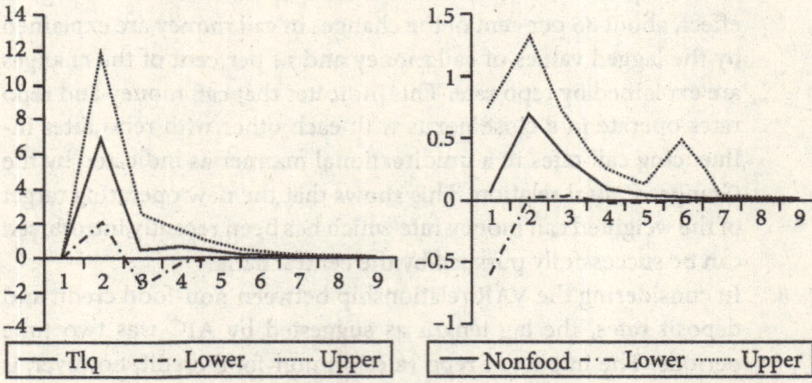

The important observations are:

1. A bi-causal relation is observed between the total liquidity and repo rates; however, repo has a stronger causal relationship with total liquidity. Total liquidity is estimated as a function of repo rate and non-food credit. From the variance decomposition table, during the peak effect both the repo rate and non-food credit together explain 9 per cent of the changes in total liquidity.
2. Non-food credit also reaches a peak effect in the second lag with 95 per cent of the changes being explained by the lagged values. Only 5 per cent of the changes are explained by total liquidity and repo rate together. An insignificant result was obtained between non-food credit and repo rate; indicating that non-food credit remains insulated from the influence of changes in repo rate.

Convention suggests a negative relationship between repo and non-food credit; however, in this study the sign of the non-food coefficient was positive. This is to a certain extent reflective of some disharmony between the rate and quantum/liquidity channels. Even while keeping the repo rate high or while raising the repo rate, liquidity is made available liberally through use of various instruments, such as the CRR, OMO, and LAF and credit growth is less affected through policy rate changes.

3. This confirms the stylized fact that liquidity for most part of the reference period was in surplus mode and it bore no relationship with the tightening or easing phase marked by repo rate changes.

***

Monetary policy in India operates through a combination of adjustment in policy rates and a complex set of liquidity management tools. This chapter captures the interplay between the rate and quantum channels and addressed the issue whether they work complementary to each other. The study covered the period April 2001 to May 2012 through a set of monthly data series (excepting GDP available on a quarterly basis). The study of stylized facts after dividing the period into easing and tightening phases showed that:

1. For most of the period, liquidity conditions remained in a surplus mode during both easing and tightening phases, except during the last tightening phase, when liquidity conditions were in deficit mode. As a result the interest rate conditions ruled relatively easy during most part, since the call money rate hovered around the reverse repo rate.
2. The elasticity of short-term interest rates, such as call and one-year government securities rates to repo rate changes was higher compared to ten-year government securities.
3. Bank deposit and lending rates showed concomitant changes to the repo rate and banks seemed to have been anxious to maintain their spread between deposit and lending rates.
4. Forex market operations seemed to have been contracted with other liquidity management operations as an attempt to sterilize foreign exchange operations.
5. CRR impacted money multiplier as expected.
6. Output growth and inflation seemed to have responded with a lag to policy easing and tightening. The easing phase resulted in higher

growth in GDP and industrial production and lower inflation in the subsequent tightening phase and vice versa. CPI inflation remained sticky in the last two phases.

7. The yield spread between one- and ten-year g-sec seemed to have anticipated growth in industrial production.
8. An empirical analysis using a combination of Granger Causal relationships and the VAR model confirmed that short-term responses to a change in policy rate—repo—attains a peak effect in two months' time. While one-year government securities showed a sharp response with a sudden rise and a steep fall, call money rates tend to have a distributed effect with the peak effect occurring only after four months. The long-term interest rate, ten-year government security, also responds to policy shock in two months, but the ten-year government security rate is dependent more on the lagged values of the variable, than on the repo rate.
9. Both the lending and deposit rates reaches a peak effect in two months, lending rates hovering around an interest rate achieved as a result of the policy shock, but the deposit rates drop immediately.

Both total liquidity and non-food credit take a two-month lag for the peak effect to occur. While total liquidity is explained by repo rate and non-food credit, non-food credit is dependent on the lagged values of the variable. An insignificant positive relationship was observed between the repo rate and non-food credit.

Appendix A6.1

Table A6.1 Cholesky Forecast-error Variance Decomposition Table—Model I

Equation 1 Onegs

Lags	FEVD (Onegs)	FEVD (Repo)	FEVD (Call)
1	1	0	0
2	0.94563	0.048281	0.006089
3	0.92953	0.049773	0.020691
4	0.874311	0.063282	0.062407
5	0.875071	0.059415	0.065514
6	0.868341	0.05893	0.072726
7	0.868343	0.059294	0.072364
8	0.859148	0.064351	0.076501

Equation 2 Tengs

Lags	FEVD (Tengs)	FEVD (Repo)	FEVD (Deposit)
1	1	0	0
2	0.948622	0.049168	0.00221
3	0.946051	0.051741	0.002208
4	0.923334	0.071331	0.005335
5	0.842763	0.12303	0.034207
6	0.839156	0.125855	0.034989
7	0.839104	0.126095	0.034802
8	0.8326	0.132979	0.034426

Equation 3 Lend

Lags	FEVD (Lend)	FEVD (Repo)
1	1	0
2	0.970278	0.029722
3	0.944799	0.055201
4	0.934954	0.065046
5	0.929637	0.070363
6	0.927115	0.072885
7	0.92579	0.07421
8	0.925127	0.074873

Equation 4 Deposit

Lags	FEVD (Deposit)	FEVD (Repo)	FEVD (Lend)
1	1	0	0
2	0.904604	0.051083	0.044312
3	0.885652	0.055272	0.059076
4	0.879615	0.056998	0.063388
5	0.87773	0.057517	0.064753
6	0.877131	0.057682	0.065186
7	0.876941	0.057735	0.065324
8	0.87688	0.057752	0.065368

Equation 5 Repo		
Lags	FEVD (Repo)	FEVD (Lend)
1	1	0
2	0.933966	0.66034
3	0.92213	0.07787
4	0.911984	0.088016
5	0.908594	0.091406
6	0.906476	0.093524
7	0.90553	0.09447
8	0.905016	0.94987

Equation 6 Call		
Lags	FEVD (Lend)	FEVD (Repo)
1	1	0
2	0.980021	0.019979
3	0.922876	0.077124
4	0.863374	0.136626
5	0.838173	0.161827
6	0.832466	0.187534
7	0.791183	0.208817
8	0.775602	0.224398

Equation 7 LnNonFoodCr		
Lags	FEVD (LnNonFoodCr)	FEVD (Deposit)
1	1	0
2	0.964103	0.035897
3	0.964276	0.035724
4	0.96337	0.03663
5	0.963315	0.036785
6	0.963061	0.036939
7	0.963044	0.036956
8	0.963028	0.036972

Table A6.2 Cholesky Forecast-error Variance Decomposition Table—Model II

Equation 9 TLq

Lags	FEVD (Tlq)	FEVD (Repo)	FEVD (LnNonFood)
1	1	0	0
2	0.911754	0.05038	0.037866
3	0.909084	0.0505	0.040416
4	0.908724	0.050831	0.040445
5	0.908677	0.050881	0.040443
6	0.90867	0.05887	0.040443
7	0.908869	0.050888	0.040443
8	0.908869	0.05889	0.040443

Equation 10 LnNonFood

Lags	FEVD (LnNonFood)	FEVD (Repo)	FEVD (TLq)
1	1	0	0
2	0.953154	0.027043	0.019803
3	0.947642	0.03267	0.019688
4	0.947067	0.33159	0.019774
5	0.94694	0.033278	0.019782
6	0.946921	0.033296	0.01783
7	0.946917	0.033299	0.019784
8	0.946917	0.0333	0.019784

References

Bernanke, Ben S. and Alan S. Blinder (1992), 'The Federal Funds Rate and the Channels of Monetary Transmission', *American Economic Review*, 82(4, September): 901–21.

Enders, Walter (2004), *Applied Econometric Time Series* (Wiley Series in Probability and Statistics). John Wiley & Sons, Inc. 2nd edition.

Friedman, Benjamin M. and Kenneth N. Kuttner (2011), *Implementation of Monetary Policy: How Do Central Banks Set Interest Rates?* Harvard University and Williams College.

Ghosh, Saurabh and Indranil Bhattacharyya (2009), 'Spread, Volatility and Monetary Policy: Empirical Evidence from the Indian Overnight Money Market', Macroeconomics and Finance in Emerging Market Economies, *Taylor and Francis Journals*, 2(2): 257–77.

Gokarn, Subir (2011), 'An Assessment of Recent Macroeconomic Developments', keynote address, Opening Plenary session of Confederation of Indian Industry's CFO Summit 2011, 3 December.

Khundrakpam, Jeevan Kumar (2011), *Credit Channel of Monetary Transmission in India—How Effective and Long is the Lag?* Mumbai: Reserve Bank of India.

Kramer, Charles F., Hélène K. Poirson, and A. Prasad (2008), 'Challenges to Monetary Policy from Financial Globalization: The Case of India', IMF Asia and Pacific Department.

Mohanty, Deepak (2012), 'Evidence on Interest Rate Channel of Monetary Policy Transmission in India', Reserve Bank of India, Working Paper WPS (DEPR); 6/2012, May, RBI.

Pandit, B.L., Ajit Mittal, Mohua Roy, and Saibal Ghosh (2006), 'Transmission of Monetary Policy and the Bank Lending Channel: Analysis and Evidence for India', Reserve Bank of India, Study No. 25, 16 January.

Pandit, B.L. and Pankaj Vashisht (2011), 'Monetary Policy and Credit Demand in India and Some EMEs', Indian Council for Research on International Economic Relations, Working Paper No. 256, May.

Patra, Michael Debabrata and Muneesh Kapur (2010), 'A Monetary Policy Model without Money for India': International Monetary Fund, Working Paper WP/10/183, August.

Rakshit, Mihir (2011), 'Inflation and Relative Prices in India 2006–10: Some Analytical and Policy Issues', *Economic and Political Weekly*, xlvi (16, 16 April).

RBI (2007), 'Third Quarter Review of Annual Statement on Monetary Policy for the year 2007–8', pp. 57–8, RBI.

Romer, Christina D. and David H. Romer (1990), 'New Evidence on the Monetary Transmission Mechanism', Brookings Papers on Economic Activity.

Thorat, Usha (2003), *Report of the Working Group on Instruments of Sterilisation*. Mumbai: Reserve Bank of India, pp. 10–11.

Virmani, Vineet (2004), 'Examination of Credit Channel of Monetary Transmission in India: Results from Response of Commercial Banks' Balance Sheet to a Monetary Policy Shock', Indian Institute of Management (IIM), Ahmedabad, WP 2004-09-03.

PART III

THE OPEN ECONOMY

CHAPTER 7

OPENNESS AND GROWTH IN THE INDIAN ECONOMY

SOUMYEN SIKDAR

Since the initiation of the economic reforms in 1991, India's economic policy has shifted continuously to outward orientation and market incentives. Imparting a big push to an economy struggling on a low-growth trajectory must have been among the main objectives of the architects of the policy change. Their expectations were not belied.

If we go back to 1950 and look at the performance over three successive decades, the following picture emerges. GDP growth rates (at constant prices) for the decades 1950–60, 1960–70, and 1970–80 were 3.9 per cent, 3.7 per cent and 3.1 per cent, respectively; a pretty depressing picture all through. Then came the first noticeable break away from the trend. Over 1980–90 growth jumped to 5.8 per cent and continued at this rate over the next decade too. But the miracle came later. The nine years spanning 2000–9 witnessed uninterrupted growth at 7.2 per cent and China ceased to be the sole poster boy of market reform and globalization. In the sub-period 2003–9, growth was actually up there at 8.3 per cent, second only to China's. There was a downturn, short but sharp, in 2008–9 when GDP grew by 6.7 per cent but recovery was fairly quick. It was hoped that India will soon regain its position on the path of dazzling performance. Unfortunately that did not happen and the slideback continued. Over the last three years or so the growth engine has slowed down considerably and advance estimates by the Central Statistical Organisation (CSO) has put down 6.9 per cent as the most that can be hoped for. This is not good news for sure, but the very fact that 6.9 per cent can cause dejection speaks volumes for what we have managed to achieve over the past quarter century. What was once unthinkable has come within the realm of possibility.

Openness and growth proceeded in tandem. The trade-GDP ratio (export + import/GDP), the most widely used measure of openness, increased from as low a value as 8 per cent in 1970 to 22 per cent in 2000–1, and to 48 per cent at present. Along with this current account openness Indian policymakers have taken significant steps to open up the capital account too. There are far fewer restrictions now on the movement of investible funds in and out of the country.

The objective of this chapter is to understand to what extent openness (on both current and capital accounts) has contributed to the Indian growth miracle. As is well known, the link between free trade and growth is a hotly discussed issue and no consensus has emerged from the debates. In this context the experiences of the newly industrializing countries (NICs), Hong Kong, South Korea, Singapore, and Taiwan, have been intensely studied with mixed conclusions. For some observers the key element was the successful export of labour-intensive manufactured products throughout the 1970s and 1980s. This, it is maintained, refutes conventional wisdom that industrial development and growth must take place via import substitution. Others point out that the spectacular export success was actually facilitated by previous import substitution and careful policy planning. There is a plethora of cross-country studies that investigate the growth-openness linkage. They have produced mixed results, with Sachs and Warner (1995), Frankel and Romer (1999), Dollar and Kraay (2002) on the supportive side and Harrison (1996) and Rodriguez and Rodrik (2001) strongly on the other. One major conclusion of the last study mentioned is that the robustness of the correlation between openness and growth declines as other variables are included in the model. Dodzin and Vambakidis (2004) use a panel of 92 developing countries over the period 1960–2000 and conclude that greater openness in trade raises the share of industry in value added at the expense of the agricultural sector. Thus, trade actually facilitates industrialization, contrary to the conventional infant industry argument. Rodrik et al. (2004) considered simultaneous effects of institutions, geography, and trade on per capita income and concluded that the quality of institutions matters a great deal for a positive trade-income nexus.

The trade-growth link for India after liberalization has been explored by many economists. Instead of listing them separately we refer to them in the course of our discussion.

Openness Growth Link

The major channels through which greater openness is supposed to stimulate an economy are:

1. *Demand pull and cost reduction effect*
   Net exports form an important component of aggregate demand in an open economy. Sustained rise in this component has historically played an important role in the success stories of Japan, NICs, and more recently China which has become the workshop of the world. In addition to getting an additional source of demand, home producers after trade liberalization can import cheaper and better quality inputs and capital equipment from abroad. Rising demand and falling costs give a strong boost to profits and encourage capital formation and other expansion plans.
2. *Competition effect*
   Exposure to foreign competition forces domestic firms to improve efficiency for survival. A protected domestic market tends to shelter too many firms. The car industry in Argentina in the 1980s and 1990s is a classic example. Examples from India and other developing countries can be multiplied at will. Greater competition raises average efficiency by forcing the less efficient firms to contract or shut down. Even the more efficient ones feel the compulsion to pay careful attention to the choice of products, production locations, and techniques. The industrial structure experiences salubrious 'rationalization'.
3. *Learning effect*
   Ongoing contact with partners operating with better technology, managerial skills, and marketing networks induces learning that boosts efficiency and competitiveness over time. Historically this has been one of the most prominent sources of *dynamic* gains from trade. The efficiency improvement due to combined competition and the learning effect is supposed to show up in improvement in

total factor productivity (TFP) of an open economy. TFP growth as an index of efficiency has many limitations but it remains the most widely used measure nevertheless.

The strength of the learning effect depends on the quality and other characteristics of the trade basket of an economy. For countries seeking to move up the value ladder in the international network of production and distribution, changing the export composition from resource-based (RB) low technology (LT) to medium technology (MT) or high technology (HT) products is essential.

4. *Capital inflow effect*

   Openness involves freer movement of both commodities (and services) and investible funds. Capital inflow may be either long term FDI or short term FPI. Of the two, FDI has the potential to act as a vehicle for transnational transfer of technological knowledge and managerial skills. This has positive supply side effect and tends to pull in local investments. The benefit once again should show up in TFP growth. The benefits of foreign portfolio investments (FPIs), on the other hand, are supposed to flow by improving the depth and liquidity of the stock market and by stimulating investments through a reduction in the cost of capital.

Let us now take a look at how effective these channels have been for the Indian economy. Though I shall mostly concentrate on the period since 1991 it is worthwhile to pause briefly to consider the 1980s. The general consensus seems to be that the first noticeable departure from a dismal trend happened in the early years of that decade.

The next section surveys the 1980s. Subsequent sections follow the openness–growth story in the following sequence: (a) the performance of the three sectors, services, agriculture, and industry; (b) the product structure of trade; (c) competition and productivity effects; (d) capital inflows and exchange rate policy; and (e) regional growth. The final section presents the conclusions in summary form.

The 1980s

The growth spurt over the 1980s may safely be taken as domestically driven. Policy reforms during this period mainly focused on domestic industrial liberalization rather than on foreign trade. Hardly anything was done to expose industry to external competition. Import liberalization related to inputs and components which actually raised the effective protection of final products. According to Rodrik and Subramanian (2005), in the early 1980s there was a significant attitudinal change on the part of the national leadership, signalling a shift in favour of the private sector. The fillip to business confidence and profitability stimulated investment in a big way. As a proportion of GDP, investments accounted for 18.27 per cent over 1971–80, but for 1981–90 the figure was significantly higher at 22.04 per cent. Public investments over the latter period grew at 6.89 per cent per annum while the rate for private investments was 7.60 per cent. The jump in the investment ratio was accompanied by improvements in productivity of capital as reflected in the drop in the incremental capital–output ratio (ICOR) from 5.98 to 3.65 over the same periods (Rakshit in Basu [2006]). Sectoral contributions to GDP growth during the latter period were: 27.5 per cent (agriculture), 28.9 per cent (industry), and 43.6 (services). International trade accounted for a small part of the economy with the trade ratio standing stagnant at around 14 per cent over the 1980s, an increase of a mere 4 per cent over the previous decade. Moreover the bulk of the trade, almost 80 per cent, was in goods and this was actually in deficit. Services trade was more or less balanced. All this suggests that the degree of integration with the global market was rather weak and that the growth boost was largely due to increase in domestic investments and the productivity of capital. There was to be a drastic deceleration in public investments (with an absolute decline in three successive years) in the second half of the 1990s and private investments would follow suit. In India there is strong evidence of complementarity or 'crowding in' between public and private investments, so that changes in government investments can have a significant impact on the economy's overall investment ratio and growth. No wonder then that with the deceleration in public investments continuing the domestic engine of growth became weaker and weaker. The consequences would have been really dire but for the emergence and growing power of an external engine in the form of services exports.

Many studies have econometrically examined the exports–growth nexus for the Indian economy. Pradhan (2011) may be taken as typical. Considering the period 1970–1 to 2008–9 he found evidence for both short run and long run relationships between exports and output growth. The direction of causality ran from export growth to GDP growth, but there was no reverse causation. Also, a long-run relationship could be detected between net capital flows and non-agricultural GDP.

We now turn to the narrative of sectoral performances in foreign trade, starting with the star of the show.

Services

In the 1990s, the speed and depth of integration went on increasing. The trade-GDP ratio had already reached 22.1 per cent by 2000–1. In sharp contrast to the 1980s, now goods exports failed to keep pace with imports and ran into persistent deficit while net exports of services accelerated. The chief contributory factor was our ability to capitalize on a great change in the technology of production and distribution. IT-aided modularization and fragmentation led to a dramatic reversal of the process of vertical integration and enabled MNCs to bring together resources, ideas, and skills from different regions of the world to lower the cost of producing a good or delivering a service. India, with her huge stock of scientific and technical manpower and significantly lower wage rates, naturally emerged as a leader in the export of business services. From an average of 6.2 per cent in 1980–95, the growth rate of such services rose to 21 per cent during 1996–2004, and further to 27 per cent during 2005–11. The share in world exports of commercial services climbed steadily to reach the value of almost 4 per cent in 2011. Over the same period, agriculture was nearly stagnant and industry grew at a much slower pace. Sectoral shares have been deeply impacted as a result of this pattern of uneven sectoral growth. The services component swelled and swelled and at present commands about 57 per cent share in GDP.

Export-oriented services are not the only type that have witnessed rapid growth since the early 1990s. Rate of expansion of telephone services or miscellaneous communications services have over some periods, 1992–6 for example, actually exceeded that of business services (Nagaraj 2008). But since 2006, business services have continued to dominate.

It is worth noting at this point that the Indian services sector is not homogeneous and displays a distinctive dual character. The unorganized part of it that is not directly linked to external demand actually accounts for no less than two-thirds of the total output. But recent growth (in terms of value added) in the sector has undoubtedly been dominated by growth in the organized component that responds positively to the growing global demand. In terms of growth of output, however, the unorganized sector has not been negligible. For most periods in the past two decades it has actually outpaced the manufacturing sector. These traditional services are usually provided by small enterprises and it is likely that in recent times they have been gaining in importance as sub-contractors to large firms. There are indications of significant spillover of the telecommunications revolution into the unorganized segment. This intra-services inter-linkage is still awaiting careful empirical investigation.

Agriculture and Industry

Agriculture's share in GDP has been declining continuously and quite steeply since the 1950s. In the course of the last two decades it has fallen from around 40 per cent to almost 15 per cent. This decline is a direct consequence of a persistently low rate of growth relative to the other two sectors. Greater openness of the economy has failed to provide a stimulus because agricultural exports never really picked up in the era of greater global integration. In our reforms programme industry was taken up first, then trade and then finance. Agriculture got the least attention. On the external front too, the prospects were fairly depressing. Yielding to the pressure of their immensely strong farm lobbies the developed countries did not (and still have not) opened up their markets to agricultural imports from the developing world. At home, pressure on fiscal consolidation coupled with the inability to bring down subsidies and other unproductive populist transfers led to sharp cutbacks in public investments. Agriculture and infrastructure were the worst sufferers. Possible diversification into horticulture and livestock was hampered by the poor state of cold storage, refrigerated transport, insurance, and organized marketing. Thus, the negative effect of a stagnant external demand has been reinforced by persistent decline in domestic investments and serious deficiencies in infrastructural facilities. Indeed, domestic supply side constraints being so severe it would be foolish to hope that better access to developed country markets will automatically provide the necessary fillip to dynamism and growth. For major crops both acreage and yield have tended to stagnate, as noted by the Economic Survey of 2011–12 (GOI 2012) in detail. The survey contains a long list of 'options for addressing supply side constraints', but all the action seems to end there. Nothing is said about sustained government initiative (actual or planned), either at the central or state levels for easing or removing these constraints.

Subsidies, as a proportion of agricultural GDP, have been rising steadily since the 1970s while public investment has declined almost continuously from around 1980. The bulk of public investments in agriculture are in surface irrigation. As in education, expenditure in rupee terms is a poor index of addition to real productive capacity. And whatever real capacity is created fails to be properly utilized due to inefficient local level management and poor maintenance. Spending on rural electrification, roads, storage facilities, and provision of extension services has declined sharply over the years.

Given its strong complementarity with private capital formation, the slowdown in public investment has had very serious negative consequences for overall GDP growth in general and agricultural performance in particular. The government's expectation that enough private sector funds will flow into the areas it was withdrawing from proved wildly off the mark. The explanation lies in a conjunction of factors. The public goods nature of most infrastructural services, return uncertainty, lumpiness of investment, and heightened difficulties of procuring finance in the new deregulated environment all played their part in discouraging private entry into the field. It is important to keep in mind in this context that India's emergence as a major provider of IT services undoubtedly owed much to the unleashing of private energy through deregulation and external sector liberalization, but equally important were the availability of skilled scientific and technical manpower in the major metropolitan centres and the massive extension and improvement in telecommunication facilities. In all this, planned public investment played a decisive role. Fund and infrastructure requirements of most IT units are considerably smaller than that of capital-intensive manufacturing, but in no way does it detract from the government's positive role in laying the foundations of our glorious 'services revolution'.

The relative stagnation of the manufacturing sector (it has managed to hold its sectoral share at an average of 22–3 per cent over 1980–1 to 2009–10) can be explained by the increased competition from China in the global market, larger import penetration in some important segments, persistent inefficiency and, very crucially, serious deficiencies in such basic infrastructural facilities as ports, roads, and power. Deceleration in public investments has acted as a major damper on private capital accumulation. While managing to avert the fate of agriculture, manufacturing has failed to keep pace with the burgeoning tertiary sector.

Even external capital has failed to provide adequate succour. After a brief period in the early 1990s when foreign companies took a lively interest in investing in Indian manufacturing, FDI flows dramatically shifted towards newly emerging tertiary activities in which the problems of outdated technology, poor supporting infrastructure, and inflexible labour laws (and militant trade unionism) were far less serious. In China, the workshop of the world, manufacturing continues to account for more than 70 per cent of net FDI every year. With respect to FDI in manufacturing, Thailand, Malaysia, and the Philippines are all substantially ahead of us.

In their work on FDI and the Indian economy Dua and Rashid (1998) took the index of industrial production (IIP) as the measure of economic activity. Causality tests suggested that FDI flows (approved and actual) respond to the level of industrial production, but actual flows do not cause industrial output.

The overall health and dynamics of manufacturing have also been adversely affected by the absence of a broad industrial base in the rural areas. Here the contrast with China is remarkable. Chinese Township and Village Enterprises (TVEs) formed an integral part of a vibrant rural enterprise boom triggered by the initiation of reforms in the late 1970s. Trade liberalization was successfully decentralized to provincial and local levels and TVEs participated vigorously in the growth of exports. Their efficiency, already higher than that of state owned enterprises, was boosted by sustained gains in TFP over time (Bardhan 2010; Lardy 1992). Absence of anything comparable in our countryside has without doubt weakened the ability of foreign trade to bring about broad-based industrial transformation and is also responsible in a big way for the much-lamented muted impact of reforms on rural poverty.

Product Structure of Trade

It is not merely export growth that is important but its quality as well. Stimulus to growth through exports will be stronger if the composition changes in favour of more skill-intensive and technologically more sophisticated products. Table 7.1 presents the export and import shares of four broad product groups.

In exports, the share of labour and resource-intensive goods fell substantially between 1996 and 2006. Medium and high skill products gained in importance, though not very dramatically. Table 7.2 tells a similar story.

Table 7.1 Product Structure of Exports and Imports

Product Groups	1985		1996		2000		2006	
	Export	Import	Export	Import	Export	Import	Export	Import
Labour and resource intensive	42.2	8.2	48.5	9.7	55.9	23.8	31.2	10.8
Low skill and technology intensive	2.5	8.9	6.2	5.6	5.1	3.7	9.4	10.1
Medium skill and technology intensive	5.8	17.0	6.3	16.6	6.2	7.4	7.9	7.9
High skill and technology intensive	4.2	17.0	8.6	20.4	12.3	34.7	10.1	37.3

Source: Bhat (2011).

Table 7.2 Export Composition (percentage share in exports)

Product Groups	2000–1	2010–11
Engineering goods	12.4	23.63
Petroleum products	1.66	16.59
Gems and jewellery	16.75	13.75
Textiles	24.26	9.34
Agriculture and allied	8.8	6.97
Ores and minerals	2.62	4.42
Leather and leather goods	4.41	1.59
Electronic goods	2.54	3.36
Chemical and related products	14.61	12.93

Source: Bhat (2011).

The shares of engineering goods and petroleum products have gone up and those of textiles and leather goods have come down substantially. The share of petroleum products has undergone a quantum leap from 1.6 to 16.5 over the last decade. Compared to their status in 1990–1 (8 per cent, not given in Table 7.2) chemical and related products have grown in importance. Electronic goods have looked up, but only marginally. Surge in demand from China explains the rise in ores and minerals. Gems and jewellery have held their position steady.

Though the movement up the value ladder of industrial exports has been encouraging there is much scope for improvement here. In manufacturing our comparative advantage has remained mostly stable over four decades. As part of the global supply chain, China, Malaysia, and the Philippines import components, assemble and re-export high and medium technology products on a big scale. India remains a marginal player in this field. This has slowed the process of technology upgradation and skill improvement in industry. To benefit more substantially from globalization India needs to broaden its trade beyond a narrow category of services. For that to happen our manufacturing-cum-export-oriented infrastructure has to be expanded and improved. The incentive regime still favours the domestic market and protection of inefficient industries still persists, though at a lower level compared to the pre-reforms days. Involving MNCs in Indian export activities is still relatively low and this has limited our ability to utilize their marketing networks and skills. Affiliates of multinationals in India contribute less than 5 per cent of our total exports, whereas the corresponding contributions exceed 50 per cent for China and Malaysia.

Import composition has also undergone significant change. Though petroleum and related products continue to dominate (30 per cent on average), there has been a perceptible shift away from petro-products towards crude imports following significant rise in refinery capacity. Actually from 2001–2, India has transformed itself from a net importer of finished petroleum products to a net exporter. At the same time the shares of capital goods and export related items have displayed a more or less upward trend since the 1990s. All these factors are positively correlated with growth.

A detailed study by Goldberg, Khandelwal, and Pavcnik (in Bhagwati and Panagariya [2013]) examined the role of imported inputs and product scope expansion in India during the period of trade reforms. It is shown that a large proportion of Indian manufacturing firms added new products to their production lines and these products contributed substantially to manufacturing output growth. A key driver of the process was the expansion in the range of imported intermediate inputs in the wake of substantial tariff harmonization and reduction.

It is relevant in this context that there have been important changes in India's *export destinations* with the share of the developing countries increasing at the cost of OECD. And within the developing countries it is developing Asia (China, South Korea, Hong Kong (China), Malaysia, Thailand, and Singapore) that is gaining in importance. This augurs well because these countries constitute the fastest growing region of the world economy today.

Within the category of business services there has been a noticeable shift towards more sophisticated, higher value added activities over the last decade. The share of routine programming work and maintenance accounted for 68.9 per cent of the total export revenue in 2001, this had fallen to 33.7 per cent by 2008. Share of software products and RDES (Research, Development, and Engineering Services) went up from 10 per cent to 21 per cent over the same period (Dossani in Ghani 2010).

An internal study (see GOI 2012) of our exports of the world's top import items using the latest UN commodity trade data shows that: (a) in the top 100 imports of the world in 2010 India had only six items with a share of 5 per cent and above and only 15 items with a share of 2 per cent and above, (b) among the top 100 items there are many where the country has acquired competence, but the share continues to be very low. Most of these are simple items like taps, cocks, valves, suitcases, briefcases, school satchels, musical instrument cases, various types of containers, flat rolled iron and steel products, and simple electric motors and generators.

Clearly there is enormous scope for greater export basket diversification and movement into more sophisticated, more valuable industrial products. A lot needs to be done to have a perceptible share in the leading items of world trade. This may, however, be difficult to achieve without greater involvement of multinationals.

Competition and Productivity Effects

A large number of studies for developing economies have concluded that increased exposure to foreign competition causes profit margins or price-cost mark ups to decline, with the largest effect in the most concentrated industries. Thus, liberalization imposes discipline on domestic business and forces it to develop its competitive muscle. Has the disciplining device worked for India?

Balakrishnan et al. (2002: 831–7) worked with data on more than 3,000 firms over the period 1988–9 and 1997–8 and found that in the post-reforms period the mark up declined for some types of products (rubber, plastic, petro products, machinery, and transport equipment) while it increased for others (food products, chemicals, basic metals, and metal products). Kambhampati and Parikh (2003) covered 280 firms over 1980–98. Their conclusion is that for firms with an above average export-sales ratio profit margins improved during 1992–8 compared to 1980–90, but fell in the relatively less export oriented firms. In Goldar and Aggarwal (2005) the competitive effect of the lowering of tariff and non-tariff barriers to manufacturing imports was examined in detail. Evidence for a significant pro-competitive impact (decline in the price-cost margin) was found, particularly for the more concentrated industries. Concomitantly, there was a significant drop in labour's share in value added in the post-reforms years beyond what can be explained by changes in capital intensity.

It is to be noted that even if in the short run the impact of trade liberalization on profitability is adverse, over a longer horizon the damage may be repaired, partially or even fully, if the affected firms succeed in raising their efficiency through restructuring of production, closures and relocations, scaling down of the labour force, mergers and amalgamations, and improvements in organizational management (reduction in X-inefficiency) in general. Such adjustments, if successful, should show up in improvements in TFP (or its rate of growth), which, despite serious limitations (see Balakrishnan 2011a), continues to be widely used as the indicator of efficiency gain in almost all empirical work.

What is the evidence for India? Table 7.3 gives an idea.

Table 7.3 Sources of Growth by Major Sectors (percentage change per annum)

Period	Output	Output per worker	Factor productivity
Agriculture			
1978–93	2.7	1.3	1.0
1993–2004	2.2	1.5	0.5
Industry			
1978–93	5.4	2.1	0.3
1993–2004	6.7	3.1	1.1
Services			
1978–1993	5.9	2.1	1.4
1993–2004	9.1	5.4	3.9

Source: Bardhan (2010).

Annual rate of growth of industrial output between 1978 and 1993 was 5.4 per cent; it was 6.7 per cent between 1993 and 2004. Corresponding TFP growth rates were 0.3 per cent and 1.1 per cent. There was considerable expansion of the varieties of imported inputs as well as of new domestic products following reductions in import tariffs on inputs. Goldberg et al. (2013) contains a detailed discussion on this very important gain reaped by Indian firms after trade liberalization. In Harrison et al. (2011), all the estimated increase in sectoral productivity is due to the scaling down of input tariffs. According to Topalova and Khandelwal (2011), a 10 per cent reduction in tariff leads to a 0.5 per cent increase in TFP of a typical firm.

Table 7.3 shows that the services sector in India experienced the most significant growth. TFP in this field jumped from an annual average of 1.4 per cent in 1978–93 to 3.9 per cent in 1993–2004. So there is a strong correlation between openness and productivity in this vibrant area of the economy.

Balakrishnan et al. (2000) failed to find any significant rise in productivity growth in manufacturing since 1991. Goldar and Kumari (2003) concluded that the post-reforms deceleration in TFP growth in industry should not be attributed to import liberalization. They suggested gestation lags in industrial projects, under-utilization of capacity, and fall in agricultural growth as possible factors contributing to the deceleration.

In principle, FDI is capable of transforming a developing economy by promoting capital formation and boosting efficiency by bringing over knowledge of new techniques and managerial methods. These beneficial effects, real as they are, are notoriously difficult to isolate and capture in empirical work. Serious as it is, data availability may not be the major problem here. Usually external sector liberalization forms just one component of a whole gamut of policy reforms that may directly or indirectly impact productivity at the firm level. Disentangling the contribution of foreign investment becomes very difficult as a result. Also fuzziness of results may be due to the imprecision of the measures of openness or foreign investment or efficiency. A detailed study by Pallikara (2002) contained in a survey report brought out by the Asian Productivity Organization failed to find any significant link between FDI and TFP growth in India. There was little evidence that openness had any significant implications for R&D expenditure. It is interesting to report in this context Ng's (2006) work on eight East Asian countries. Over the period 1970–2000 there was evidence of FDI causing TFP growth in only two of them. Replacing TFP by other measures of efficiency also did not change the results much. Actually, most studies on East Asian economies have failed to find much evidence for significant TFP growth in their years of miraculous growth.

Several studies have demonstrated that the power to assimilate new technology and ideas requires a critically high stock of human capital that determines the absorptive capacity of an economy (Easterly 2001). Only beyond that level of human capital does FDI's impact on growth becomes discernible. This seems to be a good explanation of the weak FDI-growth link in India (and much of Africa). Also, it is the *quality* of human capital that is critical. Conventional measures of education, such as literacy or school enrolment or expenditure on education are generally very poor guides to the quality of education imparted.

Capital Inflows and Exchange Rate Policy

Despite sincere efforts by the Government of India to encourage FDI, capital inflows into the country remain heavily tilted in favour of portfolio investment by foreign institutional investors (FIIs). The share of FPI in total net foreign investments in 2009–10 was almost 58 per cent, in 2010–11 the total was lower but FPI's share was more than 70 per cent of that. In 2008–9 in the wake of the global crisis net portfolio inflow actually turned negative while FDI stood practically steady. In 2010, however, FPI was the first to recover from the shock and continued on more or less an upward trend till it swerved dramatically down again in the second half of 2011. This underscores the volatility of such flows.

A closer look at FDI inflows reveals that on average a substantial portion (as high as 29 per cent between 2004 and 2007 according to Nagaraj 2008) goes into acquiring managerial control in domestic companies, which does not add to real capital stock. Also a high percentage consists of 'reinvested earnings' which does not represent fresh flow of funds. Our national accounts show that both the gross domestic saving ratio and the gross investment ratio have been rising steadily over time in close correspondence with each other. Over the period 2006–7 to 2009–10, for example, both rates hovered around an average value of 33–4 per cent with the investment rate maintaining a slender lead over most of the years. The implication of this close match between the two critical ratios is that increases in domestic investment have been almost entirely financed by domestic resources with foreign capital playing a modest role at best. It is worthy of note in this context that it is the household segment, and not the private corporate sector, that is chiefly responsible for the sharp rise in domestic savings and investments.

Given the prominence of portfolio funds in total funds inflow into the economy, an important question concerns their contribution to the nation's growth. The beneficial effects of greater portfolio flow into underdeveloped financial markets are supposed to operate through three main routes: (a) it lowers the cost of capital by raising stock prices (and hence the price-earning ratio) and thereby stimulates new investment; (b) it lowers transaction costs by enhancing the depth of the stock market; and (c) it encourages savings by providing a new equity instrument to savers. What is the scenario for India?

The doors of the Indian capital market were thrown open to portfolio flows in 1992. It was followed by considerable stock market growth. Both the Sensex and the 'depth index' (stock market capitalization/GDP) rose steadily during the early 1990s. Rising share prices combined with rising rates of interest (which were deregulated under financial liberalization) induced a big shift in corporate financing towards equity. But the trend did not last long. Using a dataset for 300 companies over 1990–2001 Khanna (2002) found that cost of capital declined initially but started on a reverse trend after 1994. In 2001 it was back at its 1991 level. Meanwhile interest rates had started falling. Rising cost of capital and falling interests restored the previous status of debt as a more attractive source than equity. A study by Chandrasekhar and Pal (2006) concludes that the promised benefits of portfolio inflows have failed to materialize for the Indian economy. Over time FII activities have come to be mostly confined to the secondary market for blue chip company shares and direct contact with the real sector seems to have been lost. Empirical research has failed to unearth any strong link between stock indices and private corporate investment in the Indian context.

It was hoped that development of the stock market would encourage the household sector to save and invest more in the newly available equity instruments, but this hope too was belied. After an initial burst of enthusiasm, domestic savers began to lose interest in the stock market rapidly chiefly because they became aware of widespread malpractices in share trading and company audits. In recent years the scenario has changed for the better under the Securities and Exchange Board of India's (SEBI's) stricter supervision, but the general public's confidence in stock related activities has failed to revive. Large swings in stock prices continue to act as a damper on the enthusiasm of individual investors. As a result the domestic investor base remains weak and instead of gaining in maturity and depth our stock market continues to be unhealthily dominated by a small number of big players.

Short-term portfolio flows driven mainly by the prospect of capital gains have enhanced the *volatility* of the stock market. This has been reflected in the volatility of the exchange rate. As a precaution against sudden outflow of short-term capital (hot money) and the consequent turmoil in the forex market, RBI has decided to maintain a large stock of foreign reserves mainly invested in low yielding US T-bills. The paradoxical implication is that capital poor India is providing cheap loan to capital rich USA. Obviously, this perversity is creating serious growth costs. China is doing the same on a much bigger scale. There is an important difference though. Most of China's reserves are 'earned' through a positive trade balance whereas our reserves are basically 'borrowed', generated by surplus in the capital account.

The growth costs of reserves are, however, counterbalanced by their insurance or buffer value in an environment of highly volatile cross-border flow of short term funds (hot money). A comfortable position with respect to foreign assets is taken by international credit rating agencies as an indicator of good health and enables the country to access the international capital market on more favourable terms.

Addition to the stock of foreign reserves directly translates into growth of high powered money. Fear of inflation led RBI to undertake sterilization on a substantial scale to sever the balance of payments-money supply link. But sterilization entails significant costs. In particular, contraction of domestic credit on a big scale in a situation of excess capacity and demand constraints has had a serious adverse impact on growth. Over the past few years RBI has scaled down its forex intervention considerably and this negative effect of the exchange rate policy has been mitigated to that extent.

International evidence is mixed on the important issue of the impact of capital inflows on the volatility of stock returns. In the Indian context Coondoo and Mukherjee (2004) considered three aspects of the volatility implicit in a given time series data: strength (S), duration (D), and persistence (P). The sample period is from January 1999 to May 2002. The S measure is consistently largest for FIIS (sale by FIIs), followed by FIIN (net FII), and FIIP (purchase by FIIs). In terms of D, FIIN tended to be in a volatile state for the largest proportion of days in a given period. In terms of P, for all the variables volatility is found to persist for a small spell only.

Openness bestows on an economy the capability to invest beyond its domestic savings by utilizing the savings of foreigners through the current account deficit. Under a flexible exchange system greater capital inflows potentially boost investment by widening the deficit. A policy that reduces the flexibility of the exchange rate blocks this route or makes it narrower. From this perspective RBI's policy of heavy intervention in the forex market has entailed some growth cost. This, however, is not easy to quantify. It is worth repeating that the intervention was undertaken primarily to counter volatility and 'maintain orderly conditions' in the forex market. Volatility and the consequent need for RBI action would have been much lower had the flows come to our shores more in the form of long term, stable FDI.

The experience of East Asia has amply demonstrated that inflows intermediated through commercial banks may lead to credit expansion which, instead of stimulating investment, may trigger a consumption boom (with a strong import bias) or a speculative asset bubble (mainly in equity or real estate). Capital takes flight en masse when the bubble inevitably bursts. To avert disasters of this type RBI has kept a close watch on bank intermediation of inflows. Kohli (2010) examined the impact of inflows on India's banking sector and found that it has not been very strong. Bank assets as a proportion of GDP underwent a modest growth of 3 per cent over 1990–2000 and has not risen significantly thereafter. The new prudential norms have induced banks to enlarge their holding of safe government securities to improve the quality of their portfolios, but actual investments in such securities is substantially in excess of prudential requirements. Heightened risk aversion in an environment of heightened financial turbulence has undoubtedly played an important role here. Private domestic credit has expanded much more slowly. Bank financed asset speculation and the resultant banking crises have been successfully prevented, but large-scale fund diversion to safe government bonds has impacted private investment adversely. The drying up of credit has been particularly disastrous for small scale enterprises. Their export operations have suffered heavily in consequence.

Regional Growth

An overwhelming majority of studies in the vast trade-growth literature have worked with country-level income or per capita income. On the other hand research on regional growth in India has for the most part concentrated on issues of convergence or divergence without paying attention to the role of external sector integration in the process. Dholakia (2009), for example, analyses regional sources of growth acceleration in considerable detail without bringing in the factor of openness at all.

In a novel attempt Maiti and Marjit (2009) constructed three indices, the export intensity index, import intensity index, and regional openness index, to scrutinize the impact of export orientation and import penetration on regional trade and disparity across 15 major Indian states during 1980–2004. It is indeed very important for a massively heterogeneous country like India to know whether greater openness has had an equalizing impact or not. Their major conclusion is that more open states grew faster by 1–1.5 per cent per annum. States that were able to change their production structure towards export production showed greater change in growth. And this ability was strongly correlated with the quality of institutions and the prevailing investment climate. Per capita net state domestic products all grew over the period but at different rates, exacerbating regional inequality. Dispersion in regional openness seems to have been a major contributory factor.

* * *

The major ideas can be summarized as follows. Openness to current account trade has indeed played a significant role in India's growth surge. The main drivers have been the lowering of trade restrictions on a wide range of imported technologies and inputs and a spectacular acceleration in the export of commercial IT-enabled services in more recent times. The pull effect of foreign demand has been much weaker for manufacturing and non-existent for agriculture. Manufacturing has suffered from intense Chinese competition no doubt, but domestic deficiencies, such as inadequacy and low quality of basic infrastructure (barring telecommunications), persistence of inefficiency, and declining public investments (in both industry and agriculture) have been more important contributors.

On the export front a movement up the value ladder is noticeable and import composition too has broadly changed for the better. But there is considerable scope for improvement along both dimensions.

Supply side effects of greater openness working through heightened competition and efficiency improvement have been rather muted and difficult to measure. But there is evidence to show that TFP growth has been stimulated and the boost given by reduction in the cost of importing inputs and technical knowledge has been substantial. Inefficient domestic firms continue to enjoy protection by the government. But for this the dynamic efficiency gains would have been greater.

FDI has failed to effect any major supply side change. This is not surprising given its low share and the deficiencies of complementary local inputs, such as physical infrastructure and human capital. FPI has been confined mostly to the secondary market and has on the whole not succeeded in stimulating real capital formation through any significant reduction in the cost of capital. The stock market remains shallow, dominated by a few big sellers. In spite of better regulation and lower frequency of scams, participation of domestic agents continues to be low and the promised stimulus to household savings has not materialized. On the positive side, strict supervision of banks in their handling of foreign funds has successfully prevented the occurrence of financial crises that have caused terrible growth disruption in a large number of developing countries.

The objectives of maintaining orderly conditions in the forex market in the face of a volatile FPI and sustaining the confidence of global investors in the Indian economy have led RBI to run up huge foreign reserves. Attendant sterilization programmes generated by fear of inflation have had a negative impact on growth. Overall, lifting of capital account restrictions has been less beneficial than greater openness on the current account.

The gains from openness have not been shared evenly by the heterogeneous regions of the country. External liberalization may have added to regional disparity.

With better infrastructure, better human capital, less corruption, better management of credit supply to the small scale sector, a broader industrial base in the countryside, a more diversified export basket, closer integration with the global supply chain, and a more favourable FDI-FPI mix, the positive impact of greater openness on growth would have been much higher, more solidly founded, and the fruits of prosperity more evenly shared throughout the economy. Nagging anxiety over the sustainability of current export-led growth would also have been far less acute in that case.

References

Balakrishnan, P. (2011a), *Economic Growth in India*. New Delhi: Oxford University Press.

——— (2011b), *Economic Reforms and Growth in India: Essays from the Economic and Political Weekly*. New Delhi: Orient Blackswan.

Balakrishnan, P., K. Pushpangadan, and S. Babu (2000), 'Trade Liberalization and Productivity Growth in Manufacturing: Evidence from Firm Level Panel Data', *Economic and Political Weekly*, 35(41): 831–7.

———(2002), *Trade Liberalization, Market Power and Scale Efficiency in Indian Industry*. Centre for Development Studies, WP 336.

Bardhan, P. (2010), *Awakening Giants, Feet of Clay*. Princeton, New Jersey: Princeton University Press.

Basu, K. (ed.) (2006), *India's Emerging Economy*. New Delhi: Oxford University Press.

Bhagwati, J. and A. Panagariya (eds) (2013), *Reforms and Economic Transformation in India*. New York: Oxford University Press.

Bhat, T.P. (2011), *Structural Changes in India's Foreign Trade*. New Delhi: ISID, November.

Chandrasekhar, C.P. and P. Pal (2006), 'Financial Liberalization in India: An Assessment of its Nature and Outcomes', *Economic and Political Weekly*, 41(11): 975–88.

Coondoo, D. and P. Mukherjee (2004), 'Volatility of FII in India', *ICRA Bulletin*, 2: 85–102.

Dholakia, R. (2009), 'Regional Sources of Growth Acceleration in India', *Economic and Political Weekly*, 44(47): 67–74.

Dodzin, S. and A. Vambakidis (2004), 'Trade and Industrialization in Developing Countries', *Journal of Development Economics*, 75: 319–28.

Dollar, D. and A. Kraay (2002), 'Trade, Growth and Poverty', *Economic Journal*, 114(493): F22–49.

Dossani, R. (2010), 'Software Production: Globalization and Its implications', in E. Ghani (ed.), *The Service Revolution in South Asia*, pp. 181–223. New Delhi: Oxford University Press.

Dua, P. and A. Rashid (1998), 'Foreign Direct Investment and Economic Activity in India', *Indian Economic Review*, 33(2): 153–68.

Easterly, W. (2001), *The Elusive Quest for Growth*. Cambridge, Massachusetts: MIT Press.

Frankel, J. and D. Romer (1999), 'Does Trade Cause Growth?', *American Economic Review*, 89(3): 379–99.

Ghani, E. (ed.) (2010), *The Service Revolution in South Asia*. New Delhi: Oxford University Press.

Goldar, B. and A. Kumari (2003), 'Import Liberalization and Productivity Growth in Indian Manufacturing in the 1990s', *The Developing Economies*, 41(4): 436–60.

Goldar, B. and S. Aggarwal (2005), 'Trade Liberalization and Price-Cost Margin in Indian Industry', *The Developing Economies*, 43(3): 346–73.

Goldberg, P.K., A. Khandelwal, and N. Pavcnik (2013), 'Variety In, Variety Out', in J. Bhagwati and A. Panagariya (eds), *Reforms and Economic Transformation in India*, pp. 168–99. Oxford University Press.

Government of India (GOI) (2012), Economic Survey 2011–12. New Delhi: Oxford University Press.

Harrison, A. (1996), 'Openness and Growth: A Time Series Cross-country Analysis for Developing Countries', *Journal of Development Economics*, 48(2): 419–47.

Harrison, A., L. Martin, and S. Nataraj (2011), 'Learning vs Stealing: How Important are Market-share Reallocations to Industrial Productivity Growth?', NBER Working Paper No. 16733.

Kambhampati, U. and A. Parikh (2003), 'Disciplining Firms: The Impact of Trade Reforms on Profit Margins in Indian Industry', *Applied Economics*, 35(4): 461–70.

Khanna, S. (2002). 'Has India Gained from Capital Account Liberalization? Private Capital Flows and the Indian Economy in the 1990s', Paper presented at a conference on International Money and the Developing Countries in Tamil Nadu, December.

Kohli, R. (2010), *Liberalizing Capital Flows; India's Experience and Policy Issues*. New Delhi: Oxford University Press.

Lardy, N. (1992), *Foreign Trade and Economic Reform in China, 1978–1990*. Cambridge, UK: Cambridge University Press.

Maiti, D. and S. Marjit (2010), 'Regional Openness, Income Growth and Disparity across Major Indian States during 1980–2004', Institute of Economic Growth Working Paper 304.

Nagaraj, R. (2008), 'India's Recent Economic Growth: A Closer Look', *Economic and Political Weekly*, 43(15): 55–61.

Ng, T. (2006), 'Foreign Direct Investment and Productivity: Evidence from the East Asian Economies', UNIDO Working Paper 03.

Pallikara, R, (2002), *Chapter on India in TFP Growth: Survey Report*. Tokyo: Asian Productivity Organization.

Pradhan, N. (2011), 'Openness and Growth of the Indian Economy: An Empirical Analysis', EXIM Bank Occasional Paper 150.

Rakshit, M. (2006), 'Some Macroeconomics of India's Reform Experience', in K. Basu (ed.), *India's Emerging Economy*, pp. 83–113. New Delhi: Oxford University Press.

Rodriguez, F. and D. Rodrik (2001), *Trade Policy and Economic Growth: A Sceptic's Guide to the Cross-national Evidence*. NBER Macroeconomics Annual.

Rodrik, D. and A. Subramanian (2005), 'From "Hindu Growth" to Productivity Surge: The Mystery of the Indian Growth Transition', *IMF Staff Papers*, 52(2).

Rodrik, D., A. Subramanian and F. Trebbi (2004), 'Institutions Rule: the Primacy of Institutions over Geography and Integration in Economic Development', *Journal of Economic Growth*, 9(2): 131–65.

Sachs, J. and A. Warner (1995), 'Economic Convergence and Economic Policies', *Brookings Papers on Economic Activities*, 3.

Topalova, P. and A. Khandelwal (2011), 'Trade Liberalization and Farm Productivity: the Case of India', *Review of Economics and Statistics*, 93(3): 995–1009.

CHAPTER 8

FINANCIAL GLOBALIZATION IN INDIA

opportunity and volatility

RENU KOHLI*

Financial globalization is an important development in the world economy in the past three decades.[1] The phenomenon—broadly described to mean the extent to which countries are linked through cross-border financial holdings (IMF 2007)—is in itself not new, having earlier been observed in the nineteenth century wave of globalization. A novel feature of the current round of financial globalization, however, is the change in the operational environment: technological progress and financial liberalization policies across countries have completely altered the landscape in which financial markets operate, making it infinitely riskier (Rajan 2005). The outcome of financial globalization is mixed; the verdict has never been unequivocal. Financial crises and volatility have been on the ascendancy, while the gains remain nebulous. With outbreak of the global financial crisis in 2008 the debate has reached a flashpoint, prompting academics

* I am grateful to an anonymous referee and Ashima Goyal (IGIDR) for helpful comments on an earlier version of this article.

[1] The terms financial globalization, international financial integration, financial openness, free capital mobility, and capital account liberalization are used interchangeably to mean free trade in assets.

and policymakers to question the wisdom of unfettered financial globalization. The need to balance risks and benefits has imparted fresh importance to the pursuit of right financial sector policies.

In theory, countries gain from financial globalization in several dimensions. Growth benefits arise from both direct and indirect channels (Prasad et al. 2003 provide a comprehensive survey). Summarily, foreign capital directly impacts growth through technology spillovers, competition, and learning effects to raise the efficiency and productivity of capital; by augmenting domestic savings, foreign capital eases financing constraints and lowers the cost of funds, increasing investment levels and output growth; finally, it enables international risk-sharing and consumption smoothing by helping tide over temporary economic fluctuations through foreign borrowings. Recent work focuses on the indirect or 'collateral' benefits of financial globalization. These include promoting development of the domestic financial sector, improving institutional quality by providing incentives for better corporate governance, and disciplining macroeconomic policies in recipient countries (Kose et al. 2008, 2009).

The posited advantages are countered by empirical evidence to a considerable extent. The literature is vast but the broad finding is that aggregate linkages between financial globalization and growth are nebulous and inconclusive[2] (Kose et al. 2006; Rodrik and Subramanian 2008 are useful surveys). For developing countries, Prasad et al. (2003) assess empirical evidence to conclude that financial globalization benefits once countries cross a certain threshold; once countries reach the threshold, bulk gains from financial globalization can be realized (Kose et al. 2009). Recent research studies are more counter-intuitive: non-industrial countries that rely on lesser foreign capital have clocked higher growth rates on average in the long-run (Prasad et al. 2007); countries financing more of their investments domestically have, on average, grown much faster (Aizenman et al. 2007); and capital seems to flow more to countries that invest and grow less or the 'allocation puzzle' where countries with faster productivity growth appear to attract less foreign capital (Gourinchas and Jeanne 2007).

International risk-sharing gains are found non-existent or insignificantly low (Gourinchas and Jeanne 2003; Lewis 1996) and restricted

[2] Empirical research on this is beset by a number of problematic issues regarding measures, reverse causation, substantially different institutional settings across countries, different patterns of financial liberalization followed by countries, and so on (Prasad et al. 2007).

to industrial countries (Kose et al. 2007) although increasing over time (Sørensen et al. 2007). Emerging market economies appear to have not realized higher risk-sharing outcomes despite higher levels of financial integration (Kose and Terrones 2009). Similarly, there is little systematic evidence that financial globalization disciplines macroeconomic policies although a cross-country aggregate study finds an association with low inflation (Tytell and Wei 2004). Institutional quality and governance are observed to improve as countries undertake reforms in response to financial liberalization (Kaminsky and Schmukler 2003); and financial market development is observed after basic legal and institutional structures develop (Chinn and Ito 2006).

Empirical proof on different types of foreign capital is more insightful. Foreign direct investment (FDI) or stable, long-term flows are more positively associated with growth through micro-linkages (Javorcik 2004) and under certain conditions (Aizenman et al. 2011). The effects of portfolio capital are differentiated. Equity market liberalization is found positively linked to higher investments and growth (Alfaro and Hammel 2007; Bekaert et al. 2005; Henry 2000, among others) but other influences cloud such causality. Debt flows, especially short-term, are decisively found to yield no obvious benefits to the recipient (Berg et al. 2004) and are systematically linked to an increased likelihood of financial crises (Eichengreen et al. 2006).

How does financial globalization relate to volatility? Most studies indicate a striking rise in GDP and consumption correlations with increased financial integration, that is, the more integrated a country, the more synchronized is its business cycle with the global one. Kose et al. (2003a, 2003b) find significant effects on both output correlations and the ratio of total consumption to income volatility, while Bekaert et al. (2006) find significant effects on consumption volatility; both findings are non-robust. The association with macroeconomic volatility also depends on a country's financial development and the quality of its institutions (Dell' Ariccia, 2008) and higher output volatility is linked to higher financial risk, that is, the ability of a country to pay its official, commercial, and trade debts (Meller 2011).

Financial globalization has also coincided remarkably with a higher frequency in the occurrence of financial crises, especially in emerging and developing countries; for example, the Latin American debt crisis in the 1980s, the prolonged Japanese recession and banking sector problems since the late 1980s, the Nordic banking crisis in early 1990s, the European exchange rate mechanism crisis in 1992–3, the Mexican crisis in 1994–5, the East Asian crisis in 1997, the Russian crisis of 1998 and the long-term capital management fund collapse in the US, the Argentinean and Turkish crises in 2001, and the global financial crisis of 2008–9. These crises underlined the changing nature of global capital flows, which are highly pro-cyclical and prone to sudden stops or reversals, herding behaviour, and speculative attacks (Calvo and Reinhart 1999).

The merits of financial globalization have always attracted criticism, notably from Bhagwati (1998), Rodrik (1998), Rodrik and Subramanian (2008), and recently Jeanne et al. (2012), who question unfettered movements of global capital, discarding the analogy with free trade in goods. With the global financial crisis of 2008 testing the trade-offs in costs and benefits, opinion has converged to a more qualified view of financial globalization as the crisis engulfed even advanced countries that had hitherto remained relatively immune. Although contrarian views on the causes of the global crisis exist,[3] academics and policymakers nonetheless acknowledge that excessive, unbridled financial flows need restraint.[4] There's evidence that financial globalization played a role in amplifying credit and asset price booms—caused by ultra-loose monetary policy in the United States—across different countries during the 2008 crisis with devastating consequences (BIS Annual Report 2012). In an up-to-date assessment of such links, Lane (2012) establishes that financial globalization amplified the costs of policy and regulatory failures in preventing the crisis and its management thereafter.

What does this imply for liberalizing emerging and developing countries? Having burnt their fingers previously, these countries have undoubtedly fared better than their advanced country peers in this round, having developed and bolstered their financial systems, banks, and financial markets to better manage capital flows in response to earlier crises; these policies helped protect and enabled them to cope with the current crisis (Lane 2012). While the global financial crisis has only reinforced this caution, that international opinion is now more favorably inclined towards the management of capital flows, including endorsement of capital controls as an additional tool, is helpful (IMF 2011). The role of

[3] Briefly, one view holds the global imbalances through steady accumulation of current account surpluses as the root cause of the crisis. A contrasting view upholds excessive financialization, lax regulation, and supervision combining with easy global liquidity from the US Federal Reserve's ultra-loose monetary policy responsible. See UN (2009) and IMF (2009) in this regard.

[4] See for instance, Turner Review (2009). Or consider the Dodd-Frank Act's proposals currently under discussion in the US.

financial sector policies has gained further importance (BIS 2012). The way forward for financial globalization lies in designing global, regional, and national policy frameworks to cope with high levels of international financial integration, suggests Lane (2012).

All these issues have a bearing for India, which has been a gradual but steady liberalizer of its financial markets for over two decades now. It belongs to the set of countries whose financial opening coincided with the trend towards increasing financial globalization. Prolonged surges in capital inflows have challenged its markets and institutions too, testing its macroeconomic responses on occasions. This chapter addresses such issues. The next section describes India's pattern of liberalization while the section that follows examines its experience with financial globalization. The section after that discusses how the challenges have been managed so far, while the last section concludes with an appraisal, raising questions for the future.

Financial Globalization of India: An Overview

Before 1991, India had a closed capital account. Barring trade, all external transactions between private residents and non-residents were prohibited; capital movements were mostly official transactions leaving the government as the only effective borrower abroad (Reddy 2000). A balance of payments crisis in 1991 prompted the restructuring of economic policies that also led to opening the economy to private foreign capital in 1992–3.[5] Then, the principal objectives were to prevent the future recurrence of another crisis, encourage foreign capital inflow into the country, reduce dependence on foreign currency deposits by Indian non-residents, and shift towards risk-sharing foreign capital like direct and portfolio equity investments.

Its approach towards capital account liberalization has been as follows. Inflows of foreign capital have been liberalized before outflows; non-resident capital flows have taken precedence over residents; amongst residents, the preference hierarchy is corporates, non-bank financial

[5] See relevant Economic Surveys 1991–2 onwards for details (Government of India).

intermediaries, banks, and individuals; and equity figures ahead of debt (Kohli 2005; Reddy 2000). Several factors contributed to this choice:

- Unlike most developing countries, India had a reasonably well-developed equity market when liberalization began in the 1990s, due to historical developments and a series of measures taken in the 1980s that established a sound institutional base for intermediating foreign capital with relative ease (RBI 2007).
- The 1991 balance of payments crisis reinforced the urgency to reduce foreign currency debt and re-orient the country's external financing pattern from expensive debt-financing towards cheaper equity-financing, along with risk-sharing. These factors effectively shifted the weight of liberalization towards foreign portfolio equity capital, as even FDI at the time depended critically on other economic reforms, including the sustainability and certainty of economic policies to inspire the confidence of long-term commitment of foreign investors.

The objective of avoiding another macroeconomic crisis has been guiding India's strategy with regard to its capital account opening policy since the early 1990s. First articulated in Tarapore Committee I (1997) and restated in Tarapore Committee II (2005), the aim is to strike a balance between fulfilling the country's foreign capital needs while ensuring balance of payments sustainability. The two reports clearly linked the dismantling of key capital account transactions with the achievement of macroeconomic objectives, like reducing inflation, fiscal consolidation, and monetary-fiscal separation. Since such critically-interdependent reforms are slow to come about, in contrast to relatively easier-to-implement financial sector reforms, capital account liberalization has been a slow, evolving process (Kohli and Belaisch 2012). Therefore, the cautious opening to foreign investors of the domestic debt markets echoes the country's slow pace of fiscal consolidation and strong dependence on the domestic banking system for financing at a reasonable cost. In the early stages of liberalization, India's large fiscal deficit, traditionally financed by the vast public sector banking system through 'financial repression', ruled out the opening of the domestic debt market to foreigners before reforms like interest rate deregulation and a reduction in fiscal dominance was achieved (Kletzer and Kohli 2001). But foreign participation in the debt market has been increased incrementally to support public debt issuance needs, while implementing a fiscal responsibility framework.

The sequencing of capital account liberalization must be understood in this historical context, reflecting the management of macroeconomic and external vulnerabilities (Reddy 2000).

- In view of the external financing gap, restrictions on capital inflows have been removed before those on capital outflows—in times of surpluses, outflows have been liberalized fairly fast.
- Non-debt creating inflows have been preferred to debt-creating inflows to minimize liquidity and interest rate risks for firms.
- Long-term borrowings have been favoured over short-term ones to enhance the productive capacity of the economy and lessen liquidity and rollover risks from a sudden reversal.
- Fear of capital flight and the non-readiness to make the currency convertible can explain why non-residents' flows have been liberalized more than those of residents. Resident transactions are relatively easier to monitor and can be readily restricted should the need arise, without affecting credibility in international markets. On the contrary, non-resident transactions can be discouraged by sudden policy reversals, damaging sovereign credibility, and creating regulatory uncertainty. Residents thus remain the most restricted investor category to date. Within this class, the removal of restrictions for firms has preceded that for individuals.

Restrictions on the capital account still remain.[6] These reflect the order and sequencing of capital account liberalization that India followed. After successive reviews of the liberalization process in India, the capital account has remained not fully open and debt flows are tightly managed. Mohan (2008) gives a clear account of the logic behind this approach: the government considers that capital inflows in excess of the domestic absorptive capacity can lead to overheating in the economy and create asset price bubbles. Abrupt reversals of short-term debt inflows, in particular, can be detrimental to the real economy. Regulation discriminates against debt flows in two ways:

- Foreign investors' participation in the domestic government bond market is capped.

[6] For a comprehensive listing of these, see Kohli and Belaisch (2012).

- Indian corporates can borrow abroad above a minimum maturity and below a maximum interest cost. These limits vary per economic sector, depending on perceived needs.

The pace of capital account opening—slow and gradual—has often been commented upon by observers. This is not specific to capital account liberalization alone; much of India's reform process is characterized by gradualism (Ahluwalia 2002). When compared with major OECD countries, however, the pace of liberalization in India has not been that slow. From adopting the OECD code on capital movements in the early 1960s to the complete dismantling of controls in the 1980s, Japan, the United States, the United Kingdom, and Germany took, on average, 20–25 years to fully liberalize their capital accounts (Griffith-Jones et al. 2000).

Historical experience does not obviously make the case that India's choices are different from others. However, it is hard to argue with the evidence that financial openness remains limited in India today, particularly when compared with many other emerging market economies. Measuring financial globalization is inherently difficult and there are many measures, *de jure* and *de facto* (Prasad 2009); the former often shows conflicting results for India, for example, an oft-quoted index, the Chinn-Ito index of financial openness which measures a country's degree of financial openness,[7] accorded India a score of −1.13—the lowest, or the least capital openness—in 2007, compared to 0.99 for Brazil, 1.18 to Indonesia, −0.09 to Malaysia, 0.14 to the Philippines, and −1.13 to Thailand. Mohan and Kapur (2009) question the validity of this index though as it remains unchanged for India since 1970 save for a minor blip in 2000 despite a large change in India's external openness.[8] In contrast, Prasad (2009) compares India's openness vis-à-vis different measures to find that it lies mostly at the low end of the distribution in 1995, moving up significantly in a decade, according to some other measures.

[7] The index measures a country's degree of financial development. It is based on binary dummy variables that codify the tabulation of restrictions on cross-border financial transactions reported in the IMF's Annual Report on Exchange Arrangements and Exchange Restrictions (AREAER). It takes into account the following four categories of restrictions: (i) presence of multiple exchange rates; (ii) restrictions on current account transactions; (iii) restrictions on capital account transactions; and (iv) requirement of the surrender of export proceeds.

[8] They note that likewise, indices for Thailand, Korea, and the Philippines also suffer inertia for extended periods. They attribute it to the fact that such studies and the IMF's AREAER view capital account openness as a binary event: either open or closed, when in fact it should be seen as a process.

The Experience: Opportunity and Volatility

How has India benefitted from its rising level of financial globalization? What opportunities has it created? There are a few existing studies that attempt a wholesome, in-depth appraisal although several studies examine one or another aspect, for example, efficiency gains from stock market integration (Joshi 2008) and greater vulnerability in times of distress from increased market integration levels (Mukhopadhyay 2009) among others. An early account of macroeconomic effects of financial opening is Kohli (2003); Prasad (2009) offers a comprehensive and recent macroeconomic perspective while Kohli and Belaisch (2012) specifically examine the real and financial effects of capital inflows and the role of capital controls in that context. Comparative India–China experiences can be found in Rogoff (2003) and Lane and Schmukler (2006).

This section attempts to fill this gap, but in a simple, broad brush assessment against the backdrop of the first section and without any claim to causality where applicable. Descriptive statistics are used for the purpose. The measure of financial globalization is gross capital flows, which is a good measure of the gross underlying exposure of an economy to cross-border financial flows as it accurately captures the stress that emerging economies can face in surges and a drought of liquidity.

Figure 8.1 depicts India's rising financial integration over time in gross terms; net capital flows bring out the capital flows' cycles more clearly. Foreign capital levels are observed to steadily rise after 2001. This is followed by a surge in the build-up to the global financial crisis in 2008; a sharp reversal thereafter; the return of the tide in 2010 and then again, a drought. As share of GDP, gross capital flows more than doubled between 2005 and 2007 to US$ 770 billion, a 10-fold increase over 2000 levels. The net capital account more than doubled from 4 per cent of GDP in 2004–5 to 9.3 per cent of GDP in 2007–8, reflecting the fast pace of integration with global financial markets.

This boom turned into bust when foreign capital reversed following the 2008 crisis; net capital flows collapsed to 0.6 per cent of GDP. Post-crisis, India's gross exposure is about 50 per cent of GDP with the net capital account averaging 3.5 per cent of GDP. Figure 8.2 dissects the quality of foreign capital entering India. Portfolio and loans, relatively more volatile categories, dominate with more than two-fifth shares in overall net capital

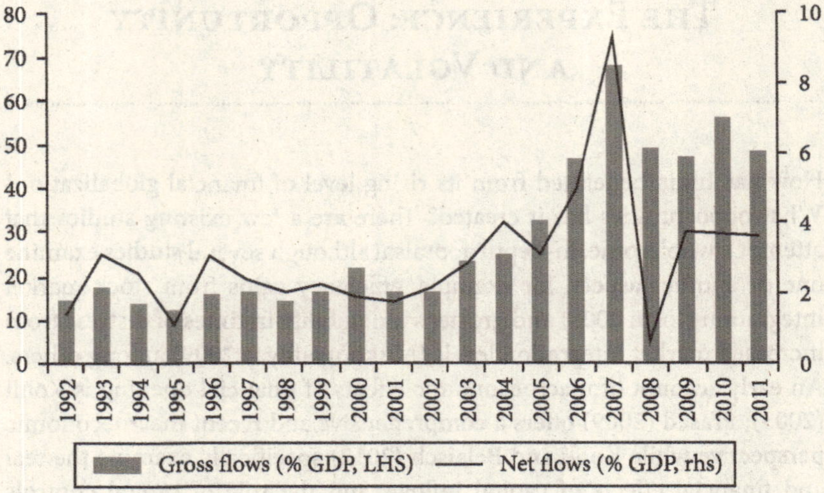

FIGURE 8.1 India: Capital Flows (percentage of GDP)

Source: RBI & author's calculations.

flow on average. Stable and long-term flows like foreign direct investment have lagged with an average 30 per cent share in net capital flows since 2005–6.

How has this benefitted India? There is little doubt that high growth rates and low, stable inflation and interest rates accompanied this financial globalization (Figure 8.3 and Table 8.1). During 2000–2 and 2010–11, financial openness almost trebled to about 50 per cent of GDP while average GDP growth rates nearly doubled from 4.5 to 8.9 per cent. But this does not necessarily imply an association as the period is characterized by significant structural changes in many spheres of India's economic policy. Global GDP grew at a brisk 5 per cent on average from 2004 to 2007 and global inflation remained below 4 per cent, a phase commonly described as the Great Moderation.[9]

Nonetheless, growth-inducing channels of financial globalization that work through an expanded pool of resources and lower cost of capital to

[9] A phrase, originally attributable to James Stock and Mark Watson who used it to describe the reduction in economic volatility from the mid-1980s ('Has the Business Cycle Changed and Why?, *NBER Macroeconomics Annual*), but then popularized to suggest improved monetary policy by advanced countries' central banks, particularly of the US Federal Reserve (Bernanke, 'Ben The Great Moderation', remarks before the Eastern Economic Association, Washington, DC, 20 February 2004).

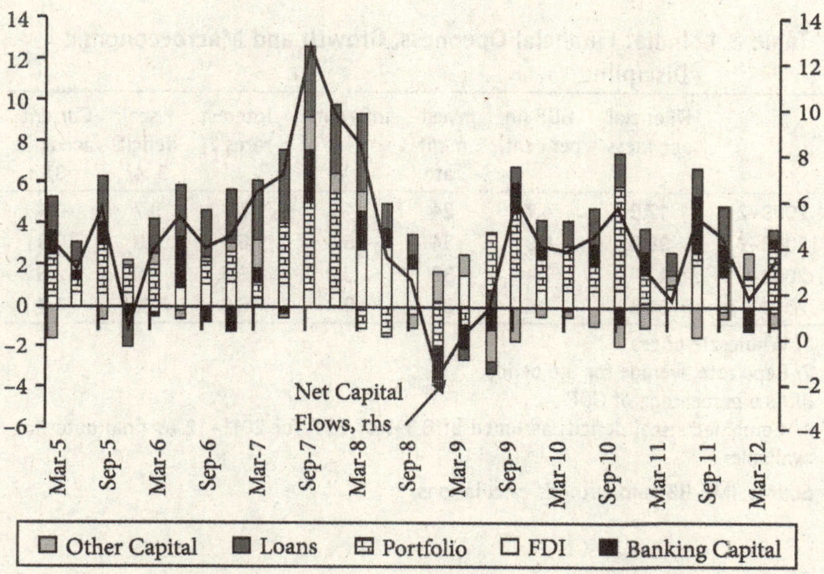

FIGURE 8.2 India: New Capital Account and Components (percentage of GDP)
Source: RBI, CEIC database and author's calculations.

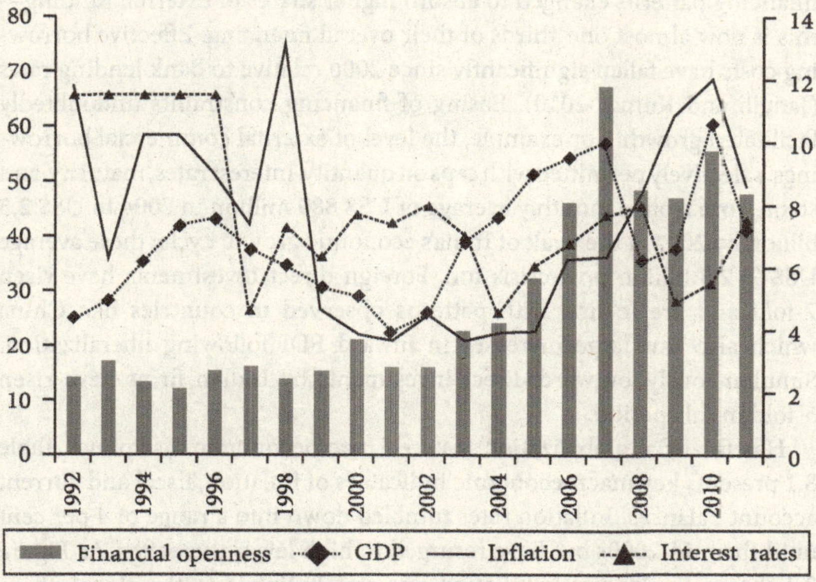

FIGURE 8.3 India: Financial Globalization, Growth and Inflation (percentage)
Source: IMF and author's calculations.

Table 8.1 India: Financial Openness, Growth and Macroeconomic Discipline

	Financial openness	GDP (in per cent)	Invest-ment rate	Inflation1/	Interest rates 2/	Fiscal deficit 3, 4/	Current account 3/
2000–2	17.9	4.7	24	4.7	7.7	9.7	0.4
2003–7	38.6	8.9	34	5.5	6.4	6.3	−0.3
2008–9	47.8	7.4	37	6.0	6.5	9.0	−2.6
2010–11	51.8	7.5	32	9.3	6.6	7.83/	−3.4

1/ Wholesale prices
2/ Repo rate average for the period
3/ As a percentage of GDP
4/ Combined fiscal deficit; assumed at 8.3% of GDP for 2011–12 as final data not available

Source: IMF, RBI and author's calculations.

raise investment-GDP shares and output can be observed in the Indian case. Illustratively, investment rates rose from 24 per cent at the start of the 2000s to a peak of 38 per cent of GDP by end-2010. Alongside, corporate financing patterns changed to absorb higher shares of external funding—this is now almost one-thirds of their overall financing. Effective borrowing costs have fallen significantly since 2000 relative to bank lending rates (Jangili and Kumar 2010). Easing of financing constraints undoubtedly facilitated growth. For example, the level of external commercial borrowings, selectively permitted with caps on quantity, interest rates, maturity, and so on, rose from a monthly average of US$ 880 million in 2004 to US$ 2.5 billion by 2007 at the peak of India's economic growth cycle; these average US$ 2–2.5 billion post-crisis too. Foreign direct investments have risen 7-fold and are in line with patterns observed in countries like China which also saw large increases in inward FDI following liberalization. Simultaneously, outward direct investments by Indian firms have risen 5-fold in this period.

Has financial globalization fostered macroeconomic discipline? Table 8.1 presents key macroeconomic indicators of inflation, fiscal and current account balances. Inflation rates tumbled down into a range of 4 per cent until the mid-2000s but have resurged to high levels thereafter. As Figure 8.4 shows, low domestic inflation was closely linked to the global phase of low inflation, but as the commodity cycle turned up, domestic inflation surged. This was additionally fuelled by domestic supply constraints in relation to overall demand. Likewise, fiscal balances that shrank to 6.3 per cent of GDP on average in 2003–7, have rebounded to unsustainably high levels since the crisis. The current account gap, which widens with higher growth rates, has expanded unsustainably in the last decade with rising dependency on short-term financing from abroad. *Prima facie* therefore, there is little evidence of the disciplining effect of financial globalization in India.

Has financial globalization led to higher volatility? The increasing co-movements of output, price, and interest rate (Figure 8.4) indisputably reflect the synchronization of the Indian business cycle with the global one. Specifically, Ang (2011) finds consumption volatility to rise after financial liberalization, consistent with other findings. A quick statistical preview on the behaviour of these aggregates over 1997–2002 and 2003–11 (quarterly data) shows that GDP volatility—measured by the coefficient of variation—more than doubled from 0.12 to 0.31, while private consumption was nearly three times as volatile (0.11 and 0.30 respectively). Inflation

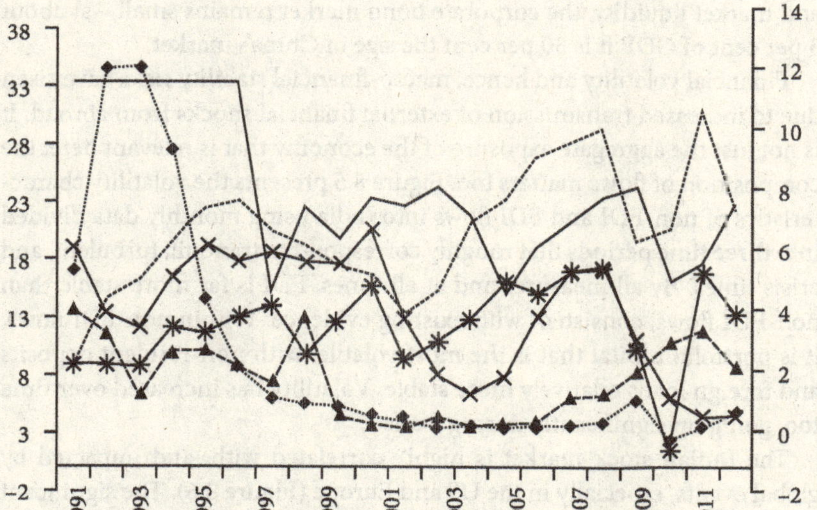

FIGURE 8.4 India: Global Macrolinkages

Source: IMF, RBI and author's calculations.

volatility was range-bound (0.38–0.44) throughout. Real exchange rate variability increased significantly; measured by the standard deviation of the monthly percentage change, nominal exchange rate volatility was double (3.0) in 2011 relative to 2002.

Development of financial markets has accompanied financial globalization for sure, although it is hard to attribute this to openness as major policy efforts also took place simultaneously (Mohan 2008). The stock market, first to be opened to foreign investors, grew in size; market capitalization (in US dollar terms) rose three-fold between 1991 and 2000, and seven times thereafter to US$ 1 trillion in 2011. The base is wider as the number of listed firms more than doubled in two decades to 2011; it has acquired depth and liquidity, comparing favourably with advanced and emerging country markets (ibid). But India's bond market—mostly closed to foreign investors who hold under 5 per cent of the public debt stock—is neither very deep nor liquid, remaining under-developed (Gopinath 2010). While the government bond market is well developed—at about 30 per cent of GDP, comparing well with countries like the US and Singapore (42 and 28 per cent of GDP)—and has a liquid yield curve, high turnover volumes, and market liquidity, the corporate bond market remains small—at about 3 per cent of GDP it is 30 per cent the size of China's market.

Financial volatility and hence, macro-financial stability risks have risen due to increased transmission of external financial shocks from abroad. It is not just the aggregate exposure of the economy that is relevant here; the composition of flows matters too. Figure 8.5 presents the volatility characteristics of non-FDI and FDI flows into India using monthly data divided into three time periods that roughly correspond to tranquil, turbulent, and crisis times. By all measures and at all times, FDI is far more stable than non-FDI flows, consistent with existing evidence. Within non-FDI flows, it is portfolio capital that is the most volatile, with non-resident deposits and foreign loans relatively more stable. Volatility has increased over time too, going up significantly during a crisis.

The Indian stock market is highly correlated with, and impacted by global events, especially in the US and Europe (Figure 8.6). The significant influence exerted by foreign portfolio capital (Batra 2003; Chakrabarti 2001; Raj and Dhal 2008) points towards the rising contagion and spillover risks that inevitably accompany financial globalization. The stock market is increasingly a conduit for the transmission of external shocks, find Kohli and Belaisch (2012), who find a standard liquidity channel at play via the stock market, the most open segment of the financial system. In turn, capital flows and stock market volatility also explain a larger part of

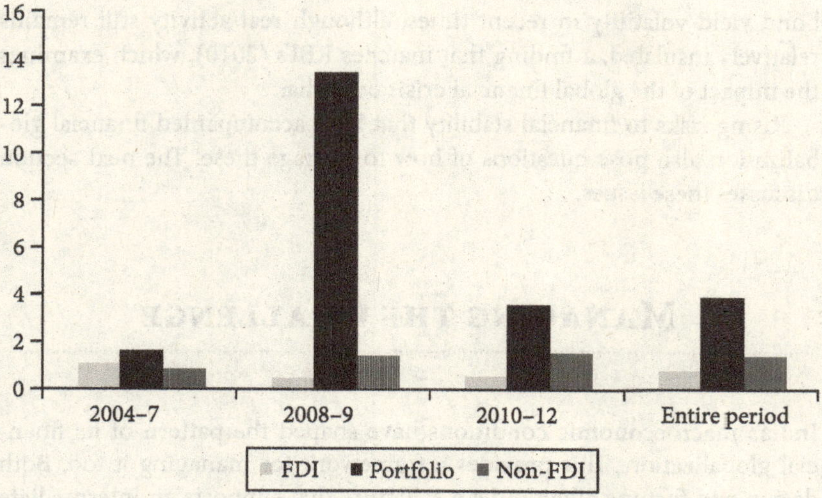

FIGURE 8.5 India: Volatility of Types of Capital Flows (Coefficient of Variation)
Source: Author's calculations with data from RBI.

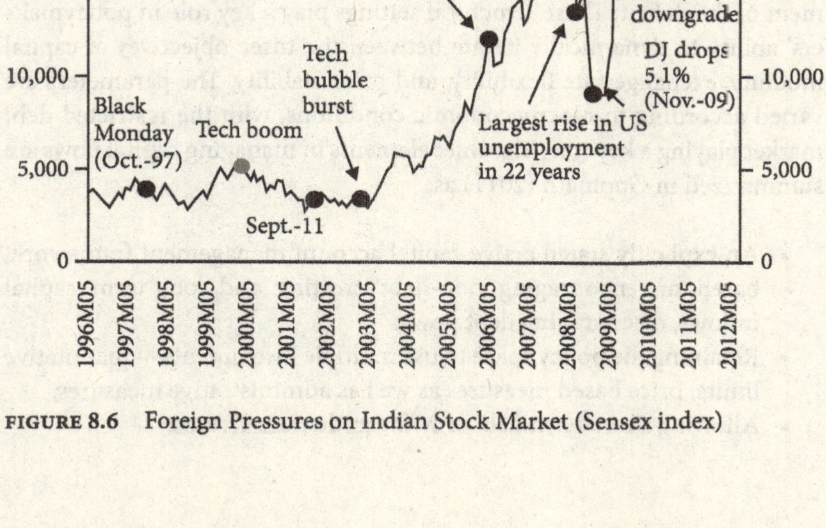

FIGURE 8.6 Foreign Pressures on Indian Stock Market (Sensex index)

bond yield volatility in recent times, although real activity still remains relatively insulated, a finding that matches RBI's (2010), which examines the impact of the global financial crisis on India.

Rising risks to financial stability that have accompanied financial globalization also pose questions of how to manage these. The next section discusses these issues.

Managing the Challenge

India's macroeconomic conditions have shaped the pattern of its financial globalization. This provides a framework for managing it too. Both design and fortune allow India a structure that supports an intermediate exchange rate regime. A partially-closed capital account and a reasonable absorptive capacity, that is, current account deficit, enable resolution of the trilemma, or the inability to simultaneously realize the three goals of free capital mobility, a fixed exchange rate, and a monetary policy devoted to domestic objectives.

The macro-monetary framework is characterized by significant capital controls, notably, on debt flows, which help maintain the domestic-foreign interest rate wedge. Controls also provide a policy tool for calibrating short-term capital flows. The second structural feature that supports simultaneous balancing of the exchange rate and price stability goals is a deficit on the current account. This helps moderate real exchange rate appreciation pressures; conversely, exchange rate flexibility assists adjustment of the deficit. These structural settings play a key role in policymakers' ability to dynamically iterate between the three objectives of capital mobility, exchange rate flexibility, and price stability. The parameters are varied according to macroeconomic conditions, with the restricted debt market playing a key role. The chief elements in managing capital flows are summarized in Gopinath (2011) as:

- An explicitly stated active capital account management framework, based on encouraging non-debt creating and long-term capital inflows, discouraging debt flows;
- Retaining the policy space to use multiple instruments—quantitative limits, price based measures as well as administrative measures;
- Allowing short-term debt only for trade transactions;

- Avoiding the 'original sin'—excessive foreign currency borrowings by domestic entities, especially the sovereign;[10]
- Prudential regulations to prevent excessive dollarization of balance sheets of financial sector intermediaries, particularly banks;
- Caution towards liability dollarization by domestic entities; and
- Significant liberalization of permitted outward investments by residents.

Under this approach, Indian policymakers have so far managed capital flows through a combination of policy responses—reserve accumulation-cum-sterilization, part feedback into money supply, exchange rate flexibility, liberalization of outflows, and occasional use of capital controls in extreme situations, but only for domestic residents so as to not impact foreign investments (Kohli 2011).

Accumulation of reserves, along with partial feedback into money supply, has been an important first-round response. Table 8.2 shows the substantial increase in foreign exchange reserves (US$ 57 billion) by 2006–7 over previous levels, reflecting accumulation of capital account surpluses in excess of absorptive capacity. The monetary impact of foreign currency purchases, that is, forex intervention, is countered through sterilization. For example, between March 2007 and December 2007 when capital inflows surged, almost 43 per cent of net foreign exchange purchases were sterilized by the central bank on average, with partial feedback into money supply. There is a cost associated with this response—the interest rate differential between the foreign and domestic currencies—that devolves on the government balance sheet; illustratively, sterilization costs were 0.42 per cent of GDP (US$ 4.9 billion) in March 2008 from a small 0.02 per cent of GDP in January 2006. Exchange rate flexibility or adjustments through a change in the value of the currency has been another tool. India's exchange rate regime is progressively flexible with a shift to a more flexible exchange rate regime in 1997–8. This has assisted managing the increasing financial integration of the economy (Figure 8.7). An index measure of exchange rate flexibility[11] derived from the relationship between the

[10] Originally proposed by Barry Eichengreen and Ricardo Hausmann in 1999 to refer to the inability of countries to borrow abroad in their domestic currencies.

[11] Index calculated as the standard deviation of change in the nominal exchange rate (monthly average of daily difference vis-à-vis the US dollar) with respect to its sum with monthly change in foreign exchange reserves as ratio to change in monetary base (one-month lag). It takes values from zero to one, with lower values signifying relative inflexibility.

Table 8.2 India: A Decomposition of Reserve Buildup
(in billlions of US$)

	1998–2000	2001–5	2006–7	2008–9	2009–11	Changes			
						2001–5 -1998–2000	2006–7 -2001–5	2008–9 -2006–7	2009–11 -2008–9
Increase in foreign reserves	4.4	21.7	79.1	–57.7	14.1	17.3	57.3	–136.8	71.9
Current account balance	–3.8	2.3	–12.7	–27.9	–54.1	6.1	–14.9	–15.3	–26.2
Current account balance	9.2	17.9	75.9	7.4	60.5	8.7	58.0	–68.5	53.1
FDI, net	2.6	3.4	11.8	22.4	16.5	0.8	8.4	10.6	–5.9
Errors and omissions, net	0.1	0.1	1.1	0.4	–1.8	0.0	1.1	–0.7	–2.3
Non-FDI capital account balance (incl. errors & omissions)	6.7	14.6	65.2	–14.5	42.2	7.8	50.7	–79.8	56.7

Sources: RBI and authors' calculations.

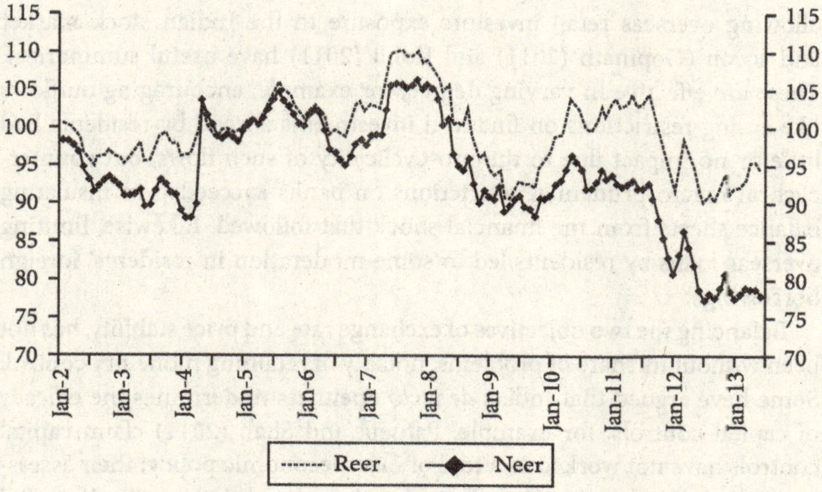

FIGURE 8.7 India: Exchange Rate Flexibility

Source: RBI.

nominal exchange rate and foreign exchange reserves shows that the index increased from 0.85 in April 2006 to 0.91 May 2007 onwards, reflecting a rise in flexibility relative to historical values, and in relation to advanced and emerging economies (Kohli 2011).

Monetary management and exchange rate flexibility are supplemented by macro-prudential measures and occasionally, capital controls. Macro-prudential tools range from varying risk weights and provisioning requirements for bank credit to the property sector; sector exposure limits for bank credit to sensitive sectors, for example, the capital market; loan-to-value ratios applying to real estate; and margin requirements and the build up of foreign currency liabilities in segments vulnerable to sharp price fluctuations (RBI 2012). These were especially used ahead of the 2008 crisis to restrain asset price inflation and a credit boom and were effective in preventing build-up of financial vulnerabilities. When the crisis struck, banks in India emerged unscathed with healthy balance sheets; households and firms were neither over-leveraged nor overtly hit by the fall in the stock prices that followed.

Capital controls have also been used after other options have been exhausted or overused. *Inter alia*, these include curbs on residents' access to overseas borrowings and/or capping conversion to domestic currency; restricting participatory notes (PNs), an offshore derivative products allowing overseas retail investors exposure to the Indian stock market and so on (Gopinath (2011) and Kohli (2011) have useful summaries). These are effective in varying degree, for example, encouraging outflows like easing restrictions on financial investments abroad by residents had little or no impact due to the pro-cyclicality of such flows, but counter-cyclical macro-prudential restrictions on banks succeeded in insulating balance sheets from the financial shock that followed. Likewise, limiting overseas loans by residents led to some moderation in residents' foreign borrowings.

Balancing the two objectives of exchange rate and price stability, has not been without its share of problems, notably of retaining monetary control. Some have argued that India's *de facto* openness undermines the efficacy of capital controls, for example, Patnaik and Shah (2011) claim capital controls have not worked as a tool of macroeconomic policy; their assessment, however, is subjective. The correct approach is to verify if capital mobility is successful in bridging the domestic-foreign market segmentation that it is designed to achieve; as long as the interest rate wedge is maintained, capital controls are binding. There is evidence that domestic-foreign interest differentials are significant and persistent in India (Hutchison et al. 2010; Ma and McCauley 2007); convergence, though increasing, is as yet incomplete (Kohli 2009); and incomplete financial integration due to a restricted presence of foreign investors in the bond market provides a degree of short-term monetary autonomy to the central bank (Kohli and Belaisch 2012). IMF (2010) mentions India among countries where capital controls are effective, not the least because of its implementation capacity, that is, institutional and administrative structures, for their enforcement.

In a post-crisis review of lessons from international finance for developing countries, Obstfeld (2009) cites India and China as examples of how imperfect mobility of capital can resolve the trilemma. Besides the conflict between monetary and exchange rate objectives, capital controls have implications for trade policy. For example, export earnings' repatriation, quantitative caps, end-use restrictions on residents' foreign borrowings and investments, and foreign investments in asset and some goods' markets do influence real economic activity, although below a threshold level of financial development the trade-off might well be of lesser risk. Last, market participants are tempted to take on more risk in the presence of capital controls, like exploitation of temporary opportunities for cross-border arbitrage through non-deliverable forward markets for rupee-dollar trades that have arisen in Singapore and Dubai, disguised re-entry of foreign loans raised by domestic firms as portfolio equity inflows, non-resident Indian deposits and build-up of unhedged positions driven by expectations of exchange rate fluctuations.

Conclusion and Appraisal

Concluding with an appraisal of India's experience with financial globalization, especially in the light of the financial crisis of 2008 that exposed its several undesirable dimensions, is useful. Many assumptions underlying the functioning of financial markets have become questionable post-crisis, while regulation and supervision of financial markets and participants has come under severe scrutiny (Turner Review 2009).[12] A number of perspectives therefore illuminate India's experience in this regard.

One standpoint of assessment is the reversal in the approach of international organizations towards handling of global financial flows. This has now reversed to incorporate capital controls and emphasize macro-prudential measures in a revised framework (IMF 2011) that closely mirrors India's capital account management framework; this is a testimony of the resilience and success of India's structure. Another perspective is of 'limited financial globalization'. Rodrik[13] observes that countries that were least globalized financially were the least hit by the crisis. McCauley and Ma (2009) document that throwing 'sand in the wheels of finance' helped Asian countries like China, India, South Korea, and Thailand insulate them from the crisis. Among the tools they identify are limited roles of foreign banks in the domestic banking system and restriction of cross-border arbitrage in foreign currency, money, and bond and equity markets.

Yet another measure of appraisal is the counter-factual: How has India fared when deviating from its intervention-reserve accumulation-limited exchange rate appreciation strategy? Table 8.2 illustrates such a departure from 2009. Despite a recovery in capital flows in 2009–11 after the crisis, India's reserves' increase was US$ 72 billion over a negative change of US$ 139 billion, that is, the US$ 58 billion erosion in reserves in 2008–9

[12] See Turner Review (2009) for a full discussion on these issues (The Turner Review: A regulatory response to the global banking crisis, March 2009, Financial Services Authority, UK).

[13] http://rodrik.typepad.com/dani_rodriks_weblog/2008/11/can-you-resist-financial-globalization.html, 7 November 2008.

was never fully recouped as the central bank followed a hands-off exchange rate policy from 2009, reversing a policy of managed float. The currency adjusted fully to heavy capital inflow; illustratively, the non-FDI capital account balance swelled by US$ 57 billion over 2008–9 levels with higher purchases of debt and equity securities stocks by foreign investors as the two main contributors. Exchange rate appreciation—significant in both real and nominal terms (Figure 8.7)—led to a steadily expanding current account deficit that doubled in 2009–11 over 2008–9 levels (Table 8.2). This was fed excessively by short-term capital, which reversed suddenly as the risk sentiment deteriorated over feeble US and euro zone recoveries in mid-2011. The currency value had plunged more than 20 per cent with adverse macroeconomic consequences, notably of financing a current account deficit of proportions as large as 4–4.5 per cent of GDP by March 2012.

Looking ahead at future challenges that financial globalization poses for India, this experience is illustrative. Above all, it exposes the severe external financing risks that India courts in following a hands-off exchange rate policy at a stage of development when it is unable to finance its import needs through sufficient export earnings and its fiscal position precludes long-term, stable financing of its internal and external deficits. It also highlights the severity of risks arising from short-term, speculative capital flows that are destabilizing, excessively volatile, and disruptive to real economic activity. And it underlines the importance of reserves' accumulation as an essential tool in the armoury to tackle foreign capital purely driven by risk sentiments that can switch suddenly.

It would be fair to say then that a cautious, gradual attitude towards financial globalization that balances the financial and real development of the economy is the best course for India. This of course, is the pre-crisis approach that helped protect the country from too-adverse a hit. This now needs supplementing with enough policy space to combat the increased risks to financial instability from global financial flows. The policy range includes fiscal and monetary responses for which both fiscal deficit and inflation need to be kept at prudent, manageable levels. Alongside, building of reserves needs to return, while some capital controls—notably on debt flows—need to be retained until such time when India's macroeconomic foundations are sustainably strong, the development of financial markets reaches sophistication levels observed in advanced countries and is supplemented with better regulation and supervision. Finally, international regulations to restrict short-term, speculative capital movements will be a useful area for coordination by the country.

REFERENCES

Ahluwalia, M.S. (2002), 'Economic Reforms in India since 1991: Has Gradualism Worked?' *Journal of Economic Perspectives*, 16(3): 67–88.

Aizenman, Joshua, Brian Pinto, and Arthur Radziwill (2007), 'Sources for Financing Domestic Capital—Is Foreign Saving a Viable Option for Developing Countries?' *Journal of International Money and Finance*, 26(5): 682–702.

Aizenman, Joshua and Vladyslav Sushko (2011), 'Capital Flow Types, External Financing Needs, and Industrial Growth: 99 Countries, 1991-2007', National Bureau of Economic Research Working Paper 17228, July.

Alfaro, L. and E. Hammel (2007), 'Capital Flows and Capital Goods', *Journal of International Economics*, 72(1): 128–50.

Ang, J. (2011), 'Finance and consumption volatility: Evidence from India', *Journal of International Money and Finance*, 30(6): 947–64.

Batra, A. (2003), 'The Dynamics of Foreign Portfolio Inflows and Equity Returns in India', ICRIER Working Paper, No. 109. New Delhi: ICRIER.

Bekaert, G., C.R. Harvey, and C. Lundblad (2005), Does financial Liberalization Spur Growth? *Journal of Financial Economics*, 77(1), 3–56.

———— (2006): 'Growth Volatility and Financial Liberalization', *Journal of International Money and Finance*, 25(3): 370–403.

Berg, A., E. Borensztein, and C. Pattillo (2004), 'Assessing Early Warning Systems: How Have They Worked in Practice?' IMF Working Paper 04/52. Washington: International Monetary Fund.

Bhagwati, Jagdish (1998), 'The Capital Myth—The Difference between Trade in Widgets and Dollars', *Foreign Affairs*, 77(3): 7–13.

Bank of International Settlements (BIS) (2012), Annual Report. Available at http://www.bis.org/publ/arpdf/ar2012e.htm

Calvo, Guillermo and Carmen Reinhart (1999), 'Capital Flow Reversals, the Exchange Rate Debate and Dollarization', MPRA Paper 8951. Germany: University Library of Munich.

Chakrabarti, Rajesh (2001), 'FII Flows to India: Nature and Causes', *Money and Finance*, 2(7).

Chinn, M. and H. Ito (2006), 'What Matters for Financial Development? Capital controls, Institutions and Interactions', *Journal of Development Economics*, 81(1): 163–92.

Dell 'Ariccia, Giovanni (2008), *Reaping the Benefits of Financial Globalization.* Washington DC: International Monetary Fund.

Eichengreen, Barry, Eduardo Borensztein, and Ugo Panizza (2006), 'Debt Instruments and Policies in the New Millennium: New Markets and New Opportunities', RES Working Paper 4456, Inter-American Development Bank, Research Department, Washington DC.

Gopinath, Shyamala (2010), 'Pursuit of Complete Markets—The Missing Perspectives', Inaugural address at the *FEDAI Annual Conference*, 28 February 2010, Kenya.

Gopinath, Shyamala (2011), Approach to Capital Account Management—Shifting Contours Keynote Address at the *Annual Conference of the Foreign Exchange Dealers' Association of India (FEDAI)*, 18 February, Thimpu.

Gourinchas, Pierre-Olivier and Olivier Jeanne (2003), 'The Elusive Gains from International Financial Integration', NBER Working Paper No. 9684, May.

Gourinchas, Pierre-Olivier and Olivier Jeanne (2007), 'Capital Flows to Developing Countries: The Allocation Puzzle', NBER Working Paper No. 13602, November.

Griffith-Jones, S., R. Gottschalk, and X. Cirrera (2000), 'The OECD Experience with Capital Account Liberalization', Paper presented at the *UNCTAD Workshop on Management of Capital Flows*, Cairo, Egypt, 20–21.

Henry, P.B. (2000), 'Do Stock Market Liberalizations Cause Investment Booms?' *Journal of Financial Economics*, 58(1–2): 301–34.

Hutchison, Michael, Jake Kendall, Gurnain Pasricha, and Nirvikar Singh (2010) 'Indian Capital Control Liberalization: Evidence from NDF Markets', MPRA Paper No. 21771, posted 30 March 2010. Available online at: *mpra.ub.uni-muenchen.de/21771/1/MPRA_paper_21771.pdf*.

IMF (2007), 'Reaping the Benefits of Financial Globalization', IMF Discussion Paper, June.

———— (2009), 'The Debate on the International Monetary System', IMF Staff Position Note SPN/09/26, 11 November.

———— (2010) 'Capital Inflows: The Role of Controls', IMF Staff Position Note SPN/10/04, 19 February.

———— (2011), 'Recent Experiences in Managing Capital Inflows—Cross-Cutting Themes and Possible Policy Framework', February, Washington DC.

Jangili, Ramesh and Sharad Kumar (2010), 'Determinants of Private Corporate Sector Investment in India', *Reserve Bank of India Occasional Papers*, 31(3): 67–90.

Javorcik, B.S. (2004), 'Does Foreign Direct investment Increase the Productivity of Domestic Firms? In Search of Spillovers through Backward Linkages', *American Economic Review*, 94(3): 605–27.

Jeanne, Olivier, Arvind Subramanian, and John Williamson (2012), *Who Needs to Open the Capital Account?* Peterson Institute, Washington DC, 21 May.

Joshi, Prashant (2008), 'Market Integration and Efficiency of Indian Stock Markets: A Study of NSE'. Available online at: http://www.nseindia.com/content/research/ResearchPaper_198.pdf (last accessed on June 2012).

Kaminsky, G.L. and S. Schmukler (2003), 'Short-run pain, long-run gain: the effects of financial liberalization', NBER Working Paper 9787. Cambridge, MA: National Bureau of Economic Research.

Kletzer, Kenneth and Renu Kohli (2001), 'Financial Repression and Exchange Rate Management in Developing Countries: Theory and Empirical Evidence for India', IMF Working Paper WP/01/103, 4 September.

Kohli, Renu (2003), 'Capital Flows and their Macroeconomic Effects in India', IMF Working Paper WP/01/192, 1 December.

Kohli, Renu (2005), *Globalization: Liberalizing Capital Flows—India's Experience & Policy Issues*. New Delhi: Oxford University Press.

———(2009), 'Financial Integration, Capital Controls and Monetary Independence', *Economic and Political Weekly*, 44(26–27): 57–61.

——— (2011), 'India's Experience in Navigating the Trilemma: Do Capital Controls Help?' *Journal of International Commerce, Economics and Policy*, 2(2): 351–71.

Kohli, Renu and Agnes Belaisch (2012), 'Do Capital Controls Matter in India?' India Policy Forum 2011–12, NCAER-Brookings. New Delhi: Sage Publications.

Kose, M.A., E.S. Prasad, and M.E. Terrones (2003a), 'Financial Integration and Macroeconomic Volatility', IMF Staff Paper 50: 119–42.

———(2003b), 'How Does Globalization Affect the Synchronization of Business Cycles?', *American Economic Review*, 93(2): 57–62.

Kose, M. Ayhan, Eswar Prasad, Kenneth Rogoff, and Shang-Jin Wei (2006), 'Financial Globalization: A Reappraisal', NBER Working Paper No. 12484, August.

Kose M. Ayhan, Eswar Prasad, Macro E. Terrones (2007), 'How does Financial Globalization Affect Risk Sharing?' IZA Discussion Paper No. 2903.

Kose, Ayhan, Eswar Prasad, and Ashley Taylor (2008), 'Thresholds in the Process of Financial Integration', Manuscript, IMF and Cornell University.

Kose, Ayhan, Eswar Prasad, Kenneth Rogoff, and Shang-Jin Wei (2009), 'Financial Globalization and Economic Policies', Global Economy & Development Working Paper 34, April.

Kose M., E. Prasad and M. Terrones (2009), 'Does Financial Globalization Promote Risk Sharing?' *Journal of Development Economics*, 89(2): 258–70.

Lane, Phillip (2012), 'Financial Globalisation and the Crisis', Paper Prepared for the 11th BIS Annual Conference on The Future of Financial Globalisation, Lucerne, 21–22 June.

Lane, Philip R. and Sergio L. Schmukler (2006), 'The International Financial Integration of China and India', CEPR Discussion Paper 5852.

Lewis, Karen (1996), 'What Can Explain the Apparent Lack of International Consumption Risk-Sharing?' *Journal of Political Economy*, 104: 267–67.

Ma, Guonan and Robert N. McCauley (2007), 'Do China's Capital Controls still Bind? Implications for Monetary Autonomy and Capital Liberalisation', BIS Working Paper No. 233.

McCauley, R. and G. Ma (2009), 'Resisting Financial Globalisation in Asia', in *Financial globalization and Emerging Market Economies*, Proceedings of an International Symposium organized by the Bank of Thailand, Bangkok, 7–8 November, pp. 177–222.

Meller, Barbara (2011), 'The Two-sided Effect of Financial Globalization on Output Volatility', *Deutsche Bundesbank, Discussion Paper Series 2*: Banking and Financial Studies No. 07/2011.

Mohan, Rakesh (2008), 'Capital Flows to India', in Financial Globalisation and Emerging Market Capital Flows, BIS Paper No. 44.

Mohan, Rakesh and Muneesh Kapur (2009), 'Managing the Impossible Trinity: Volatile Capital Flows and Indian Monetary Policy', Stanford Center for International Development Working Paper No. 401, November.

Mukhopadhyay, Bappaditya (2009), 'Financial Market Integration—The Indian Experience', *Review of Market Integration*, 1 (1, April): 37–60.

Obstfeld, Maurice (2009), 'International Finance and Growth in Developing Countries: What Have We Learned?' NBER Working Paper No. 14691, January.

Patnaik, Ila and Ajay Shah (2011), 'Did the Indian Capital Controls Work as a Tool of Macroeconomic Policy?' NIPFP Working Paper 2011–87. New Delhi: National Institute of Public Finance and Policy, April.

Prasad, Eswar S. (2009), 'Some New Perspectives on India's Approach to Capital Account Liberalization', *Brookings India Policy Forum*, 5 (2008/09), July.

Prasad, E., Kenneth Rogoff, Shang-Jin Wei, and M. Ayan Kose (2003), 'Effects of Financial Globalization on Developing Countries: Some Empirical Evidence', IMF Occasional Paper 220, September.

Prasad, E., Raghuram Rajan, and Arvind Subramanian (2007), 'Foreign Capital and Economic Growth', Brookings Papers on Economic Activity, September.

Raj, J. and Sarat Dhal (2008), 'Integration of India's Stock market with Global and Major Regional Markets', BIS Paper No. 42.

Rajan, R. (2005) 'Has Financial Development Made the World Riskier?' NBER Working Paper 11728, November.

Reddy, Y.V. (2000), 'Operationalising Capital Account Liberalisation: Indian Experience', Presentation by Dr. Y.V. Reddy, Deputy Governor, Reserve Bank of India at the Seminar on Capital Account Liberalisation: The Developing Country Perspective, at the Overseas Development Institute, London, 21 June.

RBI (2010), *Report on Currency and Finance, 2007–8*. Mumbai: RBI.

——— (June 2012), *Financial Stability Report*, Issue no 5.

Rodrik, Dani (1998), 'Who Needs Capital Account Convertibility?' *Essays in International Finance* No. 207, International Finance Section, Department of Economics, Princeton University, May.

Rodrik, Dani and A. Subramanian (2008), 'Why did Financial Globalization Disappoint?' *Manuscript*, Harvard University, March.

Rogoff, Kenneth S. (2003), 'Financial Globalization: The Case of India versus China', Lecture delivered at ICRIER, 16 July, New Delhi.

Sørensen, Bent, Yi-Tsung Wu, Oved Yosha, and Yu Zhu (2007), 'Home Bias and International Risk Sharing: Twin Puzzles Separated at Birth', *Journal of International Money and Finance*, 26(4): 587–605.

Turner Review (2009), *A Regulatory Response to the Global Banking Crisis*. UK: Financial Service Authority, March.

Tytell, Irina and Shang-Jin Wei (2004), 'Does Financial Globalization Induce Better Macroeconomic Policies?' IMF Working Paper 04/84. Washington: International Monetary Fund.

United Nations (2009), *Report of the Commission of Experts of the President of the United Nations General Assembly on Reforms of the International Monetary and Financial System*. New York: United Nations, 21 September.

CHAPTER 9

REFORMS AND GLOBAL ECONOMIC INTEGRATION OF THE INDIAN ECONOMY

emerging patterns, challenges, and future directions

NAGESH KUMAR*

A major liberalization of the trade and investment regimes has taken place since 1991 as a part of the package of reforms undertaken to deepen integration of the Indian economy with the world economy as a whole. Peak tariff rates had come down from 150 per cent in the early 1990s to just 10 per cent by 2007. The quantitative restrictions on imports were phased out and a bulk of the tariff lines (over 70 per cent) have been bound under the World Trade Organization (WTO). Most sectors of the economy are today open to foreign direct investment (FDI) with up to 100 per cent foreign

* An earlier version was issued in the UNESCAP-SSWA's Development Paper Series. The author thanks Ashima Goyal, Matthew Hammill, Chris Garroway, and an anonymous reviewer for comments. The author is grateful to Helene Meurisse, Quentin Roblin, Neha Aggarwal, and Vinod Soman, ESCAP-SSWA interns in 2012, for their competent research assistance. The United Nations or its member states are not responsible for the views expressed, which should be attributed to the author alone.

ownership, although sectoral ownership limits apply in service sectors. Since 1992, foreign institutional investors (FIIs) have also been allowed to invest in India. The Indian rupee was made convertible in the current account and the capital account is being opened gradually, including a gradual liberalization of the regime governing outward FDI from India.

These economic reforms have led to industrial restructuring in the country with a focus on competitiveness and global economic integration. The growing economic integration of the Indian economy is reflected in various indicators including the rising share of trade in the economy. The structure and direction of trade have changed over time along with growing magnitudes. An important and more dynamic aspect of India's integration with the world economy is through the growing trade in services. India has emerged as a hub for outsourcing of IT software and other business services, such as business process outsourcing (BPO). India is also attracting attention from major multinational enterprises (MNEs) around the world wishing to make India a hub for knowledge-based services to tap the availability of high-quality low-cost trained human resources as well as scientific and technological infrastructure. Another aspect of growing global integration is through FDI—both inward and outward. With a liberal FDI policy regime and a large and growing domestic market among other advantages, India is attracting increasing attention of MNEs even as Indian enterprises are also developing global ambitions and undertaking outward investments in increasing numbers and magnitudes.

India is known for an impressive turnaround of the external sector from a foreign exchange crisis faced in 1991, when the current account deficit touched 3 per cent of GDP, to a current account surplus during 2001–4 and the build-up of large foreign exchange reserves. Today, however the economy has once again entered a period of balance of payments stress in the wake of the global financial crisis of 2008–9, which still continues to rattle the world economy in 2013. Besides the urgent attention of policymakers to the balance of payments situation, the global financial crisis has warranted another major rebalancing in the trade structure away from traditional trade partners in the west to increasingly greater reliance on the fast growing Asia-Pacific economies. These Asia-Pacific economies are emerging as the centre of gravity of the world economy due to the inability of the western advanced economies to act as global growth engines in the medium term (UN-ESCAP 2012). With a visionary Look East Policy (LEP) pursued since 1992, India is well placed in this respect, having engaged ASEAN and other East Asian countries through a growing web of free trade agreements (FTAs). Indeed, India is an important part of an incipient broader regional economic arrangement bringing together 16 of the region's largest and fastest growing economies. Therefore, regional economic integration is likely to play an increasingly important role in the global economic integration of the Indian economy in the coming years.

Against that backdrop, this chapter considers the changing trade and investment profile of the Indian economy highlighting major emerging trends and patterns and the external sector challenges faced and concludes with a few policy lessons to address them.

MERCHANDISE TRADE

Growth of Merchandise Trade

The reforms of the 1990s led to a rapid expansion of India's trade. The growth rates of India's exports and imports averaged over 10 per cent during the 1990s but stepped up to an average of 22 per cent in the past decade. Imports generally grew at faster rates (24 per cent) than exports (20 per cent) as shown in Table 9.1. Rapid growth of trade is reflected in the rising share of trade in India's GDP. The share of merchandise trade in GDP more than doubled between 2001–2 to 2011–12 from 21.2 to 43.8 per cent. In fact, the global integration of the economy crossed 60 per cent if trade in services is also included (Figure 9.1).

Table 9.1 India's Merchandise Trade Growth Rates and Balance (million US$)

	2001–2	2011–12	Average Annual Growth Rate (2001–11)
Exports	43,827.0	304,624.0	20%
Share in GDP	9.4	16.8	
Imports	51,413.0	489,417.0	24%
Share in GDP	11.8	27.0	
Total trade	95,240.0	794,041.0	
Share in GDP	21.2	43.8	
Balance of trade	−7,586.6	−184,793.9	

Source: Extracted from RBI (2012).

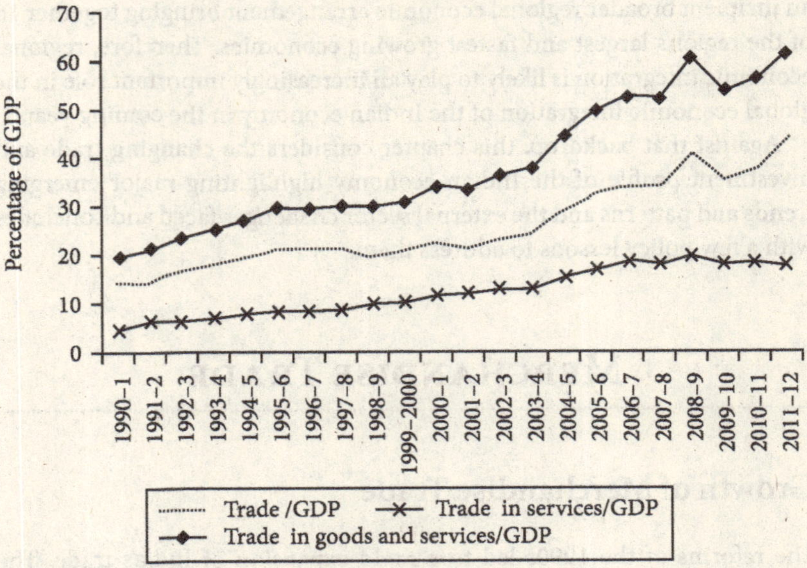

FIGURE 9.1 Growing Importance of Trade in the Economy
Source: Author's calculations based on RBI (2012).

The other noticeable trend is the widening deficit in balance of trade with imports growing at a faster rate than exports. The trade deficit snowballed from US$ 5–6 billion a year in the beginning of the last decade to US$ 185 billion in 2011–12, which amounts to over 10 per cent of GDP (Table 9.1, Figure 9.2). The widening trade deficit has created balance of payments challenges for the economy even after taking care of a substantial surplus in invisibles or services trade, as observed later.

Changing Structure of Trade

The export structure is expected to change with the level of development from one dominated by primary products to one dominated by products with greater value added. Diversification of the export structure also makes the exporting country less vulnerable to external shocks compared to a country with a more concentrated export structure. Table 9.2 summarizes some important shifts in the patterns of India's export structure over 1995–2012. Firstly, as expected, the share of primary products including

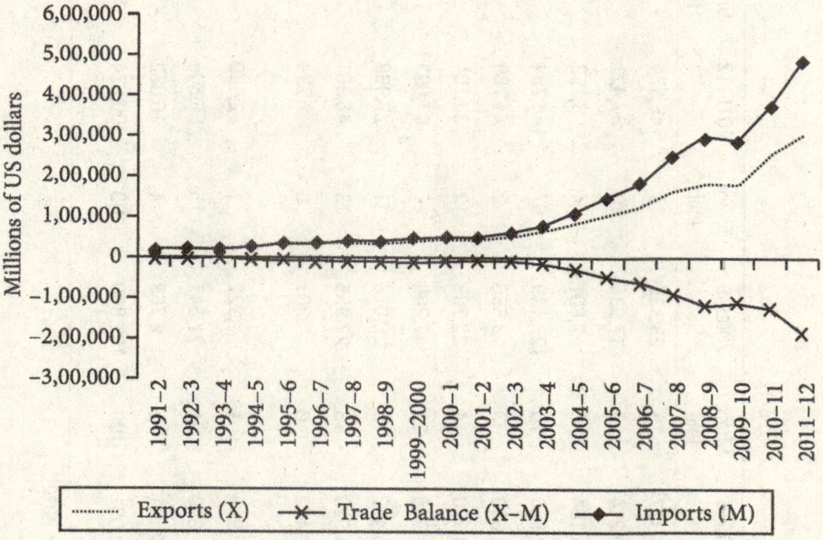

FIGURE 9.2 Trends in Balance of Trade, 1991–2012

Source: Author's calculations based on RBI (2012).

agricultural and mineral products declined steadily from nearly a quarter of India's merchandise exports to just 15 per cent over 1995–2012. However, the declining share of India's manufactured exports is a matter of concern, with manufactures steadily decreasing from a peak of 77 per cent of merchandise exports in 2000–1 to 60 per cent in 2012. However, this decline can be seen as a statistical artifact due to the emergence of India as a petroleum refining hub. Exports of refined petroleum products rose from virtually nothing in 1995–6 to 18 per cent of India's exports by 2012. If refined petroleum products are considered as value added products like other manufactured and processed products, then the share of manufactured goods in exports will be nearly 78 per cent in 2011–12, which is roughly at the level of 2000–1.

There is also a slight reorganization of exports of manufactured products as the share of conventional products like textiles and clothing has come down from 25 per cent to just 9 per cent since 1995–6 while leather products declined to 2 per cent, which is only a third of what it was in 1995–6. Gems and jewellery also lost its importance slightly from a 17 per cent share to 15 per cent. At the same time, the share of engineering goods

Table 9.2 Structure of India's Exports from 1995 to 2012

Commodity / Year	1995–6	Share (%)	2000–1	Share (%)	2005–6	Share (%)	2008–9	Share (%)	2011–12	Share (%)
I. Primary Products	7,257	23	7,126	16	16,377	16	25,335	14	45,574	15
Agriculture and Allied Products	6,082	19	5,973	13	10,214	10	17,535	10	37,421	12
Ores and Minerals	1,175	4	1,153	3	6,164	6	7,801	4	8,153	3
II. Manufactured Goods	23,747	75	34,335	77	72,563	70	123,149	67	186,784	60
Leather and Manufactures	1,752	6	1,944	4	2,698	3	3,556	2	4,789	2
Chemicals and Related Products	3,597	11	5,886	13	14,770	14	22,708	12	37,191	12
Engineering Goods	4,391	14	6,819	15	21,719	21	47,286	26	67,093	22
Textile and Textile Products	8,032	25	11,285	25	16,402	16	20,016	11	27,998	9
Gems and Jewellery	5,275	17	7,384	17	15,529	15	27,955	15	46,901	15
Handicrafts (Excluding Handmade Carpets)	434	1	662	1	462	0	301	0	234	0
Other Manufactured Goods	267	1	356	1	984	1	1,327	1	2,580	1
III. Petroleum Products	454	1	1,870	4	11,640	11	27,547	15	55,604	18
IV. Others	337	1	1,229	3	2,511	2	6,768	4	16,662	5
Total Exports (million US$)	31,795	100	44,560	100	103,091	100	182,800	100	309,624	100

Source: Extracted from RBI (2012). Available at: www.rbi.org.in (last accessed in September 2012).

rose steadily from 14 per cent to 22 per cent of all merchandise exports. Among engineering goods, exports of transport equipment rose very fast from less than a billion dollars in 1995 to nearly US$ 21 billion in 2011–12.

Besides exporting vehicles and two wheelers, India has emerged as a competitive exporter of auto parts and a number of procurement groups of auto companies such as Delphi Systems (for General Motors) and Visteon (of Ford) have set up procurement subsidiaries in India. This emergence owes itself to a particular strategic intervention by the government in the form of an erstwhile performance requirement that required foreign-owned companies to balance imports by foreign exchange earnings (Kumar 2005a). Machinery and equipment has been another category that has risen in importance.

Chemicals and related products is another group of manufactured products that has improved its share in total merchandise exports even if only marginally from 11 to 12 per cent. But among chemicals and allied products, the chemicals and pharmaceuticals group gained the most. This is due to India's emergence as a major exporter of generic medicines in the world, accounting for a third of global pharmaceuticals exports by volume. A major supplier of cost effective generics to developing countries and multilateral organizations like the World Health Organization (WHO) for their healthcare programmes in developing countries, India is sometimes referred to as the pharmacy of the developing world. That success owes itself to another strategic intervention by the government in terms of adopting a patent law abolishing product patents for pharmaceuticals in 1970, which encouraged development of generics by Indian companies (Kumar 2003).

It is clear that over time India's export structure has moved from the export of primary and conventional products, such as textiles and clothing, leather products and gems and jewellery towards products with greater value added, such as transport equipment, generic pharmaceuticals, and refined petroleum products. However, the share of technology-intensive products in India's exports is still very low compared to that of East Asian countries. Recent figures suggest that the share of high-technology exports in India's export basket was only 7.2 per cent compared to 26.2 per cent for East Asian countries (UN-ESCAP SSWA 2012). India has also not been able to make a mark in fast-growing high value added segments of manufacturing, such as electronic and telecom equipment (Kumar and Joseph 2007). In fact growing imports of electronic equipment and other hardware are straining India's trade balance, as observed later. India has also not been able to exploit the job-creating potential of exports and has been unable to develop highly labour-intensive export-oriented industries such as toys and electronic assembly, among others (RIS 2006).

India's import structure has also changed over the years, as summarized in Table 9.3. Firstly, imports comprising crude oil, raw materials, and certain foods accounted for as much as 44 per cent of total merchandise imports in 2011–12 compared to 39 per cent in 1995–6. In particular, the share of petroleum, crude and products rose rapidly from 21 per cent to 32 per cent over the same period. While consumption of petroleum and crude rose in the country with growth in volumes, a part of the increase was also due to rising fuel prices over the past decade. Considering that the demand for bulk imports that are mainly raw materials and foods is relatively price inelastic, in the context of rising trade deficit, one needs to pay attention to rising imports of capital goods and others even though their overall share in total imports may have come down. Among capital goods, major categories included machinery, except electrical accounting, for US$ 30 billion, electronic goods worth US$ 33 billion, transport equipment for US$ 14 billion, and project imports for US$ 8.7 billion in 2011–12. In particular, imports of electronic goods are expected to rise to US$ 400 billion by 2020 at current trends.[1]

The demise of India's fledgling electronic hardware industry can partly be explained in terms of India's premature signing of the WTO's Information Technology Agreement, 2000. It exposed Indian manufacturers to direct competition with established rivals in East Asian countries that have massive scales of production due to their links with multinational supply chains. It is in these categories of imports that an attempt needs to be made to pursue strategic import substitution to leverage sizeable domestic markets to develop domestic supply capabilities that will also generate value added and jobs while helping to moderate the trade deficit (Aggarwal and Kumar 2012). Gold (other than non-bulk) is yet another item imports of which are growing and were of the order of US$ 66 billion in 2011–12. While a part of the gold feeds into gems and jewellery exports, a large part is for domestic consumption and investment by households. Expansion of well-rated exchange traded funds (ETFs) might help in curbing demand by households especially for investment purposes.

[1] http://www.thehindubusinessline.com/industry-and-economy/electronic-goods-import-up-30-to-rs-157-lakh-cr-in-201112/article4512418.ece?homepage=true&ref=wl_home (last accessed on 20 September 2012).

Table 9.3 Structure of India's Imports from 1995 to 2012

Commodity / Year	1995–6	Share (%)	2000–1	Share (%)	2005–6	Share (%)	2008–9	Share (%)	2011–12	Share (%)
I. Bulk Imports	14,314	39	20,816	41	61,086	41	138,791	46	214,755	44
Petroleum, Crude and Products	7,526	21	15,650	31	43,963	29	93,672	31	154,906	32
Bulk Consumption Goods	970	3	1,443	3	2,767	2	4,975	2	11,614	2
Other Bulk Items	5,819	16	3,722	7	14,356	10	40,144	13	48,234	10
II. Non-Bulk Imports	22,361	61	29,721	59	88,080	59	160,043	54	274,663	56
Capital Goods	10,330	28	8,941	18	37,666	25	71,833	24	99,365	20
Mainly Export-related Items	5,257	14	8,059	16	18,641	12	31,931	11	54,479	11
Others	6,773	18	12,721	25	31,772	21	56,279	19	120,819	25
Total Imports (million US$)	36,675	100	50,537	100	149,166	100	298,834	100	489,417	100

Source: Extracted from RBI (2012). Available at: www.rbi.org.in (last accessed in September 2012).

Changing Geography of Trade

A major transformation has taken place in the direction of India's trade in terms of declining dependence on conventional trade partners like the European Union and the United States and diversification of trade in new and emerging markets. As Table 9.4 shows, EU's share in India's trade in 2010 was less than half of what it was in 1990. Similarly North America's share came down from 14 per cent to just 8.3 per cent over the same period. Japan's share in India's trade is now only a fourth of what it was in 1990. The trade structure is gradually diversifying in favour of emerging countries in the Asia-Pacific region and beyond. The most impressive rise is that of China from a negligible share in 1990 to over 10 per cent of India's trade by 2010, making China India's single largest trade partner.

ASEAN's share in India's trade also went up from 5.7 per cent to nearly 10 per cent in 2009 before declining marginally to 9.2 per cent in 2010. This explains the rising share of ASEAN+6 countries in India's trade from 17.70 to 26.6 per cent between 1990 and 2010. These include China, Japan, Republic of Korea, Australia, and New Zealand that are India's partners in the East Asia Summit formed in 2005. The shift in the geography of India's trade from the advanced economies of the west to East Asian economies did not happen automatically but was a result of a conscious and well thought out strategic policy pursued since 1992 called the Look East Policy, which is examined later in the chapter. Another region that is rising in prominence as a trade partner is the Middle East with a share in India's trade nearly doubling between 1990 and 2010 to 18.9 per cent, mainly on account of India's high dependence on the region for fuels. But trade with the Middle East is also increasing because of India's growing exports of manufactures, sometimes trans-shipped through the region to other countries like Pakistan. Shares of Africa and Latin America and the Caribbean have also risen very fast from rather low bases.

Decomposing Sources of Growth of India's Exports

A country's exports grow due to a growth of global markets in the products it exports (growth effect), due to improved competitiveness of its exports (competitiveness effect), due to diversification into new markets (markets effect), or due to diversification into new products (products effect). The constant market share (CMS) analysis is a technique applied to decompose the possible role of these factors in explaining countries' export growth

Table 9.4 Changing Direction of India's Trade, 1990–2010

	Percentage share in	1990	1995	2000	2005	2009	2010
North America	Imports	12.66	10.79	7.17	7.02	7.66	6.33
	Exports	16.14	18.49	23.25	18.21	12.07	11.50
	Trade	14.14	14.41	14.54	11.64	9.38	8.34
European Union	Imports	33.67	26.91	21.32	17.39	14.34	12.10
	Exports	28.87	27.62	24.38	22.43	21.14	18.64
	Trade	31.62	27.24	22.72	19.47	17.00	14.64
ASEAN	Imports	6.77	7.20	8.70	7.46	9.29	8.46
	Exports	4.27	7.77	6.45	10.10	10.51	10.32
	Trade	5.70	7.47	7.67	8.55	9.77	9.19
South Korea	Imports	1.36	2.08	1.96	3.07	3.05	2.83
	Exports	0.92	1.29	1.07	1.66	2.26	1.63
	Trade	1.17	1.71	1.56	2.49	2.74	2.37
Japan	Imports	7.51	6.48	4.00	2.76	2.48	2.36
	Exports	9.30	6.98	4.15	2.44	1.93	2.16
	Trade	8.27	6.71	4.07	2.62	2.26	2.28
China	Imports	0.13	2.35	2.88	7.10	11.19	11.78
	Exports	0.10	0.93	1.78	6.59	6.15	7.86
	Trade	0.12	1.68	2.37	6.89	9.22	10.26
Australia	Imports	3.15	2.74	2.12	3.34	4.17	3.44
	Exports	1.03	1.15	0.95	0.81	0.80	0.74
	Trade	2.25	1.99	1.58	2.29	2.85	2.39

(contd.)

Table 9.4 (*contd.*)

	Percentage share in	1990	1995	2000	2005	2009	2010
ASEAN+6 subtotal	Imports	19.17	21.03	19.84	23.86	30.35	29.07
	Exports	15.73	18.30	14.55	21.73	21.79	22.80
	Trade	17.70	19.75	17.41	22.98	27.01	26.63
SAARC	Imports	0.46	0.60	0.94	0.94	0.59	0.59
	Exports	3.06	5.11	4.28	5.41	4.52	5.00
	Trade	1.57	2.72	2.47	2.78	2.13	2.30
Middle East	Imports	13.02	18.10	6.43	5.45	17.37	20.20
	Exports	4.99	6.72	8.75	11.49	16.30	16.85
	Trade	9.60	12.76	7.50	7.94	16.95	18.90
Africa	Imports	2.80	4.57	6.07	3.18	7.33	8.36
	Exports	1.84	4.38	4.50	5.97	6.79	7.10
	Trade	2.39	4.48	5.35	4.33	7.12	7.87
Latin America & Caribbean	Imports	2.12	1.48	1.53	1.80	3.34	3.88
	Exports	0.43	1.14	2.16	2.83	2.96	4.15
	Trade	1.40	1.32	1.82	2.22	3.19	3.98
World	Imports (million US$)	23,991	34,489	50,336	139,888	257,665	350,783
	Exports in (million US$)	17813	30539	42627	98212	165186	222926
	Total trade (million US$)	41,804	65,028	92,964	238,100	422,851	573,709

Source: Extracted from IMF (2012).

(Tyszynski 1951; in India's context see Tiwari (1986)). In what follows we examine the results of an exercise done to analyse the factors contributing to India's export growth over 2000–10. The exports were grouped into ten 1-digit SITC (Standard International Trade Classification) categories and the time series was divided into two 5-year averages to suppress random yearly fluctuations. Exports to major markets, the EU, the USA, Japan, East Asia, ASEAN, China, SAARC, Africa, Central and South America, and the Caribbean, that absorb 80 per cent of India's exports, are analysed using UNCTAD data.

Table 9.5 summarizes the decomposition of different effects in the CMS analysis. The most important contributor to exports growth was the growth effect explaining 44 per cent of export growth indicating the fact India was able to benefit from the expansion of world trade over the past decade. The next most important effect accounting for 37 per cent of export growth was increased competitiveness in the products that it has been exporting. The contribution of products diversification and markets diversification is positive but is relatively modest. Therefore, the potential for the diversification of the export structure and of geography remains to be fully exploited. Although East Asia's share in India's trade improved, it was more in terms of imports than in exports. Similarly, although the product structure has changed, the share of conventional products like agricultural and mineral raw materials and textiles and clothing continues to be quite significant, as observed earlier. Furthermore, India has not been able to move up the value chain in the export of conventional products—whether it is export of iron ore, tea or textiles and clothing. One exception includes Tata Tea that acquired the Tetley brand in the UK and integrated its operations to control the entire value chain in-house (see Kumar 2008).

Table 9.5 Sources of India's Export Growth, 2000–10

	Size of the effect in million US$	Percentage share
Growth effect	56,700	44.30
Competitiveness effect	47,600	37.19
Product effect	13,200	10.31
Market effect	10,500	8.20
Total change	128,000	100.00

Source: ESCAP calculations based on UNCTAD statistics. See UN-ESCAP-SSWA (2012).

Services in India's Trade

The emergence of the services sector as the most dynamic sector driving India's growth has been accompanied by its growing importance in trade. The share of trade in services in India's GDP quadrupled from 3.3 to 14.3 per cent between 1990–2010. Table 9.6 shows that unlike in goods trade, the growth rate of services exports was higher than that for imports. There has been a striking transformation of India as a net exporter of services from being a net importer at the beginning of the decade. Exports of US$ 137 billion worth of services in 2011 left a surplus of US$ 12.5 billion after imports. Growth of trade in services in India was also faster than in other countries, tripling India's share in global services trade. The transformation of India's services trade has attracted attention in a number of studies (see Chanda 2002, Gordon and Gupta 2004, Verma 2008, and Raychaoudhuri and De 2012).

Table 9.6 Services Trade Balance

	2001	2011	Average Annual Growth Rate (2001–11) (%)
Exports (in million US$)	17,337	137,149	23
Share in global exports (%)	1.14	3.23	
Imports (in million US$)	20,099	124,566	20
Share in global imports (%)	1.31	3.05	
Balance of services trade	−2,762	12,583	

Source: Based on UNCTAD, Online database, www.unctad.org (accessed on 12 September 2012).

To understand the dynamism of services trade, Table 9.7 shows the sectoral composition of exports of commercial services. A bulk of India's commercial services exports comprise those of computers, communications, and other related services (or ICT services), which increased from 62.8 to 71.5 per cent over 2000–11 while commercial services exports of the country expanded from US$ 17 billion to US$ 137 billion. This primarily owes to the emergence of India as a hub for software development and other IT-enabled services, also referred to as business process outsourcing services (BPO). In these services India is recognized as the global leader. In the Global Services Location Index by AT Kearney, a global consultancy organization, India was ranked first globally in 2011 (Table 9.8), a position it has consistently retained since the inception of the index in 2004. Among its strength in the sector are people skills and their abundance given the large youthful workforce in the country. India's success in IT services has been attributed to, among other factors, a farsighted government policy to spot emerging opportunities and create high-end education and training facilities and computing infrastructure way back in the late-1970s (Kumar 2001). In future, this strength in ICT services needs to be leveraged to build a strong electronic goods industry.

Table 9.7 Structure of Service Exports (Percentage)

	2001	2011
Transport	12	11
Travel	19	11
Communications, computer and other services	65	71*
Insurance, financial and other business services	4	6

Source: Based on UNCTAD (2012).
Note: * relates to 2010.

Table 9.8 Ranks of Asian Countries in Global Services Location Index

Country	2004	2005	2007	2011
India	1	1	1	1
China	2	2	2	2
Malaysia	3	3	3	3
Indonesia	–	13	6	5
Thailand	13	6	4	7
Vietnam	20	26	19	8
Sri Lanka	–	–	29	21
Pakistan	–	–	30	28
Singapore	5	5	11	32
Turkey	–	–	–	48

Source: Based on atkearney.com (last accessed on 17 September 2012).

Current Account Balance

India faced a major balance of payments crisis in 1991 when its current account deficit crossed 3 per cent of GDP and the government had to mortgage its gold reserves to borrow foreign exchange to stave off a liquidity crisis. However, subsequent reforms and structural adjustment led to a major turnaround of the external sector with India running current account surpluses during the 2001–2 to 2003–4 period. But since 2004–5 the current account situation has again turned adverse with widening deficits.

Despite significant surpluses in services trade, current account deficits have been widening due to a steadily worsening merchandise trade deficit. As Table 9.9 shows, India's merchandise trade deficit widened steadily from 2.1 per cent of GDP in 2002–3 to 10.2 per cent in 2011–12, an unprecedented level in India's post-Independence history. One of the reasons for this widening was the faster growth rate of imports compared to that of exports, especially during 2002–3 to 2008–9 as is evident from Figure 9.3. Rising import intensity of Indian economy in this period, besides trade liberalization, could be because of an appreciating exchange rate during the period as the rupee-dollar exchange rate touched a new high of Rs 38 to a dollar in 2008. In terms of the real effective exchange rate, the rupee appreciated by 8.6 per cent over 2004–5 to 2007–8 as is evident from Table 9.10. By making imports cheaper in relative terms, this trend of appreciation pushed Indian corporations to outsource manufacturing of a number of their products to cheaper locations, such as China in addition to eroding the competitiveness of India's exports.

Even though the current account deficit crossed the 3 per cent threshold in 2011–12 for the first time since 1991, the key difference in 2012 was that India had sizeable foreign exchange reserves. However, there serves in terms of months of import coverage have steadily come down from 16 months in 2003–4 to seven months by 2011–12. This situation warrants immediate attention as it will not take much time for the import coverage offered by India's reserves to deplete further, especially in view of the rate at which imports are rising. Another disturbing trend is that the reserves are primarily made up of highly volatile short-term capital flows.

FII Inflows and Exchange Rate Instability

What explains the appreciation of the rupee despite the fact that India has been running a trade and current account deficit for so long? The

Table 9.9 Current Account Balance Indicators, 2000–12

Year	Trade			Invisibles			Current Account		
	Exports/ GDP	Imports/ GDP	Trade Balance/ GDP	Payments/ GDP	Receipts/ GDP	Net/GDP	CAD/GDP	Foreign Investment/ GDP	Import Cover of Reserves (in months)
2000–1	9.9	12.6	–2.7	4.9	7.0	2.1	–0.6	1.5	8.8
2001–2	9.4	11.8	–2.4	4.6	7.7	3.1	0.7	1.7	11.5
2002–3	10.6	12.7	–2.1	4.9	8.3	3.4	1.2	1.2	14.2
2003–4	11.0	13.3	–2.3	4.3	8.9	4.6	2.3	2.6	16.9
2004–5	12.1	16.9	–4.8	5.5	9.9	4.4	–0.4	2.2	14.3
2005–6	13.0	19.4	–6.4	5.9	11.1	5.2	–1.2	2.6	11.6
2006–7	13.6	20.1	–6.5	6.6	12.1	5.5	–1.0	3.1	12.5
2007–8	13.4	20.8	–7.4	5.9	12.0	6.1	–1.3	5.0	14.4
2008–9	15.4	25.2	–9.8	6.2	13.7	7.5	–2.3	2.3	9.8
2009–10	13.4	22.1	–8.7	6.1	12.0	5.9	–2.8	4.8	11.1
2010–11	14.9	22.6	–7.7	6.7	11.8	5.0	–2.7	3.4	9.6
2011–12	16.8	27.0	–10.2	5.8	11.9	6.0	–4.2	2.7	7.1

Source: Extracted from RBI (2012). Available online at www.rbi.org.in (last accessed in September 2012).

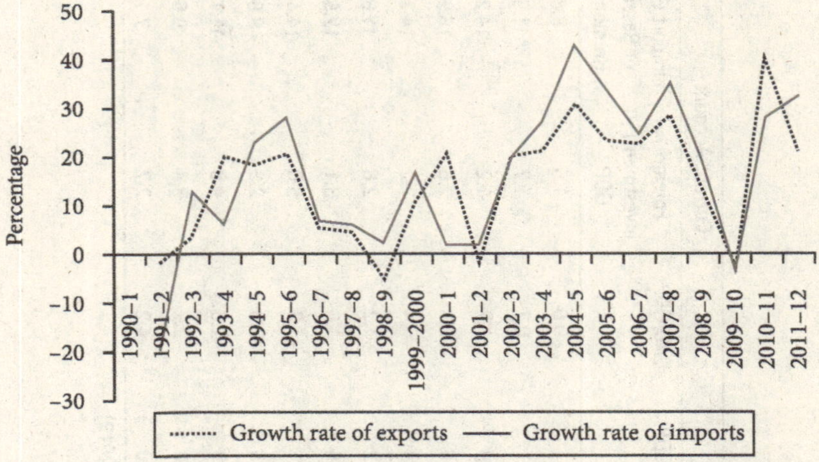

FIGURE 9.3 Growth Rates of Exports and Imports, 1991–2012
Source: Based on data from RBI (2012).

rapid rise in inflows of portfolio investments in India since 2003–4 is summarized in Table 9.11. Large magnitudes of portfolio investments in the form of short-term equity investments by foreign institutional investors (FII) flowed in as the Indian economy gathered momentum and capital markets started giving attractive returns. The annual net inflows, however, are highly volatile.

FII inflows rose to a sizeable US$ 27 billion in 2007–8 that led to not only stock prices booming, with the BSE Sensex more than doubling from under 10,000 to 20,000, but also the rupee exchange rate appreciating sharply from 47 rupees in 2006 to 38 rupees to a US dollar in 2008. In 2008–9, in the wake of the global financial crisis, there was a net outflow of FIIs to the tune of US$ 14 billion dollars that brought down the BSE Sensex from nearly 20,000 points to less than 9,000 points in the early part of 2009. Much more importantly it led to a sharp depreciation of the rupee by nearly 25 per cent in early 2009. The depreciation would have been greater if the Reserve Bank of India had not intervened in the market by selling dollars. This depleted the RBI's foreign exchange reserves by US$ 58 billion to about US$ 252 billion from US$ 310 billion from 2007–8 to 2008–9. However, as FIIs returned rapidly to the market with the onset of recovery and FII inflows to the country in 2010 were of the order of US$ 32 billion bringing the Sensex back above 20,000 points in October 2010. Despite the RBI's market intervention to offset the subsequent exchange

Table 9.10 Indices of Real Effective Exchange Rate (REER) of the Indian Rupee (36-Currency Bilateral Weights) (Financial Year-Annual Average)

Year	REER	
	Export-based Weights	Trade-based Weights
(Base:1993-4 = 100)		
1997-8	103.07	100.77
1998-9	94.34	93.04
1999-2000	95.28	95.99
2000-1	98.67	100.09
2001-2	98.59	100.86
2002-3	95.99	98.18
2003-4	99.07	99.56
2004-5	98.30	100.09
(Base: 2004-5 = 100)		
2005-6	102.74	103.10
2006-7	101.05	101.29
2007-8	108.57	108.52
2008-9	97.77	97.80
2009-10	95.26	94.73
2010-11	103.52	102.34
2011-12	100.68	99.15

Source: Extracted from RBI (2012).

rate pressure, the rupee appreciated by nearly 8 per cent although foreign exchange reserves were augmented to about US$ 284 billion. FII inflows have become primary determinants of movements in stock exchange indices and the exchange rate of the rupee (see Kumar 2011). As there are sharp movements in these inflows linked to global developments, they become channels of transmission of instability to the country's financial system. As a result, the rupee has been on a roller coaster ride: from Rs 44 per dollar in January 2007 to Rs 39 in January 2008 to an increase again to Rs 49 per dollar in January 2009 to Rs 44 in October 2010. The rupee fluctuating around Rs 54 in 2012 as FIIs showed lukewarm response to Indian capital markets.

Besides the volatility, FII inflows have a very high servicing burden. Among foreign resources such as FDI, foreign borrowings, non-resident

Indian (NRI) deposits, American Depositary Receipts (ADRs), global depositary receipts (GDRs), FII investments are the most expensive in terms of servicing burden (Kumar 2011). This is because they come to chase primarily good returns at the stock markets and exchange rate speculation. In 2007–8, the Indian stock markets were giving around 44 per cent return. This meant that for every dollar India received in FII flows, it became liable to pay US$ 1.44 in one year. As FIIs are stock price makers rather than takers, they manage to exit safely before major crashes of markets thereby precipitating declines.

One may argue that FII inflows help a country to build foreign exchange reserves. What is not appreciated very well is the fact that exposure to these inflows also enhances the need to have large foreign exchange reserves due to their highly volatile nature. Therefore, developing countries, such as India should rely for their foreign resource needs more on FDI inflows and where possible raise ADRs/GDRs and deposits from NRIs rather than relying on FIIs. In view of their high cost and their other deleterious effects, such as volatility, a number of emerging economies such as Brazil, South Korea, and Indonesia recently imposed capital controls to moderate their volatility. The unprecedented injection of liquidity by the governments in developed countries in the wake of the global financial crisis is likely to find its way to emerging economies of Asia like India to take advantage of higher returns. There is now a growing consensus on the relevance of capital controls as aspects of the policy tool kit for the governments in emerging economies (Ostry et al. 2010 and UN-ESCAP 2010). The benefits of maintaining open capital accounts, if any, are ambiguous.

Addressing BOP Stresses

Rising current account deficits pose an important challenge for policy-makers and need urgent attention. With widening merchandise trade deficits driving this trend, immediate attention needs to be paid to reviving export growth and exploiting the opportunities for import substitution. For reviving exports, whose growth rate in 2012 was negative, attention needs to be paid to strengthening their competitiveness by addressing exchange rate distortions. For an economy facing growing current account deficits, exchange rate appreciation can aggravate the situation further. Therefore, it is important to restrain volatile short-term capital flows. Export competitiveness needs to be strengthened by maintaining relative exchange rate stability with a slight tendency towards depreciation rather than appreciation. Besides that, policy distortions, such as inverted duty structures need to be removed and flow of trade finance needs to be strengthened (see Kumar and Joseph 2007 for an inventory of policy support measures).

In a situation of slowdown of the global economy as at present, a major expansion of exports can be challenging given an environment of excess capacities throughout the Asia-Pacific region, the growing threat of protectionism, and the temptation of dumping by those with deep pockets. In such circumstances, it might also be critical to look at new opportunities for strategic import substitution. As observed earlier, while large bulk imports of fuels and raw materials may be price inelastic, attention should be paid to very large and fast growing imports of electronics, non-electrical machinery, and defence equipment, among others that provide opportunities for strategic import substitution. An effort needs to be made to start domestic manufacture of these products leveraging India's large domestic market size and by targeting MNEs to set up local manufacturing facilities through creating incentives for pioneering industries, as has been done in East Asian countries like Malaysia, besides incentives in public procurement like 'buy America' programmes. These policies are part of industrial policies and infant industry protection that have been widely practiced in different developed and emerging economies (Kumar and Gallagher 2007). Strategic import substitution will also lead to a more balanced structural change by creating more manufacturing jobs (see Aggarwal and Kumar 2012). An ESCAP study analysing opportunities for building productive capacities in South and South West Asia using product space maps also found opportunities for strategic import substitution in India (Freire 2012).

Foreign Direct Investment Flows and their Quality

Besides the liberalization of trade, 1991 was also the time for substantial liberalization of the FDI policy regime for both inward as well as outward FDI. The key features of the FDI policy regime of India include up to 100 per cent foreign ownership in most sectors except those due to sensitivities

Table 9.11 FDI and Foreign Portfolio Investment Flows to India

Year	Gross Inflows/ Gross Invest-ments	Direct Invest-ment to India	FDI by India	Net Foreign Direct Invest-ment	Net Portfolio Invest-ment	Total (in million US$)
2000–1	4,029	4,029	759	3,270	2,590	5,860
2001–2	6,130	6,125	1,391	4,734	1,952	6,686
2002–3	5,035	4,976	1,819	3,157	944	4,101
2003–4	4,322	4,322	1,934	2,388	11,377	13,765
2004–5	6,051	5,986	2,274	3,712	9,291	13,003
2005–6	8,961	8,900	5,867	3,033	12,492	15,525
2006–7	22,826	22,739	15,046	7,693	6,947	14,640
2007–8	34,843	34,727	18,836	15,891	27,434	43,325
2008–9	41,873	41,707	19,364	22,343	-14,032	8,311
2009–10	37,745	33,108	15,143	17,965	32,396	50,361
2010–11	34,847	27,829	16,524	11,305	30,292	41,597
2011–12	46,553	32,955	10,950	22,006	17,171	39,177

Source: Extracted from RBI (2012).

and security concerns, such as arms and ammunition. Sectoral caps also apply to services sectors, and to the full repatriation of capital and remittances of profits, dividends, technical fees, and royalties.

FDI inflows to India have been growing since 1991 but the big break came in 2006 when annual inflows to the country nearly tripled in one year from US$ 7.6 billion to US$ 20 billion and increased from that level peaking to US$ 43 billion in 2008 before declining to US$ 24 billion in 2010 in the wake of the global financial crisis but recovering to US$ 31.5 billion in 2011. India's share in global FDI inflows nearly doubled over 2005–6 and again between 2006–9 before declining slightly (Table 9.12; Figure 9.4a). The relative importance of the flows in relation to gross fixed investment, also rose from 2.9 per cent in 2005 to 6.6 per cent in 2006. FDI's share in gross fixed investments in India has been lower than that for other developing countries but is catching up. In 2008 when FDI inflows peaked in India, this ratio at 10.1 per cent was quite close to that for developing Asia at 10.4 per cent. Afterwards it declined in the wake of the financial crisis indicating the potential for a rise in the future (Figure 9.4b).

Table 9.12 Inward Foreign Direct Investment Flows, Annual, 2001–11

(million US$) Inward FDI flows, annual 2001–11, million US$

Year	World	Developing Economies	Developing Asia	India	Share of India in Developing Asia	Share of India in Developing World	Share of India in World
2001	827,617	216,865	115,968	5,478	4.72	2.53	0.66
2002	627,975	173,283	100,083	5,630	5.62	3.25	0.9
2003	586,956	190,125	123,707	4,321	3.49	2.27	0.74
2004	744,329	291,866	177,983	5,778	3.25	1.98	0.78
2005	980,727	327,248	218,420	7,622	3.49	2.33	0.78
2006	1,463,351	427,163	290,907	20,328	6.99	4.76	1.39
2007	1,975,537	574,311	349,412	25,506	7.3	4.44	1.29
2008	1,790,706	650,017	380,360	43,406	11.41	6.68	2.42
2009	1,197,824	519,225	315,238	35,596	11.29	6.86	2.97
2010	1,309,001	616,661	384,063	24,159	6.29	3.92	1.85
2011	1,524,422	684,399	423,157	31,554	7.46	4.61	2.07

FDI Inflows as a Percentage of Gross Fixed Capital Formation

	2001	2002	2003	2004	2005	2006	2007	2008	2009	2010
India	4.7	4.6	2.8	2.7	2.9	6.6	6.2	10.1	8.1	4.5
World	12.2	9.1	7.6	8.3	9.9	13.3	15.7	12.9	9.5	9.5
Developing Economies	13.5	10.2	9.8	12.4	11.8	12.9	14.1	13.2	10.1	10.1
Developing Asia	10.3	8.0	8.4	9.9	10.4	11.7	11.5	10.4	7.9	8.0
South Asia	4.5	4.7	3.0	3.1	3.7	7.3	6.9	10.3	7.8	4.6

Source: Extracted from the UNCTAD (2012).

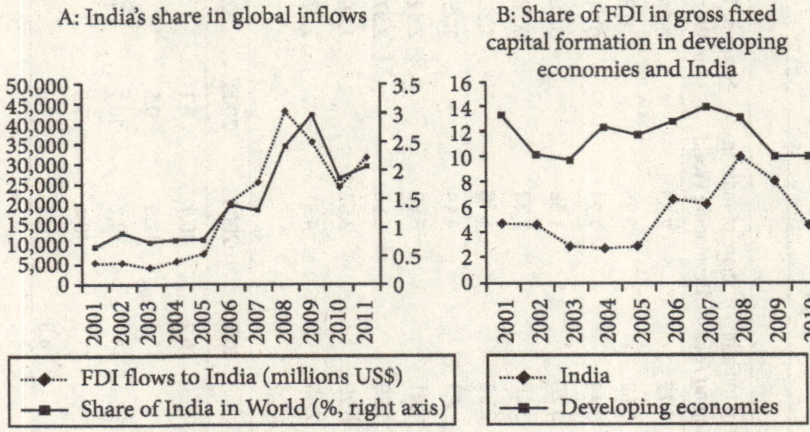

FIGURE 9.4 India's Attractiveness as a Destination of FDI Inflows

Source: Author's calculations based on Table 9.12.

The recent rise in FDI inflows since 2006 (Table 9.12) reflects an improving investment climate in India with the acceleration in the growth rate since 2003, the rise of a sizeable middle class with purchasing power, and with the recognition of India's comparative advantage in knowledge-based industries. This is not only evident from the rising magnitudes of FDI inflows but also from investor surveys conducted by global consultancy organizations. In the FDI Confidence Index published by AT Kearney, a global consultancy organization, covering 25 top destinations for FDI, India moved up from sixth place in 2003 to second place in 2005 and stayed there before swapping the third rank with the United States in 2010. In 2012, it again regained the second position in the global rankings (AT Kearney 2012). Similar upgrading in India's ranks has been reported by surveys of investors conducted by the Japanese Bank of International Cooperation (JBIC) as well as in UNCTAD's *World Prospects Survey 2012–14*, where India was ranked as the third most preferred FDI location (UNCTAD 2012). Recent reforms adopted by the country to allow FDI in multi-brand retail and civil aviation are also likely to help in realizing its potential for FDI inflows. This is in sharp contrast to the World Bank's studies on *Ease of Doing Business* based on perception surveys that tend to put India at a very poor rank of 132. It is clear therefore that foreign investors get attracted to a country by the potential of benefiting from its dynamism and are willing to put up with hardships rather than going to countries with easier business conditions but with poorer prospects of making profits. FDI inflows may also assist in a manufacturing oriented structural transformation of the economy and technological upgrading of exports that India needs by bringing technologies and other resources working together with local entrepreneurs.

Quality of FDI Inflows

There can be several indicators of the quality of FDI inflows (see Kumar 2002). In what follows, we discuss India's performance in terms of a few such indicators.

Sectoral Composition

One of the indicators of quality is the sectoral composition of FDI inflows. It matters whether FDI is going to the modern technology-intensive sectors and building productive capabilities or to conventional sectors crowding out domestic investments. In terms of the sectoral composition of FDI inflows, there has been a shift since 1991 in India's case. Earlier the bulk of FDI inflows were directed to manufacturing especially high technology industries through a selective policy. After liberalization, a substantial proportion of FDI inflows has been directed to services. Manufacturing accounted for only about 40 per cent of inflows in the post-1991 period with services accounting for about 35 per cent share. Further, among the manufacturing sub-sectors, FDI stock in post-1991 period is also more evenly distributed between food and beverages, transport equipment, metals and metal products, electricals and electronics, chemicals and allied products, and miscellaneous manufacturing. This stands in contrast to the situation prior to 1990 when there was a very heavy concentration in relatively technology-intensive sectors of machinery, chemicals, electricals, and transport equipment (Kumar 2005b).

In China, on the other hand, the bulk of FDI inflows have been directed by government policy to manufacturing (of the export-oriented type) and very little has gone to services (Yongding 2006). Of the FDI in manufacturing in China, 11 per cent went to electronics and telecommunication equipment helping it emerge as the leading producer and exporter of these products. A policy guiding FDI inflows to manufacturing helped in China's emergence as a global factory. Therefore, FDI inflows in China have been directed to assist in industrial development of the industry that has made China a global factory generating in the process billions of dollars of output and exports and millions of jobs.

Impact of FDI on Growth and Domestic Investment

FDI inflows could contribute to the growth rate of the host economy by augmenting its capital stock as well as with infusion of new technology. However, high growth rates may also attract more FDI inflows by enhancing the investment climate in the country. Therefore, the FDI-growth relationship is subject to causality bias given the possibility of a two-way relationship. What is the nature of the relationship in India? A study examined the direction of causation between FDI and growth empirically for a sample of 107 countries for the 1980s and 1990s. In India's case, the study found a Granger neutral relationship as the direction of causation was not pronounced (see Kumar and Pradhan 2005 for more details of the methodology and results).

It has also been shown that sometimes FDI projects may actually crowd-out or substitute domestic investments from product or capital markets with the market power of their well-known brand names and other resources and may thus be immiserizing (see Fry 1992 and Agosin and Mayer 2000, for evidence). Therefore, it is important to examine the impact of FDI on domestic investment to evaluate its impact on growth and welfare in the host economy. An earlier study to examine the effect of FDI on domestic investment in a dynamic setting, however, did not find a statistically significant effect of FDI on domestic investment in India's case (see Kumar and Pradhan 2005). It appears, therefore, that FDI inflows received by India have been of a mixed type combining some inflows crowding-in domestic investments while others crowding them out, with no predominant pattern emerging. In East Asian countries, such as South Korea and Thailand, the relationship clearly indicated FDI crowding-in domestic investments (Kumar and Pradhan 2005). Therefore, the quality of FDI in India with respect to its impact on growth and on domestic investments is of a mixed type and leaves scope for improvement.

Empirical studies on the nature of the relationship between FDI and domestic investments suggest that FDI's effect on domestic investment depends on the host government's policies. Governments have extensively employed selective policies and imposed various performance requirements, such as local content requirements (LCRs) to deepen the commitment of MNEs to the host economy. The Indian government has imposed a condition of phased manufacturing programmes (or local content requirements) in the auto industry to promote vertical inter-firm linkages and to encourage the development of the auto component industry (and crowding-in of domestic investments). A case study of the auto industry where such a policy was followed shows that these policies (in combination with other performance requirements of foreign exchange neutrality), have succeeded in building an internationally competitive vertically integrated auto sector in the country (see Kumar 2005a). The Indian experience in this industry, therefore, is in tune with the experiences of Thailand, Brazil, and Mexico as documented by Moran (1998).

FDI and Export-Platform Production

A number of developing countries have used FDI to exploit the resources of MNEs, such as globally recognized brand names, best practice technology or by increasing integration with their global production networks, among others, for expanding their manufactured exports. In this respect, China has had considerable success in exploiting the potential of FDI for export-oriented production. A very substantial (55 per cent) proportion of China's manufactured exports are undertaken by foreign invested enterprises, which account for as much as 80 per cent of all technology-intensive exports (UNCTAD 2005). Foreign enterprises while setting up export-oriented production bases had created 23 million jobs by 2003 making China a global factory. Export-oriented FDI also helps in bringing world's best practice technology as the affiliate has to compete globally right from the beginning. It also enhances the chances of FDI inflows crowding-in domestic investments and reducing the chances of crowding-out as the foreign affiliate will mainly cater to outside markets rather than eating into domestic firms' markets. It will also create fresh possibilities of market information spill overs for domestic firms on export possibilities.

Unlike East Asian countries, India has not been able to exploit the FDI potential for export-oriented production. The bulk of FDI inflows in India are market-seeking coming for tapping the domestic market with the share of foreign affiliates in exports being around 10 per cent. Therefore, the quality of FDI with respect to export-orientation is poorer compared to FDI received by East Asian countries. In this respect two observations can be made. The first is that recent studies of export-performance are beginning to indicate a relatively superior performance of foreign enterprises in terms of export orientation compared to early studies suggesting a poorer performance of foreign companies (see Kumar and Joseph 2007). Therefore, MNEs are beginning to exploit the potential of India as a base for export-oriented production.

The second observation is about the role of host country policies in exploiting the potential of FDI for export-oriented production. A quantitative study analysing the determinants of the patterns of export-orientation of MNE affiliates across 74 countries in seven branches of industry over three points of time shows that in host countries with large domestic markets, export-obligations were effective for promoting export-orientation of foreign affiliates to third countries (see Kumar 1998).

Export-obligations have also been employed fruitfully by many countries to prompt MNE affiliates to exploit the host country's potential for export platform production. For instance, in China which has succeeded in expanding manufactured exports with help from MNE affiliates, regulations stipulate that wholly owned foreign enterprises must undertake to export more than 50 per cent of their output (Rosen 1999: 63–71). As a result of these policies, the proportion of foreign enterprises in manufactured exports has steadily increased to over 55 per cent as observed earlier.

India has not imposed export obligations on MNE affiliates except for those entering products reserved for SMEs. However, indirect export obligations in the form of dividend balancing have been imposed for enterprises producing primarily consumer goods (since phased out in 2000). Under these policies, a foreign enterprise was obliged to earn the foreign exchange that it wished to remit abroad as dividend so that there was no adverse impact on the host country's balance of payments. Sometimes a condition of foreign exchange neutrality was imposed where the enterprise was required to earn enough foreign exchange to cover the outgo on account of imports. Therefore, these regulations have acted as indirect export obligations prompting foreign enterprises to export to earn the foreign exchange required by them. Available evidence suggests that such regulations have prompted foreign enterprises to undertake exports. In the case of the auto industry, in order to comply with their export commitments to comply with the foreign exchange neutrality condition, foreign auto majors have undertaken export of auto components from India which have not only opened new opportunities for Indian component manufacturers but in that process have also found profitable opportunities for business (Kumar 2005a). Hence, exports of auto components from India are now growing rapidly and exceeding the obligations several times over. These regulations have acted to remove the information asymmetry existing about the availability of quality components in India among foreign auto majors. In that respect India's experience is very similar to that of Thailand that has emerged as a major auto hub of South East Asia (as documented by Moran 1998 and Kumar 2005a).

R&D and Other Knowledge-Based Activities and Local Technological Capability

A comparison of R&D intensity of foreign firms in India and in other countries has not been possible due to lack of data. Within the country, foreign firms appear to be spending more on R&D activity in India than local firms although the gap between their R&D intensities has tended to narrow down. A study analysing the R&D activity of Indian manufacturing enterprises in the context of liberalization found that after controlling for extraneous factors, MNE affiliates revealed a lower R&D intensity compared to local firms, presumably on account of their captive access to laboratories in their parent and associated companies. The study also observed differences in the nature or motivation of R&D activity of foreign and local firms. Local firms seem to be directing their R&D activity towards absorption of imported knowledge and for providing a back-up to their outward expansion. MNE affiliates, on the other hand, focus on customization of their parents' technology for the local market (Kumar and Agarwal 2005).

An important issue is diffusion and absorption of technology brought by foreign firms in the host countries. Some governments, for example, Malaysia have imposed technology transfer requirements on foreign enterprises. However, such performance requirements do not appear to have been very successful in achieving their objectives (UNCTAD 2003). Instead, other performance requirements such as local content requirements or domestic equity requirements may be more effective in transfer of technology. As observed earlier, local content requirements and export performance requirements have prompted foreign enterprises to transfer and diffuse some knowledge to domestic enterprises in order to comply with their obligations. Similarly, domestic equity requirements may facilitate the quick absorption of the knowledge brought in by foreign enterprises which is an important pre-requisite of the local technological capability, as is evident from case studies of the Indian two-wheelers industry where Indian joint ventures with foreign firms were able to absorb knowledge brought in by the foreign partner and eventually become self-reliant not only to continue production but even to develop their own world class models for the domestic market and for exports on their own (see Kumar 2005a). Some have expressed the view that domestic equity requirements may adversely affect the extent or quality of technology transfer (Moran 2001). However, it has been shown that MNEs may not transfer key technologies even to their wholly owned subsidiaries abroad fearing the risk of dissipation or diffusion through mobility of employees. Furthermore, even if the content and quality of technology transfer is superior in the case of a sole venture than in the case of a joint venture, from the host country point of view, the latter may have more desirable externalities in terms of local learning and diffusion of the knowledge transferred.

India as An Emerging Source of FDI Outflows

Another important emerging trend with respect to FDI in India is its emergence as a significant source of FDI outflows. Like FDI inflows the major turnaround in outflows came in 2006 when outflows more than quadrupled in one year to US$ 14 billion and peaked to nearly US$ 20 billion in 2007 before declining to around US$ 15 billion in subsequent years in the wake of global financial crisis (Table 9.13). The big break came with Indian enterprises using their outward investments to acquire larger companies in the advanced economies as a part of their efforts to augment their bundles of strategic assets including known brand names, proprietary knowledge, and global marketing networks in order to jump start

Table 9.13 Foreign Direct Investment (FDI) Outflows Originating in India

(million US$)

Year	World	Developing Economies	Developing Economies: Asia	India
2001	747,657	83,087	49,155	1,397
2002	528,496	47,484	34,987	1,678
2003	570,679	46,668	23,961	1,876
2004	925,716	122,792	91,404	2,175
2005	888,561	132,507	86,425	2,985
2006	1,415,094	239,336	151,400	14,285
2007	2,198,025	316,863	228,154	19,594
2008	1,969,336	328,121	223,116	19,257
2009	1,175,108	268,476	210,925	15,927
2010	1,451,365	400,144	273,033	13,151
2011	1,694,396	383,754	280,478	14,752

Source: Extracted from UNCTAD (2012).

their global orientation. The past few years have seen several multibillion-dollar acquisitions of western firms by Indian companies including Tata Steel-Corrus, Tata Motors-Jaguar/Land Rover, and Handalco-Novelis.

A recent analysis of India's outward FDI flows shows that among the emerging markets, there lative scale of India's outward FDI was quite significant (Kumar 2008). The emergence of Indian enterprises on the global scene is striking considering their origin in a lower middle-income country. Their ability to acquire much larger enterprises in the developed world reflects their confidence in managing the newly acquired entities successfully. It has been argued that the source of their ownership or competitive advantage lies in their accumulation of skills for managing large multi-location operations across diverse cultures in India and in their ability to deliver value for money with their 'frugal engineering skills' honed up while catering to the larger part of the income pyramid in India. (Kumar 2008)

Considering that nearly all the Indian enterprises undertaking outward investments had their origins in import substitution-based industrialization strategies and a selective FDI policy regime, it would appear that a policy of infant industry protection with supportive institutional framework can assist in enterprise development by giving them access to the domestic market to grow and build capabilities (Kumar 2008). However, the protection needs to be phased out once the capabilities are built to expose the enterprises to international competition and sharpen their competitiveness. In fact the reforms of 1991 sparked a considerable restructuring of Indian industry which emerged from it leaner, more efficient, and competitive. The exposure also gave Indian firms global ambitions and also the confidence to pursue them. In some ways the Indian experience follows in the Japanese and Korean tradition of enterprise development policies and may have lessons for other developing countries.

The acquisition-based strategy of internationalization adopted by Indian enterprises in recent years by acquiring strategic assets such as technology, known brands, access to customers, and global footprints for jump starting their internationalization, is challenging as it involves managing across diverse cultures and winning over the confidence of the workforce to successfully exploit the synergies. Indian enterprises can face this challenge by relying on their experience and their skills in cross-cultural management honed in India, their emphasis on corporate social responsibility, and their sensitivities to workers' rights from the beginning (Kumar 2008).

Regional Economic Integration

India generally pursued multilateralism faithfully in its trade policy with very few exceptions till the end of the last century. However, it has begun to pay due respect to regionalism in its trade policy increasingly since the turn of the century following the emerging trend globally. Among the early schemes for regional cooperation, India has been a member of one of the earliest preferential trading arrangements in Asia and the Pacific—the Asia-Pacific Trade Agreement (APTA) earlier known as the Bangkok Agreement negotiated under the auspices of ESCAP in 1975. India has also been a member of the South Asian Association for Regional Cooperation (SAARC) formed in 1985 that adopted the SAARC Preferential Trading Agreement (SAPTA) in 1993 that eventually evolved in the SAARC Free Trade Agreement (SAFTA) in 2004, implemented in the decade from 2006. In 1998, India also signed a bilateral FTA with Sri Lanka that has been operational since 2000. India also has trade and transit agreements with Bhutan and Nepal that provide to them non-reciprocal free access to the Indian market.

Since 1992 in the wake of economic reforms, a new thrust was given to India's approach to regional cooperation as a part of what is called the Look East Policy. As a part of this policy, India became a sector dialogue partner of ASEAN. India was made a full dialogue partner by ASEAN in 1995 and was accorded a membership of the ASEAN Regional Forum in 1996. The ASEAN-India dialogue partnership was further upgraded to an annual summit level dialogue from 2002. Therefore, the India–ASEAN partnership saw a remarkable transformation from a sectoral dialogue partnership to a summit-level interaction within a decade (1992–2002). At their second summit in October 2003, ASEAN and India signed a Framework Agreement on Comprehensive Economic Cooperation (CEC) providing a free trade arrangement. At the Laos Summit in 2004, they signed a long-term Partnership for Peace, Progress and Shared Prosperity based on the work done by the think-tanks in ASEAN and India. CEC is usefully complemented by a Comprehensive Economic Cooperation Agreement (CECA) signed between India and Singapore in 2005. Since 2004, the early harvest scheme of the India–Thailand bilateral FTA has been operational. India has also signed a bilateral FTA with Malaysia and is negotiating one with Indonesia. The India–ASEAN FTA was also concluded in 2009 and negotiations are currently undergoing for a services agreement. The India–ASEAN partnership is also complemented by Mekong-Ganga Cooperation (MGC), and BIMSTEC (Bay of Bengal Initiative for Multi-sectoral Techno-Economic Cooperation) which combines seven South and South East Asian countries. India has been assisting the new ASEAN countries Cambodia, Laos, Myanmar, and Vietnam (CLMV) as a part of the ASEAN's Initiative for ASEAN Integration (IAI). India is assisting them, particularly with capacity-building by setting up centres for entrepreneurship development, ICT, and English language training, among other areas. High-level interactions between India and ASEAN countries have steadily grown in both the directions. In December 2012, India hosted an India-ASEAN Summit in New Delhi to commemorate the tenth anniversary of their summit level dialogue.

India's Look East Policy started with engagement with ASEAN but is not confined to it. As a part of it, India has also engaged East Asian countries like the Republic of Korea and Japan concluding Comprehensive Economic Partnership Agreements with both of them. Negotiations are on with Australia and New Zealand. India's engagement of ASEAN and the East Asian countries led to her inclusion in the East Asia Summit established in 2005 as an annual summit-level forum between ASEAN and its six dialogue partners (Kumar et al. 2008). In 2011 it was joined by the US and Russia. Within the framework of EAS, a Comprehensive Economic Partnership of East Asia (CEPEA) bringing together ASEAN and its six FTA partners into a single trade agreement was proposed and was accepted in principle in the 2009 Hua Hin Summit and four working groups were set up to take the negotiations forward. In 2011 at the Bali Summit, ASEAN proposed a framework on Regional Comprehensive Economic Partnership of East Asia (RCEP) with the six partners. RCEP was formally launched at ASEAN's Phnom Penh Summit in November 2012.

India has therefore become a key partner in the emerging broader regional trading arrangement RCEP. The latter would be the largest such arrangement in the world. Combining 16 of the fastest growing and largest economies of the Asia and the Pacific region, RCEP has the potential of becoming the third and more dynamic pillar of the world economy besides EU and NAFTA. In a new changed post-crisis international context where the advanced economies of the west will not be able to play their role as the engines of growth in view of compulsions of unwinding their huge debt accumulations, a rebalancing of external orientation in favour of regional economic integration is clearly important with the Asia-Pacific region emerging as the centre of gravity of the world economy (ESCAP 2012). In that respect the Indian Look East Policy of turning attention to East

Asia was farsighted. Hopefully business enterprises in the country will be able to take advantage of the preferential markets access made available through the emerging RTAs in some of the fastest growing markets of the world in the coming years to address the balance of trade concerns.

***

The reforms pursued since 1991 have led to much deeper integration of the Indian economy with the global economy in terms of rising share of merchandise trade and an even more dramatic transformation of services trade and India's emergence as one of the most attractive destinations for FDI, as well as an important source of FDI outflows. The trade structure has changed in terms of product composition and destinations. However, a quantitative analysis using the constant market share analysis suggests that much of the export growth benefited from expansion of world trade and enhanced competitiveness while potential of products diversification and markets diversification remains to be fully exploited. Diversification into technology-intensive higher value adding goods or labour-intensive goods could be helpful for sustaining growth of exports while also creating more industrial jobs.

Despite healthy trade surpluses earned by services as India emerged as a global hub for ICT outsourcing, the balance of payments situation has again entered into a period of stress due to a widening merchandise trade deficit. While India now has the comfort of sizeable foreign exchange reserves unlike in 1991, this is an important policy challenge which needs an immediate response before situation turns difficult. Export competitiveness needs to be strengthened through appropriate exchange rate management and opportunities for strategic import substitution need to be exploited by leveraging India's large domestic market size. This large domestic market has already led to growing and sizeable imports in several products like electronic goods, non-electrical machinery, and other equipment including defence equipments, among others. To exploit these opportunities a number of policy measures that are normally grouped as industrial policy including infant industry protection, pioneer industry incentives, public procurement preferences, and a special targeting of multinational enterprises to establish local manufacturing facilities, as employed extensively by the developed countries in the past and emerging countries in more recent times may be fruitful. Revival of manufacturing to substitute these lumpy imports will not only help in addressing the current account deficit but will also create jobs for skilled and unskilled workers helping in poverty reduction.

Finally, in the context of the dramatically changed international context in the aftermath of the global financial crisis, when advanced economies are not able to provide growth stimulus to Asian economies, a rebalancing of growth in favour of domestic and regional sources of demand is imperative. India has already moved towards integration with the East Asian economies with a number of bilateral and regional FTAs and is a part of the Regional Comprehensive Economic Partnership (RCEP) of East Asia that seeks to create a broader Asia-Pacific regional trade arrangement covering 16 of the region's largest and fastest growing economies. Indian industry should aggressively exploit export opportunities provided by preferential access to East Asian markets provided by these agreements rather than only using these FTAs to import duty free from the partners.

References

Aggarwal, Aradhna and Nagesh Kumar (2012), 'Structural change, industrialization and poverty reduction: The Case of India', ESCAP-SSWA Development Papers 1206. Available at: http://sswa.unescap.org/meeting/documents/Dev-Challenges/SSWA_Development_Papers_1206_October2012.pdf (last accessed on 27 September 2012).

Agosin, M.R., and Ricardo Mayer (2000), 'Foreign Investment in Developing Countries: Does it Crowd in Domestic Investment?' UNCTAD Discussion Paper No. 146, Geneva: UNCTAD.

AT Kearney (2012), FDI Confidence Index 2012. Available at: www.atkearney.com.

Chanda, Rupa (2002), *Globalization of Services: India's opportunities and constraints*. New Delhi: Oxford University Press.

ESCAP (2012), *Growing Together: Economic Integration for an Inclusive and Sustainable Asia and the Pacific Century*, Bangkok: United Nations.

Freire, C. (2012), Structural Transformation for Inclusive Development in South and South-West Asia, ESCAP-SSWA Development Papers 1204. Available at: http://sswa.unescap.org/meeting/documents/Dev-Challenges/SSWA_Development_Papers_1204_August2012.pdf (last accessed on 27 September 2012).

Fry, Maxwell J. (1992), 'Foreign Direct Investment in a Macroeconomic Framework: Finance, Efficiency, Incentives and Distortions', PRE Working Paper. Washington DC: The World Bank.

Gordon, J. and Poonam Gupta (2004), 'Understanding India's Services Revolution', IMF Working Paper No. WP/04/171. Washington DC: IMF.

IMF (2012), *Direction of Trade Statistics*. Available online at: www.imf.org (last accessed in September 2012).

Kumar, Nagesh (1998), 'Multinational Enterprises, Regional Economic Integration, and Export-Platform Production in the Host Countries: An Empirical

Analysis for the US and Japanese Corporations', *WeltwirtschaftlichesArchiv* 134(3): 450–83.

——— (2001), 'National Innovation Systems and Indian Software Industry Development', Paper prepared for UNIDO. Available at: http://www.unido.org/fileadmin/import/userfiles/hartmany/idr-kumar-paper2.pdf (last accessed on 11 September 2012).

——— (2002), *Globalization and the Quality of Foreign Direct Investment*. New Delhi: Oxford University Press.

——— (2003), 'Intellectual Property Rights, Technology and Economic Development: Experiences of Asian Countries', *Economic and Political Weekly*, 38(3): 209–26.

——— (2005a), 'Performance Requirements as Tools of Development Policy: Lessons from Experiences of Developed and Developing Countries', in Kevin Gallagher (ed.), *Putting Development First: The Importance of Policy Space in the WTO and International Financial Institutions*. London: Zed Press, pp. 179–94.

——— (2005b), 'Liberalization, Foreign Direct Investment Flows and Development: Indian Experience in the 1990s', *Economic and Political Weekly*, 40(14): 1459–69.

——— (2008), 'Internationalization of Indian Enterprises: Patterns, Strategies, Ownership Advantages and Implications', *Asian Economic Policy Review*, 3(2): 242–61.

——— (2011), 'Capital flows and Development: Lessons from South-Asian Experiences', in Raghabendra Jha (ed.), *Handbook of South Asian Economies* (pp. 238–57). London and New York: Routledge.

Kumar, Nagesh and Aradhna Agarwal (2005), 'Liberalization, Outward Orientation and In-house R&D Activity of Multinational and Local Firms: A Quantitative Exploration for Indian Manufacturing', *Research Policy*, 34(4): 441–60.

Kumar, Nagesh and J. Pradhan (2005), 'Foreign Direct Investment, Externalities and Economic Growth in Developing Countries: Some Empirical Explorations', in Edward M. Graham (ed.), *Multinationals and Foreign Investment in Economic Development* (pp. 42–84). USA: Palgrave.

Kumar, Nagesh and Kevin P. Gallagher (2007), 'Relevance of "Policy Space" for Development: Implications for Multilateral Trade Negotiations', RIS Discussion Papers 120. Available at: http://www.ris.org.in/publications/discussion-papers/508 (last accessed on 28 September 2012).

Kumar, Nagesh and K.J. Joseph (eds) (2007), *International Competitiveness and Knowledge Based Industries*. New Delhi: Oxford University Press and RIS.

Kumar, Nagesh, K. Kesavapany and Yao Chaocheng (eds) (2008), *Asia's New Regionalism and Global Role: Agenda for the East Asia Summit*. New Delhi and Singapore: ISEAS and RIS.

Moran, Theodore H. (1998), *Foreign Direct Investment and Development*. Washington, DC: Institute for International Economics.

——— (2001), *Parental Supervision: The New Paradigm for Foreign Direct Investment and Development*. Peterson Institute: Washington, DC.

Ostry, Jonathan D., Atish R. Ghosh, Karl Habermeier, Marcos Chamon, Mahvash S. Qureshi, and Dennis B.S. Reinhardt (2010), 'Capital Inflows: The Role of Controls', IMF Staff Position Note SPN/10/04.

Raychaudhuri, Aajitava and Prabir De (2012), *International Trade In Services In India.* New Delhi: Oxford University Press.

RBI (2012), *Handbook of Statistics on Indian Economy 2012.* Mumbai: Reserve Bank of India. Available at www.rbi.gov.in (last accessed on 29 September 2012).

RIS (2006), *Towards an Employment-Oriented Export Strategy: Some Explorations.* New Delhi: Research and Information System for Developing Countries.

Rosen, D. (1999), *Behind the Open Door: Foreign Enterprise Establishment in China.* Washington, DC: Institute for International Economics.

Tiwari, T.S. (1986), 'Constant market share analysis of export growth: the Indian case', *The Indian Economic Journal,* 33(3): 70–80.

Tyszynski, H. (1951), 'World Trade in Manufactured Commodities, 1899–1950', *The Manchester School* 19(3): 272–304.

UNCTAD (2003), *Use and Effectiveness of Performance Requirements: Select Case Studies.* New York: United Nations.

———— (2005), *World Investment Report 2005.* New York: United Nations.

———— (2012), *World Investment Report 2012.* New York: United Nations.

UN-ESCAP (2010), *Economic and Social Survey of Asia and the Pacific.* Bangkok: UN-ESCAP.

———— (2012), *Growing Together: Economic Integration for an inclusive and Sustainable Asia-Pacific Century.* Bangkok: UN-ESCAP.

UN-ESCAP-SSWA (2012), *Regional Cooperation for Inclusive and Sustainable Development: South and South-West Asia Development Report 2012–13.* New York, New Delhi and London: UN Publications and Routledge.

Verma, R. (2008), 'The Service Sector Revolution in India, A Quantitative Analysis', Research Paper No. 2008/72. Helsinki: United Nations University, UNU-WIDER, September.

Yongding, Yu (2006), 'The Experience of FDI Recipients: The Case of China', in Shujiro Urata, Chia Siow, and Fukunari Kimura (eds), *Multinationals and Economic Growth in East Asia* (pp. 423–52). London and New York: Routledge.

PART IV

INCLUSION: EQUALITY AND OPPORTUNITY

CHAPTER 10

POVERTY AND INEQUALITY

*redesigning intervention**

RAGHBENDRA JHA AND ANURAG SHARMA

Despite 20 years of economic reforms, poverty and inequality remain issues of enduring concern in India. In particular, there is substantial disquiet about persistence of mass poverty and perceived rising inequality even in the presence of accelerated rates of economic growth. This chapter shows that during the post-reforms period, inequality has grown and poverty has fallen according to the existing yardsticks of assessing these. However, legitimate questions have been raised about the accuracy of these yardsticks. There is widespread spatial variation in both inequality and poverty. The chapter also indicates that having adequate nutrition, the traditional rationale for the poverty line has not recorded impressive gains. The chapter indicates that the most important means of lowering poverty is by creating jobs for poor and unskilled workers in both rural and urban sectors on a mass scale, an area in which the economic reforms programme has not had a good track record. The chapter also advances arguments and suggestions for better targeting of anti-poverty interventions, for improving nutritional outcomes, and for reducing inequality.

* We are grateful to Raj Bhatia for expert statistical help and to Ashima Goyal and three anonymous referees for helpful comments on an earlier draft. The usual caveat applies.

Poverty and inequality are issues of enduring concern in India. In particular, there is substantial disquiet about the persistence of mass poverty and perceived rising inequality even in the presence of accelerated rates of economic growth, particularly since about 2001. An oft-repeated question in academic and policy circles has been: 'have reforms led to an accelerated fall in poverty?' The evolution of economic inequality in India has followed the first half of the Kuznets Curve pattern, that is, inequality has risen with rising per capita income. Will this rise be moderate and will the second half of the Kuznets Curve, that is, falling inequality with further increases in per capita income, come sooner rather than later?

Needless to say, there is voluminous literature on these concerns. For recent analyses of these issues, see The World Bank (2011), Kurosaki (2011), and Jha (2004). Some basic statistics on the growth and poverty performance of the Indian economy (using international poverty lines given by The World Bank) are reported in Table 10.1 which reports decadal growth rates of real GDP, real GDP per capita and their respective standard deviations along with head count ratios (HCR) and poverty gaps at US$ 2 purchasing power parity (PPP) a day and US$ 1.25 PPP a day. With the onset of economic reforms, growth rates have, by and large, accelerated and become more stable over time. During a particularly high growth phase (2005–10), HCR at US$ 2 PPP per day fell by about 7 points whereas HCR at US$ 1.25 PPP per day fell by about 9 points. These figures lend strong credence to the hypothesis that higher economic growth leads to sharp reduction in poverty.

However, The World Bank's global poverty lines, like those reported in Table 10.1, have been widely criticized. Thus, Pogge and Reddy (2010) argue that this poverty line is arbitrary and unrelated to any conception of what poverty is. The measure of purchasing power used is also deemed to be an inaccurate measure of purchasing power 'equivalence' and extrapolates incorrectly from limited data, rendering its estimates highly prone to error. Srinivasan (2010) is also sharply critical of the Bank's poverty lines. This leads us to explore inequality and poverty using national poverty lines.

Two Controversies Relating to the National Poverty Line

As indicated by Srinivasan (2007), the original poverty line for India developed by Dadabhai Naoroji in the late nineteenth century was based

Table 10.1 Real GDP Growth, Real GDP Per Capita Growth, and Poverty in India

	Real GDP Growth (Average)	Standard Deviation of Real GDP Growth	Real GDP Per Capita Growth (Average)	Standard Deviation of Real GDP Per Capita Growth	Poverty HCR at US$ 2 a day (PPP) (Percentage of Population)	Poverty HCR at US$ 1.25 a Day (PPP) (Percentage of Population)	Poverty Gap at US$ 2 a Day (PPP) (Percentage)	Poverty Gap at US$ 1.25 a Day (PPP) (Percentage)
1961–70	6.519	5.811	4.281	5.690				
1971–80	3.086	4.279	0.699	4.172				
1981–90	5.567	1.847	3.252	1.826				
1991–2000	5.475	2.065	3.519	2.070				
2001–10	7.689	2.181	6.085	2.197				
1978					88.97	65.89	44.59	23.22
1983					84.79	55.51	38.20	17.24
1988					83.77	53.59	36.74	15.81
1994					81.73	49.40	34.11	13.56
2005					75.62	41.64	29.49	10.51
2010					68.72	32.67	24.45	7.49

Source: Authors' computations based on The World Bank database. (available online at http://databank.worldbank.org/data/views/reports/tableview.aspx)

on calorie requirements. After Independence, the poverty line using calorie requirements was recast in 1961 and extended over time. Thus, in 1973–4, based on a survey of consumer behaviour by the National Sample Survey (NSS), a consumption basket was proposed that would ensure, on an average, 2,100 calories per person per day in urban areas and 2,400 calories per person per day in rural areas. The poverty lines established for 1973–4 were Rs 49 per person per month for rural areas and Rs 57 per person per month for urban areas. These poverty lines were regularly updated using the consumer price index for agricultural labourers (CPI-AL) for rural areas and the consumer price index for industrial workers (CPI-IW) for urban areas. State-level poverty lines were also determined and poverty rates were routinely calculated using these measures.

These poverty lines were heavily criticized for concentrating exclusively on food consumption norms, with no allowance being made for expenditure on health, education, and other basic needs. The Tendulkar Committee Report (henceforth TCR) submitted in 2009 was geared towards addressing this shortcoming. However, prior to that another controversy had affected the computation of poverty rates—in the fifty-fifth round of the NSS conducted in 1999–2000. This survey marked a departure from the earlier practice in two important ways—first, food items were canvassed on a dual recall period of 7 days as well as the standard 30 days. Second, items on which only infrequent expenditures are made, such as medical goods, were only canvassed on a 365 day recall instead of the dual 30 day and 365 day recall in the previous 'thick' round. Earlier experiments with reference periods indicated this change could potentially halve the measured rate of poverty. Further, this change came exactly as reliable statistics were required to gauge the impact of India's 1991 economic reforms on the poor. A wide literature has evolved analysing and correcting the data from this round. Morten (2006) and, particularly, Deaton and Kozel (2005) provide a review of this literature. In the next 'thick' round of the NSS (the sixty-first round conducted in 2004–5), recall periods were set as per previous norms making results from this round comparable to those from rounds earlier than the fifty-fifth.

Reacting to TCR, the Planning Commission fixed the poverty line for data relating to the sixty-sixth round of the NSS, conducted in 2009–10, for the country at Rs 672.8 per person per month (that is, Rs 22.42 per person per day) for rural areas and Rs 859.6 per person per month for urban areas (that is, Rs 28.65 per person per day) for urban areas. In 2011, this was revised to Rs 26 per day for rural areas and Rs 32 per day in urban areas in view of price inflation between 2009–10 and 2011.

When these figures were released, there was an immediate outcry from both the press and economists as these figures did not even guarantee bare subsistence. The ensuing course of events is well known with the Government of India appointing a new committee (under the chairmanship of C. Rangarajan) to construct a new poverty line to replace TCR's recommendations.

It now behoves us to inquire what is wrong with TCR's recommendations. A casualty in this prolonged process is, of course, that we do not yet have an accurate idea of the extent and depth of poverty in India since we do not have a widely accepted poverty line.

TCR is an attempt to address these deficiencies of the traditional approach. TCR suggests that the old urban poverty line for 2004–5, suitably adjusted, is adequate to meet today's requirements, both rural and urban, with respect to nutrition, education, and health. TCR then makes a major methodological change by constructing new price indices to compare rural and urban prices in different states and the state-level prices indices with all-India price indices. Using the existing urban poverty line for 2004–5 and these 'new' prices, a revised rural poverty line is calculated. This raised the proportion of the poor in the rural population below the official poverty line but it worked with a very flawed methodology. The poverty line that it proposes actually amounts to reduced calorie consumption, and fails to provide for reasonable household expenditures on schooling and health. A deeper issue is that by divesting the poverty line from its calorie requirement moorings, it robs the poverty line of any policy significance. Indeed, some people have legitimately argued that the poverty line is so low that it could barely buy one or two items of a subsistence basket.

Another related but distinct argument is that delinking of subsistence requirements from calorie norms is mistaken, if not misguided. If the poverty line is anchored to a calorie norm, given changes in activity patterns and lifestyles, and improvements in the epidemiology of infectious diseases, it will have greater credibility in identifying the poor.

TCR's claims about education and health are also fallacious. TCR states that in 2004–5, 90 per cent of the children aged 5–14 years belonging to households at the poverty line level of expenditure in urban areas, were in school. TCR then assumes that the median cost of sending a child to school sets a desirable level of expenditure on a child in school but little justification is provided for this assumption except to say that the average expenditure on education per child among households in the poverty line expenditure class was higher than the median cost of schooling per child.

On this basis, TCR surmises that actual expenditure is adequate to ensure that children are in school. However, in actual practice, the median cost may be completely inadequate to cover all the costs of proper schooling for all children. It should also be noted that, given the high degree of inequality of expenditure on education in urban India, the median cost is likely to be lower than the mean cost. If TCR had used the mean cost of education, the poverty line would have been higher and so would be the head count ratio of poverty. Moreover, the mere fact that a child is in school does not guarantee that all his/her schooling requirements, including learning materials and school uniform are met.

Exactly the same criticism applies to TCR's arguments with respect to health expenditure. Using data for 2004, TCR calculates the median cost of non-institutional healthcare and institutional healthcare/hospitalization. TCR again relies on median healthcare expenses but, just as in the case of educational expenses, and, given the high inequality in health expenditure, median health expenditure is likely to be well below the mean health expenditure. Further, median health expenditures may not guarantee adequate healthcare.

Thus, both generalizations of the traditional poverty line by TCR are deeply flawed and, therefore, misleading. In reality, the TCR methodology actually under-estimates the number of poor (Swaminathan 2010).[1]

Hunger, Inequality, and Poverty in India

Against this background we are justified in asking the question: what of calorie deprivation (hunger)—the original motivation behind constructing the poverty line? Deaton and Dreze (2009) have shown that despite rapid economic growth in India per capita calorie intake has declined, as has the intake of many other nutrients. More than three quarters of the population lives in households whose per capita calorie intake is less than 2,100 in urban areas and 2,400 in rural areas—calorie intakes regarded as 'minimum requirements' in India. Anthropometric indicators tell an equally dismal story and some of these indicators are the worst in the

[1] See also Subramanian (2011).

world. For instance, according to the National Family Health Survey[2] the proportion of underweight children remained virtually unchanged between 1998–9 and 2005–6—from 47 to 46 per cent for the age-group 0–3 years. Yet, the government allows thousands of tonnes of food grains to rot with no end in sight to this state of affairs.

Apart from its nutritional and human costs, such hunger also has strong implications for productivity, wages, and economic growth. If workers are nutritionally deprived, they will have low productivity whence they will get low wages. Low wages, in turn, will mean that workers will be unable to buy the entire nutritional intake they need, which will then complete this vicious cycle. In economics literature, this is called the poverty nutrition trap (PNT). Jha et al. (2009a) establish the existence of a PNT for rural India for calories and various micronutrients for various types of agricultural operations by male and female workers. In particular, women, more than men, are subject to PNT.

In the poorer districts in India the incidence of hunger is much more acute. For 2007–8, Jha et al. (2011a) collected primary data for 500 households each in Rajasthan, Maharashtra, and Andhra Pradesh (AP) and show that the incidence of deprivation of both macronutrients (calories and protein) as well as a number of micronutrients is very high, in several cases 80 per cent or above. Hence, there is a huge hunger crisis in India which is not being picked up by 'falling' poverty—no matter which poverty line is used. This reaffirms the case for rooting poverty lines on nutritional norms to discover what the people of India probably already know—that nutritional deprivation is widespread and deep and probably worsening!

Against this background,[3] Table 10.2 depicts the evolution of the inequality, measured by the Gini coefficient, in the rural and urban sectors of major individual states and the country as a whole between 1993–4 and 2009–10. Comparable figures for 1993–4, 2004–5, and 2009–10 are given and states and the country are ranked according to increasing inequality. Figures for 1999–2000 are also given as well as those for 2004–5 that are comparable to the 1999–2000 magnitudes. In the rural sector for the country as a whole, the Gini rose between 1993–4 and 2004–5 and stayed unchanged in 2009–10. For the urban sector, however, there was a steady rise in the Gini coefficient from 0.34 in 1993–4 to 0.37 in 2004–5, and 0.39 in 2009–10. Thus, the rise in urban inequality in the 5-year period from

[2] The source for this data is the website http://www.rchiips.org/nfhs/

[3] The results on poverty that follow are subject to the critique of the traditional poverty line discussed earlier.

Table 10.2 Gini Coefficient of Distribution of Consumption for Select States and All India

1993–4 (50th Round)				1999–2000 (55th Round)				2004–5 (61st Round) Uniform Reference Period (comparable with 1993–4)			
State/India	Rural	State/India	Urban	State/India	Rural	State/India	Urban	State/India	Rural	State/India	Urban
Assam	0.18	Haryana	0.28	Jammu & Kashmir	0.17	Jammu & Kashmir	0.22	Assam	0.19	Jammu & Kashmir	0.24
Bihar	0.22	Jammu & Kashmir	0.28	Assam	0.20	Rajasthan	0.28	Bihar	0.20	Gujarat	0.31
Jammu & Kashmir	0.23	Punjab	0.28	Bihar	0.21	Gujarat	0.29	Jharkhand	0.22	Assam	0.32
Gujarat	0.24	Assam	0.29	Rajasthan	0.21	Haryana	0.29	Jammu & Kashmir	0.24	Himachal Pradesh	0.32
Odisha	0.24	Gujarat	0.29	West Bengal	0.22	Odisha	0.29	Rajasthan	0.25	Uttarakhand	0.32
West Bengal	0.25	Rajasthan	0.29	Gujarat	0.23	Punjab	0.29	Karnataka	0.26	Bihar	0.33
Punjab	0.26	Odisha	0.30	Himachal Pradesh	0.23	Himachal Pradesh	0.30	Gujarat	0.27	Jharkhand	0.35
Rajasthan	0.26	Bihar	0.31	Andhra Pradesh	0.24	Andhra Pradesh	0.31	Madhya Pradesh	0.27	Odisha	0.35
Karnataka	0.27	Andhra Pradesh	0.32	Haryana	0.24	Assam	0.31	West Bengal	0.27	Haryana	0.36
Himachal Pradesh	0.28	Karnataka	0.32	Karnataka	0.24	Bihar	0.32	Odisha	0.28	Karnataka	0.36
Madhya Pradesh	0.28	Uttar Pradesh	0.32	Madhya Pradesh	0.24	Karnataka	0.32	Punjab	0.28	Tamil Nadu	0.36
Uttar Pradesh	0.28	Madhya Pradesh	0.33	Odisha	0.24	Kerala	0.32	Uttarakhand	0.28	Andhra Pradesh	0.37
India	0.28	West Bengal	0.33	Punjab	0.24	Madhya Pradesh	0.32	Andhra Pradesh	0.29	Maharashtra	0.37
Andhra Pradesh	0.29	Kerala	0.34	Uttar Pradesh	0.25	Uttar Pradesh	0.33	Chhattisgarh	0.29	Rajasthan	0.37
Kerala	0.29	Tamil Nadu	0.34	Maharashtra	0.26	West Bengal	0.34	Uttar Pradesh	0.29	Uttar Pradesh	0.37
Haryana	0.30	India	0.34	India	0.26	India	0.34	Himachal Pradesh	0.30	India	0.37
Maharashtra	0.30	Maharashtra	0.35	Kerala	0.27	Maharashtra	0.35	India	0.30	West Bengal	0.38
Tamil Nadu	0.31	Himachal Pradesh	0.43	Tamil Nadu	0.28	Tamil Nadu	0.38	Maharashtra	0.31	Madhya Pradesh	0.39
Jharkhand		Jharkhand		Jharkhand		Jharkhand		Haryana	0.32	Punjab	0.39
Chhattisgarh		Chhattisgarh		Chhattisgarh		Chhattisgarh		Tamil Nadu	0.32	Kerala	0.40
Uttarakhand		Uttarakhand		Uttarakhand		Uttarakhand		Kerala	0.34	Chhattisgarh	0.43

2004–5 (61st Round) Mixed reference period (comparable with 1999–2000)				2009–10 (66th round) (comparable with 1993–4 and 2004–5 uniform reference)			
State/India	Rural	State/India	Urban	State/India	Rural	State/India	Urban
Assam	0.17	Jammu & Kashmir	0.24	Bihar	0.23	Jammu & Kashmir	0.31
Bihar	0.17	Himachal Pradesh	0.26	Rajasthan	0.23	Assam	0.33
Jharkhand	0.20	Assam	0.30	Jammu & Kashmir	0.24	Bihar	0.34
Jammu & Kashmir	0.20	Rajasthan	0.30	Karnataka	0.24	Gujarat	0.34
Rajasthan	0.20	Uttarakhand	0.30	West Bengal	0.24	Karnataka	0.34
Uttarakhand	0.22	Bihar	0.31	Assam	0.25	Tamil Nadu	0.34
Karnataka	0.23	Gujarat	0.32	Gujarat	0.26	Haryana	0.37
Uttar Pradesh	0.23	Punjab	0.32	Maharashtra	0.27	Madhya Pradesh	0.37
Andhra Pradesh	0.24	Jharkhand	0.33	Odisha	0.27	Uttar Pradesh	0.37
Madhya Pradesh	0.24	Odisha	0.33	Tamil Nadu	0.27	Punjab	0.38
Chhattisgarh	0.24	Andhra Pradesh	0.34	Uttar Pradesh	0.27	Andhra Pradesh	0.39
West Bengal	0.24	Tamil Nadu	0.34	Andhra Pradesh	0.29	Rajasthan	0.39
Gujarat	0.25	Uttar Pradesh	0.34	Madhya Pradesh	0.30	West Bengal	0.39
Odisha	0.25	Kerala	0.35	Punjab	0.30	India	0.39
India	0.25	Chhattisgarh	0.35	India	0.30	Odisha	0.40
Himachal Pradesh	0.26	Maharashtra	0.35	Haryana	0.31	Himachal Pradesh	0.41
Punjab	0.26	India	0.35	Himachal Pradesh	0.31	Maharashtra	0.42
Tamil Nadu	0.26	Haryana	0.36	Kerala	0.44	Kerala	0.52
Maharashtra	0.27	Karnataka	0.36	Jharkhand		Jharkhand	
Kerala	0.29	West Bengal	0.36	Chhattisgarh		Chhattisgarh	
Haryana	0.31	Madhya Pradesh	0.37	Uttarakhand		Uttarakhand	

Source: For 1993–4, 1999–2000, and 2004–5 Planning Commission, Government of India, Databook for DCH; April 2012.

2004–5 to 2009–10 was comparable to that in the 11-year period from 1993–4 to 2004–5. Hence, urban inequality has become a concern.

There was wide spatial variation in the evolution of inequality. Thus, in 1993–94 rural inequality was higher than the national Gini in AP, Kerala, Haryana, Maharashtra, and Tamil Nadu whereas it was below the national Gini in Assam, Bihar, Jammu and Kashmir (JK), Gujarat, Odisha, West Bengal (WB), Punjab, Rajasthan, and Karnataka. Urban inequality was higher than the national Gini in Himachal Pradesh (HP) and Maharashtra and below the national Gini in Haryana, JK, Punjab, Assam, Gujarat, Rajasthan, Odisha, Bihar, AP, Karnataka, Uttar Pradesh (UP), Madhya Pradesh (MP), and WB. In 2004–5, rural inequality was lower than the national Gini in Assam, Bihar, Jharkhand, JK, Rajasthan, Karnataka, Gujarat, MP, WB, Odisha, Punjab, Uttarakhand, AP, Chhattisgarh, and UP. Urban inequality was higher than the national Gini in Maharashtra, Haryana, Tamil Nadu, and Kerala. In 2009–10 rural inequality was lower than the national Gini in Bihar, Rajasthan, JK, Karnataka, WB, Assam, Gujarat, Maharashtra, Odisha, Tamil Nadu, UP, and AP whereas it was higher than the national HCR in Haryana, HP, and Kerala. Urban inequality was below the national Gini in JK, Assam, Bihar, Gujarat, Karnataka, Tamil Nadu, Haryana, MP, UP, and Punjab, whereas it was higher than the national Gini in Odisha, HP, and Maharashtra.

Table 10.2 does not give information on inequality between the rural and urban sectors. Further, it gives an indication of consumption inequality and not income or wealth inequality, essentially because household level income and wealth data for India are mostly unavailable and notoriously unreliable. Typically, income and wealth inequality are higher than consumption inequality.

Table 10.3 reports on the evolution of poverty in India using the traditional poverty line. HCRs are reported for 1993–4 and 2004–5 and HCRs, poverty gap, and square poverty gaps are reported for 2009–10. Table 10.4 reports Planning Commission data on HCR for 2004–5 and 2009–10 using the TCR criterion. All poverty rates are reported according to increasing magnitudes.

HCR for the rural sector has fallen steadily from 37.3 per cent in 1993–4 to 28.3 per cent in 2004–5 and, more rapidly, to 22.2 per cent in 2009–10. In the urban sector poverty fell from 32.4 per cent in 1993–4 to 25.7 per cent in 2004–5 and, more rapidly, to 22.2 per cent in 2009–10. In the rural sector in 1993–4 Maharashtra, MP, WB, UP, Assam Odisha, and Bihar had HCR higher than the national HCR whereas Punjab, AP, Gujarat, Kerala, Rajasthan, Haryana, Karnataka, HP, JK, and Tamil Nadu had lower HCR than the national average. In the urban sector in 1993–4 Bihar, Maharashtra, UP, AP, Tamil Nadu, Karnataka, Odisha, and MP had higher poverty than the national HCR whereas Assam, HP, JK, Punjab Haryana, WB, Kerala, Gujarat, and Rajasthan had lower poverty than the national average.

In the rural sector in 2004–5, JK, Punjab, HP, AP, Kerala, Haryana, Rajasthan, Gujarat, Karnataka, Assam, and Tamil Nadu had lower poverty than the nation as a whole whereas WB, Maharashtra, UP, MP, Chhattisgarh, Uttarakhand, Bihar, Jharkhand, and Odisha had higher poverty than the national average. In the urban sector in 2004–5 Assam, HP, Punjab, JK, Gujarat, WB, Haryana, Jharkhand, Kerala, and Tamil Nadu had lower poverty than India as a whole whereas AP, UP, Maharashtra, Karnataka, Rajasthan, Bihar, Uttarakhand, Chhattisgarh, MP, and Odisha had higher poverty than the national average.

In 2009–10 in the rural sector JK, Punjab, AP, HP, Kerala, Rajasthan, Haryana, Gujarat, Tamil Nadu, Karnataka, and Maharashtra had lower poverty than the national HCR whereas WB, MP, Assam, UP, Odisha, and Bihar had higher poverty than the national HCR. In the urban sector in 2009–10 Punjab, Assam, JK, HP, Haryana, WB, Gujarat, AP, Kerala, Rajasthan, and Tamil Nadu had lower poverty than the national HCR whereas Maharashtra, Karnataka, UP, MP, Bihar, and Odisha had higher poverty than the national HCR.

For the sake of completeness, Table 10.3 also reports the poverty gap and squared poverty gap as indicators of depth of poverty and Table 10.4 reports on computations of HCR[4] by the methodology of TCR for 2004–5 and 2009–10. Table A10.1 in Appendix A10 provides information on poverty lines used by the Planning Commission in its approach to implementing TCR. As many as 354,680,000 Indians (278,210,000 in the rural sector and 76,470,000 in the urban sector) were poor in 2009–10 according to the Planning Commission. Jha et al. (2012) indicate that, at least in rural India, there is very high incidence of transient poverty with only 10 per cent of the population chronically poor. Thus, covariate and idiosyncratic shocks form a good proportion of the explanation for poverty.

Our analysis here has shown that aggregate GDP growth matters in poverty alleviation, measured traditionally or as per TCR, but agricultural growth matters more (despite a sharp reduction in its contribution to GDP) since most of the poor are in agriculture. Agricultural growth makes four contributions to poverty alleviation: its direct growth component, its

[4] These are subject to the critique of the TCR discussed earlier.

Table 10.3 Poverty Estimates Using Traditional Poverty Line Methodology for Select States and All India

1993–4 (50th Round)				2004–5 (61st Round)			
State/India	Rural	State/India	Urban	State/India	Rural	State/India	Urban
Punjab	12	Assam	7.7	Jammu & Kashmir	4.6	Assam	3.3
Andhra Pradesh	15.9	Himachal Pradesh	9.2	Punjab	9.1	Himachal Pradesh	3.4
Gujarat	22.2	Jammu & Kashmir	9.2	Himachal Pradesh	10.7	Punjab	7.1
Kerala	25.8	Punjab	11.4	Andhra Pradesh	11.2	Jammu & Kashmir	7.9
Rajasthan	26.5	Haryana	16.4	Kerala	13.2	Gujarat	13
Haryana	28	West Bengal	22.4	Haryana	13.6	West Bengal	14.8
Karnataka	29.9	Kerala	24.6	Rajasthan	18.7	Haryana	15.1
Himachal Pradesh	30.3	Gujarat	27.9	Gujarat	19.1	Jharkhand	20.2
Jammu & Kashmir	30.3	Rajasthan	30.5	Karnataka	20.8	Kerala	20.2
Tamil Nadu	32.5	India	32.4	Assam	22.3	Tamil Nadu	22.2
India	37.3	Bihar	34.5	Tamil Nadu	22.8	India	25.7
Maharashtra	37.9	Maharashtra	35.2	India	28.3	Andhra Pradesh	28
Madhya Pradesh	40.6	Uttar Pradesh	35.4	West Bengal	28.6	Uttar Pradesh	30.6
West Bengal	40.8	Andhra Pradesh	38.3	Maharashtra	29.6	Maharashtra	32.2
Uttar Pradesh	42.3	Tamil Nadu	39.8	Uttar Pradesh	33.4	Karnataka	32.6
Assam	45	Karnataka	40.1	Madhya Pradesh	36.9	Rajasthan	32.9
Odisha	49.7	Odisha	41.6	Chhattisgarh	40.8	Bihar	34.6
Bihar	58.2	Madhya Pradesh	48.4	Uttarakhand	40.8	Uttarakhand	36.5
Chhattisgarh		Chhattisgarh		Bihar	42.1	Chhattisgarh	41.2
Jharkhand		Jharkhand		Jharkhand	46.3	Madhya Pradesh	42.1
Uttarakhand		Uttarakhand		Odisha	46.8	Odisha	44.3

Poverty Head Count Ratio, Poverty Gap and Squared Poverty Gap in 2009–10 66th Round

Head Count Ratio				Poverty Gap				Square Poverty Gap			
State/India	Rural	State/India	Urban	State/India	Rural	State/India	Urban	State/India	Rural	State/India	Urban
Jammu & Kashmir	4.36	Punjab	6.27	Punjab	0.42	Punjab	0.92	Punjab	0.067	Punjab	0.21
Punjab	4.9	Assam	6.93	Jammu & Kashmir	0.66	Jammu & Kashmir	1.09	Jammu & Kashmir	0.19	Assam	0.23
Andhra Pradesh	6.4	Jammu & Kashmir	7.91	Andhra Pradesh	0.97	Assam	1.1	Himachal Pradesh	0.26	Jammu & Kashmir	0.23
Himachal Pradesh	6.8	Himachal Pradesh	8.01	Himachal Pradesh	1	Haryana	1.42	Andhra Pradesh	0.27	Haryana	0.36
Kerala	9.6	Haryana	9.69	Rajasthan	1.2	Himachal Pradesh	1.6	Rajasthan	0.28	Himachal Pradesh	0.42
Rajasthan	10.4	West Bengal	12.31	Gujarat	1.5	Gujarat	2.18	Gujarat	0.3	Gujarat	0.56
Haryana	11.3	Gujarat	12.76	Kerala	1.63	West Bengal	2.37	Haryana	0.48	West Bengal	0.68
Gujarat	12	Andhra Pradesh	15.44	Haryana	1.8	Andhra Pradesh	2.78	Kerala	0.49	Andhra Pradesh	0.77
Tamil Nadu	13.46	Kerala	16.06	Maharashtra	2.22	Kerala	3.23	Tamil Nadu	0.53	Kerala	0.95
Karnataka	14.67	Rajasthan	18.49	Tamil Nadu	2.23	Tamil Nadu	3.48	Maharashtra	0.56	Tamil Nadu	1.01
Maharashtra	14.7	Tamil Nadu	19.84	Karnataka	2.7	Rajasthan	3.6	Karnataka	0.76	Rajasthan	1.09
India	22.2	India	20.67	India	4.29	India	4.53	Assam	1.04	India	1.48
West Bengal	24.61	Maharashtra	22.43	Assam	4.3	Maharashtra	5.55	India	1.26	Maharashtra	1.91
Madhya Pradesh	26.5	Karnataka	23.45	West Bengal	4.59	Karnataka	5.84	West Bengal	1.27	Uttar Pradesh	1.96
Assam	27.3	Uttar Pradesh	27.69	Uttar Pradesh	5.3	Uttar Pradesh	6.17	Uttar Pradesh	1.45	Karnataka	2.01
Uttar Pradesh	30	Madhya Pradesh	31.97	Madhya Pradesh	5.6	Bihar	8.36	Madhya Pradesh	1.7	Bihar	2.84
Odisha	34.48	Bihar	32.46	Odisha	8.2	Madhya Pradesh	8.54	Bihar	2.6	Odisha	3.02
Bihar	39.3	Odisha	36.35	Bihar	8.4	Odisha	8.8	Odisha	2.8	Madhya Pradesh	3.17
Chhattisgarh		Chhattisgarh		Chhattisgarh		Chhattisgarh		Chhattisgarh		Chhattisgarh	
Jharkhand		Jharkhand		Jharkhand		Jharkhand		Jharkhand		Jharkhand	
Uttarakhand		Uttarakhand		Uttarakhand		Uttarakhand		Uttarakhand		Uttarakhand	

Source: For 1993–4 and 2004–5, Planning Commission (2012). For 2009–10 authors' computations.

Table 10.4 Poverty in India and its States (2009–10 and 2004–5) Using TCR Methodology

2009–10 Rural			2009–10 Urban			2009–10 Total		
State/India	Percentage of Person	No. of Persons (lakhs)	State/India	Percentage of Person	No. of Persons (lakhs)	State/India	Percentage of Person	No. of Persons (lakhs)
Puducherry	0.2	0.0	A& N Islands	0.3	0.0	A & N Islands	0.4	0.0
A & N Islands	0.4	0.0	Puducherry	1.6	0.1	Puducherry	1.2	0.1
Delhi	7.7	0.3	Lakshadweep	1.7	0.0	Lakshadweep	6.8	0.0
Jammu & Kashmir	8.1	7.3	Sikkim	5.0	0.1	Goa	8.7	1.3
Himachal Pradesh	9.1	5.6	Goa	6.9	0.6	Chandigarh	9.2	1.0
Chandigarh	10.3	0.0	Chandigarh	9.2	0.9	Jammu & Kashmir	9.4	11.5
Goa	11.5	0.6	Tripura	10.0	0.9	Himachal Pradesh	9.5	6.4
Kerala	12.0	21.6	Mizoram	11.5	0.6	Kerala	12.0	39.6
Punjab	14.6	25.1	Kerala	12.1	18.0	Sikkim	13.1	0.8
Uttarakhand	14.9	10.3	Himachal Pradesh	12.6	0.9	Delhi	14.2	23.3
Meghalaya	15.3	3.5	Jammu & Kashmir	12.8	4.2	Punjab	15.9	43.5
Sikkim	15.5	0.7	Tamil Nadu	12.8	43.5	Meghalaya	17.1	4.9
Haryana	18.6	30.4	Delhi	14.4	22.9	Tamil Nadu	17.1	121.8
Nagaland	19.3	2.8	Andhra Pradesh	17.7	48.7	Tripura	17.4	6.3
Tripura	19.8	5.4	Dadra & Nagar	17.7	0.3	Uttarakhand	18.0	17.9
Tamil Nadu	21.2	78.3	Gujarat	17.9	44.6	Haryana	20.1	50.0
Lakshwadeep	22.2	0.0	Punjab	18.1	18.4	Nagaland	20.9	4.1
Andhra Pradesh	22.8	127.9	Maharashtra	18.3	90.9	Andhra Pradesh	21.1	176.6
Karnataka	26.1	97.4	Karnataka	19.6	44.9	Mizoram	21.1	2.3

Arunachal Pradesh	26.2	2.7	Rajasthan	19.9	33.2	Gujarat	23.0	136.2
Rajasthan	26.4	133.8	India	20.9	764.7	Karnataka	23.6	142.3
Gujarat	26.7	91.6	West Bengal	22.0	62.5	Maharashtra	24.5	270.8
West Bengal	28.8	177.8	Madhya Pradesh	22.9	44.9	Rajasthan	24.8	167
Maharashtra	29.5	179.8	Haryana	23.0	19.6	Arunachal Pradesh	25.9	3.5
Mizoram	31.1	1.6	Chhattisgarh	23.8	13.6	West Bengal	26.7	240.3
India	33.8	2,782.10	Meghalaya	24.1	1.4	India	29.8	3,546.80
Daman & Diu	34.2	0.2	Arunachal Pradesh	24.9	0.8	Daman & Diu	33.3	0.8
Odisha	39.2	135.5	Nagaland	25.0	1.4	Madhya Pradesh	36.7	261.8
Uttar Pradesh	39.4	600.6	Uttarakhand	25.2	7.5	Odisha	37.0	153.2
Assam	39.9	105.3	Odisha	25.9	17.7	Uttar Pradesh	37.7	737.9
Jharkhand	41.6	102.2	Assam	26.1	11.2	Assam	37.9	116.4
Madhya Pradesh	42.0	216.9	Jharkhand	31.1	24.0	Jharkhand	39.1	126.2
Manipur	47.4	8.8	Uttar Pradesh	31.7	137.3	Dadra & Nagar	39.1	1.3
Bihar	55.3	498.7	Daman & Diu	33.0	0.5	Manipur	47.1	12.5
Dadra & Nagar	55.9	1.0	Bihar	39.4	44.8	Chhattisgarh	48.7	121.9
Chhattisgarh	56.1	108.3	Manipur	46.4	3.7	Bihar	53.5	543.5

(contd.)

Table 10.4 (*contd.*)

2004–5 Rural			2004–5 Urban			2004–5 Total		
State/India	Percentage of Person	No. of Persons (lakhs)	State/India	Percentage of Person	No. of Persons (lakhs)	State/India	Percentage of Person	No. of Persons (lakhs)
Lakshwadeep	0.4	0.0	A & N Islands	0.8	0.0	A & N Islands	3.0	0.1
Daman & Diu	2.6	0.0	Nagaland	4.3	0.2	Lakshwadeep	6.4	0.0
A & N Islands	4.1	0.1	Himachal Pradesh	4.6	0.3	Nagaland	8.8	1.7
Nagaland	10.0	1.5	Mizoram	7.9	0.4	Daman & Diu	8.8	0.2
Meghalaya	14.0	2.9	Puducherry	9.9	0.7	Chandigarh	11.6	1.1
Jammu & Kashmir	14.1	11.6	Chandigarh	10.1	0.9	Delhi	13.0	19.3
Delhi	15.6	1.1	Jammu & Kashmir	10.4	2.9	Jammu & Kashmir	13.1	14.5
Kerala	20.2	42.2	Lakshadweep	10.5	0.0	Puducherry	14.2	1.5
Punjab	22.1	36.7	Delhi	12.9	18.3	Mizoram	15.4	1.5
Puducherry	22.9	0.8	Daman & Diu	14.4	0.1	Meghalaya	16.1	4.1
Mizoram	23.0	1.1	Dadra & Nagar	17.8	0.1	Kerala	19.6	62.0
Haryana	24.8	38.8	Kerala	18.4	19.8	Punjab	20.9	53.6
Himachal Pradesh	25.0	14.3	Punjab	18.7	16.9	Himachal Pradesh	22.9	14.6
Goa	28.1	1.8	Tamil Nadu	19.7	59.7	Haryana	24.1	54.6
Sikkim	31.8	1.5	Gujarat	20.1	42.9	Goa	24.9	3.4
Andhra Pradesh	32.3	180.0	Assam	21.8	8.3	Tamil Nadu	29.4	194.1
Arunachal Pradesh	33.6	3.2	Goa	22.2	1.7	Andhra Pradesh	29.6	235.1
Chandigarh	34.7	0.2	Haryana	22.4	15.9	Sikkim	30.9	1.7
Uttarakhand	35.1	23.1	Tripura	22.5	1.5	Arunachal Pradesh	31.4	3.8

Rajasthan	35.8	166.4	Andhra Pradesh	23.4	55.0	Gujarat	31.6	171.4
Assam	36.4	89.4	Arunachal Pradesh	23.5	0.6	Uttarakhand	32.7	29.7
Karnataka	37.5	134.7	Jharkhand	23.8	16.0	Karnataka	33.3	186.5
Tamil Nadu	37.5	134.4	West Bengal	24.4	60.8	West Bengal	34.2	288.3
West Bengal	38.2	227.5	Meghalaya	24.7	1.2	Assam	34.4	97.7
Gujarat	39.1	128.5	India	25.5	814.1	Rajasthan	34.4	209.8
Manipur	39.3	6.7	Maharashtra	25.6	114.6	India	37.2	4,072.20
India	42.0	3,258.10	Karnataka	25.9	51.8	Manipur	37.9	9.0
Uttar Pradesh	42.7	600.5	Sikkim	25.9	0.2	Maharashtra	38.2	392.4
Tripura	44.5	11.9	Uttarakhand	26.2	6.6	Tripura	40.0	13.4
Maharashtra	47.9	277.8	Chhattisgarh	28.4	13.7	Uttar Pradesh	40.9	730.7
Jharkhand	51.6	116.2	Rajasthan	29.7	43.5	Jharkhand	45.3	132.1
Madhya Pradesh	53.6	254.4	Uttar Pradesh	34.1	130.1	Madhya Pradesh	48.6	315.7
Chhattisgarh	55.1	97.8	Manipur	34.5	2.3	Dadra & Nagar Haveli	49.3	1.3
Bihar	55.7	451.0	Madhya Pradesh	35.1	61.3	Chhattisgarh	49.4	111.5
Odisha	60.8	198.8	Odisha	37.6	22.8	Bihar	54.4	493.8
Dadra & Nagar	63.6	1.1	Bihar	43.7	42.8	Odisha	57.2	221.6

Source: Planning Commission (2012).

Notes: 1. Population as on 1 March 2010 has been used for estimating number of persons below poverty line (interpolated between 2001 and 2011 population census). For population in 2004–5, data as on 1 March 2005 has been used for estimating the number of persons.

2. Poverty line in Tamil Nadu is used for Andaman and Nicobar Islands; urban poverty line in the Punjab is used for both rural and urban areas of Chandigarh.

3. Poverty line in Maharashtra is used for Dadra & Nagar Haveli; poverty line in Goa is used for Daman & Diu.

indirect growth component, the participation of the poor in the growth of this sector, and its size in the overall economy.

Reducing Poverty, Inequality, and Hunger: Policy and Targeting Issues

There is large literature on the association between economic growth and poverty reduction. Just as a tide raises all boats higher, economic growth makes everyone better off, goes the refrain, to which James Tobin had responded: not if the boats have leaks! India's anti-poverty policy certainly has more than its fair share of leaks. Two basic principles of an effective anti-poverty strategy, even against the backdrop of high rates of economic growth, are fairly straightforward. Since 78.43 per cent of the poor reside in the rural sector any successful anti-poverty policy must focus on the agricultural sector and, second, since the poor have only one asset—their labour—any anti-poverty strategy must involve a sharp and sustained increase in the demand for labour, particularly in the rural sector. The performance of the Indian economy with regard to both has been lacklustre. Balakrishnan et al. (2008) consider stagnant public investment in agriculture, even as agricultural subsidies have gone up, and continuous fragmentation of landholdings as two of the principal reasons for lagging productivity and employment in agriculture. These trends must be reversed, in particular, the quality of public investment must be improved and a new blueprint for engaging the private sector in meaningful public-private partnerships, evolved. Agricultural growth is important for its own sake since although agriculture accounts for a relatively small portion of GDP it still employs more than 60 per cent of the labour force. Further, agricultural growth will also dampen the double-digit food price inflation that has recently taken place and further the cause of macroeconomic stabilization. In addition, non-agricultural growth both in the rural and urban sectors should be enhanced and labour markets made more flexible to ensure rapid growth of employment. Not surprisingly, the golden age of rural poverty reduction was the 1980s when the adoption of Green Revolution technology led to sharp rises in agricultural growth, employment, and incomes.

The NSS estimated aggregate unemployment at 8.28 per cent on a current daily status (CDS) basis for 2004–5 but the first survey on employment and unemployment (Ministry of Labour and Employment 2010) estimated 2009–10 unemployment in the economy as a whole at 9.4 per cent with 7.3 per cent of the urban labour force unemployed whereas rural unemployment stood at a staggering 10.1 per cent. Further, there is the burden of large-scale underemployment. Hence, basic problem with the current growth experience is that not enough productive jobs for unskilled and semi-skilled workers are being created. Unless this problem is attacked front and centre, rapid reduction of mass poverty will remain a mirage in India, although gradual and slow improvements will take place.

India has instituted a number of anti-poverty measures but a large number of them are subject to considerable errors of targeting, that is, Tobin's leaking boats. Thus, Jha et al. (2009b) showed that one of the most popular and widely discussed anti-poverty interventions, the National Rural Employment Guarantee Scheme (NREGS), was subject to capture by wealthier elements in a relatively well-off state like Andhra Pradesh.

The government's own statistics indicate that NREGS' performance across four criteria: (a) average number of days of employment per household; (b) percentage of households completing 100 days of employment under NREGS; (c) percentage of expenditure against total available funds; and (d) percentage of work completed in 2009–10 and 2011–12, was very disappointing and deteriorated over time (Jha and Gaiha 2012).

NREGS is an example of a broad class of rural public works programmes (RPWs). RPWs have been widely cited as a crucial tool for poverty alleviation, particularly in the rural sector (The World Bank 2001). Properly designed RPWs provide employment to the unemployed (hence reducing poverty) and build the much-needed rural infrastructure. Besides, as RPWs are designed to peak in seasonally slack periods, they help stabilize incomes. Since they stimulate rural incomes and, therefore, demand, RPWs have the potential of stimulating the rural economy and, hence, act as a counterfoil to contracting demand during recessions. RPWs have been used in many countries. But, Jha et al. (2011b) compare the capture of RPW and food for work (FFW) programmes for the 1993–4 and 2004–5 NSS and find a high degree of capture of programmes meant essentially for the poor, by non-poor groups. This capture is often in return for contributions made by the rural rich to politicians. These programmes are often meant to target socially backward groups such as Scheduled Castes (SC) and Scheduled Tribes (ST). In particular, targeting among SC worsened significantly between 1993–4 and 2004–5. Since these results are based on all-India samples, they call into question the entire basis of targeting by social class; income-based targeting is likely to yield much better results.

Further, there is an urgent need to increase low-skill manufacturing employment. India has a natural comparative advantage in low value added manufacturing but, because it has not taken advantage of international production networks, this sector of the Indian economy has stagnated. This is particularly true in comparison to China although India has a substantial labour cost advantage. Thus, Anukoonwattaka and Mikic (2011) report that the monthly wage of a typical manufacturing worker in India was US$ 23.80 in 2002, while for China the figure was US$ 110.80. This wage gap has only widened since then because wages in China have grown very substantially in the aftermath of a long period of rapid economic growth. Indeed, other economies such as the Philippines have stepped in to take advantage of high labour costs in China and have become integral parts of the international production network. Thus, it appears that India has not yet utilized its labour cost advantage to create more employment opportunities in the manufacturing sector. Two policy measures are urgently needed to facilitate India's rapid integration into such networks: a) assured infrastructural services, and b) flexible labour laws so that small and medium sized firms can plan production in response to changes in international patterns of demand.

India's targeted public distribution system (TPDS) is another programme notorious for its inefficiency, leakages, poor targeting of the poor, and a huge food subsidy bill. Consequently, for 2010–11 the food subsidy bill jumped by 27 per cent over the previous year to Rs 742.310 billion (US$ 16.495 billion at Rs 45 = US$ 1). However, Khera (2011) has indicated that there is considerable variation across states in TPDS' efficiency. In relation to the functioning of TPDS, essentially leakages from the TPDS, and some other characteristics revealed by household data over the period 1993–4 to 2004–5, states could be categorized into three groups: (i) functioning (all the southern states, Himachal Pradesh, and Maharashtra); (ii) reforming (Chhattisgarh, Madhya Pradesh, Odisha, and Uttar Pradesh; and (iii) languishing (mostly eastern states including Bihar, West Bengal, and Jharkhand). States with 'functioning' TPDS systems had low leakages throughout this period whereas 'reforming' states improved their performance on these criteria. 'Languishing' states performed poorly in 1993–4 and 2004–5. The improved performance of the 'reforming' states was itself driven by two factors: (a) increased food subsidy contribution from the central government, and (b) a rising gap between the open market price and the TPDS price of food grains which led to increased off-take from

TPDS. High food price inflation makes a significant contribution to the persistence of poverty and it will be unfair to characterize the whole PDS as dysfunctional. However, if the impact of food price inflation is not addressed any recent gains in poverty alleviation could be reduced, if not wiped out.

Careful attention must be given to reducing transaction costs—long distances to be travelled, long queues and waiting periods, and underweighing by fair price shops (FPS). A better network of FPS, higher margins, and adequate supplies will go a long way in making the TPDS more cost effective. A real culprit is the Food Corporation of India with its abysmal inefficiency in procuring, storing, and distributing food. Above all, top priorities include livelihood expansion opportunities in rural areas, and food price stabilization—two areas in which the government's track record has been and continues to be unimpressive. Indeed a revamped TPDS on a smaller scale combined with more sensible policies that aim to augment productivity in agriculture, avoid market imperfections that come in the way of remunerative farm gate food prices, and expand livelihood options may lead to fulfilment of food entitlements in a more economical and effective manner.

Further, best practices in TPDS need to be adopted on a sub-national level for TPDS to improve. In line with economist Raj Krishna who once advocated that Sikh farmers be asked to relocate to all parts of the country to teach others the benefits and practices of adopting the Green Revolution technology, it may be advisable to relocate bureaucrats from the states where TPDs is functioning well to states where TPDS is reforming or languishing. A complementary policy initiative will be raising the margin made available to retailers in FPS so as to reduce their incentive to divert TPDS stocks to the open market.

To address the hunger crisis, first and foremost food entitlements must be increased and guaranteed. For various reasons, most importantly that it will reduce farmers' incentives to expand output and grossly inflate the food subsidy bill, the Food Security Bill is not an answer to this issue. Ensuring rapid and efficient supply of food grains and eliminating all waste of food is certainly a part of the answer. Nutrition science suggests that one-third of the nutritional status of a child is determined in the mother's womb, before the child is born. Hence, ensuring adequate nutrition for women is a critical issue and must be addressed on a war footing. Social safety nets, if properly administered, can have a very strong impact on under-nutrition. Thus, Jha et al. (2011a) show for a household data set for 2007–8 for the states of Andhra Pradesh, Maharashtra, and

Rajasthan that a transfer of as little as Rs 100 per capita per month through TPDS and, in many cases, NREGS, can substantially reduce under-nutrition in all major categories of macro and micro nutrients. Hence, the potential impact of social safety nets is very high—a fact that strongly underscores the importance of proper targeting and avoiding leakages. Administrative reforms in these areas and the active involvement of the private sector and civil society organizations are the key to success.

Some economists have advocated replacing TPDS with food stamps, or even cash payments to below poverty line households. Under this scheme, FPS will go, households will buy in regular stores, and get compensated by transfers to their bank accounts, which much of the poor do not yet have. However, study after study, has indicated that directly subsidized food improves nutrition more than an equal amount of cash or food stamps (Gentilini 2007). Moreover, the value of such cash aid can be easily eroded by inflation. In some cases, food stamps can be used to supplement a successful TPDS programme but should not replace it.

Finally, when it come to inequality, India's excessive reliance on regressive commodity taxation and the handing out of current subsidies which are largely garnered by the non-poor need to be addressed. Moreover, under fiscal pressure, public provision of services, including essential services such as health and education, are stagnating, if not in decline. The spectre of increasing inequality does not bode well for increasing political support for the economic reform programme.

***

This chapter argued that more than 20 years since the current phase of the economic reforms programme was initiated, inequality has grown and poverty has fallen according to the existing yardsticks of assessing these. However, legitimate questions have been raised about the accuracy of these yardsticks. There is widespread spatial variation in both inequality and poverty. Having adequate nutrition, the traditional rationale for the poverty line, has not recorded impressive gains.

We indicated that the most important means of lowering poverty is by creating jobs for poor, unskilled, and semi-skilled workers in both rural and urban sectors. The chapter advances arguments and suggestions for better targeting of anti-poverty interventions, for improving nutritional outcomes, and for reducing inequality.

APPENDIX A10.1

Table A10.1 State-specific Poverty Lines for 2009–10 (Rs per capita per month)

State/India	Rural	Urban	State/India	Rural	Urban
Andhra Pradesh	693.8	926.4	Mizoram	850.0	939.3
Arunachal Pradesh	773.7	925.2	Nagaland	1,016.8	1,147.6
Assam	691.7	871.0	Odisha	567.1	736.0
Bihar	655.6	775.3	Puducherry	641.0	777.7
Chhattisgarh	617.3	806.7	Punjab	830.0	960.8
Delhi	747.8	1040.3	Rajasthan	755.0	846.0
Goa	931.0	1025.4	Sikkim	728.9	1,035.2
Gujarat	725.9	951.4	Tamil Nadu	639.0	800.8
Haryana	791.6	975.4	Tripura	663.4	782.7
Himachal Pradesh	708.0	888.3	Uttar Pradesh	663.7	799.9
Jammu & Kashmir	722.9	845.4	Uttarakhand	719.5	898.6
Jharkhand	616.3	831.2	West Bengal	643.2	830.6
Karnataka	629.4	908.0	A & N Islands		
Kerala	775.3	830.7	Chandigarh		
Madhya Pradesh	631.9	771.7	Dadra & Nagar Haveli		
Maharashtra	743.7	961.1	Daman & Diu		
Manipur	871.0	955.0	Lakshwadeep		
Meghalaya	686.9	989.8	India	672.8	859.6

Source: Planning Commission (2012).

REFERENCES

Anukoonwattaka, W. and M. Mikic (eds) (2011), 'India a New Player in Asian Production Networks', UNESCAP Studies in Trade and Investment 75, Bangkok.

Balakrishnan, P., R. Golait, and P. Kumar (2008), 'Agricultural Growth in India since 1991', Development Research Group Study No. 27, Department of Economic Analysis and Policy. Mumbai: Reserve Bank of India.

Deaton, A. and J. Dreze (2009), 'Food and Nutrition in India: Facts and Interpretations', *Economic and Political Weekly*, XLIV: 42–65.

Deaton, A. and V. Kozel (2005), 'Data and Dogma: The Great Indian Poverty Debate', *World Bank Research Observer*, 20(2): 177–99.

Gentilini, U. (2007), *Cash and Food Transfers: A Primer*. Rome: World Food Programme.

Jha, R. (2004), 'Reducing Poverty and Inequality in India: Has Liberalization Helped?' in G.A. Cornia (ed.), *Inequality, Growth and Poverty in an Era of Liberalization and Globalization* (pp. 297–326). Oxford and New York: Oxford University Press.

Jha, R., R. Gaiha, and A. Sharma (2009a), 'Calorie and Micronutrient Deprivation and Poverty Nutrition Traps in Rural India', *World Development*, 37(5): 982–91.

Jha, R., S. Bhattacharyya, and R. Gaiha (2009b), '"Capture" of Anti-poverty Programs: An Analysis of the National Rural Employment Guarantee Program in India', *Journal of Asian Economics* 20(2): 456–64.

——— (2011a) 'Social Safety Nets and Nutrient Deprivation: An Analysis of the National Rural Employment Guarantee Program and the Public Distribution Scheme in India', *Journal of Asian Economics* 22(2): 189–201.

——— (2011b), 'Temporal Variations of Capture of Anti-poverty Programs: Rural Public Works and Food for Work Programs in rural India', *International Review of Applied Economics* 25(3): 349–62.

Jha, R. and R. Gaiha (2012), 'India's National Rural Employment Guarantee Program as It is—Interpreting the Official Data', Australia South Asia Research Centre, Working Paper 2012/12.

Jha, R., W. Kang, H. Nagarajan, and K. Pradhan (2012), 'Vulnerability as Expected Poverty in Rural India', Australia South Asia Research Centre, Working Paper 2012/04.

Khera, R. (2011), India's Public Distribution System: utilisation and impact', *Journal of Development Studies*. online publication DOI: 10.1080/00220388.2010.506917 (last accessed on 16 March 2013).

Kurosaki, T. (2011), 'Economic inequality in south Asia', in Raghbendra Jha (ed.), *Routlege Handbook of South Asian Economics*. London and New York: Routledge, pp. 61–75.

Ministry of Labour and Employment (2010), *Report on Employment and Unemployment Survey (2009–10)*. New Delhi: Labour Bureau, Government of India.

Morten, M. (2006), 'Indian Poverty during the 1990s: Resolving Methodological Issues from the 55th NSS Round', Australia South Asia Research Centre Working Paper: 2006/07, Australian National University.

Planning Commission, Government of India (2012), Data for DCH, April.

Pogge, T. and S. Reddy (2010), 'How Not to Count the Poor', in S. Anand, P. Segal, and J. Stiglitz (eds), *Debates in the Measurement of Poverty*. Oxford: Oxford University Press, pp. 42–85.

Srinivasan, T. (2007), 'Poverty Lines in India: Reflections after the Patna Conference' *Economic and Political Weekly* 42(41): 4155–165.

——— (2010), 'Irrelevance of the US$ 1 a Day Poverty Line', in S. Anand, P. Segal, and J. Stiglitz (eds), *Debates in the Measurement of Poverty* (pp. 143–53).

Oxford: Oxford University Press, Planning Commission, Government of India (2012), Databook for DCH, April.

Subramanian, S. (2011), 'The Poverty Line: Getting It Wrong Again', *Economic and Political Weekly*, XLVI(48): 37–42.

Swaminathan, M. (2010), 'The New Poverty Line: A Methodology Deeply Flawed', *Indian Journal of Human Development* 4(1): 121–5.

The World Bank (2001), *World Development Report 2000*. New York: Oxford University Press.

———— (2011), *Perspectives on Poverty in India: Stylized facts from Survey Data*. Washington, DC: The World Bank.

CHAPTER 11

POLICY DESIGN FOR FOOD SECURITY IN INDIA

ensuring stable supplies and economic access

SHIKHA JHA AND P.V. SRINIVASAN*

High economic growth rates and sufficient food supplies have failed to improve the food security situation in India.[1] The country has been slow in achieving its Millennium Development Goals (MDGs), particularly with respect to poverty and hunger reduction. India ranked 67 among the 81 countries ranked by the Global Hunger Index in 2011 (GHI 2011). Between 1990 and 2011 its status remained at the bottom, changing only from extremely alarming to alarming. The proportion of undernourished as measured by calorie deficiency continues to be high, increasing from over 55 per cent in 1999–2000 to more than 60 per cent in 2009–10

* The views expressed in this chapter do not necessarily reflect the views or policies of the ADB, its board of governors, or the governments they represent. The authors are grateful to Ashima Goyal and an anonymous reviewer for useful comments and suggestions. Pilipinas F. Quising provided excellent research support. Responsibility for any remaining errors, however, rests with the authors.

[1] Food security is achieved when all people have physical and economic access to food that is sufficient to lead an active and healthy life. It is an important determinant of the nutritional status of a person along with other factors, such as access to safe drinking water and sanitation.

(GoI 2012).[2] All this is despite the fact that the country boasts one of the largest food subsidy programmes in the world, covering over a billion people.

The government engages extensively in procurement, storage, and distribution of food grains from surplus to deficit states. The Food Corporation of India (FCI)—a central government agency—procures food grains from farmers at a minimum support price (MSP) to provide incentives for producing cereals and maintains buffer stocks in the 'central pool' to stabilize prices through open market sales of grain. The central government issues grains to state governments at the central issue price (CIP) for subsidized distribution to consumers.

India's food policy, though successful in achieving national-level self-sufficiency in food grains, has failed to translate it into household-level food security. To a large extent this indicates lack of economic access to food. High unemployment and poverty, backward agriculture, weak infrastructure and markets, rising and volatile food prices, and high inflation are among the reasons for this outcome. Reducing purchasing power due to price shocks increases the risk of under-nourishment with long-term implications for an individual's welfare and for the productivity of the economy at large. Sustained high food prices in recent years pushed food out of the reach of poor consumers.

Providing economic access to food to the poor and vulnerable households is thus one of the major challenges facing India's food policy apart from sustaining output growth in light of increasing pressure on resources, such as land, water, and energy; rising uncertainty in weather outcomes; adverse impact of climate change on agricultural productivity; and promotion of bio-fuel production. Ironically even people who depend on agriculture for their livelihoods either as landless labourers or those cultivating small plots are most often food insecure.

Agriculture's dependence on the monsoons leads to instability in output and prices. Volatile food prices harm both consumers and producers by increasing uncertainty and making it difficult for households to budget for food consumption and for farmers to plan for production. Hence, managing food price volatility is another major challenge faced in ensuring food security.

[2] According to the NSS Sixty-sixth Round (July 2009–June 2010) the proportion of households with calorie intake less than 2,700 kcal per consumer unit per day grew from 56 per cent in 1999–2000 to 62 per cent in 2009–10 in rural India. The corresponding increase for urban India was from 57 to 63 per cent.

This chapter considers elements of an appropriate design for an efficient and effective food-based safety net programme. Its focus is on the two main staple food grains—rice and wheat, which provide a bulk of daily calorie intake for Indian households. The plan of the chapter is as follows. The next section puts in perspective the current state of affairs in India's food grain sector by analysing trends in its production and productivity and consumption. The chapter then discusses the prevailing food policy and related issues. The section that follows presents possible alternatives to current policies for an efficient food subsidy programme and effective mechanisms to support farmers and manage food price volatility. The last section makes some concluding observations.

Growth and Stability in Production and Consumption

Introduction of green revolution technology, farm price support policy, and subsidies on inputs such as fertilizers, irrigation, and power improved the supply situation of food grains dramatically over the last half a century, transforming the country from one that faced massive food shortages with heavy dependence on imports and aid in the 1960s into one that is now self-sufficient. The price support policy helped farmers by reducing price risk and generating returns from modern technology. For the past five decades, rice and wheat production in India have generally been on an upward trend, exceeding consumption in recent years (figures 11.1 and 11.2). In particular, total production of milled rice and wheat in the 2000s more than doubled vis-à-vis that in the 1970s. Similarly, per capita production of the two grains has also increased steadily (Figure 11.3). India is currently ranked amongst the world's leading producers of rice and wheat and an occasional exporter and importer.

Until the early 1970s, rising cultivated area was the main driver of production growth. With the advent of high-yielding varieties (HYV) of food grains, supported by the green revolution, growth in yields became the major driving force from late 1970s. The yields of rice and wheat continued to improve markedly well into the 1990s but they plateaued in the next decade. Presently, Indian yields are low compared with other major producers even though 90 per cent of the wheat area and 70 per cent of rice area in India is planted with HYV. Average wheat yields in major

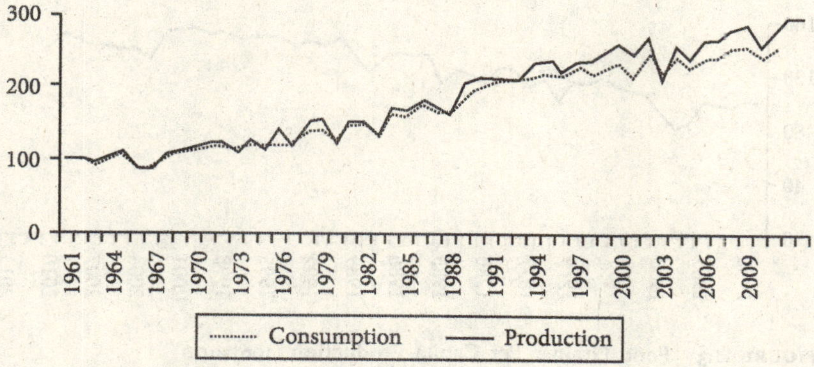

FIGURE 11.1 Rice Consumption and Production[1] (1961=100)

Source: USDA production, supply, and distribution online database. Available at: http://www.fas.usda.gov/psdonline/psdQuery.aspx

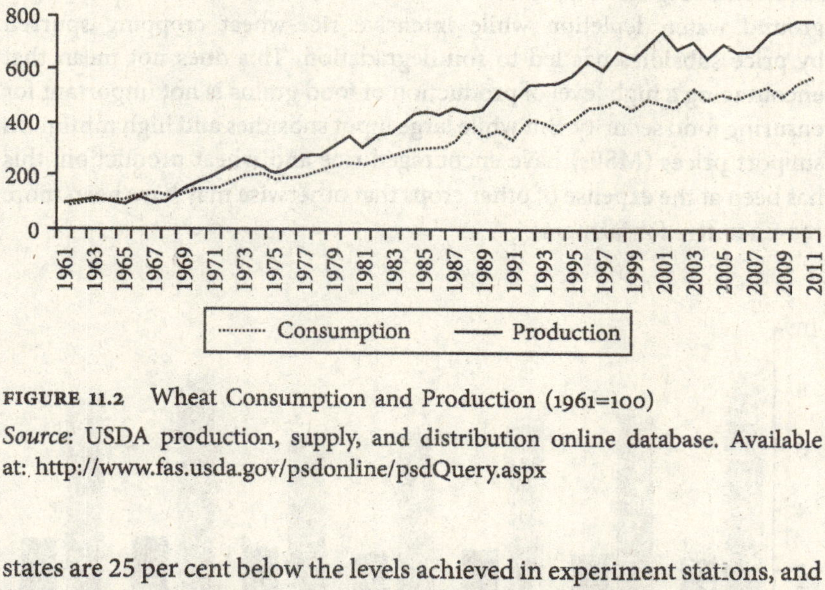

FIGURE 11.2 Wheat Consumption and Production (1961=100)

Source: USDA production, supply, and distribution online database. Available at: http://www.fas.usda.gov/psdonline/psdQuery.aspx

states are 25 per cent below the levels achieved in experiment stations, and for rice, as much as 50 per cent below (Jha et al. 2007). As future demand for food grains is likely to grow in India the importance of increasing productivity cannot be over-emphasized if dependence on imports is to be reduced.

Non-price factors responsible for this situation include declining scope of HYVs and stagnant or declining public investment in irrigation, research, and extension, except for a spike in 2009 in response to the global

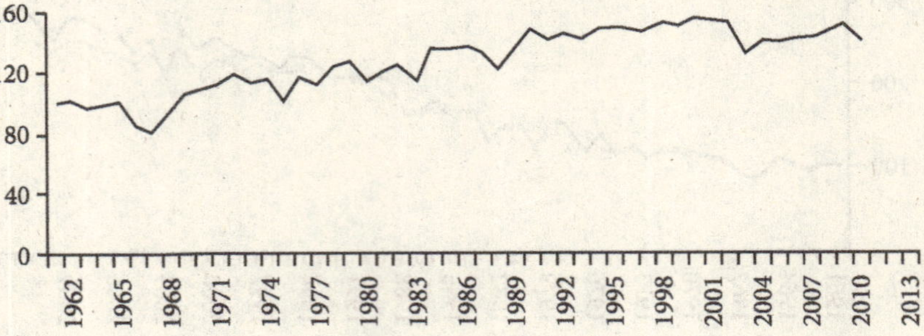

FIGURE 11.3 Food Grains* Per Capita Production (1961=100)

Source: USDA production, supply, and distribution online database. Available at: http://www.fas.usda.gov/psdonline/psdQuery.aspx

Note: * Pertains to total milled rice and wheat production.

food crisis (Figure 11.4). Water and electricity subsidies have encouraged ground water depletion while intensive rice-wheat cropping spurred by price subsidies has led to soil degradation. This does not mean that encouraging a high level of production of food grains is not important for ensuring food security. But while large input subsidies and high minimum support prices (MSPs) have encouraged rice and wheat production, this has been at the expense of other crops that otherwise may have been more remunerative for farmers.

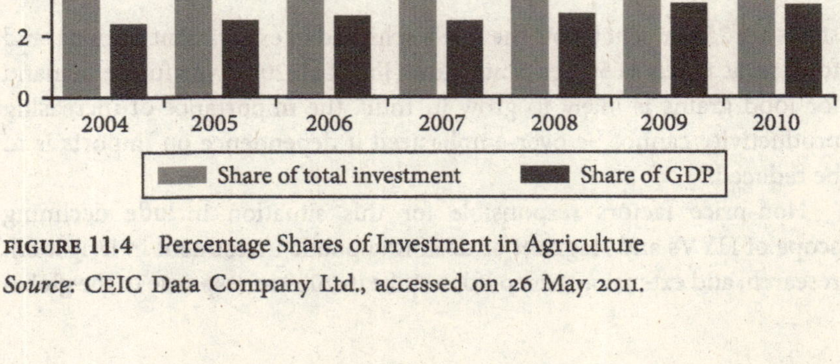

FIGURE 11.4 Percentage Shares of Investment in Agriculture

Source: CEIC Data Company Ltd., accessed on 26 May 2011.

Per capita consumption of food grains shows a declining trend over the past decade (Figure 11.5). To some extent, this trend can be explained by changes in consumption preferences towards non-cereals. Household expenditure data reveals that consumption patterns have shifted markedly in favour of high value foods, such as milk and milk products and fish and meat, driven by urbanization and rising urban incomes (Table 11.1). Other factors include stagnating incomes of the rural poor since the 1990s and lack of increase in subsidized rice distribution in the late 1990s and early 2000s (Kubo 2011). One-third of the country's population earns less than US$ 1.25 a day and a large number of households remain poor and vulnerable

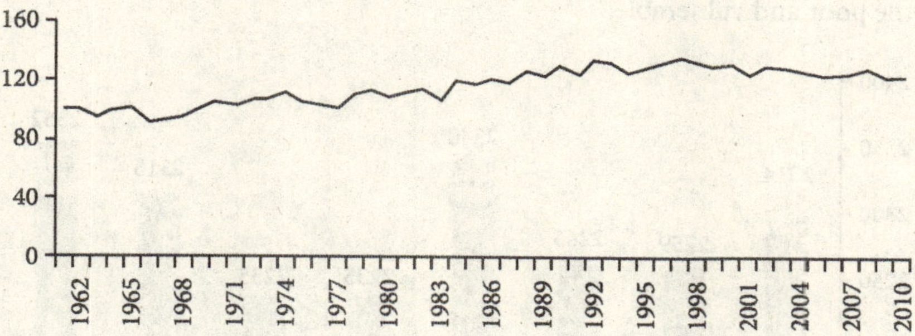

FIGURE 11.5 Food Grains* Per Capita Consumption (1961=100)

Source: USDA production, supply, and distribution online database. Available at: http://www.fas.usda.gov/psdonline/psdQuery.aspx

Note: *Pertains to total milled rice and wheat production.

Table11.1 Item-wise Share of Expenditure to Total Food Expenditure

	Rural		Urban	
	1987–8	2009–10	1987–8	2009–10
Cereals	41.1	29.1	26.6	22.4
Pulses and products	6.3	6.9	6.0	6.6
Milk and products	13.4	16.0	16.8	19.2
Egg, fish, and meat	5.2	6.5	6.4	6.6
Vegetables	8.1	11.6	9.4	10.6
Sugar	4.5	4.5	4.3	3.7
Food total	100	100	100	100

Source: Economic Survey (2011–12: Chapter 8). Available at: http://www.indiabudget.nic.in/survey.asp

to income and price shocks. Further, demand for cereals remains sensitive to prices among low-income consumers.

Consumption as measured by per capita availability of kilocalories per day has been less stable than what might be desired. For instance, between 2000–7, daily per capita food supply suffered serious dips in 2001–2 and in 2004–5 when it declined by roughly 5 per cent (Figure 11.6). During this period, it was far below the prescribed daily per capita calorie requirements for the rural populace (at 2,400 calories per capita per day), and only slightly met that for the urban populace (at 2,100 calories per capita per day). Hence, not only is there a need for incentives to increase food output but also for a well-functioning food based safety net to protect the poor and vulnerable.

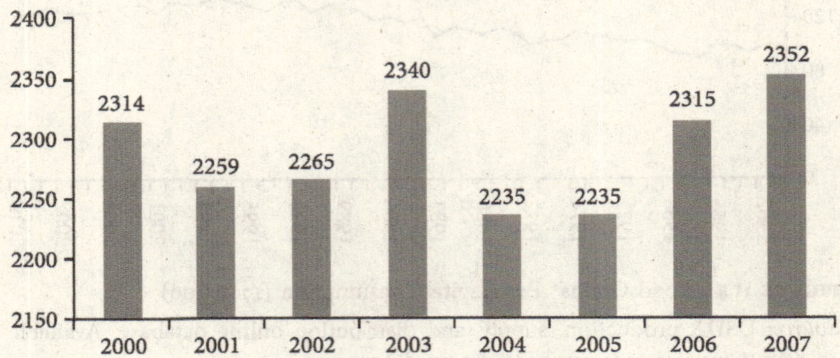

FIGURE 11.6 Food Supply (kcal/capita/day)

Source: FAOSTAT online database. Available at: http://faostat.fao.org/site/610/default.aspx#ancor

Although at the aggregate level per capita cereal consumption is on a downward trend a large proportion of the population remains undernourished, indicating lack of adequate purchasing power in the hands of the poor, who spend a major part of their incomes on buying food. There is large-scale prevalence of food insecurity even among people who depend on agriculture for their livelihood. For example, poverty incidence among small farmers (who are usually net purchasers of food) with less than one hectare of cultivated area is thrice compared to those with more than 4 hectares of cultivated area (Panda 2007). Gains from higher MSPs are restricted to only a few states where they go mainly to the medium and large farmers who have marketable surplus (Umali-Deininger et al., 2005). Even though farm productivity is higher for smaller-sized farms the landholding size is so small that food output fails to meet the household needs. As shown by Chand et al. (2011), a minimum 0.8 ha of land area is needed to keep a farm family above the poverty line, if it is the sole source of income whereas over 60 per cent of the farmers in India have less than 0.8 ha of cultivable land.

The Prevailing Food Policy and Persisting Issues

The government's food policy interventions, originally built around the objective of transferring grains from surplus to deficit areas, were extended over time to directly subsidize consumers, support farmers, and stabilize prices, thus pervading all aspects of the food grains market.

Demand-side Policies

The Public Distribution System (PDS) for food grains is a major safety net programme for providing food security to consumers.[3] It evolved from the 'rationing' system introduced by the British in 1939 as a measure to ensure equitable distribution of food grains to urban consumers in the face of rising prices (FAO 1994; Planning Commission 2005). The system involved sale of a fixed quantity of ration (rice or wheat) to entitled families (ration card holders) in specified cities/towns. The objective was to manage India's food economy and to ensure everyone access to food at affordable prices through subsidized distribution. Although initially designed as a universal food entitlement scheme, PDS was redesigned in 1997 as a targeted scheme to address the concerns of rising costs and its inefficient and ineffective functioning.

For the purpose of targeting, households are classified into those Above Poverty Line (APL), Below Poverty Line (BPL), and the 'poorest of the poor' (POP). BPL and POP households are entitled to a monthly quota of 35 kg of rice or wheat at subsidized prices. The quota for APL households is usually lower, ranging from 10 kg to 35 kg per household

[3] Other programmes, such as employment generation and public works programmes, try to protect the poor against income shocks in productive ways.

per month depending on the availability of food stocks in the central pool. BPL households receive 50 per cent subsidy on the government's economic cost whereas APL households have no subsidy entitlements. Prices for POP households have no direct reference to economic costs and are set below BPL prices.

However, subsidies reaching the poor are low because of targeting errors, leakages, and illegal diversions of grain from the system even as the costs of the PDS programme have been rising rapidly and becoming unsustainable. Targeting has been ineffective. In selecting beneficiaries for the programme two types of errors can occur. Type I or an exclusion error occurs when a deserving household or individual is denied benefits. Type II or an inclusion error occurs when a non-deserving household or individual receives the benefits. Household survey data for 2004–5 show that only 40 per cent of the rural poor households and 27 per cent of the urban poor households possessed either a BPL or a POP entitlement (ration card). Moreover, almost 40 per cent of rural and 23 per cent of urban poor households who did have BPL or POP entitlements could not use the system due to uncertain ration supplies, irregular hours, and inconvenient locations of PDS shops. Such factors raise the participation costs of the poor. At the same time, 68 per cent of BPL/POP beneficiaries in rural areas and 51 per cent in urban areas were not poor. The programme also suffers from enormous waste reflecting the economic inefficiency of the system (Jha and Ramaswami 2012). Major governance and implementation problems add to these challenges.

Substantial differences between the market and subsidized prices creates opportunities for illegal arbitrage and diversion. Leakage of food grains out of the system has been high due to outright theft or through use of ghost ration cards. However, there has reportedly been a reduction in such diversion of grains in recent years (from about 54 per cent in 2004–5 to 44 per cent in 2007–8) due to expanded coverage, de-privatization of shops selling PDS grains, use of information technology, and an increase in commissions for shop dealers (Khera 2011). Nevertheless, targeted PDS continues to suffer from large-scale leakages due to targeting errors as revealed by the latest household-level data (Table 11.2). PDS rice and wheat are patronized more by households above the poverty line, as indicated by an inclusion error of around 60 per cent. That is, 60 per cent of those who have access to PDS are non-poor whereas only around 40 per cent are poor. Only 51 per cent of the poor benefit from PDS. Pro-poor bias is lower in rural areas as compared to urban areas. In urban areas, the percentage of PDS beneficiaries among the poor is 71 per cent higher than the percentage of beneficiaries in the total urban population. In rural areas the corresponding figure is 21 per cent. This probably indicates that urban poor are relatively more empowered and have a greater voice. There is ample room for improvement as far as participation in PDS is concerned, as it has an overall access of 39 per cent only.

Table 11.2 Access to PDS Rice and Wheat (2009)

Indicator	Total	Urban	Rural
HCR	0.30	0.21	0.34
Overall access	0.39	0.28	0.43
Proportion of the poor who are beneficiaries	0.51	0.48	0.52
Proportion of beneficiaries who are poor	0.40	0.35	0.41
Under-coverage	0.49	0.52	0.48
Leakage to the non-poor	0.60	0.65	0.59
Pro-poor bias (per cent)	30.7	71.4	20.9

Source: Author's computations based on NSS Survey on household consumption expenditure Sixty-sixth Round (2009–10).

Notes: Under-coverage denotes the proportion of poor who have no access to PDS (exclusion error); leakage to non-poor indicates the proportion of beneficiaries who are non-poor (inclusion error); and pro-poor bias indicates the percentage by which access to PDS among the poor exceeds the access to PDS in the general population.

State-level household data for 2009 show that overall access to PDS is notably low in some of the poorest states in India (Table 11.3). In Bihar, where the headcount poverty ratio is the highest at 54 per cent, overall access to PDS stands at only 14 per cent. In the same vein, overall access to PDS is only 9 per cent in Manipur, where the headcount poverty is 47 per cent. The share of poor who have access to PDS too is quite low in these states (8 per cent in Manipur and 20 per cent in Bihar). Under-coverage or exclusion error is also higher in states with higher poverty (92 per cent in Manipur, 80 per cent in Bihar, 45 per cent in Dadra and Nagar Haveli, 61 per cent in Jharkhand, and 63 per cent in Uttar Pradesh to name a few). However, inclusion error (leakages to non-poor) is lower and the pro-poor bias higher in poorer states (Figure 11.7). These results indicate that efforts by the government to scale up PDS operations in poorer states will have to first ensure that exclusion errors are reduced.

Table 11.3 Access to PDS Rice and Wheat by State (2009)

State	HCR	Overall access	Ratio of poor with access to total poor	Ratio of poor among beneficiaries	Under-coverage: Exclusion error	Leakage to non-poor: Inclusion error	Pro-poor bias
	P/T	Ta/T	Pa/P	Pa/Ta	1–Pa/P	1– Pa/Ta	(Pa/P)/(Ta/T)–1
Andaman & Nicobar	0.01	0.74	0.00	0.00	1.00	1.00	–1.00
Andhra Pradesh	0.21	0.77	0.95	0.26	0.05	0.74	0.24
Arunachal Pradesh	0.26	0.49	0.61	0.32	0.39	0.68	0.25
Assam	0.38	0.30	0.48	0.61	0.52	0.39	0.60
Bihar	0.54	0.14	0.20	0.77	0.80	0.23	0.44
Chandigarh	0.09	0.12	0.27	0.21	0.73	0.79	1.30
Chhattisgarh	0.50	0.61	0.83	0.68	0.17	0.32	0.36
Dadra & Nagar Haveli	0.46	0.36	0.55	0.72	0.45	0.28	0.55
Daman & Diu	0.32	0.29	0.61	0.69	0.39	0.31	1.15
Delhi	0.14	0.10	0.18	0.24	0.82	0.76	0.73
Goa	0.10	0.55	0.82	0.15	0.18	0.85	0.49
Gujarat	0.23	0.28	0.44	0.36	0.56	0.64	0.56
Haryana	0.20	0.17	0.35	0.42	0.65	0.58	1.11
Himachal Pradesh	0.09	0.86	0.90	0.10	0.10	0.90	0.05
Jammu & Kashmir	0.09	0.68	0.90	0.12	0.10	0.88	0.32
Jharkhand	0.39	0.23	0.39	0.67	0.61	0.33	0.69
Karnataka	0.24	0.61	0.87	0.34	0.13	0.66	0.43

Kerala	0.12	0.62	0.88	0.17	0.12	0.83	0.43
Lakshadweep	0.11	0.93	1.00	0.11	0.00	0.89	0.07
Madhya Pradesh	0.37	0.42	0.63	0.56	0.38	0.44	0.49
Maharashtra	0.25	0.35	0.61	0.44	0.39	0.56	0.75
Manipur	0.47	0.09	0.08	0.43	0.92	0.57	-0.09
Meghalaya	0.17	0.61	0.73	0.20	0.27	0.80	0.21
Mizoram	0.22	0.94	0.99	0.23	0.01	0.77	0.05
Nagaland	0.21	0.00	0.00	0.00	1.00	1.00	-1.00
Odisha	0.37	0.55	0.80	0.54	0.20	0.46	0.46
Puducherry	0.01	0.59	0.96	0.02	0.04	0.98	0.62
Punjab	0.16	0.19	0.42	0.35	0.58	0.65	1.21
Rajasthan	0.25	0.18	0.29	0.41	0.71	0.59	0.65
Sikkim	0.14	0.46	0.75	0.22	0.25	0.78	0.62
Tamil Nadu	0.17	0.87	0.99	0.20	0.01	0.80	0.13
Tripura	0.18	0.75	0.86	0.21	0.14	0.79	0.14
Uttaranchal	0.17	0.35	0.56	0.27	0.44	0.73	0.60
Uttar Pradesh	0.38	0.23	0.37	0.61	0.63	0.39	0.61
West Bengal	0.27	0.34	0.46	0.37	0.54	0.63	0.37

Source: Author's computations based on NSS survey on household consumption expenditure Sixty-sixth Round (2009–10).

Notes: P denotes population that is poor; T the total population; Ta denotes the total population (poor plus non-poor) that has access to PDS and Pa denotes poor having access to PDS.

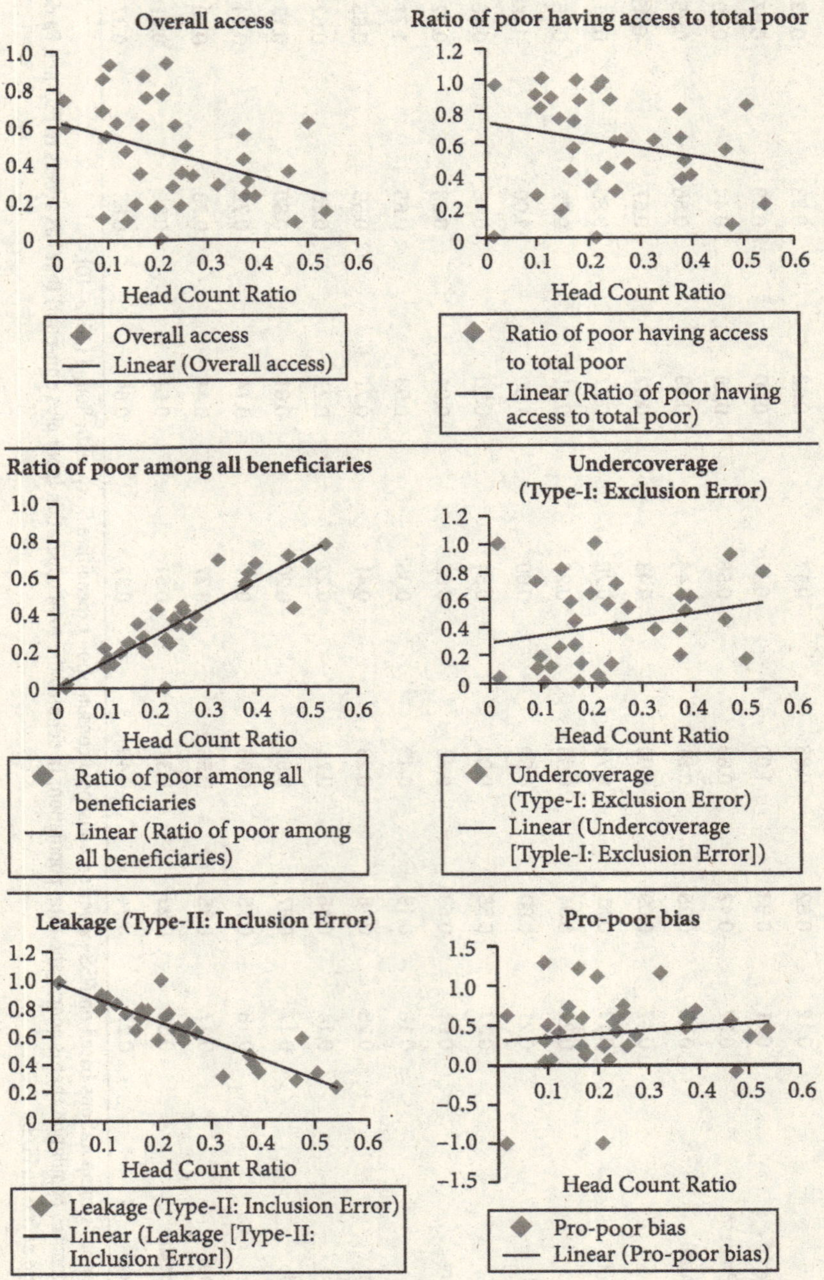

FIGURE 11.7 State-wise Access to PDS Rice and Wheat by Level of Poverty (2009)

Source: Authors' computations.

To improve the coverage of the poor, the government has enacted National Food Security Act 2013 by adopting a rights-based approach to food security.[4] At the time of writing this, the Act was under implementation. The Act envisages disbursement of food subsidy in the form of food coupons or cash transfers to improve economic access of the poor to PDS. It provides legal right to subsidized food grains for up to 75 per cent of rural population and up to 50 per cent of urban population. The extremely poor—'priority'—households are entitled to 5 kg of food grains per person per month at highly subsidized prices. Other households eligible for PDS are entitled to subsidized food grains at prices not exceeding Rs 3 per kg for rice, Rs 2 for wheat and Rs 1 for coarse grains for first 3 years and thereafter not exceeding the MSP. The act has provisions for reducing leakages in the system through doorstep delivery of food grains (to improve physical access), use of ICT including end-to-end computerization, and use of the unique identification number—'*aadhaar*'—for identification of beneficiaries (to eliminate bogus ration cards). Provisions have also been made for transparency and accountability including disclosure of records relating to the PDS, social audits, and establishment of vigilance committees and other mechanisms to redress grievances.

Supply-side Policies

To prevent food deficits, the government encourages higher domestic production by supporting farmers' prices. It guarantees purchase of all grains offered for sale by farmers at the MSP, so long as the required specifications are met. In addition, input subsidies are provided to encourage farmers to adopt high yielding variety (HYV) crops for improving yields.

MSP is set by the government based on recommendations by the Commission for Agricultural Costs and Prices (CACP), taking into account production costs, input–output price parity, demand and supply conditions, international prices and cost of marketing and cost of living, among others.[5] Due to an influential farm lobby, MSP has been regularly revised upwards to cover the rise in production costs. Between 2004–5 and 2010–11, MSP for paddy, wheat, and pulses went up by as much as 75 per cent to 125 per cent. For 2011–12, MSP for wheat was raised by about 15 per cent and for rice by about 8 per cent. Beyond the fiscal year

[4] National Food Security Act, 2013. Available online at http://egazette.nic.in/WriteReadData/2013/E_29_2013_429.pdf (accessed 24 October 2013).

[5] See 'Determination of MSP'. Available online at http://cacp.dacnet.nic.in/ (accessed on 24 October 2013).

2011–12, MSP for rice was increased further by over 15 per cent to end-June 2012. Farmers in the largest surplus states of Punjab and Haryana benefit the most from MSP as they receive greater priority as compared to other states including surplus states, such as Uttar Pradesh and Andhra Pradesh. Since MSP effectively sets the floor price in the open market, continually rising MSPs push up open market prices as reflected in rising trends in retail and wholesale prices of wheat and rice. This adversely affects consumers, particularly poor consumers who are out of PDS on account of targeting errors. This shows the interlinked nature of demand and supply side policies.

Open-ended purchases have led to a large build-up of stocks, which have added significantly to storage costs. The high level committee on long-term grain policy attributed the ballooning of the fiscal cost of the food subsidy to the sharp rise in carrying costs of stocks (GoI 2002). The cost of carrying and maintaining the central pool of buffer stocks together with rising costs of consumer subsidy due to increasing difference between CIP and MSP raised the food subsidy bill by over three and a half times between 2001–2 (Rs 17,494 crore) and 2010–11 (Rs 62,930 crore). This is one of the main reasons why the move to targeted PDS failed to cap the government's rising food subsidy expenditure. Moreover, food price inflation has remained high despite high food stocks since the government lacked effective mechanisms for the release of food grains in the market (Basu 2011).

Building buffer stocks acquired renewed interest in India due to the global food crisis in 2007–8. Prior to the crisis many countries were comfortable with low stock levels as they could cover their domestic crop shortfalls by buying in world markets. This was a result of greater openness to trade following WTO agreements and was evident from the declining levels of global food stocks in recent years. International trade facilitated price stabilization within individual countries as well as of global food prices since agricultural cycles in different countries occur at different periods during the year. However, as crop failures occurred simultaneously in many exporting countries it led to a food crisis. When weather shocks hit commodity markets in 2006 and 2007, stocks of many agricultural commodities were too low to prevent the severe price rises. As a result of this, several countries began to re-examine the merits of self-sufficiency policies, holding adequate buffer stocks and the use of trade controls for price stabilization. While trade taxes are useful in stabilizing domestic prices, outright ban on exports may undermine producer incentives and may not be in the interest of long run output growth.

In India, beginning April 2005, the minimum buffer norms in the central pool were fixed at levels shown in Table 11.4. The stock of food grains in the pool started rising steeply since January 2008, more than doubling between 2008 and 2011 (Figure 11.8). The stock of food grains has been more than twice the prescribed buffer norms since October 2009 except in January 2010, and January 2011 when the ratio of actual stock to buffer norms was slightly below 2 (Figure 11.9). As of January 2012, the stock of food grains stood at 55 million tonnes, 15 per cent higher than the available storage capacity of roughly 48 million tonnes with the Food Corporation of India (FCI). Part of the storage is cover and plinth (CAP) storage, where grains are stored in the open in conditions highly susceptible to theft, pests, and deterioration resulting in higher carrying costs and damage to grain. FCI is forced to rent storage space for more grain due to its own inadequate capacity.

Table 11.4 Minimum Buffer Norms (in lakh tonnes)

	Wheat	Rice	Total
1st April	70	142	212
1st July	201	118	319
1st October	140	72	212
1st January	112	138	250

Source: Department of Food and Public Distribution, Annual Report (2010–11).

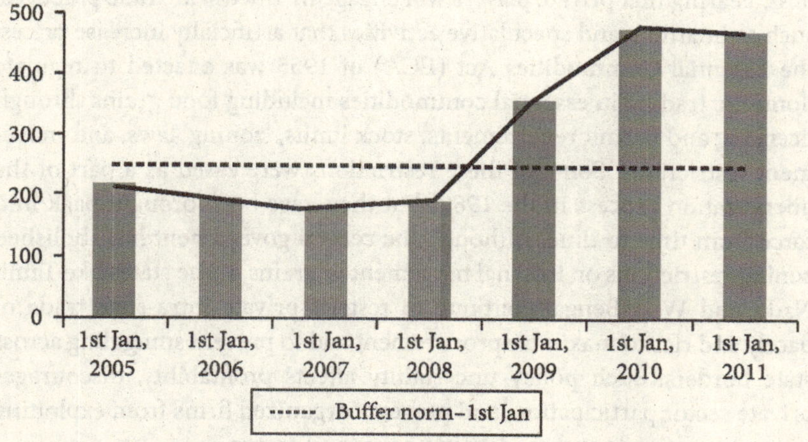

FIGURE 11.8 Total Stock of Food Grains in the Central Pool (lakh tonnes)
Source: Department of Food and Public Distribution, Annual Report 2010–11.

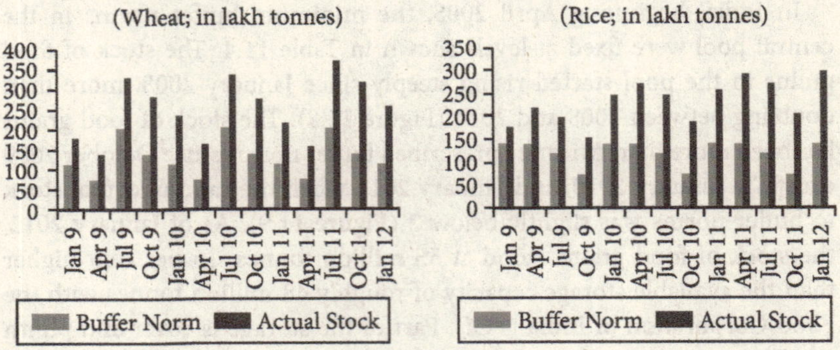

FIGURE 11.9 Buffer Norm & Actual Stock

Source: Economic Survey (2011–12: Chapter 8). Available at: http://www.indiabudget.nic.in/survey.asp

Large-scale intervention by FCI in the food market, with its procurement exceeding a third of total food grains production, undermines incentives for private sector participation. Accelerated increases in MSPs make it difficult for the private sector to compete with the government in procurement. Expectations of low future prices due to a large build-up of public stocks create a disincentive for private storage operations. Release of stocks for subsidized sale in the export and domestic open markets depresses market prices, thus limiting opportunities for profitable business. Fearing that private players will engage in 'unethical' trade practices, such as hoarding and speculative activities that artificially increase prices, the Essential Commodities Act (ECA) of 1955 was enacted to regulate domestic trading in essential commodities including food grains through licensing and permit requirements, stock limits, 'zoning' laws, and movement restrictions. Some of these restrictions were eased as a part of the liberalization process in the 1980s but they have been brought back into force from time to time. Although the central government has abolished zoning restrictions on internal movement of grains, some states like Tamil Nadu and West Bengal continue to restrict private intra-state trade of paddy and rice to maximize procurement and to prevent smuggling across state borders. Such policy uncertainty affects profitability, discourages private sector participation, and prevents organized firms from exploiting economies of scale and modernizing the food sector.

Despite such controls private traders have been shown to operate with lower margins than public agencies. Trading costs and wholesale marketing margins of private traders in 2000–1 were about half those of FCI for wheat and about three quarters for rice. FCI operated at higher costs than the private sector despite enjoying various preferential treatments from the government (Gulati et al. 2000; Jha and Srinivasan 2004). Data for 2004–5 show that due to inefficiencies of government operations, its cost of procuring, transporting, and distributing food grains to different stock points plus the additional distribution cost to retail outlets exceeded retail price of rice by 20 per cent and that of wheat by 8 per cent even after controlling for seasonal and spatial variation in market prices (Jha and Ramaswami 2012).

Policy Alternatives for Effective Food Security

Options for a Cost-effective Consumer Subsidy Program

There are several desirable factors for making safety net programmes successful, which have been analysed in a number of studies.[6] Experience of safety net programmes across a number of countries shows that the following design elements are important for successfully and efficiently reaching the poor:

- low level of programme cost as a per cent of the total budget to ensure fiscal sustainability;
- modest size of transfer to minimize 'incentive costs' from behavioural responses;
- low transaction costs of participation for the poor;
- targeting to ensure sustainable, efficient, and non-distortionary subsidies;
- balancing the cost of fine-tuned targeting with the risk of leakage to the non-poor; and
- minimizing economic waste in the system.

[6] See, for example, the World Bank 2011; Coady et al. 2004; Rogers and Coates 2002; and Subbarao et al. 1997.

It has often been argued that in-kind transfers under PDS should be replaced with cash-based transfers for higher efficiency in reaching the poor and reducing the scope for leakages. There are several other advantages with a system of cash transfers. A cash-based programme does not distort market prices and its administrative costs are likely to be lower as compared to those involved in physical handling, storage, and distribution of grains by the government. Whereas food is subject to pilferage, leakages can be minimized in the case of cash transfers with the help of information and communication technology (for example, smart cards). While it may be argued that cash may be diverted to consumption of items other than food it is seen that when the cash transfer is directed towards women it is likely that a larger share of it is spent on food. Evidence from conditional cash transfer programmes in Latin America and the Caribbean indicates that cash transfers directed at women not only increase the quantity of food intake but there is also a qualitative improvement in terms of more diverse food intake (Handa and Davis 2006). Cash transfers increase the purchasing power of the poor and give them flexibility in making decisions such as the freedom to purchase grain at their convenience and avoid missing their food entitlements due to liquidity constraints. Such flexibility is particularly useful for daily wage earners and migrant workers who may not be able to purchase their entire entitlement at one time. However, this freedom of choice will only be effective if private food grain markets function efficiently.

In physically isolated places where private markets do not function or function inefficiently there might be a case for in-kind transfer of food subsidies. If markets are disrupted people may not be able to obtain food even with cash in hand. Markets, for example, may not function in an effective way during periods of famines or crises; when populations are displaced, the existing food distribution network collapses, or food is not locally available with ease. For example, among Asian economies, it is estimated that in 2004 there were 0.6 million internally displaced persons in Azerbaijan, 0.2–0.5 million in Bangladesh, 0.7 million in India, 0.5 million in Indonesia, 0.6–1million in Myanmar, and 0.4–0.5 million in Sri Lanka (Johns Hopkins and the International Federation of Red Cross and Red Crescent Societies 2008). There may be excessive hoarding by traders and panic buying by well off consumers, which can lead to high prices. In such situations distribution of food as opposed to cash transfers would be more helpful to the poor. Under normal circumstances, well-functioning government structures are the first choice for food distribution but in emergencies it is important to mobilize other local sources including non-governmental organizations (NGOs) and UN agencies which have the capacity in terms of technical and human resources and infrastructure to respond. The situation can be addressed by procurement and targeted and equitable distribution of an adequate quality and quantity of food by local government officials working in coordination with these agencies. Because of long waiting time and high transportation and storage costs of imported food, food should be procured locally as much as possible. Imports will only be justified when the country is in food deficit or when it is not practical to move available surpluses to the areas in need (Johns Hopkins et al. 2008).

Food subsidies in kind have the potential to be self-targeting, especially if the food provided through transfer is inferior. If the objective is to meet specific targets of food intake, direct food distribution or food stamps or coupons might be more appropriate than general cash transfers, assuming resale of stamps and coupons is costly. Use of in-kind transfers will also avoid the erosion of benefits due to inflation. The choice for India is thus not whether to have a food-based or a cash-based programme but a judicious combination of the two depending on how efficient the markets are and how well the prices are stabilized. An appraisal of local markets is important in determining the right combination of the most efficient and effective interventions.

Whether transfers are in cash or in kind, targeting errors will exist since identifying target beneficiaries is a major implementation challenge in either case. The issues of keeping the list of eligible households up to date and monitoring the effectiveness and integrity of the procedures used for identifying beneficiaries will persist. Involving community actors (as in the case of the conditional cash transfer programme in Mexico) can however help keep the administrative costs low. Considering the difficulties involved in identifying the poor it is best not to attempt fine targeting of subsidies. A larger coverage of the population will help reduce exclusion errors. Although this may increase the costs, these can be compensated by reducing leakages under a better-governed system. Geographical targeting of food subsidies involving universal coverage in areas with high concentration of poverty can be another effective way of reaching the subsidy to more of the poor. For example, universal provision of PDS subsidies may be the preferred option for poorer states, such as Bihar, Odisha, Rajasthan, and Madhya Pradesh where most of the districts are 'poor' or 'very poor' (Jha and Srinivasan 2001). In other states, where poverty is not geographically concentrated, self-targeting mechanisms or other direct targeting criteria based on recipients' characteristics, such as landlessness, old age, and widowhood could also be used.

Policy Alternatives for Price Stability

Ever-rising MSPs and costs of procuring, storing, and distribution have led to enormous budgetary outlays, and even larger amounts of bank credit tied up in food grain stocks. This policy regime proved effective in maintaining producer incentives and increasing supplies of food grains at stable prices as India progressed from a deficit to surplus position in food grains. However, the policy has not been that effective in reducing the prevalence of under-nourishment. It has failed to benefit small farmers with little marketable surplus and producers in states where the MSP is not operative. Moreover, rising MSPs can contribute to food price inflation possibly resulting in a chronic cost-push inflationary process (Goyal 2010).

Price volatility creates uncertainty and risks that can threaten agricultural performance and negatively impact the income and welfare of farmers and the rural poor. However, use of MSP to cope with the uncertainty and risks associated with price volatility has proved to be fiscally expensive and created serious market distortions, thus affecting growth and competitiveness of Indian agriculture. The objective of MSP ideally is to act as insurance by protecting farmers' incomes when market prices become less remunerative, falling below a threshold level due to a bumper crop or cheaper international prices. Even in the case when MSP is based on cost of production, it should depend on the output situation. In a good crop year since the yields are higher, the average costs of production are likely to be lower and the opposite is the case in a bad year. Whatever the basis for fixing the MSP it is ideally meant to provide a floor to market prices when they tend to crash due to a glut in the market. Any sale of grain by farmers at this price to the government will be voluntary. The reality, however, is that MSP is fixed at such a high level that farmers prefer to sell their grain to the government rather than in the open market.

Market performance is a crucial factor in determining the case for government intervention. The case is weak when markets work well in the absence of interventions. Now we explore options for supporting farmers that do not distort markets and provide a greater role for the private sector. Policy options may include revisions to existing policies, such as an overhaul of the MSP policy (to make a distinction between support price and procurement price), or adoption of new alternatives based on policies used effectively in other countries, for example, deficiency payments and storage loans used in the United States to protect its farmers.

Deficiency Payments

Deficiency payments (also referred to as counter-cyclical payments) are used to provide price support to farmers and stabilize farm income.[7] Payments are made to producers with eligible historical production of a crop whenever the current price is less than a specified target price, which is typically set above recent market prices. In the US, these payments cover 85 per cent of the base acreage and farmers are guaranteed at least the support price for the portion of their crop that is eligible. To qualify for a deficiency payment a farmer must have planted that crop on at least 75 per cent of some specified portion of the farm for the past five consecutive years. A farmer's base acreage for a crop is the 5-year average of acreage planted in that crop. The payment amount is calculated as the product of the payment rate (difference between the target and market prices), the payment acres (85 per cent of base acres), and the payment yield. This payment is only issued if the market price for a commodity is below the target price. In practice, in place of market price, the effective price of commodity is used which takes into account benefits from other support programmes.

When market prices exceed the target prices, farmers have to refund advance deficiency payments to the government. Such refunds are also requested from farmers who are not able to meet programme-planting requirements due to weather or other conditions by deadline for repayment with no interest. However, farmers have the option to off-set repayment against any advanced deficiency payments for the next crop. Also, a farmer can be considered for special hardship treatment allowing up to three years to repay the advance. In principle, deficiency payments can be highly cost effective compared to MSP and the public storage policy in India since they avoid physical handling and marketing activities by the government and give an adequate role to the private sector in food grain marketing. They could also help prevent the problem of recycling of food grain procurement, a phenomenon where traders buy grains released

[7] See greater details of counter-cyclical payments at http://www.ers.usda.gov/topics/farm-economy/farm-commodity-policy/program-provisions/counter-cyclical-payments.aspx (accessed 24 October 2013).

from government storage at a low price and sell it back to it in the next procurement season. Under the deficiency payment programme, the government can still hold buffer stocks and stabilize prices by managing the sales and procurement of grains at appropriate times but it will not be an open-ended procurement. The advantage with this option is that it will be open to all farmers and not only to those in surplus states. However, given the large number of farmers in India, the administration and monitoring of such a programme could prove to be a challenge considering the lack of proper land records and tenancy contracts.

In effect, the deficiency payments scheme provides price insurance to farmers. Alternatively farmers can be encouraged to directly purchase price insurance from the market by participating in futures markets. The premium will be the price of the commodity futures option. However, a high volume of speculative trading on commodity futures markets can lead to increased volatility in spot prices of commodities. This can be a useful option if appropriate regulation can control excessive volatility in these markets.

Storage Loans

Storage loans can also provide price support to farmers, whereby the government sets a floor price (the loan rate) for covered crops, guaranteeing farmers this price for their crops. These are known as *non-recourse* loans in the US and are administered as marketing assistance loans and loan deficiency payments. The United States Department of Agriculture's Farm Service Agency administers these loans for producers of commodities, such as wheat and corn through the Commodity Credit Corporation.[8] To be eligible for such a loan, a farmer must keep the produce from a contract farm as collateral to pledge for this loan. Without collateral, the programme can be a failure. In practice, farmers borrow at the loan rate, with their crops as collateral against the loan. The loan is intended to be a marketing tool that allows farmers to temporarily store some of their crops and to sell it over a period of a few months for better returns, thus avoiding any glut in the market which can result in steep drops in market prices. If market prices remain below the loan rate (the support price) a farmer can choose to forfeit the crop instead of repaying the loan. This can be a good alternative to the current practice of MSP in India since it can

[8] For greater details see: http://www.ers.usda.gov/topics/farm-economy/farm-commodity-policy/program-provisions/marketing-assistance-loans-loan-deficiency-payments.aspx (accessed 24 October 2013).

avoid the costs of grain procurement, although it will still incur storage costs on the forfeited collateral, which will be much less compared to those under the MSP scheme. To reduce the default rate, granting of a loan in one year can be linked to loan repayment for the previous year. While keeping track of such transactions will add to administrative costs, it is still likely to be cheaper than the current system. In short, storage loans provide a promising option in the Indian case.

As excessive production of food grains puts increasing pressure on the government to provide price support it may become necessary to encourage farmers to switch to other crops, especially when there is diversification of consumer preferences in consumption. In principle, the system can be formalized through a properly designed programme for promoting cultivation of other crops in line with demand forecasts for the coming years.

Variable Levies on Trade

External trade can be an alternative to buffer stocks for stabilizing domestic supplies. A fall in domestic output can be at least partly off-set by an increase in imports or fall in exports and vice versa. Thus liberalized trade can help cushion domestic consumption against domestic supply shocks (see, for example, Gouel 2012). In the case where private external trade is permitted, variable levies, that is, taxes/ subsidies on imports/exports can be used for stabilizing domestic prices. That is, prices are prevented from going above a ceiling level by either subsidizing imports or taxing exports depending on the trade status. Similarly, prices are stopped from falling below the floor level by either taxing imports or subsidizing exports depending on whether net imports are positive or negative.

A comparison between policy alternatives can be based on the extent to which the price stabilization objective is achieved and at what cost. Different policy mixes will have different stabilization effects and different cost implications. The costs of buffer stocking include net purchase and operational costs apart from storage costs and losses. The main cost of trading in international markets relates to fluctuations in world prices, availability of trade finance, and exchange rate fluctuations. Simulation exercises show that the option of variable levies dominates public buffer stocks as a tool for price stabilization (Table 11.5). However, such levies may increase revenue instability, suggesting the need for some form of monetary buffer, such as the IMF's food financing facility for the success of such policies. Maintaining such a facility will cost less than maintaining food stocks. However, this option involves the risk of disruptions to trade due to political reasons or external factors. Moreover, depending entirely on trade for stabilizing supplies can be a risky proposition considering that international markets can be unreliable in crisis situations, necessitating some level of reliance on domestic buffer stocks.

Table 11.5 Cost Effectiveness of Buffer Stocks versus Variable Levies for Price Stabilization (10 per cent price band around target price)

Policy variable/effect	Buffer stocks	Variable levies
Reduction in price variability from the level of no intervention	1.25	8.28
Government's cost of price stabilization (Rs crore per annum)	1588	2803

Source: Srinivasan and Jha (2001).

Notes: The target price is the equilibrium price that will prevail on average with normal rainfall.

Apart from these alternatives for MSP based price stabilization, other policy reforms, such as rationalization of input subsidies can reduce the need for a high MSP. In general, supply and demand side policies are interrelated. High MSP, for example, raises the subsidy costs of PDS. Similarly, if consumer demand is increased either through cash transfers to the poor or better targeting of subsidized grain to the poor it may reduce the need for price support to farmers. Greater role for market mechanisms is possible if food grains for PDS are procured at market prices or if food subsidy is in the form of cash transfers. Further, procurement at market prices will send the right signals to farmers.

***

This chapter argued for a holistic approach to reforms by bringing together the cost and benefits of the entire food system taking into account both supply and demand sides instead of a piecemeal approach to reforms. In particular, it highlighted key policy choices that can help farmers deal with output and price uncertainty and ensure that poor consumers have adequate access to food at all times at reasonable prices. Increasing the supply of food grains through appropriate incentives, providing consumer subsidies for the poor, and stabilizing prices are equally important for ensuring food security.

The current system of food grain procurement combined with PDS is inadequate in meeting the nutrition requirements of a majority of the poor. Despite switching over to a targeted programme, PDS continues to suffer from large inclusion and exclusion errors of targeting, pilferage, and inefficiencies. A shift to subsidizing consumers through cash transfers has the advantage that it does not distort market prices, costs less to operate, and can minimize leakages and diversions with the use of technology (for example, smart cards). However, when food grain markets do not function efficiently, there is a case for food-based programmes. Even here delivery mechanisms can be made more efficient with the use of information and communication technology.

So long as poverty persists and households remain vulnerable to income shocks, social safety net policies will play an important role in ensuring the poor's physical and economic access to food. However, since lack of adequate purchasing power of the poor is the root cause of undernutrition, policies for raising their income levels are of utmost importance. At the macroeconomic level, policies that raise economic growth rates and employment levels can help improve the food security situation. At the micro and sector levels, policies that help raise agricultural productivity in general will be necessary to improve farm incomes. Smallholder productivity, for example, can be improved through access to quality seeds and agricultural R&D tailored to their needs; and improved agricultural practices for decreasing the risk of diseases and rural infrastructure (for example, irrigation, roads, and electricity). Increased efficiency of value chains can increase prices received by farmers. By increasing the purchasing power of poor farmers, these policies can eventually reduce the need for public safety nets.

Though the MSP-based procurement policy has helped improve the aggregate supply situation of food grains, the benefits have not been evenly distributed among farmers in different regions. This policy has not only been cost ineffective and resulted in burgeoning subsidy bills but it has also distorted price signals in the market thereby discouraging private trade, efficient markets, and production of other crops. Price support operations through the MSP programme have led to large buffer stocks, which have become unsustainable. Excessive public stockholding reduces incentives for private storage. Over time it has a multiplier effect and the government ends up with ever-rising stocks to provide price support. This situation can be avoided by allowing private traders a greater role in the market by, for example, procuring food grains for PDS in the open market.

Other options for supporting farmers include commodity programmes, such as deficiency payments and storage loans to farmers. Production can be increased more efficiently if instead of offering high MSPs, public spending is utilized for investments in agricultural technology and R&D, irrigation facilities, quality seeds, and improved access of small and marginal farmers to formal credit. Private sector participation in the food grains market can supplement government efforts in the areas of agricultural technology, R&D, supply chain development, food processing, handling, and packaging activities.

Price stability is equally important since higher food prices severely impact poor consumers by cutting into their budgets. Thus, the government can maintain buffer stocks purely for price stabilization purposes. Depending on external trade for price stabilization through variable trade taxes/subsidies may be more cost effective compared to buffer stocks. But considering that international markets are not always reliable, a judicious combination of these two alternatives will be better in practice than any individual option to stabilize prices.

References

Basu, K. (2011), 'India's food grains policy: An economic theory perspective', *Economic and Political Weekly* XLVI(5): 37–45.

Chand, R., P. Prasanna, and A. Singh (2011), 'Farm size and productivity: Understanding the strengths of small holders and improving their livelihoods', *Economic and Political Weekly* XLVI(26 and 27): 5–11.

Coady, David, Margaret Grosh, and John Hoddinott (2004),' Targeting of Transfers in Targeting of Transfers in Developing Countries: Review of Lessons and Experience', Regional and Sectoral Studies, the World Bank.

FAO (1994), 'Indian experience on household food and nutrition security', Regional Expert Consultation, 8–11 August, Regional Office for Asia and the Pacific, FAO-UN Bangkok (Thailand).

GHI (2011), *Global Hunger Index 2011, The Challenge of Hunger: Taming price spikes and excessive food price volatility*. Washington, DC: International Food Policy Research Institute.

GoI (2002), *Report of the high level Committee on long-term grain policy*. New Delhi: Department of Food and Public Distribution, Ministry of Consumer Affairs, Food and Public Distribution, Government of India.

——— (2012), *Nutrition intake in India*. NSS 66th Round (July 2009-June 2010), National Statistical Organization, Report No. 540 (66/1.0/2). New Delhi: Government of India.

Gouel, Christophe and Jean Sébastien (2012), 'Optimal Food Price Stabilization in a Small Open Developing Country', Policy Research Working Paper 5943, the World Bank.

Goyal, A. (2010), 'Inflationary pressures in South Asia', *Asia-Pacific Development Journal* 17(2): 1–42.

Gulati, A., Satu Kähkönen and P.K. Sharma (2000), 'The Food Corporation of India: Successes and failures in Indian food grain marketing', in Satu Kähkönen and Anthony Lanyi (eds), *Institutions, Incentives and Economic Reform in India*. Thousand Oaks, New Delhi, and London: Sage Publications India Pvt. Ltd, Chapter 10.

Handa, Sudhanshu and Benjamin Davis (2006), 'The Experience of Conditional Cash Transfers in Latin America and the Caribbean', ESA Working Paper No. 06–07, May. Agricultural and Development Economics Division, The Food and Agriculture Organization of the United Nations, Rome, Italy.

Jha, Shikha and Bharat Ramaswami (2012), 'The Percolation of Public Expenditure: Food Subsidies and the Poor in India and the Philippines', in Shekhar Shah, Barry Bosworth, and Arvind Panagariya (eds), *India Policy Forum 2011–12, Volume 8*. New Delhi: Sage Publications, pp. 95–138.

Jha, Shikha and P.V. Srinivasan (2001), 'Taking the PDS to the Poor: Directions for Further Reform', *Economic and Political Weekly*, 36(39, 29 September): 3779–786.

——— (2004), 'Achieving Food Security in a Cost Effective Way: Implications of Domestic Deregulation and Reform under Liberalized Trade', MTID Discussion Paper No. 67. Washington, DC: IFPRI.

Jha, Shikha, P.V. Srinivasan, and M. Landes (2007), 'Indian Wheat and Rice Sector Policies and the Implications of Reform', USDA Economic Research Service, Economic Research Report No. 41.

Johns Hopkins and the International Federation of Red Cross and Red Crescent Societies (2008), *Public Health Guide for Emergencies*, 2nd ed, Chapter 9: Food security and nutrition in emergency.

Khera, Reetika (2011), 'Trends in Diversion of PDS Grain', Centre for Development Economics, Delhi School of Economics, Working Paper No. 198.

Kubo, Kensuke (2011), 'India; The burden of domestic food policy', in Shinichi Shigetomi, Kensuke Kubo, and Kazunari Tsukada (eds), *The World Food Crisis and the Strategies of Asian Rice Exporters*, Chapter 2. Spot Survey No.32, Institute of Developing Economies, Japan External Trade Organization, February 2011. Available at http://www.ide.go.jp/English/Publish/Download/Spot/32.html (last accessed on 24 October 2013).

Panda, M. (2007), 'The Role of Agriculture in Poverty reduction: Case study on India', in Fabrizio Bresciani and Alberto Valdés (eds), *Beyond Food Production*. Cheltenham, UK and Massachusetts, USA: Food and Agricultural Organization of the United Nations and Edward Elgar, Chapter 5.

Planning Commission (2005), *Performance Evaluation of Targeted Public Distribution System*. New Delhi: Programme Evaluation Organization, Government of India.

Rogers, Beatrice Lorge and Jennifer Coates (2002), 'Food-Based Safety Nets and Related Programs', Social Protection Discussion Paper Series No. 0225, the World Bank.

Srinivasan, P.V. and Shikha Jha (2001), 'Liberalized trade and domestic price stability: The case of rice and wheat in India', *Journal of Development Economics* 65(2): 417–41.

Subbarao, Kalanidhi, Aniruddha Bannerjee, Jeanine Braithwaite, Soniya Carvalho, Kene Ezemenari, Carol Graham, and Alan Thompson (1997), *Safety net Programs and Poverty Reduction: Lessons from Cross-Country Experience, Directions in Development*. Washington, DC: The World Bank.

The World Bank (2011), *Social Protection for a Changing India*, Volumes I and II. Washington, DC: The World Bank.

Umali-Deininger, D., M. Sur and K.W. Deininger (2005), 'Foodgrain Subsidies in India: Are they Reaching the Poor?', American Agricultural Economics Association Annual Meeting.

CHAPTER 12

HARNESSING THE DEMOGRAPHIC DIVIDEND IN INDIA

*can primary education deliver?**

RUKMINI BANERJI AND WILIMA WADHWA

Demographic Dividend in India

In recent years, there has been a lot of talk about India's demographic dividend. The share of the working age population in total population has been rising steadily since the 1960s. The proportion of the Indian population in the age group of 15–59 years rose from 53.3 per cent in 1961 to 57.8 per cent in 2001. Projections for the next 30 years put the working age population at almost 65 per cent of the total population by 2040 (Aiyar and Mody 2011). The UN (2009) estimates that in the next 30 years India will gain about 300 million workers making it the largest contributor to the global workforce.

How does having a young population lead to growth? The relationship between population and economic growth is essentially an empirical one since theoretical growth models suggest that the relationship can go either way depending on different conditions. Further, earlier debates on growth

* Evidence from Annual Status of Education Report (ASER) 2005–11. ASER has been explained in the section titled 'Universalizing Education in India'.

and population did not take into account the age structure of the population. Once we do that, a population bulge in a particular age group can affect living standards and conditions (Bloom et al. 2003). For example, a relatively young population results in an increase in the working age ratio—the proportion of population that is in the working age group. This could translate into growth through two channels. First, young workers produce more than they consume. This can lead to generation of savings and accumulation of physical capital. Second, as human capital accumulates, the supply of skilled workers rises, leading to innovation and technical progress, which further spurs growth.

While empirical evidence for such a dividend exists, it is found to be contingent on the existence of the right kind of incentives and a favourable policy environment (Bloom and Canning 2004). Intuitively, for the demographic dividend to actually bear fruit two conditions must be met: (a) the additional labour force is productively employed; and (b) the quality of the labour force is such that it can be productively employed. Namely, both demand and supply have to be in sync to unleash the benefits of the demographic dividend.

On the demand side, the Indian picture looks rosy. India has been one of the fastest growing economies in the world for the last three decades—second only after China. Growth accelerated in the 1980s when the economy shifted to a higher growth path. Average rate of growth, which had hovered below 4 per cent in the three decades prior to 1980, jumped to above 5 per cent in the 1980s, and further increased to about 6 per cent in the 1990s. Since 2003, the rate of growth of the Indian economy has consistently been in excess of 6 per cent with it being close to 10 per cent in many years.

However, when we look at the growth process more closely, the picture does not look as rosy. Indian manufacturing has not traditionally created jobs. This is reflected in the limited movement of labour from agriculture to other more productive sectors of the economy. Even today, in excess of 50 per cent of India's labour force is engaged in low productivity agriculture. The limited movement out of agriculture has predominantly been to low productivity sectors of construction, trade, and transportation. As a result, growth has not been particularly 'pro-poor' and India continues to house the largest number of the world's poor.[1] As Kotwal et al. (2011: 1196) conclude, 'there are two Indias: one of educated managers and engineers

[1] See Kotwal et al. (2011) and Eswaran et al. (2009) for a more detailed discussion about India's growth process.

who have been able to take advantage of the opportunities made available through globalization and the other—a huge mass of undereducated people who are making a living in low productivity jobs in the informal sector—the largest of which is still agriculture.'

Further, given India's growth pattern, a looming bottleneck is a possible 'talent crunch'. The rising education premia certainly point in this direction. Since most of the fast-growing sectors are completely dependent on skilled manpower, unless the supply of such manpower keeps up with demand, the growth process is likely to be seriously constrained. A related issue is that of quality. According to a report by Diana Farrell et al. (2005: 23, 43), 'India's vast supply of graduates is smaller than it seems once their suitability for employment by multinational companies is considered'. The report stresses that the government must 'adjust the country's educational policy to ward off the looming squeeze on talent'.

This brings us to the supply side. Is India's labour force educated? Well trained? Productive? Here too, on the face of things, the situation looks very good. In excess of 96 per cent children in the age group of 6–14 are enrolled in school.[2] In addition, The Right of Children to Free and Compulsory Education Act (RTE), introduced in 2010, will ensure 100 per cent enrolment, improved infrastructure in schools, and reasonable pupil–teacher ratios. While government spending on education remains far less than the suggested 6 per cent of GDP, the government has been steadily increasing its spending on primary education under its flagship primary education programme, the Sarva Shiksha Abhiyan (SSA). In 2007, a similar programme for the universalization of secondary education, Rashtriya Madhyamik Shiksha Abhiyan (RMSA) has also been launched. Both SSA and RMSA focus primarily on providing school inputs and improving access.

To reap the demographic dividend we need a well-trained and productive labour force. How do we measure the quality of the labour force? Do years of schooling adequately capture this quality? Does enrolment translate into learning? Does better school infrastructure lead to better learning outcomes? If a better 'quality' education is the final goal, then does it matter who the provider is? These are some of the questions that we will explore in the context of primary education in this chapter. While it is important to build skills at all levels, unless the basic foundations of

[2] The Government of India reports a net enrolment ratio (NER) of 98.3 per cent for 2009–10. According to ASER (2011), 96.7 per cent of all children in the 6–14 year age group were enrolled in schools.

primary education are built for all, additional human capital accumulation is going to be constrained. Therefore, while improving the state of our education system may not be sufficient for reaping the demographic dividend, it is a necessary first step.[3]

Universalizing Education in India

In the last 50 years universalizing education has been one of the most important policy goals in developing countries. This has resulted in a huge expansion of public schooling across the developing world, driven by the thinking that given the externalities associated with human capital accumulation, the state had to intervene to ensure that adequate investments were made. For a long time, therefore, education policies in developing countries were driven by providing adequate access. Even as recently as 2000, the MDG for education was defined in terms of universalizing enrolment. India is no different in this regard and has made great strides in this area. This is evident from the fact that today more than 95 per cent children are enrolled in schools; close to 90 per cent villages have a primary school within a 1 kilometre radius; and teacher absenteeism has been falling (ASER 2011); all in all educational inputs seem to be in place.

While inputs are necessary and are easier to define, target, and monitor, if we believe that 'education' entails more than just being enrolled in school, then we need to have a set of outcomes that we expect the education process to lead to. However, the obvious outcome measure— 'learning'— is difficult to define and therefore measure. A natural proxy for learning outcomes is children's test scores on standardized tests. In developed countries, where data on test scores is routinely collected, a lot of work has been done on the effectiveness of school inputs. In the US, the debate started with the Coleman Report (Coleman et al. 1966) which found that academic achievement was less related to the quality of school inputs as compared to a child's home and family background. Results for developing countries are mixed, with some studies finding support for school effects (Heyneman and Loxley 1983) and others for parental characteristics (Fuller 1987).

[3] We thank an anonymous referee for pointing out this point.

For India, a lot of data is available on school inputs. However, until recently, very little information was available on outcomes in the education sector. School-based evaluations done by the government are not done annually and are often not in the public domain. The assumption has always been that if we build enough schools, appoint enough teachers, and get children in school, then the expected outcome of 'learning' will happen.

Since 2005, there has been steadily accumulating large-scale data on learning outcomes.[4] An important contributor to this body of evidence has been Pratham's Annual Status of Education Report (ASER). ASER is based on a nationally representative survey that tests children across rural India in basic reading and math. ASER has been brought out annually since 2005 and, therefore, provides comparable data on learning outcomes over time. In this chapter, we present evidence from various rounds of ASER to study trends in primary education in rural India and attempt to understand what ASER and other evidence says about implications for harnessing the demographic dividend in India.

THE DATA: THE ASER

This chapter uses primary data collected in ASER, the largest annual data collection effort with children in rural India. Since 2005, when it was first introduced, every year the report presents estimates of enrolment and basic reading and arithmetic learning outcomes for every district in rural India. The latest ASER is available for 2011, the seventh year of the survey.[5]

ASER uses a two-stage sample design. In the first stage, 30 villages are selected from each district from the Census 2001 village listing using PPS (probability proportional to size) sampling. In the second stage, 20 households are sampled randomly in each of the selected villages. All children in the age group of 3–16 years in the selected households are surveyed and children in the age group of 5–16 years are tested. This gives a sample size of 600 households and approximately 900–1,200 children

[4] Noteworthy are the efforts by Education Initiatives, Muralidharan and Kremer (2008) with their work in Andhra Pradesh, and a series of studies done by JPAL (The Abdul Latif Jameel Poverty Action Lab), among others.

[5] At the time of writing this chapter.

per district. At the national level, ASER visits about 16,000 villages, 300,000 households, and 700,000 children each year.

Every year the core set of questions in ASER, regarding schooling status and basic learning levels remains the same. However, a set of new questions is added in order to explore different dimensions of schooling and learning in the elementary stage. ASER 2006 and 2007 tested reading comprehension for different kinds of readers. ASER 2007 introduced testing in English and asked questions on paid tuition. ASER 2008 had questions on telling time and oral math problems using currency. In addition, ASER 2008 incorporated questions on village infrastructure and household assets. Investigators were asked to record whether the village visited had a tarred road leading to it, whether it had a bank, a ration shop, etc. In the sampled households, information on assets like type of house, telephone, and television was recorded.

Recent ASERs have brought together elements from various previous ASERs. English testing was repeated in 2009. Questions on paid tuition, household, and village characteristics have been retained since 2009. While some of the information available in ASER, like enrolment, is available from other sources, it remains the only annual exercise in the public domain to provide data on learning outcomes, which makes it an invaluable policy tool.

Testing Tools

The instruments used for the ASER survey test language and math skills of children in the age group of 5–16 years. The tools have been extensively used and piloted and provide good estimates for learning levels at the state and district levels (Ramaswami and Wadhwa 2010). Each test takes about five minutes to administer and is done so on a one-on-one basis.

There are five levels in each of the ASER tests of language and math. The highest level in the language test is reading at the level of Grade 2. In math, the highest level is being able to do a simple division problem which is in the curriculum in most states by Grade 4. Figures 12.1 and 12.2 give sample language and math tools used in ASER.

ASER tests are floor-level tests. The same tests are administered to all children, regardless of which class they are enrolled in. Once a child is at the highest level of the test, they do not tell us what else the child is capable of. Therefore, although these tests are useful for evaluating early reading and basic math ability and are able to capture changes in these parameters,

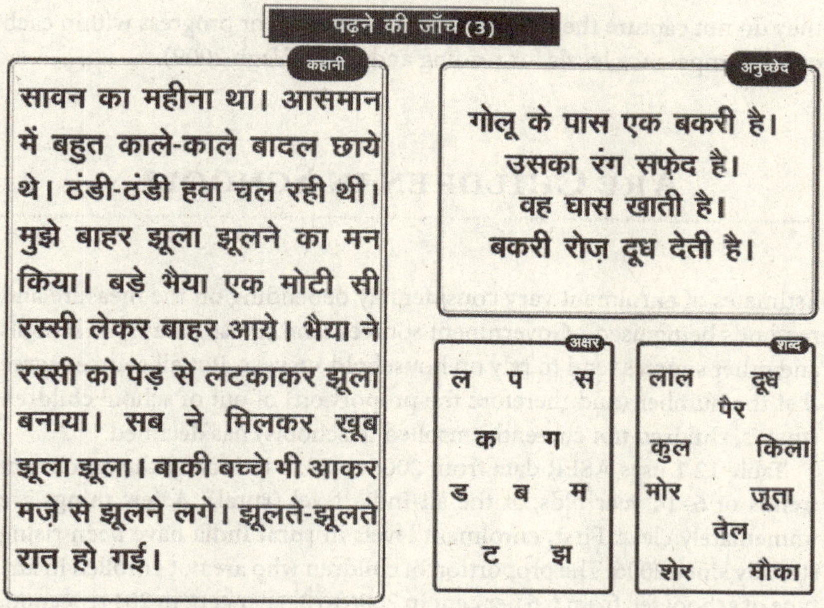

FIGURE 12.1 Sample ASER Language Tool in Hindi

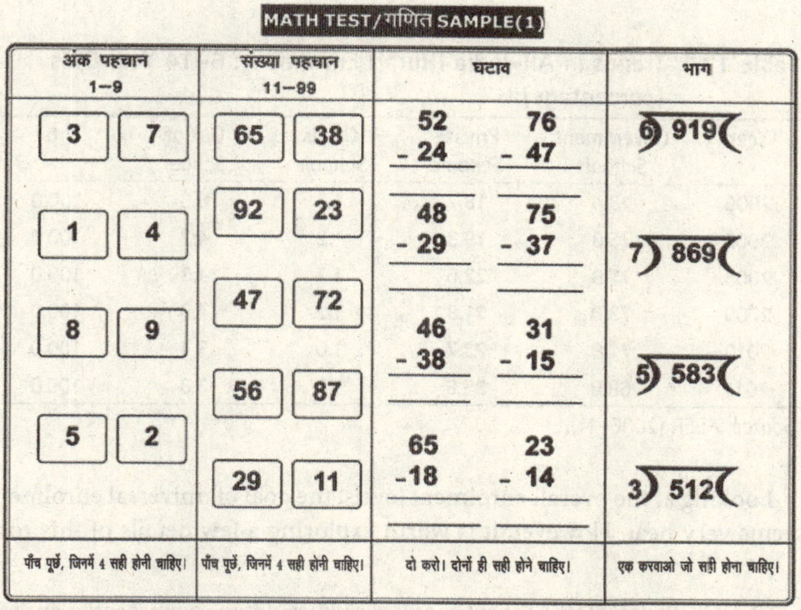

FIGURE 12.2 Sample ASER Math Tool

they do not capture the full spectrum of variation or progress within each of the competency levels for reading and math (Vagh 2009).

Are Children in School?

Estimates of enrolment vary considerably depending on the measure and methods being used.[6] Government sources tend to use data from schools and other sources tend to rely on household surveys. But all sources agree that the number (and therefore the proportion) of out of school children (that is, children not currently enrolled in schools) has declined.

Table 12.1 uses ASER data from 2006 to 2011 to look at the enrolment trends of 6–14 year olds, at the all-India level (rural). A few things are immediately clear. First, enrolment levels in rural India have been rising steadily since 2006. The proportion of children who are not enrolled in any type of school fell from 6.6 per cent in 2006 to 3.3 per cent in 2011. Second, there is a clear shift towards private schools in enrolment. For the rural sector as a whole, enrolment in private schools rose by almost 40 per cent between 2006 and 2011.

Table 12.1 Trends in All-India (Rural) Enrolment: 6–14 Year Olds (percentage)

Year	Government Schools	Private Schools	Other Schools	Out of School	Total
2006	73.4	18.7	1.3	6.6	100.0
2007	75.3	19.3	1.2	4.2	100.0
2008	71.8	22.6	1.3	4.3	100.0
2009	73.0	21.8	1.2	4.0	100.0
2010	71.8	23.7	1.0	3.4	100.0
2011	69.9	25.6	1.1	3.3	100.0

Source: ASER (2006–11).

Looking at the overall enrolment levels, the goal of universal enrolment seems very near. However, it is worth exploring a few details of this rosy

[6] A UNICEF (2012) study of out of school children does a comprehensive analysis of all data sources.

picture. First, are these enrolment trends visible for older children as well? And, second, do girls fare as well as boys—is there any evidence of a gender gap in enrolment? Table 12.2 provides the out of school numbers for different age groups disaggregated by gender.

Table 12.2 Proportion of Out of School Children in Rural India (percentage)

Year	7–10 Year Olds			11–14 Year Olds			15–16 Year Olds		
	All	Boys	Girls	All	Boys	Girls	All	Boys	Girls
2006	4.7	4.1	5.4	8.9	7.7	10.3	21.2	20.2	22.6
2007	2.6	2.4	2.8	6.6	6.0	7.3	19.4	18.3	20.8
2008	2.7	2.5	2.9	6.3	5.5	7.2	18.6	17.3	20.1
2009	2.6	2.4	2.9	6.0	5.3	6.8	17.4	16.8	17.8
2010	2.2	2.1	2.4	5.2	4.8	5.7	16.1	15.7	16.6
2011	1.9	1.8	2.1	4.8	4.4	5.2	15.3	14.6	16.1

Source: ASER (2006–11).

As expected, the proportion of children who are out of school was much higher in older age groups than in younger age groups. However, what Table 12.2 shows is that while the percentage of out of school children in the 15–16 year age group remained above 15 per cent even in 2011, there was a steady decline in out of school numbers over time, even in that age group. This is particularly noteworthy since it is much easier to boost enrolment levels among younger children. Governments routinely use enrolment drives to get children in school and these are typically aimed at younger children. Further, since learning deficits are likely to be smaller for younger children it is far easier to get them back into school as compared to older children. Perhaps incentives, such as scholarships for high school and distribution of bicycles have helped to build and sustain enrolment in higher grades.

If we compare enrolment rates of girls and boys, more girls than boys were out of school in all age groups, and the difference was largest for the 11–14 years age group. However, by 2010 this gender gap seems to have practically disappeared. Therefore, on the enrolment front, things look very good. Most children are in school and previously existing gaps are closing. But India is a very large country and there are huge variations across states. Table 12.3 presents the enrolment scenario across states.

In 2006, states like Bihar, Rajasthan, Jharkhand, and Odisha had close to or more than 10 per cent children out of school as compared to a

Table 12.3 Trends in School Enrolment (Rural India) by State: 6–14 Year Olds (percentage)

States (Rural)	Children Currently not Enrolled in School		Drop (in Percentage Points)	Children Currently Enrolled in Private Schools		Increase (in Percentage Points)
	2006	2011	2006–11	2006	2011	2006–11
Jammu & Kashmir	4.7	2.5	2.2	32.0	37.7	5.7
Himachal Pradesh	1.3	0.6	0.7	19.0	26.6	7.6
Punjab	3.2	1.6	1.6	41.5	39.6	-1.9
Uttarakhand	2.4	1.1	1.3	21.0	31.3	10.3
Haryana	4.9	1.4	3.5	43.1	43.4	0.3
Rajasthan	10.8	4.5	6.3	25.2	35.1	9.9
Uttar Pradesh	6.0	6.1	-0.1	30.3	45.4	15.1
Bihar	12.8	3.0	9.8	11.5	5.5	-6.0
Assam	4.4	4.2	0.2	9.6	14.5	4.9
West Bengal	7.8	4.3	3.5	3.5	6.3	2.8
Jharkhand	8.9	4.7	4.2	11.3	12.8	1.5
Odisha	9.1	3.7	5.4	4.3	5.0	0.7
Chhattisgarh	7.3	2.4	4.9	8.5	11.0	2.5
Madhya Pradesh	3.8	2.2	1.6	11.5	17.2	5.7
Gujarat	5.6	2.7	2.9	5.1	10.8	5.7
Goa	1.6	0.0	1.6	43.0	39.3	-3.7
Maharashtra	3.8	1.1	2.7	18.3	30.3	12.0
Andhra Pradesh	4.2	2.8	1.4	18.5	34.7	16.2
Karnataka	4.9	2.8	2.1	16.0	20.0	4.0
Kerala	0.4	0.1	0.3	46.8	60.8	14.0
Tamil Nadu	2.1	0.9	1.2	19.5	27.0	7.5
Arunachal Pradesh	7.6	3.8	3.8	15.7	17.0	1.3
Nagaland	5.0	2.0	3.0	48.7	40.9	-7.8
Manipur	5.6	1.1	4.5	58.7	71.1	12.4
Mizoram	3.7	0.6	3.1	23.2	13.7	-9.5
Tripura	5.2	1.3	3.9	5.3	5.0	-0.3
Meghalaya	6.8	5.8	1.0	42.8	54.3	11.5
Daman & Diu	1.0	0.0	1.0	23.2	22.3	-0.9
Dadra & Nagar Haveli	6.3	1.2	5.1	17.2	5.5	-11.7
Puducherry	0.3	0.0	0.3	26.2	45.0	18.8
All India	6.6	3.3	3.3	18.7	25.6	6.9

Source: ASER (2006–11).

national average of 6.6 per cent. By 2011, this percentage had fallen below 5 per cent in all these states. Two contrasting states stand out: the first is Bihar, where the proportion of out of school children fell from a staggering 13 per cent to 3 per cent between 2006 and 2011. In comparison, Uttar Pradesh which was slightly under the national average in 2006 remained completely stagnant with no change in this figure.

As mentioned earlier, apart from the sustained decline in the proportion of children out of school, the other major trend in enrolment was the steady increase in the fraction of all children who are enrolled in private schools. Here again there are variations across states. Table 12.3 gives the figures for enrolment in private schools in 2006 and 2011 by state. In 2011, private school enrolments varied between a low of 5 per cent in Odisha to a high of 71 per cent in Manipur. However, irrespective of the level of enrolment, most states saw an increase in the proportion of children enrolled in private schools during this period.

To summarize, two clear trends emerge from the discussion. First, a vast majority of Indian children are enrolled in schools. This increase in enrolment is observed for older as well as the younger age groups and depending on the age group, the gender gap narrowed significantly if not disappeared completely. The picture across states is similar with only Uttar Pradesh lagging behind. Second, there is a clear shift towards private schools across the country.

Evidence on Learning Outcomes—'The Big Stuck'[7]

In the past, much of the literature, whether in economics or in education, was focused on enrolment or years of schooling completed. In fact, the Human Development Index still includes years of schooling as a major component,[8] the assumption being that 'years of schooling' is a good proxy for 'education'. There are at least two issues that need to be kept in mind when using years of schooling as a measure for education. First, in many

[7] The term 'big stuck' has been coined by Lant Pritchett.

[8] Until 2011, the index included the adult literacy rate and gross enrolment rate of all levels of education. From 2011 onwards, the education component of the index is based on mean years of schooling and expected years of schooling.

countries, both developed and developing, a certain number of years of schooling are mandated by law. For example, in India, the 2010 Right to Education Act guarantees eight years of schooling with universal admission for children aged 6–14 years, and automatic promotion till Grade 8. Under such conditions it is likely that all children until a certain age will have to be in school thereby making 'years of schooling' a much weaker measure than before. Second, and more importantly, research done by Hanushek and Woessmann (2008, 2009) strongly suggests that it is what is learned in school that is important for economic productivity rather than simply years spent in school. Muralidharan (2012: 2) summarizes this work to say that 'the share of basic literates as well as the share of high performers has independent and significant effects on growth and that these types of human capital complement each other.'

Is there evidence from India that supports or refutes the arguments that Hanushek and Woessmann and Muralidharan have put forward? How does education in India lead to employment? Are there difficulties with respect to employability or productivity even after many years of education?

Using information from the National Association of Software and Services Companies, Anand (2011) points out that 'although there has been a quantum leap in graduates (engineering colleges in India now have seats for 1.5 million students, nearly four times the 390,000 available in 2000), 75 per cent of technical graduates and more than 85 per cent of general graduates are unemployable by India's high-growth global industries, including information technology and call centers.'

Citing figures from the IMF and the World Bank, the article shows a comparative view of growth across countries. Unlike many other countries, India's growth has not come from increase in the manufacturing sector. The contribution of industry to India's GDP remained stable, at 25.8 per cent in 1991 and 28.3 per cent in 2009. Agriculture shrunk from 29.7 per cent to 17.1 per cent in the same period while services increased from 44.5 per cent to 56.6 per cent. If we look at the contribution of different countries in the share of the world-total GDP based on purchasing power parity (PPP), we see that India went from 3.1 per cent in 1991 to 5.3 per cent in 2010 while China went from 4.2 per cent to 13.21 per cent in the same period.

Given these background statistics, it is clear that India's growth pattern is threatened if the services sector cannot find the workers it needs with requisite skills. Even though in a relative sense, the proportion of Indian children who make it to college is still very small, the absolute numbers are growing. The real challenge is why are they not learning enough and not acquiring adequate skills to become productive members of the work-force. The answer to this lies at the core of the Indian education system. Although school enrolment levels are high, what children learn is woefully inadequate.

While there was a paucity of data on learning outcomes in the past, the last decade generated several national studies on student assessment. What does this research tell us about 'value added' for each year spent in primary school? There have been several large-scale studies of student learning outcomes in the last five years. While each study uses a different set of tools and samples children in different ways, they all point to the fact that learning outcomes are well below where they should be, whether measured by Indian curricular standards or international benchmarks.

ASER is the only source that provides annual district-level estimates for basic learning (reading and arithmetic) every year since 2005. This massive annual effort surveys over 700,000 rural children across the country each year and brings out some disturbing facts.[9] For example, the latest report—ASER 2011 found that across rural India, more than 60 per cent of all children in Grade 5 and over 30 per cent of all children in Grade 8 could not solve a simple three digit by one digit division problem. ASER 2010 used a set of everyday arithmetic tasks in which children had to apply their skills to simple everyday computation problems. ASER 2010 found that 50 per cent of the children in rural India in Grade 8 could not solve a simple problem for calculating area (this kind of arithmetic problem is usually seen in textbooks in Grades 4 or 5). ASER 2009 showed that only a quarter of all Indian children could read a simple sentence in English in Grade 5 and about 60 per cent could read it in Grade 8.

What About the 'Value Added' in School from Year to Year?

The availability of ASER data allows us to track trends over time. Since the ASER tests are designed for primary grades, in this analysis we concentrate on Grades 3 and 5. Table 12.4 gives language and math learning outcomes for children enrolled in these grades at the all-India level.[10] The picture is

[9] ASER results from 2005 to 2011 can be found on www.asercentre.org and on www.pratham.org.

[10] In Table 12.4, children are not disaggregated by type of school.

dismal—50 per cent children in Grade 5 could read a Grade 2 level text in their own language and even fewer could do a division problem which was typically part of Grade 3 or 4 curriculum. The numbers were similar for Grade 3. What is even more worrisome about the picture is that while there was a slight improvement in learning outcomes between 2006 and 2008, there seems to be a steady decline thereafter, with most of the decline concentrated between 2010 and 2011.[11]

Table 12.4 Trends in All-India (Rural) Learning Levels: All Schools

	Language		Math	
Year	Percentage of Grade 3 Children Who Can at Least Read a Grade 1 Level Text	Percentage of Grade 5 Children Who Can at Least Read a Grade 2 Level Text	Percentage of Grade 3 Children Who Can at Least Do a Two-digit Subtraction Problem with Borrowing	Percentage of Grade 5 Children Who Can at Least Do Division (3 digit by 1)
2006	48.02	53.09		
2007	49.04	58.77	42.38	42.40
2008	50.39	56.17	38.73	36.98
2009	46.61	52.80	38.97	38.00
2010	45.65	53.66	36.28	36.15
2011	40.25	48.20	29.86	27.55

Source: ASER (2006–11).

At the all-India level, not only were learning levels low, but not much improvement is visible over the last six years. Most children are at least two grades behind, and the gap is not closing; instead it seems to be growing over time.

Further, work done by Pritchett using ASER data suggests that learning profiles of children through elementary school are flat (Pritchett and Beatty 2012). This implies that if a child does not learn some of the basic skills in early years, it is unlikely that he or she will learn them later. Thus,

[11] It is too early to say what happened during 2010–11. ASER testing is done between September and November each year. This is period is chosen so as to give children a chance to settle in after the summer vacations. The assumption is that children would have overcome any learning loss, which is commonly observed after the summer break. One possible explanation is that the Census of India 2011 was conducted in two phases, from April to September 2010 and from February to March 2011. While neither of these periods coincides with ASER testing, one can speculate that government school teachers, who are used as enumerators, may have been away for much longer periods than is usually the case during the school year.

learning delayed is learning denied. This is an issue for concern because it implies that for a majority of the children each year in school does not lead to much 'value added'.

However, there is considerable variation across states. For example, Table 12.5 presents trends in reading and arithmetic ability of Grade 5 children in three states of Punjab, Uttar Pradesh, and Andhra Pradesh.[12] These three states managed to maintain their reading levels—in fact Punjab even showed a slight improvement. The case of Punjab is particularly interesting. In 2006, the reading levels of Grade 5 children in Punjab were at the national average. However, by 2011 children in Punjab were more than 20 percentage points ahead. The point here is that change is possible and that too in a short period of time.[13]

Table 12.5 Rural State-wise Trends in Learning Levels: All Schools

Year	Language: Percentage of Grade 5 Children Who Can Read a Grade 2 Level Text or More			Math: Percentage of Grade 5 Children Who Can Do Division or More		
	Punjab	UP	AP	Punjab	UP	AP
2006	53.45	37.18	42.27			
2007	64.70	46.89	71.45	54.10	29.57	46.65
2008	63.14	43.51	59.99	43.51	23.58	36.12
2009	64.71	37.65	56.63	49.75	21.11	44.20
2010	69.69	44.07	60.27	69.82	25.04	40.53
2011	71.86	43.25	60.09	61.32	21.36	38.24

Source: ASER (2006–11).

There is one more factor that is common among these three states, which is that all three have large proportions of children in private schools. While both Uttar Pradesh and Punjab have had high enrolments in private schools since 2006, in Andhra Pradesh private school enrolment doubled between 2006 and 2011 (Table 12.3). So is it the case that these states have been able to maintain their learning outcomes because of the presence of private schools? Is it the case that if we disaggregate learning outcomes by type of school, a completely different picture will emerge?

[12] Detailed learning outcomes for all states are available in the annual ASER reports which can be accessed at www.asercentre.org.

[13] During this period the Punjab government collaborated with Pratham (a large-scale NGO in India) to carry out a statewide programme to boost basic learning (reading and arithmetic).

Tables 12.6 and 12.7 present learning outcomes at the all-India level by type of school management. The first thing to note is that in both language and math, learning outcomes are consistently higher in private schools relative to government schools. Second, in language the huge drop observed in reading abilities in primary schools seems to be coming from government schools. In math, there is a drop in learning levels in both government and private schools; however the drop is much larger in government schools. What this suggests is that the observed shift to private schools seems to be justified—the perception that private schools provide a 'better quality' education, indeed, seems to be the case.

Table 12.6 Trends in All-India (Rural) Learning Levels: Language

Year	Language			
	Percentage Percentage of Grade 3 Children Who Can Read a Grade 1 Level Text or More		Percentage of Grade 5 Children Who Can Read a Grade 2 Level Text or More	
	Government	Private	Government	Private
2006	45.83	58.36	51.42	60.82
2007	46.70	61.73	56.70	69.03
2008	46.90	63.86	53.09	67.86
2009	43.84	58.24	50.30	63.09
2010	42.46	57.56	50.69	64.21
2011	35.19	56.33	43.81	62.68

Source: ASER (2006–11).

Table 12.7 Trends in All-India (Rural) Learning Levels: Arithmetic

Year	Math			
	Percentage of Grade 3 Children Who Can do Subtraction or More		Percentage of Grade 5 Children Who Can do Division or More	
	Government	Private	Government	Private
2007	40.21	53.87	40.99	49.44
2008	35.42	51.75	34.40	47.06
2009	36.46	49.69	36.07	46.18
2010	33.18	47.79	33.88	44.19
2011	25.21	44.60	24.49	37.72

Source: ASER (2006–11).

Are Private Schools the Answer?

Both these points are important, though for different reasons. In 2010, The Right of Children to Free and Compulsory Education Act (RTE) came into effect. The Act guarantees free education to all children in the age group of 6–14 years. However, given the provisions of the Act, 'education' is synonymous with 'enrolment'. Since we are already at almost universal enrolment, the obvious question is what more does the act give us? The second question that the earlier analysis raises is why are parents shifting their children to private schools? Anecdotal evidence tells us that parents perceive the 'quality' of education to be better in these schools as compared to public schools. That is the reason they are willing to pay fees (over free education in government schools) to send their children to private schools. But is this really the case?

The debate on whether private schools provide better quality primary education relative to government schools is an old one. In India, the debate has been heating up in recent years. On the one hand, for over ten years through Sarva Shiksha Abhiyan, the government has intensified the move towards universalizing elementary education and The Right of Children to Free and Compulsory Education Act (RTE) came into effect in 2010. This push has led to impressive increases in provision and enrolment. At the same time, ASER as well as other data show a clear rising trend in private school enrolment in rural India.

At the all-India level, private school enrolment increased from 16.3 per cent in 2005 to about 25.6 per cent in 2011—an increase of almost 60 per cent.[14] As Table 12.3 shows, there is considerable variation across states. At one end of the spectrum are states like Uttar Pradesh, Haryana, Punjab, and Kerala where private school enrolment was 40 per cent or more; at the other end are states like Bihar and West Bengal with enrolment in private schools being closer to 5 per cent. However, across all states, enrolment in private schools has been increasing over time.

What has led to this shift towards private schools in rural areas? Government schools provide free schooling, have more qualified and higher paid teachers, and better infrastructure. On the other hand, private schools charge a fee, their teachers typically are less qualified, and get paid

[14] Other data sources give similar numbers for private school enrolments in rural India. According to DISE (District Information System for Education) (2008–9) private school enrolment was about 29 per cent for children below 14 years (Grades 1–8).

far less than their public school counterparts. Yet, the perception is that private schools provide better quality education. The reasons cited for this advantage include lower teacher absenteeism in private schools, smaller class sizes since they can hire more teachers at lower salaries, and more accountability in hiring and firing staff based on performance (Kingdon 1996; Muralidharan and Kremer 2008; Tooley et al. 2007). Until recently, there was very little evidence available on the 'quality' of education in private schools. The assumption was that the factors cited here would translate into 'better' education. However, since 2005 ASER provides annual estimates of learning outcomes in government and private schools and there is evidence from other studies as well.

At first glance, the ASER data seems to validate the private school advantage. As discussed in the previous section, and as Tables 12.6 and 12.7 demonstrate, private schools have better learning outcomes compared to government schools. In 2011, in Grade 5, the percentage of children who could read at least a Grade 2 level text was 50.7 in government schools. The corresponding figure in private schools was 64.2—a whopping 13.5 percentage point advantage. However, this difference in learning outcomes does not take into account factors that affect school choice and a child's learning levels. For instance, it is well established that a mother's education has a positive impact on the probability that a child goes to school as well as her learning ability. Supplemental help offered at home, in the form of paid tuition or by family members, also improve learning outcomes of children, regardless of whether they go to government or private schools. If any of these factors is positively correlated with the probability of going to a private school, their impact will show up as enhanced learning outcomes in private schools.

For instance, richer households can afford to pay for additional tuition for their children. It is also well established that a larger proportion of children from more affluent homes attend private schools.[15] In this case, part of the observed learning differential between government and private schools would be due to the extra help that private school children were getting at home and not because of the better quality of education being imparted in private schools. Therefore, to identify the school effect, the endogeneity of school choice has to be taken into account.

[15] ASER 2007 and 2009–11 show that a greater proportion of children in private schools availed of paid tuition, though more and more government school children have been resorting to paid tuition since 2009.

Once these different factors are taken into account, the debate is far from settled. After controlling for observed family and child characteristics, Muralidharan and Kremer (2008) find that children in private schools had higher test scores of about 0.4 standard deviations. Desai et al. (2008) and French and Kingdon (2010) find similar results[16]—while the private school advantage narrows after controlling for observed child and family characteristics, test scores of private school children remain higher than those of children in government schools.

However, there are large variations across Indian states and the picture is not that clear once an analysis is done at the state level. Goyal and Pandey (2009) look at variations in learning outcomes across government and private schools in Uttar Pradesh and Madhya Pradesh. They find that in these states, to start with private schools have a very small advantage in terms of learning outcomes. However, even this advantage is explained away once family and school factors are controlled for. Like Muralidharan and Kremer (2008), they also find that private schools have smaller class sizes but lesser qualified and trained teachers. However, they find that school and teacher characteristics account for very little variation in quality between schools, and in particular, teacher effort is at best weakly correlated with their qualifications, training, and experience.[17]

Wadhwa (2009) and Mukerji and Wadhwa (2011) using ASER data for 2009 find similar results as Goyal and Pandey (2009). Once demographic, locational, and other child characteristics are controlled for, two-thirds of learning differentials in reading between government and private schools can be attributed to factors other than the type of school. At the state level, they find that for reading in the local language, in many cases most of the learning differentials disappear once other factors are controlled for. In some states, where government schools had higher learning levels to start with, the gap widened once other factors were taken into account.

Evidence from India strongly suggests that learning levels are low and inadequate across the board. A large majority of rural children still go to government schools and while there may be a small learning advantage in private schools, those levels too are lower than what is needed for Indian children to complete the elementary curriculum in India in a satisfactory way.

[16] French and Kingdon (2010) use ASER data for 2005–7. Desai et al. (2008) use scores from the ASER tool that was employed as part of a separate large-scale survey.

[17] Bhattacharjea et al. (2011) have a similar finding for government school teachers in a sample of five states.

Will the New Law RTE Improve Learning Outcomes?

The RTE Act came into effect in 2010, and not surprisingly has come under attack from various quarters. With enrolment levels already as high as 95 per cent in most states, many feel that the government has done too little too late. Proponents of 'low cost' private schools feel that it imposes an unnecessary burden, in terms of infrastructure norms, on these schools.[18]

Since 2010, ASER has reported data on various RTE norms, compliance with which can be easily observed during school visits.[19] The RTE specifies clear norms for enrolment, access, school infrastructure, teacher appointment, TLM, and pupil teacher ratio (PTR). Most of these relate to school infrastructure and are easily observable. However, where RTE norms are fuzzy is in the area of children's learning achievements. Phrases like 'building up child's knowledge, potentiality and talent' and 'development of physical and mental abilities to the fullest extent' are used. In many ways, RTE norms continue to reflect the age old government tradition of focusing on inputs rather than outcomes.

Table 12.8 provides figures for compliance with RTE norms from ASER 2010 and 2011. In almost all indicators compliance is in excess of 50 per cent and unlike the case of learning outcomes, here we see improvement year on year. In the case of most physical infrastructure indicators, compliance improved between 2010 and 2011. The biggest jump was seen in the provision of girls' toilets and libraries. The one indicator that was lagging behind is the pupil–teacher ratio. RTE has detailed norms regarding government schools depending on enrolment, type of school, etc. Essentially the norm boils down to a maximum PTR of 30. By 2011, only 40 per cent of rural schools had PTRs which were 30 or less. But there is huge pressure on all states for teacher recruitments and so over time with the influx of teachers into schools, especially in states that have had chronic shortages of teachers, the situation is likely to improve.

[18] This section draws heavily from Wadhwa (2010).

[19] Every alternate year, ASER surveyors visit a government primary or upper primary school in each sampled village. The school information is recorded either based on observations (such as attendance or usability of the facilities) or with information provided by the school (such as grants information). School observations were reported in 2005, 2007, and 2009–11.

Table 12.8 Compliance with RTE Norms in Rural Government Schools

	2010	2011
Number of schools visited	14,240	14,283
Percentage of schools complying with:		
Pupil–teacher ratio	38.90	40.65
Teacher–classroom ratio	76.18	74.25
Percentage of schools that have:		
Office/store/office-cum-store	74.00	74.14
Playground	61.98	62.64
Boundary wall	50.91	54.07
Drinking water provision and available	72.70	73.51
Girls' toilets available	68.83	77.41
Girls' toilets available and useable	32.93	43.77
Kitchen sheds for cooking mid-day meals	82.05	83.69
Library books available	62.51	71.44
Library books in use by children	37.87	42.33
TLM observed in Grade 2	80.71	82.07
TLM observed in Grade 4	76.41	78.15

Source: ASER (2010–11).

While RTE lays down detailed infrastructure norms, here too it stops short. For instance, consider the norm regarding provision of girls' toilets. According to RTE, all government schools are required to have a separate girls' toilets, presumably to reduce girls' dropout rates as well as for improving their attendance. And a substantial 80 per cent rural government schools are in compliance with this norm. However, ASER looks not only at provision but also at usability. For example, what good is a girls' toilet if it is locked and/or not useable? In 2010, only a third of government school girls' toilets were actually useable. By 2011, this number was still under 50 per cent.[20] Libraries is another case in point. A majority of the schools had library books available as mandated by RTE. However, in only about 40 per cent of the schools were children observed using library books. Data on tracking physical infrastructure suggests improvements in provision even from one school year to the next. The use of facilities is also improving although government measurements usually focus on provision rather than usability.

[20] ASER investigators are asked to check both availability and usability of school facilities.

Wadhwa (2010) finds that learning outcomes in government primary schools are not correlated with infrastructure facilities in the school, and are negatively correlated with PTR. However, once a child's demographic and other characteristics are controlled for, even this latter correlation disappears. Bhattacharjea et al. (2011), find that teacher qualifications are also not correlated with learning outcomes.

Inputs and infrastructure are necessary for the good functioning of schools. They are easy to target and monitor. However, it is important to measure how inputs translate into outcomes and the efficacy of this process. The outcome is 'learning', defined in some manner, and its necessary pre-requisite is 'attendance' of both teachers and children in schools. Unless children and teachers attend school and instruction takes place, learning, however defined, will not take place no matter how many classrooms, toilets, and playgrounds are built. While RTE specifies many norms regarding inputs, it falls short in specifying expected outcomes of a child being enrolled in school or what will be guaranteed in terms of learning.[21]

RTE was heralded as a landmark piece of legislation. However, as we have seen, it falls short on many counts. As states rush to spend large sums of public money to make schools compliant with the RTE norms of inputs and infrastructure, we need to look at the evidence and figure out what the purpose of the act is. Is it to guarantee enrolment? Or something more than that? If it is just to make sure that every child is enrolled in school, then we are practically there. Nothing more needs to be done. However, if the goal is to guarantee that every child in the country receives 'quality' education, that provides her with the necessary skills to be a productive member of society, then we have a long way to go. To reap the demographic dividend, simply meeting RTE norms will not be enough.

Economic Growth, Demographic Dividend, and Education in India

ASER deals with children from rural India. Many in India look at ASER results with the belief that this is all about rural India, children from unschooled families, and poorly performing government schools. However a recent study throws harsh light on elite urban schools as well. Conducted

[21] The RTE does specify that teachers 'maintain regularity and punctuality in attending school' but 'regularity' and 'punctuality' are not clearly defined.

by Education Initiatives in 2006, this study covered 32,000 children in a set of English medium elite schools in metros; most of these children came from India's best educated families. The study found that while these children do well on questions which require textbook knowledge, they flounder badly when asked to apply what they know to solve problems that are a little bit different from what is usually in the textbooks.[22] A more recent wave of this study finds similar results.

India selected two states, Tamil Nadu and Himachal Pradesh, to participate in the PISA 2009+ tests (PISA stands for OECD's Program for International Student Assessment). Overall there were 75 participants including these two states from India. PISA results put the Indian students at the bottom of the list. PISA rankings show Kyrgyzstan at number 75 and the two Indian states at number 73 and 74.

As Chavan and Banerji (2012) suggest, just the ranking is not enough to understand how bad the situation is. PISA has five levels of reading and math literacy ranging from 1 to 5. On this ladder, the nodal score of Indian students is at 1b, the *lowest possible* for reading literacy, and at 1 for math literacy. Further, it is important to understand that the sample for the PISA assessment was drawn from those 15-year-olds who have survived in school up to this age. So, those who had discontinued their education for one reason or another were not even a part of the sample. Only about 17 per cent of the sampled students were found to be at the threshold of acceptable reading and math literacy as per international standards. That would make it about 7–8 per cent of all Indian children of age 15.[23]

Putting all of this together, where do we stand? What are the implications for harnessing the demographic dividend in India? All the evidence points to the fact that as a country India is not able to 'ensure' or 'guarantee' even basic levels of reading or arithmetic in primary schools. Thus, the essential skills of critical thinking, expression, comprehension, and problem solving in higher grades are weak. The primary problem with our education system is that we do not build the basic foundations of learning in early grades and do not stress the importance of critical thinking and application in upper primary or middle schools. This weakness runs through the entire education system from schools to colleges.

The two major trends that characterize the Indian education system today—move to private schools and the government's thrust on more inputs—are unlikely to make a major headway on the main issue that

[22] http://www.ei-india.com/exec-summ.pdf.

[23] This section draws from Chavan and Banerji (2012).

needs urgent nationwide attention—namely improving learning levels. Without immediate acceleration in basic learning levels and large-scale remedial efforts in primary schools, India's demographic advantage will dribble away. The potential for harnessing growth through the unique and unprecedented population bulge is getting squandered by not focusing on one of the highest national priorities—effective investment in children's education.

References

Aiyar, S. and A. Mody (2011), 'The Demographic Dividend: Evidence from the Indian States', IMF Working Paper WP/11/38.

Anand, G. (2011), 'India Graduates Millions, but Too Few Are Fit to Hire', *Wall Street Journal*, 5 April 2011. Available online at http://online.wsj.com/article/SB10001424052748703515504576142092863219826.html?mod=WSJ_hp_mostpop_read.

Bhattacharjea, S., W. Wadhwa, and R. Banerji (2011), *Inside Primary Schools: A Study of Teaching and Learning in Rural India*. New Delhi: Pratham Mumbai Education Initiative.

Bloom, D. and D. Canning (2004), 'Global Demographic Change: Dimensions and Economic Significance', NBER Working Paper No. 10817.

Bloom, D., D. Canning, and J. Sevilla (2003), *The Demographic Dividend: A New Perspective on the Economic Consequences of Population Change*. Santa Monica, California: RAND.

Chavan, M. and R. Banerji (2012), 'The Challenge of Achieving Desirable Levels of Learning in Elementary Education', *Journal of Governance*, IC Centre for Governance, 5: 33–46.

Coleman, J., E. Campbell, C. Hobson, J. McPartland, A. Mood, F. Weinfall, and R. York (1966), *Equality of Educational Opportunity*. Washington, DC: Department of Health, Education and Welfare.

Desai, S., A. Dubey, R. Vanneman, and R. Banerji (2008), 'Private Schooling in India: A New Educational Landscape', *India Policy Forum*, 5: 1–58.

Eswaran, M., A. Kotwal, B. Ramaswami, and W. Wadhwa (2009), 'Sectoral Labour Flows and Agricultural Wages in India, 1983–2004: Has growth trickled down and How?' *Economic and Political Weekly*, 44(2): 46–55.

Farrell, D., M. Laboissière, J. Rosenfeld, S. Stürze, and F. Umezawa (2005), *The Emerging Global Labor Market: Part II—The Supply of Offshore Talent in Services*. New York: McKinsey Global Institute.

French, R. and G. Kingdon (2010), 'The Relative Effectiveness of Private and Government Schools in Rural India: Evidence from ASER Data', Institute of Education, DoQSS Working Paper 1003.

Fuller, B. (1987), 'What School Factors Raise Achievement in the Third World?' *Review of Educational Research*, 57(3): 255–92.

Goyal, S. and P. Pandey (2009), 'How do Government and Private Schools Differ? Findings from Two Large Indian States', World Bank South Asia Human Development Sector Report No. 30.

Hanushek, E. and L. Woessmann (2008), 'The Role of Cognitive Skills in Economic Development', *Journal of Economic Literature*, 46(3): 607–88.

——— (2009), 'Do Better Schools Lead to More Growth: Cognitive Skills, Economic Outcomes and Causation', IZA Discussion Paper No. 4575.

Heyneman, S. and W. Loxley (1983), 'The Effect of Primary-School Quality on Academic Achievement Across Twenty-nine High- and Low-Income Countries', *The American Journal of Sociology*, 88(6): 1162–94.

Kingdon, G. (1996), 'Private Schooling in India: Size, Nature and Equity effects', *Economic and Political Weekly*, 31(51): 3306–14.

Kotwal, A., B. Ramaswami, and W. Wadhwa (2011), 'Economic Liberalization and Indian Economic Growth: What's the Evidence?' *Journal of Economic Literature*, 49(4): 1152–99.

Mukerji, S. and W. Wadhwa (2011), 'Do Private Schools Perform better than Public Schools? Evidence from Rural India', mimeo, ASER Centre.

Muralidharan, K. (2012), 'Priorities for Primary Education Policy in India's 12th Five-year Plan', Paper presented at the India Policy Forum, July.

Muralidharan, K. and M. Kremer (2008), 'Public and Private Schools in Rural India', in P. Peterson and R. Chakrabarti (eds), *School Choice International: Exploring Public-Private Partnerships*, pp. 91–110. Cambridge: MIT Press.

Pritchett, L. and A. Beatty (2012), 'The Negative Consequences of Overambitious Curricula in Developing Countries', Centre for Global Development Working Paper 293.

Ramaswami, B. and W. Wadhwa (2010), 'Survey Design and Precision of ASER Estimates', mimeo, ASER Centre.

Tooley, J., P. Dixon, and S.Gomathi (2007), 'Private Schools and the Millennium Development Goal of Universal Primary Education: A Census and Comparative Survey in Hyderabad, India', *Oxford Review of Education*, 33(5): 539–60.

UNICEF (2012), *Global Initiative on Out of School Children*. Draft India Report.

United Nations (2009), *World Population Prospects: The 2008 Revision*. New York: Department of Economic and Social Affairs, Population Division, United Nations.

Vagh, S. (2009), 'Evaluating Read India: Development of Tools for Assessing Hindi Reading and Writing Ability and Math Skills of Rural Indian Children in Grades 1–5', mimeo, ASER Centre.

Wadhwa, W. (2009), 'Private Schools: Do They Provide Higher Quality Education?' in *Annual Status of Education Report*. New Delhi: Pratham Resource Centre and ASER Centre, pp. 6–8.

——— (2010), 'RTE Norms and Learning Outcomes', in *Annual Status of Education Report*. New Delhi: Pratham Resource Centre and ASER Centre, pp. 8–10.

CHAPTER 13

HEALTH SECURITY

GITA SEN*

Assuring health security to citizens (and non-citizens) is at the centre of major global debates about health, social security, and poverty today. The strategic importance of universal health coverage at the heart of the challenge of health security is being increasingly recognized, for instance, at the World Health Assembly in May 2012, as well as in ongoing discussions about the post-2015 global development agenda, and in many related and independent forums among health policymakers, development organizations, and civil society. India is no exception to the growing attention to this challenge. In October 2010, as part of the preparatory work for the Twelfth Five-Year Plan, the Planning Commission of India appointed a high level expert group (HLEG) with a specific mandate to focus on the direction that the country should follow to achieve universal health coverage. HLEG's report (High-Level Expert Group on Universal Health Coverage 2011) was submitted roughly a year later, and a major national debate has ensued in relation to the drafting of the chapter on health in the Twelfth Plan.

While India strives to be among the powerful new engines for global economic growth, its health indicators tell a sadly different story of a country where human development has lagged drastically behind economic

* I am grateful for discussions in the High Level Expert Group on Universal Health Coverage set up by the Planning Commission of India in preparation for the Twelfth Five-Year Plan. Needless to say, all errors of interpretation are mine alone. I am also grateful to Dr Aditi Iyer for critically reading and commenting on the draft paper and to Bhavya Reddy, Mridula Shankar, and Altaf Virani for research support.

performance. Table 13.1 provides some comparisons with three other Asian countries, large, medium, and small, showing the extent to which key Indian health indicators lag behind these countries.

Table 13.1 Health Indicators Compared

	Infant Mortality Rate, 2009	Under 5 Mortality Rate, 2009	Full Immunization, 2011	Skilled Birth Attendance, 2000–10
India	50	66	66	47
China	17	19	95	96
Thailand	12	13	98	99
Sri Lanka	13	16	99	97

Source: World Health Organization (2011), cited in the HLEG report (2011: Table 2; p. 182).

While there are many factors within and outside the health sector that are responsible for India's relatively weak performance in addressing the health needs of its people, this chapter discusses the challenges to the health system through a focus on three central aspects of health security—affordability, access, and acknowledgement—which may be called the three As. The three As look at the problem of health security from the perspective of people by asking whether healthcare is affordable; whether it can be accessed easily; and whether health problems are even acknowledged as such within families and/or the health system. The chapter addresses issues of equity and the social determinants of health in examining the features and evolution of the three As in the Indian context. Finally, it raises some critical policy questions and points to possible directions towards greater accountability at the end. In doing this, there are many health related issues that are of great importance to the future of the health system but which the chapter makes no attempts to cover in depth.

An Evolving Environment for Health

Both the demographic and epidemiological transitions in the country are at present incomplete. While birth and death rates have fallen in the decades since Independence, the former has declined more slowly than the latter with a resultant ballooning of the young population in the country. In 2010, Indians under the age of 15 years accounted for 31 per cent of the total population (United Nations 2010; Figure 13.1). Bloom et al. (2003) have argued that such a young population with its economically productive years still ahead holds a potential demographic dividend.

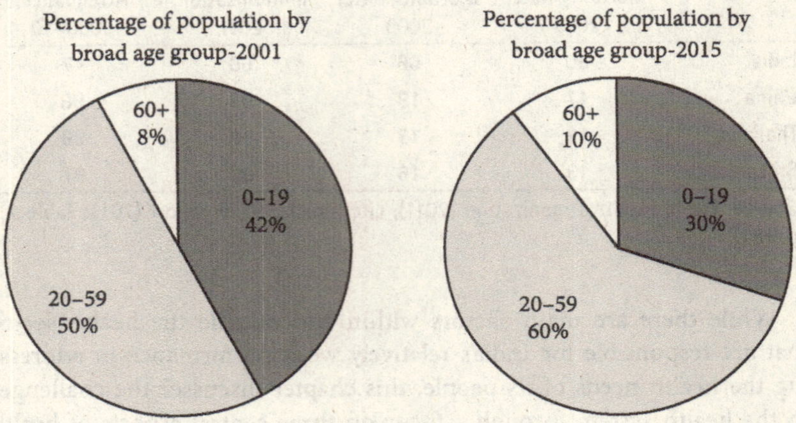

FIGURE 13.1 Age Distributions, 2001 and 2015 (projection)

Source: Office of the Registrar General and Census Commissioner India (2006: Table 19; p. 145).

By 2015, the population in the productive ages of 20–59 years is projected to be 60 per cent of the total. However, this potential can only be reaped if young people are educated and healthy. For young girls and women entering their reproductive years, the challenge of the inter-play of health needs and gender inequality can constitute a serious burden, one that is only partly recognized or acknowledged in public debates about health security. Problems of maternal morbidity and mortality, illnesses of infancy and childhood, and of many other less well-acknowledged health problems of girls and women (Bang et al. 2010) add a major load to the overall burden of illness in the country.

The prevalence and continuing high incidence of infectious diseases compound this burden. Infectious diseases contributed 38 per cent of the total disease burden in 2005 according to the National Commission on Macroeconomics and Health (2005b), and maternal and perinatal ill-health added another 12 per cent—together half of the total burden. Much of this is because major problems of unsafe water, sanitation, and serious under- and malnutrition have not been resolved, even while some broad social determinants, such as pasteurization of milk have made progress. As a result, the infectious diseases problem in the country continues to be a serious one despite other advances, such as a significant fall in family size (despite the incomplete demographic transition) such that the south and west of the country are at or close to replacement level fertility and progress has also been made in this direction in many of the other states (Visaria and Visaria 2003).

A point worth noting about the history of infectious diseases is that, in many of the currently high income countries, the decline in the nineteenth and twentieth centuries was *inter alia* driven by better nutrition, water treatment, improved sanitation, reduced urban crowding, and lower family sizes. Vaccines played a role in speeding up this decline after it was well on its way, and after they became an accepted part of preventive public health. The decline could sometimes be very steep as for example in the US, where deaths due to infectious diseases fell from around 800 per 100,000 population in 1900 to low double-digit figures 50 years later (Armstrong et al. 1999). This points to the critical role played by the social determinants of health in addressing the burden of ill health (Commission on Social Determinants of Health 2008).

In India, as is true for some other low/middle income countries, the incomplete epidemiological transition characterized by a high incidence of infectious diseases has gone hand in hand with a growing incidence of non-communicable diseases (NCDs). This burden has been rising rapidly and accounts for 34 per cent, while injuries (including traffic accidents) account for another 16 per cent (Figure 13.2). Assuring health security in the country therefore means addressing the dual burden of preventing and treating NCDs, such as diabetes and cardiovascular problems (not only among the well-off but also among poor people) without yet having transitioned out of communicable diseases or poor maternal and reproductive health. NCDs often require long-term or lifelong care and make greater demands on funds, human support, and facilities of both families and the health system at large.

Since India and China are viewed among the dynamic economies of Asia and the world, it is worth noting some of their differences in this regard. Table 13.2 shows that China has completed the demographic transition (Bloom 2010; Bloom et al. 2010) and is now facing the problem of ageing while India's population is much younger. But China, despite various health reform challenges (Cao et al. 2003; Dummer and Cook 2007; Hsiao 1995; Wagstaff et al. 2009; Yip et al. 2009), has also nearly completed

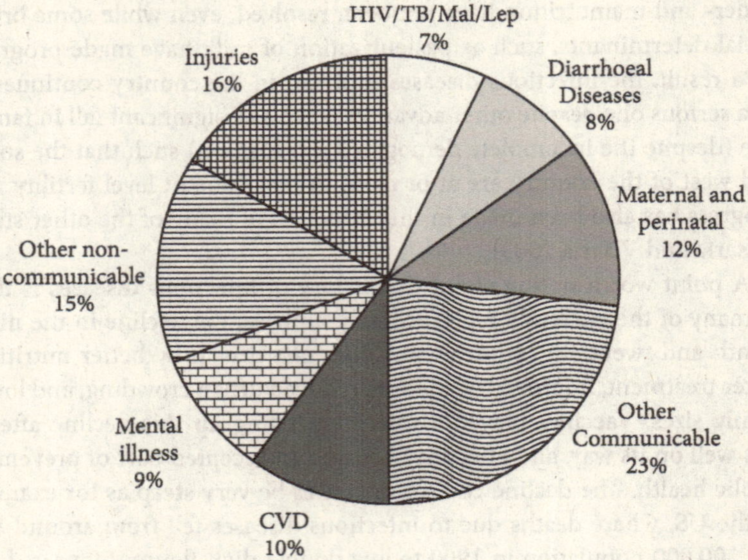

FIGURE 13.2 Distribution of the Disease Burden, 1998

Source: Peters et al. (2001), cited in National Commission on Macroeconomics and Health (2005b: Table 1; Page 2).

its epidemiologic transition with infectious diseases accounting for less than 25 per cent of the total burden of illnesses. In India, on the other hand, the share of infectious diseases and NCDs is each over 40 per cent as can be seen in Figure 13.2.

Table 13.2 India versus China—Some Key Indicators

	China	India
Population >64 years (2010)	8.2%	4.9%
Population <15 years (2010)	19.5%	30.6%
Total fertility rate (2010)	1.56	2.54
Life expectancy at birth (2010)	72.7	64.2
Maternal mortality ratio (per 100,000 live births) (2008*)	38	230
% of infants with low birth weight (2006–2010)	3	28
Communicable diseases (2000)	<25%	>40%

Source: United Nations (2011: p. 325, p. 513, Table S.14; pp. 116–17, Table S.16; pp. 122–3); UNICEF (2011); Peters et al. (2001) cited in National Commission on Macroeconomics and Health (2005b: Table 1; p. 2); Sen (2012: p. 47).

These differences imply that the approaches to health security and to health system reforms may not be identical in the two countries, either in the past or at present.

Table 13.3 provides a comparison of ageing in India versus that in China and Japan, showing the impact of a faster demographic transition in Japan and China as compared to India. However, there are some states in India, notably Kerala, where ageing is a more important issue because of the more rapid demographic transition.

Table 13.3 Ageing—India, China, Japan

% population 60+ years	1950	2010	2050
India	<10	8	20
China	<10	12	31
Japan	<10	30	40

Source: Bloom (2010, Figure 1.4, p. 125).

Evolution of the Health System

Most health analysts trace the modern Indian health system to its antecedents in the report of the Bhore Committee of 1946 followed by a number of subsequent committees—the Sokhey Sub-committee (1948), Mudaliar Committee (1962), Chaddha Committee (1963), Kartar Singh Committee (1973), Srivastava Committee (1975), and the ICMR–ICSSR Joint Panel (1980). Each of these addressed all or particular aspects of the system, and their recommendations together resulted in what we have today—a three-tier system of health centres for primary, secondary, and tertiary care in the public sector, along with a growing private sector ranging from unlicensed practitioners at one end to large corporate hospitals at the other (Sen 2012). In addition to the reports of these committees, the government enunciated two versions of a National Health Policy (1983 and 2002), and a National Population Policy (2000) which together provided a framework for health and population policies.[1] Two relatively recent reports—the report of the

[1] Since health is a state subject according to the Indian Constitution's delineation of powers, the government at the centre can enunciate framework policies and also negotiate with state governments to move the policy agenda forward. This is not, however, binding on states, which can choose to follow the centre or take their own directions.

National Commission on Macroeconomics and Health (2005a), and of the HLEG on Universal Health Coverage (2011) have also focused on an analysis and recommendations for the health system overall.

Around the time of Independence, there was only a very small private sector providing western medical care. Early planners, therefore, argued for the creation of a national public health service and for mobilizing the needed resources. The Bhore Committee (1946) also argued that attention should be on rural areas, with a focus on preventive measures and training of 'social physicians'. The Sokhey Sub-committee of the National Planning Committee (1948) supported the Bhore Committee by suggesting that there should be one community health worker for every 1,000 rural population. Although both Bhore and Sokhey gave importance to building human resources, the first two Five-Year Plans focused instead much more on building physical infrastructure.

Worse, the idea of an integrated system was challenged by the starting of vertical disease control programmes, useful though some of them undoubtedly were, for example, the smallpox eradication programme. One of the most problematic of the vertical programmes was on family planning, resulting in a serious long-term rupture between the sexual and reproductive health of people and the provision of birth control services. The emergence of contraceptive method-specific programme targets in the late 1960s drove the family planning programme further and further towards overwhelming reliance on female sterilization, distortionary incentives for field workers, and non-recognition, at times amounting to violation, of health needs and human rights (Ramachandran and Visaria 1997; Sen 2003).

The Alma Ata Declaration of 1978 provided some reverse momentum towards a more integrated and comprehensive health system. This was reflected in the report of the ICMR–ICSSR Joint Panel (1981) which called once more for such a system to be developed under the framework of a national health policy. As a result of the pressure, the government did enshrine the Alma Ata vision in a National Health Policy in 1983, but failed to follow it up with sufficient investments in human or other resources. Thus, instead of comprehensive primary care, the actual direction of the programme remained vertical, supplemented by only selective primary healthcare. This was also the root of rapid expansion of the private sector in health on the grounds that the public sector was inadequate for the health needs of the country (Duggal n.d.). This private expansion was largely unregulated, a situation that continues until today.

The 1980s also saw a sustained erosion of drug price controls in line with the policy climate of liberalization of controls after the mid-1980s. The reduction in price control from a peak of over 300 price-controlled drugs in the 1970s has had a major implication for the affordability of healthcare, as discussed later.

The growth of the private sector in health accelerated during the period of economic liberalization and privatization that took off in the 1990s, through the provision of tax and other incentives, such as land for setting up private clinics and hospitals. While the quid pro quo for getting these benefits was a requirement of reserving a share of beds and services for poor patients, the general perception is that this is flouted with impunity as there are really no mechanisms to ensure accountability.[2] Meanwhile, the public sector remained starved of funds; critical health sector positions, such as those of auxiliary nurse midwives (ANMs) were left unfilled; public infrastructure deteriorated; and the impact was felt in terms of rising inequalities in health access, a point we return to later. There were growing rural–urban disparities in health infrastructure, a severe shortage of personnel, especially doctors, and absence of minimum quality standards for medical establishments. All this was pointed out in the government's second major statement of policy intention—the National Health Policy (2002).

Coming as it did after a decade of economic liberalization, the new National Health Policy (2002) argued for an increased role for the private sector, especially for those who can afford to pay, and for more public–private partnerships (PPPs). But it also called for raising government health spending to 2 per cent of GDP. Once again, the government ignored the last recommendation and went ahead with the first two. As a result, the ratio of public spending on health to GDP continued to stagnate at around 1 per cent—one of the lowest ratios in the world. The recent rise to 1.4 per cent is largely due to the pay increases mandated by the Sixth Pay Commission. Other recommendations of the policy, such as refocusing on primary care, decentralization, or starting a cadre of licensed medical practitioners also received little attention.

A recent international comparison by the HLEG (2011: 96) shows that while a measure of fiscal capacity—total public spending as a per cent of GDP—is higher in India (at 34 per cent) by around 10 percentage points

[2] An example is the case of Apollo Hospitals in Delhi which has been pulled up for violations of these requirements by the Delhi High Court (*The Hindu* 2009).

than the corresponding figures for China, Thailand, and Sri Lanka, public spending on health is much lower. It argues that '...public spending on health as a per cent of GDP is low in India because the state and central governments have chosen so, not because of fiscal constraints.' Public spending is also skewed towards urban areas. '...30% of public health expenditure (both from the centre and states) is allocated to urban allopathic services while rural centres receive less than 12%' (ibid.).

Cross-cutting the travails of the health system were developments related to a key element of overall health—sexual and reproductive health and population policy. For roughly the first two decades after Independence, the government experimented with both community-oriented and clinic-based approaches to family planning. By the middle of the 1960s, concerns about rapid population growth and the demands it would make on the country's resources led to a shift in strategy towards a more focused vertical programme.

That India's population is growing is something no one can deny. From around 350 million at the time of Independence to around 1.2 billion at present is a tripling of the number of people whose livelihoods, schooling, and health have to be assured. At the same time, the growth *rate* of population has been falling steadily as has the number of children that the average woman in India can expect to have in her lifetime—from six in 1951 to only 2.7 on average by 2009 and still falling. Many states have already reached or gone below the replacement level total fertility rate of 2.1 (Visaria and Visaria 2003). Continuing population growth even with replacement level fertility is due to what demographers have called the *momentum* effect (Bongaarts 1994), the effect of a young age structure.[3]

According to Visaria and Visaria (2003), only 6 per cent of the population growth in India in this century will be because women actually want to have more than two children. Almost 70 per cent will come from momentum. The rest, roughly 24 per cent, will be due to the fact that people do not have access to contraceptives or because the government's family planning programmes are avoided because of poor quality or coerciveness, or because gender power within households denies to women (especially if they are young daughters-in-law) the ability to make decisions. Even in northern states that have higher than average fertility rates, such as Bihar,

[3] This *momentum* effect refers to the growth in population that continues to occur even if overall fertility drops to replacement level (that is, each couple only has the number of children needed to replace itself), because a younger population will include a larger number of such childbearing couples.

Madhya Pradesh, and Rajasthan, momentum will contribute over half of the growth in this century while the effect of a desire to have many children will be much less (well below a quarter of the total growth).

Policy implications of the importance of momentum are profound. It means that, both from a perspective of population stabilization and from that of health and human rights, harping on persuading women to have fewer children is simply akin to flogging an already running horse. Focusing on how to improve the quality of services and to address momentum by supporting girls through ensuring their secondary and higher education, and providing jobs so that they can marry later, as well as promoting later first pregnancies and more spacing methods are likely to be far more effective. Such measures are certainly more human rights compliant than targets, disincentives, or incentives.

However, population policy in India has tended to take a very different tack. Contraceptive method-specific programme targets became the approach of choice in the late 1960s, coupled with incentives and disincentives to health and other government workers, as well as to women and their families. The distortions that this approach introduced into the health system (for example, ANMs who were incentivized for family planning but not for maternal health focused, not surprisingly, on the former and ignored the latter), the problems of human rights abuses and coercion in sterilization camps, and the fragmentation of health services have been extensively documented and analysed (Ramachandran and Visaria 1997; Sen 2010). Coercion can take the form of actually forcing people into sterilization camps, or it can take more subtle forms, such as telling poor families that they cannot get access to the full benefits of welfare programmes for jobs or food or healthcare, including for maternal health, or that they cannot exercise the citizen's right to hold electoral office unless they meet a pre-determined norm for family size.

The experience of coercion through forced sterilizations during the political emergency in the mid-1970s left an indelible mark on family planning in the country. Politicians distanced themselves from the programme for almost two decades and the government changed its name from Family Planning to Family Welfare. Civil society organizations were active in pushing for a more health and rights-based approach that would privilege women's autonomy, bodily integrity, and the right to make decisions about their health.

This social movement was reinforced by a global shift in the paradigm for population policy that was concretized at the United Nations International Conference on Population and Development (ICPD) held in Cairo in 1994. Strengthening health systems to improve service access and quality so that the sexual and reproductive health needs and rights of people can be met; empowering women to have greater voice in sexual and reproductive decisions; transforming male attitudes and behaviour; and addressing the information and service needs of increasingly younger or older populations—were all central to the change in the global population paradigm. However, the challenge was how to move forward to meet this agenda in the face of crumbling health systems, inadequate funding, the rapidly spreading HIV pandemic, and a right-wing backlash against women's human rights, gender equality, and sexual rights.

In India, ICPD's paradigm change was embodied in the government's National Population Policy (2000) which, despite some ambiguities, turned away from the old approach of sterilization camps, targets, and disincentives. Two barriers came in the way of a more sustained shift in this new direction. First, the family welfare programme was the quintessential vertical health programme, and could not be easily reintegrated into the rest of the health service delivery without a serious revamping of the overall health system itself in this direction. Second, a backlash from the bearers of the old population control mindset found supporters and adherents at both the centre and in the states and this kept targets, sterilization camps, and disincentives on the anvil even if under new guises and names.[4]

The establishing of the National Rural Health Mission (NRHM) in 2005 was an attempt to come to grips in a mission mode with some of the problems bedeviling the health sector, especially lack of focused attention to high maternal mortality and morbidity. As such, it is driven by the Health Ministry at the centre but depends on the health infrastructure in the states. While NRHM contains many improvements on the supply side on, *inter alia*, infrastructure, a new cadre of health activists (ASHAs), and the management-information system, it has become known particularly for its demand side innovations. The Janani Suraksha Yojana cash transfer programme is one of the largest of its kind, conditional on a woman having her delivery in an institution. The jury is still out on whether NRHM has genuinely helped reintegrate health services through its many programmatic initiatives, or whether it is simply functioning as a large umbrella with many disparate and largely independent programmes under it. The family welfare programme certainly appears to be one such, continuing to belie the promise of National Population Policy (2000).

[4] For instance, government documents speak of 'expected levels of achievement' instead of targets.

Recent years have also seen the rapid rise of publicly funded health insurance through the Rashtriya Swasthya Bima Yojana (RSBY) and other insurance schemes promoted by different state governments. Their pros and cons are discussed in the next section. The consequences of this evolution of health strategies and the health system in the country for health security are also examined in the next section.

KEY ASPECTS OF HEALTH SECURITY—THE THREE A'S

Affordability

Sustained low public spending on health (HLEG 2011: Chapter 1; passim) means that ordinary people bear the bulk of the burden of health expenditure. Private out-of-pocket (OOP) spending accounts for 67 per cent of total health spending—one of the highest figures in the world (Table 13.4).

Table 13.4 Share of Out-of-pocket in Total Health Expenditure, 2009

	Total Health Expenditure (PPP $)	OOP Health Expenditure (PPP $)	OOP As Percentage of Total
India	132	89	67
China	309	154	50
Thailand	345	84	24
Sri Lanka	193	106	55

Source: HLEG (2011: 96–7).

Three quarters of this OOP spending is for outpatient treatment (74 per cent), and largely for drugs (72 per cent of OOP). One might call this the deadly 70–70–70 syndrome of medical poverty in India. Drug price deregulation has led to the cost of drugs going up more than three-fold between the mid-1990s and the mid-2000s (HLEG 2011) in the country. Protection against medical impoverishment is very weak. According to the National Family Health Survey (NFHS 3), barely a tenth of all households had at least one member covered by health insurance.

The Bhore Committee had enunciated back in 1946 the principle that 'nobody should be denied access to health services for his inability to pay' (Goel 2008). That principle has largely been observed in the breach in India. There is evidence of growing impoverishment due to healthcare costs, particularly in the period after economic liberalization began (Sen 2010; Sen et al. 2002; Selvaraj and Karan 2009). As discussed in the previous section, the health system already had many problems consequent on inadequate public investment prior to the 1990s. However, even as late as the mid-1980s, there were a number of drugs still under price control, and this together with the flourishing generic drugs industry in the country (through reverse engineering, prior to India signing the WTO TRIPS agreement) kept drugs relatively cheap and available. All this changed as drug price decontrol took hold. Current insurance schemes typically do not cover the cost of drugs, diagnostics, or outpatient care.

According to the National Sample Survey (2006), 28 per cent of rural residents and 20 per cent of urban residents had no funds for healthcare. More than 40 per cent of hospitalized persons had to borrow money or sell assets in order to pay for care, while more than 35 per cent of hospitalized persons fell below the official poverty line. As is to be expected, the distribution of such persons is highly skewed. Around 40 per cent of both women and men (taken separately) gave financial barriers as the main reason for non-treatment of illness in the bottom two quintiles of the population, compared to about half that number in the upper three quintiles.

An analysis of three rounds of the National Sample Surveys (NSS 1992, 1998) on morbidity and patterns of use of health services (forty-second round—1986–7, fifty-second round—1995–6, and the sixtieth round—2004) shows that not only non-treatment of illness but also discontinuation of treatment (even without the patient's recovering) went up sharply over these two decades along with a substantial increase in the role of financial reasons for non-treatment. Significant gender gaps in treatment existed in the pre-reforms period and these have continued, except for the poorest quintile of men who have become as relatively badly off as the poorest women. Economic gradients of inequality and gender gaps in access to healthcare became sharply worse in the 1990s and continued into the next decade (Sen et al. 2002; Sen 2010). Unaffordability of health expenditures compounds the loss in income that illness entails for a vast majority who are in informal employment (Berman et al. 2010). It means that households often have to go into debt, pawn prized possessions, such as jewellery, sell assets, and fall below the poverty line. Health expenditures have been cited in field surveys as one of the main reasons for households falling into poverty (Krishna 2004).

Access

There are three critical elements in access to services: overall availability, urban-rural differentials, and the distribution of services across expenditure quintiles. Another important dimension of health differentials is the variation in access across states, widely known to be substantial. However, barring a few studies, health researchers have not to date mined the available data adequately to analyse the causes of inter-state health inequalities (Joe et al. 2008; Roy et al. 2004).

By any token, overall availability of both beds for patients and medical personnel is woefully low. Table 13.5 again puts India at the bottom relative to comparator Asian countries we have been using in this chapter.

Table 13.5 Beds per 1,000 Population, 2011

India	0.9
China	3.0
Thailand	2.2
Sri Lanka	3.1

Source: World Health Organization (2011), cited in HLEG (2011: Table 4; p. 188).

As a ratio to the population, there are four times as many health workers in urban as in rural areas. Furthermore, over 40 per cent of self-proclaimed allopathic doctors in rural areas are quacks who have no medical training (Table 13.6). There are 11.3 qualified doctors per 10,000 urban population as compared to 1.9 for the rural population (HLEG 2011: Chapter 3).

Table 13.6 Urban–Rural Differences

	Rural	Urban
Percentage of hospitals	40	60
Percentage of dispensaries	25	75
Percentage of doctors	20	80
Percentage of population	69	31

Source: Sen (2012: 48); Chandramouli (2011: 1).

A third challenge to access is a by-product of the creation of a 2-tier system in public hospitals that despite their often poor quality services have long been the basis of access for the poor. But these have now become tilted towards the better-off in the rural areas according to the NSSO's sixtieth round (NSS 2006). While those below the poverty line are supposed to get free services and drugs (although this rarely happens), the non-poor are expected to pay some charges which can then be used by the facility as a flexible pool for smaller expenses including maintenance. Hospital administrators greatly appreciate this flexibility and it has drawn the better-off into public hospitals especially in rural areas. But it has meant that the share of the poor has fallen sharply in a period when overall availability in public facilities has not increased significantly (Sen 2010). Rising inequality in access has been documented by a number of studies (Acharya et al. 2011; Garg and Karan 2005; Sen et al. 2002).

Government funded health insurance has emerged as one popular method for addressing problems of both affordability and access. The Rashtriya Swasthya Bima Yojana (RSBY) programme and its 'turbo' counterparts in states—Andhra Pradesh, Tamil Nadu, Karnataka, Kerala, Maharashtra, and a growing number of others—provides government funded health insurance. Targeted initially at households below the poverty line (and spreading to many groups in the informal economy), these schemes are popular because they promise to give people access to secondary and tertiary care in private facilities at much lower cost.

One question is about the functioning of these insurance programmes. Are they genuinely inclusive, and are they relatively free of fraud or exclusion/inclusion errors (Rathi et al. 2012; Selvaraj and Karan 2012)? Recent scandals about large numbers of hysterectomies, some among girls as young as 14 years, have taken some of the sheen off RSBY. Some improvements can come through better management and the use of information technology. However, a more serious concern is that such schemes are biased in favour of secondary and tertiary care and against more financially viable preventive and primary care. There are few incentives for effective gate-keeping at primary levels in these insurance programmes. As a consequence, '...these schemes become unviable very quickly because of the large reservoir of untreated illness, because of the targeting which works against risk pooling, and because all the incentives are in favour of more and expensive treatment for which the government has to foot a sharply growing bill, as has been the experience of Andhra Pradesh' (Sen 2012: 49).

Acknowledgement

The third and lesser known (but no less important) of the three As of health security is acknowledgement. In societies such as India's, where health security for all is obstructed by social hierarchies (such as caste and gender) that compound the problems posed by economic inequality, the concept of acknowledgement can pick up aspects of health insecurity that might not be captured otherwise. By acknowledgement we mean whether a health problem is recognized as being a problem at all, how seriously it is taken, and whether it is responded to as it should be by individuals, families/communities they live in, or by policymakers. Social hierarchies, such as gender and caste operate through deeply ingrained and institutionalized norms that affect not only broad world views but also the specifics of how all actors view health problems and potential solutions.

We can identify three paths by which lack of acknowledgement works. The first is whether ill-health is recognized as such by women or Dalits themselves or their families. While the fact that poor people often under-report illnesses in self-reported morbidity surveys such as those of the NSSO is known, the fact that women also may do so is much less recognized. Detailed probing of answers to health surveys can reveal astonishing increases in morbidity rates (Madhiwalla et al. 2000). Women often suffer ill health in silence and do not consider it to be morbidity. Sensitive field investigations often find that women are silent about a range of problems—not only reproductive health problems, such as pelvic inflammatory diseases or white discharge, but also chronic back pain, sustained low grade fevers, etc. (Bang et al. 2010). Often women keep on at their routine work schedules until they literally cannot stand any longer. Part of this is because, especially if they are poor, they often do not have any one to take over the care of families and domestic work if they are ill. But it is also because a certain amount of regular pain, illness, and discomfort are often viewed as inherent in being a woman. The internalization of gender biased norms has been documented, *inter alia*, by Das Gupta (1995) and Harris (1995). Sen and Iyer (2012: 1807) found in an analysis of a large field survey in the poor district of Koppal in northern Karnataka that among reasons given for non-treatment of illness, '... the reason "I/family did not think it necessary" was much more important for women than for men. In particular, this reason accounted for as many as 62% of *non-poor* women who did not start treatment of any kind. Yet, two thirds of these women had ailments that were severe enough to cause difficulty in work for a median duration of two years' (emphasis added). Poverty clearly was not the reason in this case.

A second path to non-acknowledgement is the normalization of ill health by health providers themselves. '... Failures in acknowledgement take place for multiple reasons. Sometimes they exist due to explicit bias, as women's needs are deemed illegitimate. At other times recognition exists, but a lack of acknowledgement still persists due to neglect, as other issues claim more priority. Bias of this kind can be institutionalized into indifference in health systems through the design of budget lines, supervision systems, staffing patterns, drug allocations, training curricula, etc...' (George et al. 2005: 20). Shankar and Reddy (2012) document the complete normalization of moderate anaemia (haemoglobin: 7–8 grams) to the point that health providers often do not initiate or recommend any kind of response.

A third level at which health problems are not acknowledged is among health policymakers and managers. It is striking how little of the large global literature on health system reforms, universal healthcare, and the social determinants of health pays specific attention to the problem of social inequalities and their intersection with economic inequality[5] in shaping what we think of as a health problem, and who we think of as needing attention. HLEG report (2011) recommends actions in four areas to address the challenges posed by gender inequality: improving access for women and girls to health services (going beyond maternal and child health), to recognizing and supporting women' s central role in healthcare provision in both the formal health system and in homes; to building the capacity of the health system to recognize, measure, monitor, and address gender concerns; and to provide broad support for girls and women to be empowered (HLEG Report 2011: Chapter 9; passim).

An important policy step in this direction will be fully integrating the steps needed in the family welfare programme and in its umbrella Reproductive and Child Health programme with policies for improving the overall health system so that they do not continue to function as ineffective and expensive silos.

Which Way Forward?

We have argued in this chapter that India's health system faces critical challenges in assuring health security to people. Serious under-investment in public health, ill-conceived and unregulated privatization, the expansion of fragmented health services and programmatic silos, and inattention to economic and social inequalities and the social determinants of

[5] For more on the analysis of such intersections, see Sen et al. (2009).

health, despite six decades of policy pronouncements to the contrary, have created a crisis of serious proportions. The consequences are being felt by people, especially the socially subordinate and the poor, through a breakdown in access and affordability, and a continuing problem of insufficient acknowledgement of core health problems.

Building on the data, analysis, and recommendations contained in the earlier 3-volume report of the National Commission on Macroeconomics and Health, as well as the inputs of many others from civil society, academia, professional bodies, bilateral and multilateral agencies, and international experts, HLEG attempted to set forth an agenda for universal health care in the country. It specifically addressed, in line with its terms of reference, the issues of financing, management, and regulation, and community mobilization (the how's), along with human resources, health norms and standards, and drugs (the what's). It also provided some discussion specifically on the social determinants of health and on gender.

Arguably, all these elements are linked to each other, and together can affect how ordinary people experience whether their health is secure or insecure. But specific elements are likely to impact on particular aspects of health security.

First, would people be able to afford care when they are unwell? Two of HLEG's broad recommendations—a significant step-up in public investments through the tax route, and a major effort for providing generic drugs free of cost through the public system are the ones most likely to have an impact on the affordability of care. However, the global economy is still in the throes of a financial slowdown and the continuing European financial crisis does not bode well for the growth rate of the Indian economy in the near future. In the period while the HLEG report was being written, an increase in public investment to 2.5 per cent of GDP was well on the cards. This has slipped significantly and the government appears to now have agreed to a maximum of 1.85 per cent of GDP. How much can be done by way of strengthening the public sector in health will have to be seen.

HLEG had advocated providing of free generic drugs through the public system as the 'low hanging fruit' among its recommendations. Providing free drugs is eminently doable following the highly successful experience over more than a decade of the Tamil Nadu Medical Services Corporation (TNMSC). Furthermore, India is one of the world's largest suppliers of cheap generic drugs, and drugs account for around 70 per cent of out-of-pocket expenses. The central government has therefore moved rapidly to implement this recommendation, and the impact on healthcare seekers should begin to be felt soon. One challenge, however, is how to ensure corruption-free management of the system of providing drugs. A sobering thought is that although the Tamil Nadu 'model' has been known for some time, almost no other state has actually followed its example, and the fear is that other states do not wish to put in place TNMSC's transparency conditions. Corruption is known to be rampant in the field of drugs procurement and supply. Whether the central government's new initiative will be able to avoid this remains to be seen.

Second, will health facilities of acceptable quality be within relatively easy access of all?

Affirming the public sector as the bedrock of a well-integrated health system, HLEG called, *inter alia*, for strengthening the public sector's services with particular attention to preventive and primary care. The bulk of the stepped up public investment is meant for this purpose so that the government can ensure adequate numbers of trained healthcare providers and technical healthcare workers at different levels, giving priority to the provision of primary healthcare. This should result in an increase in the number of ASHAs, the starting of a three-year medical programme that has been stalled until now by opposition by the doctors' lobby, and creating a cadre of public health professionals. But increases in investment also need to be backed by significant management reforms. Supportive supervision mechanisms, competency-based training and deployment, and creating a health management cadre are needed in order to raise the quality of human resources for health, for strengthening the management of health institutions, and for better matching skills and competencies with expected functions.

Even this will not be enough to raise the quality of public and private services unless there is a serious attempt to improve accountability on the part of both public and private health providers through a strong regulatory architecture backed by community mobilization. While civil society has long recognized the importance of regulation, neither the private nor the public health providers are in favour of it, for obvious reasons. Effective and independent regulation of both public and private providers is essential to ensure the meeting of norms and standards, quality assurance and value for money, as well as transparent processes by which the private sector may be contracted to provide services, redress complaints, and undertake cost control.

Most of the health regulatory measures that exist in India are 'soft' measures that are largely without teeth. A number of older professional bodies exist but they have increasingly come to function like trade unions. HLEG was clear that these kinds of soft measures are not fit for the purpose of actually ensuring quality, cost control, or grievance redress in either the private or the public sectors, or in the context of public private partnerships. HLEG therefore proposed a new regulatory architecture for health, statutorily empowered to regulate and monitor/audit both the public and the private sectors and ensure enforcement and redress. As recommended, a new National Health Regulatory and Development Authority (NHRDA) would be responsible, *inter alia*, for overseeing and enforcing contracts, accrediting health providers; formulating legal and regulatory norms for facilities, staff, scope, access, quality, and rationality of services, and costs of care with clear norms for payments; standard treatment guidelines and management protocols in order to control entry, quality, quantity, and price development; enforcement of patients' charter of rights, including ethical standards and institutions and ensuring adherence to standard protocols for treatment with the involvement of professional organizations; and establishing and ensuring a system of regular audit of prescriptions and inpatient records, death audits, and other peer review processes (Sen 2012).

Three units are envisioned under NHRDA: a system support unit responsible for developing norms and protocols; an evaluation unit to evaluate the performance of both public and private providers; and a medical facilities accreditation unit. HLEG also proposed that the Drugs and Medical Devices Regulatory Authority be strengthened.

Third, how can we ensure that the health needs of all, especially those subordinated by gender, caste, or other oppressive social relationships, are recognized as such, and that the health system is inclusive and genuinely universal? HLEG implicitly addressed this question by highlighting the need to put in place measures for people's participation through citizen councils and assemblies, although such bodies may not be inclusive unless they are required to be so. It also recommended that the bottom up institutions for complaint redress be linked to ombudspersons envisaged in the regulatory authority so as to close the accountability loop. An important additional recommendation was setting up a National Health Promotion and Protection Trust in order to promote better health through information dissemination, and to conduct health impact assessments of the social determinants of health. Specific recommendations for systematically and substantially addressing gender concerns have been mentioned earlier in the chapter.

Broad strands of the HLEG's recommendations go to the heart of the challenge of health security. Whether or not the government follows its specific recommendations, it will need to move urgently in this broad direction if the crisis in the three As of health security—affordability, access and acknowledgement—is not to reach a tipping point.

References

Acharya, D., G. Vaidyanathan, V.R. Muraleedharan, D.S. Dheenadayalan, and U. Dash (2011), 'Do the Poor Benefit from Public Spending on Healthcare in India? Results from Benefit (Utilisation) Incidence Analysis in Tamil Nadu and Orissa', Consortium for Research on Equitable Health Systems Report. Available at: http://www.crehs.lshtm.ac.uk/India_BUIA.pdf (accessed on 15 October 2012).

Armstrong, G.L., L.A. Conn, and R.W. Pinner (1999), 'Trends in Infectious Disease Mortality in the United States in the 20th Century', *Journal of the American Medical Association*, 281(1): 61–66.

Bang, R., S., Khorgade, and R. Chinai (2010), *Putting Women First: Women and Health in a Rural Community*. Kolkata: Stree-Samya Publications.

Berman, P., R. Ahuja, and L. Bhandari (2010), 'The Impoverishing Effect of Healthcare Payments in India: New Methodology and Findings', *Economic and Political Weekly*, 45(16): 65–71.

Bloom, D.E. (2010), 'Population Aging and Economic Growth', in K. Eggleston and S. Tuljapurkar (eds), *Aging Asia: Economic and Social Implications of Rapid Demographic Change in China, Japan, and South Korea*. Stanford: Stanford University Walter H. Shorenstein Asia-Pacific Research Center series with Brookings Institution Press, Chapter 2.

Bloom, D.E., D. Canning, and J. Sevilla (2003), *The Demographic Dividend: A New Perspective on the Economic Consequences of Population Change*. Arlington: RAND Program of Policy-Relevant Research Communication.

Bloom, D.E., D. Canning, L. Hu, Y. Liu, A. Mahal, and W. Yip (2010), 'The Contribution of Population Health and Demographic Change to Economic Growth in China and India', *Journal of Comparative Economics*, 38(1): 17–33.

Bongaarts, J. (1994), 'Population Policy Options in the Developing World', *Science*, 263(5148): 771–76.

Cao, S., X. Wang, and G. Wang (2003), 'Lessons learned from China's fall into the poverty trap', *Journal of Policy Modeling*, 31(2): 298–307.

Chandramouli, C. (2011), *Census of India 2011: Rural Urban Distribution (Provisional Population Totals)*. New Delhi: Office of the Registrar General and Census Commissioner. Available at: http://www.censusindia.gov.in/2011 prov-results/paper2/data_files/india/paper2_1.pdf (accessed on 3 October 2012).

Commission on Social Determinants of Health (2008), *Closing the Gap in a Generation: Health Equity through Action on the Social Determinants of Health, Final Report of the Commission on Social Determinants of Health*. Geneva: World Health Organization.

Das Gupta, M. (1995), 'Life Course Perspectives on Women's Autonomy and Health Outcomes', *American Anthropologist*, 97(3): 481–91.

Duggal, R. (n.d.). *A New Health Policy for Health Sector Reforms*. Mumbai: Centre for Enquiry into Health and Allied Themes. Available at: http://www.cehat.org/go/uploads/Publications/a87.pdf (accessed on 7 October 2012).

Dummer, T.J.B. and I.G. Cook (2007), 'Exploring China's rural health crisis: Processes and policy implications, Health implications', *Health Policy*, 67(3): 329–43.

Garg, C.C. and A.K. Karan (2005), *Health and Millennium Development Goal 1: Reducing out of pocket expenditures to reduce income poverty—Evidence from India.* Working Paper No. 15. Equitap Project, New Delhi.

George, A., A. Iyer, and G. Sen (2005), *Maternity in crisis: gendered health system experiences from Koppal, Karnataka.* IDS Sussex Working Paper No. 253. Sussex: Institute of Development Studies.

Goel, S. (2008), 'From Bhore Committee to National Rural Health Mission: A Critical Review', *The Internet Journal of Health*, 7(1): DOI: 10.5580/ffa.

Government of India (1948), *Sokhey: Report of the Sub-Committee.* Bombay: National Planning Committee, Government of India.

——— (1962), *Report of the Health Survey and Planning Committee (August 1959–October 1961).* New Delhi: Ministry of Health, Government of India.

——— (1963), *Chadha Committee Report.* New Delhi: Ministry of Health, Government of India.

——— (1973), *Kartar Singh Committee Report. Report of the Committee on Multipurpose Workers under Health and Family Planning Programmes.* New Delhi: Ministry of Health, Government of India.

——— (1975), *Srivastava Committee Report. Health Services and Medical Education: A Programme for Immediate Action.* New Delhi: Allied Publishers Pvt. Ltd.

——— (1983), National Health Policy, 1983. New Delhi: Ministry of Health and Family Welfare, Government of India.

——— (2000), *National Population Policy, 2000.* New Delhi: Department of Family Welfare, Ministry of Health and Family Welfare, Government of India.

——— (2002), *National Health Policy, 2002.* New Delhi: Ministry of Health and Family Welfare, Government of India.

——— (2007), *National Family Health Survey (NFHS 2) Volume II*, Mumbai: Indian Institute of Population Sciences.

Harris, B. (1995), 'The intrafamily distribution of hunger in South Asia', in J. Dreze, A. Sen, and A. Hussain (eds), *The political economy of hunger: Selected essays.* Oxford: Clarendon Press, pp. 224–97.

Health Survey and Development Committee, Government of India (1947), *Bhore Commission: Report of the Health Survey and Development Committee.* New Delhi: Manager of Publications.

High Level Expert Group on Universal Health Coverage (2011), *High Level Expert Group Report on Universal Health Coverage for India.* Submitted to the Planning Commission of India. New Delhi: High Level Expert Group on Universal Health Coverage. Available at: http://planningcommission.nic.in/reports/genrep/rep_uhc0812.pdf (Accessed on 5 October 2012).

Hsiao, W.C.L. (1995), 'The Chinese health care system: Lessons for other nations', *Social Science and Medicine*, 41(8): 1047–55.

Indian Council of Social Science Research and Indian Council Medical Research (1981), *Health for All: An Alternative Strategy*. Pune: Indian Institute of Education.

Joe, W., U.S., Mishra, and K. Navaneetham (2008), 'Health inequality in India: evidence from NFHS 3', *Economic and Political Weekly*, 43(31): 41–48.

Krishna, A. (2004), 'Escaping Poverty and Becoming Poor: Who Gains, Who Loses, and Why?', *World Development*, 32(1): 121–36.

Madhiwalla, N., S. Nandraj, and R. Sinha (2000), *Health, Households and Women's Lives: A Study of Illness and Childbearing among Women in Nashik District, Maharashtra*. Mumbai: Centre for Enquiry into Health and Allied Themes.

National Commission on Macroeconomics and Health (2005a), *Report of the National Commission on Macroeconomics and Health*. New Delhi: Ministry of Health and Family Welfare, Government of India.

——— (2005b). *Background Papers: Burden of Disease in India*. New Delhi: Ministry of Health and Family Welfare, Government of India. Available at: http://www.who.int/macrohealth/action/NCMH_Burden%20of%20disease_(29%20Sep%202005).pdf (accessed on 5 October 2012).

National Sample Survey (1992), *Morbidity and Utilisation of Medical Services. (NSSO 42nd Round, 1986–1987*') *National Sample Survey Organisation*. New Delhi: Ministry of Statistics and Programme Implementation, Government of India.

——— (1998), *Morbidity, and Treatment of Ailments (NSSO 52nd Round, July 1995–June 1996*') *National Sample Survey Organisation*. New Delhi: Ministry of Statistics and Programme Implementation, Government of India.

——— (2006), *Morbidity, Health Care and the Condition of the Aged (NSSO 60th Round, January–June 2004*') *National Sample Survey Organisation*. New Delhi: Ministry of Statistics and Programme Implementation, Government of India.

Office of the Registrar General and Census Commissioner India (2006), *Census of India 2001: Population Projections for India and States 2001-2026*. New Delhi: Office of the Registrar General and Census Commissioner India. Available at: http://www.statehealthsocietybihar.org/survey_reports/Population_Projection_Report_2006.pdf (Accessed on 5 October 2012).

Ramachandran, V. and L. Visaria (1997), 'Emerging issues in reproductive health', *Economic and Political Weekly*, 32(36): 2244–8.

Rathi, P., A. Mukherji, and G. Sen (2012), 'Rashtriya Swasthya Bima Yojana: Evaluating Utilisation, Roll-Out and Perceptions in Amaravati District, Maharashtra', *Economic and Political Weekly*, 47(39): 57–63.

Roy, T.K., S. Kulkarni, and Y. Vaidehi (2004), 'Social inequalities in health and nutrition in selected states', *Economic and Political Weekly*, 39(7): 677–83.

Selvaraj, S. and A.K. Karan (2009), 'Deepening Health Insecurity in India: Evidence from National Sample Surveys since 1980s', *Economic and Political Weekly*, 44(40): 55–60.

Selvaraj, S. and A.K. Karan (2012), 'Why Publicly-Financed Health Insurance Schemes are Ineffective in Providing Financial Risk Protection', *Economic and Political Weekly*, 47(11): 60–68.

Sen, G. (2003), 'Population: a new paradigm for old and new concerns', in R. Sengupta and A.K. Sinha (eds), *Challenge of Sustainable Development: the Indian Dynamics*. Kolkata: Indian Institute of Management Calcutta and Manak Publishers, 61–80.

——— (2010), 'Family Planning and Sexual and Reproductive Health and Rights: the Past as Prologue?', *Studies in Family Planning*, 41(2): 143–46.

——— (2012), 'Universal health coverage in India: a long and winding road', *Economic and Political Weekly*, 47(8): 46–52.

Sen, G. and A. Iyer (2012), 'Who gains, who loses, and how: leveraging gender and class intersections to secure health entitlements', *Social Science and Medicine*, 74(11): 1802–811.

Sen, G., A. Iyer, and A. George (2002), 'Structural Reforms and Health Equity: A Comparison of NSS Surveys of 1986–87 and 1995–96', *Economic and Political Weekly*, 37(14): 1342–52.

Sen, G., A. Iyer and C. Mukherjee (2009), 'A methodology to analyse the intersections of social inequalities in health', *Journal of Human Development and Capabilities*, 10(3): 397–415.

Shankar, M. and B. Reddy (2012), 'Anaemia in pregnancy still a major cause of morbidity and mortality: insights from Koppal district, Karnataka, India', *Reproductive Health Matters*, 20(40): 67–68.

The Hindu (2009), 'Medicines also included in free treatment quota'. *The Hindu*, [online] 22 September. Available at: http://www.thehindu.com/news/cities/Delhi/article23698.ece?textsize=large&test=1 (accessed on 15 October 2012).

UNICEF (2011), Available at: http://www.unicef.org/infobycountry/china_statistics.html and http://www.unicef.org/infobycountry/india_statistics.html (accessed on 3 October 2012).

United Nations Department of Economic and Social Affairs/Population Division *World Population Prospects: The 2010, Volume II: Demographic Profiles*. Available at: http://esa.un.org/wpp/documentation/pdf/WPP2010_Volume-II_Demographic-Profiles.pdf (accessed on 5 October 2012).

Visaria, L. and P. Visaria (2003), 'Long term population projection for major states, 1991–2101', *Economic and Political Weekly*, 38(45): 4763–75.

Wagstaff A., W. Yip, M. Lindelow, and W.C. Hsiao (2009), 'China's health system and its reform: a review of recent studies', *Health Economics*, 18(2): S7–23.

World Health Organization. (WHO) (2011), *World Health Statistics 2011*. Geneva: World Health Organization. Available at: http://www.who.int/whosis/whostat/2011/en/index.html.

Yip W., A. Wagstaff, and W.C. Hsiao (2009), 'Economic analysis of China's health care system : turning a new page', *Health Economics*, 18(2): S3–6.

CHAPTER 14

CASTES, GENDER, AND CLASS

dynamism or stasis?

ASHWINI DESHPANDE

The Indian economy, in the last three decades, has seen rapid and far-reaching changes resulting from globalization and liberalization. Given the multiple axes along which the Indian society is divided, an investigation into how these fissures are changing in response to the growing integration of the Indian economy with the global economy is an extremely complex exercise. This chapter makes an attempt to capture a few key economic dimensions of the contemporary nature of caste, class, and gender disparities, with a larger focus on caste, while recognizing at the outset that there are many other critical identities, such as religion and region, which shape economic outcomes of individuals as well as group antagonisms just as significantly. The reason for focusing on three social identities is that affirmative action programmes in India are designed along caste and gender lines, thus providing an official acknowledgement of their salience. A strict space constraint does not allow the discussion to go beyond these three, and also precludes a comprehensive, in-depth assessment of each of these three fissures.

There is a view that as the Indian economy liberalizes, becomes more market-oriented, and increases its integration with the global economy, inter-group disparities are likely to reduce due to several reasons. One, labour market discrimination on account of social identity is expected to decline, and two, because the creation of newer types of jobs is likely to provide an impetus to the members of marginalized groups to acquire new skills and to break out of traditional, caste-based, dead-end, oppressive, and stigmatizing occupations. The argument that discrimination is likely to reduce is based on the belief that market-orientation is likely to give primacy to profit maximization, and more generally, to efficient allocation of resources on the part of employers, a process in which the social identity of workers ought to be irrelevant. The implicit assumption in this argument is that foreign agents, especially, are less likely to be concerned with local hierarchies and the accompanying prejudices. The argument that employment avenues will expand and become more diverse is based on the premise that globalization will provide an impetus to certain sectors which will grow faster. This will induce a demand for skilled labour, among other things, which will open up avenues of employment, hitherto either limited or unavailable to the domestic population and, given the local labour market discrimination, out of reach for marginalized groups in society.

Contrary to this set of arguments is the view that traditionally marginalized groups might be at a disadvantage even in this new scenario, given the legacy of exclusion from the kind of education that would be needed to take advantage of these emerging opportunities. Also, multinational corporations (MNCs) do not work in a vacuum; their hiring decisions are taken by local managers who are as aware of local social cleavages and are driven by the same prejudices as hiring managers of domestic firms. Foreign agents are not likely to disturb domestic norms and practices, or rock the boat, unless it is absolutely essential, since their bottomline is profits. Economic theory shows how maximization of profits and discrimination on account of social identity are not incompatible.[1] Indeed, recent research in the mechanics of the hiring process in urban formal labour markets (Deshpande and Newman 2007; Jodhka and Newman 2007) indicates that lip-service to merit notwithstanding, managers show a deep awareness of the overlapping and complex categories of caste, class, religion, and gender, and of the strong stereotypical beliefs that merit is distributed along axes defined by these social identities. This is as true for private domestic firms as it is for MNCs.

Additionally, cross-national comparisons of inter-group disparities have highlighted that there seems to be no straightforward relationship between relative prosperity of a country (or the level of its market orientation) and the severity of disparities (or the prevalence of discrimination).

[1] See, for instance, Akerlof (1984), Arrow (1971), and Becker (1957).

Darity and Deshpande (2003) summarize the major general findings that have emerged from these comparative inquiries. Specifically, they point out that inter-group disparity is persistent and significant in countries at all levels of development, whether development is measured narrowly by per capita income or more broadly by a more encompassing index of well-being, like the Human Development Index (HDI). Also, higher rates of economic growth do not invariably close economic gaps between racial and ethnic groups nor does lower economic growth inevitably widen the gap. This is relevant to the Indian discussion in that it suggests that India's high rate of growth in the post-liberalization era is not sufficient to close the gaps, just as a lower rate of growth would not necessarily widen the gaps.[2] We can apply this analogy to different states in India. We find lack of a clear pattern: inter-group disparity does not seem to be systematically related with growth, or the lack of it (Deshpande 2011).

In what follows, we briefly assess a few economic aspects of three contemporary group divisions—caste, class, and gender. The discussion is aimed at providing an overview of the critical aspects, and interested readers can follow the references at the end for more discussion on specific aspects.

Caste

Each renewed controversy over affirmative action inevitably rekindles the debate over the continued relevance or otherwise of caste as a category shaping *economic* outcomes in contemporary India. There is also the related issue of whether the primacy accorded to caste in public discourse actually keeps the (presumably considerably weakened, even dying) institution alive, whereas it needs to be given a quiet burial (Beteille 2012). This question also illustrates an interesting contrast between discussions on religion and caste: for some inexplicable reason, the legitimacy of the former is not questioned, either on the grounds of the institution being antiquated or on the grounds of promoting sectarian, communual

[2] At the time of writing, the Indian economy had experienced a distinct slowdown in its aggregate rate of growth, thus highlighting the fact that greater integration with the global economy is not an unmitigated bonus. It also makes the domestic economy more vulnerable to international trends, for example, recession.

mindsets. This is despite the fact that religious schisms have erupted into extremely violent conflicts, with disturbing regularity, in virtually all parts of the country. The contrast between the discourse on caste and religion is reflected, for instance, in the collection of macro data. Starting with the national census, all datasets have data for individual religions, but not for castes. At the moment, availability of data on caste categories is dictated by the needs of the affirmative action policy, such that data are collected by broad aggregate groups which contain within them several diverse jatis and tribes, not separately enumerated: Scheduled Castes (SCs), Scheduled Tribes (STs), Other Backward Classes (OBCs) and Others (the residual).[3] Interestingly, the Indian census till 2001 did not count OBCs separately, even though affirmative action for OBCs had been a part of individual state policies for decades and had become a part of central government policies in 1991. That is, perhaps, the only instance of affirmative action anywhere in the world where a group being recognized as deserving affirmative action was not counted in the national census.

Caste Disparities and Discrimination

The primary source of economic disparities between castes is the traditional link between caste and occupation. The caste system, since its inception, has seen enormous mutations as new castes got created through fission, fusion, migration, inter-marriages, and so forth. The operative form of contemporary caste divisions is jati, and it shares some of the characteristics of the ancient varna system; but jatis are not clear sub-sets of varnas. The occupational distribution inherent in the varna system indicates a rudimentary economy; the jati system is more complex, but over the centuries, while occupational divisions have undergone a complete transformation with the modernization of the Indian economy, the mutations in jati divisions have not kept pace. Additionally, after Indian Independence in 1947, legally, there is supposed to be no link between caste and occupation, in that it is illegal to deny a job to an applicant simply on the basis of caste (for that matter, on account of any social identity, for example, religion or gender). Thus, formally, the link between caste and occupation is broken and indeed a whole range of occupations in the modern economy, both in the public and private sectors, are not

[3] The 2011 census has conducted an accompanying socio-economic and caste census but the data are not available yet.

caste-based. However, an examination of the persistence or weakening of the link between caste and occupation has to be done at two levels: one, traditional caste-based jobs, especially at the top and bottom ends of the traditional hierarchy (for example, scavengers, sweepers, or priests in temples), being allocated randomly, with no clear caste pattern; two, there any overlap between position in the traditional caste hierarchy and in the modern occupational spectrum? Data indicate that the overlap between caste and status in the modern occupational spectrum persists. Castes that are lower in the traditional hierarchy are disproportionately represented in lower paying modern occupations, whereas the opposite is true of high castes (Deshpande 2011). Thus, one finds persistent disparities in occupational attainment, with inter-state variations, between the broad caste groups of SCs (or STs) and Others. It should be noted that any disparity based on this broad comparison actually *understates* the disparity between the top and bottom ends of the caste hierarchy, as Others is an omnibus, extremely heterogeneous category, containing castes and communities only marginally higher than SCs in the social and economic hierarchy.

Given that income data are notoriously difficult to collect in India, one of the standard ways of examining disparities is to look at differences in average monthly per capita expenditure (MPCE) between the broad caste groups using NSS data. Based on NSS employment–unemployment surveys for 1983, 1993–4, 1999–2000, and 2004–5, we find that for rural and urban India, at the national level, the ratio of SC–ST MPCE to Others' MPCE registered a sharp decline between the first two rounds, to pick up gradually over the remaining rounds.[4] However, the all-India ratio in 2004–5 was not back to its 1983 level. Hnatkovska et al. (2012) find a strong convergence between SCs and Others in educational and occupational attainment as well as in consumption and wages and suggest that the convergence is driven by the narrowing of educational gaps. The picture, however, is complicated, not the least because while educational attainment at lower levels is converging, gaps from secondary education onwards are not necessarily converging. Coming back to the ratio of MPCE, the all-India pattern contains within it a great deal of interstate variations, which are different for rural and urban India. For instance, in urban Bihar and Uttar Pradesh, there is a dip in the ratio between the

[4] For the last two rounds, data on OBCs was available separately, but the ratio has been calculated by clubbing the OBCs and Others categories, so that it is comparable to the Others category in the earlier round, when OBC data was not available.

first and second rounds, an increase in the third round, followed by a dip again between 1999–2000 and 2004–5. Thus, there is fluctuation over the four rounds, with a downward trend, overall.

Elsewhere I have created a 'Caste Development Index' (CDI) based on five indicators of standard of living (educational attainment, occupational attainment, land ownership, livestock ownership, and consumer durable ownership) (Deshpande 2001), and calculated CDI values using the three rounds of the National Family and Health Survey (NFHS) data for each of the caste groups, by state. The gap between CDI for SCs and CDI for Others can be seen as a rough measure of inter-caste disparity (Deshpande 2011). Table 14.1 shows the ranking of some major states by three measures: per capita state domestic product (SDP), CDI for SCs, and disparity between SCs and Others.

Table 14.1 illustrates the lack of a clear pattern in the relationship between the material prosperity of a state, the material well-being of SCs, and inter-caste disparity.[5] Tamil Nadu is ranked number 6 in the per capita real SDP rankings in all the three years, qualifying it as a relatively rich state among the 18 states. However, with no change in its relative ranking in per capita real SDP, its ranking on disparity (gap in CDI between Others and SCs) was 11 in 1992–3 and increased to 1 (implying highest disparity) in the other two years. In terms of CDI for SCs (the indicator for the absolute standard of living for SCs), it was the lowest among the Indian states in 1992–3 and rose to number 13 in the next rounds. These movements seem to be independent of SDP levels; moreover, despite being a relatively rich state, it fares poorly on CDI for SCs and has fairly high disparity.

Uttar Pradesh, with a ranking of 16, 17, and 16 in per capita real SDP rankings across the three rounds, is one of the poorest states in India. However, inter-caste disparity has steadily increased across the three rounds: from being the state with the lowest inter-caste disparity, it moved up to number 11 by 1998–9 and to number 7 in 2004–5, demonstrating that just as being a relatively rich state (for example, Tamil Nadu or Delhi) is no guarantee for lower disparity, being poor is not a guarantee either (witness Uttar Pradesh or Bihar). In terms of CDI for SCs, its ranking remains relatively stable: 12, 14, and 13, respectively, across the three rounds. One can find other examples to illustrate the basic point being made here: the relative prosperity of a state (or the lack of it) does not appear to be a

[5] The same lack of relationship can be seen if one uses rate of growth of different states, instead of real SDP.

Table 14.1 Per Capita SDP, CDI for SCs and Disparity between SCs and Others, Major Indian States

Ranks	PC Real SDP			Disparity			CDI SC		
	1993–4	1998–9	2002–3	1992–3	1998–9	2003–4	1992–3	1998–9	2003–4
1	Delhi	Delhi	Delhi	Haryana	Tamil Nadu	Tamil Nadu	Himachal Pradesh	Delhi	Delhi
2	Punjab	Punjab	Maharashtra	Delhi	Madhya Pradesh	Rajasthan	Jammu	Maharashtra	Gujarat
3	Maharashtra	Maharashtra	Punjab	Punjab	Karnataka	Madhya Pradesh	Rajasthan	Punjab	Maharashtra
4	Haryana	Gujarat	Haryana	Bihar	Bihar	Bihar	Delhi	Gujarat	Assam
5	Gujarat	Haryana	Gujarat	Himachal Pradesh	Andhra Pradesh	Delhi	Punjab	Jammu	Himachal Pradesh
6	Tamil Nadu	Tamil Nadu	Tamil Nadu	Jammu	Haryana	Gujarat	Assam	Haryana	Jammu and Kashmir
7	Kerala	Karnataka	Himachal Pradesh	Madhya Pradesh	Orissa	Uttar Pradesh	Madhya Pradesh	Himachal Pradesh	Haryana
8	Himachal Pradesh	Himachal Pradesh	Karnataka	Maharashtra	Punjab	Punjab	Gujarat	Assam	Punjab
9	Karnataka	Kerala	Kerala	Orissa	New Delhi	Andhra Pradesh	Haryana	Kerala	Rajasthan
10	Andhra Pradesh	Andhra Pradesh	West Bengal	Andhra Pradesh	Gujarat	Orissa	Uttar Pradesh	Madhya Pradesh	Madhya Pradesh
11	West Bengal	West Bengal	Andhra Pradesh	Tamil Nadu	Uttar Pradesh	Haryana	Maharashtra	Rajasthan	Uttar Pradesh

12	Madhya Pradesh	Rajasthan	Rajasthan	Karnataka	Rajasthan	Kerala	Karnataka	Uttar Pradesh	Kerala
13	Jammu & Kashmir	Madhya Pradesh	Madhya Pradesh	Rajasthan	Kerala	Himachal Pradesh	West Bengal	Tamil Nadu	Tamil Nadu
14	Rajasthan	Jammu & Kashmir	Assam	Gujarat	West Bengal	Jammu and Kashmir	Orissa	Karnataka	West Bengal
15	Assam	Assam	Orissa	West Bengal	Himachal Pradesh	Maharashtra	Andhra Pradesh	West Bengal	Andhra Pradesh
16	Uttar Pradesh	Orissa	Uttar Pradesh	Kerala	Assam	Karnataka	Kerala	Andhra Pradesh	Karnataka
17	Orissa	Uttar Pradesh	Bihar	Assam	Jammu and Kashmir	West Bengal	Bihar	Bihar	Orissa
18	Bihar	Bihar	N/A	Uttar Pradesh	Maharashtra	Assam	Tamil Nadu	Orissa	Bihar

Source: Deshpande (2011: 90–1).

Note: Source of PC SDP: www.indiastat.com: table 51676.

Disparity and CDI are author's own calculations from NFHS I, II and III.

Only those states that are common to all three rounds have been retained in this table.

good predictor either of inter-caste disparity or of the absolute level of development of SCs.

Deshpande (2011: 93) also reports correlations between CDI-SC and per capita real NSDP which is positive and has become stronger over the three NFHS rounds, from 0.09 to 0.72, between CDI-SC and the rate of growth of per capita real NSDP, which was very low but positive in the first round, but turned negative in the latter two rounds, with the strength of the negative correlation declining from 0.09 to −0.27 to −0.16. The correlation between disparity and per capita NSDP was positive in the first round (0.54), but declined to an insignificant −0.03 in the third round; the correlation between disparity and the rate of growth of real per capita NSDP fluctuated in direction and magnitude and was ambiguous overall. Deshpande (2011) also discusses the relationship between overall inequality (as measured by the Gini coefficient calculated over MPCE) and both CDI-SC and disparity. States with higher disparity also have higher Gini but also higher CDI-SC.

FDI and Inter-group Disparities

Coming back to the debate outlined in the beginning of this section about the possible impact of liberalization and globalization on inter-group disparities, one of the possible ways of examining this relationship is through an examination of foreign direct investment (FDI) data. Disaggregated data, which will allow us to identify the location of the project, are available only for FDI approvals, not for realized FDI.[6] An examination of this data, where the location of the proposed project can be identified by district, reveals a great deal of spatial clustering.[7] Thus, whatever the magnitude of new jobs created, they are limited to a small number of geographical clusters, limiting access to the local population or those who are willing to migrate. The next question is whether this employment generation is evenly distributed across social groups and between men and women, according to their share in the state's population. NCAER (2009: 18) suggests that India's attractiveness as an investment destination rests on the following factors: 'large and growing market, world-class scientific,

[6] A large part of FDI comes in through the automatic route and does not require prior approval.

[7] I am grateful to the Ministry of Commerce, Government of India, for allowing me access to this data.

technical and managerial manpower, cost-effective and highly skilled labour…, a large English speaking population…'. Sectoral distribution of FDI projects confirms this picture in that the labour demand generated by FDI will be for workers with a specific educational and skill profile, and especially with a knowledge of English. Given the existing educational disparities by caste, prima facie, it appears that a large section of Dalits and women will not be prime candidates for these jobs.[8] Additionally, research into the pathways through which caste plays a role in urban, formal sector labour markets suggests that Dalits face direct and indirect discriminatory barriers even after they acquire higher education from reputed, elite institutions (Deshpande and Newman 2007).

Of course, this static picture could change. Growth in certain kinds of jobs could provide the requisite incentives to acquire higher education and English-language skills over time. The educational levels of the labour force could thus be both a cause and an effect of FDI (for example, certain kinds of FDI tend to get concentrated in areas that already have the labour force with requisite education and English skills, which then provide further incentives for increasing this skill acquisition). Unless the dynamic spreads to other areas, this could lead to further clustering of FDI. Deshpande (2013b) finds that based on district level data for FDI approvals between 1995 and 2010, a greater number of FDI approvals were associated with *lower* relative wages of Dalits versus Others. This result is obtained after controlling for the relative proportions of Dalits versus Others with secondary education or more (the section which will be eligible for FDI-induced jobs), and the relative proportion of those in regular wage/salaried jobs, as well as district-specific fixed effects. This suggests that earnings' gaps are more likely to widen, rather than diminish, controlling for other factors.

The Larger Impact of Globalization

The creation of new and new types of jobs through FDI is only one channel through globalization and liberalization that is likely to affect caste

[8] The designation of English as the new 'Dalit goddess', as the vehicle which will eventually lead to Dalit emancipation is easier to understand in the context of the huge advantage that knowledge of English gives in the labour market [http://www.indianexpress.com/news/happy-birthday-lord-macaulay-thank-you-for-dalit-empowerment/15423/0 (accessed on 27 February 2011)].

disparities, either positively or negatively. The broader argument for the emancipatory effect of globalization has several contours; it hinges on the fact that globalization will make the market salient as well as unleash competition between Indian and foreign firms, impacting Dalits positively in many dimensions. FDI and MNCs will be an implicit and important, but not the only, part of this process. It has been argued that one of the ways in which globalization empowers Dalits is by 'universalising access to aspirations'. The reference is to the process of certain consumer goods being plentifully and cheaply available (for example, colour televisions, mobile phones, refrigerators, and air conditioners) and within the reach of the Dalits, goods that are supposed to be 'material markers of pride'. It is argued that this has broken the exclusivity of the 'predominantly Upper Caste Consumer Club', a process aided also by the rise of Dalit entrepreneurs.[9] Omvedt (2005) argues that globalization is inevitable, already a reality for India and it has many positive aspects. Thus, instead of taking a blind anti-globalization position (as she argues the Left and ecologists in India take), she suggests that we need to think about a comprehensive and nuanced response of Dalits and Adivasis to these changing realities. This sentiment is echoed by others in that Dalits are asked to view globalization as an opportunity rather than as a threat.[10]

Kapur et al. (2010: 39), on the basis of a survey of all Dalit households in two blocks of two districts in Uttar Pradesh, argue that the shift from a state-led to a market-led path of development has changed patterns of interaction between castes, leading to a 'rapid erosion in discriminatory practices that stigmatized Dalits'. They also find large shifts in the pattern of economic life, both within and away from the village. They see this change manifesting itself both in terms of a change in occupational patterns, with Dalits moving away from traditional occupations, as well as in the nature of contracts between Dalits and upper castes, such that practices such as bonded labour that tied Dalits to generations of servitude appear to have become obsolete.

It is not immediately apparent to what extent the study of two blocks in one state can be generalized to the rest of the country. There have undoubtedly been significant changes in consumption patterns in contemporary India over the last 2–3 decades,[11] but these changes are neither confined to

[9] http://www.chandrabhanprasad.com/frmGlobalization.aspx (accessed in February 2011).

[10] Chandra Bhan Prasad, see footnote 9.

[11] See, for instance, Meenakshi (1996).

Dalits, nor is it clear that Dalits exhibit a differential pattern of *changes* in consumption compared to upper castes.

Another channel through which liberalization will have implications for caste disparity is privatization. At the moment, affirmative action in India takes the form of quotas for SCs, STs, and OBCs in public sector jobs and government-run educational institutions. As the economy privatizes and more jobs get created in the private sector, the scope for affirmative action in its present form is likely to shrink. Deshpande (2013a) discusses the impact of the affirmative action programme in detail; suffice it to say here that while affirmative action has not been able to eliminate inter-caste disparity, partly because it is not designed for that purpose and partly because of inadequate implementation, there are compelling reasons to believe that the gaps will be larger in the absence of affirmative action.

Overall, the impact of globalization on caste disparities is complex, and contains many inter-woven strands, not necessarily easy to disentangle. What is noteworthy is that this debate over whether globalization will be favourable to Dalits or not, by and large, is *not* backed by hard empirical facts. Much more empirical work, based on smaller studies in different parts of India as well as on macro all-India data, needs to be undertaken before we can etch out the contours of the multi-dimensional impact of globalization on caste disparities.

Class

The rapid growth of the economy in the last two decades has resulted in a noticeable expansion in the group of 'high net worth individuals' (HNIs, individuals with investible assets of US$ 1 million or more), or extremely affluent Indians. India's HNI population grew at 20.8 per cent to 1,53,000 in 2010 compared with 1,26,700 in 2009, according to the 2011 Asia-Pacific Wealth Report by Merrill Lynch Global Wealth Management and Capgemini. The cumulative wealth of Indian HNIs grew by 22 per cent in 2009–10 to Rs 28,60,000 crore from a year ago.[12] These are globally connected individuals who enjoy lifestyles comparable to the elite

[12] http://businesstoday.intoday.in/story/india-high-networth-hni-population-grows-by-20-per-cent/1/19634.html (accessed in July 2012).

in developed countries, and visibly shape patterns of conspicuous consumption in urban India, especially in metropolitan cities.

The growth of this elite segment, which is small in proportion but large in numbers and purchasing power, should be separated from the growth of the Indian middle class. There has been a lot of attention on the growth of the middle class signalling the rapid growth of a domestic market; however, it should be noted that there is no official estimate of the size of the Indian middle class and estimates vary from 25 to 300 million. The variations in estimates come from different databases, but more importantly from how the middle class is defined. The middle class, by definition, should be defined as having an income within some interval which includes the median. Ravallion (2009) discusses the diverse and ad hoc ways in which the upper and lower bounds of this interval have been defined and suggests that a common way to define the middle class in developed countries is those having incomes between 75 and 125 per cent of the median of that country.[13] A key issue in the definition of the middle class is whether it is appropriate to use the same definition for both rich and poor countries.

Ravallion (2009: 6) suggests a 'developing world's middle class' defined as those who are not poor by the standards of developing countries but might be poor by the standards of developed countries. He suggests a lower bound of US$ 2 a day, which is double the official poverty line in India (and also China). His upper bound is US$ 13 a day, which is the US poverty line at 2005 PPP.[14] A person will have entered the 'Western middle class' if earning more than the US poverty line. Using this definition for India, based on NSS data, he finds only 3 million people not poor by US standards. Correcting for possible under-reporting of consumption expenditure in NSS data by increasing all consumption expenditures by 50 per cent, the count of Indians who are not poor by US standards rises to only six million (Ravallion 2009: 9). However, the growth of the segment which he defines as the 'developing country middle class' (proportion living between US$ 2 and US$ 13 a day) has been substantial between 1990 and 2005: an extra 117 million people joined this group in India. He argues that this is linked to a reduction in poverty, as the bulk of the increase in the middle class came from an increase in the US$ 2 to US$ 6 segment, rather than from an increase in the upper middle class.

[13] This is a relative definition; Ravallion (2009) discusses other definitions which have absolute lower and upper bounds.

[14] These bounds are similar to those suggested by Banerjee and Duflo (2008).

Inequality and Class Conflict: The Growth of the Maoist Movement

One side of the Indian growth story is reflected in the growth of the super rich and the middle class. However, the other side of the story is rising inequality reflected in growing class discontent which has found expression through the rise of the Maoist movement, which has spread to several states in India, including Bihar, Jharkhand, Chhattisgarh, Madhya Pradesh, Odisha, Maharashtra, and Karnataka. Today, this movement, christened 'left wing extremism' (LWE) by the Indian state, poses a challenge major enough for Prime Minister Manmohan Singh to express concern about the fact that 'not a day passes without an incident of Left Wing Extremism taking place somewhere or the other … [making LWE] probably the single biggest security challenge to the Indian state'.[15]

The rapid spread of the movement over large parts of central and south India in the last decade reinforces the need for a rigorous assessment of both the causes and consequences of this conflict. In one of the early empirical exercises, Borooah (2008) finds that the probability of Naxalite activity in a district increased with a rise in its poverty rate, and decreased with a rise in its literacy rate. In addition, districts with a smaller coverage of safe drinking water were more likely to have Naxalite activity, compared to districts where a greater proportion of the habitants had access to safe drinking water, clearly hinting at high poverty and lack of development as factors contributing to Maoist violence.

In a cross-country study of violence in South Asia (not only Maoist conflict but including all other conflicts in the region), Iyer (2009) finds a clear divergence between 'leading' and 'lagging' regions in the post-2001 period, in that incidents of violence increased sharply in the lagging regions, while they remained steady in the leading regions. She defines regions as leading or lagging based on per capita income levels in 2004. According to this definition, the lagging regions in India were Assam, Bihar, Chhattisgarh, Jharkhand, Madhya Pradesh, Manipur, Mizoram, Meghalaya, Nagaland, Odisha, Rajasthan, Uttar Pradesh, Uttarakhand, and West Bengal. She finds that this trend further intensified after 2004, with lagging regions displaying a continued increase in conflict and leading regions showing a slight decline. This is mirrored in counter-terrorism

[15] Prime Minister Manmohan Singh's speech to the Conference of Chief Ministers on Internal Security, 20 December 2007. Available at: http://www.satp.org/satporgtp/countries/india/document/papers/20071220pmspeech.htm (accessed on 13 May 2012).

activities, proxied by the number of terrorists killed by security forces, which has been declining in leading regions after 2005, possibly a reflection of lower levels of extremist activity in those areas, whereas the trend in lagging regions continues to rise.

Going further into the causes of conflict (again, note that her analysis is not confined to, but includes, the Maoist conflict) using district level data, Iyer finds that conflict is higher in poorer regions, with a large effect: an increase in poverty by 10 percentage points is associated with 0.26 incidents of conflict per district. This is quite high compared to an average of 0.77 incidents per district. A 10 percentage point increase in poverty is associated with 0.39 more deaths for an average district (compared to the mean level of 0.60 deaths per district). She also finds a significant positive relationship between intensity of conflict and the extent of mountain and forest cover. Exploring the impact of social diversity (proxied by the relative presence of members of disadvantaged groups in the population (fractions of SCs, STs, and Muslims) and institutional quality (proxied by a measure of historical property rights based on whether land tenure was historically controlled by landlords), she finds that areas with lower historical land inequality have a lower incidence of conflict, but the relationship is not statistically significant and the presence of disadvantaged communities is not significantly associated with conflict intensity.

Thus, evidence suggests that poverty, illiteracy or more broadly, underdevelopment, combined with inequality in land ownership are the key factors responsible for the sustained growth of the Maoist movement in the last decade or so. Geography plays a role in two ways: one, that forested terrains facilitate guerrilla activity and two, these are regions where tribals form a substantial proportion of the population but where there is disaffection due to lack of control over forest land and/or mineral wealth. The question which remains to be answered is whether the movement is working as a Robin Hood state, redistributing to the poor what they believe is justly due, given the perception that the state is an instrument to protect the interests of the rich landlords; or whether the movement is more like an extortionist mafia, which in return for extortion provides protection and some community services, again hinting at state failure. Also, whether the Maoist strategy of individual annihilation (of those deemed to be class enemies) will fundamentally alter the material conditions of the marginalized and the dispossessed can be debated; the point being made is that there is sufficient material deprivation to fuel further growth of Maoism.

Official Response to LWE

Official references, including journalistic accounts in the print media, regard LWE as an extremist menace, with frequent references to 'Naxalite infested' areas. The Prime Minister's 2007 speech, quoted earlier, confirms this official view by resolving that 'we cannot rest in peace until we have eliminated this *virus*' [emphasis added]. While the movement and its sympathizers view themselves as spearheading a revolution for radical social transformation in response to deprivation and inequality, the official view inverts the cause and effect and sees the movement as *causing* deprivation in order to sustain its ideology.

The Indian government's assertion is not unique to the LWE context. Indeed, the idea that conflict *causes* deprivation has been forcefully made in other international contexts. For instance, it has been suggested in the cases of Rwanda, Angola, Congo, and Sudan that war has resulted in a destruction of physical infrastructure as well as human capital, leading to a lowering of per capita incomes in war-affected countries; this being one of the factors in the growing gap between the world's richest and poorest nations (Blattman and Miguel 2009: 3).

Following directly from this view, the mainstream official view is towards the elimination of the movement through force. Increased Maoist activity has been met by increased police repression, resulting in heavy casualties on both sides. Since 2005, the Chhattisgarh state government has sponsored a counter-insurgency operation called 'Salwa Judum' (literally, the purification hunt), which is touted as a spontaneous people's reaction to the excesses of Naxalism (Sundar 2006). This outfit has killed several suspected Maoists and displaced thousands of people. There have been several reports of the terror unleashed by Salwa Judum, including sexual attacks on women. What is especially dangerous is that this is supposedly a civil society initiative but is completely state-sponsored and not accountable to any agency.

State-sponsored counter-violence, bypassing the due process of law and justice is now a matter of serious concern, as in addition to Salwa Judum, there are suspected underground counter-insurgency forces acting in several states. Additionally, special counter-insurgency forces have been created which are targeted towards Maoists. In Andhra Pradesh, an elite security force, called the Greyhounds, was launched in 1989. Though the size of the force is small, it consists of a highly trained cadre and to match the highly trained force all police capacities have been augmented. Harris

(2010: 12) describes how the Greyhounds operate very much like the Naxalites' own squads and are 'bound by no law including the constitution of India'. Thus, the approach is very clearly one of suppression by sheer force, reflecting the state's attitude which regards Maoism as a menace or at best, a 'law and order' problem.

While this is the dominant approach, attempts have been made through the appointment of commissions, most notably through the formation of an expert group set up by the Planning Commission in 2008, to examine the 'Development Challenges in Extremist Affected Areas'. The group's report comprehensively outlines multi-faceted sources of discontent in areas of Maoist activity, with a detailed outline of the multiple class–caste–gender disadvantages of Dalits, Adivasis, and women. It highlights, in particular, the sources of tribal alienation and a deep sense of exclusion, since despite several special and targeted policies, a majority of the Scheduled Tribes live in conditions of serious deprivation and poverty. The conflict between Adivasis and the Indian state is seen not only in Maoist areas, but in the north-eastern states as well, such that the deep-rooted discontent gets manifested in various insurgent forms. In addition to poverty and illiteracy, the expert group highlighted the following causes of tribal discontent: 'absence of self-governance, forest policy, excise policy, land related issues (forced evictions from land, displacement) ... political marginalisation (p. 8). The report also points out that 'failure to implement protective regulations in Scheduled Areas, absence of credit mechanism leading to dependence on money lenders and consequent loss of land and often *violence by the State*' is rampant (emphasis added).

The right to forest land is a central part of the tension between the Adivasis and the state. The lip service to symbiotic relationships notwithstanding, the actual use of forests by communities traditionally dependant on forests for livelihoods, with traditional practices which preserve the ecological balance, has been regularly circumscribed. A related issue is large-scale displacement of tribals due to large development projects. Odisha, Jharkhand, and Chhattisgarh, in particular, have seen massive displacement of tribals on account of mining projects, and these have led to widespread protests. The expert group points out that unless tribals are resettled in scheduled areas, they will lose their special rights and are likely to be further marginalized.

Each of these issues is vital and complex, and will need to be assessed separately in complete detail, taking all the nuances into account. The point of this brief discussion is that the Indian state has access to a perspective which highlights the multiple causes of discontent and suggests very forcefully that the Maoist 'menace' is a political problem, not only a law-and-order one. Yet, the mainstream approach continues to be a security-based one. The danger with this approach is that the discontent can actually multiply manifold, as in addition to the already existing dissatisfaction against material deprivation and the resulting alienation, the local populations will now also have to deal with the consequences of repression and violence by the state.

It will be useful to recall that historically there have been specific episodes during the Naxalite movement which have seen political solutions. For instance, at the time of the first Naxalbari uprising, the United Front government was in power in West Bengal. The Revenue Minister, Hare Krishna Konar of the CPI (M), used Mao Zedong's theory of 'fish in water'—the disgruntled peasantry was the water in which the fish of militancy was bound to grow, as long as the distress of the peasantry continued. Thus, the strategy to move the peasantry away from the militants took the form of government acquiring ceiling-surplus land of zamindars and big landlords and redistributing it to landless peasants. This was an important part of the anti-Naxalite strategy which proved effective in weaning a section of the peasantry away from Naxalites; of course, this was accompanied by conventional law-and-order measures.

Gender

Gender disparities in educational and occupational attainment have been a persistent feature of Indian society and the subject of a great deal of academic and policy attention (Rao et al. 2010). Considerable concern and attention is also centred on the adverse and declining sex ratio and the phenomena of sex-selective foeticides and infanticides and overall neglect and malnutrition of the girl child. In the limited space of this chapter, I would like to focus on one specific aspect—gender wage gaps, in order to comment on the nature of economic discrimination faced by women workers.

A standard way of estimating discrimination in labour markets is by decomposing the average wage gap into an 'explained' (by wage earning characteristics) part and the 'residual', which is part of the wage gap that remains even after all possible explanatory factors are accounted for. The residual is taken as the measure of discrimination in the labour market.

Both, the average wage gap as well as its decomposition, are useful in that they provide a summary measure of discrimination. However, a newer technique of quantile regressions allows us to assess how returns to wage earning characteristics vary over different quantiles or over different parts of the wage distribution (so it allows us to answer questions, such as 'what happens where'). Using quantile regressions we can see if wage gaps are higher at the top or bottom ends of the wage distribution. In other words, do women face a 'glass ceiling' or a 'sticky floor'?

Estimating quantile regressions separately for men and women also allows for separate decompositions for each quantile. Specifically, these quantile decompositions allow us to answer the following question: do high earning women face greater discrimination (greater residual or a greater unexplained part) as compared to low wage earning women? Based on the sixty-sixth round of the NSS employment–unemployment survey data corresponding to 2009–10, Khanna (2012) finds that one, among regular wage/salaried workers, the gender log wage gap is positive through wage distribution. This means that men earn more than women at all percentiles of wage distribution. Two, he finds that the gender log wage gap is higher at the lower parts of wage distribution and narrows as one goes up the wage distribution. This means that women in India face the 'sticky floor', rather than a glass ceiling. While the mean wage gap is 0.4 (from the standard decomposition technique, corresponding to a raw wage gap of 50 per cent), the log wage gap is 0.79 at the 7th percentile (which corresponds to a raw wage gap of 120 per cent) and 0.04 at the 84th percentile. This means that men get paid twice as much as women at the bottom of the distribution. This finding of a sticky floor is in sharp contrast to labour markets in developed countries which typically find a glass ceiling or increasing gender wage gaps across quintiles. Also, the sticky floor in India is much stronger or stickier, as the decline in wage gaps from the bottom to the top of the distribution is much more drastic for India as compared to the international experience.

Comparing these gaps with the two earlier rounds, Khanna finds that between 1999–2000 and 2004–5, the average log wage gap worsened to improve by 2009–10, mainly due to gains made by women in the middle range of the distribution. Overall for the decade 1999–2010, the gender log wage gaps at the two ends of the distribution (highly paid and poorly paid workers) remained virtually unchanged. This sticky floor phenomenon is seen in both rural and urban sectors, but is higher in magnitude in the rural sector. The sticky floor phenomenon persists even after decompositions based on quantile regressions are carried out separately for different quantiles. For 2009–10, he finds that discrimination (the unexplained part of the wage gap) is highest among low wage earners. For instance, in the first decile, men earn wages that are 82 per cent higher than women purely due to discrimination. This decreases as one goes up the wage distribution, such that gender wage gaps due to discrimination are about 22 per cent at the seventh decile and 10 per cent at the ninth decile.

An important reason for the high gap at the lower ends of wage distribution is due to the fact that as many as 42 per cent of women (amounting to 43 lakh women) in the *regular wage salaried category* earn less than the statutory minimum wage. One can imagine how much worse this situation will be among casual and informal workers. So a clear and straightforward lesson from this picture will be strict implementation of minimum wages.

* * *

The recent slowdown notwithstanding, the Indian economy over the last two decades has been characterized by momentous changes. The translation and impact of these changes on inter-group disparities has been uneven. Caste inequality shows very strong inter-state variations and some convergence, but no clear relationship between growth and convergence. In other words, it is not necessarily the case that richer or faster-growing states have seen lower caste disparity (or vice versa). Gender wage gaps are substantial and surprisingly, these are greater for the lower part of wage distribution. A decomposition of these gaps between 'explained' and 'residual' components indicates that the discriminatory component is greater among the bottom four wage deciles, indicating the presence of a 'sticky floor', rather than a 'glass ceiling' for women. While the incidence of poverty has reduced, class inequality has increased sharply, particularly in certain parts of the country, leading to protracted armed insurgency, which has brought to the fore questions of control over forests and natural resources. Ironically, as the economy becomes more market oriented, it appears that the state has to step in decisively to act on a strategy of redistribution in order to quell discontent and to ensure that the gains from growth are distributed more equitably across the diversity of India's population. While this is a longer-term need, the state needs to immediately improve provision of public goods and make the policy framework as well as governance structures accountable, transparent, and inclusive.

References

Akerlof, George (1984), 'The Economics of Caste and of the Rat Race and Other Woeful Tales', in *An Economic Theorist's Book of Tales.* Cambridge: Cambridge University Press, pp. 23–44.

Arrow, Kenneth J. (1971), 'The Theory of Discrimination', Working Paper 403, Princeton University, Department of Economics, Industrial Relations Section.

Banerjee, Abhijit and Esther Duflo (2008), 'What is Middle Class about the Middle Classes Around the World?' *Journal of Economic Perspectives* 22(2): 3–28.

Becker, Gary S. (1957), *The Economics of Discrimination.* Chicago: The University of Chicago Press.

Beteille, Andre (2012), 'The Peculiar Tenacity of Caste', *Economic and Political Weekly* XLVII(13).

Blattman, Christopher and Edward Miguel (2009), 'Civil War', National Bureau of Economic Research Working Paper Series, Working Paper 14801. Available at: http://www.nber.org/papers/w14801.

Borooah, Vani K. (2008), 'Deprivation, Violence, and Conflict: An Analysis of Naxalite Activity in the Districts of India', MPRA Paper No. 19425. Available at: http://mpra.ub.uni-muenchen.de/19425/, (accessed on 17 March 2012).

Deshpande, Ashwini (2001), 'Caste at Birth? Redefining disparity in India', *Review of Development Economics* 5(1): 130–44.

—— (2011), *The Grammar of Caste: Economic Discrimination in Contemporary India.* New Delhi: Oxford University Press.

—— (2013a), 'Affirmative Action in India', in *Oxford India Short Introductions.* New Delhi: Oxford University Press.

—— (2013b): 'Liberalisation and Inter-group disparities in India', mimeo.

Deshpande, Ashwini and William Darity Jr. (2003), 'Boundaries of Clan and Color: Cross National Comparisons of Inter-group Inequality'. London: Routledge.

Deshpande, Ashwini and Katherine Newman (2007), 'Where the path leads: the role of caste in post university employment expectations', *Economic and Political Weekly* 42(41): 4133–40.

Harris, John (2010), 'The Naxalite/Maoist Movement in India: a review of recent literature', ISAS Working Paper No. 109, Institute for South Asian Studies, National University of Singapore.

Hnatkovska, Viktoria, Amartya Lahiri, and Sourabh Paul (2012), 'Castes and Labor Mobility', *American Economic Journal: Applied Economics* 4(2): 274–307.

Iyer, Lakshmi (2009), 'The Bloody Millennium: Internal Conflict in South Asia', Harvard Business School Working Paper, 09–086.

Jodhka, Surinder and Katherine Newman (2007), 'In the Name of Globalisation', *Economic and Political Weekly* 42(41): 4125–32.

Kapur, Devesh, Chandra Bhan Prasad, Lant Pritchett, and D. Shyam Babu (2010), 'Rethinking inequality: Dalits in Uttar Pradesh in the Market Reform Era', *Economic and Political Weekly* XLV(35): 39–49.

Khanna, Shantanu (2012), 'Gender Wage Discrimination in India: Glass Ceiling or Sticky Floor', Centre for Development Economics Working Paper No. 214, July.

Meenakshi, J.V. (1996), 'How Important are Changes in Taste? A State-Level Analysis of Food Demand', *Economic and Political Weekly*, 31(50): 3265–9.

National Council of Applied Research and Training (NCAER) (2009), *FDI in India and Its Growth Linkages*. New Delhi: NCAER.

Omvedt, Gail (2005), 'Capitalism and Globalisation: Dalits and Adivasis', *Economic and Political Weekly*, 40(47): 4881–5.

Ravallion, Martin (2009), 'The Developing World's Bulging (But Vulnerable) "Middle Class"', Policy Research Working Paper 4816, World Bank Policy Research Group.

Rao, Nitya, Ashwini Deshpande, Arjan Verschoor, and Amaresh Dubey (2010), 'Gender Caste and Growth Assessment—India, Report to Department for International Development', DEV Reports and Policy Paper Series, The School of International Development, University of East Anglia, UK.

Sundar, Nandini (2006), 'Bastar, Maoism and Salwa Judum', *Economic and Political Weekly*: 3187–92.

PART V

GOVERNANCE

CHAPTER 15

GOVERNMENT TAXES AND EXPENDITURES

experience and reform

PARTHASARATHI SHOME*

India can be said to have progressed through its fiscal experience in fits and starts though, on the whole, for a fiscally federal country, where the Constitution guarantees both the centre and the states their own taxation assignments and shares in revenue, it has emerged on the winning side in comparison with similarly organized nations. On the expenditure side, success has been more ephemeral, with short-term gains in holding back or rationalizing expenditures being routinely reversed by deficient policies driven mainly by political economy motivations. In recent years, two challenges that have over-ridden the policy side have emerged from the corner of poor implementation, both in tax administration and expenditure management and control. They may be said to have overwhelmed any progress made on the policy side.

These developments have occurred in a milieu of continually changing global and domestic economic environments that have had an impact on the rate of economic growth, whether they were, at one end a global financial crisis that culminated in an economic crisis, or poor monsoons in a primarily rain driven agriculture, with the rural sector providing sustenance to two-thirds of India's population. Despite the central bank helping

* All opinions are the exclusive responsibility of the author. He appreciates the research assistance provided by B. Karan Singh.

insulate the economy relatively successfully from the vagaries of runaway international finance, such exogenous shocks and influences sometimes appear to have been used for relaxing a fledgling conservative fiscal stance while statistics indicating leakages from allocated expenditures for irrigation, education, or health have made the obvious revelation of how challenging the implementation problem is in India. At the moment India stands at another crossroads for correcting its lost trajectory towards responsible fiscal policy and governance, the four pillars of which comprise tax policy, expenditure policy, tax administration, and expenditure management and control. The role of these pillars in fiscal sector outcomes was delineated in Shome (2002), demonstrating the intrinsic mutual connection among them.

In what follows, we first provide a survey of India's prevailing economic environment, setting the overall fiscal outcomes in that light. This is followed by an analysis of the tax policy, revenue outcomes and their composition, and a review of overall expenditure outcomes, their composition and selected aspects of the quality of expenditure. Further on, the chapter analyses the extent to which the central government has been successful in consolidating its overall fiscal position and goes on to examine the revenue and expenditure components. Subsequently, it deals with the ever increasing importance of tax administration as well as the latest challenges in tax policy reforms as India integrates into the global economy and braces domestic challenges in a constitutionally guaranteed fiscal federal system of tax assignment and revenue sharing among national and sub-national levels of the government. Concluding remarks follow.

The Role of Economic Environment

India's economic environment has experienced a number of crucial turning points driven by transformations in domestic policy from a strategy of self-reliance, to a realization that in moving from autarky to opening up international trade, there is a need to align the economy to global practices and processes. Economic exigencies, internationally driven or domestic, have also affected the environment. In the early 2000s—2004–8 in particular—India achieved what could be termed a golden age of fiscal prudence. Tax revenue growth reached a real rate of above 20 per cent per annum, higher than ever achieved historically before or after that period, either at home or internationally. Figure 15.1 puts total revenue growth rates against Figure 15.2. They show that the increase in overall tax revenue was achieved despite a significant decline in revenue growth rates from distortionary indirect taxes—customs and excise—which was a policy driven outcome. The government's goal of reducing the fiscal deficit to 3 per cent of GDP over five years was almost achieved. Then, as the visage of an international economic crisis loomed on the horizon, India loosened its fiscal stance. The reason for the extent to which the loosening occurred, however, remains a matter of contention.

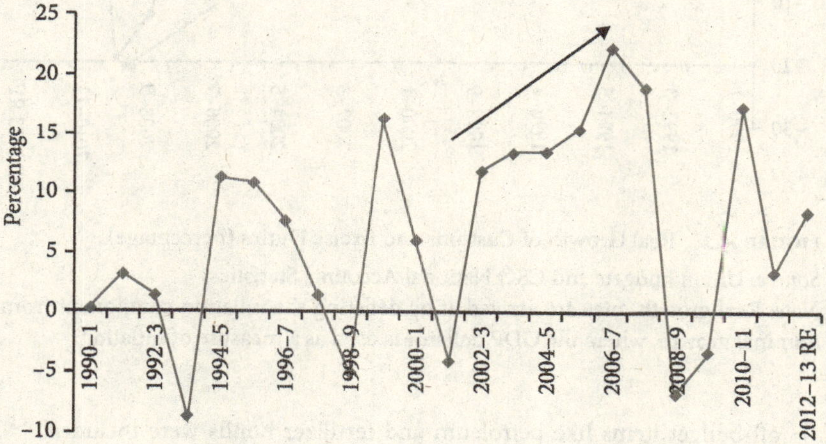

FIGURE 15.1 Real Growth of Gross Tax Revenue (percentage)
Source: Union budgets and CSO National Accounts Statistics.
Note: Real growth rates are arrived at by deflating the inflation component from nominal growth, where the GDP deflator is used as a measure of inflation.

Views on the matter differ. Mundle et al. (2010: 4) have claimed:

> A strong fiscal stimulus became necessary in the second half of FY 2008-2009 and again in FY2009-2010 to help revive growth. The positive impact of this stimulus became evident especially during the last two quarters of FY 2009-2010. At the same time the stimulus entailed a further deterioration of the fiscal condition.

Acharya's (2012: 14) opinion is different:

> [T]he central government's fiscal deficit for 2008/9 went from the 2.5 per cent of GDP budgeted in February 2008 to over 6 per cent in the actual accounts and to an even higher 8 per cent of GDP when the

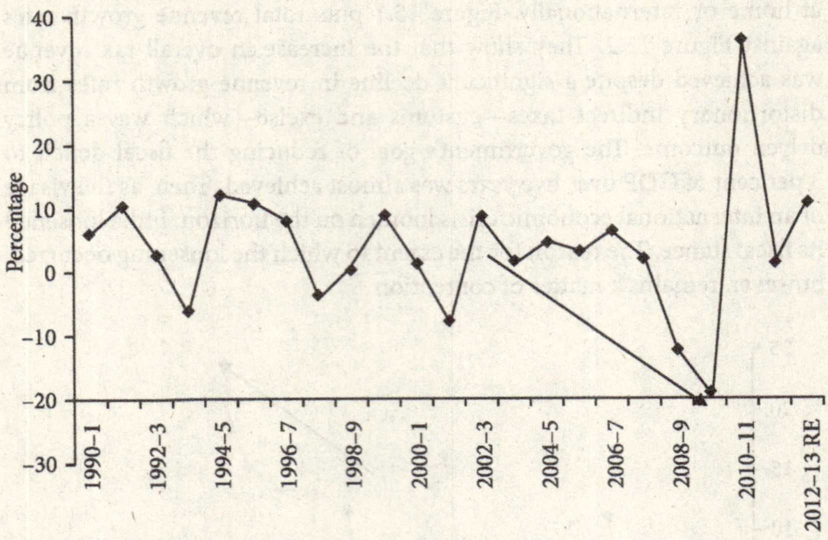

FIGURE 15.2 Real Growth of Customs and Excise Duties (percentage)

Source: Union budgets and CSO National Accounts Statistics.
Note: Real growth rates are arrived at by deflating the inflation component from nominal growth, where the GDP deflator is used as a measure of inflation.

> off-budget items like petroleum and fertilizer bonds were included. This massive fiscal overshoot more than wiped out in a single year all the hard-won fiscal consolidation achieved between 2003/4 and 2007/8. While storing up fiscal and inflationary problems for the future, it had the salutary effect of countering the deflationary shock from the global financial and economic crisis. Whether this order of fiscal stimulus (or profligacy) was really necessary remains debatable. What is clear is that the composition of the fiscal expansion, in the form mainly of higher government salaries, much larger subsidies for fuel, fertilizer and food and the ramping up of entitlement programs, seriously constrained the scope for subsequent fiscal retraction.

Acharya (2012: 14) continues:

> 2008 happened to be a year of extraordinary fiscal profligacy, influenced, no doubt, by the imminence of the general election of spring 2009. Well before the dramatic collapse of Lehman Brothers in September 2008, spending by India's central government was running far above budget levels on account of government pay increases (resulting from the adoption of Sixth Pay Commission recommenda-

tions), fertilizer and food subsidies, the new farm loan waiver scheme and the National Rural Employment Guarantee program (NREG).

It appears to be safe to conclude that a deficit expansion of 3.5 per cent of GDP could not have been necessary to counter the prevailing global recessionary conditions, and that much of it reflected political considerations.

Rakshit (2010), in a critique of the fiscal adjustment programme (FAP) of the Thirteenth Finance Commission (THFC), did put forward arguments in favour of a higher fiscal deficit but, by and large, those elements did not comprise the type of loosening that has taken place since 2008. Rakshit's (2010: 41) postulates are worth a visit, for he rationalized systemic needs over counter-cyclical fiscal policy.

> The basic strategy behind the FAP, it is emphasised, is not to compress development expenditure, but to 'raise both public and private investment'. The policies advocated, however, are not different from those suggested by the Eleventh and Twelfth Finance Commissions. The 'golden rule' is invoked in support of reducing revenue deficit to zero or negative levels. Limits on fiscal deficits are imposed for avoiding 'crowding out'. Disinvestment is to form an important source of augmenting government investment. However, the rationale behind the three policies is not as sound as is generally believed.

Rakshit (2010: 42) argues that before the fiscal deficit is reined in:

> [T]he role of fiscal policies for triggering cumulative and inclusive growth lies primarily in removal of major constraints on development. The most important of these constraints are: (a) a gross underdevelopment/segmentation of the credit market; (b) a dismal state of education and a high incidence of morbidity; and (c) a severe shortage of infrastructural facilities. Since state intervention in removal of these constraints is essential, for a constructive critique of the THFC FAP it is important to examine the nature of the optimal fiscal road map for meeting the objective.

While Rakshit's identification of the three constraints, which he develops cogently in the paper, is not falsifiable, it has to be reckoned that mere additional resource allocation in the three areas is unlikely to reverse their prevailing unimpressive outcomes. Achieving success is, increasingly, a matter of reforms in implementation and closing of leakages. Acharya (2012: 19) has argued that infrastructure gaps have resulted essentially on two grounds. First, the provision of gas and electricity has been tainted by 'scams and scandals ... pertaining to the allocation of 2G telecom spectrum industry ... government land and mining rights'. Second, the government has not been able to garner support for appropriate policies. In electricity, while power generation by private companies had been encouraged, 'much of the new generation capacity remained unutilised (in 2012) ... because the necessary fuel linkages to gas or coal failed to materialise or because the state distribution companies lacked funds....because of massive underpricing to farmers and other users and large scale thefts from the network'. Clearly, more allocation and disbursement of funds from the exchequer are not the solution to hem in the much needed infrastructure. The solution lies, instead, in a big push in correcting the pricing policy, reforming implementation, and closing leakages.

An examination of the trajectory of the fiscal deficit of the general—centre and states—government over the last three decades yields some interesting conclusions. Shome (1996) undertook a comprehensive analysis of the first half of this period.[1] For example, for two years after the imposition of an IMF supported economic stabilization programme in 1991, the fiscal deficit was controlled. Immediately with the repayment to the Fund, the fiscal deficit shot up in 1993–4, again to be contained to some extent for the next two years. Leaping over a decade, a similarly alternating overall fiscal stance continued into the 2000s. Perhaps the most striking observation that may be made is the rapid control of the combined fiscal deficit between 2003–4 and 2007–8 and its sharp increase thereafter (Figure 15.3). The levels of government are separated, as shown in Appendix A15 (Figures A15.1 and A15.2), which reveal comparable efforts and subsequent laxity in both levels of government.

An examination of the changes in the combined fiscal deficit depicted in Shome (2013: Figure 15.2),[2] helps identify periods of consolidation and loosening that have alternated over the last three decades. It is as if after a period of rule-making, such as the Fiscal Responsibility and Budget Management (FRBM) Act of the most recent period and the resolve to adhere to a path of deficit reduction, that steady policy was set aside for some extraneous, almost inexplicable, reason and years of gain were lost, to be picked up again as a new fiscal crisis appeared on the horizon. In turn, the uncertainty that is associated with it gets reflected in a diminution in India's international ratings and, consequently in an increase in the cost of borrowing and lower inflow of capital. In other words, significant

[1] Information presented in table 1 in Shome (1996) has been updated and extended here in Tables A15.1 and A15.2 that form the analytical base of the current chapter.

[2] Derived from Figure 15.3.

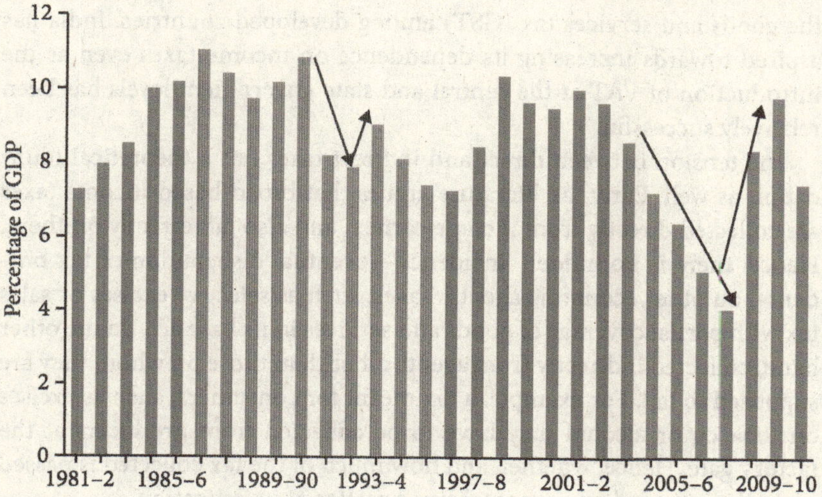

FIGURE 15.3 Combined Fiscal Deficits of Central and State Governments (percentage of GDP)

Source: RBI database on the Indian economy and CSO National Accounts Statistics.

costs to the economy get associated with fluctuating fiscal policy that India has employed over the last several decades.

Tax Policy and Revenue Outcomes

India's tussle between direct and indirect tax revenue generation is noteworthy. In tax development literature, there is an adage that developing economies transit from heavy dependence on customs duties and excises to income taxes as development occurs (Shome 1992; Tanzi 1991). In recent years, as income taxes—in particular, corporate income tax—have become increasingly complex, there is a shift towards greater dependence on broad-based consumption taxes with a mechanism for comprehensive input tax credit to minimize cascading,[3] such as value added tax (VAT) or

[3] When taxes paid in upstream stages of manufacturing and distribution are not credited out and therefore get embedded in downstream stages, it results in those taxes becoming a part of the final product price. Thus, when sale value in downstream stages is taxed, the value of the tax paid in the upstream stages gets taxed (over and above the value of the product). This 'tax on tax' impact is called cascading of a tax.

the goods and services tax (GST) among developed countries. India has aspired towards increasing its dependence on income taxes even as the introduction of VAT at the central and state government levels has been relatively successful.

The tension between direct and indirect taxes has a theoretical foundation as well. Early tax literature argues that broad-based income taxes are collected directly from income earners and also fall directly on them. Hence, there is no hidden 'incidence'—eventual distribution of tax burdens—on other economic agents. Taxes, such as selective excises or sales tax with partial coverage of goods and services in its base are, on the other hand, collected indirectly from agents other than those on whom they are supposed to fall. For example, a tax meant for consumers, such as excises on tobacco or alcohol may have to be collected from producers at the factory gate. Hence, whether, and how much of the tax collected is passed on to the intended taxpayer remains a matter of investigation.

However, looking at the matter from another angle, the basis of directness of income tax has been, and continues to be, questioned, mainly from two perspectives. First, usually income tax rates for labour and capital are different. A tax on labour income tends to increase a taxpayer's choice of leisure (Herber 1979; Musgrave 1959), so that a higher tax rate on labour than on capital should exacerbate the choice. Second, a tax on capital income may be partial rather than being broad-based. For example, corporate income tax does not fall, at first glance, on capital employed as a whole; rather, it is restricted to capital in the corporate sector at least at the point of collection. This leads to ripple effects since corporate capital tends to move out and has to be absorbed in the non-corporate sector (Harberger 1974). Such forceful absorption will tend to reduce the return to capital. The issue becomes contentious since even more than 100 per cent of the tax may be borne by capital through relative price adjustments. Hence, capital will tend to move abroad. Thus, it has become increasingly necessary to unilaterally harmonize the corporate tax rate and structure with global trends.

The non-neutrality of corporate income tax can go even deeper. Since the non-corporate sector is primarily land-intensive (agriculture and real estate), land should also ideally be recognized as a specific factor of production in the non-corporate sector. In this case, non-corporate land, being an inelastic factor, has to eventually absorb a part of the tax on corporate capital (Shome 1981). Thus, the veracity of income taxes being more direct in their collection and incidence, has not quite withstood tests of theory or the field. Indeed, some developed countries including the United Kingdom are expressing a shift in policy stance in favour of moving towards a broad-based consumption tax—that is termed 'indirect' by them. The emphasis on income tax appears to be receding, reflecting continually emerging challenges in monitoring income taxpayers who operate globally through complex corporate structures. To successfully do so while keeping at bay overzealous tax administrations that have revenue, rather than economic growth, in mind and training, remains a crucial roadblock for policymakers.

Tax Revenue Trends

With this backdrop, we now examine the direct and indirect tax revenue trends in India. Figure 15.4 depicts direct and indirect tax revenue of the general central and state governments, revealing a diminution in the indirect-direct tax revenue gap. As Figure 15.5 further reveals, as far as the central government is concerned, direct tax revenue has overtaken indirect tax revenue since 2006–7 even though the margin is narrowing once again. The difference in the experience of the general government and the central government simply reflects the fact that state government tax revenue is classified as indirect tax.

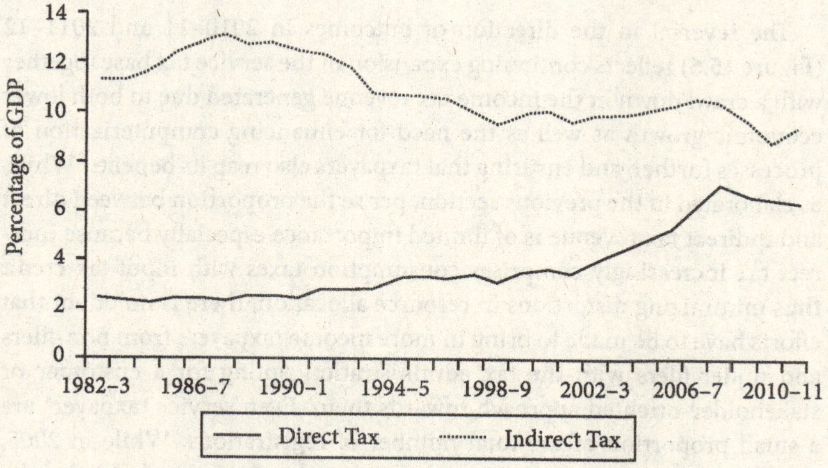

FIGURE 15.4 Direct and Indirect Tax Revenues of Central and State Governments (percentage of GDP)
Source: RBI database on Indian Economy and CSO National Accounts Statistics.

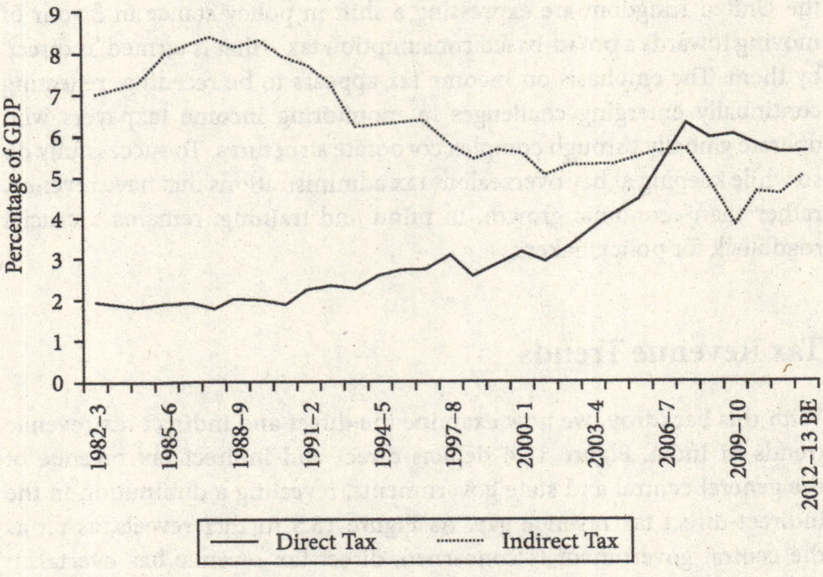

FIGURE 15.5 Direct and Indirect Tax Revenues of Central Government (percentage of GDP).
Source: Union budgets and CSO National Accounts Statistics.

The reversal in the direction of outcomes in 2010–11 and 2011–12 (Figure 15.6) reflects continuing expansion of the service tax base together with a crawl down in the income tax revenue generated due to both lower economic growth as well as the need for enhancing computerization of processes further, and ensuring that taxpayers also reap its benefits. While, as elaborated in the previous section, per se the proportion between direct and indirect tax revenue is of limited importance especially because indirect tax increasingly comprises consumption taxes with input tax credit thus minimizing distortions in resource allocation, there is no doubt that efforts have to be made to bring in more income taxpayers from non-filers and under-filers with the tax administration opting for a customer or stakeholder-oriented approach towards them. Even service taxpayers are a small proportion of the total number of registrations. While in 2005, small service taxpayers were moved below a raised threshold thereby eliminating 80 per cent of service taxpayers, it is time to revisit the issue since several of them may now be well within the population of coverable taxpayers.

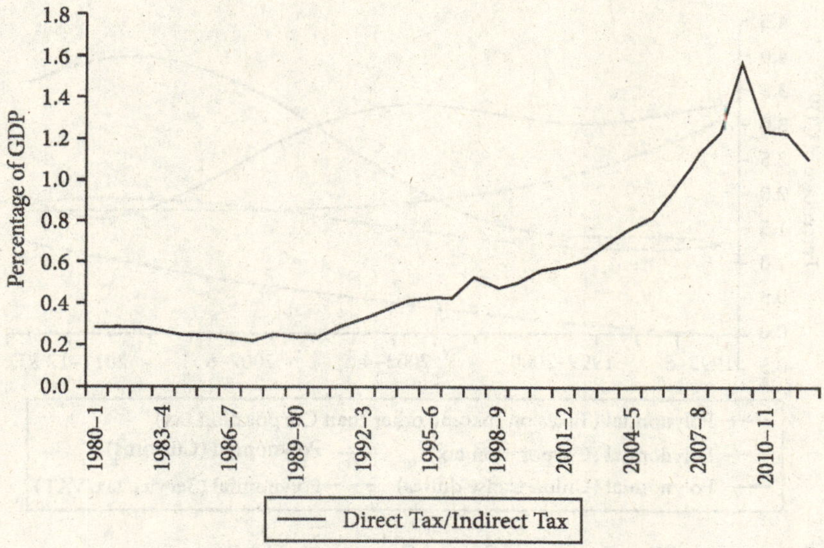

FIGURE 15.6 Proportion of Direct Taxes to Indirect Taxes: Central Government
Source: Union budgets and CSO National Accounts Statistics.

For an emerging economy with a quarter of its population below the poverty line (BPL) and a small proportion that can be called middle class, India's tax/GDP ratio is not low. The central government's ratio hovers between 10 and 11 per cent of GDP while the states collect about 6 per cent. If one assumes that this 17 per cent is being collected from non-BPL GDP, then the effective tax/GDP ratio is about 23 per cent. If one assumes that the 17 per cent is being collected from non-subsistence GDP, then the effective tax/GDP ratio approaches 28 per cent. These indicators are increasingly important in an economic environment in which the cost of doing business is considered to be among the higher ones in cross-country comparisons (The World Bank 2012).[4]

[4] Economies are ranked from 1 to 183 by the ease of doing business index. For each economy the index is calculated as the ranking on the simple average of its percentile rankings on each of the 10 topics included in the index in 'Doing Business 2012': starting a business, dealing with construction permits, getting electricity, registering property, getting credit, protecting investors, paying taxes, trading across borders, enforcing contracts, and resolving insolvency. India ranked low overall in the doing business assessment 2012, with its rank improving marginally from 139 to 132 between the 2011 and 2012 reports. Globally, India stands at 147 in the ranking of 183 economies on the ease of paying taxes.

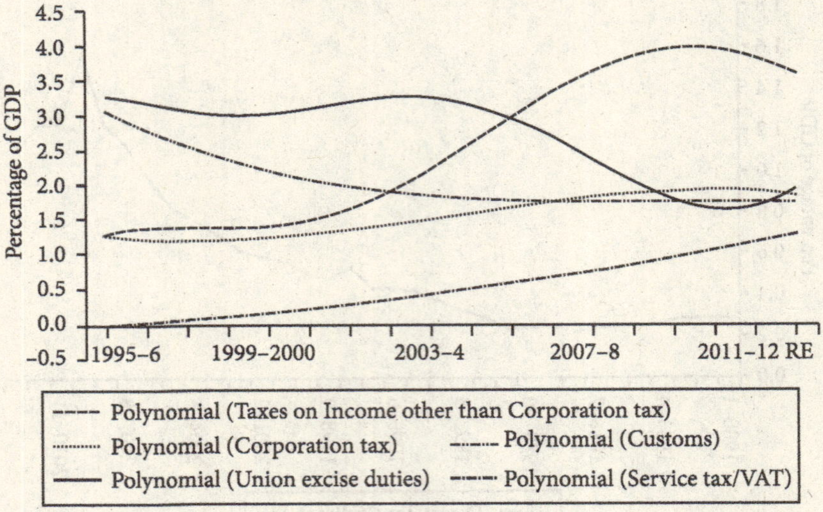

FIGURE 15.7 Major Sources of Central Government Tax Revenue
Source: Union budgets and CSO National Accounts Statistics.

Composition of Tax Revenue

The composition of central government's tax revenue, expressed in proportion to GDP, is shown in Figure 15.7 that fits a non-linear polynomial function for each tax considered from the mid-1990s.[5] It reveals certain trends. First, reflecting structural changes in reducing the level and dispersion of tax rates, excise and customs revenue have lost their high share and, since the mid-2000s, have had a comparable share as corporate income tax which has steadily increased. Second, the share of individual income tax has increased significantly, except in the most recent years. This is the major development in the composition of tax revenue and has occurred through an expansion of the taxpayers' base from around 18 million to 35 million as well as due to administrative improvements, such as widespread use of third party information and expansion in electronic filing.

[5] A linear trend could not comprehensively capture revenue variations; hence the use of a non-linear function seems appropriate. Polynomial functions are used to estimate the trend for different taxes. The degree of the functions is chosen based on the criteria of minimizing the deviation between the actual data and the trend line.

This was pointed out by Shome in Berry and Panagariya (2006: 115) during the general discussion:

> Shome went on to note that India's tax policy was moving 'briskly' from (distortionary) indirect taxes to direct taxes. For the first time, this year the government budgeted more than 5 percent of GDP from direct taxes. Also, for the first time, revenue from direct taxes would be higher than the revenue from production taxes and import taxes.

Third, service tax revenue, while continuing to remain the least represented in terms of share, has had a steady increase since its introduction in the mid-1990s as its base has been expanded. In the last two years these trends have been arrested as the growth in the share of direct taxes has abated somewhat.

Figure 15.8 shows the shares at the state government level, between state-level excises and VAT (and sales tax prior to the introduction of VAT in 2005). While the share of state excises has remained steady, it is interesting that VAT's share increased for a few years after its introduction and has since declined. Dasgupta (2012) has claimed that this is due to VAT evasion. There is no doubt that a lot needs to be achieved in terms of mechanising the VAT administration as well as the taxation mechanisms of inter-state trade.

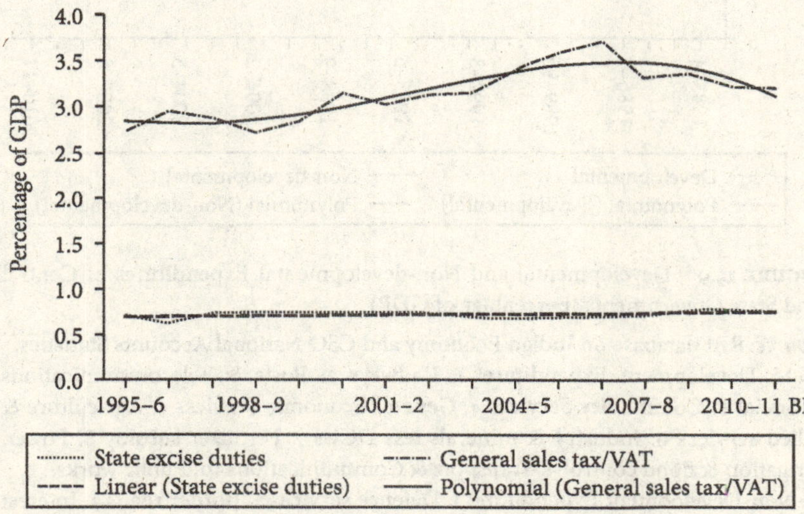

FIGURE 15.8 Major Sources of State Government Tax Revenue

Source: RBI database on Indian Economy and CSO National Accounts Statistics.

Expenditure Trends and Policies

Expenditure trends of the general government shown as a polynomial fit from the early 1980s in Figure 15.9 reveal a clear decline in development expenditure vis-à-vis non-development expenditure (as defined in Figure 15.9). Figure 15.10 also unveils the reality that at the central government level, non-developmental expenditures actually overtook development expenditures from the mid-1990s. Even under the capital and revenue expenditure nomenclature, the decline in the former compared to the rise in the latter prevails at the central government level as

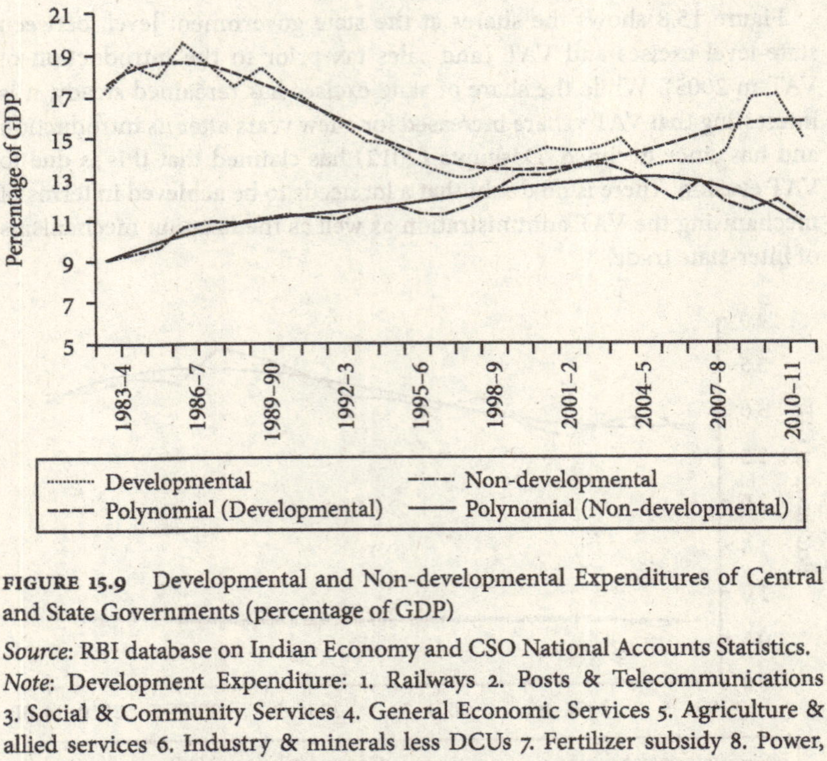

FIGURE 15.9 Developmental and Non-developmental Expenditures of Central and State Governments (percentage of GDP)

Source: RBI database on Indian Economy and CSO National Accounts Statistics.

Note: Development Expenditure: 1. Railways 2. Posts & Telecommunications 3. Social & Community Services 4. General Economic Services 5. Agriculture & allied services 6. Industry & minerals less DCUs 7. Fertilizer subsidy 8. Power, irrigation & flood control 9. Transport & Communications 10. Public works.

Non-Development Expenditure: 1. Defence services 2. Border roads 3. Interest payments 4. Fiscal services 5. Administrative services 6. Organs of State 7. Pension & other retirement benefits 8. Relief on account of natural calamities (NP) 9. Technical & economic cooperation with other countries 10. Compensation & assignment to local bodies 11. Food subsidy 12. Social security & welfare (NP).

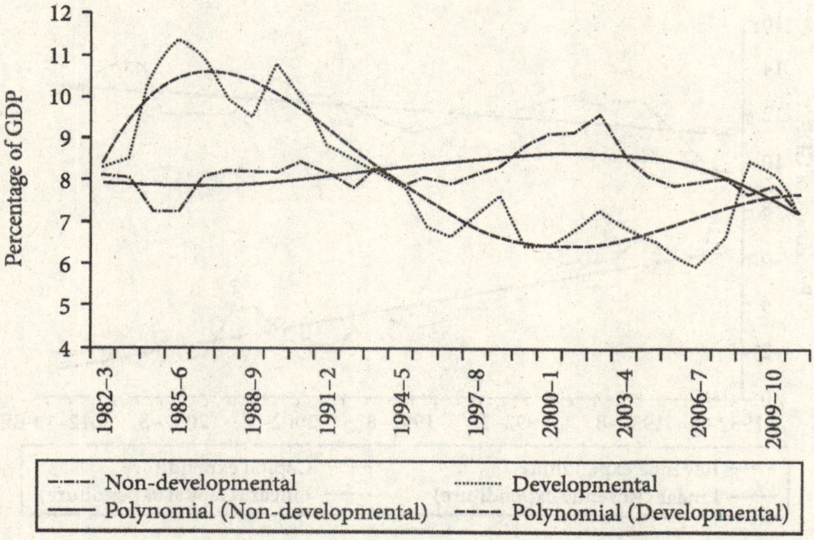

FIGURE 15.10 Developmental and Non-developmental Expenditures of Central Government (percentage of GDP)

Source: RBI database on Indian Economy and CSO National Accounts Statistics.

shown in Figure 15.11. This is repeated at the state government level (not shown here). Clearly the quality of expenditure has suffered a worsening long-term trend. Dev and Mooij (2002: 853) in a comprehensive analysis pointed towards the decline in expenditure allocation in social sectors, such as education and health in the 1990s as compared to the 1980s and also that it was less than that of most developing countries: 'With India ranking 115th in the Human Development Index, there is an obvious need to step up social sector expenditure and improve fund utilisation.' Thus, despite a very recent reversal towards the right direction, there lurks an immense future challenge to get the composition of expenditure right.

The worsening expenditure composition primarily reflects the compulsions of raising current and non-developmental expenditures comprising of administration including public sector salaries, operations and maintenance, and subsidies Interest payments also rose considerably until they declined due to lowering of interest rates and some curtailment of public debt. Bagchi (2006: 4118) pointed out:

> [T]he adverse turn in state budgets had resulted from several factors not within their control, particularly the rise in the interest rates following financial liberalisation and the fallout of the central pay

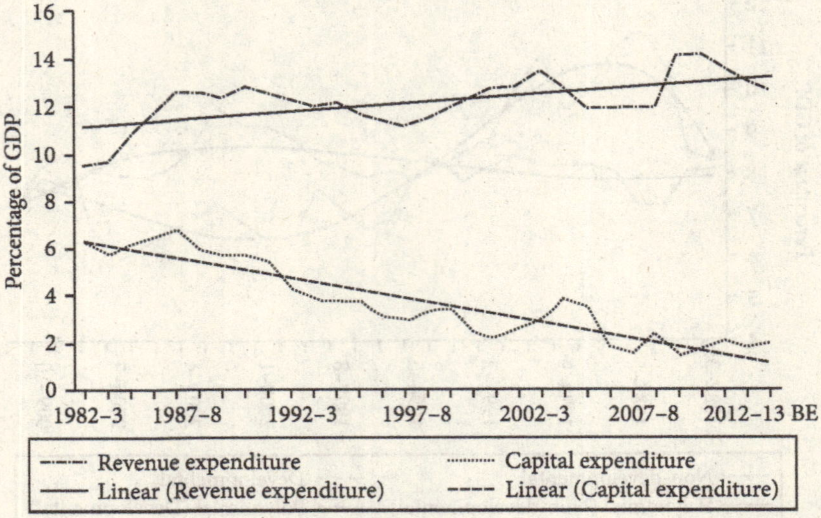

FIGURE 15.11 Revenue and Capital Expenditures of Central Government (percentage of GDP)

Source: Union budgets and CSO National Accounts Statistics.

> commission report raising the emoluments of employees heftily apart from the fall in transfers from the centre.
>
> The Twelfth Finance Commission's (TFC) review revealed an alarming state of the states' finances and how they had deteriorated between 1993–6 and 2003–6 .... A particularly worrying aspect of the fiscal situation was that an increasingly large proportion of the fiscal deficits was on account of the revenue deficits.

It was only when interest rates began to be scaled back that the interest burden declined. To give one instance, the 'Financial Express' reported on 19 January 19 that , 'The Centre has initiated debt swap scheme to replace high-cost loans with low-cost debts to states. Moreover, interest rate on loans to states was slashed from 10.5% to 9%'.

The trend for state level development expenditures is not as discouraging as for the centre, given that some of the central government's transfers to the states are for development purposes. To quote Garg (2006: 4977):

> The central government's gross budgetary support (GBS) to the Plan is divided into two broad classes—the central Plan and central assistance to the state and union territory (UT) Plans .... The specific purpose discretionary Plan expenditure of the centre on development schemes

> in areas falling in the states' domain, usually referred to as Centrally Sponsored Schemes (CSS) or the State Sector Central Plan Schemes, forms part of the GBS for the central Plan. These CSS are designed by the centre and are subject to detailed guidelines. Fund allocation to individual states... are specific to schemes. Actual releases are based more on the 'actual performance' and therefore final transfers to the states may very substantially from the original allocations. Central government spending on CSS is constantly increasing.

Indeed, the percentage of CSS to GBS increased from 31.3 to 38.6 to 41.6 in the Ninth, Tenth, and Eleventh Plans respectively (Planning Commission 2011).

An examination of the composition of the centre's revenue expenditure in Figure 15.12 reveals that the share of interest payments ballooned from the early 1980s until the early 2000s when the FRBM policy reduced the interest burden during the few years of a golden age of overall fiscal stance of both high tax revenue growth and responsible expenditure control. Thus, since then, the share of interest payments has declined, an experience that has also been replicated in the states (Figure 15.13). The share of subsidies declined slightly in the 1990s and rose considerably again after the golden age years. Though it was budgeted to decrease in 2011–12, a rise in petroleum subsidies resulted in a failure to reduce the overall share

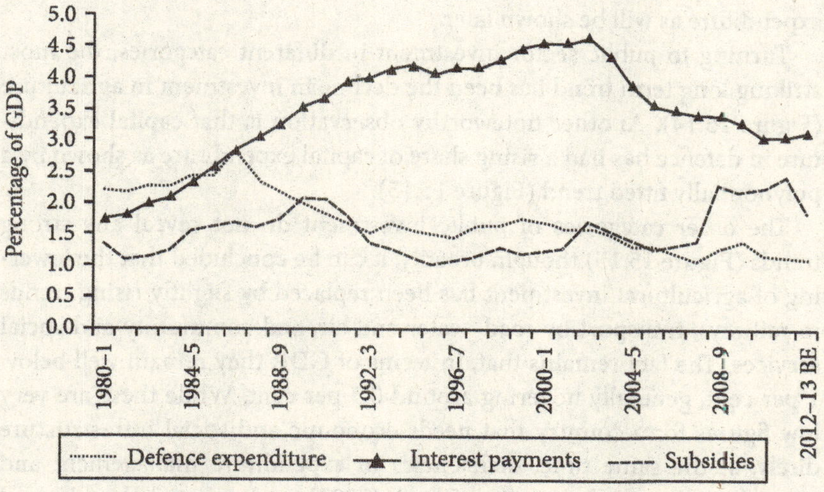

FIGURE 15.12 Major Revenue Expenditure of Central Government (percentage of GDP)

Source: Union budgets and CSO National Accounts Statistics.

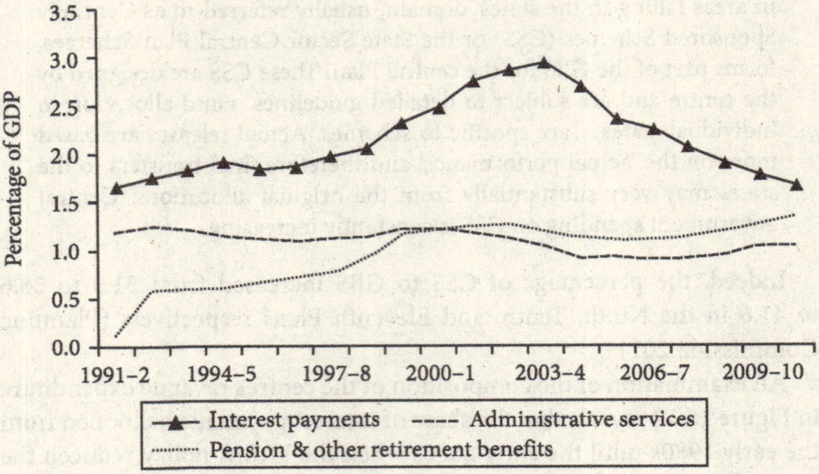

FIGURE 15.13 Major Revenue Expenditure of State Governments (percentage of GDP)

Source: RBI database on the Indian Economy and CSO National Accounts Statistics.

of subsidy. It is again budgeted to decline in the 2012–13 budget. Note that revenue expenditure on defence has declined, but its increase is in capital expenditure as will be shown later.

Turning to public sector investment in different categories, the most striking long term trend has been the decline in investment in agriculture (Figure 15.14). Another noteworthy observation is that capital expenditure in defence has had a rising share of capital expenditure as shown by a polynomially fitted trend (Figure 15.15).

The other categories of public investment do not reveal any strong trends (Figure 15.15) though, broadly, it can be concluded that the lowering of agricultural investment has been replaced by slightly rising trends in railways, transport by road, water and air, and community and social services. The fact remains that, in terms of GDP, they remain well below 1 per cent, generally hovering around 0.5 per cent. While these are very low figures for a country that needs economic and social infrastructure direly, at the same time, deficiencies in expenditure management and control are deep and pervasive. Ghosh (1997) made a detailed analysis of expenditure management and control based on his experience in India's defence department that still remains a forward looking exercise on the direction in which reforms should occur.

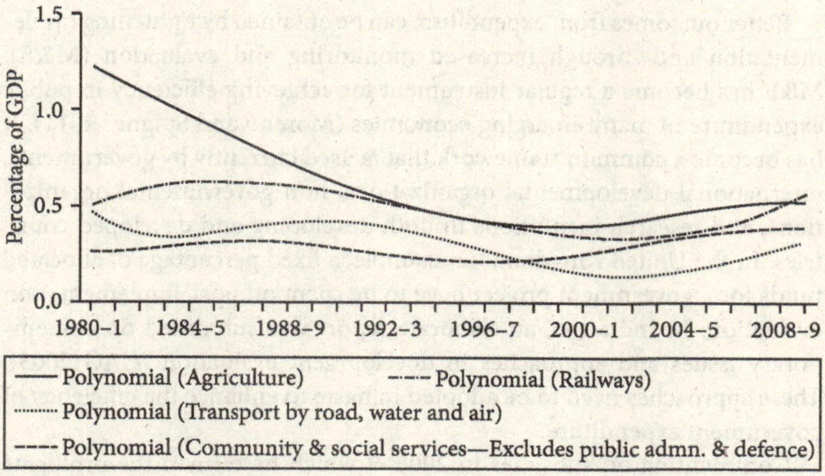

FIGURE 15.14 Public Sector Investment in Selected Sectors (percentage of GDP)

Source: CSO National Accounts Statistics.

Note: Public Sector: Under public sector, all the three institutional sub-sectors, namely government administration, departmental commercial undertakings (DCUs), and non-departmental commercial undertakings (NDCUs) are covered for compiling the gross fixed capital formation estimates.

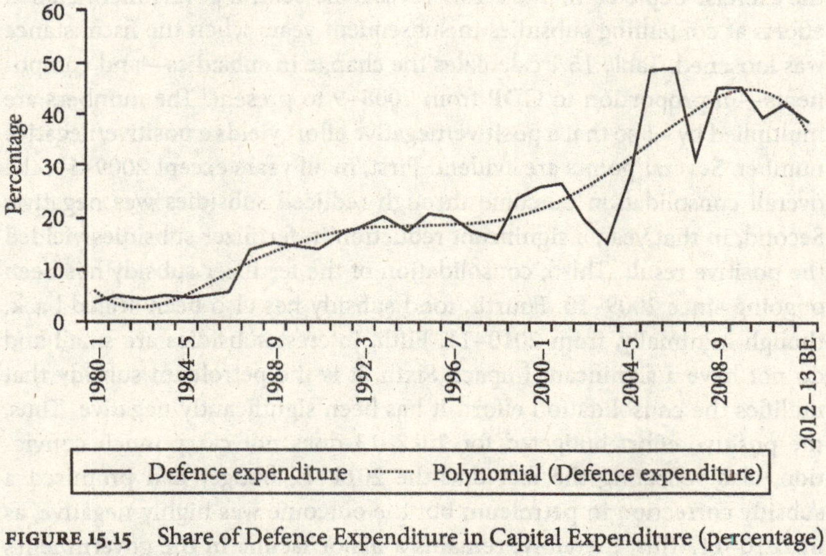

FIGURE 15.15 Share of Defence Expenditure in Capital Expenditure (percentage)

Source: Union budgets and CSO National Accounts Statistics.

Better outcomes from expenditure can be obtained by tightening implementation and through increased monitoring and evaluation (M&E). M&E has become a regular instrument for achieving efficiency in public expenditure in many emerging economies (Moreno and Spigner 2011). It has become a common framework that is used currently by governments, international developmental organizations, non-governmental organizations, and research institutions in both developing and developed countries. In the United Kingdom, for example, a fixed percentage of allocated funds for a government project have to be spent on post-implementation evaluation. In India too, an elaborate report was submitted on contemporary issues and approaches in development evaluation (CAG 2003). These approaches need to be adopted in haste to enhance the efficiency of government expenditure.

Commenting on subsidies in 2008–9 which he termed the profligate year, Acharya (2012: 14), has been more direct by commenting:

> [F]ertiliser and oil subsidies were the result of the international commodity price boom which hit the Indian economy from early 2008, with government choosing to hold down controlled prices, and explicit and implicit (through oil and fertilizer bonds) subsidies soared.

Shome (2012a) pointed towards India's relatively successful efforts at subsidy containment during the few years of the golden age. However, the exercise depicted in Table 15.1 reveals the central government's failed efforts at containing subsidies in subsequent years when the fiscal stance was loosened. Table 15.1 calculates the change in subsidies—and components—in proportion to GDP from 2008–9 to present. The numbers are multiplied by −1 so that a positive/negative effort yields a positive/negative number. Several points are evident. First, in all years except 2009–10, the overall consolidation outcome through reduced subsidies was negative. Second, in that year, a significant reduction in fertilizer subsidies yielded the positive result. Third, consolidation of the fertilizer subsidy has been ongoing since 2009–10. Fourth, food subsidy has also been scaled back, though minimally, from 2010–11. Fifth, interest subsidies are small and do not have a significant impact. Sixth, it is the petroleum subsidy that nullifies the consolidation effort. It has been significantly negative. Thus, the positive effort budgeted for 2012–13 does not carry much conviction, also reflecting the fact that the 2011–12 budget had promised a subsidy correction in petroleum but the outcome was highly negative, as in 2010–11. This, therefore, remains a major lacuna in the government's consolidation efforts against subsidies.

Table 15.1 Break-up of Central Government Subsidies

	2008–9	2009–10	2010–11	2011–12	2012–13 BE
			(Δ % to GDP) ×-1		
Fertilizer Subsidy	-0.71	0.41	0.14	0.06	0.15
Food Subsidy	-0.15	-0.13	0.07	0.01	0.08
Petroleum Subsidy	0.01	-0.18	-0.27	-0.27	0.34
Interest Subsidies	-0.02	0.02	-0.02	0.00	-0.01
Other Subsidies	-0.01	-0.01	0.01	0.03	0.00
Total Subsidies	-0.88	0.11	-0.07	-0.17	0.56

Source: Union budget (2012–13).
Note: + Tighten/- Loosen.

Central Government's Consolidation Efforts

The same tool as in the case of subsidies is used here to analyse consolidation efforts in expenditure and revenue. These are presented in Tables 15.2 and 15.3. First, the worst year for both Plan and non-Plan expenditure was 2008–9 when, together they accounted for a worsening of almost 1.5 per cent of GDP. Second, moving beyond that year, non-Plan expenditure seems to have improved through some belt tightening since 2010–11 in particular in defence, police, and pensions. Third, Plan expenditure on the capital account has not been consolidated though this is one category in which an analyst will not necessarily look for a cutback. But, fourth, Plan expenditure's revenue account also fails to show any identifiable trend, with positive and negative efforts alternating in the recent years under consideration. Nevertheless, overall, there has been a limited amount of success in consolidation efforts since 2010–11.

The same exercise, when carried out on the tax revenue side, also yields some interesting results (Table 15.3). First, what is most remarkable is that income tax—both corporate and individual—has declined in terms of GDP when the years since 2008–9 are considered together. Second, customs revenue has also declined in terms of GDP as will be expected from a policy viewpoint as India opens up its economy further. However, what is alarming is the higher effort in customs in the 2012–13 budget, revealing an increase in customs revenue when clearly it should be scaled

Table 15.2 Expenditure Consolidation of the Central Government

	2008–9	2009–10	2010–11	2011–12	2012–13 BE
	(Δ % to GDP) ×–1				
Non-plan Expenditure					
1. Interest Payments & Debt Servicing	0.02	0.11	0.25	–0.04	–0.05
2. Defence Expenditure	–0.19	–0.17	0.19	0.09	0.01
3. Subsidies	–0.88	0.11	–0.07	–0.17	0.56
4. Pensions	–0.10	–0.28	0.12	0.12	0.01
5. Police	–0.07	–0.05	0.05	–0.02	0.02
6. Other Non-plan Expenditures	0.60	–0.08	–0.03	0.67	–0.08
Total	–0.63	–0.36	0.50	0.65	0.46
Plan Expenditure					
On Revenue Account	–0.69	0.24	–0.16	0.21	–0.25
On Capital Account	–0.09	–0.05	–0.08	–0.06	–0.09
Total	–0.78	0.19	–0.24	0.15	–0.34

Source: Union budget (2012–13).

Note: 1) + Tighten/- Loosen.

Capital expenditure consists of investments on acquisition of assets like land, buildings, machinery, equipment, as also investments in shares, etc. It includes capital expenditure on social services, economic services, rural development, irrigation, industry, minerals, energy, transport, tourism, repayment of internal debt, and loans and advances to public enterprises.

Revenue expenditure (non-plan) is for the normal running of government departments and interest charges on debt, subsidies, etc. These expenditures may not result in the creation of assets. Revenue Plan expenditure mostly relates to current expenses on projects, programmes, and schemes which are revenue in nature.

back. Third, domestic consumption and production taxes, first, in the form of the central VAT (or excise), have also been negative on the whole, although since 2010–11, there has been a small attempt at improvement; and, second, as far as service tax is concerned, on the whole there has been a slightly positive effort. The sum total of all this, however, has been a lowering of the tax–GDP ratio by almost 1.5 per cent of GDP.

This is how the inexorable worsening in the fiscal deficit—by about 3 per cent of GDP—has occurred since 2008–9, with expenditure and tax revenue to blame in almost equal measure. Thus, steady and deliberate gains made in the preceding golden age of steadfast containment of the

Table 15.3 Revenue (Tax) Consolidation of Central Government

	2008–9	2009–10	2010–11	2011–12	2012–13 BE
			(Δ % to GDP)		
		Gross Tax Revenue			
1. Corporation Tax	–0.08	0.00	0.10	–0.22	0.00
2. Taxes on Income other Corporation Tax	–0.17	0.01	–0.08	0.06	0.00
3. Customs	–0.31	–0.48	0.48	–0.05	0.12
4. Union Excise Duties	–0.55	–0.33	0.20	–0.11	0.22
5. Service Tax	0.05	–0.18	0.02	0.14	0.15
6. Other Taxes	–0.08	–0.10	–0.05	–0.04	0.00
Total	–1.14	–1.08	0.66	–0.22	0.49

Source: Union budget (2012–13).
Note: + Tighten/- Loosen.

deficit through a thorough tax policy and administration measures and some restraint on the expenditure side were whittled away; a rationale to that mystery has not yet unfolded.

Tax Policy and Administration

No analysis of India's fiscal aspects can be complete without touching upon its ongoing reform efforts in tax policy and the status of its tax administration. In terms of tax policy, the crux of the reforms has to be on providing a level playing field to producers in all sectors. Big ticket reforms are certainly GST and the direct taxes code (DTC). In addition, there are existing tax policy structures in place that obstruct the efficiency of operations of economic agents. Some of these also must be touched upon.

Instances of Tax-generated Distortions in Production and Export

Perhaps the most visible tax-generated distortions are caused by tax incentives of various sorts. The deleterious ramifications of most forms of incentives have been recounted recently by Shome (2012b: 311). He concludes:

> – they distort relative prices, thus affecting the equilibrium allocation of resources, i.e. causing 'inefficiency' in resource allocation;
> – they treat preferentially, selected sectors that can be inequitable since it implies a heavier burden on non-preferred sectors, for raising the same revenue;
> – they distort the allocation of resources since non-preferred sectors pay more taxes;
> – monitoring costs are high, implying a more complex tax administration; and
> – they could increase tax evasion in the resultant system that becomes more complex, with high selectivity and administrative discretion and control. One can conclude that more often than not, tax incentives are unable to achieve their objectives.
>
> Thus, it is generally better to have a well administered tax system—with an overall low tax rate—that is certain and simple, and would be preferred by investors. It should also be noted that foreign investment responds to home country treatment of repatriated profits.

Yet, India ventured into a special economic zone (SEZ) Act that provides a panoply of tax incentives to all and sundry investors. It has become comparable to East Asian practices of the 1960s and 1970s rather than of modern tax systems. For example, investors are unwilling to locate in a state unless given SEZ treatment and free land. If the investment were non-viable in the first place, investors should rethink such investment in any event. Some already existing enterprises were converted to SEZs. The rules to administer a large SEZ that comprises both incentive and taxable activities are so complex that the revenue department needs to employ thousands of additional inspectors to separate out such activities. Since 2006–7, the central budget annually presents the tax expenditure, or revenue loss, from existing direct and indirect tax incentives, and that loss is growing.

India's export strategy led to policies to ensure that exports have 'free trade' status. Yet, the constraints that exporters have to face in the form of administrative processes are monumental. Thus, what could be the salient role of SEZs' in the presence of such constraints? To illustrate, Shome's discussion in Berry and Panagariya (2006: 115–16) indicated that India's export orientation

> led to numerous schemes to free the exports from customs duties on imported inputs. Thus there were advance licenses that allowed inputs

to be imported free of duty. There were duty drawbacks whereby the company paid the duty but later received drawbacks against it. Then there was the passbook scheme organized by the Ministry of Commerce, where companies had accounts from which they could automatically deduct the customs duties they paid. In addition, there was a target zero tax scheme, linked to how much exports increase each year. Under yet another scheme, a company that exported a certain amount could import capital goods without paying duty.

The reason for citing this small example is that while India stands at the edge of undertaking major tax reforms, the reality in the field is that there are binding constraints and obstacles for producers and exporters that add to their business costs, and convert India increasingly into a high cost location to invest and operate. This has encouraged even traditional Indian investors to seek destinations abroad as better environments to take their capital.

Goods and Services Tax

The reform of the centre's CENVAT (or central excises) *pari passu* with the states' VAT has been a challenging exercise since the announcement of a goods and services tax (GST) in the 2006 union budget to replace state VAT, and the centre's CENVAT and service tax.

The first GST report was submitted in December 2007 to the empowered committee (EC, VAT) and to the union Finance Minister by a committee co-convened by officials of both branches. That recommended that GST will have two parallel chains, the CGST for the centre and SGST for the states. Each chain will include both goods and services. Ideally, they should have single rates and wide tax bases with few exemptions. Subsequent discussions eroded the ideal, yet practical, GST structure that was recommended in that report.

The currently prevailing proposal for the GST structure has much to desire. These points are now described so that they may be addressed individually towards a better final formulation for a GST.

The rate structures for CGST and SGST have not been agreed upon. One possibility that has been discussed apparently is: (1) for states, dual rates of 6 and 12 per cent for goods, and 8 per cent for services, and (2) for the centre, either a single rate or dual rates for goods, and 8 per cent for services. The deepest flaw here is having different rates for goods and services. The whole point of a GST is *not* to have to differentiate between goods and services and, instead, to have a seamless relationship that negates all judicial cases over disagreements in classification. Having different rates for goods and services will be quite inconsistent with global practices on VAT or GST. India must follow global practices for its GST to be internationally meaningful.

The GST base should be as broad as possible. Instead, almost half the revenue coverage—petroleum, tobacco, and alcohol products—are planned to be kept out of the GST base. The advantage of keeping them within the GST base is that tax administrations at the central and state levels will have the necessary information on the complete upstream to downstream process of production and distribution. Therefore, it is important to bring in petroleum and alcoholic products into the GST base. What countries do in order to get more revenue from these products, since tobacco is a demerit good and petroleum is a depletable resource, is to levy additional excises on them over and above the GST rate. This should be done in India also.

Government departments should also ideally be within the GST base, as is the case in many countries, again to structure GST in a seamless manner. However, if political economy considerations make it impossible to cover defence, for example, then it has to be accepted (defence has essentially remained outside central excises also).

GST should be a consumption based tax. Therefore, for SGST, a method has to be found such that the revenue from inter-state trade goes to the state that imports and consumes rather than to the state that produces and exports a good or service. The appropriate method is for the producer/exporter state to collect the revenue from the purchaser/dealer (from an importing state) and to pass on that revenue to the importer state's exchequer. This can be facilitated by putting the collected money in a clearing house and, from there, to transfer the money to the importing/consuming state.

Theoretically, the clearing house can be the central government itself, that is, the states send in the collected revenue to the central government which, in turn, sends the revenue stored with it to the various importing states. The practical questions are, first, who will finance the creation of this clearing house and, second, how long will an importing state wait for its due revenue to arrive? A list of designated banks could also act as clearing houses but for this arrangement also, banks will have to be compensated as service providers. Whether it is the banking system or the central government that acts as a clearing house, a computerized system needs to be developed for it. It has to be capable of distributing revenue collected in one exporter state to all states where the goods have gone to be consumed (and it has to repeat this exercise for every exporting state, and continuously over time). Such a comprehensive computer system is not yet in place.

What is continuing now is a 2 per cent tax on inter-state trade called the central sales tax (CST) and the revenue is being retained by exporting states. These states want compensation from the centre if they remove CST (which is necessary to make GST into a consumption based tax). The central government cannot feasibly compensate states forever for the abolition of CST which is what is being effectively asked by the states. It may be recalled that when state level VAT was introduced, compensation for revenue loss by the centre for the states was kept at only Rs 5,000 crore and that too for a finite period of three years based on a formula for diminishing compensation. This aspect of diminishing revenue compensation from the centre to the states has not been worked out for the abolition of CST. CST has been brought down from the original 4 per cent rate to 2 per cent in anticipation of a consumption based GST. But given the lack of computerization to monitor inter-state trade, reports indicate that VAT evasion has grown by attributing more to inter-state trade which has only a 2 per cent CST rate than declaring it as within-state sale (which faces a higher VAT rate).

A pilot project in Maharashtra that is examining if a taxpayer reports the same turnover in tax returns for different taxes—income tax, excise and customs, service tax, VAT—apparently reveals that reported turnover can be very different for different taxes by the same taxpayer. Thus, measures to minimize tax evasion must be installed before GST is introduced or CST is abolished.

There are other unresolved issues between the centre and the states. State level VAT and the centre's CENVAT have thresholds over which these taxes apply. These are Rs 10 lakh for states and Rs 1.5 crore for the centre. The centre prefers to bring down its threshold but the states basically think of it as encroachment into their small taxpayers that they prefer to keep as exclusively theirs. Ideally, they should not have any restriction in the centre's decision regarding its own threshold.

The list of exemptions from both states and the centre should be further reduced under GST. The centre still has more than 350 while the states have almost 100 (even though the numbers are changing) exemptions. If India has to have GST, these exemptions are too high.

One issue is, in what manner will the current service tax be subsumed, and what its effects will be under GST. The states will also tax services under GST (within their chain of SGST). But they remain unconvinced about the revenue potential from this. This is because under the current state level VAT, while there is no revenue coming from service tax (since this tax remains outside state VAT), under a future GST, SGST will obtain revenue from service tax but also give input tax credit for service tax paid by taxpayers. So the states are not confident about how much net revenue they will get by being able to tax services under SGST.

Finally, the mechanism of decision making in the GST council has to be carefully structured. The original proposal was flawed since a simple majority of states present at meetings could amend the rules. That would have allowed a handful of small states to be able to change fundamental operations. Now, as is being interpreted, the new proposal requires a consensus that can result in too strict a requirement for changing rules. Therefore, this matter has to be recalibrated.

To conclude, GST should be patiently reformulated. The objective should be to achieve a simple and rational rate and base structure, with effective and transparent administrative rules, supported by a fully installed, world class computer system at the central, state, and inter-state levels, while being fully cognizant of modern taxpayers' (or customers') concerns.

Income Tax Reform and Tax Administration

Another major tax reform effort has been in the income tax area through the circulation of a DTC in 2009. Its subsequent transformations have, however, depleted the original version and the immediate need is to re-examine DTC in a new light with the objective of responding to rapid changes in the international scenario with respect to income tax. International capital—including from India—is ready to move out unless a level playing field is provided as in other destinations. Given India's current account deficit in the balance of payments at higher than 4 per cent of GDP, there is a significant need to have a positive capital account. That desire for capital reflects the continuing need for machinery, equipment, and raw materials as well as technology.

Pari passu with tax reforms, tax administration too has to modernize itself rapidly. Shome (2012c: 159) has pointed to three pillars of a modern tax administration following emerging and developed economies that have followed such benchmarked postulates

> [t]he clever use of analysis and fostering specialised knowledge in a tax administration are linked closely to three pillars. These comprise, first, installing new technology in the form of a data warehouse that makes possible an analytical base for policymaking; second, state-of-the-art management techniques to produce quality customer service by maintaining the taxpayer as the primary focus as if he or she were a customer of a private firm; and third, developing an administrative structure that is based on functional groupings within an administration rather than merely a geographical one. The central strategy should be analysis that could help drive changes in administration policy through evidence, provide analytically sound internal measures of performance, and enable a more sophisticated understanding of customers, their expectations and their compliance behaviour.

India is yet to embark meaningfully on its journey to modernize the tax departments including the possibility of amalgamating them into one as other countries have done to reap the benefits of more composite information from taxpayers while providing the latter one-window service for all taxes.

Several countries, including emerging ones such as South Africa, benchmark themselves against one another in an ongoing international exercise. To quote Shome (2012c: 163–4):

> A big gap in Indian tax administration is the lack of comparison with the performance of other tax administrations. An international exercise, spearheaded by the UK that originated as a concept at OECD's Forum for Tax Administration in 2006 in Seoul, attempts to compare benchmarks for participating tax administrations. In the first round, Australia, South Africa and the UK participated. Several other tax administrations are expected to join in the second round. The exercise attempts to compare the performance of call centres, the self-assessment process, ease of VAT registration and audit and risk assessment. Tax administrations are at different stages of development and possess different levels of data availability; hence, comparisons may not be fully consistent or meaningful. Nevertheless, participation in such a cross-country exercise has intrinsic value since it indicates areas of improvement, their feasibility as well as the constraints. India should seriously consider joining the international benchmarking exercise. If these hallmarks of change, reflecting the successes and failures from international experience, in particular the UK and Brazil, are taken up, Indian tax administration would put itself on a roadmap of rapid reform.

Thus, India should join the cross-country group to perceive where its differences lie with global practices and how it can quickly achieve comparability.

* * *

India's overall fiscal experience in recent years has been one that could be characterized as unstable, with periods of fiscal conservatism followed by loosening in both taxation and expenditure. When expanding, the authorities have tended to set aside already established policy, for example, on fiscal responsibility and budget management.

Good policies have also been undertaken, for example, in the taxation area. Distortionary indirect taxes on domestic production and distribution as well as on international trade have been scaled back while direct taxes on income and assets have been increased through expanding the and taxpayer bases rather than merely through increasing tax rates. On the other hand, high compliance costs are associated with income tax regimes. Indirect taxes are more difficult to avoid than direct taxes (Shome 1995) and though indirect taxes could result in greater excess burden through deadweight losses to the economy (Harberger 1974), their lower compliance costs keep the distortions resulting from poor administration at lower levels. Gaps in Indian tax administration make high compliance costs a reality in the Indian taxation environment so that the relative emphasis on income versus consumption tax becomes relevant in terms of the tax administration policy.

A uniform and broad-based value added tax (VAT) or goods and services tax (GST) that is a more general tax on all factor payments is increasingly judged to be better in aiding investment and growth than selective profit taxes. In efficiency terms, it lowers real wages and discourages work effort but does not distort relative prices and releases more resources for investment (more so with a VAT or GST of the consumption type which allow credit for taxes paid on purchases of capital goods and raw materials). India too has been steadily moving towards such broad-based VAT of the consumption type with the ongoing efforts to introduce GST.

Thus, broad-based consumption orientation is being given to taxation in the form of a state-level VAT and a central VAT (CENVAT) and, in further improvement, there are ongoing efforts to implement a national GST.

The government has had less success on the expenditure side. Non-development expenditures have overtaken development expenditures in terms of GDP. Revenue expenditures have had a rising trend while capital expenditures have plunged in terms of GDP. Public sector investment in agriculture declined in terms of GDP and, despite some improvement in recent years, remains well below that in the 1980s. Small successes in containing some subsidy components, such as on food and fertilizers have been overwhelmed by petroleum subsidies.

Overwhelming challenges in structural policies remain in the areas of tax administration and expenditure implementation. In a 2012 World Bank ranking of 183 countries, India stood at 147 on the ease of paying taxes, and 132 on the ease of doing business. Modernizing the tax administration and bringing it up to benchmarks being established in a cross-section of countries including emerging economies such as South Africa are of essence. Regular use of M&E techniques on expenditure programmes and projects remain crucial even as cogent and instructive CAG reports have been placed on the table and international examples exist as good practices. Experts increasingly believe it is in enhancing administration and monitoring, in tipping leakages and ridding Indian society of corruption, that India's future economic success lies.

The most recent period of extreme loosening has been from 2008–9 in what has been claimed to comprise the fiscal stimulus policy to counter global economic recession, even though there is little agreement among experts regarding the extent to which such a stimulus was needed. All fiscal indicators comprising tax revenue and other fiscal outcomes have collapsed. Some scholars have gone to the extent of calling 2008–9 a year of profligacy. Others have viewed this period as worse than 1991 when India faced a balance of payments crisis and had little option other than to enter into an IMF supported economic stabilization programme. It appears that in order to finally counter the inexorable worsening in fiscal outcomes, the government subsequently introduced some draconian counter measures for which the organized sector was not prepared. The reaction was no less than an outcry and the authorities have been obliged to reconsider several policies. The ramifications of those earlier policies as well as of the subsequent corrections are yet to fully unfold. It is proven time and again that once the path of fiscal rectitude which usually takes years to design and then implement, is abandoned, it may take longer to get back on a comparable path, leave alone demonstrate the wherewithal to adhere to it.

Appendix A15.1

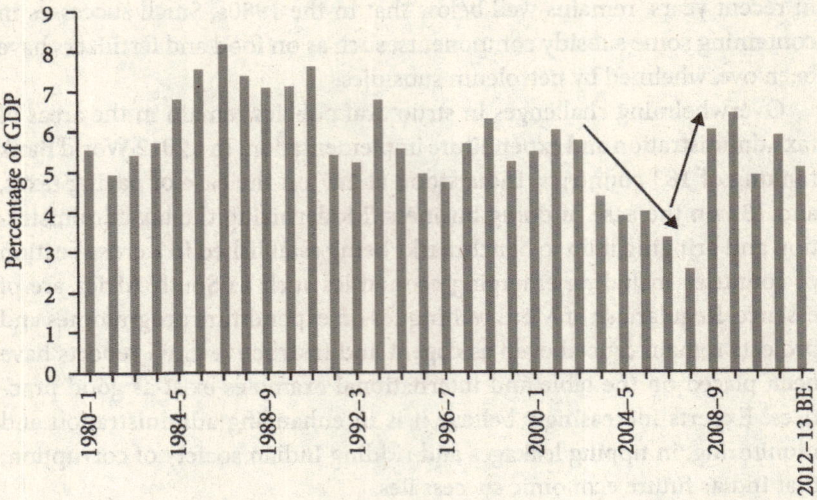

FIGURE A15.1 Central Government Fiscal Deficits (percentage of GDP)

Source: RBI database on the Indian Economy and CSO National Accounts Statistics.

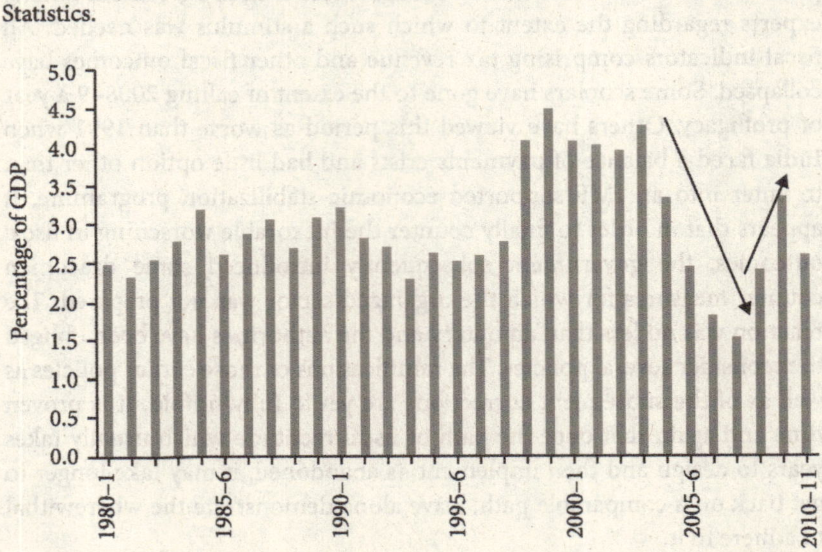

FIGURE A15.2 State Governments Fiscal Deficits (percentage of GDP)

Source: RBI database on the Indian Economy and CSO National Accounts Statistics.

Table A15.1 Fiscal Scenario of the Central Government (percentage of GDP)

	1990–1	1995–6	2000–1	2004–5	2005–6	2006–7	2007–8	2008–9	2009–10 RE	2010–11 BE
A. Tax Revenue	7.34	5.77	5.82	6.93	7.32	8.18	8.81	7.87	7.20	6.96
1. Direct Taxes	1.18	1.57	2.11	4.08	4.40	5.24	6.26	5.68	5.89	5.51
A) Corporation Tax	0.91	1.16	1.07	2.55	2.74	3.36	3.87	3.79	3.95	3.93
B) Share of Taxes on Income other than Corporation Tax	0.21	0.30	1.01	1.52	1.65	1.87	2.24	1.88	1.94	1.57
C) Other Direct Taxes	0.05	0.10	0.03	0.01	0.01	0.01	0.15	0.01	0.01	0.01
2. Indirect Taxes	6.16	4.20	3.72	5.33	5.52	5.79	5.63	5.07	3.91	4.22
A) Customs	3.52	2.52	1.45	1.78	1.76	2.01	2.09	1.77	1.31	1.50
B) Share of Union Excise Duties	2.41	1.56	2.12	3.06	3.01	2.74	2.48	1.93	1.58	1.72
C) Service Tax	0.00	0.06	0.08	0.44	0.62	0.88	1.03	1.08	0.90	0.89
D) Other Indirect Taxes	0.24	0.06	0.06	0.06	0.12	0.16	0.04	0.28	0.12	0.12
3. States Share Excluded from Consolidated Fund (Including NCCF)	0.00	0.00	0.01	2.47	2.60	2.85	3.08	2.88	2.60	2.77
B. Non-Tax Revenue	2.04	1.98	2.39	2.46	2.10	1.93	2.04	1.66	1.66	1.89
1. Net Contributions by PSUs	0.18	0.29	0.67	0.76	0.86	0.87	0.84	0.79	0.86	0.73
2. Interest Receipts	1.49	1.30	1.40	1.00	0.60	0.50	0.48	0.38	0.30	0.25
3. Fiscal Services	0.10	0.07	0.04	0.03	0.05	0.00	0.00	0.00	0.00	0.00
4. General Services (Excluding Defence Receipts)	0.09	0.09	0.11	0.13	0.12	0.10	0.05	0.12	0.14	0.11
5. Social & Community Services	0.01	0.01	0.01	0.01	0.04	0.01	0.01	0.01	0.01	0.01
6. Economic Services	0.06	0.14	0.13	0.45	0.36	0.38	0.60	0.31	0.31	0.77
7. External Grants	0.10	0.08	0.03	0.08	0.08	0.06	0.05	0.05	0.05	0.03
Total Revenue Receipts (A+B)	9.38	7.75	8.21	9.40	9.42	10.11	10.85	9.54	8.86	8.85
Total Capital Receipts	5.89	3.83	4.83	4.99	2.27	2.44	3.22	3.30	7.15	5.49

(contd.)

Table A15.1 (*contd.*)

A. Non-Developmental Expenditure	3.67	3.53	4.23	3.92	3.59	3.50	3.39	3.41	3.40	3.24
1. Interest Payments	2.63	1.89	2.11	2.34	2.18	1.99	1.84	2.03	2.11	1.92
2. Defence Services (Net)	0.49	0.43	0.57	0.54	0.54	0.50	0.44	0.55	0.59	0.47
3. Administrative Services	0.36	0.30	0.61	0.56	0.55	0.51	0.49	0.59	0.65	0.56
4. Pension & Other Retirement Benefits	0.42	0.38	0.51	0.72	0.62	0.56	0.63	0.78	0.87	0.72
5. Subsidy to FCI	0.78	0.76	0.48	0.59	0.53	0.53	0.63	0.77	1.07	0.66
6. Other Non-Developmental Expenditures	5.90	3.37	3.91	4.41	4.74	5.10	6.10	6.80	6.54	6.18
B. Developmental Expenditure	1.10	0.83	1.07	1.16	1.26	1.28	1.36	1.61	1.56	1.58
1. Social & Community Services	0.37	0.27	0.37	0.44	0.52	0.59	0.58	0.68	0.63	0.65
Of which										
i) Education, Art & Culture	0.22	0.15	0.18	0.23	0.22	0.21	0.20	0.22	0.24	0.24
ii) Scientific Services & Research	0.13	0.11	0.13	0.16	0.17	0.17	0.18	0.20	0.25	0.26
iii) Medical, Public Health, Santination & Water Supply	0.69	−0.02	0.05	0.06	0.09	0.14	0.94	0.13	0.40	0.58
2. General Economic Services	0.55	0.64	0.36	0.50	0.65	0.71	0.89	1.17	1.04	1.02
3. Agriculture & Allied Services	0.75	0.44	0.59	0.50	0.53	0.61	0.65	1.36	0.82	0.65
4. Fertilizer Subsidy	0.53	0.19	0.17	0.14	0.12	0.17	0.13	0.16	0.17	0.15
5. Power, Irrigation & Flood Control	0.61	0.27	0.73	0.72	0.82	0.80	0.76	0.76	0.88	0.79
6. Transport & Communications	1.21	0.81	0.75	1.00	0.96	1.06	1.15	1.27	1.20	1.10
7. Grants to States & UTs	0.45	0.20	0.20	0.32	0.30	0.33	0.22	0.35	0.47	0.31
8. Other Developmental Expenditures	0.58	0.37	0.49	0.37	0.68	0.66	0.53	0.48	0.46	0.43
C. Statutory Grants to States	2.38	1.25	0.41	−1.03	0.02	−0.20	0.03	0.12	0.17	0.17
D. Loans & Advances	17.21	12.28	13.33	12.42	13.45	13.15	14.08	15.54	15.87	14.34

Source: Ministry of Finance, Indian Public Finance Statistics (various issues).

Table A15.2 Fiscal Scenario of the State Government (percentage of GDP)

	1990–1	1995–6	2000–1	2004–5	2005–6	2006–7	2007–8	2008–9	2009–10 RE	2010–11 BE
A. Tax Revenue	7.54	6.56	6.91	8.26	8.57	8.93	8.49	8.25	7.96	7.92
(i) Direct Taxes	0.89	0.95	0.92	1.27	1.34	1.54	1.67	1.61	1.55	1.60
1. Share of Income Tax	0.68	0.79	0.58	0.44	0.49	0.52	0.62	0.57	0.49	0.48
2. Other Direct Taxes	0.21	0.16	0.34	0.83	0.85	1.01	1.05	1.05	1.06	1.13
(ii) Indirect Taxes	6.65	5.61	5.99	6.99	7.23	7.40	6.82	6.64	6.41	6.31
1. Share of Union Excise Duties	1.72	1.26	0.95	0.70	0.69	0.61	0.56	0.46	0.34	0.36
2. State Excise Duties	0.82	0.61	0.67	0.68	0.71	0.71	0.71	0.75	0.77	0.75
3. General Sales Tax	2.81	2.38	2.91	3.41	3.60	3.73	3.32	3.37	3.24	3.22
4. Other Indirect Taxes	1.30	1.37	1.45	2.21	2.23	2.34	2.23	2.06	2.07	1.99
B. Non-Tax Revenue	0.94	1.26	0.86	0.91	0.93	1.24	1.09	0.98	0.99	0.91
1. Net Contributions by PSUs	−0.24	−0.05	−0.22	−0.28	−0.15	−0.12	−0.16	−0.18	−0.27	-0.21
2. Interest Receipts	0.41	0.41	0.48	0.29	0.29	0.31	0.28	0.32	0.30	0.26
3. General Services	0.33	0.54	0.25	0.34	0.32	0.52	0.52	0.38	0.46	0.35
4. Social & Community Services	0.10	0.08	0.10	0.11	0.13	0.16	0.15	0.13	0.12	0.14
5. Economic Services	0.35	0.27	0.24	0.45	0.35	0.37	0.30	0.34	0.38	0.38
C. Grants from the Centre	2.11	1.46	1.59	1.76	2.10	2.23	2.15	2.25	2.78	2.35
D. Transfer from Funds	0.11	0.01	0.09	0.16	0.17	0.16	0.09	0.09	0.10	0.12
Total Revenue Receipts (A+B+C+D)	10.70	9.28	9.44	11.10	11.77	12.56	11.82	11.58	11.83	11.29
Total Capital Receipts	3.14	1.16	3.95	3.64	3.38	0.54	1.77	2.35	2.62	2.23

(contd.)

Table A15.2 (*contd.*)

A. Non-developmental Expenditure	4.51	4.54	5.50	6.33	5.94	5.73	5.21	5.19	5.63	5.29
1. Interest Payments	1.48	1.54	2.14	2.73	2.34	2.22	1.90	1.73	1.71	1.59
2. Administrative Services	1.12	0.89	0.96	0.92	0.91	0.89	0.86	0.89	1.04	1.06
3. Pension & Other Retirement Benefits	0.52	0.56	1.05	1.15	1.10	1.09	1.07	1.10	1.28	1.17
4. Other Non-developmental Expenditures	1.39	1.55	1.35	1.53	1.58	1.53	1.38	1.47	1.61	1.47
B. Developmental Expenditure	8.45	6.65	7.17	7.39	7.77	8.27	7.83	8.43	9.07	8.15
1. Social & Community Services	4.43	3.49	3.98	3.98	4.02	4.15	3.99	4.44	5.17	4.76
Of which										
i) Education, Art & Culture	2.68	2.06	2.41	2.21	2.20	2.19	2.02	0.20	2.54	2.42
ii) Medical, Health, Santination & Water Supply	1.02	0.79	0.92	0.89	0.91	0.91	0.87	0.89	0.94	0.82
2. Agriculture & Allied Services	1.57	0.98	1.01	0.98	0.99	1.03	0.97	1.11	1.08	1.01
3. Power, Irrigation & Flood Control	1.19	1.28	1.27	1.44	1.61	1.70	1.54	1.56	1.43	1.24
4. Transport & Communications	0.54	0.44	0.51	0.56	0.73	0.85	0.80	0.83	0.85	0.69
5. Public Works	0.17	0.13	0.14	0.13	0.13	0.15	0.16	0.14	0.19	0.16
6. Other Developmental Expenditures	0.56	0.34	0.26	0.30	0.30	0.38	0.37	0.34	0.36	0.30
C. Loans & Advances by States & UTs (Net)	0.73	0.34	0.19	0.33	0.22	0.22	0.19	0.14	0.23	0.20
D. Transfer to Funds	0.18	0.01	0.19	0.30	0.21	0.20	0.11	0.09	0.12	0.12
Total Expenditure	13.87	11.54	13.06	14.34	14.14	14.42	13.34	13.84	15.05	13.76

Source: Ministry of Finance, Indian Public Finance Statistics (various issues).

REFERENCES

Acharya, S. (2012), 'India and the Global Crisis', in C. Fred Bergsten and Randy Henning (eds), *Global Economics in Extraordinary Times: Essays in Honor of John Williamson*. Washington, DC: Peterson Institute of International Economics.

Bagchi, A. (2006), 'India's Fiscal Management Post-liberalization: Impact on the Social Sector and Federal Fiscal Relations', *Economic and Political Weekly*, 41(39): 4117–21, September 30.

Berry, S., B. Bosworth, and A. Panagariya (eds) (2006), 'General Discussion', in *India Policy Forum: 2005–6*. (pp. 114–18) New Delhi: Sage Publications.

Comptroller and Auditor General of India (CAG) (2003), 'Development Evaluation in India: Contemporary Issues and Approaches', Report submitted by the Core Group Constituted by CAG, International Centre for Information Systems and Audit, Office of Comptroller and Auditor General of India, Noida, February.

Dasgupta, A. (2012), 'An Assessment of the Revenue Impact of State-Level VAT in India', *Economic and Political Weekly*, XLVII(10), March 2.

Dev, S.M. and J. Mooij (2002), 'Social Sector Expenditures in the 1990s: Analysis of Central and State budgets, '*Economic and Political Weekly*, 37(2): 853–66.

Garg, S.C. (2006), 'Transformation of Central Grants to States: Growing Conditionality and Bypassing State budgets,' *Economic and Political Weekly*, 41(48): 4977–84.

Ghosh, A.K. (1997), 'Effective Budgetary Control for Expenditure Management and its Ramifications for Public Policy and Governance', in Parthasarathi Shome (ed.), *Fiscal Policy, Public Policy & Governance*. New Delhi: National Institute of Public Finance and Policy, Centax Publications Pvt. Ltd., pp. 230–72.

Harberger, Arnold C. (1974), *Taxation and Welfare*. Chapter 3, 'The Measurement of Waste', pp. 69–85. and Chapter 7, 'The Incidence of the Corporation Income Tax', pp. 135–62. Boston: Little Brown and Co.

Herber, Bernard P. (1979), *Modern Public Finance*, Figure 8–1, 'Work-leisure Trade-offs under Alternative Personal Income Tax Rate Structures', p. 161. Homewood, Illinois: Richard D. Irwin Inc.

Moreno Leguizamon, C. and C. Spigner (2011), '*Monitoring and evaluating well-being projects*', in *Understanding Wellbeing: An Introduction for Students and Practitioners of Health and Social Care*. Banbury, pp. 50–66. UK: Lantern Publishing/Scion Publishing.

Mundle, S., N. Bhanumurthy, and S. Das (2010), 'Fiscal consolidation with high growth: A policy simulation model for India', Working Paper 10/73, National Institute of Public Finance and Policy.

Musgrave, Richard A. (1959), *The Theory of Public Finance*, Chapter 11, 'Adjustments in Work Effort', pp. 232–45. New York/Tokyo: McGraw-Hill Inc./ Kogakusha.

Planning Commission (2011), *Report of the Committee on Restructuring of Centrally Sponsored Schemes* (CSS). New Delhi: Government of India, September.

Rakshit, M. (2010), 'Fiscal Consolidation and Inclusive Growth: The Finance Commission Approach', *Economic and Political Weekly*, 45(48): 38–45.

Shome, P. (1981), 'The General Equilibrium Theory and Concepts of Tax Incidence in the Presence of Third or More Factors', *Public Finance*, 36(1): 22–38.

——— (1992), 'Trends and Future Directions in Tax Policy Reform: A Latin American Perspective', *Bulletin for International Fiscal Documentation*, Amsterdam, September. Reprinted in Spanish in *Cuadernos de Economía*, National University, Bogota, Colombia, May 1994.

——— (1995), 'Comprehensive Tax Reform: The Colombian Experience', Occasional Paper 123, Appendix II (VAT) and Appendix V (Income Tax). Washington DC: International Monetary Fund, March.

——— (1996), *Fiscal Policy in the 1990s: Needed Reforms and Ramifications for the Financial Sector*. Mumbai: Sir Purshotamdas Thakurdas Memorial Lecture, Indian Institute of Bankers.

——— (2002), *India's Fiscal Matters*. New Delhi: Oxford University Press.

——— (2012a), 'Fiscal Stimuli and Consolidation', in Olivier J. Blanchard, David Romer, Michael Spence, and Joseph E. Stiglitz (eds), *In the Wake of the Crisis: Leading Economist Reassess Economic Policy*. Cambridge, Massachusetts: International Monetary Fund, MIT Press.

——— (2012b), 'Tax Incentives: Forms, Merits and Demerits—The Asian Experience', *Asia-Pacific Tax Bulletin, IBFD*, 18(4): 308–11.

——— (2012c), *Tax Shastra: Administrative Reforms in India, United Kingdom and Brazil*. New Delhi: Business Standard Books.

——— (2013), 'Rebalancing and Structural Policies—An Indian Perspective', *Oxford Review of Economic Policy*, 28(3): 587–602.

Tanzi, V. (1991), *Public Finance in Developing Countries*. New York: Edward Elgar.

The World Bank (2012), *Doing Business 2012*. Washington DC: The World Bank Group.

CHAPTER 16

THE DYNAMICS OF URBAN GOVERNANCE IN INDIA

ABHAY PETHE, VAIDEHI TANDEL, AND SAHIL GANDHI

Following Latin America, urbanization is set to take off in Asia (Mohan and Dasgupta 2005). While many Asian countries have a significant proportion of their population living in urban areas, in India this proportion continues to be modest, although in terms of magnitude the numbers are large (Mohan 2007). According to the 2011 Census, India is 31 per cent urban.[1] Much of this population is concentrated in large metropolises; as per the 2011 Census 43 per cent of India's urban population lives in 53 million plus cities. However, a concomitant trend in the last decade has been a growth in the number of towns and small cities. Many of the new towns have come up in close proximity to large metropolises (Lall 2011) thus drawing attention to the need for land and infrastructure management in peri-urban areas and governance at a metropolitan level. The record of service delivery in urban areas is poor. Most cities have not been able to realize their economic potential due to major infrastructure bottlenecks. The problem has been further compounded by the existence

[1] This remarkably low level of urbanization is likely to be a statistical artefact due to the way 'urban' and 'rural' are defined in India (Lall 2011).

of exclusionary practices and unequal access to services and spaces.[2] With the urban population for India in 2031 projected to be 600 million by the high-powered expert committee on urban infrastructure and services (HPEC 2011), there remains no doubt that the future of India is decidedly urban. The challenges before policymakers are addressing poverty and inequality, meeting the infrastructure demand arising due to backlog as well as future requirements in urban India, and making Indian cities globally competitive. It is in this milieu that we write this chapter in order to assess whether the existing governance system is able to meet the challenges of urbanization.

Governance is a complex entity, comprising a set of institutions that shape interactions among various actors leading to certain outcomes (see Ostrom 2010). It has been well recognized that governance goes beyond the government to include all stakeholders involved in the co-production, provision, and consumption of public goods and services (Pethe et al. 2011). The existing urban governance system in India suffers from several deficiencies due to the nature of the underlying institutions that do not foster right incentives but rather create vested interests and hence impede efficient delivery of goods and services. Government interventions, policies, and reforms for addressing the lacunae in the processes and outcomes of infrastructure delivery by not taking into account the existing inter-governmental interactions, protocols, informal networks, and elite coalitions, have also failed to achieve their objectives. This chapter examines the urban governance system using the analytical apparatus from New Institutional Economics and attempts to unravel the reasons for persistence of sub-optimal outcomes and policy failures. The chapter is divided into six sections, including the introduction. The next section provides an overview of New Institutional Economics and discusses its relevance for understanding governance. The section that follows examines the nature of multi-level urban governance in India while the next section discusses issues pertaining to land management. In particular it illustrates—using the case of Mumbai—how well intentioned pro-poor policies are subverted by a few powerful elite. The next section highlights recent developments in the supervisory space in urban governance. The last section provides a conclusion.

[2] Some of these practices can be discerned from the 'crowding out' of a large proportion of the urban population from formal housing (Annez et al. 2010; Gandhi 2012) and overall marginalization of migrants belonging to low economic and social strata (Kundu 2011: 12).

New Institutional Economics and Governance

A governance system can be termed 'good' or 'bad' depending on its performance in delivering public goods and services and managing common pool resources, which is assessed, based on certain pre-defined evaluative criteria. The local governance system in India is characterized by sub-optimal outcomes, such as under-provision, low accountability, unequal access, corruption, leakages, and gridlocks. Why do inefficiencies in the system persist? Why do policies aimed at reforms do not achieve their stated objectives? What is the rationale for different arrangements for public goods delivery, such as contracting out, public–private partnerships, and co-production by municipalities? The rich analytical tools provided by New Institutional Economics are useful for understanding such questions.

New Institutional Economics, built on the contributions of Ronald Coase, Douglass North, and Oliver Williamson, has had a profound impact on the way in which economists perceive economic and political activity. It has challenged the fundamental neo-classical assumptions of complete rationality and costless transactions. The basic premise of New Institutional Economics is that individuals are endowed with bounded rationality, characterized with limited cognition and foresight and that all transactions incur significant costs. Williamson (1981, 1985, 1996) pioneered the theory of Transactions Cost Economics, which holds that the nature of governance is affected by asset specificity, uncertainty, and frequency of transactions. The governance structure that ultimately evolves is one that economizes on transaction costs. This phenomenon explains the existence of different modes of organization, such as markets, firms, and private ordering.

Individuals devise institutions, or rules, in order to mitigate transaction costs. These institutions, defined by North (1994: 360) as 'humanly devised constraints that structure human interactions', may be formal or informal in nature. While formal institutions include laws, regulations, and other written codes, informal institutions comprise norms, culture, and beliefs.[3] Dixit (2004) highlights the complementary relationship

[3] New Institutional Economics makes a distinction between institutions and organizations. Although the two are closely related, North (1994) identifies institutions as the rules of the game and organizations as players of the game.

between formal and informal institutions. According to him, even when formal institutions exist and are well functioning, private ordering continues to thrive under the shadow of the formal system. This is because private ordering is relatively less costly and recourse to a formal system is possible when private contracts fail. However, formal systems fail when they are unable to protect property rights and enforce contracts and these functions are then assumed by a mafia. Over time, such an arrangement becomes common knowledge and hence the norm, which may be changed with an exogenous shock. However, when exogenously implanted institutions aimed at reforms do not take into consideration the existent endogenous institutions, they might be severely limited in achieving their goals (Boettke et al. 2008). As we see later, land markets in Mumbai have a well functioning informal system with a powerful land mafia and a strong politician-builder nexus, and reforms to improve land market outcomes have been unsuccessful.

In order to understand the nature of local governance in India it is imperative to take into account the political institutions that determine distribution of powers across levels of government (see Rodden and Rose-Ackerman 1997), redistributive policies (Arulampalam et al. 2009), checks and balances (see Bardhan 2009), dissemination of information to voters (Banerjee et al. 2011), and inter-governmental interactions (Pethe et al. 2012a). New Institutional Economics recognizes the importance of political institutions and their crucial role in shaping economic activity. North (1994) highlights that political institutions, by protecting property rights and enforcing contracts, determine how the economic market would function.[4] New Institutional Economics is also concerned with understanding the functioning of political markets. Dixit (1996: 48) provides the perspective of transaction cost politics to understand the nature and workings of political contracts. According to him, in transaction cost politics, 'the parties to a political contract are citizens (individuals or interest group organizations), on the one hand, and politicians (individuals or parties) or administrators (regulatory agencies, etc.), on the other.' He avers that political actors take decisions to mitigate political transaction costs and political efficiency rather than economic efficiency is their main objective. These transactions costs are borne out of political uncertainty, information asymmetry, and multiple agency relationships between different actors. Transaction cost politics provides a useful analytical tool to

[4] In fact, Acemoglu and Robinson (2012) show that divergence between economic performances of countries is a result of differences in the nature of political institutions that support economic institutions.

study the alternative modes of arrangements between public officials and citizens for public goods and service delivery. Kwon et al. (2010) apply transactions cost politics to local public goods and service provision to understand how delivery arrangements for public services in cities are determined. They find that public service delivery arrangements are a result of bargaining between political actors—elected officials, administrators, and constituents—who seek to minimize their costs. Changes in production arrangement depend on political institutions and the economic situation of the constituents (ibid.).

Nature of Multi-level Urban Governance in India

Urban governance in India has evolved as a response to changing conditions, ideas, and urbanization impulses. Municipal corporations were first created during the British colonial rule for better city administration. Post-Independence, the Constitution created a federal structure with division of legislative powers between the centre and the states, and local governments formed a part of the state list. These municipalities were therefore subsumed under the state governments and were treated as creatures of the state. Local governments differed widely in sizes and functions. The third tier of local governments was constitutionally recognized in the aftermath of the economic reforms of 1991. It was hoped that decentralization will be a good way to cede power to local authorities for better governance. However, state governments, influenced by the legacy overhang, have been reluctant to devolve power and continue to exert a strong influence over urban local governments.

Over time, the rate of urbanization started increasing although urbanization was top-heavy, with most urban population being concentrated in a few large cities. Large metropolises expanded beyond their municipal boundaries leading to increased commuting and economic linkages with peripheries, which brought the focus on metropolitan regions. Given the absence of government at the metropolitan level and the existence of many municipal governments along with rural local governments within the region, it was usually the state government—through its parastatals in charge of planning and development—that governed the region as a whole. In recent decades, central interventions in urban governance have been on the rise. This is in part due to the recognition that urbanization needs to be sustained through provisions of adequate infrastructure and in part due to a greater ability to incur expenditure at the central level as compared to the state and local levels. Thus, to speak of urban governance in India would be to recognize the multi-tiered arrangements between different governments within the fiscal federal set-up.

Urban Local Bodies

Urban local bodies (ULBs) were constitutionally recognized as the third tier of government with the passing of the Seventy-fourth Constitutional Amendment Act (CAA) in 1992. The Act mandated compulsory elections for all urban local governments, that is, municipal corporations and municipal councils, along with enumerating a list of functions for them to undertake. Over the two decades since the act was passed, the success of decentralization has been uneven across states (see Oommen 2006). However, the general experience is that state governments continue to exercise excessive control over ULBs and limited autonomy has rendered decentralization ineffective. An assessment of the nature of devolution of functions, finances, and functionaries to ULBs attests this.

The 12th Schedule of the Constitution lists the various functions to be performed by ULBs. These include providing local public goods and services, such as hospitals, primary education, solid waste management, sanitation, fire fighting along with general functions, such as land use planning, improving slums, and promoting culture and education. Most ULBs have been unsuccessful in fulfilling these functions, thus resulting in tremendous deficit of basic local goods and services in many towns and cities. According to the 2011 Census, approximately 30 per cent of India's urban population does not have individual connections for water whereas 13 per cent of urban households do not have latrine facilities. Storm water drains exist for less than 20 per cent of the road network; 18 per cent of urban households do not have access to drainage and disposal methods for solid waste generated in urban regions continue to be obsolete. Inadequate provisions by ULBs have given rise to parallel systems for providing local goods and services operated by private individuals. The inability of urban local governments in effectively undertaking their functions is largely attributed to inadequate fiscal autonomy.

Along with devolving functions, the 74th CAA specified the devolution of revenue handles to ULBs. Besides their own revenues, ULBs were to be provided grants from the state and central governments for meeting their expenditure requirements. An assessment of the overall financial position of ULBs reveals that they face severe budget constraints which in turn affect their capacity to carry out the mandated functions. The combined expenditure of ULBs declined from 1.74 per cent of gross domestic product (GDP) in 1998–9 to 1.54 per cent of GDP in 2007–8 (Government of India 2010).

Revenue handles with ULBs include both tax and non-tax sources. Property tax is the most important tax handle with ULBs. Property tax revenues in 36 of India's largest cities were estimated to be Rs 4,522 crore (Government of India 2010). For these cities, on an average, revenues from property taxes account for 23 per cent of total municipal revenues and 28.5 per cent of own source revenues (ibid.). Further, there is considerable variation in property tax collections among ULBs and they have not been able to exploit the complete potential of this tax source (ibid.). The contribution of other tax revenues was much lower, except for ULBs in Maharashtra which rely on octroi as an important revenue source. Non-tax revenue collections of ULBs have also been poor; in 2010 these amounted to a meagre 0.13 per cent of GDP (Rao and Bird 2010). There was a decline in the own revenues of ULBs from 63 per cent in 2002–3 to 53 per cent in 2007–8 (Government of India 2012). In a study of 25 municipal corporations, Mohanty et al. (2007) found that only two corporations could recover more than 75 per cent of the costs of service provision through fees. Rao and Bird (2010) argue that user charges need to be rationalized not only for buttressing own revenues but also because these indicate the scarcity value of the services to consumers and demand for the services from providers.

Besides own sources, most ULBs rely heavily on tied and untied grants from the state and central governments. The 74th CAA mandated setting up of state finance commissions (SFCs) to devolve grants to local bodies. However, the performance of SFCs in this regard has been dismal. Pethe et al. (2009) observe that in many states, SFCs are not appointed regularly and the timing of their appointment is not synchronous with central finance commissions. Moreover, the recommendations of SFCs are either rejected or there is considerable delay in their implementation (ibid.). Central finance commissions also devolve grants to local governments, but these have been on an ad hoc basis. The Thirteenth Finance Commission recommended dividing grants to be devolved into a basic component and performance based component (Government of India

2010). Other grants from the state and central governments are part of specific schemes and are tied in nature.

Most ULBs lack the capacity to borrow for financing their activities, which prevents them from undertaking large capital projects. Until recently, ULBs only borrowed from public institutions such as the Housing and Urban Development Corporation or the Life Insurance Corporation (Rao and Bird 2010). Once credit rating was introduced for municipal corporations, they were able to access the capital market through the issue of municipal bonds. The Ahmedabad Municipal Corporation was the first to access the capital market in 1998 without state guarantee and since then, funds raised through municipal bonds have amounted to Rs 1,200 crore (Government of India 2010). Municipal borrowing is mostly undertaken by large municipal corporations (Pethe and Lalvani 2006: 637). Smaller ULBs find it difficult to access capital markets since they lack borrowing capacity. As a result, municipal borrowing in India remains a fairly recent and under-explored source for infrastructure finance. In summary, the financial position of ULBs in India is weak, with a few buoyant tax handles, inefficient collection of user fees and charges, low borrowings, and over-reliance on inter-governmental transfers.

Besides functions and finances, the role and appointments of functionaries also affect the nature of decentralization. In India, ULBs may be classified as municipal corporations or municipal councils, with the criterion for distinction between the two being the size of the population. Councillors are directly elected to corporations for a period of five years, while the mayor is usually indirectly elected. The corporations are headed by a Municipal Commissioner, who is a bureaucrat appointed by the state government. An exception is the Kolkata Municipal Corporation which has a Mayor-in-Council system where the council is akin to cabinets in the state and central governments. Under this system, the Municipal Commissioner is under the supervision and control of an empowered Mayor. A common critique of the organization of municipal corporations is that the mayor lacks any authority and all power is vested with a state appointed bureaucrat. The Commissioner's incentives lie in acting in accordance with the state government's diktats. Without an empowered Mayor, there is no single, autonomous authority which is in charge of the city and can be held accountable for public goods and service delivery.

Although, theoretically, decentralization has several merits, the experience of decentralization as adopted by many countries, differs vastly (see Treisman 2002). Tanzi (2001) cautions that for developing countries, adopting decentralization could prove to be deleterious if requisite supportive institutions are absent. Bardhan (2002) opines that decentralization might be disadvantageous in developing countries as weak institutions for local accountability make local governments prone to elite capture. India's experience with decentralization has been disappointing primarily because it has not been accompanied by institutions that result in better empowerment, autonomy, and accountability for the third tier of government.

Metropolitan Governance

The significance of metropolitan regions in India is on the rise primarily due to greater integration of large primate cities and contiguous smaller cities, towns, and villages. This integration is reflected in travel patterns of daily commuters, production linkages, and high population growth in the peripheries beyond the city's municipal boundaries. This trend entails greater coordination among local and metropolitan level authorities for planning and delivery of public goods and services. In other words, there is a need to pay special attention to metropolitan governance for improving the provision of public goods and enhancing the competitiveness of the metropolitan region.[5] This section focuses on assessing metropolitan governance in Mumbai, Kolkata, Bangalore, Chennai, and Hyderabad.

The question of which system of metropolitan governance would be best suited for metropolitan regions has received considerable attention among scholars in the west. Much of the literature on this subject is based on a study of metropolitan governance in the US. The early view regarding the organization of government in metropolitan regions was that it resembled a 'crazy quilt pattern' with too many governments and that the solution to this 'pathological phenomenon' was consolidating the different governments towards a single government at the metropolitan level (Ostrom et al. 1961: 831). However, in their seminal paper in 1961, Ostrom et al. opine that a polycentric governance system having 'many centers of decision making that are formally independent of each other' (ibid.) is ideal for metropolitan regions.[6] The rationale is that an arrangement with multiple public organizations having overlapping jurisdictions

[5] Bahl (2013) discusses the various possibilities of organizing metropolitan governance depending on the objectives and considerations for minimizing costs.

[6] Ostrom et al. (1978) studied police services to provide an empirical validation for polycentric governance.

and functional scopes will allow reaping the benefits of economies of scale, competition, cooperation, and conflict resolution (Ostrom 1999; Pethe et al. 2011). Such a system is also considered to be more democratic as it facilitates citizen participation in decision making, caters to heterogeneous populations, and has a built-in system of checks and balances (Pethe et al. 2012b).

Metropolitan governance in India resembles a polycentric system owing to a multitude of public organizations involved in the delivery of public goods and services. The extant system is a complex entity resulting out of ad hoc measures undertaken by different governments as a response to continuous delineation of metropolitan and municipal boundaries and to challenges in service provision at a metropolitan level. Besides urban local governments that have constitutional recognition under the 74th CAA and have to perform mandated functions of providing basic goods and services at the local level, there exist numerous state and central level parastatals involved in providing services throughout the metropolitan region. Utilities such as water supply, sewerage, power, and roads, which enjoy economies of scale or whose delivery requires inter-municipal coordination are provided by these parastatals. In some cases, even mandated functions of ULBs, such as solid waste management, are undertaken by specially created parastatals. The predominance of parastatals in metropolitan regions is evident from the fact that between 2005–6 and 2007–8, their share in public investments in the Mumbai Metropolitan Region amounted to 55 per cent (Pethe 2013).

All the five metropolitan regions have a special development and planning authority set up under the state government to oversee and plan for the development of the metropolitan region. These authorities also play a crucial role in coordinating activities, undertaking investments in infrastructure, and acting as the nodal agency for centrally sponsored schemes. Recognizing the need for metropolitan level coordination, the 74th CAA mandates the setting up of metropolitan planning committees (MPCs). MPCs comprise elected councillors from local bodies, ministers from state governments, and other officials in order to foster cooperation and coordination for delivery of services in the metropolitan region. However, many states are still to constitute an MPC, possibly fearing that the metropolitan development authorities—which are the state governments' creatures—will lose their importance in metropolitan affairs. There are instances of inter-municipal arrangements in Chennai, Kolkata, and Bangalore Metropolitan Regions for jointly undertaking provision of certain services, albeit in a limited sense and in an ad hoc fashion. Increasingly, we find a greater involvement by the private sector in infrastructure provision in metropolitan regions. This participation is either in the form of public private partnerships or due to local governments outsourcing some of their functions to the private sector.

The existing governance system has been ineffective in addressing the needs of the metropolitan regions. Serious deficiencies continue to exist in service provision and access to basic utilities is often iniquitous. There is little effort to dovetail the various regional, local, and master plans created by the various planning agencies. Despite having a multi-level, multi-functional, multi-sector governance structure, the system does not result in 'true' polycentricity. This is largely because of missing institutions and high political transaction costs that preclude effective competition, cooperation, and conflict resolution (see Pethe et al. 2011). Multiplicity of authorities combined with no accountability reduces incentives for public officials in ensuring efficient provision. Absence of accountability and transparency has been a major cause of inefficient management of public land, owing to conflicts among different various public authorities over the ownership and use of public land (Pethe et al. 2012b). The state government, through its various parastatals and departments, has a dominant presence in metropolitan regions. Not only does the state government undertake many of the functions for provision of utilities in the metropolitan region, it also resolves inter-governmental/organizational conflicts that may arise in the region.

MPCs—wherever they are present—are given little importance in facilitating inter-municipal coordination (Sivaramakrishnan 2011). Thus, instead of multiple independent decision-making authorities, one finds most of the authorities subsumed under the state government and excessive power vested with the chief minister. A fractured polity, with different political parties ruling at the state and city levels along with an empowered Mayor could have infused some checks in the system. However, in Chennai, Hyderabad, Bangalore, and Kolkata we find that the same political party is in power both in the city and in the respective states.[7] Thus checks in the system that would have existed with multiple powerful organizations having conflicting interests are subverted and the advantages from the resultant creative conflicts remain unrealized. In

[7] As in 2013, the ruling party in Chennai and Tamil Nadu was the All India Anna Dravida Munnetra Kazhagam (AIADMK), in Hyderabad and Andhra Pradesh it was the Indian National Congress, in Bangalore and Karnataka it was the Bharatiya Janata Party, and in Kolkata and West Bengal it was the All India Trinamool Congress.

the case of Mumbai, the Indian National Congress–Nationalist Congress Party coalition is in power at the state while the Shiv Sena–Bharatiya Janata Party coalition is in power in the Municipal Corporation of Greater Mumbai. However, there is no creative conflict between the corporation and the state government controlled Mumbai Metropolitan Region Development Authority since the administrative heads of both the organizations are appointed by the chief minister and the elected local councillors have no actual power over the actions of the authority (Pethe et al. 2012a). Instead, political rivalry only thwarts cooperation between the two, which is vital for providing various services (ibid.).

The inefficiencies in the existing metropolitan governance system prompt the question whether institutional reforms should be directed towards greater consolidation or polycentricity at the metropolitan level. Moving towards either will incur significant transaction costs. There has been an active debate in policy circles regarding the organization of government at the metropolitan level (see Sood 2013). A recent proposal is to undertake the necessary amendments and introduce new provisions in the Constitution to create a metropolitan council headed by an elected person, having a specific mandate and jurisdiction, and comprising politicians, bureaucrats, private sector representatives, and civil society organizations (Sivaramakrishnan 2013). As discussed in Boettke et al. (2011), the debate among consolidationists and polycentrists regarding the ideal system for provision of public goods is relevant even today. Understanding the possible merits and demerits of such a metropolitan council will require a deeper analysis.

Central Interventions

The recognition of the inevitability of urbanization, the rising growth of urban poor, and the serious infrastructure deficiencies facing cities prompted the central government to introduce programmes and policies for better management of urbanization and for adequate infrastructure provision. The most noteworthy scheme, both in terms of the financial and functional magnitude, in the sphere of urban governance is the Jawaharlal Nehru National Urban Renewal Mission (JnNURM) launched in 2005. The mission targeted 65 cities and comprised two sub-missions called the Urban Infrastructure and Governance and the Basic Services for Urban Poor. The duration of the mission was for seven years and it was allotted Rs 66,085 crore. For financing projects under JnNURM, ULBs have to raise a certain proportion of the project cost and the rest of the cost is covered through grants from the state and central governments. The funds from the state and centre are disbursed to ULBs via a nodal agency appointed by the state government. Cities became eligible for funds from JnNURM only after the ULBs prepared detailed city development plans and the state governments fulfilled the conditions of undertaking the mandated structural reforms. However, JnNURM has only moderately succeeded in achieving its objectives. In an appraisal of JnNURM, the Twelfth Plan report noted that 'despite some good examples in some cities, the overall progress in improving service delivery standards have been unsatisfactory' (Government of India 2012: 323).

The introduction of JnNURM has important implications for the nature of inter-governmental interactions. The mandated reforms that state governments are required to undertake to avail funds under JnNURM include repealing the Urban Land Ceiling Act and amending the Rent Control Act. Since land is a subject in the constitutional state list, such reforms are seen to be an encroachment on the autonomy of state governments. Further, the mission is silent about building capacities of ULBs to undertake infrastructure projects and to strengthen their revenue sources. Much of the funds earmarked under the various components of JnNURM have remained unutilized because relatively smaller and weaker ULBs have been unable to put up their share of required finances. It is possible that central interventions like JnNURM when not accompanied by measures to bolster the ULBs' own revenues will make the latter even more dependent on such grants. Finally, the nodal agencies for disbursing funds and undertaking functions, such as appraisal of projects submitted by ULBs, releasing funds to ULBs, and monitoring the progress of sanctioned projects are appointed by state governments. State governments usually appoint state parastatals and development authorities, such as the Mumbai Metropolitan Region Development Authority, the Directorate of Municipal Administration, or the Tamil Nadu Urban Finance and Industrial Development Corporation Limited as nodal agencies, thereby allowing the states to exercise a greater control over ULBs. Whilst requirements, such as reforming property tax, introducing e-governance for ULBs, and adopting better accounting practices are intended to strengthen local governance, the top-down nature of governance reforms under JnNURM is, perhaps, further undermining decentralization.

Besides JnNURM, centrally sponsored schemes also include the Swarna Jayanti Shahari Rozgar Yojana, the National Slum Development Programme, the Integrated Low Cost Sanitation Programme, and the recently introduced Rajiv Awas Yojana (RAY) which aims to create a 'slum free India'. As per the recommendations of the Twelfth Plan, RAY will become a component of JnNURM and existing schemes for the urban poor such as the Basic Services for Urban Poor and Integrated Housing and Slum Development Programme will be subsumed under RAY (Government of India 2012). The main thrust of RAY is *in-situ* slum rehabilitation and providing property rights to slum dwellers. The design of the scheme allows maximum flexibility to the states and cities at all stages of slum up-gradation. Under RAY, the centre provides project-based allocations up to 50 per cent of the project cost. The scheme also emphasizes the need for creating rental housing, inclusionary housing, community participation, and partnerships with the private sector. Assigning property rights to slums on prime land could pose difficulties for RAY (Kundu and Samanta 2011). Further, many cities already have policies for slum up-gradation and affordable housing. In Mumbai, for instance, affordable housing is provided by the Maharashtra Housing and Area Development Authority while the Slum Rehabilitation Schemes provide free housing to slum dwellers. The policies pursued by such authorities have given rise to entrenched positions of certain groups, such as builders and politicians, who are keen for the policies to continue despite ample evidence that they have not succeeded. Dovetailing these policies to RAY will be a major challenge as it will involve significant political transaction costs.

Urban Land Governance: The Case of Mumbai

A well-functioning land market essays a vital role in a city's growth. Clearly defined property rights, transparent procedures for ownership and titling, well maintained land records, and flexible land use encourage investments and support economic growth. On the flip side, the high responsiveness of land values to business cycles and changes in production structures of the economy, as well as possibilities of extracting rents make land most susceptible to speculation and capture by elite groups, such as politicians and builders. Urban land in India has been characterized by inefficient management giving rise to bitter contestations, multiple claims by various stakeholders, and collusions to capture rents. Inefficient management arises largely out of the complex nature of land regulations, faulty reform policies that do not take into account incentives of stakeholders, and the highly adaptive nature of informal institutions that subverts reform measures in order to maintain the status quo.

Land is a state subject under the Constitution of India and all legislative and executive powers pertaining to land are vested with state governments. As a result state governments have the authority to plan and manage land. However, the Seventy-fourth CAA mandates ULBs to prepare land use plans for their jurisdictions. Thus, although plans are prepared by ULBs they are vetted by the state governments who have the ultimate veto in all land related matters. Besides ULBs, the state governments also create special planning authorities for specific purposes, such as townships or commercial complexes. These special planning authorities are in charge of planning and development within their jurisdiction. However, coordination and dovetailing the various plans is often neglected. Besides these organizations, several central level authorities such as the defence and railway boards and port trusts, own and manage significant tracts of urban land.[8] Thus, regulation of land is characterized by multiple public actors and uncoordinated plans.

Mumbai, with some of the highest real estate prices in the world, more than 50 per cent of the population living in slums, and complex land regulations, is perhaps the best example of inefficient land management in India and an inquiry into the problems of land management will be well worth undertaking given the rich lessons it could provide to policymakers as well as for other growing Indian cities. The following sub-sections provide an analysis of the failure of land reforms.

Effective urban land management in the wake of larger macroeconomic transformations prompts policy reforms to ensure that the process is inclusive. Given the fact that much of urban land is under the control of a few powerful actors, reforms are likely to lead these actors to re-position themselves in order to continue their hold on this resource. As Acemoglu (2010: 27) states, 'large-scale shocks and policy interventions will create political economy responses from those who see their economic or political rents threatened or from those that see new options to increase their rents'. Such responses must be anticipated and policy design should take cognizance of the informal ways in which bargaining among the stakeholders can subvert the objectives of reforms. We focus

[8] Multiple organizations owning land in the city often do not pay taxes to ULBs (see Pethe et al. 2011).

on the case of a land regulation and a land reform to highlight the political economy of land governance.

Development Control Regulation (DCR) 58

Urban regeneration and renewal brings to the fore the need for land use plans—known as development plans—to be able to allow for land use changes while taking into consideration the impact on the environment as well as on the poorer sections of the population. Following economic reforms, the early 1990s witnessed a rapid decline in textile manufacturing (D'Monte 1998) and a real estate boom with prices at an all-time high and intense construction activity in Mumbai. With builders and developers looking for avenues to profit from the boom, there was tremendous pressure for redevelopment of the vast mill land that was lying vacant and unused. At that point in time, land use in Mumbai was governed as per the development plan of 1991. The development plan provides reservations for land use and is accompanied by DCRs to guide all building activity in the city. Redevelopment of the mill land was to take place as per DCR 58, which stated that existing open land and land that would be made available on demolition had to be divided roughly into three equal parts with one-third being given to the Municipal Corporation of Greater Mumbai for open spaces and amenities, one-third being handed over to the state government for affordable housing, and one-third to be made available for development/sale by mill owners. Accordingly, several mill lands were sold in the early 1990s and subsequently converted to high rise commercial and residential complexes. This period also witnessed bitter contestations between labour unions and mill owners (D'Monte 2002) and an increased involvement of the mafia in the sale of mill land (Weinstein 2008). Mill owners often resorted to relying on the mafia for infiltrating the labour unions to intimidate workers into agreeing to the mill owners' terms. However, in 1995, there was a drastic decline of property prices and mill owners as well as developers, in order to stop their profits from falling, lobbied the government to change the DCR (see D'Monte 2002). Accordingly, in 2001 the Government of Maharashtra amended DCR 58 by the powers vested in it under the Maharashtra Regional and Town Planning Act 1966, to remove the phrase 'land becoming open upon demolition' so that only the existing open land could come under the one-third rule of dividing mill land (Adarkar and Phatak 2005). In a rare display of solidarity, the amendment went unopposed by any political party. The amendment was challenged in the high court through a public interest litigation. The high court passed a judgement in favour of the litigants and stayed the sale of mill lands. However, the Supreme Court later overturned the judgement and allowed mill redevelopment as per the amended DCR. As a result, instead of 33.3 per cent, 94 per cent of 600 acres of redundant industrial land became available for private development (Weinstein and Ren 2009). Thus, while the city lost out on much needed land for affordable housing and open spaces, the builders and mill owners continued to profit from mill redevelopment.

The case of DCR 58 brings to light several issues in the political economy of cities in developing countries and the nature of decentralization. It clearly points to the fact that the management of land was in a state of de facto lawlessness, which saw the unbridled control of the mafia in collusion with builders, mill owners, and politicians. The rents that accrued from this arrangement were shared between these powerful actors. The control of the builder lobby over the state government is not surprising given the synergistic relationship between the two (see Kapur and Vaishnav 2011). Further, despite the mill land being an intrinsic part of the local urban fabric, decisions regarding their sale and use, instead of being taken by the local corporation were taken at the state level. This weakened accountability since those taking the decision at the state level were elected from constituencies outside Mumbai. Their re-election did not depend on the citizens of Mumbai and hence perhaps, they did not feel answerable to those who their decisions were affecting.

Introduction and Repeal of Urban Land Ceiling and Regulation Act (ULCRA)[9]

In India, the dominant political thinking has historically influenced the nature of distributional reforms. ULCRA was introduced in 1976 during the heyday of socialism and nationalization in order to acquire excess privately owned land and use it for public purposes. The objective of the act was 'to prevent the concentration of urban land in the hands of few persons and speculation and profiteering therein and with a view to bringing about an equitable distribution of land in urban agglomerations to sub-serve the common good' (The Urban Land (Ceiling and Regulation) Act, 1976). The Act, therefore, mandated acquisition of vacant private land in excess of a

[9] This section draws heavily from a study on ULCRA by Pethe (2010).

set ceiling by a competent authority in the state government and using it for certain social purposes, such as low income housing, public utilities, and industries, among others. Compensation to landowners as per the Act was set at Rs 10 per sq mt or Rs 200,000 whichever was higher. Exemptions could be granted if the land was to be used for a public purpose, if it was to be used for low income housing, or if it caused the landowner undue hardship. Besides these conditions, discretionary powers were vested with the competent authority for granting exemptions.

The ULCRA legislation contained several lacunae that severely affected its implementation. There was no comprehensive plan or a time-line for using the acquired land for the various public purposes. The compensation that was stipulated was extremely arbitrary and so low that it would not incentivize the landowners to give up their land voluntarily. Exemptions provided a means for landowners to use as loopholes. Discretionary powers with the competent authority were a potential tool for extracting rents. Bribes were paid by large landowners to politicians and bureaucrats for being exempted. Exemptions were also used by networked actors who declared that the excess land would be used for public purposes, such as education (read profiteering colleges and private schools) or charitable purposes (read private hospitals and guest houses). Many large landowners encouraged encroachment of squatter settlements on their lands. Where such strategies were not possible the matter was contested in court, which resulted in long drawn legal battles. The acquired vacant surplus land was doled out to various government organizations who were vying for it irrespective of whether they required the land. In the Mumbai Metropolitan Region, 17,000 acres of land was declared as surplus vacant land, of which nearly 13,000 acres was exempted. Of the remaining, around 2,000 acres of land was held up in litigation. Ultimately, about 262 acres of land, that is 1.5 per cent of the potential, was acquired by 2007.

The economic reforms of 1991 and direction towards liberalization, privatization, and globalization, a change in the perception of the role of the government from a provider to an enabler, and the dismal performance of ULCRA, all contributed to the central government repealing the Act in 1998. However, the state governments did not immediately repeal the Act given the entrenched practices and incentives of various actors. Maharashtra repealed ULCRA in 2007. Primarily the repeal was a precondition in order to avail funds under JnNURM. One of the important consequences of ULCRA was that it created a shortfall in the supply of land and thus was one of the contributing factors to increasing property prices in the city. It was expected that the repeal of ULCRA would result in considerable land entering the market and a price correction. This expectation had resulted in considerable speculation regarding the extent of land that would be released and lobbying to repeal the Act. However, after the repeal there was little change in the situation. This was largely due to the fact that the amount of land actually acquired was very less, much of the land remained locked in litigation or encroached upon by squatter settlements, the land parcels were scattered over different parts of the city which confined the impact to only a few localities, and also because the market players had already discounted the information about the repeal. Property prices did not fall nor was there a glut of newly available land in the market and the problem of affordable housing continued to be a major cause for concern.

Thus, a reform that was introduced to meet certain redistributive objectives was unable to do so and, after its repeal, did not result in expected outcomes. 'The entire episode related to ULCRA, from promulgation to its repeal is an exercise in futility, as it traverses from point of dysfunction to another state of dysfunction' (Pethe 2010: 31). ULCRA is an archetypal example of well-intentioned yet wrong-headed reforms that create perverse incentives and vested interests. Such reforms are bound to fail because they neglect the high political transaction costs of redistribution and under-estimate the ability of informal institutions to quickly adapt in order to maintain the existing power structures.

New Developments

The principal–agent problem in political economy—that is further made complex by multiple agency relationships—can be mitigated with the introduction of supervisors who monitor the agents (Laffont 2000). In India, the supervisory role is essayed by diverse actors, such as the media, judiciary, and civil society. It has been recognized that monitoring the agents, that is public officials, is made effective by creating channels for dissemination of information. Banerjee et al. (2011) show that access to information about legislators' performance considerably affected voting patterns of slum dwellers in urban India. In particular, they find that access to information about politicians' performance led to increased turnout and more votes for incumbents who were performing better and who were relatively more qualified. Thus, political institutions that create formal channels for information sharing and creating data banks are crucial for better governance.[10] In this regard, the Right to Information Act has played an important part in providing access to the citizens regarding the delivery of public goods and services. The media and the civil society—that is, non-governmental organizations (NGOs), community based organizations, and citizen's groups, among others—have used to act to obtain information about the performance of public organizations, and any discrepancies, especially instances of corrupt practices. The Adarsh housing society scam was brought to light by an NGO, based on information that it obtained through a Right to Information application. Increasingly, NGOs with the mandate of improving urban governance and increasing accountability are gaining prominence in the supervisory space. Besides creating awareness through publicizing information, the civil society lobbies the government to meet its demands, acts as liaison between the government and the citizens, and often collaborates with the government for facilitating the delivery of public goods and services. For instance, the Society for the Promotion of Area Resource Centres was involved with slum inhabitants for building community toilet blocks under the Slum Sanitation Programme—a demand driven programme implemented in Mumbai by the Municipal Corporation of Greater Mumbai and funded by the World Bank (McFarlane 2008; Sharma and Bhide 2005). Recent years have seen a great involvement of residential welfare associations, advanced locality management, and similar citizens' groups in local governance. Although initially these groups were created to organize solid waste collection in different localities and to maintain a clean environment, they have forayed into providing other utilities, such as storm water drainage, neighbourhood beautification, and are increasingly influencing decision makers especially on issues related to slum settlements and illegal hawking (Zérah 2009). But the growing activism of the middle and upper middle classes and their contestations with the poor has resulted in a fragmented civil society.

The Indian judiciary has often acted as a watchdog over the executive and legislature. However, its chief disadvantage has been a substantial backlog in terms of pending cases—exacerbated by the large number of vacant positions for judges—resulting in high transactions costs (both time and money) in approaching the judiciary (Patibandla 2013). Nonetheless judicial activism has gained prominence post-1990s, after public interest litigations' jurisdiction started to focus on governance

[10] Pande (2011) cautions that whether politicians' ability to overturn the impact of better information will be limited or amplified depends on other political institutions.

and the control of corruption (Thiruvengadam and Joshi 2012: 330–1). Incidences of judicial intervention in local governance have been on the rise with local courts often being sensitive to local governance issues. Higher level courts, on the other hand, are often at an arm's length and hence are more conservative in interpreting the laws. As seen in the case of DCR 58, this has often resulted in higher courts overturning the stays ordered by lower courts. Judicial activism is especially high in sensitive issues of environment protection, and informal housing and livelihoods (such as hawking). However, judicial intervention in these areas is not unbiased, raising questions of differential access and right to the city. For instance, the anti-poor judicial orientation of the courts has resulted in the sanctioning of slum demolition drives in Delhi (Dupont 2008; Ghertner 2008). Zérah (2007) points to the case where courts took an anti-poor and pro-environment stance in the case of illegal encroachment in the Sanjay Gandhi National Park. Moreover, the courts targeted encroachments made by the poor whereas illegal constructions by the more affluent sections were not probed (ibid.).[11]

It is clear that although the supervisory role is gaining prominence, the class of supervisors is highly fragmented. Nonetheless, the creation of a supervisory space has infused the governance system with some participatory character. It is a significant development since it has considerably changed the rules of engagement among different actors.

***

The fact that India is urbanizing and this process is realized in a particular way leading to a specific nature of Indian urbanization is in itself a challenge to the psyche seeped in the received wisdom that India lives in her villages and calls for a mind-set change. That such a change further calls forth special skills in governing and managing urban spaces is fortunately being recognized. The delivery of public goods and services in urban India suffers from serious deficiencies in terms of inadequate service provision, unequal access, corruption, and leakages, drawing attention to the nature of governance. We strongly believe that in this context, governance is the key to improving the state of affairs. Urban governance in India is a complex emergent entity, evolving as a response to changing conditions,

[11] As an aside, albeit relevant to the overall governance system, we may mention that specifics apart, judicial activism often encroaches (especially when it takes *suo moto* cognizance) into areas that legitimately fall in the executive's domain and this may not be good in the long run.

ideas, and urbanization impulses. This chapter attempted to understand the reasons for the persistence of suboptimal outcomes and policy failures in urban governance by using analytical tools from New Institutional Economics. The specific aspects examined were the nature of multi-level governance, urban land management, and the supervisory space in urban governance. We find that the multi-level governance is characterized by weak decentralization, excessive interventions by state governments through their parastatals, absence of true polycentricity in metropolitan governance, and top-down reforms induced through centrally sponsored schemes. Using the case of urban land management in Mumbai, we saw how a high valued resource such as urban land is prone to capture by a few elite groups. The examples of DCR 58 and ULCRA were used to illustrate how reforms are bound to fail when they neglect the high political transaction costs and under-estimate the ability of informal institutions to quickly adapt to maintaining existing power structures. Although the rise of supervisory actors, such as civil society and judiciary are a positive development and have infused the governance system with some checks, they suffer from serious lacunae. Civil society is highly fragmented while approaching the judiciary involves significant time and monetary costs. In sum, the existing urban governance system is unable to efficiently deliver public goods and services because of deficient political institutions that vest too much power with few authorities; missing institutions for information dissemination, accountability, and transparency; elite capture; a fragmented civil society and an overburdened judiciary; and high political transaction costs that preclude effective competition, cooperation, and conflict resolution among the various public organizations. Any reforms attempted to ameliorate the situation must be implemented after careful deliberation. Political economy responses must be anticipated and the design should take cognizance of the informal ways in which bargaining among the stakeholders could subvert reforms.

There have been many encouraging cases of reforms pertaining to improvements in municipal finances and infrastructure provision. A much talked about success story has been the property tax reforms undertaken by Bangalore, which have resulted in increased collection efficiency and thus bolstered municipal finances. The Municipal Corporation of Greater Bangalore undertook property tax reforms through innovative and participatory means, such as self-assessment schemes for self declaration of property tax, use of geographical information systems to identify all the properties, and engaging with taxpayers through media and citizens' groups to make the reforms acceptable (Ahluwalia 2011; Rao 2013). There is ample scope for similar property tax reforms to be undertaken in other Indian cities. The institution of the Tamil Nadu Urban Development Fund could be imbibed by other states for enabling pooled financing by ULBs and thus empower them to undertake investments in infrastructure. Besides municipal finances, innovative solutions are being implemented for better service delivery. For instance, the Pune Municipal Corporation has undertaken various measures for revamping the processes for solid waste management and is making extensive use of technology for converting waste to energy (Ahluwalia 2012). The Town Planning Schemes implemented in Gujarat for pooling lands in urban peripheries for providing and financing infrastructure such as roads are highly successful. The scheme can be replicated in other agricultural areas that are witnessing pressures of urban development. Such successful practices offer lessons for crucial reforms that must be implemented in other urban areas in India.

We can flag a few of the many crucial arenas which require urgent policy initiatives. These will be the very nature of urban planning suited to the particular Indian dynamic, the removal or reforms of archaic rent control, the organization of government for metropolitan scale issues, and generally to carry out reforms so as to ease the difficulties in doing business (which will bring in much needed public, private, and foreign investment in infrastructure). In attempting these reform initiatives, lessons have to be learnt so that wrong-headed policies are not pursued since they have the potential not only for causing specific harm but will also ramify through the management of expanding urban spaces throughout the country. With urban spaces in India already contributing overwhelmingly to the national income, urban policy reforms and management emerge as the numero uno issue facing the country. Unleashing growth through such measures is surely the way for addressing the issues of poverty and vulnerabilities of a large number of Indians in a positive manner. We are at a cusp and failure to attend to the issues of urban governance will push the economy into an abyss and given the heightened aspirations of the citizens, will cause much harm to the socioeconomic fabric of the nation. There will be, perhaps, no second chances; the tipping point is upon us.

References

Acemoglu, D. (2010), 'Theory, General Equilibrium, and Political Economy in Development Economics', *Journal of Economic Perspectives*, 24(3): 17–32.

Acemoglu, D. and J. Robinson (2012), *Why Nations Fail: The Origins of Power, Prosperity, and Poverty*. New York: Crown Business.

Adarkar, N. and V.K. Phatak (2005), 'Recycling Mill Land: Tumultuous Experience of Mumbai', *Economic and Political Weekly*, 40(51): 5365–368.

Ahluwalia, I.J. (2011), Property Tax Reform Can Fund Our Cities. Indian Express, 29 June.

——— (2012), 'Clean It Like Pune'. *Indian Express*, 31 October.

Annez, P.C., A. Bertaud, B. Patel, and V.K. Phatak (2010), 'Working with the Market: Approach to Reducing Urban Slums in India', Policy Research Working Paper No. 5475. The World Bank.

Arulampalam, W., S. Dasgupta, A. Dhillon, and B. Dutta (2009), 'Electoral goals and center-state transfers: A theoretical model and empirical evidence from India', *Journal of Development Economics*, 88(1): 103–19.

Bahl, R. (2013), 'The Decentralization of Governance in Metropolitan Areas', in R. Bahl, J. Linn, and D. Wetzel (eds), *Metropolitan Government Finances In Developing Countries*. Cambridge Massachusetts: Lincoln Institute of Land Policy (forthcoming).

Banerjee, A., S. Kumar, R. Pande, and F. Su (2011), 'Do Informed Voters Make Better Choices? Experimental Evidence from Urban India', Working Paper, Harvard Kennedy School.

Bardhan, P. (2002), 'Decentralization of Governance and Development', *Journal of Economic Perspectives*, 16(4): 185–205.

——— (2009), 'India and China: Governance Issues and Development', *The Journal of Asian Studies*, 68(2): 347–57.

Boettke, P.J., C.J. Coyne, and P.T. Leeson (2008), 'Institutional Stickiness and the New Development economics', *American Journal of Economics and Sociology*, 67(2): 331–58.

——— (2011), 'Quasimarket failure', *Public Choice*, 149(1): 209–24.

Dixit, A.K. (1996), *The Making of Economic Policy: A Transaction Cost Politics Perspective*. Cambridge, MA: MIT Press.

——— (2004), *Lawlessness and Economics: Alternative Modes of Governance*. Princeton: Princeton University Press.

D'Monte, D. (1998), 'Redevelopment of Mumbai's Cotton Textile Mill Land: Opportunity Lost', *Economic and Political Weekly*, 33(6): 283–90.

——— (2002), *Ripping the Fabric: The Decline of Mumbai and its Mills*. New Delhi: Oxford University Press.

Dupont, V. (2008), 'Slum Demolitions in Delhi since the 1990s: An Appraisal', *Economic and Political Weekly*, 43(28): 79–87.

Gandhi, S. (2012), 'Economics of Affordable housing in Indian Cities: The case of Mumbai', *Environment and Urbanization Asia*, 3(1): 221–35.

Ghertner, D.A. (2008), 'Analysis of New Legal Discourse behind Delhi's Slum Demolitions', *Economic and Political Weekly*, 43(20): 57–66.

Government of India (2010), *Report of the Thirteenth Finance Commission (2010–2015)*. New Delhi: Finance Commission of India, Government of India.

——— (2012), *Twelfth Five Year Plan (2012–2017)*. New Delhi: Planning Commission, Government of India.

HPEC (2011), 'Report on Indian Urban Infrastructure and Services', New Delhi: MoUD. Available at: http://niua.org/projects/hpec/FinalReport-hpec.pdf (accessed on 20 March 2013).

Kapur, D. and M. Vaishnav (2011), 'Quid Pro Quo: Builders, Politicians, and Election Finance in India', Working Paper No. 276, Center for Global Development.

Kundu, A. (2011), 'Politics and Economics of Urban Growth', *Economic and Political Weekly*, 46(20): 10–12.

Kundu, D. and D. Samanta (2011), 'Redefining the inclusive urban agenda in India', *Economic and Political Weekly*, 46(5): 55–63.

Kwon, S.W., I. Lee, and R. C. Feiock (2010), 'Transaction Cost Politics and Local Service Production', *International Review of Public Administration*, 14(3): 37–52.

Laffont, J.J. (2000), *Incentives and Political Economy*. Oxford: Oxford University Press.

Lall, S. (2011), *Urbanization Beyond Municipalities: Urban Review India*. Washington, DC: The World Bank.

McFarlane, C. (2008), 'Sanitation in Mumbai's Informal Settlements: State, "Slum" and Infrastructure', *Environment and Planning A*, 40(1): 88–107.

Mohan, R. (2007), 'Asia's Urban Century: Emerging Trends in a book', in Gregory K. Ingram and Yu-Hung Hong (eds), *Land Policies and Their Outcomes* (pp. 239–58). Cambridge, Mass. Lincoln Institute of Land Policy.

Mohan, R. and S. Dasgupta (2005), 'The 21st Century: Asia Becomes Urban', *Economic and Political Weekly*, 40(3): 213–23.

Mohanty, P.K., B.M. Misra, R. Goyal, and P.D. Jeromi (2007), 'Municipal Finance in India: An Assessment', *Development Research Group Study No. 26*. Mumbai: Department of Economic Analysis and Policy, RBI.

North, D.C. (1994), 'Economic Performance through Time', *American Economic Review*, 84(3): 359–68.

Oommen, M.A. (2006), 'Fiscal Decentralisation to the Sub-State Level Governments', *Economic and Political Weekly*, 41(10): 897–903.

Ostrom, E. (2010), 'Beyond Markets and States: Polycentric Governance of Complex Economic Systems', *American Economic Review*, 100(3): 641–72.

Ostrom, E., R.B. Parks, and G.P. Whitaker (1978), *Patterns of Metropolitan Policing*. Cambridge, MA: Ballinger Publishing Company.

Ostrom, V. (1999), 'Polycentricity (Part I)', in M. McGinnis (ed.), *Polycentricity and Local Public Economies. Readings from the Workshop in Political Theory and Policy Analysis*. Ann Arbor: University of Michigan Press, pp. 52–74.

Ostrom, V., C.M. Tiebout, and R. Warren (1961), 'The Organization of Government in Metropolitan Areas: A Theoretical Inquiry', *The American Political Science Review*, 55(4), 831–42.

Pande, R. (2011), 'Can Informed Voters Enforce Better Governance? Experiments in Low-Income Democracies', *Annual Review of Economics*, 3(1): 215–37.

Patibandla, M. (2013), 'New Institutional Economics: Its Relevance to Curbing Corruption', *Economic and Political Weekly*, 48(9): 55–63.

Pethe, A. (2010), 'Collusion, Conflicts, Informal Systems & Rent Seeking: The Great Prototype Indian Story of Urban Land Management in Mumbai', Synthesis report of a study undertaken for the World Bank presented at Urban Design and Research Institute, Mumbai, 10 December.

——— (2013), 'Metropolitan Public Finance: The Case of Mumbai', in R. Bahl, J. Linn, and D. Wetzel (eds), *Financing Metropolitan Governments in Developing Countries*, Cambridge Massachusetts: Lincoln Institute of Land Policy (forthcoming).

Pethe, A. and M. Lalvani (2006), 'Towards Economic Empowerment of Urban Local Bodies in Maharashtra', *Economic and Political Weekly*, 41(7): 635–41.

Pethe, A., B.M. Mishra, and P.B. Rakhe (2009), 'Strengthening Decentralization—Augmenting the Consolidated Fund of the States by the Thirteenth Finance Commission: A Normative Approach', *Development Research Group Study No. 29*. Mumbai: Department of Economic Analysis and Policy, RBI.

Pethe, A., S. Gandhi, and V. Tandel (2011), 'Assessing the Mumbai Metropolitan Region: A Governance Perspective', *Economic and Political Weekly*, 46 (26 & 27): 187–95.

Pethe, A., V. Tandel, and S. Gandhi (2012a), 'Understanding Issues Related to Polycentric Governance in the Mumbai Metropolitan Region', *Public Finance and Management*, 12(3): 182–203.

——— (2012b), 'Anatomy of Ownership and Management of Public Land in Mumbai: Setting an Agenda Using IAD Framework', *Environment and Urbanization Asia*, 3(1): 203–20.

Rao, M.G. (2013), 'Property Tax System in India: Problems and Prospects of Reform', Working Paper No. 2013–114. New Delhi: National Institute of Public Finance and Policy.

Rao, M.G. and R.M. Bird (2010), 'Urban Governance and Finance in India', Working Paper No. 2010–68. New Delhi: National Institute of Public Finance and Policy.

Rodden, J. and S. Rose-Ackerman (1997), 'Does Federalism Preserve Markets?', *Virginia Law Review*, 83(7): 1521–72.

Sharma, R.N. and A. Bhide (2005), 'World Bank Funded Slum Sanitation Programme in Mumbai: Participatory Approach and Lessons Learnt', *Economic and Political Weekly*, 40(17): 1784–9.

Sivaramakrishnan, K.C. (2011), 'Urban Development and Metro Governance', *Economic and Political Weekly*, 46(31): 49–55.

——— (2013), 'Revisiting the 74th Constitutional Amendment for Better Metropolitan Governance', *Economic and Political Weekly* 48(13): 86–94.

Sood, A. (2013), 'Urban Multiplicities: Governing India's Megacities', *Economic and Political Weekly*, 48(13): 95–101.

Tanzi, V. (2001), 'Pitfalls on the Road to Fiscal Decentralization', Carnegie Endowment for International Peace Working Paper No. 19. Washington, DC: Carnegie Endowment.

Thiruvengadam, A.K. and P. Joshi (2012), 'Judiciaries as Crucial Actors in Southern Regulatory Systems: A Case Study of Indian Telecom Regulation', *Regulation and Governance*, 6(3): 327–43.

Treisman, D. (2002), 'Defining and Measuring Decentralization: A Global Perspective', Unpublished manuscript.

Weinstein, L. (2008), 'Mumbai's Development Mafias: Globalization, Organized Crime and Land Development', *International Journal of Urban and Regional Research*, 32(1): 22–39.

Weinstein, L. and X. Ren (2009), 'The Changing Right to the City: Urban Renewal and Housing Rights in Globalizing Shanghai and Mumbai', *City & Community*, 8(4): 407–32.

Williamson, O.E. (1981), 'The Economics of Organization: The Transaction Cost approach', *American Journal of Sociology*, 87(3): 548–77.

——— (1985), *The Economic Institutions of Capitalism: Firms, Markets, Relational Contracting*. New York: Free Press.

——— (1996), *The Mechanisms of Governance*. USA: Oxford University Press.

Zérah, M.H. (2007), 'Conflict between Green Space Preservation and Housing Needs: The Case of the Sanjay Gandhi National Park in Mumbai', *Cities*, 24(2): 122–32.

——— (2009), 'Participatory Governance in Urban Management and the Shifting Geometry of Power in Mumbai', *Development and Change*, 40(5): 853–77.

CHAPTER 17

ISSUES IN FEDERALISM AND DECENTRALIZATION

T.R. RAGHUNANDAN

The Justice Punchhi Commission on Centre–State relations was constituted by the United Progressive Alliance (UPA) 1 government to recommend reforms to the constitutional arrangements for centre–state relations. The commission submitted a seven-volume report to the Government of India (GoI) in early 2010. Since then, nothing much has been heard of the report and, in all probability, the hope that the commission's recommendations would contribute to the future of India's federal structure might be well and truly dead.

While kick-starting its deliberations in early 2008, the commission held a meeting of intellectuals and luminaries from a wide range of fields in Delhi. I was a second row occupant, representing the central Ministry of Panchayati Raj. One of India's most respected legal minds, Mr F.S. Nariman was also present. Following a brief introduction, Justice Punchi requested Mr Nariman to advise the commission on the broad direction that it ought to take. For all his modesty, Mr Nariman is a commanding presence at any gathering. He made probably one of his shortest speeches ever: 'Just follow the Constitution', he said. 'It is a very detailed and well deliberated document and all one needs to do to run the country well is to follow it, in letter and spirit'. That was all.

The hall fell silent. Many were nonplussed with Mr Nariman's simple advice and half expected him to clear his throat and launch into a longer elaboration. Yet, that was all he had to say. The more I thought about what Mr Nariman had said, the more it made sense to me. He was bluntly warning us against India's greatest governance failure, that in designing and running our government, we were often breaching our Constitution and those breaches had gone unrecognized and unchallenged.

Both lay persons and experts observing India's governance architecture are sure to be confused by the layers upon layers of institutions at the centre, state, and local levels, each with its own complex management structure. To make matters worse, these institutions interact with each other in diverse and mysterious ways. In practical terms this means that many government services, even a matter as mundane as obtaining a building license from the local municipality, requires dealing with a large number of bodies and levels within them, each brandishing a volume of regulations that can disorient the most meticulously organized individual. Little wonder then that most of us see the government as a large black hole which is best left alone as far as possible. The practical way out is to bribe everyone in sight, so that institutions and people with little to do except getting in each other's way and causing the maximum inconvenience to people can be bought out.

Robust institutions are an essential ingredient of a well-functioning democracy. Three pre-conditions are essential for institutions to be strong and responsive. First, they must have a precise and exclusive role. Second, there must be a way by which people can hold them accountable for the performance of that role. More precisely, there should be a way in which they can be punished if they do not perform their responsibilities. Third, there must be a clear network of relationships that mesh different institutions together. These might be relationships of command and subordination—these are not always dirty words—or relationships of partnership, collaboration, and complementarity.

There are several adverse effects if institutional roles are imprecise. On the one hand, hazy functional definitions leave institutions confused and ill-equipped to perform their responsibilities and leave them open to criticism. Yet, on the other hand, such confusion also allows institutions to escape accountability, because they can always resort to the alibi that someone else had to do what they are accused of not doing. In the government's context, role clarity would mean that the centre, states, and local governments (the panchayats and municipalities) ought to have precise and exclusive functions, regardless of the larger order issue of how much power and authority should be ideally handled at each level. Yet, a good exercise of defining roles does not mean that subjects matters of governance, for example, health or education, are devolved wholesale; they need to be unbundled into activities and assigned to different levels of government at the level of such disaggregation. When responsibilities are disaggregated into activities and each activity is assigned precisely to one level of government and none other, then these levels have the incentive to seek out and obtain the capacity to perform these responsibilities. Only when role precision drives the acquiring of competencies for effective performance, can an institution be held accountable for the performance of its responsibilities.

Accountability is a slippery term, vulnerable to being used to mean many things. An authority on the subject, Staffan Lindberg (2009)[1] avers that the need for accountability is best captured in Bentham's principle: 'The more strictly we are watched, the better we behave'. Lindberg points out Nietzsche's observation, that we give an account only when it is requested and only when that request is backed by power. Thus, only actors with some discretion to make authoritative decisions can be the object of accountability relationships. Lindberg observes that this is best captured in Burke's succinct statement on representative accountability: 'Your representative owes you not his industry only, but his judgment; and he betrays, instead of serving you, if he sacrifices it to your opinion'. Continuing the same train of thought, he points towards the need for an identifiable locus of authority, as argued famously by J.S. Mill, that 'responsibility is null and void when nobody knows who is responsible.... there must be one person who receives the whole praise of what is well done, the whole blame of what is ill'. Thus, a strong system of accountability requires that the distinction between performers and those who hold them to account ought to be real and tangible. In short, accountability is possible only when those who govern are separated from the governed.

There is yet another principle that needs to be considered before we explore the issue of whether India's institutional framework meets these fundamental principles. This is the one of hierarchies of institutions. Common sense and logic suggest that constitutional institutions stand on a higher footing than institutions created through statute. Similarly, statutory institutions have a stronger basis than those that are created through executive orders.

India's governance architecture is replete with instances where these fundamental principles of design for a good multi-order system of

[1] Accountability: the core concept and its sub-types (Lindberg 2009).

governance have been ignored or overtly violated. This is the fundamental reason why our institutions do not function well. Yet, these flaws buried in the DNA of governance are rarely considered by lay persons, even though they suffer the consequences of system dysfunctionality in nearly every transaction with the government. The following examples illustrate some instances of how institutional structures in India do not meet these fundamental precepts and highlight how these infirmities adversely affect governance at all levels.

History

The genesis of our institutional design lies in our Constitution. It is a long one, meticulously detailed and the history of its evolution is well known. While many lofty principles contained in it, such as the fundamental rights drew inspiration from the ideals of the freedom struggle, in many ways the details of the institutional design followed its imperial predecessor, the Government of India Act of 1935. That has often led to the view that the Indian Constitution is more centralized than federal. The Supreme Court has on more than one occasion, described our country as being a quasi-federal one. Pranab Bardhan (2002: 185, 205) quotes Stepan, who made a 'useful distinction between "coming-together federalism" like the United States, where previously sovereign polities gave up part of their sovereignty for efficiency gains from resource pooling and a common market, and "holding-together federalism" like the multi-national democracies of India, Belgium and Spain, where the emphasis is on redistributive or compensating transfers to keep the contending polities together'. The trend towards 'holding together' in India's federal history is clear if one observes historical trends since we became a republic.

In 1950, Prime Minister Jawaharlal Nehru, inspired by the centralized Soviet model, established the Planning Commission, a body that was to formulate the national Five-year Plans. In 1952, a resolution was passed at a meeting of all chief ministers of states convened by the union government, to establish a National Development Council (NDC) chaired by Nehru and comprising all the cabinet ministers and chief ministers of states. This was the era when centralized planning was at its ascendancy and Nehru's personality towered over our nation building strategy like a colossus. The function of the council was to guide the preparation of

India's Five-year Plans. The NDC was positioned as a general body to the Planning Commission and was also entrusted the task of considering and approving the national plan prepared by the Planning Commission and to review its implementation. In this endeavour, the council could also deliberate on important national social and economic policy issues. The rationale for this arrangement was institutionalizing a centralized planning process, which Nehru considered essential for India's balanced development. The first meeting of the NDC was held in 1952. An interesting feature of both the NDC and the Planning Commission is that both institutions have no constitutional or statutory basis. Indeed, there is no central law that mandates national planning and the only foundation for these institutions remains the executive decision to set up the Planning Commission and the resolution passed more than 60 years ago by all the chief ministers under the tutelage of Nehru, to establish the NDC.

In 1983, following the recommendations of the Sarkaria Commission on centre–state relations, the Constitution was amended to provide for an inter-state council (ISC) chaired by the Prime Minister and comprising of the chief ministers of all states and union territories (UTs) and administrators of UTs without legislatures and six central cabinet ministers. In addition, four more central cabinet ministers could be inducted as permanent invitees to ISC. There is a remarkable similarity between the composition of the NDC and ISC. The council has been positioned as a recommendatory body with the duty of investigating and discussing subjects in which some or all of the states or the union and one or more of the states have a common interest, as may be brought up before it, making recommendations on any such subject, in particular recommendations for better coordination of policy and action with respect to that subject; and deliberating on such other matters of general interest to the states as may be referred by the chairman to the council. Clearly, ISC's constitutionally mandated scope of responsibility is wider than that of the Planning Commission and could easily include approval of the national plan. The most important feature of the ISC is that it has been given a constitutional status, whereas both the NDC and the Planning Commission survive on the basis of executive orders.

Quite easily, the NDC could have morphed itself into the ISC and the Planning Commission could have been positioned to become the ISC's secretariat. This would have ensured a natural evolution of the idea of having a deliberative body in our federal set-up. Yet, the reality continues to be otherwise. The NDC continues to exist and function as a separate body; in 2011, it held its 55th meeting. One would imagine that the Planning

Commission would have faded away in importance with the advent of liberalization. However, paradoxically, the Planning Commission is probably stronger today than ever before in terms of its capability to influence government expenditures across all levels from the central to the local. Even as the economy was opened up, government expenditure decisions have become more centralized and this contradiction has gone unnoticed. In stark contrast, the ISC lives in a gilded cage. It has a permanent secretariat, with a senior officer heading it. There is little for its staff to do, so it holds seminars and discussions. In the unlikely event that a commission such as the Justice Punchi Commission is established, it stirs out of its sleep and functions as the secretariat.

In recent years, the Planning Commission has started having increasing influence over GoI's expenditure decisions. Appreciating this requires an understanding of India's inter-governmental fiscal transfer system, the pipelines through which money is transferred from the centre to the states and local governments. Typically, fiscal transfers between government tiers fall into four categories. First, the money collected as taxes by one level of government could be shared with other levels of governments. The second is a related measure; a particular level of government can be entrusted the powers to levy, collect, and keep for itself tax revenues. Third, one level of government can give grants in aid to another without conditionalities. Fourth, the central government can entrust specific performance responsibilities to the State or the local governments and transfer funds to them, with detailed conditions on how they are to be used. To enable tax sharing, grants in aid, entrustment of taxation power and specific purpose transfers, India's Constitution provides for eight pipelines, illustrated in Figure 17.1.

Sharing of tax revenues in India is provided by A, B, E, and F, in Figure 17.1. A refers to the sharing of central tax revenues with the states. Every five years, a Central Finance Commission (CFC) is to be set up, which recommends the share of the central tax pool that ought to be shared with the states and the *inter-se* proportion in which the states' shares are to be allocated among them. Though the CFC report is only recommendatory, India has largely followed the convention of accepting these reports in toto and implementing them. Currently, the report of the Thirteenth Finance Commission is under implementation. B and F together constitute an inter-connected pipeline, through which the centre can augment states' finances from central revenues in order to supplement the resources of panchayats and municipalities. Following the Seventy-third and Seventy-fourth Amendments, the Constitution was amended to enlarge the CFC's

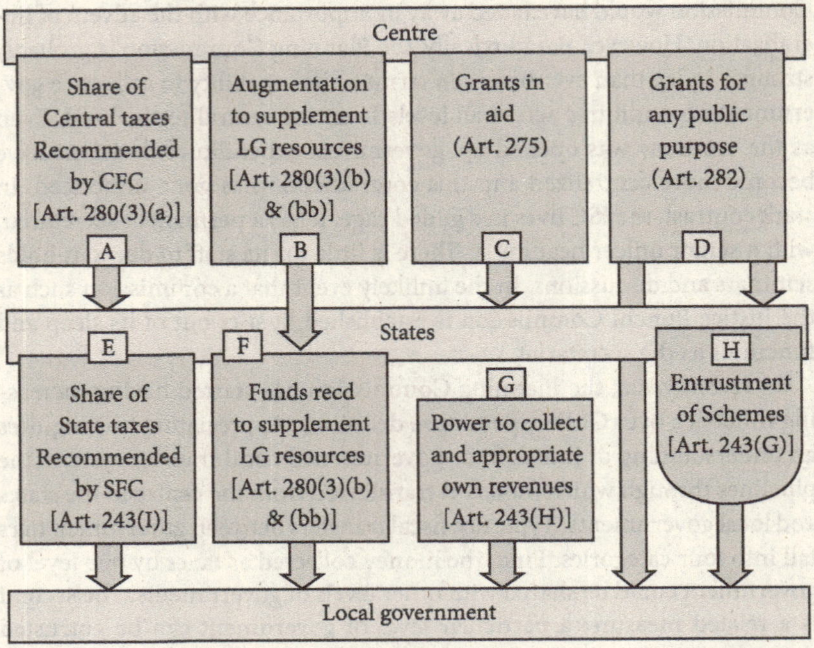

FIGURE 17.1 Constitutional Framework for Inter-governmental Fiscal Transfers

responsibility to recommend a share from the central tax resource pool for local governments (LGs). These transfers are, however, not given directly to LGs, but are deposited with the states with the condition that they ought to be transferred to LGs in turn. Earlier, states diverted these funds for their own purposes, but CFC has now set strict conditionalities to prevent these funds from being delayed or diverted. The Thirteenth Finance Commission has broken new ground by allocating a percentage of central revenues for LGs. Typically, these funds are allocated without conditionalities, but there has been a recent tendency for both the centre and the states to impose conditionalities that restrict the use of these funds by LGs, or force them to collect more local revenue and adopt robust standards of accounting.

E refers to a similar measure as A, operating at the state level. Every state is to set up State Finance Commissions (SFCs) to recommend the share of state taxes that ought to be given to local governments. A few states have followed the good convention of setting up these institutions regularly and following their recommendations, but this is more the exception than the rule.

G refers to the assignment of taxation powers to LGs by law. Typically, these taxation powers include property taxes, user charges for water supply and sanitation services, professional taxes, taxes on advertisement boards, ferries, parking fees, and entertainment tax on non-cinematographic shows.

As indicated in C, CFC is also tasked with recommending grants in aid for especially disadvantaged areas and states under Article 275. For example, such grants are given to tribal areas by the central government on CFC's recommendations.

However, over and above these routes for making normative transfers from the centre to state and local governments, there is yet another route for transfer, namely, D and H. D refers to Article 282 of the Constitution, under which the centre or the state can give grants for 'any public purpose' to anyone, even if the centre or the state as the case may be, does not have the competence to legislate on the subject matter concerned. Article 282 has a long history; it dates back to a similar clause, Section 150(2), in the Government of India Act of 1935. Clearly, Article 282 is meant to be used as an exception clause, to be used in the rare circumstances where transfers are required to be made by the centre or the states, for example, in case of an emergency such as a natural calamity where aid has to rapidly reach the recipients regardless of where it might originate. The clear giveaway that Article 282 is not part of the fiscal transfer system but is an exception, is that it does not appear in the chapter that deals with distribution of revenues between the centre and the states (Articles 268 to 281), but in a separate chapter termed 'Miscellaneous Financial Provisions'.

Over time, this small window of discretion in the Constitution, clearly meant to be used in exceptional circumstances where the normal fiscal transfer route might not be flexible enough, has been used to create a huge universe of non-normative transfers from the centre to states and local governments that rivals the normative route in the volume of funds transferred (see Table 17.1). Though the Planning Commission is a non-statutory and extra constitutional body, it presides over this large empire of funding, edging out the sharing of revenues between the centre and the states and the grants in aid based on the recommendations of CFC under Articles 280 and 275 respectively.

At first sight, it is bewildering why the exception clause of Article 282 in the Constitution is relied on to transfer huge volumes of funds from the centre to the states and local governments. Protagonists of the Planning Commission route justify transferring funds through centrally sponsored schemes (CSSs) and Central Plan Assistance in the interest of

Tabhle 17.1 Centre to State Fiscal Tranfers*

Centre to State Fiscal transfers made under Art. 280 & 275						Centre to State Fiscal transfers made under Art. 282					
Sl	Item	Amt (Rs. Cr)				Sl	Item	Amt (Rs. Cr)			
		2009-10	2010-11	2011-12	2012-13			2009-10	2010-11	2011-12	2012-13
1	States' share of Taxes and Duties [Art. 280(3)(a)]	164832	219303	255414	301921	1	Central Assistance for State and UT Plans (Planning Commission)	84490	93079	105197	129998
2	Non-Plan Grants & Loans [includes grants under Art. 275(1)]	46029	49875	55397	64296	2	Assistance for Central and Centrally Sponsored Schemes (Planning Commission)	24475	30606	37126	41592
						3	Direct release to State/UT implementing agencies (MPLADS)	1532	1533	2950	3955
						4	Direct releases to State/ District level autonomous bodies/implementing agencies	90521	118740	112803	133359

Note: * I am grateful to Dr Pinaki Chakraborty, Professor NIPFP, who compiled this data at my request.

equity and efficiency. CSSs contain conditionalities that ensure that the funds flow precisely where gap filling is required, as in the case of specific purpose transfers, such as the Sarva Shiksha Abhiyan and the National Rural Health Mission. CSSs also enable flexibility in funding, they argue. However, on closer examination, these justifications hold little water. First, the normative route of Article 275 clearly enables exactly the same kind of specific purpose transfer that is now being undertaken under Article 282. One cannot help but wonder at the real reason for resorting to Article 282 for making fiscal transfers from the centre to the states: Is it that it permits a wide latitude of discretion to the Planning Commission and the central line ministries to move funds across programmes and states? This view is also corroborated by many respected academicians. Bagchi (2003) mentions that the transfers by various finance commissions were directed in such a way that ensured the goal of equity but other forms of transfers showed discretion. He also adds a note of caution, that if the central government continues to increase inter-governmental fiscal transfers in Plan programmes that relate to subject matters that fall squarely in the functional ambit of the states, then this is an open invitation to fiscal indiscipline, as states develop an increasing dependence on inter-governmental fiscal transfers.

The bulk of the fiscal transfers made by the centre to the states under the exception clause of Article 282, are designed and operated by the Planning Commission and central line ministries. These fall into three categories: Centrally Sponsored Schemes, Central Schemes (CSSs), and Additional Central Assistance. CSSs are funding allocations meant for specific purposes, such as running education, anti-poverty, or health programmes. Elaborate guidelines are given by central ministries, which devise these schemes, based on the overall strategic advice given by the Planning Commission. Typically, these conditionalities include stipulations that the states must also contribute a certain percentage, typically between 10 to 25 per cent, to the scheme. Central Schemes are similar, often the only difference being that the centre contributes the entire amount for the scheme. Over the years, the corpus of CSSs has enlarged multi-fold. In 2004, the number of centrally sponsored schemes was around 230, with a total allocation of Rs 36,000 crore. In 2011, the number of schemes had been reduced to around 120, but the annual allocation had gone up to Rs 160,000 crore.

Another feature of CSSs is the skewed nature of funding. A few leviathan schemes account for a bulk of CSS allocations; the ten largest schemes, led by the National Rural Employment Guarantee (NREG) Programme account for nearly 90 per cent of the funding of CSSs and the remaining 110 of them only stream a little more than 10 per cent of the funding to states and local governments. CSSs are also highly skewed in favour of a few ministries, which then become enormously powerful in determining how funds are channelized from the centre to the states. Chakraborty and Isaac (2008) observe that in 2006–7, around 93 per cent of this flow was through three central ministries, namely, the Ministry of Rural Development (57 per cent), the Ministry of Human Resource Development (22 per cent), and the Ministry of Health and Family Welfare (13 per cent). Out of this, transfers on account of Sarva Siksha Abhiyan (SSA) and NREGS together constituted almost half of the total.

The other large windows of discretionary funding are the Special and Additional Central Assistance programmes. Historically, apart from tax shares and Article 275 grants recommended by the Finance Commission, the Planning Commission also dispensed a normative allocation based on a formula of *inter se* sharing between states, known as the Gadgil Formula, which has been in operation since the Fourth Five-year Plan (1969). This was considered as central assistance for state plans managed by the Planning Commission, as contrasted with CSSs, which though approved by the Planning Commission, were operated by central ministries. Under the current revised version of the Gadgil Formula, known as the Gadgil-Mukherjee Formula, 30 per cent of the amount is allocated for 11 special category states to enable them to fill gaps in funding their budgets. The remaining money is given to the other states on the basis of a formula in which 60 per cent weightage is given to the states' share in total population as per the 1971 Census—so the states which have controlled their populations since then are not penalized—25 per cent on per capita income and 7.5 per cent on performance covering criteria on tax effort, fiscal management and progress in achieving national objectives in population control, reduction of infant mortality, increasing female literacy, on-time completion of externally aided projects and undertaking land reforms. Finally, 7.5 per cent is allocated on a discretionary basis for tackling special problems in different states.

Yet, over time, the block grants given under the Gadgil Formula have been whittled away by a new instrument—Additional Central Assistance programmes. This stream of funding started as a trickle, as the Planning Commission began to fund development programmes primarily focused on hill, border, and tribal areas. The justification for tying funds that were hitherto given under the Gadgil Formula, was that the Planning Commission needed to allocate specific grants to deal with activities that are spread over many departments and sectors within a region, which are not easily allocable by a ministry or department of the central government as a central sector or CSS. From 1996 onwards, this trickle began to turn into a flood. The Additional Central Assistance programmes started burgeoning at the expense of the block allocations under the Gadgil Formula. Today, they comprise large programmes, such as the Accelerated Irrigation Programme, the Rajiv Gandhi Vidyutikaran Yojana, the Backward Regions Grant Fund, and the Jawaharlal Nehru Urban Renewable Mission. By operating Additional Central Assistance (ACA), the Planning Commission has now stepped outside its primary role as a strategic advisor, to behave as if it were a central ministry directly operating schemes and programmes. Chakraborty and Isaac (2008: 86) state the situation as:

> The provision for the periodic appointment of an independent finance commission, with a semi judicial character to limit the scope of discretion of the centre in the matter of resource flows to the states was a key stone of the basic fiscal structure envisaged in the Constitution. However, this basic structure is being undermined due to proliferation of transfers through various other channels outside the statutory transfers recommended by the finance commissions. Many of these transfers are not only discretionary; they are directly going to district authorities and societies bypassing the state budgets. Multilateral and bilateral lending institutions are also entering in a big way in determining state level fiscal policy through various sectoral and structural adjustment lending linked to fiscal reforms.

To sum up, we have the Planning Commission, a non-statutory, extra constitutional authority, which advises the centre on planning and prepares and approves national plans. This commission acts as the advisor and secretariat for the NDC, which too is an institution created through an executive fiat. Now the Planning Commission is sitting at the apex of a funding empire of massive proportions and through CSSs and ACAs, it allocates more money to states and LGs than the shares of central revenue that flow to the latter on the basis of the Finance Commission's recommendations, though the Finance Commission is a constitutionally mandated institution. Of course, there is the Cinderella of the federal arrangement, ISC, a constitutionally mandated institution that ought to have stepped into the shoes of the NDC, waiting for her fairy godmother to turn up.

Yet, the normative fiscal grants through the Finance Commission route and the schematic transfers presided over by the Planning Commission are not the only ways by which central funds are transferred. We have the

MP and MLA Local Area Development Schemes, which is a travesty of any rational norm-based approach to allocating public funds. Legislators voting for themselves a budget for garnering public funds and then using it ostensibly for 'constituency development' is not a new phenomenon. Pork barrel schemes, as they are known, were common in many democracies, such as the US and Australia in their early periods of development before they were discredited and were given up in favour of norm-based fiscal transfers. In South Asia, the affliction of such schemes is relatively new. Maharashtra was the first state to introduce such individually controlled public fund allocations in the early 1990s.

The Government of India put in place the Members of Parliament Local Area Development Scheme (MPLADS) in December 1993, barely two weeks after the Parliament passed the Seventy-third and Seventy-fourth Amendments giving constitutional status to panchayats and municipalities respectively. The need for an MP's constituency development fund was vociferously argued for by Ram Naik, MP from Maharashtra. The then Prime Minister Narasimha Rao succumbed to the pressure easily; it was rumoured that this was a tactical gambit to allay fears that giving constitutional status to local governments would erode the hitherto unchallenged hegemony of MPs and MLAs over the local political structure. The scheme had modest outlays to begin with; each MP was allocated Rs 5 lakh every year to enable him/her to identify small capital works and create durable community assets based on locally felt needs in their constituencies. Once the cat was out of the bag, the disease of patronage funding windows quickly spread. The initial allocation of Rs 5 lakh in 1993–4 was increased to Rs 1 crore per annum from 1994–5 per MP, and was further stepped up to Rs 2 crore from 1998–9. In 2011, the allocation was increased to Rs 5 crore per MP. All states have followed suit and created similar Member of the Legislative Assembly Local Area Development Scheme (MLALADS), which vary in allocation from Rs 40 lakh to Rs 2 crore per annum.[2]

From the outset, civil society representatives, the media, political commentators, and academics have been critical of MPLADS, as incentivising patronage politics. A study led by a former MP, Era Sezhiyan of the DMK, revealed several insights into the manner of expenditure of these funds by MPs (Sezhiyan 2005). A sting operation in 2007 also exposed MPs taking bribes in return for sanctioning projects from these funds. Yet, this scheme continues with increased allocations. Such schemes across all states and

[2] The highest allocation of Rs 2 crore per MLA is in Jharkhand, which has also not had panchayat elections since 1978 (when the state was part of undivided Bihar state).

covering Parliament members now channelize more than Rs 25,000 crore of public funds per annum to programmes that are decided by MPs and MLAs. Not only are legislators not accountable for the implementation of the schemes, the running of the programme diverts their time from their core responsibility of being lawmakers and drives them to behave as local executive officers, determining how local programmes should be implemented.

PRACTICE

Apart from fund allocations violating the constitutional spirit of federalism, the manner of actually sending these funds down is also a transgression of the constitutionally envisaged pattern. The Constitution provides for how funds ought to flow from the centre to the states and local governments. Under Article 266, the centre and each state are to set up 'consolidated funds' which comprise of all revenues, loans, and other money received by way of repayment of loans. Under Article 266, it naturally means that all fiscal transfers received by the state should also be deposited in the consolidated fund. The Article also mandates that no expenditure from the consolidated fund can be appropriated without legal sanction. In practice, without exception, revenue shares as recommended by the Finance Commission strictly flow through the consolidated funds of the states. Even the central revenue shares destined to reach local governments, are deposited in state consolidated funds with the stipulation that these ought to be deposited with the LGs within a specified period of time.

Yet, this constitutionally mandated path of transferring funds downward is largely bypassed in sending down a bulk of scheme based allocations by the Planning Commission and central ministries. There was a rationale for this conscious bypassing of state consolidated funds in the past. In earlier days, when states' financial positions were precarious and the centre was upping the ante on spending money on activities that fell within the states' domain, a genuine dilemma faced by the centre was how to prevent states from delaying fiscal transfer or worse, diverting funds given for specific purposes, for other imperatives determined by fiscal stress. For example, how could the central Agriculture Ministry ensure that its allocation for fertilizer purchase was not diverted by a state to pay teachers' salaries? The solution was simple; GoI ministries began to insist through their schematic guidelines that states must create state or district-level societies, which could open bank accounts into which central allocations and state contributions could be deposited, bypassing the state consolidated funds. This was welcomed by all as a simple and swift way of ensuring that funds reached implementing authorities in time, without the possibility of being hijacked along the way by cash starved states. One of the first such bodies was the Small Farmers' Development Agency (SFDA), created in 1979 by the then fledgling Rural Development Ministry. SFDA metamorphosed into the District Rural Development Agency (DRDA) and was quickly joined by many such specific purpose institutions, which included societies for control of malaria, blindness, promotion of horticulture, undertaking watershed development, and running education and health programmes. Today, a bulk of the CSS allocations is routed through these parallel structures and is insulated from the state budget. While these parallel structures have diverse objectives, they share one common feature; nearly all of them are headed at the district level by that ubiquitous officer, the District Collector, another stellar example of India's institutional mess.

The office of the District Collector, also known as the Deputy Commissioner or District Magistrate, is an anachronism dating back to colonial days. Starting as an institution that was primarily created to settle and measure land and assess and collect revenues, the office of the collector grew to being an outpost of the empire in the district, vested with powerful magisterial and law and order responsibilities as well. One would have expected that following Independence this colonial institution, which finds its equivalent across erstwhile British colonies in Asia and Africa would have faded away, but the reality is that it became stronger. Before Independence, the collector did little more than keep a watchful eye on the natives, to see that they did not step out of line. Today this office has metamorphosed into an all-powerful fulcrum of regulation and development in the district, without whose knowledge or approval, nothing much can happen.

The job of being District Collector is reserved—the right term is 'encadred'—for officers belonging to the Indian Administrative Service (IAS). High visibility is part of the job. It is tremendously challenging for the incumbent; indeed in the IAS, no other job defines an officer's potential any better than whether she has been a good collector. The aura that surrounds the collector is also the single most important motivator for joining the IAS. This is particularly true of provincial and small town

India, where the collector's office, his sprawling bungalow, and wireless bedecked white ambassador car are enduring symbols of state power. The collector is seen everywhere, visiting hospitals, schools and dutifully at the arm of the district minister on the occasions when the latter visits. The collector could on the same day, organize heroic raids to check irregularities in fair price shops and sand quarries, and then inaugurate vasectomy camps in the evening, before retiring for the night with a couple of hundred files.

It is not therefore surprising that no other institution is as fiercely protected from change by the IAS as that of the collector. The lore of the infallible collector is ingrained into fresh recruits in the IAS training academy at Mussoorie where senior officers relate their collector days' exploits to wide eyed probationers. Incidentally, every senior officer has his favourite collector story, most of which grow rosier and more improbable with the passage of years. All this makes for good fun; it is good for the morale of the service and for building an *esprit de corps*, in a manner quite similar to regimental traditions and stories in the army.

However, on a more serious note, the question is whether this is good for the country. For several reasons, the institution of the collector has become a huge bottleneck in unlocking the potential for development in most places across India. First, there is an excessive concentration of power in the collector; apart from their statutory roles under several regulatory legislations, collectors are entrusted with the responsibilities of heading a large number of district missions, meetings, and coordination committees, trying to make sense of a confusing and complex pattern of institutional overlaps. Collectors chair anything from 62 to 110 committees depending on the state concerned, including several powerful central level parallel structures. Most of a collector's roles require full time attention. For instance, the collector is often the District Programme Coordinator of MGNREGA (Mahatma Gandhi National Rural Employment Guarantee Act), the District Mission Chief for the Horticultural Mission, the Health Mission and so on. It is therefore impossible for a collector to do full justice to all her tasks.

Second, the twin phenomenon of the creation of new districts and a decade long reduction in recruitments commencing from the mid-1990s has resulted in very junior officers being posted as collectors. They do not command the same respect that they used to, particularly from middle level management officers of technical departments, such as chief engineers, additional directors, and conservators of forests. Third, in some states, the collectors are getting increasingly short tenures.

However, trying to change things is easier said than done. Suggesting any diminishing of the role of the collector is treated as heresy by the IAS; phrases such as 'time tested', 'historic and traditional', 'proven', 'universally recognized', and 'providing leadership' are bandied about. Yet, most of the aura surrounding a collector is ephemeral, of doubtful validity, and hardly shared by the people at large, outside the inner circle of departmental courtiers.

While the IAS is surely entitled to be a little sentimental about the post of a collector, to assert that the entire population of India shares that sentimental attachment is wishful thinking and naivety at its worst. To prescribe reforms is just about everything else, while arguing that the post of the collector must remain inviolate, just does not hold water.

In 1987 when Karnataka went in for its big bang devolution, Shri Abdul Nazeer Saab, the then minister of RDPR in Karnataka, successfully implemented a new system of district administration. The Deputy Commissioners (DCs) were fully divested of any development role and only handled revenue, law and order, elections, calamities, and district protocol. Far more senior officers were posted as 'Chief Secretaries' (CS) of the zilla parishads (ZPs). The CS was answerable to the elected body and its president was authorized to write his annual confidential report. This prompted several doomsday predictions from traditionalists that the district administration would crumble and that people would be totally confused, put to great inconvenience, and then they would agitate. Sage advice was given that a state must have only one person named the 'Chief Secretary', to ensure discipline and control. What happened next amply proved these traditionalists wrong. There were no widespread agitations against the separation of the development and regulatory functions of collectors. Nobody sat on a dharna demanding reinstatement of a DC as the head of the district administration. People quickly adjusted to the new reality and 'DC avaru' ('avaru' meaning 'respected') was replaced with 'CS avaru', in the district development lingo. People almost immediately recognized the CS as the de facto leader of the district development administration.

Sadly, this logical system was not allowed to continue. In mid-1991, ZPs were superseded on the excuse that a constitutional amendment for Panchayati Raj was imminent. Overnight, in a twin move, officers senior to CSs were posted as DCs and administrators of ZPs. The 'natural order', in the eyes of the IAS, was restored and it continues to be so till today. Incidentally, there was still the lingering matter about the use of the 'Chief Secretary' term. That was replaced with the more acceptable 'CEO', following the new Panchayati Raj Act of 1993. However, the use of the term 'CS avaru' among the common people, MLAs and even ministers still continues, more than 15 years after it was dropped.

Institutionally speaking, regulators cannot be service providers; there will be huge conflicts of interest. Second, there is just too much to do; it is both unfair to the incumbent of the post and the people at large to entrust so much work to one individual. The wide concentration of formal and informal power in the office of the District Collector would perhaps not be so starkly recognized if it were not for the establishment of panchayats and municipalities as constitutionally mandated institutions of local government. The Seventy-third and Seventy-fourth Amendments were supposed to herald a new era, under which the local elected councils and municipalities were to take over a wide range of development responsibilities and socioeconomic planning. Like with any other process of transfer of power, the transition ought to have been managed by realigning the plethora of institutions that pre-dated the LGs, the parallel structures, societies, and various development authorities that were under the control and superintendence of the District Collector—to become support systems to LGs. Yet, the vested interest of the bureaucracy has delayed and prevented this transfer from happening on the specious ground that LGs lack 'capacity'. It does not occur to the bureaucracy—or it chooses to ignore the obvious reality—that LGs can easily acquire the capacity to perform, if the capacities of erstwhile institutions that were performing the same functions are transferred to them.

One might ask if there are not enough politicians and bureaucrats who see this audacious distortion in non-constitutional bodies gaining ascendancy over constitutional institutions and attempts to rationalize institutional frameworks so that they conform with the Constitution's spirit and design. Two examples will suffice to show how difficult it is for well-intentioned reformers like Naseer Saab, to pilot and actualize change.

In October 2002, in a meeting of chief ministers chaired by then Prime Minister Atal Behari Vajpayee, there was consensus that release of funds under CSSs ought not to be sent directly to districts, or to separate societies set up for the purpose, bypassing state consolidated funds. The meeting agreed unanimously that henceforth, all releases under CSSs should be made through the consolidated funds of states. As a safeguard against the possibility of delay or diversion of funds by state governments, it was also agreed that as pre-condition, the states will pass on the funds to end users within a stipulated time of three weeks and inform GoI's administrative ministry of having done so. As a follow up to this high-level consensus decision, Finance Minister Jaswant Singh issued orders in January 2003 directing all concerned central ministries or departments to implement this decision forthwith. All hell broke loose. central ministries such as health and rural development began actively opposing this decision. This author remembers that as Secretary, Rural Development in Karnataka, he was summoned to a review meeting where the Secretary of the central Rural Development Ministry did everything but raise the banner of open revolt against the decision of his own government, making ill-concealed suggestions that state secretaries of rural development should write to the centre opposing the move to send funds through state consolidated funds. The Finance Minister could not resist the pressure from his ministerial colleagues and a few months later, the Finance Ministry directive was withdrawn and 'order' was restored; funds began to again flow through the parallel structures and banking channels, bypassing state consolidated funds.

The union budget does not make any special effort to conceal the massive fiscal transfer that bypasses the constitutional route of transfer to state consolidated funds. A separate table in the budget lists out these items of funding and at the latest, the amounts sent directly to implementing agencies at the state and district levels exceeds Rs 100,000 crore. Apart from the bureaucracy-controlled parallel bodies that gain from this arrangement, the other vested interest in continuing the current off-budget method of transferring funds is banks. At any given time, banks obtain the benefit of around Rs 50,000 crore of public money in the pipeline, lying idle in scheme specific bank accounts held by implementing parallel structures across the country. The losers are state governments, which do not have any precise idea of the funding that swirls around them en route to the field and the LGs, which are starved of funds even as these are parked in parallel structures.

While Finance Minister Jaswant Singh actually operationalized the change from the parallel system to the consolidated fund route for some time, other reform recommendations in this direction lie forgotten. In 2005, the Planning Commission appointed a committee chaired by the former Petroleum Secretary, Arvind Verma to develop concrete proposals for restructuring CSSs. Verma, a laconic man to say the least, presented a short report that did not beat around the bush. The key recommendation of the committee was that no CSS should have an allocation of less than Rs 300 crore. By that yardstick, the committee recommended that only 25 schemes were required and more than 130 small schemes could be closed with only a marginal impact on the fiscal transfer system. The committee also endorsed that CSS guidelines should not contradict the assignment of functions to local governments by state law and that the funds for CSSs should be routed through the consolidated funds of states. Predictably, the report was salted away, never to be considered. The Planning Commission's website also does not have a copy of the report. A more recent report authored by a sitting member of the Planning Commission, B.K. Chaturvedi, which says more or less the same thing, is poised to suffer the same fate.

Another report that makes a pointed recommendation to wind up parallel bodies is still hanging fire. The central Ministry of Rural Development mandates the setting up of DRDAs in every district, to which huge volumes of funds relating to central Rural Development programmes are channelized. Since the setting up of panchayats, pressure has risen to dismantle DRDAs and merge them with district panchayats. It is interesting to note that the Chairperson of the UPA, Sonia Gandhi, wrote a letter in the late-1990s requesting the government to abolish DRDAs, stating that their continuation as independent parallel structures hampered the full development of panchayats as institutions of self-government. However, DRDAs still continue, in spite of a recent report of a high-level committee recommending their dissolution and merger with district panchayats.

Clearly, no will exists to ensure that constitutional institutions perform their rightful duties. Those who seek that the formal structure works as envisaged are rendered impotent in the face of a complex web of relationships between second order institutions that often do not have constitutional or legal status. The examples cited in this chapter are only the tip of the iceberg. Institutional overlapping lurks everywhere. If one observes the urban governance firmament, the situation is even more chaotic. Urban local governments are hemmed in by all manners of special institutions, such as planning authorities, urban development authorities, and water and sewerage boards with which they have no relationship or over which they have very little control.

Despondency might lead a rational observer to ask whether there is any point at all in electing local governments in these circumstances. Why not accept the reality and do away with local governments and run the system as a vertically integrated hierarchy of higher level governments and their institutions? Why do we need this sham of devolution of power to local governments?

There are two reasons why our politicians and bureaucrats wish to keep local governments, even in their truncated and reined in status, alive. From a political point of view, decentralization is a good thing around which a politician can weave rhetoric. For the bureaucracy, the local governments perform an important role, that of being scapegoats for governance failures. When a District Collector who controls real power fails, he can always blame the panchayats. And if the panchayats succeed, then one can rest assured that it will be the collector who will make PowerPoint presentations about what 'he did' for the people, before admiring audiences. It is not an accident that most social audits are arranged by district authorities to arraign Panchayat-elected representatives before their own people. No District Collector or MLA or MP has ever exposed their executive actions to a social audit by local government-elected representatives, or the people directly.

The symptoms of institutional failure are everywhere. Roads that do not get built, bridges that collapse, garbage that does not get collected, and expensive pipelines for water and sewage that leak into each other. There are other less visible, but equally serious failures, such as the failure to control infant and maternal deaths, or to supply food grains or ensure nutrition. An administration that has not been able to run these programmes well through the centralized hierarchical ways and parallel structures is never blamed for these failures or punished for them. It is always the panchayats that can be pulled up, by the press as also by the people themselves, who target the most proximate level of government for their ire. When formal and informal powers do not converge in the same institution, accountability suffers. The real sufferers are the people.

What then, is the answer to India's institutional mess? If this issue is considered too esoteric to be discussed and resolved by people directly and if expert and rational opinion does not cut any ice with the government, where do we go for a resolution of these issues? Typically, the last resort could be legal action. Two issues arise in this connection. First, is an appeal to clear up institutional irrationalities in government a justiciable matter and second, if so, are courts willing to take the bold step of giving directives to the government on how institutions ought to align with the constitutional design?

Remedies: Courts

On the first question, it is worthwhile to consider whether there is a constitutional case for winding up institutions that have lost their relevance, or which have been overtaken by the creation of new institutions entrusted with the same functions. A good ground to test this premise of institutional succession, is the constitutional provisions for setting up local governments.

The Constitution was amended in 1993 through the Seventy-third and Seventy-fourth Constitutional Amendment Acts to provide a constitutional status to local governments in rural and urban areas respectively. These amendments provided for an elaborate framework for ensuring inclusion of all people in the electoral representation system. However, as the subject of local bodies was (and is) a subject matter that comes within the legislative ambit of states, the Constitution left it to the states to determine the range of functions that local governments will perform.[3]

The Constitution further states that notwithstanding anything in it,[4] any provision of any law, relating to LGs in force in a state immediately before the commencement of the Seventy-third and Seventy-fourth Amendment Acts, which is inconsistent with the provisions of these amendments shall continue to be in force until amended or repealed or until the expiration of one year, whichever is earlier.

Read along with the other clauses in the Seventy-third and Seventy-fourth Amendments, Articles 243N and W might give some handle for courts to direct restraint and to ensure that institutional functions do not overlap. However, two recent decisions of the Supreme Court throws light on how courts have tended to interpret issues relating to institutional overlaps. The outcomes are not ideal. The first concerns the constitutional validity of MPLADS. Following the sting operations that exposed the rampant corruption and kickbacks taken by some MPs for sanctioning works under the MPLADS, several writ petitions were filed in the Supreme Court, questioning the constitutional validity of the scheme. The Supreme Court clubbed these and heard them together as the Bhim Singh vs. Union of India case (the MPLADS case):[5] Before the Supreme Court, the petitioners made the submission (among others), that MPLADS, by giving works to individual MPs, is contrary to the Seventy-third and Seventy-fourth Amendments to the Constitution of India, which entrusts the entire area of local self-government to panchayats and municipalities. The choices

[3] Article 243G with respect to panchayats and 243W for municipalities.

[4] Article 243N for panchayats and 243ZF for municipalities.

[5] The judgement was delivered on 6 May 2010. The bench consisted of J. Panchal, P. Sathasivam, D. Jain, R. Raveendran, K. Balakrishnan, JJ.

and functions of the panchayats and municipalities are denuded by it. The petitioners argued that Article 282 contemplates that identifying a public purpose should precede the making of a grant, because in the absence of this exercise, no decision can be taken on the extent of the proposed grant. Under MPLADS, it was contended that the grant precedes the identification of the particular public purpose, and this is contrary to Article 282. The petitioners also submitted that MPLADS is a permanent scheme for transfer of funds each year, which can be done only under Article 275 of the Constitution and not under Article 282, which is a 'Miscellaneous Financial Provision', intended to meet an emergency or an unforeseen situation. They contended that if Article 282 were intended to be used regularly as a second channel for transfers from the centre to the states then it should have found a place along with Articles 268 to 281, under the heading 'Distribution of Revenues between the Union and States'. The petitioners pointed out that any expansion of the scope of Article 282 would necessarily result in the corresponding abridgement of the scope of Article 275, which could not have been intended by the makers of the Constitution. Therefore, it was contended that though Article 282 can be used to transfer money/provide grants to states for use for particular public purposes which may be in the state list, it cannot apply to MPLADS in which an MP exercises executive powers within a state on matters in the state list.

The state averred that the scheme is not inconsistent with the various other schemes of panchayats and municipalities. On the other hand, it only supplements the welfare measures taken by them. There is no violation of the concept of separation of powers.

The court held that MPLADS is *intra vires* the Constitution. With respect to this argument, it held that the Indian Constitution does not recognize strict separation of powers. The constitutional principle of separation of powers will only be violated if an essential function of one branch is taken over by another branch, leading to a removal of checks and balances. It held that LGs have also not been denuded of their role or jurisdiction by the scheme as due place has been accorded to them by the guidelines in the implementation of the scheme. It concluded that under the scheme, though the district authority[6] is given the power to identify the agency through which a particular work recommended by the MP should be executed, Panchayati Raj Institutions (PRIs) will be the

[6] The guidelines show a distinct preference for the District Collector/Deputy Commissioner to be the district authority, as opposed to the district panchayat.

preferred implementing agency in rural areas, through the chief executive of the respective PRI, and implementing agencies in urban areas would be urban local bodies, through the commissioners/chief executive officers of municipal corporations, municipalities. For that reason, the court felt that the scheme did not erode the powers of the LGs.

Another judgement of the Supreme Court relates to the constitutional validity of parallel structures. The Bondu Ramaswamy vs. Bangalore Development Authority case (The Arkavathi case)[7] arose out of the action of the Bangalore Development Authority (BDA) in attempting to acquire land for forming a new layout to the north of Bangalore city. Several writ petitions were filed challenging the acquisition before the Karnataka high court. The petitioner, among other contentions, averred that BDA had no jurisdiction or authority to take up a development scheme in the light of the fact that the Brihat Bangalore Mahanagar Palika (BBMP) was the constitutionally mandated local government having the required jurisdiction. A learned single judge of the Karnataka high court[8] allowed the writ petitions and quashed the entire acquisition holding *inter alia*, that BDA had no jurisdiction or authority to take up any development scheme in the Bangalore Metropolitan Area having regard to parts IX and IXA of the Constitution. Following the overturning of the judgment of the single judge before a division bench of the high court, the matter went in appeal to the Supreme Court. On the question of whether BDA's legitimacy to exist following the constitution of BBMP as a local government, the court held that the benefit of Article 243ZF, prohibiting other institutions that clash with municipal laws, will be available only in regard to laws relating to 'municipalities'. The court took the reasoning that since BDA is not a municipality referred to in Article 243ZF, this article has no relevance to test the validity of the BDA Act. The court observed that Part IX-A seeks to strengthen democratic political governance at the grass-roots level in urban areas by providing constitutional status to municipalities, and Article 243ZF was inserted to provide continuity for some time and an opportunity to state governments to bring the respective enactments relating to municipalities in consonance with the provisions of Part IX-A. The court declared that the object of Article 243ZF was not to invalidate any law relating to or development authorities which operate with reference to a specific and specialized field of planned development of cities by forming

[7] The judgement was delivered on 6 May 2010. The Bench comprised R.V. Raveendran J. and K.G. Balakrishnan CJ.

[8] Gopala Gowda J., as he then was, by order dated 15 April 2005.

layouts and making available plots/houses/apartments to members of the public. The court held that BDA's scope and ambit is separate and distinct from that of a municipality and therefore, Article 243ZF will not come in the way of BDA's existence. The court concluded that merely because a Municipal Corporations Act duly amended to bring it in conformity with Part IX-A of the Constitution exists, that alone will not nullify or render redundant, the BDA Act.

It is in the matter of interpreting the scope of the functional ambit of local governments that the Supreme Court judgements in MPLADS and Arkavathy cases are disappointing. There seems to have been a poor appreciation of the implications of Parts IX and IX-A of the Constitution. It is not appreciated that these amendments have dramatically altered the democratic polity of the country by mandating a third level of government. In the MPLADS case, the judgement states that 'the amendment to the Constitution sought to strengthen the Panchayat system by giving a uniform constitutional base so that the Panchayats become vibrant units of administration in the rural area by establishing strong, effective and democratic local administration so that there can be rapid implementation of rural development programmes'. There is not a word about municipalities and panchayats being institutions of local self-government.

Not considering the implications of the Seventy-third and Seventy-fourth Amendments to be significant is also manifest in the way that the contention that MPLADS denudes the powers of LGs has been rejected. Without entering into an examination of Articles 243N and 243ZE, the court felt that there was no substance in the contention on the sole ground that the MPLADS scheme stated that municipalities and panchayats are 'Preferred agencies' for implementation.[9]

Reading the MPLADS and Arkavathy cases together also can raise cynical smiles; in the MPLADS case, while interpreting whether the Indian system was a true federation or otherwise, the court quoted a previous judgement of itself[10] in support of its conclusions as follows: 'The Constitution is not an ephemeral legal document embodying a set of legal rules for the passing hour. It sets out principles for an expanding future and is intended to

[9] A reading of the MPLADS guidelines will also show that this means nothing. In the guidelines, it is LG's CEO, who is responsible for implementation, not the LG itself. This distinction is a real one, as most CEOs are appointed by the government and see a clear difference between their actions as CEOs of LGs and as individual agents of higher level governments.

[10] M. Nagaraj vs. Union of India (2006) 8 SCC 212.

endure for ages to come and consequently to be adapted to the various crises of human affairs. Therefore, a purposive rather than a strict literal approach to the interpretation should be adopted. A constitutional provision must be construed not in a narrow and constricted sense but in a wide and liberal manner so as to anticipate and take account of changing conditions and purposes so that a constitutional provision does not get fossilised but remains flexible enough to meet the newly emerging problems and challenges.' However, such sentiments were noticeably absent in the approach taken in the Arkavathy case, where a literal and restrictive interpretation of Article 243ZF was adopted in coming to the conclusion that the BDA Act is not one that relates to municipalities, even though BDA's activities significantly overlap with BBMP's functional ambit.

Several conclusions made in the Arkavathy and MPLADS cases seem to be an incorrect appreciation of facts. In the Arkavathy case, the court does not accept the contention that BDA is not a representative body and states that it has several elected representatives on it. Immediately thereafter, the judgement proceeds to list the representatives and discovers that of the 22 board members only four are nominated from amongst elected members, two MLAs, and two Bangalore city corporators. It then changes track and observes that BDA's membership pattern is more suited to fulfil the requirements of a specialist agency executing development schemes. The court seems unaware of the fine distinction between an elected body and a body to which a few elected representatives are nominated. In the MPLADS case, the court avers that there is a system of accountability inherent in the scheme. Any reader of the scheme's guidelines will be hard put to find a convincing system therein.

One of the disturbing aspects of the findings of the Arkavathy case is its conclusion that the BDA Act is not relatable to municipalities and therefore the question of inconsistency with Part IXA does not arise. If this position is maintained then it is possible to argue that most of the parastatals dealing with several of the items in the Eleventh and Twelfth Schedules operate in a field different from panchayats and municipalities and therefore are not relatable to Parts IX and IX-A. If so, the stipulation of inconsistency under Articles 243N and 243ZF cannot ever be invoked against all the missions and societies that implement schemes in the functional domain of LGs. This will eventually denude the functional domain of the local bodies to the barest minimum. We will then have panchayats and municipalities as formal shell institutions, without any substance, with real power being wielded by a plethora of parallel structures that ultimately are not accountable for failure to deliver.

It is clear that the courts at the moment see LGs as nothing more than agencies of higher-level governments, within a largely centralized polity. It is this absence of an appreciation that panchayats and municipalities are local governments, and not merely agencies of higher levels of government that permeates both the MPLADS and the Arkavathy judgements. The endorsement of systems of overlapping responsibilities between governments and the acceptance that MPs can engage in pork barrel schemes, spells a dismal augury for the future of accountability and fixing of responsibility on the appropriate level of government for failures of governance. These judgements can open the floodgates in the sanction of new patronage based schemes, or enlargement of older ones.

***

What then, is the answer? Policy recommendations for institutional euthanasia are all in place. Yet the centre and the states are disinclined to clear the field and have few strong institutions with clearly defined responsibilities and with robust accountability structures. Clearly, they are the beneficiaries of weak accountability structures and hence the disinclination. Courts too do not seem overly bothered by this grievous fault in our governance DNA and the recent judgements in the MPLADS and Arkavathy cases are disappointing auguries for the future. The only hope left is to continue to point out the absurdities and contradictions in these arrangements. The other hope is for LGs to assume their roles as governments and not agencies; to occupy the vacuum that higher level governments and their ramshackle welter of institutions have left. As long as LGs continue to look upward and beseech higher levels to transfer power, they will be at the latter's mercy. On the other hand, if they assume powers and perform as effective and responsive agents of those who elect them, they will gain the credibility that will move the higher levels to recognize the new emerging power structure and concede ground. Last, citizens will need to learn the basics of governance and at the very least, understand which level of government is responsible for what categories of responsibilities so that they can apply pressure on the right authority for improving the services that that authority delivers.

References

Bagchi, A. (2003), 'Fifty Years of Fiscal Federalism in India: An Appraisal', NIPFP Working Paper, No. 02, New Delhi.

Bardhan, Pranab (2002), 'Decentralization of Governance and Development', *Journal of Economic Perspectives*, 16(4): 185–205.

Chakraborty, P. and T.M.T. Isaac (2008), 'Intergovernmental Transfers: Disquieting Trends and the Thirteenth Finance Commission', *Economic and Political Weekly*, 43(43): 86–92.

Lindberg, Staffan I. (2009), 'Accountability: The Core Concept and Its Subtypes', Working Paper No. 1, published on behalf of the Africa Power and Politics Programme (APPP) by the Overseas Development Institute, London. Available at: http://www.dfid.gov.uk/R4D//PDF/Outputs/APPP/APPP-WP1.pdf (last accessed on 2 November 2012).

Sezhiyan, Era (2005), *MPLADS—Concept, Confusion and Contradictions*. New Delhi: The Institute of Social Sciences.

CHAPTER 18

LAW AND REGULATION

towards social control of economic activities in india

A.V. RAJA AND

FRANCIS XAVIER RATHINAM

It is now widely recognized that institutional arrangements of countries have a significant impact on creating the incentives for, or obstacles to, the development process. The presence of asymmetric information, moral hazard, opportunistic behaviour, and externalities in economic activities necessitate institutional arrangements to deter such behaviour and reduce undesirable effects. There are many ways in which this can be done. Essentially, a country can adopt private law to exercise social control of economic activities, or use regulation (public law) or hand over ownership of resources to the government.

At low levels of economic development, both the judiciary and the regulatory structure may be susceptible to capture by interest groups. As the economy moves up the development ladder, either of the mechanisms, or any mix thereof, would work better. The choice of which mix of these forms will dominate or be chosen will depend on civic capital, the characteristics of the industry concerned, the relative power of interest groups, and the state of economic development itself. This chapter explores whether, and to what extent, the legal system and regulation determine the social control of economic activities, and hence economic development in

India. We assess, for specific sectors of the Indian economy, how law and regulation help in building a stronger governance structure and help in furthering the development process. The chapter focuses on the financial sector and environmental regulations in India.

The quality of legal protection of creditors and investors, and the extent and effectiveness of financial sector regulations were shaped by political choice in India. The interests of the political class and the industry, primarily the ones subjected to central planning, were well aligned to keep the banking sector tightly regulated. On the other hand, dominant forces in the new fast-growing services sector and high-tech manufacturing industry, which relied more on equity finance, sought for more market oriented reforms in equity markets. In sum, there was considerable support for equity market reforms and not as much support for debt market reforms (creditor rights, insolvency laws, and banking entry regulation). This unique difference in the demand for legal protection by the industry, well aligned with the interest of the government, led to a spectacular growth of equity markets, while the banking sector, though resilient during crises, was still impaired by lack of competition and excessive government back-up and bail-outs (Acharya and Kulkarni 2012; Armour and Lele 2009; Buiter and Patel 2005). The judiciary, constrained by backlogs, procedural hurdles, and archaic laws that emphasized banning of financial products rather than regulating them (GoI 2012), played only a limited role. The government proposed several reforms to speed up recovery and reduce court backlogs. The Supreme Court upheld major creditor protection reforms that helped credit recovery due to banks, but reforms in contract enforcement in general and those in bankruptcy procedures are yet to materialize.

The second is the quality of the environment. Protection against environmental harm is primarily given in the Indian tort law. However, during the 1970s and 1980s the government constituted several environment regulatory agencies to enact and enforce standards on hazardous waste, micro-organisms, noise, toxic chemicals, and air, water, and vehicular pollution. The agencies wielded vast powers including the right to initiate proceedings without affected party complaints. We argue that the regulation of the environment was largely captured by interest groups and forced the government to legislate weak laws and/or allowed lax enforcement (Rathinam and Raja 2011). Due to rational apathy and/or lack of access to justice by the affected sections of society, the law in the books did not translate well into law on the street. Regulatory failure and the problem of access to justice, however, did not go unnoticed by the judiciary. The court's initiative to improve access to justice, the public interest litigation, also offered an alternative to the failure of the executive to carry out its regulatory obligations. This interaction of the courts, the government, and civic bodies is analysed from case law in the context of the environment.

This chapter is organized as follows: the next section discusses the relative role of courts and regulation in shaping the financial sector, especially the role of interest groups, the changing political dynamics that led to reforms, and the role of, or rather lack of presence of the judiciary in the recent growth story. The next section discusses the role of the executive and the courts in environmental regulation in India, especially the executive's failure in checking the depletion of forests and urban air pollution, and the efficiency and desirability of subsequent court intervention. The conclusion follows.

Law and Regulation in Financial Sector in India

This section analyses the nature, choice, and role of regulation (administrative rules), and courts (precedents) in defining the rules of the game for the financial sector in India. The financial sector requires a strong institutional apparatus—a central authority, usually the government, to enforce disclosure, supervision and deposit insurance, and a legal apparatus for contract enforcement. However, the government's involvement in the financial sector may be motivated more by political survival than any economic rationale or public interest. The incumbent firms will support financial repression that serves as a barrier to entry in non-financial markets. In this section we analyse how dominant interest groups shape the rules using recent reforms in the financial sector and the role played by the judiciary.

Political Economy of Financial Sector Regulation in the Planning Era

In the early years of Independence, as the government needed to mobilize savings for developmental expenditure and channel resources to priority sectors, financial repression, as practised in many catch-up countries, was inevitable. First, the government ensured rent for banks by restricting competition within the banking sector by entry restrictions for new and foreign banks and virtually eliminated competition from direct financial markets—securities and corporate bond markets.[1] Second, prudential measures and lending requirements and restrictions on banks helped channel the resources into government hands for public spending. The central bank, RBI, was subordinated to government with quasi-fiscal responsibilities (Chandavarkar 2005).

The Indian business elite, a handful of well-organized family-owned industrial houses, extracted considerable influence through various channels—election and individual contributions and organized industry associations (Kochanek 1987). Industrial houses in the large manufacturing sector, relying mainly on internal sources and bank relational lending for their investment needs, were well served by the repressed financial sector.

The planning era had also given rise to new interest groups, such as bureaucrats, white-collar government employees and organized labourers, and politically well-connected large and medium farmers. As the beneficiaries of the planning regime, they supported government control in all walks of life: it meant license-issuing power and corrupt income for bureaucrats; job security for white-collar and organized labourers; and cheap credit, and more often than not credit waivers for large and medium farmers (Bardhan 2011). The resultant political equilibrium—a network of subsidies, concessional credit, tax exemption on agricultural incomes and wealth, and write-offs of loans to farmers; over-staffing in the public sector including financial institutions; failure to wind up sick firms; and populous freebies—was built on a repressed financial system.

Captured banking sector resources were directed to politically powerful industrial houses and to more numerous and vocal large and medium farmers. For example, government-owned financial institutions lent more to large industrial houses and, hence, these firms raised fewer resources from internal sources in the 1970s vis-à-vis the 1960s (Bardhan 2011; Uppal 1986); farmers received politically motivated loans from public

[1] Controller of capital issues (CCI) required prior permission to issues shares and dictated the price and quantity of shares to be issued; hence, it made raising capital through equity markets non-viable (Thomas 2005) while scores of structural factors, such as poor legal apparatus and administrative hurdles crippled the bond market (Khanna and Varottil 2012).

sector banks before elections and loan waivers after election victories which did not bear any positive impact on agricultural output (Cole 2009); and Banerjee and Duflo (2004) show that the small and new firms were under-served by banks.

In sum, the interest of dominant players—government, incumbent industry, bureaucrats, white-collar government employees, organized labourers, and large and medium farmers—were well aligned. As the economy was struck in a low-equilibrium trap, there were extensive arrangements, such as subsidies and cheap credit to share the spoils among interest groups. Financial repression was integral to this scheme.

Regulation in the Post-reforms Era

Many things changed in the economic landscape in the 1980s. A large pool of technically educated Indians with relatively less opportunities in a stagnant manufacturing sector and the availability of technology import through joint ventures led to the emergence of high-tech manufacturing and services, especially the newer sunrise small- and medium-scale industries, such as software, electronics, and high-tech manufacturing as a new powerful industrial group; the emergence of powerful regional political parties, coalition politics, and the subsequent state-dominant political scenario led to considerable competition among states to outgrow one another where the states with a head-start lobbied for faster market-friendly reforms. There was also significant change in the upper echelons of the bureaucracy, where the view that the government had over-reached and needed to scale back gained considerable support.

The changing political interest groups had directed a specific path to financial sector reforms. Newly emerging high-tech and software industries that typically relied on equity rather than debt favoured quick equity market reforms. Among the traditional industry coalitions, breaking up of northern and southern manufactures, who were typically smaller firms, supported faster liberalization as they relied on external capital more than their larger cousins in the parent association (Kochanek 1987; Pedersen 2000). Equity markets, still in their nascent stages in the late 1980s, did not have many interest groups—except traditional brokerage houses that benefited from the erstwhile mutualized exchange set-up—opposing the reforms. The Securities and Exchange Board of India (SEBI), as against RBI, was free of conflicts of interest in functioning by virtue of being a newcomer and also enjoyed relative independence from the Ministry of Finance. Many of the reform efforts came as by-laws and rules enacted by SEBI which did not require government enactment. Hence, they went unnoticed on the political radar; it was regulation by stealth rather than by brokering an overarching political consensus (Bardhan 2011).

Major equity market reforms include, first, a national platform that widened the participation, electronic order matching, and guaranteed settlement through centralized counter-parties; and second, reforms in the organizational structure of exchanges to enable competition and transparency. The result was quite dramatic: liquidity and daily turnover went up; brokerage fees was slashed; transaction costs decreased to international standards; and it also set the tone for further reforms and innovations in other financial markets (Thomas 2005).

While equity markets came as by-laws, banking reforms required a mix of new laws by the government and rules by the regulator. As the need for external finance was growing, RBI had introduced a series of steps to ensure more transparency and prudence in bank management and independence of banks in deciding interest rates and credit allocations. Historical weaknesses, such as inadequate legal apparatus for enforcing contract was partially corrected by a series of Acts—the Recovery of Debt Due to Banks and Financial Institutions Act, 1993 and the Securitization and Reconstruction of Financial Assets and Enforcement of Security Interest Act, 2002 (SARFAESI)—which allowed financial institutions to quickly recover the bad debt or sell it to asset reconstruction companies. This process was swifter as *de novo* private banks backed faster creditor protection reforms.

Banking sector reforms in general lacked vigour vis-à-vis stock market reforms, especially in enhancing competition and efficiency and hence depth. First, the dominance of public sector banks in the industry slowed down the pace of reforms to their convenience. Further, poor incentives for the management inherent in the public banking system, and the fear of a bad debt evoking vigilance enquiries, were also a drag on public banks' ability to respond to a changing environment and reforms. While any act of commission may come under the scanner of the enforcement agencies, the act of omission (read inaction) would go unnoticed creating built-in incentives in the system for lazy banking, which in turn worked well for the government that used the banks as quasi-fiscal instruments (Banerjee et al. 2005). There was also complementarity between the dominance of public financial institutions and the lack of impetus for reforming institutional bottlenecks, such as bankruptcy and collateral laws. With explicit government back-up, public sector banks did not need swift legal reforms, while private sector banks did not grow to be a threat without adequate legal reforms. In sum, the Indian banking sector remains a passive conduit for channelling resources rather than allocating capital to its best use (Buiter and Patel 2005).

The Indian financial sector, however, came out unscathed during the financial crisis of 2008–9. This was mainly attributed to stringent regulations and the presence of public sector banks. It is argued that selective deregulation, especially limiting access to international financial markets—restrictions such as eligibility criteria, caps, minimum maturity period, and end user criteria—prevented excessive exposure to international markets despite domestic distortions (Goyal 2012). While prudential regulation is absolutely essential for financial stability, it is important to note that RBI's excessive interventions in bank investment decisions, lack of competition, and the dominant presence of government in the banking sector did not help in allocating resources efficiently. Public sector banks, though fared well against private sector banks during the crisis: they raised more deposits, lent more, and their stock earnings were superior. This, however, may not be read as public banks' ability to be resilient vis-à-vis private banks, as public banks' performance could be attributed to explicit government guarantees (Acharya and Kulkarni 2012). Public sector banks remain more fragile in terms of systemic risk measured by marginal expected shortfall (MES)—the tail dependence of each firm on the stock market as a whole.

The political choice of reforms and the resultant financial structure meant that the main source of investment for non-financial firms were retained earnings followed by bank credit, equity, and corporate bonds (RBI 2007). Studies using firm-level data confirm the same pattern. The most important financing channel is internal finance, though in the 1990s during the equity boom external finance was dominant; of external sources, banks and financial institutions are dominant followed by trade dues and other current liabilities (financing from other sources including the informal sector). Small and medium enterprises (SMEs), in particular, rely on the informal sector for about 50 per cent of their funding needs (Allen et al. 2012). This points to that fact that the informal financing sector is still a dominant factor for small firms which is possibly costlier than bank and market finance. The poor legal apparatus for credit recovery played a role in constraining the expansion of the formal financial sector.

The Role of Courts on Resolving Financial Disputes

The judiciary in India is fairly independent of the executive. It was the bulwark of upholding the fundamental and property rights of citizens against the arbitrariness of the government. Judicial review was an effective check on all executive actions, such as enactment and implementation.[2] Though there was ample scope for the judiciary to play a wider role in shaping the financial sector, it did not play a significant role. Financial contract enforcement and insolvency matters were the prerogative of the courts. Unsustainable and ever-increasing backlogs crippled court activism in financial disputes.[3] Further, using courts to solve a dispute is not the first choice for firms, both financial and non-financial. For example, in a survey conducted by Allen et al. (2012), about 80 per cent of the respondent firms indicated that recourse to courts would not be their first choice in case of a breach of contract. Though this is true for all firms, irrespective of their size and age, there is complete absence of a legal deterrence among small firms.

Inadequate court activism and the firms' reluctance to use courts as an enforcer is striking as India provides world class substantive laws for protecting investors and creditors. La Porta et al. (1998) rank India among the top in creditor rights and anti-director rights. The quality of enforcement, however, is below par: in the legal formalism index constructed by Djankov et al. (2003) and the legality index of Berkowitz et al. (2003), India ranks well below the English common-law origin countries—a poor 3.51 and 11.35, respectively (Table 18.1). India provides good substantive law on paper, but weak enforcement and judicial delays are major lacunae.

Following the recommendations of the Rajamannar Committee (1977) and the Tiwari Committee (1981) and Narasimhan Committee (1991) to constitute a specialized court to resolve cases involving bank and financial institution loan defaults, a specialized tribunal—the Debt Recovery Tribunal (DRT)—was constituted as a quasi-judicial entity under the executive arm of the government. Unlike civil courts, DRT follows a summary procedure for fact-finding, speeding up the process of summoning,

[2] However, there were many conflicts between the judiciary and the government on land reforms, credit market reforms, etc.

[3] Financial cases, especially default cases due to financial institutions, directed to civil courts were pending for approximately 8 to 10 years (Law Commission of India 1988). This delay was mainly attributed to the lacunas in the Code of Civil Procedures (1908) which allowed for excessive appeals and re-appeals.

Table 18.1 Investor and Creditor Protection in India: A Comparison

	Creditor Rights‡	Anti-director Rights‡	Legal Formalism Index#	Legality Index*
India	4	5	3.51	11.35
Average of EMs	1.47	3.64	4.07	10.25
La Porta et al. (1998) country groups				
English-origin Ave.	2.28	4.19	3.02	15.56
French-origin Ave.	1.31	2.91	4.38	13.11
German-origin Ave.	2.33	3.04	3.57	15.53
Nordic-origin Ave.	1.75	3.8	3.32	16.42

Source: Compiled by Allen et al. (2012); ‡ La Porta et al. (1998); # Formalism index proposed by Djankov et al. (2003) measure the level of intervention in the judicial process for eviction of a tenant where higher the number slower the courts; * Legality index of Berkowitz et al. (2003) is a principal component combining five legal proxies (efficiency of the judiciary, rule of law, absence of corruption, risk of expropriation, and risk of contract repudiation) where the higher the number indicates better legal environment.

hearing and execution of decrees, and allowing only one further appeal to the appellate tribunal.

The Act has evoked a huge debate on the constitutional validity as DRTs enjoy exclusive jurisdiction to pass decrees and execute proceedings in recovery cases due to banks and other financial institutions. The Delhi high court in the Delhi Bar Association vs. UOI (AIR 1995 Del 323), maintained that the Act is unconstitutional as it erodes the rights of the high court; the procedures are unreasonable and the limits to appeal and mandatory deposit of 75 per cent of the disputed value are arbitrary and unjustifiable. However, the Supreme Court of India overruled the verdict of the Delhi high court stating that constituting tribunals, now an effective part of the justice delivery system, do not erode the independence of the judiciary. With the new amendment, the Act is just as it promotes swift recovery of debts; further, the decisions of DRT and appellate tribunals are not final as they can be subjected to judicial review (Union of India vs. Delhi High Court Bar Association (2002) 4 SCC 275).

Similarly, the Supreme Court upheld the validity of the SARFAESI Act.[4] These were, however, reforms pertaining only to credit due to banks and financial institutions. The role of courts as an enforcer of financial

[4] Mardia Chemicals Ltd. vs. Union of India, (2004) 4 SCC 311.

contract in general is not effective due to huge backlogs and complex laws governing bankruptcy and liquidation. However, recent initiatives such as the National Legal Mission and the approach paper issued by the Financial Sector Legislative Reforms Commission (FSLRC) augur well for consolidating financial sector laws and speeding up disposal rates.

The Report of the Working Group for the Twelfth Five-year Plan (2012–17) that proposed the National Legal Mission suggested several promising initiatives, such as enhancing a judge-population ratio and court infrastructure, rationalizing government litigation, and set of procedural overhauling—constituting small cause courts, pre-litigation and alternate dispute resolution systems, and introducing a manual for summary trial procedures and providing a life span for trials depending on their complexity. Other initiatives to speed up bankruptcy procedures, especially the proposed National Company Law Tribunal (NCLT) that would consolidate the powers conferred in the Companies Act, Sick Industrial Companies Act, and high courts, are promising but yet to materialize. The other initiative, FSLRC, is set out to create a consistent framework for consolidating multiple laws and multiple regulatory agencies covering various segments in financial markets to eliminate regulatory gaps and overlaps (GoI 2012).

In sum, the Indian legal apparatus—a strong substantive law, complex procedures, and weak enforcement—to enforce financial contracts is inadequate at present. But the proposed reforms are promising.

Law, Environment, and the Judiciary

In this section, we focus on the role of regulations and the rise of judicial activism in the field of environmental regulation in India. The questions that we address here have more to do with the implementation of environmental regulations rather than on the laws relating to the environment per se. As in the previous section we take the larger political economy question into account, namely the role of the government in a democracy.

The Central Problem of the Environment: Depletion, Degradation, and Pollution

Regulation, or the need for it, depends on the nature of the problem. The basic framework for understanding depletion and degradation pertains to property rights (Ostrom 1999), whereas the problems of pollution revolve around the problem of correcting negative externalities.

Depletion and Degradation of Environmental Resources

Property rights are a bundle of rights to ownership, use, and transfer of any property. The basic argument is that the problems of the environment stem from mis-specification of property rights. When property rights change, the rights to use, own, and transfer also change. This can create conditions for the degradation or depletion of the resource. For example, it is well known that open access resources, ones in which it is difficult to exclude agents from the using them, will lead to depletion of the resources. Mainstream literature argues that lack of property rights leads to the famous 'tragedy of the commons'. The usual prescription is to reinstate specific, unambiguous property rights over the resource, in other words, privatize the resource. However, it is now understood that common property resources need not result in the tragedy of the commons as it was earlier thought. Indeed a distinction is to be made between common property resources and open access resources. Community held ownership of resources, which is closely related to the common property concept, can be more efficient in the management of the resource under certain conditions. The state plays an important role since in such contexts there is a need to regulate efficiently and prevent resources from becoming open access regimes. If monitoring property by the state is weak, then such resources will de facto become open access resources, leading to their degradation or depletion. The second aspect of the problem is that the state may be 'captured' by powerful stakeholders who will pressure it to enact laws that will favour them rather than cater to public interest.

The Problem of Pollution

Typically, pollution is regarded as a negative externality and therefore a market failure manifests itself. Taxation (such as an emission tax or a green tax) is the suggested method to 'correct' for the market failure. However, correcting for externalities requires information about the costs that the externality has inflicted. In the case of environmental pollution (whether it be air, water, or ground soil) this information is hard to obtain. In many cases it is difficult to identify polluters, damages are diffused, and their effects are felt over a long period of time. In such cases, regulation by the state in the form of setting up environmental standards, such as ambient air quality standards, is the remedy. Regulatory measures are typically enforced through the coercive powers of the state. The state is assumed to act in public interest by enforcing regulations. However, literature on public choice theory questions this assumption. Environmental pollution and its effects are diffused and there is a weak link between state regulation and pollution levels. Hence, the state can shirk in carrying out its duties, especially if the polluters are large industries that may significantly contribute to election funds. This chapter analyses the role of the judiciary in the light of these problems. The fundamental role that the judicial system plays in strengthening institutions in India is analysed with respect to the problems of degradation and depletion of forests in India and to the problem of air pollution in urban cities.

The Case of Depletion and Degradation of India's Forests

The twin problems of degradation and depletion of natural resources stem from a mis-specification of the property rights regimes. We analyse how property rights related to forests in India are defined, the problem of depletion of forest cover (due to unregulated felling of trees), and the degradation of forest land due to alternative activity (such as agriculture). The Forest Act of 1865 empowered the government to declare forests as government land (reserved forests). However, the government found the 1865 Act inadequate as the prevalence of customary rights came in the way of imposing state control over forests (Balooni and Inone 2009). The legislation of 1878 to the Forest Act of 1865 and, later, the National Forest Policy of 1894, stipulated that:

> Forests which are the reservoirs of valuable timbers should be managed on commercial lines as a source of revenue to the State '... wherever an effective demand for cultivable land exists and can only be supplied [by a] forest area, the land should ordinarily be relinquished without hesitation.

This changed the property rights regime of these resources. For example, forests, which were used by tribes, had their informal property rights over the forest taken away from them. Communally owned property of villages became government property.[5] The Government of India's resolution

[5] 'Common property regimes controlling access and harvesting from local streams, forests, grazing areas, and inshore fisheries had evolved over long periods of time in all parts of the world, but were rarely given formal status in the legal codes of newly independent countries' (Ostrom 1999: 336).

(No. 13/52/F) dated 12 May 1952 formulated a forest policy for the protection of forests in the country. However, in the National Forest Policy of 1988, it was acknowledged that:

> Forests in the country have suffered serious depletion. This is attributable to *relentless pressures* arising from ever-increasing demand for fuel-wood, fodder and timber; inadequacy of protection measures; diversion of forest lands to nonforest uses without ensuring compensatory afforestation and essential environmental safeguards; and the tendency to look upon forests as revenue earning resource (emphasis added).

This may refer to the pressures emanating from other stakeholders who may be large, and more powerful, and capable of twisting the decisions towards their ends. The permissions given for projects in the name of 'development' which encroach on forest lands is an example. The second deficiency is the lack of a reliable inventory of forests:

> There is no reliable assessment of the growing stock of trees at state level.[6] Other deficits include a lack of data on different products from forests and a lack of increment and biomass data. It is difficult to make economic assessments and set policies without quality data and information on both the tangible and intangible benefits of forests.[7]

The third failure relates to 'illegal felling of trees' that somehow elude the state's monitoring mechanisms. Thus, there is sufficient evidence that the state has not been able to prevent the depletion of forest cover in recent years. Forests in many states have thus become de facto open access resources.

Role of the Judiciary—The Godavarman Case

Large-scale illegal felling of timber and denuding of the forests in Gudalur taluka in Nilgiri which went unchecked even though it was under the purview of the state government of Tamil Nadu. This prompted the filing of a Civil Writ Petition (T.N. Godavarman Thirumulpad vs. Union of India and Others (W.P. (C) No. 202/1995)) in 1995. This single case started what would be the largest judicial intervention by the Supreme Court on the

[6] Here the word state refers to the different states in India delimited by legal boundaries.

[7] The Challenges for the Indian Forestry Sector International Institute for Systems' analysis and TIFAC Policy brief #5 (February 2009).

use and conservation of forests in India. Although the initial writ referred only to the particular region, the counsel brought to the notice of the court many such instances of violations on the use of forests. The court reacted by enlarging the scope of the petition to include all forests in India. The notice issued to all chief secretaries of all state governments in 1996 made the state a party to all the petitions of a similar nature that were filed.

The Apex Court observed that there was no explicit mention of the nature of ownership of forests in the Forest Act.[8] The first reinterpretation of the Act was clarifying on ownership issues. The court stated that that the act was applicable to all forests irrespective of ownership or classification (TGS, p. 8). This effectively put to rest various claims of ownership or interpretations of what constitutes a forest.

The court ordered that all decisions on the use of forests must have prior approval of the central government and would be subject to the scrutiny of the Apex Court. This was done with the help of appointing various expert committees, *amicus curiae*, filing of bi-monthly action taken reports (ATRs), and imposing costs and contempt proceedings against erring officials. Thus, other dimensions of property rights become an important consideration and will have to take into account others rights such as the right to use when taking decisions on the use of forests. Earlier, since regulatory authorities were the various state governments, right to use was given based on the bargaining powers of the users, now that power wielded over ineffectual regulators was curtailed.

The upshot of this is that the judiciary has stepped in to correct 'government failure'. However, since all governments are subject to capture, the judiciary cannot exercise control on all government decisions. Alternative institutions that evolved as a result of a large number of conflicts can be seen as a result of state failure as well as the limitation of judicial interventions in the matter.

The Joint Forest Management (JFM) policy that has evolved over the years in India is a promising alternative for managing forests by primary stakeholders rather than by the state and has emerged due to the state's failure to manage forests. Over the years there have been around 84,000 such JFM committees in 27 states that manage forest at a micro-level (Balooni and Inone 2009). This shows that the way forward for sustainable management of common property resources is in evolving a property

[8] This section is based on material provided by ELDF and WWF India 2009, Protection of Forests in India—The Godavarman Story, New Delhi. Referred to as TGS hereafter.

rights regime that gives back to some of the primary stakeholders the rights to use which were taken away by the state.

The Case of Air Pollution

Problems of pollution control are due to the diffused nature of damages and uncertain causal links. In all such cases the choice of regulation is formulating ambient air quality standards and appointing a regulator to monitor it. In India, the government appointed several bodies such as the Pollution Control Board of India to carry out this task. However, as in the case with forests, there has been evidence that many of the regulatory agencies were not effective in controlling pollution (Rathinam and Raja 2011). There are two problems associated with this failure. Regulatory capture can be either at the time of enacting the standards themselves (ex ante legislative capture) wherein the state may enact legislation that is weak and leaves many loopholes for interest groups to exploit, or it can be at the time of enforcement (ex post executive capture).

The problem of ineffective regulation can be checked in several ways. The first is through private litigation. However, this presumes that the litigant is the affected party and hence has *locus standi* in the case. Second, it also assumes a level of awareness of such issues and awareness of one's own rights. Those who have this awareness are also those who have the means of protecting themselves and hence do not find it worthwhile to take up the cause.

The second check could be through civil society actions if civil society is strong enough and has the right information about pollution levels and their effects on health. India is a country where such environmental awareness is largely lacking. This also gives a corridor of non-accountability to the state to shirk and/or cater to interest groups (for example allowing industry to pollute).

Public Interest Litigations and the Role of the Judiciary

Once again, the judiciary played a role in dealing with executive inaction. The resulting changes in law that helped in making judicial intervention in controlling pollution effective did not stem from environmental considerations but from a concern regarding *access to justice* to those who do not have the means to do so. The innovation in the law was to relax the locus standi requirements so that the court can be moved by any individual or individuals who are not directly affected by the problem. This innovation, referred to as public interest litigations (PILs), has played a major role in controlling environmental pollution.

A case study on Delhi air pollution wherein a PIL was filed against the Delhi municipality by M.C. Mehta is an example. Rathinam and Raja (2011) uncovered several interesting facets of the case. First, PILs are filed only in the higher courts thus mitigating the problems of long drawn-out court cases and capture of the judiciary at the lower levels. Second, since a PIL can be filed by any public spirited citizen, there cannot be the possibility of buying out of potential litigants by polluters thereby only partially internalizing the externality. The third interesting feature is that PILs themselves generate a significant interest in the media thus exposing the failure of the state in doing its public duty. This exerts pressure on governments and acts as an informal regulation of the regulators. A study of documents pertaining to the New Delhi pollution case, show regulatory capture at both the legislative level as well as in execution. Using auto regressive distributed lag models and univariate structural break models, the study clearly shows two results: the first is that the series of orders that the Supreme Court handed down to the Delhi Municipal Corporation on air pollution were effective in getting the regulator to enforce the standards. The second is that the spillover effect that the case generated in the media did correlate with the controlling of pollution levels. Once again judicial intervention did help in getting the state to act.

Faure and Raja (2010) undertook a deeper study on PILs and have several reservations on this kind of judicial intervention. First, it is not clear that public spirited citizens who have the welfare of the affected parties at hand will come forth in large numbers. Second, relaxing the locus standi in itself can lead to frivolous litigation. Third, PILs can at best be a second best solution to efficient legislation. However, in the light of the problems that are peculiar to developing countries and to India in particular, the study does acknowledge that judicial intervention did bring about changes in the circumstances for the better.

***

This chapter argued that law and regulation are complementary in social control of economic activities. However, the choice of using courts and/or regulators, though influenced by many factors, such as the state of economic development, civic capital, and industry characteristics, is predominantly political. Interest groups, through a grand political bargain, choose the mix that serves their best interests. Here, we highlighted the role of interest groups in determining the nature of social control in India using financial and environmental regulations and commented on the role of the judiciary in circumventing the problems of capture.

The choice of level, and type, of financial regulation is determined by politicians, incumbent industry, and other interest groups. The changes in the relative power of these constituencies will determine the specific course of action, that is, financial liberalization or re-regulation and determine who stands to gain more. During the quota–licence era, the interests of pressure groups were well aligned to keep the financial sector repressed and the spoils were shared. Emergence of new interest groups, especially sunrise industries that needed external finance led to swift equity market reforms and *de novo* private banks lobbied for creditor protection reforms, at least those pertaining to financial institutions. Further reforms, especially ensuring competition in the banking industry and kick-starting the corporate bond market that require a mixture of tough reforms in laws governing collaterals, creditors other than financial institutions, bankruptcy law and labour laws, have not witnessed much progress.

Environmental cases involve victims who are unaware of their rights, the extent of harm inflicted upon them, and are too numerous and marginally affected to come together for a solution. This inability of the victims makes it easier for the well-organized and politically powerful beneficiaries to capture environmental law-making and implementation. Hence, judicial intervention in the best interest of the public is a quick fix solution. The case studies in this chapter show clearly that the judiciary has been actively pursuing issues that were best left to the executive. In many cases it has succeeded in bringing about a change but in many cases this has been limited. The criticisms of judicial activism are many. First, the judiciary does not have the expertise to deal with all issues. Second, it intervenes in areas that blur the separation of power between the three branches of the government. However, as participatory democracy is still not strong enough in India, until such time when the state is made more accountable to the people, interest groups will continue to further their own interests. If judicial activism is a reaction against a dysfunctional executive, then we may conclude that the judiciary will continue to be the watchdog of the actions of the government.

References

Acharya, V. and N. Kulkarni (2012), 'What Saved the Indian Banking System: State Ownership or State Guarantees?', *The World Economy*, 35(1): 19–31.

Allen, F., R. Chakrabarti, S. De, and J. Qian (2012), 'Financing firms in India', *Journal of Financial Intermediation*, 21(3): 409–45.

Armour, J. and P. Lele (2009), 'Law, Finance and Politics: The Case of India', *Law and Society Review*, 43: 491–526.

Balooni, K. and M. Inone (2009), *Joint Forest Management in India: The Management Change Process*. Bangalore: IIMB Management Review.

Banerjee, A.V. and E. Duflo (2004), 'Do Firms Want to Borrow More? Testing Credit Constraints Using a Directed Lending Program', mimeo, MIT.

Banerjee, A.V., S. Cole., and E. Duflo (2005), Banking Reform in India'. *India Policy Forum*, 1: 277–323.

Bardhan, P. (2011) [1984], *The Political Economy of Development in India*. New Delhi: Oxford University Press.

Berkowitz, D., K. Pistor, and J. Richard (2003), 'Economic Development, Legality, and the Transplant Effect', *European Economic Review*, 47: 165–95.

Buiter, W and U. Patel (2005), 'Excessive Budget Deficits, a Government-Abused Financial System, and Fiscal Rules', *India Policy Forum*, 2(1): 1–54.

Chandavarkar, A. (2005), 'Towards an Independent Federal Reserve Bank of India: A Political Economy Agenda for Reconstitution.' *Economic and Political Weekly*, 40(35): 3839–45.

Cole, S. (2009), 'Fixing Market Failures or Fixing Elections? Agricultural Credit in India', *American Economic Journal: Applied Economics*, 1(1): 219–50.

Djankov, S., R. La Porta, F. Lopez-de-Silanes, and A. Shleifer (2003), 'Courts', *Quarterly Journal of Economics*, 118: 453–517.

Faure, M. and A.V. Raja (2010), 'Effectiveness of Environmental Public Interest Litigation in India: Determining the Key Variables', *Fordham Environmental Law Journal*, XXI(2): 239–94.

GoI (2012), *Approach Paper, Financial Sector Legislative Reforms Commission*. New Delhi: Ministry of Finance, Government of India.

Goyal, A. (2012), 'The Future of Financial Liberalization in South Asia', *Asia-Pacific Development Journal*, 19(1): 63–96.

Khanna, V. and U. Varottil (2012), 'Developing the Market for Corporate Bonds in India'. Available at: SSRN: http://ssrn.com/abstract=2021602 (accessed on 25 July 2012).

Kochanek, S.A. (1987), 'Briefcase Politics in India: The Congress Party and the Business Elite', *Asian Survey*, 27(12): 1278–301.

La Porta, R., F. Lopez-de-Silanes, A. Shleifer, and R.W. Vishny (1998), 'Law and Finance', *Journal of Political Economy*, 106(6): 1113–55.

Ostrom, E. (1999), 'Private and Common Property Rights', in Boudewijn Bouckaert and Gerrit De Geest (eds), *Encyclopedia of Law and Economics: The History and Methodology of Law and Economics, Volume I*, pp. 332–79, Cheltenham: Edward Elgar.

Pedersen, J.D. (2000), 'Explaining Economic Liberalization in India: State and Society Perspectives', *World Development*, 28(2): 266.

Rathinam, F. and A.V. Raja (2011), 'Courts as Regulators: Public Interest Litigation in India', *Environment and Development Economics*, 16(2): 199–219.

RBI (2007), *Report on Currency and Finance 2005–6*. Mumbai: Reserve Bank of India.

Thomas, S. (2005), 'How the Financial Sector in India Was Reformed', mimeo, IGIDR.

Uppal, J.S. (1986), 'Public Financial Institutions and Economic Concentration in India, *Journal of Development Economics*, 20(1): 135–44.

CHAPTER 19

THE EVOLVING SYSTEM OF CORPORATE GOVERNANCE IN INDIA*

JAYATI SARKAR AND SUBRATA SARKAR

Corporate governance, the set of mechanisms by which publicly held corporations are directed and controlled, has been a major issue of policy discourse since the 1990s. The need for such mechanisms is rooted in agency problems with the nature of the problem being largely dependent on the ownership and control structure of the corporation in question.

In corporations with diffused ownerships, agency problems arise due to the separation of ownership and control between dispersed shareholders and professional managers (vertical agency problems). Managers, who are entrusted with the responsibility of running a corporation by shareholders, have incentives to engage in self-seeking behaviour due to their informational advantages vis-à-vis the shareholders (asymmetric information) as well as their unobservable effort (moral hazard). Due to free-riding behaviour, dispersed shareholders, each with a small stake, have little incentive to organize themselves and monitor the management (Hart 1995).

* This chapter was written prior to the passage of the Companies Bill, 2011. This Bill was passed by the Lower house of the Indian parliament (Lok Sabha) on 18 December 2012 and by the upper house of the Indian parliament (Rajya Sabha) on 8 August 2013 and received the President's assent on 29 August 2013 and became known as the Companies Act, 2013. The main points of the chapter, however, remain qualitatively same even after taking the final legislation into account.

In corporations with concentrated ownerships where ownership and management control are typically concentrated in the same hands, the nature of the agency problems changes to conflicts between controlling inside shareholders and minority outside shareholders (horizontal agency problems), whereby the controlling shareholders seek to extract private benefits expropriating minority shareholders.

While vertical agency problems are largely prevalent in the US and UK, horizontal agency problems are considered to be more common in other parts of the world, especially in developing economies. Whatever the nature of agency problems, there is universal recognition of the need to focus on devising both internal and external corporate governance (CG) mechanisms through which outside investors of a corporation can exercise control over insiders to mitigate agency problems.

A review of burgeoning literature on governance reveals that there is considerable subjectivity regarding the scale and scope of these governance mechanisms. At one end of the spectrum is the rather narrow definition of governance from a corporate finance perspective, focusing on the various ways in which suppliers of finance to a public corporation can assure themselves of getting a return on their investment (Shleifer and Vishny 1997). On the other end is the all-encompassing view that 'corporate governance involves a set of relationships between a company's management, its board, its shareholders and other stakeholders. Corporate governance also provides the structure through which the objectives of the company are set, and the means of attaining those objectives and monitoring performance are determined (OECD, 2003: 11).

Irrespective of the difference in scope, the point of commonality across the variety of definitions is that CG essentially involves a system of internal and external mechanisms that seek to provide managers and controlling owners proper incentives, especially in non-competitive product and labour markets, to mitigate agency costs and thereby maximize shareholder/stakeholder value. Internal mechanisms of governance consist of the board of directors, the presence of large shareholders, executive compensation packages, and the financial structure of firms. Among the important external governance mechanisms are the market for corporate control, product market competition, a managerial labour market, and the legal and institutional environment in which a firm operates.

The problems of governance can be traced back to the origins of the corporate form as early as in 800 BC (Khanna 2005), and more recently to the prototype modern corporation of Berle and Means (1932). However, the increasing importance of CG comes from a large body of empirical and theoretical research that highlights that a well-functioning governance system is critical for economic growth and development. Governance systems can have economy-wide effects through increasing access to low cost external finance thereby spurring investment, growth, and employment; improving the allocation of resources by positively impacting a firm's performance; reducing the risk of financial crises; and in general by strengthening relationships with stakeholders that go beyond simple economic objectives (Claessens and Yortoglu 2012). Such relationships include improving social and labour harmony and contributing to larger social goals like environmental protection and alleviation of poverty and inequality.

The renewed focus on CG since the 1990s has to a large extent been dictated by the spate of corporate scandals in countries like the UK and US with more mature governance systems, and later by systemic failures during the East Asian crisis and more recently by the financial crisis of late 2000s. Each of these developments has resulted in the strengthening of governance reforms, examples being the setting up of the Cadbury Committee on the Financial Aspects of Corporate Governance in the UK in 1991, enactment of the path breaking Sarbanes–Oxley Act of 2002, and the over arching Dodd-Frank Act of 2010 in the United States.

In emerging economies like India and China, the increased focus on governance came not from concerns about corporate failures but in response to structural reforms initiated in the real and financial sectors. Reforms ushered in increased investment opportunities and created opportunities for corporations to access external sources of finance both in domestic and international markets. This in turn required strengthening of governance systems to increase confidence among both domestic and foreign investors. By 2009, 23 developed countries and 43 developing/emerging economies had come up with best practice governance codes and principles either through private or government initiatives, some mandatory, some non-mandatory. Subsequent to the first round of codes, almost all countries followed up with other codes, either updating the older codes, or issuing fresh ones.

An examination of CG institutions across countries reveals that there are essentially two prototype governance systems—the market-based Anglo Saxon system and the bank-based Continental system with some countries adopting a combination of these two systems. The Anglo Saxon system prevalent in countries like the US and UK is characterized by widely held corporations, liquid capital markets, an active market for corporate control; the securities markets play a centre-stage in the supply of investment finance. The bank-based Continental system prevalent in countries such as Germany and Japan is, on the other hand, characterized by greater concentration of shareholder power, fewer listed companies, less liquid capital market, and the banks play a lead role in mobilizing savings and channelizing investments.

With agency problems in the two systems inherently different, the modes of controlling these problems are typically different. Whereas governance mechanisms in market-based systems are a combination of internal and external mechanisms, in bank-based systems greater reliance is placed on internal control mechanisms. The prevalence of a specific governance system in a country at any point of time is the product of its history. Country level experiences have shown that changes in the economic environment as well as changes in cultural, political, and legal institutions have impacted the evolution of ownership structures and governance systems. In general, as several scholars have argued, a country's pattern of ownership structure and national governance systems are path dependent, being politically and historically contingent and continuously shaped by the 'shadow of their unique histories' (Gilson 1996). An important implication of such path dependency in the context of reforming governance systems, particularly in emerging economies, is that while the general approach has been to imbibe international best practices, a host of political, economic, cultural, and other informal institutions have militated against their convergence to such practices. This is highlighted in cross-country evidence (Khanna et al. 2006) which shows that while there have been *de jure* similarities in systems between countries whereby both developing and developed countries adopt similar governance standards, there is no statistical evidence to suggest *de facto* convergence of CG in terms of implementation of standards.

Using this discussion on issues pertaining to CG in a dynamic economy as the backdrop, this chapter examines the evolving system of governance in India with particular focus on developments since India embarked on the path of economic liberalization in the early 1990s. The chapter is organized into the following sections. The next section provides an overview of the various committees and codes that have shaped governance standards in India in the last two decades. A discussion on the evolution of standards of some of the important governance mechanisms along with a comparative assessment with international standards is undertaken in the next section. The section that follows reports on the quality of CG attained in India in terms of the extent of convergence to best practices and its evolution in terms of trends in key governance indicators and as reflected in an overall CG index. The last section concludes the chapter.

Governance Regulations in India since Liberalization

Backdrop

Like other countries, laws and regulations on corporate governance in India are primarily geared towards listed companies registered in the various stock exchanges in the country, primarily the Bombay Stock Exchange (BSE) and the National Stock Exchange (NSE). Since the liberalization of capital markets, the number of listed companies on BSE increased from 2,556 in 1991 to 4,946 in 2008 (SEBI 2009). Regulation of unlisted registered companies, estimated to be around 745,000 in 2007, is primarily through the Companies Act, 1956 (Sarkar and Sarkar 2012).

While formal institutions of corporate governance in India have been in place for a number of years, governance issues came to the forefront following the adoption of the structural adjustment and globalization programme. Policy changes led to changes in the economic and institutional set-up, in response to which the governance system evolved with a positive feedback. With a spurt in private sector investment opportunities and an increase in the number of listed companies, many of which were keen on tapping international sources of finance through cross-listing, public concerns started becoming more focused on effective investor protection, on transparency of operations in business and industry, and on the need to attain international standards for disclosure of company information. Recurrent corporate scandals, even in countries with relatively well developed governance systems also brought home the need for strengthening existing governance mechanisms.

One of the key characteristics of listed companies in India that has influenced much of the evolution of the governance framework is the dominance of family-owned firms with concentrated ownership and insider control. Estimates for a sample of around 2,000 listed companies as of 2006, show that almost 93 per cent of these firms had at least one shareholder with controlling votes. Further, dominant among controlling insiders were promoters and promoter groups, which, on the average, had ownership stakes ranging anywhere between 45–50 per cent (Sarkar and Sarkar 2012). Additionally, anecdotal and empirical evidence have consistently pointed out to the complexity of insider ownership and control structures manifested in control pyramids and cross-holdings, the combined effect of which has been to exacerbate agency problems between majority and minority shareholders. All major committees that were set up to recommend governance reforms recognized such agency problems and the potential for promoters to benefit at the expense of minority shareholders.

CG reforms in India have by and large involved: (i) improving the functioning of capital markets, (ii) ensuring more effective protection of minority investors through promoting greater transparency of operations and higher standards of information disclosure and enforcement, (iii) reforming company board structures and operational systems to make the board of directors more accountable to the shareholders, and (iv) reforming governance mechanisms of financial institutions. CG initiatives have come from the government via government legislations involving several amendments to the Companies Act of 1956; from SEBI in the form of statutory regulations; and through self-disciplining and voluntary initiatives taken by industry chambers and business associations, professional bodies, and the companies themselves.

Committees and Reports

The first formal attempt at formalizing a CG code came from the Confederation of Indian Industries (CII), which, in 1998, published the Desirable Code of Corporate Governance (CII 1998) that recommended several best practices to improve the governance of Indian companies. Alongside, several companies voluntarily initiated in-house reviews of their existing governance practices, particularly their board structures, operational mechanisms, and information disclosure norms. Notwithstanding these initiatives, the need of putting in place some statutory governance regulations to legally formalize CG standards was felt increasingly. It is in this context that the securities markets regulator, the Securities Exchange Board of India (SEBI) set up the Kumar Mangalam Birla Committee on Corporate Governance (SEBI 1999) in May 1999 to suggest measures, both mandatory and voluntary, to improve CG standards of listed companies, particularly with respect to disclosure of material financial and non-financial information, responsibilities of independent and outside directors on company boards, and to suggest safeguards against insider trading. As a follow up, a second committee, the Narayana Murthy Committee on Corporate Governance was set up in 2002 (SEBI 2002) to further review and further reform CG procedures.

In parallel, the Ministry of Corporate Affairs (MCA) in the Government of India set up a study group in May 2000 to operationalize 'the concept of corporate governance/excellence' to make India more globally competitive (MCA 2000). It also set up the Naresh Chandra Committee on Corporate Audit and Governance in 2002 (MCA 2002) to reform the auditing and accounting norms of Indian companies. Finally, in a major initiative to revise, modify, and rationalize the existing Companies Act, 1956 in light of continuing changes in domestic and international business operating environments, MCA set up the Expert Committee on Company Law (the J.J. Irani Committee) in December 2004. Drawing on the recommendations of the Irani Committee in 2005 (MCA 2005), the Companies Bill, 2009 (now Companies Bill, 2011) was drafted and introduced in Parliament for deliberations and passage. Recognizing that the passage of the bill will take some time, MCA issued two guidelines in December 2009, first, the Corporate Governance Voluntary Guidelines and second, the Corporate Social Responsibility Voluntary Guidelines to urge the corporate sector to voluntarily conform to high standards of governance and social responsibility (MCA 2009). The timeline of key reform initiatives is presented in Figure 19.1.

While the terms of reference of the different committees are distinct in some respects, all have subscribed to shareholder value maximization while catering to stakeholder interests, although the weight assigned to shareholders and stakeholder welfare have varied across committees (Sarkar and Sarkar 2012). The recommendations have primarily focused on strengthening both external and internal governance mechanisms with a view to mitigating horizontal agency problems arising from concentrated ownership and control structures of Indian companies. In particular, all committees have emphasized the importance of a board structure and board functioning in protecting shareholder value, highlighting the need for the board's independence from promoter influence, board expertise, an independent audit committee, and the need for regular board and audit committee meetings to monitor management. Additionally, all governance codes have emphasized the need to have adequate disclosures on related party transactions that are significant for Indian companies, and the need to strengthen external market-based institutions of governance by specifying a tight and transparent takeover code.

Clause 49 of Listing Agreement

Clause 49 of the Listing Agreement was a landmark CG regulation introduced by SEBI effective 21 February 2000, based on the recommendations

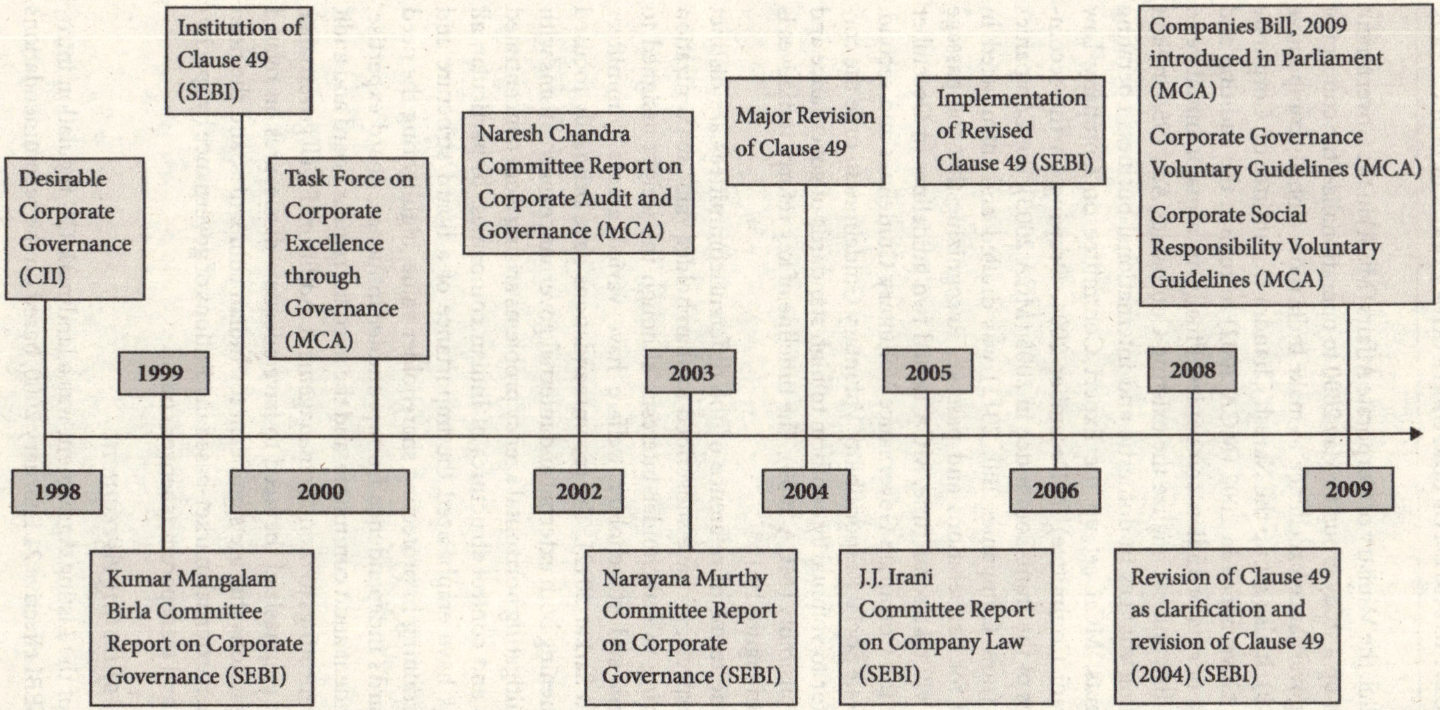

FIGURE 19.1 Timeline of Corporate Governance Initiatives in India

Source: Constructed by the authors.

of the Kumar Mangalam Birla Committee. These CG principles were made applicable in a phased manner and all the listed companies with a paid up capital of Rs 3 crore and above or net worth of Rs 25 crore or more at any time in the history of the company, were covered as of 31 March 2003. The compliance of companies to Clause 49 is monitored by the stock exchanges through monitoring cells, and compliance reports have to be filed with SEBI within a stipulated period. Subsequent to its introduction in 2000, Clause 49 underwent several modifications, sometimes incremental, sometimes substantial, the most important one being in October 2004, based on the recommendations of the Narayana Murthy Committee report and the feedback received on the original version.

The path-breaking feature of Clause 49 is that listed companies are required not only to comply with a set of CG regulations but they also have to disclose their compliance with these regulations in a separate section on corporate governance in their annual reports. Thus, with the institution of the Clause 49, for the first time CG compliance became an explicit yardstick for shareholders and stakeholders to evaluate a listed company in India. The compliance philosophy behind the clause was a hybrid of the 'comply or explain' and 'comply or else' approaches to governance regulations, with certain key regulations being mandatory and some others that were non-mandatory. Mandatory compliance is with respect to: (i) the board of directors, (ii) the audit committee, (iii) subsidiary companies, (iv) disclosures including those on related party transactions, (v) CEO/CFO certification, (vi) report on corporate governance, and (vii) compliance. Non-mandatory requirements include setting up a remuneration committee, training board members, and audit qualifications. In the compliance report, non-compliance if any, of the mandatory requirements under Clause 49 is required to be reported and explained while the adoption of any non-mandatory requirements is to be highlighted.

Companies Bill, 2009

The activities of all registered Indian companies, listed and unlisted, are regulated through the Companies Act, 1956 which is by far the largest legislation enacted by the Indian Parliament, comprising 658 sections and 14 schedules. The statues in the Act aim at ensuring that the interests of creditors and shareholders are adequately protected and that shareholders' voice is adequately represented in the management of companies. Since 1956, the Companies Act, 1956, has been amended as many as 24 times. Given the 'proliferation and diversity' of amendments to the Act over time, it was felt that it was imperative that the law be re-codified. With this objective, MCA set up the Expert Committee on Company Law (the Irani Committee referred to earlier) which culminated in the drafting of the Companies Bill, 2009 which is currently awaiting Parliament's approval.

The Companies Bill, 2009 marks a departure from the Companies Act, 1956, by drawing up extensive CG provisions for all registered companies independent of their listing status. These have been with respect to management and board oversight covering important governance aspects like the obligations of the board, the desired board size (relaxing the existing requirement in company law to have a minimum number of directors), and board independence (not specified in the existing law) with at least one-third of the board consisting of such directors. Other provisions of the bill have important implications for CG as well corporate sector developments. These include, among others, buy-back of securities, an investor education and protection fund, postal ballot, audit committee, directors responsibility statement, and secretarial compliance certificate. Significantly, the bill places greater focus on empowering minority investors in corporate governance through various provisions, such as the option for electing a director by small shareholders, envisaging a positive role for investors' associations/NGOs in protecting investor rights, and providing for class action and derivative suits on behalf of depositors and shareholders.

Subsequent to the drafting of the Companies Bill, 2009, the Standing Committee on Finance submitted its report on 'The Companies Bill, 2009' on 31 August 2010 (MCA 2010). The Bill was revised in light of the recommendations and renamed as Companies Bill, 2011 and is in the last stages of consideration before being presented to Parliament for approval.

Comparative Assessment of Governance Standards

Governance reforms, based on the recommendations of various committees, have been comprehensive, covering a wide range of CG mechanisms. However, there have been three areas on which reform efforts have been particularly focused—the board of directors, audit committees, and auditor independence. This section focuses on the evolution of standards in these three areas from a comparative international perspective.

Board of Directors

Board regulations for all registered companies in India are laid down by the Companies Act, 1956, and additional regulations applicable to the sub-set of listed companies as laid down by SEBI under Clause 49. While matters, such as minimum board size, appointments and rotation of directors, limits on directorships, board procedures, and responsibilities of board members are laid down in detail under the Companies Act of 1956, those regarding board independence, financial disclosures, board procedures, and in general the entire gamut of issues relevant to a board's governance role relevant to listed companies come under Clause 49.

In particular, Clause 49 contains provisions relating to: (a) composition of the board, (b) non-executive directors' compensation and disclosures, (c) other provisions applicable to the board and its sub-committees that specify the frequency of meeting of the board of directors and the number of multiple directorships that board members can hold in other companies, and (d) code of conduct for board members. Many of these provisions have been refined over time to bring in greater clarity so as to increase their effectiveness and to facilitate their implementation. For instance, the definition of an independent director was made more objective and key terms like 'nominee directors' and 'senior management' were incorporated in the first major revision of the clause in October 2004. Such changes have brought in increasing convergence with best practices existing in countries with more mature governance systems.

Board Composition

One of the most important provisions of Clause 49 pertains to making the board of directors (BoD) sufficiently independent of the management by specifying the requirements of both non-executive and independent directors. All listed companies are required to have at least 50 per cent of its board comprised of non-executive directors. Additionally, regulations prescribe a minimum percentage of independent directors, the requirement of which varies based on whether the company has an executive or non-executive chairman. The original regulations of February 2000 required that 'in case of a non-executive Chairman, at least one-third of the board must comprise of independent directors, and in case of an executive Chairman, at least half of the board should comprise of independent directors.' However, such a requirement did not consider the possibility that in many Indian companies, especially those related to business groups, the non-executive chairman may be related to the promoters and may be as much an insider as an executive chairman is deemed to be. This anomaly was corrected subsequently in April 2008 where the more stringent requirement of at least half of the board being comprised of independent directors was extended to boards with 'non-executive chairman who is a promoter of a company or is related to any promoter or person occupying management positions at the Board level or at one level below the Board.'

The emphasis of Clause 49 on having a significant presence of independent directors in company boards is in line with general practices around the world that require or recommend majority or substantial presence of independent directors on corporate boards. For example, the New York Stock Exchange (NYSE) listing standards require all public companies to consist of a majority of independent directors, while the UK Combined Code on Corporate Governance and the Australian Stock Exchange recommend a majority of independent directors on corporate boards. Similar recommendations come from various institutional investors like CalPERS (California Public Employees' Retirement System) and the OECD principles of corporate governance. Emerging economies, such as Brazil, Hong Kong, and Singapore too seem to be moving towards the constitution of more independent boards (Sarkar and Sarkar 2012).

Definition of Independent Directors

One of the challenging issues among policymakers and academics has been defining the 'independence' of a director as much as possible in objective terms based on 'relationship standards'. The usual way of defining 'independent' directors in most regulations has been to first state that an independent director is one for whom any material relation with the company is absent, and then identifying conditions which prima facie suggest that material relations could be present. Any person who does not fall under these conditions is then deemed to be independent. The laws in various countries differ according to: (i) the list of the presumptive conditions that lead to a material relation and hence lack of independence, and (ii) the authority which makes this determination.

In the original version of Clause 49, both the identifications of conditions that can foreclose independence as well its determination were left to the board. Under the clause, independent directors are those 'who apart from receiving director's remuneration, do not have any other material pecuniary relationship or transactions with the company, its promoters, its management or its subsidiaries, *which in the judgement of the board* (emphasis added) may affect the independent judgement of the director.' However, as the Naresh Chandra Committee recognized, such a broad definition of independence while pragmatic and flexible, is 'circular and tautological' and hence recommended a more rigorous definition. Subsequent revisions to Clause 49 have addressed such concerns, putting in place a more stringent and objective set of criteria that a director has to satisfy to be deemed independent. These revisions came closely on the heels of the enactment of the Sarbanes–Oxley Act (SOX Act) of 2002 in the US and the incorporation of a set of 'bright line' tests for independent directors by NYSE in its new listing standards in 2003.

Notwithstanding their similarities, there are interesting differences between NYSE regulations and the revised Clause 49 with respect to determining of 'independence'. NYSE regulations define an independent director as one who 'has no material relationship with the listed company' which is similar to the original version of Clause 49 enacted by SEBI. However, NYSE regulations require an affirmative determination of independence of each director by the board by considering 'all relevant facts and circumstances' unlike the original version of Clause 49. In addition, NYSE regulations specify several exclusion conditions using 'relationship standards' with a 'look-back' period of three years which automatically disqualifies a person from being an independent director. Thus, in NYSE regulations, only a part of the conditions of independence, or the lack of it, is made by the regulator, leaving the onus of specifying and determining the remaining conditions that may hinder independence, to the board.

In contrast, SEBI's revised Clause 49 does not require any affirmative determination of independence. Instead, the clause specifies a broader set of criteria which if violated leads to automatic disqualification as an 'independent' director. These criteria are a combination of the exclusion restrictions of NYSE plus a set of conditions which SEBI has determined to hinder independence. Thus, SEBI seems to have proactively set all the standards that can potentially affect independence and left only the task of verifying these conditions to the board. It has not given companies the flexibility to deviate from the laid down conditions through affirmative determination.

An important issue that arises for independent directors is how to incentivize these directors without compromising their independence. One view is that incentives can be provided through significant stock ownership that is more likely to align the interests of these independent directors with that of the shareholders. This seems to be the view of the NYSE regulation which 'does not view ownership of even a significant amount of stock, by itself, as a bar to an independence finding'. In contrast, Clause 49 regulations automatically disqualify a person with stock ownership in excess of 2 per cent as an independent director. This is perhaps motivated by SEBI's concern of weak insider trading rules that prevent easy prosecution in case a director acts in self interest, based on private information. The other way of incentivizing independent directors is by offering them commissions based on performance. However, offering cash incentives based on current performance, as is prevalent in India now, may promote short-term goals and compromise independence. A better option is offering stock options with long vesting periods.

Nominee Directors

A particular issue on the constitution of the board that is unique to India and has been the subject of much debate is whether to treat nominee directors as independent directors. Nominee directors are appointed by financial institutions having significant equity and debt holdings in a company. Clause 49 waives all tests of independence for nominee directors and considers them to be independent directors by default. However, most governance committees take a contrary view and recommend that nominee directors should not be deemed independent. The Kumar Mangalam Birla Committee was the first to note the conflict of interest inherent in nominee directors participating in board decisions while being major players in the stock market as well as being debt holders. Subsequently, the Naresh Chandra Committee recommended that while nominee directors could be present on the board, they should not be considered as independent directors. The Narayana Murthy Committee was more forceful in its recommendation and suggested doing away with the concept of nominee directors altogether by noting that these directors claim to be accountable only to their institutions. The J.J. Irani Committee also recommended that nominee directors should not be deemed to be independent directors. The collective opinion of all these committees has been reflected in the Companies Bill, 2009 which has formally proposed excluding nominee directors in computing the independence requirement of the board.

Audit Committee

The audit committee is the ultimate body that provides oversight of the workings of both the internal and external auditors and ensures that all the relevant disclosures are made by the company in accordance with legal requirements. It plays a vital role in ensuring the independence of the audit process. These functions are adequately recognized under Clause 49 which requires all listed companies to have an audit committee of at least three directors of which two-thirds should be independent. The chairman of the audit committee is required to be an independent director. Clause 49 requires the audit committee to meet at least four times a year with the gap between two successive meeting not exceeding four months. The regulation tries to ensure the quality of the audit committee by requiring that all audit committee members be 'financially literate' with at least one member having 'accounting or related financial management expertise'. In addition, Clause 49 regulations contain detailed guidelines regarding the role and powers of the audit committee that include oversight, integrity, and credibility of the company's financial reporting process, recommendation to the board regarding the appointment, re-appointment, and removal of the statutory auditor, fixing the audit fees, and approval of non-audit services.

In general, regulations regarding size, composition, and expertise of the audit committee under Clause 49 mirror NYSE regulations in many respects, but there are two important differences. First, while Section 303A.07 of NYSE regulations also requires the audit committee to be have a minimum of three members, it requires all of them to be independent directors unlike the two-thirds rule under Clause 49. Second, the NYSE regulation specifically discourages audit committee members to serve on more than three audit committees. In case a member serves on more than three audit committees, the NYSE regulation requires the company to make an affirmative determination of the ability of the member to effectively discharge his/her responsibilities. No such limits or affirmative determination are specified under Clause 49.

Another area of difference is in the power of the audit committee vis-à-vis the board. Under Clause 49 regulations it is not specified whether the audit committee's recommendations relating to hiring, oversight, compensation, and firing of the outside auditor are binding on the board. However, Section 158 (9) of the Companies Bill of 2009 (and currently under Section 292-A of the Companies (Amendment) Act, 2000) states that if the board does not accept the recommendations of the audit committee, reasons therefore should be communicated to the shareholders. This is in contrast to the regulation in the US where under the SOX Act of 2002, and implemented by SEC under Rule 10A-3, the audit committee is 'directly responsible for the appointment, compensation, retention and oversight' of the statutory auditor and each such statutory auditor 'must report directly to the audit committee'.

Auditor Independence

The quality of financial information is integral to good corporate governance. The statutory auditors of a company are considered to be lead actors in ensuring quality through providing independent oversight to financial reporting by companies. Poor quality of financial information exacerbates agency problems through increasing informational asymmetries, thereby increasing investment risks and the cost of capital. Empirical evidence does show that firms with less transparent earnings and more independent audit committees have lower cost of capital.

Auditors scrutinize and verify the accounts and certify that the financial systems are prepared in accordance with the prescribed principles and that the accounts are free from material misstatements and give a true and fair view of a company's financial status. Currently issues related to auditor independence in India are governed by the Chartered Accountants Act, 1949 which governs the accountancy profession, and Sections 224–33 of the Companies Act, 1956. The Chartered Accountants Act of 1949 lays down a detailed code of ethics which members of the Institute of Chartered Accountants of India (ICAI) are required to follow. The codes closely follow the guidelines on Professional Ethics for the Accountancy Profession issued by the International Federation of Accountants (IFAC). As in the case of other CG regulations, accounting standards have evolved over the years in consonance with changing circumstances, with ICAI periodically revising the codes of ethics—the eleventh code of ethics being announced in February 2009.

The code of ethics while laying down the fundamental principles of integrity, objectivity, professional competence and due care, confidentiality, professional behaviour, and technical standards, do not list conditions which lead to assumption of lack of independence. Likewise, the codes do not contain a list of prohibited non-audit services which are deemed to create conflict of interest and jeopardize auditor independence. Section 226 of the Companies Act does specify some conditions which automatically disqualify an audit firm or a person to render audit services, such as prohibiting an officer or employee of a company or a company shareholder with voting rights from rendering audit services. However, the act does not impose restrictions on family members or other close relatives of the audit firm's members from occupying senior management positions in the audited company and vice-versa. Similarly, like the code of ethics, the Companies Act does not have any specific restrictions on the type of non-audit services that audit firms can render along with regular audit services.

In summary, neither ICAI's code of ethics nor the provisions of the Companies Act, 1956 have any tightly defined norms for auditor independence. As such, auditor independence in India is currently largely dependent on self regulation and the practice of subjective guidelines. In this respect, the Naresh Chandra Committee in 2002 provided a number of recommendations relating to objective criteria for determining qualifications for audit assignments, including company-auditor independence, specification of prohibited non-audit services, audit partner rotation and cooling off periods for both the audit firm and the audited company, powers, responsibility and accountability of auditors, and independent oversight of the auditors. The recommendations are in line with best practices in many mature economies. Most of the recommendations have been incorporated in the Companies Bill, 2009. When enacted into law, this will be one more step forward in improving governance.

The Quality of Governance: A Report Card

The adoption of Clause 49, the 'big bang' in the CG system in India, set in motion reform processes in all relevant areas of governance. This section presents a report card of the progress made in governance reforms and the quality attained from two perspectives—one at the systems level in terms of select international benchmarks, and the other at the firm level in terms of trends in the three governance indicators discussed in the previous section and that of a composite corporate governance index.

The State of Best Practices

A qualitative assessment of the quality of governance in Indian corporations in accordance with the OECD Principles of Corporate Governance and in terms of important governance indicators set out by the World Bank, reveals the beneficial effect of CG reforms within a short period. The positive transformation has happened in terms of improved levels of responsibility/accountability of insiders, fairness in dealing with minority shareholders and stakeholders, improved board practices, and increased transparency. As Table 19.1 shows, of the different gradations in the assessment, most of the OECD principles are observed or largely observed. This is the case especially with respect to shareholder and stakeholder rights as well as board functioning. Specifically, a comparison of minority investor and creditor rights across countries shows India to be very much at par with UK and US (Table 19.1).

Table 19.1 Summary of Observance of OECD Corporate Governance Principles in India

Principle	O	LO	PO	MO	NO
Rights of Shareholders					
Basic shareholder rights	X				
Right to participate in fundamental decisions	X				
Shareholder's AGM rights	X				
Disproportionate control disclosure		X			
Markets for corporate control should be allowed to function	X				
Cost/benefit to voting				X	
Equitable treatment of shareholders					
All shareholders should be treated equally			X		
Prohibit insider trading			X		
Board/ managers disclose interests			X		
Role of stakeholders in corporate governance					
Stakeholder rights respected	X				
Redress for violation of rights			X		
Performance enhancement	X				
Access to information	X				
Disclosure and transparency					
Disclosure standards		X			
Standards of accounting and audit		X			
Independent audit annually			X		
Fair and timely dissemination	X				
Responsibilities of the board					
Acts with due diligence and care		X			
Treats all shareholders fairly		X			
Ensures compliance with law	X				
The board should fulfil certain key functions		X			
The board should be able to exercise objective judgements			X		
Access to information	X				

Source: Compiled from ROSC (2004).

Note: (O) Observed; (LO) Largely Observed; (PO) Partially Observed; (MO) Materially not Observed; (NO) Not Observed.

In general, many of the important governance institutions in India have *de jure* convergence with Anglo Saxon countries. This is not surprising given that governance institutions in India date back to the mid-nineteenth century and the fact that most of the related legislation was fashioned around English law. However, compared to these countries India is considered to lag in enforcement of CG laws and regulations despite making significant strides in reforming governance mechanisms. There have been compliance gaps, and enforcement and implementation of laws and regulations have remained 'important challenges' (ROSC 2004). This has been particularly so with respect to investor rights (rule of law, corruption, risk of expropriation), and with regard to accounting and disclosure standards. The received wisdom is that rules in the book have not necessarily translated into rules on the ground, thereby preventing *de facto* convergence of best practices at the system level.

Trends in Governance Indicators: Firm-level Analysis

This section reports the trends in the three governance indicators discussed in the previous section and a composite corporate governance index for the period 2003–8. The trends are based on the sample of the top 500 listed companies in terms of their market capitalization as on March 2008. Recall that in 2003 all listed firms came under Clause 49 regulations followed by the revised Clause 49 that came into effect from 31 December 2005. Accordingly, 2006 represents the year by which all firms should have complied with the revised regulations.

Board Structure

- The board of a typical large Indian company consists of nine directors with about 30 per cent of them being executive or inside directors while 70 per cent are non-executive or outside directors (Table 19.2).
- Twenty per cent of the outside directors are grey directors[1] and 50 per cent are independent directors.

[1] Grey directors are non-executive directors who have some non-pecuniary or pecuniary relationship with the firm, which is associated with the board membership. For example, non-executive directors who are former officers of the company, relatives of the company officers, or those who have existing business relationships with the company such as investments bankers and lawyers are classified as grey directors.

Table 19.2 Board Composition of Top 500 Listed Indian Companies: 2003–8

		2003	2004	2005	2006	2007	2008	All Years
Board Size	Mean	9.80	9.56	9.01	9.11	9.20	9.41	9.34
	Median	10.00	9.00	9.00	9.00	9.00	9.00	9.00
	Max	19.00	19.00	22.00	19.00	23.00	21.00	23.00
Companies with Board Size greater than 12	Mean	0.08	0.08	0.04	0.07	0.08	0.08	0.07
Companies with Board Size less than 7	Mean	0.08	0.09	0.11	0.16	0.17	0.10	0.12
Percentage of Inside Directors	Mean	28.61	29.31	30.86	29.43	28.14	28.23	28.99
Percentage of Outside Directors	Mean	71.39	70.69	69.14	70.57	71.86	71.77	71.01
Percentage of Grey Directors	Mean	17.87	18.40	18.53	21.54	21.91	19.90	19.93
Percentage of Independent Directors	Mean	53.52	52.29	50.61	49.03	49.95	51.87	51.08
Company has Nominee Director	Mean	0.32	0.34	0.33	0.22	0.20	0.21	0.26
Proportion of Nominee Director	Mean	21.74	20.18	20.44	19.25	18.17	18.29	19.72

Source: Authors' calculations based on data from annual reports available in the SANSCO database.

- The composition of inside and outside directors has remained stable over time. However, within outside directors the proportion of grey directors has increased and the proportion of independent directors has decreased.
- A disaggregated analysis shows that this change is driven largely by group companies which registered a fall of 4 percentage points in the proportion of independent directors between 2003 and 2008, with standalone companies actually registering a two point increase over the same period (Sarkar and Sarkar 2012).
- The mean percentage of independent directors is above 50 per cent suggesting that overall compliance is high. However, sorting the companies by the status of the chairman presents a different picture.
- As of March 2008 all companies with a non-executive chairman, barring 1 per cent, have complied with the Clause 49 requirement of having at least one-third of the board as independent directors (Table 19.3).
- In contrast, as of March 2008, 12 per cent of the companies with an executive chairman had failed to comply with the Clause 49 requirement of having at least 50 per cent of the board of independent directors.

Table 19.3 Board Independence and Compliance of Top 500 Listed Indian Companies: 2003–8

Proportion of Independent Directors in Board	2003	2004	2005	2006	2007	2008
Panel A: Companies with Executive Chairman						
Less than 1/3	2.86	6.56	7.50	6.55	3.95	0.00
1/3 to Less than 1/2	20.95	18.85	13.33	10.12	12.43	11.89
1/2 to Less than 3/4	65.71	59.84	70.00	76.19	79.66	84.32
3/4 to 1	10.48	14.75	9.17	7.14	3.95	3.78
Total Number of Companies	105	122	120	168	177	185
Panel B: Companies with Non Executive Chairman						
Less than 1/3	0.00	2.52	3.76	1.00	1.00	0.98
1/3 to Less than 1/2	42.59	41.51	46.62	51.74	50.25	49.51
1/2 to Less than 3.4	42.59	42.14	36.84	43.78	42.79	41.67
3/4 to 1	14.81	13.84	12.78	3.48	5.97	7.84
Total Number of Companies	162	159	133	201	201	204

Source: Authors' calculations based on data from annual reports available in the SANSCO database.

- However, compliance in 2008 was better than in 2003 and 2004 when almost one-fourth of the companies with executive chairmen did not comply with Clause 49 requirements.

NOMINEE DIRECTORS

- Nearly one-third of the companies had a nominee director present on the board in 2003, with the proportion declining significantly by 2006 and stabilizing in ensuing years (Table 19.2).
- In companies where nominee directors were present, they accounted for one-fifth of board strength on an average.
- Many of these companies had an executive chairman requiring at least 50 per cent independent directors on their boards.
- The significant presence of nominee directors in these companies is indicative of the fact that companies have been meeting the statutory requirement of board independence by virtue of having nominee directors on their boards.
- This observation acquires importance in view of the debate on whether nominee directors should be counted as independent directors.

PROMOTER INFLUENCE

- In 2003, two out of every five companies had a promoter on their boards with their presence increasing significantly over the years with a noticeable jump in 2006. By 2008, every three out of five Indian companies had a promoter on their boards (Table 19.4).
- Promoters are more likely to be present on the board as inside directors than as outside directors. In 2003, while 32 per cent of the companies had a promoter present as an outside director, 40 per cent of the companies had a promoter present as an inside director.
- In companies where promoters were present as directors, they exerted a significant influence on the board, occupying three out of every ten seats as of 2003. This proportion remained the same over the years with a slight decrease in 2007 and 2008.
- Board seats of promoters were almost equally split between inside and outside positions in the early years of 2003 to 2005. However, it has shown a relative shift towards inside positions since 2006.
- When promoters are present on the board, they occupy key board positions. In 2003, 80 per cent of the companies where promoters were present on the board, occupied the position of either the

Table 19.4 Promoter Influence in Company Boards in Top 500 Listed Indian Companies: 2003–8 (Sample Means)

	2003	2004	2005	2006	2007	2008	All years
Board Size	9.80	9.56	9.01	9.11	9.20	9.41	9.34
Proportion of Companies Having							
A Promoter Director	0.40	0.45	0.54	0.63	0.56	0.59	0.54
A Promoter as an Executive Director	0.32	0.37	0.41	0.50	0.44	0.47	0.43
A Promoter as a Non-executive Director	0.26	0.28	0.37	0.41	0.32	0.33	0.33
In Companies with a Promoter Director Proportion of Board Seats Held by							
Promoter Directors	0.31	0.31	0.33	0.30	0.29	0.28	0.30
Promoter Executive Directors	0.17	0.17	0.17	0.17	0.16	0.16	0.17
Promoter Non-executive Directors	0.14	0.14	0.16	0.13	0.12	0.12	0.13
In Companies with a Promoter Director Proportion of Companies where							
Promoter is Chairman or Managing Director	0.81	0.82	0.92	0.94	0.94	0.95	0.91
Promoter is Chairman	0.72	0.73	0.85	0.87	0.85	0.86	0.83

Source: Authors' calculations based on data from annual reports available in the SANSCO database.

chairman or the managing director. This percentage increased very significantly to 95 per cent in 2008.

- In summary, promoters have increasingly taken up board positions in their companies occupying key management positions. Correspondingly, the percentage of companies with executive/promoter chairmen has increased significantly since 2006 (Sarkar and Sarkar 2012). Judged in this context, the insistence of Clause 49 on a higher percentage of independent directors for companies with executive/promoter chairmen is a proactive step by SEBI to ensure higher board oversight for these companies.

Audit Committee

- All companies have complied with Clause 49 regulations that require all listed companies to have an audit committee with a minimum of three members (Table 19.5).
- However, a majority of the companies have constituted their audit committees with the minimum size required under regulations, with

Table 19.5 Trends in Audit Committee Size and Independence Distribution of Companies: 2003–8

	2005	2006	2007	2008
Size				
Less than 3	0.30	2.19	0.51	1.25
3	57.19	50.27	51.39	49.87
4	29.64	33.61	34.43	36.84
5	7.78	9.02	9.87	8.02
More than 5	5.09	4.92	3.80	4.01
Mean Size	3.62	3.66	3.66	3.65
Fraction of Independent Directors				
Less than 2/3	8.16	15.32	12.76	10.35
2/3 to Less than 3/4	18.43	18.11	22.45	23.48
3/4 to Less than 1	18.43	33.84	25.51	28.28
1	54.98	43.73	39.29	37.88
% of Independent Directors	85.00	78.00	78.00	79.00
% of Companies with an Executive Director present in Audit Committee	19.51	19.70	19.90	22.47

Source: Authors' calculations based on data from annual reports available in the SANSCO database.

one-third of the companies adding one extra member. Companies that have audit committees with more than five members are few.

- The percentage of independent directors in a typical audit committee is around 80 per cent which is above the Clause 49 requirement that all audit committees have at least two-thirds of their members as independent directors.
- In 2006, 15 per cent of the companies did not comply with the regulations. However, non-compliance decreased to just over 10 per cent by 2008.
- There is a steady decline in the percentage of companies with fully independent audit committees. While in 2005 more than half the companies had voluntarily chosen to have a fully independent audit committee, this percentage steadily declined to just over one-third by 2008.
- There is a very steady move to have audit committees which are in accordance with the minimum independence requirement that is prescribed under law.
- A disaggregated analysis for different sizes of audit committees confirms that this decline is true for of all sizes of audit committees though the decline is more pronounced for audit committees which are bigger in size (Sarkar and Sarkar 2012).

Auditor Independence

- In 2005, the statutory auditor was also rendering non-audit services in about 90 per cent of the companies. There was an 11-percentage-point decline in this number by 2008 (Table 19.6).
- The percentage of non-audit fees to audit fees in all the four years was well below the statutory limit of 100 per cent.
- The percentage of non-audit to audit fees declined from 68.75 per cent in 2005 to 35.65 per cent in 2008.
- The percentage of non-audit fees to audit fees was higher in larger companies for all the years. However, all companies, irrespective of size, showed a significant decline in non-audit fee percentage from 2005 to 2008.

Corporate Governance Index

While an analysis of trends of specific governance mechanisms like the board of directors, audit committees, and auditor independence is a

Table 19.6 Non-audit Services and Non-audit Fees in Top 500 Listed Indian Companies: 2003–8

	2005	2006	2007	2008
Companies in which Auditors Rendering Non-audit Services—%	90.86	90.36	80.00	79.40
Non-audit to Audit Fees—Median %	68.75	71.38	46.67	35.65
Non-audit to Audit Fees According to Size—Median %				
Small (< Rs 750 crore)	65.90	57.43	48.33	35.42
Medium (Rs 750–Rs 3,400 crore)	72.77	79.33	41.43	33.50
Large (> Rs 3,400 crore)	75.00	77.36	55.36	44.44
All Companies	68.75	71.38	46.67	35.65

Source: Authors' calculations based on data from annual reports available in the SANSCO database.

valuable exercise, this does not quantify the overall state of corporate governance of companies. However, quantifying the overall state of governance is not an easy task. In part, the difficulty comes from the all-encompassing nature of the definition of CG that covers a wide range of internal and external mechanisms. With internal mechanisms, the ownership structure of the firm, the board of directors, the auditor and the audit committee, and other committees of the board like nomination committee and remuneration committee acquire special significance. Within external mechanisms, the market for corporate control and product market competition play a significant role in improving CG. Internal and external mechanisms in turn are shaped by the overall legal and institutional structures of the country. Given the large number of facets that are covered by corporate governance, an overall corporate governance index (CGI) that adequately summarizes the different aspects of governance with a composite number becomes highly useful both in terms of comparing governance quality across companies as well as over time.

Research focusing on the construction of CGI for Indian corporations has recently picked up. One of the first attempts in this regard was an index constructed by Balasubramanian et al. (2010) based on survey responses of senior management of 360 Indian listed companies for 2006. While this exercise has been instructive, the index based on survey data may be subject to a self-reporting bias. In a later and a more comprehensive attempt, Sarkar et al. (2012) constructed a corporate governance index for 500 large listed firms in the Indian corporate sector for each year for the period

2003 to 2008 using information contained in the corporate governance reports filed by companies under the statutory requirement of Clause 49 regulations. Given the year-wise estimates, incorporating four important CG mechanisms namely, the board of director, ownership structure, audit committee, and the external auditor, the index becomes particularly useful in examining the evolution of the state of corporate governance in India over the time period when a large number of CG reforms have taken place. Table 19.7 presents some of the descriptive statistics of this index where a higher values of the index, the way it has been constructed, proxies for better governance (for details, see Sarkar et al. 2012).

- In 2008, the mean value of CGI was 64.09 which is two-thirds of the maximum value for the index. The mean and median were similar suggesting that the distribution of CGI was symmetric.
- The difference between the lowest (31) and the highest (83) value of the index is quite high at 52, suggesting that there were both well and poorly governed companies in the sample.
- The board index as well as the ownership index exhibit similar characteristics as CGI. Compared to these two indices, the audit committee index and the auditor index exhibited much more variation.
- The audit committee index was skewed to the right suggesting that companies with lower values of the index outnumbered companies with higher values of the index. The standard deviation (not reported) was much higher at 14.55 and the range was 70.

Table 19.7 Descriptive Statistics of the Corporate Governance Index and its Components: 2003 and 2008

	2003			2008		
	Lowest	Highest	Mean	Lowest	Highest	Mean
Board Index	36.00	91.00	66.48 (67.00)	32.00	89.00	66.03 (67.00)
Ownership Index	27.00	83.00	57.77 (61.00)	22.00	83.00	61.97 (61.00)
Audit Committee Index	15.00	95.00	69.32 (75.00)	30.00	100.00	71.84 (75.00)
Auditor Index	15.00	90.00	56.34 (60.00)	15.00	90.00	59.38 (60.00)
Corporate Governance Index	15.00	85.00	59.91 (60.00)	31.00	83.00	64.09 (66.00)

Source: Sarkar et al. (2012).

Note: Sample: Top 500 listed companies. Figures in brackets denote medians.

- The auditor index exhibited even more variation, with a standard deviation of 16 and a range of 75.
- CG standard improved over the years with GCI value increasing from 59.91 in 2003 to 64.09 in 2008.
- Both the range and the standard deviation of CGI in 2008 were lower than in 2003 suggesting that there was an improvement across the board with the distribution of the index becoming tighter.
- The minimum value of the index increased from 15 in 2003 to 31 in 2008 which is more than a 100 per cent improvement.
- All components of the index, except for the board index contributed to GCI's improvement. In particular, the audit committee index showed the maximum improvement when judged in terms of reduction in the range and standard deviation.

The Road Ahead

This chapter provided an overview of the evolution of corporate governance standards in India since the late-1990s following the liberalization of the Indian economy. In particular, in the context of India's transformation from a controlled into an increasingly market-oriented globalized economy, the chapter examined how governance standards dynamically evolved towards international best practices, yet at the same time being suitably adapted to the institutional specificities of the Indian economy especially those related to concentrated and pyramidal ownership and control structures. With respect to the quality of the evolving governance system in India, trends in important governance mechanisms and a corporate governance index show an improvement in governance practices. At the same time, there is a tightening of the distribution of the index over the years implying that companies are moving close to each other in terms of governance standards.

With regard to evaluating quality by benchmarking governance institutions in India with select international standards, the issues are somewhat complex. The present chapter reveals a mixed picture. While on paper, the fundamental framework continues to be in line with governance practices elsewhere related to board independence, auditing quality, and disclosure standards, there are some noticeable differences too. In some cases, Indian regulations are more demanding, and in some cases these fall short of international best practices. As existing research on CG institutions points out, apart from economic considerations, political economy compulsions, cultural factors, and the like can possibly explain the divergence.

A debate that is pertinent and yet unresolved in the context of measuring governance quality, either in the Indian context or elsewhere is whether existing deviations from 'best practices' either at the firm level or with respect to international benchmarks are necessarily efficiency reducing, or whether it is the case that one size does not fit all? For instance, should existing governance regulations, such as those under Clause 49, be mandatorily adopted by companies of all hues, that is, a 'comply or else' approach, or should this be based on a 'comply or explain' approach as in the UK and South Korea. The latter is based on the presumption that given differences in company characteristics, a one-size-fits-all philosophy may prevent firms from taking optimal decisions resulting in sub-optimal governance structures which can hurt company performance.

Finally, while the corporate governance system in India has made substantial strides in a relatively short time span, it is important to recognize that rules in the book do not necessarily translate into rules on the ground. In the last two decades, while the CG framework in India has emerged to improve governance standards, protect individual investors, and enhance their confidence, there is scope for improvement in the enforcement of rules. Matching rules-on-the-ground with rules-in-the-book is paramount to establishing the link between better governance systems and better economic outcomes.

References

Balasubramanian, N., B. Black, and V. Khanna (2010), 'The Relation between Firm Level Corporate Governance and Market Value: A Case Study of India', *Emerging Markets Review*, 11(4): 319–40.

Berle, A.A. and G.C. Means (1932), *The Modern Corporate and Private Property*. New York: Harcourt, Brace and World.

Claessens, S. and B.B. Yortoglu (2012), *Corporate Governance and Development: An Update, Focus 10*. Washington, DC: Global Corporate Governance Network, IFC.

CII (1998), *Desirable Corporate Governance: A Code*. New Delhi: Confederation of Indian Industry.

Gilson, Ronald J. (1996), 'Corporate Governance and Economic Efficiency: When Do Institutions Matter?' *Washington University Law Quarterly*, 74(2): 327–45.

Government of India (2003), *Naresh Chandra Committee Report on Corporate Audit and Governance 2002*. New Delhi: Department of Company Affairs,

Government of India. Available at: http://www.nfcgindia.org/library.htm (last accessed on 17 October 2004).

——— (2009), *Companies Bill, 2009*. New Delhi: Department of Company's Affairs, Government of India. Available at: http://www.mca.gov.in/Ministry/actsbills/pdf/ Companies_Bill_2009 _24 Aug2009.pdf (last accessed on 13 June 2011).

Hart, Oliver (1995), 'Corporate Governance: Some Theory and Implications', *The Economic Journal*, 105: 678–89.

Khanna, Vikramaditya S. (2005), 'The Economic History of the Corporate Form in Ancient India', Working paper, University of Michigan Law School.

Khanna, T., J. Kogan, and K. Palepu (2006), 'Globalization and Similarities in Corporate Governance: A Cross Country Analysis', *Review of Economics and Statistics*, 88: 69–90.

MCA (2000). *Report on Corporate Excellence on a Sustained Basis to Sharpen India's Global Competitive Edge and to Further Develop Corporate Culture in the Country*. New Delhi: Department of Company Affairs, Government of India.

——— (2002). *Naresh Chandra Committee on Corporate Audit and Governance*. New Delhi: Government of India.

———(2005), *J.J. Irani Report, 2005*. New Delhi: Ministry of Corporate Affairs, Government of India.

——— (2009). *Corporate Governance Voluntary Guidelines 2009*. Available at: http://www.mca.gov.in/Ministry/guideline_archieve.html (last accessed on 13 June 2010).

——— (2010), Available at: http://www.nfcgindia.org/pdf/21_Report_Companies_Bill-2009.pdf (last accessed on 16 June 2011).

NYSE Stock Exchange, Listed Company Manual. Available online at http://nysemanual.nyse.com/lcm (last accessed on 23 December 2006).

OECD (2003), *White Paper on Corporate Governance in Asia*. Paris: OECD.

ROSC (2004), *Report on the Observance of Standards and Codes (ROSC): Corporate Governance Country Assessment (India)*, World Bank, Washington D.C.

Sarkar, Jayati and Subrata Sarkar (2012), *Corporate Governance in India*. New Delhi: Sage India Publishers.

Sarkar, Jayati, Subrata Sarkar, and Kaustav Sen (2012), 'A Corporate Governance Index for Large Listed Companies in India', Working Paper, Indira Gandhi Institute of Development Research, Mumbai, India.

SEBI (1999), *Kumar Mangalam Birla Committee Report, 1999*. Mumbai: Securities and Exchange Board of India.

——— (2003), *Recommendations of the Narayana Murthy Committee on the Revised Clause 49*. Available at: http://www.sebi.gov.in/Index.jsp?contentDisp=Section&sec_id=5.

——— (2009), *Handbook of Statistics on the Indian Securities Market 2009*. Mumbai: SEBI.

Shleifer, A. and R.W. Vishny (1997), 'A Survey of Corporate Governance', *The Journal of Finance*, 52(2): 737–83.

PART VI

INFRASTRUCTURE

CHAPTER 20

A GOVERNANCE ANALYSIS OF TRANSPORTATION IN INDIA

S. SRIRAMAN

The Governance Factor in Delivering Transportation Services

Lack of adequate transportation constrains the growth process and limits the reach of development to different areas in any economy. The Indian economy has also been subjected to such constraints. It is now recognized that the traditional approach of removing bottlenecks as and when they arise should be replaced by a more proactive process which prepares plans as well as implements them well ahead of requirements. While this may not be easily feasible in a developing country likes India, there is no doubt that supply of facilities must at least keep up with the demand if not precede it. At the same time, it is also known that existing facilities are not adequately utilized for a variety of reasons, including inappropriate pricing, poor regulation, and inefficient operating practices. It has often been pointed out that this is due to lack of effective governance practices relating to investment and pricing, legislation, and absence of coordinated efforts. In fact, it is said that if existing transport capacity were better utilized, it would take care of a good part of emerging requirements. While investment for expansion purposes is necessary, better governance practices, resulting in better return to existing facilities, are equally significant.

The traditional model of publicly owned and operated public utility appears to have under-performed, especially in the context of most developing economies. These monopolies suffered from low labour productivity, deteriorating fixed facilities and equipment, poor service quality, chronic revenue shortages, and inadequate investments. The adequacy of existing transport governance, institutional arrangements, and strategies for governments to facilitate the implementation of action plans that resolutely deal with economic development, has come for serious questioning by many critics.

In the last few decades, there has been a paradigm shift that has involved the emergence of public–private partnerships (PPPs) which has emphasized a continuing public sector responsibility for strategic network and locational planning of utilities, while, at the same time, enabling the private sector to contribute to the financing, building, and operation of facilities for a given period of time. The emergence and spread of this paradigm, especially in the context of a significant need for investment, have impacted provision in recent decades to some extent, but fundamental questions of larger social interests, especially those relating to the sustainability of such developments, have been hardly addressed in an effective manner. As a result, it has been recognized that there is need for greater attention to governance of transport—the processes, institutions, and other stakeholders that determine how decisions are made and implemented. In other words, conventional patterns of decision making in the transportation sector are no longer being accepted today, given the paradigm shift in the thinking and methods of provision of infrastructure and services resulting from an emerging desire of the stakeholders, especially users, to play a more active role in processes that have till now been within the jurisdiction of legislation and governments who have also largely served as regulators, on the basis of which bureaucrats, technocrats, and businessmen have carried forward the implementation of policies without much regard for user concerns as stakeholders.

Given the new approach, the issue is whether there has (or is) emerged (or emerging) a new scheme for governance of the transport sector in terms of its various dimensions, which is contributing to the system being more efficient, viable, and with greater accessibility to all concerned, while also being environmentally sustainable. There have been attempts to define qualitative standards of governance in the form of characteristics or principles that 'governance' ought to reflect for it to be good or ideal, which could perhaps be viewed in terms of the following criteria:

- Coordination (improving the overall national policy framework with regard to road, rail, transit traffic);
- Efficiency (decentralization with a view to increasing efficiency);
- Effectiveness (sound public finance management and institutional capacity development);
- Accountability (to improve the standard of public services); and
- Equity.

The objective of this chapter is to understand the changes in governance structures that have taken place (or that are needed), given the new approach to the provision of transport infrastructure and services, with emphasis not only on policymaking but also on effective implementation. Alternatively, it attempts to outline the transport governance framework with a view to highlighting inherent systemic strengths and weaknesses. A broad framework of an ideal governance mechanism is followed by a brief description of the institutional framework for governance as it has evolved. We then examine specific issues with regard to the two dominant modes of transport in India—railways and road transport—and also briefly report a case study with regard to the governance of urban transport in Mumbai.

About Governance and Dimensions of Governance

UNDP (2002) defines governance as a system of values, policies, and institutions by which a society manages its economic, political, and social affairs, through interactions within and among the state, civil society, and the private sector. Rodriguez et al. (2013), while attempting to define governance, hold that governance is the exercise of authority and institutional resources to manage activities in society and in the economy. It concerns the public as well as the private sectors, but tends to apply differently, depending on whether it is public or private interests which are at stake. In both cases a significant concern is performance, which is how effectively available resources are used.

The Government of India outlined a governance approach to development in its National Human Development Report (GoI 2001). Here, governance is viewed as involving a continuous interplay of three elements, each representing a specific set of deliberate arrangements that include:

- Institutions—adopted or created arrangements, both formal and informal, to bring about predictability, stability, and efficiency in managing the social, economic, or political transactions in any society;
- The delivery mechanism—including the executive apparatus adopted or evolved by the institutions for implementing the agenda and objectives for which the said institutions have been created; and
- The supportive and subordinate framework of legislations, rules, and procedures—formulated for delivering and meeting the stated responsibilities of the concerned institutions.

In this approach, the role of the civil society and the market in governance is recognized as being critical for sustaining human development. While the state is responsible for creating a conducive political, legal, and economic environment for building individual capabilities and encouraging private initiative, the market is expected to create economic opportunities.

According to SOCG (2007), governance has many facets. Conceptually, governance can be broken into five broad dimensions, each of which can be further broken down into components, which are basically a group of inter-related aspects which together make up the dimension. Each component can be viewed as a basic unit of governance. Figure 20.1 provides a view of the dimensions and their components.

Given that there are specific sector-based characteristics, some studies (The World Bank 2012) have revealed the need to further specify the roles of different stakeholders in the governance of that particular subsector. This can be outlined in terms of different phases of a 'governance cycle' appropriate to, say, the transport sector, as described in Figure 20.2. Given the public utility nature of a transport facility, while the policy and planning design and budgeting phases form part of the public policy framework, it becomes equally necessary to ensure that other phases at the

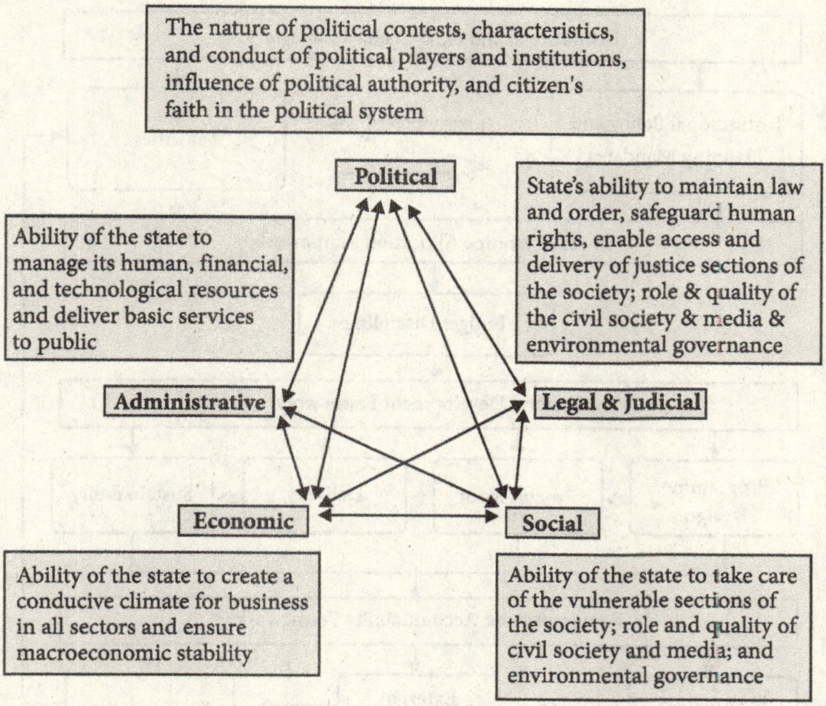

FIGURE 20.1 Governance Dimensions

Source: SOCG (2007).

user level—namely, information processes, delivery, and, above all, due regard to a sense of accountability—are well laid out. The conflict between interests (national, regional, and local) and strategic policy objectives is often cited in most cases as a major reason for varied policy outcomes in the transport sector. The challenges range from adapting organizational approaches to policy transfer processes to strategic efforts in achieving balance and integration between social, environment, economic, and political aspirations, in terms of both functional delivery and investment. While it is true to say that the objectives of the national transport policy are being developed today by taking into account the expanded role of regional–local governance structures, it is admitted that, in most cases, local and regional authorities are too small or weak. So transport delivery, in terms of both infrastructure and services, is impacted by this weak integration and coordination between transport organizations and planning bodies.

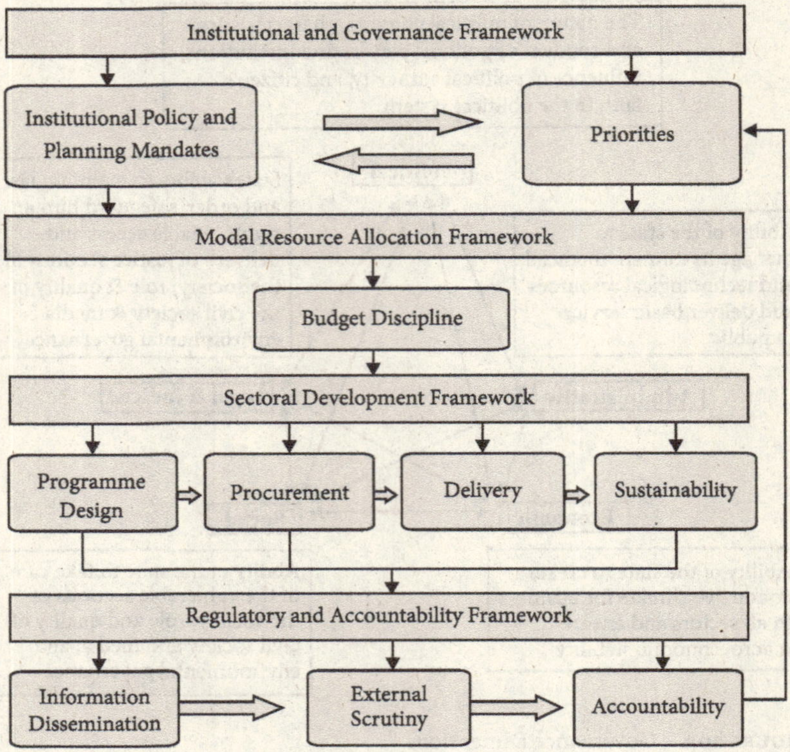

FIGURE 20.2 A Governance Cycle Framework Based on Transport Planning, Management, and Oversight

Source: The World Bank (2012).

The Institutional Governance Framework for Transport Sector in India

The Sector Structure as it Evolved in India

India's transport sector has been traditionally organized along a mixed pattern of public and private sector ownership with the constitutional responsibilities for the provision of transport services vested in both the central and state governments. Broadly speaking, for nearly four decades the central government was responsible for providing railways, national highways, civil aviation, domestic and international air transport services, and international shipping and major ports, whereas states held the responsibility for all roads except national highways, all minor ports, coastal shipping and inland water transport, and urban transport.

Indian Railways has been owned and managed departmentally by the Ministry of Railways as a government monopoly, though there has been some relaxation on provision of rail transport in urban areas which, since 1985, has been the responsibility of the central Ministry of Urban Development.

Providing domestic air transport was deregulated in the 1990s thereby allowing private sector operators to compete with public operators. This was followed by the entry of private operators in international air transport during the early 2000s. Since then airports have also gone into a private sector scheme with some new Greenfield ones coming up and some older ones being upgraded by private sector parties.

The road freight sector has always been in private hands but road passenger bus transport services were opened for nationalization by the state governments under an enabling Act, called the Road Transport Corporations (RTC) Act, passed by the Indian Parliament in 1950. Under this Act, some states opted for complete nationalization of road bus passenger transport while others adopted a mixed ownership pattern, allowing both public and private sector participation. Water transport services, both domestic and international, have been largely operated by private and public sectors. The port sector has also been attempted to be reformed with many up-gradations of facilities at existing ports taking place with some role for the private sector but under supervision and control of the public sector. At the same time, some new ones have emerged (involving minor ports or non-major ports as they are called now) under the scheme of public–private partnerships with the some of the individual maritime states participating actively in this process.

The transport sector as a whole has been one of the principal recipients of budgetary support with public sector transport undertakings depending heavily on the public exchequer to finance their development programmes as well as their operating losses. The new economic policy adopted in the 1990s required that these undertakings generate sufficient resources internally to meet their operating costs as well as finance their expansion plans. But transport undertakings in India, as in many others, generally had no control on their pricing and investment decisions and have traditionally lacked the power to run their business on commercial lines despite provision in the legal framework to do so. Equally serious has been the problem of bearing the burden of a host of public service obligations without receiving any explicit financial compensation from the governments. All these have imposed unnecessary burden on their financial positions. With the new economic policy in place, crucial governance issues, such as the extent to which these undertakings will be allowed to determine their pricing and investment policies, obligations to carry out social obligations on behalf of the government, and the extent of compensation, have come to the forefront and are still being debated even after about two decades.

Policy and Planning Mandates

The development of a correct transport planning model for a country should begin with an examination of the broad socioeconomic policy of the government and the objectives and priorities of its macroeconomic plan so that the development of transport proceeds in close conformity with the needs of the country. India has a unique distinction among developing countries in that it has since the early 1960s developed a very sophisticated macroeconomic planning model using a highly disaggregated inter-sector input–output matrix, which can simultaneously treat both output and demand targets within an integrated framework. This adoption made the task of transport modelling easy as well as difficult—easy in that the model could straightway start with traffic generation and distribution stages, and difficult since it was extremely time consuming to generate meaningful and consistent traffic flows for such a large number of sectors using the standard models, while, at the same time, providing for the spatial dimensions of movement thereby neglecting regional dimensions. The most obvious effect of this neglect was the failure to correctly forecast the volume of traffic demand in terms of traffic leads—which was nevertheless done but based on arbitrary assumptions. Consequently, right from the time the planning process began, while the volume of originating traffic has invariably been over-estimated, the average traffic leads have been under-estimated for most of the commodities. This inability to systematically take into account traffic leads has been considered by many experts as one of the main reasons why planners failed to make adequate provisions for investment in the transport sector, especially the railways. As a result, a most disconcerting development in the Indian transport scenario has been the emergence of road transport as a dominant mode. Further, the lack of coordinated efforts between various elements of the system has contributed to misallocation of resources which has resulted—especially so within a liberalized economic framework regime adopted since the 1990s—in severe mismatches even within every transport mode in terms of developing transport infrastructure and the growth of service provision.

The central purpose of a policy and planning coordination mechanism is to create such technical, economic, and other conditions for the growth of transport and distribution of traffic between different modes so that it will help in ensuring, to the greatest extent feasible, that facilities in each mode are developed and operated keeping in view the need to satisfy the overall requirements of traffic at minimum cost to the community. The result hoped for is not complete coordination but a framework of economic policy and institutions conducive to coordination between modes of transport, especially rail and road. While the Committee on Transport Policy and Coordination (GoI 1966) strongly felt that this role was best done by the Planning Commission, subsequently, the National Transport Policy Committee (GoI 1980) recommended the setting up of a National Transport Commission to coordinate attempts at the macro level in terms of policies required for investment, pricing, fiscal strategies, regulatory mechanisms, and above all for the integration of modes. The committee also recommended the setting up of transport authorities in major urban conglomerations in the country to tackle issues of coordination at the micro level. Though the ideas of the commission never materialized, a nodal Ministry of Transport was established at the central level in the mid-1980s with a supposed objective of attempting at some coordination between the various modes. Though no formal analysis of this attempt at coordination was ever undertaken, some findings indicated that the purpose of having a nodal ministry was never achieved in any sense, with each ministry chartering its own course and the experiment being abandoned soon after. All through, the Planning Commission continued its feeble attempts only to be taken lightly by the concerned authorities. This situation has not changed. We now examine a few issues.

Some Emerging National Issues

Modal Share and Modal Split

In the 1950s, Indian Railways (IR) had a near monopoly in inland transport of goods. In 1950–1, its share amounted to nearly 90 per cent in total of inland land movement of goods. IR could achieve this premier role not only because of its capability to cater to traffic in small and wagon loads as well as train loads but also owing to lack of competition from road transport, which, at that point of time, lacked necessary infrastructure in terms of roads and moving units to provide an alternative. IR had its share of increasing investments in developing infrastructure flowing from enhanced provisions in the first three Five-Year Plans for strengthening the transport sector. The impact of improvements in infrastructure was reflected in the 63.7 per cent decadal growth in originating traffic for 1950–1 to 1960–1. The historical growth of railway freight traffic is given in Table 20.1.

Table 20.1 Historical Performance of Originating Traffic on Indian Railways (IR)

Year	Tonnes Originating (Million Tonnes)		Net Tonne-Km (Million)		Average Lead (km)
	Revenue Earning Traffic	Total Traffic	Revenue Earning Traffic	Total Traffic	
1950–1	73.2	93.0	37,565	44,117	470
1960–1	119.8	156.2	72,333	87,680	561
1970–1	167.9	196.5	110,696	127,358	648
1980–1	195.9	220.0	147,652	158,474	720
1990–1	318.4	341.4	235,785	242,699	711
1996–7	409.0	423.4	277,567	279,992	661
1997–8	429.4	445.5	284,249	286,771	644
1998–9	420.9	441.6	281,513	284,270	644
1999–2000	456.4	478.2	305,201	308,039	644
2000–1	473.5	504.2	312,371	315,516	626
2001–2	492.5	522.2	333,228	336,445	644
2002–3	518.7	542.7	353,194	356,027	656
2003–4	557.4	581.4	381,241	384,074	661
2004–5	602.1	626.2	407,398	411,280	657
2005–6	666.5	682.4	439,596	441,762	647
2006–7	727.75	744.56	480.993	483,000	661

Source: RITES (2009).

However, inadequate allocations in the ensuing three Five-Year Plans led to an increasing gap between demand and supply. Its impact could be seen in the progressive decline in the decadal growth of rail traffic from 40.2 per cent during 1960–1 to 1970–1 and subsequently to 16.7 per cent during 1970–1 to 1980–1.

In the early 1980s, IR, under pressure for transporting increasing volumes of bulk commodities facing capacity constraints, decided to do away with small and wagon-load traffic and resorted to origin-destination runs of single commodity rake loads. As a result of this change in the pattern of movement, IR could carry significantly higher volumes of traffic which was reflected in the decadal growth of 62.5 per cent achieved till 1991. However, in the process, IR practically lost most of the piecemeal wagon-load traffic (including parcels) to a growing road transport system. GoI (1980), in formulating its policy recommendations, had accorded an over-riding priority to the objective of energy conservation, particularly the conservation of petroleum products whose import bill absorbed over 50 per cent of India's foreign exchange earnings during the late 1970s. The committee suggested a package of policy measures to conserve the use of petroleum products in transport. These measures intended, first of all, to divert traffic from roads to railways through pricing and fiscal policies. Second, they envisaged a greater use of electricity as a powerful motive for transport by encouraging measures such as the electrification of the railways. The railways, by the early 1990s, had completed, to a large extent, the electrification targets but other measures were not undertaken with almost nothing having been done to change the pricing and fiscal policies to discourage energy-intensive use of transport. This scenario that emerged was the reverse of what had been expected or desired by policymakers. This had very serious implications for the country not only from the point of view of energy conservation or the balance of payments problem—the objectives traditionally pursued—but also for the pursuit of what are now globally considered the most crucial objectives, which any modern transport policy should seek to achieve as part of a sustainable development strategy, namely, the control of environmental impact and reduction in the number of deaths and injuries in transport. These impacts have, in recent years, assumed such alarming proportions that they have almost everywhere threatened the lives of users and non-users of the system.

While a major part of the traffic has shifted to road transport, substantial quantities of petroleum, oil and lubricant products (POLs) have shifted to pipelines. Movement of cargo by coastal shipping has also been on the increase. Inland water transport (IWT) accounts for a small share of traffic. During the past decade, however, IR has adopted various policy initiatives and innovative measures which have resulted in improved productivity of assets and given a boost to the traffic-handling capability of the railways. The historical performance of different modes in terms of share in total originating tonnes is given in Table 20.2.

Table 20.2 Historical Modal Performance (inter-regional traffic)

(Million tonnes)

Year	Total Originated Tonnes (Million)	Modal Shares in Total Originating Tonnes (Million)					
		Railways	Highways	Coastal Shipping	Airlines	Pipelines	IWT
1950–1	82.2*	73.2 (89%)	9.0 (11%)	–	–	–	–
1978–9	283.40**	184.70 (65%)	95.60 (34%)	3.10 (1%)	–		
1986–7	484.9**	255.40 (53%)	224.00 (46%)	5.50 (1%)	–		
2007–8	2,555.35	768.72 (30.08%)	1,558.87 (61.01%)	59.10 (2.31%)	0.28 (0.01%)	113.50 (4.44%)	54.88 (2.15%)

Source: RITES (2009).

Note: * Exclusive of coastal shipping, airways, pipelines, and IWT.

** Exclusive of airways, pipelines, and IWT.

The modal share of the railways as given by RITES (2009) is just about 60 per cent. A useful exercise undertaken as part of this study was related to an examination of the resource cost of movement by each of the modes in order to understand the break-even distances up to which each mode has a comparative resource advantage. Break-even distance in this context refers to a point of cost indifference when it come to a choice between two modes. The misallocation resulting from a divergence from an optimal modal mix in favour of roads was to the extent of around Rs 40,000 crore in 2007–8, indicating that the railways had an allocative efficiency advantage in various markets over other modes in providing transportation services, especially for bulk items which need to be tapped through appropriate and effective governance practices.

Mode-wise Analysis of Certain Governance Issues

The following sections attempt to address issues related to resource mobilization through better governance practices. We take up the examples of the Indian Railways and State Road Transport Undertakings in India.

Both these examples underscore the fact that resource mobilization is possible through improved governance strategies aimed at greater internal resource generation in terms of removal of inefficiencies and appropriate pricing of services to a significant extent. As part of the new paradigm involving public–private partnerships in transport, we also look at PPPs in terms of provisions for proper governance and their implementation (Sriraman and Roy 2009).

Indian Railways

INTERNAL RESOURCE GENERATION

In attempting to raise internal resources the railways could normally seek:

i. to reduce the costs of its services;
ii. to increase the price of its services; and
iii. to reduce its social obligations.

REDUCTION IN COSTS

Increase in productivity arising from better utilization of existing capacity by improved operating and scheduling practices can result in substantial cost savings. While examining the extent of supply gap in rail freight services in the 1970s and 1980s, Rao and Sriraman (1985) observed that it would be very pertinent to concentrate on developing effective operating policies to augment the short- and medium-run supply potential. Anand (2004) noted the prevalence of both excess capacity as well as sub-optimal input use on the Indian Railways. More specifically, it would be necessary to:

(a) keep loaded wagons moving for longer hours per day,
(b) reduce the delays in loading, classification, unloading, etc., by imposing a tariff rate per wagon utilized per day rather than tonnage, and
(c) improve wagon allocation procedures by appropriate scheduling and reduction in the movement of empty wagons (Sriraman 1988).

Since the mid-1980s, productivity increases have been observed on the Indian Railways, in terms of both capital and labour inputs (Dalvi 1997). This has been achieved by better utilization of assets like rolling stock and motive power as is indicated by various indices. However, the accumulation of arrears of track renewals, rolling stock replacement, and under-investment in line-haul facilities, have set a limit to better utilization of facilities (GoI 1993). Wagon usage levels as, measured by the turnaround time, have gone up substantially (turnaround time has been reduced to nearly six days in the recent past compared to eight days in 1997–8 and to 12 days in 1990–1). NCAER, (2001: 5) observed 'Cost reduction and the increased speed of freight movement over the past few decades have been increasingly based on multi-modal transport involving containerization which requires interactive coordination by shippers across rail, port, air and road freight modes. These developments provide yet another challenge to IR, calling for a basic change in their approach to freight transportation'. Some remarkable changes followed in the next five or six years in the form of innovative managerial strategies which saw a steep growth in freight revenue after 2004. The increase in freight revenue can be traced to three factors: (i) increased axle load, (ii) reduced wagon turnaround, and (iii) market-oriented tariffs and schemes. The first two managerial actions increased IR's capacity to move higher volume of goods while the third action—market-oriented tariffs and schemes—helped raise the per unit revenue from freight and passenger movements. While the first two factors contributed to a reduction in costs and thereby net revenue, the third factor, namely, market-oriented tariffs and schemes rationalized tariffs and helped in better revenue realization.

How is this development sustainable? Limitations to these strategies of better utilization of assets and the fact of rising inputs costs have made it imperative to move tariffs in alignment with costs especially passenger fares in order to correct the imbalance between freight and passenger traffic. Productivity per employee has no doubt been improving steadily. However, progressive increases in staff-related costs have had a negative impact on staff productivity if staff costs are taken into account. In other words, it will be possible to sustain the achieved 'turnaround' only if some policy strategies are in place, especially with regard to pricing and reorientation of the cross-subsidization policy which, in its current form, can lead to a collapse of the system given the huge social burdens that the organization is required to bear even today. We now turn to these issues.

Pricing of Services

In determining prices for multi-product firms like the railways, policymakers have, for a long time, faced a number of issues that relate to the basic economic characteristics of the industry. The endemic economies of scale and scope imply that straightforward measures of cost cannot be used to dictate pricing. Economies of scale imply that marginal cost pricing will not allow firms to break even. Further, shared costs that are a result of economies of scope cannot be unambiguously identified with individual products without being arbitrary. Arbitrary measures, such as fully distributed costs, cannot be substitutes for marginal cost measurements as decision rules for proper pricing. Alternatively, there are sound pricing principles which promote economic efficiency while simultaneously removing impediments to appropriate reforms for operators. These principles lead to differentiated prices, sometimes referred to as Ramsey prices, which apportion all unattributable fixed and common costs of railways among its services on the basis of the value of those services to consumers—mathematically expressed as their elasticities of demand. By providing that each service is priced at a mark-up over marginal costs, which is inversely related to the elasticity of demand for that service, economically efficient differential pricing combines cost and demand factors in an optimal manner (Baumol and Bradford 1970). Hence, where the demand for a service is highly inelastic, a substantial addition must be made to the marginal cost. Where demand is perfectly elastic, revenue above the short-run marginal cost can be used to meet the financial target without distorting the allocation of traffic between services. These principles result in lower prices generally by establishing a set of rates, which encourage the purchase of more rail transportation services, thereby creating a larger base over which unattributable costs can be, apportioned (Kessides and Willig 1995).

Historically, these principles have served as the theoretical basis for what has been popularly termed the 'value of service pricing principle' which has been adopted by a number of railway systems including IR. But it must be noted that such an approach was feasible in the absence of any effective competing mode. However, the rapid expansion of road transport services, over a period of time, has severely limited the scope of discriminatory pricing, which used to provide adequate returns to capital earlier. Essentially, the point is that railway user charges (especially on high-valued items) cannot be raised beyond the level at which the elasticity of demand for railway transport works against the interests of the railways. In other words, there is no evidence to bear out that the value of the service pricing principle, which is justified on theoretical grounds, is the kind that is found to be practised in IR. This is obvious from the observation that the rate-making process has been highly insensitive to changes in the relative advantages of modes. Following the recommendations of the Railway Tariff Enquiry Committee (GoI 1980), there were sharp increases in tariffs over the past two decades. (GoI 1993: 189) observed 'the scope for mobilising large-scale internal surpluses by raising tariffs is limited due to proven shift away from the railways'. NCAER (2001: 98) observed 'In the Eighth Plan, 18 per cent of the total plan spending was raised by additional resources mobilized. An unprecedented proportion of this share was from freight tariff revisions and this had other consequences'. Dalvi and Sriraman (1998) pointed out large gaps between costs incurred by the railways and prices charged by it, especially with respect to passenger services.

There has, thus, been an argument in favour of increasing passenger fares. This may have been specifically true for traffic in the second-class mail/express component (mainly long-distance, inter-city, and non-suburban). This segment has normally accounted for nearly 55 per cent of the passing per km and 58 per cent of the revenue generated. Even a marginal increase per passenger-km could, it has been argued, result in huge additional earnings. It has also been a widespread belief that there will not be a response to fare rise (in other words, inelastic demand). NCAER (2001: 70) has pointed out that the 'railways have a virtual monopoly on a large range of travel options in the middle of the transportation hierarchy. This represents an opportunity to increase usage of higher class services'. The recommendation was that rebalancing passenger tariffs will require an annual adjustment of 10 per cent in second class sleeper fares and 8 per cent in second ordinary fares on a continual basis for about five years. At the same time, upper class fares were to be raised by 1–2 per cent a year. The railway budget for 2002 attempted a modest beginning but this exercise ended then, and the subsequent budgets have avoided any passenger fare increases (Sriraman 2009; Sriraman and Anand 2004). It is an emerging feeling that the potential to tap the middle segments of the transportation price and distance hierarchies with regard to passenger traffic may be severely limited in the years to come with the commissioning of the upgraded National Highway sections fully in place.

Social Burdens

A major factor impacting the financial performance of IR is its social burden. Conceptually, social burdens can be categorized into five different forms: (i) Those arising from cross-subsidization; (ii) Those arising as a result of the government's equity-distributional policies; (iii) Those which result because rail transport is supplied as a public good; (iv) Those which result from the external effects of the transport system; and (v) Those incurred in the form of welfare measures for the benefit of railway employees. At the operational level, these are categorized as: (a) losses on transport of essential commodities; (b) losses on coaching services; (c) losses on uneconomic branch lines; and (d) losses on strategic lines. In 2002–3, the net social service obligation borne by IR was assessed at Rs 3,908 crore, while in 2011–12, it was assessed at Rs 17,651.62 crore excluding the staff welfare cost (Rs 3,842.50 crore) and law and order cost (Rs 2,4945.04 crore). It has often been stated that if they IR was relieved of its social burden, it would not have to depend on budgetary support to finance its Plan outlays and that tariffs levels could be lower even after meeting the dividend liabilities.

As observed, losses were earlier covered by a process of cross-subsidization. The existence of considerable cross-subsidization, as it happens extensively in infrastructure, exposes public operators to selective private competition, which greatly deteriorates the supplier's financial position. The policy of cross-subsidization for IR has resulted in freight rates of several commodity groups reaching unreasonably high levels, resulting in diversion of traffic to other modes, especially road transport, with attendant social costs in terms of higher energy consumption and environmental damage. The continually increasing levels of subsidization in passenger fares are also generating excessive demand, leading to extreme congestion and deterioration of services. Excessive demand for passenger traffic displaces freight and reduces the speed at which freight can be transported by the railways. The benefit of subsidized services also does not always accrue to genuine passenger but is appropriated as 'rent' by intermediaries.

Economists are unanimous in their view that the social burdens carried on equity distribution grounds (such as provision of subsidized services to students, suburban travellers or even to remove regional imbalances) have no justification on allocative efficiency grounds. It is normally argued that these burdens should be properly quantified and, in all fairness to the IR, passed on to the exchequer. The same point can be made about obligations borne because of the 'public good' characteristics of IR (to meet defence needs, or to maintain law and order). There is no conceivable logic why the railways should support the losses it incurs on these movements. However, there could be an externality argument which introduces an altogether different dimension in the case for cross-subsidization; if the railways are causing less environmental damage vis-à-vis other modes of transport, such as road, railway services can be under-priced and the resultant losses met by increasing the prices charged by environmentally more damaging modes of transport and not by the railways (as a cross-subsidy) or general body of taxpayers. It is a fairly, widely accepted proposition that losses incurred on suburban rail services should be met by charging road users the full costs, including pollution costs of road services.

The kind of investment that is envisaged in the growth scenario requires an exceptional commitment from IR to reform and reinvent the organization's pricing practices.

State Road Transport Undertakings in India

A scrutiny of the financial performance of 34 State Road Transport Undertakings (SRTUs) (GoI 2011) for 2010–11 reveals that the total losses of all SRTUs taken together was around Rs 5,492.28 crore compared to Rs 4,737.10 crore in 2009–10. Five out of 34 reporting SRTUs posted profits during the fiscal year 2010–11. While the Karnataka State Road Transport Corporation (KSRTC) posted the highest profit of Rs 62.05 crore, Delhi Transport Corporation incurred the highest losses of Rs 2,286.54 crore.

In a study undertaken for the Eleventh Finance Commission, Sriraman (2000) examined these issues in detail within the framework of an analytical model which investigated the impact of physical performance on the financial performance of SRTUs. The optimal price for achieving profit maximization differs from that needed to maximize social welfare or sales revenue. If there is more than one objective to attain, some of these are treated as goals while others are treated as constraints. The objectives he goals and constraints is usually a political decision. Thus, the problem of SRTUs, for example, is one of constrained maximization where the objective function is revenue maximization based on fares while the constraints spell out social obligations. In practice, government approval is necessary for tariffs to be implemented. The government has the power to modify the recommended tariffs and even if no modifications are made, its approval, it is observed, is accorded after a long delay. The delay in approval often means that the relationship between costs and tariffs, on which the recommendations were made, is no longer valid (the case of IR is different since tariffs automatically come for review at the time of preparing the Railways, annual budget proposals).

Exercises based on simulation of the base-year model (1997–8) for the different SRTUs revealed three scenarios. Scenario 1 related to the case of undertakings in Tamil Nadu that are registered under the Companies Act. All of them achieved a high level of physical efficiency and had high load factors. This performance did not get reflected in the financial performance since fares were low. A uniform tariff for units across the state, in spite of varying sizes and characteristics and low levels of such tariffs, resulted in huge losses for these undertakings. Under Scenario 2, high fare levels but low physical efficiency performance contributed to losses in states like Maharashtra and Gujarat. Improving performance to optimal levels could have seen the emergence of huge surpluses. In Scenario 3, undertakings needed to take care of both price increases as well as promoting efficiency. Exercises undertaken for 34 SRTUS in 2010–11 (GoI 2011) reveal a similar picture. The load factor (LF) and a critical fare level were significant influences on the financial performance of an SRTU. SRTUs will need to effective tackle the problem of low load factors in a variety of ways. It must be understood that while LF is mostly demand driven, it is also supply-induced. Once this is realized, an appropriate fare strategy is required to set the organization on a long-term growth path. For this to happen, these SRTUs need to function on 'business-led principles' (as directed in the RTC Act of 1950).

Experiences under the Current Policy Framework: JnNURM and PPPs in Bus Transport—Case Studies[1]

THE VADODARA EXPERIENCE

Vadodara Municipal Corporation (Vadodara Municipal Seva Sadan, or VMSS) took up the initiative of organizing a city bus service on the basis of a public–private partnership. It defined the bus routes, bus stops, and fare structure, and also the quality of service in terms of frequency. It had to follow guidelines for city bus services as per state urban development, was responsible for getting a no objection certificate from Gujarat State Road Transport Corporation (GSRTC) stopping the current services, and for get ting the Road Transport Authority's (RTA's) sanction for stage carriage permits under the Motor Vehicles Act. The private partner procured, owned, operated, and maintained the buses. In lieu of the rights given to the operators for collecting fare, VMSS got a premium on a yearly basis from the operators. The bus stops were built by VMSS on a Build-operate-transfer (BOT) basis with another private party supporting bus services on the basis of advertisements.

[1] Sriraman 2013.

With 41 routes and 100 buses, VMSS's income increased from bus operations as also from bus stands. It was recognized that the success of this venture could be attributed to:

(1) quick approvals from the state government;
(2) quick decisions regarding tariffs, routes, frequency;
(3) overall monitoring by VMSS;
(4) transparent selection of operators; and
(5) continuous consultation with stake holders—public, police, etc.

VMSS encountered several challenges in terms of the phenomenal growth in three wheelers and personalized vehicles (two wheelers and cars) which created difficulties in bus movements. A move towards heavy occupancy vehicle lanes and then towards a bus rapid transit system could pave the way for an improved system to emerge.

THE JALGAON EXPERIENCE

The motivation behind the application of the PPP model in Jalgaon was provided by the poor services provided by the then existing public operator, the Maharashtra State Road Transport Corporation (MSRTC). MSRTC sustained continued losses from the business and its demand for compensation from the Jalgaon Municipal Corporation did not receive any response. As a result, operations were discontinued in August 2009. The municipal corporation wanted to provide bus services but had neither the resources nor the requisite expertise to do so and hence there was no option but to go in for the PPP model.

A special purpose vehicle (SPV)—JMTU (Jalgaon Municipal Transport Undertaking) was formed which floated tenders for bus services which received one response from Prasanna Bus Links (PBL). PBL began operations with a fleet of buses with rates of Rs 3 for the first 2 km and Rs 0.60 per km thereafter. This system adopted e-enabled measured, such as a GPRS fleet tracking system, an electronic ticketing system, LED and LCD displays in buses and stops, and smart card passes. The frequency on all routes was 15 minutes. As a result, the carrying capacity increased by 400 per cent while average occupancy rose to 55 and there was a revenue increase of 500 per cent. All these were achieved due to sustained marketing efforts, more revenue from advertising, motivation of man-power thereby providing high-quality services, and, above all, achieving high levels of operational efficiency.

However, a little more than a year later, the services were withdrawn due to a number of reasons significant among them being the lack of infrastructure provision as provided in the agreement between the public and private partners. Non-cooperation on the part of MSRTC did not permit use of a terminal that has been lying unused ever since MSRTC stopped city operations. The absence of a bus terminus and depot space resulted in significant additional expenditure for diesel for bus turnaround on every trip and empty movement at the start and close of the day. While the tendering process had specified 15 routes to be bid for, only five were offered for, with the remaining not being offered for, at the insistance of MSRTC. It is our understanding that even the routes that were proposed were never planned which meant that there is need for rationalization of routes based on a comprehensive study that needs to be undertaken to examine origin-destination movements and also to categorize routes as trunk and feeder routes. 'There is need for planning of transport facilities/ routes which are a vital part of the urban planning and development process for any town and region. This is currently not being given any particular attention in most of our cities. Further, it is being realized that in the absence of a model concession agreement prepared by the central government for use specifically for bus operations in urban areas (as was done for roads, ports, airports), there are no clear signals to the operators on what is expected from them. Addressing these issues of institutional weakness and the capacity building constraints of urban local governments needs much more serious attention from policymakers.

A Mumbai Case Study involving the Mumbai Urban Transport Project (MUTP) II[2]

The MUTP II has been an extremely complex project—not only in formulation and implementation but also in terms of its sustainability. The World Bank, with its experience, played a big role in designing the project; what it could not easily do, however, is to select an agency that could implement this complex project efficiently. This was the biggest risk in MUTP with the risk analysis of the project by the World Bank team noting that cooperation between various stakeholders of the project and from other government departments was weak with an additional (perhaps less pessimistic) remark that this risk would be mitigated by the creation of a high power steering committee and a project coordination committee.

[2] Based on Mukhopadhyay (2006) and Sriraman (2012).

Even a cursory examination of the then existing administrative structure reveals that there was virtually no coordination between the agencies involved in managing traffic and transportation in Mumbai. The municipal corporation had no set up to deal with road traffic issues till under MUTP conditionalities, the Municipal Act was amended so that a traffic management unit (TMU) could be set up in the corporation. As of today, it is the Police Department that manages the traffic, but only as a reactive measure; it has no sense of carrying on a traffic survey from time to time and suggesting policy changes, particularly on modal issues. Similarly, the most important component of railways is being handled by a new corporation, the Mumbai Rail Vikas Corporation (MRVC) because the existing system did not allow the execution of what MUTP had envisaged. However, the understanding in many quarters is that MRVC was merely to be involved in carrying out construction of railway projects and was not to be involved in operations. It is our considered view that the proposed institutional changes have not been adequate in establishing a rational transport operations and management system in the Mumbai metro region even though it may have been just about adequate to implement the current MUTP. MUTP has at best been a temporary reactive and fire-fighting project. But it has afforded an opportunity to reform the system effectively. What Mumbai needs is a statutory local transport authority that will not only execute similar projects in the future but will actually be on top of the problem on a continuous basis and come up with planning, policy changes, and implementation ideas as the situation becomes more complex and difficult. We now explain the rationale and outline the framework of such an authority.

A LOCAL TRANSPORT AUTHORITY IN MUMBAI

MUTP II was expected to serve as a basis for some limited expansion of the rail system. A major component of the project, that is, the expansion of rail capacity projects aims at relieving congestion on the existing suburban rail system so as to make commuting comfortable and safe. This is to be attempted by providing extra suburban rail capacity by segregating suburban traffic from long-distance traffic. An economic evaluation of these projects conducted in 1999–2000 revealed that high returns could be expected in the corridor between Santacruz and Borivali and that between Kurla and Thane. However, the return on lines beyond Borivali is expected to be much lower. This evaluation considered the benefits that are expected to accrue to consumers in terms of waiting time, reduction in discomfort, and also marginal savings in operating costs of vehicles by those who will benefit by reduced congestion. However, what needs to be noted is that even after the completion of these projects, a rake (nine car) will still be expected to cater to about 3,000 users (on an average) which will definitely be lower than what is being handled today (in excess of 4,000), but will still be higher than the carrying capacity of a rake, that is, around 2,000. From a financial perspective, the evaluation pointed out to almost no return on investments from any of the projects. To generate a financial return of 15 per cent, it was found that very steep hikes in fares would be required. Obviously, the revenue gap that could arise would have to be taken care of by other means.

In the context of the Brihanmumbai Electric Supply and Transport (BEST), it is well known that there is cross-subsidization of bus deficits by surpluses of the electricity division. With a growing inability to pass on tariff increases continuously and indiscriminately in the electricity sector, it has been found that the range for discrimination of tariffs has narrowed down. BEST has, it appears, finally become a victim of such a process whereby it is no longer able to tap surplus electricity consumers. One also needs to take into consideration the implications of the provision of the Electricity Act of 2003 relating to cross-subsidization. Under section 51 of the Act, it is provided that the distribution licensee (which is what BEST is) shall maintain a separate account for each business undertaking to ensure that the distribution business neither subsidizes such business undertaking in any way, nor encumbers its distribution assets in any way to support such a business. Accordingly, surpluses generated by the electricity division will soon not be available for subsidizing the bus division. Moreover, fixing tariffs is vested with an appropriate regulatory commission. With competition and control of a regulatory authority, the amount of surpluses generated by the electricity division can be expected to come down considerably. In the present framework, deficits can still be met by transferring surpluses from the municipal corporation's other budgets to BEST. However, the independence in relation to all aspects of functioning of BEST that has been ensured till now may no longer be feasible. It is in this context, that organizations, like the BEST, which, though within the framework of the municipal corporation of Greater Mumbai, need to be supported. In recent years, when the organization has faced deficits (in an overall sense), capital requirements have been met partly by accessing the capital market in terms of long-term borrowings. However, this has been very limited. Accordingly, only replacements provided through depreciation have been attempted to be ensured. But the expansion of the network (electricity and bus divisions) has suffered (Sriraman and Mukhopadhyay

2003). Thus, in the case of bus transport also, the revenue gap is to be covered from other sources.

It is observed that institutional weaknesses are the sources of many failures in public service delivery in the case of many urban areas, including in Mumbai. The need to integrate policies between several activities within an urban area, in general, and also within the transport sector in particular, calls for an approach completely different from the past. In the context of the suburban rail system, as has been pointed out earlier it would be preferable to have a local authority to deal with the provision of transport facilities given the localized nature of benefits and the intrinsic inter-dependence with other transit modes like the bus system.

Coverage and Framework of Such an Authority

Such an authority will enable the system to cater to the diversified transport needs through a harmonized unified system of transport output mix. It is most likely that such a system will respond to changing local needs and preferences, flexibly and receptively. Further, the authority need not be bound by other constraints arising out of national or state considerations. Assuming that this idea is accepted, the relevant issues that emerge are:

- Identifying the optimum area under the authority; and
- Sources of finance.

Evidently, in the context of the Mumbai metropolitan region, the area of the authority cannot be coincidental with that under one local government. In fact, it should compass areas under several local bodies pooled together.

The question of finance is complex and calls for innovative methods. As suggested earlier, the issue is one of identifying beneficiaries within the region, who should be made to pay for maintaining and growing the system. The beneficiaries can be broadly classified as:

- Users per se;
- Employers of users;
- Property owners in the region;
- Users and occupants of lands/buildings; and
- Local authorities like municipal corporations, councils, etc.

These groups taken together should pay for the costs of the efficient operations of the system. Users, per se, pay directly for services. Setting public transport prices and raising the necessary finance raises problems due to multiple objectives faced by decision makers. The primary objective is to generate revenues that can ensure an efficient and adequate supply of services. In typical bus operations, over 90 per cent of the costs vary with respect to either the number of vehicles employed or the number of bus-km run. Short-run marginal cost pricing will nearly cover the full cost. The same is not the case for rail systems where typically only 50 or 60 per cent of costs are directly related to the service provided. In such conditions, the most efficient way may be involving different levels of total cost coverage by the modes and transfers between them. But public transport pricing may also be expected to help in reducing congestion, to provide for efficient coordination between public transport modes, etc. In order to be able to do this, user prices cannot be expected to cover the full costs. We have already pointed out this issue both in the context of the suburban rail system and BEST. The other beneficiaries may be expected to pay for the rest of the costs. The present system hardly provides for such alternative methods of financing. These can be explored and exercised more easily and accurately by a local transit authority. With the establishment of the special purpose vehicle—the Mumbai Rail Vikas Corporation—it was expected that the first step towards the constitution of a local transit authority had been taken. However, this does not seem to be the case as explained earlier. What needs to be done as a first step is to provide for treatment of the suburban rail system as a distinct entity (maybe that is what MRVC should be) with clearly earmarked allocation of fixed assets and semi-variable and variable costs that are attributable and imputable under transparent costing principles. In other words, the suburban rail system ought to be accorded autonomy as a separate accounting unit and an autonomous profit centre.

It is widely recognized that despite all the limitations posed by the budgetary process (resulting from being a constituent unit of the municipal corporation), BEST has been able to maintain its independence in providing quality services. Besides its relative independence in terms of budgetary processes, the fact that it is a professional organization with a fairly high standard of governance is another factor (perhaps the more important one) responsible for its efficient functioning. The two dimensions have perhaps acted on each other to give rise to an outcome vastly different from that found in other typical municipal transport corporations. However, as pointed out earlier, the organization needs support in the future and this could perhaps be derived best within the framework of a local authority that we have proposed.

Concluding Remarks

Given that the traditional model is slowly giving way to a new approach, the issue is whether there has (or is) emerged (or emerging) a new scheme for governance of the transport sector in terms of its various dimensions which have contributed to the system being more efficient, viable with greater accessibility to all concerned while also being environmentally sustainable. Recent debates on transport policy have inclusively focused on how to maximize efficiency and achieve sustainability in transportation The delivery ability of the transportation system is associated with the adequacy and quality of the available transportation supply (infrastructure, roads, railway lines, rolling stock, etc.) organized and managed by a hierarchy of public organizations called 'institutional arrangements'. A review of the good practices in rail, road, and urban transport delivery indicates that well structured governance (institutional) arrangements are imperative to a successful delivery of policy objectives.

References

Anand, V. (2004), 'Pricing, Cost and Efficiency on Indian Railways', Unpublished PhD thesis submitted to the Faculty of Arts (Economics), University of Mumbai.

Baumol W. and D. Bradford (1970), 'Optimal Departures from Marginal cost Pricing', *American Economic Review*, 60(3): 265–83.

Dalvi, M.Q. (1997), *Transport Planning and Policy in India*. Mumbai: Himalaya Publishing House.

Dalvi, M.Q. and S. Sriraman (1997), 'Indian Railways' Tariff Policy', *Indian Economic Journal*, 45(2): 1–28.

GoI (1966), *Report of the Committee on Transport Policy and Coordination*. New Delhi: Planning Commission, Government of India.

——— (1980), *Report of the National Transport Policy Committee*. New Delhi: Planning Commission, Government of India.

——— (1993), *Report of the Fare and Freight Committee*. New Delhi: Ministry of Railways (Railway Board), Government of India.

——— (2001), *National Human Development Report*. New Delhi: Planning Commission, Government of India.

——— (2011), *Review of the Performance of State Road Transport Undertakings*. New Delhi: Transport Research Wing, Ministry of Road Transport and Highways, Government of India.

Kessides, I. and R. Willig (1995), *Restructuring Regulation of the Rail Industry for the Public Interest*. Washington DC: The World Bank.

Mukhopadhyay, U.K. (2006), 'Urban Governance with special reference to Transport in Mumbai', thesis submitted to Faculty of Arts (Economics), University of Mumbai.

NCAER (2001), *The Indian Railways Report: Policy Imperatives for Reinvention and Growth*. New Delhi: National Council of Applied Economic Research.

Rao, T.V.S.R.M. and S. Sriraman (1985), *Disequilibrium in Rail Freight Services*. New Delhi: Ajanta Books International.

RITES (2009), 'Total Transport System Study', Report of study submitted to the Planning Commission, Government of India, New Delhi.

Rodrigues, J.P., C. Comtois, and B. Slack (2013), *The Geography of Transport Systems*. New York: Routledge.

SOCG (2007), 'State of Governance: A Framework for Assessment', Mimeo, Centre for Good Governance, Hyderabad.

Sriraman, S. (1988), 'Empty Wagon Movement in India', *Artha Vijnana*, 30(1): 1–54.

——— (2000), 'State Road Transport Undertakings in India', Report submitted to the 11th Finance Commission, Government of India, New Delhi.

——— (2009), 'Railway Budget: Lack of a Long-term Strategy', *Economic and Political Weekly*, 44(30).

——— (2012), 'Urban Transport Governance with special reference to Mumbai', *Journal of Governance*, 4: 86–104.

——— (2013), 'An Approach to a National Urban Transport Policy Framework for India', *Journal of the Indian School of Political Economy*. Pune: Indian School of Political Economy (forthcoming).

Sriraman. S. and U.K. Mukhopadhyay (2003), *The MMC and BEST Budgets, India Infrastructure Report, 3i Publication*. New Delhi: Oxford University Press.

Sriraman, S. and V. Anand (2004), 'Railway Budget 2004–5', *Economic and Political Weekly*, 39 (31 August).

Sriraman, S., and S. Roy (2009), 'Financing Transport Infrastructure and Services, RBI DRG Study No. 28', Reserve Bank of India, Development Research Group.

The World Bank (2012), 'Transport Governance Indicators for Sub-Saharan Africa', Sub-Sahara Africa Transport Policy Program, Working Paper No. 95. Washington, DC: The World Bank.

UNDP (2002), *Governance Indicators: A User's Guide*. Oslo: UNDP Governance Centre.

CHAPTER 21

INFRASTRUCTURE

source of growth or bottleneck?

RAM SINGH AND PARAM JIT*

There is a strong relationship between infrastructure and the economic growth rate, though some disagreement remains on the direction and magnitude of the causality between the two.[1] A large number of empirical studies demonstrate that infrastructure investment has positive and significant economic effects. A sub-set of these works argues that infrastructure has macroeconomic effects in terms of growth rate as well as employment levels.[2] Some other studies show that infrastructure contributes to growth by increasing the efficiency of firms via reducing their inventories and other input costs, and by increasing overall capacity utilization.[3] Apart from being a key determinant of the growth rate, infrastructure also plays a significant role in achieving other economic objectives, such as poverty reduction and promotion of education.

It is not difficult to understand the importance of infrastructure for economic growth. For instance, commodities, such as coal, petroleum,

* We are grateful to Ashima Goyal, the editor of this volume, and an anonymous referee for providing extremely useful comments and suggestions on the first draft of this chapter.

[1] For a discussion on the issue see Qian et al. (2009), Michaels (2008), Chandra and Thompson (2000), and Fernald (1998), among others.

[2] See, for example, Démurger (2001), Chandra and Thompson (2000), and Donaldson (2010).

[3] See, Shirley and Clifford (2004), and Dutta (2012). For India-centric studies see Majumdar (2003), and Hong and Ahmed (2009).

cement, iron ore, and steel are crucial ingredients of the growth engine. Timely and low cost transportation of these inputs from their supply sources to demand centres is a pre-requisite for sustainability of growth, which in turn requires a network of extensive and efficient infrastructure. Moreover, infrastructure services act as an input for other sectors of the economy. Congested and inefficient infrastructure increases transportation costs and lowers the competitiveness of the economy. Therefore, the growth rate is an obvious victim if infrastructure is inefficient. Simply put, an adequate and efficient infrastructure is needed to increase productivity of all sectors, and thus to expand the growth potential of the entire economy.

Transport infrastructure in India is inadequate even for meeting the existing demand. Roads are congested and of poor quality. As a result, for passengers, as well as freight traffic, road services are very costly in terms of lost time, wasted fuel, additional pollution, and wear and tear of vehicles. Similarly, railways and ports infrastructure has been stretched to its limits. The railways and ports sectors are not in a position to meet the current demand for their services. For instance, several power plants are unable to secure sufficient and timely supply of coal partly because of inadequate capacity in these sectors. For similar reasons, steel plants are also facing problems in ensuring timely supply of iron ore. In fact, efficient transportation of 'basic goods' has emerged as a serious challenge for the economy. Even to keep pace with the current growth rate of 7–8 per cent, the economy needs much more extensive infrastructure.

The magnitude of the problem is simply confounding. For instance, assuming unit elasticity for traffic growth (which is a conservative assumption by all accounts) a growth rate of 7 per cent means that the traffic will expand by a factor 4 during the next 20 years. Similarly, the demand for transportation of coal, iron ore, steel, and cement will increase at least in equal measures. Unless road and railways infrastructure is expanded considerably, we could be looking at a really messy situation. Most of our demand for petroleum products is met through imports. Therefore, it is crucial to expand the ports' handling capacity. If the recent controversy over allocation of coal mines is anything to go by, it is very unlikely that domestic production will be able to meet the national demand for coal. Therefore, a significant fraction of demand will have to be met through imports, putting additional burden on the ports' infrastructure. Thus, it is essential that the capacity of our roads, ports, airports, and waterways be expended drastically and without further delay.

Besides, we need to improve the utilization of the existing infrastructure, which is not being used efficiently. This is a consequence of the ad-hoc approach to infrastructure planning in the past. Very little attention has been paid to externalities across the sector. Given the resource constraints, it is crucial that infrastructure investments are planned keeping in view the nature of traffic across various modes of transportation. Moreover, prices of infrastructure services should be determined to minimize transportation and the related costs for the entire economy. Also, it goes without saying that in order to provide world class infrastructure, both the centre as well as the state governments need to contribute in tandem.

In this chapter, we analyse the state of infrastructure in India. We focus on the issues and challenges facing transport infrastructure, especially on inter-modular planning, infrastructure delivery systems, private funding, public–private partnerships (PPPs), and the associated risks and problems. The rest of the chapter is organized as follows. The next section explores the issues and challenges faced by infrastructure sectors, particularly transport infrastructure sectors. The following section analyses the problems with the infrastructure project delivery systems in India. The focus of the section that follows is on PPPs. This addresses questions, such as what are PPPs? How do they differ from the traditional method of providing infrastructure? Whether they are a desirable means of infrastructure procurement? The last section gives a conclusion by proposing an integrated approach involving public and private sectors for the provisioning of infrastructure.

Issues and Challenges

Inadequate Investment

Since the beginning of the planning era, infrastructure investment has been awfully inadequate. Infrastructure investment has increased over time, but rather slowly. As a result, as late as in 2006–7, that is, at the end of the Tenth Five-Year Plan, the total infrastructure investment was just about 5 per cent of GDP. During the first four years of the Eleventh Five-Year Plan, infrastructure investment accounted for only 5.6 per cent of GDP.[4] Similarly, investments in crucial transport sectors have been

[4] Source for the data presented: Planning Commission (2011).

inadequate. During 2007–11, the transport sector accounted for only 2.6 per cent of GDP and 47 per cent of the total infrastructure investment. Even for the entire Eleventh Plan period, the total investment is expected to be less than the revised target. According to revised projections made by the Planning Commission, Rs 20,54,205 crore was expected to be invested during the Plan period. As much as one-third of this was to come from the private sector. However, due to the reasons discussed later, the actual private investment has been much lower than the targets in several sectors, especially in railways, roads, water supply, and sanitation. As a result, the actual investments are going to be well below targets.

Low investments are one of the main reasons behind inadequate infrastructure. The quantum of infrastructure investments needed to sustain growth obviously depends on growth targets. Various estimates suggest that investment in infrastructure should be at least 8–9 per cent of the GDP, if the growth rate of 7 per cent or above is to be sustained. For infrastructure to facilitate and spur growth, the investment needs to increase significantly. For instance, according to the Planning Commission a growth rate of 9 per cent requires that infrastructure investment for the Twelfth Plan be targeted at 9.95 per cent of GDP. This means a total investment of about Rs 40,99,240 crore (at 2006–7 prices) (Planning Commission 2011) is required. According to the Approach Paper for the Twelfth Plan, the required investment is over 45 lakh crore. It seems the policymakers have realized the necessity of a significant increase in infrastructure investment. According to the Planning Commission's estimates, the transport sector-wise investment targets for the Twelfth Plan are: Rs 9,20,071 crore for roads and bridges; Rs 5,57,673 for railways and metro rails; Rs 1,60,559 crore for ports and inland waterways; and Rs 71,000 crore for airports. For all sectors combined, the target is to increase the infrastructure investment to over 10 per cent of GDP by the end of the Twelfth Plan (Planning Commission 2012a), which is a tall order by all accounts.

Investments of this order will require an innovative approach towards financing infrastructure. There is need to mobilize funding through non-conventional sources, for example, user fee, and private sector funding. User fee is a less-distortionary source than taxation. Moreover, for a large number of infrastructure projects it can be a reliable source. However, this source remains largely untapped, except for projects implemented through private sector participation for which the private party is allowed to charge a user fee. Even for projects where government collects user fee, the choice of commission-based contracts has resulted in poor collection and maintenance of project assets. We discuss this issue in greater detail later in this chapter. In order to make adequate provision of infrastructure, public funding can and should be increased. Private funding can also be tapped. However, the question whether infrastructure funding should be public or private warrants serious attention. Besides, there is need to review extant project planning and delivery mechanisms. Indeed, unless concerted efforts are made to combine increased funding with a superior project delivery structure, the actual investment will remain well below the ambitious targets as it has in the past.

Desirability of Private Investment?

From the Tenth Plan onwards there has been an increase in reliance on private funding of infrastructure. The Tenth Plan targeted to attract 20 per cent of infrastructure investments from the private sector. The actual private investment during the Plan was about 24 per cent of the total investment; that is, 4 per cent greater than the targeted level. Encouraged by this outcome, the Eleventh Plan increased the share of private sector to 30 per cent. During the first two years of the Plan, private investment surpassed annual targets.[5] As per the revised estimates, actual private investment in the electricity and telecom sectors is going to be much greater than the targets. Accordingly, during the Eleventh Plan as a whole, about 36 per cent of infrastructure investments will be funded by the private sector. However, in several sectors private investments were way below annual targets for the last three years of the Eleventh Plan. The projected investment has been revised downward in road and bridges, railways, irrigation, water supply and sanitation, ports, and storage sectors. The main reasons behind a decline in private investment are discussed later in this chapter.

As to the desirability of private investment, in principle, it has several benefits. For one, it has great potential to augment the infrastructure network. Besides, when it comes to selection of contractors, private funding can have an advantage over public funding. Due to oversight on the part of the funding bank, private funding leads to better selection of contractors. Otherwise, there is greater risk that 'bad faith' bids will be selected

[5] During 2007–8 the total infrastructure investment stood at Rs 3,03,907 crore against the target of Rs 2,70,273 crore. Similarly, in 2008–9 the actual total investment, Rs 3,59,192 crore, was significantly greater than the targeted sum of Rs 3,21,579 crore. See Planning Commission (2011).

over genuine but costlier bids. Moreover, private sector participation can increase the efficiency of infrastructure services and delivery systems. Generally, private firms have greater contractual options available to them. Also, they have greater flexibility in adjusting their resources (personnel, equipment, and materials) to constantly changing circumstances. Naturally, private firms have stronger motivation to earn good returns on their investments. There are claims that private firms can manage the demand and supply curves in a more rigorous way than the public sector. Therefore, wherever there is scope for financing a project through direct user fee, private investors can use provision of toll-fee in a more efficient way to recoup their investments. As discussed later, the incentive to increase revenue from user fee is inter-connected with the incentive to ensure quality of the construction of assets and their subsequent maintenance. The use of private funding, along with a suitably designed procurement contract, can achieve alignment of incentives of the contractor with that of society. This can give incentives to the contractor to do right things during the contraction, as well as the operation and maintenance (O&M) phases of a project.

At the same time, private funding is generally associated with delegation of project designing, building, and operational rights to investors. As discussed later in this chapter, the delegation of decision rights poses several risks and problems. Besides, the cost of raising funds from the market is relatively high for the private sector. The cost of funds has increased significantly during the ongoing economic slowdown. Moreover, under PPPs, the government is required to make annuity payments to investors or forgo the right to charge a toll fee from users. Therefore, the decision whether to opt for private funding should be taken only after comparing the costs and benefits of the options available. Yet, given the fiscal constraints facing the centre as well as the states, private funding is more of a necessity than a matter of choice. Indeed, it is due to the paucity of funds with the public sector that from the Tenth Plan onwards there has been an increase in reliance on private funds for infrastructure. About 50 per cent of the targeted total investment for the Twelfth Plan is expected from the private sector. Moreover, the share of private investment is aimed at about one-third of the total investment in roads and bridges, 40 per cent in metro rails, 80 per cent in airports, and as much as 85 per cent in ports (Planning Commission 2012a).

Given the inevitability of private financing of infrastructure, the need of the hour is to facilitate private funding of infrastructure while protecting social interests.

Inter-modular Planning of Investment and Traffic

As argued earlier, the demand for infrastructure services is huge and expanding by the day. At the same time, there is shortage of funds needed to provide adequate infrastructure. Such a scenario calls for a two-fold response: firstly, prioritization of investment across transport infrastructure sectors; and secondly, an optimal allocation of traffic among the available modes of transportation. So far infrastructure planning has been marked by an ad-hoc and disjointed approach. For instance, there is no effective coordination among the ministries responsible for planning roads, railways, and ports. The recent plans for new expressways by the Ministry of Road Transport and Highways, and of dedicated freight corridors (DFCs) by the Railways amply illustrate a total lack of coordination. Given our heavy reliance on imported fuel, inefficient use of infrastructure is a luxury we can ill-afford.

Given the inter-dependence and complementarities across transportation sectors, the objectives of minimizing travel time and costs for goods and services can be achieved only by adopting multi-modular planning for a pan-India transportation network. Such an exercise will automatically reduce the carbon intensity of the economy. Moreover, it will have several other collateral benefits as well. For instance, transportation cost of coal is an important determinant for the locations of power plants. The location of a plant in turn affects transmission losses and other costs related to the distribution of electricity. Indeed, efficient inter-modular planning has the potential to reduce costs and losses involved in transmission and distribution of power. In contrast, inefficient use of transport modes aggravates infrastructure constrains and thereby reduces the competitiveness of the economy and lowers the production possibility frontier.

There is a need for optimal allocation of traffic among various modes of transportation, such as roads, railways, shipping, and air-based transportation. Optimum allocation of traffic across available traffic modes is crucial in a scenario of ever expanding traffic. Unfortunately, the issue has not received deserved attention from policymakers.

True determination of the optimum traffic-mix across sectors is inevitably a counter-factual inquiry and involves some value judgment. However, the existing mix of freight and passenger traffic seems to be far from optimal. For instance, it needs no persuasion that the share of railways and waterways should be much more than that of roads. Nonetheless, since Independence, these modes of transportation have accounted for a rather small fraction of passenger, and also freight, traffic. Moreover, their share has declined over time. Railways and waterways have advantages over roads in terms of transportation, environmental and other social costs. Therefore, the trend of declining shares of these sectors needs to be reversed without any delay. This will require optimum pricing of infrastructure services, an issue addressed later.

In the meanwhile, the government should take up the expansion and upgradation of railways and waterways. There should be a long-term plan for these modes along the lines and in complementarity with the National Highways Development Project (NHDP). Expansion of railways is especially crucial. On the one hand, it will increase the competitiveness of the economy by reducing transportation costs for steel, iron ore, coal, cement, and other engines of growth. On the other hand, by creating addition demand for steel, wagons, and equipment, it will spur growth. While DFCs have been planned on the Delhi–Kolkata and Delhi–Mumbai routes, there are no such plans for the equally congested Kolkata–Mumbai and Kolkata–Chennai routes.

Efficient use of infrastructure requires integration of roads, railways, ports, and airports networks and smooth transition of freight across these modes. Containerization of cargo is crucial here.[6] The process of containerization of cargo in India is far behind the levels observed in developed and some developing economies such as China. In the absence of containerization the potential gains from NHDP and DFCs cannot be captured fully. To reap the full benefits of containerization, it is crucial to increase the number of state-of-the-art container freight stations and inland container depots.

Logistic parks and warehouses are also crucial links of the logistic chains. The efficiency of transport infrastructure depends on the availability and managerial efficiency of the links. Though recent years have experienced increased investments in infrastructure, investment in logistic parks and warehouses has not increased in similar proportions. We need to develop advanced logistic parks and cargo interchange points, especially on DFC and NHDP routes. Similarly, there is a need to develop air cargo complexes for an efficient handling of exports and imports of perishable commodities, pharmaceuticals, and other valuable commodities.

[6] Containerization of freight transport entails use of shipping containers that are built to standardized dimensions to ensure smooth loading, unloading, stacking and transferring of containers from one mode of transport to another.

Pricing of Infra Services

To determine the optimum traffic mix, one needs to start with estimating the traffic growth in all segments as well as the relative costs of the competing modes of transportation. However, optimal allocation of traffic across modes and sub-modes can actually be realized only if the pricing of infrastructure services makes it compatible for users to use the intended mode. Currently, the relative prices are not optimally determined. Thus, actual traffic allocation is socially inefficient. As argued earlier, from a social efficiency perspective the railways are a better mode of transportation than roads. However, roads account for an unduly large share of freight traffic. Why? Capacity constraints and inefficient handling of traffic by the railways is surely one of the reasons. Roads will account for a disproportionately large share of traffic, even if the railways had enough capacity. Indeed, there is more to the issue than what meets the eyes.

One after the other, railway ministers have preferred political expediency of the budget over the long-term interests of the sector. Over and over again, freight tariffs have been used as a tool to cross-subsidize passenger traffic. Unsurprisingly, the railways per km earning from one tonne of freight is as much as four times that from an average passenger.[7] On top of it, most of the road stretches are not tolled and the fuel (diesel) is subsidized. The result is that the cost of using roads is less than that of using the railways. Predictably, the share of railways in freight traffic has declined over time. Some estimates suggest a steep decline, from some 65 per cent in the 1970s to below 30 per cent currently.

Compared to public transportation, within the road sector also, there is excessive use of private vehicles, especially diesel cars. Lack of reliable public transportation is surely one of the underlying factors. However, subsidy on diesel is an equally important contributory factor. To get the traffic balance right, an appropriate pricing of infrastructure services is indispensable.

Infrastructure Delivery Systems: Inadequate and Inefficient

Delay and cost over-runs have become a hallmark of infrastructure delivery systems in India. Even high-priority programmes are no exception.

[7] The 2009 white paper by the Railways admits that its freight rates are extremely high. Also see Sriraman (2002).

NHDP highlights several problems with the planning and execution of infrastructure projects. The contracting process for NHDP's Phase I got over by 2003 and the execution of the contracts was to be completed by November 2004. However, for several of these projects, the implementation is not yet fully complete. Similarly, most of the contracts for Phase II were awarded by 2007 and execution was planned to be completed by December 2009. But, development of about 1,300 km is still unfinished. A majority of the projects under implementation are experiencing delays. Some projects have been delayed by four or more years. While most of the delayed projects are non-PPPs, some PPPs are also experiencing delays. Unsurprisingly, in recent times, the highest construction rate has been 13.2 km per day in 2009–10, against the ambitious target of 20 km per day. During 2010–11, the Ministry of Roads and Surface Transport and the National Highways Authority of India (NHAI) together could achieve a construction rate of 10.8 km. Due to a decline in the number of awarded build-operate-transfer (BOT) contracts—technical name for PPP contracts—the construction rate for 2011–12 decreased to 10.15 km per day, resulting in a decline in the total length constructed by 6 per cent (SBICAP Securities 2012).

Given the recent slowdown in the contract awarding activity, the coming years are also unlikely to see a significant increase in the construction rate. Otherwise also, without resolution of the implementation phase problems, there is no way that the official target of building 6,000 km per year can be achieved in the near future.

Projects in several other sectors especially power, ports, and railways also experience long delays. The project delivery system of the railways is the worst among all sectors. Compared to other sectors, railways projects exhibit long delays and higher cost over-runs. There are several problems with the project delivery system of the railways. Projects take unnecessarily long during tendering and contracting phases. Besides, the railways award different works to different contractors which leads to serious coordination problems among contractors and the department. Another issue is the fund allocation procedure in railways. Funds for railways projects are allocated on a yearly basis, which are generally available for use only in the latter half of the year.[8]

Table 21.1 provides summary statistics on delays and cost over-runs for infrastructure projects for 17 infrastructure sectors. The data pertain to projects completed between April 1992 and June 2009. As is evident from the statistics, there are wide-ranging variations across sectors in terms of

[8] For more on the issues of delays and cost over-runs see Singh (2011).

Table 21.1 Summary Statistics (all infrastructure sectors)

Sector	Number of Projects	Percentage of projects with positive cost over-runs	Percent age of Cost Over-run (CO)				Percentage of projects with positive time over-runs	Percent Time Over-run (TO)			
			Mean	Std. Dev.	Min	Max		Mean	Std. Dev.	Min	Max
Atomic Energy	12	25.00	15.05	113.12	-84.89	265.12	91.67	301.02	570.48	-3.13	2033.33
Civil Aviation	51	41.70	-2.07	38.97	-80.32	109.18	90.80	67.20	56.01	-12.20	289.29
Coal	102	22.30	-11.42	91.72	-99.73	466.23	62.10	30.42	69.70	-93.33	359.57
Fertilizers	16	25.00	-12.57	28.92	-67.75	50.13	62.50	26.53	41.80	-18.18	109.30
Finance	1	100.00	132.91	-	132.91	132.91	100.00	302.78	-	302.78	302.78
Health and Family Welfare	2	100.00	302.30	92.96	236.56	368.03	100.00	268.04	208.63	120.51	415.56
I & B	7	42.86	14.00	62.97	-34.60	134.64	100.00	206.98	140.57	101.67	491.43
Mines	5	0.00	-33.16	20.65	-62.78	-9.88	80.00	42.44	36.23	-2.78	98.11
Petrochemicals	3	33.33	-12.22	25.92	-28.40	17.68	100.00	74.43	3.05	70.91	76.19
Petroleum	125	20.73	-15.82	29.12	-80.87	106.77	79.20	38.52	50.31	-41.67	242.86
Power	108	46.72	51.09	271.36	-61.83	2603.96	60.70	33.55	54.89	-50.00	202.08
Railways	130	82.70	94.06	178.33	-65.49	1287.98	98.36	118.05	141.13	-2.17	1100.00
Road Transport and Highways	169	53.10	14.50	61.09	-93.86	416.72	84.00	46.48	54.66	-28.26	317.39
Shipping and Ports	61	31.15	-1.35	84.35	-90.37	574.38	95.08	118.64	276.79	-7.14	2150.00
Steel	44	18.52	-15.41	47.32	-91.85	235.88	81.35	50.49	60.08	-25.00	305.56
Telecommunications	74	15.41	-33.82	56.22	-98.40	279.46	90.07	248.82	253.98	-18.18	1200.00
Urban Development	24	41.67	12.31	50.27	-48.81	144.00	100.00	66.44	44.58	3.60	166.67
Total	934	40.69	15.06	131.26	-99.73	2603.96	82.24	79.46	152.98	-93.33	2150.00

Source: Various quarterly reports on project implementation published by Ministry of Statistics and Programme Implementation (MOSPI), Government of India.

the number of projects, average percentage delays, and cost over-runs, and their standard deviations. However, in most sectors delays and cost over-runs are too frequent and too large.

Singh (2010a and 2011) throws light on the underlying factors behind delays and cost over-runs. He shows that both time and cost over-runs remain a source of major concern, even though there has been some decline in both since the 1980s. Moreover, other factors as fixed, delays are one of the crucial causes behind cost over-runs. *Ceteris paribus*, cost over-runs increase with the project size. Relatively big projects—in terms of project cost and the planned implementation phase—tend to experience much higher cost over-runs in absolute as well as percentage terms. Compared to other sectors, projects from road, railways, urban development sectors, as well as those from civil aviation, shipping and ports, and power sectors have experienced much longer delays and significantly higher cost over-runs.[9] The railways have the worst record (see Singh 2011).

Further, the study argues that poor project planning is a major reason behind delays and cost over-runs. Poor planning necessitates large variations in the scope of the project as well as the number of project works, leading to frequent delays and cost over-runs.

What can be called a 'regulatory hold-up' also greatly aggravates the problem of delays and cost over-runs. Implementation of a typical infrastructure project requires several regulatory clearances and further needs cooperation of several departments in shifting of power, water and sewer lines, and other utilities. These departments rarely do what is required of them. However, they can use a cobweb of complicated rules and procedures to pass the blame for delays on each other. The problem is so serious that even when a contractor causes delays, it is almost impossible to punish him since he can easily prove a contributory negligence on the part of one or the other government department. It will help if activities like land acquisition, provision of regulatory clearances, and shifting of utilities can be completed either before or within a pre-scheduled time after the award of contract. In that case, contractors can be put on high-powered incentives to deliver on time.

The project planning and awarding processes adopted by the project sponsoring department also have a bearing on delays and cost over-runs. Rather than awarding different works of a project to different contractors,

[9] For detailed analysis of these issues see Singh (2010a).

it is better to bundle and award most of the relevant construction works to one contractor.[10]

Poor quality of infrastructure assets is another area of concern. For instance, the roads have to be repaired after every monsoon season. Here, a part of the blame lies with the nature of the traditionally used contracts. Under these contracts, neither the contractor nor the authorities have incentives to deliver on time, cost, or quality. Serious rethinking is required on this issue. As we discuss in the next section, the choice of the contract has a significant bearing on the quality of construction and the maintenance of projects.

PPPs: The Better Way Out?

The private funding for infrastructure mentioned earlier is to be channelized through what are called public–private partnerships (PPPs). Under a PPP, the government contracts out to the private sector the tasks of building, operating, and maintaining public assets, such as state or national highways, ports, airports, schools, and hospitals. A PPP contractor is also called a concessionaire.

PPPs have been projected as an antidote to the problems with infrastructure projects discussed earlier, namely, delays, cost over-runs, and the poor quality of assets. It is believed that PPPs can reduce the cost of public goods and ensure speedier delivery of infrastructure projects. The recently released draft of the National Public Private Partnership Policy (NPPPP) amply exhibits this belief in the superiority of PPPs over traditional procurement. The objective of PPPs is stated to 'Harness private sector efficiencies in asset creation, maintenance and service delivery ... provide focus on life cycle approach for development of a project, involving asset creation and maintenance over its life cycle....'[11]

Do PPPs actually induce an infrastructure delivery system so that it is superior to the traditional approach? To answer this question, it is important to analyse the differences between PPPs and the traditional method. First of all, under a typical PPP project, the construction and maintenance expenses are borne by the concessionaire, though the government may

[10] For more on this issue see Singh (2011).

[11] See MoF (2011: 8).

contribute partially.[12] Funding is a mix of equity and the debt raised by the investor-contractor. In contracts, under the traditional approach toward infrastructure procurement, the construction and maintenance works are publically funded through budgetary support and taxation. The contracts used under the two approaches are also very different. Under the traditional approach, construction is done by a contractor. The contract used is called the traditional or the 'item rate' (IR) contract, popularly known as *cash contract*. The contractor is paid according to the amount of work done. An increase in project works means more income for the contractor. Under PPP, in contrast, the construction is the full responsibility of the concessionaire. So, the private partner in the PPP does not receive additional payments if there is an increase in project works, as long as the scope of the project is not changed by the government.[13] There are several major differences between PPP contracts and IR contracts.

Under IR contracts there is no bundling of project tasks, such as construction, O&M, and collection of user fee. These tasks are performed by different entities. The construction contractor is responsible only for the construction and related project works. O&M is done either by the relevant department or by some other contractor hired for the purpose. So, the construction contractor is compensated only for construction works. In contrast, under a PPP contract, construction and maintenance tasks are bundled together and are required to be performed by the concessionaire/PPP contractor. Therefore, the private partner needs to be compensated for construction-related as well as maintenance-related expenses. Depending on the context, the payment is either in the form of annuity payments promised by the government, or, the user fee collected by the PPP contractor.

Besides, risk allocation is significantly different under the two contract types. Under IR, the contractors bear only some of the construction cost related risks; maintenance and commercial risks stay with the government. Under a PPP, by contrast, most of the construction- and maintenance-related risks are transferred to the PPP contractor. Many a time, commercial risks are also passed on to the PPP contractor.

[12] The PPPs in railways are slightly different; in that the construction task is generally a responsibility of the public sector entity. For example, for the PPP between Delhi Metro Rail Corporation (DMRC) and Reliance Infrastructure Limited (RIL) over the airport express line, the construction works were performed by the contractors hired by the DMRC.

[13] The 'scope' of the project specifies the output features of the project. For example, for highway projects, it specifies the number of flyovers, service lanes, distance, etc. If the government changes the scope, then the concessionaire is entitled to additional compensation.

As a result of these differences, a PPP entails a greater delegation of control and decision rights to the contractor. Generally, PPP contracts are design, build, finance, operate, and maintain (DBFO&M) contracts, as the decision and control rights with respect to these activities are delegated to the concessionaire-contractor. These rights over project assets revert back to the government at the end of the contract period. Moreover, under a PPP contract, the time period of construction is included in the contract period itself. An earlier completion of the project enables the concessionaire to increase the total toll/user fee revenue from the project. In case of annuity-based contract, the concessionaire is not paid annuity for the delay period. So the PPP contractor has strong interest in completing the project as soon as possible, as the project revenue flows can start only after its completion. In contrast, under IR there is no such provision. These differences allow us to make the following inference: *other factors as fixed, shorter delays are expected in PPP projects.*

Since, under a PPP contract, the tasks of project designing, construction, and maintenance are bundled together, most of the risks associated with these tasks are borne by the contractor. This bundling naturally encourages the contractor to focus on the life-cycle costs of the project, rather than just the construction costs. So, *compared to non-PPPs, total project costs—construction costs plus the O&M costs—are expected be lower for PPP projects.*[14]

Besides, the PPP contractor has an incentive to make quality investments during the construction phase, since an increase in the quality of construction of an asset lowers O&M costs and therefore the total life-cycle costs of the project. Under IR, contractors do not have such incentives. On the contrary, wherever possible, they like to reduce their construction costs, which can result in higher O&M costs and greater wear and tear of vehicles, and thereby higher total costs for society. Therefore, *PPPs can lead to better quality of assets.*

In principle, better quality of the construction and proper upkeep of project assets leads to better quality service, which in turn, increases demand from users. Therefore, the PPP contractor stands to gain by improving the quality of assets and services. However, if there are no competing facilities supplying the same service, PPP contractors may not have sufficient incentives to invest in the quality of service. In the next

[14] As discussed later, the real challenge here is to make sure that these savings on project costs are appropriated by the public sector.

sub-section, we verify whether these conjectures are corroborated by the Indian experience with PPPs.

Experience So Far

Table 21.2 shows that by now, a large number of PPPs have been formed across sectors; a majority of them by state governments. Several sectors, such as ports, energy, tourism, and urban development have attracted a fairly large number of PPPs. On the other hand, the number of PPPs is rather small for several sectors such as railways and civil aviation.

Table 21.2 PPPs in India

Sector	Number of PPPs
Airports	6
Education	19
Health	13
Energy	77
Ports	62
Road	457
Railways	9
Tourism	52
Urban Development	181
Total	878

Source: PPP database by MoF, GoI.[15]

This dataset does not permit a comparison of the performance of PPPs with non-PPPs, with regard to issues relating to delays, cost over-runs, and quality of services, since most of the projects in this dataset are still under implementation. Moreover, in most sectors, with the exception of road ways, PPP as well as non-PPP projects vary greatly. Fortunately, road projects are helpful in comparing the performance of PPPs with non-PPP projects. While several state agencies have awarded PPPs for state highways and other roads, a majority of the PPPs have been awarded by NHAI. Table 21.3 provides summary statistics on project time and costs

[15] Available at: http://www.pppindiadatabase.com/Screens/frmSearch.aspx?AUTHORISEDUSER=N&ACTIONTAG=VIEW (accessed on 8 September 2012).

for the completed national highways projects for which relevant data are available.

Table 21.3 Summary of Delays and Cost Over-runs for National Highways Projects

	PPPs	Non-PPPs	All Projects
Number of projects	50.00	145.88	195.00
%age of projects with positive time over-runs	74.00	78.62	77.44
Mean of the ration of actual time to planned time	117.49	149.30	141.14
%age of projects with positive cost over-runs	74.00	55.17	60.00
Mean of the ratio of actual to expected construction cost	121.39	105.98	109.93

Source: NHAI Data (www.nhai.org, accessed on 17 November 2012).

As expected, PPP projects have experienced shorter delays; on an average, PPPs have taken 17 per cent extra time (See Table 21.3). By comparison, traditionally procured projects have taken 49 per cent extra time.

As far as cost over-runs are concerned, on the face of it the results seem to be striking as the actual costs of PPPs is 21per cent higher than estimated costs. This difference is smaller for non-PPPs. The unverified conjecture is that at least a part of this is on the account of quality investment in PPPs (as argued earlier). PPP contracts give incentives to contractors to make quality investments during the construction phase. Under IR, there is no such incentive for contractors. From another perspective it can be argued that under PPPs there is a desirable absence of quality-shading efforts on the part of contractors. In contrast, under IR contracts, the contractor has a strong incentive to dilute the quality of construction in order to reduce costs.[16] These inferences have been corroborated by CAG reports on NHDP.[17] In these reports, most of the IR projects were found to be deficient in quality. The quality of most of the PPP projects was found to be satisfactory.

[16] The construction-cost-cutting efforts by the IR contractors make them bid aggressively, leading to lower contracted costs for the government department, NHAI in this case.

[17] See, for example, CAG Report No. 7 of 2005 (PSUs) and CAG Report No. PA 16 of 2008. Also see Lok Sabha (2006).

At the same time, our results and the Indian experience with PPPs so far highlights the following concerns about PPP contracts:[18] PPPs are not a panacea against delays during the construction phase. As Table 21.3 shows, as many as 74 per cent of PPP projects experienced delays. Since PPP contractors cannot benefit from these delays, they are largely attributable to official hold-ups of projects during the construction phase. Moreover, PPPs can shift delays from the construction to the procurement phase. It is true that PPPs have performed better than non-PPPs in term of time management during the construction phase. However, PPP projects take much longer during the pre-construction phase. Award of PPP contracts is a protracted process. As a result, PPPs are shifting the delays from the construction to the procurement phase.[19] Of course, these delays also increase project costs, which go unreported in the standard data on cost over-runs.

To sum up, PPPs do offer an opportunity to augment the stock of funds for the purpose of public goods. However, this path poses its own risks and challenges, an issue discussed in next sub-section.

Risks and Challenges

Procurement of infrastructure services is a long and complex process.[20] Compared to IR contracts, procurement through PPPs is even more complex, since the contract covers not only the project development and construction phases, but also the operation and maintenance phase. Besides, PPPs often involve revenue-sharing arrangements between private and public partners. Therefore, problems of corruption and mismanagement are potentially more acute. Indeed, corruption in PPP procurement is a matter of great concern worldwide. It is extremely important to ensure transparency and efficiency at each stage of PPP procurement.

The process of selecting a PPP contractor is crucial for reducing corruption and enhancing economic efficiency of production. Generally,

[18] The case studies of 16 projects also corroborate our findings. See NCAER (2011).

[19] For example, for the Bengaluru International Airport, there was a gap of nearly four years between the bidding and the actual signing of the concession contract.

[20] It requires several activities, such as bidding for the contract, selection of contract clauses, execution of contract, quality control during construction phase, etc. Each of these activities is vulnerable to corruption.

competitive bidding is believed to be the best option to secure 'value for money' to the public sector. Competitive bidding is highly desirable in many procurement contexts, especially those involving procurement of goods with well-defined features, such as wagons, engines, and air craft. In such contexts, competitive bidding not only ensures economic efficiency—the most efficient suppliers are chosen—but also the best value for money as the good is purchased by the public sector at the minimum possible price. For such goods, competitive bidding works well because the good can be fully specified in the bid and contract documents.

However, for infrastructure projects, competitive bidding per se can guarantee neither efficiency nor value for money for the public sector. For competitive bidding to deliver desired results, it is crucial that the nature of the item to be procured can be described completely, and that the terms of the contract are not changed after it is signed. This means that for infrastructure projects, there should be no changes in the project scope and contract terms after the signing of the contraction contract.

Ex post changes in the scope and other terms seriously undermine the benefits of competitive bidding. To see why, note that any ex post changes in the project scope and contract terms are negotiated at a time by which the discipline imposed by a competitive bidding has been removed. So during renegotiations, the contractor is unlikely to offer good value for money to the sponsoring department. There is empirical evidence to back this claim.[21] Moreover, when the ex post changes in the scope or design are substantial, the final project can become very different from the one for which initial bids were invited. As a result, it is possible that the selected contractor may not turn out to be the most efficient one for the project. So, ex post changes are problematic even in the absence of corruption. Of course, contract renegotiations are highly vulnerable to corrupt practices.

Due to greater complexity, there is more scope for PPP contractors to use ex post contractual changes to their advantage. Recent disputes between the Delhi Metro Rail Corporation (DMRC) and Reliance Infrastructure Limited's (RIL) Delhi Airport Metro Express Private Limited (DAMEPL) is an illustrative case in point—the two entities had formed a partnership for the airport line. Vaguely drafted terms can only exacerbate the problem. The experience with PPPs for Delhi and the Mumbai airports

[21] For example, a comprehensive study of PFIs in the UK shows that in most cases, the sponsoring department fails to get value for money when a change in scope is undertaken during the construction phase.

amply demonstrate this tendency among contractors. For instance, the GMR-led consortium for the Delhi International Airport Limited (DIAL) used vague contract terms to trade low-rentals for high upfront security deposits from investors in the 250-acre hospitality district.[22]

In the past, the government's willingness to renegotiate the terms of the contract enabled the contractors to pass some of the construction-related risks back to users. To cite a few instances, the government granted permission to DIAL to extract Rs 1,827 crore from passengers by levying an airport development fee. In a similar move, Mumbai International Airport Limited (MIAL) was allowed to collect development fee of up to Rs 1,543 crore, which has led to a legal dispute, with the Supreme Court stepping in to stop the charging of the fee. In the context of the road sector, the government increased the concession period for several road projects to allow investors to charge toll for five additional years. Moreover, the acceptance of the BK Chaturvedi Committee report by the government has resulted in major changes in the contractual obligations of contractors. Through such renegotiations, the concessionaires have been able to pass some of the commercial risks back to the taxpayer. In the long term, such manipulation will seriously undermine the justification for the PPP route. The government must send a credible signal that demand for renegotiations will be considered only in the rarest of rare cases, such as, *force majeure*.

The Indian experience has brought to the fore some more problems with PPPs. The first concerns revenue-sharing arrangements. Most of the PPPs for which user fee is charged, require sharing of revenue between the concessionaire and the sponsoring department. However, very few departments have effective mechanisms in place to monitor the revenue stream. Without such mechanisms, there is every risk that society will not get its due benefits from PPPs. Overly optimistic traffic forecasts too have emerged as a serious problem. There seems to be a tendency among bidders for user-fee-based PPPs to exaggerate the demand, as in most cases the actual demand has turned out to be less than the forecasts. However, concessionaires tend to use low demand as grounds to renegotiate the contract in order to extract more concession from the sponsoring department. The dispute between DMRC and DAMEPL is mainly due to this reason. Finally, there are concerns over the quality of services provided. While PPP contractors have an incentive to build quality assets, they may not

[22] As per the contract, only rentals are to be shared with the government and not the security deposits. Therefore, the government has lost out in the process.

have an incentive to do the other things needed to provide quality service. The problem is serious where the users do not have any alternatives available. The PPP over the Delhi–Gurgaon Expressway is an illustrative case in point. Since there is no competing facility, the concessionaire, Delhi–Gurgaon Super Connectivity Ltd. (DGSCL), does not have any incentive to reduce congestion to an acceptable level. As a result, users have to spend a lot of time waiting at the toll plaza.[23]

The Way Forward

Facilitate Private Investment

Given the fiscal and technical constraints faced by the centre and the states, building world class infrastructure will require the public and the private sectors to work together. The objective should be to facilitate private investment while protecting the interests of the taxpayers. So far, the official performance has been deficient on both the counts. Several factors limit the attractiveness of infrastructure for private investors. As discussed earlier, during the Eleventh Five-year Plan the actual private investment in transport sectors was less than what was expected. As a result, the targets were revised downwards. For example, for the ports sector, the total investment target was downsized to Rs 40,647 crore against the original target of Rs 87,995 crore. For the roads and bridges, the revised target, Rs 2,78,658 crore is significantly less the original target of Rs 3,14,152 crore (Planning Commission 2011).

Private investors' lacklustre response is attributable to factors including policy paralysis, regulatory hurdles during the construction phase, and systemic constraints on bank-lending for infrastructure projects. Due to mid-way policy changes, the roads and ports sectors registered a decline in private investments even before the advent of the economic slowdown. For instance, during 2008, national highways projects worth at least Rs 70,000 crore fell prey to detrimental mid-course changes made in the request-for-qualifications and the request-for-proposal rules (see Singh

[23] The Punjab and Haryana high court has taken serious note of the callous attitude of the concessionaire. However, as on 16 November 2012, the matter was lying pending before the court, among allegations and counter-allegations made by NHAI and DGSCL.

2010b). Things are much worse for the railways sector. For the roads and ports sectors, at least the model concession agreements (MCAs)[24] have been prepared. Unfortunately, the railways minister has failed to even to come out with a clear policy on private investment. Predictably, private investment in the sector has been disappointingly low—during the first three years of the Eleventh Plan the actual private investment was less than Rs 2,400 crore, against the target of Rs 50,354 crore (Planning Commission 2011). So far, only 16 PPPs have been formed for operating container trains. The plans for upgrading 50 stations, developing logistical parks, and an elevated rail system for Mumbai and other cities on a PPP basis, are hanging in limbo.

The economic slowdown and the international financial crisis of 2008–9 have made things worse. The appetite for risk among investors has decreased drastically. To illustrate, during the first quarter of 2012–13, NHAI was able to form PPPs covering only 288.6 km against a target of 1,785 km (SBICAP Securities Ltd 2012). Reportedly, even for the awarded projects, the investors are finding it difficult to raise debt.

Though it is difficult to separate the effect of factors collectively responsible for the decline in private investments, it seems that the economic downturn and the international financial crisis are only the aggravating factors. Several systemic factors dampen the attractiveness of infrastructure projects for private investors. These projects are inherently risky and have long gestation periods. Therefore, lending to infrastructure companies is a risky business as such. Regulatory uncertainties, ambiguous tax rules, and official hold-ups, as discussed later, have unnecessarily increased the risk profile of infrastructure projects. The result is the reduced willingness on the part of investors and banks to invest in these projects. On top of this, several structural problems restrict the scope of lending to infrastructure projects. Though the total domestic saving rate is fairly high, long-term savings constitute only about 4 per cent of GDP. Therefore, lending to infrastructure projects creates an assets–liability mismatch for the banking sector. Also, PPP funding is generally non-recourse funding as SPVs formed to implement PPPs typically do not have recourse to the assets of their parent companies. On top of all this, SPVs do not have a credit history of their own to draw upon while seeking loans. These aspects increase the risk profile of banks' lending to SPVs. The fact that the services provided by infrastructure projects are non-tradable also reduces the scope of international funding for these projects.

[24] MCA is the basic contract document for PPPs.

Though insurance companies and pension funds are ideally placed to fund PPPs, Indian insurance companies are unable to process funds for PPPs due to their small sizes.[25] Moreover, insurance companies and pension funds are generally risk-averse and therefore tend to invest in government securities, rather than in riskier long-term assets. Then there are also official restrictions which also reduce the scope for insurance companies and funds to invest in infrastructure projects and companies. This situation needs to change. Promoters account for about 80 per cent of the equity investment in PPPs (see Lall and Anand 2009). So, there is scope for pension funds and insurance companies to invest in these projects, especially in those that have already completed their construction phases. Similarly, private equity investment in such projects needs to be facilitated. All this calls for developing a debt and corporate debt market, which in turn requires institutions for efficient inflow of funds in these markets.

However, in the interim the government can promote PPPs by strengthening its initiatives, such as the India Infrastructure Project Development Fund (IIPDF), viability gap funding (VGF), resources for annuities, and long-term lending. Moreover, it can expand the scope and magnitude of refinancing of loans through the India Infrastructure Finance Company Ltd. (IIFCL). IIFCL's mandate needs to be changed. Instead of being a direct lender, it should focus on enabling flow of non-bank long-term debts to infrastructure. Several recommendations of the Deepak Parekh Committee on Financing of Infrastructure can help increase the attractiveness of infrastructure for PPPs by reducing the costs of raising funds for investors. For instance, IIFCL should use its experience to issue guarantees for bonds issued by private infrastructure companies. It should provide subordinate debt only up to 10 per cent of the project costs. Direct landing should be restricted to cases where banks and non-bank finance companies (NBFCs) will not provide the required funds. Moreover, 'group exposure limits' on lending can be removed. As long as equity stakes for investors are kept undiluted during the construction phase, these measures need not worsen the problems of adverse selection—during the bidding and contracting phase—and moral hazards during the contraction phase.

Project risks and therefore the cost of private financing can be reduced by resolving issues relating to taxation/general anti-avoidance rules (GAAR) making regulatory laws and rule predictable, and by improving the project delivery systems as discussed later. Lastly, funding costs can

[25] Insurance penetration in India is still small, compared to developed countries where it accounts for 9–10 per cent of GDP (see Lall and Anand 2009).

also be reduced by a competition among funders, once the bidder has been chosen. Since, the bidder has already been selected it may be possible to find cheap funders for the project. There also seems to be scope for significant savings through such competitions, especially for projects in energy, ports, etc.

Improve Project Delivery Systems

As the earlier analysis shows, the choice of contract matters, since different contracts provide different incentives to contractors in terms of contract management and timely completion of the project. With a suitable choice of contracts, it is possible to manage time better, reduce frequency and intensity of cost over-runs, and improve the quality of infrastructure services. PPP contracts have in-built incentives for contractors as far as delivery time and quality of assets are concerned. However, in India, PPPs as such are not the ultimate solution against delays during the construction phase. In all sectors, PPPs frequently encounter construction delays. Since the contractor does not stand to gain from these, construction delays are due to the regulatory hold-ups discussed earlier. The case of Delhi Airport Express Metro is a case in point.

Many projects experience delays on account of land acquisition. A significant fraction of such delays are attributable to disputes and litigation over compulsory land acquisition. These problems have been triggered by the gross misuse of the ambiguous and archaic Land Acquisition Act (1894) by the states. Today, land acquisition, even for genuine public purposes, sparks off popular protests. Moreover, relevant regulatory frameworks for the infrastructure sector are vague in terms of conditions to be met by project sponsors. Similarly, there is a complex overlap of responsibilities and domains of individual departments and ministries. Consequently, project files go back and forth among ministries and departments within ministries. The result is an 'official hold-up'. There have been strange instances in which the Ministry of Environment and Forests has gone back on its decisions and held up projects even after providing clearances.

To overcome these problems, the centre has proposed the setting up of the National Investment Board. The objective is to expedite clearance for big projects. The proposal has already met with resistance from expected quarters, including the Ministry of Environment. Clearly, there is every case for putting the stalled infrastructure projects back on track, especially when achieving of even 5 per cent growth rate for 2013–14 has become a challenge. However, instead of adopting a selective and shortcut approach, there is need to overhaul the policy frameworks on land acquisition and regulation of infrastructure. If the land acquisition law is transparent and its use is restricted to clearly defined public purposes, it will go a long way in reducing resistance against land acquisition.[26] Similarly, the regulatory structure needs to be made clear and consistent. It should provide for time bound clearances from the ministries involved. Moreover, if a project receives regulatory clearances, individual ministries should not be allowed to put further objections. Such a commitment is crucial for the success of the centre's ambitious infrastructure development plans.

Moreover, PPPs experience longer delays during the pre-construction phase. For example, for the Bengaluru International Airport, there was a gap of nearly four years between the bidding and the actual signing of the concession contract. A study on private finance initiative (PFI) in UK shows that that depending on the complexity of the project a period of 18–24 months is enough for pre-construction activities, that is, project identification, development, and tendering.[27] The official responsible should be held to account in the event of delays during these phases.

Inadequate official capacity to handle PPPs seems to be a leading factor behind shortage of bankable projects offered under the programme. It also means that the projects that are actually offered to the market are poorly planned and developed projects. The importance of proper project planning cannot be overstated. Poor project designing is one of the leading causes behind the need for change in the scope and contract terms during the construction phase which, in turn, leads to delays and cost overruns. Moreover, as discussed earlier, contract renegotiations seriously undermine the utility of competitive bidding for PPPs. Therefore, the official capacity needs to expand, especially in the railways.

Project monitoring is also crucial for PPPs as well as non-PPPs. Currently, the project identifiers are different from their planners who, in turn, are different from the people responsible for monitoring the tendering and construction processes. As a result, if things go wrong, it is difficult to fix responsibilities. This also means that project planners have no incentive to put in the required efforts. It will help if the same set of

[26] For a detailed analysis of problems with land acquisition and the possible ways out, see Singh (2012).

[27] See NAO, UK (2007). The study shows that for some of the complex projects, project planners were able to complete the tasks of project identification, development, and tendering within 18 months.

officials/engineers is required to see the project through from the very beginning till the end of the contraction phase. In case of changes in the scope, the official responsible for planning should be required to explain the same. This measure will also help generate and provide reliable time and cost estimates for the bidding process.

Revamping of the project delivery system for publicly funded projects is of equal importance. Under the traditionally used (IR) contracts, neither the contractor nor the officials from the sponsoring department have an incentive to monitor a project's progress during the construction phase. It will help if these contracts are replaced with an appropriate version of what are called engineering procurement contracts (EPCs). Some of the problems with traditional contracts will be overcome if the contractor is made responsible for project design and its maintenance for 4–5 years. Also, the contract should provide for bonus for timely project delivery and penalties for delays.

Other Helpful Measures

To get the traffic balance right, there is need to estimate the medium- and long-term demands for various infrastructure services. Besides, an appropriate pricing of infrastructure services is indispensable. This means that the user fee and relative service charges should reflect the social costs of the competing modes of transportation. Moreover, other relevant taxes, such as excise duty on diesel cars should be determined with an objective to minimize the social costs of transportation. Determining an optimum traffic mix and relative prices are complex exercises. To achieve these goals, the nation must enhance decision-making capabilities of policymakers, scientists, engineers, designers, and maintenance staff in all sectors. In this regard, the recommendations of the interim report of the National Transport Development Policy Committee (headed by Rakesh Mohan) are laudable. The committee identified the following priority areas for capacity building: engineering and mathematical modelling to assess freight and passenger traffic; statistical and sociological studies on safety issues; survey and operational techniques on the operation and management of infrastructure, and modelling and instrumentation techniques to assess environmental health effects of various modes.[28]

[28] For this purpose, the report has proposed the setting up of national-level institutions; namely, Indian Institute for Transport Research and Indian Institute for Transportation Statistics. See Planning Commission (2012b).

Moreover, there is need to have an infrastructure regulator. As discussed earlier, political economy considerations rather than social interests dominate the pricing of infrastructure services in several sectors, especially railways. It will help if decision-making powers regarding service prices and user fee are delegated to the regulator. Moreover, the regulator can ensure that demands for contract renegotiations are considered only in the rarest of rare cases and as per the contract's provisions.

Finally, it is important to remember that PPPs as a means of public procurement are feasible only under limited circumstances. In many situations, PPPs are not viable or are simply not feasible. This is especially true of the user-fee-based PPPs. Such PPPs can work only if there is significant demand for the service offered by the PPP combined with the willingness to pay on the part of users. For instance, a study on PPPs on national highways in India shows that PPPs are likely to work only for projects located close to big cities in richer states (see Anant and Singh 2009). This means that infrastructure development in the countryside and the other backward regions, such as the North-East will have to be publically funded. The centre as well as state governments need to mobilize more resources for this purpose. The country can ill-afford the decline in the tax–GDP ratio from 12 per cent in 2007–8 to 10 per cent in 2011–12.

References

Anant, T.C.A. and Ram Singh (2009), 'Distribution of Highways Public Private Partnerships in India: *Key Legal and Economic Determinants' CDDRL Stanford University Paper* No 100. Available at: http://iis-db.stanford.edu/pubs/22651/No_100_AnantSingh_Highways_Public_Private_India.pdf (accessed on 17 November 2012).

Chandra, Amitabh and E. Thompson (2000), 'Does Public Infrastructure Affect Economic Activity? Evidence from the rural interstate highway system', *Regional Science and Urban Economics*, 30: 457–90.

Démurger, Sylvie (2001), 'Infrastructure Development and Economic Growth: An Explanation for Regional Disparities in China?' *Journal of Comparative Economics* 19: 95–117.

Donaldson, Dave (2010), 'Railroads of the Raj: Estimating the impact of transportation infrastructure', NBER Working Paper No. 16487. October.

Dutta, Saugato (2012), 'The impact of improved highways on Indian firms', *Journal of Development Economics*, 99: 46–57.

Fernald, J.G. (1998), 'Roads to Prosperity? Assessing the Link between Public Capital and Productivity', *The American Economic Review*, 89, 619–38.

Hong, Huqui and Sadiq Ahmed (2009), 'Government Spending on Public Goods: Evidence on Growth and Poverty', *Economic and Political Weekly*, XLIV(31): 102–8.

Lall, Rajiv B. and Ritu Anand (2009), 'Financing Infrastructure', IDFC Paper. Available at: http://idfc.com/pdf/white_papers/bs_infra_funding.pdf (last accessed on 11 November 2012).

Lok Sabha (2006) '*Fourteenth Report' of Committee on Public Undertakings (2006–7)*. New Delhi: Lok Sabha Secretariat.

Majumdar, Rajarshi (2003), 'Infrastructural Facilities in India: District Level Availability Index', *Indian Journal of Regional Science*, 35(2): 58–71.

Michaels, Guy (2008), 'The Effect of Trade on the Demand for Skill: Evidence from the Interstate Highway System', *The Review of Economics and Statistics*, 90(4): 683–701.

MoF (2011), 'National Public Private Partnership Policy' (Draft). New Delhi: Department of Economic Affairs, Ministry of Finance, Government of India.

NAO (2007), *Improving the PFI tendering process*. UK: National Audit Office.

NCAER (2011), *Seeking Efficiency and Excellence in the Implementation of Infrastructure Projects in India*. New Delhi: Holcim Ltd. and NCAER.

Planning Commission (2011), *Investment in Infrastructure During the Eleventh Five Year Plan*. New Delhi: Planning Commission.

——— (2012a), *Interim Report of the High Level Committee on Financing of Infrastructure* (the *Deepak Parekh Committee*). New Delhi: Planning Commission.

——— (2012b), *Interim Report of the National Transport Development Policy Committee* (the *Rakesh Mohan Committee*). New Delhi: Planning Commission.

Qian, Nancy, Abhijit Banerjee, and Esther Duflo (2012), 'On the Road: Access to Transportation Infrastructure and Economic Growth in China', NBER Working Paper No. w17897. Available at SSRN: http://ssrn.com/abstract=2014590.

SBICAP Securities Ltd. (2012), *Report on Infrastructure—Roads and Highways Sector*. Mumbai.

Shirley, Chad and Winston Clifford (2004), 'Firm Inventory Behavior and the returns from highway infrastructure investments', *Journal of Urban Economics*, 55: 398–415.

Singh, Ram (2010a), 'Delays and Cost Overruns in Infrastructure Projects in India: *Extents, Causes and Remedies*', *Economic and Political Weekly*, XLV(21): 43–54.

——— (2010b), 'A High-handed Approach to National Highways', *Economic and Political Weekly*, 45(08): 19–21.

——— (2011), 'Determinants of Cost Overruns in Public Procurement of Infrastructure: Roads and Railways', *India Policy Forum* 7: 97–158.

——— (2012), 'Inefficiency and Abuse of Compulsory Land Acquisition: An enquiry into the way forward,' *Economic and Political Weekly* XLVII(19): 46–53.

Sriraman, S. (2002), 'Indian Railways Finances—A Critical Review of Basic Issues and Emerging Options', *Journal of Indian School of Political Economy*, 14(3): 377–94.

CHAPTER 22

PRIVATE PARTICIPATION IN POWER DISTRIBUTION REFORMS

SIDHARTH SINHA*

The power sector in India requires large investments in electricity generation, transmission, and distribution. A significant proportion of the investment is expected to come from the private sector. According to the approach paper to the Twelfth Five-Year Plan (Planning Commission 2011a) about 33 per cent of the total incremental capacity during the Eleventh Plan is expected to come from the private sector. This share is expected to increase further to about 50 per cent in the Twelfth Plan. The approach paper goes on to point out that 'since the financial viability of the power sector as a whole depends upon the revenues collected at the distribution end, it is absolutely vital that the distribution system is made financially viable'.

Distribution utilities have consistently incurred losses and faced shortage of funds for growth and even for maintaining existing assets. According to the recent Power Finance Corporation report on power utilities (Power

* I am grateful for useful comments from an anonymous referee; Daljit Singh of Prayas Energy, Pune; and the editor Ashima Goyal.

Finance Corporation 2011) the distribution sector incurred losses of Rs 27,489 crore during 2009–10. Most of these losses were financed by state governments and public sector banks.

As a part of the reforms process, most states have unbundled and corporatized the integrated state electricity boards (SEBs) into separate transmission, generation, and one or more non-overlapping distribution companies, with state regulatory commissions determining tariffs. Distribution has been privatized, with transfer of 51 per cent ownership, in Odisha and Delhi. Distribution companies in a few states have entered into franchise agreements for managing specific urban regions. In all the states distribution continues to be a monopoly of one or more non-overlapping distribution utilities, which are required to purchase power through a 'single buyer'. Attempts to introduce competition through 'open access', which allows large consumers to contract directly with generators for supply of power, have not been successful.

The experience of privatizing distribution has been mixed. While Odisha's privatization failed to deliver promised results, Delhi's privatization is considered largely successful, though there have been severe regulatory problems in recent years. The limited experience of franchise arrangements is generally considered positive. The report of the high level panel on financial position of distribution utilities (Planning Commission 2011b) has recommended the distribution franchisee arrangement as the way forward for power distribution reforms. However, most states continue to attempt reforms *without* any private participation, with significant success in some states, such as Andhra Pradesh and Gujarat.

This chapter examines the evolution and the future role of private participation in power distribution reforms. The chapter is organized as follows. It begins with a brief overview of the current state of distribution utilities and highlights the major problems. it then examines the privatization experience in Odisha and Delhi and the distribution franchisee experience of Bhiwandi in Maharashtra. It also briefly discusses the case of Andhra Pradesh which has made substantial progress without privatization. In the section that follows, it discusses reform efforts in rural areas—feeder separation and the use of distribution franchisees. Finally, it provides a conclusion with some ideas on the future of distribution reforms and the role of private participation, on the basis of the experience so far.

State of the Power Distribution Sector

Audited information on the operating and financial position of distribution utilities is not readily available. According to the report of the high-level panel on the financial position of distribution utilities (Planning Commission 2011b: 3), 'a true and fair picture of the electricity sector is simply not available because accounts have been in arrears, books of accounts have not been maintained, a number of statements made as part of the accounts are inaccurate and it cannot be said that reliable information is provided by the Distribution utilities'. The Power Finance Corporation, a Government of India undertaking, brings out reports on the power sector obtaining information from audited accounts, provisional accounts, and resource plans submitted to the Planning Commission. We use the report brought out in September 2011 covering the three years 2007–8 to 2009–10 (Power Finance Corporation 2011). There are three important aspects of the performance of distribution utilities—profitability and financial position, technical and commercial losses, and adequacy of regulated tariffs.

Profitability and Financial Position

Table 22.1 shows that the total financial losses for distribution utilities, even after accounting for subsidies, increased over the period 2007–8 to 2009–10. Tamil Nadu, Uttar Pradesh, Madhya Pradesh, and Jammu and Kashmir, together account for almost 75 per cent of the total losses of all distribution utilities. Cash losses, after adjusting accounting profits for less than 100 per cent collection and less than 100 per cent of the booked subsidy received in the year, amounted to Rs 44,402 crore in 2009–10.

Distribution companies receive subsidies for agriculture and domestic sales. Subsidies have been increasing both in aggregate terms as well as a percentage of revenues. Booked subsidy is the amount shown in audited accounts. However, the entire subsidy booked in a year may not be received in that year. In 2009–10 subsidy booked for all distribution utilities was Rs 34,000 crore, equal to about 20 per cent of revenue from sale of power. Out of this amount only Rs 19,075 crore was received during the year.

Table 22.1 Income, Expenditure, and Profitability for Utilities Selling Directly to Consumers

(Rs crore)

	Total income excluding subsidy	Total expenditure	Profit after tax (including booked subsidy)	Cash profit revenue and subsidy received basis
2007–8	149,622	183,595	(14,751)	(16,612)
2008–9	171,639	223,403	(22,607)	(36,973)
2009–10	190,948	252,125	(27,489)	(44,402)

Source: Power Finance Corporation (2011: Annexures 1.2.1, 1.2.2, and 1.2.3).

Andhra Pradesh (AP), Haryana, Punjab, and Rajasthan had the largest subsidies booked. Together they accounted for almost 75 per cent of the total subsidies. In these four states the share of agriculture to total sales was more than 30 per cent. Utilities in Rajasthan received only about 7 per cent and in AP they received about 45 per cent of the subsides booked in 2009–10. In general there is a problem of timely transfer of subsidy amounts from the government to the distribution companies. This results in financing problems and additional financing costs which may not be approved by regulators.

Losses have been increasing not only in aggregate terms but also in terms of per unit of power input. Table 22.2 gives the gap per unit KWh input. This is defined as the difference between the average revenue and the average cost to supply (ACS).

Table 22.2 Gap (Rs/KWh of Total Electricity Input) for Utilities Selling Directly to Consumers

Year	Gap (subsidy booked basis)	Gap (subsidy received basis)	Gap (subsidy/revenue on realized basis)
2007–8	0.23	0.28	0.37
2008–9	0.35	0.55	0.67
2009–10	0.38	0.59	0.73

Source: Power Finance Corporation (2011: annexures 1.6.1, 1.6.2, and 1.6.3).

As a result of the accumulated losses of the distribution utilities the net worth of the power sector as a whole declined to 4 per cent of total capital employed in 2009–10. The share of banks and financial institutions in the total capital employed increased to almost 70 per cent. State governments have been extending substantial guarantees to state utilities. According to the Thirteenth Finance Commission Report (2009) the overall outstanding guarantees extended by the states to power sector utilities as on 31 March 2008 amounted to Rs 88,385 crore. At the end of 2009–10 distribution utilities also had payments worth about Rs 42,500 crore outstanding for purchase of power, equal to almost three months (84 days) of power purchases. This created financial problems for the generating companies.

Aggregate Technical and Commercial (AT&C) Losses

Electricity losses are normally measured as the difference between energy produced and dispatched by power plants and the energy sold (billed) to end customers. This is referred to as T&D (transmission and distribution) losses. With unbundling of T&D activities the distribution utility is responsible for losses in the distribution system. Total distribution losses have two components: technical and non-technical (commercial) losses. Technical losses occur naturally and consist mainly of power loss in the electricity system components, such as transmission and distribution lines, transformers, and measurement systems. Commercial losses consist primarily of electricity theft, non-payment by customers, and errors in accounting and record-keeping (The World Bank 2009).

In India, energy sold to consumers cannot be measured accurately as most of the agricultural consumption and some rural consumption is unmetered. Even in the case of metered consumers there are problems of faulty and non-working meters. Traditionally, utilities have over-estimated unmetered sales to show lower T&D loss measures.

An additional problem is that bills are often not collected for long periods and consumers continue to remain connected. In response to this problem regulators use a measure called the aggregate technical and commercial (AT&C) loss which can be expressed as:

$$AT\&C\ Loss = 1 - \frac{Units\ billed}{Input\ units} \times \frac{Amount\ collected}{Amount\ billed}$$

This measure adjusts the T&D loss measure for collection efficiency.

The overall AT&C losses were high and declined marginally from 29 per cent in 2007–8 to 27 per cent in 2009–10. AP had the lowest AT&C

losses at 16 per cent. However, the losses were 40 per cent in states, such as Uttar Pradesh, Odisha, and Madhya Pradesh even after several years of reforms and privatization in the case of Odisha.

Tariffs

Regulators are required to set tariffs such that distribution utilities can earn a reasonable return on equity. The regulator determines the aggregate revenue requirement (ARR) for the utility based on forecasts of consumption for different consumer categories; estimates of power purchase costs; estimates of technical and commercial losses; estimates of other costs and capital expenditure; and the required return on capital. Tariffs are then set to enable the utility to realize ARR.

A critical determinant of ARR is estimates of AT&C losses. Unmetered supply and the prevalence of defective meters often lead to irreconcilable differences in loss estimates between the regulator and distribution utilities. Similarly, targets for loss reduction cannot be based on a sound analysis given the critical role of the government law and order machinery and employee related problems in controlling losses. This is a major reason why regulated tariffs are often inadequate for covering actual costs (Forum of Regulators 2010a).

The cross-subsidy in tariffs can be seen from Table 22.3, which gives the average revenue per unit sale for different consumer categories. This does not include subsidies.

Table 22.3 Revenue per Unit Sales (Rs)

	Domestic	Commercial	Agricultural	Industrial	Total
2007–8	2.34	5.22	0.77	4.09	2.99
2008–9	2.48	5.93	0.85	4.20	3.19
2009–10	2.64	5.58	0.89	4.49	3.26

Source: Power Finance Corporation (2011: annexures 5.2.1 to 5.2.6).

Tariffs with a cross-subsidy can distort consumption patterns. For achieving the objective that tariffs progressively reflect the cost of supply of electricity, the Tariff Policy (Ministry of Power 2006) required the state regulator to notify a roadmap for ensuring that by the end of 2010–11 all tariffs were within ± 20 per cent of the average cost of supply.

Evolution of Private Participation

Privatization or divestiture which transfers controlling ownership of a distribution company to private investors is the most commonly understood form of private participation. This is the approach adopted in Odisha and Delhi. In this case the private investor bears significant risks and has the most incentive to perform. However, given the state of the sector, private investors may not be willing to take on such risks like the risks of rural and agriculture distribution or tariff risks dues to regulatory uncertainty. There are other forms of private participation which do not involve transfer of ownership, with transfer of only limited control and risks to the private investor. One such arrangement that has emerged in the Indian context is a distribution franchisee. This approach was first adopted in Bhiwandi, Maharashtra and then in several other cities in Uttar Pradesh and Maharashtra. This section describes the process of evolution of private participation as captured by the experience in Odisha, Delhi, and Bhiwandi.

Odisha: Classic Privatization[1]

Odisha became the first state in India to launch an ambitious power sector reforms programme, based on unbundling, privatization, and implementation of a new regulatory framework. The Odisha power sector was unbundled and corporatized during 1995–6. Four distribution companies were set up and distribution assets and employees were transferred to these four companies. The transmission company, GRIDCO, was the single buyer for power for all the distribution companies and it also held the government's share of equity in these companies.

The reforms process was largely based on the approach outlined in a report on power sector reforms issued by the World Bank in 1993 (The World Bank 1993: 7, para. 1.21). One of the issues that the World Bank confronted was the sequencing of the reforms process. The 1993 World Bank policy promoted commercialization/corporatization *before* privatization, an approach influenced by reforms in Chile, England, and Wales, which were the only experiences available for analysis at that time.

[1] For an early discussion of the Odisha reforms see Sinha (2002).

However, based on subsequent experience the World Bank concluded that commercial standards in the power sectors could not be achieved in the presence of poor governance and state ownership in most World Bank client countries (The World Bank 2003). Consistent with this approach the Staff Appraisal Report of the Odisha Power Sector Restructuring project (The World Bank 1996) argues that, 'while theoretically possible, it is very difficult to introduce, in the public sector at the state level, the required management and operational autonomy and performance incentives, that are essential to successfully address the fundamental issues in power distribution in India.' While the Report questioned Odisha's capability to develop and manage the new utilities and the regulatory commission, it also expressed optimism that these problems could be dealt with 'by transferring responsibility for distribution to specialized private companies whose survival depends on their success in addressing Orissa's current problems in distribution.'

The four distribution companies were privatized with transfer of 51 per cent stake to private operators in April 1999. The Bombay Suburban Electric Supply Company (BSES) acquired three distribution companies and US firm AES, partnering with an Indian company, acquired the fourth company called Central Electricity Supply Company (CESCO). However, at the end of five years of the reforms process in Odisha, T&D entities were financially insolvent. The privatized distribution companies did not have adequate cash flows to even pay salaries. AES abandoned its distribution company and the Odisha Electricity Regulatory Commission (OERC) issued an order for vesting management control of CESCO in a government nominee.

The major problem was the gap between the highly optimistic efficiency and cost targets used by the regulator to determine tariffs and those achievable by the licensees. In early 1996, the World Bank had assessed Odisha State Electricity Board's (OSEB's) T&D losses at 43 per cent for 1995–6. Based on this, OERC decided to allow T&D losses of 35 per cent for 1997–8. Later during the project implementation, with the availability of detailed information and data, the 1996 base figures for OSEB's last year of operation was raised to 52–3 per cent. In spite of this revision, OERC persisted with the 35 per cent T&D loss benchmark and the initial loss reduction trajectory in subsequent tariff orders.

Overall, after privatization, efficiency improvements were marginal and T&D losses continued to be high. Since the regulator refused to allow the high levels of T&D losses while setting tariffs, regulated tariffs were inadequate for the distribution companies to cover their costs and earn a return. The state had stopped subsidy payments to distribution companies after privatization. With no transition financing plan in place neither the private investors nor the government were willing to finance the losses.

According to the World Bank completion report (The World Bank 2004a: 20, 23, 24):

> The private firms must take significant responsibility for failing to undertake adequate due diligence. BSES/Reliance in particular singularly failed to put adequate managerial resources on the ground, and also failed to invest risk capital beyond the initial purchase of its 51 per cent stakes in the three companies. Only by the end of the project, nearly five years after operational transfer, did BSES/Reliance Energy make concerted and effective moves to put robust management teams in place.

The completion report also provided the views of the distribution companies, as expressed by AES, which had to abandon CESCO's management:

> At every turn, GRIDCO and GoO (Government of Orissa) made CESCO's job nearly impossible by interfering in the management of CESCO's operations, including forced transfer and redeployment of employees (even for political activities unrelated to CESCO) and preventing necessary commercial practices like the disconnection of defaulting customers, and finally agitating a multiple number of litigations against AES before multiple fora i.e. Arbitrator, Courts and OERC on a single frivolous issue that CESCO's dues to GRIDCO to be assumed by AES as an investor in CESCO.
>
> Unfortunately, World Bank could not make GoO accountable for the reform. Despite World Bank continuing to provide Structural Adjustment Loan to GoO for its fiscal correction, GoO till date failed to setup any special court and adequate number of police stations to deal with theft of electricity as per Electricity Act 2003. GoO dues to CESCO on account of energy bill have been piling up as before. (pp. 20, 23, 24)

The completion report assessed the overall performance of the bank and the borrower as 'Unsatisfactory' and the government performance as 'Highly Unsatisfactory'. The report concluded that private participation in the distribution business cannot overcome flawed policy and regulatory approaches.

Delhi: Privatization with a Transition Plan[2]

Delhi's power sector reforms were designed and implemented during 1999–2002, with a lag of a few years relative to Odisha reforms. While the approach for the reforms was based on the Odisha model there was no direct involvement of the World Bank. According to Jagdish Sagar, the then chairman of Delhi Vidyut Board and the architect of the reforms design and implementation, the primary concern that needed to be addressed in the Delhi's privatization related to regulatory uncertainty (Sagar 2004: 170):

> Something would have to be done to mitigate regulatory uncertainty, since in Orissa decisions regarding the extent of T&D losses that would be allowed in the Annual Revenue Requirements (ARRs) filed by the distribution companies were left entirely in the hands of the Orissa Electricity Regulatory Commission, which not only failed to allow reasonable and achievable targets but also each year, left uncertain what it would do the following year. It would be impossible for an investor to prepare a business plan, as the basis for his bidding, if this kind of uncertainty were now to be repeated in Delhi.

The core of the Delhi distribution privatization was a five-year transition plan. The Delhi government recognized that a successful transition plan would require the Delhi Electricity Regulatory Commission (DERC) to issue a multi-year tariff plan to provide a measure of certainty to private investors. However, the commission argued that a multi-year tariff approach would be suitable only for a mature and stable environment, which was not the situation in Delhi.

Since the commission refused to lay down long-term tariff setting principles, the Delhi government issued a statutory policy directive binding the regulator to a set of tariff setting principles during the transition period 2002–7. According to the policy directive, the loss reductions to be achieved by private operators would be determined through competitive bidding. The successful bidders would then be offered 51 per cent equity shares at face value. The winning bid for loss reduction would form the basis for tariff determination purposes during the transition period. Only if the distribution companies achieved the loss reduction as per their bids,

[2] For an initial discussion of the Delhi reforms, see Sinha (2003), and Singh and Sinha (2004).

would they be able to earn the 16 per cent rate of return. In addition, if the loss reduction of a distribution company was better than the minimum loss levels stipulated by the government, the company would be allowed to retain 50 per cent of the additional revenue resulting from such better performance and the balance 50 per cent would be counted as revenue for the purpose of fixing tariffs. This would enable the regulator to fix lower tariffs than would be possible otherwise. In order to avoid a 'tariff shock', especially in the initial years, the Government of Delhi committed to providing a subsidy of approximately Rs 2,600 crore over the five-year period.

Following the bidding and negotiations, BSES took over two of the distribution companies and Tata Power the third. As a part of the negotiations government support was increased from Rs 2,606 crore to Rs 3,450 crore. The privatization process was largely successful during the transition period. In most cases, loss reduction targets were exceeded, providing additional room for the regulator to manage tariffs.

However, there was serious confrontation in the post-transition period between the regulator and distribution companies. In response to complaints of unfair treatment by the regulator by distribution companies, the government ordered DERC to hold back the ready to release tariff order for 2010–11. The government order was challenged in the Delhi high court through a public interest litigation. BSES distribution companies had filed an appeal earlier before the Appellate Tribunal for Electricity against the orders passed by DERC for 'true-up'[3] of the 2007–8 tariffs and determining tariffs for 2009–10. The appeals covered issues similar to those addressed in their representations to Delhi government.

It emerged that the source of the problem was a disagreement over the tariff orders between DERC chairman and other commission members resulting in a breakdown of communications. Matters were resolved only when the chairman's term expired in September 2010. The commission, under a new chairman, agreed to most of the complaints of the licensees. The Appellate Tribunal also upheld many complaints of BSES distribution companies.

During this period, the two BSES companies had defaulted on payments and had received a number of warnings from generation and transmission companies. BSES companies attributed their financial position to inadequate tariffs and asked for government financial support. With a

[3] 'True-up' is a process by which the regulator makes up to the distribution companies for differences in estimated and actual revenues and costs due to 'uncontrollable factors'.

looming threat of a power blackout, the Delhi government agreed to bail out the two companies by infusing equity worth Rs 500 crore. Reliance Infrastructure, the private promoter of the two companies, announced infusion of its share of financial equity of around Rs 520 crore. Meanwhile, the Tata company, NDPL, also sought similar benefits.

This experience highlights the problem of regulatory uncertainty. The high court, in its order, was extremely critical of the government, the commission, and private operators, for their approach to the tariff dispute:[4]

> Keeping the statutory role ascribed to it and the jurisdiction determined by the Apex Court, the Commission has to function with responsibility, intellectual integrity, consistent objectivity and transparent functionalism appreciating the essential nature of the regulatory body. We emphasize on intellectual integrity and transparent functionalism as we are totally dissatisfied with the way the Commission has proceeded with the manner of determination. ...
>
> We may also note here that if a state of chaos and anarchy has ushered-in in the Commission the State Government is also responsible by unjustifiably intruding and encroaching on the functions of the Commission by interdicting. ...
>
> We will be failing in our duty if we do not express our views on the conduct of the distribution companies. ...The manner in which they submitted the representation to the State Government requiring its interference at a stage when the regulatory body was proceeding with the determination was totally unwarranted.

Bhiwandi: Distribution Franchisee

The Electricity Act of 2003 allows the holder of a distribution license to contract out some or all distribution activities to a franchisee. This enables state-owned distribution companies to benefit from private management in a specific problem area for a limited term by awarding distribution areas to private companies through the franchisee route. This is more manageable and convenient than the statewide approach to privatization in the Odisha or Delhi models. It also does not involve the political fallout associated with privatization of a state-owned utility. The arrangement is attractive for franchisees because it has little or no exposure to regulatory

[4] Judgement of the High Court of Delhi, pronounced on 23 May 2011, W.P.(C) No. 4821/2010 (paras 72 and 73).

uncertainty and strong incentives to reduce losses quickly and increase metering and collection. However, there is ambiguity about the long-term role and status of the franchisees.

The Maharashtra State Electricity Distribution Company (MSEDCL), the state-owned distribution licensee in Maharashtra, appointed Torrent Power AEC Limited (TPAL) as the franchisee for the distribution circle in the town of Bhiwandi, about 48 km north-east of Mumbai, in January 2007 for a period of ten years. At that time TPAL was the distribution licensee for the cities of Ahmedabad, Gandhinagar, and Surat in Gujarat. Bhiwandi is a small, primarily urban area with high levels of customer and load densities and minimal agriculture consumption. It is a major textile hub in western India accounting for about one-third of the country's powerlooms. According to the Draft Bhiwandi Information Docket (MSEDCL 2005), in 2005, powerlooms accounted for almost 55 per cent of total sales of electricity in the circle and 30 per cent of consumers; domestic consumers accounted for 4 per cent of sales and 50 per cent of consumers. Loss levels were high and collection efficiency low as reflected in AT&C losses, transformer failure rates, and the number of faulty meters.

In the Input-based Distribution Franchisee Agreement[5] the franchisee is responsible for all obligations of the distribution licensee in the franchise area. There is no transfer of assets or shares. A joint audit of key parameters and assets is conducted prior to the handing over of the circle to the franchisee. The agreement also provides for independent audits of the financial and operating performance of the franchisee.

The franchisee is given full autonomy for planning and executing its capital expenditure. The value of any assets added has to be certified by MSEDCL as acceptable. MSEDCL is required to make termination payments upon expiry of the contract, at the depreciated value of the distribution assets created by the franchisee.

MSEDCL employees in Bhiwandi were given the option to work on deputation with the franchisee on equal or better terms. Employees had the right to return to MSEDCL and the franchisee had the right to cancel the deputation of any MSEDCL employee. The cost of employees on deputation was borne by the franchisee, but the right to their promotion remained with MSEDCL. The franchisee was free to hire new employees, but there MSEDCL had no reemployment obligations.

[5] This description is based on the Ministry of Finance (2010); IDFC Ltd. (2009); and Prayas (Energy Group) Pune (2009).

Franchisee Cash Flows

MSEDCL is committed to providing a minimum level of energy input linked to the actual level in the preceding year. The franchisee makes payments to MSEDCL for supply of power at a pre-determined tariff, referred to as the 'input rate', adjusted for changes in the average billing rate (ABR) for consumers in the Bhiwandi circle. The input rate is the key bidding parameter, determined at the time of evaluation of bids. The payment by the franchisee to MSEDCL in a particular year is given as:

$$\textit{Input Energy Units} \times \textit{Input Rate} \times \frac{ABR\ (n)}{ABR\ (base)}$$

ABR(n) is the average billing rate in the franchise area in a given year (n) and ABR (base), is defined as the rate for a base year. The ratio is referred to as the tariff indexing ratio. This method of indexing the input rate to changes in tariffs and consumer mix is a method for sharing of the change in revenue due to change in tariffs. The standard franchise agreement issued by the Forum of Regulators (2010b) provides for a more direct sharing mechanism as:

$$\textit{Input Energy Units} \times \textit{Input Rate} + TS$$

Tariff share (TS) is determined in the following manner: If there is an increase in revenue due to increase in the average billing rate, 75 per cent of the increase goes to the licensee and 25 per cent to the franchisee. If there is a decrease in revenue due to decrease in the average billing rate, 100 per cent of the decrease is borne by the licensee. The rationale behind allowing the franchisee to retain 25 per cent of the increase in revenue on account of change in tariff or consumer mix is that with every increase in revenue, the collection and bad debt losses of the franchisee could go up in absolute terms.

Bhiwandi's consumers are charged the same tariff as applicable to other MSEDCL consumers. The franchisee collects the tariffs and retains the balance after remitting the security deposit for new connections and electricity taxes and duties to MSEDCL. The state government provides subsidy on electricity tariffs for powerloom customers to MSEDCL. This subsidy amount is then passed on to the franchisee.

The net effect of these transactions is providing the franchisee a cash flow which is largely insulated from tariff changes. On the other hand, the franchisee reaps the full benefits of loss reduction and increased cost efficiency relative to the levels built into the input rate bid.

Input Rate Bidding

Bidders were required to quote the annual input rate for power supplied by MSEDCL. The bids had to built in a minimum reduction of 30 per cent in distribution losses and improvement of 33 per cent in collection efficiency by the end of the contract period. Through this structure, the incentive and penalty mechanism for over- and under-achieving the specified performance trajectory was perceived to be implicitly in-built. In contrast, the standard franchise agreement (Forum of Regulators 2010b) included a specific loss reduction trajectory, approved by the regulator, to be achieved by the franchisee during the term of the agreement.

Outcome[6]

MSEDCL began the handover of operations to TPAL in July 2006. Although MSEDCL had set a period of 90 days for this handover, the duration finally got extended to six months mainly because of differences over opening level of data including those on distribution losses and collection efficiency.

AT&C losses declined from 58 per cent in December 2006, just before the handover, to 24 per cent (12-month moving average) at the end of FY 2008–9. The annual value of reduction in AT&C losses was about Rs 170 crore, as against a capital investment of about Rs 250 crore by the franchisee over this period.[7] TPAL focussed on three important areas—upgrading the network, reducing losses, and consumer services. Immediately after the handover, it initiated a process of regularizing illegal connections and metering. It replaced all existing meters with accurate and tamper-proof ones. TPAL also improved customer services by introducing a call centre facility, online collection centres, user-friendly bills, extending the operating time for customer care centres, and public awareness and community development activities.

In Maharashtra, during 2011 three divisions in the Nagpur urban circle, two divisions in Aurangabad, and the city of Jalgaon were also handed

[6] This is based on Ministry of Finance, Government of India (2010). The calculation assumes the pre-franchisee energy input of 2,500 GWh for the Bhiwandi circle and using a per unit rate of Rs 2/KWh.

[7] This is based on the pre-franchisee energy input of 2,500 GWh for the Bhiwandi circle and using a per unit rate of Rs 2/KWh as stated in Ministry of Finance (2010).

over to distribution franchisees. Meanwhile, in Uttar Pradesh, the cities of Agra and Kanpur were given to TPAL under a franchise agreement.

Andhra Pradesh: Reforms without Private Participation[8]

As pointed out most earlier, the states are following a reform process that does not include privatization or private participation, beyond outsourcing of specific routine activities such as meter reading and billing. Andhra Pradesh is considered an example of a state which has done well without privatization.

The Andhra Pradesh State Electricity Board (APSEB) was unbundled and restructured into a power generation company (APGENCO), a transmission and bulk supply company (APTRANSCO), and four distribution companies for retail power supply. This was completed by 2001. The reform process was funded by the World Bank (The World Bank 1999).

In the three rankings of state power sectors prepared for the Ministry of Power jointly by ICRA and CRISIL, Andhra Pradesh was first during 2003 and 2006 and marginally second to Delhi in 2004. Andhra Pradesh's success can be attributed to government support and the functioning of the Andhra Pradesh Electricity Regulatory Commission (APERC).

According to the completion report (The World Bank 2004b: 5, para. 4.13):

> The APERC has set a good track record of operating through transparent regulatory processes, with the involvement of stakeholders and public, and has demonstrated its ability to take independent decisions. It has issued important regulatory orders and has set precedent in defining several regulatory approaches in the country. In the important area of tariff reforms a transparent process with a distinct role of regulator and the government has been established.

The state government also provided serious support to the reform process. Andhra Pradesh was the first state to enact an anti-theft legislation in July 2000 which stipulated penalties that include mandatory imprisonment for electricity theft. This was enforced seriously and resulted in a quantum jump in the registration of theft cases and a large number of

[8] For a comparison of the Delhi and Andhra Pradesh approaches to reforms see Singh and Sinha (2004).

arrests of consumers and employees. According to the completion report (The World Bank 2004b):

> The government's support is evident from (i) the support provided for financial restructuring, (ii) full and timely payment of the subsidy committed as per the regulatory directives, (iii) non-interference and support to the utilities in controlling electricity theft and collection of dues from the consumers, including the government departments, (iv) support for improving corporate governance by allowing appointment of senior managers through a transparent and competitive selection process and (v) non-interference in the regulator's jurisdiction and in implementing the regulatory directives.

However, the completion report cautioned that 'sustainable improvements in the financial viability are unlikely unless tariff reforms for the subsidized consumer categories are accelerated and government continues its support for improving sector governance'. Table 22.4 shows the current aggregate performance of distribution companies in Andhra Pradesh. Andhra Pradesh had the lowest level of AT&C losses in 2009–10 but had large subsidies.

Table 22.4 Performance of Andhra Pradesh Distribution Companies (Rs crore)

	Total income (excluding subsidy)	Total expenditure	Profit after tax	Subsidy booked	AT&C losses (per cent)
2007–8	13,808	16,557	107	2,866	16
2008–9	14,783	22,684	44	7,980	13
2009–10	17,451	24,122	65	6,709	16

Source: Power Finance Corporation (2011).

Management of Power Supply to Rural India[9]

Expanding coverage and improving the quality of electricity in rural India is a challenging task. According to a World Bank report on rural access to electricity in India (The World Bank 2004c) the lower density

[9] For a detailed discussion see Sinha (2004, 2005).

of consumers in rural areas and low levels of household demand result in high grid expansion costs, high losses, and high average unit cost of supply. For large centralized utilities, retaining and supervising a cadre of technical staff members is more costly and difficult in rural settings. Greater distances and poor transport infrastructure make supervision difficult and expensive, resulting in lower quality of maintenance, higher levels of corruption, and higher rates of absenteeism.

In rural India, two specific types of customers have to be served—households and commercial establishments, and farmers with pumps for irrigation of agriculture. Agriculture consumption is estimated to account for almost 30 per cent of total sales of distribution companies. During the mid-1970s to early 1980s, most states shifted away from metering electricity sales to agricultural consumers and introduced flat-rate tariffs based on the capacity of pumps. This shift was apparently a matter of administrative convenience meant to minimize costs involved in metering, billing, and collection from agriculture consumers scattered in remote areas. However, flat-rate tariffs were generally sticky upwards. They did not keep up with the increasing consumption and cost of power. Hence, state governments subsidized agriculture consumption. Most regulators asked for a phased programme of 100 per cent metering of agriculture pump sets. However, farmers continue to resist the installation of meters. Unmetered supply to agriculture has also created an opportunity for camouflaging T&D losses as supply to agriculture.

With flat-rate unmetered tariffs, rationing of power supply for agriculture is inevitable. The only option available to distribution companies is to switch on the distribution lines serving the agricultural area only for a limited period each day, based on seasonal water requirements. In most villages since the supply to both households as well as agricultural water pumps is provided by the same transformer, other electricity users in the village also receive electricity only for the same number of hours each day as the agricultural water pumps. This has led to a situation where the rural communities do not benefit by the availability of electricity for household use and for small industrial or commercial activities. The only way for rationing power supply to agriculture without affecting supply to other rural consumers is to physically separate the distribution network for supply to agriculture from other rural supply. This is also referred to as agriculture 'feeder separation'.[10] With metering at appropriate points in

[10] For a detailed discussion see the World Bank (2001) and the Asian Development Bank (2011).

the distribution system this also enables measuring the power input to agriculture. This can be used to obtain more reliable figures for T&D losses for the non-agriculture network.

Gujarat is the first state to complete separation of agriculture and rural feeders through a state financed scheme called Jyotigram. The Jyotigram scheme (JGS) was launched initially in eight districts in the state on a pilot basis in 2003. By 2006 all the existing electrified villages had been covered under the scheme. This resulted in significant improvements in power supply to rural households and commercial establishments.[11] However, even though feeder separation has been implemented, tariff orders (Gujarat Electricity Regulatory Commission 2010) are still based on estimates of agriculture input.

The feeder separation scheme is being implemented in many other states like Madhya Pradesh with Asian Development Bank's (ADB's) support (Asian Development Bank 2011).

Beyond the separation of feeders, there is broad consensus on the need for a separate organization for delivering power to agriculture. The expert committee on state-specific reforms (Ministry of Power 2002: 23, para. 3.3) recommended carving out of states into 'concentrated' and other zones. Concentrated zones are in areas of high load density and relatively compact distribution networks, such as urban and industrial centres and their immediate periphery. These concentrated zones can be privatized. For the rural zones the committee recommends:

> The Government would ring-fence the subsidy that is targeted towards the rural zones and deploy it diligently through a combination of innovative solutions such as minimum subsidy bidding and involving user co-operatives and local franchisees, and fostering of institutions to provide quality advice to these franchisees on financial, technical and managerial matters.

This approach is reflected in the Rajiv Gandhi Grameen Vidyutikaran Yojana (RGGVY). The scheme requires deploying franchisees for managing rural distribution in projects financed under the scheme (Rural Electrification Commission 2008). However, as pointed out by the working group on power for the Twelfth Plan (Planning Commission 2012) most of the states have not been able to adopt franchisee systems as mandated in the scheme. It is likely to take time to develop and implement such schemes.

[11] For a detailed discussion see Shah et al. (2008).

The Future of Power Distribution Reforms

The viability of the distribution sector depends not only on the management of the distribution utility but also on the performance of the state government and the regulator. The government must provide support of the law and order machinery for preventing power thefts; make prompt payments of subsidies; provide funds for capital expenditure; and refrain from interfering in the day-to-day functioning of distribution companies. The regulator must determine tariffs that allow utilities to recover costs and make necessary investments for reducing losses, subject to well defined and reasonable efficiency targets. If full-cost tariffs are unreasonably high during the transition period when legacy AT&C losses are high then the government needs to provide necessary financial support as a part of a comprehensive plan to reduce losses. Only if the government and regulator fulfill their obligations can the management of the distribution utility be held accountable for performance. Otherwise the management can even attribute its poor performance to failures of the government and the regulator. Therefore, irrespective of government or private control, the government and the regulator will have to play a major role in ensuring successful reforms, especially during the initial transition period.

The primary reason for attracting private participation in the management of distribution utilities is the incentive for performance created by the profit motive.[12] In general, a competitive market is required to align the private profit motive with consumer welfare. However, power distribution is considered a natural monopoly even though there is potential for introducing competition in the retail service component, for example, through open access provisions. This presents the regulator with the challenging task of providing the discipline of competitive markets while ensuring that distribution companies earn a reasonable rate of return.

The performance of states, such as Andhra Pradesh and Gujarat, is evidence that it is possible to achieve viability without private management if government and regulator support is available. However, to the extent that these achievements are the result of specific political leaders[13] or regimes

[12] For a discussion on the role of incentives in improving efficiency of improving public rail and air transport systems in India see Goyal (2008).

[13] For example, the then Chief Minister of Andhra Pradesh, N. Chandrababu Naidu.

they may be vulnerable to changes in political regimes and not sustainable in the long term. Moreover, to the extent regulation works by providing incentives and penalties through profits, it is likely to be less effective for public sector utilities. For example, given their performance evaluation structures, managers of public sector utilities may not put in additional effort even if the regulator provides higher revenues to the company for reducing AT&C losses. Similarly, managers may be less likely to challenge regulatory decisions which hurt their profitability.

Irrespective of public or private management it is necessary to separate the subsidized rural and agriculture distribution business from urban and industrial distribution. This is especially important for privatization since private investors are unlikely to be interested in the rural and agriculture distribution business given the high costs and low revenues of rural distribution and the large subsidies in supply of power to agriculture. This is referred to as 'concentrated zoning' by the expert committee on state-specific reforms (Ministry of Power 2002: 21, para. 3.3). This involves creating 'concentrated areas of high load density and relatively compact distribution network, such as urban and industrial centres and their immediate periphery' which could be privatized. The distribution franchisee approach is based on this principle.

The success of the distribution franchisee mechanism in Bhiwandi has generated significant interest by both distribution companies and private investors. For example, the high-level panel on distribution utilities (Planning Commission 2011b) makes a number of recommendations on the role of the government, tariff setting by regulators, and management and corporate governance of utilities. However, it concludes:

> Given the magnitude of losses, the several far reaching measures required to reduce them and the high Capex required to do so, it is unlikely that the measures outlined above would succeed in radically reducing the losses during the next plan period. In recognition of this unfortunate conclusion the HLP recommends the introduction of the Franchisee model detailed in the report on an urgent basis. This should be extended by the States during the next few years to at least 255 towns (including peripheral areas) listed state wise which seem to account for over 40 per cent of consumption.

The distribution franchisee approach is attractive for private investors because it is less risky than privatization. Since the franchisee is not subject to a rate of return regulation there is also a significant upside. On the other hand the downside is limited since there is no up-front investment for acquiring an ownership stake in the business. Distribution companies also find it attractive because it can be targeted at specific zones and promises quick improvements.

However, there are several issues that need to be addressed by distribution companies. A distribution company will need to develop skills for developing contracts, generating bidder interest, negotiations, and monitoring the performance and regulatory compliance of the franchisee. For example, MSEDCL has set up a franchisee management cell to undertake all activities on distribution franchising in the state (IDFC 2009). Franchising will also result in surplus employees since the franchisee is unlikely to take all the existing employees on deputation.

The initial Bhiwandi agreement was for 10 years but more recent agreements are for longer time periods. For example, the Agra agreement is for 20 years and other MSEDCL agreements are for 15 years. It appears that the franchising arrangement is being seen as a long-term arrangement and not merely a short-term attempt to increase efficiency. If this is true then the distribution utility needs to develop a plan for the long-term organizational form and function of the distribution company. For example, if it were to follow the recommendations of the high-level panel (Planning Commission 2011b) it could become an organization which manages a number of distribution franchisees in urban areas and directly serves rural areas. Over time, some of the rural areas could also be integrated into the distribution franchisee zones. It will then need to develop capabilities consistent with its long-term vision.

References

Asian Development Bank (2011), 'India: Madhya Pradesh Energy Efficiency Improvement Investment Program, Initial Environmental Examination for Feeder Separation Project' (Tranche1), Project Number 43467.

Finance Commission of India (2009), Report of the Thirteenth Finance Commission (2010–15), December.

Forum of Regulators (2010a), 'Tariff revision assessment for financial viability of DISCOM and comparison of approaches, Final Report—Phase 2', Crisil Advisory services, New Delhi, India.

——— (2010b), 'Final Report on Standardisation of the Distribution Franchise Model', Prepared by Feedback Ventures, New Delhi, India.

Goyal, Ashima (2008), 'Governance in India's Public Transport Systems: Comparing Indian Railways and Airlines', *Economic and Political Weekly*, XLIII(28): 119–27.

Gujarat Electricity Regulatory Commission (2010), *Tariff Orders for 2010–11*. Ahmedabad, India: Gujarat Electricity Regulatory Commission.

IDFC Ltd. (2009), 'The Bhiwandi Electricity Distribution Franchisee Model: A Resolute Step in Distribution Reforms', Policy Group Quarterly, June.

MSEDCL (2005), 'Draft Bhiwandi Information Docket'. Available at: www.mahadiscom.in/consumer/bhiwandi_info_docket.pdf (last accessed on 28 October 2013).

Ministry of Finance (2010), *Public-Private Partnership Projects in India, Case Study 14: Bhiwandi Electricity Distribution Franchisee*. New Delhi: PPP Cell, Department of Economic Affairs, Ministry of Finance, Government of India.

Ministry of Power (2002), 'Expert Committee on State-Specific Reforms: Structuring of APDRP, Reform Framework and Principles of Financial Restructuring of SEBs', (Under the Chairmanship of Shri Deepak Parekh), September.

——— (2006), *Tariff Policy*. New Delhi: Ministry of Power, Government of India.

Planning Commission (2011a), *Approach to the 12th Five Year Plan*. New Delhi: Planning Commission, Government of India (October).

——— (2011b), *Report of High-Level Panel on Financial Position of Distribution Utilities* (Under the Chairmanship of Shri V.K. Shunglu). New Delhi: Planning Commission, Government of India (December).

——— (2012), *Report of The Working Group on Power for Twelfth Plan (2012–17)*. New Delhi: Planning Commission, Government of India (January).

Power Finance Corporation (2011), *Performance of State Power Utilities for the years 2007–8 to 2009–10*. New Delhi, India.

Prayas (Energy Group) (2009), *Review of the Distribution Franchisee Model Implemented by MSEDCL in the Bhiwandi Circle*. Pune: Prayas.

Rural Electrification Commission (2008), 'REC Guidelines for Franchisee Development'. Available at: recindia.nic.in/download/franchisee_guidelines.pdf (last accessed on 28 October 2013).

Sagar, Jagdish (2004), *Ensuring Value For Money, Chapter 7.3, Why And When Do State Governments Reform: The Case Experiments In Electricity In Delhi*, India Infrastructure Report, 3iNetwork. New Delhi: Oxford University Press.

Shah, T., S. Bhatt, R.K. Shah, and J. Talati (2008), 'Groundwater Governance through Electricity Supply Management: Assessing an Innovative Intervention in Gujarat, western India', *Agricultural Water Management*, 95(11): 1233–242.

Singh, Daljit and Sidharth Sinha (2004), *Improving the Performance of the Distribution Sector: An Evaluation of two Approaches, India Infrastructure Report 2004*, 3iNetwork. New Delhi: Oxford University Press, pp. 174–84.

Sinha, Sidharth (2002), *Orissa Power Sector Reforms: Getting Back On Track*, India Infrastructure Report, 2002, 3iNetwork. New Delhi: Oxford University Press, pp. 260–71.

——— (2003), *Transition Plans for Power Sector Privatization: The Case of Delhi and Karnataka*, India Infrastructure Report, 2003, 3iNetwork. New Delhi: Oxford University Press, pp. 269–79.

——— (2004), *Management of Power Supply to Agriculture*, India Infrastructure Report, 2004, 3iNetwork. New Delhi: Oxford University Press, pp. 208–17.

——— (2005), 'Introducing competition in the power sector: Open access and cross subsidies', *Economic and Political Weekly*, XL(no. 7, 12 February): 631–37.

The World Bank (1993), 'The World Bank's Role in the Electric Power Sector: Policies for Effective Institutional, Regulatory and Financial Reform—A World Bank Policy Paper', Report No. 11676.

——— (1996), 'Staff Appraisal Report, Orissa Power Sector Restructuring Project', Report No. 14298-IN, April.

——— (1999), 'Project Appraisal Document on a Proposed Loan in the Amount of US$ 210 Million Equivalent to India for a Andhra Pradesh Power Sector Restructuring Project in Support of the First Phase of The Andhra Pradesh Power Sector Restructuring Program', Report No. 18849, 25 January 1999, Energy Sector Unit, South Asia Region.

——— (2001), 'India: Power Supply To Agriculture, Volume 2, Haryana Case Study', 15 June 2001, Energy Sector Unit, South Asia Regional Office.

——— (2003), 'Private Sector Development In the Electric Power Sector, A Joint OD/OEG/OEU Review of the World Bank Group's Assistance in the 1990s', Report No. 26427, 21 July.

——— (2004a), 'Implementation Completion Report, on a Loan in the amount of US$ 350 million to the Government of India for Orissa Power Sector Restructuring Project', Report No. 30269, 9 December.

——— (2004b), 'Implementation Completion Report, Andhra Pradesh Power Sector Restructuring Project (APL I)', Report No. 27775, Energy and Infrastructure Unit, South Asia Region.

——— (2004c), 'Rural Access to Electricity: Strategy Options for India', Discussion Paper, South Asia Energy and Infrastructure Unit.

——— (2009), 'Reducing Technical and Non-Technical Losses in the Power Sector', Background paper for the World Bank Group Energy Sector Strategy, July.

CHAPTER 23

PROMOTING SEZs AS A STRATEGY OF INDUSTRIALIZATION AND LESSONS LEARNT

ARADHNA AGGARWAL

It is widely recognized that industrialization is critical for economic growth and development. Evidence suggests that economies that have successfully made the transition from low-income to medium- and high-income status owe their growth to rapid industrialization (Kuznets 1955; Lewis 1954; Rodrik 2012; Szirmai 2011). Industrialization has therefore been targeted as a route to economic growth in most developing countries. However, industrial transformation is a complex process which involves significant institutional and social transformation. It requires identifying the drivers of industrial development and forming well-designed policies to push these drivers (Chang 2002; Shapiro 2005).[1] Developing countries, being late entrants, face an even more complex and daunting set of circumstances than that faced by now advanced countries when they embarked on industrialization. These countries are characterized by numerous production failures and bottlenecks. As a result, markets by themselves cannot lead to efficient outcomes (Lin and Chang 2009). State-led policy instruments designed to address these bottlenecks are therefore a critical

[1] Chang (2002) argued that all major developed countries used interventionist economic policies in order to get industrialized.

element in the process of industrial development in these countries (Lin 2010; Lin and Chang 2009; Rodrik 2005; Stiglitz 1998). One such policy instrument that has become increasingly popular within developing countries is the creation of special economic zones (SEZs). A growing number of countries are increasingly focusing on SEZs as engines of industrialization. According to ILO (2007), the number of SEZs increased from a mere 79 across 29 countries in 1975 to 3,500 across 130 countries in 2006. Not only has the number of SEZs increased, but so have the varieties of SEZs. New varieties of zones have evolved and are subsumed within the broad category of SEZs (Aggarwal 2012a). Evidence, however, suggests that the success of these zones has not been unequivocal across countries. While they have been associated with significant industrial transformation in China, Korea, Taiwan, and Malaysia, they have failed miserably in many other countries (Madani 1999). This chapter examines India's SEZ experience. The objective of the chapter is to examine the formation and evolution of the SEZ policy,[2] and analyse its contribution to the process of industrialization in India in different phases of its evolution. In doing so, it essentially aims to draw lessons for the recently launched new variety of zones: national investment and manufacturing zones (NIMZs). It examines important dimensions of the policy surrounding NIMZs and identifies SEZ practices that linger and need to be addressed with urgency if the new zones are to be successful.

NIMZs are conceptualized as integrated industrial townships with state-of-the-art infrastructure which will offer relaxed investment regimes to attract industrial investments. In that sense, they have a close resemblance with SEZs. However, while SEZs are meant exclusively for exports, NIMZs are aimed at boosting both export and domestic manufacturing. They are typically hybrid SEZs which are also sub-divided into general industrial parks open to all industries regardless of their export orientation and separate areas reserved for export-oriented enterprises.[3] An assessment of the strengths and weaknesses of the existing SEZ framework will, therefore, have important policy implications for the new zones.

The rest of the chapter is organized as follows. The next section presents theoretical links between SEZs and industrialization. The section that

[2] The analysis focuses only on SEZs; export-oriented units (EOUs) and software/electronic hardware technology parks (STPs/EHTPs) which also share commonalities with SEZs are out of the purview of this study.

[3] Sri City, Mundra, and Mahindra World City are some of the hybrid SEZs in India.

follows it describes the evolution of the SEZ policy in India since 1965 with the next section examining arguments for and against the contribution of SEZs to industrialization in India. The next section outlines key lessons useful in planning zone initiatives that have emerged from the experience of the SEZ programme in India. The section following it addresses what is new in the NIMZ policy. It also reviews the practices that have been continuing as legacies of the past and that need to be addressed. The last section gives concluding observations.

SEZ and Industrialization

An export-processing zone is a government-promoted industrial cluster of firms that specializes in manufacturing for export. It offers firms favourable investment and trade conditions as compared with the rest of the host country. It provides for importing raw materials, intermediate products, and equipment and machinery required for export production on a duty-free basis and offers a liberal regulatory environment. It is believed that SEZs can provide the 'engine of growth' to propel the economy into industrialization by augmenting trade and investment and promoting agglomeration economies. But there are costs associated with promoting industrialization via SEZs. In what follows, we discuss the SEZ-induced channels of industrialization and associated costs in detail.

SEZ-induced Channels of Industrialization

Augmenting Trade

The primary objective of SEZs is promoting exports. Exports are closely associated with industrial development in both import-substituting and export-oriented regimes. In an import-substituting regime, exports have to be promoted in order to earn foreign exchange to finance import requirements for industrialization in the domestic economy. In an export-oriented regime, on the other hand, exports act as an important engine of growth not only by contributing to a more efficient allocation of resources based on comparative advantages but also by dynamically shifting the whole production possibility frontier of countries outwards. Dynamic shifts arise from more investment and faster productivity growth based on scale economies and inflows of new technologies and their diffusion within the economy.

Promoting Export-oriented FDI

In the contemporary economy, multinational corporations (MNCs) are increasingly restructuring their operations to avail economies of scale and scope by internalizing the economies of specialization through an integration of assets, production, and marketing activities across countries to advance their core competencies in the global markets (see Aggarwal 2012a for discussion). They seek locations where they can offshore a part of their activity most efficiently (UNCTAD 1998: 11). SEZs offer strategic locations that can attract export-oriented foreign direct investment (FDI) by offering an enabling investment climate.

This type of investment brings in technology and know-how that is compatible to the host country's level of development and enables local suppliers and competitors to benefit from spillovers generated through demonstration effects, on-the-job training, and learning by doing and copying, thus diffusing technology and knowledge in the host country. In particular, it is expected to fill the gaps in technical, marketing, and managerial know-how that a developing country's firms face and that constrains their growth. According to Johansson and Nilsson (1997), this has a catalytic effect on the domestic economy raising exports in the host economy beyond the level which is produced within the SEZ sector. They find that the estimated effects of SEZs on total exports are significantly larger than the exports of SEZs in Malaysia, which they argue is an indicator of the prevalence of FDI's catalyst effect in SEZs (see also, Basile and Germidis 1984).

Promoting Integration of Domestic Firms within Global Values/Supply Chains

As discussed earlier, it is becoming increasingly rare that a good or a service is entirely produced at one location and then exported to a final consumer. MNCs are restricting their businesses not only to offshore a part of their activity, as discussed earlier, they are also outsourcing an increasing share of their non-core manufacturing and service activities to other firms internationally. These arrangements have come to be known as global value chains. The growth of world trade is closely associated with the emergence of these chains. They have opened a new industrialization path. Today, nations can industrialize by joining a supply chain—there is no need to build one. The integration of local firms within global value chains is an essential way of strengthening their competitiveness and building their productive capacities (see Baldwin 2011; Coxhead and Jayasuriya 2010; Szirmai 2011 for some recent references). Producers gaining access to the chain have good prospects for upgrading. They start at the low end of the market and then, as a consequence of 'learning by exporting', move up the value chain and target more sophisticated market segments, such as design, marketing, and branding. However, market forces alone cannot ensure an effective integration of domestic firms in these chains. Global competition is so intense that unless deliberate policies are introduced to foster a favourable investment climate in terms of improved infrastructure, simplified rules, and harmonized processes; regulations; and standards with domestic, bilateral, regional, and international practices, firms in these economies may not be able to avail of the opportunities to integrate within these networks. SEZs are a useful policy instrument to create an enabling investment climate for domestic firms to reap the benefits of supply chains.

Encouraging Domestic Investment

In this globalized era, capital is highly mobile. An uncertain business/investment climate in developing countries underscores domestic investors' reluctance to invest in the domestic economy. SEZs, by offering a conducive investment climate and newer opportunities, may prove to be instrumental in reversing this tendency. SEZs are established to drive down the cost of doing business and remove roadblocks in undertaking investment activities. They can thus motivate professionally qualified and enterprising local entrepreneurs to undertake investment. Zones offer them the opportunity to introduce new technologies, new products, or new ways of doing businesses and use their talent to spin success stories of entrepreneurship. In that sense, they can serve as a fertile ground for technocrat/professional first generation entrepreneurs.

Promoting Technology and Skill Transfers

Technology and skill transfers within SEZs spillover through backward and forward linkages to the rest of the economy and promote knowledge and upgrade the productive structure of the economy. Backward linkages occur when SEZ firms source intermediates locally and/or outsource a part of their activity to local firms. These linkages can stimulate the production of intermediate inputs in the local economy, leading to an increase in national income and welfare. Further, learning and knowledge created in SEZs is eventually transmitted to domestic firms supplying to SEZ firms when the companies within an SEZ buy inputs from the host country. Forward linkages are established when final products produced in the zone are sold in the domestic market (Warr 1989). There are two other important channels (Aggarwal 2012a) that promote forward linkages between the zones and the domestic mainland: one, when firms set up production units in the domestic mainland to cater to domestic markets after succeeding in export markets, they introduce new products and new technologies in the domestic mainland; and two, trade bodies, manufacturers associations, and export marketing bodies provide a valuable forum for information sharing and spillovers and act as catalysts. There is evidence that being part of production networks can result in welfare gains for producers and consumers in host countries (Feenstra et al. 2002; Moran 2002).

SEZs and Agglomeration Economies

An important benefit of creating SEZs is in promoting agglomeration economies. SEZs are, essentially, highly geographically concentrated government-promoted agglomerations of internationally competitive enterprises. Economic literature suggests that geographic concentrations of similar/related firms generate externalities which are termed 'agglomeration (or localization) economies'. These externalities arise from labour market pooling, knowledge interactions, specialization, and the sharing of inputs and outputs, and are associated with economic benefits for member firms in the form of access to specialized human resources and skills, lower input and service costs, knowledge spillovers, and pressure for higher performance enhancing productivity and competitiveness of firms, regions, and nations (Fujita et al. 1999). According to Porter (1990), these externalities can take place in all clusters, but 'traded' (export-oriented) clusters such as SEZs which are agglomerations of trade-oriented highly competitive firms, have better prospects of generating externalities. The concentration of outward-oriented firms, rivals, suppliers, and customers fosters important linkages, complementarities, and knowledge and technology spillovers and thus stimulates innovative activity, raising productivity, and competitiveness.

The new economic geography theory takes this argument forward and argues that trade gains are higher when goods are subject to agglomeration economies because the concentration of world production in a single location allows greater exploitation of external economies and, hence, raises efficiency.

There is a stream of literature that shows that internationally competitive clusters in host countries act as a pull factor for inward FDI (Amiti and Javorcik 2008; Debaere et al. 2010; Nachum and Keeble 2000; Ng and Tuan 2006) and more domestic firms (Kaldor 1966; Myrdal 1957), thus launching a process of chain reactions. This promotes further expansion and specialization.

Conditions for SEZ-induced Industrialization

SEZ-induced industrialization has taken place in some countries, but it is not a universal phenomenon. It is conditional upon several factors:

- In general, the success of SEZs in attracting investments and generating economic activity is critical for an initial push to the generation of economic activity which can set the conditions for the subsequent process of growth.
- The composition of zone activity is another critical factor for industrialization-promoting effects. If zones are, for the most part, labour-intensive, low-tech assembly firms, with no access to advanced technology, their role in technology transfers and diffusion remains limited.
- Finally, the zone might be providing avenues for foreign direct investors, enterprising entrepreneurs, and technology transfers but its effectiveness as an instrument for achieving long-term industrial development will largely depend on the degree of backward and forward linkages created with the domestic economy. Benefits of SEZs accrue to the domestic economy through these linkages. Linkages define the ability of SEZs to develop productive relationships through exchange of information and resources. These linkages in turn are conditional on the industrial base of the host country, SEZ policies, and the technology gap between SEZs and local firms.

Empirical evidence thus suggests that the contribution of SEZs to industrialization cannot be said to be uniform across the board (Madani 1999). It varies across countries, within countries across zones, and more specifically, over time. The benefits that they yield depend on a complex inter play of three major factors: the quantum of activities generated by their establishment, the composition of zone activity, and the extent of backward economic integration into the economy. These, in turn, depend on government policies, and a host of other host country-, region- and zone-specific factors.

Costs of Zone-based Industrialization

Distortions in the Economy

According to the neo classical economists, SEZs are essentially grafted on to host economies; they do not reflect or feed into the actual or potential strengths of the host economies distorting them completely. As a result, international capital inflows promoted by SEZs with tax and tariff incentives can divert the resources of the labour-abundant host country towards more capital-intensive production and, hence can work against the country's comparative advantage. This can reduce the country's welfare.[4] This line of research is based on international trade theoretic models and has been pursued by Hamada (1974), Rodriguez (1976), Hamilton and Svensson (1982), and Devereux and Chen (1995) leading to similar results.

While countering the basic theoretical premise that SEZ production can be more capital-intensive, Balasubramanyam (1988) argues that SEZs represent a move to exploit a country's comparative advantage which may in reality be welfare-enhancing. However, according to him, SEZs can reduce national welfare by creating a dual economic structure in which a highly protected, import-substitution-oriented domestic economy, marked by the concentration of investments in the production of capital-intensive goods, coexists with an export-oriented enclave where investments are in the production of labour-intensive goods.

Political Rents

For political economists, SEZs are an outcome of the politics of interest groups. SEZs are established to generate rents to a few capitalists and MNCs by offering them tax incentives and other benefits at the cost of the rest of the population. These groups make investments anyways but due to large stakes involved, they incentivize government officials to influence policy in their favour. SEZs are thus tax shelters which induce relocation or diversion of economic activity from domestic areas to SEZs causing huge cost to the state exchequer with no net addition to investment and economic activity. This results in massive revenue forgone in tax incentives.

[4] If SEZ production is labour-intensive then it can improve national welfare by improving resource allocation.

Dependency Argument

According to this argument, the primary function of SEZs is the use of cheap labour, rather than tax and tariff privileges. According to this approach, production systems largely driven by transnational corporations (TNCs) benefit from differences in labour costs and are an outcome of capitalist industrialization. The main argument is that the fragmenting of production processes and relocating some of them to developing countries has divided the world economy into a core of dominant nations and a periphery of dependent ones (Frank 1967; Fröbel et al. 1978; Lacharrière 1969). The division of labour is such that research and management is controlled by the core or developed countries while assembly line work is relegated to periphery countries. In this system, SEZs are world factories performing assembly line work with dramatically lower wages augmenting the dependency of developing countries on dominant nations.

Diseconomies of Agglomerations

Agglomerations also generate substantial costs called diseconomies of agglomeration (Krugman 1991; Marshall 1890). These involve congestion, environment degradation, and regional imbalances. In the case of government-promoted estates, these costs can also arise from large-scale displacement of population involved in agriculture. Also, there are widespread concerns that SEZs will lead to uneven growth, thereby aggravating regional inequalities, dirty growth, and will have adverse social impact through the acquisition of land in large chunks.

Figure 23.1 depicts both the SEZ channels of industrialization and associated costs in this framework. The proposed framework is used in this chapter to assess the contribution of SEZs in India through different policy regimes.

Evolution of the SEZ Policy in India

The Initial Phase

After Independence in 1947, the government adopted a strategy of import substitution with emphasis on establishing basic and heavy industries for the rapid industrialization of the economy. It was believed that the

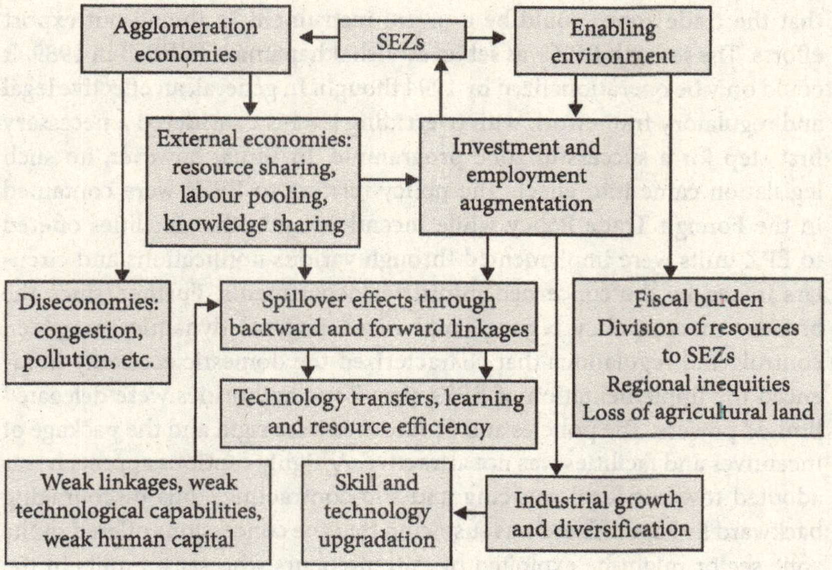

FIGURE 23.1 SEZ Channels of Industrialization and Associated Costs
Source: Adapted from Aggarwal (2011).

country should first develop a sound industrial base by creating domestic capabilities in investment goods industries and then extend this to produce a wide range of sophisticated consumer-manufactured items. In order to finance import requirements for heavy industrialization, the government pursued export promotion through fiscal incentives, import entitlement schemes, and other promotional measures, such as creating infrastructure for information dissemination on export opportunities and marketing development. As part of its export promotion measures, the government set up Asia's first export processing zone (EPZ) in Kandla as early as in 1965. This was followed by the second EPZ, the Santa Cruz Electronics Export Processing Zone (SEEPZ), set up in Mumbai in 1974.[5] In the mid-1980s, the central government set up four more zones at Noida (NEPZ), Madras (MEPZ), Cochin (CEPZ), and Falta (FEPZ) in the belief

[5] This EPZ was developed specifically for processing electronics goods and was expected to accelerate the progress of nascent electronics manufacturing in India to take advantage of the growing electronics world market. In 1987, the zone was opened to the gems and jewellery sector also.

that the trade zones could be a useful instrument in the all-out export efforts. The seventh EPZ was set up at Vishakhapatnam (VEPZ) in 1989. It could only be operationalized by 1994 though. In general, an effective legal and regulatory framework with overriding laws is considered a necessary first step for a successful zone programme. In India, however, no such legislation came into effect. The policy relating to EPZs were contained in the Foreign Trade Policy while incentives and other facilities offered to EPZ units were implemented through various notifications and circulars issued by the concerned ministries/departments. Further, since the broader macro-policy regime emphasized internal dynamics, umpteen controls and regulations that characterized the domestic economy influenced the implementation of EPZs also. Zone authorities were delegated limited powers. The policies and procedures were rigid and the package of incentives and facilities was not attractive. A highly cautious approach was adopted towards local sourcing and sub-contracting, thus discouraging backward linkages. There was suspicion that the concessions offered in the zone sector might be exploited by entrepreneurs who set up units in the zone for their own benefits. The problems were compounded by budgetary constraints and a lack of proper planning.

In 1991, India began to reorient its existing industrial strategy from import substitution to export promotion. This affected the government's attitude towards EPZs, also with major reforms introduced in this sector as well. Fresh initiatives were launched by the government to revamp the EPZ scheme. The focus was on:

- delegating powers to zone authorities,
- providing additional fiscal incentives,
- simplifying policy provisions, and
- providing better facilities.

Further, prior to 1990, the EPZ policy allowed only manufacturing activities. The scope and coverage of the EPZ/EOU scheme was enlarged to include agriculture, horticulture and aquaculture, and animal husbandry in 1992; floriculture, pissiculture, sericulture, viticulture, etc., in 1994; poultry, reconditioning, repair, testing, calibration, quality improvement, reengineering and upgradation of technology in 1995; and finally all services in 1999.

In an effort to spur the establishment of EPZs, a 1994 reform permitted the development and operation of EPZs by state governments, autonomous agencies, and the private sector. Until then, the central government was solely responsible for the setting of EPZs. However, complex bureaucratic red tape, administrative procedure, rigid labour laws, and poor infrastructure continued to affect the investment climate adversely within the EPZs.

Transitional Phase: 2000–6

In a major initiative to boost export-led growth and motivated by the success of Chinese SEZs, the government replaced the EPZ scheme with the 'SEZ scheme' in 2000. SEZ is defined as a self-contained area with high-class infrastructure for commercial as well as residential inhabitation. The main difference between SEZ and EPZ is that the former is an integrated township with fully developed infrastructure according to international standards whereas the latter is just an industrial estate. SEZs enjoy some features which distinguish them from the then existing EPZs. For instance, while EPZs had been set up by the central government, SEZs were proposed to be set up in the public, private, or joint sector or by state governments. Further, EPZs were small (less than 120 hectares)[6] trade enclaves essentially located in backward regions near port areas; on the other hand, the minimum size of SEZs was initially envisaged to be 400 to 500 hectares. Unlike the former, the latter were also given locational flexibility in the sense that their location was to be decided by the developer and not the government. EPZs were subject to fulfilment of minimum net foreign exchange earnings but this condition was done away with in the SEZ policy. It was expected that FDI, which was getting diverted to other Asian countries, would be attracted to India by these SEZs. In a move to promote backward linkages with the domestic economy, it was announced in 2003 that domestic sales to SEZs will be treated as exports and the suppliers would get all export-related benefits on these sales.

During this phase, both EPZs and SEZs coexisted. By 2003, all the existing EPZs had been converted to SEZs, and with that the EPZ policy ceased to exist and the transition from the EPZ to the SEZ regime was complete. In addition, 12 new SEZs became operational; most were set up by the state government initiatives. The policy failed to generate enough confidence among private investors to commit substantial funds for infrastructure development.

[6] Kandla is the only exception with an area of 404 hectares.

The Take-off Phase: 2006 Onwards

With a view to instill confidence in investors and to signal the government's commitment to a stable SEZ policy regime, an SEZ Act was enacted in 2005. This was the first time that a legal framework with special overriding laws and legislation was formulated to provide the necessary regulatory foundation for SEZs/EPZs. The Act became operative with effect from 10 February 2006 when SEZ Rules were also finalized. This Act, along with SEZ Rules, provides a comprehensive SEZ policy framework to satisfy the requirements of all principal stakeholders in an SEZ—the developer and operator, occupant enterprise, out-zone supplier, and residents. In addition to the central government's SEZ Act, there are SEZ Acts of state governments also which cover state subjects.

Under this Act, the central government is responsible only for the broad policy framework and monitoring of the scheme; it is not expected to set up new SEZs. Further, unlike the earlier EPZ/SEZ model, SEZ Rules provide for different minimum land requirements for different classes of SEZs. The minimum size stipulated for a greenfield SEZ for a multi-product zone, for instance, is 1,000 hectares. Within each zone, the processing area is distinguished from the non-processing area. The processing area is designated for production activities whereas the non-processing area is intended to provide support facilities and social infrastructure. The minimum processing area stipulated in the SEZ Act of 2005, was 25 per cent of the total area. This was extended to 50 per cent by introducing an amendment to the Act. The Act also has special provisions for promoting backward linkages by encouraging local sourcing and sub-contracting. There is no limitation on Domestic Tariff Area (DTA) sales with full-duty payment, subject to the fulfilment of positive net foreign exchange earnings over five years.

The Act offers a highly attractive fiscal incentive package, which ensures an attractive corporate tax holiday, exemption from custom duties, central excise duties, service tax, central sales taxes, and securities transaction tax to both the developers and the units. While the SEZ units enjoy tax benefits for 15 years, 100 per cent tax exemption for five years, 50 per cent for the next five years, and 50 per cent of the ploughed back export profits for the next five years,[7] developers are ensured 100 per cent income tax exemption for 10 years in a block period of 15 years.

7 This is applicable to SEZ units who begin their operations during the previous year relevant to any assessment year commencing on or after 1 April 2006.

Finally, the Act claims to provide world-class infrastructure and expeditious and single-window clearance mechanisms. The development commissioner is the nodal officer for SEZs who helps in resolving problem, if any, faced by units/developers.

The enforcement of the SEZ Act has led to tremendous growth in the establishment of SEZs in India and has completely transformed the SEZ sector in terms of size, structure, composition, and contribution. Table 23.1 shows that during the EPZ regime of 1965–2000, only seven zones were set up by the central government, locking a land area of 894 hectares with 95,000 people employed. During the transitional phase (2000–6), 12 new zones, mostly sector-specific, were set up. Of these, five were set up by the respective state governments while the rest were in the private sector. Despite expansion, the SEZ sector remained rather small in terms of land area covered and employment. As on 10 February 2006, India had 19 operational EPZs with a combined area of 1,817.5 hectares and employment of 1,23,000.

Table 23.1 Structure of India's EPZ/SEZ Sector

Period	Number	Ownership	Area (in hectare)	Type of zone
1995–2000	7	Central government: 7	894.40	Multi-product: 1 Bi-product zones: 1
2000–6	12	State government: 5 Private sector: 7	1,817.50	Multi-product, Sector-specific, service zones
2006–11	581	State governments: 119 Private sector: 462	63,608.27	Multi-product: 24; sector-specific: 164; service: 371; FTWZ: 22

Source: Data compiled by the author.

The SEZ scenario completely changed in the post-SEZ Act period. An unprecedented rush for setting up SEZs ensued following the passage of the act. By December 2006, that is, within 18 months of the Act, 237 new SEZs had been granted formal approval. This number increased at a steady pace in 2007 and 2008. As on 23 February 2009, 560 new SEZs had been granted formal approvals of which 286 had been notified. SEZ expansion slowed down thereafter. As on 17 July 2012, the number of formal SEZs stood at 589. Of them, 389 had been notified and were in different stages of development/operation. These 'newly notified zones' SEZs covered an area of 71,502 hectares.

The proliferation in the number of SEZs triggered a fierce nationwide debate over the usefulness of the SEZ policy in the country. Massive intellectual support for this criticism of SEZs came from the media, activists, and academia from both the right and the left. The whole debate that still rages on is usurped by anti-SEZ rhetoric. It touches upon almost every aspect of SEZs from macroeconomic issues related to their impact on government revenue, employment, trade, and foreign exchange earnings to social issues like land acquisition, labour rights, regional inequities, and environmental protection. The anti-SEZ obsession is so widespread that it has become cult-like. The government responded to the controversy by diluting not only the policy but also its support to SEZ investors. Many states started dragging their feet and adopted the policy of 'go slow'. The centre put on hold clearances for new SEZs for a few months in 2007 and started reconsidering the tax incentives offered to them. These populist measures sent wrong signals across the world regarding the sincerity of the government with respect to its policy in the initial phase of their evolution.

Further, the SEZ policy itself is fraught with some major challenges (Aggarwal 2012a). Some of the issues that have eroded the credibility of the policy include ambiguity in the provisions of the act, different interpretations by different authorities of a single act, lack of a clear-cut vision in promoting SEZs, involvement of different authorities in the government decision-making system, absence of an accountable governance model, and absence of a well-designed redressal system. A major challenge faced by policy-makers is how to ensure single-window governance. The implementation of the policy involves multiple departments and ministries both at the centre and state levels who must work jointly for achieving the objectives of the policy. However, there has been a lack of both horizontal and vertical coordination.

Despite raging protests, policy gaps, and uncertainty in the policy regime, SEZs continued to flourish when the economy was booming. In 2008, however, the global recession set in, hitting export demand. The vulnerability of investors was further aggravated by the policy decision of imposing minimum alternative tax and dividend distribution tax on SEZs in 2010–11. With the direct taxes code being considered by the Parliament which proposes to do away with profit-linked income tax exemption given to them and instead links tax sops to investments made in them, the demand for space in SEZs has declined sharply. As a result, there has been a growing demand for denotification or surrendering of SEZ status. Of the 589 formal approvals as on 17 July 2012, 36 have already been surrendered.

Against this background, in what follows, we analyse the contribution of SEZs to the process of industrialization.

Promoting Industrialization through SEZs: the Indian Experience

Quantitative Indicators

Attracting Investment

Investment is a key driver of industrialization and, as discussed earlier, SEZs can offer a viable platform for attracting both domestic and foreign investments. But the total EPZ investments remained abysmally small till the late 1980s.[8] According to official data procured from the Ministry of Commerce and presented in Table 23.2, total investments in 1988 stood at Rs 897.1 million. In the 1990s, when the investment climate in EPZs improved somewhat, investments started increasing. By 2000, they had grown to Rs 17.84 billion, almost 20 times in 10 years. The policy shock of 2000 further impacted on the magnitude of investments attracted by SEZs. In the post-SEZ Act (2005) period, however, the investment scenario in SEZs has completely changed. The sector registered an overwhelming growth in terms of investments and employment. Total investments multiplied several times to reach the level of Rs 2,018.75 billion (as on 31 March 2012) from a modest Rs 49.4 billion worth of investments in February 2006. Increase in investments has not only been due to the emergence of new zones; economic activity in those SEZs that came into force prior to the act has also shown an impressive growth after 2005. FDI forms only 12.8 per cent of this investment. Apparently, SEZs offer domestic entrepreneurs fertile grounds to flourish in India. There has been an exceptional rise in outward FDI by Indian entrepreneurs particularly since 2000 (RBI 2012). While this is an indicator of their increasing competence, there are apprehensions that overseas investment by the Indian corporate is at the cost of domestic investment. One of the obstacles for companies to undertake domestic investment is the poor investment climate in India (RBI 2012). In this scenario, SEZs, by overcoming constraints of doing

[8] One caveat: data on capital employed is not available for India for all the years. Therefore, the series is largely constructed using the available data.

Table 23.2 Direct Employment and Investment in SEZs

Type of SEZ	Employment (Number)					Investment (Rs billion)				
	1988	2000	February 2006	March 2011	March 2012	1988	2000	February 2006	March 2011	March 2012
Central government	25,625	81,372	158,197	210,434	213,853	8.97	17.84	33.51	104.53	114.86
Transition phase	-	-	20,566	66,031	79,015	-	-	16.08	77.16	76.38
Newly notified	-	-	-	400,143	552,048	-	-	-	1,846.41	1,827.51
Total	25,625	81,371	129,704	676,608		8.97	17.84	49.50	2,028.05	2,018.75

Source: Based on the Ministry of Commerce database procured directly by the author.

business in India, can offer domestic investors useful platform to invest within the country.

What is worrisome is that the share of FDI in total SEZ investment remains abysmally small. But more worrisome is that even the proposed FDI in SEZs has been declining. It declined from Rs 345,090 million as on 31 December 2009 to Rs 309,640 million in September 2010, and then further to Rs 269,844 million as on 31 March 2012. SEZs could offer a useful platform for foreign investors who were looking at India as a regional hub of manufacturing, trade, and logistics. But academic, political, and civil society resistance that followed in the initial phase of the implementation of the SEZ Act seems to have adversely affected the prospects of attracting FDI. Domestic investment growth also waned during 2011–12 (Table 23.3). As a matter of fact, the overall SEZ investment had declined in 2011–12. It has somewhat recovered in 2012–13. Uncertainty around the policy appears to have ruined the future prospects of SEZs.

Table 23.3 Annual Growth Rates of SEZ Exports and Total National Exports*: 2005–6 to 2011–12

Year	National	SEZ (Rs billion)	Share (%)
2005–6	4,657.48	228.40	3.17
2006–7	5,828.71	346.14	3.78
2007–8	6,680.00	663.38	6.43
2008–9	8,580.00	996.89	7.41
2009–10	8,633.00	2,207.11	16.76
2010–11	11,395.00	3,158.68	18.11
2011–12	14,825.00	3,644.78	16.32

Source: Calculations based on data from the Ministry of Commerce available at http://www.sezindia.nic.in/about-ep.asp and *Handbook of Statistics on Indian Economy 2011–12*, Reserve Bank of India.

Note: * Total national exports are inclusive of service exports.

Augmenting Trade

During the EPZ regime, the contribution of EPZs in the overall exports remained minuscule in India due to convergence of the EPZ export growth rate with the export growth rates of the overall economy at an early stage of evolution of the EPZ programme. This is evident in Figure 23.2 which shows growth rates of real exports (nominal exports deflated by unit value) in EPZs and outside them.

During the initial years, the growth rate in exports was as high as over 65 per cent per annum. This was due to a very low base at which

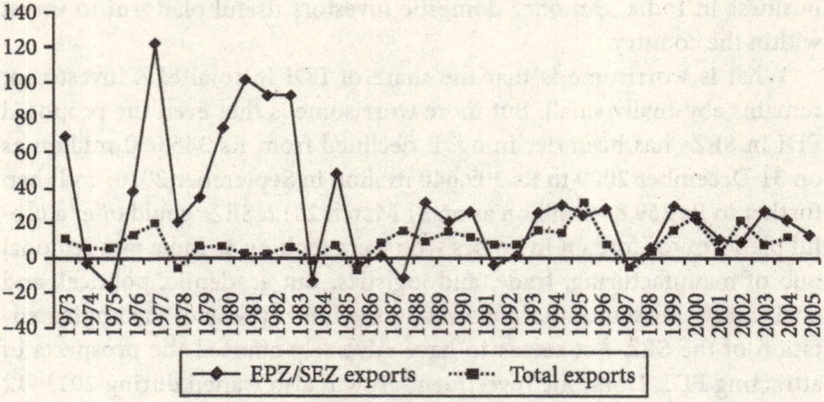

FIGURE 23.2 Growth Rates of SEZ and Total Exports in India over the Period 1966–2006 in Real Terms

Source: Author's calculations based on the SEZ Division, Ministry of Commerce database procured by the author and *Handbook of Statistics on Indian Economy 2011–12*, Reserve Bank of India.

production started. It became negative by the early 1970s. In 1974, another SEZ became operational in Santa Cruz, giving a push to exports. Further, in 1978, a bilateral trade agreement between the former Soviet Union and India based on 'rupee/ruble payment' became effective. Several companies used Kandla and Santa Cruz EPZs as a base for exports to Russia. This led to a quantum jump in the export growth of EPZs (Kumar 1989). By the mid-1980s, however, the growth rate of such exports had started slowing down. In the late 1980s, when the USSR collapsed, several zone units shut down and EPZ exports declined sharply. Post-1991 reforms did not yield significant results for reasons discussed earlier. During 2002–4, the average annual growth rate zoomed up to 23 per cent per annum in terms of US dollars but stabilized again in 2005. In 2005–6, the share of SEZs in total exports stood at a mere 3.2 per cent. Clearly, the EPZ or even the SEZ regime introduced in 2000 failed to induce significant dynamism.

The enactment of the act provided a major push to SEZs' export performance. The share of SEZs in total national exports (both merchandise and service) increased from a mere 3.2 per cent in 2005–6 to around 17 per cent by 2011–12.[9] The possibility of relocating export units from

[9] The ministry's claim that the share of SEZs in total exports is 30 per cent is based on merchandise exports, rather than total exports.

the domestic mainland to SEZs cannot completely be ruled out. Aggarwal (2012a) finds evidence of relocation of large IT firms to SEZs. However, as we discuss later, the argument of additionality is myopic and has been over emphasized in the context of industrial growth.

In 2008–9, when the global crisis had ravaging effects on the export sector and the overall merchandise exports recorded a single-digit growth of 3.4 per cent in dollar terms and services' export growth crashed to 12.4 per cent against 22 per cent in 2007–8, SEZs registered an impressive growth in exports. SEZs further improved their performance in 2009–10. While national merchandise exports declined by 13.7 per cent over their 2008–9 level, SEZ exports registered an impressive growth of 121.4 per cent. This continued to increase in 2011 at the rate of 43 per cent. However, in 2012, consequent on the global economic turndown and withdrawal of key benefits offered to SEZ units, SEZs' performance also deteriorated.

Foreign Exchange Earnings

The share of SEZ trade surplus in the national trade balance is an indicator of the contribution of SEZs to foreign exchange earnings. In India, trade surplus has remained routinely negative. On the other hand, it has always been positive in SEZs. To estimate the contribution of SEZs to foreign exchange earnings, we examine how much total import outgoings are covered by trade surplus in SEZs (Figure 23.3). Until 1990, the contribution of EPZs to import bills remained less than 0.50 per cent given the small magnitude of trade from EPZs. Thereafter, it started rising. In 2010–11,

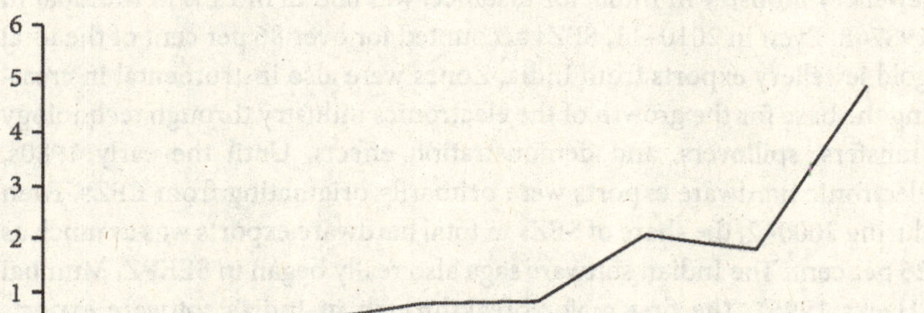

FIGURE 23.3 Share of Trade Balance in EPZs/SEZs to Total Import Bills in Selected Years between 1975–6 and 2010–11

Source: Author's calculations based on the SEZ Division, Ministry of Commerce database procured by the author and *Handbook of Statistics on Indian Economy 2011-12*, Reserve Bank of India.

it stood at 5 per cent. This implies that 5 per cent of the national imports were funded by the surplus generated in SEZs in 2010–11.

Industrialization and SEZs: Qualitative Analysis

While most analysts assess the contribution of SEZs in terms of macro-indicators, such as investment, employment, and exports, what is more important is their impact on technological and industrial sophistication in the host country. In a large economy such as India, SEZs may not constitute a significant proportion of total exports or employment but can still have important spillover effects on the process of industrialization. Madani (1999: 6) finds, 'even at the height of their influence, EPZs never acquired a prominent role either in terms of exports value or employment creation in S. Korea or Taiwan.' The following analysis focuses on the contribution of SEZs to the upgradation of the industrial sector in India.

Introduction of New Industries

A micro-level analysis of the zones' contribution to industrialization efforts in India reveals that EPZs had been instrumental in inserting domestic firms in global value chains of new industries which in turn had a catalytic effect in promoting new production sectors, exporting new products, and in building the country's image in certain products in international markets (Aggarwal 2006a). The foundation of the modern jewellery industry in India, for instance, was laid in SEEPZ in Mumbai in 1987–8. Even in 2010–11, SEZs accounted for over 86 per cent of the total gold jewellery exports from India. Zones were also instrumental in creating the base for the growth of the electronics industry through technology transfers, spillovers, and demonstration effects. Until the early 1980s, electronic hardware exports were primarily originating from EPZs. Even during 2000–2, the share of SEZs in total hardware exports was as much as 26 per cent. The Indian software saga also really began in SEEPZ, Mumbai (Heeks 1996). The first major breakthrough in India's software exports came in 1977 when the Tatas established a unit in SEEPZ in partnership with Burroughs, an American company, to export software and peripherals. A further breakthrough in the progress of the industry occurred when, in 1985, Citibank established a 100 per cent foreign-owned, export-oriented, offshore software company in SEEPZ. This company drew attention to the possibilities available for offshore software development in India. Soon after, Texas Instruments and Hewlett-Packard established subsidiaries in Bangalore in 1986 and 1989, respectively, and the rest is history. Rubber gloves are another story of successful industrial transformation. In the late 1980s, the US made it mandatory for doctors to use the gloves when they came in touch with patients. This led to a tremendous increase in the demand for the product and eventually to offshoring of production. It was in the Cochin SEZ that the 'automated line dipping technology' was first introduced with the help of Malaysian companies. Eventually, Indian firms became technological competitive. But *anecdotal evidence notwithstanding*, the erstwhile EPZs could not replicate the success stories of South East Asia.

In the post-2005 act period, several new technology- and knowledge-based industries have come up in SEZs. These are, for instance, electronics manufacturing services industry (EMS), aerospace industries, alternative energy industries, and bio tech industries, to name a few. These industries are capital-and scale-intensive and can immensely benefit from the externalities associated with agglomerations, such as lower costs of inputs and services, access to skilled labour, and knowledge spillovers (see Aggarwal 2012a for a discussion). Their growth will, however, call for vision and a set of clear-cut policies to promote such industries. There have been no discussions in policy circles on how to exploit these opportunities. Even the benefits of SEZs which relate to transfer of advanced technology, managerial techniques and know-how, skill upgradation, and export diversification have completely been ignored in the SEZ policy document.

Entrepreneurial Development

The development of private entrepreneurship is a pressing issue in developing countries. Entrepreneurs create new ways, new businesses, and new industries, which are essential for development. Our research shows that the erstwhile EPZs proved to be a fertile ground for technocrat/professional first generation entrepreneurs in India. Zones offered them an opportunity to execute their ideas and use their talent to spin success stories of entrepreneurship. These zones offered standard design factories (SDFs) on the basis of highly subsidized annual rent. Starting businesses in SDFs is based on the 'plug in' concept. Basic infrastructure facilities like developed land, power, water, and customs clearance facilities were developed within the zone. This significantly reduced the gestation period and hence the cost of the project. Constructing one's own factory was also cheaper due to tax exemptions on all construction materials, office equipments, and fixtures. Further, they offered a somewhat relaxed industrial regime when the domestic regime was rather strict and thus acted as an incubator to help new entrepreneurs to start, *grow*, and succeed. One of the most successful stories is that of Deepak Puri. As a mechanical engineer, Deepak Puri started Moser Baer in 1983 in technical collaboration with the Swiss firm Moser Baer AG, which was into time solutions. Later, when he started manufacturing floppy diskettes for export, he was given a license to manufacture 50,000 units per month during the License Raj. Puri realized that competing with global players with such a low-capacity output was not feasible. Since these restrictions were not applicable to zone units, he moved to the Noida export processing zone. From then on, the growth of the company zoomed. By 2004, Moser Baer had grown to become the world's second largest optical media manufacturer and one of the largest tech hardware exporters from India, shipping to 82 countries.[10] Rajiv Seth,[11] a technocrat and gemologist was instrumental in laying down the foundation of the modern jewellery industry in SEEPZ. He later established his company Tara Jewels in SEEPZ. The company has been one of the top exporters of studded jewellery from EPZ and EOU complexes in India.[12] Javed Hassan, a technocrat from Kerala with 21 patents in semiconductor technology[13] and the president of AMP Global Communications Group, founded the NeST (Network Systems and Technologies) Group in 1990. In 1991, he chose the Cochin EPZ to set up an outsourcing arm of AMP due to a better investment climate within the EPZ than outside it. This almost laid the foundation of the electronics industries in Cochin. Workers were sent for training to the US and Japan and when they came back they trained the others. They expanded phenomenally within the zone and outside it. Ashoke Mukherjee, an engineering student from Roorkee University initiated the manufacturing of amplifiers and speakers in India when he released stereo amplifiers in the 1970s. In 1982, a 100 per cent export-oriented division, Sonodyne International Ltd., was established in SEEPZ, Mumbai to manufacture professional audio and power electronics equipment as an OEM for European and American houses. In the early 1990s, when competition heated with the entry of global giants, he took a step back from domestic sales and focused on developing technological

[10] Information available online at http://www.moneycontrol.com/smementor/news/technology/moser-baer-has-allshut-down-738420.html (last accessed on 2 October 2012).

[11] Our interview with Ms Nalini Jayaraman, the Vice-President of the company and the material given by her.

[12] **Source:** Gems and Jewellery Export Promotion Council.

[13] Our interview with Mr Shamsuddin, joint director and the material provided by him.

capabilities through technology transfers by concentrating only on exporting activities in SEEPZ. Eventually, he successfully re-launched the company in the domestic market.

Unfortunately, the newly notified SEZs do not share this feature with the erstwhile EPZs. While they do offer a good investment climate, they charge premium prices for space for international standards that they have created in SEZs. Further, most of them (including the state governments) are offering large plots above some threshold level to investors, encouraging large investors. Also, they do not offer a plug-n-play facility within SEZs. There is no reserved space for SDFs for leasing it out to SMEs or new entrepreneurs for incubation of their ideas. This is a serious gap in the policy that needs attention.

Scale Advantage and SEZs

Since 1991 government policies in India have been directed at encouraging large-scale production. However, capital market rigidities, constraints on availability of land, and labour market rigidities have not allowed companies to reap the benefits of scale economies. Most of these constraints are directly addressed by the new SEZs. As a result, they have been instrumental in promoting several large enterprises. The Apache footwear company in the Apache SEZ, for instance, has a large facility with around 6,549 employees. Similarly, the Lotus footwear company has set up a large facility in Cheyyar (Tamil Nadu) which employs over 4,500 workers. The Jamnagar SEZ refinery, together with its sister company, has emerged as the world's largest single-location refinery with a combined refining capacity touching 1.2 million barrels per day, which is 5 per cent of the world's capacity. The Moser Baer SEZ unit is poised to be the world's second largest such unit after Phoenix, a US-based company. These large, and often single-enterprise SEZs, are expected to act as Hirschman's growth poles and have the potential of being instrumental in forming regional clusters by generating backward and forward linkages. This will not, however, be an automatic process. It requires a holistic and multi-disciplinary approach to create an enabling environment in regional economies to promote industrialization.

Promotion of Agglomeration

Most SEZs are coming up in strategic locations which can reinforce regional agglomeration economies. A large number of SEZs, privately owned in particular, are developing in or around natural clusters or industrial complexes and are expected to augment and reinforce them. Most SEZs in Uttar

Pradesh and Haryana, for instance, are in the information technology (IT) sector and are clustered in the existing IT hubs of Noida and Gurgaon. The Uttar Pradesh state government has also been promoting two handicrafts SEZs in the natural clusters of Moradabad and Bhadohi; other state-promoted SEZs are proposed to be located in the industrial town of Kanpur. In Andhra Pradesh, Kerala, and Tamil Nadu, many IT-based private SEZs are clustered near the IT hubs of Hyderabad, Thiruvananthapuram, Kochi, and Chennai, respectively. In Maharashtra, most private SEZs are being set up in the industrially developed belt of the state, namely, Nashik-Pune-Mumbai. The Gujarat state government has identified six regions that have already acquired industrial capabilities. Most SEZs are located in these regions to revitalize their core competencies and transform them into internationally competitive hubs by generating positive synergies between them. These are Ahmedabad (pharmaceuticals and textiles), Gandhinagar (information technology), Bharuch (chemicals), Vadodara (engineering), Jamnagar (petrochemicals), and Kutch (heavy metals and logistics). The Rajasthan government's handicraft SEZs in Jodhpur and the gems and jewellery SEZ in Jaipur and Kerala's food park and animation and gaming SEZs are carved out of existing industrial estates. The Andhra Pradesh government has also created some SEZs (Mehaboobnagar, for instance) in the existing growth centres. In an increasingly knowledge-intensive and globalized world, many inward-looking clusters and industrial estates are facing serious challenges in terms of technology flows, skills, environment, and quality control. The strategy of situating SEZs in and around them will create synergies and augment the inward-looking clusters/estates by creating opportunities for mutual learning and innovations with the presence of outward-looking clusters in close proximity.

In some places several small SEZs are clustered in a region and have been reinforced by developing industrial estates in the proximity. In Andhra Pradesh, for instance, new industries such as gems and jewellery, bio-tech, engineering, sports shoes, and the high-end pharmaceutical industry are being implanted by promoting large-scale production facilities through clustered SEZs. Following a similar strategy, the Tamil Nadu government is using SEZs to move up the value chain in industrial production. It is promoting 'Industrial Corridors of Excellence' and using SEZs to kick-start their development. In the first phase, the Chennai-Manali-Ennore and the Chengalpattu-Sriperumbudur-Ranipet corridors will be developed, with several SEZs clustered in this belt supported by industrial and IT parks, research and development (R&D) institutions, universities, and social infrastructure like housing, healthcare, and schools.

It has now been envisaged to synthesize the setting up of SEZs with the development of industrial corridors. Several SEZs are projected to be located in investment regions, industrial hubs, and multi-model logistic hubs planned along the upcoming Delhi–Mumbai industrial corridor. Each hub will have world-class infrastructure, business centres, transport facilities, and good connectivity. This will create synergies between sectors looking at the domestic market and outward-looking SEZs and between various SEZs in the same region. These synergies, drawing on both local production systems and global resources, will enhance regional competitiveness.

Large original brand manufacturing companies (OBM), such as Nokia, Suzlon, Gitanjali, and Uniparts have been developing integrated industrial parks to cut the cost of logistics. They use SEZs to attract upstream and downstream links in the global value chain within an SEZ and forge an industrial chain by creating all the necessary backward and forward linkages of the firms. This process of localization of international chains enhances industrial efficiency by reducing transport and inventory costs and ensures all the advantages of vertical integration.

Efforts are thus directed at augmenting the benefits of SEZs by locating them close to existing clusters/industrial estates, or clustering them in one location, or creating large-scale integrated production facilities.

Regional Diversification

As discussed earlier, there are instances where SEZs are being created as industrial estates clustered in one location to promote new industries and diversifying the economic base. Several electronics products-based SEZs, for instance, are being developed along the Sriperumbudur-Oragadam belt. They cover the full spectrum of different tiers of suppliers in the supply chain network. Similarly, Sri Ranga Reddy district in Andhra Pradesh—a large barren and rocky tract of land near Hyderabad—is being promoted by the state government as an IT hub with several IT SEZs clustered in the region. Surat in Gujarat is known as the synthetic city but with the setting up of an apparel park, textile industry has also been introduced in the region. It is also known for diamond trading, but with gems and jewellery SEZs, the jewellery manufacturing industry has been introduced in the region. SEZs have also facilitated the emergence of the IT sector in new locations, such as Mohali in Punjab, Gandhinagar in Gujarat, and Jaipur in Rajasthan. SEZs can thus be used strategically to move industrial areas from low value added activities up to high-end activities and promoting industrial activity in under developed regions.

Shift of Production Activity from Unorganized to Organized Sectors

SEZs have the potential to transform unorganized industry clusters into organized parks driven by innovation and design. For instance, the introduction of the gems and jewellery industry in Santacruz SEZ (then EPZ) in 1986–7 proved to be a turning point for the industry. Under the new policy, handicrafts and brassware SEZs are being promoted to repeat the Santacruz EPZ miracle. However, the incentive structure is not conducive for the growth of labour-intensive small industries in SEZs with its thrust on promoting large-scale businesses (Aggarwal 2012a).

Costs of SEZ-linked Industrialization

Loss of Agricultural Land

The diversion of land from agriculture to industrial use is the most contentious issue in the SEZ debate which even led to violent protests against SEZs in the initial phases of their evolution (Banerjee et al. 2007; Basu 2007; Bhaduri 2007; Levien 2011; Palit and Bhattacharjea 2008). From the national economy perspective, it means loss of fertile agricultural land, which has serious implications for food security. From the landowners' perspective, if meager compensation is paid for the land and they are displaced with no alternative means of livelihood, this will have poverty enhancing effects. One can, however, argue that this issue is not SEZ-centric, any large development project is bound to face it. It requires identifying and institutionalizing innovative methods to deal with the challenges faced in land acquisition for development projects. Even from the investors' perspective, acquiring land for large projects from a large number of sellers is expensive and time-consuming; a few strategically located owners may hold up the entire project discouraging investments in such projects.

Revenue Losses

The revenue foregone on account of direct tax sops for the period 2006–7 to 2009–10 as calculated from the annual receipt budgets of the Ministry of Finance is Rs 148.8 billion. The total investment in SEZs (including investment in infrastructure) as on 31 March 2010 was over Rs 1,284 billion, mostly in the private sector. This implies considerable savings for the government in infrastructure development. Further, the generation of economic activity outside SEZs will also generate tax revenue producing net benefits (Aggarwal 2012a). Critics, however, argue that there has been a large-scale relocation of existing units and diversion of new economic activities from non-SEZ to SEZ areas and that there is very little new addition to economic activities. A counter-argument is that capital has become increasingly mobile across borders and that with most countries adopting pro-industrialization strategies with generous benefits to their industries, competition to attract industrial investment, both domestic and foreign, has intensified. In this scenario, SEZs might have been instrumental in attracting such large investments which would otherwise not have come. It can also be argued that the concern for additionality itself is over-emphasized. Growth does not mean only augmentation of physical resources, it also means knowledge, technology, and learnings. The New Economic Geography focuses on rearranging resources which can contribute to productivity and economic growth. The clustering of competitive firms in SEZs can initiate the process of evolutionary dynamics and attract more foreign and domestic investment, as discussed earlier. This in turn augments resources and economic activity (Aggarwal 2012a).

Regional Disparities

There are widespread concerns that SEZs will lead to uneven growth, thereby aggravating regional inequalities. A state-wise analysis of notified SEZs indicates that, as on 31 March 2010 the five most industrialized states of Andhra Pradesh, Tamil Nadu, Karnataka, Gujarat, and Maharashtra accounted for over 69 per cent of all (notified) SEZs and over 89 per cent of the land tied up in them. In contrast, the industrially backward states of Bihar, the North East, and Jammu and Kashmir did not have a single approval. Literature suggests that industries tend to be located where they find a pro-business attitude and policies of the regional government, they have easy access to major infrastructure (main highways, electricity, gas, communication), services (financial services, public agencies), and trade infrastructure. This line of thinking underscores the role of the government in creating enabling conditions for industrialization. There are instances, in particular in Andhra Pradesh and Tamil Nadu, where SEZs are being used to diversify backward regions by giving them a big push through the creation of several small SEZs clustered in the these regions and reinforcing them by developing industrial estates in the proximity.

Labour and Environment Standards

There are concerns over welfare-reducing effects of the relaxation of labour and environmental laws for SEZ units (Sen and Dasgupta 2009). These costs seem to be exaggerated in the Indian context, given that these standards are not diluted in SEZs and that the zones are dominated by high-tech and skill-intensive activities. Further, there are severe pressures by international buyers on companies to meet labour and environment standards. They insist on a global standard like SA 8000 that has both labour and environmental norms and ISO 14000 which has implication for environment norms.

Sectoral Imbalance and Skewed Export Base

Many criticize SEZs on the ground that the policy seeks to promote manufacturing but more than 55 per cent of the zones are IT-specific. Data reveal that while IT and ITES SEZs dominate in numbers, they accounted for only approximately 10 per cent of the area under SEZs and 29 per cent of the total SEZ investments as on 31 March 2012. Interestingly, despite the fact that IT zones have far outnumbered other zones, manufacturing accounted for almost 50 per cent of their total physical exports in 2008–9; its share increased to over 77 per cent in 2009–10. In 2011–12, manufacturing exports took a hit and their share declined to 58 per cent though it still remained more than that of the IT exports.

It has also been pointed out that the distribution of exporting companies is rather skewed. In 2011, the Jam Nagar refinery alone accounted for over 50 per cent of the total exports. Two things may be noted here. One, SEZs have been undergoing internal and external vulnerabilities since their inception. Despite that they have proliferated in terms of numbers and investment. Two, the evolution of SEZs involves time. Farole (2011) argues that even the biggest SEZ success stories like China and Malaysia started slowly and took at least 5 to 10 years to build momentum. Manufacturing zones in particular have long gestation periods.

The upshot is that while SEZs do entail costs, in some contexts these are exaggerated and in others, they can be addressed through a long-run vision, strong commitment, a pragmatic and flexible approach, and dynamic learning and institution-building (Aggarwal 2006b). The experiences of South Korea, Taiwan, Malaysia, and China reveal that a crucial element in the success of SEZs is a strategic policy intervention that includes vision, strong commitment, legal and institutional frameworks, and a continuously unfolding and dynamic set of policies (Aggarwal 2012b). In India however, sensationalization of SEZ-related issues has created an inflated public perception of their costs mainly due to deficiencies/gaps in the policy formulation and implementation. Amidst widespread public misconceptions about the policy, the ruling party appears to be convinced that SEZs have no public appeal. Since it perceives no political returns in promoting zones, instead of systematically addressing the challenges to carry the policy forward, it has backtracked, creating uncertainty and confusion regarding SEZs. In a major policy reversal, MAT and DDT were imposed on SEZs. The global recession that set in 2008 has also affected exports and SEZs adversely. Today, the ministry that conceived the idea and implemented the scheme also seems to have moved on, and is promoting the concept of NIMZs under the recently introduced National Manufacturing Policy. This will completely ruin the future prospects of the SEZ policy and will harm the credibility of the government for future programmes.

The National Manufacturing Policy: Lessons Learnt from SEZs

While SEZs with an investment of Rs 200,000 crore have been facing uncertainty over their future, the government proposed to set up NIMZs under the National Manufacturing Policy (NMP). NMP has an ambitious objective of enhancing the share of manufacturing in GDP to 25 per cent within a decade and creating 100 million jobs. NIMZs are conceptualized as integrated industrial townships of at least 50 sq. km (5,000 hectares) with state-of-the-art infrastructure catering to manufacturing for both the domestic market and exports. The government has notified nine NIMZs—one each in Haryana, Uttar Pradesh, Gujarat, and Madhya Pradesh; two in Rajasthan; and three in Maharashtra. They will have 'high class' physical infrastructure with areas earmarked for manufacturing units ('processing areas') as well as for residential, commercial, and other facilities ('non-processing areas'). The processing areas may contain export-oriented units and even SEZs. Apparently, NIMZs are proposed to be established on a premise similar to the SEZs—that 'world-class' infrastructure, a business friendly 'single window' to the government, and relaxed regulatory regime will accelerate the establishment of new enterprises and the growth of exports. As stated earlier NIMZs resemble hybrid SEZs. Even the promises made in the policy are similar to the ones made when the SEZ Act was passed.[14] Experts argue that NIMZs are just another re-branding attempt in the backdrop of SEZ activities increasingly becoming tepid. Indeed NIMZs have been set within the overall framework of the earlier zones. Yet, the new policy has some new dimensions that were missing in the SEZ Act.

New Dimensions of the Policy

Administration: Public–Private Partnership

Developing and managing NIMZs will be through an SPV, a company set up for this specific purpose and having management representation from the government, public sector, and private parties according to financial stakes and at least one director from the Government of India. Public–private partnership in zone administration is an important dimension of the new zone policy. The special purpose vehicle (SPV) will plan, build, and maintain the internal infrastructure of the zone and allot sites to units. The company will have the right to levy user charges against the services it provides. The functions and responsibilities of the SPV are similar to those assigned to developers in the case of SEZs. It will play the role of a facilitator in getting clearances from the central and state governments. However, it will have no authority to issue these clearances on behalf of the government at any level. This means that dependence on the bureaucratic system outside the zone will continue.

Fiscal Incentives

Another distinctive feature of the policy is that government support and incentives offered are not generic. They are essentially targeting environment and technological development activities. For instance, relief from capital gains tax on sale of plant and machinery of a unit located in a NIMZ will be granted in case of re-investment of sale consideration within a period of three years for purchase of a new plant and machinery in any other unit located in the same NIMZ or in another NIMZ. Similarly, venture capital funds with a focus on SMEs in the manufacturing sector will be granted tax pass-through status to facilitate financing of SMEs. Broadly, the objective is to target market failures directly (Rodrik 2007: 7–28).

[14] The SEZ Act was also passed in 2005 with the ambitious goal of attracting a total investment of about Rs 1,484.40 crore including FDI and create additional 15,46,569 jobs by December 2009.

Exit Policy for Companies

An important feature of NIMZ is that it will have an exit policy which will facilitate the expeditious redeployment of assets belonging to non-viable units, while giving full protection to the interests of employees. It provides for workers' insurance which will create a safety net for workers in the event of job loss. Under the SEZ policy framework there was no exit mechanism for SEZ firms. This issue was addressed by the Ministry of Commerce in April 2013, when, as part of the policy reforms for SEZs, it provided for exit rules for these firms.

Environment and Labour Laws Relaxation

To relax the regulatory regime, the new Manufacturing Policy (NMP) allows the central/state governments to delegate environment related inspection power as allowed by the relevant statutes to an official of the State Pollution Control Board (SPCB) posted in the manufacturing zone (NIMZ). Similarly, the powers of inspection and enforcement of labour laws will be delegated to the CEO of the SPV who will be a senior government official. While the policy has been notified by the Ministry of Environment, the Labour Ministry has yet to notify it. The provision of labour inspections by development commissioners (DCs) was a part of the SEZ policy announced in 2000 but could not find favour to be included in the SEZ Act. It is now voluntary for state governments to delegate these powers to DCs.

Technology Development

Another new feature of NMP is its emphasis on skill-building and technology development. India is exposed to the full weight of international competition. Success in manufacturing will rely on a continuing commitment to be at the forefront of future technologies, innovation, and development of the industry. The National Manufacturing Policy proposes to offer several incentives to promote green technologies to ensure clean industrialization. A Technology Acquisition and Development Fund will be established for acquisition of appropriate technologies including environment friendly technologies; creating a patent pool; and developing domestic manufacturing of equipments used for controlling pollution and reducing energy consumption. Further, the policy highlights the need for skill building by encouraging the setting up of institutional infrastructure for vocational training, design, and quality. It also emphasizes on vocational education with 'farm-to-work' and 'school-to-work' programmes. These dimensions are missing in the SEZ policy. The SEZ Act does not have as its objectives the diversification of the productive structure, strengthening value chains, and technology transfers. The emphasis has been only on employment generation. Indeed, several private developers have taken voluntary initiatives to upgrade skill availability (Aggarwal 2012a). But these initiatives are not institutionalized in the act.

Promotion of MSMEs

Unlike its predecessor (the SEZ policy), the National Manufacturing Policy (NMP) offers sops targeting micro and small enterprises in particular, to facilitate financing, technology acquisition, creating patent tools, and developing manufacturing equipment. The objective is to provide finance for investment, and if suitably implemented, this will further the capability of MSMEs.

Continuing Practices

Regulatory Framework

The regulatory and policymaking mechanisms of NIMZ are guided by the bureaucratic model of policymaking. The government has established four regulatory bodies. At the apex is the Manufacturing Industry Promotion Board (MIPB) for matters pertaining to the implementation of NMP. MIPB has been tasked to periodically review the implementation of NMP in general and the development of NIMZs in particular. MIPB will have the secretaries of various concerned central government departments. The industry secretary will serve as the member secretary, while the Commerce and Industry minister will serve as the chairman.

A high-level committee (HLC) under the chairmanship of secretary, industry with secretaries from all the concerned ministries, and state governments has also been notified to resolve coordination issues among central ministries on the one hand and state governments on the other. HLC will monitor the implementation of policy provisions on a regular basis and resolve inter-ministerial issues.

Another key regulatory mechanism is the Board of Approval (BOA) for matters pertaining to NIMZs. It will examine applications for establishing NIMZs and recommend such proposals for consideration to HLC as are found to be meeting the requirements of NMP. A Green Manufacturing Committee (GMAC) for matters pertaining to environment related issues and a Technology Acquisition and Development Fund (TADF) under NMP have also been notified with all bureaucrat members.

It shows that the government does not recognize the role that the private sector can play in effective policymaking. There is a need to recognize mutual interdependence between the government and business sectors; an alliance of government and business can contribute to the development of more effective strategies than if they are addressed by bureaucrats only, particularly in the context of mutual distrust.

Coordination

Coordination within the government and between governments has been a major weakness of the SEZ policy. It continues to be a weak point in the new policy also. The policy, for instance, has been stuck due to failure of the Labour Ministry to issue notifications on the new policy despite the union cabinet clearing it in June 2012. Clearly, one department can hold up the policy jeopardizing plans. Setting up of an autonomous board could be a way forward.

Diversification and Innovations

A dynamic vision continues to be missing in the NIMZ policy. Market positioning, diversification of the productive structure, strengthening productive chains, export diversification with more value added, and innovations are some of the issues which have remained unaddressed in the context of the new zones. Zones are not merely about creating new infrastructure and attracting investments. The vision of the zone policy is to boost manufacturing activity in the domestic mainland through them. This vision continues to be elusive in this document. This has been the weakness of all other zone policies in India with NIMZs being no exception.

Financing Gaps

There are challenges in financing the zones, which can slow the pace of infrastructure development. NMP is silent on financing zone infrastructure development. Earlier the RBI policy of not treating SEZs as infrastructure projects had badly hit the SEZ development programme due to a resource crunch. A lesson learnt is that there is a need for clear financing and PPP implementation arrangements for infrastructure investments to enhance the attractiveness of the zones for private investors.

Land Acquisition

The issue of land acquisition remains unaddressed in the new policy even while each zone requires a minimum of 5,000 hectares of land.

Land acquisition is therefore an important issue which needs urgent attention. The Land Acquisition, Rehabilitation and Resettlement Act, 2013, with its extremely complicated procedures and provisions for any future land acquisition, will seriously jeopardize the NIMZ take-off. There is a need for innovative practices for land acquisition. The community land trusts (CLTs) is an equitable and sustainable model of land acquisition and development that emerged in the late 1960s and has slowly spread throughout the United States, Canada, and the United Kingdom. Creating an autonomous National Land Board to monitor and oversee the process may also go a long way (see Aggarwal 2012a).

Legal Framework

The analysis presented earlier in the chapter shows that the legal apparatus is a necessary pre-requisite for the success of a policy which has huge investment implications. The SEZ policy became a rage with investors after the act came into force to support it. Despite that learning, new zones are being promoted without a well designed legal framework. There is no 'special' legal and regulatory framework to facilitate such large multi-use zones. It is instructive to note that even the SEZ Act passed by Parliament has not been implemented in its entirety and has been subjected to policy reversals. In this backdrop, once high-level political backing is withdrawn from NIMZs, the projects will be completely stranded.

Spirit of Experimentation

In a democratic set-up when the normal social, economic, or political routine is disturbed due to the introduction of a new law, people often react initially with strong, emotion-laden feelings and opinions. Given the internal dynamics, multiple interest groups emerge. The emergence of interest groups may act as an element that balances the system. But it may also create chaotic situations in which these groups pull bureaucrats and politicians in different directions. This essentially happens when the policy affects people at the grassroots level. Effective implementation of a policy that aims at giving a shock to the economy therefore requires broader mobilization of public opinion. This in turn requires an experimental policy approach. The SEZ concept sparked-off unprecedented turmoil largely due to clearances given to a large number of projects disturbing the social and economic systems of rural areas. The idea should have been to start with a handful of SEZs and if these proved to be a success, to increase them carefully. NIMZs seem to be going the same way. Initially the proposal was to set up six NIMZs. Currently, nine NIMZs have already been notified. Now, more states are clamouring to have their own zones. It must be recognized that policy solutions are *contextual* in nature. This calls for an approach that is explicitly *experimental*. This lesson learnt from the SEZ policy must not be ignored.

To recapitulate, SEZs did prove to be a testing laboratory for large-scale industrialization in the country. Some of the weaknesses of the earlier programme have been addressed in NMP and these advances are encouraging and major. However, one also sees serious limitations, some of which are legacies from the past and will continue to harm the policy. The success of the programme will depend on how these challenges are addressed in the future. What ultimately counts is the continuity of government support over political cycles. Each new minister/top bureaucrat/government negates the policy and programmes of its predecessor and introduces a new programme without evaluating what worked and what did not earlier. This is the perfect recipe for the failure of large projects. The secret of a successful zone programme lies in a strategic vision, dynamic learning, and political will power. Large projects typically tend to have long gestation periods. There is need for strong commitment to these zone projects from the government and from developers. Developers and the government need to be responsive to the challenges facing the zones. Key implementation challenges need to be addressed through innovative methods for improving outcomes.

References

Aggarwal A. (2006a), 'Special Economic Zones: Revisiting the Policy Debate', *Economic and Political Weekly*, 41(43–4): 4533–6.

——— (2006b), 'Performance of Export Processing Zones: A Comparative Analysis of India, Sri Lanka and Bangladesh', *Journal of Instaflag Institute*, 30(1): 33–122.

——— (2011), 'Promoting Agglomeration Economies and Industrial Clustering through SEZs: Evidence from India', *Journal of International Commerce, Economics and Policy*, 2(2): 201–27.

——— (2012a), *Social and Economic Impact of SEZs in India*. New Delhi: Oxford University Press.

——— (2012b), 'SEZ-led Growth in Taiwan, Korea, and India: Implementing a Successful', Strategy *Asian Survey*, 52(5): 872–99.

Amiti, M. and B.S. Javorcik (2008), 'Trade costs and location of foreign firms in China', *Journal of Development Economics*, 85(1–2): 129–49.

Balasubramanyam, V.N. (1988), 'Export Processing Zones in Developing Countries: Theory and Empirical Evidence', in D. Greenaway (ed.), *Economic Development and International Trade*. pp. 157–65, London: Macmillan.

Baldwin R.E. (2011), 'Trade and Industrialisation after globalisation's 2nd Unbundling: How Building and joining a supply chain are different and why it matters', NBER Working Paper 17716.

Banerjee, A.V., P. Bardhan, K. Basu, M.D. Chaudhury, M. Ghatak, A.S. Guha, M. Majumdar, D. Mookherjee, and D. Ray. (2007), 'Beyond Nandigram: Industrialisation in West Bengal', *Economic and Political Weekly*, 42(17, 2 April): 1487–9.

Basile, A. and D. Germidis (1984), *Investing in Export Processing Zones*. Paris: OECD.

Basu, P.K. (2007), 'Political Economy of Land Grab', *Economic and Political Weekly*, 42(14, 7 April): 1281–7.

Bhaduri, A. (2007), 'Alternatives in industrialisation', *Economic and Political Weekly*, 42(18, 5 May): 1597–601.

Chang, H.J. (2002), *Kicking Away the Ladder: Development Strategy in Historical Perspective*. London and New York: Anthem Press.

Coxhead, I. and S. Jayasuriya (2010), 'China, India and the Commodity Boon: economic and environmental implications for low income countries', *The World Economy*: 525–51.

Debaere, P.M., J. Lee, and M. Paik (2010), 'Agglomeration, Backward and Forward Linkages: Evidence from South Korean Investment in China', *Canadian Journal of Economics*, 43(2): 520–46.

Devereux, J. and L.L. Chen (1995), 'Export Zones and Welfare: Another Look', *Oxford Economic Papers*, 47(4): 704–13.

Farole, T. (2011), *Special Economic Zones in Africa: Comparing Performance and Learning from Global Experience*. Washington, DC: The World Bank.

Feenstra, R.C., G.H. Hanson, and S. Lin (2002), 'The Value of Information in International Trade: Gains to Outsourcing through Hong Kong', Working Paper No. 932, National Bureau of Economic Research (NBER) Massachusetts.

Frank, A.G. (1967), *Capitalism and Underdevelopment in Latin America*. New York: Monthly Review Press.

Fröbel, F., J. Heinrichs, and O. Kreye (1978), *The New International Division of Labour*. UK: Cambridge University Press.

Fujita, M., P. Krugman, and A. Venables (1999), *The Spatial Economy: Cities, Regions, and International Trade*. MIT Press: Cambridge, Massachusetts.

Hamada, K. (1974), 'An Economic Analysis of the Duty Free Zone', *Journal of International Economics*, 4(3): 225–41.

Hamilton, C. and L.E.O. Svensson (1982), 'On the Welfare Effects of a Duty-Free Zone', *Journal of International Economics*, 13(1): 45–64.

Heeks, R. (1996), *India's Software Industry: State Policy, Liberalization, and Industrial Development*. New Delhi: Sage Publications.

International Labor Organization (ILO) (2007), *Export processing zones statistics*. Geneva: International Labor Organization. Available online at http://www.ilo.org./public/english/dialogue/sector/themes/epz/stats.htm (accessed on 10 August 2009).

Johansson, H. and L. Nilsson (1997), 'Export Processing Zones as Catalysts', *World Development*, 25(12): 2115–28.

Kaldor, N. (1966), *Causes of the Slow Rate of Growth of the United Kingdom*. Cambridge: Cambridge University Press.

Krugman, P.R. (1991), 'Increasing Returns and Economic Geography', *Journal of Political Economy*, 99(3): 483–99.

Kumar, R. (1989), *Indian Export Processing Zones: An Evaluation*. New Delhi: Oxford University Press.

Kundra, A. (2000), *The Performance of India's Export Zones: A Comparison with the Chinese Approach*. New Delhi: Sage Publication.

Kuznets, S. (1955), 'Economic Growth and Income Inequality', *The American Economic Review*, 45(1): 1–28.

Lacharrière, L. de. (1969), *La nouvelle division internationale du travail*. Geneva: Droz.

Lewis, W.A. (1954), 'Economic Development with Unlimited Supplies of Labor', *Manchester School of Economic and Social Studies*, 22(2): 139–91.

Levien, M. (2011), 'Rationalising Dispossession: The Land Acquisition and Resettlement Bills', *Economic and Political Weekly*, 46(11, 12 March): 66–71.

Lin, J.Y. (2010), *New Structural Economics: A Framework for rethinking development and policy*. Washington, DC: The World Bank.

Lin, J.Y. and H.J. Chang (2009), 'Should industrial policy in developing countries conform to comparative advantage or defy it?' *DPR Debate between Justin Lin* and *Ha-Joon Chang Development Policy Review*, 27(5): 483–502.

Madani, D. (1999), 'A Review of the Role and Impact of Export Processing Zones, Policy Research Paper No. 2238'. Washington, DC: The World Bank.

Marshall, A. (1890), *Principles of Economics*. London: Macmillan.

Moran, M.T.H. (2002), *Strategy and Tactics for the Doha Round: Capturing the Benefits of Foreign Direct Investment*. Manila: Asian Development Bank.

Myrdal, G. (1957), *Economic Theory and Underdeveloped Regions*. London: Duckworth Press.

Nachum, L. and D. Keeble (2000), 'Localized clusters and the Eclectic and David Keeble Paradigm of FDI: Film TNCs in Central London', *Transnational Corporations*, 9(1): 1–38.

Ng, C. and L.F.Y. Tuan (2006), 'The Place of FDI in China's Regional Economic Development: Emergence of the Globalized Delta Economies', *Journal of Asian Economics*, 18(2): 348–64.

Palit A. and S. Bhattacharjee (2007), *Special Economic Zones in India—Myths and Realities*. India: Anthem Press.

Porter, M.E. (1990), *The Competitive Advantage of Nations*. New York: The Free Press.

RBI (2012), 'Outward Indian FDI—Recent Trends & Emerging Issues', Address delivered by H.R. Khan, Deputy Governor, Reserve Bank of India at the Bombay Chamber of Commerce & Industry, Mumbai on 2 March 2012. Available online at http://rbi.org.in/scripts/BS_SpeechesView.aspx?Id=674 (last accessed on 4 November 2013).

Rodrik, D. (2005), 'Growth Strategies', in A. *Philippe and S. Durlauf* (eds), *Handbook of Economic Growth*, Vol. 1. Amsterdam: Elsevier, pp. 967–1014.

——— (2007), 'Industrial Development: Stylized Facts and Policies', *Industrial Development for the 21st Century.* New York: The United Nations.

——— (2012), *No More Growth Miracles.* Available online at http://www.project-syndicate.org/commentary/no-more-growth-miracles-by-dani-rodrik (last accessed on 23 September 2012).

Rodriguez, C.A. (1976), 'A Note on the Economics of the Duty-Free Zone', *Journal of International Economics*, 6(4): 385–88.

Sen, S. and B. Dasgupta (2009), *Unfreedom and Waged Work: Labour in India's Manufacturing Industry.* India: Sage Publications.

Shapiro, H. (2005), 'Industrial Policy and Growth', Background Paper in World Economic and Social Survey, 2006.

Stiglitz, J. (1998), 'More Instruments and Broader Goals: Moving Towards the Post-Washington Consensus', Address to the WIDER Annual Lecture, Helsinki, 7 January.

Szirmai, A. (2011), 'Industrialisation as an engine of growth in developing countries, 1950–2005', *Structural Change and Economic Dynamics*, 23(4): 406–20.

UNCTAD (1998), *World Investment Report 1998: Trends and Determinants.* Geneva: UNCTAD.

Warr, P.G. (1989), 'Export processing zones: The economics of enclave manufacturing', *The World Bank Research Observer*, 9(1): 65–88.

PART VII

SECTORS

CHAPTER 24

AGRICULTURE IN INDIA

performance, challenges, and opportunities

S. MAHENDRA DEV, SRIJIT MISHRA, AND VIJAY LAXMI PANDEY*

In 2012, a delay in rains and the possibility of drought reiterated the risks of monsoon-dependent agriculture in India. It brought into focus the discourse on the crisis in Indian agriculture, observed since the early 1990s. Two symptoms of this crisis were non-serviceable debt and increasing incidence of farmers' suicides. These symptoms point out the adverse implications on the livelihood of people dependent on agriculture—the agrarian crisis. The crisis was also associated with stagnation in the growth of production and productivity—the agricultural crisis. The latter is intertwined with the former. There seems to have been revival in the agricultural growth in recent years, which we elaborate in the next section, in our analysis of the performance of Indian agriculture. What is more,

* This chapter draws from related recent work by the authors, including Dev (2012), Dev and Pandey (2013), Mishra (2012), Mishra and Reddy (2011), and Reddy and Mishra (2009, 2010) among others. The chapter is written as part of the 'Tackling the Agriculture: Nutrition Disconnect in India (TANDI)-Phase II', an initiative by Bill & Melinda Gates Foundation. The authors are thankful to an anonymous peer reviewer and the editor for their insightful comments and to Rishi Kumar and Ritika Palit for a careful reading. For remaining omissions and commissions, usual disclaimers apply.

despite these improvements, the incidences of farmers' suicides continue to remain a matter of concern and it is premature to visualize a positive outcome in the livelihood of those dependent on agriculture. A true measure of success should be the implications on smallholders, which we discuss in the section that follows, who constitute more than four-fifths of the cultivating households. To address these, as the next section suggests, it is particularly important to leverage new technologies, build institutions, and emphasize on low external input sustainable agriculture (LEISA) so as to help improve incomes and reduce risks without compromising on yield.

Performance of Indian Agriculture

Recent discourses have pointed out relatively lower growth in agriculture in the post-1990s than prior to that (Desai et al. 2011; Dev and Pandey 2013; Mishra 2012; and Mishra and Reddy 2011, among others). Some of them do point to a reversal during recent years, that is, sometime after 2004–5. Keeping this is mind, this chapter proposes to calculate growth rates by using triennium ending (TE) time series data, a standard practice to smoothen out fluctuations in agricultural production, to separate the experiences of the recent years (TE 2004–5 to TE 2010–11) with that of the immediate post-reforms period (TE 1993–4 to TE 2004–5) while contrasting the experience of the latter with the pre-reforms period (TE 1981–2 to TE 1993–4). The choice of TE 1981–2 as a start year is a standard practice in the analysis of Indian agriculture; the years TE 1993–4 and TE 2004–5 have been chosen as one observed some changes in broad trends around these years. Our calculations are based on a double-kinked exponential curve following Boyce (1986).[1]

[1] Growth rates have been computed using the double-kinked exponential curve, $Ln(Y_t)=a+b_1D_1+b_2D_2+b_3D_3+u_t$; Y_t refers to TE average data, t begins with 0 for TE 1981–2 and increases by one unit for every year such that it is 29 for TE 2010–11. D_1 begins with 0 and increases by one unit for every year till TE 1993–4 and for this as also all subsequent years it is 12. $D_2=0$ from TE 1981–2 till TE 1993–4 and then increases by one unit for every year till TE 2004–5 and for this as also all subsequent years it is 11. $D_3=0$ from TE 1981–2 till TE 2004–5 and then increases by one unit for every year till TE 2010–11. Growth rates of the three sub-periods are b_1, b_2 and b_3, respectively.

Growth in Agricultural Gross Domestic Product

An analysis of agricultural gross domestic product (GDP) shows a significant decline in the growth rate of agriculture and allied sector GDP from 3.29 per cent in the pre-reforms period to 2.72 per cent in the immediate post-reforms period; a matter of concern because the overall economy was going very strong during this period. Thus, the measures taken under the rubric of economic reforms during 1991–2 were not of much help to agriculture (Bhalla 2004; Chand 2004; Kumar 2002). However, in recent years, the agriculture sector, specifically crop and livestock, is showing some signs of revival (Table 24.1). Agricultural GDP from crop and livestock, improved to 3.08 per cent in TE 2004/5–2010/11 from 2.68 per cent during TE 1993/4–2004/5, but the improvement in growth rate was not statistically significant.

Table 24.1 Growth Rate of Agricultural Gross Domestic Product

Items	TE 1981/2–1993/4		TE 1993/4–2004/5		TE 2004/5–2010/11	
Agriculture and allied sectors	3.29	**	2.72	**†	2.95	**
Agriculture (crop & livestock)	3.36	**	2.68	**†	3.08	**
Forestry sector	0.06	**	1.72	**†	1.93	**†
Fishery	6.29	**	4.27	**†	3.54	**†

Source: CSO (2012a and 2012b).

Note: ** significant at the 1 per cent level (or 99 per cent confidence interval), † significantly different from the first period at a 95 per cent confidence interval. TE is triennium ending. Growth rates have been computed using a double-kinked exponential curve. All data are in 2004–5 prices.

This growth could be attributed to different initiatives taken by the government since late 2005, due to which the ratio of gross fixed capital formation in agriculture to agricultural GDP improved from 13 per cent in 2004–5 to 20 per cent in 2010–11 (Ministry of Agriculture, hereafter MoA 2012). Total investments, especially public investments firmed up (Table 24.2), public expenditure in agricultural research and extension was boosted (Table 24.3). However, it may be noted that public investment in agriculture mostly relates to medium and major irrigation projects where substantial resources are put without much critical scrutiny (Government of India 2011; Vaidyanathan 2010). There is also a lag effect of public investments in agriculture growth. Therefore, impacts from these will be felt more in the long run and will depend on the nature and composition of the investment. Besides, since the mid-2000s, private investments by individual farmers as well as by other entities who develop infrastructure from an agri-business perspective, have increased significantly and this can also have positive implications.[2] It may also be noted that the share of private sector in total agricultural investment is 70 to 75 per cent (MoA 2012). There is complementarity between public and private investments. The terms of trade for agriculture, based on GDP-implicit price deflators, seem to have improved considerably during the recent period; they increased from 100 in 2004–5 to 126 in 2009–10 (Dev and Pandey 2013).

The forestry sector showed a gradual improvement in the growth rate whereas the fishery sector registered a gradual decline over the three periods (Table 24.1). Now, we take up a crop-wise analysis of growth in value of output as also in area, production and yield.

Table 24.2 Investment in Agriculture

Items	TE 1981/2–1993/4		TE 1993/4–2004/5		TE 2004/5–2010/11	
Investment, agriculture	2.23	**	6.43	**†	8.52	**†
Public investment, agriculture	-4.46	**	2.25	**†	12.50	**†‡

Source: CSO (2012a and 2012b).

Note: ** significant at the 1 per cent level (or 99 per cent confidence interval), † significantly different from the first period at a 95 per cent confidence interval, ‡ indicates significantly different from the second period at a 95 per cent confidence interval. TE is triennium ending. Growth rates have been computed using double-kinked exponential curve. All data are in 2004–5 prices.

Crop-wise Analysis

The performance of different segments of agriculture show that growth rates in the value of output of crops and livestock declined in the immediate post-reforms period (Table 24.4). But the growth rates were relatively

[2] Note that certain types of public investment will crowd-in private investments that supplement them and have multiplier effects and doing away with such public investments could have disastrous consequences. For instance, a decline in public investments on irrigation led to an increase in private investments on borewells that not only had an adverse debt and cost implication on the farmer, but also led to a depletion of ground water in many areas—a tragedy of the commons.

Table 24.3 Growth of Real Government Expenditure on Agricultural Research, Education, and Extension in India (2004–5 prices)

Items	TE 1981/2–1992/3	TE 1993/4–2004/5	TE 2005/6–2009/10
Research and education	4.25	6.28	9.00
Extension	6.15	0.93	5.14
Total	4.68	5.14	9.75

Note: Estimates provided by Suresh Pal and Alka Singh from the Indian Agricultural Research Institute, New Delhi through a personal communication.

higher in more recent years. Growth rates for most of the individual crops except for fruits and vegetables are similar. They declined in the immediate post-reforms period as compared to the pre-reforms period and are showing improvements in the recent years. During recent years, the period TE 2004–5 to 2010–11, a significantly higher growth was observed for cotton, maize, pulses, and oilseeds. Cereals also registered some improvement over the post-reforms period growth rates.[3] The significantly higher growth of cotton coincides with the introduction of *Bacillus thuringiensis* (Bt) cotton towards the end of our second period and its spread in usage during the same period is worth noticing. However, one should be cautious in attributing reasons for this entirely to the introduction of this genetic modification because of the absence of appropriate counter-factuals that separate out the impacts on account of new hybrid varieties and the lower incidence of specific pest attacks (see Gaurav and Mishra 2012).

Indian agriculture has been witnessing diversification over time. Though the growth rate for value of output from fruits and vegetables declined in recent years (Table 24.4), its share in total value of output increased from 19 per cent in 1981–2 to 27 per cent in 2010–11 whereas the share of cereals declined from 34 per cent to 29 per cent in the same period (Central Statistical Organization, hereafter CSO 2012a, 2012b). Change in cropping patterns is also evident. There has been a decline in the area under other cereals and a decline in the growth rate of area for rice and sugarcane. However, area under pulses and oilseeds that had declined in the post-reforms period reversed in recent years and the improvement

[3] An interesting initiative with regard to rice cultivation is the spread of an alternative cultivation practise called the system of rice intensification (SRI), which involves civil society as also some public policy initiatives (Thiyagarajan and Gujja 2012).

Table 24.4 Value of Output from Different Crops and Livestock

Items	TE 1981/2–1993/4		TE 1993/4–2004/5		TE 2004/5–2010/11	
Crops	2.74	*	2.32	*	2.68	*
Cereals	3.28	*	0.98	*†	1.90	*†
Paddy	3.77	*	0.80	*†	1.71	*†
Wheat	4.02	*	1.67	*†	1.75	*†
Maize	2.49	*	3.31	*	5.98	*†‡
Pulses	1.53	*	-0.03	†	2.48	*†‡
Oilseeds	6.07	*	0.46	†	4.79	*‡
Sugarcane	3.52	*	1.70	*	1.83	§
Cotton	4.08	*	1.02	†	13.69	*†‡
Fruits and Vegetables	2.84	*	4.79	*†	2.88	*†
Livestock	4.42	*	3.39	*	4.11	*
Milk group	4.96	*	3.73	*†	3.45	*†
Meat group	5.15	*	2.92	*†	5.50	*†
Eggs	6.25	*	3.61	*†	6.48	*†

Source: CSO (2012a and 2012b).

Note: * significant at 5 per cent level (or a 95 per cent confidence interval), § indicates significant at 15 per cent, † significantly different from the first period at a 95 per cent confidence interval, ‡ indicates significantly different from the second period at a 95 per cent confidence interval. TE is triennium ending. Growth rates have been computed using double-kinked exponential curve. All data are in 2004–5 prices.

in the growth rate of area is also significant (Table 24.5). The increase in production of other cereals is attributable to yield growth only. In case of pulses, oilseeds, and cotton, both area and yield growth are responsible for increase in the growth rate of production in recent years. Improvements in recent years can be attributed to various initiatives including the National Food Security Mission (NFSM) launched in 2007–8 and a favourable monsoon in almost all the years except 2009–10 and also a price or terms of trade that favoured agriculture. It would be worthwhile to take up an analysis across states.

Analysis Across States

An analysis of agricultural gross state domestic product (GSDP) shows that it increased in 11 of the 15 major states during TE 2004–5 to 2010–11

Table 24.5 Growth in Area, Production, and Yield

Items	Area			Production			Yield		
	TE 1981/2–1993/4	TE 1993/4–2004/5	TE 2004/5–2010/11	TE 1981/2–1993/4	TE 1993/9–2004/5	TE 2004/5–2010/11	TE 1981/2–1993/4	TE 1993/9–2004/5	TE 2004/5–2010/11
Food Grains	-0.27 *	-0.27 *†	0.46 *†‡	3.05 *	1.00 *	2.18 *	3.31 *	1.27 *	1.72 *
Rice	0.65 *	0.18 §†	0.02	3.79 *	0.92 *†	1.87 *†	3.15 *	0.73 *†	1.88 *†‡
Wheat	0.76 *	0.72 *	0.95 *	4.04 *	1.67 *†	1.75 *†	3.28 *	0.95 *†	0.80 *†
Other Cereals	-2.05 *	-1.55 *	-0.28 †‡	0.52 *	0.31	3.60 *†‡	2.57 *	1.84 *	3.93 *‡
Total Pulses	-0.13	-0.45 *	1.50 *†‡	1.51 *	-0.40 §†	3.04 *‡	1.64 *	0.03 †	1.58 *‡
Oilseeds	3.16 *	-0.46 †	1.72 *‡	5.83 *	0.57 †	4.93 *‡	2.69 *	1.01 †	3.25 *‡
Cotton	1.09 *	0.61 *	3.98 *†‡	3.67 *	2.84 *	14.27 *†‡	2.59 *	2.22 *	10.24 *†‡
Sugarcane	2.17 *	1.39 *	1.31 *	4.01 *	1.15 *†	1.79 *	1.84 *	-0.26 †	0.48 *†

Source: MoA (2012).

Note: * significant at 5 per cent level (or a 95 per cent confidence interval), § indicates significant at 15 per cent, † significantly different from the first period at a 95 per cent confidence interval, ‡ indicates significantly different from the second period at a 95 per cent confidence interval. TE is triennium ending. Growth rates have been computed using double-kinked exponential curve.

as against the post-reforms period of TE 1993–4 to 2004–5; the increase was significant in seven of these states (Table 24.6). States like Kerala, Uttar Pradesh, and West Bengal recorded a decline in agricultural GSDP, but the decline was significant in Kerala alone. Some states recorded a gradual improvement in agricultural GSDP over the three periods; the improvements were significant in Andhra Pradesh and Odisha. In recent years, the highest growth rate for agricultural GSDP was recorded by Andhra Pradesh followed by that in Maharashtra and then Madhya Pradesh.

Table 24.6 Growth of Agricultural Gross State Domestic Product

States	TE 1981/2–1993/4		TE 1993/4–2004/5		TE 2004/5–2010/11	
Andhra Pradesh	2.44	*	3.34	*	6.22	*†‡
Bihar	1.69	*	3.60	*†	3.85	*
Gujarat	1.85	*	3.80	*	4.57	
Haryana	4.25	*	1.83	*†	3.84	*‡
Himachal Pradesh	0.12	*	0.10	*	0.06	
Karnataka	3.99	*	0.55	†	4.71	*‡
Kerala	4.40	*	1.36	*†	-0.42	†‡
Madhya Pradesh	3.78	*	1.40	*†	5.34	*‡
Maharashtra	5.12	*	3.48	*†	5.91	*‡
Odisha	−0.26		0.63		4.99	*†‡
Punjab	4.15	*	1.84	*†	2.20	*†
Rajasthan	4.12	*	2.57	*	3.77	*
Tamil Nadu	4.53	*	0.58	*†	4.13	*‡
Uttar Pradesh	3.35	*	2.11	*†	2.01	*†
West Bengal	5.44	*	2.71	*†	1.36	*†

Source: CSO (1999, 2007, 2010, 2012c).

Note: * significant at 5 per cent level (or a 95 per cent confidence interval), § indicates significant at 15 per cent, † significantly different from the first period at a 95 per cent confidence interval, ‡ indicates significantly different from the second period at a 95 per cent confidence interval. TE is triennium ending. Growth rates have been computed using double-kinked exponential curve.

These growth rates suggest an overall improvement in agricultural performance with respect to agricultural GSDP during recent years (TE 2004–5 to 2010–11) when compared with the post-reforms period (TE 1993–4 to 2004–5). It is therefore important to understand from an equity point of view, whether instability in agriculture increased or decreased and if the states were converging towards the national average or diverging from it. Table 24.7 shows that volatility reduced from 6.28 per cent during the post-reforms period to 3.03 per cent in recent years at the all-India level for net domestic produce from agriculture. Even in the case of states it was observed that for almost all the states, fluctuations in net state domestic produce reduced in recent years as against the post-reforms period, except for Himachal Pradesh and Maharashtra. An analysis of β-convergence, based on the linear regression of growth rates for net state domestic produce from agriculture (NSDPA) per hectare on their respective initial NSDPA per hectare, shows an overall convergence during the period 1980–1 to 2009–10. Despite this positive note on reductions in volatility and an increase in convergence across states, it should be borne in mind that more than half the workforce and their dependents still depend on agriculture for their livelihood and a large majority of them are small and marginal farmers. It is therefore imperative that we take up a discussion from their perspective.

Table 24.7 Instability in Net Domestic Produce and Net State Domestic Produce from Agriculture Using Ray's Instability Index

States	TE 1981/2–1992/3	TE 1993/4–2004/5	TE 2005/6–2009/10
All India	6.39	6.28	3.03
Andhra Pradesh	8.93	13.19	6.03
Bihar	14.51	14.10	12.13
Gujarat	45.38	26.69	13.75
Haryana	13.09	6.03	5.76
Himachal Pradesh	13.11	9.13	14.22
Karnataka	9.36	12.58	7.84
Kerala	7.19	9.31	7.60
Madhya Pradesh	11.16	20.44	6.58
Maharashtra	18.62	9.75	14.47
Odisha	20.51	15.69	4.40
Punjab	4.61	3.97	1.16
Rajasthan	25.02	29.68	14.96
Tamil Nadu	13.21	13.46	9.34
Uttar Pradesh	3.70	4.22	1.65
West Bengal	7.43	5.06	3.98

Source: CSO (1999, 2007, 2010, 2012a, 2012b, 2012c).

Note: Ray Instability Index- Standard Deviation of Ln $\{(Y_{t+1})/(Y_t)\}$ where Y_t is net domestic produce or net state domestic produce from agriculture.

Small and Marginal Farmers: Role, Challenges, and Opportunities

The objective of this section is to examine the role and challenges of agricultural small holdings in achieving agricultural growth, food security, and livelihoods in India. It may be noted that Indian agriculture is the home of small and marginal farmers. Therefore, the future of sustainable agricultural growth and food security in India depends on the performance of these farmers. Agricultural census data shows that there were about 129 million agricultural holdings in India in 2005–6. Small and marginal farmers were around 108 million. The average size of holdings declined from 2.3 hectares (ha) in 1970–1 to 1.23 ha in 2005–6. Small and marginal farmers account for more than 80 per cent of the total farm households, but their share in the operated area is around 41 per cent. Thus, there are significant land inequalities in India.

The role of small farms in development and poverty reduction is well recognized (Lipton 2006). The global experience of growth and poverty reduction shows that GDP growth originating in agriculture is at least twice as effective in reducing poverty as GDP growth originating outside agriculture (The World Bank 2008). Small holdings play an important role in agricultural development and poverty reduction.

Farm Size, Output, and Productivity

There has been debate in India on the relationship between farm size and productivity. The results of the situation assessment survey (SAS) of farmers, in the National Sample Survey Fifty-ninth Round (2003) empirically established that for the agricultural year 2002–3, small farms continued to produce more in value terms per hectare than medium and large farms. The value of output per hectare was Rs 14,754 for marginal farmers, Rs 13,001 for small farmers, Rs 10,655 for medium farmers, and Rs 8,783 for large farmers. It shows that from the efficiency point of view, small holdings were equal to or better than large holdings.

It is being observed that small holdings have higher productivity than medium and large farms. But, returns are not enough to compensate for the disadvantage of the small area of holdings. The cost of cultivation per hectare is also high on small and marginal farms as compared to medium and large farms.[4] At the all-India level, net farm income per hectare for small holdings is higher than large holdings. Across 20 major states, the results are similar to the all India pattern in 11 of these states. But, in the remaining nine, the reverse was true—net farm income per hectare was high in large holdings than in small holdings.

However, the monthly income and consumption figures across different size class of landholdings show that marginal and small farmers had dis-savings (expenditure higher than income) compared to medium and large farmers. According to SAS, the monthly consumption of marginal farmers was Rs 2,482 and monthly income was Rs 1,659 (Figure 24.1). This shows that they had dis-savings of Rs 823. The dis-savings for small farmers were Rs 655. For large farmers, monthly income and consumption was Rs 9,667 and Rs 6,418 respectively with a savings of Rs 3,249. As National Commission for Enterprises in the Unorganized Sector (NCEUS 2008:12) suggests, '... consumption expenditure of marginal and small farmers exceeds their estimated income by a substantial margin and presumably the deficits have to be plugged by borrowing or other means.' NCEUS (2008) also indicates that poverty for small holding farmers was much higher than that for other farmers. The need for increasing productivity and incomes of small holdings and promoting of non-farm activities for these farmers are obvious.

Access to Inputs and Markets

There are many issues and challenges for small holding agriculture in India. They face several challenges in their access to inputs and marketing. They need a level playing field with large farms in terms of accessing land, water, inputs, credit, technology, and markets. Small holdings also face new challenges on integration with value chains, liberalization and globalization effects, market volatility, other risks and vulnerability, and adaptation of climate change (Thapa and Gaiha 2011).

SAS 2003 brought out many issues relating to small and marginal farmers (NSSO 2005). Based on this survey, NCEUS (2008: 7) said that:

> Some of the general issues that confront marginal-small farmers as agriculturalists are: imperfect markets for inputs/product leading to smaller value realizations; absence of access to credit markets or

[4] On returns to farming, see Gaurav and Mishra (2011).

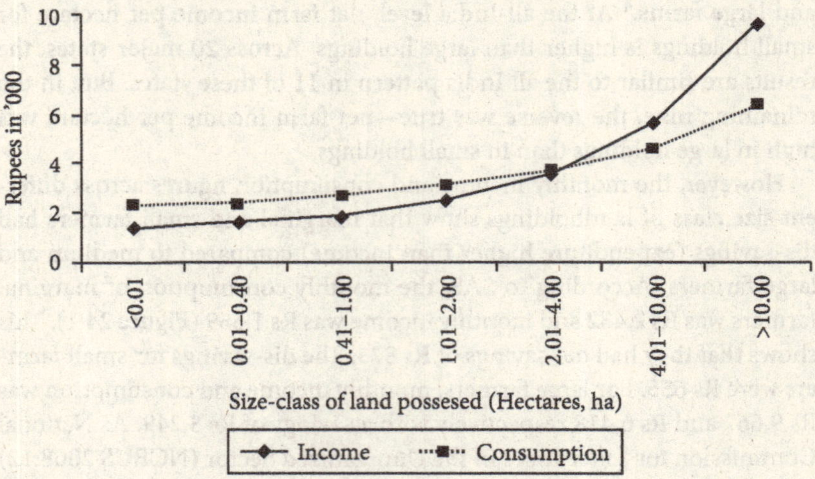

FIGURE 24.1 Income and Consumption by Size-class, India, 2002–3

Source: NSSO (2005: 21–22).

imperfect credit markets leading to sub-optimal investment decisions or input applications; poor human resource base; smaller access to suitable extension services restricting suitable decisions regarding cultivation practices and technological know-how; poorer access to 'public goods' such as public irrigation, command area development, electricity grids; greater negative externalities from poor quality land and water management, etc.

Increasing globalization has added to the problems faced by the small holding agriculture. The policies of huge subsidies and protection by developed countries have negative effects on small holding farmers in developing countries.

Credit and Indebtedness

Small holdings need credit for both consumption and investment purposes. As discussed in Mishra (2012), we reiterate some of the recent policy discourses. A report by a working group, Reserve Bank of India (RBI) (2006), pointed out the relevance of both credit and non-credit factors. But, some important observations are that agriculturists continue to be bothered with inadequate amount, untimely disbursement and other hassles while borrowing credit from formal sources; that the system fails to differentiate between wilful and non-wilful defaulters; and that no credit guarantees exist to facilitate non-wilful defaulters.

The report of the expert group on agricultural indebtedness indicates that farmers are increasingly depending on informal sources of credit; share of debt of farmer households from formal sources showed a secular increase from 7.3 per cent in 1951 to 66.3 per cent in 1991 and then it declined to 61.1 per cent in 2002 (Government of India 2007). Dependence on informal sources is higher for marginal and small farmers (Figure 24.2) and that too at a higher interest burden because 75 per cent of the debt by farmer households from non-institutional sources has an interest rate of more than 20 per cent, of which more than half (overall 38 per cent) have an interest rate of more than 30 per cent per annum (Government of India 2007).

Shetty (2009) further observes that: (a) there was a decline in the number of rural bank branches from 32,981 in 1996 to 31,967 in 2005, (b) there was a decline in the number of agricultural borrowal accounts from 277 lakh in March 1992 to 198 lakh in March 2001, and (c) there was a decline in agricultural credit as per cent of net bank credit from

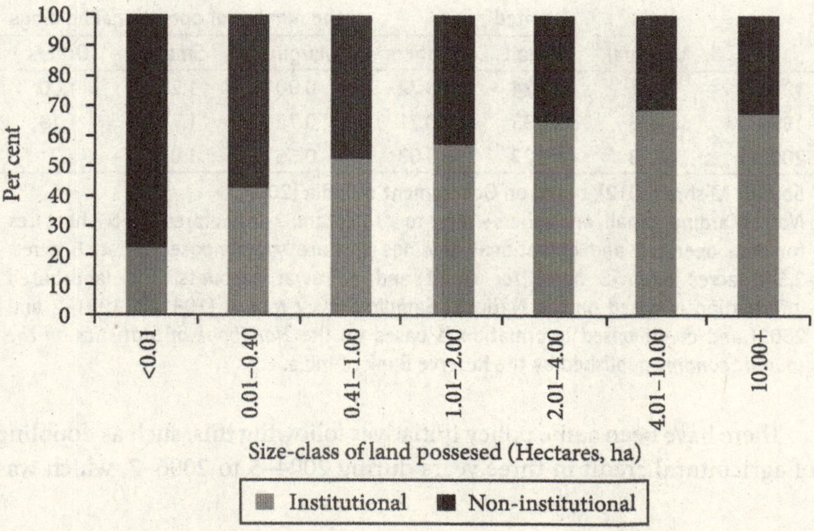

FIGURE 24.2 Share of Loan Amount from Institutional and Non-institutional Sources of Credit by Size-class of Land Possessed, 2002–3

Source: Reddy and Mishra (2010).

18 per cent in the 1980s, which is the statutory requirement, to 11 per cent in 2004.[5]

The ratio of the share of credit disbursed to the share of area operated and the ratio of the share of the number of borrowal accounts to the share of the number of operational holdings indicate that both have been declining for marginal holdings (those with less than one hectare) (Table 24.8). For small holdings, both the ratios increased in the 1980s, but in the 1990s it was only the borrowal accounts to operational holdings ratio that increased whereas the credit disbursed to area operated ratio decreased. For the others category of holdings, the credit disbursed to area operated ratio showed a slight decline in the 1980s, but all the ratios increased in the 1990s. In other words, there was a shift in favour of small holders in the 1980s, which seems to have been reversed in favour of the other (medium and large) holdings in the 1990s.

Table 24.8 Ratio of the Share of Credit Disbursed to the Share of Area Operated and the Ratio of the Share of the Number of Borrowal Accounts to the Share of the Number of Operational Holdings

Year	Ratio of the share of credit disbursed to the share of area operated			Ratio of the share of the number of borrowal accounts to the share of the number of operational holdings		
	Marginal	Small	Others	Marginal	Small	Others
1981–2	2.41	1.24	0.72	0.90	1.28	1.00
1991–2	1.85	1.33	0.71	0.72	1.77	1.19
2002–3	0.98	1.22	0.93	0.56	1.85	2.21

Source: Mishra (2012), based on Government of India (2007).

Note: Marginal, small, and others+ refer to <1 hectare, 1–2 hectares and >2 hectares for area operated and operational holdings and are superimposed on <2.5 acres, 2.5–5 acres and >5 acres for credit and borrowal accounts. The land-based information is based on the National Sample Survey rounds (1981–2, 1991–2 and 2003) and credit-based information is based on the *Handbook of Statistics on the Indian Economy* published by the Reserve Bank of India.

There have been some policy initiatives following this, such as doubling of agricultural credit in three years during 2004–5 to 2006–7, which was

[5] Using Basic Statistical Returns, Chakrabarty (2012) points out that outstanding credit from scheduled commercial banks to agricultural occupation as per cent of adjusted net bank credit (ANBC) was as follows: 16.7 per cent in 1981, 15 per cent in 1991, 9.6 per cent in 2001 and 11.3 per cent in 2011. The statutory requirement of priority sector lending being calculated from ANBC is as per RBI (2012a).

achieved but this did not increase the proportion of agricultural credit as a per cent of adjusted net bank credit (ANBC) that stood at 16.1 per cent in March 2011.[6] There was an Agricultural Debt Waiver and Debt Relief Scheme (ADWDRS) in 2008, which helped banks' books by reducing their non-performing assets, but as a study by the National Bank for Agriculture and Rural Development (NABARD) indicates this did not automatically improve access to credit of all farmers because 50 per cent of active farmers are not likely to have a kisan credit card (Samantara 2010). Some other initiatives are the introduction of no frills accounts and use of business correspondents to improve access to banking services.

A report on credit-related issues of farmers (Government of India 2009; also see Mehrotra 2011) refers to regional inequalities—the eastern region's share in credit disbursed was much lower than its share in gross cropped area, the southern region with a history of good branch banking had a higher share of credit and the amount was spread across a large number of borrowal accounts with the average amount disbursed per borrowal account at Rs 41,331 in June 2008 being lower than the eastern region (Rs 66,812), the western region (Rs 113,387), and the northern region (Rs 176,179). This raises issues of inclusion or rather exclusion in the latter areas. The report also points to a seasonal anomaly with nearly one-fourth of the credit being disbursed during March and another 10–20 per cent being disbursed during January and February, when even rabi activities are by and large over, raising questions on the timeliness and the 'purpose' behind these disbursals. All these do raise concerns on the livelihoods and opportunities for agriculture in general and that of the small and marginal farmers in particular. We now take up some further discussion on technological and institutional innovations for agriculture.

Opportunities: Technological and Institutional Innovations

There are many opportunities in the form of technological and institutional innovations which can enable marginal and small farmers to raise

[6] RBI (2012b) indicates that the credit disbursed for agriculture and allied activities as per cent of gross bank credit declined from 13.5 per cent in March 2010 to 12.3 per cent in March 2011 to 12.0 per cent in March 2012.

agricultural productivity and increase incomes through diversification and high value agriculture. Research and extension should give importance to reducing costs without reducing yields. Therefore, new technological innovations with approaches focusing on LEISA that do not use chemical fertilizers, pesticides or genetically modified organisms. It counters the argument of 'there is no alternative' (TINA) by affirming that there are multiple alternatives that are situation specific, but they are not mainstream practices because to promulgate them one needs the support of appropriate knowledge, resources, and also appropriate leveraging with new advances in marketing opportunities and information technology.

Information Technology

Changes in information technology will help in a big way in improving agri-business and incomes of small farmers. Indian private companies and non-governmental organizations (NGOs) are global leaders in providing information to farmers, as a spin-off from India's meteoric rise as a world leader in information and communications technology (ICT). E-choupals have expanded access to internet in rural areas. Up to 6,400 internet kiosks were set up between 2000 and 2007 by ITC Limited, one of the largest agricultural exporters. They reached about 4 million farmers growing a range of crops—soybean, coffee, wheat, rice, pulses, or shrimp—in over 40,000 villages. They get free information in their language about local and global market prices, weather forecasts, farming practices, and crop insurance. They serve as a purchase centres, cutting marketing costs and allowing farmers to obtain a bigger farm price.[7] The M.S. Swaminathan Research Foundation established knowledge centres in Puducherry in 1997. With the support of the Indian Space Research Organization (ISRO), centres in each village are connected by satellite to a hub at Villianur. Women self-help groups (SHGs) use the centres' computers to manage their business accounts and coordinate their activities using video links with other villages. The declining costs of ICTs are giving small farmers much greater access to information. Mobile phone coverage in India is expanding and has an important function of linking farmers to markets.

[7] A caveat is that there have been some second generation problems with e-Choupal and their success in scaling-up or reproducing the same in other regions have not been as smooth.

Institutions for Marketing

A number of innovative institutional models are emerging to link farmer groups to bargain together in the input and produce markets. For small and marginal farmers, marketing of their products is an important problem apart from credit and extension. In recent years, there has been some form of contract arrangements in several agricultural crops, such as tomatoes, potatoes, chillies, gherkin, baby corn, rose, onions, cotton, wheat, basmati rice, groundnut, flowers, and medicinal plants. There is a silent revolution in institutions related to non-cereal foods. New production-to-market linkages in the food supply chain are: spot or open market transactions, agricultural cooperatives, and contract farming (Joshi and Gulati 2003).

There is a need to revamp some of the legal hurdles for agro-processing and the Agriculture Produce Market Committee (APMC) Act. Several state governments have already amended their APMC Acts, allowing varying degrees of flexibility. However, several states are yet to notify the relevant rules that would make the amendment fully operational (Patnaik 2011). These steps should be speedily completed to provide a boost to promoting direct marketing, contract farming, and setting up of markets in private and cooperative sectors.

There are different models for marketing collectively by small and marginal farmers: the SHG model, cooperative model, small producer cooperatives, and contract farming. *Apni mandi*s in Punjab, *rytu bazar*s in Andhra Pradesh, and dairy cooperatives are some of the successful cases in marketing. The real challenge lies in organizing small and marginal farmers for marketing and linking them to high value agriculture. Thus, group approach is needed for getting benefits from marketing. Most important problem for the small farmers is output price fluctuations. There is a big gap between producer prices and consumer prices.

Small farmers can also benefit from the emerging supermarkets and value chains. In a study on food supply chains in India, Reardon and Minten (2011) indicated a rapid change in supply food chains in the past two decades. A modern sector is emerging in the wholesale sector with the growth of modern logistics firms and specialized modern wholesalers. Along with this, the traditional segment of the wholesale sector is also transforming with reductions in supply chains, declining role of village brokers as farmers sell directly to mandis, and an expansion of cold storages that seem to be taking up wholesale functions including providing credit. However, it is the medium and small farmers who take advantage of this dynamism with the marginal farmers being at a disadvantage because of less marketable surplus. They also point out infrastructural constraints on account of poor roads, unavailability of electricity, limited access to credit, less education, and no tube wells.

In India, the expansion of modern retailing has the potential to spark investments in marketing efficiency and processing that yield benefits to both producers and consumers. In those cases where small producers have been able to integrate into the supplying chains, supermarkets have offered enhanced security and considerably higher margins than traditional clients, such as wholesalers and groceries. However, there is scope for exploitation in contract farming and supermarkets if rules are not properly framed or not properly implemented.

While recognizing the advantages of contract farming, Singh (2012), as also Narayanan (2012), point out that its evaluation has to be situation specific, as contracts depend on the type of firm, the farmer, the crop being grown, and the nature of contract, among others. Singh (2012), further adds that the success of contract farming should be assessed based on its impact on reducing market risks for small and marginal farmers, and its impact on the resource base because of implications on future incomes and the environment.[8] Next, we discuss a cultivation practice that could ensure some of these advantages.

Non-pesticide Management

Non-pesticide management (NPM) is one of the approaches that reduces costs and adverse implications on the environment. As the term suggests, it tries to manage pests without the use of chemical pesticides and if feasible, tries to avoid the use of fertilizers. This technology is knowledge-centric, and hence, its success as also scaling-up depends a lot on appropriate extension services. A successful intervention, as discussed in Mishra and Reddy (2011), is community-managed sustainable agriculture (CMSA) under the aegis of the Society for Elimination of Rural Poverty (SERP) in Andhra Pradesh.[9] A major emphasis of this is on retaining soil health through natural processes that enhance microbial activity and replenish

[8] For a discussion on technological changes giving higher net returns, which happen to be facilitated through contract farming and can add rather than reduce exposure to risks, see Mishra (2008).

[9] The continuing effectiveness and further scaling-up of NPM under SERP in Andhra Pradesh also needs constant interventions in terms of knowledge, human resources, physical capital, and monitoring and evaluation.

nutrients to sustain productivity. NPM has a number of non-negotiable practices that include 'deep summer ploughing, community bonfires, seed treatment, bird perches, border crops, trap crops, yellow and white plates, intercrops, light traps, pheromone traps, delta traps in groundnut, alleys in paddy, and cutting of the tips in paddy at the time of transplantation among others' (Mishra and Reddy, 2011, p. xx).

Under CMSA, farmer field schools comprising 15 to 20 members meet every week for on-site observations that help them understand the ecological systems—the life cycle of pests and their predators. If pest infestation is observed then there is discussion with the resource person as also with other groups in the village to gauge the intensity of the problem and plan a course of action. Bio-pesticides are used only as a last resort. In addition to pest management, nitrogen fixation and soil nutrient deficiencies are addressed through locally available resources. Some of the other important aspects are setting up of community seed banks and promoting an appropriate cropping pattern and crop rotation practices. Local youth are encouraged to start micro-enterprises with forward and backward linkages to facilitate availability of inputs or marketing of produce.

There are other similar experiments. For instance, Revitalizing Rainfed Agriculture Network (RRA-N) comprising a number of civil society groups working in the field. An aspect of their interventions is that they are refined as per local conditions with focus on natural resource management and integrated other measures to help adapt to rainfed conditions as also to the increasing vagaries of the monsoon.[10] This is particularly important because more than three-fifths of the geographical and more than two-thirds of the gross cropped area are in rainfed regions (Planning Commission 2011a). This calls for an alternative policy discourse on agricultural intervention, which has been indicated in the approach paper to the Twelfth Five-year Plan (Planning Commission 2011b; also see Mishra et al. 2013). It suggests initiatives in the form of comprehensive pilots spread across different agro-ecological conditions that focus on integrating interventions in water, soil, seed, livestock, fisheries, credit, and institutions, among others. This will require knowledge interventions from each perspective. RRA-N has already started some pilots on their own from kharif 2012 and the Planning Commission is likely to supplement these initiatives. It will also help identify specificities as also similarities to help scale-up such interventions in the future.

[10] For an analysis showing changes in monsoon with greater intensity of rainfall in shorter wet spells and longer dry spells, see Singh and Ranade (2010).

Federation of Self-help Groups

Beginning with 400 acres in 2004–5, the programme under NPM in Andhra Pradesh covered 18.15 lakh acres in 2009–10 and they are likely to have been further scaled up after that. This has to be understood under the institutional arrangement of federation of women SHGs that SERP had built to improve the livelihood of poorer households. Interactions with SHGs and their federations made SERP evaluate livelihood problems associated with agriculture and the need for reducing costs in cultivation led to NPM. The success in Andhra Pradesh has now been extended to the national level under the National Rural Livelihoods Mission (NRLM) through a programme called the Mahila Kissan Sashaktikaran Pariyojana (MKSP).[11] The agricultural intervention also tried to involve NGOs like PRADAN (Professional Assistance for Development Action) who as part of their livelihood facilitation have been independently forming federations of women SHGs in poorer districts of the country for nearly two decades.[12]

The institutional imperative articulated in the federation of SHGs and other successful experiments, such as the Grameen Bank in Bangladesh and the Peoples Participation Programme of the Food and Agriculture Organization (FAO) in Sri Lanka, Thailand, and Zambia (see Rouse 1996), give some lessons. These, as indicated in Mishra and Reddy (2011), point to restricting the number of members to 20–5 per farmer group (or about 15 per SHG) and drawing members from homogenous groups to avoid conflicts. The focus should be on local problems identified by the group and the involvement of outside promoters should be limited to enabling or facilitating processes so that the members take over as soon as possible. Training and capacity building for 4–5 years, including hand holding in the initial stages, should be part of the long-term process of building sustainable small-marginal federated farmer groups. A sound organizational structure should be built from below with female membership and participation being insisted upon from the group level itself. Building institutions also requires developing democratic processes that are sensitive to inequities at every level. Once these are put in place and capacities of individuals and their institutions augmented, then groups and their federated institutions become self-sustaining and, over time,

[11] The scaling-up of the programme under MKSP has been slow and one has to gauge its effectiveness across states in due course of time.

[12] For an evaluation of PRADAN's interventions, see Mishra and Sengupta (2013).

they could slowly graduate to addressing the other requirements of the community.

***

The analysis in this chapter tried to contextualize our understanding of Indian agriculture by an evaluation of its performance, the roles and challenges for small holders, and some opportunities. Its performance appraisal delineates recent years (2004/5–2010/11) from the immediate post-reforms period (1993/4–2004/5) and the pre-reforms period (1981/2–1993/4). Our growth estimates, using a double-kinked exponential curve, reiterates a turnaround in agriculture in recent years. This is also because of some changes in public investments in agriculture as also increased public expenditure in agricultural education, research and extension, initiatives for improving availability of credit from formal sources, and a slew of normal monsoons in almost all but for one of the recent years. The turnaround is particularly evident for maize, pulses, oilseeds, and cotton in terms of their growth in value of output as also in production and yield. There have also been significant yield increments in rice in recent years. An analysis of agricultural GSDP across major states also shows significantly higher growth in recent years for most of them; there also seems to be a decline in volatility and convergence across states.

A matter of concern is the implications on small holders, particularly so when SAS, a nationally representative survey in the 2002–3 agricultural year, points to income being less than expenditure for farmer households with less than four hectares, that is, 95 per cent of the operational holdings. What is worrying is that this difficulty in livelihood sustainability remained in spite of the fact that per hectare returns were higher for them—there continues to be an inverse relationship between size-class and returns. Nevertheless, small holder farmers have had to bear a greater risk burden because of higher per unit cost, limited access to credit despite new initiatives, and a lower bargaining power in the input and produce markets among others. These problems get aggravated in bad years like 2012 when the monsoon plays truant and that too when nearly two-third of Indian agriculture is rainfed.

To address some of these concerns, some opportunities identified are effective use of information technology, whether to know about monsoon patterns or be informed about new knowledge on agricultural production and management or on the prevailing prices in different markets. The alternatives of RRA-N and NPM through CMSA under SERP are people-centred initiatives through the involvement of small and marginal farmers through SHGs and field schools. The need of the hour is to organize farmers at different levels and empower them. On the knowledge front, it is equally important that technologies that reduce costs, and hence risks, while not compromising on production or yield and make use of locally available resources, are encouraged.

References

Bhalla, G.S (2004), *Globalisation and Indian Agriculture, State of the Indian Farmer: A Millennium Study*, Vol. 19. New Delhi: Academic Publishers.

Boyce, J.K. (1986), 'Kinked Exponential Models for Growth Rate Estimation', *Oxford Bulletin of Economics and Statistics*, 48(4): 385–91.

Central Statistical Organisation (CSO) (1999), *State Domestic Product, 1980–81 Series*. New Delhi: Ministry of Statistics and Program Implementation, Government of India. Available at: http://mospi.nic.in/Mospi_New/upload/NAS12.htm (accessed on 30 August 2012).

——— (2007), *State Domestic Product, 1993–94 Series*. New Delhi: Ministry of Statistics and Program Implementation, Government of India. Available at: http://mospi.nic.in/Mospi_New/upload/NAS12.htm (accessed on 18 August 2012).

——— (2010), *State Domestic Product, 1999–2000 Series*. New Delhi: Ministry of Statistics and Program Implementation, Government of India. Available at: http://mospi.nic.in/Mospi_New/upload/NAS12.htm (accessed on 18 August 2012).

——— (2012a), *National Accounts Statistics, 2011 (Back series)*. New Delhi: Ministry of Statistics and Programme Implementation, Government of India. Available at: http://mospi.nic.in/Mospi_New/upload/back_series_2011.htm (accessed on 18 August 2012).

——— (2012b), *National Accounts Statistics*. New Delhi: Ministry of Statistics and Program Implementation, Government of India. Available at: http://mospi.nic.in/Mospi_New/upload/NAS12.htm (accessed on 18 August 2012).

——— (2012c), *State Domestic Product, 2004–05 Series*. New Delhi: Ministry of Statistics and Program Implementation, Government of India. Available at: http://mospi.nic.in/Mospi_New/upload/NAS12.htm (accessed on 18 August 2012).

Chakrabarty, K.C. (2012), 'Revised Guidelines on Priority Sector Lending: Rationale and Logic', Address at FIBAC 2012 organized by FICCI and the Indian Banks' Association at Mumbai on 4 September. Available at: http://www.rbi.org.in/scripts/BS_SpeechesView.aspx?id=727 (accessed on 10 September 2012).

Chand, R. (2004), 'Agricultural Growth during the Reforms and Liberalization: Issues and Concerns', Policy Brief No. 20. New Delhi: National Centre for Agricultural Economics and Policy.

Desai, B.M., E. D'Souza, J.W. Mellor, V.P. Sharma, and P. Tamboli (2011), 'Agricultural Policy Strategy, Instruments and Implementation: A Review and the Road Ahead', *Economic and Political Weekly*, 46(53): 42–50.

Dev, S.M. (2012), 'Small Farmers in India: Challenges and Opportunities', IGIDR Working Paper No.WP-2012-014. Mumbai: Indira Gandhi Institute of Development Research.

Dev, S.M. and V.L. Pandey (2013), 'Performance and Key Policy Issues of Indian Agriculture, in S. Mahendra Dev (ed.), *India Development Report, 2012–13*. New Delhi: Oxford University Press, pp. 79–92.

Gaurav, S. and S. Mishra (2011), 'Size Class and returns to Cultivation in India: A Cold Case Reopened', IGIDR Working Paper No.WP-2011-027. Mumbai: Indira Gandhi Institute of Development Research.

——— (2012), 'To Bt or Not to Bt? Risk and Uncertainty Considerations in Technology Assessment', IGIDR Working Paper No.WP-2012-001. Mumbai: Indira Gandhi Institute of Development Research.

Government of India (2007), *Report of the Expert Group on Agricultural Indebtedness* (Chairperson: R. Radhakrishna). New Delhi: Ministry of Finance.

——— (2009), *Report of the Task Force on Credit Related Issues of Farmers* (Chairperson: Umesh Sarangi). New Delhi: Ministry of Agriculture.

——— (2011), *Report of the Expert Committee on Improvement of Agricultural Statistics* (Chairperson: A. Vaidyanathan). New Delhi: Department of Agriculture and Co-operation. Available at: http://eands.dacnet.nic.in/Vaidiyanathan-CommitteeReport.pdf (accessed on 22 May 2013).

Joshi, P. K. and A. Gulati (2003), 'From Plate to Plough: Agricultural Diversification in India', Paper presented at the workshop on 'Dragon and Elephant: A Comparative Study of Economic and Agricultural Reforms in China and India', New Delhi, 25–6 March.

Kumar, P. (2002), 'Agricultural Performance and Productivity', in S.S Acharya and D.P. Chaudhri (eds), *Indian Agricultural Policy at the Crossroads*. Jaipur: Rawat Publications, pp. 353–428.

Lipton, M. (2006), 'Can Small Farmers Survive, Prosper, or be the Key Channel to cut Mass Poverty', *Journal of Agricultural and Development Economics*, 3(1): 58–85.

Mehrotra, N. (2011), 'Agriculture Credit: The Truth behind the Aggregate Numbers', *Economic and Political Weekly*, 42(42): 22–6.

Ministry of Agriculture (2012), *Agricultural Statistics at a Glance, 2011*. New Delhi: Directorate of Economics and Statistics, Department of Agriculture and Cooperation, Government of India. Available at: http://eands.dacnet.nic.in/latest_2006.htm (accessed on 19 August 2012).

Mishra, S. (2008), 'Risks, Farmers' Suicides and Agrarian Crisis in India: Is There a Way Out?' *Indian Journal of Agricultural Economics*, 63(1): 38–54.

——— (2012), 'Crisis in Indian Agriculture: Where Do We Stand?' *Artha Beekshan*, 20(4): 94–107.

Mishra, S., A. Ravindra, and C. Hesse (2013), Rainfed 'Agriculture: For an Inclusive, Sustainable and Food Secure India', IIED Briefing Paper 10041. Available at: http://pubs.iied.org/pdfs/10041IIED.pdf (accessed on 22 May 2013).

Mishra, S. and D.N. Reddy (2011), 'Persistence of Crisis in Indian Agriculture: Need for Technological and Institutional Alternatives', in Dilip M. Nachane (ed.), *India Development Report 2011*. New Delhi: Oxford University Press, pp. 48–58.

Mishra, S. and N. Sengupta (2013), *Impact Assessment Study of PRADAN's Interventions at the Grassroots*. Mumbai: Indira Gandhi Institute of Development Research.

Narayanan, S. (2012), 'The Heterogeneous Welfare Impacts of Participation in Contract Farming Schemes: Evidence from Southern India', IGIDR Working paper No.WP-2012-019. Mumbai: Indira Gandhi Institute of Development Research.

National Commission for Enterprises in the Unorganised Sector (NCEUS) (2008), *A Special Programme for Marginal and Small Farmers*. New Delhi: NCEUS.

National Sample Survey Organisation (NSSO) (2005), *Situation Assessment Survey of Farmers: Income, Expenditure and Productive Assets of Farmer Households*. NSS 59th Round (January-December 2003), NSS Report No. 497 (59/33/5).

Patnaik, G. (2011), 'Status of Agricultural Marketing Reforms', Paper presented at the workshop on 'Policy Options and Investment Priorities for Accelerating Agricultural Productivity and Development in India'. New Delhi: Indira Gandhi Institute of Development Research, Mumbai and Institute for Human Development, 10–11 November.

Planning Commission (2011a), *Report of the XII Plan Working Group on Natural Resource Management and Rainfed Farming*. New Delhi: Government of India. Available at: http://planningcommission.nic.in/aboutus/committee/wrkgrp12/agri/wg_NRM_Farming.pdf (accessed on 23 May 2013).

——— (2011b), *Faster, Sustainable and More Inclusive Growth: An Approach to the Twelfth Five Year Plan (2012–17)*. New Delhi: Government of India.

Reardon, T. and B. Minten (2011), 'The Quiet Revolution in India's Food Supply Chains', IFPRI Discussion Paper 01115. Washington, DC: International Food Policy Research Institute, August 2011.

Reddy, D.N. and S. Mishra (eds) (2009), *Agrarian Crisis in India*. New Delhi: Oxford University Press.

——— (2010), 'Economic Reforms, Small Farmer Economy and Agrarian Crisis', in R. S. Deshpande and S. Arora (eds), *Agrarian Crisis and Farmers' Suicides*. New Delhi: Sage, pp. 43–69.

Reserve Bank of India (RBI) (2006), *Report of the Working Group to Suggest Measures to Assist Distressed Farmers* (Chairperson: S.S. Johl). Mumbai: RBI.

——— (2012a), *Report of the Committee to Re-examine the Existing Classification and Suggest Revised Guidelines with regard to Priority Sector Lending Classification and Related Issues*. Mumbai: RBI.

——— (2012b), *Annual Report, 2011–12*. Mumbai: RBI.

Rouse, J. (1996), *Organizing for Extension: FAO Experiences in Small Farmer Group Development.* Rome: Sustainable Development Department, Food and Agriculture Organization.

Samantara, S. (2010), 'Kisan Credit Card—A Study', Occasional Paper 52. Mumbai: National Bank for Agriculture and Rural Development.

Singh, N. and Ranade, A. (2010), 'The Wet and Dry Spells across India during 1951–2007', *Journal of Hydrometeorology*, 11(1): 26–45.

Singh, S. (2012), 'Contract farming for sustainable agricultural development in India: A smallholder perspective', Revised version of paper presented at the workshop on 'Policy Options and Investment Priorities for Accelerating Agricultural Productivity and Development in India'. New Delhi: Indira Gandhi Institute of Development Research, Mumbai and Institute for Human Development, 10–11 November.

Shetty, S.L. (2009), 'Agricultural Credit and Indebtedness: Ground Realities and Policy Perspectives', in D.N. Reddy and S. Mishra (eds), *Agrarian Crisis in India.* New Delhi: Oxford University Press, pp. 61–86.

Thapa, G. and R. Gaiha (2011), 'Smallholder farming in Asia and the Pacific: Challenges and Opportunities', Paper presented at the Conference on new directions for small holder agriculture. Rome, International Fund for Agricultural Development (IFAD), 24–5 January.

The World Bank (2008), *World Development Report: Agriculture for Development.* Washington, DC: The World Bank.

Thiyagarajan, T.M. and B. Gujja (2012), *Transforming Rice Production with SRI (System of Rice Intensification) Knowledge and Practice: Reducing Agriculture Footprint and Ensuring Food Security*, AgSri. Available at: http://www.agsri.com/images/documents/sri/SRI_Book_Final_Version.pdf (accessed on 10 September 2012).

Vaidyanathan, A. (2010), *Agricultural Growth in India: Role of Technology, Incentives and Institutions.* New Delhi: Oxford University Press.

CHAPTER 25

NEW SOURCES OF DYNAMISM IN THE INDUSTRY

BANDI RAM PRASAD*

The landscape of the global economy is undergoing rapid change. Developing countries are outpacing developed countries in terms of growth and diversity. Globally, the composition of the industrial sector is changing. Aspects, such as technology, efficiency, the environment, and competitiveness are emerging as key determinants of growth and performance. The changing patterns of economic growth are giving way to new segments and sectors. The fastest growing industry sectors at present are found to be: (a) office, accounting and computing machinery; and (b) radio, television, and communication equipment in which countries such as Thailand, Taiwan, Malaysia, Turkey, Philippines, and Saudi Arabia have a larger share in the manufacturing value added in the developing world. The ranking of countries in the top league of industrial growth, performance, and competitiveness have undergone rapid change. China has emerged as the second biggest in terms of global manufacturing value added, displacing several developed economies. During the period 2005–9,

* The author thanks Dr Jinesh Panchali, M. Ravindran, Suprabhat Kumar, and his colleagues at FTKMC for research and editorial support. Views presented in this chapter are the author's own in his individual capacity and do not reflect, in whatsoever manner that of the organization in which he employed. The views are author's own.

countries that made a rapid jump in the ranking of the Competitive Industrial Performance Index of the United Nations Conference on Trade and Development (UNCTAD) include countries such as Kuwait, Syria, Swaziland, Vietnam, Gambia, Egypt, Latvia, Romania, Oman, and Slovakia.

This chapter broadly presents an overview of the major trends in Indian industry in regard to growth and structure, with particular emphasis on the financial sector that has emerged as an important stimulus and a source of dynamism. In this context, the chapter discusses certain aspects of Indian industry in regard to: (a) evolution of industrial policies; (b) growth trends in output; (c) changes in the structure; (d) a brief assessment on the growth trends following economic liberalization; and (e) international perspectives on the emergence of Indian industry, etc. It also discusses the role of financial sector reforms in the Indian industry and the corporate sector, with particular reference to a wide range of instruments that have emerged as new sources of dynamism helping further progress of the industry.

Much of the discussion in this chapter is from the perspective of financial markets' practice reflecting on the author's engagement with it over a long period of time. The chapter is prepared with the purpose of narrating the multi-dimensional growth of the financial sector in terms of numerous products and options (Figure 25.1) that have emerged as important sources of dynamism for the Indian economy in general, and the industry in particular.

Evolution of Indian Industry

Industrial development in India was governed by licensing policies that came into being in 1948. The first comprehensive Industrial Policy Resolution of 1956 classified industries into three categories with the state being given the primary role of industrial development and the private sector expected to supplement the efforts of the state. Industrial Policy Resolution of 1970 classified industries into four categories: core sector, heavy investment sector, the middle sector, and the de-licensed sector with the first three categories confined to large business houses and foreign companies. The Industrial Policy Statement of 1973 gave preference and thrust to the growth of small and medium enterprises (SMEs). The

NEW SOURCES OF DYNAMISM IN THE INDUSTRY

Policy Framework	Domestic Capital Markets	Indian Banking Sector	Non-Bank Finance	New Opportunities	Political environment
Delicensing and deregulation. Promotion of competition. Conducive environment for growth of the private sector. Foreign direct investment. Promotion of capital markets. Liberal access for corporates to tap foreign markets for resource mobilization. Scope for global acquisitions. Deregulation of the financial sector. New manufacturing policy. Promotion of special zones for export.	Liberalization of interest rates. Reform of the public capital markets. Foreign portfolio investment to strengthen secondary capital markets. Thrust on debt capital markets. Introduction of hedging and risk management products in the form of financial derivatives in equities, commodities, currencies, and fixed income. International listing opportunities for corporates in global exchanges in the form of Global Depository/ American Depository Receipts.	Deregulation of interest rates and greater functional autonomy for banks in regard to lending. Access to capital markets for the state-owned banks to bolster capital levels to sustain the pace of lending. Growth in loan products, including consortium lending. Provision for corporate loan restructuring.	Non-bank financial companies expanded operations with thrust on financing of machinery, farm equipment (such as tractors), and transport equipment giving thrust to the related industries.	Economic reforms and liberalization have given new opportunities to expand in the realm of certain key industries such as automobiles, engineering machinery, telecommunications, infrastructure, etc.	One of the largest democracies in the world. Political and consultative decision making. Continuity of reforms irrespective of political party in power.

Skills and Expertise	Access to International Finance	Foreign Investment	Domestic Demand	India as a Hub for Exports	Social Sector
Capacity building in education with greater emphasis on study of engineering, computer science, and information technology that have generated human resource inputs at a fairly competitive costs benefiting the industry. Setting up of National Skill Development Council to augment the skills.	India is one of the leading emerging markets to access global financial markets to raise resources for expansion, new acquisitions, and pursue domestic and global growth aspirations.	Liberalized norms of foreign direct investment and foreign portfolio investment. Liberal entry norms for foreign companies. Foreign collaborations by domestic industrial houses.	Surge in domestic demand in the background of liberalization of lending norms for personal finance, including loans for housing, personal consumption, consumer durables, cars, etc., which have fuelled growth in industrial activity.	In view of the cost-effective resources and labour, India emerged as an attractive avenue for development centers of major companies as also back office functions that led to creation of infrastructure and demand for related industries.	Rising literacy and education levels across society. One of the largest wage-earning young population. Society is relatively open to adopt new technologies and customs.
CHALLENGES OF IMPLEMENTATION					
• Challenges to meet priority sector lending • Microfinance credit is still in developing state • Private and unorganized private credit association like chit funds, etc.	• Relatively low proportion of savings invested in financial markets • Slow pace of reforms in debt market and lack of retail participation • Sluggish pace of reforms in the judicial sector	• Scale and scope restriction in the manufacturing sector • Lack of enabling infrastructure for domestic and foreign venture capital and private equity • Lack of reforms in the agriculture sector	• Uncertainty over fulfillment of political commitments • Low degree of financial inclusion • Lack of social security and basic social infrastructure		• High level of fiscal deficit • Lack of alignment in monetary and fiscal policies • Concern over the level of corruption

Source: Author's presentation

FIGURE 25.1 New Sources of Dynamism in the Industry

Industrial Policy Statement of 1977 further promoted decentralization with an increased role for small-scale, tiny, and cottage industries. The Industrial Policy Statement of 1980 placed greater thrust on promotion of competition in the domestic market, technological upgradation, and modernization of industries. The Industrial Policy Statement of 1991 that came in the backdrop of major economic reforms stated that 'the government will continue to pursue a sound policy framework encompassing encouragement of entrepreneurship, development of indigenous technology through investment in research and development, bringing in new technology, dismantling of the regulatory system, development of the capital markets, and increased competitiveness for the benefit of common man'. While import substitution policies were predominant in 1950s, the 1980s witnessed surging export promotion strategies and the 1990s saw major tariff liberalization.

The evolution of industrial policies can be assessed from the decade of the 1950s when the state had monopoly over basic and key industries to the years following reforms that restricted compulsory licensing to only six industries with just three industries reserved for the public sector.

Economic reforms in India in the last 20 years have contributed significantly in expanding the scope and significance of Indian industry. The focus of the reforms with particular reference to the industry sector, was to: (a) maintain a sustained growth in productivity; (b) enhance gainful employment; (c) achieve optimal utilization of national resources; (d) attain international competitiveness; and (e) transform India into a major partner and player in the global arena (Government of India 2010–11). The focus of the industrial policy[1] is centered on deregulation of the Indian industry, allowing it the freedom and flexibility in responding to market forces, including greater interaction with the financial sector and providing a policy regime that facilitates and fosters the growth of Indian industry.

[1] Major policy measures include liberalization of the industrial licensing policy under which at present only five industries are under compulsory licensing mainly relating to environmental, health, safety, and strategic considerations and only two industries are reserved for the public sector; Industrial Entrepreneurs Memorandum (IEM) under which industries are not covered under compulsory licensing are required to file an IEM to the Secretariat for industrial assistance; Policy for Small Scale Industries is categorized on the basis of the value of investment in plant and machinery.

Indian Industry: Growth Trends

The average annual growth rate of industry (Banga and Das 2012) which remained around 5.8 per cent in the 1950s and the 1960s, fell to 5 per cent in the 1970s and returned to 5.8 per cent in the 1980s. Reforms in the 1990s led to improvement in the value-added growth rate of the manufacturing sector, taking it to 6 per cent. The 2000s witnessed a number of measures in reducing tariffs and quantitative restrictions that led industrial growth to climb to an annual average of 8 per cent. Corresponding with value addition, industry also witnessed a huge spurt in external trade. The average annual growth rate of manufacturing real exports surged from 5 per cent in the 1980s to 9.7 per cent in the 1990s and increased further to 12 per cent in 2000s. The average annual growth rate of real imports increased from 5.4 per cent in the 1980s, to 11 per cent in the 1990s, and to 16 per cent in the 2000s. Sectoral contribution of manufacturing exports witnessed major change. Trends with regard to growth in organized and unorganized sectors, however, varied slightly. Value added in organized manufacturing, which showed an average annual growth (at 1999–2000 constant prices) of 6.3 per cent (Table 25.1) in the 1950s, rose to 7 per cent in the 1960s, fell steeply to 4.1 per cent in 1970s, and picked up to 8 per cent in the 1980s. Following the reforms, the value-added average annual growth rate adjusted at 5.9 per cent in the 1990s but quickly rose to 7.8 per cent in the 2000s. In contrast, value added in unorganized manufacturing that showed an average annual growth of 5 per cent (Table 25.1) in 1950s remained in the realm of 4 per cent in the next four decades and moved up to 6.6 per cent in the decade of 2000s.

Table 25.1 Decadal Growth in Value Added in Manufacturing Sector of India at Constant Prices (in percentage)

	Manufacturing Sector	Organized Manufacturing	Unorganized Manufacturing
1950s	5.6	6.3	5.0
1960s	5.4	7.0	3.9
1970s	4.2	4.1	4.3
1980s	6.0	8.0	3.4
1990s	5.4	5.9	4.4
2000–7	7.4	7.8	6.6

Source: Banga and Das (2012).

Structure of the Indian Industry

The share of the industry in GDP remained more or less stagnant, between 24.3 per cent in 1983 and 25.2 per cent in 1993–4, and 27 per cent in 2011–12. The share of manufacturing in GDP too remained steady between 14.5 per cent in 1983 and 15.3 per cent in 2011–12. The share of industry in employment, however, moved up from 13.8 per cent in 1983 to 22.4 per cent in 2010. The share of industry value added as percentage of GDP at 27 per cent was low as compared to countries such as China (44 per cent), Korea (39 per cent), Malaysia (44 per cent), and Thailand (45 per cent). Similarly, the share of manufacturing value added as a percentage of GDP for India at 14 per cent is quite low as compared to China (31 per cent), Korea (31 per cent), Thailand (36 per cent), and Malaysia (26 per cent). The record of India in terms of employment in industry as percentage of total employment, however, compares favourably with countries, such as China (27 per cent), Korea (17 per cent), and Thailand (20 per cent).

There is wide diversity in the growth of manufacturing in the last three decades (Table 25.2). For instance, coke and petroleum products have hardly had any growth in the 1980s and 1990s whereas the growth jumped to 19.4 per cent a year in 2000s. In contrast, radio, television, and communication equipment that showed annual growth of 28.1 per cent in the 1980s fell to 1.8 per cent in the 2000s. Sectors in the manufacturing industry that showed high growth during the 1980s included (annual growth in real value added in organized manufacturing sector), radio, television, and communication equipment (28.1 per cent); food products and beverages (18.6 per cent); wearing apparel, dressing, and dying of fur (14.3 per cent); medical, precision, and optical instruments (11.6 per cent); and chemicals and chemical products (11.1 per cent). In the 1990s, the top sectors with regard to growth were furniture and other manufacturing (29.7); basic metals (17.5); electrical machinery and apparatus (15.8 per cent); wearing apparel, dressing, and dyeing of fur (15.5 per cent); and motor vehicles, trailers, and semi-trailers (14.8 per cent). The top performing sectors with regard to growth in the 2000s were coke, petroleum and nuclear fuel (19.4 per cent); motor vehicles, trailers, and semi-trailers (16.55 per cent); fabricated metal products (15.5 per cent); wood and wood products (14.8 per cent); and furniture and other manufacturing (13 per cent). The high growth industries in the 2000s included coke, petroleum products, and nuclear fuel; motor vehicles, trailers, and semi-trailers; electrical machinery and apparatus; fabricated metal products and food products and beverages, whereas the sectors in which growth declined were non-metallic mineral products; chemicals and chemical products; basic metals; wearing apparel, dressing, and dyeing of fur and textile products.

Table 25.2 Sectoral Average Annual Growth in Real Value Added in Organized Manufacturing Sector (in percentage)

	1980s	1990s	2000s
Radio, television, and communication equipment	28.1	14.8	1.8
Food products and beverages	18.6	8.6	11.1
Wearing apparel, dressing, and dyeing of fur	14.3	15.5	9.0
Medical, precision, and optical instruments	11.6	0.7	10.5
Chemicals and chemical products	11.1	10.1	3.8
Basic metals	0.5	17.5	3.3
Electrical machinery and apparatus	9.7	15.8	12.3
Motor vehicles, trailers, and semi-trailers	6.9	14.8	16.5
Fabricated metal products	1.9	13.4	15.5
Wood and wood products	7.5	−13.5	14.8
Furniture and other manufacturing	4.1	29.7	13.0
Coke, petroleum products, and nuclear fuel	−0.1	0.6	19.4
Textile Products	4.9	12.8	8.0

Source: Banga and Das (2012).

Indian Industry: Global Perspectives

A few of the major trends that explain the growing stature of Indian industry are summarized here.

India is positioned to be a major beneficiary in the process of the gradual shift taking place in global manufacturing production. Specific advantages in terms of cheaper labour, improved infrastructure, lower costs, and large markets that India is bestowed with are likely to further intensify the pace of the shift.

According to a report of the United Nations Industrial Development Organization (UNIDO), world-manufacturing value added (MVA) peaked at US$ 7,390 billion in 2010 (18.2 per cent of the global GDP) after a sharp drop in 2009. During 1990–2010, the MVA in developing countries showed a remarkable 5.6 per cent annual growth rate as compared to 1.7 per cent in developed countries. The share of developing countries in world GDP rose from 20 per cent in 1990 to 30 per cent in 2010. The share of developed countries in the MVA fell from 79.3 per cent in 1990 to 64.4 per cent in 2010. Though the financial crisis caused a setback in this pace, the MVA continued to grow in developing countries. China increased its share in world MVA from 6.7 per cent in 2000 to 15.4 per cent in 2010, becoming the second largest manufacturer after the US. India with its focus more on the services sector also fared quite well accounting for 1.8 of global MVA in 2010 moving from 14th to 9th in the rankings. The report adds, 'Global manufacturing has been shifting from developed to developing economies even faster, with economies such as China, India and Taiwan Province of China building strong manufacturing sectors.'

Globalization and reforms have changed the structure of industry in more than one way. Globalization has led to diffusion of industrial production from developed countries to developing nations, which have enabled disaggregation of production of individual components. Competitiveness of developing countries enabled them to emerge as attractive locations for global corporates for production of certain components that benefit companies in developed markets through lower costs and in developing markets with newer opportunities in industrial production. A recent UNIDO report (2009), which examined this aspect, observed that 'where this process has been successful, the resulting so called "trade in tasks" has had a dramatic impact in promoting industrial and economic growth, reducing poverty and generating social progress'. India has been a beneficiary of the 'trade in tasks' in areas, such as information technology, telecommunications, and pharma, etc. (UNIDO 2009).

Manufacturing in developing economies is highly concentrated, with 15 leading economies accounting for 83 per cent of the total production in 2010, up from 73.2 per cent in 1990. China tripled its share of developing countries' MVA over the period 1990–2010 from 13 per cent in 1990 to 43.3 per cent in 2010. India overtook Mexico and Brazil to become the second leading manufacturer among developing economies with a share of 5 per cent of MVA in 2010.

Per capital manufacturing value added in India grew from US$ 80 (in US$ at 2000 prices) in 2005 to US$ 99 in 2009. India's share of world manufacturing value added rose from 1.38 to 1.69 per cent during this period. Per capita manufacturing exports rose from US$ 77 to US$ 124, and share of manufactured exports to total exports increased from 87.84 to 88.17 per cent.

India's leadership in the manufacturing sector is reflected in industries, such as electrical machinery and apparatus, other transport equipment, and basic metals. India accounted for 44 per cent of the developing world MVA in electrical machinery and apparatus, 18 per cent in other transport equipment, and 25 per cent in basic metals. In terms of world MVA, India's share is 5 per cent with respect to electrical machinery and apparatus and 3 per cent in basic metals. Average MVA in India withstood the impact of the global recession by showing resilience in growth. India's exports of manufactured goods rose from US$ 26 billion in 1995 to US$ 37 billion in 2000, to US$ 87 billion in 2005, to US$ 150 billion in 2009.

In the 1960s, on the basis of total factor productivity (TFP), India was ranked 98 with a TFP of 19 (as against 100 of US, which was in the top position). In 2000, India's rank moved up to 73 with a TFP of 25. India's rank in UNIDO's competitive industrial performance index moved up from 51 in 2000 to 42 in 2009. Global studies rank India as a country catching up with the US during the period 1960 to 2000 with regard to TFP.

South and Central Asia in which India leads in terms of size and significance showed highest growth after East Asia in terms of the average annual growth rate during 2001–10. Average annual growth in manufacturing value added posted by this region was in the range of 7 per cent throughout the decade.

Corporate performance in both public and private sector companies in India, showed improvement. Companies in the public sector have been making steady improvement in their commercial and operational performance which resulted in the public sector's saving rate growing from –2 per cent of GDP in 2001–2 to 3.2 per cent of GDP in 2006–7 (Mohan 2008). The investment rate in the public sector also increased from 6.9 per cent of GDP in 2001–2 to 7.8 per cent in 2006–7. During 2001–7 public sector savings–investment gap reduced from 8.9 per cent of GDP to 4.5 per cent. Foreign direct investment (FDI) as a percentage of GDP rose from 0.05 in 1991–2 to 3.27 per cent in 2008–9 and foreign portfolio flows rose from 0.05 per cent to 1.98 per cent. Indian companies investing abroad also increased with FDI outflow from India rising from about US$ 25 million in the early 1990s to $ 14 billion in 2007, with the number of projects approved rising from 395 in 1999–2000 to 1,595 in 2007–8. Indian companies also began to acquire foreign companies in a significant manner in the realm of IT services, software development, pharmaceuticals, and telecommunications. Foreign acquisitions by Indian companies intensified with Tata Tea acquiring UK-based Tetley in the year 2000, for a value of US$ 341 million increased in scope and size with the US$ 7.6 billion acquisition of Anglo-Dutch steel company (CORUS Group) by the Tatas in 2006 and the US$ 10.7 billion acquisition of Zain Telecom by Bharti Airtel in 2010. Listed and unlisted companies together announced 1,995 (Mohan 2008) overseas acquisitions during 2001–12 involving an investment of nearly $ 116 billion.

Reduction in corporate tax from 45 per cent in 1992–3 to 30 per cent by 2005–6, reduction in the peak customs duty on non-agricultural goods reduced gradually from 150 per cent in 1991–2 to 10 per cent in 2007–8, a conducive monetary policy, a regime of reduced or moderate interest rates, and financial restructuring of firms led to increased profitability of the private corporate sector. The private corporate sector's profit after tax recorded an average annual growth of 47 per cent per annum over the four-year period ended 2006–7. The private corporate sector's saving rate rose from 3.8 per cent in the 1990s to almost 8 per cent in the late 2000s and the investment rate from 5.4 per cent of GDP in 2001–2 to 14.5 per cent in 2006–7, showing increased prospects for the private corporate sector.

In view of the paramount importance of industry for strong and sustained economic growth, the Department of Industrial Policy announced a National Manufacturing Policy (NMP) that has set an objective of enhancing the share of manufacturing in GDP to 25 per cent by the start of the next decade and creating 100 million additional jobs. The policy is based on the principle of industrial growth in partnership with the states, where the Central government will create an enabling policy framework. The specific objectives of the policy are:

- Increase manufacturing sector growth to 12–14 per cent a year over the medium term.
- Increase the rate of job creation in manufacturing to create 100 million additional jobs by 2022.
- Create appropriate skill sets between rural migrants and urban poor to make growth inclusive.
- Increase domestic value addition and technological depth in manufacturing.
- Enhance global competitiveness of Indian manufacturing.
- Ensure sustainability of growth, particularly with regard to the environment, optimal utilization of resources, and restoration of damaged and degraded ecosystems.

An assessment of the Indian industry by UNIDO (2005) captures the essence of industrial growth in India:

> Industrial growth averaged 7.1 per cent per annum in the 1980s. It accelerated slightly to 7.6 per cent per year in the first five years following the beginning of the economic policy reform process in 1991. In the second half of the 1990s industrial growth trended lower at around 5 per cent per annum. However, since 2002–3 industrial growth has accelerated markedly on the back of strong GDP growth. Rising disposable incomes, easy access to finance and the changing attitudes of India's rapidly rising middle class (with a traditional focus on savings) have resulted in a consumer-lending boom. Industrial growth rose above 8 per cent in 2004–5, with consumer durables and non-durables showing exceptionally strong growth. Capital-goods production has been growing at double-digit rates since 2002–3, suggesting increased investment in the industrial sector and the economy as a whole.

Recent Growth Trends in the Indian Industry

The growth of the Indian industry has been sluggish in the recent period due to global economic recession compounded by uncertainties in the domestic economy. An assessment by the Reserve Bank of India (2013) on macroeconomic conditions in the third quarter of FY 2013 observed:

> Growth decelerated further during Q3 of 2012–13, with the slowdown extending to the services sector, which has been the mainstay of India's high growth. Mining and manufacturing activity continued to stall while agriculture output was impacted by deficient rainfall during the monsoon season. Domestic policy uncertainties, sluggish external demand and the lagged impact of the earlier monetary tightening policy reduced growth. Global growth decelerated in 2012 and is expected to remain weak in 2013 also. As business sentiments remain weak and structural impediments still constrain activity levels, recovery during 2013–14 may be modest.

Growth of the Indian Industry: An Assessment

In the background of the prominence of the services sector in India, studies on Indian industry with regard to growth, structure, efficiency, and productivity have attracted the interest of academic research. A study (Kumari 2005) that decomposed output growth into four sources (domestic demand expansion, export expansion, import substitution, and intermediate demand expansion due to change in input-output coefficient) found that output growth in the manufacturing industry has been mainly driven by domestic demand expansion, followed by contribution of export expansion during both pre-liberalization and post-liberalization, but after liberalization the contribution of both domestic demand expansion and export expansion have increased. A study (Aggarwal and Kumar 2012) on structural change, industrialization, and poverty reduction noted: '[S]ignificantly India's pattern of growth has not been characterized by a change in the structure of employment towards manufacturing with the share of the structure in total employment stagnating and recently declining despite growth of output. The mismatch between sectoral patterns of value added and employment has led to wide wage differentials across sectors. This raises an important question about the impact of growth on poverty'. A study (Ray 2012) on selected manufacturing industries in India (iron and steel, aluminium, cement, glass, fertilizers, chemicals, and paper and pulp, etc.) during 1979–80 to 2003–4 showed that 'output growth in selected Indian manufacturing industrial sectors is driven mainly by inputs accumulation while the contribution of TFP growth remains either minimal or negative'. A study on the industrial performance during 1991–2008 (Nagaraj 2011) noted:

> In spite of the dismantling of the much criticized 'Permit license raj', industrial growth rate has not accelerated, nor has the growth rate of labor intensive consumer goods gone up; but there has been no de-industrialization either, as the critics fear: the shares of industrial employment and output in the total have not declined (as had happened in Latin America and Africa after the debt crisis in 1980). The structural transformation of work force has continued at the same pace after the reforms though the work force has gone into the services and not manufacturing. Within industry, the incremental workforce has gone into construction. Measured by investment, the reforms were

not a setback for industrialization as the manufacturing sectors' share in total fixed investment has gone up from around 27 per cent in the 1980s to about 40 per cent in the current decade.

Growth and Financial Markets Relationship

Walter Bagehot (1873), Joseph Schumpeter (1912), and John Hicks (1969) to Merton Mellor (1988) observed the important role of finance in promoting growth (Ray). Ross Levine (Park 2011) identified the functions of the financial sector under five broad categories: (a) producing information about potential investment opportunities; (b) mobilizing savings to the most productive investment; (c) monitoring firms and exerting corporate governance; (d) promoting risk diversification and sharing across, individuals, firms, and countries, and (e) facilitating the exchange of goods and services. Development of the financial sector is envisaged to reduce the cost of collecting information, enforcing contracts, and transactions, thereby increasing efficiency of allocation and promoting economic growth. Financial intermediation can affect growth through three channels (Aziz and Deunwald 2012): (a) it can increase the marginal productivity of capital by collecting information to evaluate alternative investment projects and by risk sharing; (b) reducing the resources absorbed by financial intermediaries (borrowing/lending spreads, commission, etc.) and thus increasing the efficiency of financial intermediaries; and (c) it can raise the private savings rate. A recent study (International Monetary Fund 2012) on the relationship between financial structures and economic outcomes observed: '[O]n financial development and growth, there have long been two schools of thought with sharply differing perspectives on the potential importance of finance. One school sees financial intermediation playing a key role in economic activity and growth. Another school believes that causality is reversed: economies with good growth prospects develop institutions to provide the funds necessary to support the expected growth—the economy leads and finance follows'.

Notwithstanding the cause and effect, the evolution of Indian finance in the post-reforms period has been quite useful and relevant to the growth of the Indian industry in providing new sources of dynamism, certain aspects of which this chapter will endeavour to discuss.

Some studies on the financing pattern of the Indian corporate sector (Beena 2011) during 1990–2009 observed that: (a) the Indian private sector mobilized a large share of resources through external sources although there was an increasing trend in the share of internal financing since 1990; (b) borrowings were the major source of external financing; (c) the share of resources mobilized through the capital market has sharply declined since the mid-1990s; (d) Indian acquiring firms mobilized large funds through external sources although the share of the retained profit was quite substantial; and (e) revenue foregone through various tax concessions is still found to be a major source of corporate growth during the liberalization period. Studies on the efficiency (Oura 2008) of the Indian financial system on corporate financing patterns observed that firms were increasingly relying on external funds to finance their investments in most recent years. Capital markets in general were found not to be contributing much to the resource mobilization of companies.

However, it might not be right to assess the role of capital markets solely on the basis of resource mobilization. Lower resource mobilization from the capital market could be due to issues with regard to the absence of a proper alignment with the market framework in terms of ownership control (higher incidence of family ownership and control), lack of enough transparency and disclosure; and shortcomings in the quality of corporate governance, that might have limited some companies with access to stock markets. Though some studies may point out that capital markets have not provided enough resources to industry, what cannot be overlooked is that Indian stock exchanges have over 5,000 listed companies, the highest for any stock market in the world.

The development of capital markets that has taken place in India in the last two-and-a-half decades might have helped Indian companies in several ways other than just resource mobilization in primary markets. A few of them include:

- The listing opportunities provided by capital markets enhanced investor awareness about the companies in domestic and international markets, which helped them in business expansion and resource mobilization from various other instruments.
- Capital markets not only helped companies to raise resources but also provided a vital platform to divest government shareholding in state owned enterprises. All over the world, capital markets have played a major role in promoting and further privatization programmes of governments. Globally, around US$ 410 billion was raised through

privatization in the period 1990–2003. In India, the Government, through the sale of minority stakes in central public sector enterprises, raised Rs 1.4 trillion during the period 1992–2013.

- Secondary capital markets that provided trading in securities and liquidity of stocks are very important for companies to strengthen integrated treasury management, which helps in generating liquidity.
- Listing in domestic capital markets will be an essential feature for companies to tap international capital markets to issue global instruments such as Global Depository Receipts (GDRs) and American Depository Receipts (ADRs).
- Listing reflects the regulatory compliance aspect of companies that elevate their position in global markets in various areas of business and resource mobilization.
- Well-performing companies in stock markets form a part of the global and domestic indices of markets in which significant fund management activity takes place, the benefits of which will accrue to corporates in their efforts in resource mobilization.
- Private and venture capital segments, which showed sizeable growth in the post-reforms period, have given access to funding to new enterprises and those yet not ready for listing in stock markets.
- Banks have designed several products that enhance efficiency of cash management and other resource flows.
- Foreign direct investment in India which increased significantly following the reforms, paved the way for Indian corporates to raise money in international markets in the form of equity and debt.

Thus, the contribution of the capital market in relation to benefits to corporates should be assessed on a wider canvas rather than that of a single perspective of resource mobilization in primary markets though the latter remains a primary objective of the capital market.

The financial sector as a whole showed rapid growth in India. After information technology, the prowess of the country is recognized more for the maturity and diversity of its financial sector. Assets (Park 2011) of deposit taking institutions in the financial sector as a percentage of GDP rose from 60 per cent in 2000 to 98 per cent in 2010; and that of non-banking financial institutions more than doubled from 15 per cent of GDP in 2000 to 35.2 per cent in 2010. Market capitalization of the stock market made a sharp jump from 32 per cent of GDP in 2000 to 69 per cent to 97 per cent in 2010; total bonds outstanding from

23.7 per cent of GDP in 2000 to 54.4 per cent in 2010; government bonds outstanding as a per cent of GDP rose from 23.3 per cent to 43.3 per cent during the ten-year period and corporate bonds from almost nothing to 11.1 per cent during 2000–10.

Financial intermediation (Bank for International Settlement) has also strengthened in a big way. During 1997–2008 (Mohanty and Turner 2010), domestic private bank credit doubled from 25 per cent of GDP to 52 per cent and domestic private debt securities' outstanding increased from 1 per cent to 3 per cent. Nominal increase in bank deposits (Mohanty, Schnabel, and Garcia-Luna 2006) during the period 1995–2001 (as a percentage of cumulative nominal GDP) which was 6.6 per cent rose to 9.4 per cent during 2001–7 and domestic bank credit to the private sector which was 3.7 per cent during 1995–2001 rose to 7.8 per cent during 2001–7 (Bank for International Settlement). Marginal propensity to save, which was at 31 per cent during 1990–96 rose to 47.8 per cent during 2000–7 and marginal propensity to invest rose from 22.7 per cent to 48.8 per cent.

Developments in the Indian Financial Sector

A few of the major developments that have brought Indian finance closer to resource requirements of the Indian industry include.

- Banking reforms led to setting up of new banks in the private sector and deregulated the interest rate regime, enabling banks to design numerous financial products and services relevant and useful for the industry. A rise in the number of foreign banks operating in India and the growth of international presence of Indian banks also helped Indian corporates find useful support in international ventures.
- Capital market reforms ushered in new opportunities in raising equity and debt that enhanced the scope of resource mobilization as also managing risks arising from interest rate and currency that proved vital for overcoming challenges of volatility. The quality of Indian capital markets in terms of regulation and governance and administration of stock exchanges that followed a major part of the reforms provided credibility to Indian corporates in their pursuit of resource mobilization in international markets.

- Liberalization of foreign financial flows enabled corporates to raise international finance by way of external commercial borrowings and American depository receipts (ADRs)/Global depository receipts (GDRs) listed in international exchanges. Also financial flows in terms of foreign direct investment greatly benefited corporates in terms of new investment flows and foreign institutional investors (FIIs) evinced interest in the stocks of well performing companies that had a very distinct and strong impact on company valuations.
- Special attention for small and medium enterprises (SMEs) led to focused and targeted lending to this sector. Separate capital markets for SMEs were also established by the national level stock exchanges.
- Private equity markets began to take shape following reforms that provided vital access to finance for those companies and start-ups, which are not yet ready to tap the public markets for initial public offerings. The value chain in this regard included angel investors, venture capital firms, and private equity firms that provided resources to the new companies in various stages of evolution and growth.
- Emergence of structured products enabled corporates to enhance the scope of risk management and resource utilization.
- Risk management embedded in financial market products and services enabled companies to adopt useful risk management strategies and solutions that enhanced their scope of functioning including pursuing international aspirations.

A few benefits of financial sector reforms brought to the industry are explained in Table 25.3.

India is a constituent of BRICS forum (Brazil, Russia, India, China, and South Africa), which is gaining momentum and pursuing global influence. An important agenda of BRICS is to actively consider promoting a BRICS Development Bank in which India is expected to play an important role given the extensive presence of its institutions and instruments.

India today has a wide matrix (Figure 25.2) of financial institutions and instruments that provide functions of wholesale banking, public equity markets, private equity markets, international borrowing, alternative markets, securitization, and structured products markets, which provide important services of access to finance to Indian industry or enable it to enhance the efficiency of financial management.

A report on the Indian capital markets observed, 'India's capital markets have experienced sweeping changes since the beginning of the last decade (Deutsche Bank Research 2007). India boasts a dynamic equity

Table 25.3 Benefits to Industry from the Reforms in Financial Sector

Nature of the Financial Sector Reform	Specific Benefits to the Industry
Liberalization of Entry and Expansion of Banks	Range of products and quality of services vastly improved due to competition.
Interest Rate Deregulation	Better performing companies were able to borrow at prime lending rates, which induced others to scale up quality of operations.
Liberalization of Lending Norms	Spurred huge growth in the companies engaged in businesses pertaining to consumer durables, automobiles, and real estate, for which obtaining personal finance was made easier and quicker.
Loan Targets for Priority Sector Lending	Special allocations ensured adequate resource flows to the vital sectors of the economy, including agriculture, cottage industries, SMEs, and corporates dependent on these sectors.
Reforms in the Primary Capital Markets	Enabled growth-oriented companies to access capital markets for Initial Public Offerings/Follow-On Offerings to raise/enhance capital without restrictions on the issue price.
Reforms in the Secondary Capital Markets	FIIs began to show interest in Indian companies that have positive impact on the liquidity and tradability of shares of companies, leading to better valuations that benefited them significantly.
Reforms in the External Finance	Issuance of capital in the international markets grew substantially with major companies coming up with GDRs/ADRs and External Commercial Borrowings (ECBs).
Development of Mutual Fund Industry	Several new institutions in the realm of mutual funds management emerged, and their resource flows to the stock markets helped improve the liquidity of the listed stocks.
Introduction of Derivatives Markets	Enabled corporates to hedge various aspects of risk, including equity, commodities, interest rate, and foreign exchange.
Special Focus on SME Development	Special concessions for promotion and development of SMEs. SME Capital Markets set up by the national stock exchanges.
Introduction of Structured Products	Enabled companies to realize revenues through securitization of assets, leading to better management of the balance sheet.
Corporate Restructuring	Induced corporates to undergo transformation in tune with the challenges of the global markets and pursue mergers and acquisitions.
Corporate Debt Restructuring	Relief provided by the banks to the corporates that are facing resource crunch to restructure loan obligations and payment schedules.

Private Equity	A source of funding for companies, which are not yet ready for listing in the public markets. Major source of finance for new enterprise in the realm of technology, e-commerce, and related businesses.
Venture Capital	Funding for the start-up companies and commercialization of new ideas that have business potential.

Source: Author.

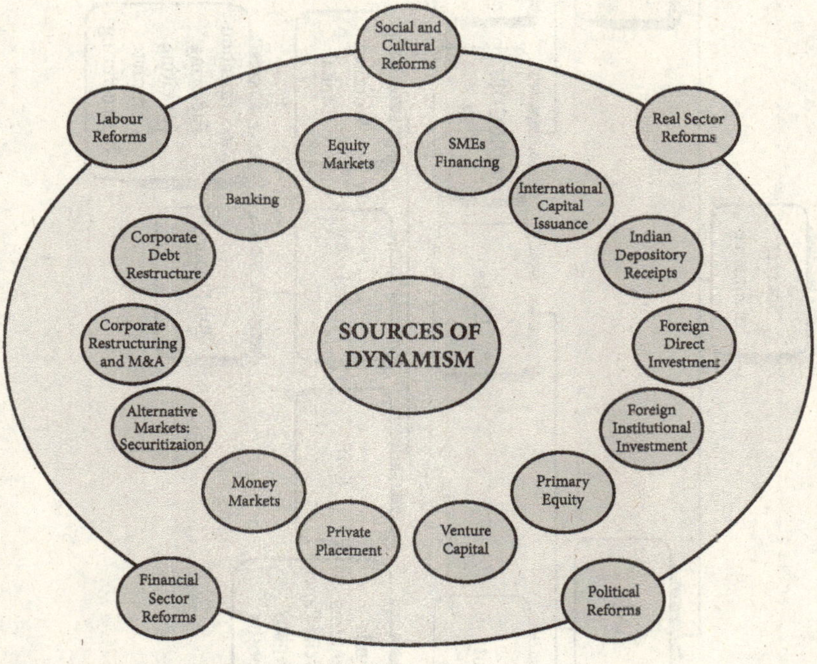

FIGURE 25.2 Sources of Dynamism

Source: Author's presentation.

market; innovative products such as securitized debt and fund products based on alternative assets are starting to break ground; and a vibrant, well-developed capital market has been facilitating investment and economic growth.'

Finance for Industry

A wide range of financial resources to which the Indian industry has reach and access is summarized in Figure 25.3.

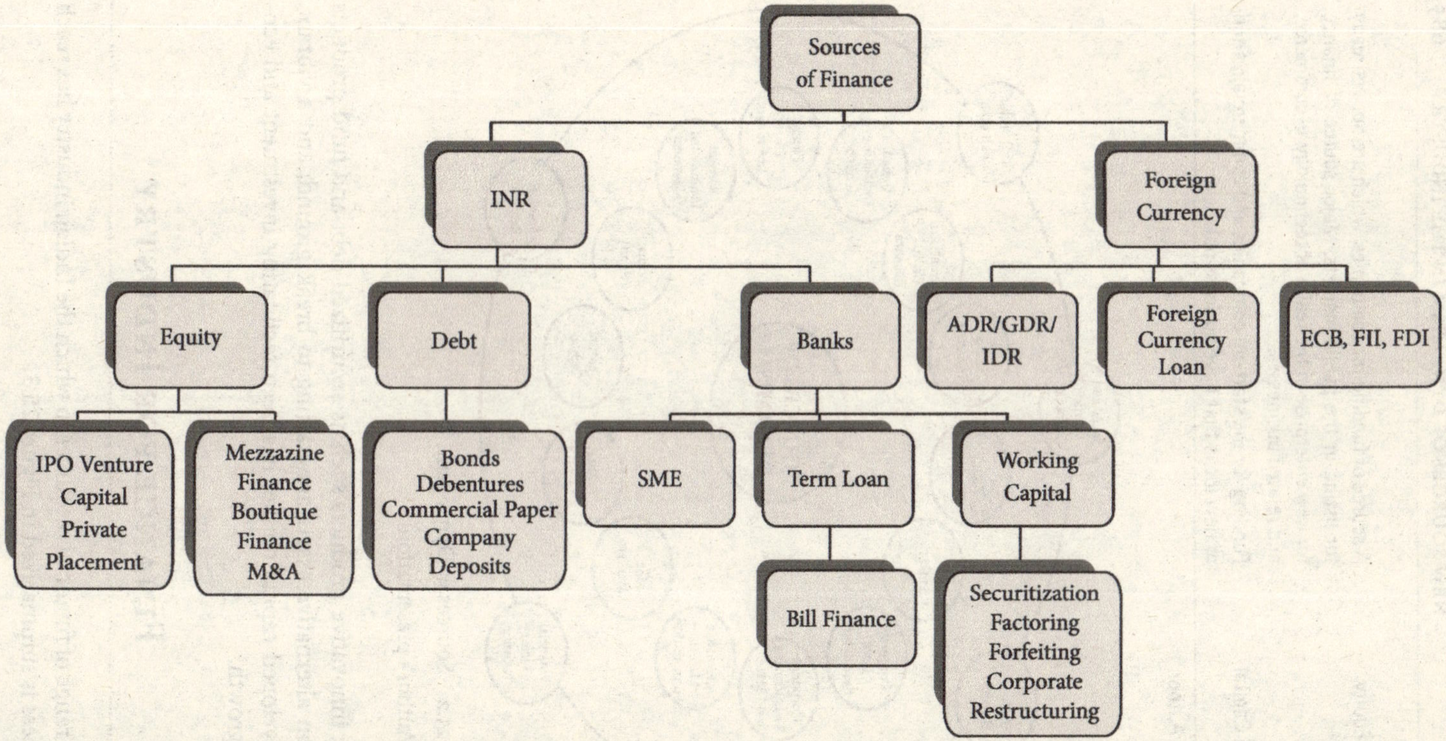

FIGURE 25.3 Sources of Finance for Industry

Source: Author's presentation.

The following is a brief description of the aspects of growth of specific sectors in the financial sector that will have an important role in strengthening resource flows to industry.

Banking Sector

Following the liberalization of the banking sector and greater functional autonomy to state-owned banks, a number of services useful for the corporate sector have emerged, which include infrastructure financing (extended to infrastructure projects), project financing (for greenfield industrial projects), dealer financing (for corporate distribution networks), channel financing (funding necessities along the supply chain), structured finance (assembling unique credit configurations to meet large industrial and complex infrastructure projects), and equipment leasing (for greenfield projects). Outstanding bank credit as on 21 February 2014 was Rs 58,617 billion of which Rs 57,551.7 billion is non-food credit. Of the total industrial credit outstanding at the end of 2011 of Rs 18,585 billion, 63 per cent was in the manufacturing sector followed by 32 per cent in infrastructure, and the remaining in construction (3 per cent) and mining (2 per cent). Growth of bank credit to the commercial sector rose from 28.7 per cent of GDP in the first decade of reforms to 42.9 per cent in the next decade to rise up to over 50 per cent during 2008–11. Non-food credit grew at an average rate 15.95 per cent (1990–1 to 1999–2000)in the first ten years of the reforms that further rose to 21 per cent (Table 25.4) in the next decade. During the last two decades the credit deposit ratio rose from 55.1 per cent to 75.7 per cent (Table 25.4) and the credit-GDP ratio from 21 per cent to 50 per cent (Table 25.4).

With effect from 1 July 2010, the following measures have been evolved to strengthen credit flow to industry—all categories of loans to industries are to be priced only with reference to the base rate; in case of restructured loans, lending below the base rate can be granted for purposes of viability; all loan applications for small and medium enterprises (SMEs) up to Rs 5 lakh to be processed within four weeks; and banks are mandated not to accept collateral security up to Rs 10 lakh for loans extended to units in the SME sector; public sector banks have been advised to open at least one specialized branch in each district to assist industrial financing, etc. To provide further boost to bank lending with particular focus on financial inclusion, the Reserve Bank of India has invited applications for new bank licenses and the process of selection of eligible institutions to open new banks is under progress.

Table 25.4 Average Growth in Bank Credit

	Average 1990–1 to 1999–2000	Average 2000–1 to 2009–10	Average 2003–4 to 2007–8	2008–9	2009–10	2010–11
Bank credit (per cent change)	15.9	21.8	25.5	17.5	16.9	21.5
Non-food credit (per cent change)	15.4	22.4	26.7	17.8	17.1	21.3
Credit–deposit ratio (per cent)	55.1	64.8	68	72.4	72.2	75.7
Credit–GDP ratio (per cent)	20.6	37.7	39.5	49.7	49.5	50

Source: RBI Annual Report, various issues.

Equity Markets

A wide range of reforms in primary markets (capital issuance) and secondary markets (trading, settlement, and payment systems) have taken India to be among the top 20 stock markets in the world in terms of market capitalization. The stock market in India is emerging as competitive, setting a new trend in emerging markets with the active presence and functioning of three national-level stock exchanges: the Bombay Stock Exchange, the National Stock Exchange, and the MCX Stock Exchange.

The stock market in India, in the background of several reforms, has evolved to become a significant source of finance for companies. A number of reforms carried out in primary and secondary markets have completely transformed the functioning of the equity market, making it one of the best in the world in terms of regulation, investor protection, and technology adoption. Market infrastructure (SEBI 2012) is quite extensive with 19 stock exchanges (three national and the remaining regional), 8,922 brokers, 1,738 foreign institutional investors, 19 custodians, 2 depositories, 823 merchant bankers, 6 credit rating agencies, 205 venture capital funds, 267 portfolio managers, 60 mutual funds, etc., During the period 1990–1 to 2012–13 (Table 25.5), nearly 6,000 public issues came out, amounting to Rs 3.2 trillion. Other forms of resource mobilization, such as debt offers, rights issues, private placement of debt, and commercial paper were of sizeable magnitude. The banking and power sectors raised a major portion of the resources (Table 25.6) though a large number of industries accessed capital markets for resource mobilization.

Table 25.5 Resource Mobilization in Capital Markets

Resource Mobilization	1990–1 to 2012–13 (as on 30 Sep. 2012)	
	No. of Issues	Amount (Rs billion)
Public Issues[1]	5,993	3,169.59
Public Debt Offers[1]	151	1,028.06
Rights Issues	2,578	1,347.39
Debt Private Placement[2]	9,728	16,400.31
Commercial Paper[3]	14,874	9,093.21
Takeover Open Offers[4]	1,258	1,156.47
Buyback Offers[5]	260	356.33

Source: Prime Datatbase. http://www.primedatabase.com/

[1] 1989–90 to 2012–13 (30 September 2012);
[2] 1995–96 to 2012–13 (30 September 2012);
[3] 2003–04 to 2012–13 (30 September 2012);
[4] 1997–98 to 2012–13 (30 September 2012);
[5] 1998–99 to 2012–13 (30 September 2012).

Table 25.6 Industry-wise Mobilization of Resources from Capital Market

Industry	Capital Raised (1993–2011)		Percentage of the capital raised	
	No.	Amount (Rs billion)	No.	Amount
Banking/FIs	181	1,064.06	3	26
Cement & Construction	152	133.36	2	3
Chemical	439	89.62	7	2
Electronics	110	42.41	2	1
Engineering	166	67.44	3	2
Entertainment	50	71.79	1	2
Finance	1,320	309.23	20	8
Food Processing	560	76.23	9	2
Healthcare	370	67.82	6	2
Information Technology	243	131.47	4	3
Paper & Pulp	67	20.35	1	0
Plastic	125	16.11	2	0
Power	44	455.57	1	11
Printing	7	4.03	0	0
Telecommunication	12	49.55	0	1
Textile	631	112.71	10	3
Others	2,085	1,371.07	32	34
Total	6,562	4,082.82	100	100

Source: Prime Datatbase. http://www.primedatabase.com/

Corporate Bond Market

Debt markets are a vital component of financial markets, particularly for a developing economy like India. In countries, such as Korea and Malaysia, corporate bonds account for a major share of the total bonds issuance ranging from 40 to 60 per cent. The scope for corporate bonds market in India is huge in the context of the enormous need for infrastructure development and new projects. However, the corporate bonds market in India has not developed to the extent that it was expected to. As the corporate sector expands and Indian financial markets get progressively integrated with the rest of the market, the three national stock exchanges—BSE, NSE, and MCX-SX have set up exclusive debt market segments to promote the growth of exchange-traded bonds market. Though the size of corporate debt market in India (US$ 179 billion) has grown in the recent years (ADB 2012), it is still below the levels of China (US$ 696 billion outstanding) and Korea (US$ 687 billion).

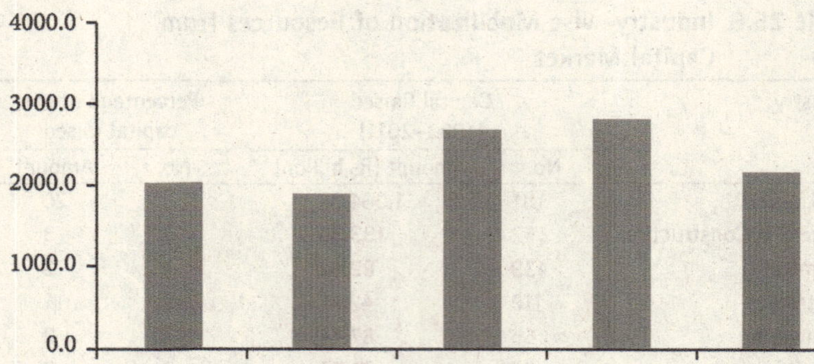

FIGURE 25.4 Corporate Bond Issuance in India (Rs billion)

Source: SEBI.

SME Markets: SME Financing

Economic integration and technological breakthroughs warrant the need to make SMEs globally competitive. As per data released by the Ministry of Micro, Small, and Medium Enterprises (MSMEs) there are about 26.1 million units in this sector. The sector accounts for 45 per cent of manufactured output and 8 per cent of GDP. MSMEs contributed close to 40 per cent of all exports from the country and employed nearly

59.7 million people, which is next only to the agricultural sector. MSMEs primarily rely on bank finance for their operations. In addition to bank financing, national level stock exchanges such as NSE and BSE have started SME capital market segments to promote listing of SMEs. About 30 SMEs from India are listed in the AIM of the London Stock Exchange. In 2011 and 2012, SMEs raised Rs 0.68 billion in 11 issues from the SME capital markets in India. Bombay Stock Exchange has, by the early 2014, 50 companies listed under the SME platform.

International Capital Issuance: ADRs/GDRs/ECBs

Indian companies began to access global financial markets in a big way to raise resources for domestic expansion of business as also international acquisition of business. Companies that accessed global capital markets in the form of GDRs/ADRs during 1992–3 raised resources of US$ 30.1 billion. ECBs, which were about US$ 10 billion in 1991 rose to US$ 104 billion with their share in the total external debt of the country increasing from 12 per cent in 1991 to 30 per cent in 2012. During the four year period of 2008–9, Indian companies made international investments of $ 60 billion with a major chunk of it being in the realm of manufacturing (40 per cent) and financial services (29.4 per cent). Corporates in the hotels, hospitals, and software sectors permitted ECB up to US$ 100 million per financial year.

Indian Depository Receipts

Indian depository receipts (IDRs) are an instrument denominated in the Indian rupees in the form of depository receipts created by a domestic depository against the underlying equity of the issuing company to enable foreign companies to raise funds from the Indian securities markets. The size of an IDR issue should not be less than Rs 0.5 billion. The foreign issuing company should have paid-up capital and free reserves of at least US$ 50 million and have a minimum average market capitalization (during the last three years) in its parent country of at least US$ 100 million and a track record of distributable profits for at least three out of the immediately preceding five years and listed in its home country. The Indian securities market saw its first IDR from Standard Chartered Plc. in May 2010 for an issue size of US$ 240 million. This instrument is yet to catch up in a big way.

Foreign Direct Investment and Foreign Institutional Investment

Indian companies gained significant benefit from the global financial flows in the form of foreign direct investments (FDI) and foreign institutional investments. According to the data published in the Economic Survey (various years), foreign investments received into industry amounted to US$ 167 billion during 1991–2000 and US$ 110 billion during 2000–10. In the next three years, another US$ 59 billion was received. Gross capital inflows plus outflows as a per cent of GDP rose from an average of 15.1 per cent during 1990–1/1999–2000 to 33.6 per cent in the next ten years. For 2010–11, the figure was 54 per cent. The level of FDI rose from an average of $ 1.6 billion in 1990–1/1999–2000 to US$ 16.3 billion in the next 10 years, rising to a high of US$ 37 billion in 2008–9. Foreign institutional investment rose from an average of US$ 1.3 billion during the first ten years of reforms (1990–1/1999–2000) to US$ 16.3 billion in the next ten years reaching a level of $ 30 billion in 2009–10 and 2010–11. A comparison of foreign investment flows into various emerging market economics is given in Table 25.7.

Table 25.7 FIIs' Investment Flows

FII inflows (equity) US$ billion

Year	India	Indonesia	Korea	Taiwan	South Africa	Brazil
2000	1.57	0.09	10.13	3.02	2.47	−1.16
2001	2.75	0.43	5.79	7.49	3.47	0.46
2002	0.71	0.87	−2.26	−0.11	−0.62	−0.46
2003	6.67	1.12	11.80	15.89	−1.00	2.51
2004	8.62	2.20	9.32	8.05	5.21	0.66
2005	10.70	3.40	−2.76	19.19	7.33	2.21
2006	8.37	1.88	−11.81	17.11	11.00	1.17
2007	17.82	3.55	−29.22	2.24	8.89	−1.92
2008	−12.17	1.87	−33.37	−15.38	−5.57	−12.02
2009	17.63	1.39	24.83	13.72	8.99	10.03
2010	28.71	2.33	18.56	8.69	4.83	3.60
2011	−0.54	2.60	−6.72	−9.34	−2.00	3.62
Total	90.86	21.73	−5.69	70.58	44.00	8.70

Source: GoI (2012).

Private Markets

Private equity refers to any type of equity investment in an asset in which the equity is not freely tradable on a public stock market. There has been a rise in private equity, partly due to the smaller impact of the economic crisis on India and partly due to better prospects for economic growth. The proportion of investors' total private equity commitments is showing a positive trend. The size of private equity was 499 deals amounting to $ 14 billion in 2007; 481 deals with a value of US$ 11 billion in 2008 and in 2011 and 460 deals with a value of US$ 10 billion. India held a major share in the deal value among the six major Asian regions in 2010, with the momentum continuing in the next year. Private equity institutions are required to be registered with the Securities and Exchange Board of India (SEBI).

Venture Capital Financing

Venture capital has developed as an important intermediary in Indian financial markets, providing capital to firms that might otherwise have difficulties in attracting finance. These firms are typically small and young, plagued by high levels of uncertainty. There is a severe problem of asymmetry of information that makes the investment risky and therefore retail investors are generally not involved in venture capital investments. There was no organized form of venture capital investing activities till the late 1980s and early 1990s, when the World Bank encouraged and provided funds for developing venture capital investing activities in India. Over the years, venture capital funds have proliferated and the investments by means of venture capital have also shown remarkable progress. Domestic venture capital funds grew from Rs 173.25 billion in 2007 to Rs 212.16 billion in 2008 to Rs 248.93 billion in 2009 to Rs 230.23 billion in 2010 and to Rs 275.92 billion in 2011. Foreign venture capital funds grew from Rs 153.84 billion in 2007 to Rs 198 billion in 2008 to Rs 268.27 billion in 2009 to Rs 332.41 billion in 2010, and to Rs 387.30 billion in 2011.

Private Placements

Raising money through public equity markets takes considerable time as it requires numerous approvals from regulatory institutions. Private placement enables companies to raise money at a shorter notice by adhering to certain guidelines. When a company makes an issue of securities to a select group of persons, not exceeding 49, and the issue is neither a rights issue nor a public issue, it is called private placement. It can be of two types: (i) preferential allotment: when a listed company issues shares or convertible securities to a select group of persons in terms of provisions of Chapter XIII of SEBI (DIP) guidelines, it is called a preferential allotment. (ii) qualified institutions placement: when a listed issuer issues equity shares or security convertible into shares to qualified institutional buyers only, in terms of provisions of Chapter XIIIA of SEBI (DIP) guidelines, it is called qualified institutional placement (QIP). Private placements showed sharp growth in the recent period. During the priod 1995–6 to 2012–13, a total 9,728 issues of private placement took place with a value of Rs 16,400.81 billion.

Money Market Instruments: Commercial Papers

Money market instruments, such as commercial paper (CP) and certificates of deposit (CD) have provided avenues for corporates to manage their short-term liquidity mismatches. Issuance norms and maturity profiles of money market instruments, such as CP and CDs have been modified in tune with changing market conditions. With respect to the preferred maturity ranges from 6 months to 1 year and non-banking financial companies like leasing and financing companies are the major issuers. CP is an unsecured money market instrument issued in the form of a promissory note and it was introduced in India in 1990 with a view to enable highly rated corporate borrowers to diversify their sources of short-term borrowings and for providing an additional instrument to investors. Subsequently, primary dealers and satellite dealers were also permitted to issue CPs to enable them to meet their short-term funding requirements for their operations. A total of 14,874 issues of CP took place during 2003–4 to 2012–13 amounting to Rs 9,093.21 billion.

Alternative Markets: Securitization

Securitization as a financial instrument has been in practice in India since the early 1990s essentially as a device of bilateral acquisitions of portfolios of finance companies and banks. Securitization has traditionally offered banks with a key source of long-term funding, and thereby allowed for improved balance sheet management. Prior to the global financial crisis, benign economic and financial conditions fuelled an explosion in securitization issuance. Capital flight and illiquidity infected the wider market for collateralized products and, consequently, securitization issuance slumped in recent years. The securitization market in India is driven, on the supply side, by growth of retail loan portfolios in banks and non-banking financial companies (NBFCs) and, on the demand side, by the increased participation of mutual funds, particularly at the short end, insurance companies, and banks to meet their priority sector lending targets. Asset-backed securities (ABS) are the largest securitization class driven by the banks' growing retail loan portfolios. Most of the securities are acquired with the intention to hold to maturity. Securitization registered a growth of 73 per cent in 2008 but later showed a slowdown. Value of ABS, which was Rs 313.2 billion (Table 25.8) in 2008 fell to Rs 135.8 billion (Table 25.8) in 2009 but rose to Rs 209.2 billion in 2011. Value of mortgage-backed securities (MBS), which was Rs 5.9 billion (Table 25.8) in 2008 rose to Rs 50.3 billion in 2011. Total retail securitization which showed a high of Rs 318.2 billion in 2008 slowed down to Rs 259.5 billion in 2011. Loan sell offs (LSO) was at a level of Rs 318.2 billion in 2008 which rose to Rs 356.1 billion in 2009 but drastically fell to Rs 43.4 billion in 2011. Total securitization proceeds were Rs 637.3 billion in 2008 but gradually reduced to reach Rs 308.3 billion in 2011.

Table 25.8 Trends in Structured Finance Volumes

(Rs billion)

Type	2007–8	2008–9	2009–10
ABS (Asset-backed securities)	313.2	135.8	209.7
MBS (Mortgage-backed securities)	5.9	32.9	62.5
CDO/LSO/SLSD	318.2	364.4	145.8
Others	13.0	11.6	7.9
Total	650.3	544.7	425.9

(CDO: Corporate Debt Obligations, LSO: Loan Sell-off, SLSD: Single Loan Sell-down)

Source: Various rating agencies like ICRA, CRISIL, etc.

Corporate Restructuring

Corporate restructuring is a process of redesigning one or more aspects of a compnay for achieving certain objectives and outcomes. Examples of restructuring include: (a) conversion of a partnership firm into a limited company (corporatization); (b) pure asset sale or pure liability transfer (subsidiarization); (c) conversion of a company into a limited liability partnership (buyback of shares); and (d) takeover of a company. The size of the corporate restructuring surged in the recent period as could be seen from the number of companies undergoing this process increased from 76 with a value of Rs 58.6 billion in 2009–10 to 103 companies with a value of Rs 187.54 billion in 2010–11. Specialized financial firms extend advisory and financial services support to corporate restructuring initiatives.

Mergers and Acquisitions

M&A is a part and extension of corporate restructuring. M&A activities are mainly driven by the strategic initiatives of companies to achieve economies of scale, both from geographical and product-offering perspectives. India witnessed big ticket merger and acquisition activity in terms of Indian companies' acquisitions overseas and overseas companies taking over Indian companies (Table 25.9). Banks and specialized financial institutions provide resources for M&A initiatives in different forms.

Corporate Debt Restructuring

Corporate debt restructuring is a specialized institutional mechanism for restructuring large exposures involving more than one lender under consortium/multiple banking arrangements. Financial restructuring for corporaties can take many forms: rescheduling (extension of maturities), lower interest rates, debt for equity swaps, debt forgiveness, indexing of interest payments to earnings, and so on. The main aims of financial restructuring are separating and treating appropriately viable and nonviable firms and creating the right incentives for operational restructuring. Restructuring is a tool to lend a hand of assistance to companies and businesses which are temporarily in distress, in particular where the distress is caused by circumstances beyond the control of the borrower. Thus, debt restructuring may be required under certain circumstances like a general downturn in the economy or in any particular sector, which results in the deterioration of the financial health of borrowers. It may also be warranted in case of emergence of legal or other issues that cause delays, particularly in cases of project implementation. External developments

Table 25.9 Top International M&A with Indian Companies

Top 10 M&A Deals since 2007 by size							
Value (US$ bn)	Year	Target	Target Nationality	Target Business Description	Acquirer	Acquirer Nationality	Acquirer Business Description
12.2	2007	Corus	Luxembourg	Steel	Tata Steel	India	Steel
10.8	2007	Hutchison Essar	India	Telecom	Vodafone	United Kingdom	Telecom
10.7	2010	Zain Africa BV	Kenya	Telecom	BhartiAirtel Ltd	India	Telecom
8.6 (4 deals)	2011	Cairn India	India	Oil & Gas	Vedanta Plc	United Kingdom	Oil & Gas
7.2	2011	Reliance Industries	India	Oil & Gas	British Petroleum	United Kingdom	Oil & Gas
6	2007	NovelisInc	United States of America	Aluminum	Hindalco Industries	India	
5	2011	Vodafone Essar	India	Telecom	Vodafone Group (Plc)	United Kingdom	Telecom
2.6	2009	Tata Teleservices Ltd	India	Telecom	NTT DoCoMo Inc	Japan	Wireless telecommunications
1.9	2011	Abbot Point Port	Australia	Shipping & Ports	Mundra Port SEZ Ltd	India	Shipping & ports
1.7	2010	Atlas Energy Inc (Marcellus Shale)	United States of America	Marcellus Shale	Reliance Industries Ltd	India	Production and distribution process for synthetic textiles

Source: Grant Thornton Dealtracker India (various issues).

may also result in a widespread impact on the financial health of borrowers and may necessitate the use of restructuring as a tool to help borrowers tide over difficult circumstances. Restructured standard advances rose from Rs 753 billion in March 2009 to Rs 1,364.3 billion in March 2010 to Rs 1,376 billion in March 2011 to Rs 2,180.7 billion in March 2012 (Table 25.10).

Managing Risks

The financial sector getting closer to industry in terms of greater resource support has also brought in better practices in accounting, transparency and disclosure, governance, and risk management. It is important for companies to move to international accounting practices and standards to get greater access to domestic and international financial markets. Financial market regulations insist on periodic disclosure of the financial performance of listed companies, rating requirements while borrowing and listing, predominance of independent directors on the board, management accountability, investor grievance redressal mechanisms, etc. Simultaneous with expansion of asset classes and financial products that proved beneficial to companies for raising resources and trading and hedging, the challenge of risk, both known and unknown, that is embedded in all asset classes and financial products has also increased. Managing risks of various nature, such as credit, interest rate, foreign exchange rate, liquidity, equity price, commodity price, legal, regulatory, reputational, and operational, has become a matter of utmost importance for corporate to sustain in their business.

Looking Ahead

Notwithstanding the rise of India on the global industrial map and its growing stature as one of the leading manufacturers in the world, it shows certain major limitations in terms of lower and stagnating share in GDP, which does not augur well for a developing country in its growth prospects as also its sub-optimal performance as compared to several other developed and developing countries. The share of manufacturing in GDP in India actually declined from 14.13 per cent in 2005 to 13.74 per cent

Table 25.10 Trends in Corporate Debt Restructuring

Particulars		March 2009	March 2010	March 2011	March 2012
Gross Advances	Gross Advances (Rs billion)	27,533.65	32,272.87	39,829.54	46,552.71
	Growth rate (per cent)		17.21	23.41	16.88
	Compounded Annual Growth Rate (2009–12) (per cent)				19.13
Restructured Standard Advances	Restructured standard advances (Rs billion)	753.04	1,364.26	1,376.02	2,180.68
	Growth rate (per cent)		81.17	0.86	58.48
	Compounded Annual Growth Rate (2009–12) (per cent)				42.54
Restructured Standard to Gross Advances	Ratio (per cent)	2.73	4.23	3.45	4.68

Source: http://www.rbi.org.in/home.aspx

in 2009. On the aspect of industrial competitiveness, India is found to be lagging begind countries like China and Korea and even several transition economies like Slovakia, Slovenia, and Poland. The concern of the slow growth of industry in India can be seen from the fact that China which had 13 per cent of the share in manufacturing value added of the developing world in 1990, catapulted to a position of having a major share of 43.3 per cent by 2010 whereas India's share at 4.8 per cent in 2000 barely moved to 5 per cent a decade later. Similarly, the share of East Asia in global manufacturing value which was about 6.3 per cent in 1990 rose to 20.9 per cent by 2010 whereas that of South and Central Asia, where India dominates just moved from 1.5 to 2.8 per cent during this period. India's share in this regard in a period of two decades moved up by a meagre one-percentage point. Slower growth in industrial production and lower share in manufacturing value added are dragging down India's the prospects of higher economic growth, which might undermine its position in the global community as well as its potential role in the BRICS community. On the aspect of technology too Indian industry seems to be losing. The share of medium and high tech production in manufacturing value added declined from 39.41 to 34.13 per cent during 2005–10.

Plan documents estimate that manufacturing in India needs to grow at 13–14 per cent a year to sustain a GDP growth rate of 9–10 per cent. The National Manufacturing Policy and the Delhi-Mumbai Industrial Corridor Project are envisaged to create integrated industrial cities that will support strong growth. Adding the current rate of inflation the government agencies estimate Rs 83.2 lakh crore as investment requirements for the Twelfth Plan period (2012–13 to 2016–17). At present banks have been the largest funding institutions for infrastructure development, which may find it difficult to maintain the same pace and momentum in view of their asset liability mismatches. Limited access to long-term funds has a bearing on the sustained growth potential of industry. The government has taken certain measures to boost long-term investments, such as hiking the automatic limits on euro commercial borrowings; refinancing of rupee loans through ECBs, allowing high net worth individuals to invest in infra-debt funds, and credit enhancement through guarantees. Simultaneously developing bonds and currency derivatives markets is taking place in a sizeable manner.

In this background, it is imperative that reforms continue at a pace that will strengthen stimulants to growth. On the side of finance, the major challenges are expanding the size and significance of key segments in terms of bank assets, new capital issuances, product innovations, designing new instruments, special focus on SME development, and a conducive environment for global expansion. The priority of industry is pursuing productivity, global competitiveness, quality, and efficiency. In addition, industry should adopt market-oriented framework that brings it closer to the easy reach of global finance. Given the great scope that exists for Indian finance and industry to grow and support each other, the combination could emerge as a potent and powerful instrument in taking India towards the next generation of growth and pride of place in the global economic community.

References

ADB (Asian Development Bank) (2012), *Asia Bond Monitor*. Manila, Philippines. Available at: http://asianbondsonline.adb.org/documents/abm_apr_2012.pdf

Aggarwal, A. and N. Kumar (2012), *Structural Change, Industrialization and Poverty Reduction: The Case of India*. United Nations Economic and Social Commission for Asia and the Pacific.

Aziz, J. and C. Duenwald (2002), 'Growth-Financial Intermediation Nexus in China', *IMF Working Paper. WP/02/94*.

Banga, R. and A. Das (2012), *Twenty Years of India's Liberalization: Experiences and Lessons*. UNCTAD and Center for WTO Studies, United Nations.

Beena P.L. (January 2011), 'Financing Pattern of Indian Corporate Sector Under Liberalisation: With Focus on Acquiring Firms Abroad', Working Paper 440, Centre for Development Studies, Thiruvananthapuram, Kerala, India.

Deutsche Bank Research (2007), 'India's Capital Markets, Unlocking the door to future growth', page 1, 14 February. Available at: http://www.dbresearch.com/PROD/DBR_INTERNET_EN-PROD/PROD0000000000205002.PDF (accessed in 2013).

GOI (Government of India) (2012), *Fact Book*. Department of Economic Affairs, Ministry of Finance. June. Available at: http://win2vin.files.wordpress.com/2012/06/india_factbook-2012.pdf.

Kumari, A. (2005), *Liberalisation and Sources of Industrial Growth in India: An Analysis Based on Input-Output Approach*. Delhi: Institute of Economic Growth, University of Delhi Enclave, North Campus.

Mohan, R. (2008), 'The Growth Record of the Indian Economy, 1950–2008: A Story of Sustained Savings and Investment.' Keynote address by Dr Rakesh Mohan, Deputy Governor, RBI, at the Conference organized by the Institute of Economic Growth, New Delhi, 14 February 2008.

Mohanty M.S., G. Schnabel, and P. Garcia-Luna, 'Banks and Aggregate Credit: What is New?', *BIS Papers No. 28*.

Mohanty, M.S. and P. Turner (2010), 'Banks and Financial Intermediation in Emerging Asia: Reforms and New Risks', BIS Working Papers No. 313, Bank for International Settlements.

Nagaraj, R. (2011). *Industrial Performance, 1991–2008: A Review in Indian Development Report*, pp. 45–7. Delhi: Oxford University Press.

Oura, H. (2008). 'Financial Development and Growth in India: A Growing Tiger in a Cage?' IMF Working Paper, WP/08/79.

Park, C.Y. (2011), 'Asian Financial System: Development and Challenges', ADB Economics Working Paper Series, Asian Development Bank.

Ray, S. (2012), 'Growth of Industrial Production in Selected Indian Manufacturing Industries: Is it Productivity Driven or Input Accumulated?' *Industrial Engineering Letters*, 2(1): 22–33.

Ray, T. *Financial Development and Economic Growth: A Review of Literature*. Calcutta, India: Indian Statistical Institute. Available at: http://www.isid.ac.in/~planning/Slides-ISI-LitReview.pdf.

RBI (Reserve Bank of India) (2013), *Macroeconomic and Monetary Developments Third Quarter Review 2012–12*, January.

SEBI (Securities and Exchange Board of India) (2012), *Handbook of Statistics*. Available at: http://www.sebi.gov.in

UNIDO (2011), 'Industrial energy efficiency for sustainable wealth creation: Capturing environmental, economic and social dividends', *Industrial Development Report*, p. 141. Available at: http://www.unido.org/fileadmin/user_media/Publications/IDR/2011/UNIDO_FULL_REPORT_EBOOK.pdf. Accessed in February 2011.

——— (2009), 'Banking In and moving Up: New Industrial Challenges for the Bottom Billion and the Middle-Income Countires', *Industrial Development Report*, p. vii. Available at: http://www.unido.org/fileadmin/user_media/Publications/IDR/2009_print.PDF. (accessed in 2010).

——— (2005), 'Indian Manufacturing Industry: Technology Status and Prospects', p. 5. Available at: http://www.unido.org/fileadmin/user_media/Publications/Pun_free/Indian_manufacturing_industry_technology_status_and_prospects.pdf. Accessed in June 2005.

CHAPTER 26

MAKING INDIAN ICT WORK FOR INDIA

ROHIT PRASAD*

The task set out in this chapter—that of identifying ways to make Indian information and communication technology (ICT) work for India—becomes relevant in the context of certain gaps that prevent a sector from achieving its full potential in an emerging economy. These include the market efficiency gap, that is, policy bottlenecks that prevent markets from working in an unfettered manner; market failures that represent the limitations of markets in achieving efficiency; and viability gaps that represent the boundaries beyond which high costs and/or lack of purchasing power prevents markets from delivering essential goods and services to citizens.

There are several features of ICT that make the identification of such gaps particularly necessary. On the supply side, the provision of ICT networks and services is characterized by economies of scale; generates positive externalities by raising the productivity of economic factors; engenders negative externalities through the carbon footprint of telecom networks, and the ecological impact of cell phone and tower radiation; and requires an enabling ecosystem that includes skilled manpower, protection of intellectual property, and trade facilitation. On the demand side, ICT consumption is characterized by network externalities, that is, the network value increases with the number of active users. In addition,

* Research assistance by Rajat Gururaj, Achin Mandotia, Angad S. Bhullar, and Shreyans Acharya is gratefully acknowledged.

except for basic telephony, adopting ICT requires developing relevant skills and attitudes in the target population, and the availability of relevant content and applications that can incentivize adoption.

Given these features, it is neither possible for the ICT industry to emerge spontaneously like a hothouse flower, nor reasonable to expect that it will distribute its largesse unbidden once it is developed. The development of both the IT and the telecommunications industries in India was facilitated by government action. The stock of high-quality engineering graduates, a legacy of choices made in the education policy after Independence; the decision to reduce levies on IT imports starting in 1995 but accelerating with the Information Technology Agreement of 1997 arrived at in the Singapore Ministerial Conference of the WTO; and the bailout of telecommunications operators after the incidence of the winner's curse in the 1995 license auctions—are some examples of the ways in which the government has played its role in developing the ICT sector (Arora et al. 2001).

Today, both IT (including the business process outsourcing industry) and telecommunications are striking success stories of post-liberalization India. The aggregate revenue of the IT-BPO industry crossed US$ 100 billion in 2012–13. Direct employment is expected to reach 2.8 million in 2013, almost 6 per cent of the organized workforce. Indirect job creation is estimated at 8.9 million. As a proportion of national GDP, the sector's revenues grew from 1.2 per cent in FY 1998 to an estimated 7.5 per cent in FY 2012. IT-BPO's share in total Indian exports (merchandize plus services) increased from less than 4 per cent in FY 1998 to about 25 per cent in FY 2012. India's market share in global outsourcing was 58 per cent in 2011 (NASSCOM 2012). The performance of the Indian telecommunications industry has been no less astonishing. By December 2011, there were 926 million subscribers, making India the second largest telecommunications market in the world after China. The industry is expected to cross the mark of 1 billion subscribers by 2014. The urban teledensity is 168 per cent, a level typical of advanced economies. The price of services is the lowest in the world, at 1 cent a minute on average (TRAI 2012a).

However, the performance of ICT as a driver of welfare has not matched its performance as a driver of GDP growth. While there are several reports that provide estimates of the positive impact of increased penetration of telephony/internet on state-level GDP (IAMAI 2012; Kathuria et al. 2009), the applicability of their results to rural pockets is questionable (Prasad 2012). Though the penetration of ICT appears to have outstripped that of other essential services like banking or power, much more can be done in order to reduce socioeconomic disparities. The total internet subscribers within the country number only 22 million, and broadband subscribers (with broadband defined at 256 kbps) number only 13 million (TRAI 2012a).[1] While the diffusion of telephony is high with an overall penetration of 77 per cent, rural penetration is only 34 per cent. Even within rural India there is a rural–rural divide with states like Bihar and Odisha lagging behind Himachal Pradesh, Kerala, and Punjab.

While the introduction of data services creates opportunities for tremendous productivity increases and for bypassing the infrastructure deficit of rural areas, the uptake of such services even in urban India is abysmally slow, and that in rural India virtually non-existent.

Further, despite having the second largest telecom market in the world, India's domestic manufacturing capability is extremely limited. The contribution of all domestic products, including products embodying foreign IP but partly assembled in India, was 12–13 per cent in 2009–10 while products with Indian IP could meet just 3 per cent of the Indian demand (TRAI 2011). Much of the equipment used for expansion of the Indian network is imported from other countries. This is an important lacuna not just in context of the need to move up the value chain but also in the interest of national security. In a similar vein, while Indian IT-BPO services are world class, Indian IT products are conspicuous by their absence. Of the total IT-BPO exports of US$ 68 billion, only US$ 1.5 billion is expected to come from software product exports.

In a stark indictment of the depth of ICT diffusion in the country, India ranked a lowly 48 out of 138 countries in terms of the network readiness index computed by the World Economic Forum (World Economic Forum 2011). A look at the details of India's network readiness score indicates an interesting split between India's readiness to use ICT and its actual adoption. In terms of readiness, that is, the capability to leverage ICT, India is ranked 33 globally owing mostly to its high score in individual readiness (rank 21).[2] However India's rank in terms of ICT usage is only 67, with individual adoption showing especially poor performance with a rank of 98.

[1] A recent Internet and Mobile Association of India research report fixes the number of internet users at 112 million. However this is deceptive as only 90 million claim to use the internet at least once a month and the numbers for moderate to heavy internet users fall further still (TRAI 2012a).

[2] Business and government readiness (rank 33 and 48, respectively) do not appear to be as high.

In sum, while India's IT-BPO industry serves world markets, a majority of India's citizens do not enjoy the benefits of internet and broadband. While telephones, that is, mobile phones, reach every corner of the country, rural citizens lag behind their urban counterparts. While broadband connectivity is reaching every citizen, citizens are not adequately empowered to adopt the new technology to improve their lives.

Awareness about the need for a wider diffusion of the benefits of ICT comes at an interesting juncture in the development of the ICT industry. The much feted growth story is itself facing challenges from global macroeconomic tremors (NASSCOM 2012). The IT-BPO industry is at an inflexion point and needs to develop new models of customer engagement, new skill sets, new industry specializations, and new geographical foci. It is estimated that almost 80 per cent of new growth in this industry in the next 10 years will come from new markets, predominantly in emerging economies. The telecommunications industry similarly needs to find ways to profitably serve the bottom of the pyramid in rural areas in India in order to grow. Thus, to some extent, the aims of growth and equity are converging in today's world.

The next two sections in this chapter provide snapshots of the IT-BPO and the telecommunications industries in which market efficiency gaps (policy bottlenecks to growth) are identified. In the next two sections, the role of public policy in overcoming market failures and viability gaps is highlighted using rural ICT and indigenous manufacturing of telecom equipment respectively as case studies. The last section provides a conclusion.

The IT-BPO Industry

The Indian IT-BPO industry is a service-oriented, export-driven industry. Software and services revenues (excluding hardware) comprise nearly 87 per cent of the total industry revenue, and were estimated at US$ 87.6 billion in FY 2012. Within services, IT services accounted for 58 per cent, BPO for 23 per cent, and enterprise R&D and software production for 19 per cent. IT-BPO exports at US$ 70 billion constitute the lion's share of IT-BPO demand.

The IT-BPO industry is quite competitive with Herfindahl–Hirschman Index (HHI) of 269.8 (see Table 26.1). One of the main causes for this is the low barrier to entry.

Table 26.1 IT-BPO Industry HHI

Category	Number	Total Market Share	Per Firm	HHI
Large	8	45	5.6	253.1
Medium	75	35	0.5	16.3
Emerging	350	10	0.0	0.3
Small	3,500	5	0.0	0.0
HHI				269.8

Source: NASSCOM 2012 and author's estimates.

However, till a few years ago, when the value proposition of Indian firms was largely driven by cost and process optimization, a large IT-BPO firm stood at a definite advantage over medium and small firms. This advantage stemmed from the ability of large firms to get large projects in which the management overheads were smaller. As a result, large firms had operating margins of around 25 per cent while small firms had operating margins of about 15 per cent. In that context, an attractive option for a small- or medium-sized firm was to get acquired. This was the route taken by Mphasis which was acquired by EDS in 2006.

Today all firms, large and small, are getting smaller projects. Customers are splitting up projects to reduce risks, and are initiating innovative but small-sized projects in order to meet the demands of their fast-changing markets (NASSCOM 2012). Hence, both small and big firms have similar overheads in their new projects. And more importantly, knowledge capital in niche areas is emerging as an important differentiator. Thus, small firms are better able to compete with large firms in today's market.

A rapidly changing technological paradigm is also playing a key role in throwing open the competitive landscape. Over the past several decades, the ability to fit larger quantities of computing power over smaller surface areas at lower price points, and the ability to transmit larger quantities of data at faster speeds over wireless networks has led to a convergence of the computing and telecommunications industries (Mulligan 2011). Cheaper handsets, the emergence of the tablet as a new device category, and the vertical integration of device manufacturers, service providers, application developers, and content providers are some manifestations of the new paradigm that enable niche players to acquire an important role.

Further, the emergence of cloud computing, that is, the possibility of accessing storage space, software applications, and content through the internet on a pay-per-use basis, has dramatically expanded the possibilities for IT use by small and medium businesses, and the prospects for small IT companies. The emergence of a new breed of start-ups like Pinterest and Instagram who can cater to millions of consumers on the internet with a skeletal IT infrastructure of their own is a result of this phenomenon.

Hence, competition in the IT industry is poised to take off and is limited only by the quality of the entrepreneurial ecosystem in India. A few points on the entrepreneurial ecosystem must suffice for this chapter.

The elements of an entrepreneurial ecosystem include venture capitalists (VCs), government schemes, incubators, academia industry linkages, and emerging geographic and vertical-based clusters. About 50 per cent of the VC investments in India are in the IT-ITeS (IT-enabled services) space (Grant Thornton 2011). VC investments are currently limited by a number of restrictive tax laws and rules on the trading of shares in secondary markets. The most notorious such law is the recent start-up tax announced in the budget of 2012–13 (Shenoy 2012). This tax requires start-ups to pay income tax on the appreciation in the value per share over the face value in the event of an investment if they are not able to convince a tax officer that the increase in valuation emanates from a genuine increment in the assets of the firm. This will be a deep blow to the VC activity in India which is still at a formative stage. It is worth noting that VC-backed companies represent 17 per cent of the GDP of the United States and generate over 10 million jobs.

The Telecommunications Industry

The telecom industry is a service-oriented industry driven by the domestic market. The total revenue of the Indian telecommunications industry was Rs 3.2 lakh crore or about US$ 66 billion in FY 2011. The market is dominated by wireless—873 million out of the 906 million subscribers are wireless subscribers. Two-third of the subscribers are based in urban areas although 70 per cent of India's total population is rural; 89 per cent of the revenues of operators come from voice services and 50 per cent of the data revenue comes from SMS.

Competition in the telecommunications industry, unlike in the IT-BPO industry, is driven by the government's licensing policy. This is on account of several distinctive features of the telecommunications industry: telecommunications is perceived as a basic need with ramifications for national security; there are high entry costs and significant scale economies; the interconnection between networks needs to be regulated; and the provision of wireless services requires the use of spectrum, a scarce resource controlled by the government.

The Indian telecommunications industry was state-owned until 1991, when the Department of Telecommunications (DoT) began the process of introducing private participation in basic telephone services by inviting bids (Desai 2006). The Indian communications market was divided into 22 licensed service areas (LSAs)[3] also known as circles, categorized as metros, category A, category B, and category C depending on revenue potential.

Mobile services using GSM technology were introduced in 1994 as per the New Telecom Policy 1994 (DoT 1994), and initially were reserved exclusively for the private sector. Mobile licenses, named Cellular Mobile Telephone Service (CMTS) licenses, were allocated through a bidding process in all circles except the metros where a process of economic and technical evaluation was used. The licenses came bundled with 4.4 Mhz of spectrum in the GSM band. Only duopoly was permitted in the beginning. Mobile operators fell prey to the 'winner's curse' and were allowed to migrate to a revenue share agreement as per the New Telecom Policy 1999 (NTP 99) (DoT 1999). Government operators, MTNL in the metros, and BSNL elsewhere became the third cellular service providers in each circle in 2000. The fourth licensee was introduced in 2001 through a bidding process, where bidders bid for an upfront payment to be made for the license, with the revenue share decided on in NTP 99 continuing to be in force.

Some basic service operators, using the limited amount of spectrum allocated to them for wireless in the local loop, began to provide virtual mobility using CDMA technology. In response, the Universal Access Service License (UASL) that permitted any service to be provided with either technology—GSM or CDMA—was introduced with effect from 2003. Mobile operators and basic service operators were migrated to this new license. The UASL for GSM came bundled with 4.4 Mhz of spectrum, and the UASL for CDMA came bundled with 2.5 Mhz of spectrum. The amount of spectrum could be increased to 6.2 Mhz and 5 Mhz in GSM and CDMA, respectively, on demonstration of need. The number of mobile service providers in each circle now rose to 6–7 in number.

In 2008, a new category of dual technology operators was admitted. These operators were permitted to hold UASLs for both GSM and CDMA

[3] There were initially 23 circles till Chennai was merged in the Tamil Nadu circle.

technologies. Further, 4–5 new GSM operators were introduced in each circle. This took the number of licensees in each circle to 12–13. The Indian mobile market has HHI of about 1900 (Sridhar and Prasad 2011).

The gradual increase in the level of competition in concert with facilitative policies like the migration to revenue share in 1999, and the introduction of calling party pays in 2003 led to first a steady and then a galloping growth in the number of subscribers (see Figure 26.1) although the sustainability of this growth is questionable given the high level of spectrum and market fragmentation (Prasad and Sridhar 2009). However, there were questions raised about the process used to grant the licenses in 2008. The ensuing uproar culminated in the formulation of the New Telecom Policy 2012 (DoT 2012) and the cancelation of 122 licenses issued in 2008 by the Supreme Court in 2012 (Supreme Court of India 2012).

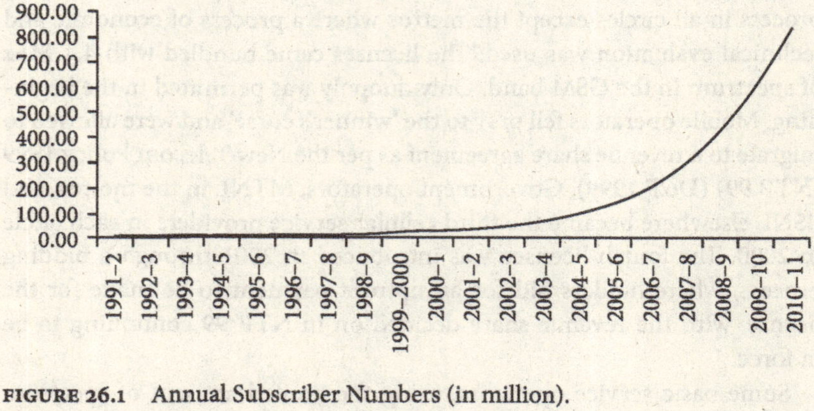

FIGURE 26.1 Annual Subscriber Numbers (in million).
Source: TRAI 2012a.

Ever since the allocation of the fourth cellular license in 2001 through a bidding process, new licensees (including dual technology operators) continued to pay the same upfront fee that emerged as the final price in the 2001 auction even though the value of the spectrum bundled into the license had increased manifold.[4] While the low prices of licenses arguably aided in the rapid spread of services (Prasad 2010), there are allegations that the discretionary power inherent in the process was misused.

Henceforth, the UASL is to be delinked from spectrum and all spectrum is to be auctioned. TRAI (2012b) has also advocated liberalizing the

[4] The spectrum bundled in the license is to be used with 2G technology, either GSM or CDMA. 3G spectrum in the 2100 Mhz band was allocated through the auction mechanism in 2010.

use of spectrum, no longer mandating the use of certain bands for specific technologies. Spectrum auctions are expected to be held by early 2013.

The Proposed 2G Spectrum Auction

As per the proposed design of the auctions, only two new entrants can obtain up to 5 Mhz in order to continue to provide services. While India has 12–13 licensed operators, as per licensed shared access (LSA), countries other than India have an average of only four license holders (Sridhar and Prasad 2011). A look at the 2G licenses issued in the Europe indicates that the maximum number of licenses issued in any country is five (Whalley and Curwan 2006). Moreover, all the countries added only one or two licenses when introducing 3G technologies. In any case, most of the new entrants in 2008 have not shown the capability to sustain themselves and there does not appear to be a need to free more spectrum for new entrants. However, two important aspects of the proposed auction will have a material impact on competition: first, the reserve price; and second, the benchmarking of the price of spectrum already held by operators.

TRAI benchmarked the reserve price of 1800 Mhz to the price discovered for the 2100 Mhz spectrum in the 2010 auction (discussed later). This comes to Rs 18,100 crore for a 5 Mhz block of spectrum at a pan-India level. DoT reduced the reserve price to Rs 14,000 crore but retained the ascending pattern of spectrum usage charges, instead of moving to a uniform, low charge in a phased manner as recommended by TRAI.

The reserve price in any auction is based on an estimate of the value of the object being auctioned and the discount applied in order to give sufficient room for the market to arrive at the true value through the bidding process without incurring the risk of collusion. In TRAI's auction design, the estimate of the value of 1800 Mhz draws on the accompanying recommendation of TRAI to liberalize the use of spectrum, allowing any band of spectrum to be used with any technology. From this policy stance, and from the availability of LTE (an acronym for long-term evolution, that is, 3G) handsets in the 1800 Mhz band, TRAI concludes that the relative value of 1800 Mhz, traditionally associated with 2G, and 2100 Mhz, traditionally associated with 3G, spectrum is linked only to their relative propagation capability with the 1800 Mhz band having 1.2 times the propagation characteristics of the 2100 Mhz band. It then applies an average prime lending rate of 12.63 per cent to the 2010–11 price of the 2100 Mhz band to arrive at the current estimate of the value of the 1800

Mhz spectrum. It finally applies a discounting factor of 0.8 to determine the reserve price.

The benchmarking of the value of the 1800 Mhz spectrum to the price discovered in the auction for the 2100 Mhz spectrum is flawed for a number of reasons. As shown in the TRAI (2012b) recommendations, LTE devices in the 1800 Mhz band are far fewer in number than LTE devices in the 2100 Mhz band. Further, the 1800 Mhz band suffers from fragmented assignment, compared to that of the 2100 Mhz band. It is premature to conclude that a fragmented band with such a low number of devices can be treated at par with a harmonized band with a highly developed device ecosystem.

Hence, at this stage, it is appropriate to reduce the duration of the spectrum holding to 10 years, and apply a conservative estimate based on the continued use of GSM technology in the 1800 Mhz band. The present reserve price especially discriminates against new entrants who will be bidding for start-up spectrum while incumbents bid for incremental spectrum. This is because the value of start-up spectrum is lower than that of incremental spectrum on account of scale economies. Hence, the high reserve price is conceptually flawed and militates against competition in the sector.

Further, in order to benchmark the value of all spectrum held to the market, and to ensure a level playing field, all licensees will have to pay either for: (i) all the spectrum they hold, or (b) spectrum beyond 4.4 Mhz in the case of GSM or 2.5 Mhz in the case of CDMA, or (c) spectrum beyond 6.2 Mhz in the case of GSM or 5 Mhz in the case of CDMA, in line with the price discovered in the auction for the remaining period of their licenses. This clause makes the auction extremely complex as new entrants will have to assess the trade-off between bidding low in order to win at the lowest price and bidding high in order to force a larger capital outflow by incumbents for the spectrum that they already hold. Incumbents, on the other hand, would want the final price to be as low as possible. Such a design does not appear suitable to discover the market value of unencumbered 1800 Mhz, one of the purported goals of the action. However, given the importance given to the 'level playing field' it is not clear how the issue can be addressed.

Competition in Higher Generation Services

With urban areas reaching saturation and rural areas in need of high speed access for the provision of basic services, the stage is set for higher generation services. 3G services were kicked off with the auction of 2100 Mhz-3G spectrum in 2010. Winners of spectrum were required to acquire a UAS license prior to rolling out services if they had not already done so. The auctions resulted in unexpectedly high revenues with a block of 5 Mhz of 3G spectrum in the 2100 Mhz band priced at Rs 16,670 crore (Kumar 2011). No private operator has pan-India spectrum.

The rollout of 3G services is mired in litigation. Operators are claiming that as per their license terms they are entitled to sign up customers even in circles where they do not possess 3G spectrum. This will allow them to function as virtual pan-India operators. However DoT has ruled that this is not permissible (Press Trust of India 2011).

Under the circumstances, obtaining 3G spectrum in circles where they do not possess this spectrum—either in the 2100 Mhz band or the soon to be 're-farmed' 800 Mhz and 900 Mhz band, or obtaining BWA (broadband wireless access) spectrum in the 2300 Mhz band, or 4G spectrum in the 700 Mhz band—has acquired strategic importance for operators. The recent announcement that Airtel has acquired a 49 per cent stake in Qualcomm, which possesses BWA spectrum in four circles, is of interest in this regard (Shetty 2012). More such deals are expected to follow. Some 'pure-play' entities with spectrum only in the 2300 Mhz band are also expected to acquire 2G spectrum. In future, operators will use a combination of spectrums to service each customer for their different needs of voice, data, and applications.

Here again the TRAI recommendation on reserve price could be a show stopper as the reserve price in the 800 Mhz and 900 Mhz bands have been fixed at twice the value of the reserve price of 1800 Mhz, and the reserve price of 700 Mhz at four times the value of the 1800 Mhz band.

License Rationalization

The percentage of annual revenue that is charged as license fees differs for different categories of license holders. For example, ISP (internet service provider) license holders who do not offer internet telephony pay Rs 1 as license fees while UASL holders who provide the predominant share of ISP services are liable to pay 10 per cent in metros, 8 per cent in Category A and Category B circles, and 6 per cent in Category C circles.[5] Telecom tower

[5] Even if spectrum and license is delinked as per NTP 2012, the proposed license fees of Rs 20 crore to cover administrative costs is much higher than the fees due from ISPs.

companies hold an IP-1 license and are not covered by the license fees. TRAI is of the view that the differential license fee gives rise to arbitrage opportunities. Accordingly, it has recommended (TRAI 2010) that license fees should be uniform across all telecom licenses and service areas.

Contestability

While the Indian telecommunications market is highly competitive as measured by HHI, there is scope to increase contestability. Contestability (Baumol 1982) is a broader measure of market power than the traditional market-share-based measures. In perfectly contestable markets new entrants will not face any disadvantage vis-a-vis incumbents, there are no sunk costs, and the entry lag is less than the price adjustment lag. In such markets even a monopolist will be constrained to price competitively. No telecommunications market can be perfectly contestable. However, measures to increase the level of contestability are possible in the Indian context. The introduction of mobile number portability in 2011 was one such measure. The introduction of Mobile Virtual Network Operators who can lease network time from existing network providers and provide services is another necessary step that needs to be taken.

Measures to bridge market efficiency gaps mentioned earlier will certainly facilitate the growth of the IT-BPO and telecommunications industries. However, there is further room for public policy on account of market failures and viability gaps inherent in the ICT industry. Two areas of focus—rural ICT and the development of indigenous manufacturing—are highlighted.

Rural ICT

On the supply side, the challenges to the provision of rural services include high cost of network due to inhospitable terrains and far-flung habitations; discontinuous electricity supply with a majority of rural India either off the grid or having access to erratic and limited power; non-existent content in local languages; paucity of relevant software applications; and inadequate supply of skilled personnel to set up and maintain the networks.

On the demand side, subscribers in the rural hinterland have low per capita incomes leading to lower ARPUs. They are largely recipients of calls, rather than originators of calls. They rarely travel outside their cluster of villages and hence do not use the roaming facility. They have little or no awareness of the internet. Their demand is as volatile as their incomes.

Hence, the government must step in to bridge the viability gap. India's record in this sphere has been rich in pious intentions but less than abundant in outcomes. This is a result of certain conceptual and systemic policy failings. Three of these are highlighted through the case studies that follow: a technology-led development paradigm that under-emphasizes the necessity of complementary 'soft' inputs; unwarranted faith in the market mechanism for awarding projects and ensuring the percolation of their benefits to the common citizen; and unthinking transference of urban solutions to rural areas.

Universal Access to Telephony

The National Telecom Policy of 1994 targeted full coverage of all 600,000 villages by 1997 (Swaminathan 1997). The goal of universal access started off by being driven by basic service operators. License holders were given a rural obligation towards the objective of universal access. Up to March 1999, basic service providers had provided only 12 of the 42,856 village public telephones (VPTs) to which they had committed. By 2002, Tata Teleservices had provided 1,314 of the 9,635 VPTs to which it had committed, and Reliance 502 of its committed 8,635 (Mukherji 2005).

In 2003, after observing continuing slow progress toward targets, the universal service fund was formed and the universal service levy instituted. From the license fees paid by all licensed telecom operators, 5 per cent of the annual revenue was appropriated toward the fund. The rural obligation was removed from the license terms of wireline operators and became the responsibility of the Universal Service Obligation Fund (USOF) administration under DoT (Jain and Raghuram 2010).

With mobile service penetration exceeding that of fixed lines, the regulator as well as the government decided to include mobile communication services under the ambit of USOF in 2006. In 2007, the first of a two-part tender was floated for creating a mobile infrastructure in rural areas. The tender was divided into two sections—Part A for the provision of towers, and Part B for the provision of services using the towers—with up to three operators allowed on each tower. For towers, USOF prescribed maximum subsidy ranged from Rs 3.68 to 5.07 lakh per site per year for five years. However, the final bid price was much lower, ranging from Rs 0.66 to 2.75 lakh per site per year. In Part B, the bidding for services resulted in a zero or in some cases negative subsidy even though provision of services requires a service provider to provide backhaul connectivity, a highly capital-intensive activity (Prasad 2009).

While the scheme certainly seems to have reduced the subsidy burden of the government, there is a question on whether the desired service was satisfactorily provided after the auction. For instance, two of the largest operators in India, after winning the bid in 2007, approached the government in 2011 seeking an early exit without fulfilling the commitment they had made. One of them had less than 500 base stations active out of about 8,000 committed by it. In the second phase of the tender, which never got off the ground, there were many schemes proposed including creating 3G infrastructure in villages in order to provide access to high-speed data services.

The USOF collected Rs 37,223.92 crore in the period 2002–3 to 2010–11. The accumulation of funds has far outstripped disbursal, raising questions about the size of the levy as well as the speed of use.

Overall, the architecture chosen for the rural rollout mimicked the energy-intensive architecture of urban areas. Due to the poor and erratic supply of grid power in areas of operation, operating costs were exorbitant. The absence of an adequate road network made diesel costs high. Auctions were unable to yield the correct level of subsidy and operators fell prey to the winner's curse. As a result, policy targets were not met.

The National e-Governance Plan

India adopted the national e-governance action plan on 18 May 2006. The vision was to 'make all Government services accessible to the common man, through common service delivery outlets, and ensure efficiency, transparency, and reliability of such services at affordable costs to realise the basic needs of the common man.'

The common service centre (CSC) scheme, approved by the government in September 2006 with an outlay of Rs 5,742 crore over a period of four years, is a strategic cornerstone of the national e-governance plan. It is the largest such project in the world and aims to establish 100,000 (now expanded to 300,000), rural internet kiosks across the country at the rate of one for every six villages (now expanded to one for every village panchayat). Telecentres are to be set up as delivery points for e-governance services as well as other B2C and B2B services 'for the common man' (Department of Information Technology 2013). It is the largest such project in the world.

The design of the scheme is symptomatic of a paradigm of development that believes that 'optimal' financial provisioning for basic services (and that too the hardware component of basic services, telecentres in this case) constitutes the most important, if not the only aspect of the role of the government. The amount of the subsidy, the choice of the provider, and the subsequent outcome of the provision of services in terms of reaching the intended beneficiaries are to be left to market forces.

Under the scheme, states have been divided into one or more zones. There is one private entity, the service centre agency (SCA), selected through bidding at a zonal level. Each zone consists of around 100 telecentres. SCA is charged with a certain pace of rollout and a minimum number of hours of internet up-time. The government has prescribed one important rule of operation, namely that the SCA operates telecentres through village level entrepreneurs (VLEs). The minimal specification of requirements seems to be based on the premise that a commercially oriented telecentre will automatically achieve development goals for the 'common man'.

The government has promised to provide two complementary inputs for the running of telecentres: a broadband network for connectivity and state data centres to provide the necessary inputs for e-governance services. In most states, the broadband network is being built by the government telecom operator BSNL. The state data centres are the responsibility of the respective state governments. There is no penalty on the government for not meeting targets.

The financial contribution of the government is in the form of a revenue subsidy that is decided on the basis of bidding. The subsidy is meant to tide over SCAs for four years at which point it is expected that e-government services will be operationalized and the subsidy will no longer be required.

The performance of the scheme is poor (Prasad and Ray 2012). While the pace of rollout is more or less as per schedule, there have been instances of the failure of SCAs in Andhra Pradesh, Haryana, Maharashtra, Madhya Pradesh, Tamil Nadu, Uttar Pradesh, and Uttarakhand. Many of the CSCs reported to be open are shuttered (10 per cent according to IMRB (2009)), several have no internet connectivity, and a majority are struggling for financial viability. The reasons include the slow rollout of the promised broadband network and e-governance projects, the low level of relevant content and applications on the internet in local languages, low level of awareness of the internet, and high operational costs. It has been observed that given the lack of oversight on the SCA-VLE relation, some of the SCAs are transferring the impact of the poor business performance on VLEs.

The way forward needs to be a combination of hardware systems and complementary inputs, markets and planning, solutions developed for urban markets and rural-centric innovations. Currently there is a proposal for the USOF to be used to provide optic fibre connectivity to the panchayat level. The following features of optic fibre need to be considered while designing the scheme: the provision of optic fibre will take time, while the task of providing digital connectivity must happen immediately. The level of basic services enabled by an optic fibre network is far beyond the level that the government is obliged to provide. Hence, part of the payment for the optic fibre must come from private parties. The speed of connectivity provided by an optic fibre is far beyond the foreseeable absorption capacity of rural areas. Therefore, it will be a lasting solution whose deployment needs to begin immediately.

In parallel with the optic fibre network, a wireless network closely aligned to the absorptive capacity of the target population needs to be built and complementary inputs including electric power, digital capability, content, and e-governance applications need to be provided. The wireless network will serve to immediately mainstream the rural population and prepare it for the coming of the optic fibre network. Every care should be taken to deploy an architecture that takes the unique challenges of rural areas into account. This should not be done through the selection of a technology by the government but by specifying requirements that reflect a realistic assessment of the rural population's needs and capabilities in the present and the near future.

The use of auctions is unavoidable but care should be taken to study rural conditions and design the auction in order to minimize uncertainty. The recent move of the Department of Information Technology to invite bids for setting up common service centres after guaranteeing a fixed monthly payment for connectivity, salary of the local entrepreneur, and power is a step in the right direction. The announcement that the Prime Minister's Office is setting up a cell to coordinate schemes related to rural areas across different ministries is also promising.

Development of Indigenous Telecom R&D and Manufacturing

The government of India founded the Centre for Development of Telematics (C-DOT) in 1984 to develop domestic R&D and manufacturing capabilities in telecommunications. However, C-DOT focused on wireline solutions and rural exchanges. The growing importance of wireless in the Indian telecommunications landscape and the inability to promote universal connectivity through the wireline route, led to a gradual decline of C-DOT, although it appears to be reviving on account of the proposed optic fibre rollout in rural areas.

As of now, India has developed the world's second largest telecommunications market but needs to import close to 90 per cent of its requirement of telecommunications equipment. TRAI has set an ambitious goal of meeting 70 per cent of our requirements from indigenous sources by 2020.

The further growth of the telecommunications industry will not spontaneously lead to the growth of domestic manufacturing capability. The global telecom equipment market is dominated by 4–5 multinational vendors who are tightly coupled with telecom operators. Operators are able to convert their capital expenses into operating expenses using the managed services model (pioneered in India), under which vendors manage the networks of operators. The vendors automatically upgrade networks based on new technological developments. The R&D costs of vendors are supported by a mammoth installed base of equipment. All these features make it difficult for a new entrant, even one with competing R&D in some product niche, to break into the market. It thus becomes necessary for public policy to create a protective wall in a selective, time-bound manner to enable the growth of local industry.

While the task of developing an indigenous industry is daunting, it is one that cannot be ignored. The Nobel Prize winning economist Robert Solow identified technological progress as the key factor in the growth of a country's per capita income. The large domestic market represents an important opportunity to move up the value chain by seeding a high-value domestic manufacturing capability. Such a high technology industry will have a host of beneficial economywide spillover effects. Further, telecom networks are critical elements of the security infrastructure of a country given the possibility of international powers using their national telecom vendors to infiltrate the networks of other countries. Finally, India's share in global ICT and electronics (ICTE) equipment consumption is projected to rise from just above the present 2 per cent to 5.5 per cent in 2010 and 11.5 per cent in 2015 thus touching US$ 380 billion (combined estimates of Indian Semiconductor Association-Frost & Sullivan, CII, and others). At the present rate of growth of the domestic industry, ICTE imports will gallop to surpass India's oil imports.

All the major telecom equipment manufacturers—Ericsson in Sweden, Nokia in Finland, Qualcomm in the US, Alcatel in France, and Huawei and ZTE in China—are products of carefully designed national, regional, and sectoral innovation systems that provided support in the form of finance, creation of national laboratories, technical education, and preferential market access. As Ren Zhenfei, CEO of the Chinese equipment manufacturer Huawei said: 'Huawei was naïve to enter telecom-equipment space. The rivals were internationally renowned companies. If there had been no government policy to promote national companies we would no longer exist' (CSIS Hills Program on Governance 2013).

Strengths, Weaknesses, and Possible Approach

The following are some of the strengths of the Indian economy that could feed into the policy (TRAI 2011). India has a large pool of highly skilled manpower and experienced technical people to work in production and R&D areas; and strong management experience in critical functions, such as supply chain management, high-tech manufacturing systems, and operational management. Telecommunications equipment is now largely software driven and India can leverage its strengths in software to gain a point of entry. The country is now also exhibiting competency in the chip design industry. A number of big names in semiconductor manufacture are outsourcing their design work to India. This booming semiconductor design industry promises 3.5 million jobs by 2015, according to a report by the Indian Semiconductor Association. Aside from sector-specific strengths, India has a favourable FDI regime with a 74 per cent cap in telecom and 100 per cent FDI permissible in some areas like provision of infrastructure and ISPs without gateways. India's weaknesses include very low level of investment in R&D, non-existent ownership of critical IPRs by Indian telecom companies, absence of component manufacturing capability, and lack of testing and accreditation facilities.

A linear innovation strategy proceeds in an incremental manner through the stages of assembly, component manufacturing, product redesign, and new product development. However, in order to leapfrog into the realm of advanced manufacturing nations and achieve the ambitious goals, we must follow a non-linear strategy (Prasad 2011). As the Austrian economist Schumpeter pointed out, the fact that every country is a beginner for a newly emerging techno-economic paradigm implies that latecomers can catch up by leapfrogging or direct innovations at the technology frontier. A non-linear growth path requires the government to identify techno-economic frontiers where indigenous capacity is beginning to gain traction, and put its weight behind one or two companies in each area.

If we look at market demand, it is concentrated in the area of handsets, active infrastructure for mobile telephony, wireless broadband, and wireline broadband. Besides, there is also a large demand for customer-premises equipment (CPE) modems for wireline broadband. We also have a booming market for optical fibre and the associated multiplex/terminal equipment.

There are several domestic companies which have made significant investments in some of these technology areas. Our endeavour should be to identify the front runners and create national champions. With our talent pool in chip design, we should aim to develop chips for the telecom industry and establish foundries for chip manufacturing, or alternatively outsource the manufacturing to global foundries like Taiwan and South Korea, to begin with. Some of the big foreign companies are already doing this by locating their design shops in India.

On the one hand, we need to move forward with this near-term strategy to provide the telecom manufacturing industry a point of entry and infuse confidence in the minds of the operators about the suitability, reliability, and interoperability of domestic products. On the other hand, we need to identify some core technology areas which will address evolving futuristic trends and promote companies who can develop world-class technologies to meet global needs. Some of the areas could be IP-based new generation soft switches, transport systems, next generation mobile wireless technology, security and surveillance, and non-conventional energy sources and their applications in telecom to meet the global challenges on environment sustainability.

Present Initiatives on Preferential Market Access

If the volume of policy activity is an indicator of intent, India has much to cheer in the field of ICT. New national policies on electronics (DIT 2012), and telecom (DoT 2012) have been released close on the heels of the national manufacturing policy (Ministry of Commerce and Industry 2011). Supplementing these policy documents is the detailed roadmap laid out by TRAI's recommendations on national telecom manufacturing (TRAI 2012a). The Department of Information Technology is in the process of issuing guidelines reserving 30 per cent of the total procurement of specified products for domestic manufacturers, who are defined as those whose value addition from domestic sources exceeds a certain amount.

In order to avoid excessive bureaucratization of procurement, the list of products should be narrowed down to include those which either represent an area of comparative advantage for India, or are critical from a security point of view. As far as the ability of the domestic manufacturing industry to deliver on the reserved quotas is concerned, it is routine for tenders to switch to the general sourcing route in case of lack of domestic supply. The performance of the domestic industry can be used to recalibrate the list of products and the percentage of reservations every few years (Prasad and Kakkar 2012).

While Indian products should be expected to compete on quality, they should not be expected to compete on price due to the economies of scale enjoyed by leading telecom vendors. In order to promote domestic manufacturing, we should define a small business based on global (not just Indian) revenue. A bidding credit in line with the perceived handicap (15–20 per cent) should be provided. The credit will need to be budgeted through the creation of a fund as recommended by TRAI. Such preferences are granted in the FCC spectrum auctions in the United States to small businesses, businesses owned by women and minorities, and rural telephone companies.

While WTO has strictures on laws promoting local content in procurement, these provisions do not apply in the case of security issues. The physical and financial security of a country depends on its telecom infrastructure. Unless the country gradually develops its domestic knowledge base and expertise in the important aspect of system design and architecture, it will not be able to deeply analyse the issues and challenges with respect to security and offer suitable safeguards.

Classic import substitution with haphazard and open-ended protection for all activities with no regard to efficiency, breeds inefficiency and technological sloth. Hence, preferential access for Indian products must be reasonably time bound. Further, we must also build in export orientation through export subsidies. Facing world competition builds capability and export markets are a source of technological information.

One area of innovation at the techno-economic frontier is rural telecom where the task of connecting over 2 lakh remote villages has barely begun. The low addressable market per tower, highly variable incomes, unavailability of grid power, and lack of relevant content make the task much more complicated than one of merely providing access. Some Indian companies have developed innovative solutions and will benefit if USO specifies its targets for rural areas in an appropriate manner. A significant export market for such products also exists in the form of the 2 billion people all over the globe with highly variable or absent power supply.

* * *

The growth of the Indian ICT sector while remarkable has not adequately contributed to welfare goals. The failure is partly a result of the understandable preoccupation with growth in the nascent stages of the industry and partly a result of conceptual flaws and policy limitations. Given the challenges facing the growth of the ICT industry, the time is ripe to bring welfare into the mainstream of the business plans of companies aided by a smart public policy. This chapter offered some ideas towards this goal with special reference to market efficiency gaps, rural ICT and telecommunications, R&D, and manufacturing.

Many other themes, including a greater use of ICT in the domestic industry, an enhanced role of industry associations, accelerated skill development, and coordinated management of spectrum across ministries could have been addressed. As a chapter in a book on India, this exercise is, by its nature, selective and thematic, not comprehensive. A more elaborate treatment of the issues awaits another forum.

References

Arora, A., V.S. Arunachalam J. Asundi, and R. Fernandes (2001), 'The Indian software services industry', *Research Policy*, 30(8): 1267–87.

Baumol, W. (1982), 'Contestable Markets: An Uprising in the Theory of Industry Structure', *The American Economic Review*, pp. 1–15.

CSIS Hills Program on Governance (2013), *China's Competitiveness: Myths, Realities, and Lessons for the United States and Japan*. Available at: http://csis.org/files/publication/130215_competitiveness_Huawei_casestudy_Web.pdf (accessed on 25 October 2013).

Department of Information Technology (2012), *Policy to Drive a National Agenda on ICTE*. Available at: http://india.gov.in/allimpfrms/alldocs/16392.pdf (accessed on 20 June).

——— (2013), *Common Service Centre Scheme*. Available at: http://www.csc-india.org/ (accessed on 25 July 2011).

Department of Telecommunications (1994), *The New Telecom Policy 1994*. Available at: http://www.dot.gov.in/ntp/ntp1994.htm (accessed on 20 June 2012).

——— (1999), *The New Telecom Policy 1999*. Available at: http://www.dot.gov.in/ntp/ntp1999.htm (accessed on 20 June 2012).

——— (2012), *The New Telecom Policy 1999*. Available at: http://www.dot.gov.in/ntp/NTP-06.06.2012-final.pdf (accessed on 20 June 2012).

Desai, A.V. (2006), *India's Telecommunications Industry*. New Delhi: Sage Publications.

Grant Thornton (2011), *The Fourth Wheel—Private Equity in the Indian Corporate Landscape*. Available at: http://www.indiavca.org/pdf/The-Fourth-Wheel-a-Grant-Thornton-Report-.pdf (accessed on 20 June 2012).

IAMAI (2012), *India—The Impact of Internet*. Available at: http://www.iamai.in/rsh_pay.aspx?rid=hDRaoEQvrnY= (accessed on 13 August 2012).

IMRB (2009), *Mid-term Assessment of the CSC Plan*. Available at: http://www.imrbint.com/index.php?option=com_content&view=article&Itemid=6&id=15 o:e-governance (accessed on 25 July 2011).

Jain, R. and G. Raghuram (2010), 'The role of the universal service obligation fund in rural telecommunications services: Lessons from the Indian experience', *Journal of Telecommunications Management*, 3(2): 181–96.

Kathuria, R., M. Uppal, and Mamta (2009), 'An econometric analysis of the impact of mobile', Vodafone Policy Paper Series Number 9. Available at: http://www.icrier.org/pdf/public_policy19jan09.pdf (accessed on 13 August 2012).

Kumar, A. (2011), '3G Spectrum Auctions in India: A Critical Appraisal', *Economic and Political Weekly*, February 2011. Available at: http://papers.ssrn.com/sol3/papers.cfm?abstract_id=1764882 (accessed on 25 October 2013).

Ministry of Commerce and Industry (2011), *National Manufacturing Policy*. Available at: http://india.gov.in/allimpfrms/alldocs/16395.pdf (accessed on 20 June 2012).

Mukherji, R. (2005), 'Regulatory Evolution in Indian Telecommunications', ISAS Working Paper, No. 7, 25 January.

Mulligan, Catherine E.A. (2011), 'The Communications Industries in the Era of Convergence', Routledge Studies in Global Competition. Routledge.

NASSCOM (2012), *The IT-BPO Sector in India—Strategic Review 2012*. Available at: http://www.nasscom.org/itbpo-sector-india-strategic-review-2012-0 (accessed on 13 August 2012).

Prasad, R. (2009), 'Poll Promises and the USO Fund', *Economic Times*, 16 April. Available at: http://articles.economictimes.indiatimes.com/2009-04-16/news/29403948_1_usof-providers-towers (accessed on 20 June 2012).

Prasad, R. (2010), 'The Value of 2G Spectrum in India', *Economic and Political Weekly*, 45(4): 25–28.

———(2011), 'Non-linear Innovation for Telecom Growth', *Mint*, 10 November. Available at: http://www.livemint.com/articles/2011/11/10230506/Nonlinear-innovation-for-tele.html (accessed on 20 June).

——— (2012), 'Rainbow Bridge to Broadband', *Economic Times*. Available at: http://articles.economictimes.indiatimes.com/2011-12-15/news/30520451_1_broadband-internet-access-high-speed-access (accessed on 13 August 2012).

Prasad, R. and R.S. Ray (2012), 'Critique of the Common Service Centre Scheme', *Economic and Political Weekly*, XLVII(6): 18–23.

Prasad, R. and S. Kakkar (2012), 'Boosting Indigenous Telecom', *Economic Times*, 17 April. Available at: http://articles.economictimes.indiatimes.com/2012-04-17/news/31355598_1_value-addition-public-procurement-bom (accessed on 20 June 2012).

Prasad, R. and V. Sridhar (2009), 'Allocative efficiency of the mobile industry in India and its implications for spectrum policy', *Telecommunications Policy*, 33: 521–33.

Press Trust of India (2011), *DOT Asks Bharti, Vodafone, Idea to Stop 3G Roaming*. Available at: http://www.business-standard.com/india/news/dot-asks-bharti-vodafone-idea-to-stop-3g-roaming/153664/on (accessed on 20 June 2012).

Shenoy, Deepak (2012), *The Startup Tax*. Available at: http://capitalmind.in/wp-content/uploads/downloads/2012/03/The-Startup-Tax.pdf (accessed on 20 June 2012).

Shetty, A. (2012), *Bharti Airtel, Qualcomm seal 4G partnership*. Available at: http://tech2.in.com/news/mobile-services/bharti-airtel-qualcomm-seal-4g-partnership/309932 (accessed on 20 June 2012).

Sridhar, V. and R. Prasad (2011), 'Towards a new policy framework for spectrum management in India', *Telecommunications Policy*, 35(2011): 172–84.

Supreme Court of India (2012), Available at: http://articles.economictimes.indiatimes.com/2012-02-03/news/31021473_1_crore-in-corporate-guarantees-telecom-licences-dent-investor-confidence (accessed on 15 May 2012).

Swaminathan, R. (1997), 'Functioning Anarchy: India's National Telecommunications Policy and the Development of Basic Telephone Services', *Columbia Journal of Asian Law*, 11: 393–433.

TRAI (2010), *Recommendation on Spectrum Management and Licensing Framework*. Available at: http://www.trai.gov.in/WriteReadData/Recommendation/Documents/FINALRECOMENDATIONS.pdf (accessed on 15 May 2012).

———(2011), *Recommendations on Telecom Equipment Manufacturing Policy*. Available at: http://www.trai.gov.in/WriteReadData/Recommendation/Documents/Recommondation_teleco.pdf (accessed on 20 June 2012).

——— (2012a), *The Indian Telecom Services Performance Indicators October–December 2011*. Available at: http://www.trai.gov.in/WriteReadData/PIRReport/Documents/Indicator%20Report-dec-2011.pdf (accessed on 20 June).

TRAI (2012b), *Recommendations on Auction of Spectrum*. Available at: http://www.trai.gov.in/WriteReadData/Recommendation/Documents/Finally%20final%20recommendations230412.pdf (accessed on 13 August 2012).

Whalley, J. and P. Curwan (2006), 'Third generation new entrants in the European mobile telecommunications industry', *Telecommunications Policy*, 30: 622–32.

World Economic Forum (2011), *Global Information Technology Report 2010–11*. Available at: http://www3.weforum.org/docs/WEF_GITR_Report_2011.pdf (accessed on 20 June 2012).

CHAPTER 27

URBAN INFORMAL SECTOR

functioning, constraints, and mobility

ARUP MITRA*

An informal sector in the context of the developing countries, particularly India, is a popular term which cuts across almost all the activities ranging from agriculture to manufacturing and various components of the services arena. Most of the agriculture is located in the informal sector. But issues relating to agricultural growth, sluggish or no expansion in employment opportunities and prevalence of a high incidence of poverty are not independent of the failure of some of the larger initiatives concerning land redistribution, technological progress, irrigation development, and diversification of agriculture. The present chapter, however, does not consider these aspects. Instead, it refers to the informal sector that comprises non-agricultural activities only. Between rural and urban areas, we consider the latter as the urban informal sector has claimed much greater significance in literature. Some of the important issues that we take up in the analysis include the structure of the informal sector, its functioning, the constraints it faces, linkages between the formal and informal sectors, the changes that are taking place within the informal sector over time,

* The author would like to thank Professor Ashima Goyal for her detailed comments and suggestions on the chapter.

particularly after globalization, job search procedures followed by workers in the informal sector, and the scope for upward mobility.

The term 'informal sector' has been used extensively, particularly in empirical literature, in spite of the difficulties involved in defining the term.[1] The informal sector in India is seen to absorb surplus labour residually in low-productivity activities resulting from the sluggish growth of employment in high-productivity activities. As poor person cannot afford to remain unemployed for long, so the phenomenon of the 'working poor' is prevalent. Meagre earnings reduce the poor people's accessibility to decent living conditions. In other words, there are considerable overlaps among informal sector employment, poverty, and slum dwelling (Mitra 1994).

Some of the defining characteristics of the informal sector used in literature are in terms of the smallness of the size of operating units, poor levels of technology, perfect competition prevailing in both factor and product markets, the lack of protection by the government to units/workers, and the lack of unionization of the workforce (see Mitra 1990 and Papola 1981).[2] The working definition, however, cannot be based on all the criteria—usually the size and ownership criteria are used in estimating the share of the informal sector in total employment (see Mitra 1994, 2001). Most of the earlier studies noted that at least 50 per cent of the city workforce was engaged in the urban informal sector (Papola 1981; Mitra 1990, 1994). Also, in terms of composition, a large majority of the informal sector workers were employed in low-productivity tertiary activities. We now examine the size of the informal sector for the more recent years.

It may be further noted that informal sector employment is only a subset of informal employment (see Papola 1981; Mitra 1994; Sastry 2004). The latter includes informal sector employment as well as those engaged informally in the formal or organized sector. In an attempt to avoid strict labour laws and reduce labour costs, firms have taken recourse to hire-and-fire practices and state governments in the fear of losing revenue have extended indirect support to these practices (Tendulkar 2004; Uchikawa 2003).

[1] See Peattie (1987) for details.

[2] ILO (1991) laid down the following characteristics of the informal sector: condition of free entry into the product market, dependence on traditional resources, family ownership of enterprises, small scale of operations, low level of technology characterized by a low capital–labour ratio, skills acquired outside the formal school system, and unregulated and competitive factor markets.

The overlaps between informal sector employment and poverty are significant (Mitra 1994, 2001). Based on the NSS data (1999–2000), Sastry (2004) shows that the incidence of poverty as well as the intensity of poverty among households sustaining on employment in the informal sector was higher in urban areas as compared to rural areas. Also the incidence and intensity of poverty among those sustaining on informal sector employment was higher than in their counterparts among the general population in the urban areas of the country.

Broad Features

The changes that we get to observe within the manufacturing component of the informal sector are noteworthy. Many petty enterprises, especially in the garment, leather, and gems and jewellery-related industries are now connected to large units falling in the domain of the formal sector. Since the large units provide raw materials, etc., to the small units the uncertainty component faced by the small informal sector units in carrying out their operations may have declined. They are not required to explore possibilities for credit assistance or production-outlets, rather they have the supplies of raw materials and work consignments, etc., available at their doorsteps. All this is likely to contribute to a smooth and efficient functioning of the units. From this, one may further conjecture that the positive effects of growth experienced by the large units get transmitted to micro units through the process of subcontracting and ancillarization and thus globalization is expected to be pro-poor as well. However, our field visits in the Sundar Nagari area bring out startling results to which we will turn later in the chapter. At the moment what is worth mentioning is that manufacturing is only a single component within the informal sector—there are many other activities within this sector (Table 27.1). Much of the informal sector is located in the services segment comprising trade, transport and community, and social and personal services (Maiti and Mitra 2011).

The incidence of informal sector employment defined as the proportion of informal sector employment to total employment in a given activity is high across most of the non-agricultural activities and between 1999–2000 and 2004–5 it increased considerably. The rate of growth of employment in the informal sector was much faster than that in the formal sector. What

Table 27.1 Relative Size of the Informal Sector in Percentage: All-India

Year	Manufacturing	Construction	Trade, Hotel	Transport	Finance	Service	Aggregate Non-agriculture
1999–2000	77.91	69.70	88.78	67.37	53.45	33.07	68.46
2004–5	84.54	81.95	94.44	77.38	69.16	67.12	82.05

Source: Based on NSS employment–unemployment data.

is also worth mentioning is that the supply-push component within the informal sector is much larger than the demand-induced component, implying that much of the growth in the informal sector is of residual type (Maiti and Mitra 2011). Within the services segment, linkages between formal and informal sectors are also evident as some of the high-wage employment in the services sector generates secondary effects (Joshi 2009). But the relative size of such a dynamic component is modest and much of the informal-services sector employment is characterized by low productivity, resulting in meagre earnings (Mitra 1994).

Based on a slum survey[3] in four Indian cities, we can draw more inferences related to the composition of the informal sector. The occupational distribution of slum workers was prepared on the basis of detailed lists of activities collected through the survey. Along with this, the nature of employment was also listed.

The occupational distribution of slum workers shows that sales and trade accounted for the largest percentage (27 to 30 per cent) of the total slum workers except in Ujjain (Table 27.2). The category of labour comprised of nearly 34 per cent of the total in Ujjain. The total services sector accounted for a predominant share of the total slum workers in all the four cities, which is in conformity with the patterns observed in Table 27.1 at the aggregate level from NSS data. On the other hand, Ludhiana being an industrial city showed a higher share of manufacturing than its corresponding shares in Jaipur and Mathura. However, Ujjain, which is not an industrial town, too showed a figure comparable to that of Ludhiana. It is important to mention here that similarities in terms of broad occupation category do not mean similarities in terms of economic activities carried out by the individuals. For example, in Ujjain a large percentage of the

[3] The slum survey was conducted in four cities by the Institute of Economic Growth, Delhi, under a UNDP-Government of India project on urban poverty.

Table 27.2 Percentage Distribution of Workers by Occupations and Nature of Employment: All Four Cities Combined

Present Occupation	Distribution of each category of workers across occupations				Workers in each occupation by nature of employment			
	Daily Wage	Regular Wage/ Salaried	Self-employed	All Workers	Daily Wage	Regular Wage/ Salaried	Self-employed	Total
Semi-professional	0.22	22.81	2.31	8.47	1.01	91.61	7.38	100
Sales & Trade	8.77	24.06	54.93	26.22	13.00	31.20	56.77	100
Personal Services	2.85	14.70	4.72	7.39	15.00	67.69	17.31	100
Manufacturing & Repair	17.31	14.70	11.43	14.83	45.40	33.72	20.88	100
Commerce & Security	1.53	5.76	1.36	2.93	20.39	66.99	12.62	100
Transport	8.98	5.60	8.07	7.59	46.07	25.09	28.84	100
Tailoring	7.96	5.60	6.18	6.68	46.38	28.51	25.11	100
Construction	14.68	2.92	1.78	7.19	79.45	13.83	6.72	100
Labour	35.28	1.50	0.21	14.29	96.02	3.58	0.40	100
Others	2.41	2.34	9.96	4.43	21.15	17.95	60.90	100
Total	100.00	100.00	100.00	100.00	38.89	34.01	27.10	100

Source: Slum Survey (2006–7) under the UNDP-GoI project.

workers were engaged in the production of incense sticks which raised the percentage share of manufacturing in total workers.

As per Table 27.2, a sizeable percentage of workers was engaged as daily wage earners. Particularly, in the cities of Jaipur and Ujjain, nearly half of the workers were employed in daily wage employment. On the other hand, Ludhiana, an industrial city, showed only one-fifth of the workers in this category while nearly half the workers were employed in regular wage or salaried jobs. Hence, the city's economic structure was a major determinant of the occupations that the low-income households were engaged in. In other words, the nature and structure of the informal sector were determined by the size and composition of the formal sector which tended to vary across cities. The second finding relates to the significant variations in the nature of employment across occupation categories in the informal sector. While some of the occupations were largely characterized by regular wage or salaried jobs, certain others comprised of self-employed or daily-wage workers to a large extent.

However, a very large majority of slum workers were actually in informal jobs. That is because in addition to self-employed and casual wage employees, a significant proportion of workers were in contractual jobs. Tables 27.1 and 27.2 may underestimate their proportion since we preferred to place the workers in the way they wanted to define themselves. In other words, even those who reported to be in regular wage jobs were actually in contractual employment in the informal as well as formal sectors. Since in contractual jobs most of the workers receive a monthly salary, and the short-term contracts are renewed from time to time without a break, the respondents have a tendency to interpret their jobs as regular wage employment. On the whole, a very large percentage of workers seemed to have been engaged in informal employment, and labour laws are hardly applicable to provide protection to these workers.

It is widely believed that the old labour regulations need to be substantially reformed as they often create major hindrances to employment creation in the formal sector. And to avoid stringent labour laws, employers prefer to adopt the route of informalization. While labour market reforms may facilitate employment generation in the formal sector it is still debatable as to whether labour will be able to get a fair deal in the absence of labour laws. Even in the presence of protective measures employers have already worked out mechanisms for avoiding labour laws and thus in their absence labour may be worse-off. The National Commission on Unorganized Sector Enterprises, therefore, recommended a series of benefits for informal sector workers which are essential if labour reforms are to be introduced on a large scale. As a large majority of the workers from poor households are engaged in the informal sector, social safety nets for these workers will naturally be conducive to reducing poverty.

The distribution of workers by type of education indicates that many of them in the slums were either illiterate or had studied only up to the primary level (Table 27.3), and this pattern seems to be quite uniform across cities. Other vocational training, which we tried to capture in terms of non-formal education, does not seem to be significantly present as only a nominal percentage of workers (except in Jaipur) reported possessing this attribute. One of the common activities in which a significant percentage of the illiterate workers were engaged was sales and trade. Besides, city-specific differences existed. In Jaipur the other important activities for illiterate workers were personal services, construction, and transport while manufacturing appeared to be important in the rest of the three cities. The category of unskilled labour pursuing menial jobs also constituted a sizeable percentage of illiterate workers in Mathura and Ujjain.

Average income figures varied considerably across cities (Table 27.4). Ujjain being the least developed town, the incomes were at the lower end. Also there was a relationship between education and income. For example, the percentage of illiterates in total workers engaged in semi-professional jobs was on the low side and these activities also revealed higher incomes across cities. On the other hand, in personal services, the proportion of illiterate workers to total workers was quite high and income figures were also relatively low. Based on these findings, it may be deduced that education and skill formation may have a positive role in the context of upward mobility even within the informal sector. Surprisingly, except in Jaipur, manufacturing did not show a high level of average income. Transport, construction, and commercial services possibly offered relatively high-income jobs though in Ujjain the corresponding figures were found to be much lower than those in other cities. Tailoring, on the other hand, in which workers used informal networks to a large extent, yielded low incomes. Hence, keeping in view the importance of networks and the average income figures across activities, it will be difficult to suggest that networks help enhance earnings. They may, at the most, provide accessibility to jobs and thus can be interpreted as a crucial component of survival strategies. Of course, the type of network is an important determinant of accessing higher income jobs. Besides, the network diversification, particularly the shift from informal to formal or within the informal, the shift from relatives to co-employees is pertinent. Besides, self-initiative is more

Table 27.3 Distribution of Workers by Occupation and Education: All Four Cities Combined

Occupation	Each category of workers by occupation				Workers in each occupation by education				
	Illiterate	Non-formal	Primary	Secondary	Illiterate	Non-formal	Primary	Secondary	Total
Semi-Professional	3.55	6.16	4.89	21.82	12.79	2.95	24.26	59.67	100
Sales & Trade	24.55	29.45	27.30	25.42	28.78	4.58	44.03	22.60	100
Personal Service	11.91	7.53	5.95	4.20	49.06	4.12	33.71	13.11	100
Manufacturing & Repair	14.36	13.70	16.59	13.07	29.37	3.72	46.65	20.26	100
Commerce & Security	1.09	4.11	3.11	4.68	11.54	5.77	45.19	37.50	100
Transport	8.82	10.96	6.94	6.47	35.66	5.88	38.60	19.85	100
Tailoring	4.55	8.22	8.06	6.59	20.92	5.02	51.05	23.01	100
Construction	6.55	10.96	8.53	5.16	27.69	6.15	49.62	16.54	100
Labour	19.82	7.53	15.07	6.83	42.41	2.14	44.36	11.09	100
Others	4.82	1.37	3.57	5.76	33.76	1.27	34.39	30.57	100
Total	100.00	100.00	100.00	100.00	30.61	4.06	42.10	23.21	100

Source: Slum Survey (2006–7) under the UNDP-GoI project.

Note: Figures in each of the first four columns (workers by occupation and education) adds up to 100 per cent whereas the rest (workers by education) are relative to row totals.

profitable as compared to informal networks (Mitra 1994). We will return to these issues on network later in the chapter.

Table 27.4 Average Monthly Income of Workers in Different Occupation Categories (in Rs), 2006–7 Prices

Present Occupation	Jaipur	Ludhiana	Mathura	Ujjain	All Four City
Semi-Professional	4,701	3,859	5,756	3,427	4,538
Sales & Trade	3,018	2,859	2,475	1,551	2,550
Personal Services	2,798	2,590	2,861	1,841	2,545
Manufacturing & Repair	3,177	2,721	2,115	951	2,052
Commerce & Security	3,018	3,032	3,162	1,888	2,778
Transport	3,540	2,836	3,118	2,307	3,165
Tailoring	2,290	2,797	2,161	1,609	2,479
Construction	3,231	3,067	2,675	1,936	2,896
Labour	2,555	2,807	2,275	1,366	1,734
Others	3,179	3,149	3,788	2,465	3,244
All Occupations	3,787	2,999	3,053	1,659	2,864

Source: Slum Survey (2006–7) under the UNDP-GoI project.

Presuming that the wage rate of regular wage employees was a proxy for formal sector earnings at the lowest level and the earnings of the self-employed and casual workers represent the informal sector, we calculated the inter-sectoral earnings ratio across activities. The ratio of informal sector to formal sector earnings was less than unity. However, the ratio was higher in cities like Ludhiana compared to Ujjain, and Jaipur compared to Mathura and this is true across most of the activities, implying that informal sector activities were relatively more productive in the industrialized or otherwise dynamic cities.

Informal Manufacturing Sector

On the whole, as observed earlier, manufacturing constituted only a small percentage of total workers in the informal sector and further, informal manufacturing was not necessarily characterized by higher levels of income compared to the other components within the informal sector. In this section we focus on value added and employment in the informal manufacturing sector, as brought by the enterprise surveys of the National Sample Survey Organisation (NSSO).

One important structural change that has been occurring for a long time in Indian manufacturing is the decline in the share of household enterprises—their share in manufacturing employment dropped from 55 per cent in 1961 to 32 per cent in 1981, and further to 23.7 per cent in 1991 (Ramaswamy1994). This trend seems to have been arrested to a large extent in the post-reforms period though not entirely. Household enterprises are covered under the own account manufacturing enterprises (OAME) segment of the unorganized[4] or informal manufacturing sector. The share of OAME in unorganized manufacturing employment declined by 4.4 percentage points only (from 69.4 per cent to 65 per cent) between 1989–90 and 2005–6. On the other hand, there was an increase in the share of non-directory manufacturing enterprises (NDME) and directory manufacturing enterprises (DME) within unorganized manufacturing over the same period.[5]

Table 27.5 gives the share of OAME, NDME, and DME in unorganized manufacturing employment and value added in rural and urban areas. The share of employment in rural areas was the maximum in OAME, about 80 per cent in 1989–90 which fell to around 77 per cent in 2005–6. In the urban areas also, OAME's employment share was larger than the shares of NDME and DME, but it was below 45 per cent in both 1989–90 and 2005–6. In terms of value added, OAME's share was the largest in rural areas in both 1989–90 and 2005–6, though this share declined over the years. In urban areas, the share of value added was the maximum in DME in both 1989–90 and 2005–6.

Two broad conclusions may be drawn by examining the distribution of value added in rural and urban areas by type of enterprise, OAME, NDME, and DME, across various industry groups in 1989–90 and 2005–6: (1) In rural areas, OAME's share in value added declined in general between 1989–90 and 2005–6, except in paper and chemicals. (2) In urban areas, DME's share in value added generally improved except in non-metallic minerals and transport equipment. In other words, own account enterprises which are quite dominant in rural areas are on the decline as they are not able to compete. On the other hand, DME which are relatively dynamic in urban areas are able to expand. Structural changes, assessed

[4] This is a working definition of the informal sector adopted by NSSO, based on the Factories Act, 1948. Registered-unregistered is a broad proxy, particularly in terms of an operational definition of the formal-informal dichotomy.

[5] Establishment with 1 to 5 workers (household and hired together) fall in the domain of the NDME segment; the DME segment in the informal sector comprises units with 6 to 9 workers and units with 10 to 19 workers without using power.

Table 27.5 Employment and Value Added (percentage share) in Unorganized Manufacturing, 1989–90 and 2005–6

Sector	Employment				Value Added			
	Rural		Urban		Rural		Urban	
	1989–90	2005–6	1989–90	2005–6	1989–90	2005–6	1989–90	2005–6
OAME	79.7	76.8	44.1	43.6	65.3	49.5	23.1	18.6
NDME	8.6	10.2	25.2	26.2	15.3	16.9	31.7	29.7
DME	11.7	13.0	30.6	30.2	19.4	33.6	45.2	51.7
Unorganized Manufacturing	100.0	100.0	100.0	100.0	100.0	100.0	100.0	100.0

Source: Computed from NSS data on unorganized manufacturing enterprises (see Goldar et al. 2011).

in terms of employment and value added, in unorganized manufacturing between 1989–90 and 2005–6 showed that some of the labour-intensive industries like food products witnessed a decline in a relative sense while some other groups like textiles gained significance (Table 27.6). Hence, the changes were not invariably in favour of labour-intensive industries.

In the backdrop of this, we would like to bring out certain results from our field survey on the unorganized sector. Particularly keeping in view the fact that the textiles group performed better, workers' gains in this sector may be assessed. The field survey in the Sunder Nagari area in Delhi identifies workers in three types of activities: tailoring and embroidery, jewellery-making, and packaging. Most of them received work consignments through contractors who supplied the products to large as well as small shops. While some of the products carried the name of certain specific companies, others were sold without any such liaison. Contractors supplied the raw materials and collected the final products at regular intervals and as per the workers there was no dearth of work consignments. However, the wage rate which was offered on a piece rate basis was extremely low in comparison to the efforts put in. In fact, there is evidence to suggest that the real wage rate has declined over time. Thanks to the supply of work consignments, workers' levels of living have not witnessed any deterioration, implying, however, that much more labour is spent to earn the same magnitude of real income. The workers did not take the initiative to sell the products directly to shopkeepers as none were willing to buy from them. This helped the middlemen to extract large sums of profit. To bypass the middlemen, marketing assistance has to be provided to these units by the government and by civil society.

Table 27.6 Structural Change in Employment and Value Added in Unorganized and Organized Manufacturing, 1989–90 to 2005–6

Industries	Employment				Value Added			
	1989–90		2005–6		1989–90		2005–6	
	Unorganized	Organized	Unorganized	Organized	Unorganized	Organized	Unorganized	Organized
Food Products, Beverages and Tobacco	28.27	22.52	28.93	21.52	24.63	12.98	20.86	8.85
Textiles and Leather	24.42	22.76	32.29	23.37	22.64	14.69	26.28	8.73
Paper and Paper Products	1.85	3.84	2.10	3.48	4.26	3.82	3.16	2.57
Chemical and Chemical Products	2.56	11.20	3.19	13.85	5.11	23.25	3.57	30.34
Non-metallic Mineral Products	8.65	6.11	6.41	6.21	5.96	5.01	7.55	4.89
Basic Metals	0.34	8.29	0.35	6.87	1.16	12.34	1.40	18.54
Metal Products	3.53	3.04	4.55	3.79	6.52	2.53	10.28	2.23
Machinery and Equipment	3.47	13.34	2.42	9.51	6.33	16.55	6.39	9.93
Transport Equipment	0.44	6.65	0.56	6.18	1.46	7.26	1.21	9.48
Other Manufacturing including Wood	26.47	2.25	19.20	5.23	21.93	1.57	19.30	4.45
All Industries	100.00	100.00	100.00	100.00	100.00	100.00	100.00	100.00

Source: Computed from NSS data on unorganized manufacturing enterprises (see Goldar et al. 2010).

For some of the products which were sold under the name of certain specific companies quality-consciousness existed and thus the better performers tended to receive consignments abundantly and regularly. However, this process did not lead to any rise in the wage rate as the better performers were still large in number. In fact, it is a buyers' market—the contractors set the price and no negotiation is possible to revise it in any manner. 'Take it or leave it' is the principle followed widely. The role of civil society in this context is important. Some of the organizations are able to offer a much higher piece rate than what the contractors do. But since the work consignments collected by civil society groups are highly negligible, the workers naturally get drawn to private contractors and civil society's interventions are not able to make any dent on the rates offered by contractors.

There is no formal or informal union of workers though each one of them is aware of the going rate. While further exploitation by offering a lower rate to any of the workers is not possible, raising the rate from the workers' side is almost impossible as collective bargaining does not take place due to lack of coordination. On the other hand, different contractors have a strong nexus which does not allow any upward revision of the rate. Since the contractors supply the raw materials, the workers do not have sufficient motivation to access credit or marketing assistance directly so as to establish an independent enterprise.

Some of the companies which have good reputations in the market and are also able to get export consignments have followed the practice of sub-contracting and much of the products are manufactured by home-based workers. But the benefits of growth do not percolate down partly because of excess supplies of workers and partly because of the middlemen's role. As quality is a strong criterion for success, these companies prefer to engage the same workers on a long-term basis instead of adopting a high labour turnover policy. To do this, economic theory suggests that the employers will have to pay higher wages to retain the workers and thus mutual benefits are assured. But there is hardly any evidence suggesting a pattern favourable to informal sector workers. There is no indication of a rise in the piece rate on the basis of which the payment is made in the informal sector. The only benefit that the workers are able to experience is regularity in employment. The so-called informal sector which is known for irregular employment is emerging to offer regular employment though only in certain specific sub-sectors. This pattern of regularity is expected to result in a positive effect in the long run. Workers taking advantage of stability in employment conditions may get an opportunity to develop market contacts and acquire more proficient skill to develop entrepreneurship in the long run, which in turn may contribute to productivity growth in the informal sector. However, some of these positive developments seem to get neutralized by the informalization process in many activities in the formal sector. Incidentally, several segments within the formal sector have adopted the informalization process at various levels though in some of the activities the process has been followed only at the lower rungs (for example, labourers in industries and class four employees in various organizations including in universities and government offices).

Informal Trade, Transport, and Services

The informal sector comprises a great deal of trading, transport, and other activities falling in the domain of services. In fact, as observed from macro data these activities constitute a very large percentage of informal sector employment (Mitra 2010). Even from the micro-surveys we noted that a large percentage of slum workers was employed in the trade, transport, and services segment of the informal sector. Though some of the transport jobs (such as auto-rickshaw driving) were seen to be generating higher incomes in a relative sense, there were still a number of jobs characterized by pitiably low incomes, comprising most of the urban poor located in the informal sector. Lack of skills and education, lack of on-the-job training, poor bargaining powers, and excess supplies of labour do not allow the wage rate to rise in these activities. At least those who are younger can benefit from education and skill formation which can help them graduate to high-productivity activities and experience upward mobility.

Some of the informal sector activities are linked with the growth of the modern sector. For example, metro connectivity in Delhi has generated demand for cycle rickshaws plying between a metro station and adjoining residential areas. In many areas in Delhi, where cycle rickshaws were not allowed earlier, they are now being used extensively, providing livelihood to a number of informal sector operators. The informal unionization of workers in fixing the rates as per the distance has been effective in reducing fluctuations in individual earnings. Many of the cycle rickshaw pullers now live in rented rooms in pucca buildings instead of sleeping on pavements. Though this may be taken to represent an improvement in the quality of life, many of these buildings actually do not have proper living conditions in terms of sanitation and ventilation leading to poor health outcomes. In fact, these structures are nothing but new types of slums. On the whole, while livelihood opportunities are increasing, urban space for informal sector workers is shrinking phenomenally. In certain localities owners of open spaces are deliberately allowing a number of households to settle in without providing any access to proper sanitation and other basic amenities. This not only allows the owners to earn substantial rents but also a kick-back from the operation of economic activities that these households carry out. More importantly, the owners use these households as vote banks during the time of elections which in turn facilitates their participation and accessibility to the power structure. The nexus between builders, politicians, and local muscle-men is on the rise reducing the supply of land to the urban poor. Though this process might provide livelihood opportunities to migrants from agriculturally poor rural areas, from the point of view of citizenship formation, hardly any progress seems to have been made. First of all the means of livelihood are not sustainable in the long-run and secondly in spite of being used as vote banks these workers are not in a position to bargain for better deals that would enhance their economic well-being. At the most, they are able to secure limited access to sanitation and drinking water with the help of local political leaders (Edelman and Mitra 2006).

By and large, informal sector activities including those in the trade, transport, and services components are relatively more productive in the industrialized or otherwise dynamic cities compared to stagnant ones. However, a large number of urban settlements in India are actually devoid of an adequate infrastructure base and much of the public and private investment, therefore, is concentrated in a few pockets (Mitra and Mehta 2011). To make the informal sector vibrant and the livelihood opportunities sustainable, infrastructural investments have to be stepped up in several of the stagnant urban centres. With increases in the paying capacity of the population the demand for informal sector services can then be stepped up. With improvements in human capital formation, workers in petty activities can actually start pursuing innovative methods to initiate productive jobs. For example, the younger lot selling products as street vendors in small towns can access bank loans, add value to the products with better packaging and skills, and hire shopping space at nominal rents in complexes built by government institutions. Similarly, rickshaw pullers can graduate to become auto-rickshaw drivers. Even in the context of garbage collection, private operators with improved techniques can come up with jobs that will offer better money and have no adverse health implications. The new rich class has created demand for a variety of services which did not exist earlier. How the informal sector will be able to take advantage of this and offer better employment opportunities is an important challenge.

Interlinkages

Interlinkages among the formal and informal sectors exist but they are not necessarily favourable to informal sector workers always (see Mitra 1994; Shaw 1990). Through subcontracting from the formal to the informal sector, intersectoral input linkages and recycling of waste products generated by the formal sector, informal sector workers earn their livelihood but often they are not in a position to dictate the terms of transactions, and hence the trickle-down effects of growth are limited. At times informal sector workers are seen to work within this sector for almost their entire working life without being able to graduate to the formal sector though within the informal sector they have experienced upward mobility (Mitra 2003).

Papola (1981) argues that the size of the informal sector is large in situations of both limited industrial spread and rapid industrialization. In the former case it is mainly a manifestation of residual absorption of labour whereas in the latter case a complementary relationship exists between the industrial and informal sectors. Also, in this situation the informal sector is no more seen to be one of low productivity by virtue of its close linkage with the industrial sector and income percolating from this sector to the rest.

Based on the city-level data, Mitra (1994) observed that the partial elasticity coefficients of informal sector employment with respect to different components of formal sector employment, including organized industry were extremely low in magnitude though positive in sign. And this will explain why, in relative terms, there is a negative relationship between the organized/formal industry and informal sector employment. The inverse relation between industrialization and the informal sector is indicative of the lack of strong interlinkages and the absence of possibilities of a complementary relationship between the sectors (Mitra 2001). However, based on the NSSO's estimates of the informal sector, the effect of industry and urbanization both on the former is found to be statistically insignificant (Table 27.7). In other words, states which are highly industrialized and urbanized and states, which are not so, both show a large size of the informal sector in the rural as well as urban areas. This is in conformity with the view which Papola (1981) suggested: the large size of the informal sector in states with low level of industrialization is mostly of a residual type whereas the same in industrialized states reveals a complementary relationship between industry and the informal sector, that is, the possibilities of subcontracting result in a large size of the informal sector in industrialized states. All this implies statistical insignificance of the coefficient of industrialization as seen in Table 27.7. If wages in some of the informal sector activities have shown an increasing pattern in the recent past, the linkage effect as perceived by Papola (1981) can be a possible explanation.

There are several other factors which contribute to the growth in incomes in the informal sector. Availability of physical, financial, and social infrastructure enhances total factor productivity growth. The issue of collective bargaining is also important for informal sector workers in getting them better deals. Assistance for accessing information on demand generated by the households belonging to the middle- and high-income groups can help diversify and improve the quality of the products manufactured in the informal sector. Similarly, products with high exportability can be manufactured by micro-enterprises once they have the information on demand and access to vocational training and skill improvement programmes. Mementos sold in European cities and made in China constitute the best lesson for the Indian informal sector. Quality improvement in informal sector products and services can enhance demand and with cost advantages the informal sector will be able to capture a large market share.

Table 27.7 The Effect of Industry and Urbanization on the Informal Sector

Exp. Var.	INFR1	INFR2	INFU1	INFU2
INDUS	0.34	−0.55	0.44	−0.19
	(0.38)	(−1.22)	(1.33)	(−0.42)
URBAN	−0.81	0.45	−0.16	0.005
	(−1.16)	(1.28)	(−0.61)	(0.01)
Intercept	70.43	62.52	41.77	59.62
	(4.78)*	(8.42)*	(7.59)*	(8.22)*
Adj. R^2	−0.01	−0.01	0.004	−0.14

Note: INFR1 and INFR2 are the two alternative estimates of the informal sector in the rural areas (1999–2000). Similarly INFU1 and INFU2 are for urban areas. INDUS and URBAN are estimates of the organized industry's share in net state domestic product and the percentage of population residing in the urban areas respectively.
* represents significance at the 5 per cent level.

How do Informal Sector Workers Access Jobs?

An important question is how informal sector workers access jobs. Since most of the workers do not possess higher levels of education the possibility of utilizing formal methods of accessing information about the job market is rather weak. The percentage of workers accessing informal networks across occupations is given in Table 27.8 based on our survey of slum workers in four cities. Tailoring and manufacturing are some of the activities in which workers used networks to a larger extent than they did in the other activities. On the other hand, those working as construction workers and labourers (excluding Jaipur) seemed to be using networks relatively less. Figure 27.1 shows the percentage of workers using networks and it brings out this point sharply. Since the construction sector is dominated by contractors and it operates on the basis of the daily wage labour market, the requirement for networks could be rather less. However, the nature of the city could also be a determinant of network use. A large city with greater economic opportunities attracts larger supplies of labour and accessibility to labour markets from an individual point of view becomes more difficult. Even the possibility of accessing public space to squat is more difficult in a large city as compared to a small one (Edelman and Mitra 2006). Hence, operating through networks among workers is an effective solution.

The importance of informal networks for accessing jobs in the urban labour market is enormous. In fact this is an indispensable part of the job search process without which an entry to the urban labour market is almost impossible. But prevalence of networks—given the specialization of activities in different parts of the city leading to heterogeneity in its economic structure—leads to market information asymmetry resulting in physical segmentation of the labour market (Mitra 2004). Further, excess supplies of labour in certain activities reduce the possibility of upward movement in incomes. Also, in the long run, the scope of experiencing upward income mobility remains quite modest as contact persons and new migrants both pursue their jobs in similar activities and in the same neighbourhoods. Surplus resources, which can be utilized for productive channels, are often spent on social commitments, which may be reducing uncertainties relating to housing, income, consumption, and health. But the lack of direct investment in productivity-enhancing projects and

Table 27.8 Distribution of Workers by Occupation and Network

Occupation	Jaipur		Ludhiana		Mathura		Ujjain		All Four Cities	
	Self	Networks	Self	Networks	Self	Networks	Self	Networks	Self	Networks
Semi-professional	45.57	54.43	70.37	29.63	74.12	25.88	70.59	29.41	64.26	35.74
Sales & Trade	44.17	55.83	62.78	37.22	56.65	43.35	71.74	28.26	57.14	42.86
Personal Services	47.22	52.78	72.50	27.50	59.18	40.82	72.58	27.42	58.80	41.20
Manufacturing & Repair	40.24	59.76	66.45	33.55	44.04	55.96	67.03	32.97	57.25	42.75
Commerce & Security	41.38	58.62	70.59	29.41	60.00	40.00	75.00	25.00	62.50	37.50
Transport	58.62	41.38	81.63	18.37	76.71	23.29	78.57	21.43	69.12	30.88
Tailoring	41.89	58.11	64.41	35.59	50.00	50.00	47.37	52.63	54.39	45.61
Construction	63.57	36.43	65.71	34.29	76.09	23.91	90.24	9.76	69.23	30.77
Labour	34.48	65.52	79.49	20.51	75.00	25.00	88.89	11.11	81.71	18.29
Others	51.61	48.39	71.43	28.57	61.70	38.30	76.19	23.81	64.97	35.03
Total	48.33	51.67	67.77	32.23	62.64	37.36	77.57	22.43	63.49	36.51

Source: Slum Survey (2006–7) under the UNDP-GoI project.

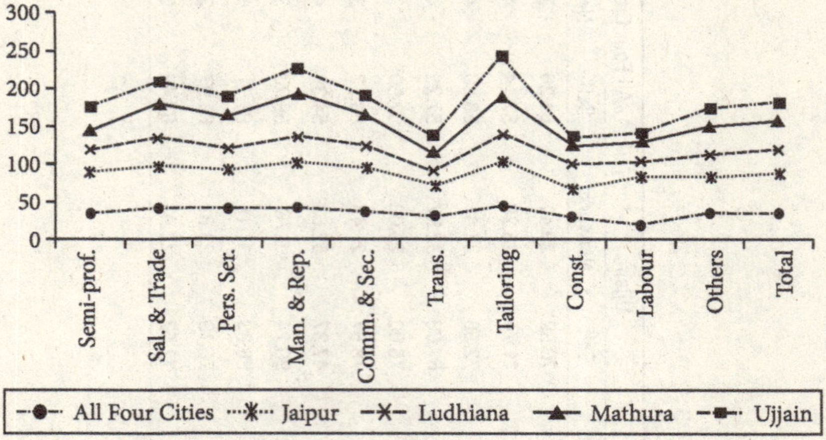

FIGURE 27.1 Percentage of Workers Using Networks Across Occupations
Source: Slum Survey (2006–7) under the UNDP-GoI project.

human capital formation restricts the scope for upward mobility to a much larger extent than what indirect gains may usher in. Also, social ties often do not release these people from the close cohorts that they have formed and do not allow them to diversify their job search across space. Hence, the trade-offs between social intermingling and economic gains may turn out to be substantive. Elliott (1999) noted that for less educated workers the use of informal contacts results in significantly lower wages.

Kono (2006) demonstrates that hiring workers through employee-referrals reduces a new applicant's pay-offs while a diversification of networks can raise their pay-offs. In a market with information asymmetry, the 'lemon effect' (that is decrease in the market equilibrium wage induced by the increase in network density) (Montogomery 1991) is caused by network extension or pursuing similar networks while network diversification raises referral wages through the bargaining effect (Kono 2006). Empirically, Munshi and Rosenzweig (2006) note that male 'working-class-lower-caste-networks' in Mumbai continued to channel boys into local language schools that led to a traditional occupation although returns to non-traditional white-collar occupations rose substantially in the 1990s. On the whole, benefits of the network come with social obligations (Luke and Munshi 2006) and thus may result in sluggish or no upward mobility of both contact persons and new entrants. Munshi (2003) observed that there is an externality associated with an individual's migration decision: members of Mexican migrants in the US face strong pressure to remain in low-skill jobs that have traditionally been chosen to maintain the stability of the network. In other words, stability of the network has implications in terms of low levels of education and low-skill occupations. In the context of upward mobility, Mitra (2010) noted no strong evidence to confirm possibilities of improving earnings through networks. On the contrary, traditional networks tended to reduce the possibility of upward mobility by creating an information asymmetry and excess supplies of labour in certain pockets and activities within a given city. However, younger workers were able to form new networks, particularly through new communication technologies. As a result of this, the duration of job search seems to have come down though with increased competition between young and elderly workers who have been forced to participate in the labour market in search of livelihoods, real income levels have not increased widely. Hence, government intervention is important from the long-term developmental point of view. These interventions can be manifested in terms of housing support, provision of health, skill formation and education, dissemination of job market information (pertaining to the informal sector) through effective channels, and a range of livelihood support schemes including marketing and credit assistance and assurance of minimum wages.

* * *

In this chapter, we focused on the relative size and structure of the informal sector, its functioning, the constraints it faces, the linkages between the formal and informal sectors, the changes that are taking place within the informal sector over time, job search procedures followed by workers in the informal sector, and the scope for upward mobility.

The incidence of informal sector employment is high across most of the non-agricultural activities and it has been increasing considerably. The rate of growth in employment in the informal sector has been much faster than that in the formal sector. Much of the expansion is supply-push and this residual type of employment results in meagre earnings. However, the nature and structure of the informal structure are also determined by the size and composition of the formal sector which tends to vary across cities. Population growth, including migration to the cities leading to vast supplies of labour, limited spread of the large-scale industrial sector, and adopting capital-intensive technologies and the lack of dynamism affecting the growth of high productivity trade, transport and services in cities are some of the factors which lead to a residual absorption of labour in low productivity activities in the informal sector. On the other hand, lack of demand—both domestic and international—for informal sector products, inadequate credit support, inaccessibility to market, and operations of a number of intermediaries and contractors are some of the factors which do not make informal sector units viable and keep the workers' earnings at a meagre level.

Besides, the nature of employment tends to vary considerably across occupation categories within the informal sector. While some of the occupations are largely characterized by regular wages or salaried jobs, certain others comprise of self-employed or daily-wage workers to a large extent. As a large majority of the workers from poor households are engaged in the informal sector, social safety nets for them will naturally be conducive to reducing poverty.

Through ancillarization and subcontracting the positive effects of growth experienced by large units are expected to get transmitted to micro-units and thus globalization is expected to be pro-poor. But there is hardly any evidence suggesting a pattern favourable to informal sector workers. It is not indicative of a rise in the piece rate on the basis of which payments are made in the informal sector. The only benefit that some of the workers are able to experience is regularity in employment. The so-called informal sector which is known for irregular employment is emerging to offer regular employment though only in certain specific sub-sectors.

Lack of skills and education, lack of on-the-job training, poor bargaining powers, and excess supplies of labour do not allow the wage rate in the informal services sector to rise. At least those who are young can benefit from education and skill formation which can help them graduate to high productivity activities and experience upward mobility. The nexus between builders, politicians, and local muscle-men is on the rise reducing the supply of land to the urban poor. Though the possibility of settling in a slum might have provided livelihood opportunities to migrants from agriculturally poor rural areas, from the point of view of citizenship formation hardly any progress seems to have been achieved.

To make the informal sector vibrant and livelihood opportunities sustainable, infrastructural investments have to be stepped up in several stagnant urban centres. There is little evidence on upward mobility to confirm possibilities of improving earnings through networks. On the contrary, traditional networks that informal sector workers use for job searches tend to reduce the possibilities of upward mobility by creating an information asymmetry and excess supplies of labour in certain pockets and activities within a given city. All this reiterates the importance of government interventions which can be initiated in a number of ways.

References

Elliott, James (1999), 'Social Isolation and Labour Market Isolation: Network and Neighbourhood Effects on Less-Educated Urban Workers', *Social Quart*, 40(2): 199–206.

Edelman, B. and Arup Mitra (2006), 'Slum Dwellers' Access to Basic Amenities: The Role of Political Contact, Its Determinants and Adverse Effects', *Review of Urban and Regional Development Studies*, 18(1): 25–40.

Goldar, B. Arup Mitra, and Anita Kumari (2011), 'Performance of Unorganised Manufacturing in the Post-reforms Period', in K. Das (ed.), *Micro and Small Enterprises in India: The Era of Reforms*. pp. 67–97, New Delhi: Routledge.

International Labour Office (1991), *The Dilemma of the Informal Sector.* Report of the Director General (Part-I), 78th Session, Geneva.

Joshi, Seema (2009), 'IT and ITES as an Engine of Growth: An Exploration into the Indian Experience', Working Paper Series No. E/294/2009. New Delhi: Institute of Economic Growth.

Kono, Hisaki (2006), 'Employment with Connections: Negative Network Effects', *Journal of Development Economics*, 81(1): 244–58.

Luke, Nancy and Kaivan Munshi (2006), 'New Roles for Marriage in Urban Africa: Kinship Networks and the Labour Market in Kenya', *The Review of Economics and Statistics*, 88(2): 264–82.

Maiti, D. and Arup Mitra (2011), 'Informality, Vulnerability and Development', *Journal of Developmental Entrepreneurship*, 16(2): 199–211.

Mitra, Arup (1990), 'Duality, Employment Structure and Poverty Incidence: The Slum Perspective', *Indian Economic Review*, 25(1): 57–73.

——— (1994), *Urbanisation, Slums, Informal Sector Employment and Poverty: An Exploratory Study.* Delhi: B.R. Publishing Corporation.

——— (2001), 'Employment in the Informal Sector', in A. Kundu and A.N. Sharma (eds), *Informal Sector in India: Perspectives and Policies*. pp. 85–92, New Delhi: Institute for Human Development and Institute of Applied Manpower Research.

——— (2003), *Occupational Choices, Networks and Transfers: An Exegesis Based on Micro Data from Delhi Slums.* Delhi: Manohar.

——— (2010), 'Migration, Livelihood and Well-being: Evidence from Indian City-Slums', *Urban Studies*, 47(7): 1371–1390.

Mitra, Arup and B. Mehta (2011), 'Cities As the Engine of Growth: Evidence from India', *Journal of Urban Planning and Development*, 137(2): 171–83.

Montgomery, J.D. (1991), 'Social Networks and Labour Market Outcomes: Towards an Economic Analysis', *American Economic Review*, 81: 1408–18.

Munshi, K. (2003), 'Networks in the modern economy: Mexican migrants in the U.S. labour market', *Quarterly Journal of Economics*, 118(2): 549–99.

Munshi, K. and Rosenzweig, M. (2006), 'Traditional institutions meet the modern world: caste, gender, and schooling choice in a globalizing economy', *American Economic Review*, 96(4): 1225–52.

Papola, T.S. (1981), *Urban Informal Sector in a Developing Economy.* New Delhi: Vikas Publishing House.

Peattie, Lisa (1987), 'An Idea in Good Currency and How it Grew: The Informal Sector', *World Development*, 15(7): 851–988.

Ramaswamy, K.V. (1994), 'Small-Scale Manufacturing Industries: Some Aspects of Size, Growth and Structure', *Economic and Political Weekly*, 29(9), 26 February.

Sastry, N.S. (2004), *Estimating Informal Employment and Poverty in India.* New Delhi: Human Development Resource Centre, UNDP.

Shaw, A. (1990), 'Linkages of Large Scale, Small Scale and Informal Sector Industries: A Study of Thane-Belapur', *Economic and Political Weekly*, 17–24 February.

Tendulkar, Suresh D. (2004), 'Organised Labour Market in India: Pre and Post Reform', Paper presented at a Conference on Anti Poverty and Social Policy in India, Alwar, 2–4 January.

Uchikawa, S. (2003), *Labour Market and Institution in India: 1990s and Beyond.* Delhi: Manohar.

CHAPTER 28

THE UNORGANIZED SECTOR AND ACCESS TO FINANCE IN RURAL INDIA

SAIBAL KAR AND MEGHNA DUTTA*

Economic and financial liberalization in India, as has been argued in various places, was a reaction to the imminent external crisis that the country was experiencing at the beginning of the 1990s. The reasons put forth by the ruling government at that time have been contested in different forums and it has also been stated that the reforms should have begun much earlier. Nonetheless, whatever might have been the driving force behind the economic and financial reforms, there is little doubt that the country was unprepared to adopt them at that time. In fact, the polity expected that the depth and spread of various other distortions in the country would automatically correct themselves once the more prominent sources were dealt with. For example, while trade and financial reforms aimed at removing some of the distortions responsible for the known maladies within the formal sector, the evolving conditions of the large unorganized sector were little known to the academic and policy communities in

* The authors are grateful to the editor and an anonymous reviewer for comments and suggestions. Saibal Kar wishes to thank Shrabani Saha and the School of Accounts, Finance and Economics, Edith Cowan University, Australia for their generous support during this research. The usual disclaimer applies.

the country, despite recognition of the fact that the unorganized sector employed approximately 90 per cent of the working population including those in the agricultural sector (NCEUS 2009). Thus, the reforms brought in a watershed, in the way various sectors in the 'formal' economy functioned, and presently offer a natural experiment to observe if the changes were significant enough for some of the crucial sectors in the country in the presence of large informal counterparts. In this connection, we focus on a specific aspect of the rural economy that continues to be of prime importance in the development discourses in India and might offer related inferences for other developing countries.

In India, financial liberalization was implemented at a time when the rural credit market was marked by imperfections and fragmentations. Therefore, much of the benefits of liberalization, in terms of coverage, ease of access, and lower as well as fairer repayment conditions, failed to reach the rural poor. It is well known that sections of the population in a developing country, particularly those in the labour-surplus agricultural sector, are comparatively more vulnerable to credit malpractices as compared to their urban counterparts. Hence, the burden of indebtedness in rural India was on those who resorted to informal credit institutions as the most important source to borrow from.[1] Despite major structural changes in credit institutions and forms of rural credit, the engagement of the rural masses with the informal credit market has been one of the most exploitative and persistent features of rural India (Basu 2006). In this connection, Jeromi (2007), for example, discusses the undesirable aspects of informal moneylending in Kerala and its overall impact on the society. Needless to mention, the predicament of rural borrowers is a historical phenomenon in India, as one observes from earlier documents. Among others, Sinha (1976) presents a worrisome account of the rule of moneylenders in rural societies in Dhanbad. In the same vein, the Rural Financial Access Survey (RFAS) (2003) indicates that 70 per cent of marginal and landless farmers do not have bank accounts and about 87 per cent have no access to credit from a formal source. The study also found that 48 per cent of marginal and landless farmers had borrowed from an informal source at least once in the previous 12 months, at interest rates averaging 48 per cent per year. On the other hand, the National Sample Survey Office (2007b) reports that informal sources accounted for about

[1] Informal credit institutions imply those that are not regulated by a public authority. The terms and conditions associated with such loans are personalized and vary according to the bargaining power of the borrower on a case-to-case basis.

44 per cent of outstanding loans taken by unorganized manufacturing enterprises.

Consequently, efforts have been made to disentangle borrowers from the clutches of informal lenders. In addition, some of the measures that the government resorted to in an attempt to arrest the adverse effects of liberalization included expansion of the institutional structure and coverage of formal sector-lending institutions, initiation of directed lending, and providing for concessional or subsidized credit (Basu 2006). In the period between nationalization and liberalization, banks had opened more rural branches in states having fewer branches per capita as of 1961. This trend was, however, reversed after liberalization (Burgess and Pande 2004). The number of branches of scheduled commercial banks (SCBs) in rural areas increased from 1,833 in 1969 to 34,791 in 1990. On the other hand, between 1990 and 2012, only 862 new branches were opened (RBI 2012). However, note that according to the Reserve Bank of India (2006), during 2005–6, the credit advanced by scheduled commercial banks rose by 36 per cent. The government also accepted the recommendations of the task force formed under Professor Vaidyanathan in a bid to revive short-term rural cooperative banking institutions. In view of their importance as lenders, supporting banks were encouraged to merge with regional rural banks (RRBs) that they sponsored, state-wise, in order to strengthen them. By 2006, the government had issued notifications providing for amalgamation of 93 RRBs into 27 new RRBs, sponsored by 15 banks in 12 states (RBI 2006).

The EPW Research Foundation (2007) subsequently shows how the objective of a rapid credit expansion is stifled without the expansion of the rural branch networks of dominant public sector banks. In fact, studies have found a positive impact of branch expansion in rural areas and greater positive impact of access to finance on poverty (Banerjee and Newman 1993; Burgess et al. 2005). However, the steady reduction in the number of branches in rural areas and increasing demand by banks for collaterals tends to invalidate and wither the benefits that were envisaged by policymakers before bank nationalization (Nair 2000). The reversals were so severe that it led the RBI (2006: 55) to report, 'despite the spread of banking facilities in rural areas and availability of bank finance at reasonable rates, farmers in several areas are still in distress', and proposed the formation of a working group to suggest measures for assisting distressed farmers, including provision of financial counselling services and introduction of a specific Credit Guarantee Scheme under the Deposit Insurance and Credit Guarantee Corporation (DICGC) Act.

The All-India Debt and Investment Survey (AIDIS) by NSSO also reveals that the loans taken from moneylenders in the total credit stock of rural households increased from 17.5 per cent in 1991 to 29.6 per cent in 2002. This indicates an increase in indebtedness of rural households over the past decade to informal lending institutions. However, this can also mean increased access to credit. According to AIDIS (1991) (cited in NSSO 1991, 2002), just 16 per cent of rural households had formal loan outstandings. Based on the World Bank-NCAER Rural Financial Access Survey (2003), the corresponding number was 21 per cent (Basu 2006).

Several other factors, such as the amount of processing time required to obtain a loan and the bribes that need to be paid, makes access to credit from the formal sector a difficult alternative. Evidently, it raises the effective cost of borrowing for poor credit-starved households. According to RFAS (2003) (Table 28.1), 26.8 per cent households reported paying bribes for getting a loan from banks. Bribes paid as a per cent of the loan amount was 10.1 per cent for banks, 18.2 per cent for RRBs, and 19.9 per cent for cooperatives. For RRBs, which were established by the Government of India through an ordinance and then by a legislation to improve credit accessibility of the poor, the average time taken to process a loan application was as long as 28.5 weeks. Most of the loans given by commercial banks, RRBs, and cooperatives required collaterals; 89 per cent of the households who borrowed from RRBs, and 87 per cent of the households who borrowed from commercial banks reported that they had to provide collateral. The value of collaterals required as a proportion of the loan, however, remains relatively low in the case of banks and RRBs, at under 10 per cent, but high in the case of government schemes (see Table 28.1).

Table 28.1 Sources of Formal Borrowing and Associated Costs, 2003

Indicators	Banks	RRBs	Coope-ratives	Government Schemes	Others
Interest rate (median) % p.a.	12.5	11.0	11.0	14.0	14.0
Loan amount received as % of amount applied	91.8	88.2	83.5	86.6	93.9
Percentage of households reporting bribes	26.8	27.0	9.7	27.27	23.21
Bribe as % of amount approved	10.1	18.2	19.9	42.3	8.3
Time taken to process a loan application (weeks)	33.0	28.5	24.0	8.9	14.3
Collateral required (as % of loan)	87.0	89.3	72.9	58.3	83.1
Value of collateral (as % of loan)	9.1	9.5	11.0	26.8	24.3

Source: RFAS (2003).

The performance of scheduled commercial banks and other bank-based financial intermediaries since nationalization, and up to 2000, are given in Table 28.2. It is evident that priority sector lending,[2] which had been an important agenda of the government since 1968, suffered a setback after liberalization. Priority sector lending by SCBs as a proportion of total credit advanced increased significantly from 14 per cent in 1969 to 34.4 per cent in 1993. However, between 1993 and 2011, it declined to 33.9 per cent.

Based on some of these facts and figures, we attempt to discuss the degree of financial inclusiveness of the rural population in various states in India. It should be borne in mind that the rural sector in India is largely composed of the agricultural sector and rural formal and informal industries, albeit the share of the formal sector, is quite thin. Therefore, in order to understand the role of the current financial system, we examine the two major sectors separately in the rural areas, namely, agriculture and unorganized manufacturing. While literature talks extensively about the supply of credit to agriculture (Basu 2006; Chavan 2005; Jagan Mohan 2004), an in-depth analysis of the rural unorganized manufacturing sector remains somewhat neglected. This chapter also attempts to fill this gap.

With the unorganized manufacturing sector emerging as a substantive and growing sector within the total manufacturing sector per se, its contribution to the rural economy can hardly be neglected. According to the National Sample Survey Office (NSSO) of India, during 2005–6, an estimated 17 million unorganized manufacturing enterprises were in operation at the all-India level, of which 71 per cent were located in rural areas. This bears out the fact that rural unorganized manufacturing enterprises play a non-trivial role in the development of the rural economy. This primarily motivates us to discuss the financial linkages and inclusiveness of rural organizations outside of agriculture.

[2] Advances to priority sectors consist of advances to: (1) agriculture and allied activities, (2) small-scale industries including loans for setting up industrial estates, (3) small road and water transport operators, (4) small businesses, (5) professional and self-employed persons, (6) retail trade, (7) state-sponsored organizations for Scheduled Castes/Scheduled Tribes, (8) education, (9) housing, (10) self-help groups (SHGs)/non-governmental organizations (NGOs), (11) consumption loans granted under the consumption credit scheme, (12) net funds provided to sponsored RRBs, (13) advances to software industry units having credit limit up to Rs 1 crore, (14) advances to food and agro-based processing sector which do not satisfy small-scale industry norms, (15) credit offered to weaker sections under different schemes, and (16) investments in venture capital.

Table 28.2 The Extent of Commercial Banking in India, Various Years

Indicators	June 1969	1993	1995	1999	2000	2011
No. of Commercial Banks	89	276	284	303	297	169
(a) Scheduled Commercial Banks	73	272	281	302	297	165
Of which: Regional Rural Banks	–	196	196	196	196	82
(b) Non-Scheduled Commercial Banks	16	4	3	1	–	4
Number of Bank Offices in India	8,262	61,169	62,367	64,939	65,412	92,063
(a) Rural	1,833	35,389	33,004	32,857	32,734	34,208
Population per office (in thousands)	64	14	15	15	15	13.1
Deposits of scheduled commercial banks in India (Rs in crore)	4,646	274,938	386,859	714,025	851,593	5,207,969
Credit of scheduled commercial banks in India (Rs in crore)	3,599	154,838	211,560	368,837	454,069	3,942,082
Scheduled commercial banks' Advances to Priority Sector (Rs in crore)	504	51,739	69,209	126,309	155,779	133,733
Share of Priority Sector Advances in Total Credit of scheduled commercial banks (%)	14	34.4	33.7	35.3	35.4	33.9
Share of Priority Sector Advances in Total Non-food Credit of scheduled commercial banks (%)	15	36.1	35.8	37	37.4	34.5

Source: Reserve Bank of India bulletin (various years).

The chapter is organized as follows. We discuss the data sources in the next section followed by a brief analysis of the agricultural sector. In the section after it, we discuss the rural unorganized manufacturing sector as the focus of this study. The section that follows deals with volatility in the informal sector as a whole and income volatility in the unorganized manufacturing sector in particular. The next section discusses micro-credit organizations as a link between formal credit and informal manufacturing units in rural India. The chapter then provides a conclusion.

Agriculture and Finance

Data Sources

The data for this study is obtained from the sixty-second round of the Unorganized Manufacturing Enterprise Survey by NSSO, the All-India Debt and Investment Survey by NSSO, the survey conducted by the National Council of Applied Economic Research and the World Bank of India (a survey of 6,000 households and micro-enterprises in two states—Andhra Pradesh and Uttar Pradesh), Reserve Bank of India (RBI), and National Bank for Agricultural and Rural Development (NABARD). As stated earlier, we begin by discussing financial issues in the agricultural sector and subsequently that of the rural unorganized manufacturing sector. We define the 'rural' unorganized manufacturing sector as those unorganized manufacturing enterprises[3] (OAME, NDME, and DMEs taken together) that the NSSO reports to be located in rural areas. We also follow the same definition of 'rural areas' as followed by NSSO.

Agricultural Sector

There are various reasons why farm households need loans. Ray (1998) has identified demand for fixed capital at the household level to start up new

[3] The unorganized manufacturing sector is defined by NSSO as: 'all manufacturing enterprises except those registered under section 2m(i) and 2m(ii) of Factories Act, 1948 and Bidi and Cigar Workers (conditions of employment) Act, 1966, and all manufacturing enterprises except those run by Government (Central Government, State Governments, Local Bodies)/Public Sector Enterprises' (see Appendix A28.2 for the various sub-clauses under Factories Act, 1948).

production or to improve and modernize existing production techniques. On the other hand, it is also observed that the demand for working capital comes mainly from the need to buy raw materials, such as seeds, fertilizers, and pesticides, to carry the output to the market, and as consumption credit, comprising the three important sources of demand for credit. However, there are several bottlenecks in the credit supply chain. Formal lending institutions are less keen to lend to the poor because agriculture is inherently risky, and if the crop fails there is very little option through which the farmer can repay the loan. To combat this problem, institutional agencies demand collateral, but the collateral offered by poor farmers is often not acceptable to banks. For, example, a landless labourer might offer his labour as collateral (which an informal lender will accept), but a formal financial institution like a bank obviously cannot accept. It also clearly suggests that the practice of bonded labour continues in relation to informal financial facilities in rural India. Again, a small farmer may offer his land as collateral but the bank might not find it profitable because the cost of selling it in case of a default could be too high (Ray 1998). This is over and above the usual moral hazard of monitoring and policing a borrower that restricts formal financial institutions from offering extensive credit facilities. Many of these aspects have been discussed in detail in Basu (1997) and therefore do not require further deliberation.

Nevertheless, statistics on indebtedness in farm households in India shows greater reliance on institutional credit over the last few decades although the share of moneylenders continues to be reasonably high. But during the last decade, there has been a decline in the share of institutional credit as a source of debt in farm households. For farm households, the proportionate share of debt from institutional sources fell from 66.3 per cent in 1991 to 61.1 per cent in 2002 (Table 28.3).

Table 28.3 Percentage Share of Debt of Cultivator Households from Different Sources of Credit in India, 1951–2002

Source of Credit	1951	1961	1971	1981	1991	2002
Institutional	7.3	18.7	31.7	63.2	66.3	61.1
Cooperative Societies/Banks	3.3	2.6	22.0	29.8	30.0	30.2
Commercial Banks	0.9	0.6	2.4	28.8	35.2	26.3
Non-institutional	92.7	81.3	66.3	36.8	30.6	38.9
Moneylenders	69.7	49.2	36.1	16.1	17.5	26.8
Unspecified	–	–	–	–	3.1	–
Total	100.0	100.0	100.0	100.0	100.0	100.0

Source: Lok Sabha Unstarred Question No. 857 (dated 25 February 2011).

Figure 28.1 also displays the proportion of loans taken by cultivator households from institutional and non-institutional sources. Loans taken from institutional sources show a steady increase in the total loan taken by these households. However, the share of formal sources has declined since 1991. The clear withdrawal of formal lending institutions from rural areas, as shown earlier, after liberalization, has been explained as a systematic design to remain profitable. It is well known that borrowers in rural areas often do not have sufficient assets to provide as collaterals. Consequently, in case of non-recovery of a loan it leads to loss/NPAs (non-performing assets) for banks with reportedly technical restraints in capturing and selling off the collaterals. Moreover, under direct finance schemes of lending, the crop produce is regularly kept as collateral. This becomes extremely risky as, in case of a crop failure the entire amount of the loan proves to be a bad debt for the bank. Lending institutions argue that in a bid to remain competitive, the banks have started looking away from the rural sector as part of their strategic decisions.

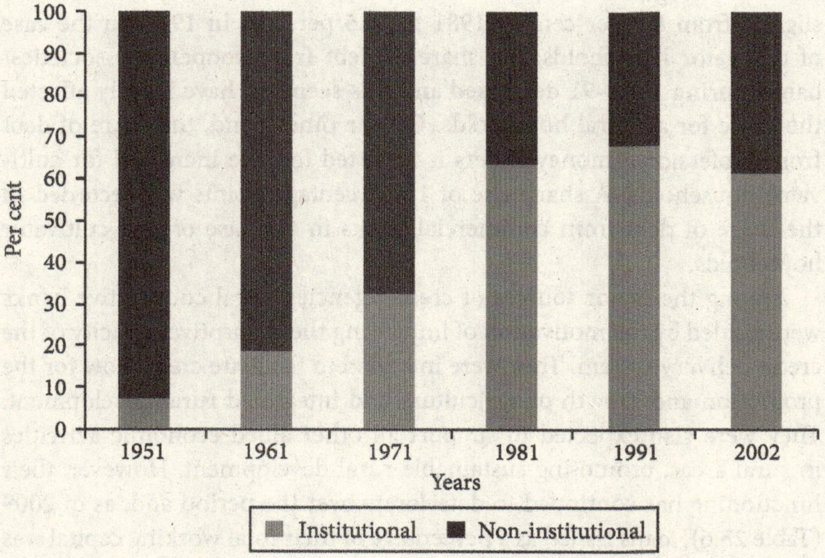

FIGURE 28.1 Percentage Share of Debt of Cultivator Households by Source of Credit in India

Source: Reserve Bank of India bulletin (various years).

A study of the distribution of farm households across states by source of loan (Table 28.4) shows that Andhra Pradesh accounts for the highest number of farmer households indebted to moneylenders (at 57 per cent) followed by Tamil Nadu (at 52 per cent). In states where the dominance of moneylenders is low, traders emerge as a substitute for lending agencies. Traders account for 88 per cent, 51 per cent, 30 per cent, and 70 per cent of the loans contracted in Jammu and Kashmir, Nagaland, Mizoram and Sikkim, respectively. At the all-India level, 29 per cent of farm households were indebted to moneylenders whereas only 27 per cent took loans from banks.

Contextualizing this data with the objectives of both nationalization and liberalization leads one to conclude that those sections of rural India that heavily depend on agriculture for their livelihood remain extremely starved for credit. Moreover, the share of credit from cooperative societies decreased by 7 percentage points to 21.6, during the same period (Table 28.5). This drop was, however, compensated partly by the rise in the share of commercial banks (5.7 percentage points) and partly by direct government interventions (2.1 percentage points). Among non-institutional agencies, the share of debt to professional moneylenders rose slightly from 8.3 per cent in 1981 to 10.5 per cent in 1991. In the case of cultivator households, the share of debt from cooperative societies/banks during 1981–91 decreased and this seems to have mainly affected the share for all rural households. On the other hand, the share of debt from professional moneylenders is reported to have increased for cultivator households. A sharp rise of 10 percentage points was recorded in the share of debt from commercial banks in the case of non-cultivator households.

Among the major sources of credit agencies, rural cooperative banks were guided by the motivation of improving the absorptive capacity of the credit delivery system. They were intended to facilitate credit flow for the promotion and growth of agriculture and integrated rural development. They were also expected to support all other allied economic activities in rural areas, promoting sustainable rural development. However, their functioning has continued to deteriorate over the period and, as of 2009 (Table 28.6), loans issued as a percentage of their total working capital was as low as 6.5 per cent for district cooperative banks and 16.75 per cent for state cooperative banks, for the north-eastern regions of the country. At the all-India level, loans granted by district and state cooperative banks accounted for less than 50 per cent of their total working capital. Punjab, however, was a case where the state cooperative banks issued loans more than their total working capital.

Table 28.4 Number per 100 Distribution of Indebted Farmer Households, by Source of Loans and States, 2003

State	Govt.	Coop society	Bank	Moneylender	Trader	Relatives & Friends	Doctor, Lawyer	Others
Andhra Pradesh	3	20	31	57	9	6	1	4
Arunachal Pradesh	4	0	10	0	33	49	0	21
Assam	3	3	9	10	17	54	1	6
Bihar	2	4	17	44	5	26	2	7
Chhattisgarh	2	37	27	20	17	12	2	5
Gujarat	0	40	23	8	10	29	1	1
Haryana	2	44	30	29	9	9	2	1
Himachal Pradesh	5	24	28	5	22	32	2	4
Jammu & Kashmir	4	1	4	1	88	5	0	0
Jharkhand	6	0	38	22	8	28	1	1
Karnataka	2	23	32	34	5	12	1	3
Kerala	8	46	42	16	6	12	1	5
Madhya Pradesh	4	37	23	22	23	17	2	2
Maharashtra	2	61	29	7	6	11	2	4
Manipur	4	0	2	25	11	57	0	6
Meghalaya	2	0	0	6	0	91	0	0
Mizoram	10	2	21	0	30	37	0	0
Nagaland	4	2	14	0	51	28	0	0

(contd.)

Table 28.4 (*contd.*)

State	Govt.	Coop society	Bank	Moneylender	Trader	Relatives & Friends	Doctor, Lawyer	Others
Odisha	2	30	36	23	4	16	0	3
Punjab	1	38	19	28	18	21	1	2
Rajasthan	2	15	21	40	23	14	2	2
Sikkim	6	0	12	5	70	14	0	2
Tamil Nadu	3	33	23	52	2	11	0	2
Tripura	11	3	32	2	29	20	0	4
Uttar Pradesh	4	13	30	26	9	28	3	4
Uttaranchal	8	17	40	7	5	25	0	7
West Bengal	10	19	22	15	29	23	2	4
Group of UTs	9	15	18	30	9	31	0	1
India	3	26	27	29	12	18	2	3

Source: NSSO (2003).

Table 28.5 Distribution of Cash-debt According to Credit Agencies, 1971–91 (%)

Credit Agency	Rural Households								
	Cultivators			Non-cultivators			All Households		
	1971	1981	1991	1971	1981	1991	1971	1981	1991
Institutional	31.7	63.2	66.3	10.8	36.7	55.3	29.2	61.2	64.0
Government	7.1	3.9	5.7	3.4	4.5	7.6	6.7	4.0	6.1
Cooperative Society	22.0	29.8	23.6	6.0	13.9	14.2	20.1	28.6	21.6
Commercial Banks	2.4	28.8	35.2	0.8	17.3	27.9	2.2	28.0	33.7
Insurance	0.1	0.4	0.2	0.2	–	0.6	0.1	0.3	0.3
Other Institutional Agencies	–	–	1.1	–	–	3.4	–	–	1.6
Non-institutional	68.3	36.8	30.6	89.2	63.3	40.6	70.8	38.8	32.7
Landlord	8.1	3.7	3.7	12.6	8.4	4.9	8.6	4.0	4.0
Agriculturist Moneylender	23.0	8.3	6.8	23.8	11.4	8.2	23.1	8.6	7.1
Professional Moneylender	13.1	7.8	10.7	18.7	13.4	9.8	13.8	8.3	10.5
Trader	8.4	3.1	2.2	10.9	5.8	3.6	8.7	3.4	2.5
Relatives/Friends	13.1	8.7	4.6	19.0	14.4	8.8	13.8	9.0	5.5
Others	2.6	5.2	2.6	4.2	9.9	5.4	2.8	5.5	3.2
Unspecified	–	–	3.1	–	–	4.0	–	–	3.3
Total	100.0	100.0	100.0	100.0	100.0	100.0	100.0	100.0	100.0

Source: RBI bulletin (various issues).

Table 28.6 Loans Issued by State Cooperative and District Cooperative Banks as a Proportion of their Total Working Capital, by Regions, 2009 (%)

Regions	District Cooperative Banks	State Cooperative Banks
Haryana	56.3	81.65
Delhi	N.A.	24.02
Chandigarh	N.A.	2.94
Himachal Pradesh	24.4	21.94
Jammu & Kashmir	10.5	5.26
Punjab	78.4	125.05
Rajasthan	56.9	48.82
North Zone	**58.0**	**69.86**
Arunachal Pradesh	N.A.	0.00
Assam	6.5	35.44
Manipur	N.A.	17.06
Meghalaya	N.A.	6.80
Mizoram	N.A.	13.56
Nagaland	N.A.	16.03
Tripura	N.A.	12.56
North East Zone	**6.5**	**16.75**
Andaman & Nicobar	N.A.	8.05
Bihar	14.1	16.39
Odisha	2.5	45.14
Sikkim	39.6	17.72
West Bengal	35.6	27.99
East Zone	**32.5**	**32.62**
Chhattisgarh	56.4	13.68
Madhya Pradesh	51.4	66.73
Uttar Pradesh	47.1	77.61
Central Zone	**48.5**	**60.14**
Goa	N.A.	47.12
Gujarat	41.0	32.64
Maharashtra	32.9	40.36
West Zone	**34.6**	**39.43**
Andhra Pradesh	32.4	44.21
Karnataka	58.9	52.60
Kerala	71.3	48.70
Puducherry	N.A.	85.40
Tamil Nadu	77.3	47.33
South Zone	**62.4**	**48.72**
Total	**47.8**	**48.97**

Source: Authors' calculations from NABARD data.
Note: N.A. = Not Available

The government of India issued an ordinance and later transformed it into legislation in order to provide support to the rural population that struggles to arrange for minimum start-up capital. This legislation, essentially, led to the formation of RRBs in India. A study of their performance reveals that though there has been an increase in the ground-level credit disbursed by RRBs, they are still outperformed by cooperative banks (Table 28.7). This seems to be a commendable achievement on the part of cooperative banks. It also confirms that the purpose of setting up RRBs remains far from fulfilled. Note that, the general situation in the agricultural sector is likely to affect rural credit alternatives in various ways, which is why the financial inter-linkage can be of significance. On the production side, however, Foster and Rosenzweig (2004) previously argued that whenever there was a productivity increase in Indian agriculture, the consequent higher rural wages discouraged rural industrialization. Thus, the supply side effect could not be compensated by greater demand for local goods through the increased income effect. Currently, the provision of rural employment guarantee schemes for all the states and union territories should also impart an artificial upward pressure on rural wages and affect industrialization. Nevertheless, the increased demand for local goods is strong enough to encourage the setting up of local unorganized industries.

The Rural Unorganized Manufacturing Sector

Not enough studies have been done on the credit options available to the unorganized sector. Unorganized manufacturing enterprises that are located in rural areas produce the same goods as their urban counterparts. In fact, NSSO gives the same industry groups for both the rural and urban enterprises. In earlier attempts, Marjit and Kar (2011) modeled various forms of interactions between the formal and the informal sectors using empirical observations available from NSSO. Amongst other things, they show that informal wage may depend critically on the degree of capital mobility between the formal and informal sectors when there is a greater degree of homogeneity between the goods produced in formal and informal units spread across regions. It also suggests that depending on sectoral complementarity, mobility of capital may raise informal

Table 28.7 State-wise Ground-level Credit (GLC) disbursed by Cooperative and Regional Rural Banks as a Proportion of Total Credit Disbursed by these Institutions for Production (Crop Loan) States, Regions and India (% and Rs lakh)

States/UTs/Region	2008-9		2009-10		2010-11	
	Cooperative Bank	RRB	Cooperative Bank	RRB	Cooperative Bank	RRB
Chandigarh	0.0	0.0	0.0	0.0	0.0	0.0
Delhi	100.0	0.0	100.0	0.0	100.0	0.0
Haryana	74.6	25.4	71.6	28.4	68.7	31.3
Himachal Pradesh	72.3	27.7	77.6	22.4	63.0	37.0
Jammu and Kashmir	40.4	59.6	37.6	62.4	0.9	99.1
Punjab	87.1	12.9	87.6	12.4	84.5	15.5
Rajasthan	56.2	43.8	54.8	45.2	57.7	42.3
Northern Region	**76.2**	**23.8**	**74.6**	**25.4**	**71.7**	**28.3**
Arunachal Pradesh	0.0	100.0	0.0	100.0	5.5	94.5
Assam	2.8	97.2	4.3	95.7	0.5	99.5
Manipur	0.0	100.0	0.0	0.0	100.0	0.0
Meghalaya	25.7	74.3	18.0	82.0	46.1	53.9
Mizoram	15.3	84.7	0.0	100.0	1.9	98.1
Nagaland	69.8	30.2	74.0	26.0	93.1	6.9
Tripura	1.8	98.2	1.8	98.2	1.8	98.2
Sikkim	100.0	0.0	100.0	0.0	100.0	0.0
North eastern region	**6.4**	**93.6**	**8.9**	**91.1**	**7.4**	**92.6**
Bihar	18.7	81.3	17.4	82.6	19.5	80.5
Jharkhand	0.0	100.0	0.0	100.0	0.0	100.0
Odisha	77.2	22.8	83.2	16.8	85.9	14.1

West Bengal	65.9	34.1	70.1	29.9	69.9	30.1
Andaman and Nicobar Islands	69.8	30.2	100.0	0.0	100.0	0.0
Eastern Region	**51.5**	**48.5**	**59.5**	**40.5**	**61.9**	**38.1**
Madhya Pradesh	62.8	37.2	66.6	33.4	69.7	30.3
Chhattisgarh	73.0	27.0	77.7	22.3	74.8	25.2
Uttar Pradesh	28.6	71.4	29.9	70.1	31.5	68.5
Uttarakhand	77.5	22.5	79.9	20.1	85.3	14.7
Central Region	**44.2**	**55.8**	**48.0**	**52.0**	**51.8**	**48.2**
Dadra and Nagar Haveli	0.0	0.0	0.0	0.0	0.0	0.0
Daman and Diu	0.0	0.0	0.0	0.0	0.0	0.0
Gujarat	81.6	18.4	82.0	18.0	81.3	18.7
Goa	100.0	0.0	100.0	0.0	100.0	0.0
Maharashtra	92.8	7.2	93.3	6.7	93.0	7.0
Western Region	**87.2**	**12.8**	**89.0**	**11.0**	**88.7**	**11.3**
Andhra Pradesh	40.9	59.1	51.3	48.7	52.9	47.1
Karnataka	60.1	39.9	53.9	46.1	50.0	50.0
Kerala	68.3	31.7	66.4	33.6	36.0	64.0
Lakshadweep	0.0	0.0	0.0	0.0	0.0	0.0
Puducherry	85.2	14.8	26.6	73.4	14.0	86.0
Tamil Nadu	64.6	35.4	62.4	37.6	56.7	43.3
Southern Region	**58.9**	**41.1**	**58.4**	**41.6**	**50.1**	**49.9**
India	4,023,003	2,241,269	5,694,569	2,980,236	6,452,724.41	3,780,824

Source: NABARD.

wages. Notwithstanding such possibilities, credit scarcity remains a major problem for this sector. The need for larger start-up capital (compared to agriculture) makes this sector more dependent on the vagaries of credit agencies. According to NSSO, in 2005–6, a majority of rural unorganized manufacturing enterprises (42.4 per cent) reported shortage of capital as the most crucial problem. A meagre 3 per cent and 2 per cent rural manufacturing enterprises received institutional and non-institutional loans respectively.

A state-wise analysis of unorganized manufacturing enterprises shows that the proportion of enterprises obtaining institutional loan was the highest in Dadra and Nagar Haveli (23 per cent), and the proportion of enterprises obtaining loans from non-institutional sources was the highest in Puducherry, at 7.3 per cent (Table 28.8). This implies that access to credit is extremely limited for unorganized enterprises in rural areas.

An analysis at the level of each manufacturing industry in each state further shows that the highest amount of loans from moneylenders was taken in Chandigarh, followed by Delhi (Table 28.9). States and union territories, such as Mizoram, Nagaland, Goa, Jharkhand, Sikkim, Daman and Diu, and Dadra and Nagar Haveli did not have predominance of moneylenders. The interesting feature that emerges from this analysis is that the prevalence of typical moneylenders was lower in those states where apart from formal institutions, credit was also available from suppliers or contractors. In such a situation it may be interesting to identify the type of contracts that owners of the enterprises enter into with suppliers and contractors, in view of the high volatility that these units are usually exposed to.

Not surprisingly, therefore, according to the reports of National Commission for Enterprises in the Unorganized Sector (NCEUS 2009) the overall availability of credit to small unorganized enterprises as a percentage of net bank credit (NBC) of SCBs declined from 15.5 per cent in 1996–7 to 6.6 per cent in 2007–8. NCEUS finds that the growth in credit to small-scale industries (SSIs) that includes micro-enterprises or informal sector enterprises has not kept pace with the growth in NBCs. In 2007–8, the share of SSI credit was only 6.6 per cent of NBC compared to 15.2 per cent in 1994–5 (Table 28.10).

Next, we compare the per worker value of total emoluments, outstanding loans, gross value added (GVA), fixed capital, and assets of the organized as well as unorganized manufacturing sectors. Not surprisingly, we observe that the proportion of outstanding loans compared to GVA and the fixed assets of the unorganized sector are much lower than that of

Table 28.8 Number per 1,000 of Rural Enterprises by Source of Loans, by States and All-India, 2005–6

State/Union Territory	Loans		Total estimated no. of enterprises
	Institutional	Non-institutional	
Andhra Pradesh	51	37	1,085,242
Arunachal Pradesh	4	2	541
Assam	4	5	333,006
Bihar	6	4	663,379
Chhattisgarh	15	7	172,610
Delhi	67	18	3,639
Goa	167	19	4,546
Gujarat	26	4	300,753
Haryana	54	11	119,687
Himachal Pradesh	75	11	100,437
Jammu & Kashmir	7	2	140,468
Jharkhand	13	3	540,250
Karnataka	46	25	663,211
Kerala	133	49	492,777
Madhya Pradesh	15	7	564,463
Maharashtra	92	51	556,168
Manipur	11	8	35,797
Meghalaya	0	0	34,513
Mizoram	17	0	3,291
Nagaland	17	34	7,167
Odisha	14	11	870,877
Punjab	27	5	150,208
Rajasthan	28	9	400,875
Sikkim	15	0	3,684
Tamil Nadu	24	45	850,353
Tripura	11	10	38,900
Uttaranchal	60	3	53,940
Uttar Pradesh	15	8	1,704,516
West Bengal	14	20	2,223,768
A & N Islands	82	37	1,872
Chandigarh	95	0	753
D & N Haveli	230	0	797
Daman & Diu	3	0	1,464
Lakshadweep	18	47	255
Puducherry	118	73	4,058
All India	30	19	12,128,266

Source: NSSO (2007b).

Table 28.9 Outstanding Loans per Rural Manufacturing Enterprise on the Date of Survey and Annual Interest Payable per Enterprise by Source Agency of Loan for Each State/UTs (in Rs), 2005–6

State/UT	Central and state-level lending institution		Other institutional agencies		Money-lenders		Business partner		Supplier/ contractor	
	Amount	Interest	Amount	Interest	Amount	Interest	Amount	Interest	Amount	Interest
Andhra Pradesh	853	217	210	28	641	181	510	61	90	11
Arunachal Pradesh	7,391	355	0	0	9	0	0	0	1,715	133
Assam	361	63	104	16	81	88	3	2	15	1
Bihar	120	22	0	0	7	4	0	0	5	3
Chhattisgarh	19,187	2,499	21	3	205	264	769	45	2	0
Delhi	43,765	19,699	18	7	5,897	530	0	0	0	0
Goa	124,854	16,880	4,445	629	0	0	0	0	934	0
Gujarat	833	247	567	645	209	14	254	26	0	0
Haryana	23,003	3,197	2,348	264	4,134	3,479	4,549	503	1,337	60
Himachal Pradesh	5,475	1623	483	127	214	32	205	39	89	7
Jammu & Kashmir	705	95	67	66	0	0	2	1	280	2
Jharkhand	189	26	0	0	0	0	0	0	0	0
Karnataka	1,948	540	109	33	175	63	1	0	9	0
Kerala	12,892	1,615	13,622	838	1,947	485	19	2	301	7
Madhya Pradesh	1,384	476	5	1	147	125	116	8	40	3
Maharashtra	7,449	1,260	319	85	160	80	1,124	124	117	3
Manipur	0	0	4	3	85	51	0	0	0	0
Meghalaya	45	33	4	3	4	3	0	0	0	0

Mizoram	1,567	331	0	0	0	0	0	0	0	0
Nagaland	150	87	0	0	0	0	1	1	229	0
Odisha	571	82	196	24	111	25	0	0	3	0
Punjab	4,055	571	69	44	693	93	262	31	30	1
Rajasthan	2,303	465	671	50	1,953	472	382	34	16	4
Sikkim	2,828	741	0	0	0	0	0	0	0	0
Tamil Nadu	3,016	893	317	166	1,586	416	120	12	33	3
Tripura	963	569	0	0	62	23	29	0	102	0
Uttaranchal	16,337	2,657	0	0	24	7	167	5	0	0
Uttar Pradesh	723	292	2	2	174	87	134	61	88	0
West Bengal	1,611	253	164	9	102	55	47	7	109	17
A & N islands	5,500	543	0	0	235	118	0	0	3	0
Chandigarh	1,909	10,981	0	0	8,219	54,795	0	0	0	0
D & N Haveli	280	83	0	0	0	0	0	0	0	0
Daman & Diu	43	18	0	0	0	0	0	0	0	0
Lakshadweep	105	11	0	0	2,343	844	0	0	0	0
Puducherry	84,404	9,585	18,889	2,351	5,504	852	12	1	487	0
All India	2,654	495	736	82	454	164	220	30	83	6

Source: NSSO (2007b).

Table 28.10 Flow of Credit from Commercial Banks to SSI Sector, 1994–2008

Year	Net Bank Credit (Rs Crore)	Annual Growth (%)	Credit to SSI (Rs Crore)	Annual Growth (%)	SSI credit as % of NBC
1994–5	192,424	–	29,175	–	15.2
1995–6	228,198	18.6	34,246	17.4	15.0
1996–7	245,999	7.8	38,196	11.5	15.5
1997–8	297,265	20.8	45,771	19.8	15.4
1998–9	339,477	14.2	51,679	12.9	15.2
1999–2000	398,205	17.3	57,035	10.4	14.3
2000–1	467,206	17.3	60,141	5.4	12.9
2001–2	535,063	14.5	67,107	11.6	12.5
2002–3	668,576	25.0	64,707	-3.6	9.7
2003–4	664,244	-0.6	71,209	10.0	10.7
2004–5	877,708	32.1	76,592	7.6	8.7
2005–6	1,266,689	44.3	101,285	32.2	8.0
2006–7	1,763,709	39.2	127,323	25.7	7.2
2007–8	2,361,913	39.2	155,804	22.0	6.6

Source: NCEUS (2009).

the organized sector. It also shows that the total emolument per worker is proportionately high for the organized sector (Table 28.11).

One of the interesting results that we come across is that in all the states and union territories the 'ratio of GVA to outstanding loans' as well as 'ratio of fixed assets to outstanding loans' is much higher in the informal sector as compared to the formal sector.[4] Despite the fact that the gross value added and the value of fixed assets are often quite significant in the informal sector (Table 28.12), the existence of such a sector in the grey area between legality and illegality usually hinders free flow of formal capital. If the problem of interpretation that comes with the legal ambivalence of the informal sector can be minimized via appropriate institutional interventions, it may also be possible to use the fixed assets per informal unit as collateral against loans. In fact, for states and union territories, such as Bihar, Jharkhand, Meghalaya, Manipur, Dadra and Nagar Haveli,

[4] In the absence of data on amounts of loans taken, we consider outstanding loans as a proxy for the amount of loans obtained by the enterprises.

Table 28.11 Per Worker Details of Rural Unorganized Sector and Organized Sector, 2005–6

State / UT	Total Emoluments*		Outstanding Loans		GVA		Fixed Capital/Fixed Asset	
	Unorganized	Organized	Unorganized	Organized	Unorganized	Organized	Unorganized	Organized
Andhra Pradesh	3,434	64,341	1,293	341,888	19,540	175,588	17,998	479,734
Arunachal Pradesh	13,995	N.A.	2,471	N.A.	199,637	N.A.	46,361	N.A.
Assam	3,254	55,315	491	258,245	20,341	276,560	12,401	683,445
Bihar	542	51,409	97	688,241	14,882	30,764	13,980	513,791
Chhattisgarh	3,047	171,672	9,742	956,978	18,719	700,127	19,200	1,867,088
Delhi	77,022	127,136	11,581	266,946	4,432,648	274,610	113,879	298,318
Goa	25,604	153,824	45,192	769,611	143,609	973,248	124,249	1,308,519
Gujarat	7,493	113,944	1,180	773,064	46,391	568,555	21,210	1,785,980
Haryana	12,695	118,367	22,154	275,060	73,667	374,605	79,371	605,874
Himachal Pradesh	4,896	121,474	4,982	1,060,384	17,649	1,210,626	47,108	1,947,297
Jammu & Kashmir	3,174	65,621	1,132	271,379	43,907	280,565	35,471	362,363
Jharkhand	1,188	198,748	125	508,594	12,845	967,791	8,543	1,655,050
Karnataka	6,090	112,845	1,265	486,579	33,482	348,158	21,960	876,363
Kerala	12,926	66,150	14,784	135,560	31,360	127,906	46,930	265,816
Madhya Pradesh	2,553	108,824	919	602,728	18,329	344,410	12,345	1,146,271
Maharashtra	8,829	17,212	6,096	721,630	46,895	735,241	36,145	1,159,745
Manipur	3,524	23,414	108	30,969	19,712	52,191	22,174	48,847
Meghalaya	10,843	81,594	73	516,074	36,281	556,108	14,877	892,088

(contd.)

Table 28.11 (*contd.*)

State / UT	Total Emoluments*		Outstanding Loans		GVA		Fixed Capital/Fixed Asset	
	Unorganized	Organized	Unorganized	Organized	Unorganized	Organized	Unorganized	Organized
Mizoram	3,097	N.A.	1,042	N.A.	40,111	N.A.	27,583	N.A.
Nagaland	1,533	33,483	1,122	152,587	34,786	134,868	31,039	118,045
Odisha	1,037	127,377	476	927,352	8,646	437,987	5,471	2,141,695
Punjab	5,146	73,390	3,961	246,105	46,644	150,790	57,405	397,032
Rajasthan	8,476	88,929	3,331	484,314	39,564	284,077	28,357	715,368
Sikkim	8,589	N.A.	1,733	N.A.	55,941	N.A.	40,857	N.A.
Tamil Nadu	8,891	78,357	2,492	354,413	36,482	199,022	33,040	541,468
Tripura	13,896	20,824	402	52,438	27,366	57,718	5,137	70,159
Uttaranchal	10,462	124,927	9,697	374,417	27,265	579,428	48,029	783,538
Uttar Pradesh	3,216	96,999	704	482,457	18,896	260,486	16,331	751,805
West Bengal	3,094	98,800	1,303	620,359	13,965	171,590	1,073	629,964
A & N Islands	18,666	91,844	10,876	1,637,589	49,915	-36,170	58,411	2,590,071
Chandigarh	17,260	166,129	5,232	487,966	70,894	267,787	148,319	553,507
D & N Haveli	16,613	98,727	139	1,073,063	48,507	541,344	38,309	1,310,824
Daman & Diu	32,866	105,844	10	400,933	145,257	700,457	73,911	677,400
Lakshadweep	11,106	N.A.	1,645	N.A.	34,316	N.A.	21,541	N.A.
Puducherry	24,560	115,274	30,160	331,332	326,083	840,490	180,059	705,245

Source: Calculated from NSSO (2007a) and Annual Survey of Industries (ASI) data.

Note: * = Total emoluments are calculated for all workers at the rates obtained by hired workers.

N.A. = Not Available.

Table 28.12 Per Worker Ratio of GVA and Fixed Capital/Fixed Assets to Outstanding Loans for Organized and Unorganized Sector, 2005–6

State / UT	Fixed Capital or Asset/Loans		GVA/Loans	
	Unorganized	Organized	Unorganized	Organized
Andhra Pradesh	13.9	1.4	15.1	0.5
Arunachal Pradesh	18.8	N.A.	80.8	N.A.
Assam	25.2	2.6	41.4	1.1
Bihar	143.6	0.7	152.8	0.0
Chhattisgarh	2.0	2.0	1.9	0.7
Delhi	9.8	1.1	382.8	1.0
Goa	2.7	1.7	3.2	1.3
Gujarat	18.0	2.3	39.3	0.7
Haryana	3.6	2.2	3.3	1.4
Himachal Pradesh	9.5	1.8	3.5	1.1
Jammu & Kashmir	31.3	1.3	38.8	1.0
Jharkhand	68.4	3.3	102.8	1.9
Karnataka	17.4	1.8	26.5	0.7
Kerala	3.2	2.0	2.1	0.9
Madhya Pradesh	13.4	1.9	19.9	0.6
Maharashtra	5.9	1.6	7.7	1.0
Manipur	205.2	1.6	182.4	1.7
Meghalaya	202.8	1.7	494.6	1.1
Mizoram	26.5	N.A.	38.5	N.A.
Nagaland	27.7	0.8	31.0	0.9
Odisha	11.5	2.3	18.2	0.5
Punjab	14.5	1.6	11.8	0.6
Rajasthan	8.5	1.5	11.9	0.6
Sikkim	23.6	N.A.	32.3	N.A.
Tamil Nadu	13.3	1.5	14.6	0.6
Tripura	12.8	1.3	68.0	1.1
Uttaranchal	5.0	2.1	2.8	1.5
Uttar Pradesh	23.2	1.6	26.8	0.5
West Bengal	0.8	1.0	10.7	0.3
A & N Islands	5.4	1.6	4.6	0.0
Chandigarh	28.3	1.1	13.5	0.5
D & N Haveli	275.5	1.2	348.9	0.5
Daman & Diu	7,515.3	1.7	14,769.8	1.7
Lakshadweep	13.1	N.A.	20.9	N.A.
Puducherry	6.0	2.1	10.8	2.5

Source: Calculated from NSSO and ASI data.

and Daman and Diu, fixed assets belonging to informal enterprises seem much better than what is reflected by their realized creditworthiness. The same applies if one analyses the GVA to outstanding loans in such enterprises. Overall, it seems that the problem of interpretation significantly stifles access to credit for rural enterprises located in the informal sphere.

Volatility in the Rural Informal Sector

It has been discussed earlier that the business of lending to rural informal organizations is a high-risk proposition for banks. Uncertainty with regard to income sources of the rural informal sector and evaluating assets remain the foremost predicament for banks. The repayment capacity of rural borrowers, with their irregular and volatile income streams and expenditure patterns is also of serious concern that formal lending agencies cannot ignore. Secondly, the transaction costs of rural lending in a country like India are high, mainly due to small loan sizes, the high frequency of transactions, the large geographical spread, the heterogeneity of borrowers, and widespread illiteracy. Thirdly, collaterals, which rural borrowers lack, usually push them out of the purview of formal lending institutions. Borrowers from the rural informal sector either keep the produced output or their land as collateral. As we have already discussed, the volatility of crops (for cultivators) and manufacturing goods (for owners of small manufacturing enterprises) make these goods unacceptable to banks. Fourthly, the government's policies have worsened the lending conditions facing the banks in general, and in rural areas in particular. High fiscal deficits and statutory pre-emptions imposed on banks crowd-out credit to the private sector. Persistent interest rate restrictions—floors on short-term deposit rates and lending rates, ceiling on small loans, etc., act like an 'implicit tax' on banks (Basu 2006).

From the perspective of the rural poor too, dealing with formal sector banks proves to be immensely complex and problematic. Firstly, rural banks lack the flexibility of providing loans for goods and services that form the consumption basket given the diminutive income and expenditure patterns of small rural borrowers. Secondly, the transaction costs of dealing with formal banks are high. Procedures for opening an account or seeking a loan are cumbersome and costly (with high rejection rates). It is indicated by RFAS (2003) that clients often have to pay hefty bribes (ranging from 10 to 20 per cent of the loan amount) to receive a loan. This makes the ultimate costs to borrowers very high. It takes, on average, 33 weeks for a loan to be approved by a commercial bank. Moreover, the predominance of land as collateral automatically excludes a huge section of tenant and marginal cultivators.

While much has been written about the lack of credit facilities for agriculture in general, the reasons behind the lack of credit offered to the rural manufacturing sector are relatively under-explored. One conjecture, as we have discussed in the preceding sections, is the uncertainty of output and the associated transaction costs which could be an important reason behind the lack of access to credit. What we offer next, therefore, is a brief account of the extent of volatility in rural informal manufacturing organizations in India to identify the reasons behind their lack of access to formal credit. Clearly, this is only one of the possible barriers facing formal financial institutions, the more well-known ones have been studied in substantial detail in various places.

Measuring Income Volatility of Rural Manufacturing Enterprises

To identify what causes banks to consider unorganized manufacturing enterprises as unworthy creditors, we tried to obtain an indicator of volatility of the unorganized manufacturing industries. To this end, we calculated the coefficient of variation in the fixed assets and gross value added (GVA) of unorganized manufacturing industries between 2000–1 and 2005–6. This measure of dispersion helped us in identifying industry groups which have a volatile asset and volatile production base. It is well known that the coefficient of variation measures the extent of variability in relation to the mean of the population. The coefficient of variation is computed only for data measured on a ratio scale, which are measurements that can only take non-negative values.

Table 28.13 shows that across various industry classifications, the degree of volatility is quite high in terms of GVA. Industries, such as cotton ginning, cleaning and baling, publishing, printing and reproduction of recorded media, electrical machinery and apparatus, radio, television and communication equipments, medical precision and optical instruments, motor vehicles, trailers and semi-trailers, and recycling, show

Table 28.13 Measure of Volatility of Fixed Assets and GVA, by Industry

Industry	Coefficient of variation of assets	Coefficient of variation of GVA
Cotton ginning, cleaning and baling	0.19	1.21
Food products and beverages	0.33	0.47
Tobacco products	0.00	0.25
Textiles	0.26	0.50
Wearing apparel, dressing and dyeing of fur	0.17	0.53
Tanning and dressing of leather	0.45	0.71
Wood and of products of wood and cork	0.36	0.10
Paper and paper products	0.42	1.06
Publishing, printing and reproduction of recorded media	0.38	1.07
Coke, refined petroleum products and nuclear fuel	0.58	0.65
Chemicals and chemical products	0.12	0.72
Rubber and plastic products	0.54	0.83
Other non-metallic mineral products	0.04	0.35
Basic metals	0.82	0.85
Fabricated metal products, except machinery and equipment	0.42	0.64
Machinery and equipment N.E.C.	0.44	0.72
Electrical machinery and apparatus N.E.C.	0.23	1.05
Radio, television and communication equipment	0.80	1.32
Medical, precision and optical instruments, watches and clocks	0.80	1.18
Motor vehicles, trailers and semi-trailers	0.30	1.24
Other transport equipment	0.54	0.67
Furniture, Manufacturing N.E.C.	0.42	0.81
Recycling	1.12	1.09

Source: Authors' calculations from NSSO data.
Note: N.E.C. = Not elsewhere classified.

high volatility in their gross value added over the years.[5] On the other hand, industries, such as paper and paper products, tanning and dressing of leather, coke (coal), refined petroleum products and nuclear fuel,

[5] Note that these classifications of rural industries are directly obtained from NSSO surveys of the rural informal manufacturing sector in India.

radio, television and communication equipments, medical precision and optical instruments, and recycling, have high volatility in their fixed asset base. Comparing these with the loans outstanding for each enterprise by source agencies for each industry (see Appendix A28.1), we observe that the industries for which the availability of loans is low are also the ones which have a volatile asset base and are seldom the ones which have a highly volatile GVA. Thus, it seems banks, while lending tend to consider the asset base of these enterprises more important than their GVA. Since in case of informal manufacturing, units banks cannot hold output as collateral they tend to offer loans on the basis of the fixed assets of the units. Therefore, it can be concluded, at least from this exercise, that while volatility of GVA does not significantly explain the lower availability of loans to informal enterprises,[6] the volatility in the asset base may be responsible for the lack of access to formal credit. As the asset bases of rural unorganized manufacturing industries are quite low and volatile at the same time, banks, in turn, do not consider them creditworthy. It seems that in order to help these industries grow, the government may play the role of a guarantor. It involves some risk-sharing arrangements between the banks and the government and may turn out to be a better policy than loan write-offs or subsidies *en masse* that the government often pursues. It certainly requires more efficient and dedicated bureaucratic interference and management, which does not seem a stumbling block, given the vividly laid out rural and panchayat (local self-government) institutions in India. It may also device contracts or schemes specifically for the rural manufacturing sector to supply banks with greater information and hence, greater confidence in the borrowers.

Given the current trend of shifting from agriculture to manufacturing and services, it is also evident that the rural unorganized manufacturing sector forms the spine of the rural economy. In such a situation, the government must facilitate the credit accessibility of these industries from banks and cooperatives.

[6] Here we do not look into the general equilibrium aspects of linkages between rural industries and other sectors such as agriculture. Therefore, we do not delve into the causes of volatility of GVA of the unorganized manufacturing sector and consider the source of volatility to be exogenous.

The Micro-credit Linkage and Concluding Remarks

On the more traditional front, to mitigate some of the persistent obstructions in accessing credit in rural India, the role of micro-credit or the system of peer-group lending seems to be a convenient way to nullify the problem of moral hazard pertaining to individual creditworthiness of the rural people. Therefore, it is no surprise that in the absence of dedicated information, historically, micro-credit became an important avenue through which the government tried to provide easy credit to the rural poor. In the event of withdrawal of formal banks from rural areas, the link between banks and SHGs ensures some relief in terms of access to cheap credit. The increased financial alienation of the rural poor and its consequent effect on poverty and inequality led the government to launch a pilot programme by NABARD in 1992, in an endeavour to increase the outreach of formal lending institutions, by linking 255 SHGs with commercial banks. Apart from direct institutional loans provided to the unorganized sector, micro-credit entails a flow of indirect credit that is made available to unorganized sector enterprises (NCEUS 2009). Micro-credit is mainly disbursed through two different sources, first through the SHG bank Linkage Programme and the second through micro-finance institutions (MFIs) (Table 28.14).[7] While over 84 per cent of the micro-credit is through SHG-bank linkages, the remaining 16 per cent is routed through MFIs (NCEUS 2009). Therefore, officially micro-credit remains an important linkage between formal sources of loans and the unorganized sector.[8] However, data on micro-credit, other than that provided by

[7] The government also started the Swarnajayanti Gram Swarojgar Yojana in the SHG method in April 1999. Under this scheme, credit is provided to SHGs formed by the rural poor to establish micro-enterprises (GoI 2008).

[8] Note that, micro-credit is often used for personal consumption rather than production. See Coleman (1999), Kaboski and Townsend (2005), McKernan (2002), Pitt et al. (2003), and Pitt and Khandker (1998) for developing countries in general. These studies focus on micro *entrepreneurial* credit rather than on consumer credit. However, it appears that there are strong overlaps between small, closely-held businesses and the households that run them. This gives rise to the possibility that micro-entrepreneurial loans are often used for consumption smoothing (Morduch 1998, 1999).

official sources, remains scarce and erratic. Nonetheless, almost all sources agree to an increase in share of micro-finance over the last two decades. Presently, we do not have the scope to discuss the role of micro-credit in much detail.

Table 28.14 Number of SHGs Financed by Banks and the Amount of Loan Disbursed under the SHG-bank Linkage Programme (Number and Rs crore)

Years	No. of SHGs financed by banks	Bank Loan
1992–3	255	0.29
1993–4	365	0.36
1994–5	1,502	1.79
1995–6	2,635	3.62
1996–7	3,841	5.78
1997–8	5,719	11.92
1998–9	18,678	33.31
1999–2000	81,780	135.91
2000–1	149,050	287.89
2001–2	197,653	545.47
2002–3	255,882	1,022.33
2003–4	361,731	1,355.53
2004–5	539,365	2,994.26
2005–6	620,109	4,499
2006–7	1,105,749	6,570
2007–8	1,227,770	8,849.26
2008–9	1,609,586	12,253.51
2009–10	1,586,822	14,453.30
2010–11	1,196,134	14,547.73

Source: NABARD.

In spite of the fact that SHGs helped credit outreach to the rural poor extensively and helped ensure more stable businesses and livelihoods, the performance of SHGs remains a moot subject. The existence of private players who provides micro-credit apart from commercial banks is often reported to have led to the exploitation of SHGs' members by charging usurious rates of interest. In fact, studies on the performance of micro-finance remain diverse. Some have cited equity, outreach, and good recovery rate as the major affirmative aspects of SHGs, whereas several others indicate the exploitative effects of usurious rates of interest that they charge.

It should be remembered, however, that micro-credit through SHGs does not automatically address the problems of enforcement and collateral directly. The success of micro-credit depends heavily on the monitoring pressure from the peer groups, which often fails to act as a perfect substitute for the collateral against group loans. It nevertheless, lowers the burden of moral hazard quite successfully as has been epitomized by the success of Grameen Bank in Bangladesh. On the same note, the functioning of micro-credit as the most vibrant link between formal credit and rural unorganized industries may suffer from institutional inefficiencies, whereby the credit disbursement mechanism may itself be faulty and biased. In a well-known study for the Philippines, Ashraf et al. (2006) show that micro-finance was targeted only at the already established units, neglecting the prospective businesses completely in the process. Consequently, these units got access to more capital, made more profits, and even laid-off the relatives and dependents who they had initially considered as their social responsibility.

The present chapter, therefore, discussed many such findings and tried to delineate the linkage between the rural unorganized sector and the sources of formal finance. We also offered a cross-industry study of the degree of volatility faced by rural unorganized firms and how that might affect access to finance. Interestingly, the volatility of the asset base in the rural unorganized sector appears to be a major stumbling block as to why formal lending agencies do not find them attractive. In this regard, we wish to reiterate that for developing countries like India, there is a long-standing problem of the enforcement of property and legal rights, which has a strong bearing on the functioning of businesses and entrepreneurship and consequently on access to credit and formal linkages. The not-so-unusual business, bureaucracy, and corruption nexus often helps to bypass the problems of rights and enforcement in poor countries via use of money or power. However, the general condition remains worrisome. It is hard to see how the economic environment of a country can continue to remain de-linked from pressing aspects in legality and governance, which seem to be at the core of the formal–informal argument critically influencing the observed production organization associated with it. These highlight some of the directions in which this debate may enrich itself for developing countries in general.

Appendix A28.1

Table A28.1 Outstanding Loan per Enterprise on Date of Survey by Source Agency of Loan for Each Industry, Rural India, 2005–6 (in Rs)

Industry	Central and state-level lending institution	Other institutional agencies	Moneylenders	Business partner	Supplier/ Contractor	Friends and Relatives	Others	Total
Cotton ginning, cleaning and baling	7915	0	954	91	2162	760	0	11882
Food products and beverages	4664	3387	821	349	182	583	334	10320
Tobacco products	20	0	22	0	2	1	1	47
Textiles	2046	57	315	2	83	228	32	2763
Wearing apparel, dressing and dyeing of fur	457	81	92	10	9	97	2	749
Tanning and dressing of leather	2075	0	1012	0	44	55	40	3225
Wood and of products of wood and cork	499	76	182	18	29	83	16	903
Paper and paper products	3734	29	212	3245	36	1038	1	8296
Publishing, printing and reproduction of recorded media	14439	827	3111	553	9	2156	333	21428
Coke, refined petroleum products and nuclear fuel	69918	0	2191	0	0	115	9751	81974
Chemicals and chemical products	5029	1177	654	21	250	1505	212	8848

(contd.)

Table A28.1 (*contd.*)

Industry	Central and state-level lending institution	Other institutional agencies	Moneylenders	Business partner	Supplier/ Contractor	Friends and Relatives	Others	Total
Rubber and plastic products	68530	12801	4927	9818	1411	23352	457	121296
Other non-metallic mineral products	6432	1044	2389	826	83	830	610	12214
Basic metals	221303	5287	13829	8373	5768	5808	2121	262489
Fabricated metal products, except machinery and equipment	5168	210	387	12	48	559	24	6407
Machinery and equipment N.E.C	3544	324	601	1153	500	3479	271	9873
Electrical machinery and apparatus N.E.C	14310	220	794	11850	756	778	401	29110
Radio, television and communication equipment	406133	0	11743	0	0	2	0	417878
Medical, precision and optical instruments, watches and clocks	157052	455	1374	0	3195	15338	75	177488
Motor vehicles, trailers and semi-trailers	81394	1800	5809	0	0	6828	0	95832
Other transport equipment	7443	7	889	0	8	1847	370	10563
Furniture, Manufacturing N.E.C	3154	88	842	28	98	540	102	4852
Recycling	6460	0	2798	0	0	390	0	9647

Source: NSSO.

Appendix A28.2

The definition of factories in Factories Act, 1948, is as follows (also adopted by NSSO):

2m(i) and 2m(ii) of Factories Act, 1948 describe a 'factory' as any premises including the precincts thereof

(i) whereon ten or more workers are working, or were working on any day of the preceding twelve months, and in any part of which a manufacturing process is being carried on with the aid of power, or is ordinarily so carried on, or

(ii) whereon twenty or more workers are working, or were working on any day of the preceding twelve months, and in any part of which a manufacturing process is being carried on without the aid of power, or is ordinarily so carried on, but does not include a mine subject to the operation of the Mines Act, 1952 (35 of 1952), or a mobile unit belonging to the armed forces of the Union, a railway running shed or a hotel, restaurant or eating place.

References

Ashraf, N., D. Karlan, and W. Yin (2006), 'Tying Odysseus to the Mast: Evidence from a Commitment Savings Product in the Philippines', *Quarterly Journal of Economics*, 121(2): 635–72.

Banerjee, A. and A. Newman (1993), 'Occupational Choice and the Process of Development', *Journal of Political Economy*, 101: 274–98.

Basu, K. (1997), *Analytical Development Economics: The Less Developed Economy Revisited*. New Delhi: Oxford University Press.

Basu, P. (2006), 'Improving Access to Finance for India's Rural Poor', Report No. 36448. Washington, DC: The World Bank.

Burgess, R. and R. Pande (2004), 'Can Rural Banks Reduce Poverty? Evidence from the Indian Social Banking Experiment', *American Economic Review*, 95: 780–95.

Burgess, R., R. Pande, and G. Wong (2005), 'Banking for the Poor: Evidence from India', *Journal of the European Economic Association*, 3(2–3): 268–78.

Chavan, P. (2005), 'How "Inclusive" Are Banks under Financial Liberalisation?', *Economic and Political Weekly*, XL(43): 4647–9.

Coleman, B. (1999), 'The Impact of Group Lending in Northeast Thailand', *Journal of Development Economics*, 45: 105–41.

EPW Research Foundation (2007), 'Rural Credit Structure Needs Genuine Revitalisation', *Economic and Political Weekly*, 42(20): 1802–08.

Foster, A. and M.R. Rosenzweig, (2004), 'Agricultural Productivity Growth, Rural Economic Diversity, and Economic Reforms: India, 1970–2000', *Economic Development and Cultural Change*, 52: 509–42.

Government of India (2008), *A Report on the Success and Failure of SHG's in India—Impediments and Paradigm of Success*. New Delhi: Planning Commission, Government of India.

Jagan Mohan, V. (2004), 'Regional Rural Banks (RRBs): The Vehicles for Bridging the Banking Divide', *State Bank of India Monthly Review*, XLIII: 21–41.

Jeromi, P.D. (2007), 'Regulation of Informal Financial Institutions: A Study of Money Lenders in Kerala', *Reserve Bank of India Occasional Papers*, 28(1). Available online at http://rbidocs.rbi.org.in/rdocs/Publications/PDFs/82931.pdf

Kaboski, J. and R. Townsend (2005), 'Policies and Impact: An Analysis of Village-Level Microfinance Institutions', *Journal of the European Economic Association*, 3(1): 1–50.

Marjit, S. and S. Kar (2011), *The Outsiders: Economic Reforms and Informal Labor in a Developing Country*. New Delhi: Oxford University Press.

McKernan, S.M. (2002), 'The Impact of Microcredit Programs on Self-Employment Profits: Do Non-credit Program Aspects Matter?' *Review of Economics and Statistics*, 84(1): 93-115.

Morduch, J. (1998), 'Does Microfinance Really Help the Poor? New Evidence on Flagship Programs in Bangladesh', MacArthur Foundation project on inequality, Princeton University, draft.

——— (1999), 'The Microfinance Promise', *Journal of Economic Literature*, 36: 1569–614.

Nair, T. (2000), 'Rural Financial Intermediation and Commercial Banks: Review of Recent Trends', *Economic and Political Weekly*, 35(5): 299–306.

National Bank for Agricultural and Rural Development (2002–3), *Annual Report*. Mumbai.

National Commission for Enterprises in the Unorganised Sector (2009), *The Challenge of Employment in India—An Informal Economy Perspective*. New Delhi: Government of India.

National Sample Survey Office (1991), *All India Debt and Investment Survey*. Mumbai: NSSO.

——— (2002), *All India Debt and Investment Survey*. Mumbai: NSSO.

——— (2007a), 'Unorganised Manufacturing Sector in India: Input, Output and Value Added 2005–6', 62nd Round, Report No. 526(62/2.2/3). Mumbai: NSSO.

——— (2007b), 'Operational Characteristics of Unorganised Manufacturing Enterprises in India 2005–6', 62nd Round, Report No. 524(62/2.2/1). Mumbai: NSSO.

Pitt, M. and S. Khandker (1998), 'The Impact of Group-Based Credit Programs on Poor Households in Bangladesh: Does the Gender of Participants Matter?', *Journal of Political Economy*, 106(5): 958–96.

Pitt, M., S. Khandker, O. Haider Chowdhury, and D. Millimet (2003), 'Credit Programs for the Poor and the Health Status of Children in Rural Bangladesh', *International Economic Review*, 44(1): 87–118.

Ray, D. (1998), *Development Economics*. New Jersey: Princeton University Press.

Reserve Bank of India (2006), *Annual Policy Statement for the year 2006–7*. Mumbai: RBI.

———(2012), *Database of the Indian Economy*. Available at: http://dbie.rbi.org.in/DBIE/dbie.rbi?site=home (accessed in August 2012).

Rural Financial Access Survey (2003), Published by National Council of Applied Economic Research (NCAER), India.

Sinha, A. (1976), 'Moneylenders' Reign of Terror', *Economic and Political Weekly*, 11(3): 53.

PART VIII

FACTORS: TECHNOLOGY, LABOUR, AND FINANCE

CHAPTER 29

INNOVATION AND DEVELOPMENT IN INDIA

changing paradigms and trajectories

K.J. JOSEPH AND

KIRAN KUMAR KAKARLAPUDI*

India has the distinction of being one of the pioneering developing countries that explicitly recognized science, technology, and innovation as a key factor in development. In fact, even before Independence, there existed an active discourse on the adverse effect of colonialism and colonial science on nation building and the role of modern science and technology and self reliance therein for the development of the country (Krishna 2013).[1] No

*An earlier version of this chapter was delivered as the valedictory address by the first author in an international conference on Developments and Innovation in Emerging Economies, organized by Centre for Development Economics and Innovation, Punjabi University, Patiala on 16–18 November 2012. We are thankful to the conference participants, especially Lakhwinder Singh and Rajeswari Raina for their feedback. We have also benefited from the comments from an anonymous referee and helpful comments by Ashima Goyal. The usual disclaimers apply.

[1] The discourse was spearheaded mainly in *Science and Culture*, an Indian journal published during 1938–47 and dealt with science and technology, which was edited by Professor M.N. Saha, an eminent Indian physicists and the founder of Saha Institute of Nuclear Physics, Kolkata.

wonder, in India's development planning led by the first Prime Minister Jawaharlal Nehru, who believed that science alone could solve the problems of hunger and poverty, insanitation and illiteracy, superstition, deadening custom and tradition, and vast resources running waste of a rich country inhabited by starving people, the prime of place was assigned to science and technology.

Each technological paradigm or outlook defines the trajectory or the normal problem-solving activity (Dosi 1982). One aspect of natural trajectories, whether specific to a particular technology or more general, whether nineteenth century or contemporary, Nelson (1993) observed, is certain underlying knowledge. The science and technology paradigm for India was laid down unambiguously by the Science Policy Resolution (SPR) passed by the Indian Parliament in 1958 which underlined the need for pursuing self reliance in technology when it stated 'in industrializing a country heavy price has to be paid in importing science technology and early and large scale development of science and technology in the country could there for greatly reduced the drain on capital'. Hence, SPR aimed to 'foster, promote, and sustain, by all appropriate means, the cultivation of science and scientific research in all its aspects—pure, applied and educational'.

Pursuit of the paradigm of technological self reliance was manifested in different Five-year Plans, especially with the third Plan (1961–6) and the comprehensive science and technology plan (1974–9), for the first time in India, being closely integrated with the Fifth Five-year Plan of the country (Parthasarathi 2007) along with the Science Policy Statement of 1983. The technological paradigm and the trajectory, however, have been subjected to major changes. The observed changes need to be seen in the context of changes in our understanding of the process of technological change and its bearing on growth and development along with the changes that took place in the development strategy followed by the state. This chapter is an attempt at mapping these changes[2] in India against the backdrop of our knowledge base on the role that science, technology, and innovation play in growth and development.

The remainder of this chapter is organized as follows. The next section presents the broad contours of the evolution of changing foundations of the economics of technology. Here we locate major changes in the way

[2] See Perez (2009) for an analysis of the bearing of technological revolutions on techno-economic paradigms, the causal mechanisms that bring them about, and their impact on the economy and institutions and their relevance for an economic analysis.

in which economics of technological change and innovation has been viewed in relation to growth and development. Against this background, the next section examines the changes in the S&T paradigm and India's trajectory as evidenced from the organizational architecture and institutional arrangements through a survey of studies, with no claim of being exhaustive. The last section summarizes the major findings and presents the concluding observations.

TECHNOLOGY, INNOVATION, AND CATCHING UP

Though Schumpeter may be considered as having invented what we today call economics of innovation,[3] economics of technological change is said to have emerged as an offshoot of the 'search for the residual'.[4] While Schumpeter was concerned with a broader issue of understanding the dynamics of capitalist development, scholars searching for the residual took up a rather narrow issue (why growth rates differ?) and therefore their concern was more with R&D and growth.[5] The search for the residual in the neo-classical tradition considered technology as exogenous to the system and involving the linear process of invention, innovation, and diffusion. The burgeoning literature that emerged as a distinct area of enquiry at the crossing of the economics of growth, industrial organization, regional economics, and the theory of the firm, has become a well-identified area of competence in economics specializing not only on the analysis of the effects of the introduction of new technologies, but also in understanding the process of technological change (Antonelli 2007).

We can locate six different heuristic paradigms that evolved with varying focus. The central concern of the first four (classical legacies, the Schumpeterian paradigm, Arrovian legacy, and endogenous growth models) to great extent was on understanding growth in developed

[3] Please note that for Schumpeter, innovation is a broader process involving a new product, new process, new market, new organization, and others.

[4] As is well-known, Solow (1957) found that only around 12.5 per cent of the observed growth of labour productivity in the US economy during 1911–56 could be explained by increments in the stock of capital, the remaining 87.5 per cent being a 'residual' accounted for by 'technological change'.

[5] For an exhaustive survey of studies, readers are referred to Stoneman (1995).

countries and that of the last two (technological capability approach and National Innovation System approach) was on development with much relevance to developing countries. Hence the latter two have been dealt with in some detail in this chapter.

Smith and Marx's heritage made significant contributions towards understanding the contribution of technological change to economic growth, mainly at the aggregate level. The demand-pull hypothesis building up on Smith and induced approach to technological change building on Marx and the role of learning constitute the core contributions of this line of analysis (Antonelli 2007). The Schumpeterian legacy led to the exploration of the relationship between innovation and competition with important implications for the theory of the firm and the theory of the markets. Pioneering contributions by Arrow led to an analysis of knowledge as an economic product, characterized by non-appropriability, non-excludability, non-rivalry, and non-divisibility (Arrow 1962a). Arrow (1962a), while being in agreement with the neo-classical view of the production function as an expression of technological knowledge, opened a new field of inquiry when he stated that all that has to be added is the obvious fact that knowledge is growing in time. He concluded that the aggregate amount of investment under the competitive model will fall short of the socially optimum level. Building on Arrow's contribution, the late 1980s saw the emergence of endogenous growth models pioneered by Romer (1986) and Lucas (1988) and subsequent developments therein highlighting the role of human capital, technology spillovers, and other factors.

Technology, Innovation, and Developing Countries

In the context of developing countries, the 1970s witnessed a discourse on the choice of technique, broadly within the neo-classical framework, suggesting that the pattern of technological choice is to be governed by relative factor prices. This also implied that for developing countries, the key issue is one of choice and not of developing technology as the required technologies are available from the international technology shelf.

The 1970s also witnessed the drafting of a the Sussex manifesto (Singer et al. 1970) which underlined the need for bringing technology generation at the centre of the development discourse and called for redirecting science and technology to meet the needs of low income countries. Its main proposition was that developing countries that accounted for only about 10 per cent of global R&D should have their own scientific and technological capability both for increasing production and for improving the capacity to produce. Apart from calling for greater access to developing countries for technologies from advanced countries by establishing an international technology transfer bank, the manifesto also required the developing countries to raise their own R&D expenditure to 0.5 per cent of GDP. Although the manifesto was not accepted by its UN sponsors, it turned out to be a highly influential document among policymakers in developing countries like India and induced the developing countries to allocate greater resources for R&D.

Technological Capability-building in Developing Countries

In the context of a growing interest in bringing about technological change by developing countries, there has been a growing body of literature that has dealt with the technological capability-building process in the newly industrializing countries (NICs) (Bell and Pavitt 1992, 1997; Bell et al. 1982; Cooper 1980; Dahlman 1984; Dahlman and Westphal 1982; Enos 1982; Fransman 1986; Katz 1984; Kumar and Siddharthan 1997; Lall 1982, 1987; Patel 1995; Subrahmanian 1995). These studies, by analysing the 'inducement mechanisms and focusing devices' along with the process involved and the outcomes of innovation in the NICs, have thrown up significant insights that are highly relevant even today.

Literature on technological capability in NICs have highlighted that the inducement for innovation has been the need for generating basic production capabilities wherein 'know how' rather than 'know why' has been the focal point.[6] Yet there are a number of instances wherein countries have successfully developed both. Kim (1980), for example, captured in a 3-stage process of mastery of technology—imitation, assimilation, and improvement. Katz (1984) showed that innovation follows a sequence of simple to more difficult activities—product design engineering, process engineering, and production planning engineering. There is also evidence to show that government policies acted as a major source of inducement in promoting the innovation process and capability-building, especially in the first phase (imitation) of technological mastery (Kim 1980). Other studies have also

[6] While the former is the capability of operating or imitating the production of a particular machine, the latter involved knowledge of the underlying scientific and design principles.

highlighted the importance of government policies by providing a stable and large demand along with easy credit, R&D subsidy, among others, and helping acquisition of technology (Enos 1982; Fransman 1986; Kumar 1998; Patel 1995; Subrahmanian 1995, among others).

Studies on technological capability in NICs also highlighted two different, but inter-related, processes involved in technological capability building (Katrak 1994, 1997). The first one related to the transfer of technology—mediated by the market with an active role for foreign firms (for example, technology licensing) and non-market mediated means and with a passive role for the foreign firms (for example, imitation) from developed countries (Dahlman and Westpal 1982). As Freeman (1986) has pointed out, technological knowledge, because of its complexity, cannot be transferred in its entirety. The result is that the purchaser of technology always receives a less complete information set than what is possessed by the seller. This forces technology importing countries to develop local technological capability through an R&D effort. Moreover, since the technology imported has been generated in the developed economy context the effective use of technology transferred calls for adaptations to suit local conditions like scaling down (Katrak 1985) and unavailability of the needed raw materials and spares (Desai 1984; Katz 1980; Page Jr 1979) or the need to diversify the products and to increase capacity utilization. The second process in technological capability-building, therefore, involved domestic R&D effort, mostly adaptive, by developing countries.

These adaptive R&D efforts by firms, along with interactions, though limited, with other actors like universities and R&D laboratories, resulted in innovations specific to developing countries. These innovations, following Freeman (1986) have been in the nature of incremental improvements in products and processes in contrast to radical innovations which were noticed often. The underlying processes that facilitated such innovations included learning by doing, using and interaction (Jensen et al. 2005) along with promotion of R&D and creating access to explicit codified knowledge. Though incremental in nature, as a result of their cumulative effect some of the NICs have built up significant capabilities and even emerged as technology exporters (Lall 1980, 1981, 1983, 1992).

National Innovation Systems Approach

The decade of the 1980s also witnessed the emergence of the National Innovation Systems approach towards understanding innovation and technological change. By the late 1980s, disenchanted with the neo-classical paradigm[7] and building on the work of List (1841)[8] and Freeman (1987), and drawing from the theoretical insights from evolutionary theory (Nelson and Winter 1982) and institutional economics, Lundvall (1992) and Nelson (1993) evolved the concept of National Innovation System (NIS). These scholars went beyond the narrow confines of product and process innovation and considered innovation as an interactive learning process involving different actors in an evolutionary manner, emphasizing the inter-dependence and non-linearity wherein institutions played the central role (Edquist 1997; Joseph 2006).[9] Literature got further enriched by the subsequent developments focusing on systems of innovation at regional (Asheim and Gertler 2004), local (Lastres and Cassiolato 2005), sectoral (Malerba 2004), and technological (Carlsson and Stankiewitz 1995) levels.

NIS can be viewed both from a narrow and a broader perspective. From a narrow perspective (or the science, technology, innovation mode), in tune with the earlier analyses of national science systems and national technology policies (Mowery and Oxley 1995; Nelson 1993), NIS aimed at mapping indicators of national specialization and performance with respect to innovation and R&D efforts by science and technology (S&T) organizations. The policy issues raised were almost exclusively in the realm of explicit S&T policy focusing on R&D. But the broader approach to NIS, which is of much relevance to developing countries, takes into account social institutions, macroeconomic regulations, financial systems, education and communication infrastructures, and market conditions, as far as these have an impact on learning, innovation, and competence-building systems and process (Gu and Lundvall 2006). An important contribution of the concept is towards building a powerful bridge between development economics and innovation studies in contrast to the endogenous

[7] As noted by Lundvall (2007a), the most important weakness of neo-classical theory is not that it is too abstract. *It is rather that it makes the wrong abstractions.* In a context where knowledge is the most important resource and learning the most important process, neo-classical theory tends to abstract from the very processes that make a difference in terms of the economic performance of firms and for the wealth of nations (Lundvall 2007b: 21).

[8] Here it may be noted that the central concern of the List was how to achieve catch up of a less developed country (Germany at that time) with a developed country (England).

[9] For a growing number of studies on innovation systems readers are referred to papers presented in 10 Globelics conferences available at www.globelics.org (accessed on 4 May 2013).

growth models that linked technology and economic growth. Conceptual advancements in terms of *regional/local innovation systems* in which the boundary is the region, *technological systems*, in which the focus is on technologies, and sectoral systems of innovation have contributed towards strengthening this bridge. Using bibliometric evidence, Fagerberg and Sapprasert (2011) have shown that by now NIS literature has emerged as the most important work on innovation published during the last two decades which coincided with an upturn in scholarly interest in innovation and development. However, the conceptual origins of NIS are based on empirical evidence from developed countries wherein the concept was used to describe, analyse, and compare relatively strong and diversified systems with well developed institutional and infrastructure support (see Lundvall 2002 and Arocena and Sutz 2000). But in the case of developing countries not only the institutional context but also the nature of innovations is significantly at variance with developed countries. However, there have been a number of attempts to characterize innovation systems in developing countries (Gu 1999; Intarakamnerd et al. 2002; Razavi and Maleki 2004; Lundvall 2002; Joseph 2006; Arocena and Sutz 2000; Srinivasan and Sutz 2008 to list a few). In a careful review of such studies, Razavi and Maleki (2004) find two sets of studies on NIS in developing countries. The first group of studies have suggested important revisions to the concept of NIS for its application in developing countries (Edquist 1997; Mathews 2001; Viotti 2001) and called for new a terminology as an alternative to the NIS concept that was being used for rich countries. A second group of authors basically took its applicability to developing countries for granted and preferred to deploy the concept of NIS for both developed and developing countries (Alcorta and Peres 1998; Radosevic 1999). Joseph (2006) argued that not only the context, wherein developing countries innovate today, but also the content of innovations is different from the earlier catch-up episodes and called for evolving a southern perspective within the NIS framework. In a similar vein, Arocena and Sutz (2000) point out that industrial innovation in developing countries is highly informal and Srinivasan and Sutz (2008) have made a case for a scarcity-induced innovation framework in developing countries. While considering the relevance of NIS and addressing issues in developing countries the latest development has been an attempt at exploring the link between innovation, poverty, and inequality (Cozzens and Kaplinski 2009). Broadly the attempt is to build bridges between human development in general and specifically with capabilities and freedoms as articulated by Amartya Sen (Lundvall et al. 2009; Capriati 2013). The new direction needs to be seen in the context of higher growth in some of the developing countries coinciding with accentuating poverty and inequality and heightened concern with inclusive development. These explorations have led to studies on systems of innovation for inclusive development and factors and forces that give rise to varied spaces of exclusion and policy options in addressing them (Arocena and Sutz 2012; Das 2010; Joseph 2012; Raina 2012).[10]

Changing Paradigms and Trajectories: Evidence from India

The discussion in the previous section highlighted the broad contours of changing paradigms in the economics of innovation. In the light of this discussion, this section seeks to locate the changes in the innovation paradigm as reflected in the policies and major discourses on the issue of harnessing science, technology, and innovation for development in India. To the extent that the issue at hand warrants an evolutionary picture, there is the need for a periodization. A universally acceptable and undisputable periodization, however, is rather difficult as different perodizations are possible depending on the purpose at hand. Nonetheless, even at the risk of inviting controversy, we propose two broad phases in the evolution of the science, technology, and innovation paradigm, and the trajectory that emerged. The first phase, covering the period up to 1990, is marked by the pursuit of self reliance orchestrated by the state and with limited play of market forces. The second phase, covering the last two decades, has been marked by a process of a globally integrated innovation process.

Phase 1: Pursuit of Self Reliance, as Orchestrated by the State

As noted earlier, the Science Policy Resolution (SPR) of 1958 was at the core of the science, technology, and innovation paradigm in India at least

[10] Readers are referred to, among others, studies undertaken at the instance of IDRC sponsored China–India joint research project on Systems of Innovation for Inclusive Development available at http://www.siid.org.in/ (accessed on 4 May 2013).

up to 1990. The paradigm was further articulated in the exclusive science and technology plan coinciding with the Fifth Five-year Plan and the Technology Policy Statement of 1983, with its basic objective of developing indigenous technology and efficient absorption and adaptation of imported technology appropriate to national priorities and resources. These documents are well discussed in literature (for example, Joseph and Abrol 2009). For the present discussion, it is sufficient to say that the paradigm seems to have been influenced by the scientific achievements of erstwhile USSR under central planning, Arrovian legacy, and the Sussex manifesto, along with the studies of technological capability in newly industrializing countries in general and those pertaining to India in particular. Within the technological self reliance paradigm, the trajectory involved attempts towards building up of S&T infrastructure under the public sector, providing access to foreign technology along with domestic R&D efforts to adapt the imported technology to local conditions.

Presumably, under the influence of the Sussex manifesto, there was a marked increase in investment in science and technology as envisaged in the comprehensive science and technology plan. By the end of the Fifth Five-year Plan, Rs 13,800 million was invested against an outlay of Rs 18,500 million—amounting to an almost 4-fold increase in investment in S&T as compared to Rs 3,730 million spend in the Fourth Five-year Plan (1969–74). What is more the outlay for R&D during the last year of the Plan (1978–9) constituted 0.84 per cent of GDP against a target of 0.95 per cent (Parthasarathi 2007).

Towards building the S&T infrastructure, a separate Ministry of Scientific Research and Cultural Affairs, was set up under the Prime Minister. At the instance of this ministry, elaborate scientific and technical infrastructure has been set up over the years under CSIR, ICMR, ICAR, and various government departments like the Department of Atomic Energy, Department of Space, Department of S&T, Defense Research and Development Organization, and others. As Patel (1993: 34) observed 'the maze of institutions for science and technology is an outstanding testimony to the wide spread of the scientific and technology infrastructure. India has no rival in the whole third world for the vastness of infrastructure and even many among the highly development countries could not be able to rival India in the number and the spread of the institutions'. These institutions, apart from their wider contribution in the fields of their specialization, became the largest source of experienced scientists/technologists for in-house R&D activities in the country (Desai 1980).

The policy for foreign technology and capital, which was relatively liberal up to the mid-1960s, became more restrictive from then to the early 1980s, following the recommendation of the Mudaliar Committee on foreign collaborations in 1966. The Foreign Investment Board (FIB) was set up to deal with all cases involving foreign investment of less than Rs 20 million and those within the 40 per cent equity limit.[11] The maximum ceiling for royalty payment was fixed (normally 5 per cent of sales) and duration specified (normally 5 years). In general, foreign collaborations were restricted and FDI was allowed only in core industries where no alternative local technologies were available (Kumar 1987; Pathasarathi 1987). The result has been a marked decline in the reliance on foreign technology—the annual average number of foreign collaborations approved during the early 1970s was less than half of those approved in the early 1960s. More importantly, the number of cases involving foreign equity participation declined sharply from 165 in 1961 to 27 in 1971.

In tune with the generally held practice in other countries (Kumar and Siddharthan 1997), fiscal incentives were offered to promote industrial R&D. As early as in 1974, the government started a scheme of recognizing in-house R&D units of industrial firms. The number of such registered units had increased from 106 in 1973 to over 900 by the early 1980s. These units were given easier access to imported equipments, raw material, and various tax concessions.[12] The various fiscal incentives provided by the state continued in the 1980s and 1990s notwithstanding major changes in government policy approach towards technology development.

The Patent Act of 1970 has been considered as the most innovative initiative in pursuit of indigenous development of technology. Comprehensive and extensive, the Act aimed at protecting the nascent domestic industry and was a role model for many developing countries. The new Patent Act (of 2005) abolished product patents in food, chemicals, and drugs. It also reduced the life of patents from 14 to 5 years from the date of sealing of the patent or 7 years from the date of filing, whichever was earlier. The Act had many other features to facilitate indigenous development of technology like adopting process patenting instead of product patenting in the area of chemicals, powerful compulsory licensing provisions, enabling state intervention in pricing of patented products, and so on.

[11] Collaborations that exceed this limit were to be referred to the cabinet committee on foreign investment.

[12] For example, expenditure incurred on scientific research was 100 per cent deductible from profit for the purpose of income tax calculations.

Subsequent to the Technology Policy Statement of 1983, new initiatives like the Programme Aimed at Technological Self Reliance (PASTER)—now known as the Technology Development and Demonstration Programme (TDDP), the Technology Absorption and Adaptation Scheme, National Register on Foreign Collaboration, Technology Development Fund, Science and Technology Entrepreneurship Parks, jointly with financial institutions, state governments, and academic institutions, and a full-fledged Ministry of Science and Technology, was created in 1985, with the earlier Department of Science and Technology (DST) and a new Department of Scientific and Industrial Research (DSIR) as its constituents (Richardson 2002).

A key element of the trajectory followed in this phase pertains to technology missions, within a sectoral perspective, covering telecom, drinking water, oil seeds, literacy, and others, for promoting technological applications for civilian development and their diffusion in society. Important positive outcomes obtained from these missions in terms of technology development and diffusion in the fields of rural telephone exchanges developed by CDOT, and improvement in literacy targets to the extent of almost 10 per cent, may be considered as examples of what could be achieved through technology missions. Technology missions for societal development were not pursued consistently after 1991 (Joseph and Abrol 2009).

In the context of the trajectory that was manifested in the varied state initiatives involving building organizational and institutional architecture for prompting R&D and facilitating technology import, studies in the Indian context dealt with specific issues like bearing of technology import on domestic R&D, cost of technology import (Kumar 1990; Subrahmanian 1986; Parthsarathi 1987), FDI and technology transfer (Subrahmanian and Pillai 1977; Kumar 1996 for a survey), technological strategies of firms (Basant 1997), and the role of the state in building technological capability (Lall 1992; Siddharthan 1988a, 1988b) in general. Studies on the impact of technology import, either through licensing or FDI on technology capability dealt with two sets of issues. The first one related to the nature of interface between the two and the second dealt with the effect of imported technology on knowledge and productivity spillovers along with export[13] and profitability.

[13] On exports, please see, among others, Agarwal (2002) and on growth, Narayanan (2004).

With respect to the first issue while one set of studies considered technology import and R&D as substitutes, others considered them as complements. Subrahmanian (1991) and Joseph (1995) observed that under regulation, firms build up technological capability by supplementing technology imports with domestic R&D, whereas, in the liberalized context of the 1980s, the tendency was to have continued reliance on imported technology indicating that the technology import and R&D are substitutes. Similar conclusions were drawn by Fikkert (1993), based on an empirical analysis of firm behaviour in terms of in-house R&D and technology import during 1974–5 and 1977–88. The study noted a significant negative relationship between the two and argued that India's restrictive policy towards FDI and technology import had had the desired outcome of promoting domestic R&D.

Scholars like Desai (1980, 1985) and Lall (1983) observed that R&D by Indian firms was by and large adaptive in nature and that unlike goods, import of technology and local R&D were complementary. Desai (1985) made a strong case for shifting emphasis from regulating the import of technology to encouraging the diffusion of all technology—local and foreign—in the country and its translation into greater efficiency and exports. Further, technology imports, apart from their bearing on the market structure, are also influenced by the domestic market structure and called for greater government neutrality as between state-owned and private firms, large and small firms, and efficient and inefficient firms, if imported technology was to be more fully exploited. Empirical investigation by other scholars like Siddharthan (1988a, 1992), Katrak (1985, 1989), Alam (1985), Deolalikar and Evenson (1989), and Agarwal (2000) also confirmed the complementary relationship between technology import and R&D.

However, Kumar (1987) argued that the relationship between the two is greatly influenced by the mode of technology import, apart from other factors. Thus viewed, technology imported through FDI need not necessarily lead to a complementary relation between the two. A similar finding was reported was Lall (1992). Kumar and Saquib (1994), in their analysis of the technology behaviour of firms, observed inter-firm variations in the relationship between technology import and R&D wherein neither complimentarity nor substitutability dominated. Similarly Basant (1997) observed that R&D and foreign technology licensing were neither perfect substitutes nor perfect complements of each other. If the circumstances permitted, a firm may choose one than the other.

Basant and Fikkert (1996) in their analysis of R&D spillovers using panel data for Indian manufacturing firms for 1974–5 to 1981–2 observed a high private rate return to expenditure on both technology purchase and R&D although the effect of the latter was statistically insignificant. Further, the return to technology purchase was higher than that of R&D by 44 per cent. Positive spillovers of foreign R&D have also been reported by Lakhwinder Singh and Evenson (1997). But Evenson and Joseph (1999) observed that while foreign technology licensing has had a positive effect on firm-level profits, such a positive relationship was not observed in the case of exports.

Lall (1992) argued that apart from the domestic technological effort, the extent and nature of a country's reliance on foreign technology was also directly relevant to national technological capability. Further, the development of capabilities was the outcome of a complex interaction of incentive structures with human resources, technological effort, and institutional factors. Partial explanations of national technological capability development, which concentrate exclusively on market-driven incentives, on the one hand, or on capability-building measures, on the other, are apt to be misleading for analytical and policy purposes. Indicating the influence of an innovation system, Lall (1992) argued that it is the interplay of all these factors, in particular, country settings, that determine at the firm level how well producers learn the skills and master the information.

Phase II: Globally Integrated Innovation for International Competitiveness

During the 1990s there was a paradigm shift in technology and innovation involving the harnessing of all possible external sources for stimulating domestic capability-building for fostering an internationally competitive economy. While theoretical support for such a paradigm shift could be discerned from the endogenous growth models and new trade theories, empirical support was provided by the studies highlighting the complementary role of foreign technology in augmenting domestic R&D and spillover benefits associated with foreign technology (Kathuria 2010 among others).

The new trajectory that derived from the new paradigm was marked by free access to foreign technology—both embodied and disembodied—and foreign direct investment—both inward (Kumar 2009) and outward (Pradhan 2005, 2007; Kumar 2007; Lakhwinder Singh and Jain 2009; Hattari and Rajan 2010)—in the production of goods and knowledge (FDI in R&D). The Micro, Small and Medium Enterprise Development

(MSMED) Act of 2006 also made a strong case for external orientation of small firms and enhancing firm competitiveness (Das 2010).

While technology licensing was left to be governed by the commercial considerations of enterprises and regional governments entered into incentive competition for FDI, inflow of FDI as well as technology collaborations increased at an unprecedented rate. Simultaneously, given the larger access to highly skilled manpower and the facilitating policy environment, India emerged as one of the attractive locations for R&D (Basant and Mani 2012). With a view to translating these into domestic technological capability, there was unprecedented focus on revamping the higher education sector, *inter alia*, by increased state investment (with an almost 7-fold increase in the outlay for higher education during Eleventh Five-year Plan) and private sector participation along with a renewed emphasis on academia industry interaction. With the new Patent Act of 2005, the weak patent regime was done away with and was made compliant with World Trade Organization's (WTO's) Agreement on Trade Related Aspects of Intellectual Property Rights (TRIPS) regime.[14] In 2003, the new science and technology policy was announced which underlined the need for infusing new vitality to the S&T system such that it played a central role in raising the quality of life of the people, particularly of the disadvantaged sections of society. The new policy also highlighted the need for being globally competitive, utilizing natural resources in a sustainable manner and in ensuring national security.

With respect to innovation performance under liberalization, while some of the studies have noted evidence suggesting an improvement (Dutz 2007; Office of the Adviser to the Prime Minister 2011; and Mani 2010), the overwhelming evidence tends to suggest that with the adoption of a globally integrated approach towards innovation, domestic innovation capability at the national, regional, and sectoral level has been lagging behind (Krishnan 2010). Moreover, NISTADS (2009) shows that while the actual plan investment in S&T by core central ministries exceeded the outlay in all the Five-year Plans beginning with the Fifth Plan, in case of the Ninth Plan (1997–2002) the actual and outlay just matched where as in Tenth Plan (2002–7) the actual was only a little over 93 per cent of the outlay. R&D expenditure as a per cent of GDP still remained less than one per cent and lagged much behind other emerging countries.

[14] See Abrol (1994a) for a critical appraisal and Sudip Chaudhuri (2005) for a detailed account of pharmaceutical sector under WTO.

For most enterprises in India, the acquisition of global knowledge is found more important for productivity than in the creation of domestic knowledge (Dutz 2007). In the similar vein Mani (2010) argued that domestic enterprises, barring a few notable exceptions, were not innovative and Balakrishnan et al. (2000) did not find any evidence of acceleration at the firm-level productivity in industries with significant tariff reduction during the decade following 1987. Further, much of the innovative activities were contributed by MNCs and the National System of Innovations was dominated by the sectoral innovation system of the pharmaceutical industry (Mani 2006; Mani 2010). With respect to spillovers of technology, Kathuria (2002) observed that only those domestic firms, which invested in R&D to decode the spilled knowledge, could benefit.

While the country emerged as a major player in the export of software services, the diffusion of Information and Communication Technology (ICT) in the domestic sectors remained less impressive and the intra-national digital divide (read as rural–urban divide) in the use of internet and mobiles remained a major challenge (Joseph and Abrol 2009). Moreover, most firms operated in a low-tech environment leading to the domination of low technology goods in the export basket (Kumar and Pradhan 2007). Therefore, despite having technologically sophisticated cities and world-class firms, the economy-wide level of technological achievement remained as much to be desired. Even within sectors, there existed significant inter-firm variations such that there were sectors wherein the most sophisticated firms used technologies and achieved levels of productivity that rivaled world leaders, but a vast majority of the firms operated at levels of productivity that were less than one-fifth those of the top performers (Krishnan 2010; Dutz 2007). No wonder the country has had to live with a near stagnant manufacturing sector and its share in GDP has remained almost flat at around 16 per cent since 1991 (GoI 2012).

When it comes to agriculture, the emerging picture appears more discouraging. Raina (2011) has shown that technological capacities, embodied in the national agricultural research system (NARS) have grown steadily since the mid-1960s, when the state decided that a central line of authority and control was necessary to generate technologies for the Green Revolution. However, during 1990–2009, the formal knowledge-generation (agricultural research) component received less than 0.4 per cent of agricultural GDP, while the subsidy for inputs ranged from 8 to 11 per cent of agricultural GDP (Raina 2012). What is more, the rate of growth of public expenditure in research and education declined from 6.3 per cent during the 1980s to 4.8 per cent during 1990–2005 and that of extension and training declined from 7 per cent to 2 per cent (Balakrishnan 2010). In such a context though the gross input subsidy accounted for 88 per cent of the total Plan outlay for agriculture in 2006–7 (Vaidyanathan 2010), there was significant stagnation in the production of rice-wheat systems—the main users of these inputs thus far (Bhalla and Singh 2010; GoI 2008). With investments in technology and innovations taking a back seat today, agriculture survives on the two key domestic policy planks of output price support and input subsidies (Ray 2007, quoted in Raina 2012). As observed by the Planning Commission (GOI 2008) and Vaidyanathan (2010) among others, notwithstanding an unprecedentedly high GDP growth rate of 7.7 per cent during the Tenth Plan (1992–7), growth of the agricultural sector that accommodated 58 per cent of India's labour force remained almost stagnant at 2.3 per cent (which increased marginally to 3.4 per cent during the first four years of the Twelfth Plan) and the country had to live with the largest number of poor and illiterates in the world.

In a context wherein the manufacturing sector in general and agriculture in particular lagged behind, much of the growth was contributed by the services sector with its implications on employment generation and poverty alleviation. To be more specific, while the share of the services sector increased by about 16 per cent during 1991–2011, its share in employment increased only by about 6 per cent which in turn contributed towards the jobless growth that characterized India's growth during globalization (Kannan and Raveendran 2009; Nagaraj 2000; Neethi 2008; Singh and Singh 2009; Uma et al. 2010).[15] Thus, reflective of Freeman (2011), structural-adjustment-induced growth was characterized by 'crises of structural adjustment' because there was also growing unemployment, a main source of inequality and poverty. Abhijit Sen and Himanshu (2005) have shown that the 1990s was the first post-independent decade when economic inequality increased sharply in all its dimensions and poverty reduction deteriorated markedly. More specifically Himanshu (2007) shows that the rate of decline in poverty during 1993–4 to 2004–5 was at a lower rate than the previous decade of 1983 to 1993–4. Thorat and Dubey (2012), using the latest NSSO Rounds, observe that consumption expenditure was more poverty reducing during 2005–10 with variations

[15] Much of the growth in employment has been accounted by contract workers in the informal sector indicating the inferior quality of employment (Sen and Dasgupta 2006; Uma et al. 2010). In case of the organized sector, wherein the quality of employment is perceived to be better, there has been a marked deceleration in employment growth from 3.44 per cent per annum during 1990–1 to 1996–7 to –0.63 per cent in 1997–8 to 2004–5.

across socio-religious groups. While the higher castes, the Muslims, other religious minorities and the Scheduled Tribes (STs) did better, poverty declined at relatively lower rates in the case of Scheduled Castes (SCs). When it comes to economic groups, self-employed, non-farm households saw a reduction in poverty at a much higher rate as compared to self-employed farmers, and the non-farm and farm wage labourers. Thus viewed, the result of a lopsided and globally integrated innovative effort has been the lopsided growth and the co-evolution of marginalization and inequalities along with higher GDP growth rates.

Innovation and Inclusive Development

Against this background, the catch-up strategy shifted from growth to inclusive growth and the paradigm swung from innovation to inclusive innovation. Coinciding with the declaration of the current decade as the decade of innovation by the President of India, the office of the Advisor to the Prime Minister, drawing insights from the NIS perspective, came up with an insightful strategy paper 'Towards a more innovative and inclusive India: Creating a roadmap for a decade of innovation'. Recognizing the limits of the myopic approach of linking innovation to R&D efforts alone, it involves innovations that go beyond the narrow competitive index, to accelerate growth and to create a more inclusive model of development which is also environmentally sustainable. The new Science, Technology and Innovation Policy (STIP) 2013, a derivative of the roadmap, made a point of departure from the earlier S&T policies when it stated 'Science, technology and *innovation* for the people' as the new paradigm of Indian STI enterprises. The roadmap along with STIP 2013 presents the broad contours of the new inclusive innovation paradigm and the trajectory therein. While the current thinking, as enshrined in these documents, has many attractive features, the present understanding of the problem is far from complete.

The roadmap has an explicit inclusive innovation strategy with a need-based approach towards creating an 'Indian model of development'. In concrete terms, the suggested strategy involves facilitating innovations that lead to frugal cost products and services that are affordable to people at low levels of income. STIP 2013, while translating the roadmap into policy action for inclusive development, calls for 'new structural mechanisms and models to address the pressing challenges of energy and environment, food and nutrition, water and sanitation, habitat, affordable health care and skill building and unemployment'. Towards ensuring access, availability, and affordability of solutions for below the pyramid population it envisages driving investment in science and investment of science-led technology and innovation in select areas of socioeconomic importance. It appears that in STIP 2013, the narrow S&T centralism prevailed over the broader innovation approach of the roadmap. No wonder, the central concern boils down to raising the R&D–GDP ratio to 2 per cent (from 0.8 per cent at present), which the roadmap considered myopic, indeed with innovative initiatives.

The new paradigm conceives inclusive development as provisioning of frugal innovations resulting in the need-based strategy. It fails to acknowledge that millions in the world during the past centuries got elevated out of poverty and deprivation through varied innovations. Strangely enough, for the new paradigm, the learning from these innovations is of little relevance in the Indian context. Hence, the one-third of the world's poor, living in India, are left to destiny until the private sector finds frugal innovations a profitable enterprise. Certainly, as Sen (2000) observes, human beings do have needs and it is good to have them met. But should people be seen only in terms of their needs (something human beings share with other animals)? Since people are the ultimate 'agents' of change, who can think and act, not just as patients who have needs that require catering, we do require a broad enough notion of inclusive development and an inclusive innovation system.

Inclusive innovation needs to be contrasted in terms of its short-term and long-term dimensions. While the need-based approach could at best have some short-term relevance, in the longer term, we need to have a broader perspective wherein there is the need to locate and address the varied spaces of exclusion in the innovation system. Here Sen's taxonomy of social exclusion is especially illuminating. Sen considers four situations: (i) constitutive exclusion happens when being excluded is in itself a deprivation which can be of intrinsic importance on its own; (ii) instrumental exclusion refers to causally significant exclusions that may not be impoverishing by themselves, but can lead to impoverishment of human life through consequences of great instrumental importance; (iii) active exclusion happens when exclusions come about through policies directly aimed at that result; and (iv) passive exclusion is the result of policies that have not been devised to bring about that result nevertheless have such consequences (Sen 2000).

We can also have transient *exclusion versus sustained exclusion*. The often adopted unbalanced development strategies might involve a certain extent of exclusion of some sectors/sections for some time leading to transient exclusion. If the excluded remain as excluded for long we have cases of sustained exclusion which is socially more painful. We could also have *subordinated inclusion and illusive inclusion* depending on how the inclusion takes place and how the returns to inclusion are being distributed (Joseph 2012). Hence, from a long-term perspective, fostering inclusive development involves competence building of people and organizations along with locating spaces of exclusion that are all pervasive.

***

India has the credit of being one of the pioneering developing countries that explicitly recognized science, technology, and innovation as a key factor in development. The outlook towards harnessing science, technology, and innovation for development as well as the trajectory that followed has undergone major changes. This chapter attempted to map the broad contours of the paradigms and trajectories. The inquiry enabled us to locate different heuristic frameworks including the classical legacies of Marx and Smith, the Schumpeterian approach, Arrovian legacy, endogenous growth models, technological capability paradigms, and the National Systems of Innovation approach. Of these the last two are particularly concerned with innovation and development in developing countries.

Broadly we located two phases in the evolution of the science, technology, and innovation paradigm and the trajectory that evolved in India. The first phase, covering the period up to 1990, was marked by the pursuit of self reliance orchestrated by the state and with limited play of market forces. The paradigm and the trajectory were influenced by the scientific achievements of erstwhile USSR under central planning, Arrovian legacy, and the Sussex manifesto along with technological capability paradigms in developing countries. The second phase, covering the last two decades, was marked by a process of innovation by greater integration with the world market under globalization. While theoretical support for the paradigm shift could be discerned from the endogenous growth models and new trade theories, empirical support was provided by the studies highlighting the complementary role of foreign technology in augmenting domestic R&D and other spillover benefits associated with foreign technology.

Within the technological self reliance paradigm, the trajectory involved attempts towards building the S&T infrastructure under the public sector and providing access to foreign technology along with domestic R&D efforts to adapt imported technology to local conditions. The trajectory also involved substantial increase in R&D investments, various initiatives towards local capability building inspired by the Technology Policy Statement of 1983, a unique patent policy, and setting up technology missions within a sectoral perspective covering telecom, drinking water, oil seeds, literacy, and others, for promoting technological applications for civilian development and their diffusion in society. While the outcome of the trajectory followed was not very impressive in terms of economic growth until the 1980s, the country managed to establish a highly diversified industrial sector along with self sufficiency in food production thanks to the state-orchestrated Green Revolution and managed to achieve significant reduction in poverty and inequality.

With the development strategy shifting towards globalization, there arose the new paradigm of globally integrated innovation that involved harnessing all possible external sources for stimulating the domestic capability building process for fostering an internationally competitive economy. The new trajectory involved liberalized access to embodied technology (capital goods) and FDI and technology, increased reliance on mergers and acquisitions, increasing participation in global innovation networks through R&D in FDI, greater reliance on outward FDI, and a new patent policy compliant with WTO's TRIPS regime.

As the paradigm shifted towards globally integrated innovation—like Latin American countries in 1980s—instead of further strengthening the learning, innovation, and competence building systems at the national, regional, and sectoral levels—like East Asian countries—the outcome was less satisfactory. While a few sectors emerged as innovative and competitive and the overall rate of growth of the economy was impressive, the mainstay of the rural economy—the agricultural and manufacturing sectors—lagged behind. Lopsided growth, therefore, resulted in increasing marginalization and growing inequality along with a discouraging performance in poverty reduction.

As the development strategy shifted from growth to inclusive growth, the paradigm shifted from innovation to inclusive innovation. The accompanying trajectory involves creating an institutional architecture at the national, regional, and sectoral levels that is geared towards creating more 'frugal, distributed, affordable, innovation' that produces more 'frugal cost' products and services that are affordable by people at low levels of incomes.

Historically, innovation has been a highly-cherished cheque for the poor as it has helped in improving the living conditions of millions in different parts of the world. At the same time, history abounds with instances, like in India, wherein the cheque repeatedly bounced and that the poor remained as poor. The real culprit was not innovation per se but the institutional (rules, laws, norms, policies a la North 1990) context which gave rise to multiple contexts of exclusion like active, passive, constitutive, and instrumental exclusion (Sen 2000). The unimpressive outcomes in the Indian context, notwithstanding the heightened concern for the poor, needs to be seen in the context wherein the innovation-induced inclusion often turned out to be illusive and at best subordinating which instead of remaining as transient, sustained over time (Joseph 2012). Without addressing the factors that give rise to the genesis and sustenance of such multiple spaces of exclusion, the poor are now offered yet another cheque leaf—frugal or below the pyramid innovation—which if it bounces will not be surprising as the strategy lacks a long-term perspective on the issues involved.

References

Abrol, D. (1994a), 'Technology & WTO' in *New Economic Policy (NEP) and Indian People*, based on Proceedings of the National Seminar on NEP, Jan Vigyan Vedika, Indian Institute of Chemical Technology, Hyderabad, August.

——— (1994b), 'Intellectual Property Rights in the Uruguay Round Negotiations: A Review of the Indian Debate', in K.R.G. Nair and Ashok Kumar (eds), *Intellectual Property Rights*. New Delhi: Allied Publishers.

Agarwal, Aradhna (2000), 'Deregulation, technology imports and in-house R&D efforts: an analysis of the Indian experience', *Research Policy*, 29(9): 1081–93.

——— (2002), 'Liberalisation, Multinational Enterprises and Export Performance: Evidence from Indian Manufacturing', *Journal of Development Studies*, 38(3): 119–37.

Alam, G. (1985), 'India's Technology Policy and Its Influence on Technology Imports and Technology Development', *Economic and Political Weekly*, 20(45/47, Special Number): 2073–80.

Alcorta, L. and W. Peres (1998), 'Innovation systems and technological specialization in Latin America and the Caribbean', *Research Policy*, 26: 857–81.

Antonelli Cristiano (2007), 'The foundations of the economics of innovation', Working paper No. 02/2007, Department of Economics, University of Torino.

Arocena, R. and J. Sutz (2000), 'Looking at National Innovation Systems from the South', *Industry and Innovation*, 7(1): 55–75.

——— (2012) 'Research and innovation policies for social inclusion: an opportunity for developing countries', *Innovation and Development*, 2(1): 147–58.

Arrow, K.J. (1962a), 'Economic Welfare and the Allocation of Resources for Invention', in Universities National Bureau (eds), *The Rate and Direction of Inventive Activity: Economic and Social Factors*. NBER, National Bureau of Economic Research, Cambridge, MA, pp. 609–26.

——— (1962b): 'The Economic Implications of Learning by Doing', *The Review of Economic Studies*, 29(3): 155–73.

Asheim, B. and M. Gertler (2004), 'The Geography of Innovation: regional Innovation Systems', in J. Fagerberg, D. Mowery and R. Nelson (eds), *The Oxford Handbook of Innovation*. Oxford, UK: Oxford University Press, pp. 291–317.

Balakrishnan, P. (2010), *Economic Growth in India: History and Prospects*. New Delhi: Oxford University Press.

Balakrishnan, P., K. Pushpangadan, and M. Suresh Babu (2000), 'Trade Liberalisation and Productivity Growth in Manufacturing: Evidence from Firm-Level Panel Data', *Economic and Political Weekly*, 35(41): 3679–82.

Basant, Rakesh (1997), 'Technology Strategies of Large Enterprises in Indian Industry: Some Explorations', *World Development*, 25(10): 1683–700.

Basant, Rakesh and Brian Fikkert (1996), 'The Effects of R&D, Foreign Technology Purchase, and Domestic and International Spillovers on Productivity in Indian Firms', *The Review of Economics and Statistics*, 78(2): 187–99.

Basant, R. and Sunil Mani (2012), 'Foreign R&D Centres in India: An Analysis of their Size, Structure and Implications', Working Paper No. 2012-01-06. Ahmadabad: Indian Institute of Management.

Beena, P.L. (2008), 'Trends and Perspectives on Corporate Mergers in Contemporary India', *Economic and Political Weekly*, Review of Industry and Management, 43(39): 48–56.

Bell, M. and K. Pavitt (1992), 'Accumulating Technological Capability in Developing Countries', Proceedings of the World Bank Annual Conference on Development Economics, pp. 257–81.

——— (1997), 'Technological Accumulation and Industrial Growth: Contrasts between Developed and Developing Countries', in D. Archibugi and J. Michie (eds), *Technology, Globalisation and Economic Performance*. Cambridge: Cambridge University Press, pp. 83–137.

Bell, M., Scott Kemmis, and W. Satyarakwit (1982), 'Limited Learning in Infant Industry: A Case Study', in F. Stewart and J. James (ed.), *The Economics of New Technology in Developing Countries*. London: Frances Pinter, pp. 138–56.

Bhalla, G.S. and Gurmail Singh (2010), 'Final Report on Planning Commission Project Growth of Indian Agriculture: A District Level Study'. New Delhi: Planning commission. Available at: http://planningcommission.nic.in/reports/sereport/ser/ser_gia2604.pdf (accessed on 19 November 2012).

Capriati, M. (2013), 'Capabilities, Freedoms and Innovations: Exploring Connections', *Innovation and Development*, 3(1): 1–19.

Carlsson, B. and R. Stankiewicz (1995), 'On the nature, function and composition of technological systems', in B. Carlsson (ed.), *Technological Systems and Economic Performance: The Case of Factory Automation*. Dordrecht: Kluwer Academic Publishers, pp. 21–56.

Chaudhuri, Sudip (2005), *The WTO and India's Pharmaceutical Industry*. New Delhi: Oxford.

Cooper, C. (1980), 'Policy Interventions for Technological Innovations in Developing Countries', Staff Working Paper No. 441. Washington, DC: The World Bank.

Cozzens, S. and R. Kaplinsky (2009), 'Innovation, poverty and inequality: cause, coincidence or co-evolution?' In B.-Å. Lundvall, K.J. Joseph, Cristina Chaminade, Jan Vang (eds) *Handbook of Innovation Systems and Developing Countries: Building Domestic Capabilities in a Global Setting*. Cheltenham: Edward Elgar, pp. 57–82.

Dahlman, C.J. (1984), 'Foreign Technology and Indigenous Technological Capability in Brazil', in Martin Fransman and K. King (eds), *Technological capability in the Third World*. London: Macmillan, pp. 317–34.

Dahlman, C. and L. Westpal (1982), 'Technological Effort in Industrial Development: An Interpretive Survey', in F. Stewart and J. James (eds), *The Economics of New Technology in Developing Countries*. London: Frances Pinter, pp. 105–37.

Das, K. (2010), 'Indian Rural Clusters and Innovation: Challenges for Inclusion', SIID Working Paper No. 9. New Delhi: Centre for Policy Research.

Deolalikar, A. and R. Evenson (1989), 'Technology production and technology purchase in Indian industry: an econometric analysis', *Review of Economics and Statistics*, 71(4): 687–92.

Desai, A.V. (1980), 'The origin and direction of industrial R&D in India', *Research Policy*, 9(1): 74–96.

———— (1984), 'India's Technological Capability: An analysis of its Achievements and Limits', *Research Policy*, 13: 303–10.

————(1985), 'Indigenous and Foreign Determinants of Technological Change in Indian Industry', *Economic and Political Weekly*, 20(45/47): 2081–93.

Dosi, G. (1982), 'Technological Paradigms and Technological Trajectories: A suggested interpretation of determinants and direction of technical change', *Research Policy*, 11: 147–62.

Dutz, Mark A. (2007), *Unleashing India's Innovation: Toward Sustainable and Inclusive Growth*. Washington DC: The World Bank for the 21st Century: Sustainable Development Perspectives. Available at: http://www.un.org/esa/sustdev/publications/industrial_development/1_2.pdf (accessed on 12 October 2012).

Edquist, C. (1997), *Systems of Innovation: Technologies Institutions and Organizations*. London: Washington: Pinter.

Enos, J. (1982), 'The Choice of Techniques v/s the Choice of Beneficiary: What the Third World Chooses', in F. Stewart and J. James (eds), *The Economics of New Technology in Developing Countries*. London: Frances Pinter, pp. 69–81.

Evenson, R.E. and K.J. Joseph (1999), 'Technology Licensing in Indian Industry: An Econometric Analysis of Choice of Partners, Terms of Contract and Effect on Licensees' Performance', *Economic and Political Weekly*, 34(27, 3 July): 1801–9.

Evenson, R.E. and Lakhwinder Singh (1997), 'Economic Growth, International Technology Spillovers and public policy: theory and empirical evidence from Asia', Working paper No. 777. Yale University: Economic Growth Center.

Fagerberg, Jan and Koson Sapprasert (2011), 'National innovation systems: the emergence of a new approach', *Science and Public Policy*, 38(9): 669–79.

Fikkert, Brian (1993), 'An Open or Closed Technology Policy? The Effects of Technology Licensing, Foreign Direct Investment, and Technology Spillovers on R and D in Indian Industrial Sector Firms', PhD Dissertation, Yale University.

Fransman, M. (1986), *Technology and Economic Development.* Brighton, Sussex: Wheatsheaf Books.

Freeman, C. (1986), *The Economics of Industrial Innovation.* London: Pinter Publishers.

——— (1987), *Technology Policy and Economic Performance: Lessons from Japan.* London: Frances Pinter.

——— (2011), 'Technology, inequality and economic growth', *Innovation and Development*, 1(1): 11–25.

Government of India (GoI) (2008), '11th Five Year Plan (2007–2012): Inclusive Growth', Vol. 1, New Delhi: Oxford University Press, Planning Commission.

——— (2012), *Economic Survey 2011–12.* New Delhi: Government of India.

Gu, S. (1999), *Implications of National Innovation Systems for Developing Countries: Managing Change and Complexity in Economic Development.* Maastricht: UNU-INTECH.

Gu, S. and B.-Å. Lundvall (2006), 'Policy learning as a key process in the transformation of the Chinese Innovation Systems', in B.-Å. Lundvall, P. Intarakumnerd, and J. Vang (eds), *Asian innovation systems in transition.* London: Edward Elgar Publishing, pp. 293–312.

Hattari, R. and R.S. Rajan (2010), 'India as a Source of Outward Foreign Direct Investment', *Oxford Development Studies*, 38(5): 497–518.

Himanshu (2007), 'Recent Trends in Poverty and Inequality: Some Preliminary Results', *Economic and Political Weekly*, 42(6): 497–508.

Intarakumnerd P., P. Chairatana, and T. Tangchitpiboon (2002), 'National Innovation System in Less Successful Developing Countries: The Case of Thailand', *Research Policy*, 31: 1445–57.

Jensen, M.B., B. Johnson, E. Lorenz, and B.-Å. Lundvall (2005), 'Forms of Knowledge, Modes of Innovation and Innovation Systems', Department of Business Studies, mimeo, Aalborg University.

Joseph, K.J. (1997), *Industry under Economic Liberalization: The Case of Indian Electronics.* New Delhi, Thousand Oaks, London: Sage Publications.

——— (2006), *Information Technology, Innovation System and Trade Regime in Developing Countries—India and the ASEAN.* New York: Palgrave Macmillan.

——— (2009), 'Sectoral innovation Systems in Developing Countries: the Case of India's ICT in India', in B.-Å., Lundvall, K.J. Joseph, C. Cristina, and Jan Vang (eds), *Handbook of Innovation Systems and Developing Countries.* Cheltenham: Edward Elgar, pp. 183–213.

——— (2012). 'In search of spaces of social exclusion in innovation systems. The case of plantation agriculture in India', Paper prepared for the international seminar on Innovation systems and Inclusive innovation, 27–8 August, organized by the Federal University of Brazil, Rio de Janeiro.

Joseph, K.J. and Dinesh Abrol (2009), 'Science, Technology and Innovation Policies in India: Achievements and Limits', in E. Cassiolato and V. Vitorino (eds), *BRICS and Development Alternatives: Innovation Systems and policies*. London: Anthem Press.

Kannan, K.P. and Raveendran, G. (2009), 'Growth sans Employment: A Quarter Century of Jobless Growth in India's Organised Manufacturing', *Economic and Political Weekly*, 44(10), 7 March.

Kathuria, V. (2002), 'Liberalisation, FDI, and productivity spillovers—an analysis of Indian manufacturing firms', *Oxford Economic Papers*, 54(4): 688–718.

——— (2010), 'Does the Technology Gap Influence Spillovers? A Postliberalization Analysis of Indian Manufacturing Industries', *Oxford Development Studies*, 38(2).

Katrak, H. (1985), 'Imports of technology, enterprise size and R&D-based production in a newly industrializing country: The evidence from Indian enterprises', *World Development*, 22(10): 1599–1608.

——— (1989). 'Imported technologies and R&D in a newly industrialising country: the experience of Indian enterprises', *Journal of Development Economics*, 31(1): 123–39.

——— (1994), 'Imports of technology, enterprise size and R&D-based production in a newly industrializing country: The evidence from Indian enterprises', *World Development*, 22(10): 1599–608.

——— (1997), 'Developing countries' imports of technology, in-house technological capabilities and efforts: an analysis of the Indian experience', *Journal of Development Economics*, 53(1): 67–83.

Katz, J. (1980), 'Domestic Technology Generation in LDCs: A review of Research Findings', Working Paper No. 35. Buenos Aires: IDB/ECLA Programme CEPAL Office.

——— (1984), 'Domestic Technological Innovations and Dynamic Comparative Advantage', *Journal of Development Economics*, 16(1–2): 13–37.

Kim, L. (1980), 'Stages of development in Industrial Technology in a Developing Country: A Model', *Research Policy*, 9: 254–77.

Krishna, V.V. (2013), 'India', in M. Scerri, M. Helena, and M. Lastres (eds) *BRICS National Systems of Innovation: The Role of the State*. New Delhi: Routledge.

Krishnan, R.T. (2010), *From Jugaad to Systemic Innovation: The Challenge for India*. Bangalore: The Utpreraka Foundation.

Kumar, N. (1985): 'Cost of Technology Imports: The Indian Experience', *Economic and Political Weekly*, 20(35): M103–14.

——— (1987), 'Technology Policy in India: An Overview of its Evolution and An Assessment', in P.R. Brahmananda and V.R. Panchamukhi (eds.), *The Development Process of the Indian Economy*, pp. 461–92. Bombay: Himalaya Publishing House.

Kumar, N. (1990), 'Cost of Imported and Local Technologies: Implications for Technology Policy', *Economic and Political Weekly*, 25(2): 103–6.

——— (1996), 'Foreign Direct Investments and Technology Transfers in Development: A Perspective on Recent Literature', Discussion Papers 06, United Nations University, Institute for New Technologies.

——— (1998), 'Technology Generation and Technology Transfers in World Economy: Recent Trends and Implications for Developing Countries', in Nagesh Kumar (ed.), *Globalization, Foreign Direct Investment and Technology Transfers: Impact on Prospects for Developing Countries*. London and New York: Routledge.

——— (2007), 'Emerging TNCs: trends, patterns and determinants of outward FDI by Indian Enterprises', *Transnational Corporations*, 16(1): 1–26. New York and Geneva: UN.

——— (2009), 'FDI and Economic Development: Indian Experience in Global Comparative Perspective', in S.R. Hashim, K.S. Chalapati Rao, K.V.K. Ranganathan, M.R. Murthy (eds), *Indian Industrial Development and Globalization: Essays in Honour of Professor S.K. Goyal*. New Delhi: ISID and Academic Foundation, pp. 409–28.

Kumar, Nagesh and Jaya Prakash Pradhan (2007), 'Knowledge-based Exports from India: A Firm-level Analysis of Determinants', in N. Kumar and K.J. Joseph (eds) *International Competitiveness & Knowledge-based Industries*. pp. 53–96, New Delhi: Oxford University Press.

Kumar, Nagesh and Mohammed Saqib (1994), 'Firm Size, Opportunities for Adaptation and In-house R&D Activity in Developing Countries: The Case of Indian Manufacturing', Working Paper No. 13, Maastricht: UNU/INTECH, The Netherlands.

Kumar, N. and N.S. Siddharthan (1997), *Technology, Market Structure and Internationalization: Issues and Policies for Developing Countries*. London and New York: Routledge.

Lall, Sanjay (1980): 'Developing Countries as Exporters of Industrial Technology', *Research Policy*, 9: 24–52.

——— (1981), 'Indian Technology Exports and Technological Development', *Annals of the American Academy of Political and Social Science*, 458: 151–61.

——— (1982), 'The emergence of Third World multinationals: Indian joint ventures overseas', *World Development*, 10(2): 127–46.

——— (1983), 'India's Technological Capacity: The Effects of Trade, Industrial Policies', in M. Fransman and K. King (eds), *Technological Capability in the Third World*.

——— (1987), *Learning to Industrialize: The Acquisition of Technological Capability by India*. New York: Palgrave Macmillan.

——— (1992): 'Technological Capabilities and Industrialization' *World Development*, 20(2): 165–86.

Lall, Sanjay (1993), 'Promoting Technology Development: The Role of Technology Transfer and Indigenous Effort', *Third World Quarterly*, 14(1): 95–108.

Lastres, H.M.M. and J.E. Cassiolato (2005), 'Innovation systems and local productive arrangements: new strategies to promote the generation, acquisition and diffusion of knowledge', *Innovation: Management, Policy & Practice* 7(2): 172–87.

List, F. (1841), *The National System of Political Economy*, English Edition. London: Longman (1904).

Lucas, Robert E., Jr. (1988), 'On the Mechanics of Economic Development', *Journal of Monetary Economics*, 22: 3–42.

Lundvall, B.-Å. (ed.) (1992), *National Systems of Innovation: Towards a Theory of Innovation and Interactive Learning*. London: Pinter Publishers.

——— (2002), *Growth, Innovation and Social Cohesion: The Danish Model*. London: Elgar Publishers.

——— (2007a), 'National Innovation Systems—Analytical Concept and Development Tool', *Industry and Innovation*, 14: 1, 95–119.

——— (2007b), 'Innovation system research: where it came from and where it might go', Globelics Working paper, No. 2007-01. Available at: www.globelics.org (accessed on 10 October 2012).

Lundvall, B.-Å., K.J. Joseph, C. Chaminade, and J. Vang (eds) (2009), *Handbook of Innovation Systems and Developing Countries*. Edward Elgar: Cheltenham.

Malerba, F. (ed.) (2004), *Sectoral Systems of Innovation: Concept, Issues and Analysis of Six Major Sectors in Europe*. Cambridge: Cambridge University Press.

Mani, S. (2006), 'The Sectoral System of Innovation of Indian Pharmaceutical Industry', Working Paper 382, Centre for Development Studies, Trivandrum, India. Available at: http://www.cds.edu/download_files/wp%5B1%5D382.pdf (accessed on 8 November 2012).

——— (2010), 'Has China and India become more Innovative since the onset of Reforms in the two countries?' Working Paper No. 430. Trivandrum: Centre for Development Studies.

Mathews, J.A. (2001) 'National Systems of Economic Learning: The case of Technology Diffusion Management in East Asia', *International Journal of Technology Management*, 22: 455–79.

Mowery, D. and J.E. Oxley (1995), 'Inward technology transfer and competitiveness: the role of national innovation systems', *Cambridge Journal of Economics*, 19: 67–93.

Nagaraj, R. (2000), 'Organised Manufacturing Employment', *Economic and Political Weekly*, 35(38): 3445–8.

Narayanan, K. (2004), 'Technology acquisition and growth of firms: Indian automobile sector under changing policy regimes', *Economic and Political Weekly*, 39(5): 460–71.

Neethi, P. (2008), 'Contract Work in the Organised Manufacturing Sector: A Disaggregated Analysis of Trends and their Patterns', *Indian Journal of Labour Economics*, 51(4): 559–73.

Nelson, R.R. (ed.) (1993), *National Innovation Systems: A Comparative Analysis.* Oxford: Oxford University Press.

Nelson, R.R. and S.D. Winter (1977), 'In Search of Useful Theory of Innovation', *Research Policy*, 6: 36–76.

——— (1982), *An Evolutionary Theory of Economic Change.* Cambridge, MA: Harvard University Press.

NISTADS (2009), *India: Science and Technology 200*, National Institute of Science, Technology and Development Studies, New Delhi.

North, Douglass C. (1990), *Institutions, Institutional Change, and Economic Performance.* Cambridge: Cambridge University Press.

Office of Adviser to the Prime Minister (2011), 'Towards a More Inclusive and Innovate India: Creating a Road Map for a Decade of Innovation', Strategy Paper. Available at: http://www.iii.gov.in/images/stories/innovation/Innovation_Strategy.pdf (Accessed on 22 February 2014).

Page Jr., J.M. (1979), 'Small Enterprises in African Development: A Survey', World Bank Staff Working Paper No. 363. Washington, DC: The World Bank.

Parthasarathi, A. (1987), 'Acquisition and Development of Technology: Some Issues', *Economic and Political Weekly*, 22(48): M131–8.

——— (2007), *Technology at the Core: Science and Technology with Indira Gandhi.* New Delhi: Pearson Education.

Patel, S.J. (1993), *Technological self-reliance in India.* New Delhi: Ashish Publications.

——— (ed.) (1995), *Technological Transformation of the Third World Vol 1.* Aldershot and Honkong: Aveburry.

Perez, C. (2009), 'Technological revolutions and techno-economic paradigms', *Cambridge Journal of Economics*, 34(1): 185–202.

Pradhan, J.P. (2005), *Outward Foreign Direct Investment from India: Recent Trends and Patterns.* Ahmedabad: Gujarat Institute of Development Research.

——— (2007), 'Growth of Indian multinationals in the world economy: implications for development', Working Paper No. 2007/04. New Delhi: Institute for Studies in Industrial Development.

Radosevic, Slavo (1999), 'Transformation of S&T systems into systems of innovation in central and Eastern Europe: the emerging patterns of recombination, path-dependency and change', *Structural Change and Economic Dynamics*, 10(3–4): 277–320.

Raina, R.S. (2011), 'Institutional Strangleholds: Agricultural Science and the State in India', in D. Narayana and R. Mahadevan (eds), *Shaping India—Economic Change in Historical Perspective.* New Delhi: Routledge, pp. 99–123.

——— (2012), 'Innovation for Development: Policy Trajectories and Reform for Rural India', SIID Working Paper No. 9. New Delhi: Centre for Policy Research.

Ray, S. (ed.) (2007), *Handbook of Agriculture in India.* New Delhi: Oxford University Press.

Razavi, M.R. and A. Maleki (2004), 'Applying National Innovation Systems Approach in the Context of Industrializing Countries: Methodological Unity and Terminological Diversity in Literature', Paper presented in the Second GLOBELICS Conference, Beijing.

Richardson, P. (2002), *New science, technology and innovation development in India*. Brussels: European Commission Directorate-General for Research.

Romer, P.M. (1986), 'Increasing Returns and Long-Run Growth', *Journal of Political Economy*, 94(5): 1002–37.

Sen, A. and Himanshu (2005), 'Poverty and Inequality in India: Getting Closer to the Truth', in Angus Deaton and Valerie Kozel (eds), *Data and Dogma: The Great Indian Poverty Debate*. New Delhi: Macmillan, pp. 306–70.

Sen, A.K. (2000), 'Social Exclusion: Concept, Application and Scrutiny', Social Development Papers No. 1. , Manila: Asian Development Bank.

——— (2012), 'Innovation for Development: Policy Trajectories and Reform for Rural India', SIID Working Paper No. 9. New Delhi: Centre for Policy Research.

Sen, Sunanda and Byasdeb Dasgupta (2006), 'Labour In India's Organized Manufacturing Sector', *Indian Journal of Labour Economics*, 41(2): 79–101.

Siddharthan, N.S. (1988a), 'In-house R&D, Imported Technology and Firm Size: Lessons From Indian Experience', *The Developing Economies*, 26(3): 212–21.

——— (1988b), 'Technology, Modernisation and Growth A Study of Indian Corporate Sector, 1975–83', *Economic and Political Weekly*, 30 July: 1587–90.

——— (1992), 'Transaction costs, technology transfer and in-house R&D: A study of the Indian private corporate sector', *Journal of Economic Behavior and Organisation*, 18: 265–71.

Singer, H., C. Cooper, R.C. Desai, C. Freeman, O. Gish, S. Hall, and G. Oldham (1970), 'The Sussex Manifesto: Science and Technology for Developing Countries during the Second Development Decade', IDS Reprints No. 101. Brighton: Institute of Development Studies.

Singh Lakhwinder and R.E. Evenson (1997). 'Economic Growth, International Technology Spillovers and Public Policy: Theory and Empirical Evidence from Asia, Working paper No. 777, Economic Growth Center, Yale University.

Singh, Lakhwinder and Baldev Singh (2009), 'National Innovation System in the era of liberalization: implications for science and technology policy for developing economies', MPRA Paper 15432. Germany: University Library of Munich.

Singh, Lakhwinder and Varinder Jain (2009), 'Emerging pattern of India's outward foreign direct investment under the influence of state policy', A macro view MPRS paper 13439. Germany: University Library of Munich.

Solow, R.M. (1957), 'Technical Change and the Aggregate Production Function', *The Review of Economics and Statistics*, 39(3): 312–20.

Srinivas, S. and J. Sutz (2008), 'Developing Countries and Innovation: Searching for a New Analytical Approach,' *Technology in Society*, 30: 129–40.

Stoneman, P. (1995), *Handbook of the Economies of Innovation and Technological Change*. Oxford, London: Oxford University Press.

Subrahmanian, K.K. (1986), 'Policy on Foreign Collaboration: Need for Change', *Economic and Political Weekly*, 3(41): 1591–93.

——— (1971), 'Determinants of Corporative R and D', *Economic and Political Weekly*, 6(48): M169–71.

——— (1991), 'Technological Capability under Economic Liberalism: Experience of Indian Industry in the eighties', *Economic and Political Weekly*, 26(35): M87–9, M91–2.

——— (1995), 'Technological Transformation: An assessment of India's Experience', in S.J. Patel (ed.), *Technological Transformation of the Third World, Vol. 1*. Aldershot and Honkong: Aveburry, pp. 59–142.

Subrahmanian, K.K. and P.M. Pillai (1976), 'Implications of Technology-Transfer in Export-Led Growth Strategy', *Economic and Political Weekly*, 11(44): 1729–35.

——— (1977), 'Rhetoric and Reality of Technology Transfer', *Social Scientist*, 5(6): 73–92.

Thorat, Sukhadeo and Amaresh Dubey (2012), 'Has Growth Been Socially Inclusive during 1993/4–2009/10?', *Economic and Political Weekly*, 47(10): 43–54.

Uma, S, Vinoj Abraham, and K.J. Joseph (2010), 'Impact of Trade Liberalization on Employment: The Experience of India's Manufacturing Industries', *Indian Journal of Labour Economics*, 49(4): 587–605.

Vaidyanathan, A. (2010), *Agricultural Growth in India, Role of Technology, Incentives, and Institutions*. New Delhi: Oxford University Press.

Viotti, E.B. (2001), 'National Learning Systems: A new approach on technical change in late industrializing economies and evidences from the cases of Brazil and South Korea', *Science, Technology and Innovation*, Discussion Paper No. 12. Cambridge, MA: Center for International Development, Harvard University.

CHAPTER 30

LABOUR MARKET

balancing freedom and protection

RUPAYAN PAL AND BIBHAS SAHA*

As India completed a decade of high growth and successfully weathered storms of global financial crises, yet another phase of turbulence—this time coming from Europe—has begun.[1] India's vast labour force remains cautiously optimistic about job creation but some old questions continue to weigh on their minds. Is the end of poverty in sight yet? Will high growth bring jobs and permanent improvements in the lives of hundreds of millions?

There is no denying that growth has not trickled down; nor have its fruits been shared widely.

Desperation of the rural economy feeds into steady streams of migration, which are turning the cities into mega-cities with unpleasant living conditions. Though migration reflects vibrancy of the urban labour market, there are persistent problems. Increased trade reforms probably have given rise to unemployment in some industries and firms are looking for flexible modes of hiring. The organized sector, in particular, has been plagued by hostile industrial relations, and the discontent of globalization is quite visible.

* We are grateful to Ashima Goyal and Errol D'Souza for their helpful comments. Any remaining errors are our responsibility.

[1] Some of the turbulence was due to internal factors, such as slowdown of economic reforms, decline in foreign investment, and food price inflation.

Through this chapter, we aim to provide a broad account of the labour market by focussing on some key aspects, such as industrial relations and labour market rigidities of the organized sector. In particular, we provide a summary of academic research on labour market rigidities, job security provisions, and the unequal effects of liberalization. For the unorganized sector we touch upon the issues of labour standards, migration, and insecurity of informal workers, though these issues deserve a separate chapter each. Broadly we try to convey that there are labour rigidities in the organized sector and that they need to be resolved by carrying out overdue labour reforms. Simultaneously the welfare of informal sector workers has to be addressed, in addition to enabling them to take advantage of new opportunities in a globalized world.

The chapter is organized as follows. In the next section we briefly discuss the key labour laws that characterize the industrial relations framework. The next section provides an up-to-date account of the trends in industrial disputes while the section that follows digs deep into academic research on labour market rigidities and the impacts of liberalization. The next two sections contain brief discussions on labour standards and migration. The main threads of the discussion are brought together in the concluding section along with some policy implications.

All figures and tables are relegated to Appendix A30.1 and Appendix A30.2, respectively.

Labour Laws

We begin with a brief overview of labour legislations that regulate industrial relations and labour welfare, predominantly for the organized sector, which have been given in the Factories Act, 1948. As per this Act, factories above a certain size must be registered and are enumerated by the Annual Survey of Industries.[2] Workers employed in these factories come under the purview of key labour legislations, which have been amended time and again by the states and the centre, as labour falls in the concurrent list of jurisdiction.

[2] This Act is applicable to firms with 10 or more workers and use electricity, or with 20 workers and do not use electricity.

Three major central Acts regulate industrial relations in India: the Industrial Employment (Standing Orders) Act, 1946 (IE in short); the Trade Union Act, 1926 (TU); and the Industrial Disputes Act, 1947 (ID). Another Act, the Contract Labour (Regulation and Abolition) Act, 1971, is also important in this respect. However, we will not be devoting much of our attention to this Act in this chapter. The states have amended various aspects of these acts, relating to their enforcement and applicability, as labour falls in the concurrent list of jurisdiction. Recently these state level variations in labour laws have been a subject of interest on which we report later.

IE Act: The IE Act requires that the status of an industrial employee, along with the conditions of recruitment, confirmation, misconduct, discharge, disciplinary action, leave, holidays, etc., be explained to the employee by the employer in the most precise terms. The Act applies to the whole of India and to all industrial establishments where 50 or more workers are employed. The Act also provides for severance pay.

TU Act: The TU Act, one of the oldest labour laws dating back to 1926, remained almost unchanged until 1964. The Act recognizes workers' freedom of association to express grievances, to engage in collective bargaining, and also to promote civil and political interests among themselves. Under section 4 of the TU Act (amended in 1964) any seven people can form and register a trade union at the factory (or establishment) level or at the industry level. They need not necessarily be the employees of that establishment because they can be classified as office bearers, and half of the office bearers can be outsiders. One crucial provision of the Act is that the union members and office bearers are protected from criminal and civil suits in relation to bona fide trade union activities.

While the immunity from prosecution clause was a possible area of abuse, there were other problems. There was no test for representativeness of a trade union, through secret ballots or otherwise. The result has been multiple unions within the same establishment as well as large centralized unions. The Act is also so general that it does not differentiate between political and industrial strikes.

The TU Act of 1964 continued to be in force for more than three decades, until major amendments were introduced in 2001 and were made effective from January 2002. After this amendment a registered trade union must have at least 10 per cent or 100 of the workers as its members, subject to a minimum of seven persons engaged or employed in the establishment or industry. The cap on the number of outsiders acting as office bearers was also reduced to one-third.[3] Certain rules and procedures have been introduced to test for the representativeness of a union. Nonetheless, collective bargaining agreements continued to be applicable to all workers covered by a particular agreement, irrespective of their individual union status, as in all 'open shop' contexts. Unlike as in many developed countries, jobs cannot be categorized as unionized jobs and non-unionized jobs in India. In the post-liberalization era, collective bargaining has taken a more decentralized character. With fewer governmental controls and steady disappearance of protection, the unions' need to maintain strong political links has diminished.

ID Act: Any dispute on the terms and conditions of work, or disagreements during negotiations over wage or any other matters come under the purview of the ID Act. First passed in 1947 to replace the Trade Disputes Act, 1929, the ID Act became the main governing legislation with respect to industrial relations all over India. As its importance grew over time, several amendments were passed in 1964, 1965, 1971, 1976, 1982, and 1984, to improve on its shortcomings and also to strengthen the interventionist role of the state.

The Act aimed at creating a legal and regulatory framework within which industrial disputes can be peacefully resolved. Among the main provisions of the Act are defining legality of strikes and lockouts; restrictive procedure for layoffs, retrenchment, and closure; compensation for layoffs and retrenchment; conciliation procedures; and a 3-tier system of adjudication.

The legality of a strike or lockout primarily hinges on the question of fair use. For example, a sudden strike or lockout in public utilities is illegal; prior notice must be served. Similar issues arise in other industries.

Rules regarding layoffs, retrenchment, and closure are far more restrictive. The IE Act permits certain types of layoffs (as contractual) or retrenchment (on disciplinary or medical ground). But if these are instigated by financial reasons, then the ID Act comes into force. Since 1976, the ID Act has made it *mandatory* for employers to seek prior permission from the government to layoff or retrench any worker, or close down a unit. Originally, firms with 300 or more permanent workers were under

[3] 'All office bearers of a registered trade union, except not more than one-third of the total number of office bearers or five, whichever is less, shall be persons actually engaged or employed in the establishment or industry with which the trade union is connected'—Trade Unions (Amendment) Act 2001.

this requirement. But later, in 1982, this requirement (codified in Chapter V-B of the ID Act) was extended to all industries employing 100 or more workers. A violation of this may lead to serious penalty on the employer, as well as reinstatement of laid-off workers. This particular provision has been criticized as too restrictive and uncommon by international standards, given that the government has been conservative in granting permissions to retrench or layoff.[4] For example, in 1997, the central government received 60 applications for layoffs/retrenchment/closures, but granted permission only in six cases. Because of this abnormally low rate of approvals, the provision of Chapter V-B continues to be seen as a major stumbling block for the restructuring of loss-making enterprises.

While large firms are restricted, relatively smaller firms can freely layoff or retrench in compliance with the IE Act (wherever it is applicable). In any event of retrenchment, the principle of 'last come first go' applies. But not all laid-off or retrenched workers are eligible for compensation. Only when they are of a permanent category and when the firm size is in excess of 50, does the compensation rule apply.

It is noteworthy that because labour falls under a joint jurisdiction, states also have modified the ID Act on various aspects of enforcement. Some states have made changes in favour of employers (such as Andhra Pradesh), while quite a few states have favoured workers (such as West Bengal). There is now a growing recognition that such divergence in labour legislations has affected the economic performance of the states in both pre- and post-liberalization periods (see Aghion et al. 2008 and Besley and Burgess 2004) which we discuss later.

Apart from the laws, social customs, and political factors also shape the workers ability to form unions (Booth 1985; Naylor 1989). In the context of 39 developing countries, Martin and Brady (2007) show that the workers' propensity to unionize rises sharply if a country has a communist legacy. In India, state-level variations in political activism and support bases play an important role in fostering or discouraging union growth. Pal (2010), using a national-level representative survey data from India, shows that the reach of the communist parties in a given state has considerable effect on the unionization probability within that state. Different propensities

4 According to the OECD employment protection database (Venn 2009), for 2008, India has the second highest level of protection of permanent workers against individual dismissal out of 40 countries. The scenario is somewhat better, if we consider overall employment protection. Nonetheless, India's rank is as high as 29 in terms of overall employment protection out of those 40 countries.

to form unions and sustain union activities have a significant impact on industrial disputes and their persistence, a topic we turn our attention to next.

Industrial Disputes in India: Patterns and Changes during 1981–2007

Over the last few decades, there has been a declining trend of the incidence of industrial disputes, that is, in the number of strikes plus the number of lockouts, during the period 1981–2007 (see Figure A30.1). Compared to very high incidences of industrial disputes in the 1970s and early 1980s (who can forget the year-long Bombay textile strike?), we have a much improved situation. However, there have been periodic reversals and inter-state variations are enormous.

During the first decade of our study, 1981–90, the average number of industrial disputes was as high as 2,045 per year, which fell by about 40 per cent in the following decade (1991–2000). The average number of man-days lost also declined by 46.28 per cent in the next decade. The situation improved further during the second decade of the post-reforms era, the beginning of which was marked by major amendments to the TU Act (see Table A30.1). During 2001–7 the average number of industrial disputes declined by more than 59 per cent from the average of 1991–2000. Despite this, the average number of man-days lost actually went up during the period (over the previous decade) suggesting that disputes that could not be resolved soon were dragged much longer, reflecting a greater intensity of disputes in recent years.

Of course, disputes include both strikes and lockouts, and they are very different types of disputes. Therefore, they deserve separate scrutiny. It is interesting to note that, on an average, incidences of lockouts increased from 418 per year during 1981–90 to 449 per year during 1991–2000, and thereafter fell to 237 per year during 2001–7. But the average number of man-days lost due to lockouts decreased by 26.34 per cent during 1991–2000 compared to that during 1981–90, but increased by 21.9 per cent during 2001–7 (see Table A30.2). Nonetheless, looking at the pattern of the annual frequency of lockouts and associated man-days lost, it seems that the number of lockouts has declined steadily since 1997 and associated man-days lost has also declined in recent years (see Figures A30.2 and A30.3). It is possible that the first wave of lockouts that occurred in the early 1990s, soon after liberalization, was due to prolonged industrial sickness. While inefficient firms were forced to shut down, either by the lockout route or by closure, efficient firms could see the benefits of reforms, particularly in the area of exports. In the second phase of liberalization, competition and restructuring of firms might have taken place along with rent dissipation. A study by Pal (2006) shows that both profit and workers per factory fell during this period, and yet the number of factories increased significantly. So the decline in the number of lockouts could be due to this overall process of rent dissipation, which is bound to occur with liberalization.

On the other hand, the frequency of strikes has more or less steadily declined over the period from 1981 to 2007 (see Figure A30.4). But, the pattern of man-days lost due to strikes over this period is not very clear (see Figure A30.5). The annual average number of strikes (man-days lost due to strikes) during the pre-reforms period was as high as 1627.2 (24.3 million), which decreased to 780.89 (9.36 million) during 1991–2000, and further decreased to 263.83 (8.54 million) during 2001–7 (see Table A30.3).

Overall, it seems that the industrial relations scenario has largely improved during the post-economic reforms era (1991–2007) in India. Similar trends are also observed in most of the states. Nonetheless, there are wide variations in terms of both incidence and intensity of industrial disputes across states in India. For example, during 2001–7, the annual average number of strikes was as low as 3.75 in Bihar, while in Tamil Nadu it was 65.5. The range of annual average number of strikes was larger in earlier decades 140.78 during 1991–2000 and 251.8 during 1981–90. However, it seems that the variation in the *number of lockouts* across states increased over time (see Table A30.2). On the other hand, the *duration of disputes* as measured by the average number of man-days lost decreased between 1991 and 2001, but increased again between 2001 and 2007.[5] Therefore, we can say that though in the post-reforms era the industrial relations scenario has improved in general, there are still significant inter-state disparities, which indicate that there might be regions with persistent problems.

[5] This is true for both strikes and lockouts. The average number of man-days lost due to strikes (lockouts) across states first decreased from 8.58 (11) million during 1981–91 to 1.97 (6.8) million during 1991–2000, and then increased to 3.43 (13.27) million during 2001–07.

Growth and Employment Impacts of Reforms

What do we know about the growth and employment impacts of liberalization? Economists generally believe that if the markets are fairly 'flexible'—a term not easy to explain—liberalization will generate strong incentives to gain efficiency. Firms will try to restructure their costs, relocate plants, explore new markets, and eventually battle it out in the marketplace to decide who will survive and who will have to exit. The whole process is fairly complex. Even if there is a net gain in aggregate employment, there might be substantial redistribution of employment between regions, between sectors, and between skill categories—none without potential frictions and disputes. But if there are rigidities in the labour market (and other markets, say for other inputs and the product market) liberalization may have unfair and unintended consequences.

The study of labour market rigidities goes back to the 1980s, when a debate broke out on the puzzling observation of the 'jobless growth' of the 1980s. During this period industrial output grew by record 9.30 per cent, but employment almost remained stagnant (grew by just 0.69 per cent).[6] While a study by the World Bank (1989) blamed the wage growth for low employment, its argument was countered by Nagaraj (1994) and Bhalotra (1998). From this debate arose the need to get a better understanding of labour market rigidities, which may prevent hiring in upswings and equally restrict layoffs during downswings.

One particular provision of the ID Act that was first introduced in 1976 and then amended in 1982 drew economists' attention. By this provision employers cannot layoff or retrench any workers if they have a firm size in excess of 100 workers; the provision is still in force. Several studies, namely Fallon and Lucas (1991, 1993), Bhalotra (1998), and Dutta Roy (2003) studied the impacts of this particular job-security provision. While Fallon and Lucas argued that the job security provision of 1976 reduced the long run industrial employment by 17.5 per cent (on the aggregate), Bhalotra (1998) and Dutta Roy (2003) found this claim to be a bit exaggerated. Of these three studies, Dutta Roy's (2003) analysis is more comprehensive and updated. She found that in some industries, labour market rigidities were

[6] Though industrial output has always grown much faster than industrial employment, their gap became the widest between 1980 and 1990.

present well before the 1976 regulation, and in many instances the 1976 or the 1982 regulations did not make things worse. An important message of this study is that there are deeper structural characteristics of the Indian industry and labour market that are more responsible for apparent labour market rigidities than the legislative provisions of job security per se.

Notwithstanding the difficulty of deciphering labour market rigidities, economists began to look at other possible impacts of economic liberalization. For example, Ramaswamy (1999) noted improvements in technology with deregulation of industries. Chand and Sen (2002) found that the productivity of the manufacturing sector improved with trade reforms. In a similar vein, Thangavelu and Rajaguru (2004) argued that import competition led to efficiency improvements in the industry. Many other authors generally echoed such positive assessments of liberalization.

A study by Pal (2006) noticed significant dynamism for the organized manufacturing sector as a whole in the decade immediately following economic reforms. There were far more new firms and overall industry output and employment were greater than in the pre-reforms period. By the end of the 1990s, the average number of factories per industry rose by 22.90 per cent; the average size of a factory (in terms of employment) and profits fell by 15 and 25.15 per cent respectively. But these contractions in individual firm size and profits were accompanied by an expansion in aggregate industry output and employment (14.73 per cent) (see Table A30.4). The number of factories increased from 105,038 in 1981–2 to 112,286 in 1991–2, an increase of over 7,000. But between 1991–2 and 1997–8 it rose to 135,549 registering an increase of over 23,000 (or 20.7 per cent).

Pal (2006) went on to study the impact of various components of reforms. His econometric analysis showed: (i) industrial reforms had increased the number of factories; (ii) trade reforms reduced the number of factories; (iii) labour market institutions also reduced the number of factories; and (iv) greater unionization and increased wage share of organized workers (which might have resulted from the absence of labour reforms) restricted growth in the number of factories.

While most economists were studying the industrial sector as a whole, two LSE economists, Tim Besley and Robin Burgess, turned our attention to divergent patterns of growth among the Indian states (Besley and Burgess 2004). However, this was not the first time that a state-level analysis received attention. For example, Dasgupta et al. (2000) studied the possibility of growth convergence among Indian states. But Besley and Burgess (2004) looked into the changes in state labour laws since

1947 and categorized the states in three groups: pro-worker, neutral, and pro-employer, and studied the co-variations in labour legislations and states' industrial (or non-agricultural) outputs.[7] They concluded that state manufacturing output showed a stronger negative relationship with (pro-) labour regulations. More interestingly, when state industrial output was disaggregated between registered and unregistered manufacturing outputs, registered manufacturing showed an even stronger negative relationship with labour regulations, while the unregistered manufacturing output showed a stronger positive relationship. Their point is that pro-worker states have lost out on registered manufacturing and at the same time encouraged a substitution in favour of the unorganized sector.

More evidence of the damaging effects of state-level labour regulations has been uncovered in Aghion et al. (2008) and Adhvaryu et al. (2012). Aghion et al. examined the unequal effects of industrial and trade reforms across states. They found that in comparison to the neutral states, the relative effects of industrial deregulation were significantly positive for those states which had (relatively) pro-employer labour legislations, and significantly negative for those states that had enacted pro-worker legislations. Though the effects of trade and industrial reforms were positive for all states, the effects as channelled through the labour market were unequal depending on their nature of past labour legislations. Adhvaryu et al. (2012) studied how firms are able to adjust their employment after an adverse demand shock in the presence of restrictive labour legislations. They found that industrial employment was more sensitive to shocks in areas where labour regulations were less restrictive or more pro-employer.

From these studies we know that pro-worker legislations that are aimed mainly at organized sector workers have several unexpected consequences; one of these is the growth of the unorganized sector. Employers try to bypass the regulations as far as possible, or look for flexibility legally or by bending the law a bit. One such development (of seeking flexibility) is contract employment. The share of contract workers in total workers in the registered manufacturing sector has steadily increased all over India. Between 1998 and 2004, among 15 major states, Bihar posted the maximum gain in the share of contract workers (53 percentage points), while Kerala posted the lowest increase (7 percentage points). Exploiting the data on contract workers in organized sector firms Saha et al. (2013) show

[7] In their sample, West Bengal had the most pro-worker labour legislations (cumulative up to 1997), while Andhra Pradesh and Tamil Nadu had the most pro-employer legislations.

that import penetration, employers' bargaining power, and pro-worker state-level legislations are all conducive to a higher proportion of contract workers. Moreover, stronger bargaining powers of an employer enhance the effects of export orientation and import penetration. That is to say, where employers have greater bargaining power, they are able to respond to import competition by hiring relatively more contract workers than those employers who have weak bargaining powers.

It is clear that apart from the ID Act there are other Acts, such as trade union Acts and contract labour Acts that are equally important. State-level variations in these Acts should also be considered. OECD has compiled a separate state-level index on the strength of these other laws. Saha et al. (2013) confirm that the OECD index bears a similar result to the Besley-Burgess index. This suggests both hope and despair. There is hope in the fact that states can take initiatives in reforming labour laws as far as possible without waiting for the centre. But there is also despair because unless central laws are changed, there is a clear limit to what states can do. There is also a danger of competitive deregulation that can harm workers' welfare.

To summarize, early researches on labour market rigidities were aggregative and less conclusive. Recent researches that have explicitly allowed for changes in legal provisions among the states are far more successful in uncovering rigidities. They also detect unequal effects of liberalization between the states and between the organized and unorganized sectors. The unorganized sector, by and large, has responded positively to reforms and globalization. Other studies that do not focus on labour markets also provide evidence of positive impacts on firm productivity and profitability, despite labour market rigidities. Such has been the force of liberalization.

Labour Standards

With rapid growth of the unorganized sector and greater reliance of firms on contract workers, issues of safety at the workplace, workers' rights, and social security for all workers assume importance. It is well argued that there should be appropriate labour standards to protect the interests of the workers, much in line with developed countries. This may be regarded as an inevitable consequence of globalization.

Existing laws in India prohibit forced labour, discrimination in work places, and promote freedom of association. Moreover, there are rules that set out guidelines regarding workplace safety, protection against accidents, working hours, etc. The question is, to what extent are these measures effective in protecting the interests of workers? How do labour standards in India compare with those in other countries?

According to the international labour standards, as prescribed by the International Labour Organization (ILO), there are 153 conventions in force and 202 recommendations, which relate to forced labour, discrimination, child labour, health and safety at the work place, social security, paid educational leave, etc. ILO conventions create legally binding obligations on countries that ratify these conventions, but ILO recommendations are non-binding and provide guidelines for formulating national policies and actions. Out of these 153 conventions, the following eight are considered core conventions. (1) Forced Labour Convention (1930), (2) Equal Remuneration Convention (1951), (3) Abolition of Forced Labour Convention (1957), (4) Discrimination (Employment and Occupation) Convention (1958), (5) Freedom of Association and Protection of the Right to Organize Convention (1948), (6) Right to Organize and Collective Bargaining Convention (1949), (7) Minimum Age Convention (1973), and (8) Worst Forms of Child Labour Convention (1999).

India is a founder member of ILO and has ratified the first four of these core conventions and another 39 non-core conventions. Nonetheless, India's position in terms of ratification of international conventions is better than that of other Asian countries. For example, China has ratified four core conventions and 29 non-core conventions so far.

India has not ratified the fifth and sixth core conventions, which concern freedom of association and collective bargaining. However, freedom of association, freedom of expression, and functional democracy are guaranteed by the Constitution of India. Moreover, according to existing labour legislations, all workers, except government servants, have the right to unionize and engage in collective bargaining. In a highly politicized trade union system, it is perhaps better for the functioning of government offices that unionization among government servants is not promoted. The other two core conventions (not ratified) are aimed at abolishing child labour. According to the Child Labour (Prohibition and Regulation) Act, 1986, no child of age less than 14 years shall be employed or permitted to work in some selected, but not all, occupations and processes in India. A further amendment to this Act in 2006 extends this to almost all occupations, and primary schooling has been made universal and compulsory.

However, the ground reality is still far from achieving the desired outcome of no child labour, particularly in hazardous jobs. Though there has been a declining trend in children's work participation rates in the age group 5–14 years in recent years,[8] more than 1.2 million children in India are still engaged in hazardous occupations. This calls for strengthening existing child development schemes, such as the National Child Labour Project, the Skill Development Initiative Scheme, and the International Programme on the Elimination of Child Labour, and a more coordinated approach to reduce child labour at a faster rate, as proposed by the working group of the Twelfth Five-year Plan (2012–17). Banning child labour by law, by ratifying the ILO conventions, without creating appropriate child development schemes, can make the situation worse for children (Basu 1999).

Several arguments have been put forward in favour of a coordinated approach to uniform global labour standards. It is argued that if countries are allowed to choose their own labour standards, competition in international trade can trigger a 'race-to-the-bottom' in labour standards, as speculated in standard tax competition models (Sengenberger 1994). Further, poor labour standards may also reduce workers' efforts in jobs and firm efficiency in the long run (Buchele and Christensen 1995; Levine 1992). However, Bhagwati (1995, 2002) argues against a coordinated approach to achieving global labour standards, because it compromises the competitive position of developing countries like India. A coordinated approach may lead to a redistribution of wage income from low-skill low-wage countries to developed countries. In his view, a coordinated approach to international labour standards essentially promotes protectionism. Nonetheless, there is continuous pressure from developed countries to impose higher labour standards on developing countries by linking international trade with labour standards since the Uruguay Round at Marrakesh in 1994. It remains a challenge for India and other developing countries to maintain their stand and successfully negate pressures from developed countries.

Though raising labour standards in one go will hurt the poor most, the importance of the issues underlying labour standards should not be discounted, especially when a vast majority of the workers is engaged in the informal sector. Indirect mechanisms that aim to provide better public goods, environment, education, and health facilities will perhaps help

[8] According to the Census of India, work participation rate of children in the age group 5–14 years declined from 5.4 per cent in 1991 to 5 per cent in 2001.

workers and contribute to better labour standards. It is worth mentioning here that the Government of India recently undertook several initiatives to address these issues. First, in 2005, the National Rural Employment Guarantee Act (NREGA) was passed to guarantee 100 days of employment per year to one member of any rural household in government-funded local employment programmes. Though NREGA suffers from problems of corruption and partial implementation, it seems that it has successfully raised wages at least in some regions in India (Banerjee and Saha 2010; Dreze and Khera 2009). Second, the Unorganized Workers' Social Security Bill (UWSSB) was passed in 2008, with an objective of delivering social security to all workers. However, how far, and to what extent, this has been implemented remain to be seen.

MIGRATION

Migration is an important arena of study for the simple fact that it reflects how people are responding to opportunities that may arise due to economic reforms (and globalization in general); through migration they also get an opportunity to change the lives of their children. A poor worker may migrate from rural Madhya Pradesh to Mumbai, and not only can he find steady income but also learn the importance of education, as a result of which his children may have a better future. Such inter-generational improvements are probably more important than short-term income gains. This may be even more important for women, who, as seen in many countries, may experience 'social emancipation' through migration, and through increased incomes, they improve their bargaining power within the household, which, in turn, can have a significantly positive impact on their children's well-being. Luke and Munshi (2011) have identified such positive effects for low-caste female plantation workers in southern India.

There are two sources of data for studying migration in India—Census and National Sample Survey Office (NSSO). A recent report of the Government of India (June 2010) puts the estimated number of Indians on the move around 325 million or around 28.5 per cent of the population. In the absence of a report based on the 2011 Census, we base our analysis on 2001 Census data which shows that 30 per cent of India's population (or 309 million people) were migrants; that is, they moved in the last six months from their earlier place of residence. This proportion was significantly higher than what it was in 1991, when it was recorded to be 22 per cent. Out of these 309 million 'migrants', females constituted 71 per cent and males 29 per cent. But for women, migration is mostly linked to marriage, and 90 per cent of the migrant women moved only within the state. For men the most cited reason for mobility was employment but their mobility was also mainly restricted within the same state; 79 per cent of the male migrants were within state migrants. Though moving outside the state is less frequent, this is nevertheless the type of migration that increased the most between 1991 and 2001. This is not surprising in an era of rapid, but disparate, growth and opportunities. Another evidence of pro-employment migration is that rural-to-urban migration is becoming far more important than rural-to-rural migration.

The NSSO migration survey (2007–8) confirms that the same pattern remained valid in recent years. It also provides further insight into the migration behaviour of various social groups. In rural areas, migration rate (proportion of people migrating out of the total population of a given group) was smallest among Scheduled Tribes (STs)—47 per 1,000 males—and highest among the 'others' group (which includes predominantly upper caste Hindus)—68 per 1,000 males. In the urban sector, however, both STs and others maintain a very high proportion—about 288 per 1,000 males, compared to other social groups. Moreover, as reported in Table A30.5, when compared to the 1999 NSSO survey we see that in the rural sector the migration rate fell for almost all groups, while in the urban sector the migration rate rose or remained unchanged. For all groups combined, the migration rate for rural males was 5.4 per cent, while for urban males it was 25.9 per cent. In general, we are seeing greater mobility among urban groupings.

Migration is a vast topic, as it not only involves moving from rural to urban areas, but also from rural to rural areas. The economics of return migration is also equally complex. In this short chapter we are not able to do justice to this topic. However, we wanted to highlight that with liberalization, the migration propensity for various economic groups has risen, and future studies should pay attention to migration behaviours of different socioeconomic groups.

***

All economic policies are a deliberate choice to interfere with the functioning of market forces. While the desired goal may be achieved and the economy steered on to a particular path, there are costs to be borne in the form of hidden or overt inefficiencies and altered incentives by pursuing an unexpected course of actions. Labour policies are no exceptions. Well meaning labour laws aim to prevent labour exploitation, but they may also create rigidity. The long-term consequences of such laws and their implementations are complex.

In this chapter we have provided an overview of the state of play of industrial disputes and a summary of academic research on labour market rigidities. While economic reforms have been positive for the economy at large, protecting only the interests of the organized workers cannot continue, and if continued the dividends of reforms will dry up. Therefore, the disparity between income and welfare levels of workers in the organized and unorganized sectors must be narrowed. The government's new welfare initiatives for unorganized workers are a positive step in this direction. But social sector interventions for health and education are also necessary. Without them the poor will not be able to take advantage of the new opportunities that globalization may bring.

Appendix A30.1

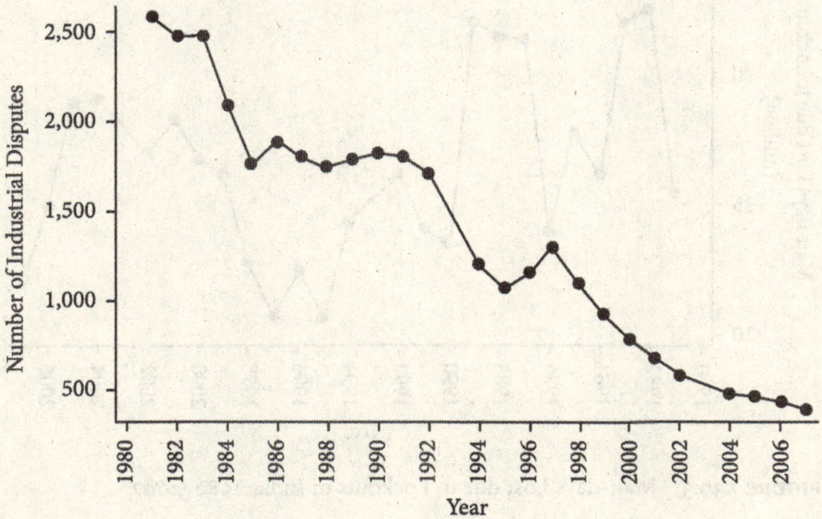

FIGURE A30.1 Incidence of Industrial Disputes in India: 1980–2007

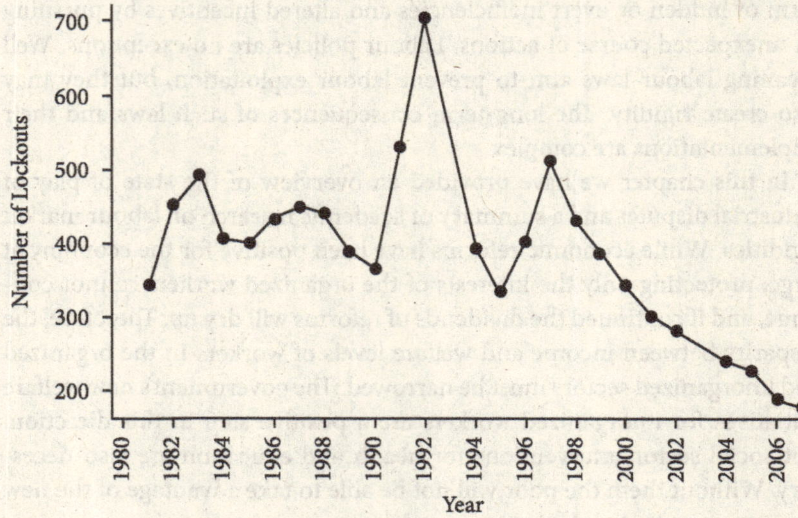

FIGURE A30.2 Incidence of Lockouts in India: 1980–2007

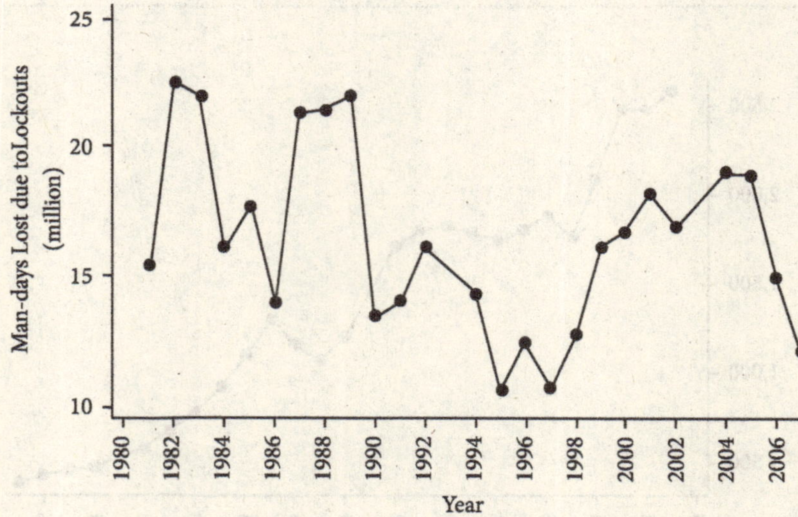

FIGURE A30.3 Man-days Lost due to Lockouts in India: 1980–2007

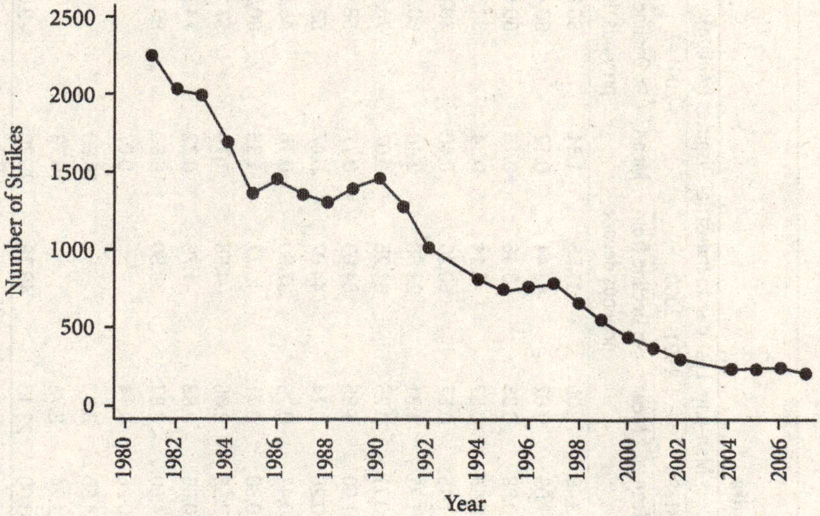

FIGURE A30.4 Incidence of Strikes in India: 1980–2007

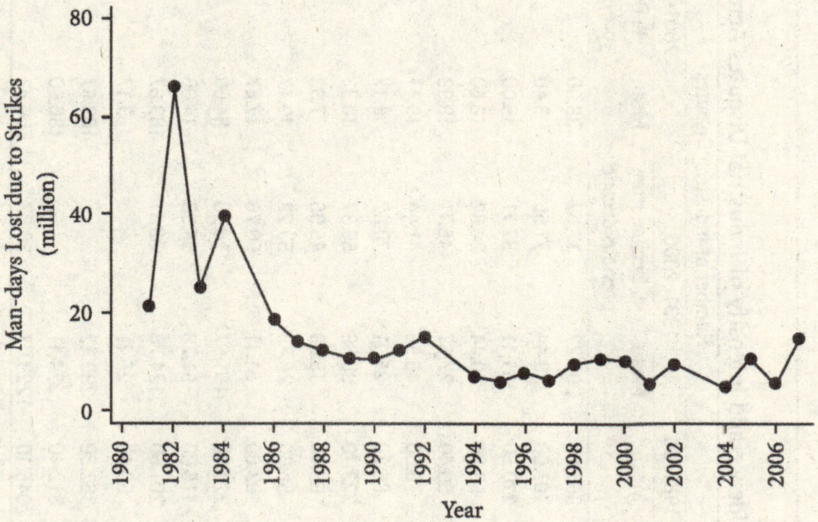

FIGURE A30.5 Man-days Lost due to Strikes in India: 1980–2007

Appendix A30.2

Table A30.1 Incidence and Intensity of Industrial Disputes Across States in India

State	Number of Industrial Disputes					Man-days Lost due to Industrial Disputes (million)				
	1981–90	1991–2000		2001–7		1981–90	1991–2000		2001–7	
	Mean	Mean	% Decline from previous decade	Mean	% Decline from previous decade	Mean	Mean	% Decline from previous decade	Mean	% Decline from previous decade
Andhra Pradesh	362.80	299.22	17.52	38.00	87.30	3.49	3.09	11.55	1.34	56.66
Bihar	107.00	30.44	71.55	3.40	88.83	1.09	0.62	43.44	0.12	80.43
Gujarat	210.50	131.11	37.71	39.00	70.25	0.88	0.85	3.46	0.16	80.86
Haryana	53.80	40.44	24.82	16.60	58.96	0.49	0.52	-5.14	0.34	34.72
Karnataka	50.40	27.67	45.11	18.33	33.73	1.15	0.57	50.20	0.40	30.75
Kerala	79.50	46.56	41.44	19.17	58.83	1.71	1.31	23.60	2.10	–60.36
Madhya Pradesh	86.20	25.11	70.87	3.17	87.39	0.71	0.25	64.25	0.07	70.59
Maharashtra	223.70	90.89	59.37	10.33	88.63	11.60	1.85	84.09	0.77	58.41
Orissa	66.40	35.89	45.95	7.33	79.57	0.26	0.14	44.07	0.07	53.17
Punjab	56.30	26.33	53.23	10.17	61.39	0.47	0.29	37.60	0.16	45.98
Rajasthan	103.80	51.11	50.76	17.67	65.43	0.80	0.71	10.77	1.35	–90.22
Tamil Nadu	229.00	191.67	16.30	84.00	56.17	2.55	2.66	–4.58	1.14	57.25
Uttar Pradesh	115.00	51.78	54.98	14.00	72.96	0.86	0.88	–1.79	0.22	74.55
West Bengal	201.60	124.78	38.11	189.67	–52.00	14.50	8.87	38.80	16.80	–89.30
Minimum	50.40	25.11		3.17		0.26	0.14		0.07	
Maximum	362.80	299.22		189.67		14.50	8.87		16.80	
Range	312.40	274.11		186.50		14.24	8.73		16.73	
All India	2045.10	1229.67	39.87	500.83	59.27	43.00	23.10	46.28	25.20	–9.09

Note: Authors own calculations, based on data from various issues of Indian labour Statistics and Indian Labour Year Book, published by Labour Bureau, Ministry of Labour and Employment, Government of India.

Table A30.2 Incidence and Intensity of Lockouts Across States in India

State	Number of Lockouts					Man-days Lost due to Lockouts (million)				
	1981–90	1991–2000		2001–7		1981–90	1991–2000		2001–7	
	Mean	Mean	% Decline from previous decade	Mean	% Decline from previous decade	Mean	Mean	% Decline from previous decade	Mean	% Decline from previous decade
Andhra Pradesh	69.00	169.89	−146.22	15.17	91.07	0.72	2.08	−188.00	0.71	66.03
Bihar	16.50	10.33	37.37	1.00	90.32	0.53	0.21	59.74	0.06	73.36
Gujarat	23.60	16.56	29.85	6.00	63.76	0.35	0.28	22.38	0.04	83.95
Haryana	8.10	5.33	34.16	2.00	62.50	0.16	0.33	−104.47	0.09	71.77
Karnataka	8.40	8.00	4.76	4.20	47.50	0.48	0.17	64.75	0.14	18.53
Kerala	20.40	18.67	8.50	4.83	74.11	0.47	0.65	-37.94	0.32	50.71
Madhya Pradesh	2.67	1.40	47.50		100.00	0.21	0.08	61.19	0.00	100.00
Maharashtra	52.00	28.44	45.30	2.40	91.56	2.83	1.35	52.15	0.44	67.57
Orissa	6.60	4.22	36.03	2.67	36.84	0.10	0.07	26.27	0.03	63.78
Punjab	4.70	3.50	25.53	3.33	4.76	0.20	0.04	78.05	0.11	−143.94
Rajasthan	19.40	13.89	28.41	7.67	44.80	0.17	0.28	-70.07	1.14	-302.61
Tamil Nadu	28.70	30.78	-7.24	18.50	39.89	0.66	0.76	-14.32	0.38	49.52
Uttar Pradesh	14.40	23.44	-62.81	4.83	79.38	0.33	0.57	-74.48	0.12	79.67
West Bengal	130.70	103.78	20.60	165.83	-59.80	11.10	6.84	38.38	13.30	-94.46
Minimum	2.67	1.40		1.00		0.10	0.04		0.03	
Maximum	130.70	169.89		165.83		11.10	6.84		13.30	
Range	128.03	168.49		164.83		11.00	6.80		13.27	
All India	417.90	448.78	-7.39	237.00	47.19	18.60	13.70	26.34	16.70	−21.90

Note: Authors own calculations, based on data from various issues of Indian labour Statistics and Indian Labour Year Book, published by Labour Bureau, Ministry of Labour and Employment, Government of India.

Table A30.3 Incidence and Intensity of Strikes Across States in India

State	Number of Strikes					Man-days Lost due to Strikes (million)				
	1981–90	1991–2000		2001–7		1981–90	1991–2000		2001–7	
	Mean	Mean	% Decline from previous decade	Mean	% Decline from previous decade	Mean	Mean	% Decline from previous decade	Mean	% Decline from previous decade
Andhra Pradesh	293.80	129.33	55.98	22.83	82.35	2.77	1.01	63.65	0.63	37.28
Bihar	90.50	20.11	77.78	3.75	81.35	0.56	0.40	27.88	0.10	74.74
Gujarat	186.90	114.56	38.71	33.00	71.19	0.53	0.57	-9.30	0.12	79.37
Haryana	45.70	35.11	23.17	14.60	58.42	0.33	0.19	43.20	0.24	–30.19
Karnataka	42.00	20.56	51.06	14.83	27.84	0.67	0.40	39.79	0.28	30.18
Kerala	59.10	27.89	52.81	14.33	48.61	1.24	0.66	47.10	1.78	–170.96
Madhya Pradesh	83.80	24.33	70.96	3.80	84.38	0.50	0.21	58.28	0.07	64.20
Maharashtra	171.70	62.44	63.63	8.33	86.65	8.74	0.49	94.36	0.40	18.43
Orissa	59.80	31.67	47.05	6.00	81.05	0.16	0.07	54.78	0.05	24.98
Punjab	51.60	23.22	55.00	8.50	63.40	0.27	0.25	5.97	0.11	58.71
Rajasthan	84.40	37.22	55.90	10.00	73.13	0.63	0.43	32.22	0.21	51.19
Tamil Nadu	200.30	160.89	19.68	65.50	59.29	1.89	1.91	–1.15	0.76	60.32
Uttar Pradesh	100.60	28.33	71.84	11.00	61.18	0.53	0.30	43.03	0.11	64.88
West Bengal	70.90	21.00	70.38	23.83	–13.49	3.32	2.04	38.73	3.49	–71.34
Minimum	42.00	20.11		3.75		0.16	0.07		0.05	
Maximum	293.80	160.89		65.50		8.74	2.04		3.49	
Range	251.80	140.78		61.75		8.58	1.96		3.43	
All India	1627.20	780.89	52.01	263.83	66.21	24.30	9.36	61.49	8.54	8.75

Note: Authors own calculations, based on data from various issues of Indian labour Statistics and Indian Labour Year Book, published by Labour Bureau, Ministry of Labour and Employment, Government of India.

Table A30.4 Industry Characteristics Before and After Reform

Sample (73 industries)	1981–2 to 1990–1 (Pre-reform period)	1991–2 to 1997–8 (Post-reform period)	Change (%)
Annual number of factories per industry	747.65	918.89	22.90
Annual real profit per factory (1981–2 prices)	Rs 4.14 million	Rs 3.1 million	–25.15 %
Effective rate of protection per industry	121.25 per cent	67.75 per cent	
Number of employees per industry per year	61,085.18	70,087.13	14.73 per cent
Man-days lost per factory	593.79	1,060	78.51 per cent
All industries			
Number of employees per industry per year	46,123	49,078	6.4 per cent
Number of employees per factory per year	142	120	–15 per cent
Annual real net value added per industry (1981–2 prices)	Rs 1,019.7 million	Rs 2,051.5 million	101 per cent

Source: Pal (2006).

Table A30.5 Number of Male Migrants per 1,000 Population

	Rural		Urban	
	55th round (1999–2000)	64th round (2007–8)	55th round (1999–2000)	64th round (2007–8)
ST	56	47	282	288
SC	64	49	225	235
OBC	65	51	237	230
Others	81	68	276	290
All groups	69	54	257	259

Source: NSSO 2008.

References

Adhvaryu, Achyuta, A.V. Chari, and Siddharth Sharma (2012), 'Firing Costs and Flexibility: Evidence from Firms' Employment Responses to Shocks in India', *Review of Economics and Statistics*, 95(3): 727–40.

Aghion, Philippe, Robin Burgess, Stephen Redding, and Fabrizio Zilibotti (2008), 'The Unequal Effects of Liberalization: Evidence from Dismantling the License Raj in India', *American Economic Review*, 98(4): 1397–412.

Annual Survey of Industries (1980–2010), various issues. New Delhi: Ministry of Industry, Government of India.

Banerjee, K. and P. Saha (2010), 'The NREGA, the Maoists and the Developmental Woes of the Indian State', *Economic and Political Weekly*, 45(28): 42–8.

Basu, Kaushik (1999), 'Child Labor: Cause, Consequence, and Cure, with Remarks on International Labor Standards', *Journal of Economic Literature*, 37(3): 1083–119.

Besley, Timothy and Robin Burgess (2004), 'Can Labour Regulation Hinder Economic Performance? Evidence from India', *Quarterly Journal of Economics*, 119(1): 91–134.

Bhagwati, Jagdish (1995), 'Trade Liberalization and "Fair Trade" Demands: Addressing the Environmental and Labour Standards Issues', *World Economy*, 18(6): 745–59.

——— (2002), *Free Trade Today*. Princeton, NJ: Princeton University Press.

Bhalotra, S. (1998), 'The Puzzle of Jobless Growth in Indian Manufacturing', *Oxford Bulletin of Economics and Statistics*, 60(1): 5–32.

Booth, Alison L. (1985), 'The Free Rider Problem and a Social Custom Model of Trade Union Membership', *Quarterly Journal of Economics*, 100(1): 253–61.

Buchele, Robert and Jens Christensen (1995), 'Productivity, Real Wages, and Workers' Rights: A Cross-national Comparison', *Labour*, 9(3): 405–22.

Chand, S., and K. Sen (2002), 'Trade Liberalization and Productivity Growth: Evidence from Indian Manufacturing', *Review of Development Economics*, 6(1): 120–32.

Dasgupta, D., P. Maiti, R. Mukherjee, and S. Sarkar (2000), 'Growth and Interstate Disparities in India', *Economic and Political Weekly*, 35(27): 2413–22.

Drèze, J. and R. Khera (2009), 'The Battle for Employment Guarantee', *Frontline*, 26(1). Available online at: http://www.frontlineonnet.com/fl2601/stories/20090116260100400.htm (accessed on 31 July 2012).

Dutta Roy, Sudipta (2003), 'Employment Dynamics in Indian Industry: Adjustment Lags and the Impact of Job Security Regulations', *Journal of Development Economics*, 73: 233–56.

Fallon, Peter and Robert Lucas (1991), 'The Impact of Job-security Regulations in India and Zimbabwe', *The World Bank Economic Review*, 5(3): 395–413.

——— (1993), 'Job-security Regulations and the Dynamic Demand for Labour in India and Zimbabwe', *Journal of Development Economics*, 40(2): 241–75.

Indian Labour Yearbook (various issues), New Delhi: The Ministry of Labour, Government of India.

Levine, David (1992), 'Can Wage Increases Pay for Themselves? Tests with a Production Function', *Economic Journal*, 102(414): 1102–15.

Luke, Nancy and Kaivan Munshi (2011), 'Women as Agents of Change: Female Income and Mobility in India', *Journal of Development Economics*, (94): 1–17.

Martin, Nathan D. and David Brady (2007), 'Workers of the Less Developed World Unite? A Multilevel Analysis of Unionization in Less Developed Countries', *American Sociological Review*, 72(4): 562–84.

Nagaraj, R. (1994), 'Employment and Wages in Manufacturing Industries: Trends Hypotheses and Evidence', *Economic and Political Weekly*, 29(22 January): 177–86.

National Sample Survey Office (2008), *Migration in India: July 2007–June 2008*, NSS Report No. 533. New Delhi: Government of India.

Naylor, Robin (1989), 'Strikes, Free Riders, and Social Customs', *Quarterly Journal of Economics*, 104(4): 771–85.

Pal, Rupayan (2006), 'Essays on Labour Contracts and Asymmetric Information', PhD dissertation, Indira Gandhi Institute of Development Research, Mumbai.

——— (2010), 'Impact of Communist Parties on the Individual Decision to Join a Trade Union: Evidence from India', *The Developing Economies*, 48(4): 496–528.

Ramaswamy, K.V. (1999), 'Productivity Growth, Protection and Plant Entry in a Deregulating Economy: The Case of India', *Small Business Economics*, 13(2): 131–9.

Saha, Bibhas, Kunal Sen, and Dibyendu Maiti (2013), 'Trade Openness, Labour Institutions and Flexibilisation: Evidence from India', *Labour Economics*, 24: 180–95.

Sengenberger, Werner (1994), 'International labour standards in a globalized economy: the issues', in W. Sengenberger and D. Campbell (eds), *International Labour Standards and Economic Interdependence*. Geneva: International Institute for Labour Studies (ILO), pp. 3–15.

The World Bank (1989), *India: Poverty, Employment and Social Services, a World Bank Country Study*. Washington, DC: The World Bank.

Thangavelu, S.M. and G. Rajaguru (2004), 'Is There an Export or Import Led Productivity Growth in Rapidly Developing Asian Countries: A Multivariate VAR Analysis', *Applied Economics*, 36: 1083–93.

Venn, Danielle (2009), 'Legislation, collective bargaining and enforcement: Updating the OECD employment protection indicators', Social, Employment and Migration Working Paper No. 89. Paris: OECD. Available at: www.oecd.org/employment/protection (last accessed on 3 September 2012).

CHAPTER 31

THE FINANCIAL SECTOR IN INDIA

an overview

RAJESH CHAKRABARTI

> We do indeed live in the age of financial capitalism. We should not regret that. Regulations and restrictions can and should be placed on financial institutions to help them function in the best interests of society, but the underlying logic and power of these institutions remains central to their role. Financial institutions and financial variables are as much a source of direction and an ordering principle in our lives as the rising and setting sun, the seasons, and the tides.
>
> —*Robert Shiller (2012)*

What is a Financial System?

In order to appreciate the Indian financial system, it is best to first lay down the nature of financial systems in general, to delineate the expectations and challenges that the system in India faces. The financial sector in any country relates to the economy it serves, much like the manner in which the circulatory system in the human body serves the entire organism. It is the job of the circulatory system—consisting of the heart, the blood and the miles of intricate vessel network—to draw nourishment from the intestines and oxygen from the lungs and relentlessly supply each cell of the body with these. Similarly, it is the task of the financial system to pick up the tiny specks of surplus that appear throughout the economy—in households spanning the entire geography, in businesses in various sectors, and sometimes even in government—and channel it to the best investment opportunity.

The circulatory system cannot be held responsible for death from starvation or asphyxiation, as the supply of food and oxygen are not its responsibility. And yet its criticality is manifest in the fact that left unattended a heart attack can kill a person in a few minutes—the immediate cause of death not being that the blood had stopped flowing but that the brain had been starved of precious oxygen for too long. The financial system is equally critical. While, in itself, it neither generates the surplus nor creates busy opportunities (outside the financial sector), a collapse of the financial sector can bring the entire economy to a complete halt, to push a society to anarchy, and can cause severe economic damage that could take years to mend. The stability of the financial system is therefore no less critical for the health of the economy than is cardiac health for the longevity of an individual. For an economy to survive and thrive it is imperative that the financial system ceaselessly transports capital form the savers to the investors and brings back the returns on the investment—in the form of dividend and interest—to the ultimate suppliers of capital.

Carrying the circulatory system analogy a little further, in all countries around the world, two systems compete with and complement each other in fulfilling this circulatory role—the banking system and financial markets. While the two channels are increasingly getting intertwined in the institutions that form part of the arteries, they differ in a fundamental way—in their style of working and information dissemination. Banks are, by their very nature, relational in their dealings while markets specialize in faceless, arm's length, and contractual transactions. Rarely is the financial flow balanced between the two channels. Some countries—notably the US and the UK—are market dominated, while others—including Germany and Japan—see a greater role for banks. The causes of this difference have puzzled economists for decades and continue to do so, though the accepted explanation today—thanks to the work of Andrei Shleifer and his co-authors—is that it is the level of investor protection in the legal system that determines which artery is more throbbing, with greater protection leading to more vibrant markets.

While the primary job of the financial system is to bridge the space between savers and investors, in doing so it fulfils several other roles. In making the twain meet, the system must ensure that varying risk appetites, size needs, information asymmetry, as well as planning horizons and liquidity needs, are reconciled at the two ends, not to speak of geographical distance. Here is where various financial institutions and products—including the oft-dreaded derivatives—play their role.

Finally, the stability of a financial system is as solid as the public faith in it. Whether it is banks or financial markets, the fact that the system functions only on the basis of complete consent, indeed eagerness, of savers to hand over their hard-earned savings to complete strangers, underlines the need for regulatory practices that are not just prudent but are perceived to be so, in order to sustain the throughput. In the ultimate analysis, of course, this faith rests on the ability of the country's legal and judicial system to enforce and maintain the sanctity of contracts.

It is with this background that we can approach the task of understanding and assessing the Indian financial system.

The Indian Financial Sector—A Systemic Assessment

The World Economic Forum provides an assessment of the relative financial development of 60 countries—ranging from the OECD countries to Nigeria and Bangladesh—in its annual Financial Development Report (WEF 2011). In its 2011 rankings, India figured at a rank of 36 with an overall score of 3.29 on a seven-point scale where the range for the 60 countries was from 2.44 to 5.16. The underlying approach behind this evaluation is a seven-dimensional rating system, presented in Table 31.1. There is an input to output progression in the dimensions. The first three criteria—institutional environment, business environment, and financial stability—constitute the 'factors, policies and institutions' set, an area where India performs particularly poorly. In both kinds of environment measures, India is at the threshold of the worst decile, confirming findings from other sources like the World Bank's Ease of Doing Business indicators that the socio-legal foundations of the financial system in India are quite poor.

The second set—'financial intermediation'—comprising banking and non-banking financial services and financial markets, shows much better relative performance. This seems to suggest that the volume of transactions supported by the system is actually larger than what one would expect given the strength of its foundations.

Table 31.1 Financial Development Index for India

Financial Development Index 2011		
	Rank (out of 60)	Score
2011 Index	36	3.3
1st pillar: Institutional environment	54	3.1
2nd pillar: Business environment	54	3.4
3rd pillar: Financial stability	47	4.0
4th pillar: Banking financial services	43	3.1
5th pillar: Non-banking financial services	5	4.2
6th pillar: Financial markets	29	2.3
7th pillar: Financial access	47	2.8

(Score is on a 1-7 scale)
Source: WEF (2011).

The last measure, financial access, is an output variable in the sense that it is a key feature desired from the system. Here too India finishes at the verge of the bottom of 20 per cent of the countries, pulled down mostly by low penetration by bank branches and ATMs and buoyed to some extent by micro-finance activity, which of late, is experiencing severe turmoil.

In terms of the relative size of the financial sector in India, financial assets amounted to 228 per cent of GDP in 2009 as opposed to 539 per cent for UK, 399 per cent for the US, 224 per cent for Thailand, and 102 per cent for Pakistan. Of the financial assets, equity markets accounted for 41 per cent, bank deposits for 31 per cent, and public debt for 23 per cent. In terms of its structure (relative dominance bank versus markets) and efficiency, Table 31.2, taken from Allen et al. (2012), indicates that India has a greater relative dominance of financial markets as opposed to banks when compared to a broad set of emerging market countries. In terms of efficiency too, the Indian financial system (banks and markets together) performs better than its counterparts in other emerging market countries but, as its comparison with developed countries shows, it has significant room for improvement.

It is perhaps relevant to note here that the Indian financial system—in the modern western institutions sense, not dating back to *hundies* and other indigenous practices but dating as far back to at least Kautilya—is one of the oldest ones in the colonial world. The oldest Asian stock exchange, for instance, is the Bombay Stock Exchange which predates the Tokyo Stock Exchange. At Independence in 1947, India inherited a fairly developed

Table 31.2 Financial System Structure in India: Bank versus Markets

This table compares financial markets and banking sector of the Indian financial system with those of other emerging countries and LLSV country groups (sorted by legal origins). All the measures are taken from Levine (2002) or calculated from the World Bank Financial Database using the definitions in Levine (2002). We use 2005 figures for all countries. The figures for other emerging countries and for all LLSV country groups are weighted averages (with the countries' GDPs in 2005 as the weights).

	Size of Banks and Markets				Structure Indices: Markets vs. Banks**				Financial Development*** (banking and market sectors)		
Measures	Bank credit/ GDP	Bank Over-based cost/ Bank assets	Value Traded/ GDP	Markets cap./GDP	Structure Activity	Structure Size	Structure Efficiency	Structure Regulatory	Finance Activity	Finance Size	Finance Efficiency
Panel A: India and Other Large Emerging Markets (EMs)											
India	0.37	0.02	0.56	0.60	0.43	0.49	−4.44	10.00	−1.57	−1.51	3.30
Argentina (F)	0.10	0.08	0.09	0.30	−0.12	1.07	−4.95	7.00	−4.70	−3.51	0.13
Brazil (F)	0.29	0.08	0.18	0.51	−0.40	0.56	−4.20	10.00	−2.88	−1.91	0.93
China	0.31*	0.01	0.26	0.32	−0.16	0.03	−5.87	16.00	−2.51	−2.31	3.19
Egypt (F)	0.45	0.02	0.28	0.66	−0.45	0.39	−5.13	13.00	−2.06	−1.22	2.61
Indonesia (F)	0.22	0.03	0.15	0.27	−0.40	0.22	−5.48	N.A.	−3.45	−2.83	1.63
Korea (G)	N.A.	0.02	1.53	0.73	N.A.	N.A.	−3.73	N.A.	N.A.	N.A.	4.57
Malaysia (E)	1.03	0.01	0.38	1.44	−0.99	0.33	−5.22	10.00	−0.93	0.39	3.30
Mexico (F)	0.15	N.A.	0.07	0.27	−0.75	0.61	N.A.	12.00	−4.60	−3.24	N.A.
Pakistan (E)	0.27	0.02	1.27	0.34	1.56	0.24	−3.58	10.00	−1.08	−2.40	4.06
Peru (F)	0.18	0.07	0.03	0.36	−1.93	0.70	−6.35	8.00	−5.39	−2.75	−0.98
Philippines (F)	0.26	0.06	0.07	0.35	−1.32	0.29	−5.51	7.00	−3.98	−2.37	0.21

S. Africa (E)	0.80	0.05	0.84	2.14	0.04	0.98	−3.12	8.00	−0.40	0.54	2.76
Sri Lanka (E)	0.30	0.04	0.05	0.20	−1.81	−0.40	−6.22	7.00	−4.24	−2.82	0.16
Taiwan (G)	N.A.	0.02	1.79	1.35	N.A.	N.A.	−3.62	12.00	N.A.	N.A.	4.78
Thailand (E)	0.73	0.02	0.51	0.68	−0.37	−0.07	−4.72	9.00	−0.99	−0.70	3.36
Turkey (F)	0.21	0.06	0.55	0.36	0.96	0.52	−3.40	12.00	−2.14	−2.57	2.21
Ave. for EMs[a]	0.32	0.04	0.62	0.65	−0.32	0.53	−4.19	7.97	−3.00	−2.15	2.55
Panel B: LLSV Country Groups											
English origin*	0.67	0.04	1.57	1.34	0.89	0.77	−2.99	1.93	−0.15	−0.10	3.72
French origin*	0.77	0.04	0.60	0.66	−0.43	−0.05	−4.02	8.50	−1.45	−1.08	2.50
German origin*	1.06	0.02	1.05	0.82	−0.16	−0.37	−4.01	9.65	−0.08	−0.27	3.90
Nordic origin*	1.05	0.02	0.99	0.85	−0.07	−0.20	−3.86	7.74	−0.08	−0.21	3.71
Sample Ave.	0.78	0.03	1.17	1.02	0.28	0.28	−3.55	8.53	−0.50	−0.50	3.48

Source: Allen et al. (2012).

Notes: [a]*weighted* (by 2005 GDP) average of other emerging market economies *without* India;

* = the figures for each legal origin group are weighted averages (GDP in 2005); English origin averages are calculated *without* India.

** Structure indices measure whether a country's financial system is market- or bank-dominated; the higher the measure, the more the system is dominated by markets. Specifically, 'structure activity' is equal to log (value traded/bank credit) and measures the size of markets relative to banks; 'structure efficiency' is equal to log (market cap ratio × overhead cost ratio) and measures the relative efficiency of markets vs. banks; finally, 'structure regulatory' is the sum of the four categories in regulatory restriction, or the degree to which commercial banks are allowed to engage in security, firm operation, insurance, and real estate: 1-unrestricted; 2-permit to conduct through subsidiary; 3-full range not permitted in subsidiaries; and 4-strictly prohibited.

*** Financial development variables measure the entire financial system (banking and market sectors combined), and the higher the measure, the larger or more efficient the financial system is. Specifically, 'finance activity' is equal to log (total value traded ratioxprivate credit ratio), 'finance size' is equal to log (market cap ratioxbank private credit ratio), and 'finance efficiency' is equal to log (total value traded ratio/bank overhead cost).

financial system, complete with legal codes for companies and banks to function.

Nevertheless, the Indian financial system virtually re-booted during the liberalization process that started in 1991 and continues to this day. The transformation in the financial system brought about by liberalization has been so vast that it practically rendered the pre-liberalization history irrelevant. For instance, the primary stock market regulator, the Securities and Exchange Board of India (SEBI), was empowered after the reforms. The leading stock exchange of the country transacting over 95 per cent of trades today, the National Stock Exchange (NSE), and the second largest bank, ICICI Bank, are both children of reforms, not to speak of the vibrant mutual fund and insurance industries that appeared since a little over a decade ago, together with derivatives trading that is a bigger market than equities. A closed system has gradually opened up to foreign participation since liberalization, with foreign institutional investors (FIIs) emerging as an important investor category in equity markets. Krishnan (2011) provides an informative contrast between the pre-liberalization state of the markets and those that prevail today. Consequently India's financial depth (financial assets/GDP) grew steadily from slightly over 100 in the 1990s to more than double the figure by the end of the first decade of the new century.

The transformation of the Indian financial system is far from over though. Indeed flux and an unfinished change agenda are key features of the Indian financial system. While multiple important bills—including one regarding the Pension Fund Regulatory and Development Authority (PFRDA), as well as the one that seeks to overhaul the Companies Act—await the Parliament's approval, the Financial Sector Legislative Reforms Commission is working on revising the very laws that constitute the foundation of the system.

The Financial System's Infrastructure

While banks and financial markets constitute the most visible parts of a financial system, they both stand on a set of infrastructure institutions that make credit and investment flows happen in an economy. We devote this section to a discussion of this infrastructure, which has at least four components, including a set of laws like the Banking Regulation Act, Companies Act, and Securities Contracts Regulation Act, that allow the financial system to exist and function in the first place, and the technology that enables it to function with increased efficiency. The other two legs are more nuanced. On the credit side, these comprise the credit information system and the insolvency and creditor rights (ICR) mechanism that help in the recovery mechanism in the case of default. On the investment side, it comprises the corporate governance system that protects a retail investor not just from rogue management but also from expropriation by controlling shareholders, typically promoters.

As in many other countries, the financial sector in India developed organically with new segments appearing with time, and regulation and legislation being done as each of these reached a certain critical mass. Consequently, the legal and regulatory system that has emerged in the country is essentially institution based—a set of rules and regulators for banks, a different set for markets, a third for insurance, and so forth. Over time, however, the sector has changed and as commercial banks cross-sell insurance and own investment banking arms and insurance companies offer market-based products, the need for a more up-to-date and holistic approach to regulation is being strongly felt. The recently constituted Financial Sector Legislative Reforms Commission (FSLRC) seeks to revisit the entire landscape with a systemic perspective and will hopefully bring forth consistent standards of regulation across sectors, creating room for a dynamic and continuously evolving financial system to function and expand with the times.

It is easy to overlook the technology that provides the foundation for all transactions in a modern financial system, but that will be a grievous error. While ATMs, net-banking and perhaps very soon m-banking (mobile banking) will form the visible face of technology in finance, equally if not more important are the Centralized Online Real-time Environment (CORE) banking networks that connect all bank branches to a central server allowing for anywhere anytime banking, the inter-bank payment gateways that enable fund transfers across banks via National Electronic Funds Transfer (NEFT) and Real-time Gross Settlement (RTGS) or the IT backbone that enables NSE to handle, on average, roughly 11,500 transactions per second. Indeed, more than anything else, it was core banking that gave the new private banks a competitive edge over their public sector counterparts till the latter caught up.

Equally important for all credit transactions is the ability of a borrower to convince a lender of his creditworthiness. In most developed countries this is achieved through credit bureaus. In India, the operations of credit information companies got a boost only with the passing of the Credit Information Companies Act (CICA), 2005. Currently there are four active credit bureaus—CIBIL, the oldest and the biggest among them, Equifax, Experian, and Highmark. Each has a leading foreign credit bureau as a co-promoter. CIBIL covers over 170 million consumer reports and 6.5 million company reports and functions on a membership basis—where a member financial institution shares data to have access to other data—rather than on a subscription basis that would open the information up to non-financial service providers as well. The quality of the data hinges on proper identification and that is where the ongoing UIDAI efforts are expected to make a big difference.

Another equally important element of credit infrastructure comprises creditor rights, referring to the ability of a lender to possess the collateral in case of default, as well as the related issue of a bankruptcy option for the defaulter. Together these issues are referred to as insolvency and creditor rights (ICR). India has traditionally witnessed very weak ICR with courts liberally issuing stay orders on creditors' right to possess collateral. The Sick Industrial Companies Act (SICA), 1985, constituted the Board of Industrial and Financial Reconstruction (BIFR) which provided protection to 'sick' companies (defined as companies that have had their net worth wiped out by accumulated losses, almost already beyond redemption). BIFR proceedings often extended to several years (REF) in effect destroying the collateral value even in cases which led to eventual liquidation. Debt recovery tribunals (DRTs) made their appearance in the mid-1990s but the situation really changed with the promulgation of the Securitization and Reconstruction of Financial Assets and Enforcement of Security Interest Act, 2002 (SRFAESI Act), that gave lenders the right to seize collateral upon default after a notice. Bankruptcy, particularly personal bankruptcy, remains an area where a lot of improvement is necessary. This is particularly important in a country where suicides have often been ascribed to default.

Just as a lender needs to be assured of the creditworthiness of a borrower and the creditor's rights in case of a default, an equity investor needs to be assured of the integrity of the management of a company he is investing in as well as his rights as a shareholder. This is where corporate governance enters the picture as a critical infrastructure input (please see Chapter 15 for a detailed discussion for corporate governance). While on paper, India enjoys one of the highest levels of shareholders' rights in the world, questions about its judicial process and its regulatory activism reduce the effectiveness of this protection. A major step in corporate governance for listed companies came in the form of Clause 49 of the listing agreements in the early 2000s with a host of governance and disclosure measures broadly in line with global reforms like Sarbanes-Oxley Act in the US. However, the widely reported Satyam crisis of 2008–9 raised several questions about the efficacy of the institution of independent directors on corporate boards as well as the other major pillars of corporate governance—auditors. On the whole though, the quality of corporate governance in India is perhaps comparable to that in most emerging markets, with significant room for improvement.

Financial Access and Inclusion

Recent research has demonstrated the strong impact of access to finance and financial inclusion on economic growth (see Beck and Demirguc-Kunt 2008). This is also an area where India has lagged behind. In 2005 McKinsey estimated that less than 50 per cent of India's household savings were captured by the formal financial system (see McKinsey 2005). Even in 2011 the number of bank accounts in India was less than half of the eligible population in India[1] and if one considers unique account holders the proportion falls to perhaps closer to a third of the population. A recent World Bank study (Demirguc-Kunt and Klapper 2012) estimates India's bank account penetration at 35 per cent, well below the developing country average in their sample of 41 per cent. To continue with the analogy of a circulatory system, the Indian financial system is a woefully low-pressure system with cold toes and fingers.

Financial exclusion leads to inferior outcomes for excluded individuals as they get poorer returns on their savings (in a country with one of the highest household savings rates in the world at above 30 per cent) and deprives the system itself of significant investible capital. Financial inclusion has formed a key part of the UPA government's inclusive growth agenda, particularly with the Committee on Financial Inclusion headed by Dr Rangarajan in 2005 and the follow-up on its recommendations of a Financial Inclusion Fund and the 'no frills' accounts in India. The

[1] See the relevant article in *DNA*, available at http://www.dnaindia.com/money/report_over-50pct-population-without-bank-account-rbi-deputy-governor_1535450 (accessed on 6 November 2013).

wide reach of MNREGA (Mahatma Gandhi National Rural Employment Guarantee Act), which seeks to make payments directly to bank accounts, is expected to improve the situation over time, though expectations of any revolutionary change in the situation remain unrealistic.

Geography remains a major challenge. India has over 600,000 villages—from tiny hamlets to those with populations exceeding 2,000 people—served by less than 22,000 rural branches of scheduled commercial banks and less than 41,000 ATMs in 2011. Rural branching in India has actually declined significantly since liberalization (from a figure exceeding 35,000 in 1993) when the 1:4 rule (whereby the RBI issued a license to open an urban branch to a bank only if it opened four rural branches) started in 1977 was discontinued.[2] Part of this change comes from re-designation of branches but the fact remains that covering remote villages through branch networks remains a distant dream.

Several innovations have occurred in recent years. The use of business correspondents—agents hired to extend banking services to outside branch premises—aided in a big way with modern ICT, as well as the thrust on ATMs and 'ATMs on wheels', and hopes of mobile banking taking financial services to the masses all underpin the hopes of a massive financial roll-out. Nevertheless, the fact remains that these have not translated from cute innovations to India-scale efforts with a national-level impact. Far from withering away, as was envisaged during bank nationalization in the 1960s, moneylenders have increased their importance as a source of financing for the poor (from about 21 per cent of rural household credit in 1990–1 to close to 30 per cent in 2002–3) in the years since liberalization (see IIEF Household Incomes and Savings Survey 2005).

Policy is often blamed for the tardy progress of inclusion innovations. RBI's rule of allowing business correspondents to operate only within 30 km of a branch (extended from the initial 15) takes the teeth out of the geographical reach imperative. Mobile phone-based banking has also been awaiting regulatory nod for a long while. But the central bank's concerns about balancing innovation with stability are also valid, although one may argue that risking a bit in rural branches where even a breach or abuse is likely to remain too small to destabilize the system may be worthwhile if more innovation-friendly policies actually help enhance financial access.

Micro-finance was widely believed to provide the solution that the formal banking system (regional rural banks included) with its much higher

[2] See relevant article in *The Hindu*, available at http://www.hindu.com/thehindu/thscrip/print.pl?file=2008032857540100.htm&date=2008/03/28/&prd=th& (accessed on 6 November 2013).

personnel costs and forbidding documentation processes failed to deliver. The 1990s and the 2000s witnessed a virtual revolution in the Indian micro-finance space with stunning growth rates (see Chakrabarti and Ravi 2011) before hitting a major roadblock in 2010 in Andhra Pradesh, the state that alone accounted for over a third of all micro-finance activity in the country. In the wake of a hugely successful IPO by the leading micro-finance provider SKS and about 30 widely publicized suicides, the Andhra Pradesh government regulated the industry extremely heavily and repayment rates dropped from near-perfect to below 30 per cent. The impression—not wholly unfounded—was that profit-hungry micro-finance operators had slowly changed from angels of development to merciless usurers in the absence of regulation, leading the poor to a fatal debt trap. Different models of micro-finance have worked side-by-side. While banks have usually followed the self-help group model, private players have tended to stress on personal loans and joint liability lending where the problems seem to have been most marked. RBI responded to the Andhra Pradesh crisis by coming out with new regulations in 2011, including an interest rate ceiling of 24 per cent and lending restrictions for micro-finance providers while continuing to give them access to priority sector funding, but the sector is currently undergoing significant turmoil and many micro-finance lenders are gasping for survival. Many find the operating costs of delivering credit to the poor to be too high—and highly variant across geographies and societies—to keep them viable within the 24 per cent ceiling. The fear that the demise or at least contraction of micro-finance will push the poor back to moneylenders—completely informal and hence unregulated or some of the non-bank financial companies (NBFCs) with questionable practices—remains strong.

As in all matters, India exhibits considerable regional variations in levels of financial inclusion with the southern states being the most inclusive financially and the north-eastern and northern states the least. Financial exclusion is not exclusively a rural phenomenon with significant parts of the urban poor remaining outside the banking system as well, largely owing to documentation needs—particularly proof of address—that make opening an account difficult. Nor is financial exclusion only an issue about credit. Indebtedness in the lowest quartile of the income-distribution often stems from financial and health emergencies. Thus, insurance products are equally, if not more, important. Old age support in the form of pension is another area where financial exclusion is extremely widespread with virtually no state pension and 85 per cent of the labour force engaged in the informal sector and excluded from employer pension plans.

Banking

No discussion of the financial system can even hope to be meaningful without a clear analysis of the nature and health of the country's banking system. However, we shall leave that formidable task to the next chapter, that is, Chapter 32, 'Banks: Financing the Future' and restrict ourselves to only pointing out a few key aspects of the Indian banking system.

Broadly speaking, India has a stable, fragmented, largely protected, public-sector-dominated banking system monitored closely by the RBI, that has performed very well in terms of stability, especially during turbulent phases of the world financial system but has featured less well in matters of inclusion and innovation. With risk-weighted capital adequacy in the range of 13–14 per cent, well above the Basel norms, Indian banks are among the safest in the world.

India's banks are also extremely fragmented. State Bank of India, India's largest bank by far, does not even make it to the top 50 of the world's largest banks (in contrast to China that has three of the world's 10 largest banks). This is not necessarily a problem and the US has an even more fragmented banking sector than India though its larger banks are among the largest in the world. But over time, the size of India's banks has fallen relative to India's large companies and individual banks are running into balance sheet constraints to serve big client businesses. There is therefore a view that consolidation may add value in a business sense.

With more than three-quarters of India's banking deposits and advances, public sector banks (in most cases listed and partially privatized) clearly dominate the banking landscape in the country. The state's role in commercial banking in India started in 1955 with the nationalization of the erstwhile Imperial Bank and creation of the State Bank of India through an eponymous act of Parliament and the two rounds of nationalization in 1969 and 1980. Liberalization saw a shift in direction with licenses for new banks being issued after a long time and these new private banks—dominated by ICICI Bank that has quickly become the nation's second largest bank—have raised standards of banking services, particularly among the urban affluent class as well as in corporate banking. Public sector banks, after lagging behind, slowly adapted to the changing environment in the mid-2000s with the adoption of core banking technology and the associated benefits that such technology makes possible. Nevertheless, a joint report commissioned by the Indian Banks Association (IBA) and executed by McKinsey found several managerial gaps between the incumbents (public sector banks) and the attackers (new private sector banks and foreign banks) particularly in terms of service quality and in attracting and retaining human resources.

While Indian banks have fared well through the storms of financial crises—whether during the Asian crisis or the global crisis—detractors have often pointed out that this is because of RBI's ultra-conservative policy of not allowing banks to get into any activity that could be potentially destabilizing. So the cost of stability has been slow progress in innovation and inclusion. Whether that cost has been commensurate with benefits remains a matter of debate.

Financial Markets

Table 31.3 presents the characterization of levels of liquidity in various financial markets as made by the Rajan Committee (High Powered Committee on Financial Sector Reforms, Planning Commission, 2008). While Indian markets have seen a lot happening in the less than four years following that report, the basic liquidity levels have probably not changed drastically from that assessment.

Table 31.3 Liquidity in Indian Financial Markets

Market	Immediacy	Depth	Resilience
Large cap stocks/futures and index futures	Y	Y	Y
Other stocks			
On the run government bonds	Y	Y	
Other government bonds			
Corporate bonds			
Commercial paper and other money market instruments			
Near money options on index and liquid stocks	Y		
Other stock options			
Currency	Y		
Interest rate swaps	Y	Y	
Metals, energies, and select agricultural commodity futures	Y		
Other commodity futures			

Source: Planning Commission (2008).

Though financial markets in India cherish a long history, they were completely revamped during the liberalization starting in the early 1990s. The dominant equity exchange, NSE, was established in 1994 and the regulator SEBI empowered in 1992. Trading in commodity forwards, which halted in the mid-1960s, resumed, and equity derivatives, that now account for a much greater trading volume than equities themselves, made their appearance in 2001. Intermediary industries like mutual funds and insurance were opened in the late 1990s and early 2000s and both sectors have exhibited unprecedented growth in the period that has followed. Currency markets have also boomed with India's share of world currency transactions—itself a rising amount—growing nine-fold between 2004 and 2011. Currency futures were introduced in 2008 and more recently currency options have begun trading on exchanges as well.

As in many other countries, the financial markets, arranged in terms of turnover in India, provide the following ordering—foreign exchange, money market, equity derivatives, equities, government securities, corporate debt. Together with a widening of the range of tradable assets, Indian markets have also witnessed a revolution of sorts in trading technology and transparency. T+2 settlements, which mean all trading is settled in two working days, standard in India now, are among the best in the world. Online brokerage accounts and dematerialized trading in equity shares have taken equity trading a long distance away from the dark days of BSE-dominated trading in the pre-liberalization period.

The first decade of the new century witnessed explosive growth in the activities of the collective investment and insurance industries, an important participant in markets. As the mutual funds industry gradually evolved from a government monopoly to a competitive industry with foreign participation, the assets under management rose from less than Rs 80,000 crore in March 2003 to over Rs 592,000 crore in March 2011, a rise of over seven times. Similarly, the insurance industry grew at an annual rate exceeding 30 per cent for the life sector and close to 16 per cent for the non-life sector between 2000 and 2010. Finally, foreign institutional investment (FII) flows, allowed since 1993, reached a cumulative figure below Rs 40,000 crore in March 2000. By November 2011, the cumulative figure exceeded Rs 543,000 crore (more than 13 times) despite significant pull-back during the global crisis as well as the Euro crisis.[3] Since March 2000, the Sensex value has risen roughly four times—from slightly below 4,000 to close to 17,000 with significant gyrations during the period. On

[3] IRDA Annual Reports (various years).

the whole then, the first few years of the current century have proved to be a period of explosive growth for Indian markets, notwithstanding global crises.

The exception to this across-the-board growth story is the corporate bonds sector. Despite close top-level policy attention to this segment, starting at least with the Patil Committee recommendations in 2005, the number of listings as well as trading volume have remained stubbornly low in this area that is becoming particularly critical with the growing need of infrastructure financing. In the absence of corporate bonds, which should have been the natural instrument to finance long-term infrastructure projects, much of the funding has come from bank lending which implies significant asset–liability duration mismatch for banks (since bank liabilities are of much shorter maturity it leaves the banks more exposed to interest risks on the asset side compared to the liability side). The reasons commonly cited for the poor performance of the sector include the charging of stamp duty, market micro-structure issues as well as restrictions on financial institutions—the primary buyers of corporate bonds—and holding debt securities of only AAA ratings.

Indian bourses, the BSE and the NSE now figure in the top ten of the world's capital markets in terms of market capitalization but in terms of liquidity they still leave a lot to be desired. The NSE has a turnover velocity (annual turnover value divided by market capitalization) of just over 57 per cent while for BSE, which boasts of maximum listed stocks anywhere in the world, the figure is merely 18 per cent. The NASDAQ by contrast has a turnover velocity of 340 per cent. It is fair to say that the lower 50 per cent of BSE stocks hardly see any movement. In terms of market participants, about half of all trading happens roughly between 450 participants, almost a third of whom are proprietary traders. Trading has become more concentrated over the years and participation in equity markets ranges between 2 to 5 per cent of the population by various estimates, and 5 to 10 per cent, if one adds mutual fund investments. Such revelations this was made in response to a question in Parliament—are often picked up by sections of the media as indicative of price-manipulation through cartelization and cheating the common investor. Such concerns, however, are likely misplaced since advanced markets also exhibit similar traits (Chakrabarti 2010).

While NSE is the virtual monopolist in the exchange space in India SEBI, of late the market watchdog has been kept busy with the issue of competition there. MCX-SX, a subsidiary of the leading commodities exchange MCX, has sought entry into the equities space, which has been denied in the wake of a controversial committee report and the unprecedented suing of SEBI by MCX, forcing a decision. Recently a court order has asked SEBI to re-look into its decision, so the matter is far from settled.

Regulation

The financial regulatory environment in India is heavily fragmented and exceedingly rule-based. As many as six different federal ministries are involved in regulating parts of the financial system. This includes the Ministry of Consumer Affairs, that controls the Forward Markets Commission charged with regulating the commodities markets, the Ministry of Labour, that controls the Employees' Provident Fund Organization, as well as the Ministry of Urban Development, that controls the National Housing Bank, a second-rung sector regulator. Among the apex regulators, RBI controls all banking and non-banking financial companies, currency-related transactions as well as bond markets, while SEBI is in charge of exchanges and actors therein and IRDA insurance. The long-awaited and recently passed PFRDA Act puts the PFRDA in charge of the pension sector.

The current set up suffers heavily from regulatory gaps and overlaps and is, at times, marked with the possibility of regulatory capture and arbitrage. Perhaps the best example of regulatory overlap emerged in the public squabble between SEBI and IRDA over control of unit-linked insurance plans (ULIPs) that the former argued were nothing other than mutual funds in disguise, getting away with much lesser regulation and transparency than applied to regular mutual funds. The regulatory gap aspect became evident in the 2010 episode involving the micro-finance sector in Andhra Pradesh discussed earlier.

The Rajan Committee had argued for a gradual movement of financial regulation in India towards a more integrated one, with a lighter, principle-based approach. Following the ULIP episode the government constituted a Financial Stability and Development Council (FSDC) chaired by the Finance Minister to coordinate among apex regulators. Another of the Rajan Committee's recommendation that has been acted upon is the constitution of the Financial Sector Legislative Reforms Commission

(FSLRC) to look into the updating and internal consistency of the various laws mentioned earlier.

A problem of the fragmented, silo-based regulatory system is the potential mis-measurement of overall risks associated with diversified financial conglomerates—the SBI and ICICI groups for instance—that span several segments of the financial sector from banking to insurance to capital markets. However, in the wake of the global financial crisis and the world-wide emphasis on monitoring large financial institutions, RBI has started producing an annual financial stability report that attempts to fill this void by taking a more comprehensive view of the financial sector.

However, as for the rules versus principles debate, not much change has happened with Indian regulation remaining largely rule-based and with the naturally conservative mandate of regulators much more tilted towards avoiding crisis than boosting market growth, the rules are geared towards keeping the worst performers in line rather than facilitating innovations in more capable players. Consequently, the regulatory response time to financial innovations has been rather large, for instance, in cases like the introduction of gold ETFs and US$–INR futures, where discussions have extended for over five years. While proponents of financial reforms consider this a serious drawback in Indian financial markets, keeping pace with the fast-changing world of finance around the globe, conservatives, particularly after the global financial crisis involving credit derivatives, continue to put caution before innovation. In any case, a move towards an exclusively principle-based regulatory approach will probably be premature in India given the level of development of its legal system, though a move towards more flexible application of rules—with pre-defined grounds of such flexibility rather than after-the-fact arbitrariness—may help encourage innovation without taking undue risks.

Stability in Times of Global Turmoil

The global financial crisis of 2007–8 as well as the more recent crises in Greece and other euro area countries revealed quite a bit about the strengths and vulnerabilities of the Indian financial system. The former caught the country after a few months of it raging in the west—giving rise to the later discredited 'decoupling' view of the Indian markets from the global economy when the Indian stock markets reached their peak with the Sensex climbing to the 21,000 levels in January 2008. However, the descent began thereafter and precipitated into a deep crash after the collapse of Lehman Brothers. Figure 31.1 provides a schematic presentation of a possible channel of impact in India flowing from FII withdrawal which may be argued as the immediate cause for the collapse of both the value of the rupee as well as the equity market. Post-Lehman fears and the severe crash also caused tremors in the money market, largely to finance the margin calls associated with such a sudden collapse. Another view proposed by Patnaik and Shah (2010) contends that Indian MNCs borrowing in India to fulfil their short-term dollar obligations abroad contributed to the choke-up in Indian financial markets, particularly the money market.

While there may still be debates over the exact channels of contagion of global disturbances into India, it is beyond dispute that the financial system in India has significant exposure to international markets and the causal relationship between FII flows and the value of the rupee is probably well-settled. The pull-back of portfolio investments from the country in 2008, when the US was viewed as a 'safe harbour', notwithstanding its being the main source of troubles, got re-enacted three years later as trouble in Greece and uncertainties in Italy, Spain, and elsewhere in Europe led to a similar withdrawal of funds in the second half of 2011 and the rupee falling from Rs 44 to Rs 52 to a dollar and beyond in a relatively short period.

The vulnerabilities notwithstanding, the global crisis also stress-tested the tenacity of Indian banks with none of the Indian banks actually ran into a crisis, owing largely to their negligible direct exposure of credit derivatives as well as low exposure to real estate lending, when, as elsewhere, property prices in India too decline sharply. A view, credible but difficult to confirm, is that the presence of a large informal (and to a large measure illegal) financial network largely insulated the formal financial system in India from a drop in real estate prices and helped the country emerge from the global crisis, not without bruises, but by and large in a better shape than many other countries.

Nevertheless, the crisis has changed key regulatory concerns for banking in India as elsewhere in the world. It has also shaken the faith in global regulators and standard-setting bodies, encouraging the demand for room for local leeway within broad trans-national regulatory norms (see Goyal 2010). India's conservative regulatory stance has also been widely credited for the system surviving the crisis with relatively less damage.

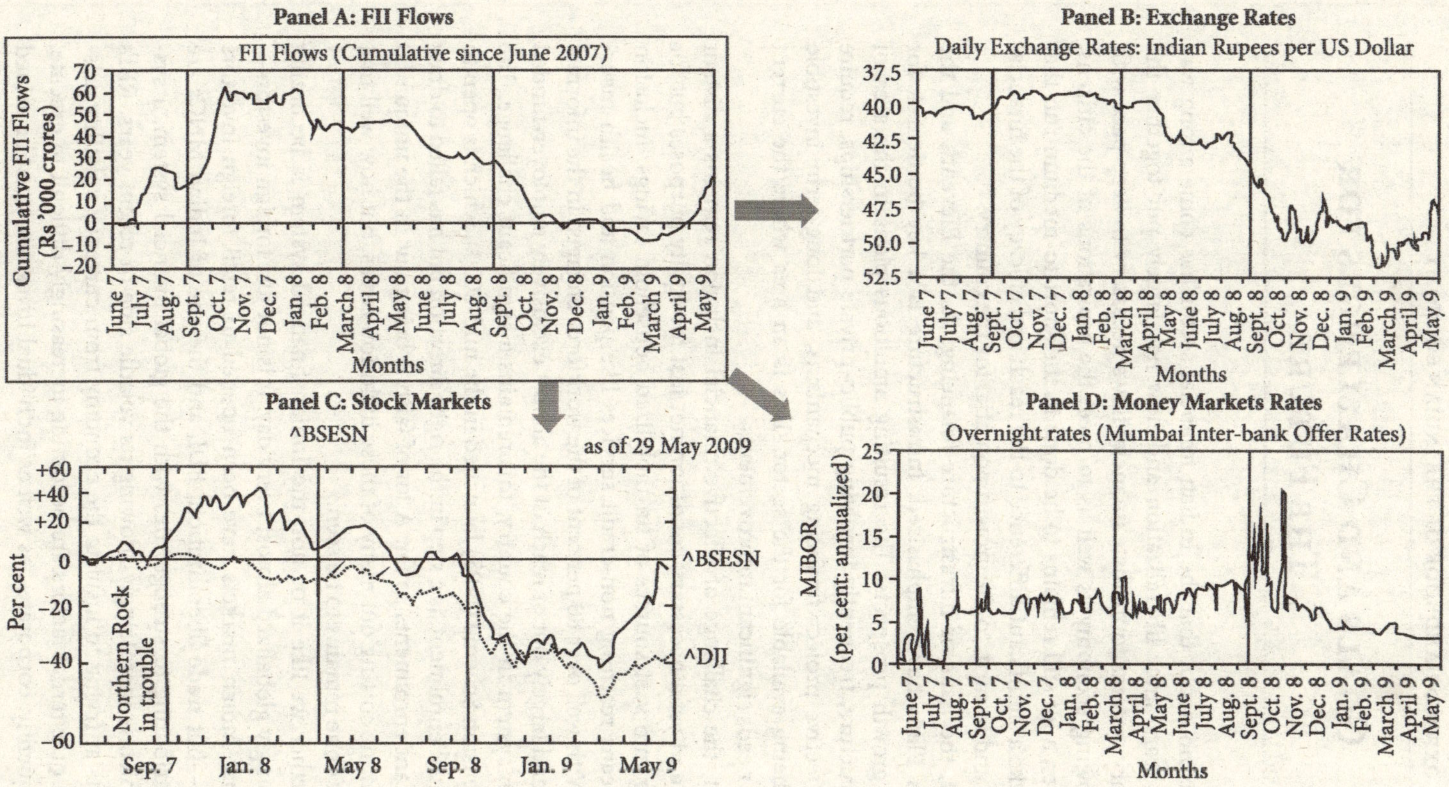

FIGURE 31.1 Contagion of the 2008 Global Financial Crisis into India—A possible characterization

Source: Author's Data

Note: The three vertical lines in each panel represent the dates of the collapse of the Northern Rock, Bear Sterns and Lehman Brothers.

Goals and Challenges for The Future

There is no doubt that the Indian financial sector has come a long way in the years since liberalization and now has largely put together the necessary systems to mediate financial flows necessary to keep pace with the growing economy as well as to meet the aspirations of the citizens. However, a lot still remains to be done in the short-to-medium run that can make a significant difference to the reach and efficacy of the financial system and in turn, to the growth potential for the country.

First, the issue of infrastructure financing. As the Eleventh and the Twelfth Plans have emphasized, infrastructure is a key bottleneck for India's growth prospects. The resulting ambitious plans in the area of infrastructure, frequently involving public–private partnerships, require very effective project financing mechanisms, and long-term investible funds being available for the sector. This is an area where the current system needs significant improvements.

Next, the challenge of effective financial inclusion remains a distant dream and yet a necessary condition not just for equity purposes but for tapping into vast sources of un-mobilized household savings. Inclusion also means reaching non-credit services like pension and health insurance. With well over 80 per cent of the workforce engaged in the informal sector and largely out of reach of the almost exclusively employer-funded pension system in the country, this remains a significant challenge. The New Pension Scheme (NPS) launched in the mid-2000s, which is open to individual enrolment, is a step in the right direction but has failed to draw significant enrolments so far. A lot of faith is being put in the unique ID programme sorting out many of these inclusion issues, but how well that will get done remains to be seen.

Whether we like it or not, the Indian financial system is becoming increasingly globalized almost every day. It is not just foreign investors—now that Indian markets have been opened to retail foreign investors as well—but trade liberalization, FDI, and the rise of Indian MNCs are all contributing to stronger ties with the global financial system, a system which is increasingly showing its volatile side in recent years. RBI's attempts at trying to insulate the economy from currency volatility arising out of external factors are becoming increasingly difficult to execute. Consequently, corporates, as well as individual investors, must be armed with instruments and the ability to hedge against the unavoidable volatility in financial markets. This is where sophisticated financial derivatives have their use. Currently such products are still far from the reach of average financial market participants.

If there is one thing that is universal and constant in the Indian financial system today, it is change. Liberalization is far from complete. Several key financial legislations are stuck in Parliament including the PFRDA Bill, and the new Companies Act. A responsive, market-friendly regulatory system is a pre-requisite for the Indian financial system to keep pace with the rapidly evolving, technology-oriented, and intricately inter-connected world of global finance.

References

Allen, Franklin, Rajesh Chakrabarti, Sankar De, Jun Qian, and Meijun Qian (2012), 'Financing Firms in India', *Journal of Financial Intermediation* 21(3): 409–45.

Beck, Thorsten and Asli Demirguc-Kunt (2008), 'Access to Finance: An Unfinished Agenda', *World Bank Economic Review* 22 (3 December).

Chakrabarti, Rajesh (2010), Should we really lose some sleep?, *Financial Express*, 28 August.

Chakrabarti, Rajesh and Shamika Ravi (2011), At the Crossroads: Microfinance in India', *Money and Finance*, (Special Issue, July): 3–6.

Demirguc-Kunt, Asli and Leora Klapper (2012), 'Measuring Financial Inclusion: The Global Findex Database', World Bank Policy Research Paper 6025.

Goyal, A. (2010), 'Regulatory Structure for Financial Stability and Development', *Economic and Political Weekly*, XLV(39): 51–61.

Krishnan, K.P. (2011), 'Financial Development in Emerging Markets: The Indian Experience', Financial Market Regulation and Reforms in Emerging Markets. Available at http://muse.jhu.edu/books/9780815704904/9780815704904-18.pdf (accessed on 6 November 2013).

Patnaik, Ila and Ajay Shah (2010), 'Why India choked when Lehman broke', *India Policy Forum*, 6: 6–9.

Planning Commission (2008), 'A Hundred Small Steps, Report of the Committee on Financial Sector Reforms', Available at: http://planningcommission.gov.in/reports/genrep/report_fr.htm (accessed on 6 November 2013).

Shiller, Robert (2012), *Finance and the Good Society*. Princeton: Princeton University Press.

World Economic Forum (2011), *The Financial Development Report 2011*. Available at: http://www3.weforum.org/docs/WEF_FinancialDevelopmentReport_2011.pdf (accessed on 6 November 2013).

CHAPTER 32

BANKS

financing the future

T.T. RAM MOHAN

India's banking system has undergone a remarkable transformation in the last decade and a half. At the commencement of banking sector reforms in 1993–4, the system's viability was in doubt and that was the provocation for reforms. The system was hopelessly antiquated. For instance, ATMs, which overseas Indian travellers were familiar with, were unknown in the system. The penetration of the banking system was poor and Indian banks seemed puny in comparison to international banks.

Today, the Indian banking system is among the most profitable in the world. A great deal that is modern in banking in terms of customer services is commonly available, including mobile banking. Penetration has increased although India remains under-banked by international standards, and banks have attained a respectable size.

But, perhaps, most worthy of celebration is that the system remained stable with not even the hint of a banking crisis throughout the period of deregulation. Even as the banks in the advanced economies reeled in the wake of the sub-prime crisis, banks in India remained stolidly unaffected. Perhaps for the first time ever, a governor of India's central bank (Y.V. Reddy), made front-page news in the *New York Times* (NYT 2008).

In what follows, we attempt to document this transformation and explain how efficiency with stability has become the *leitmotif* of Indian banking. The rest of the chapter is organized as follows. The next section outlines in brief the important reforms in the banking sector. The section that follows deals with the impact of reforms on efficiency while the impact of reforms on stability is addressed in the next section. In the section that follows we attempt to identify the factors that account for improved performance. The next section touches on a range of challenges and opportunities facing Indian banks in the years ahead. The last section gives a conclusion.

Overview of Reforms

The story of reforms in India's banking sector, especially the crucial reforms in the early stages, is well known and has been recounted in several places (for example, Rakesh Mohan 2007). Some of the key features of this regime are:

- Interest rates on deposits as well as loans were administered (there was a maximum deposit rate and a minimum lending rate).
- A high proportion of bank resources was pre-empted for financing the government through investments in government securities or what was called the statutory liquidity ratio (SLR). The ratio was 38.5 per cent at its peak. A high proportion was also pre-empted for meeting the needs of agriculture, small enterprises, and the 'weaker sections' of the community (all falling under the label of the 'priority sector').
- The interest rate on government securities itself was administratively determined (and kept at a low level to facilitate cheap funding of the government).
- Entry into the sector was restricted for foreign banks, with stringent limits on the number of branches that foreign banks could have. No private banks had been licensed subsequent to the nationalization of large private banks in 1969.
- Prudential norms for income recognition, asset classification, and capital adequacy were based on subjective considerations and were not in line with international norms.

The reasons for overhauling the system were not ideological; the compulsion to overhaul flowed from the recognition that the policy regime had ended up creating a system whose viability was in doubt with public sector banks in the aggregate reporting a negative return on net worth in the early 1990s. The reforms that followed have been divided, in official recounting, into two phases, 1991–2 to 1997–8 and 1997–8 and beyond (RBI 2008a).

Phase 1: 1991–2 to 1997–8

Starting in 1992, more stringent norms for income recognition, asset classification, and capital adequacy were introduced. Four classes were provided for assets (in place of the four that obtained): standard, sub-standard, doubtful, and loss-making, with provisioning requirements for each class. Banks were told not to include in the income interest on non-performing assets. These stipulations made for a clearer understanding of the health of India's banks.

Banks with branches abroad were told to meet the international norm of capital adequacy of 8 per cent by 31 March 1994; other Indian banks by 1996. The new provisioning requirements required banks to set aside Rs 10,000 crore. In order to meet this requirement and comply with the new capital adequacy norms, the government infused Rs 200 billion into public sector banks and also allowed banks to raise funds from the capital market.

This resulted in diversified ownership of banks, with both financial institutions and retail investors becoming holders of equity and it also paved the way for continued access to the capital market for replenishment of equity. Listings on the stock exchanges subjected public sector banks to the discipline of financial markets.

Statutory pre-emptions in the form of SLR and the credit reserve ratio (CRR) were brought down. SLR was lowered to 25 per cent and CRR had been reduced from 15 to 9.5 per cent by 1997. The long-term objective of reducing CRR to 3 per cent has not been achieved to this day though. These measures freed more funds for loans. However, thanks to reduced corporate demand and risk-aversion at a time of structural changes in the economy, banks chose at various points in time, to have a level of government securities above the statutory minimum.

Banks were allowed to set their own deposit and lending rates. In the case of deposits, the interest rate on savings deposits remained regulated. In the case of loans, interest rate on small loans (below Rs 20,000), exports, and under the differential interest rate of the scheme, remained regulated.

New private banks came to be licensed from 1994 onwards. By 1998, 10 new private banks had come into being. In addition, 22 foreign banks were granted licenses. RBI's approach conformed to the broad Indian policy of privatizing through expanding the presence of the private sector in a given sector rather than selling a controlling interest in existing public sector enterprises (PSEs). Such an approach, it may be added, is uncommon in the annals of privatization. Privatization has more often meant the transfer of public assets to private ownership. As we will document later with reference to the banking sector, this rather unique approach to privatization has helped improve the efficiency of PSEs.

In the phase under review, the Board for Financial Supervision was also set up under RBI's aegis. The intention was for improving oversight over the banking system. Another important institution created in this period was the banking ombudsman to whom customers could address complaints that had not been resolved by banks within a specified period.

Phase II: 1998–9 Onwards

In this phase, RBI decided to raise the capital adequacy norm for Indian banks from 8 to 9 per cent, thus moving ahead of international norms for capital adequacy. Income recognition and asset classification norms were tightened further. An asset was to be classified as non-performing if interest was due beyond 90 days instead of 180 days as specified earlier. Provisioning for standard assets was introduced and raised to 1 per cent over time.

Although these norms are in line with international norms, in India, there is a category of loans called 'restructured loans' for which the provisioning requirements are not as stiff as those for ordinary loans. 'Restructured loans' are loans that could have turned into non-performing assets (NPAs) but for the restructuring, the regulatory forbearance shown with respect to this category is seen by some as introducing an element of fudging into asset classification norms. However, others contend that restructuring is very often an attempt to address temporary problems in cash flows in long gestation projects and does not necessarily point to inherent lack of viability in projects.

The phase was also marked by efforts to create institutions necessary for banks to function efficiently. In 2001, the government passed a bill for setting up the Credit Information Bureau India Ltd. (CIBIL) which would collect and share data on borrowers. In 2002, the government moved to strengthen the legal framework for banks to recover their dues by enacting the Securitisation and Reconstruction of Financial Assets and Enforcement of Security Interest (SARFAESI) Act.

The licensing of new private banks in the 1990s did introduce an element of competition but it was not significant enough to make an impact: the share of new private banks in total assets was a mere 6 per cent in 2000. In the early 1990s, RBI permitted two large mergers that were to provide an impetus to competition. One was the reverse merger of the financial institution ICICI with ICICI Bank. The other was the merger of IDBI Bank, the subsidiary of another financial institution, with IDBI. (ICICI and IDBI were among three all-India financial institutions which had been set up with the purpose of focusing on long-term finance for companies. The third was IFCI).

RBI has always required banks to get its approval for opening branches. Bankers have long felt that this is a legacy of the license raj and needs to be done away with, a demand that the Committee on Financial Sector Reforms (2009), headed by Raghuram Rajan, concurred with. In 2005, RBI changed its policy from giving individual branch approvals to giving approvals for several branches at a time (and the number approved in any quarter can run into hundreds now). In July 2011, RBI decided that no approvals would be required for branches set up in Tier-3 to Tier-6 centres (which are typically towns with low bank penetration).

Through the noughties and into the present decade, RBI grappled with issues of private (domestic) and foreign ownership in the Indian banking sector. The necessity of both these forms of ownership to co-exist with public ownership had long been recognized. The challenge for RBI was one of calibrating an increase in the presence of private and foreign ownership in ways that were consistent with the stability of the banking sector.

Private ownership of banks carries with it the dangers of concentration of funds in the hands of a few, with the potential for diversion of funds to owners' other businesses. In 2005, RBI sought to address this danger by issuing a comprehensive framework for private ownership of banks. The framework mandated diversified ownership and control of banks and sought to achieve this by stipulating that no single entity or group of related entities could own more than 10 per cent of the paid-up capital of a private bank. The framework also made it clear that shareholders as well as directors of private banks must satisfy 'fit and proper' criteria.

In 2009, RBI revisited the subject of private banks by issuing a discussion paper. This was followed by draft guidelines in 2010 (RBI indicated that it would be in a position to issue final guidelines only after certain amendments to the Banking Regulation Act had been carried out). One important issue that RBI sought to grapple with in the guidelines was allowing entry to corporate houses into banking.

The clamour for allowing corporate houses into banking arises from the perception that competition in Indian banking today may not be intense enough; the time may have come to shake up the market by facilitating the entry of players which have the financial muscle of corporate houses behind them. However, allowing such entry raises the danger of inter-connected lending. RBI has sought to balance these concerns in its guidelines by putting in a number of safeguards (for instance, a proviso that the exposure of the bank to any entity in the group shall not exceed 10 per cent and to all entities in the group shall not exceed 20 per cent of the paid-up capital and reserves of the bank). We will have to await the issue of licenses before we can judge what form competition in Indian banking is likely to take in the years ahead.

Foreign banks present an equally big challenge to policymakers in emerging markets. There is pressure both from within the system and from outside, to open up to foreign banks in a big way on the grounds that the entry of large, sophisticated banks will help raise efficiency in the banking sector. However, this consideration again must be balanced against considerations of stability in domestic banks and the supervisory challenges posed by the cross-border operations of foreign banks.

In 2005, RBI announced a roadmap for foreign banks, divided into two phases. In phase I, RBI said it would go beyond the commitment made to WTO, of 12 new branches for foreign banks every year. Acquisition of private banks would be allowed only in banks identified for restructuring. In phase II, which was to commence in 2009, foreign banks could plan for mergers and acquisitions with private banks, subject to a ceiling of 74 per cent on the equity stake of foreign banks. This was, however, made conditional on a review of the experience in phase I.

The sub-prime crisis of 2007 caused RBI to put its review, planned for 2009, on hold. This was partly because the world's leading banks were embroiled in the crisis and were in no position to enter new markets and partly because the crisis had thrown up a host of issues on which clarity was required. It was only in early 2011 that RBI broached the subject through a discussion paper.

In the discussion paper RBI indicated that it was willing to go beyond its WTO commitment of approving 12 branches every year for foreign banks that operate as subsidiaries. Foreign bank subsidiaries will be free to open branches in under-banked centres (designated as Tier-3 to Tier-6 centres). They can open branches in Tier-1 and Tier-2 centres on the same conditions as domestic banks. These measures, if implemented, will amount to significant liberalization of the policy for foreign banks. However, they come with a caveat: foreign banks will not be allowed to expand beyond 25 per cent of capital in the banking system.

We must await the final guidelines on foreign banks but the broad contours of the policy on competition should be clear enough. RBI favours greater competition but, like the reforms that India has seen over two decades, it will be slow in coming and it will be measured; one cannot expect any 'big bang' opening up.

In the phase under discussion, RBI pushed ahead with other reforms. The migration of banks to the basic approaches of Basel II was done by 2009. In April 2010, RBI announced a shift from the base prime lending rate (BPLR) system to the base rate system. The prime lending rate is intended to be the rate for the best borrowers and one would expect rates for others to be at a premium above the prime lending rate.

For several reasons, however, it turned out that in the BPLR system, nearly 80 per cent of the loans were being made below the prime lending rate. This was perceived to have led to lack of transparency in interest rates in the system and an inability to gauge how bank lending rates were responding to policy rates.

The base rate computation was devised in a manner that precluded lending below this rate. In a major policy shift, RBI also announced deregulation of lending rates for small loans. Lending below BPLR was seen as making loan rates somewhat opaque; it was hard to see the link between a bank's lending rate and a borrower's creditworthiness. In this respect, the base rate is seen as an improvement. However, like BPLR, the base rate used by banks is arrived at by using a weighted average cost of funds, as distinct from the marginal cost of funds. Since the former changes more slowly than the latter, this does tend to introduce an element of inefficiency in the transmission of monetary policy.

In January 2011, RBI sought to subject the lending to micro-finance institutions to stringent regulations (including a cap on the net interest margin and on the interest rate on loans). The savings rate was deregulated in October 2011. In January 2012, RBI announced a policy on compensation for top management of private banks.

In all this, RBI showed a willingness to keep in step with international developments in regulation as well as changes in Indian market conditions. It also showed a willingness to adapt policy to Indian political and economic realities. Barring the new policies on licensing on new private banks and foreign banks that are awaited, it is fair to say that 'big bang' reforms in Indian banking are nearly done. There has been no mention in recent years of one item that was talked about in the early years of the reforms period, namely, privatization of public sector banks (PSBs). At least in the medium term, the mix of public, private, and foreign ownership seems poised to stay.

Impact of Reforms on Efficiency

Reforms were intended to usher in greater efficiency in the Indian banking system. Has this purpose been achieved? There are two ways in which this question can be looked at. One is to look at accounting measures of efficiency. Another is to look at economic measures of efficiency. One way to answer these questions is to assess whether the segment that was said to be badly wanting in efficiency at the commencement of reforms, PSBs, has improved its performance; if this has happened, it augurs well for efficiency in the system as a whole. Some of the literature on the Indian banking sector focuses on this aspect alone.

We begin by looking at trends in accounting measures of efficiency.

Has Competition Increased?

One measure of competition is the share of top five banks in assets, deposits, and profits (Table 32.1). It can be seen that on all three indicators, the share of the top five banks has declined, which points to increased competition.

Table 32.1 Share of Top Five Banks—Assets, Deposits, and Profits

	1991–2	1998–9	2001–2	2007–8	2012–13
	1.0	3.0	5.0	–	–
Assets	51.7	44.7	43.5	38.4	36.9
Deposits	49.0	44.4	43.3	37.3	35.8
Profits	54.5	49.1	41.4	37.2	42.1

Source: Report on Trend and Progress in Banking, several reports and the RBI database.

RBI (2008b) also noted that the concentration ratio in India was among the lowest after the US and the Russian Federation (Table 32.2). Further, the Herfindahl–Hirschman index, another measure of concentration, declined in India alone between 1998 and 2004 among a sample of advanced and emerging economies and was lower than in the other emerging economies chosen for comparison (Table 32.3)

Table 32.2 Trend in Banking Concentration Ratio Across Countries

Country	1991	1998	2006
1	2	3	4
Advanced Economies			
Singapore	0.86	0.81	0.99
Germany	0.55	0.63	0.72
Spain	0.71	0.74	0.75
France	0.60	0.48	0.68
Australia	0.89	0.62	0.64
Canada	0.71	0.55	0.60
United Kingdom	0.56	0.70	0.57
Netherlands	0.55	0.77	0.54
Korea Rep.	0.58	0.38	0.51
Japan	0.32	0.33	0.41
Italy	0.69	0.48	0.40
United States	0.20	0.22	0.33
Emerging Market Economies			
South Africa	0.99	0.94	0.99
Israel	0.85	0.74	0.81
China	0.91	0.83	0.70
Turkey	0.83	0.53	0.70
Indonesia	0.72	0.40	0.63
Philippines	0.83	0.65	0.60
Brazil	0.94	0.40	0.59
Malaysia	0.42	0.40	0.53
Thailand	0.56	0.51	0.51
Argentina	0.76	0.32	0.37
India	0.46	0.35	0.35
Russian Federation	0.99	0.75	0.20

Source: Report on Currency and Finance 2003–8 (Volume V).

Table 32.3 Herfindahl–Hirschman Index

Country	1998	2004
1	2	3
Advanced Economies		
US	117	157
Germany	245	283
UK	339	493
Italy	489	542
France	399	682
Spain	854	1188
Emerging Market Economies		
India	720	541#
Malaysia	1317	1334
Chile	974	1462$
Mexico	1542+	1529&
South Africa	1310++	1840#
Brazil	2164+	3352

Source: Report on Currency and Finance 2003–8 (Volume V).

Note: +: for 2000, ++: for 2001, $: for 2002, &: for 2005 and #: for 2006.

Has the Spread Declined?

One measure of spread is the ratio of net interest income (NIM) to total assets. One would expect the spread to decline consequent to deregulation. This is what deregulation is all about: it squeezes producers' margins and leads to increase in volumes. India's banking sector has been relatively impervious to this trend. Table 32.4 shows the trend in NIM in the period since deregulation. NIM was surprisingly steady from the start of deregulation until 2006–7. For three years thereafter, there was promise of a decline in NIM. In 2010–11, however, NIM rose again and was slightly above the level at the start of deregulation.

This has, of course, turned out to be a blessing for banks but it goes counter to the rationale for deregulation. It also runs counter to the experience of other banking sectors consequent to deregulation. Indeed, the pressure on NIMs and, hence, on profitability elsewhere is an important factor causing banking crises; the steadiness of NIM in India is one factor underlying the absence of a similar crisis in India.

Table 32.4 Net Interest Income (Spread) to Total Assets

Bank Group	1992–5 (Avg)	1999–2000	2000–1	2003–4	2004–5	2007–8	2008–9	2009–10	2010–11
Public Sector Banks	2.72	2.70	2.86	2.94	2.92	2.15	2.10	2.29	2.78
Old Private Sector Banks	3.24	2.33	2.51	2.60	2.70	2.43	2.60	2.56	2.95
New Private Sector Banks	1.17*	1.95	2.14	1.98	2.17	2.40	2.80	3.00	3.16
Foreign Banks in India	3.98	3.92	3.63	3.46	3.33	3.79	3.90	3.96	3.86
Scheduled Commercial Banks	2.84	2.73	2.85	2.86	2.83	2.35	2.40	2.17	2.92

Source: Report on Trend and Progress in Banking, several reports and the RBI database.
Note: * Based on Asset size of banks.

Have Returns Improved?

Efficiency, as measured by net profit to total assets, has shown an unambiguous improvement over the years and has touched the important figure of 1 per cent in recent years (internationally, a 1 per cent return on assets is considered a benchmark for good performance). It is striking that in the years following the sub-prime crisis, said to be the worst crisis in the past century, return on assets remained over 1 per cent in Indian banking (Table 32.5). This is a measure of how insulated Indian banking is and it is also a measure of the steady improvement in the fundamentals in the sector.

Have Intermediation Costs Declined?

The ratio of operating costs to total assets declined dramatically in the post-reforms years, driven largely by the decline in the ratio in the PSB group (Table 32.6). The most important reason is that the workforce remained constant in PSBs through the initial years in the face of rising volume of work, followed thereafter by a reduction caused by voluntary retirement schemes. It is only in the last three years or so that recruitment has gathered pace in PSBs. Another reason is branch rationalization. The hard work of setting up branches had been accomplished in the nationalization era, so PSBs found that they did not have to invest in branches and could, in fact, afford to close down a few.

Thus, efficiency in the system as a whole can be said to have improved, using a set of accounting measures.

We now turn to economic measures of efficiency. RBI (2008b) measured efficiency in Indian banks for 1992–2007 using a data envelopment analysis (DEA). It found that cost efficiency had improved in all three categories of banks—PSBs, private banks, and foreign banks. It noted that the improvement was greater in 1998–2007 than in the earlier period; also that PSBs had higher levels of efficiency than banks in the other two categories.

The study decomposed cost efficiency into technical efficiency and allocative efficiency. It found that gains in private banks and foreign banks were mostly with respect to technical efficiency whereas PSBs had improved on both counts. The study is significant in that it runs counter to the link between ownership and efficiency in literature, whereby public ownership is associated with lower levels of efficiency. This study found

Table 32.5 Net Profit/Total Assets (%)

Bank Group	1996–7	1997–8	1998–9	1999–2000	2000–1	2002–3	2004–5	2006–7	2008–9	2009–10	2010–11
Public Sector Bank	0.57	0.77	0.42	0.57	0.42	0.96	0.87	0.83	0.9	0.97	0.96
Old Private Sector Bank	0.91	0.80	0.48	0.81	0.59	1.17	0.33	0.70	1.0	0.95	1.12
New Private Sector Bank	1.73	1.55	1.03	0.97	0.81	0.90	1.05	0.91	1.1	1.38	1.51
Foreign Banks in India	1.19	0.96	0.69	1.17	0.93	1.56	1.29	1.57	1.7	1.26	1.74
Scheduled Commercial Bank	0.67	0.82	0.47	0.66	0.49	1.01	0.89	0.90	1.0	1.05	1.10

Source: Report on Trend and Progress in Banking, several reports.

Table 32.6 Intermediation Costs to Total Assets Ratio (Per cent)

Bank Group	1996–7	1997–8	1998–9	2004–5	2006–7	2007–8	2008–9	2009–10	2010–11
Public Sector Bank	2.88	2.66	2.66	2.09	1.77	1.54	1.50	1.61	1.70
Old Private Sector Bank	2.52	2.31	2.26	1.96	1.85	1.66	1.70	1.88	1.94
New Private Sector Bank	1.94	1.76	1.74	2.06	2.11	2.28	2.20	2.16	2.23
Foreign Banks in India	3.00	2.97	3.59	2.88	2.78	2.84	2.80	2.52	2.71
Scheduled Commercial Bank	2.85	2.63	2.67	2.13	1.91	1.78	1.70	1.78	1.86

otherwise: SBI was the most efficient bank; further, the most efficient banks were to be found in all three categories.

There is other evidence that competition and deregulation together have led to a convergence in performance between public and private sector banks. In other words that the link between ownership and performance, on which there is extensive literature, becomes weak when PSBs are exposed to competition and given the necessary freedom to compete.

Thus, Sarkar et al. (1998), looking at the data for 1993–4 and 1994–5, found weak evidence in favour of the proposition that ownership determines performance. Bhaumik and Dimova (2004) used data for a later period to examine the relationship between ownership and performance. Their results suggest that while private and foreign banks performed better than PSBs in 1995–6, no observable relationship between ownership and performance was found by 1999–2000.

This theme of a trend towards convergence in performance has been seen in several other studies. Ram Mohan (2005) provides a comprehensive comparison. He compared performance of PSBs with private and foreign banks in 1994–5 to 1999–2000 using several measures: financial ratios, Tornquist and Malmquist total factor productivity (TFP and MFP), and revenue efficiency. He also compared pre-and post-privatization performance of listed PSBs.

Using financial ratios, Ram Mohan found that PSBs' performance in the period was inferior to that of the other two categories. There was no significant difference in the performance of PSBs and the two other categories using TFP or MFP growth. In terms of revenue efficiency, PSBs' performance was superior to that of private banks but inferior to that of foreign banks.

In all, out of ten comparisons made by Ram Mohan, there was no difference in performance on four measures, PSBs did better on two, and private and foreign banks on two each. He concluded that in the aggregate efficiency in PSBs could not be said to be inferior to that of the other two categories. Ram Mohan also found that performance of PSBs improved post-privatization. Lastly, comparing returns on PSB stocks with those of private banks, he found no difference in performance, whether on an unadjusted basis or on a risk-adjusted basis.

Das (1999) also finds a trend towards convergence in performance in 1992–8. Das et al. (2005) used DEA to measure efficiency of Indian banks in 1997–2003 and found that there was not much to differentiate among the different bank categories in terms of technical efficiency, cost efficiency, or revenue efficiency. In terms of profit efficiency, SBI and its associates did better than nationalized banks, private banks, and foreign banks. Nationalized banks, they found, had improved their profit efficiency scores considerably. They concluded that it was hard to claim that privatization led to greater efficiency in the Indian context.

Sathye (2003) compared the technical efficiency of the three categories of banks for 1997–8, using DEA and using two different sets of inputs and outputs (models A and B). He found that the mean efficiency score for Indian banking was lower than the world mean efficiency score, which showed that the Indian banking system had some catching up to do. In model A, PSBs had a higher mean efficiency score than private and foreign banks. In model B, PSBs had a lower mean efficiency score than foreign banks but a higher score than private banks. He concluded that the policy of reducing non-performing assets and reducing the workforce was correct and, if continued, could help Indian banks match the world efficiency score.

Thus, whether we look at accounting measures or economic measures of efficiency, we can conclude that efficiency in the system has improved and this is, to a large extent, because of PSBs catching up with private and foreign banks on efficiency.

Impact of Reforms on Stability

A banking system that is inefficient also tends to be unstable because it means, among other things, that the system is not producing enough surplus to sustain growth (here it is necessary to enter a caveat: we need to measure efficiency correctly and efficiency must be demonstrated over a long period; it is possible for banks to show high efficiency in the form of high returns to equity but we know from the sub-prime crisis that such measures of efficiency can be deceptive at a given point in time). Indeed, it was the threat of instability arising from poor commercial performance that necessitated the sweeping reform in 1993–4. To the extent that efficiency has improved, we can say that stability has also improved.

We can judge the improvement in stability using two widely used measures: the capital adequacy ratio and the ratio of non-performing assets to total assets advances. As Table 32.7 shows that there has been an improvement in both these indicators.

Table 32.7 Soundness Indicators

Net NPAs/	1996–7	1999–2000	2001–2	2003–4	2004–5	2006–7	2009–10	2010–11
Advances	9.18	7.42	5.82	2.98	2.06	1.05	1.11	0.97
Capital adequacy (Basel I)	NA	NA	12.00	12.90	12.8	12.30	13.6	13.00

Source: Report on Trend and Progress in Banking, RBI

In recent years, RBI has been publishing a financial stability report that attempts to capture vulnerabilities in the system through stress tests. Some of the results in the most recent set of tests are worth highlighting because they give an indication of the level of stability that the Indian banking system has attained over the years (RBI 2012). The tests covered 60 banks that comprise 99 per cent of banking sector assets.

- A 100 per cent increase in NPAs causes the capital adequacy of the system to drop from 14.1 to 11.9 per cent, which is above the minimum requirement of 9 per cent. Only five banks have capital adequacy falling below the minimum and they account for just 6.7 per cent of the total banking assets.
- The capital adequacy of the system remains well above the minimum even when subjected to an interest rate shock in the form of a parallel shift in the yield curve, upwards or downwards, of 250 bps.
- An appreciation/depreciation in the exchange rate of 10 or 20 per cent and a fall in equity prices of 40 per cent likewise has no appreciable impact on capital adequacy in the system.

The resilience of the banking system in the face of macro-shocks was also tested. The level of NPAs was estimated under three scenarios: a baseline scenario, medium shock, and adverse shock. Under the baseline scenario, NPAs were expected to be in the range of 3.3–3.5 per cent by March 2013; under the medium scenario 3.7–4.1 per cent; and under the severe scenario 4.1–4.6 per cent. Capital adequacy under the severe scenario had declined to 12.5 per cent by March 2013, which is still above the regulatory minimum.

Since these tests are recent in origin, we are not in a position to document any improvements in stability but they do give a sense of the stability achieved over two decades of reforms.

The most striking aspect of stability in the Indian banking system is that is that nearly two decades after deregulation, the system has remained free from crises. Typically, deregulation sets the stage for a crisis down the road. One study estimates that the probability of a crisis rises over time, following financial liberalization (Demirguc-Kunt and Detragiache 1998).

This is because banks find their margins squeezed by greater competition and they are also forced to raise more capital to comply with stiffer regulatory requirements. Maintaining returns on equity on the higher capital base becomes difficult, so banks resort to risky lending. This creates conditions for a crisis. Such conditions have not arisen for a variety of reasons including prudent macroeconomic management as well as stringent regulations.

While this aspect of Indian banking had been commented upon earlier, stability in Indian banking came to attract more attention consequent to the sub-prime crisis when India remained one of the few oases of stability in the international banking system. We now turn to a discussion of the factors that have contributed to stability and efficiency in Indian banking.

Factors Underlying Improvement in Performance

As we saw earlier, efficiency improved in the Indian banking system consequent to deregulation; the system has also been stable. Few could have anticipated such benign outcomes given the record of deregulation elsewhere and the fragility of banking systems in general. What explains these outcomes? It is possible to ascribe the outcomes to three sets of factors: macroeconomic management; regulation and supervision; and factors specific to the Indian banking system.

Macroeconomic Management

- Strong economic growth: Banks are a play on the underlying economy. To the extent that the economy in which a bank operates is strong, the banking sector benefits. The period of deregulation in banking coincided with broader reforms in the economy leading to an acceleration in the growth rate from 6–7 per cent in the 1990s and then to 8-9 per cent in the noughties. Banks benefited from a strong demand for credit, from low levels of NPAs resulting from strong economic fundamentals, and good recovery from past NPAs.

- Caution on capital account convertibility and prudent management of capital inflows: India followed a graduated approach to capital account convertibility. To this date, there are restrictions on foreign investments in domestic debt, corporate borrowings in foreign currency, and residents moving their savings to overseas locations. The gradual removal of restrictions on capital inflows prevented asset bubbles and excessive volatility in currency, both of which have been known to lead on to banking crises.
- This has been supplemented by RBI's policy of having a 'managed float', whereby the exchange rate of the rupee is substantially but not wholly market-determined, with RBI intervening, as required, to maintain the exchange rate within a desired band.
- No large savings–investment imbalance: One of the findings of the sub-prime crisis is that large savings–investment imbalances can lead to financial crises by creating excess debt in certain countries. At some point, the debt level becomes unsustainable and a process of debt reduction—or deleveraging—becomes necessary which impacts adversely on economic growth. The G-20 meeting in Seoul in November 2010, arrived at a norm of current account imbalance of 4 per cent of GDP. Through most of the reforms period, India's current account deficit stayed below 2 per cent of GDP. Of late, it has risen to beyond 4 per cent of GDP but this may be regarded as an aberration in a long period.

Regulation and Supervision

- Imposition of global standards for capital and income recognition: RBI has laid down capital requirements in accordance with successive Basel accords (I, II and III) and it has attempted to move the banking system towards international norms for income recognition. These have had the effect of ensuring that there is a certain minimum capital in the system and that figures for income are an accurate picture of a bank's finances. In addition, RBI has had stiff norms for empanelment of statutory auditors and rotation of auditors, something not seen outside the banking sector in India.

- Caution on foreign bank entry: Rapid expansion of foreign bank presence can undermine stability in various ways. Foreign banks can take away the best customers leaving domestic banks weakened; in times of crises in the home economies, foreign banks may restrict funding of host economies creating a credit crunch in the host economies; and supervision of cross-border transactions poses serious challenges to regulators in developing economies. Thus, the advantages of increased competition and global standards of banking have to be balanced against considerations of stability. As mentioned earlier, RBI pursued a cautious policy with respect to foreign bank entry and this can be said to have contributed to stability in Indian banking.
- Restrictions on private ownership: RBI, while licensing a new set of private banks, imposed limits on private ownership. In order to ensure diversified ownership, it stipulated that no entity can, in general, have an equity stake of more than 10 per cent in a private bank. Whether this has served the purpose of limiting the control of a private bank by a promoter can be debated but it does make it necessary for the management to address the interests of institutional and retail investors and not just those of the promoter. As noted earlier, RBI has also thus far not permitted industrial houses entering banking for fear that connected lending may jeopardize the operations of the bank.
- Close monitoring and supervision by the regulator: RBI has been inclined to pursue an intrusive and rule-based approach to regulation as distinct from the principle-based or 'light touch' regulation that obtained in the UK and some developed economies. It would appear that the experience in the sub-prime crisis has vindicated RBI's approach. One example of RBI's approach is stringent limits on risky sectors—real estate, capital markets, commodities—that have traditionally proved the bane of banking. Other examples are limits on single borrowers and group exposure of banks and on inter-bank borrowings and norms for pricing of loans, such as the base PLR and the base rate. Supervision too has been intense with off-site as well as on-site surveillance underpinned by the annual financial inspection report based on the CAMELS approach.
- Imposition of counter-cyclical checks on lending as required: During the rapid growth period of 2004–8, RBI introduced the principle of higher risk weights on specific products, such as housing loans and credit cards as a means of checking excessive credit growth in these

products. The principle of counter-cyclical checks on lending has since come to be incorporated in Basel III norms.

- Norms for governance: RBI has fairly elaborate norms for governance including the creation of various board-level committees (notably, the risk management committee), 'fit and proper' criteria for appointment of CEOs and board members, norms for CEO compensation, a fixed tenure of eight years for board members, and specifications for an appropriate composition for bank boards. Whilst practices at various banks may not have measured up to expectations, the desirability of such norms cannot be questioned.

Factors Specific to Indian Banking

- As mentioned earlier, NIM remained remarkably constant through the period of deregulation, and this is an important factor making for stability in Indian banking. What explains the fact that NIM has been constant and high for such a long period?
- One can posit that a certain level of bank penetration or intermediation must take place before disintermediation occurs. India started off the reforms era with a low level of intermediation: the credit/GDP ratio was 29 per cent and the deposit/GDP ratio 40 per cent in 1991–5. The credit/GDP ratio rose to 56 per cent and the deposit/GDP ratio to 73 per cent in 2011. But credit penetration was still below the range of 80–100 per cent in a range of other emerging markets and way below that in advanced countries such as the US and the UK.
- The under-penetration of banking at the commencement of reforms meant that both credit and deposit grew faster post-reforms than before. In other words, banks have not faced any threat of disintermediation. It has also helped that savers in India prefer deposits to capital market instruments, partly because of risk-aversion at relatively low levels of income and partly because of the ups and downs in the Indian stock market. Lack of disintermediation has helped banks maintain their NIMs.
- Public ownership: This prevents runs on banks in adverse times of economic crises because of greater public confidence in deposits in the public sector. It also made possible pre-emptive recapitalization of Rs 20,000 crore post-deregulation, that is, the strengthening of banks' capital *before* they were exposed to deregulation and greater

competition. Besides, the Indian public sector tends to have strong checks on executive malfeasance, so serious financial frauds are not easy to perpetuate and this again is a safeguard against failure.

- Retail assets: Almost 20 per cent of the assets in the banking sector are retail assets. The retail market came to be tapped somewhat belatedly by Indian banks, and much of the growth in the retail market has happened in the last ten years. As banks have only scratched the surface of the market, these assets tend to be of good quality. It is these good quality assets in the retail segment that propelled credit growth of 25–30 per cent in 2004–8. As a result, high credit growth has not come at the cost of quality of assets. At the same time, NIMs in Indian banking have been high. Thanks to the peculiarities of the Indian market, therefore, Indian banks enjoy an impossible trinity: high credit growth, high quality, and high NIMs.

Thus, a combination of macroeconomic and sector-specific factors, along with sound regulation, contributed to the improved performance of the Indian banking sector in the last two decades and are responsible for its insulation from the international economic environment.

Challenges and Opportunities

In this section, we address challenges and opportunities to Indian banks in the coming years. As we shall see, some of the challenges are more perceived than real.

Lack of Global Size

Indian banks are said to lack global size. India's largest bank, SBI, was just one-sixth the size of Citigroup, the tenth largest bank in the world in December 2011 (Table 32.8). Other Indian banks look puny in comparison. Lack of balance sheet size, it is said, will come in the way of Indian banks competing with international giants once foreign banks enter India in a bigger way. How real is this problem?

First, the real measure of size is market capitalization, not balance sheet size, as debt and equity values in corporate finance are measured in market

Table 32.8 Comparison of Size by Book Value

December 2011; US$ bn

	Foreign Banks	Book Value	Indian Banks	Book Value
1	BNP Paribas	2681	State Bank Of India	322
2	Deutsche Bank	2557	ICICI Bank Ltd.	108
3	HSBC Holdings	2468	Punjab National Bank	67
4	Barclays	2328	Bank of Baroda	63
5	Royal Bank of Scotland	2266	Bank of India	61
6	Bank of America	2265	Canara Bank	59
7	Mitsubishi UFJ Financial	2177	IDBI Bank Ltd.	52
8	Credit Agricole	2131	HDFC Bank Ltd.	49
9	JP Morgan Chase	2118	Union Bank of India	43
10	Citigroup	1914	Central Bank of India	40

Source: Forbes magazine.

terms. In terms of market capitalization, the top three Indian banks are closer to international banks (Table 32.9).

India's better banks are poised to grow their earnings at 15–30 per cent annually, while most western banks will be lucky to show double-digit growth in the present troubled environment. This means that through sheer profit growth, India's banks can hope to catch up with foreign banks on market capitalization.

Table 32.9 Comparison of Banks by Market Capitalization

		Market Cap		Market Cap
1	BNP Paribas	88	State Bank Of India	36.0
2	Deutsche Bank	60	ICICI Bank Ltd.	25.0
3	HSBC Holdings	187	Punjab National Bank	5.5
4	Barclays	58	Bank of Baroda	7.5
5	Royal Bank of Scotland	75	Bank of India	7.2
6	Bank of America	146	Canara Bank	5.3
7	Mitsubishi UFJ Financial	75	IDBI Bank Ltd.	2.9
8	Credit Agricole	39	HDFC Bank Ltd.	3.6
9	JP Morgan Chase	182	Union Bank of India	1.4
10	Citigroup	133	Central Bank of India	22.4

Source: Forbes magazine.

The problem with banks whose market capitalization is very low is not lack of balance sheet size but their inability to attain a higher level of efficiency on their existing basis. This is a problem that cannot be tackled by growing bigger but by tackling revenue and cost issues at the existing scale. Several new private banks in the country have shown that it is possible to attain world class parameters in terms of return on assets, net interest margin, and cost to income ratio at a scale of less than Rs 100,000 crore. Hence, balance sheet size cannot be said to be a barrier to improved performance in the Indian context.

Greater Competition

It is said that India's banking system has done well over the years because of lack of competition, both domestic and foreign. Of late, there have been moves to usher in greater competition by licensing more domestic banks and through a more liberal regime for foreign banks. In December 2011, RBI released draft guidelines for licensing of new private banks that envisaged the issue of bank licenses to industrial houses. In January 2011, it released a discussion paper on foreign banks. One can thus expect to see new entrants in banking in the years to come.

However, movement on this front is likely to be slow. With respect to domestic banks, RBI has sought amendments to the Banking Regulation Act that will require parliamentary approval. Whenever this comes through, the process of reviewing applications and issuing licenses is likely to take time. Moreover, not many will qualify, given the stringent criteria that RBI has laid down in its guidelines. One should expect the process of granting new licenses to stretch out over two years or so. It should take another three years at least for the newly licensed banks to achieve a minimum critical scale.

As for foreign banks, the guidelines were issued a few months ago. The willingness of foreign banks to set up subsidiaries and to comply with various governance requirements stipulated by RBI in its discussion paper will be known only over time. Not many foreign banks are in a position to explore new markets in the present conditions. Thus, the expansion of foreign banks in India will also be a slow process. It is realistic to suggest that Indian banks have a window of at least five years to get their act together before new entrants pose a credible threat.

The threat from capital markets too will not become significant until banking penetration has proceeded further. However, a wild card in the banking scenario is the possible emergence of internet operators as quasi-banking intermediaries, a phenomenon that has started assuming importance in the west in recent years. These operations rely on analytics and data-crunching, so their arrival pre-supposes the existence of large databases. Nevertheless, given the dexterity with which Indians have taken to IT and the Internet, this is a threat that banks will need to factor into their long-term calculations.

Increase in Regulatory Capital Requirements

Capital requirements for banks will go up under the Basel III accord, with banks requiring more equity capital than before. Indian banks will require additional capital to sustain rapid growth in credit in the coming years. The question asked of banks everywhere is whether the requisite capital will be available; indeed, banks in the west are in a deleveraging mode partly in order to comply with stiffer capital requirements.

Given the returns that Indian banks deliver today, any international fund manager, comparing growth prospects for banks across the globe, will have to make suitable allocations for India. (It is true that returns will come under pressure in 2012–13 thanks to the economic slowdown; most analysts, however, believe that stresses in infrastructure and other sectors will at most be 1 percentage point to the gross NPA ratio of 2.9 per cent in March 2012, which will still not make the NPA position threatening). Capital from domestic investors should also be available, especially since PSBs have had a good track record of returns on IPOs. We do not see funding from capital markets as an issue for Indian banks in the years to come.

The constraint for PSBs is the government's equity share staying over 51 per cent or continued majority ownership by the government. In the difficult budgetary situation in which the government finds itself, there is certainly a question mark over its ability to provide the equity capital necessary to maintain its shareholding in PSBs at above 51 per cent. If the government is not in a position to do so, it will have to allow its shareholding to fall below 51 per cent. This is a major political decision, which will not be easily forthcoming in the present political situation and it does introduce an element of uncertainty where PSBs are concerned.

Financial Inclusion

In India, financial inclusion has long been on the agenda of policymakers. Reaching banking services—whether payments, deposits or loans—to the masses was an important motivation behind the nationalization of banks in 1969. However, the approach to financial inclusion has evolved over time and we can discern two distinct strands in it.

In the post-nationalization phase and until a few years ago, the focus was entirely on directing credit to certain sectors or groups. This came to be known as 'priority sector' lending. In more recent years, and, in particular, through the Annual Policy Statement of 2005–6, RBI focused on financial inclusion at the individual and household levels. The thrust is now on reaching basic banking services to under-banked areas and segments of the population and on such things as financial literacy and credit counselling. Here, our focus is on assessing, in brief, what these two different approaches to inclusion imply for banks in the years to come.

We begin with priority sector lending where RBI requires domestic banks to set aside 40 per cent of their credit (for foreign banks, the target is 32 per cent for banks with less than 20 branches and 40 per cent for the rest) to designated categories, such as agriculture, small and micro-enterprises, housing, education, exports, and weaker sections. Over the years, separate sub-limits have evolved, such as a limit of 18 per cent for agriculture, further broken into 13.5 per cent for direct lending and 4.5 per cent for indirect lending, and 10 per cent for weaker sections.

In the initial years, priority sector lending was seen by banks overwhelmingly as a social obligation and something that detracted from their commercial performance. However, with the inclusion of commercially attractive loans, such as housing and education in the priority sector (subject to limits that have varied over time), not all of the priority sector loans are viewed as a burden. To be sure, there has been criticism that RBI has 'diluted' the definition of priority sector in order to reduce the burden on banks.

In 2010, RBI deregulated the pricing of small loans, leaving it to banks to price these on a commercial basis; earlier, there had been regulatory limits on lending rates. The result is that for private banks, which happen to be limited in their reach, direct lending to agriculture and lending to weaker sections are the onerous elements in priority sector lending; the rest of the priority sector is not such an impediment to commercial performance.

We turn now to the more recent attempts at financial inclusion, which focus on the individual and household levels. The absence of financial inclusion has been documented in numerous surveys (for instance, the NSSO All India Debt and Investment Survey 2002) and by the report of the Rangarajan Committee on Financial Inclusion (2008). In particular, the Rangarajan Committee noted that 51.4 per cent of farmer households were financially excluded from both formal and informal sources and 73 per cent did not access formal sources of credit, statistics that highlight how much work remains to be done in the area of financial inclusion.

In the new approach to inclusion, RBI's objective is to ensure access to financial services at affordable prices. The services include access to payments and remittances, savings, loans, and insurance. The strategy includes the following elements (Thorat 2008):

- Penetration into unbanked and backward areas and encouraging intermediaries, such as NGOs, micro-finance institutions (MFIs), and business correspondents
- Strengthening cooperatives and regional rural banks
- Using technology
- Advising banks to open a 'no frills' basic banking accounts
- Emphasis on financial literary and credit counselling

An important step in the approach to financial inclusion has been the provision of micro-finance, which has involved both banks and MFIs. An important initiative is the self-help groups to bank linkage programme that was launched by NABARD in 1992. Under the scheme, banks were to provide the finance and NGOs were to serve as canalizing agencies for credit and also to build capacities of the poor.

This official route soon came to be overtaken in importance by MFIs, with some profit-oriented MFIs stealing the limelight. Prominent MFIs had access to bank funds as well as private equity and other funds. However, MFIs ran into serious problems in 2011 and this impacted on banks with significant exposures to MFIs.

One outcome appears to be that banks can no longer rely as heavily on MFIs for meeting their priority sector or financial inclusion requirements on the credit side. They will have to find ways to do this substantially on their own. They can do so through initiatives, such as closely partnering one or two MFIs (so that they exercise significant control over lending activities), setting up and using branches in creative ways, using technology in combination with business correspondents, etc. In other words, banks will not be able to escape direct responsibility for 'last mile' financing.

Banks need not be despondent on this account. There is every possibility that the new approach to financial inclusion can make commercial sense for banks as much of the earlier approach did. For one thing, MFIs have shown that very high returns on micro-credit can go hand in hand with high recoveries. The MFI model proved unsustainable because the returns were seen as extortionate and their recovery practices questionable. Banks can do better on both counts.

Unlike MFIs, banks can operate through branches where micro-finance is one of a portfolio of products that includes agriculture credit, lending to SMEs, retail credit, and savings deposits. Hence, the operational costs can be spread over several products, which, in turn, will imply that micro-finance need not be priced at the levels at which MFIs priced it. Over time, there will be opportunities for cross-selling products to micro-finance borrowers as well.

Secondly, as mentioned earlier, non-branch alternatives, such as the business correspondent model are available and can become viable with the use of appropriate technologies. There appears to be a growing realization that attaining scale is the key where these technologies are used.

For banks, the challenge is to evolve a composite model of banking that is different for financial inclusion. They will need a branch that is more utilitarian, employees who are on a different pay scale altogether and technology that is appropriate to inclusion. Banks that can address these challenges quickly should be well placed to gain in commercial terms. Moreover, accessing more of India's yet poorly intermediated savings could be the key to financing growth through domestic resources instead of borrowing from abroad.

Lack of Global Presence

India's banks lack a significant global presence. Some see this as an obstacle to Indian banks being able to compete with international banks. It is true that Indian banks cannot compete internationally with foreign banks. However, this does not mean that they cannot compete against foreign banks in India where they have an advantage in terms of branch networks, their cost structures, and their understanding of the Indian consumer.

The idea that Indian banks need to go overseas in order to improve their competitiveness or their growth prospects is mistaken. It arises partly from the steady flow of Indian manufacturing ventures abroad. What is overlooked is that there is a fundamental difference between manufacturing and banking with respect to overseas ventures.

Indian manufacturers going abroad through acquisitions or otherwise hope to reap the advantages of cheaper production in India and to use their foreign ventures for brand building and marketing. In banking, in contrast, the services will have to be produced locally. Knowledge about a customer, ability to manage local executives, offering a wide suite of products, etc., are crucial requirements. Indian banks do not measure up on these counts today and will take several more years to acquire necessary competencies.

In their overseas ventures, particularly in advanced countries, Indian banks do not have any advantage either in terms of gathering deposits or making loans. They will have to focus on Indian related business (remittances, advisory services, etc.) and on trade finance, which has assumed significant proportions in recent years. There are, however, significant downsides to be reckoned with: risky investments by the overseas subsidiary, dependence on wholesale markets for funding, regulatory risk, and disproportionate demands on the management's time.

There could be non-commercial reasons for going abroad: creating an institutional understanding of foreign markets, rewarding talented employees, etc. In general, however, the growth opportunities in the Indian market dwarf the attractions of overseas ventures. Indian banks would be well advised to think hard before committing large resources to foreign ventures.

Concluding Remarks

India's banking system has come a long way in the two decades since major reforms were initiated. The outcomes could have been scarcely predicted at the onset of reforms, nor could policymakers have imagined that these would have been as benign as they turned out to be.

One or two aspects are striking. Unlike in a number of other sectors, where the private sector has displaced the public sector in terms of importance, the public sector continues to dominate banking. This is because the introduction of competition in the sector has been more controlled than it has been in other sectors. Secondly, as in many other sectors, the public sector has improved its performance in the face of deregulation and competition.

As we have seen, improvement in efficiency in the system has gone hand in hand with increased stability, and the system has remained free from crises. The recapitalization cost in Indian banking (around 2 per cent of GDP in the aggregate) is among the lowest in the world. At the same time, the basics of social orientation in banking remain and have been strengthened in some ways by a broader definition of what constitutes financial inclusion.

We have documented the factors that we believe have contributed to these remarkable outcomes in Indian banking. Among these, tighter regulations and public ownership must stand out as distinctive factors when compared with other systems. India's policymakers have eschewed calls for 'light touch' regulations and followed a more intrusive approach to regulation, one that is coming to be embraced in the very economies that had propounded the 'light touch' approach. The benefits of having a diversified ownership structure are beginning to be appreciated elsewhere and the notion that the public sector must necessarily be a drag on the banking system is no longer self-evident. Thus, India's approach to banking reforms, more than its approach to the broader economy, can be said to be quite unique.

The challenges of improving penetration and inclusion remain and the system will be further tested when it is opened to greater competition from domestic and foreign players. However, it can be said with confidence that a sound basis exists for banking to play its role in promoting growth and equity in the Indian economy.

References

Bhaumik, Sumon Kumar and Dimova, Ralitza (2004). 'How important is ownership in a market with level playing field?' The Indian banking sector revisited', *Journal of Comparative Economics*, 32(1, March): 165–80.

Committee on Financial Sector Reforms (2007), *A hundred small steps*. New Delhi: Sage Publications.

Das, Abhiman (1999), 'Profitability of Public Sector Banks: A Decomposition Model', *Reserve Bank India Occasional Papers*, 20(1): 55–81.

Das, Abhiman, Ashok Nag, and Subhash Ray (2005), 'Liberalisation, Ownership and Efficiency in Indian Banking: A Nonparametric Analysis', *Economic and Political Weekly*, 40(12): 1190–7.

Demirguc-Kunt, Asli and Enrica Detragiache (1998), 'Financial liberalisation and financial fragility', Annual World Bank Conference on Development Economics, Fostering Growth While Containing Risk, Yale University.

NYT (2008), 'How India avoided a crisis', 19 December.

Rakesh Mohan (2007), 'India's Financial Sector Reforms: Fostering Growth while Containing Risk. Yale university speech, 3 December.

Ram Mohan, T.T. (2005), *Privatization in India: challenging economic orthodoxy*. UK: Routledge.

RBI (2008a), *Report on Currency and Finance*, Vol. 4, Chapter III. Mumbai: RBI.

——— (2008b), *Report on Currency and Finance* Vol. V, Chapter IX. Mumbai: RBI.

Report of the Committee on Financial Inclusion (2008) Planning Commission, Government of India, 2009.

Sarkar, Jayati, Subrata Sarkar, and Suman Bhaumik (1998), 'Does ownership always matter?—Evidence from the Indian Banking Industry', *Journal of Comparative Economics*, 26(2): 262–81.

Sathye, Milind (2003), 'Efficiency of banks in a developing economy: The case of India', *European Journal of Operations*, 148: 662–71.

Thorat, Usha (2008), 'Inclusive growth: the role of banks in emerging economies', RBI Bulletin, March.

CHAPTER 33

FINANCIAL INTERMEDIATION AND ECONOMIC DEVELOPMENT

evidence from Bihar

SANJAY BANERJI,

KRISHNA GANGOPADHYAY,

PRASHANT GUPTA, AND

SUSHANTA MALLICK*

Given the debate on financial inclusion as a means of achieving inclusive growth in recent years, this chapter aims to examine the overall development of the financial sector in Bihar (one of the poorest states in India), and its contribution to economic activity in the state at the district level. Essentially the underlying logic of financial inclusion is largely a greater degree of 'financial intermediation' which leads to lower poverty via higher

* The authors gratefully acknowledge the financial support from the International Growth Centre (IGC), funded by DFID, UK. We appreciate comments by Maitreesh Ghatak, Kunal Sen, and other participants at the IGC annual conference (Growth Week 2012), 24–6 September 2012, held at the London School of Economics, London, UK. We are solely responsible for any errors that might yet remain.

growth by relaxing borrowing constraints as in the occupational choice literature. According to Prasad and Rajan (2008), the solution to the lack of access to formal banking services is not more intervention but more competition between formal and informal financial institutions, including freeing up interest rates and setting up incentives for banks to make loans to priority sectors, such as agriculture rather than just mandating it. This in turn can help develop a healthy rural financial sector in order to meet the needs of agriculture, infrastructure, and the rural poor.

Overall economic activity surged greatly in Bihar with an average rate of 11.03 per cent between 2003–4 and 2008–9. This achievement is spectacular not only with respect to similar performance at the all-India level with a growth rate of 8.49 per cent in the same period. But what is striking is with respect to Bihar's past performance, when the state grew about 3.50 per cent during the period between 1999–2000 to 2003–4 (Government of Bihar 2008–9). These achievements, after decades of stagnation with negative growth rates at times, certainly sound very impressive, but may not be sustainable in the long run for two inter-related reasons. First, these growth rates have not been uniform across sectors. For example, while sectors like construction, communication, and trade, hotels, restaurants grew by 35.80, 17.68, and 17.71 per cent, respectively, over 2003–4 to 2008–9, the agriculture sector, which provides livelihood to a majority of the population, grew only by 5.58 per cent over the same period. Second, future developments may not carry on smoothly if the state's financial sector fails to mobilize current resources (savings) into investments in areas that promote growth with equality. It has also been noted that while per capita deposits in Bihar increased significantly in 2008–9 by Rs 1,437, the increase in per capita credit was only Rs 246. This constitutes a leakage in the sense that funds generated within the state are flowing to other profitable destinations. It is for this reason that we look at the credit–deposit (CD) ratio as a measure of financial intermediation, since the CD ratio reflects whether the supply of funds from depositors are channelled to borrowers by the banks, along with considering directed credit programmes such as KCC.

In this chapter we examine: (1) the pattern of CD ratio across districts in Bihar in the light of high growth performance in recent years; (2) the extent to which the CD ratio and other financial indicators in Bihar influence district-level development; and (3) sectoral developments. This exercise helps us understand to what extent the mobilized resources are allocated in the form of loans to the private sector, how do they vary across districts and across banks, and finally what their impact is on both SDP as well as on the district-level economic activities. This, in turn, will reflect the concentration of banking activity in different areas in Bihar and underline its effective contribution to the state's economic activities.

Our main findings are: The overall CD ratio shows a remarkable stability across districts and bears almost negligible correlation with economic activity. On the other hand, the impact of the CD ratio on economic growth is at best statistically insignificant, both across the state and district levels. However, when we extend our analysis to include the impact of CD ratio on sectoral output, we find its impact positive and significant for agriculture and trade but very negligible for industry and consumption loans. Public provision of working capital loans to farmers in the form of kisan credit cards (KCCs) was introduced in 1998–9 which allows credit to be provided to farmers for agricultural operations or working capital requirements for agriculture. Interestingly, we find that the KCC scheme has a positive and significant impact on the output of the agricultural sector. Since bank loans under this scheme are pre-determined, our results suggest that there may be widespread rationing of agricultural credit by banks as withdrawing the limited amount of working capital under the KCC scheme is voluntary. Also such government guarantees in this sector are probably leading the industrial sector being rationed out and thereby lack of deeper financial intermediation in the state.

The rest of the chapter is organized as follows. The next section gives a brief discussion on existing literature on financial intermediation in the context of other less developed regions and discusses the limitations of replicating such studies in this context. The section that follows presents a statistical picture of the current state of intermediation in the state with the following section introducing the empirical framework. The next section deals with the approach, data, and descriptive statistics for the ensuing analysis. The section that follows discusses the results and the next section gives details of the firm-level analysis. The last section gives a conclusion.

Financial and Economic Development—A Brief Review

A well-functioning financial system plays an important role in the process of economic growth by performing a wide range of activities including not only transferring resources from savers to investors but also helping an economy attain transformation of maturity of assets. For example, depositors would like to withdraw funds with a short notice but banks can earn higher rates of return from projects with longer term horizons. Financial markets help an economy grow by resolving this maturity mismatch by making an optimal allocation of funds between current withdrawals and investments in long-term projects (see Diamond and Dybvig 1983). In addition, banks also perform a valuable service by screening projects, monitoring borrowers, and renegotiating loan contracts in times of financial distress. The value-enhancing activities tend to increase sharply when an economy makes the transition from an interventionist financial regime to a market-led paradigm of development finance (see Levine 1997).

Although there are studies which indicate that financial markets may have contributed significantly to corporate growth in the 1980s and 1990s (Singh 1997), however, financial markets in India are yet to be fully liberalized in terms of comprehensively capturing the extent of financial inclusion in a multi-dimensional sense. The existence of macroeconomic instability, government and political intervention, and inadequate banking supervision (Fry 1997; Gupta and Lensink 1996) had made the banking sector's credit allocation being dictated not always by rational economic calculations but by considerations ranging from regional, sectoral, and political considerations.[1]

Evidence on the impact of the financial sector on the Indian economy as well as on emerging markets as a whole is mixed. It is true that there exists some relationship between banking expansion as reflected in domestic credit to the private sector (as per cent of GDP) and long-run growth, and there is also a link between stock market development and growth (Levine and Zervos 1998). There are also studies that show that the link is tenuous when alternative measures of financial development are used for examining the impact of financial markets and economic activities. See Arestis et al. (2002), who used nominal liquid liabilities to GDP and other studies that employed measures of financial sector development, included stock market capitalization, stock market turnover, the ratio of domestic credit to the private sector to GDP, and the ratio of M3 to GDP. These indicators of financial development have been used in existing studies to examine

[1] Financial liberalization and capital market growth have led partly to portfolio substitution from bank deposits to tradeable securities, with limited impact on greater aggregate national or financial savings. However, the spread of banking facilities in a developing economy has a positive impact on private savings (Athukorala and Sen 2004).

their impact on investment (see Hermes and Lensink 1996; Luintel and Khan 1999) but the link between financial market development and economic activity is ambiguous (Pentecost and Moore 2006).

Besides, in many emerging economies, 'flight to quality' in asset allocation of financial institutions and lack of willingness by financial institutions, primarily banks, to extend credit to the private sector could arise in part due to fears of default due to risks related to political and other factors, which may have affected development.[2] Blanco (2009) finds that the net effect of financial development on growth is relatively small. Ang (2010), on the other hand, explores how financial development and financial sector reforms influence the evolution of income inequality in India and finds that while financial development helps reduce income inequality, financial liberalization seems to exacerbate it.

The problem of replicating many of these studies in the context of India and for that matter towards any state in India, like Bihar, is problematic for the following sets of reasons. First, credit is also used as a tool for redistribution, and programmes like implicit government guarantees and loan waiver schemes towards priority sectors like agriculture imply that such decisions are often based on social welfare cum political criteria. Second, banks in India are often federal and link between credits granted to a particular state may or may not be strongly related to overall deposits in that state. Third, many rural regional banks are also cooperatives that also make loan decisions based on norms other than profit maximizing, which is the standard assumption made in papers that explore links between financial intermediation and aggregate economic activities.

In other words, there is a 2-way inter-dependence between financial development (measured by volume of credit, deposits, stock market capitalization, etc.) and GDP per capita. As an economy grows, financial intermediation becomes more profitable, and FIIs enter the market and mobilize resources that in turn aid the process of savings, investment, and growth which encourages intermediation activities. However, political considerations, directed-credit programmes, the cooperative nature of rural banks, the presence of nationwide banks, etc., very often make loan decisions divorced from pure economic activities in local or geographical

[2] Credit to the commercial sector not only plays an important role in influencing domestic liquidity, but it also acts as a crucial input in the production process [for a simulation exercise, see Mallick (2006)]. If credit gets channelled by the government through the banking sector to the loss-making state enterprises, such as in China and Russia, that kind of financial development reflected in the credit–GDP ratio may not indicate the true development of the financial sector.

regions and may not have a one-to-one relationship in both ways, namely credit and GDP.[3] Hence, in what follows, we would like to make variables related to credit as explanatory variables and then examine their impact on Bihar's SDP (State domestic product) as a whole as well as that of its districts.[4]

The study will help in assessing the impact of financial intermediation across districts and sectors using recent available data. Kendall (2012) is the only study which uses district-level data from India to investigate the connection between banking sector development, human capital, and economic growth in Indian districts. But the focus of this paper is on examining the effect of financial intermediation on economic development, which we examine at a more disaggregated level across districts and sectors within the poorest Indian state. Such a closer examination of micro-data can help avoid many of the omitted variable problems in cross-country studies in this line of literature.

This study therefore aims to analyse and understand the effectiveness of the banking sector in Bihar in disbursing loans to private enterprises using disaggregated district-level data, along with understanding its impact on the overall economic activity at both aggregate and sectoral levels.

Current State of Financial Intermediation in Bihar

There are three types of financial institutions that operate in the formal market for lending and borrowing in Bihar: commercial banks which mostly provide finance for both agricultural and Industrial sectors; cooperative banks; and rural banks, which mostly specialize in transactions in rural credit markets. Consistent with the current SDP growth rates, the volume of deposits rose in almost all types of banks. For example, in 2008–9 alone, total deposits increased by over Rs 18,000 crore. However, such increases in the volume of deposits are not matched by increments in the disbursement of loan size. In the same year, the overall credit in the state expanded by only Rs 3,251 crore. For example, Bihar's per capita

[3] Ang (2009) shows that significant directed credit programmes favouring certain priority sectors tend to discourage private capital formation in India.

[4] The chapter explicitly recognizes these problems in specific contexts. See Banerjee and Duflo (2012) or Burgess and Pande (2005) for use of specific instruments to deal with the problem. However, limitations of data in our study prevent us from using a specific instrument suitable for our analysis.

deposits increased significantly in 2008–9 by Rs 1437 while the increase in per capita credit was only Rs 246, which is 17 per cent of the per capita deposits. Such a gap between the volume of deposits and lending typically measured by the CD ratio is an indicator of the development of the financial sector; it also indicates the overall link between the real and financial sectors and thus gives an idea about a bank's involvement in aggregate economic activities.

We present some empirics at a descriptive level which are related to the CD ratio across various districts in the state in Figures 33.1 to 33.5 (given later) and try to capture their correlation with other important variables, such as geographical locations, degree of prosperity, availability of bank loans, number of branches across districts in the state. Our findings of the descriptive statistics regarding the state of financial intermediation are as follows:[5] First, the CD ratio in Bihar is among the lowest in the country and far behind the national average (72.6 per cent) and other states like Tamil Nadu (108.9 per cent), Maharashtra (90.8 per cent), Rajasthan (80.2 per cent), West Bengal (60.8 per cent), and Madhya Pradesh (57.4 per cent). Second, this ratio also shows a remarkable diversity across districts, across banks, and across various sectors within the economy. For example, the CD ratio in the district of Siwan is 20 per cent, while in Araria it is above 40 per cent. The CD ratio of private commercial banks varied from 1 to 38 per cent. None of these banks had any rural branches as on September 2009 except for ICICI Bank and Axis Bank, and no other bank even had a branch in semi-urban areas.

Third, this ratio exhibits some geographical concentration as well. It tends to be highest in the north-east and north-west areas and along the contagious districts in that region. These preliminary statistics at a first glance imply concentration of financial activities mostly in the northern, and some in the very poorer areas in the southern parts of the state. The high ratio is concentrated in both relatively rich (like West Champaran, Muzaffarpur) and poor districts (like Kishengaunge and Araria) in the northern belt. While among the relatively poorer districts, Khagrai and Sheonha made substantial progress in both generating a higher CD ratio and per capita GDP but the picture was far from uniform. District Patna was one of the richest in the state but it showed a stable low-level ratio over the years under study. However, these variations across various denominators suggest that the overall ratio across the state was remarkably stable over time.

[5] Further insights regarding empirical facts are also presented later in the chapter.

While description pertains mostly to financial intermediation in private and commercial banks, the history of public intervention in the process of intermediation in the state goes back to more than 100 year. The institutional credit delivery system for agriculture was started in the country with the setting up of cooperative credit societies in 1904, but the coverage of these societies towards meeting the credit requirements of farmers was limited (Kumar et al. 2011). The process of financial reforms led to novel credit intervention from financial institutions to support farmers. However, much later the state also initiated interventions with the aim of improving the farmers' credit constraints. Launching KCCs in 1998–9 was one of the innovative credit delivery mechanisms introduced in the country to promote financial inclusion. We therefore examine the effect of KCCs on per capita incomes across districts. Another major intervention in this regard was the implementation of the agricultural debt waiver and relief scheme in 2008 by the Government of India covering nearly 37 million farmers to mitigate the consequences arising out of growing indebtedness and the agrarian crisis.

High NPAs in the case of state-owned commercial banks and cooperatives do suggest that default risks are high, while in the case of private banks there are limited non-performing assets. Loan waiving together with targeted lending towards priority sectors are probably creating twin effects: (1) over-lending in some sectors but under-lending in other sectors; and (2) lack of project selection because loans made to sectors receiving waivers tend to be safer even though they might not generate the highest surplus. To sum up, our study is expected to yield insights about the effectiveness of both private intermediation and efficacy of the public programme of directed credit (in the form of KCCs) on both macro- (SDP) and micro- (district-level output) level activities in the state.

To conclude this section, we find a stagnant state in the CD ratio prevailing in the overall scenario despite some geographical variations and increasing government interventions in priority sectors including agriculture. However, in order to analyse the impact of intermediation on Bihar's economic condition, we now resort to data and an empirical analysis.

Empirical Framework

We estimate the relationships mentioned earlier by using the fixed effects panel model. The advantage of using panel data is that it contains more degrees of freedom and greater sample variability than cross-sectional data, improving the efficiency of estimates.

The panel data model takes the following form:

$$y_{it} = x_{it}\beta + \alpha_i + \delta_t + \varepsilon_{it}$$

where y_{it} is GDP per capita for district i in period t. All control variables mentioned in the earlier section are captured by the vector x_{it}. α_i is a district specific effect and δ_t, a fixed time effect. ε_{it} is a random error term that captures all other variables.

The fixed-effects estimator permits controlling for any unobserved country-specific time-invariant effects. We also follow a two-way random effects log linear regression model for period 2008–10.

Before using the random effects model, we check our model with Hausman specification test of whether there is significant correlation between the unobserved random effects and the regressors. The advantage of this test is whether the error term is uncorrelated with the time series component and the cross-sectional (group) error. We estimated both fixed and random effects models. A Hausman test showed greater support for fixed effects model, therefore the results are reported for the fixed effects estimator. Although the fixed effects estimator is designed to control for unobserved region-specific time-invariant effects in the data, it does so by conditioning them out and taking deviations from time-averaged sample means. The result of this is the removal of any long run variation in the dependent variable.

Our first model captures the effect of aggregate CD ratio in each district. In addition, we decompose the aggregate CD ratio into sectoral CD ratios, and then we measure the effects of sectoral CD ratios in each district. We plan to estimate the following log-level empirical specification:

$$y_{it} = \alpha_i + \delta_t + \beta_1 CD_{it} + \beta_i x_{it}\, \varepsilon_{it},\ t = 1, ..., T \quad (1)$$

$$y_{it} = \alpha_i + \delta_t + \beta_1 CD_{it} + \beta_2 KCC + \beta_3 CGAP_{it} + \beta_4 BBR_{i,\,2010} + \varepsilon_{it} \quad (2)$$

where subscripts: i = districts, and t = time. Equation (1) is a panel regression, while equation (2) is cross-section regression due to bank branches data being available only for one year. CGAP denotes credit gap (proportion of actual credit in targeted credit limit), and BBR refers to bank branches. δ_t refers to time fixed effect which captures business cycle effects and δ_i captures unobserved district heterogeneity like local conditions, or environment. ε_{it} is the idiosyncratic error term with IID (independently and identically distributed) properties. In equations 1 and 2, y_i is log of GDP per capita in each district, x_{it} is $1 \times K$ vector of explanatory variables which includes aggregate CD ratio across districts and CD ratios in sectors such as agriculture, industry, transport operator, professional and other services, personal loans, trade and finance & all other sectors. The value of KCC is used in log levels, δ_i in equation 1 is the unobserved time-invariant district heterogeneity like local conditions, or different policies introduced in different sectors that could affect the development level in each district.The annual credit plan (ACP) is used to capture credit deployment plan which is percentage achieved of credit allocated in priority (agriculture, small scale industries and other priority sector)and non-priority sectors.

The notations α and δ respond to district and time respectively. The GDP per capita measures the regional development level, while the CD ratio measures the financial deepening in the district and KCC measures the political preferential policies towards farmers as in Cole (2009a). The CD ratio and KCC can be thought of as the supply side of credit. δ_t is the time-fixed effects which capture business cycle effects and ε_{it} is the idiosyncratic error term with independently and identically distributed properties: *iid* $(0, \sigma^2)$.

Data and Descriptive Statistics

The assessment of the impact of financial intermediation on economic development in Bihar is done using both aggregate and firm-level information in addressing multiple dimensions of financial intermediation. Districts with higher speed of financial intermediation could have higher economic development or growth rate, or whether the rate of growth is because of enhanced credit flow.

Panel regression methods are employed to test the relationship between financial intermediation and GDP per capita at the district level. We construct sectoral CD ratios at the district level which directly measure the proportion of bank deposits in a district that is allocated as loans to different sectors. The sectoral deployment of credit can reveal the demand originating in a particular sector which could also reflect whether a sector is a high-return sector from a bank's point of view or whether there are state guarantees in place that encourage banks to create loans for that sector. We also look at other indicators of financial intermediation, for example, bank branches and their fund mobilization and deployment capacities.

After undertaking the aggregate analysis, we use firm-level data, largely covering the industrial sector, to examine the impact of the alternative sources of financing on various indicators that measure the performance of publicly listed firms located in Bihar. This approach reveals the nature and characteristics of the methods of financing and links to economic activity of the listed firms given in Appendix A33.1. Out of 56 companies, data on 46 are usable which allow us to analyse whether bank financing and equity financing are substitutes or complements.

The aggregate data used in this research mostly come from the State-level Bankers Committee (SLBC) in Bihar (http://slbc.bih.nic.in, accessed on 5 November 2013) and RBI database on Indian economy (http://www.rbi.org.in, accessed on 5 November 2013), covering all 38 districts. The CD ratios of all scheduled commercial banks as well as the regional rural banks in all the 38 districts come from SLBC. The wide variation in CD ratios across districts—for instance, 19 per cent in Siwan to 51 per cent in Kishanganj—however, indicates that the high CD ratio of districts, accumulated interests on loan and NPA (non-performing assets) of many banks prevent any increase in the credit flow in those areas. The data on KCC, ACP, number of bank branches and NPAs also come from SLBC, Bihar (several issues). GDP data at district-level for Bihar (over 10 years) are obtained from Indicus Analytics Pvt. Ltd.—an economics research firm (www.indicus.net). In addition, aggregate time series data for financial variables across districts in Bihar have been procured from RBI and SLBC in Bihar.

The KCC scheme, introduced in 1998–9, shows that the numbers of KCCs, issued by banks in Bihar during the period from 1999 through 2009, and the achievement figures were consistently high during the entire period. On the other hand, if we look at the role of banking services in Bihar, during 2009–10, 214 new branches were opened, while Bihar's share in the total bank branches in the country have remained at little less than 5 per cent during the past few years. With a share of less than 5 per cent of the total number of bank branches in India, 1500 RRB branches in Bihar mobilise about INR 1600 crore annually. But only half of it flows back to the rural economy in the form of credit. The deposits of RRBs constitute nearly 43 per cent of the total rural deposits of all scheduled commercial banks in Bihar and 6.0 per cent of all rural deposits of the scheduled commercial banks in the country. The total rural deposits of the scheduled commercial banks in Bihar amounted to Rs 24,000 crore, which is more than most other states in India. But the per capita deposits and credits in the state remain one of the lowest and the population served by a bank office one of the highest in the country, while there has been significant growth in total deposits of banks in Bihar in 2009–10 over the previous year of about Rs 14,000 crore.

An operational indicator from the supply side therefore is the CD ratio which measures 'financial deepening' in a country or local region. A low CD ratio means that for every unit of currency deposited, less credit flow could imply lower investments (see Table 33.1). For example, the total (per capita) deposits in Bihar increase in 2008–9 (Rs 1,437) by over Rs 18,000 crore while credit expanded by only Rs 3,251 crore (Rs 246, that is, 17 per cent). The CD ratio in Bihar was behind the national average of 72.6 per cent and other states like Tamil Nadu (108.9 per cent), Maharashtra (90.8 per cent), Rajasthan (80.2 per cent), West Bengal (60.8 per cent), and Madhya Pradesh (57.4 per cent). Bihar being at the lower end probably indicates failure of mobilization of resources.

It is obvious from Table 33.1 that the CD ratio in Bihar over the time period 2004–10 has never exceeded, on an average, a ratio of 33.41, indicating that credit allocation in the economy has only been just over 30 per cent of the deposits received during the period. Moreover, it seems that the trend of CD ratio in Bihar has a downward trend. With a maximum of approximately 70 per cent in 2004, The CD ratio has never reached that level since then. The CD ratio has never exceeded 58 per cent during 2006–10. Patna has always been a district with the highest GDP growth, which has one of the lowest CD ratios. Kaimur, West Champaran, etc., are districts with highest CD ratios with middle-range growth rates. The map of Bihar with CD ratios does indicate the regions with five different categories of CD ratios (see Figure 33.1).

The decline in CD ratio could indicate inefficiency in the use of credit which triggers the unwillingness of further credit to be allocated in the economy. Low CD ratios raise serious concerns about the effectiveness of the banking sector as to why banks are not lending as much as they are mobilizing in the form of deposits. There is little correlation between per capita income and the CD ratio (see Figure 33.2), implying that districts with higher CD ratios do not appear to have higher per capita incomes.[6]

If an increase in financial deepening and political preferential policies increased the development level, we would expect the estimated coefficients

[6] Since the CD ratio bears almost no correlation with economic growth, we also explore the percentage realized of the credit limit set by banks in each year.

Table 33.1 Descriptive Statistics

	2004	2005	2006	2007	2008	2009	2010
GDP (Log)	8.91	8.94	9.08	9.12	9.23	9.3	9.37
	(0.322)	(0.341)	(0.332)	(0.344)	(0.335)	(0.323)	(0.320)
KCC (Log)	8.95	9.11	8.78	9.07	9.27	9.93	10.31
	(1.527)	(0.973)	(0.751)	(0.666)	(0.594)	(0.549)	(0.646)
CD ratio	33.62	34.36	35.47	34.1	30.98	33.59	33.65
	(11.558)	(10.177)	(9.712)	(9.396)	(8.453)	(8.331)	(8.898)
Sectoral CD ratio							
Agriculture	–	–	–	–	10.79	13.53	14.64
					(5.344)	(6.205)	(5.980)
Industry	–	–	–	–	5.10	2.09	2.21
					(5.751)	(1.917)	(1.648)
Transport and operator	–	–	–	–	0.27	0.35	0.48
					(0.154)	(0.202)	(0.298)
Professional and other services	–	–	–	–	1.09	0.86	1.32
					(0.799)	(0.405)	(0.758)
Personal loans	–	–	–	–	10.57	8.22	8.38
					(3.977)	(2.587)	(2.256)
Trade	–	–	–	–	4.74	5.04	5.37
					(1.852)	(1.590)	(1.750)
Finance and all other sectors	–	–	–	–	0.81	0.59	1.03
					(0.414)	(0.294)	(0.553)
Credit gap (priority sector)					81.33	10.94	10.75
					(20.356)	(3.656)	(5.700)
Credit gap (non-priority sector)					121.97	14.52	9.69
					(51.159)	(8.040)	(5.174)
Number of Observations (N)	37	37	37	37	36	36	36

Note: (1) Standard deviations are shown in parenthesis.

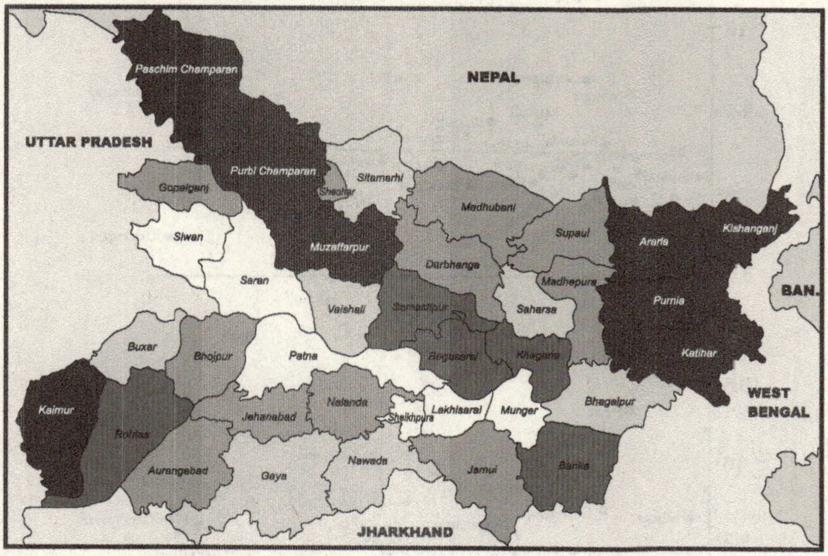

FIGURE 33.1 Map of Bihar

Source: http://d-maps.com/carte.php?num_car=8534&lang=en (accessed on 5 November 2013).

Notes: Category A: Siwan, Munger, Saran, Patna, Lakhisarai (colour code on map:).

Category B: Bhojpur, Sheohar, Darbhanga, Gopalganj, Jamui, Nalanda, Aurangabad, Sheikhpura, Jehanabad, Supaul, Madhepura (colour code on map:).

Category C: Vaishali, Arawal, Bhagalpur, Gaya, Sitamarhi, Nawada, Buxar, Saharsa (colour code on map:).

Category D: Khagaria, Banka, Rohtas, Begusarai (colour code on map:).

Category E: Samastipur, East Champaran, Araria, West Champaran, Katihar, Muzaffarpur, Purnea, Kishanganj, Kaimur (colour code on map:).

on the CD ratio and KCC to be positive. However, if credit is not efficiently utilized, its impact on development will be less and therefore we may expect the coefficient estimate on the CD ratio and KCC to be either small and insignificant or even negative. The allocated credit does not seem to have any significant positive impact on the level of development within the region (see Table 33.2 and Figure 33.3). A correlation matrix of log GDP per capita and the CD ratio denotes a negative correlation between the two key variables of interest here.

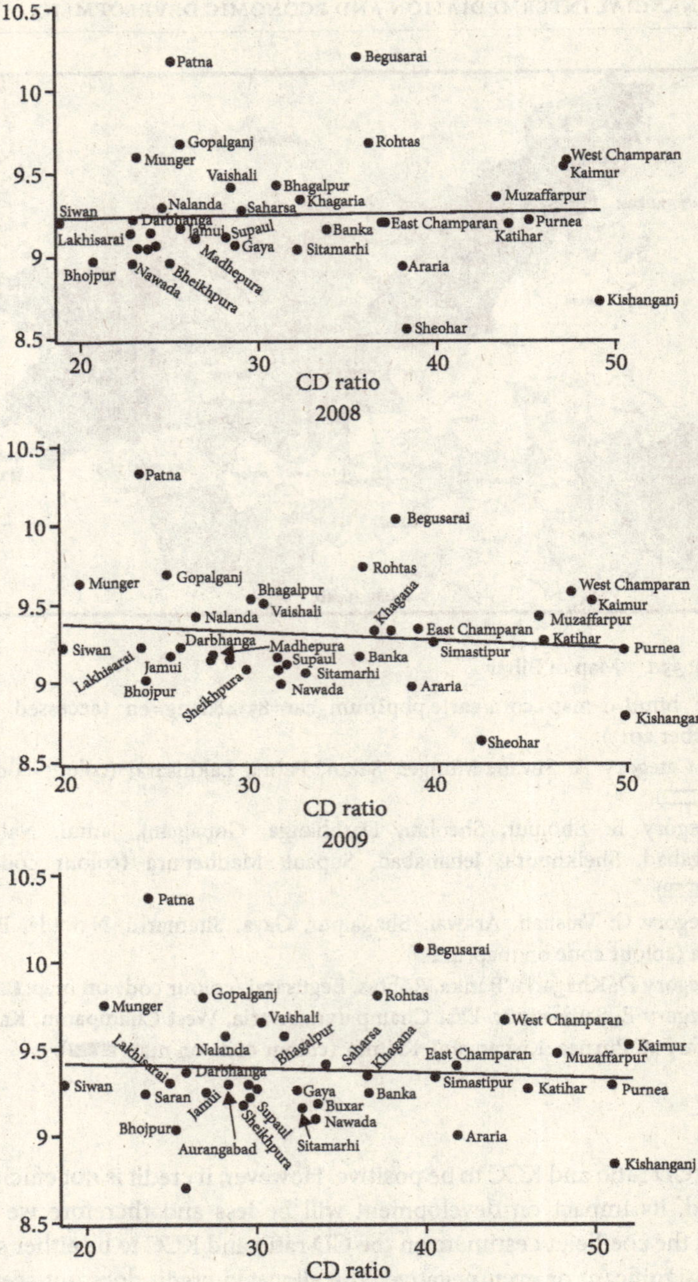

FIGURE 33.2 Scatter Plot of Credit–Deposit Ratio versus Per Capita GDP for 2008–10.

Source: Authors' calculations using data from SLBC, Bihar and RBI, Mumbai.

Financial Intermediation in Bihar—A District-level Analysis

In Bihar, SDP growth has taken place along with the development of financial intermediation but the issues of distributive concerns persist. While for these high growth districts there is a significant correlation (>65 per cent) between the GDP growth rate and CD ratio, the causality is less clear for districts with a relatively less growth rate (<9 per cent). Six of these ten high-growth districts are located in relatively prosperous and agrarian north Bihar. The four districts from south Bihar (Aurangabad, Gaya, Jahanabad, and Sheikhpura) are part of the Magadh division which has the highest MSME activities next to Patna division.

While some of these districts, which are historically prosperous due to development of agriculture and located mostly in the northern part of the state and others located near important divisions, did relatively better both in terms of generation of high output and CD ratio, for the remaining districts, the overall CD ratio was stagnating and had a negative impact on the GDP growth per capita. However, whether the stagnation in the CD ratio was driven by historical NPAs driving down the appetite of the financial intermediaries needs to be further assessed. The next section explores some of these themes in detail both at the district and sectoral levels and links these findings with proactive government policies in parts of rural areas that displayed higher growth with intermediation.

With a view to tracing the impact of financial development from the supply side (as measured by CD ratios) on per capita income, we use disaggregated data at the district level for Bihar. Panel regression methods were employed to test the relationship between financial intermediation and GDP per capita at the district level. At the aggregate level, the relationship between the level of development and the CD ratio can be tested with KCC as a control variable where KCC can be thought of as an instrument for political preferential policies towards agricultural farmers.

The heterogeneity in the relationship between GDP per capita and the CD ratio and KCC can be tested considering time-invariant district-differences along with time dimensions. We find that there is insignificant correlation between per capita income and the CD ratio across all districts on average using data from 2004 onwards (see Table 33.2). While the CD ratio is insignificant for the full sample, KCC does have a significant positive impact on per capita income. Districts with higher KCC tend to have higher per capita income, although there is regional heterogeneity across districts. As the CD ratio has declined significantly from 2004 onwards, we decided to run this regression for a reduced sample period from 2008 onwards and it is seen from Table 33.2 (column 4) that the coefficient estimate on the CD ratio is still statistically insignificant while KCC has a significant impact. This suggests that credit allocated within the state directly or indirectly does not seem to have any significant positive impact on the level of development within the region (see Table 33.2 and Figure 33.3).

Table 33.2 Regression of Per Capita Income on Credit–Deposit Ratio Across Districts

	(1) †	(2)†	(3)†	(4)††
Constant	8.8955***	7.8119***	7.8215***	7.7418***
	(0.1013)	(0.2231)	(0.2285)	(0.2104)
CD ratio	0.0014		-0.0005	-0.0015
	(0.0025)		(0.0024)	(0.0021)
KCC		0.1262***	0.1270***	0.1397***
		(0.0242)	(0.0246)	(0.0227)
N	185	185	185	258
R-squared	0.106	0.222	0.223	0.290

Note: (1) * p<0.05; ** p<0.01; *** p<0.001. (2) Robust standard errors are shown in parenthesis. (3) Unless specified, all specifications include districts and time fixed effects. (4) KCC is in log form. (5) † for period 2004–8. (6) †† for period 2004–10.

In finance and growth literature, issues have been raised with regard to dealing with identification issues with aggregate data due to problems of heterogeneity of effects across countries, measurement errors, omitting relevant explanatory variables, and endogeneity all of which tend to bias the estimated effect of the included variables. This is where micro-data at the district level with sectoral differences can help us identify sectors that are more likely to benefit from access to finance relative to other sectors with lower credit flows. Financial underdevelopment in some sectors can prevent investment in profitable growth opportunities and thereby lower per capita income. Thus, we decided to construct sectoral CD ratios. We calculated sectoral CD ratios by deriving total deposits for each district from the CD ratio, given the total credit for each district. Then the ratio of credit allocated to each sector divided by total bank deposits, as given earlier, gave us the sectoral CD ratios in each sector which directly measure the proportion of bank deposits in a district that is allocated as loans to different sectors.

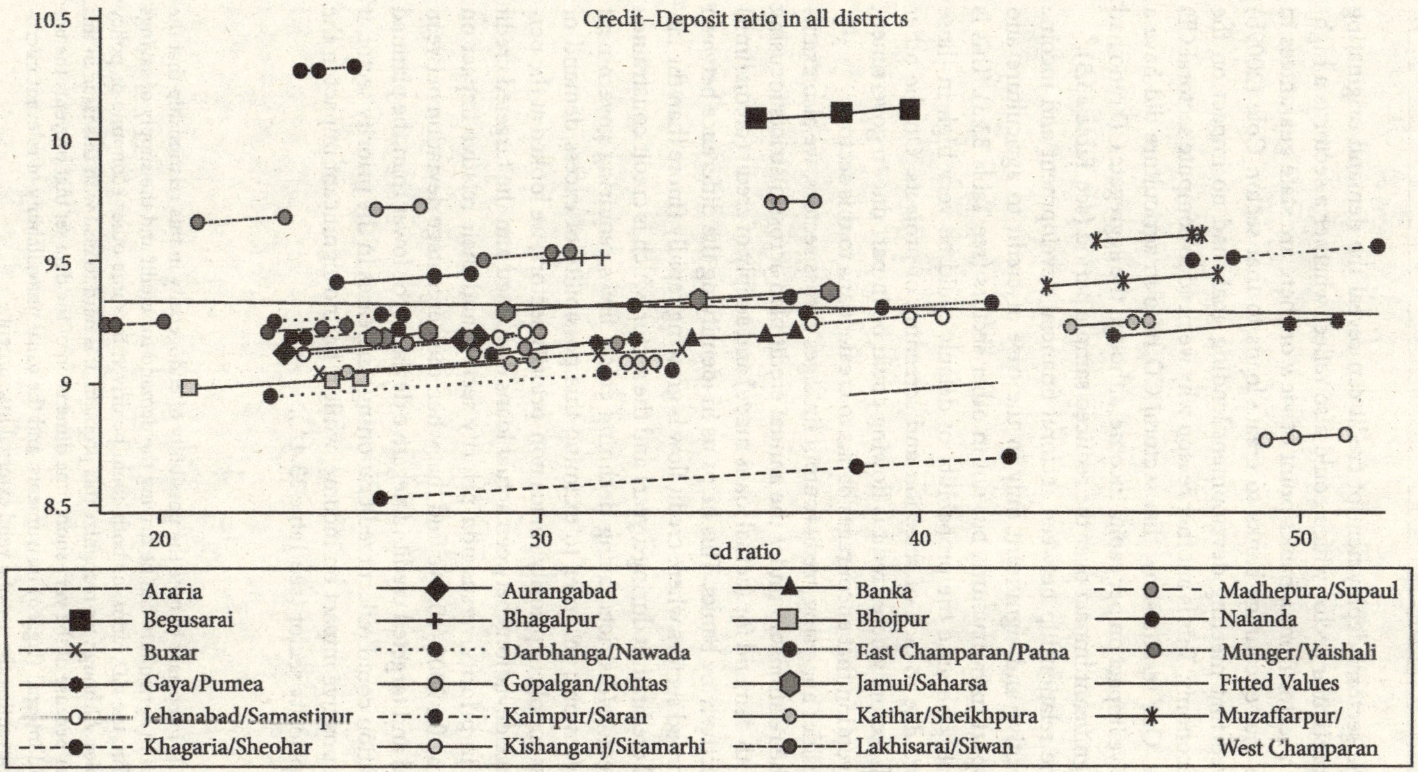

FIGURE 33.3 District-wise Estimated Relationship between Credit–Deposit Ratio and GDP Per Capita (2008–10)

Source: Authors' calculations using data from SLBC, Bihar and RBI, Mumbai.

The sectoral deployment of credit can reveal the demand originating in a particular sector which could also reflect whether a sector is a high-return sector from a bank's point of view or there are state guarantees in place that encourage banks to create loans to that sector. Cole (2009b) showed that meeting development lending goals had no impact on the real economy. This is another reason why we need to compute sectoral CD ratios. Our results show that sectoral CD ratio in agriculture did have a positive impact on per capita income, although the aggregate CD ratio had no significant impact over the reduced sample period (see Table 33.3).[7]

The relationship between sectoral financial development and income is positive and significant only in the case of credit to agriculture and transport infrastructure, but not in other sectors (see Table 33.3). This is probably because the probability of default could be very high in those sectors due to lack of selection and screening of projects. On the other hand, sectors where credit is flowing could be in part due to government intervention that encourages banks to create loans to this sector.

Besides analysing credit–output linkages across sectors, we also examine the relationship under the annual credit plan across districts focusing on both demand for (actual loans made) and supply of credit (credit limit) respectively by banks. This helps us in identifying the difference between two broad sectors where credit flow is growing rapidly (more than the targeted credit limit during a year) and the sector which is credit constrained (or sectors/districts facing declining credit flows requiring government intervention). In order to examine this possibility of excess demand or excess supply in priority versus non-priority sectors, we looked at the percentage deviations between actual loans disbursed and the targeted credit limit in priority versus non-priority sectors and their relative impact on income for 2008–10. We find that when the percentage deviation between actual and targeted credit (a negative deviation or lower than the planned allocation could reflect credit rationing) increases in the priority sector, it has a positive impact on income, while it has no significant impact in the non-priority sector (see Table 33.4A).

[7] It is important to note the possibility of endogeneity in this relationship that the growth in agriculture can be driving the demand for credit and the supply of savings therefore the CD ratios, or both could be driven by some other economic or policy variables. Although we recognize this problem, it is hard to deal with this issue in this chapter because of the very short time dimension of the data set that prevents the use of valid internal (lagged) instruments, and the usual unavailability of relevant micro-data preventing the use of a valid external instrument.

Table 33.3 Regression of GDP Per Capita on Credit Deposit Ratio of Each Sector Across Districts (2008–10)

CD Ratio								
Constant	8.846***	9.004***	8.901***	8.900***	9.087***	8.901***	8.955***	8.979***
	(0.0536)	(0.0455)	(0.0446)	(0.0562)	(0.0672)	(0.0595)	(0.0451)	(0.0796)
Agriculture	0.00834***							
	(0.0023)							
Industry		-0.0059*						−0.0033
		(0.0025)						0.0028)
Transport operators			0.142***					0.111**
			(0.0371)					(0.0381)
Professional and other services				0.0326				0.0380*
				(0.0165)				(0.0161)
Personal loans					-0.0085*			−0.0083*
					(0.0037)			(0.0035)
Trade						0.0143		−0.00465
						(0.0083)		(0.0089)
Finance and all others							0.031	0.0222
							(0.0199)	(0.0178)
Fixed effect	YES	YES	YES	YES	YES	YES	YES	YES
R^2	0.9684	0.9654	0.9690	0.9645	0.9651	0.9641	0.9638	0.9743
N	108	108	108	108	108	108	108	108

Note: (1) * p<0.05, ** p<0.01, *** p<0.001. (2) Robust standard errors are shown in parenthesis. (3) Unless specified, all specifications include districts and time fixed effects.

Table 33.4A District-wise Performance under Annual Credit Plan (ACP) for 2008–10

Constant	8.790*** (0.0899)	8.803*** (0.1050)	8.207*** (0.1680)	7.913*** (0.1750)
KCC	‡	‡	0.0632*** (0.0159)	0.0993*** (0.0170)
CD ratio	0.00570** (0.0020)	0.00466 (0.0024)	0.00443* (0.0019)	0.00248 (0.0020)
CD ratio x Credit gap in priority sectors	−0.0041*** (0.0000)	- -	−0.0019** (0.0000)	- -
CD ratio x Credit gap in non-priority sectors	- -	-0.00194*** (0.0000)	- -	0.0133 (0.0000)
Fixed effect	YES	YES	YES	YES
R^2	0.9781	0.9726	0.9826	0.9818
N	108	108	108	108

Note: (1) * p<0.05, ** p<0.01, *** p<0.001. (2) Robust standard errors are shown in parenthesis. (3) Unless specified, all specifications include districts and time fixed effects. (4) KCC is in logs. (5) ‡ no interaction (6) - - referenced category.

Table 33.4B District-wise Performance under Annual Credit Plan (ACP) for 2009–10

Constant	8.317*** (0.1201)	8.405*** (0.1261)	8.007*** (0.1790)	8.093*** (0.2003)
KCC	‡	‡	0.044* (0.0197)	0.0401 (0.0205)
CD ratio	0.0172*** (0.0029)	0.0155*** (0.0031)	0.0140*** (0.0030)	0.0132*** (0.0032)
CD ratio x Credit gap in priority sectors	0.0033 (0.0047)	- -	-0.0033** (0.0045)	- -
CD ratio x Credit gap in non-priority sectors	- -	-0.0039 (0.0032)	- -	-0.00217 (0.0033)
Fixed effect	YES	YES	YES	YES
R^2	0.9914	0.9917	0.9926	0.9925
N	72	72	72	72

Note: (1) * p<0.05, ** p<0.01, *** p<0.001. (2) Robust standard errors are shown in parenthesis. (3) Unless specified, all specifications include districts and time fixed effects. (4) KCC is in logs. (5) ‡ no interaction (6) - - referenced category.

Due to significant variations in the percentage deviation between the actual loans disbursed and the targeted credit limit in priority versus non-priority sectors in 2008 compared to 2009–10, in addition to Table 33.4A, we do a similar cross-section regression analysis for 2009–10. We find that there is a positive and significant relationship in the CD ratio across districts (see Table 33.4B) whereas in Table 33.4A, (columns 2 and 3), no correlation is found in the case of non-priority sectors. However, excluding KCC from the analysis, we find that the percentage deviation between actual and targeted credit is positively correlated in priority sectors.

Finally, we look at another financial intermediation indicator to check the robustness of our results with regard to the relationship between the CD ratio and GDP per capita at the district level, controlling for the interaction of credit gap with district-level bank branch expansion. We carry out a district-level cross-section regression including bank branches as another supply side financial intermediation variable for further robustness of our results. We use the total number of branches in a district including different groups of credit institutions (commercial banks, cooperative banks, and foreign and private banks).

The CD ratios could be higher in local regions where there are a higher number of bank branches (see Figures 33.4A and 33.4B). So we include an interaction term between credit gap in (priority versus non-priority) and bank branches to uncover any non-linearity in the data and show its

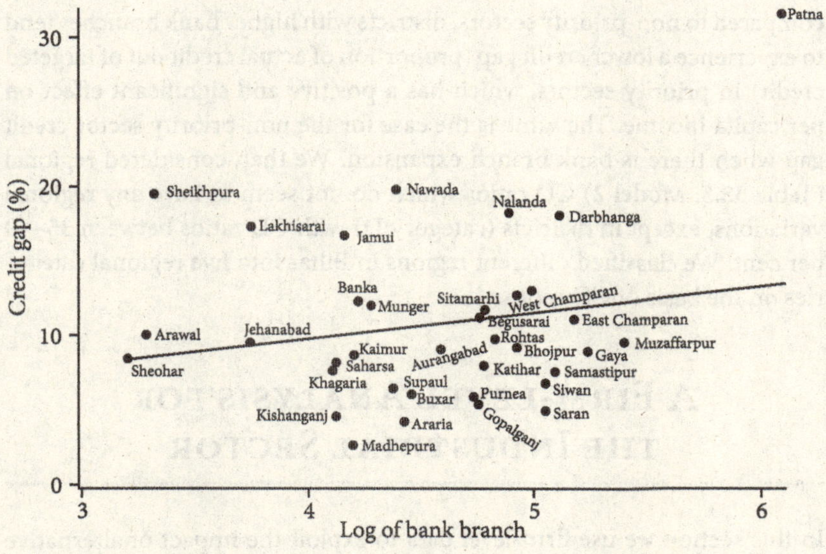

FIGURE 33.4A Credit Gap vs. Bank Branches in (priority sectors) in 2010

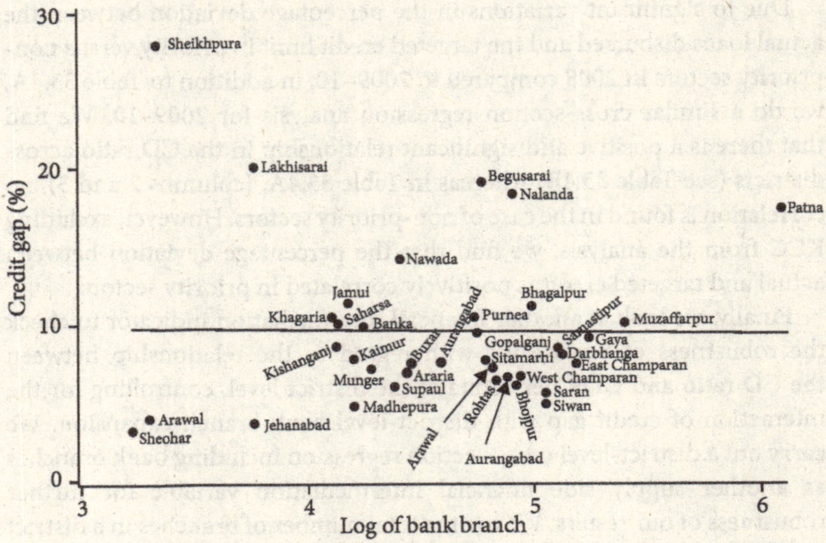

FIGURE 33.4B Credit Gap vs. Bank Branches in (non-priority sectors) in 2010

Source: Authors' calculations using data from SLBC, Bihar and RBI, Mumbai.

impact on per capita income. We find that districts with higher levels of bank branches do have a positive and significant effect on the development in those districts (Table 33.5, Model 1). As shown in Model 1 (Table 33.5), compared to non-priority sectors, districts with higher bank branches tend to experience a lower credit gap (proportion of actual credit out of targeted credit) in priority sectors, which has a positive and significant effect on per capita income. The same is the case for the non-priority sector credit gap when there is bank branch expansion. We then considered regional (Table 33.5, Model 2) CD ratios which do not seem to have any regional variations, except in districts (category D) with CD ratios between 35–40 per cent. We classified different regions in Bihar into five regional categories on the basis of CD ratios.

A Firm-level Analysis for the Industrial Sector

In this section we use firm-level data to exploit the impact of alternative sources of financing on firm level performance in Bihar, using company

Table 33.5 Effect of Bank Branches on Per Capita Income Across Sectors and Regions

	Model 1		Model 2	
	A	B	A	B
Constant	8.406***	8.289***	7.825***	7.177***
	(0.3952)	(0.3756)	(0.6531)	(1.020)
Log of bank branch	0.198*	0.254**	0.251**	0.251*
	(0.0858)	(0.0755)	(0.0897)	(0.0897)
CD ratio	−0.0053	−0.0103	0.0144	0.014
	(0.0049)	(0.0054)	(0.0185)	(0.0185)
Credit gap in priority sectors x log bank branch	0.0148*	--	0.009	0.009
	(0.0060)		(0.0071)	(0.0071)
Credit gap in non-priority sectors x log bank branch	--	0.0179*	0.005	0.005
		(0.0066)	(0.0084)	(0.0084)
Category-A			--	0.648
				(0.4460)
Category-B			−0.223	0.424
			(0.1605)	(0.3580)
Category-C			-0.383	0.265
			(0.2280)	(0.2741)
Category-D			−0.146	0.501*
			(0.6481)	(0.2296)
Category-E			-0.648	--
			(0.4461)	
R^2	0.4118	0.4333	0.5405	0.5405
N	35	35	35	35

Note: (1) * p<0.05, ** p<0.01, *** p<0.001. (2) Robust standard errors are shown in parenthesis. (3) - - referenced category.

level data from Prowess published by CMIE. We extracted 54 companies, which are located in Bihar (see the list of companies in Appendix A33.1). Data on 46 companies are usable which allow us to find whether bank-financing or equity financing are important for a company's performance. It appears that most companies resort to bank financing as shown in Table 33.6 with a higher proportion of debt share (borrowings as a proportion of total assets) rather than equity financing.

Table 33.6 Descriptive Statistics at Firm level

	Mean	Std. Dev.	Min	Max
Total income	57,735.71	31,0767.10	0.100	3,622,316.00
Borrowings	15,218.98	55,710.46	0.100	527,338.70
Equity Capital	3,177.57	13,767.33	0.500	82,455.00
Raw materials	22,491.01	122,301.20	2.000	1,428,809.00
Wages	1,388.86	4,928.77	0.200	51,919.70
Total assets	44,099.20	18,4621.40	0.300	1,868,434.00
Net fixed-assets	13,693.83	55,794.05	0.200	581,874.00
Debt share	1.63	7.11	0.001	105.34
Equity share	0.22	0.39	0.001	3.41

Source: Prowess data, CMIE.

Despite the data caveats with regard to missing/unreported values, the key question that we intend to address here is whether the alternative sources of financing have a varied impact on a firm's output in terms of its performance indicators like income, value added, profitability, and share price of the industries located in Bihar. That is, while in the earlier section, we dealt with the agricultural sector performance and credit availability in Bihar, here we consider the impact of such financial resources on the industrial sector with the analysis being carried out at the company level. Specifically, we first carried out an empirical analysis to examine the impact of the level of borrowing and equity financing on the first two performance indicators (income and value added), while controlling for firm size, with the remaining two indicators (profitability and share price) being used for robustness checks.

First, we estimated when the dependent variable is output (or gross revenue) and then we turned to using value added—gross output, net of intermediate inputs—as the dependent variable. Both total revenue and value added were used as alternative indicators of performance and the results are presented in Table 33.7. We find that borrowing and

Table 33.7 Firm-level Empirical Results

	Panel A					Panel B		
Total Income					Total Value added			
Constant	5.947***	5.293***	0.788	-0.0602	Constant	8.144***	8.174***	8.177***
	(0.3917)	(0.4022)	(0.4108)	(0.4676)		(0.3090)	(0.2907)	(0.2906)
Borrowing	0.417***	0.287***	-0.108*	0.112	Debt share	−0.0331**	0.0121	−0.0187
	(0.0380)	(0.0442)	(0.0419)	(0.0728)		(0.0110)	(0.0117)	(0.0288)
Equity capital	ǂ	0.363***	−0.246***	-0.212**	Equity share	ǂ	-2.666***	-2.499***
		(0.0674)	(0.0640)	(0.0640)			(0.3225)	(0.3524)
					Debt share squared	ǂ	ǂ	0.000284
								(0.0002)
Total assetsǂ		ǂ	1.131***	1.169**				
			(0.0640)	(0.0641)				
Borrowing squared			ǂ	-0.0236**				
				(0.0064)				
R^2	0.8774	0.8833	0.9252	0.927		0.8776	0.8918	0.8921
N	605	605	605	605		566	566	566

Source: Authors' estimates using Prowess data, CMIE, Mumbai.

Note: (1) * $p<0.05$, ** $p<0.01$, *** $p<0.001$. (2) Robust standard errors are shown in parenthesis. (3) Unless specified, all specifications include company (4) ǂ no interaction.

equity financing have a positive impact on firm output in the benchmark case, but when we control for firm size via total assets, the effect turns insignificant. When we include a squared term for borrowing to capture any non-linearity, the impact is negative confirming that firms with high level of borrowings tend to experience higher debt burden influencing their output negatively.

But when we replace gross income with value added (see Panel B, Table 33.7), the effect of borrowing (whether level or squared term) turns insignificant, regardless of whether we use the borrowing or equity capital in their log levels or as a proportion of assets. However, equity capital tends to have a negative impact on gross revenue or value added, which confirms that companies in Bihar are less dependent on equity capital (as 22 per cent of their total assets on average), while they are heavily dependent on bank borrowings for their performance as reflected through their debt share as a proportion of total assets (see Table 33.6).

When we consider the impact of borrowing as a proportion of total assets on firm profitability (defined as profits over sales) or share price, the effect is somewhat different. We find that the debt–assets ratio has a negative effect and the squared debt ratio has a positive effect, which is contrary to what one would expect in corporate finance literature. The

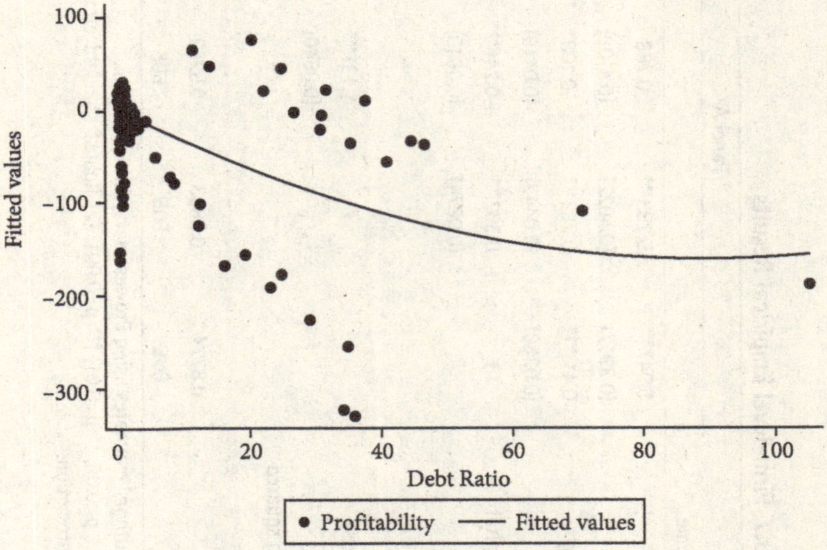

FIGURE 33.5 Relation between Corporate Borrowing over Assets and Profitability

Source: Authors' calculations using data from SLBC, Bihar and RBI, Mumbai.

plots, however, do not show a clear U-shape, implying that with very higher levels of debt, the profitability is lower but remains flat (see Figure 33.5). When we turn to share price replacing profitability as a dependent variable, we find that the effect remains the same. The share price is lower with a higher debt ratio or with a higher equity ratio. As the number of observations gets halved due to missing data, we have not presented these results in a tabular form, but they are available on request from the authors.

Since both sources of financing have a negative impact on performance, we tried to separate the firms with high and low levels of borrowings (by dividing the sample into below- and above-average borrowings). We find that there are only six firms (out of 46) which had high debt ratios (above average), and those firms' equity ratio was also above average. From this we can conclude that firms with high debt ratios tend to have high equity ratios which might explain the negative impact of equity on performance. In other words, firms which borrow too much may end up reducing their creditworthiness by increasing the possibility of bankruptcy and bankruptcy costs on their performance in the equity market, overall firm performance, and shareholder value. Thus over-borrowing and lack of creditworthiness leads companies to resort to equity financing thereby jeopardizing the value of equity. However, the number of firms on the high side is very small which basically drive the negative impact in the credit market that spills over to the equity (stock) market. Since Bihar has only a very small number of companies with higher levels of debt or equity ratios (that is, skewed at the low end), it may not be reasonable to generalize the average relationship for the whole of Bihar.

Nevertheless, directed credit policies might have helped these firms to expand their borrowing from banks, as opposed to going for equity financing which requires more disclosure on the part of firms. This explains why equity financing has not had a discernible positive effect on company performance. In a panel of 62 countries, Agnello et al. (2012) find that the removal of mandatory credit allocation has a favourable impact on an economy in terms of helping reduce income inequality. Banerjee and Duflo (2012) show that unconstrained firms will primarily use a directed credit programme to borrow more so as to substitute other sources of financing. This suggests that directed credit is probably contributing to bank loans accounting for a big proportion of a company's total assets, but as shown in our results they do not seem to translate into better company performance.

* * *

To sum up, a larger number of bank branches do imply higher credit allocation relative to targeted credit, given their combined positive impact on per capita income. But CD ratios do not provide conclusive evidence as to whether better financial intermediation can contribute to higher levels of economic activity. Our preliminary analysis of the data shows that while Bihar grew at a more rapid pace than the rest of India, much of the growth and development of the intermediation took place in the prosperous belts in the north as well as in the south and proactive government programmes like KCC helped these regions to grow both in terms of output and development of financial indices. While the rest of the regions are still languishing and under-performing with poorer indices of intermediation activities, it is confirmed that while allocation of credit certainly has a positive impact on the priority sector, the opposite holds true for the non-priority segments of the economy, including industrial sectors. We also find similar effects with respect to government guarantees or regions where there are more bank branches. However, the overall impact of financial intermediation on economic development is limited possibly due to credit market imperfections in Bihar. Companies in Bihar, however, derive a big part of their financing in the form of borrowings, although the impact of borrowing on a firm's performance remains less significant in our empirical analysis, which requires further research with data on more companies over a longer time period and better location information of companies.

APPENDIX A33.1

Table A33.1 List of Company Names and District Names

Company Names	
Alkem Laboratories Ltd.	JVL Agro Inds. Ltd.
Ambuja Electrocastings Ltd.	Kalyanpur Cements Ltd.
Ambuja Flour Mills Ltd.	Krishi Rasayan Exports Pvt. Ltd.
Ambuja Zinc Ltd.	Mcdowell & Co. Ltd. [Merged]
Balmukund Concast Ltd.	Motilal Padampat Udyog Ltd.
Bata India Ltd.	NTPC Ltd.
Belsund Sugar & Inds. Ltd.	Nacro Chemicals Ltd.
Bennett, Coleman & Co. Ltd.	Nacro Chemicals Ltd.
Bestavision Electronics Ltd.	National Jute Mfrs. Corpn. Ltd.

Bharat Wagon & Engg. Co. Ltd.
Bihar Mercantile Union Ltd.
Cawnpore Sugar Works Ltd.
Champarun Sugar Co. Ltd.
Dina Iron & Steel Ltd.
Dumraon Textiles Ltd.
Eastern India Powertech Ltd.
Eastern Sugar & Inds. Ltd.
Ganesh Foundry & Castings Ltd.
Gangotri Iron & Steel Co. Ltd.
Graphite India Ltd.
Graphite India Ltd. [Merged]
Harinagar Sugar Mills Ltd.
Hindustan Fertilizer Corpn. Ltd.
ITC Ltd.
Indian Oil Corpn. Ltd.
Indian Railway Catering & Tourism Corpn. Ltd.
JJ Exporters Ltd.
JMD Alloys Ltd.
National Textile Corpn. (W.B., Ass., Bih. & Ori.) Ltd. [Merged]
New India Retailing & Invst. Ltd.
Oudh Sugar Mills Ltd.
Progressive Steels (India) Ltd.
Pyrites, Phosphates & Chemicals Ltd.
Rameshwara Jute Mills Ltd.
Riga Sugar Co. Ltd.
SKG Consolidated Ltd.
SRP Industries Ltd.
Saraswati Steel & Alloys Ltd.
Shalimar Pellet Feeds Ltd.
Sree Behariji Mills Ltd.
Tirupati Sugars Ltd.
United Spirits Ltd.
Upper Ganges Sugar & Inds. Ltd.
Usher Agro Ltd.
Vishnu Sugar Mills Ltd.
Winsome International Ltd.
District Names in Bihar
Araria
Arawal
Aurangabad
Banka
Begusarai
Bhagalpur
Bhojpur
Buxar
Darbhanga
Gaya
Gopalganj
Jamui
Jehanabad
Kaimur
Katihar
Khagaria
Kishanganj
Lakhisarai
Madhepura
Munger
Muzaffarpur
Nalanda
Nawada
West Champaran
Patna
East Champaran
Purnea
Rohtas
Saharsa
Samastipur
Saran
Sheikhpura
Sheohar
Sitamarhi
Siwan
Supaul
Vaishali

Source: Prowess database, CMIE, Mumbai.

References

Agnello, L., S.K. Mallick, and R.M. Sousa (2012), 'Financial Reforms and Income Inequality', *Economics Letters*, 116(3): 583–87.

Ang, J.B. (2009), 'Private Investment and Financial Sector Policies in India and Malaysia', *World Development*, 37(7): 1261–73.

——— (2010), 'Finance and Inequality: The Case of India', *Southern Economic Journal*, 76(3): 738–61.

Arestis, P., P. Demetriades, B. Fattouh, and K. Mouratidis (2002), 'The Impact of Financial Liberalisation Policies on Financial Development: Evidence from Developing Economies', *International Journal of Finance and Economics*, 7(2): 109–21.

Athukorala, P.C. and K. Sen (2004), 'The determinants of private saving in India', *World Development*, 32(3): 491–503.

Banerjee, A. and E. Duflo (2012), *Do Firms Want to Borrow More? Testing Credit Constraints Using a Directed Lending Program*. MIT Economics working paper.

Blanco, L. (2009), 'The Finance-Growth Link in Latin America', *Southern Economic Journal*, 76(1): 224–48.

Burgess, R. and R. Pande (2005), 'Do Rural Banks Matter? Evidence from the Indian Social Banking Experiment', *The American Economic Review*, 95: 780–95.

Cole, S. (2009a) 'Fixing market failures or fixing elections? Agricultural credit in India', *American Economic Journal: Applied Economics*, 1(1): 219–50.

——— (2009b), 'Financial development, bank ownership, and growth: Or, does quantity imply quality?' *Review of Economics and Statistics*, 91(1): 33–51.

Diamond, D.W. and P.H. Dybvig (1983), 'Bank Runs, Deposit insurance, and Liquidity', *Journal of Political Economy*, 91: 401–19.

Fry, M.J. (1997), 'In Defence of Financial Liberalisation', *Economic Journal*, 107(442): 754–70.

Government of Bihar (2009), *Economic Survey 2008–9*, Chapter 6: Banking and Allied Sectors, pp. 207–38, Finance Department, Patna: Bihar, February.

Gupta, K.L. and R. Lensink (1996), *Financial Liberalization and Investment*. London: Routledge.

Hermes, N. and R. Lensink (1996), *Financial Development and Economic Growth: Theory and Experiences from Developing Countries*. London: Routledge.

Kendall, J. (2012), 'Local financial development and growth', *Journal of Banking and Finance*, 36(5): 1548–62.

Kumar, A., C. Yadav, S. Jee, S. Kumar, and S. Chauhan (2011), 'Financial innovation in Indian agricultural credit market: Progress and performance of kisan credit card', *Indian Journal of Agricultural Economics*, 66(3): 418–28.

Levine, R. (1997), 'Financial development and economic growth: views and agenda', *Journal of Economic Literature*, 35(2): 688–726.

Levine, R. and S. Zervos (1998), 'Stock markets, banks, and economic growth', *American Economic Review*, 88(3): 537–58.

Luintel, K.B. and M. Khan (1999), 'A quantitative reassessment of the finance-growth nexus: evidence from a multivariate VAR', *Journal of Development Economics*, 60: 381–405.

Mallick, S.K. (2006), 'Policy Instruments to Avoid Output Collapse: An Optimal Control Model for India', *Applied Financial Economics*, 16(10): 761–76.

Pentecost, E.J. and T. Moore (2006), 'Financial Liberalization in India and a New Test of the Complementarity Hypothesis', *Economic Development and Cultural Change*, 54(2): 487–502.

Prasad, E.S. and R.G. Rajan (2008), 'Next Generation Financial Reforms for India', *Finance and Development*, 45(3): 23–7.

Singh, A. (1997), Stock Markets, Financial Liberalisation and Economic Development', *Economic Journal*, 107(442): 771–82.

ABOUT THE EDITOR AND CONTRIBUTORS

Editor

Ashima Goyal is a Professor at the Indira Gandhi Institute of Development Research (IGIDR), Mumbai, and is widely published in institutional and open economy macroeconomics, international finance and governance, with 3 books and over a hundred scholarly articles. She had received many fellowships, national and international awards, is active in the Indian public debate, and has served on several boards and policy committees. Currently, she is member of the Indian Technical Advisory Committee on monetary policy and is co-editor of a Routledge journal, *Macroeconomics and Finance in Emerging Market Economies*.

Contributors

Aradhna Aggarwal is a Senior Fellow with the National Council of Applied Economic Research. She is also associated with the Policy Unit of Wadhwani Foundation as a consultant. She earned her post-graduation and PhD degrees from the Delhi School of Economics and taught at the University of Delhi for several years. She has authored several journal articles and working papers on SEZs. Her book titled *Social and Economic Impact of SEZs in India* (OUP) was released in January 2012.

Pulapre Balakrishnan is Professor and ex-Director, Centre for Development Studies, Thiruvananthapuram, India.

Rukmini Banerji is Director, ASER Centre and Pratham, New Delhi, India.

Sanjay Banerji is Professor, Finance at Nottingham University Business School in the division of Economics and Finance. Previously, he taught at Essex University, UK and McGill University, Canada. He has research interests in corporate finance, corporate governance and Indian political economy.

Laveesh Bhandari heads Indicus Analytics. He has been leading policy-oriented studies for international institutions like the ADB, The World Bank, academic organizations like Stanford, Cambridge and Harvard Universities, and non-profits like Ford Foundation and the Cato Institute. He has published extensively in books, journals, and newspapers, in India and internationally.

Rekha A. Bhangaonkar is Research Associate at School of Management, IIT-Bombay. She completed her under-graduation (St. Teresa's College, 2004) and graduation (Madras Christian College, 2007) in Economics and MPhil in Planning and Development (IIT-Bombay, 2009). Her interests are monetary economics, development economics, and agriculture economics.

Rajesh Chakrabarti is Executive Director, Bharti Institute of Public Policy and Clinical Associate Professor at the Indian School of Business. He is an alumnus of Presidency College, Kolkata, and IIM Ahmedabad and earned his PhD in Management from the University of California at Los Angeles.

Romar Correa is Reserve Bank of India Professor, Monetary Economics at the University of Mumbai. He works on the interface between micro and macro in non-neoclassical frameworks. At present, he is developing stock-flow-consistent macro models.

Ashwini Deshpande is Professor, Economics at the Delhi School of Economics, University of Delhi, India. She has worked on the international debt crisis of the 1980s, economics of discrimination and affirmative action issues, with a focus on caste and gender in India, as well as on aspects of the Chinese economy. She has published extensively in leading scholarly journals and has edited several books. She is the author of *Grammar of Caste: Economic Discrimination in Contemporary India*, OUP, 2011 and *Affirmative Action in India* (OUP, 2013). She has received national awards for her work.

S. Mahendra Dev is Director (Vice-chancellor) at IGIDR. He has written extensively on agricultural development, poverty and public policy, and other development issues, and has more than 100 research publications. One of his recent books from OUP is *Inclusive Growth in India*. He has been member of several committees and has received honours for eminence in public service.

Meghna Dutta is affiliated to the Centre for Studies in Social Sciences, Calcutta, India. A doctoral research scholar in economics at the Centre for Studies in Social Sciences, Calcutta, her research interests are in the areas of international economics and production organizations. She is currently working on a number of theoretical and empirical research papers on FDI, production outsourcing, and political economy of lobbying.

Sahil Gandhi is PhD Scholar at the Vibhooti Shukla Centre of Urban Economics and Regional Development, Department of Economics, University of Mumbai.

Krishna Gangopadhyay studied at Jawaharlal Nehru University, New Delhi and Indian Institute of Management, Kolkata. As an economist with an MBA, her interests lie in financial markets and communication technology.

Prashant Gupta is PhD candidate at the Department of Economics, Swansea University, UK. He specialises in the area of economic development, especially on issues related to social cohesion. Prashant is interested in both theoretical and empirical aspects of poverty, cohesion, and development under uncertainty. He holds an MSc in Economics and Finance from Swansea University, UK and a BSc in Mathematics from India.

Raghbendra Jha, PhD (Columbia), FWIF, is Head, Arndt-Corden Department of Economics, Rajiv Gandhi Chair Professor and Executive Director Australia South Asia Research Centre, Australian National University. He has previously taught at Columbia University and Williams College in the US; Queen's University in Canada; University of Warwick in the UK; and Delhi School of Economics, Indian Institute of Management Bangalore and Indira Gandhi Institute of Development Research in India.

His research and teaching areas are macroeconomics, public economics and development economics. He has published 28 books/monographs with reputed publishers and more than 150 papers in scientific journals and other refereed outlets.

Shikha Jha is Principal Economist at the Economics and Research Department of Asian Development Bank. She has published widely on fiscal policies, government expenditure, social safety nets, and economics of food markets. Her research and operational experience covers several countries in South Asia, South-East Asia, East Asia and Central Asia.

Param Jit teaches at the Department of Economics at Delhi School of Economics, University of Delhi. His teaching and research areas are econometrics, development and environmental issues. He has authored a book *Portfolio Diversification Behaviour—A Study of Urban Salary Earners.* He has served on several university committees. Currently, he is Deputy Dean Planning and Member of Task Force on 'Four Year Undergraduate Programme' at the University of Delhi.

K.J. Joseph is the Ministry of Commerce Chair at Centre for Development Studies. He is the author of *Industry under Economic Liberalization: Case of Indian Electronics* (1997); *Information Technology Innovation System and Trade Regime in Developing Countries: India and the ASEAN* (2006) and the co-editor of *International Competitiveness & Knowledge-based Industries in India* (Oxford University Press 2007) and *Handbook of Innovation Systems and Developing Countries Edward Elgar* (2009).

Sumita Kale is Chief Economist, Indicus Analytics, New Delhi. She has also been visiting faculty at Department of Economics, Gokhale Institute of Politics and Economics, University of Pune and National Insurance Academy. She has a number of publications and writes regularly for financial newspapers in India.

Kanagasabapathy K. is Director, EPW Research Foundation, Mumbai. Educated from Annamalai University, Indian Statistical Institute and University of Surrey (UK), he served at the Reserve Bank of India from 1977 to 2006. His areas of interests are money, banking, financial markets and international finance.

Saibal Kar is Faculty of Economics at the Centre for Studies in Social Sciences, Calcutta and is a Research Fellow at IZA, Bonn, Germany. His research interests are in the fields of labour economics, international economics and applied microeconomics. He is the Managing Editor of the *South Asian Journal of Macroeconomics and Public Finance*.

Renu Kohli, a New Delhi-based macroeconomist, currently Lead Economist, International Financial Architecture, DEA-ICRIER G20 Research Programme, consultant for foreign investors, contributor to business media. A former staff member of the International Monetary Fund and Reserve Bank of India, she has published in a number of refereed journals; she has also has authored a book—*India's Experience with Capital Account Liberalization* (OUP, 2005). A DPhil from the University of Sussex, she has several academic distinctions/ honours to her credit, including the Commonwealth Award in 1992.

Kiran Kumar is ICSSR Doctoral Fellow, Centre for Development Studies, Thiruvananthapuram, India.

Dr Nagesh Kumar is Director, UNESCAP South and South-West Asia Office, New Delhi. He was previously Director (MPDD), Chief Economist, and Acting Deputy Executive Secretary at UNESCAP headquarters, Bangkok. Before that he was Director-General, RIS, a New Delhi-based policy think-tank. Dr Kumar has served on the boards of the Exim Bank of India, ICTSD Geneva, and SACEPS, Kathmandu; and has consulted for ADB, UNCTAD, UNDP, UNIDO, World Bank, among others. A PhD from the Delhi School of Economics, Dr Kumar has published over 15 books and 90 papers, and received national and international awards for his work.

Sushanta Mallick is Professor, International Finance at the School of Business and Management, Queen Mary, University of London, UK. He holds a PhD in economics from the University of Warwick, UK, under a Commonwealth Scholarship, and has worked at Loughborough University, UK; at Chatham House, London, UK; at JPMorgan Chase Hong Kong, and at the Institute for Social and Economic Change (with a year at Indian Statistical Institute), Bangalore, India. He has over 50 peer-reviewed journal articles in the areas of international economics and finance and development studies. [see details at http://webspace.qmul.ac.uk/skmallick/].

Srijit Mishra is Subir Chowdhury Fellow at the London School of Economics and Political Science (LSE) and Associate Professor at IGIDR. His research interests are in development-related issues with a people-centric focus that cover social philosophy, analytical measurement and their applications. Some of his recent works are on farmers' suicides and he recently co-edited *Agrarian Crisis in India* published by OUP.

Arup Mitra is Professor, Economics, Institute of Economic Growth, Delhi. His research interest includes urban development, labour economics, industrialization, services sector growth and gender inequality. His recent book is *Insights into Inclusive Growth, Employment and Wellbeing in India*.

Deepak Mohanty is Executive Director, Reserve Bank of India in charge of Monetary Policy, Economic Research and Statistics. Prior to his current position, he was Senior Adviser in the International Monetary Fund (IMF). He holds master's degrees in Economics from Yale University and Jawaharlal Nehru University (JNU).

Rahul Mukherji is Associate Professor, South Asian Studies Programme at the National University of Singapore. He has edited *India's Economic Transition* published by Oxford University Press (2007, 2011) and co-authored with Sumit Ganguly *India Since 1980* (2011). His forthcoming book with Oxford University Press is titled: *Globalization and Deregulation: Ideas, Interests, and Institutional Change in India.*

Rupayan Pal is Associate Professor, Economics, Indira Gandhi Institute of Development Research (IGIDR), Mumbai, India. His research covers issues like inter-regional competition, privatization, environmental regulation, union-oligopoly bargaining, network effects, market structure and innovation, financial inclusion, growth and government efficiency. He has published in several refereed international journals.

Shruti Pandey is Research Officer with EPW Research Foundation, Mumbai. She holds MBA in Finance from ICFAI University (2012) and MA Economics from University of Mumbai with specialization in International Trade and Econometrics (2008). Her areas of interests are money, banking and macroeconomy.

Vijay Laxmi Pandey is Associate Professor at IGIDR. Her areas of interest are environmental economics, sustainable agricultural, rural studies and gender issues. She has completed many national and international research and consultancy projects. She has a large number of research publications, which include research papers in peer-reviewed journals, books, magazine articles, and policy reports.

Abhay Pethe is Chair Professor at the Vibhooti Shukla Centre of Urban Economics and Regional Development, Department of Economics, University of Mumbai.

Rohit Prasad is Associate Professor of Economics at MDI Gurgaon. He was a member of the Subodh Kumar Committee on Spectrum Allocation at the DOT, and the expert panel of the TRAI on Spectrum Pricing. His forthcoming book *The Conundrums of Thin Air* co-authored with Varadarajan Sridhar deals with the theory and practice of spectrum management with an application to the Indian case. He is the author of *Startup Sutra—What the Angels Won't Tell You About Business and Life* and a Director of the Stern Fisher Angel Network.

T.R. Raghunandan currently advises state governments, international organizations, NGOs, and research institutions on decentralized public governance and anti-corruption. A former Indian Administrative Service officer, he served as the Joint Secretary in the Union Ministry of Panchayati Raj and Secretary, Rural Development and Panchayat Raj, Karnataka between 2001 and 2009.

A.V. Raja is a professor of Economics at the School of Economics, University of Hyderabad. His Areas of Specialization are Law and Economics, Environmental Economics, and New Institutional Economics

T.T. Ram Mohan is Professor, Finance and Economics at IIM Ahmedabad, and is a graduate of IIT Bombay, IIM Calcutta and Stern School, New York. He has authored many books and been a columnist for *The Economic Times* for 15 years. He has served on important committees and boards.

Bandi Ram Prasad is President, Financial Technologies Knowledge Management Co., and has worked in senior management positions in Indian Banks Association, Bombay Stock Exchange, Dun & Bradstreet India, etc. His expertise includes banking, securities markets, rural finance and knowledge management. He carried out consulting assignments for a wide range of institutions in India and abroad on areas such as financial markets development, corporate governance, business strategy and capacity building.

Francis Xavier Rathinam is research specialist with South Asia Research Hub (SARH) at the UK Department for International Development (DFID). His areas of interest include New Institutional Economics, Law and Economics and Development Microeconomics. His recent work explores the legal, regulatory, and political economy aspects of current financial and banking sector reforms in India.

Bibhas Saha is Senior Lecturer at the University of East Anglia, England. His work on economics of betting, corruption and privatization has been published in international refereed journals.

Jayati Sarkar is Professor at the Indira Gandhi Institute of Development Research, Mumbai, India. She has a PhD from the University of Southern California, USA. Her field of specialization is institutional economics and her current research interests are in corporate ownership and governance in emerging economies, business groups, public sector enterprise reforms and performance. Her articles have been published in leading scholarly journals. She has also co-authored a book titled *Corporate Governance in India*. She is the editor of the *Journal of Interdisciplinary Economics*.

Subrata Sarkar is Professor at the IGIDR, Mumbai, India. He has a PhD in Economics from the University of Southern California. His research interests are in the areas of corporate governance, corporate finance, empirical industrial organization, and risk modelling. His articles have been published in leading scholarly journals. He is the co-author of the book *Corporate Governance in India* and is the co-editor of the journal *Macroeconomics and Finance in Emerging Market Economies*.

Gita Sen has recently retired from her position as Professor of Public Policy at the Indian Institute of Management, Bangalore. She was a member of the High Level Expert Group on Universal Health Coverage, and of the Mission Steering Group of the National Rural Health Mission, and is currently a member of the Board of the National Health Systems Resource Centre of the Government of India.

Anurag Sharma is Senior Research Fellow in Faculty of Business and Economics, Monash University, Australia. His current research interests include development economics (poverty nutrition linkages and economics of education) and health economics (hospital choice modelling and impact of taxation strategies on consumption of soft drinks and alcohol).

Parthasarathi Shome is Adviser (Minister of State) to Indian Finance Minister, and Chairman, Tax Administration Reform Commission. Earlier, Chief Economist, Her Majesty's Revenue and Customs, UK, Chief of Tax Policy, IMF, Director NIPFP and ICRIER, New Delhi. He has chaired India's Ninth and Tenth Five Year Plan Tax Policy and Administration

Task Forces, and provided technical assistance in taxation to over thirty countries.

Soumyen Sikdar studied at Presidency College, Calcutta, University of Calcutta and University of Minnesota, USA. He is currently Professor of Economics at IIM Calcutta. He taught in Presidency College, University of Calcutta and Burdwan University, was visiting faculty at Osaka University, Japan, and has authored two books: *Contemporary Issues in Globalization*, and *Principles of Macroeconomics* (both OUP India).

Ram Singh is Associate Professor at the Delhi School of Economics, University of Delhi. He holds a PhD (JNU, New Delhi) degree and Post-Doctorate (Harvard) in Economics. His areas of research interests are contract theory, public economics, public–private partnerships, and law and economics. He is recipient of Ronald Coase Fellowship in Institutional Economics, and Fulbright Senior Research Fellowship in Economics.

Sidharth Sinha is a Professor at the Indian Institute of Management Ahmedabad, India. He has a PhD in Finance from University of California, Berkeley, USA.

P.V. Srinivasan is an Evaluation Specialist at the Independent Evaluation Department of the Asian Development Bank. He has published extensively on issues related to poverty, food security, and public finance. He has been consultant to several international organizations including the World Bank, the Asian Development Bank, the African Development Bank and the Food and Agricultural Organization.

S. Sriraman is Walchand Hirachand Professor of Transport Economics, Department of Economics, University of Mumbai. He is a visiting Professor in many universities in the country and has been part of many high-powered government committees focusing on policies related to the transport sector.

Vaidehi Tandel is PhD Scholar, Department of Economics, University of Mumbai.

Wilima Wadhwa is Director, ASER Centre, New Delhi, India and is also affiliated to University of California, Irvine.

INDEX